GLEIM®

2016 EDITION

CPA Review

Regulation

by

Irvin N. Gleim, Ph.D., CPA, CIA, CMA, CFM

The AICPA formal title of this section is *Regulation*, and the AICPA acronym is REG.

Gleim Publications, Inc.
P.O. Box 12848
University Station
Gainesville, Florida 32604
(800) 87-GLEIM or (800) 874-5346
(352) 375-0772
Fax: (352) 375-6940
Internet: www.gleim.com
Email: admin@gleim.com

For updates to this 2016 edition of
CPA Review: Regulation

Go To: www.gleim.com/CPAupdate

Or: Email update@gleim.com with **CPA REG 2016-1** in the subject line. You will receive our current update as a reply.

Updates are available until the next edition is published.

ISSN: 1547-8092

ISBN: 978-1-61854-002-7 *CPA Review: Auditing and Attestation*
ISBN: 978-1-61854-003-4 *CPA Review: Business Environment and Concepts*
ISBN: 978-1-61854-004-1 *CPA Review: Financial Accounting and Reporting*
ISBN: 978-1-61854-005-8 *CPA Review: Regulation*
ISBN: 978-1-61854-010-2 *How to Pass the CPA Exam: A System for Success*

First Printing: November 2015

ACKNOWLEDGMENTS

Material from *Uniform CPA Examination, Selected Questions and Unofficial Answers*, Copyright © 1974-2015 by the American Institute of Certified Public Accountants, Inc., is reprinted and/or adapted with permission. Visit the AICPA's website at www.aicpa.org for more information.

The author is indebted to the Institute of Certified Management Accountants for permission to use problem materials from past CMA examinations. Questions and unofficial answers from the Certified Management Accountant Examinations, copyright by the Institute of Certified Management Accountants, are reprinted and/or adapted with permission.

Environmental Statement -- This book is printed on recyclable, environmentally friendly groundwood paper, sourced from certified sustainable forests and produced either TCF (totally chlorine-free) or ECF (elementally chlorine-free).

ABOUT THE AUTHOR

Irvin N. Gleim is Professor Emeritus in the Fisher School of Accounting at the University of Florida and is a member of the American Accounting Association, Academy of Legal Studies in Business, American Institute of Certified Public Accountants, Association of Government Accountants, Florida Institute of Certified Public Accountants, The Institute of Internal Auditors, and the Institute of Management Accountants. He has had articles published in the *Journal of Accountancy*, *The Accounting Review*, and *The American Business Law Journal* and is author/coauthor of numerous accounting books, aviation books, and CPE courses.

REVIEWERS AND CONTRIBUTORS

Garrett W. Gleim, B.S., CPA (not in public practice), received a Bachelor of Science degree from The Wharton School at the University of Pennsylvania. Mr. Gleim coordinated the production staff, reviewed the manuscript, and provided production assistance throughout the project.

Grady M. Irwin, J.D., is a graduate of the University of Florida College of Law, and he has taught in the University of Florida College of Business. Mr. Irwin provided substantial editorial assistance throughout the project.

D. Scott Lawton, B.S., is a graduate of Brigham Young University-Idaho and Utah Valley University. He has worked as an auditor for the Utah State Tax Commission. Mr. Lawton provided substantial editorial assistance throughout the project.

Lawrence Lipp, J.D., CPA (Registered), is a graduate from the Levin College of Law and the Fisher School of Accounting at the University of Florida. Mr. Lipp provided substantial editorial assistance throughout the project.

A PERSONAL THANKS

This manual would not have been possible without the extraordinary effort and dedication of Jacob Brunny, Julie Cutlip, Courtney McAllister, Kelsey Olson, Teresa Soard, Justin Stephenson, Joanne Strong, and Elmer Tucker, who typed the entire manuscript and all revisions and drafted and laid out the diagrams and illustrations in this book.

The authors also appreciate the production and editorial assistance of Jacob Bennet, Jessica Felkins, James Harvin, Blaine Hatton, Kristen Hennen, Jeanette Kerstein, Katie Larson, Josh Lehr, Diana León, Jake Pettifor, Shane Rapp, Drew Sheppard, and Martha Willis.

The authors also appreciate the critical reading assistance of Jared Armenti, Coryn Brewer, Ellen Buhl, Paul Davis, Jack Hahne, Bethany Harris, Nathan Kaplan, Melissa Leonard, Yating Li, Monica Metz, Tyler Rankin, Daniel Sinclair, Tingwei Su, Nanan Toure, Diana Weng, and Kenneth Wilbur.

Finally, we appreciate the encouragement, support, and tolerance of our families throughout this project.

TABLE OF CONTENTS

DETAILED TABLE OF CONTENTS

PREFACE FOR CPA CANDIDATES

This is the 2016 Edition of CPA Review. It reflects relevant business law, ethical, and federal tax pronouncements (discussed in Study Unit 1) through November 2015.

The purpose of this Gleim CPA Review study book is to help YOU prepare to pass the 2016 Regulation (also referred to throughout the rest of this text as REG) section of the CPA examination. Our overriding consideration is to provide a comprehensive, effective, and easy-to-use study program. This book

1. Explains how to optimize your grade by focusing on the Regulation section of the CPA exam.
2. Defines the subject matter tested on the Regulation section of the CPA exam.
3. Outlines all of the subject matter tested on the Regulation section in 20 easy-to-use-and-complete study units.
4. Presents multiple-choice questions from recent CPA examinations to prepare you for questions in future CPA exams. Our answer explanations are presented to the immediate right of each question for your convenience. Use a piece of paper to cover our answer explanations as you study the questions.
5. Presents several task-based simulations in each study unit to acquaint you with simulation task formats. Answer the simulations in your book. The answers and grading instructions follow each simulation.

The outline format, the spacing, and the question and answer formats in this book are designed to facilitate readability, learning, understanding, and success on the CPA exam. Our most successful candidates use the Gleim Premium CPA Review System,* which includes Gleim Instruct videos; our Access Until You Pass Guarantee; expertly authored books; the largest test bank of multiple-choice questions (presented with NEW adaptive learning technology), Task-Based Simulations, and Written Communications; Audio Lectures; and the support of our team of accounting experts. This review book and all Gleim CPA Review materials are compatible with other CPA review materials and courses that follow the AICPA Content and Skill Specification Outlines (CSOs/SSOs).

To maximize the efficiency and effectiveness of your CPA review program, augment your studying with *How to Pass the CPA Exam: A System for Success*. This booklet has been carefully written and organized to provide important information to assist you in passing the CPA examination.

Thank you for your interest in the Gleim CPA Review materials. We deeply appreciate the thousands of letters and suggestions received from CPA, CIA, CMA, and EA candidates during the past 5 decades.

If you use the Gleim materials, we want YOUR feedback immediately after the exam and as soon as you have received your grades. The CPA exam is NONDISCLOSED, and you will sign an attestation including, "I hereby agree that I will maintain the confidentiality of the Uniform CPA Examination. In addition, I agree that I will not divulge the nature or content of any Uniform CPA Examination question or answer under any circumstance . . ." We ask only for information about our materials, i.e., the topics that need to be added, expanded, etc. Our approach has AICPA approval.

Please go to www.gleim.com/feedbackREG to share your suggestions on how we can improve this edition.

Good Luck on the Exam,

Irvin N. Gleim

November 2015

* Visit www.gleimcpa.com or call (800) 874-5346 to order.

OPTIMIZING YOUR REGULATION SCORE

CBT-e Exam

CPA Exam Section	Auditing & Attestation	Business Environment & Concepts	Financial Accounting & Reporting	**Regulation**
Acronym	AUD	BEC	FAR	**REG**
Exam Length	4 hours	3 hours	4 hours	**3 hours**
Testlets:				
Multiple-Choice	3, 30 questions each (60%)	3, 24 questions each (85%)	3, 30 questions each (60%)	**3, 24 questions each (60%)**
Simulations	1 with 7 tasks (40%)	0	1 with 7 tasks (40%)	**1 with 6 tasks (40%)**
Written Communication	0	1 with 3 tasks (15%)	0	**0**

READ *HOW TO PASS THE CPA EXAM: A SYSTEM FOR SUCCESS*

Scan the Gleim *How to Pass the CPA Exam: A System for Success* booklet and note where to revisit later in your studying process to obtain a deeper understanding of the CPA exam.

1. *How to Pass the CPA Exam: A System for Success* has seven study units:

   Study Unit 1: The CPA Examination: An Overview and Preparation Introduction
   Study Unit 2: AICPA Content Specification Outlines and Skill Specification Outlines
   Study Unit 3: Content Preparation, Test Administration, and Performance Grading
   Study Unit 4: Multiple-Choice Questions
   Study Unit 5: Task-Based Simulations and Written Communications
   Study Unit 6: Preparing to Pass the CPA Exam
   Study Unit 7: How to Take the CPA Exam

2. *How to Pass the CPA Exam: A System for Success* is available as an e-book at www.gleim.com/PassCPA.

OVERVIEW OF REGULATION

Regulation is scheduled for 3 hours (180 minutes).

AICPA title:	Regulation
AICPA acronym:	REG
Question format:	72 multiple-choice questions in three testlets of 24 questions each One testlet with six Task-Based Simulations

SUBJECT MATTER FOR REGULATION

Below, we have provided the AICPA's abbreviated Content Specification Outlines (CSOs) for Regulation. The percentage of coverage for each topic is indicated. Appendix A contains the CSOs in their entirety as well as cross-references to the subunits in our text where topics are covered. Remember that we have studied and restudied the CSOs in developing our CPA Review materials. Accordingly, you do not need to spend time with Appendix A. Rather, it should give you confidence that Gleim CPA Review is the best review source available to help you PASS the CPA exam.

I. (17%) Ethics, Professional, and Legal Responsibilities
II. (19%) Business Law
III. (13%) Federal Tax Process, Procedures, Accounting, and Planning
IV. (14%) Federal Taxation of Property Transactions
V. (16%) Federal Taxation of Individuals
VI. (21%) Federal Taxation of Entities

The Regulation section tests knowledge and understanding of ethics, professional and legal responsibilities, business law, and federal taxation.

Ethics, Professional and Legal Responsibilities, and Business Law

These topics test knowledge and understanding of professional and legal responsibilities of certified public accountants. Professional ethics questions relate to tax practice issues and are based on the AICPA Statements on Standards for Tax Services, Treasury Department Circular 230, and rules and regulations for tax return preparers. Business law topics test knowledge and understanding of the legal implications of business transactions, particularly as they relate to accounting, auditing, and financial reporting. This section deals with federal and widely adopted uniform state laws or references identified in this CSO.

In addition to demonstrating knowledge and understanding of these topics, candidates are required to demonstrate the skills required to apply that knowledge in performing their responsibilities as certified public accountants. To demonstrate such knowledge and skills, candidates will be expected to perform the following tasks:

- Identify situations that might be unethical or a violation of professional standards, perform research and consultations as appropriate, and determine the appropriate action.
- Recognize potentially unethical behavior of clients and determine the impact on the tax services being performed.
- Demonstrate the importance of identifying and adhering to requirements, rules, and standards that are established by licensing boards within their state, and which may place additional professional requirements specific to their state of practice.
- Apply business law concepts in evaluating the economic substance of client transactions, including purchase agreements, loans and promissory notes, sales contracts, leases, side agreements, commitments, contingencies, and assumption of liabilities.
- Evaluate the legal structure of an entity to determine the implications of applicable laws and regulations on how a business is organized, governed, and operates.

Federal Taxation

These topics test knowledge and understanding of concepts and laws relating to federal taxation (income, gift, and estate). The areas of testing include federal tax process, procedures, accounting, and planning, as well as federal taxation of property transactions, individuals, and entities (which include sole proprietorships, partnerships, limited liability entities, C corporations, S corporations, joint ventures, trusts, estates, and tax-exempt organizations).

In addition to demonstrating knowledge and understanding of these topics, candidates are required to demonstrate the skills required to apply that knowledge in providing tax preparation and advisory services and performing other responsibilities as certified public accountants. To demonstrate such knowledge and skills, candidates will be expected to perform the following tasks:

- Evaluate the tax implications of different legal structures for business entities.
- Apply analytical reasoning tools to assess how taxes affect economic decisions related to the timing of income (expense) recognition and property transactions.
- Consider the impact of multijurisdictional tax issues on federal taxes.
- Identify the differences between tax and financial accounting.
- Analyze information and identify data relevant for tax purposes.
- Identify issues, elections, and alternative tax treatments.
- Research issues and alternative tax treatments.
- Formulate conclusions.
- Prepare documentation to support conclusions and tax positions.
- Research relevant professional literature.

WHICH PRONOUNCEMENTS ARE TESTED?

Following is the section of the AICPA's pronouncement policy that is relevant to the Regulation section:

For the federal taxation area, the Internal Revenue Code and Treasury Regulations in effect six months before the beginning of the current window may be tested on the Uniform CPA Examination.

*For all other materials covered in the Regulation and Business Environment and Concepts sections, material eligible to be tested includes federal laws in the window beginning six months after their **effective** date and uniform acts in the window beginning one year after their adoption by a simple majority of the jurisdictions.*

AICPA's NONDISCLOSURE AGREEMENT

The following is taken verbatim from the Uniform CPA Examination: Candidate Bulletin dated May 2015. It is reproduced here to remind all CPA candidates about the AICPA's strict policy of nondisclosure, which Gleim consistently supports and upholds.

Policy Statement and Agreement Regarding Exam Confidentiality and the Taking of Breaks

I hereby agree that I will maintain the confidentiality of the Uniform CPA Examination. In addition, I agree that I will not:

- *Divulge the nature or content of any Uniform CPA Examination question or answer under any circumstance*
- *Engage in any unauthorized communication during testing*
- *Refer to unauthorized materials or use unauthorized equipment during testing; or*
- *Remove or attempt to remove any Uniform CPA Examination materials, notes, or any other items from the examination room*

I understand and agree that liability for test administration activities, including but not limited to the adequacy or accuracy of test materials and equipment, and the accuracy of scoring and score reporting, will be limited to score correction or test retake at no additional fee. I waive any and all right to all other claims.

I further agree to report to the AICPA any examination question disclosures, or solicitations for disclosure of which I become aware.

I affirm that I have had the opportunity to read the Candidate Bulletin and I agree to all of its terms and conditions.

I understand that breaks are only allowed between testlets. I understand that I will be asked to complete any open testlet before leaving the testing room for a break.

In addition, I understand that failure to comply with this Policy Statement and Agreement may result in invalidation of my grades, disqualification from future examinations, expulsion from the testing facility and possible civil or criminal penalties.

HOW TO USE THE GLEIM REVIEW SYSTEM

To ensure that you are using your time effectively, we have formulated a three-step process to apply to each study unit that includes all components together. You will be guided through these steps when you access your online course.

Step 1: Diagnostic

a. Multiple-Choice Quiz #1 (30 minutes, plus 10 minutes for review) – Complete Multiple-Choice Quiz #1 in 30 minutes. This is a diagnostic quiz, so it is expected that your scores will be lower.

   1) Immediately following the quiz, review the questions you marked and/or answered incorrectly. This step is essential to identifying your weak areas. Refer to "Learning from Your Mistakes" on page 8 for tips.

Step 2: Comprehension

a. Audiovisual Presentation (30 minutes) – This presentation provides an overview of the study unit. (Use the Gleim CPA Audio Lectures instead if you're on the go!)

b. Gleim Instruct – CPA Video Series (30-90 minutes) – These videos are for customers who prefer live instruction to the slide-show style of the Audiovisual Presentations. Gleim Instruct videos include lectures featuring professors from accredited universities, multiple-choice questions, and detailed examples.

c. Focus Questions (45 minutes) – Complete the Focus Questions and receive immediate feedback.

d. Knowledge Transfer Outline (60-90 minutes) – Study the Knowledge Transfer Outline, particularly the troublesome areas identified from your Multiple-Choice Quiz #1 in Step 1. The Knowledge Transfer Outlines can be studied either online or in the books.

e. Multiple-Choice Quiz #2 (30 minutes, plus 10 minutes for review) – Complete Multiple-Choice Quiz #2 in Gleim Online.

   1) Immediately following the quiz, review the questions you marked and/or answered incorrectly. This step is an essential learning activity. Refer to "Learning from Your Mistakes" on page 8 for tips.

Step 3: Application

a. Task-Based Simulations (90 minutes, including 10 minutes for review) – Complete and review the simulation section.

b. CPA Test Prep (60 minutes, plus 20 minutes for review) – Complete two 20-question quizzes in CPA Test Prep, a component of the Mega Test Bank, using the Practice Exam feature. Spend 30 minutes taking each quiz and then spend about 10 minutes reviewing each quiz as needed.

Additional Assistance

1. Gleim Simulation Bank– For additional practice, complete task-based simulations from the Simulation Bank, a component of the Mega Test Bank, as needed.
2. Core Concepts – These consolidated documents provide an overview of the key points of each subunit that serve as a foundation for learning.

Final Review

1. CPA Exam Rehearsal (3 hours/180 minutes) – Take the Exam Rehearsal at the beginning of your final review stage. It contains three testlets with 24 multiple-choice questions each and one testlet with six task-based simulations, just like the Regulation section of the CPA exam. This will help you identify where you should focus during the remainder of your final review.

2. CPA Mega Test Bank (10-20 hours) – Use the Mega Test Bank to focus on your weak areas identified from your Exam Rehearsal. This software features adaptive learning technology and gives you access to the largest test bank of multiple-choice and task-based simulations so you can work on the topics and question-answering techniques you struggle with the most. Also, be sure to do a cumulative review to refresh yourself with topics you learned at the beginning of your studies. View your performance chart to make sure you are scoring 75% or higher.

The times mentioned above and on the previous page are recommendations based on prior candidate feedback and how long you have to answer questions on the actual exam. Each candidate's time spent in any area will vary depending on proficiency and familiarity with the subject matter.

GLEIM KNOWLEDGE TRANSFER OUTLINES

This edition of the CPA Review book has the following features to make studying easier:

1. **Backgrounds:** In certain instances, we have provided historical background or supplemental information. This information is intended to illuminate the topic under discussion and is set off in bordered boxes with shaded headings. This material does not need to be memorized for the exam.

Background

Prior to passage of the Securities Act of 1933 and the Securities Exchange Act of 1934, issuers were required to do little financial reporting. The stock market crash of 1929 and the ensuing Great Depression left many with the impression that reporting by publicly traded companies had been misleading or even fraudulent. The securities acts made two major changes: They assigned the power of accounting rule-making to the SEC and required most issuers to have their financial statements audited by independent CPAs.

2. **Examples:** Illustrative examples, both hypothetical and those drawn from actual events, are set off in shaded, bordered boxes.

EXAMPLE

Teresa, a CPA, is the paid preparer for Smith, Inc., an S Corporation. John Smith owns 80% of Smith. Smith's net income is $150,000. Thus, Teresa is a tax preparer with respect to John Smith's return.

3. **Gleim Success Tips:** These tips supplement the core exam material by suggesting how certain topics might be presented on the exam or how you should prepare for an issue.

The AICPA has tested CPA candidates on what the plaintiff needs to prove to win a judgment against a CPA in a suit under Section 11 of the 1933 act. Thus, candidates should **know and be able to cite Section 11 of the 1933 act.**

4. **Detailed Table of Contents:** This information at the beginning of the book is a complete listing of all study units and subunits in the Gleim CPA REG Review program. Use this list as a study aid to mark off your progress and to provide jumping-off points for review.

5. We have also provided additional study materials to supplement the Knowledge Transfer Outlines within the online course. For example, you will find Core Concepts for each study unit. These consolidated documents provide an overview of the key points of each subunit that serve as the foundation for learning. As part of your review, you should make sure that you understand each of them.

TIME BUDGETING AND QUESTION-ANSWERING TECHNIQUES FOR REGULATION

Expect three testlets of 24 multiple-choice questions each and one testlet with six Task-Based Simulations (TBS) on the Regulation section with a 180-minute time allocation. Study Units 4 and 5 in *How to Pass the CPA Exam: A System for Success* contain additional discussion of how to maximize your score on multiple-choice questions and simulations.

1. **Budget your time.** We make this point with emphasis. Just as you would fill up your gas tank prior to reaching empty, so too would you finish your exam before time expires.
   a. Here is our suggested time allocation for Regulation:

	Minutes	Start Time	
Testlet 1 (MC)	35	3 hours	0 minutes
Testlet 2 (MC)	35	2 hours	25 minutes
Testlet 3 (MC)	35	1 hour	50 minutes
Testlet 4 (TBS)	60	1 hour	15 minutes
***Extra time	15	0 hours	15 minutes

   b. Before beginning your first testlet of multiple-choice questions, prepare a Gleim Time Management Sheet as recommended in Study Unit 7 of *How to Pass the CPA Exam: A System for Success*.
   c. As you work through the individual items, monitor your time. In Regulation, we suggest 35 minutes for each testlet of 24 questions. If you answer five items in 7 minutes, you are fine, but if you spend 10 minutes on five items, you need to speed up.

   ***Remember to allocate your budgeted extra time, as needed, to each testlet. Your goal is to answer all of the items and achieve the maximum score possible.

2. **Answer the questions in consecutive order.**
   a. Do **not** agonize over any one item. Stay within your time budget.
   b. Flag for review any questions you are unsure of and return to them later as time allows.
      1) Once you have selected either the Continue or Quit option, you will no longer be able to review or change any answers in the completed testlet.
   c. Never leave a multiple-choice question unanswered. **Make your best educated guess in the time allowed.** Remember that your score is based on the number of correct responses. You will not be penalized for guessing incorrectly.

3. **For each multiple-choice question,**
   a. **Try to ignore the answer choices.** Do not allow the answer choices to affect your reading of the question.
      1) If four answer choices are presented, three of them are incorrect. These choices are called **distractors** for good reason. Often, distractors are written to appear correct at first glance until further analysis.
      2) In computational items, the distractors are carefully calculated such that they are the result of making common mistakes. Be careful, and double-check your computations if time permits.
   b. **Read the question** carefully to determine the precise requirement.
      1) Focusing on what is required enables you to ignore extraneous information, to focus on the relevant facts, and to proceed directly to determining the correct answer.
         a) Be especially careful to note when the requirement is an **exception**; e.g., "Which of the following is **not** an above-the-line deduction?"

c. **Determine the correct answer** before looking at the answer choices.

d. **Read the answer choices carefully.**

1) Even if the first answer appears to be the correct choice, do **not** skip the remaining answer choices. Questions often ask for the "best" of the choices provided. Thus, each choice requires your consideration.

2) Treat each answer choice as a true/false question as you analyze it.

e. **Click on the best answer.**

1) You have a 25% chance of answering the question correctly by guessing blindly; improve your odds with educated guessing.

2) For many multiple-choice questions, two answer choices can be eliminated with minimal effort, thereby increasing your educated guess to a 50-50 proposition.

4. After you have answered all the items in a testlet, consult the question status list at the bottom of each multiple-choice question screen **before** clicking the "Exit" button, which permanently ends the testlet.

   a. Go back to the flagged questions and finalize your answer choices.

   b. Verify that all questions have been answered.

5. **If you don't know the answer,**

   a. Make an educated guess, which means selecting the best possible answer. First, rule out answers that you think are incorrect. Second, speculate on what the AICPA is looking for and/or the rationale behind the question. Third, select the best answer or guess between equally appealing answers. Your first guess is usually the most intuitive. If you cannot make an educated guess, read the stem and each answer and pick the most intuitive answer.

   b. Make sure you accomplish this step within your predetermined time budget per testlet.

LEARNING FROM YOUR MISTAKES

Learning from questions you answer incorrectly is very important. Each question you answer incorrectly is an **opportunity** to avoid missing actual test questions on your CPA exam. Thus, you should carefully study the answer explanations provided until you understand why the original answer you chose is wrong as well as why the correct answer indicated is correct. This learning technique is the difference between passing and failing for many CPA candidates.

Also, you **must** determine why you answered questions incorrectly and learn how to avoid the same error in the future. Reasons for missing questions include

1. Misreading the requirement (stem)
2. Not understanding what is required
3. Making a math error
4. Applying the wrong rule or concept
5. Being distracted by one or more of the answers
6. Incorrectly eliminating answers from consideration
7. Not having any knowledge of the topic tested
8. Using a poor educated guessing strategy

It is also important to verify that you answered correctly for the right reasons (i.e., read the discussion provided for the correct answers). Otherwise, if the material is tested on the CPA exam in a different manner, you may not answer it correctly.

HOW TO BE IN CONTROL

Remember, you must be in control to be successful during exam preparation and execution. Perhaps more importantly, control can also contribute greatly to your personal and other professional goals. Control is the process whereby you

1. Develop expectations, standards, budgets, and plans
2. Undertake activity, production, study, and learning
3. Measure the activity, production, output, and knowledge
4. Compare actual activity with expected and budgeted activity
5. Modify the activity, behavior, or study to better achieve the expected or desired outcome
6. Revise expectations and standards in light of actual experience
7. Continue the process or restart the process in the future

Exercising control will ultimately develop the confidence you need to outperform most other CPA candidates and PASS the CPA exam! Obtain our *How to Pass the CPA Exam: A System for Success* booklet for a more detailed discussion of control and other exam tactics.

IF YOU HAVE QUESTIONS ABOUT GLEIM MATERIALS

Gleim has an efficient and effective way for candidates who have purchased the Premium CPA Review System to submit an inquiry and receive a response regarding Gleim materials **directly through their course**. This system also allows you to view your Q&A session in your Gleim Personal Classroom.

Questions regarding the information in this Introduction (study suggestions, studying plans, exam specifics) should be emailed to personalcounselor@gleim.com.

Questions concerning orders, prices, shipments, or payments should be sent via email to customerservice@gleim.com and will be promptly handled by our competent and courteous customer service staff.

For technical support, you may use our automated technical support service at www.gleim.com/support, email us at support@gleim.com, or call us at (800) 874-5346.

FEEDBACK

Please fill out our online feedback form (www.gleim.com/feedbackREG) IMMEDIATELY after you take the CPA Regulation section so we can adapt our material based on where candidates say we need to increase or decrease coverage. Our approach has been approved by the AICPA.

STUDY UNIT ONE
ETHICS AND PROFESSIONAL RESPONSIBILITIES

(15 pages of outline)

When a dispute or disagreement over tax issues arises, a taxpayer may have to appear before the IRS. Enrolled agents (EAs), CPAs, attorneys, and other individuals authorized to practice before the IRS may represent taxpayers. This study unit discusses the various individuals who may practice before the IRS and their standards of conduct.

1.1 CIRCULAR 230

1. **Rules Governing Authority to Practice**
   a. Practice before the **Internal Revenue Service (IRS)** includes presenting to the IRS or any of its officers or employees all matters relating to a client's rights, privileges, or liabilities.
2. **Practice before the IRS**
   a. Rules for practice before the IRS are in Treasury Department Circular 230.
      1) A person is practicing before the IRS if (s)he
         a) Communicates with the IRS for a taxpayer regarding taxpayer rights under laws and regulations administered by the IRS.
         b) Represents a taxpayer at conferences, hearings, or meetings with the IRS.
         c) Prepares necessary documents and files them with the IRS for a taxpayer.
         d) Renders written advice with respect to any entity, transaction, plan, or arrangement or other plan or arrangement having a potential for tax avoidance or evasion.
      2) The following do **not** constitute practicing before the IRS:
         a) Preparing a tax return, an amended return, or a claim for refund
         b) Furnishing information upon request of the IRS
         c) Appearing as a witness for a person
      3) **All or Substantially All of a Return**
         a) Any individual who for compensation prepares or assists with the preparation of all or substantially all of a tax return or claim for refund (1) must have a preparer tax identification number and (2) is subject to (a) the duties and restrictions relating to practice and (b) the sanctions for violation of the regulations.

3. **Persons Authorized to Practice**
   a. The following persons may practice before the IRS:
      1) Attorneys
         a) An attorney is a member in good standing of the bar of the highest court of any state, possession, territory, commonwealth, or the District of Columbia.
         b) An attorney who is not under suspension or disbarment from practice before the IRS may practice before the IRS.
      2) CPAs
         a) A CPA who is suspended from practice by the IRS Office of Professional Responsibility is not eligible to practice before the IRS.
      3) Enrolled agents and others specifically permitted
         a) An enrolled agent is an individual, other than an attorney or a CPA, who is eligible, qualified, and certified as authorized to represent another in practice before the IRS.
         b) This designation is issued by the IRS to individuals passing the EA exam.

Practice before the IRS Comparison		
Practitioners		
	Attorney, CPA, EA	**Noncertified**
Allowed Practice	Unlimited	Limited
	Preparation of return or claim for refund	
	a. All or substantially all b. Sign returns, refunds, etc., for submission	a. All or substantially all b. Sign returns, refunds, etc., for submission
	Representation	
	a. Before anyone at the IRS (e.g., revenue agents, customer service representatives, employees, appeals officers, revenue officers, counsel officers)	a. Before IRS revenue agents, customer service representatives, and employees
	b. Anytime (e.g., examination, appeals)	b. During examination
	c. Any return or refund for any period	c. Signed return or refund for the period under examination
	Tax advice	
	a. Unlimited (e.g., return preparation, tax planning)	a. Limited to return or refund preparation needs

   b. To practice before the IRS, an attorney or a CPA must
      1) File a written declaration for each party (s)he represents that (s)he
         a) Is currently qualified.
         b) Has been authorized to represent the party.
      2) Not be suspended or disbarred.
   c. Also authorized to practice before the IRS are enrolled actuaries and enrolled retirement plan agents (for limited purposes).

d. The IRS may authorize any person to represent another without enrollment. Individuals who are under suspension or disbarment from practice before the IRS may not engage in limited practice before the IRS. Listed below are a few of the situations in which representation by an individual without enrollment has been authorized:

1) Family. An individual may represent, without compensation, an immediate family member.
2) Employee. An employee may represent his or her regular full-time employer.
3) Practitioner. A practitioner, properly authorized by the taxpayer, who (a) signed a return as a preparer or (b) prepares a return but is not required (by the instructions to the return or regulations) to sign the return may represent the taxpayer with respect to tax liability for the period covered by the return.
4) Others. An individual may be authorized by the Commissioner of the IRS to represent others in a particular matter.

e. Unauthorized persons may not practice before the IRS.

4. **Rules of Conduct**

a. Rules for conduct of an attorney, a CPA, or an enrolled agent practicing before the IRS are provided in Part 10 of Circular 230. Unless otherwise indicated, a **practitioner** is a person authorized to practice before the IRS.

b. The person representing a taxpayer before the IRS must be qualified, e.g., a CPA.

c. **Conflict of Interest**

1) A practitioner may represent conflicting interests before the IRS only if
   a) All directly affected parties provide informed, written consent at the time the existence of the conflict is known by the practitioner (written consent must be within 30 days of informed consent);
   b) The representation is not prohibited by law; and
   c) The practitioner reasonably believes that (s)he can provide competent and diligent representation to each client.
2) The return preparer is not required to disclose the conflict of interest.

d. **Diligence** must be exercised in preparing and in assisting in preparing, approving, and filing returns, documents, and other papers relating to IRS matters.

1) Diligence is presumed if the practitioner (a) relies upon the work product of another person and (b) uses reasonable care in engaging, supervising, training, and evaluating the person.
2) A practitioner may not unreasonably delay the prompt disposition of any matter before the IRS.

e. **Information or records** properly and lawfully requested by a duly authorized officer or employee of the IRS must be promptly submitted.

1) However, if reasonable basis exists for a good-faith belief that (a) the information is privileged or (b) the request is not proper and lawful, the practitioner is excused from submitting the requested information.
2) A practitioner also is required to provide information about the identity of persons that the practitioner reasonably believes may have possession or control of the requested information if the practitioner does not.

f. A practitioner must **not** negotiate, including by endorsement, any income tax refund check issued to a client.

g. A practitioner who knows that a client (1) has **not complied** with the revenue laws of the U.S. or (2) has made an error or omission is required promptly to advise the client of noncompliance and the consequences of such noncompliance, error, or omission under the Code and regulations.
   1) Circular 230 does not require the practitioner to notify the IRS.
h. A practitioner may not charge an unconscionable **fee** in connection with any matter before the IRS.
   1) A practitioner may **not** charge a **contingent** fee in relation to any matter before the IRS except in relation to an IRS examination of (a) an original return, (b) an amended return, or (c) a claim for refund or credit.
i. A practitioner must return a **client's records** on request, regardless of any fee dispute. Records deemed returnable for purposes of this requirement are those records necessary for a client to comply with his or her federal tax obligations.
   1) Returns or other documents **prepared** by the practitioner that the practitioner is withholding pending payment of a fee are not included (provided state law permits retention of records in a fee dispute).
j. Circular 230 allows **advertising** and **solicitation**.
   1) False, fraudulent, misleading, deceptive, or unfair statements or claims are not allowed. Claims must be subject to factual verification.
   2) Specialized expertise may not be claimed except as authorized by federal or state agencies having jurisdiction over the practitioner.
   3) Each of the following fees may be advertised:
      a) Fixed fees for specific routine services
      b) A range of fees for particular services
      c) The fee for an initial consultation
      d) Hourly rates
      e) Availability of a written fee schedule
   4) Fee information may be communicated in professional lists, telephone directories, print media, mailings, electronic mail, facsimile, hand delivered flyers, radio, television, and any other method.
   5) A practitioner may not assist or accept assistance from any person or entity that the practitioner knows has obtained clients in violation of Circular 230's advertising and solicitation rules.

5. **Best Practices for Tax Advisors**
   a. Tax advisors should provide clients with the highest quality representation regarding federal tax issues. They should adhere to best practices in providing an opinion and preparing or assisting in the preparation of a submission to the IRS.
   b. Best practices include
      1) Communicating clearly with the client about the terms of the engagement.
      2) (a) Establishing the facts, (b) determining which facts are relevant, (c) evaluating the reasonableness of any assumptions or representations, (d) relating applicable law to the relevant facts, and (e) arriving at a conclusion supported by the law and the facts.
      3) Advising the client regarding the importance of the conclusions reached, including, for example, whether a taxpayer may avoid accuracy-related penalties under the **Internal Revenue Code (IRC)** if a taxpayer acts in reliance on the advice.
      4) Acting fairly and with integrity in practice before the IRS.
   c. Tax advisors with responsibility for overseeing a firm's provision of advice about federal tax issues should take reasonable steps to ensure that the firm's procedures for all members, associates, and employees are consistent with the best practices.

6. **Written Tax Advice**
   a. When providing written advice about any federal tax matter, a practitioner must
      1) Base the advice on reasonable assumptions,
      2) Reasonably consider all relevant facts that are known or should be known, and
      3) Use reasonable efforts to identify and determine the relevant facts.
   b. The advice cannot rely upon representations, statements, findings, or agreements that (1) are unreasonable or (2) are known to be incorrect, inconsistent, or incomplete.
   c. The advice must not consider the possibility that (1) a tax return will not be audited or (2) a matter will not be raised during the audit in evaluating a federal tax matter.
   d. When providing written advice, a practitioner may rely in good faith on the advice of another practitioner only if that advice is reasonable given all the facts and circumstances.
   e. The practitioner cannot rely on the advice of a person who (1) the practitioner knows or should know is not competent to provide the advice or (2) has an unresolved conflict of interest.
7. **Sanctions for Violations**
   a. An attorney, CPA, or enrolled agent may be censured (public reprimand), suspended, or disbarred from practice before the IRS for willful violations of any of the regulations contained in Circular 230.
   b. The Secretary of the Treasury may censure, suspend, or disbar from practice before the IRS any attorney, CPA, or enrolled agent who
      1) Is shown to be incompetent or disreputable.
      2) Refuses to comply with the rules and regulations relating to practice before the IRS.
      3) Willfully and knowingly, with intent to defraud, deceives, misleads, or threatens any claimant or potential claimant.
   c. The following is a brief list of conduct that may result in suspension or disbarment:
      1) Being convicted of an offense involving dishonesty or breach of trust
      2) Providing false or misleading information to the Treasury Department, including the IRS
      3) Negotiating a client's refund check or not promptly remitting a refund check
      4) Circulating or publishing matter related to practice before the IRS that is deemed libelous or malicious
      5) Using abusive language
      6) Suspension from practice as a certified public accountant by any state licensing authority, any Federal court of record, or any Federal agency, body, or board
      7) Conviction of any felony involving conduct that renders the practitioner unfit to practice before the IRS
      8) Attempting to influence the official action of any IRS employee by bestowing a gift, favor, or anything of value
   d. A notice of disbarment or suspension of a CPA from practice before the IRS is issued to (1) IRS employees, (2) interested departments and agencies of the federal government, and (3) state licensing authorities.

Stop and review! You have completed the outline for this subunit. Study multiple-choice questions 1 through 7 beginning on page 26.

1.2 AICPA STANDARDS FOR TAX SERVICES

1. **Statements on Standards for Tax Services**
   a. The AICPA has issued seven **Statements on Standards for Tax Services (SSTSs)**, which are enforceable under the AICPA's *Code of Professional Conduct*.
2. **Tax Return Positions**
   a. According to the **Small Business and Work Opportunity Act of 2007** (as amended),
      1) A position is treated as unreasonable unless
         a) Substantial authority exists or existed for the position or
         b) The position was properly disclosed and had a reasonable basis.
      2) A tax shelter position is treated as unreasonable unless it is reasonable to believe that the position would more likely than not be sustained on its merits.
   b. An AICPA member should advise the taxpayer of penalties associated with a recommended position.
   c. A member should not recommend a position that
      1) Exploits the taxing authority's audit selection process or
      2) Is advanced solely to obtain leverage in the bargaining process.
   d. A member has the right and responsibility to be an advocate for the taxpayer.
   e. When the standards of a taxing authority differ from AICPA standards, the member should comply with the more stringent standard.
3. **Answers to Questions on Returns**
   a. A member should make a **reasonable effort** to obtain from the taxpayer appropriate answers to all questions on a tax return before signing as preparer.
      1) An omission may reduce the quality of the return because a question may be important in calculating taxable income or loss or the tax liability.
      2) The answer may be necessary to complete the return or avoid a penalty.
      3) A member may need to sign a preparer's declaration that the return is true, correct, and complete.
   b. Reasonable grounds for omitting an answer include the following:
      1) Information is not readily available, and the answer is insignificant with respect to taxable income or loss or the tax liability.
      2) Uncertainty exists about the meaning of the question in relation to the return.
      3) The answer to the question is extensive, and the return states that the data will be supplied upon examination.
   c. A taxpayer is not required to explain on the return the **omission of an answer** when **reasonable grounds** exist for the omission.
      1) The member should consider whether the omission causes the return to be incomplete.
4. **Certain Procedural Aspects of Preparing Returns**
   a. A member may in good faith **rely, without verification,** on information provided by the taxpayer or third parties.
      1) **Reasonable inquiries** should be made if information appears to be incorrect, incomplete, or inconsistent on its face or on the basis of other facts known.
         a) Prior returns should be consulted if feasible.
   b. Inquiries should be made to determine whether the taxpayer has met the requirements for the tax treatment of an item, for example, to maintain books, records, or documentation to **support deductions**.

c. A member who prepares a return should consider information known from **another taxpayer's return** if
   1) It is relevant,
   2) Its consideration is necessary, and
   3) Its use does not violate any law or rule of confidentiality.

5. **Use of Estimates**
   a. A member may use the taxpayer's estimates if it is **impracticable to obtain exact data** and the estimates are reasonable under the facts.
      1) Estimates should be presented so as not to imply greater accuracy than exists.
      2) The taxpayer is responsible for providing the estimated data.

6. **Departure from a Position Previously Concluded in an Administrative Proceeding or Court Decision**
   a. The treatment of an item determined in an administrative proceeding or a court decision does not restrict the recommendation of a **different tax treatment** in later years.
      1) However, the taxpayer may be bound to a specified treatment in the later year, e.g., by a formal closing agreement reached in the proceeding or decision.

7. **Knowledge of Error: Return Preparation and Administrative Proceedings**
   a. The member should inform the taxpayer upon becoming aware (1) of an error in a **previously filed return**, (2) of an error in a return subject to an administrative proceeding, or (3) that the taxpayer **did not file** a required return.
      1) The member should advise the taxpayer about consequences and recommend measures to take.
      2) The member is **not obligated** to inform the taxing authority and may not do so without the taxpayer's permission, unless required by law.
      3) If the member is requested to prepare a return when the taxpayer has **not corrected a previous year's error**, the member should consider whether to continue a professional relationship with the taxpayer or withdraw.
      4) If the member prepares the **current return**, the member should take reasonable steps to ensure that the error is not repeated.
      5) **Errors** include a position, omission, or accounting method that, when the return is filed, does not meet AICPA standards. They also include positions on prior returns that no longer meet those standards because of retroactive legislation, judicial decisions, or administrative pronouncements.
         a) An error does not include an item with an **insignificant** effect.

8. **Form and Content of Advice to Clients**
   a. When providing tax advice to a taxpayer, a member should use judgment to ensure that the advice reflects **professional competence** and meets the taxpayer's **needs**.
      1) When advising or consulting on tax matters, the member should follow the guidance on tax return positions.
      2) A member is not obligated to communicate with the taxpayer when **subsequent developments** affect previous advice.
         a) However, (s)he is obligated to do so when helping to implement the plans associated with the advice or when undertaking the obligation by specific agreement.

3) Tax advice may be oral or written.

   a) But advice about important, unusual, or complicated transactions preferably should be in a writing that complies with the taxing authority's guidance.

Stop and review! You have completed the outline for this subunit. Study multiple-choice questions 8 through 13 beginning on page 28.

1.3 TAX RETURN PREPARERS

1. **Tax Return Preparers**

   a. A tax return preparer is any person who prepares for compensation, or employs one or more persons to prepare for compensation, all or a substantial portion of any return of tax or claim for refund under the **Internal Revenue Code (IRC)**.

   b. Preparation with respect to the following is within the scope of the rules governing return preparers:

Individual income tax	Corporate income tax
Individual returns	Corporate returns
Partnership returns	DISC returns
S corporation returns	Estate taxes
Employment tax	Excise taxes
Gift tax	

   c. Persons Subject to the Rule

      1) Nonpreparers

         a) Planning. A person who merely gives an opinion about events that have not happened is not a preparer.

         b) Clerical. A person who merely provides typing, reproducing, or mechanical assistance is not a preparer.

      2) A person who provides to a taxpayer or other preparer sufficient information and advice so that completion of the return is simply a mechanical matter is a return preparer.

      3) A person who has primary responsibility for the overall return or claim for refund is the **signing** tax return preparer.

      4) A **nonsigning** tax return preparer is an individual who prepares all or a substantial portion of a return or claim for refund. Examples include preparers who provide advice that constitutes a substantial portion of the return.

         a) An **insubstantial portion** is

            i) Less than $10,000 or

            ii) Less than $400,000 and also less than 20% of the gross income on the return.

         b) Whether a position is substantial also may be considered when an individual prepares entries on one return that substantially affect an entry or entries on a second return.

         c) Length and complexity of the portion are compared with the return as a whole.

      5) Preparation outside the U.S. is included.

EXAMPLE

Teresa, a CPA, is the paid preparer for Smith, Inc., an S Corporation. John Smith owns 80% of Smith. Smith's net income is $150,000. Thus, Teresa is a tax preparer with respect to John Smith's return.

6) Primary Responsibility

   a) If more than one tax return preparer is involved, the individual who has primary responsibility for overall substantive accuracy is required to sign the return or claim for refund.

EXAMPLE

Bob just passed the CPA exam and has become licensed in his state as a CPA. The managing partner asked him to prepare Ms. Daisy's return. Because the managing partner reviews Bob's work on the return and the information provided and then applies this information to the return, the managing partner is considered to be the signing preparer.

7) Compensation

   a) If no compensation is provided for a person (or for his or her employee) to prepare a return or claim for refund, the person is not subject to the return preparer rules.

   b) Without an explicit or implicit agreement for compensation, a person is not a preparer even if (s)he receives a gift, return service, or favor.

8) A person can be a return preparer without regard to educational qualifications or professional status.

d. Persons **Not** Subject to the Rule

1) The following are not return preparers according to the tax code:

   a) An employee who prepares a return for the employer by whom (s)he is regularly and continuously employed

   b) A fiduciary who prepares a return or refund claim for any person (the trust)

   c) A person who prepares a refund claim in response to a notice of deficiency issued to another

   d) A person who provides typing, reproducing, or other mechanical assistance

2. **Tax Return Positions**

a. Significant aspects of return preparation include (1) making factual inquiries and (2) taking a position relative to tax law.

b. A tax return preparer may rely, if in good faith, on information provided by the taxpayer without having to obtain third-party verification.

1) However, the preparer may not ignore the implications of the information.

2) The preparer must make reasonable inquiries if the information appears inaccurate or incomplete.

3) The preparer should make appropriate inquiries of the taxpayer to determine the existence of facts and circumstances required by an IRC section or regulations incidental to a **deduction** (e.g., substantiating documentary evidence) even if for a minimal amount.

c. A return preparer may not adopt a position without substantial authority for the position.

1) Whether a position meets the **reasonable belief of success** requirement is essentially a legal question.

   a) The issue is whether substantial authority supporting the position outweighs authority contrary to it.

b) What constitutes substantial authority is defined by statute and IRS statements.

i) A revenue ruling, for example, is legal authority that, with other authority, may be substantial.

c) A frivolous position (patently without merit) fails the test.

2) A **more likely than not** standard applies to a tax shelter or a reportable transaction.

a) Disclosure of a position may shield a preparer from liability for a nonfrivolous position when this standard is not met.

i) However, a tax return preparer theoretically is not required to notify the IRS when a taxpayer's liability is understated.

d. Circular 230 addresses the possibility of an omission from a taxpayer's tax return in Section 10.21.

1) When a practitioner discovers that a client has made an error in or omission from any document filed with the IRS, (s)he must notify the client of the error or omission immediately.

a) The practitioner also must advise the client of the consequences provided by the IRC and regulations.

3. **Procedural Requirements**

a. A return preparer is required to sign the return or claim for refund after it has been completed and before it is presented to the taxpayer [Reg. 1.6695-1(b)(1)].

b. A return or refund claim prepared by a return preparer and filed with the IRS must include the return preparer's identifying number.

c. A return preparer is required to provide a completed copy of the return or refund claim to the taxpayer no later than the time it is presented for the taxpayer's signature.

d. A person who employs one or more return preparers is required to retain a record of (1) the name, (2) identifying number, and (3) principal place of work of each employed tax return preparer [Reg. 1.6060-1(a)(l)(i)].

e. A return preparer is required to retain a completed copy of each return or claim prepared for 3 years after the close of the return period [Sec. 6107(b)].

1) An alternative is to keep a list that includes, for the returns and claims prepared, the following information [Reg. 1.6107-1(b)(1)(B)]:

a) The taxpayers' names
b) Taxpayer identification numbers
c) Their tax years
d) Types of returns or claims prepared

2) The return period is the 12-month period beginning on July 1 each year.

4. **Penalties**

a. Tax return preparers are subject to severe penalties for violations. The degree of severity varies among the penalties. Also subject to penalties are individuals with overall supervisory responsibility for advice given by a firm.

b. Taking an **undisclosed** position **without a reasonable belief** that substantial authority exists that it will be sustained on its merits results in a penalty of an amount equal to the greater of $1,000 or 50% of the income to be derived.

1) If the position is **disclosed**, its tax treatment must have a **reasonable basis**.
2) The penalty does not apply if the preparer proves the following:

a) (S)he acted in good faith, and
b) Reasonable cause exists for the understatement.

c. **Negligence**

1) Negligence includes any failure to make a reasonable attempt to (a) comply with the provisions of the internal revenue laws or (b) exercise ordinary and reasonable care in the preparation of a return.

d. If the understatement was caused by the preparer's **willful or reckless** conduct, the penalty is the greater of $5,000 or 50% of the income to be derived.

e. **Frivolous Submission** (Returns and Documents)

1) Filing a frivolous return is penalized. A frivolous return (1) omits information necessary to determine the taxpayer's tax liability, (2) shows a substantially incorrect tax or willful understatement of tax liability, (3) is based on a frivolous position (e.g., that wages are not income), or (4) is based on the taxpayer's desire to impede the collection of tax.

f. The tax code provides that any tax return preparer who endorses or otherwise **negotiates** any check issued to a taxpayer with respect to taxes imposed by the IRC is subject to a penalty. Furthermore, any tax return preparer who operates a check cashing agency that cashes, endorses, or negotiates tax refund checks for returns prepared also is subject to a penalty.

g. **Aiding or abetting** in preparation of any document is subject to a penalty if using the document would result in an **understatement** of tax liability.

1) Any act that constitutes a **willful** attempt to evade federal tax liability, even that of another person, is subject to criminal penalties, including imprisonment. Furthermore, any person who willfully aids or assists in preparation or presentation of a materially false or fraudulent return is guilty of a felony.
2) Violations of these rules may result in disciplinary action by the director of the IRS, and an injunction may be issued prohibiting the violator from acting as a tax preparer.

h. **Fraud**

1) Fraudulent transactions ordinarily involve a willful or deliberate action with the intent to obtain an unauthorized benefit.

5. **Disclosure of Taxpayer Information**

a. **Penalty**

1) A penalty is imposed on any tax return preparer who discloses or uses any tax return information without the consent of the taxpayer. But the penalty is **not** imposed if the disclosure was specifically for (a) preparing, (b) assisting in preparing, or (c) providing services in connection with the preparation of any tax return of the taxpayer.
2) The penalty is $250 per disclosure, with a maximum of $10,000 per year.
3) If convicted of knowingly or recklessly disclosing the information, a preparer is guilty of a misdemeanor and subject to up to $1,000 in fines and up to a year in prison.

b. **Exceptions**

1) The penalty for disclosure is not imposed if the disclosure was made in the following circumstances:
   a) Under other provisions of the IRC
   b) To a related taxpayer, provided the taxpayer did not expressly prohibit the disclosure
   c) Under a court order
   d) To tax return preparers within the same firm
   e) For the purpose of a quality or peer review to the extent necessary to accomplish the review

c. **Consent**

1) The taxpayer's consent must be a written, formal consent authorizing the disclosure for a specific purpose.

2) The taxpayer must authorize a preparer to

a) Use the taxpayer's information to solicit additional current business from the taxpayer in matters not related to the IRS.

b) Disclose the information to additional third parties.

c) Disclose the information in connection with another person's return.

d. **Confidentiality**

1) The confidentiality privilege is extended to certain nonattorneys.

a) The privilege may **not** be asserted to prevent the disclosure of information to any regulatory body other than the IRS.

2) In noncriminal tax proceedings before the IRS, a taxpayer is entitled to common-law protections of confidentiality with respect to the tax advice given by any **federally authorized tax practitioner**. They are the same protections a taxpayer would have if the advising individual were an attorney.

a) A federally authorized tax practitioner includes any nonattorney who is authorized to practice before the IRS, such as a CPA.

b) **Tax advice** is advice given by an individual with respect to matters that are within the scope of the individual's authority to practice before the IRS.

3) The privilege also applies in any noncriminal tax proceeding in federal court brought by or against the United States.

Stop and review! You have completed the outline for this subunit. Study multiple-choice questions 14 through 28 beginning on page 29.

1.4 LICENSING AND DISCIPLINARY SYSTEMS

1. **State Boards of Accountancy**

a. State boards of accountancy are governmental agencies that license accountants to use the designation **Certified Public Accountant**. They prohibit non-CPAs from performing the attest function.

1) **Requirements for licensure** vary from state to state. In addition to passing the CPA examination, a candidate may need to satisfy a state's educational, experience, and residency criteria.

2) Moreover, continuing professional education (CPE), peer review, and ethics standards also may vary. Meeting these standards is necessary to remain licensed.

3) State boards can suspend or revoke licensure through administrative process, for example, in board hearings.

4) **State CPA societies** are voluntary, private entities that can admonish, suspend, or expel members.

5) CPA examination questions do not test specific state disciplinary systems.

2. **AICPA Membership Requirements**

   a. The requirements for regular membership include

      1) Holding a valid and current CPA license and passing either the Uniform CPA Exam or the International Qualification Examination (IQEX),
      2) Holding a CPA license in the past that was not revoked for disciplinary reasons and passing either the Uniform CPA Exam or the IQEX, or
      3) Completing the requirements for CPA licensure as defined by the Uniform Accountancy Act (UAA) but having never been licensed.

   b. A member also must

      1) Pass an **examination** on accounting and related topics satisfactory to the AICPA.
      2) Have earned a **bachelor's degree** and at least **150 semester hours of education** at an accredited institution.
      3) Be individually, or as an employee of a firm, enrolled in an AICPA-approved **practice-monitoring program**.
      4) Meet **continuing professional education (CPE)** requirements.
         a) The basic standard is 120 hours (or equivalent) over a 3-year period. CPE compliance should be reasonably expected to maintain the member's competence in his or her area of practice or employment.
      5) Pay dues.
      6) Conform with the bylaws and *Code of Professional Conduct*.

3. **AICPA Disciplinary Mechanisms**

   a. **Professional Ethics Division**

      1) The Professional Ethics Division investigates ethics violations.
      2) It imposes sanctions in less serious cases. For example, it may require an AICPA member to take additional CPE courses as a remedial measure.

   b. **Joint Trial Board**

      1) More serious infractions come before a joint trial board, which can acquit, admonish (censure), suspend, or expel a member. It may also take such other disciplinary, remedial, or corrective action as it deems to be appropriate.
      2) The *CPA Letter* publishes information about suspensions and expulsions.
      3) A decision of a trial board panel may be appealed to the **full trial board**. The determination of this body is conclusive.
      4) Upon the member's exhaustion of legal appeals, **automatic expulsion** without a hearing results when a member has been convicted of, or has received an adverse judgment for,
         a) Committing a felony.
         b) Willfully failing to file a tax return.
         c) Filing a fraudulent tax return on the member's or a client's behalf.
         d) Aiding in preparing a fraudulent tax return for a client.
      5) **Automatic expulsion** also occurs when a member's **CPA certificate is revoked** by action of any governmental agency, e.g., a state board of accountancy.

6) Expulsion from the AICPA or a state society does not bar the individual from the **practice of public accounting**.
   a) A valid state-issued license is required to practice.
   b) Thus, violation of state law issued by a board of accountancy is more serious than expulsion from the AICPA because it may result in revocation of the CPA certificate, which prohibits public practice.
7) **Joint Ethics Enforcement Program (JEEP)**
   a) The AICPA and most state societies have agreements that permit referral of an ethics complaint either to the AICPA or to a state society.
   b) The AICPA handles matters of national concern, those involving two or more states, and those in litigation.
      i) JEEP also promotes formal cooperation between the ethics committees of the AICPA and of the state societies.

4. **Other Disciplinary Bodies**

a. The **SEC**

1) The SEC may seek an **injunction** from a court to prohibit future violations of the securities laws. Moreover, it may conduct **administrative proceedings** that are quasi-judicial.
   a) Such proceedings may result in **suspension** or permanent **revocation** of the right to practice before the SEC, including the right to sign any document filed by an SEC registrant. Sanctions are imposed if the accountant
      i) Does not have the qualifications to represent others.
      ii) Lacks character or integrity.
      iii) Has engaged in unethical or unprofessional conduct.
      iv) Has willfully violated, or willfully aided and abetted the violation of, the federal securities laws or their rules and regulations.
2) Suspension by the SEC also may result from
   a) Conviction of a felony or a misdemeanor involving moral turpitude.
   b) Revocation or suspension of a license to practice.
   c) Being permanently enjoined from violation of the federal securities acts.
3) Some proceedings have prohibited not only individuals but also **accounting firms** from accepting SEC clients. Furthermore, the SEC can initiate administrative proceedings against accounting firms.
   a) The SEC may, for example, prohibit a firm from appearing before the SEC if it engages in unethical or improper professional conduct. Such misconduct may include negligence.
4) The SEC may impose civil penalties in administrative proceedings.
   a) Furthermore, the SEC may order a violator to account for and surrender any profits from wrongdoing and may issue cease-and-desist orders for violations.

b. The **IRS**

1) The IRS may prohibit an accountant from practicing before the IRS if the person is incompetent or disreputable or does not comply with tax rules and regulations.
2) The IRS also may impose fines.

c. The **Public Company Accounting Oversight Board (PCAOB)**

1) The PCAOB was established by the Sarbanes-Oxley Act of 2002 to oversee auditors of issuers. Some of the provisions of the act are described below.
2) The SEC has oversight authority over the PCAOB, including approval of rules, standards, and budgets.
3) Public accounting firms are required to register with the PCAOB to prepare, issue, or participate in audit reports of issuers.
4) The PCAOB has **rule-making authority** regarding quality control, ethics, and auditing standards.
   a) These rules, especially those governing quality control, have great relevance to enforcement actions.
5) The PCAOB annually **inspects** registered CPA firms that regularly provide audit reports for more than 100 issuers. It inspects firms at least triennially that regularly provide audit reports for 100 or fewer issuers. Violations are reported to the SEC and state licensing authorities.
   a) All **attestation engagements** may be reviewed.
   b) The inspection also involves a **quality control assessment**.
   c) Furthermore, the inspection report must include the **firm's response**. The firm then has 12 months to correct the reported weaknesses.
6) The PCAOB has substantially the same **investigatory scope** with respect to accountants as the SEC.
   a) The PCAOB may request that the SEC issue subpoenas to third parties, and it may **deregister** any uncooperative firm.
7) The PCAOB has no power to issue injunctions, but it may initiate **administrative proceedings**.
   a) It may suspend or revoke a firm's registration or seek (1) disassociation of a person from a registered firm, (2) suspension (temporary or permanent) of the firm's registration, or (3) a penalty of up to $15 million.
8) Each registered public accounting firm must **report annually** to the PCAOB.
   a) A firm also may be required to submit **special (event-based) reports**.
      i) Annual reports must provide information about such matters as audit reports issued during the year and disciplinary history of new members of the firm.
      ii) Special reports must be filed within 30 days after reportable events, including the initiation of certain actions against the firm or certain classes of individuals.

Stop and review! You have completed the outline for this subunit. Study multiple-choice questions 29 and 30 on page 34.

QUESTIONS

1.1 Circular 230

1. Frank Maple, CPA, represents his brother Joe Maple and Joe's business partner Bill Smith. Joe Maple and Bill Smith are equal shareholders in the Joe & Bill Corporation. The Internal Revenue Service examined the corporation and determined that one of the shareholders committed fraud, but could not determine which shareholder it was. Frank has made an appointment with the Internal Revenue Service to determine which partner was guilty. Which of the following statements reflects what Frank should do in accordance with Circular 230?

A. Frank should meet with the Internal Revenue Service and try to convince the examiner that each shareholder is equally guilty.

B. Advise Joe & Bill that they should dissolve the corporation, thereby making it difficult for the Internal Revenue Service to pursue the issue.

C. Advise Joe & Bill that he cannot represent them because there is a conflict of interest.

D. Advise Joe & Bill on creating documents that will convince the Internal Revenue Service that neither shareholder is guilty of fraud.

Answer (C) is correct.

REQUIRED: The attorney's action when asked to represent a sibling in an IRS fraud investigation.

DISCUSSION: An agent may represent conflicting interests before the IRS only if all directly interested parties expressly consent in writing after full disclosure. According to Sec. 10.29(a) of Circular 230, a conflict of interest exists if

1. The representation of one client will be directly adverse to another client or
2. There is a significant risk that the representation of one or more clients will be materially limited by the practitioner's responsibilities to another client, a former client or a third person, or by a personal interest of the practitioner.

Frank Maple should determine whether a conflict of interest exists and get all appropriate consents to the representation. Because acquiring the consent of the parties is involved, it is not given as an option. Frank should advise Joe and Bill that he cannot represent them.

2. Mike is a CPA. Widget, Inc., is an accrual-basis taxpayer. In Year 3, while preparing Widget's Year 2 return, Mike discovered that Widget failed to include income on its Year 1 return that Widget received in Year 2 but that should have been included in income in Year 1 under the accrual method of accounting. What must Mike do?

A. Advise Widget of the error and the consequences of the error.

B. Include the income on the Year 2 return.

C. Refuse to prepare Widget's Year 2 return until Widget agrees to amend its Year 1 return to include the amount of income.

D. Change Widget to the cash method of accounting.

Answer (A) is correct.

REQUIRED: The action required by a CPA who knows that a client has not complied with the revenue laws.

DISCUSSION: An agent who knows that a client has not complied with the revenue laws of the U.S. is required to promptly advise the client of noncompliance as well as the consequences of noncompliance under the Code and Regulations. Under Circular 230, the agent is not required to notify the IRS.

Answer (B) is incorrect. An amended return would need to be filed, and the agent would file an amended return at the request of the taxpayer. Answer (C) is incorrect. It is the client's responsibility to request for the amended return to be filed for Year 1. Answer (D) is incorrect. Widget, Inc., may be required to maintain an accrual method of accounting due to the Code and Regulations. Also, amending the Year 1 return would be the only way to properly correct the understatement of income.

3. Which of the following statements is true with respect to a client's request for records of the client that are necessary for the client to comply with his or her Federal tax obligations?

A. The practitioner may never return records of the client to the client even if the client requests prompt return of the records.

B. The existence of a dispute over fees always relieves the practitioner of his or her responsibility to return records of the client to the client.

C. The practitioner must, at the request of the client, promptly return the records of the client to the client unless applicable state law provides otherwise.

D. The practitioner must, at the request of the client, return the records of the client to the client within 3 months of receiving the request.

Answer (C) is correct.

REQUIRED: The true statement about a client's request for records of the client.

DISCUSSION: A practitioner must return a client's records on request, regardless of any fee dispute. Records deemed returnable for purposes of this requirement are those records necessary for a client to comply with his or her federal tax obligations. Returns or other documents prepared by the practitioner that the practitioner is withholding pending payment of a fee are not includible.

Answer (A) is incorrect. The client's records are required to be returned if the taxpayer makes such a request to comply with federal tax laws. Answer (B) is incorrect. A fee dispute does not relieve the practitioner of his responsibility to return documents that the taxpayer needs to comply with federal tax laws. Answer (D) is incorrect. The practitioner must return the documents to the taxpayer as quickly as is reasonable.

4. Identify the appropriate action that a practitioner should take when (s)he becomes aware of an error or omission on a client's return.

A. Amend the return and provide it to the client.

B. Inform the IRS of the noncompliance, error, or omission.

C. Do nothing.

D. Promptly advise the client of such noncompliance, error, or omission and the consequences thereof.

Answer (D) is correct.

REQUIRED: The appropriate action when a practitioner is aware of an error or omission.

DISCUSSION: Section 10.21 of Treasury Department Circular 230 requires an attorney, a certified public accountant, or an enrolled agent who knows that a client has not complied with the revenue laws of the United States to promptly advise the client of the noncompliance, error, or omission and the consequences of the noncompliance, error, or omission as provided in the IRC and regulations.

Answer (A) is incorrect. A practitioner may not amend the return without first informing a client. Answer (B) is incorrect. A practitioner is not required to inform the IRS. Answer (C) is incorrect. A practitioner must promptly advise the client of the noncompliance, error, or omission.

5. Which of the following is **not** an example of disreputable conduct (as described in Sec. 10.51 of Circular 230) for which a CPA may be suspended or disbarred from practice before the IRS?

A. Knowingly giving false or misleading information to the Treasury Department.

B. Willful failure to make a federal tax return in violation of federal revenue laws.

C. Failure to respond to a request by the Director of the Office of Professional Responsibility to provide information.

D. Misappropriation of funds received from a client for the purpose of payment of federal tax.

Answer (C) is correct.

REQUIRED: The action for which a CPA may not be disbarred or suspended from practice.

DISCUSSION: Section 10.51 of Circular 230 lists several examples of disreputable conduct for which a CPA may be disbarred or suspended from practice before the Internal Revenue Service. Failure to respond to a request by the DP to provide information is not disreputable conduct under Sec. 10.51 of Circular 230.

Answer (A) is incorrect. Knowingly giving false or misleading information to the Treasury Department is prohibited by Circular 230. Answer (B) is incorrect. Willful failure to make a federal tax return in violation of federal revenue laws is prohibited by Circular 230. Answer (D) is incorrect. Misappropriation of funds received from a client for the purpose of payment of federal tax is prohibited by Circular 230.

6. A notice of disbarment or suspension of a certified public accountant from practice before the Internal Revenue Service is issued to which of the following?

A. IRS employees.

B. Interested departments and agencies of the federal government.

C. State authorities.

D. All of the answers are correct.

Answer (D) is correct.

REQUIRED: The parties issued a notice of disbarment or suspension of a CPA from practice before the IRS.

DISCUSSION: Sec. 10.80 of Circular 230 outlines the parties that should receive notice of disbarment or suspension. The list includes IRS employees, interested departments and agencies of the federal government, as well as the appropriate state authorities.

7. All of the following are examples of disreputable conduct for which a CPA may be disbarred or suspended from practice before the Internal Revenue Service **except**

A. Soliciting by mailings, the contents of which are designed for the general public.

B. Suggesting that (s)he is improperly able to obtain special consideration from an Internal Revenue Service employee.

C. Maintaining a partnership for the practice of tax law and accounting with a person who is under disbarment from practice before the Internal Revenue Service.

D. Failing to properly and promptly remit funds received from a client for the purpose of payment of taxes.

Answer (A) is correct.

REQUIRED: The action for which a CPA may not be disbarred or suspended from practice.

DISCUSSION: Sec. 10.51 of Circular 230 lists several examples of disreputable conduct for which a CPA may be disbarred or suspended from practice before the Internal Revenue Service. Solicitation by mailings, the contents of which are designed for the general public, is not prohibited under Sec. 10.30(a)(2) and is not disreputable conduct under Sec. 10.51 of Circular 230.

1.2 AICPA Standards for Tax Services

8. When a member of the AICPA prepares a taxpayer's federal income tax return, the member has the responsibility to

A. Be an advocate for the entity's position.

B. Verify the data to be used in preparing the return.

C. Take a position of independent neutrality.

D. Argue the position of the Internal Revenue Service.

Answer (A) is correct.

REQUIRED: The responsibility of a member of the AICPA who prepares a federal income tax return.

DISCUSSION: A member of the AICPA engaged in tax practice has the right and responsibility to be an advocate for the client with regard to any tax return position that meets legal and professional standards.

Answer (B) is incorrect. The data need not be verified unless the information seems incomplete, inconsistent, or incorrect. Answer (C) is incorrect. A member must be independent when performing attestation services, not for tax return preparation services. Answer (D) is incorrect. A member has the right and the responsibility to be an advocate of the client, not the IRS.

9. A member of the AICPA who is engaged to prepare an income tax return has a duty to prepare it in such a manner that the tax is

A. The legal minimum.

B. Computed in conformity with generally accepted accounting principles.

C. Supported by the client's audited financial statements.

D. Not subject to change upon audit.

Answer (A) is correct.

REQUIRED: The duty of a member of the AICPA in preparing a client's income tax return.

DISCUSSION: A member of the AICPA should serve to the best of his or her ability and with professional concern for the taxpayer's best interests, consistent with responsibilities to the tax system. Within the limits of the law and ethical practice, the member should strive for the legal minimum tax, not for tax evasion.

Answer (B) is incorrect. The tax is computed based on statutes and pronouncements of the taxing authority, not GAAP. Answer (C) is incorrect. The tax expense, according to the statements, is based on GAAP. Moreover, the tax preparer need not audit the client's statements. Answer (D) is incorrect. Discovery of errors may necessitate a change.

10. Which of the following is implied when a member of the AICPA signs the preparer's declaration on a federal income tax return?

A. The tax return is not misleading based on all information of which the member has knowledge.

B. The tax return and supporting schedules were prepared in accordance with GAAP.

C. The tax return was examined in accordance with standards established by the AICPA.

D. The tax return was prepared by a member who maintained an impartial attitude.

Answer (A) is correct.

REQUIRED: The implication when a member signs the preparer's declaration on a federal income tax return.

DISCUSSION: According to the Integrity and Objectivity Rule, "In the performance of any professional service, a member shall not knowingly misrepresent facts or subordinate his or her judgment to others."

Answer (B) is incorrect. The tax return and supporting schedules should be prepared in accordance with federal tax law. Answer (C) is incorrect. The member is not required to examine or review documents or other evidence supporting the taxpayer's information. Answer (D) is incorrect. A member in tax practice should take a position of client advocacy, barring any wrongdoing.

11. In accordance with the AICPA's Statements on Standards for Tax Services (SSTSs), when a reasonable basis exists for omission of an answer to an applicable question on a tax return,

A. The member-preparer need not provide an explanation for the omission on the return.

B. A brief explanation of the reason for the omission must be provided on the return.

C. The question should be marked as nonapplicable.

D. A note on the return should state that the answer will be provided if the information is requested.

Answer (A) is correct.

REQUIRED: The proper action when a reasonable basis exists for omission of an answer on a tax return.

DISCUSSION: According to SSTS No. 2, *Answers to Questions on Returns*, a member of the AICPA should sign the preparer's declaration when a question has not been answered only if the member has made "a reasonable effort to obtain from the taxpayer the information necessary to provide appropriate answers to all questions on a tax return." A possible disadvantage to the taxpayer does not justify omission of an answer. However, given reasonable grounds for the omission, the taxpayer is not required to provide an explanation on the return, although the member must consider whether the omission may cause the return to be incomplete.

Answer (B) is incorrect. Given reasonable grounds for the omission, the taxpayer is not required to provide an explanation on the return. Answer (C) is incorrect. An omission may be reasonable on grounds other than inapplicability. Answer (D) is incorrect. Given reasonable grounds for the omission, the taxpayer is not required to provide an explanation on the return.

12. According to the AICPA's standards, which of the following actions should be taken by a member tax preparer who discovers an error in a taxpayer's previously filed tax return?

A. Advise the IRS.

B. Correct the error.

C. Advise the taxpayer.

D. End the relationship with the taxpayer.

Answer (C) is correct.

REQUIRED: The proper action by a member of the AICPA who discovers an error in a previously filed tax return.

DISCUSSION: According to SSTS No. 6, *Knowledge of Error: Return Preparation and Administrative Proceedings*, a member should inform the taxpayer promptly upon becoming aware of an error in a previously filed return and "recommend the corrective measures to be taken." In the case of a material understatement, an amended return should be filed by the taxpayer. A claim for refund is appropriate for a material overstatement. The advice may be given to the taxpayer orally.

Answer (A) is incorrect. A member should not inform the IRS without the taxpayer's permission, except if required by law. Answer (B) is incorrect. A member is not responsible for correcting a discovered error unless requested to do so by the taxpayer. Answer (D) is incorrect. A member need not end the relationship with the taxpayer over the discovery of a previous error.

13. Jones, a member of the AICPA, prepared Smith's federal income tax return and appropriately signed the preparer's declaration. Several months later, Jones learned that Smith improperly altered several figures before mailing the tax return to the IRS. Jones should communicate disapproval of this action to Smith and

A. Take no further action with respect to the current year's tax return but consider the implications of Smith's actions for any future relationship.

B. Inform the IRS of the unauthorized alteration.

C. File an amended tax return.

D. Refund any fee collected, return all relevant documents, and refuse any further association with Smith.

Answer (A) is correct.

REQUIRED: The proper action of a tax preparer-member after the taxpayer improperly altered the return.

DISCUSSION: When the member discovers an error, (s)he must inform the taxpayer and recommend the corrective measures to be taken. It is then the taxpayer's responsibility to correct the error. If the IRS is likely to bring criminal charges, the taxpayer should be advised to seek legal counsel. If the error is not corrected, "the member should consider whether to withdraw from preparing the return and whether to continue a professional or employment relationship with the taxpayer" (SSTS No. 6).

Answer (B) is incorrect. The member may not inform the IRS, except if required by law. Answer (C) is incorrect. The member may not file an amended return without the taxpayer's permission. Answer (D) is incorrect. SSTS No. 6 does not mention refunding fees and returning documents.

1.3 Tax Return Preparers

14. A CPA must sign the preparer's declaration on a federal income tax return

A. Only when the CPA prepares a tax return for compensation.

B. Only when the CPA can declare that a tax is based on information of which the CPA has personal knowledge.

C. Whenever the CPA prepares a tax return for others.

D. Only when the return is for an individual or corporation.

Answer (A) is correct.

REQUIRED: The condition for signing the preparer's declaration on a federal income tax return.

DISCUSSION: Treasury Regulations require preparers to sign all the returns they prepare and to include their identification numbers. However, a preparer is defined as a person who prepares (or employs persons to prepare) for compensation any tax return, amended return, or claim for refund of tax imposed by Subtitle A of the Internal Revenue Code (which covers income taxes on all entities).

Answer (B) is incorrect. The CPA may prepare a return based on information provided by the taxpayer. Personal knowledge of the information is not required. Answer (C) is incorrect. The CPA must sign only when (s)he receives compensation. Answer (D) is incorrect. The signature requirement applies to returns and claims for refund by all income tax-paying entities.

15. Which of the following statements is **false** regarding tax return preparers?

A. Only a person who signs a return as the preparer may be considered the preparer of the return.

B. Unpaid preparers, such as volunteers who assist low-income individuals, are not considered to be preparers for purposes of preparer penalties.

C. An employee who prepares the return of his or her employer does not meet the definition of a tax preparer.

D. The preparation of a substantial portion of a return for compensation is treated as the preparation of that return.

Answer (A) is correct.

REQUIRED: The false statement about tax return preparers.

DISCUSSION: Under Sec. 7701(a)(36), a tax return preparer is any person who prepares for compensation, or employs others to prepare for compensation, any tax return or claim for refund under Title 26. A person who prepares a substantial portion of a return is considered a preparer even though someone else may be required to sign the return.

16. Joe is the trustee of a trust set up for his father. Under the Internal Revenue Code, when Joe prepares the annual trust tax return, Form 1041, he

A. Must obtain the written permission of the beneficiary prior to signing as a tax return preparer.

B. Is not considered a tax return preparer.

C. May not sign the return unless he receives additional compensation for the tax return.

D. Is considered a tax return preparer because his father is the grantor of the trust.

Answer (B) is correct.

REQUIRED: The true statement about a trustee's preparation of the annual trust tax return.

DISCUSSION: Joe is not considered a tax return preparer because he is a fiduciary who prepares the return for the trust.

Answer (A) is incorrect. Because Joe is the trustee, he is not required to obtain the written permission of the beneficiary prior to signing as a tax return preparer. Answer (C) is incorrect. Compensation is not required for Joe to prepare the tax return. Answer (D) is incorrect. Joe is not considered a tax return preparer, as he is a fiduciary who prepares the return for the trust. The fact that his father is the grantor of the trust is irrelevant.

17. Mike is a CPA. For the past 5 years, the information that Anne provided Mike to prepare her return included a Schedule K-1 from a partnership showing significant income. However, Mike did not see a Schedule K-1 from the partnership among the information Anne provided to him this year. What does due diligence require Mike to do?

A. Without talking to Anne, Mike should estimate the amount that would be reported as income on the Schedule K-1 based on last year's Schedule K-1 and include that amount on Anne's return.

B. Call Anne's financial advisor and ask him about Anne's investments.

C. Nothing, because Mike is required to rely only on the information provided by his client, even if he has a reason to know the information is not accurate.

D. Ask Anne about the fact that she did not provide him with a Schedule K-1.

Answer (D) is correct.

REQUIRED: The actions required to act in due diligence.

DISCUSSION: A tax return preparer may rely, if in good faith, upon information furnished by the taxpayer without having to obtain third-party verification. However, the preparer may not ignore the implications of the information furnished. The preparer must make reasonable inquiries if the information appears inaccurate or incomplete.

Answer (A) is incorrect. The tax return preparer is not supposed to make up numbers. The tax return preparer is required to use the actual amounts in preparing a tax return. Answer (B) is incorrect. The tax return preparer cannot contact Anne's financial advisor without Anne's consent. Answer (C) is incorrect. A tax return preparer is required to make reasonable inquiries if information provided by the taxpayer appears inaccurate or incomplete.

18. Arnie is a Certified Public Accountant who prepares income tax returns for his clients. One of his clients submitted a list of expenses to be claimed on Schedule C of the tax return. Arnie qualifies as a return preparer and, as such, is required to comply with which one of the following conditions?

A. Arnie is required to independently verify the client's information.

B. Arnie can ignore implications of information known by him.

C. Inquiry is not required if the information appears to be incorrect or incomplete.

D. Appropriate inquiries are required to determine whether the client has substantiation for travel and entertainment expenses.

Answer (D) is correct.

REQUIRED: The conditions with which a return preparer must comply.

DISCUSSION: A practitioner (i.e., a CPA) may rely on information provided by a client without further inquiry or verification. However, if the information so provided appears incorrect, incomplete, or inconsistent, the practitioner must make reasonable inquiries about the information. This requirement includes inquiry about unsubstantiated travel and entertainment expenses (Circular 230).

Answer (A) is incorrect. Arnie may rely in good faith on the client's information. Answer (B) is incorrect. Arnie may not ignore implications of information known by him. Answer (C) is incorrect. Arnie is required to make reasonable inquiries about information that appears to be incorrect or incomplete.

19. All of the following are tax return preparers **except**

A. A person who prepares a substantial portion of the return for a fee.

B. A person who prepares a claim for a refund for a fee.

C. A person who gives an opinion about theoretical events that have not occurred.

D. A person who prepares a United States return for a fee outside the United States.

Answer (C) is correct.

REQUIRED: The person who is not an income tax return preparer.

DISCUSSION: A tax return preparer is any person who prepares for compensation, or employs others to prepare for compensation, any tax return or claim for refund under Title 26. A person who gives an opinion about events that have not happened is not a tax return preparer.

Answer (A) is incorrect. A person who prepares a substantial portion of the return for a fee represents tax return preparers under the regulations. Answer (B) is incorrect. A person who prepares a claim for a refund for a fee represents tax return preparers under the regulations. Answer (D) is incorrect. A person who prepares a United States return for a fee outside the United States represents tax return preparers under the regulations.

20. Which of the following is **not** a tax return preparer?

A. Someone who does not physically prepare a tax return but offers enough advice that completion of the return is largely a mechanical matter.

B. Someone who prepares a substantial portion of a return or claim for refund under Title 26.

C. A firm who offers computer tax preparation services if the program makes substantive tax determinations.

D. Someone who prepares a return or claim for refund for his or her employer.

Answer (D) is correct.

REQUIRED: The person who is not an income tax return preparer.

DISCUSSION: Under Sec. 7701(a)(36), a tax return preparer is any person who prepares for compensation, or employs others to prepare for compensation, any tax return or claim for refund under Title 26. However, a person who prepares a return for his or her regular employer is disqualified as a tax return preparer.

21. Jane is a Certified Public Accountant who specializes in preparing federal tax returns. Which of the following returns would **not** qualify Jane as a tax return preparer?

A. Estate or gift tax returns.

B. Excise tax returns.

C. Withholding tax returns.

D. None of the answers are correct.

Answer (D) is correct.

REQUIRED: The preparation of the type of return that qualifies an individual as a tax return preparer.

DISCUSSION: A tax return preparer is any person who prepares for compensation any return of tax or claim for refund under the IRC. Estate returns, gift tax returns, excise tax returns, and withholding returns are covered by the IRC. This coverage is new since May of 2007.

Answer (A) is incorrect. Preparation of gift tax returns does qualify Jane as a tax preparer. Answer (B) is incorrect. Preparation of excise tax returns does qualify Jane as a tax preparer. Answer (C) is incorrect. Preparation of employment tax returns, including withholding tax returns, does qualify Jane as a tax preparer.

22. When must a tax return preparer provide a copy of a tax return to a taxpayer?

A. Within 45 days after the return is filed, including extensions.

B. Within 48 hours after the taxpayer requests a copy of the tax return.

C. Not later than the time the original return is presented to the taxpayer for signature.

D. None of the answers are correct.

Answer (C) is correct.

REQUIRED: The time when a preparer must provide a copy of the return to the taxpayer.

DISCUSSION: Sec. 6107(a) requires all tax return preparers to furnish a completed copy of the return to the taxpayer not later than the time such return or claim for refund is presented for the taxpayer's signature.

Answer (A) is incorrect. The taxpayer must receive a copy no later than the time the original return is presented for a signature. Answer (B) is incorrect. The taxpayer must receive a copy no later than the time the original return is presented for a signature. Answer (D) is incorrect. A correct answer choice is provided.

23. Jack, a return preparer, did not retain copies of all returns that he prepared but did keep a list that reflected the taxpayer's name, identification number, tax year, and type of return for each of his clients. Which of the following statements best describes this situation?

A. Jack is in compliance with the provisions of the tax code if he retains the list for a period of 1 year after the close of the return period in which the return was signed.

B. Jack is in compliance with the provisions of the tax code, provided he retains the list for a 3-year period after the close of the return period in which the return was signed.

C. Jack is not in compliance with the tax code since he must retain copies of all returns filed.

D. Jack is not in compliance with the tax code since he has not kept all the information required by the Code.

Answer (B) is correct.

REQUIRED: The statement that best describes the situation.

DISCUSSION: The person who is an income tax return preparer of any return or claim for refund shall "retain a completed copy of the return or claim for refund; or retain a record by list, card file, or otherwise of the name, taxpayer identification number, and taxable year of the taxpayer for whom the return or claim for refund was prepared and the type of return or claim for refund prepared." The material shall be retained and kept available for inspection for the 3-year period following the close of the return period during which the return or claim for refund was presented for signature to the taxpayer.

Answer (A) is incorrect. The list must be retained for a 3-year period. Answer (C) is incorrect. Jack is in compliance with the tax code. Answer (D) is incorrect. Jack is in compliance with the tax code.

24. Which of the following statements is true regarding records required to be maintained by return preparers?

A. Tax return preparers are required to maintain a complete copy of each return or claim for refund they have filed for 3 years after the return period.

B. Tax return preparers are required to maintain a list of the names, identification numbers, and tax years for whom returns are prepared and to keep this list for 3 years after the return period.

C. Tax return preparers are required to maintain a complete copy of each return or claim for refund they have filed for 3 years after the return period, or are required to maintain a list of the names, identification numbers, and tax years for whom returns are prepared and to keep this list for 3 years after the return period.

D. Tax return preparers are required to maintain a complete copy of each return or claim for refund they have filed for 3 years after the return period and are required to maintain a list of the names, identification numbers, and tax years for whom returns are prepared and to keep this list for 3 years after the return period.

Answer (C) is correct.

REQUIRED: The true statement regarding the records that are required to be maintained by return preparers.

DISCUSSION: A return preparer is required to retain a completed copy of each return or claim prepared for 3 years after the close of the return period [Sec. 6107(b)]. Alternatively, a list may be kept that includes, for the returns and claims prepared, the following information: (1) the taxpayers' names, (2) taxpayer identification numbers, (3) their tax years, and (4) the types of returns or claims prepared. Additionally, this list must be kept for 3 years after the return period.

25. Which of the following persons would be subject to the penalty for improperly negotiating a taxpayer's refund check?

A. A tax return preparer who operates a check cashing agency that cashes, endorses, or negotiates tax refund checks for returns he prepared.

B. A tax return preparer who operates a check cashing business and cashes checks for her clients as part of a second business.

C. The firm that prepared the tax return and is authorized by the taxpayer to receive a tax refund but not to endorse or negotiate the check.

D. A business manager who prepares tax returns for clients who maintain special checking accounts against which the business manager is authorized to sign certain checks on their behalf. The clients' federal tax refunds are mailed to the business manager, who has the clients endorse the checks and then deposits them in the special accounts.

Answer (A) is correct.

REQUIRED: The person subject to the penalty for negotiation of a refund check.

DISCUSSION: Sec. 6695(f) provides that any tax return preparer who endorses or otherwise negotiates any check issued to a taxpayer with respect to taxes imposed by the IRC will be subject to a penalty of $500 for each such check. A tax return preparer who operates a check cashing agency that cashes, endorses, or negotiates tax refund checks for returns that (s)he prepared is subject to the penalty.

Answer (B) is incorrect. The preparer's second business meets the definition of a bank. Answer (C) is incorrect. A preparer may receive checks provided (s)he does not cash it. Answer (D) is incorrect. The clients endorsed the checks.

26. Which of the following acts by a CPA will **not** result in a CPA's incurring an IRS penalty?

A. Failing, without reasonable cause, to provide the client with a copy of an income tax return.

B. Failing, without reasonable cause, to sign a client's tax return as preparer.

C. Understating a client's tax liability as a result of an error in calculation.

D. Negotiating a client's tax refund check when the CPA prepared the tax return.

Answer (C) is correct.

REQUIRED: The act that will not result in a CPA's incurring an IRS penalty.

DISCUSSION: Understating a client's tax liability as a result of an error in calculation will not result in imposition of an IRS penalty unless it is the result of gross negligence or a willful attempt to avoid tax liability.

Answer (A) is incorrect. A CPA is required to provide his or her client with a copy of the tax return. Answer (B) is incorrect. A tax preparer is required to sign the return. Answer (D) is incorrect. Any tax return preparer who endorses or otherwise negotiates a refund check issued to a taxpayer is liable for a $500 penalty.

27. A CPA who prepares clients' federal income tax returns for a fee must

A. File certain required notices and powers of attorney with the IRS before preparing any returns.

B. Keep a completed copy of each return for a specified period of time or keep a summarized list of specified return information.

C. Receive client documentation supporting all travel and entertainment expenses deducted on the return.

D. Indicate the CPA's federal identification number on a tax return only if the return reflects tax due from the taxpayer.

Answer (B) is correct.

REQUIRED: The duty of a tax return preparer.

DISCUSSION: A CPA who prepares clients' federal income tax returns for a fee meets the definition in the federal tax code of an income tax return preparer. An income tax return preparer is subject to penalties for certain types of failures. For example, for each failure to retain a copy of a prepared return, the penalty is $50. The copy must be retained for 3 years.

Answer (A) is incorrect. The IRC does not require such filing. Answer (C) is incorrect. The preparer is not required to examine documents to verify independently information provided by the taxpayer. But (s)he must make reasonable inquiry, if the information appears to be incorrect or incomplete, or determine the existence of required facts and circumstances incident to a deduction. Answer (D) is incorrect. The preparer is required to indicate his or her federal identification number on each return filed.

28. Which of the following acts, if any, constitute grounds for a tax preparer penalty?

I. Without the taxpayer's consent, the tax preparer disclosed taxpayer income tax return information under an order from a state court.

II. At the taxpayer's suggestion, the tax preparer deducted the expenses of the taxpayer's personal domestic help as a business expense on the taxpayer's individual tax return.

A. I only.

B. II only.

C. Both I and II.

D. Neither I nor II.

Answer (B) is correct.

REQUIRED: The acts, if any, that constitute grounds for a tax preparer penalty.

DISCUSSION: A penalty equal to the greater of $1,000 or 50% of the income derived is imposed on a tax return preparer if any part of an understatement of tax liability resulted from a willful attempt to understate the liability or from an intentional disregard of rules or regulations. A penalty will not be imposed if client information is disclosed under a court order.

1.4 Licensing and Disciplinary Systems

29. Which of the following professional bodies has the authority to revoke a CPA's license to practice public accounting?

A. National Association of State Boards of Accountancy.

B. State board of accountancy.

C. State CPA Society Ethics Committee.

D. Professional Ethics Division of AICPA.

Answer (B) is correct.

REQUIRED: The body with the authority to revoke a CPA's license.

DISCUSSION: A valid license is a prerequisite to the practice of public accounting. State boards of accountancy are the governmental agencies that license CPAs. Revocation or suspension of a CPA's license may be made only by the issuing board.

Answer (A) is incorrect. Only individual boards have the power to revoke licenses. Answer (C) is incorrect. State CPA societies and their ethics committees are not authorized to suspend or revoke a CPA's license. Expulsion by a state society does not prohibit the practice of public accounting. Answer (D) is incorrect. The AICPA and its committees are not authorized to suspend or revoke a CPA's license. Expulsion by the AICPA does not prohibit the practice of public accounting.

30. The SEC can suspend or revoke the right of an accountant to sign any document filed by an SEC registrant if the accountant

	Lacks Integrity	Engages in Unethical Conduct
A.	No	No
B.	No	Yes
C.	Yes	No
D.	Yes	Yes

Answer (D) is correct.

REQUIRED: The basis for discipline by the SEC.

DISCUSSION: The SEC may conduct quasi-judicial proceedings. Pursuant to such proceedings, it may suspend or permanently revoke the right to practice before the SEC, including the right to sign any document filed by an SEC registrant, if the accountant does not have the qualifications to represent others, lacks character or integrity, has engaged in unethical or unprofessional conduct, or has willfully violated the federal securities laws or their rules and regulations.

1.5 PRACTICE TASK-BASED SIMULATIONS

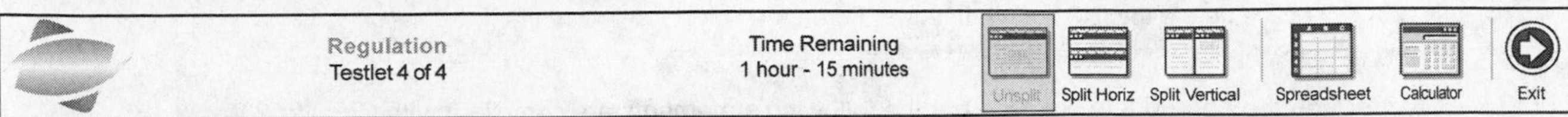

DIRECTIONS

Note: If you believe you have encountered a software malfunction, report it to the test center staff immediately.

Navigation

To navigate from task to task, use the controls at the bottom of the screen. Click on the **Next** button to advance to the next task, or the **Previous** button to go to the previous task. To go directly to any task, click on its number.

If you would like a reminder to revisit a task, or want to indicate that you are finished with it, click on the reminder flag below the task number. To clear the flag, click on it again. Reminder flags are for your use only – they do not contribute to your score.

Tabs

In this part of the examination, you will be asked to complete various tasks. Every task has one or more **Work Tabs**. Some tasks have one or more **Information Tabs**, others may have none. Every task has a **Help** tab.

If a task has **Information Tabs**, you may use the information in them to complete your responses in the **Work Tabs**.

Work tab **Information tab** **Help tab**

Work Tabs:

- **Work Tabs** are identified with a pencil icon. This is where your responses are expected.
- Each task has one or more **Work Tabs**.
- **Work Tabs** contain directions for completing the task – be sure to read these directions carefully.
- The **Work Tab** name in the example above is for illustration only – yours will differ.
- You must complete all of the **Work Tabs** in each task to receive full credit.

Information Tabs:

- The Authoritative Literature will be provided in all tasks in the AUD, FAR, and REG sections for your reference.
- Your simulation may have one or more additional **Information Tabs**. Like the Authoritative Literature tabs, **Information Tabs** do not have a pencil icon.
- If your task has additional **Information Tabs**, go through each to familiarize yourself with the task content.

Help Tab:

- The **Help Tab** provides assistance with the exam software that is used in this task. For example, if the task is to compose a memorandum, **Help** will provide information about the word processor.

The Toolbar

The toolbar at the top of the screen shows the amount of time remaining for you to complete the tasks. In addition, the following tools are available. Note that only the **Exit** button is displayed when Directions are visible - the others will appear when you begin the tasks.

Click on these buttons to split or unsplit the screen. You can split the screen vertically or horizontally.

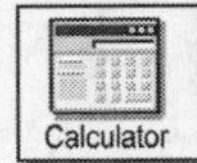

Click on this button to display the calculator; click on it again to hide the calculator. To move the calculator, click on the calculator title bar and drag the calculator to the desired location.

Click on this button to use the spreadsheet; click on it again to hide the spreadsheet. To move the spreadsheet, click on the the spreadsheet title bar and drag the spreadsheet to the desired location.

Click on this button to go on to the next part of the examination. You must complete all of the tasks to receive full credit. Once you click on **Exit** and confirm the action, you will NOT be able to return to this testlet.

= Reminder | Directions | 1 2 3 4 5 6 | Previous | Next

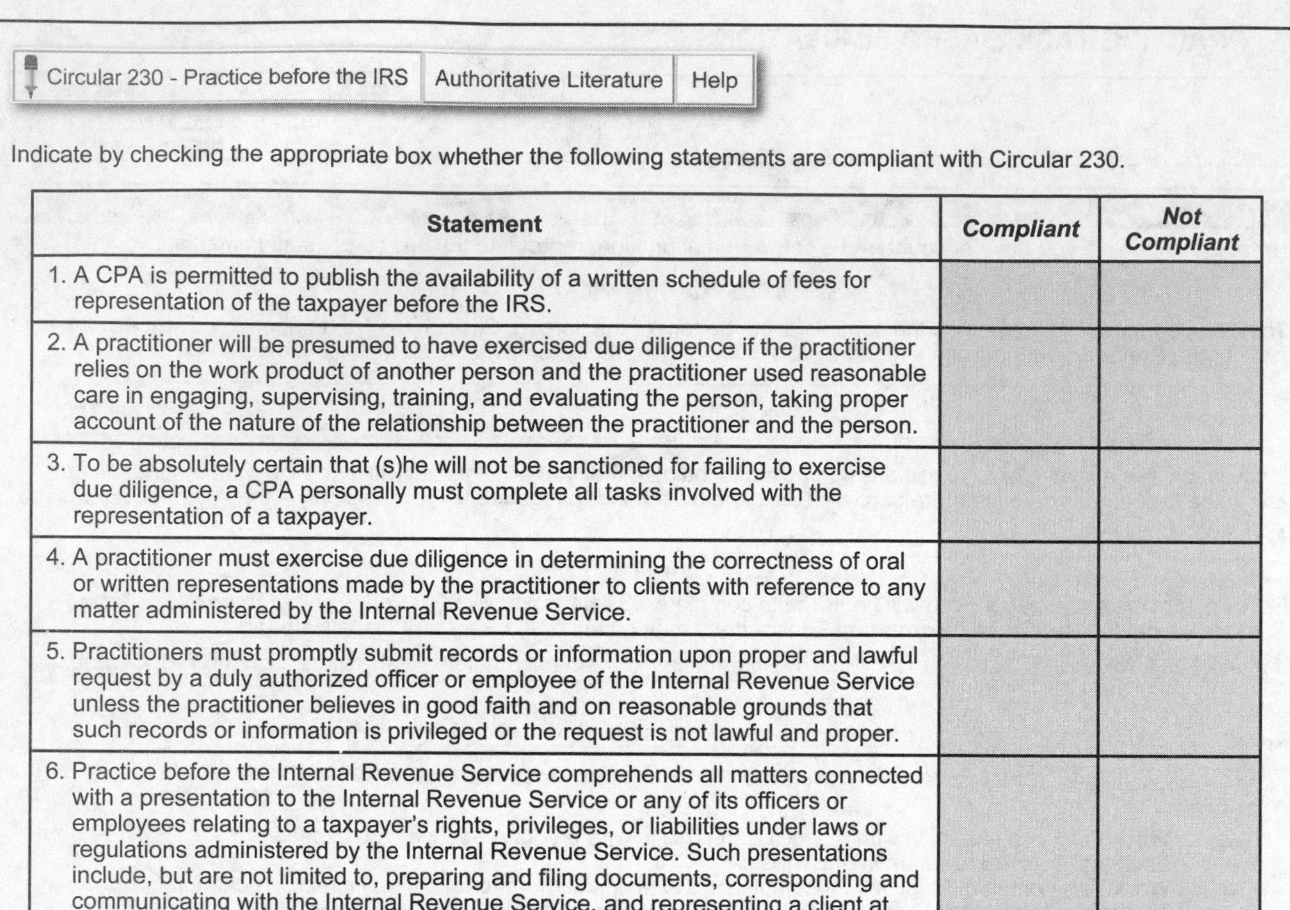

Circular 230 - Practice before the IRS | Authoritative Literature | Help

Indicate by checking the appropriate box whether the following statements are compliant with Circular 230.

Statement	Compliant	Not Compliant
1. A CPA is permitted to publish the availability of a written schedule of fees for representation of the taxpayer before the IRS.		
2. A practitioner will be presumed to have exercised due diligence if the practitioner relies on the work product of another person and the practitioner used reasonable care in engaging, supervising, training, and evaluating the person, taking proper account of the nature of the relationship between the practitioner and the person.		
3. To be absolutely certain that (s)he will not be sanctioned for failing to exercise due diligence, a CPA personally must complete all tasks involved with the representation of a taxpayer.		
4. A practitioner must exercise due diligence in determining the correctness of oral or written representations made by the practitioner to clients with reference to any matter administered by the Internal Revenue Service.		
5. Practitioners must promptly submit records or information upon proper and lawful request by a duly authorized officer or employee of the Internal Revenue Service unless the practitioner believes in good faith and on reasonable grounds that such records or information is privileged or the request is not lawful and proper.		
6. Practice before the Internal Revenue Service comprehends all matters connected with a presentation to the Internal Revenue Service or any of its officers or employees relating to a taxpayer's rights, privileges, or liabilities under laws or regulations administered by the Internal Revenue Service. Such presentations include, but are not limited to, preparing and filing documents, corresponding and communicating with the Internal Revenue Service, and representing a client at conferences, hearings, and meetings.		

= Reminder | Directions | 1 2 3 4 5 6 | Previous | Next

Disciplinary Actions | Authoritative Literature | Help

Indicate which entities may take disciplinary action by checking the appropriate box.

Activity	State Accountancy Board	SEC	PCAOB	AICPA	IRS
1. Susan, CPA, prepared a frivolous tax return for one of her clients.					
2. Jim, CPA, issued an unmodified opinion on financial statements that were not in accordance with GAAP.					
3. John, CPA, was convicted of preparing fraudulent income tax returns.					
4. Mary practiced as a CPA and represented taxpayers before the IRS. Her license as a CPA and her CPA firm's license were revoked by the state accountancy board.					

= Reminder | Directions | 1 2 3 4 5 6 | Previous | Next

Indicate by selecting the appropriate boxes whether each statement below violates Circular 230 or tax code rules, AICPA Statements on Standards for Tax Services, SEC rules, or PCAOB rules. You may select more than one answer for each statement.

Statement	***Circular 230 or Tax Code Rules***	***AICPA Statements on Standards for Tax Services***	***SEC or PCAOB***	***No Selections***
1. Jeff, CPA, discovered that his client filed a frivolous return last year, so he immediately reported it to the IRS.				
2. Jessica, CPA, returned all of her client's tax documents but did not include documents she prepared.				
3. Veronica, CPA, completed a waiter's personal tax return. This waiter explained that what the IRS did not know could not hurt them and that he did not receive any cash tips. Veronica completed the waiter's return.				
4. During a nontax proceeding, a CPA refused to divulge information the IRS requested.				
5. Bob, CPA, has a client with a strong belief that he is correct about an aggressive but creative tax position. Bob thinks otherwise and has documented his position. Bob files the tax return as his client wishes but also includes disclosure on his client's position. There is no substantial authority on this tax position. The client agrees with Bob that the position should be disclosed to the IRS.				

= Reminder | Directions | 1 2 3 4 5 6 | Previous | Next

Written Tax Advice | Authoritative Literature | Help

Eric, CPA, has a number of emails going to different clients. Select whether each email complies with or violates the requirements for written tax advice.

Email	***Complies***	***Violates***
1. Eric emails a client advising on the deductability of travel expenses to and from rental property for the purpose of making repairs to the rental property. Eric reasonably assumes the client meets the qualified rental property requirements.		
2. Eric emails a client concerning offshore bank accounts and the possibility of foreign sources of income not being repatriated to the U.S. Eric promotes his advice based on the low likelihood of a tax audit.		
3. Eric emails a client who is starting a business that will allow its investors significant losses. The client is asking for an opinion on the legality of his business. Eric's advice relies in good faith on the reasonable advice of another practitioner.		
4. One of Eric's clients has asked Eric to provide written advice on a particular matter. Eric's response relies on the advice of a practitioner with unresolved conflicts of interest.		

= Reminder | Directions | 1 2 3 4 5 6 | Previous | Next

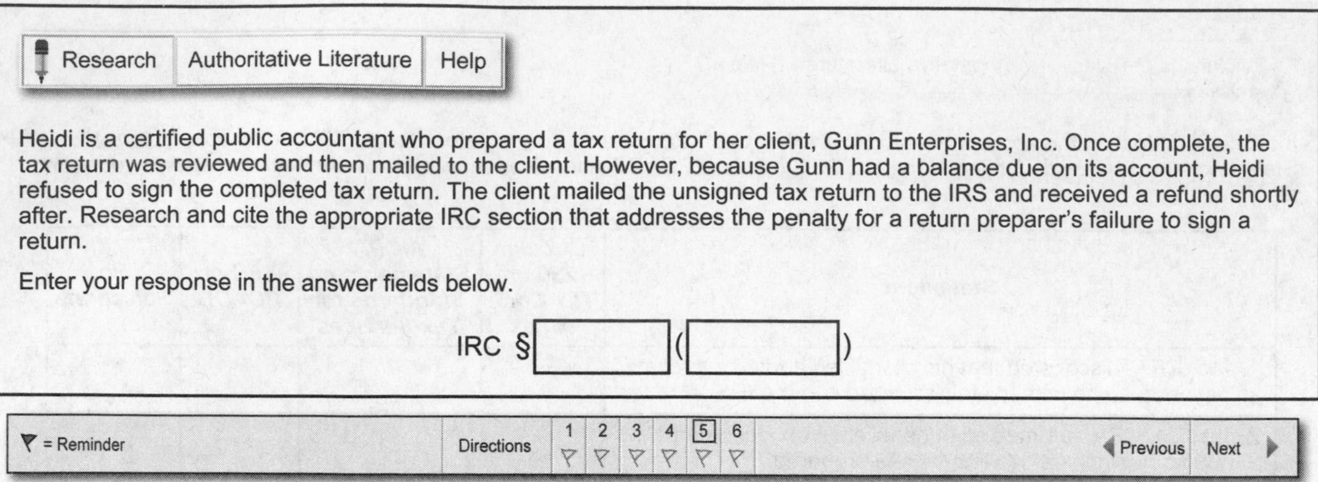

Research | Authoritative Literature | Help

Heidi is a certified public accountant who prepared a tax return for her client, Gunn Enterprises, Inc. Once complete, the tax return was reviewed and then mailed to the client. However, because Gunn had a balance due on its account, Heidi refused to sign the completed tax return. The client mailed the unsigned tax return to the IRS and received a refund shortly after. Research and cite the appropriate IRC section that addresses the penalty for a return preparer's failure to sign a return.

Enter your response in the answer fields below.

IRC § [ ] ([ ])

= Reminder | Directions | 1 2 3 4 5 6 | Previous | Next

Allowable under IRS Rules | Authoritative Literature | Help

Indicate by selecting whether each of the following situations is acceptable or unacceptable according to IRS Code or U.S. federal law.

Statement	***Acceptable***	***Unacceptable***
1. Ms. Smith hired Tom, CPA, to prepare her federal income tax return for Year 3. While gathering information to prepare the return, Tom discovered that although Ms. Smith was required to file federal income tax returns for the Year 1 tax year and the Year 2 tax year under the federal tax laws, she did not file these returns. Tom promptly advised Ms. Smith that she did not comply with the Internal Revenue laws by failing to file her federal income tax returns for the Year 1 tax year and the Year 2 tax year, and he advised her of the consequences of failing to file under the Code and regulations.		
2. On December 17 of last year, Stan, CPA, placed an ad in the local newspaper and a trade magazine that he would prepare a complex Form 1040 for $200. On January 2 of this year, the owner of Stan's office building unexpectedly increased his rent by a large amount. Stan determined he would have to charge $230 to make a profit. Stan changed his rate to $230 on January 10.		
3. Nancy, CPA, wanted to have Fay as a new client. Without invitation, Nancy approached Fay at a local fitness spa, explained how she could assist Fay with her federal tax matters, and stated that she would like to have Fay as a client.		
4. Tony, CPA, advises prospective clients that he is able to obtain approval of qualified retirement plans with unique vesting provisions because of his close relationship with the IRS territory manager of the Tax Exempt Government Entities operating unit in his locality.		
5. Joseph, CPA, has represented Stephen before the Internal Revenue Service and also prepared returns for Stephen in each of the last 3 years. Stephen was divorced last year, and his ex-wife, Lindsay, stopped by Joseph's office and asked Joseph to represent her before the Internal Revenue Service with respect to the examination of her return that she filed separately from her husband in a year in which they were separated but not yet divorced. Because the representation involved a tax return for which Lindsay filed separately and because they were separated at the time, Joseph undertook the representation of Lindsay without disclosing the situation to Stephen.		

= Reminder | Directions | 1 2 3 4 5 6 | Previous | Next

Unofficial Answers

1. Circular 230 – Practice before the IRS (6 Gradable Items)

1. Compliant. Under Circular 230, fixed fees for specific routine services, hourly rates, the range of fees for particular services, and the fee charged for an initial consultation may be advertised. The availability of a written fee schedule may also be published.
2. Compliant. Diligence must be exercised in preparing and in assisting in preparing, approving, and filing returns, documents, and other papers relating to IRS matters. Diligence is presumed when the practitioner relies upon the work product of another person if (s)he uses reasonable care in engaging, supervising, training, and evaluating the person.
3. Not Compliant. Diligence must be exercised in preparing and in assisting in preparing, approving, and filing returns, documents, and other papers relating to IRS matters. Diligence is presumed when the practitioner relies upon the work product of another person if (s)he uses reasonable care in engaging, supervising, training, and evaluating the person. Thus, due diligence can be achieved if the proper measures are taken in engaging, supervising, training, and evaluating the person.
4. Compliant. Diligence must be exercised in preparing and in assisting in preparing, approving, and filing returns, documents, and other papers relating to IRS matters. Diligence is presumed when the practitioner relies upon the work product of another person if (s)he uses reasonable care in engaging, supervising, training, and evaluating the person. A practitioner also must exercise due diligence in determining the correctness of oral or written representations made by the practitioner to clients with reference to any matter administered by the Internal Revenue Service.
5. Compliant. Circular 230 provides that no attorney, CPA, or enrolled agent shall neglect or refuse to promptly submit records or information in any matter before the IRS upon proper and lawful request by a duly authorized officer or employee of the IRS, unless (s)he believes in good faith and on reasonable grounds that such information is privileged or that the request is not lawful and proper.
6. Compliant. Practice before the IRS includes presenting to the IRS or any of its officers or employees all matters relating to a client's rights, privileges, or liabilities (Circular 230). Circular 230 states that a person is practicing before the IRS if (s)he (a) communicates with the IRS for a taxpayer regarding taxpayer rights under laws and regulations administered by the IRS; (b) represents a taxpayer at conferences, hearings, or meetings with the IRS; and (c) prepares necessary documents and files them with the IRS for a taxpayer.

2. Disciplinary Actions (4 Gradable Items)

1. State Accountancy Board, AICPA, IRS. Filing a frivolous return is a violation of IRS rules. It is also a violation of the AICPA Statement on Standards for Tax Services. Violations of generally accepted standards of practice are grounds for discipline by the state boards of accountancy. The IRS shares information concerning violations of IRS standards with the respective state board of accountancy. The AICPA and most state societies have agreements that permit mutual referral of violations of AICPA Standards. Therefore, a violation uncovered by one organization will lead to sanctions by others.
2. State Accountancy Board, SEC, PCAOB, AICPA. Violations of generally accepted standards of practice, including issuing reports on financial statements that are not in conformance with GAAP, are grounds for discipline by state boards of accountancy, the SEC, PCAOB, and AICPA.
3. State Accountancy Board, SEC, PCAOB, AICPA, IRS. All of the entities can take disciplinary action for conviction of a felony.
4. SEC, PCAOB, AICPA, IRS. Because Mary's license has been revoked by the state accountancy board, no further action would be taken by the state board unless Mary practiced public accounting after her license was revoked. The SEC requires a CPA license to be eligible to practice before them. Therefore, they would revoke Mary's right to practice. The PCAOB would deregister the firm. The AICPA requires licensure for membership. Revocation of the license results in automatic expulsion from membership. Individuals who wish to represent taxpayers before the IRS must be a CPA, an attorney, or an EA.

3. Violations of Rules (5 Gradable Items)

1. Circular 230 and SSTSs. Both Circular 230 and the AICPA Statements on Standards for Tax Services require a CPA to notify a client if the CPA discovers the client has not complied with IRS rules and to advise the client of the consequences. However, neither Circular 230 nor the AICPA's SSTSs require the CPA to notify the IRS.
2. No selections. Both Circular 230 and the AICPA Statements on Standards for Tax Services require a CPA to return the client's documents even if there is a dispute over fees. However, neither Circular 230 nor the AICPA's SSTSs require a CPA to return documents or working papers prepared by the CPA that were necessary for the CPA to complete his or her work. Therefore, Jessica does not need to return documents that she prepared to her client.
3. Circular 230 and SSTSs. Both Circular 230 and the AICPA Statements on Standards for Tax Services require a CPA to be diligent in preparing tax returns. Moreover, both ethical standards require reasonable inquiries, and if a waiter suggests that he did not receive cash tips, both ethical standards require that a CPA request documentation. In this case, Veronica should have performed more investigation rather than taking the waiter's word.
4. No selections. The IRS tax code allows any federally authorized tax practitioner a confidentiality privilege. A taxpayer is entitled to the same common-law protections of confidentiality with respect to the tax advice given by any federally authorized tax practitioner as a taxpayer would have if the advising individual were an attorney. Thus, the CPA did not violate any ethical standards.
5. SSTSs. Circular 230 requires that a CPA disclose a position that is more likely than not a position that would withstand an IRS inquiry. On the other hand, the AICPA's SSTSs require that a CPA neither prepare nor sign a tax return when the CPA does not have a good-faith belief that it will be sustained if challenged. Thus, because Bob disclosed the position to the IRS and his client allowed him to do so, Bob violated only the AICPA's SSTSs.

4. Written Tax Advice (4 Gradable Items)

1. Complies. The IRS usually allows the deduction of travel expenses to and from qualified rental property for the purpose of making repairs to the property. In providing written advice, a practitioner must base the advice on reasonable assumptions.
2. Violates. The advice must not take into account the possibility that a tax return will not be audited.
3. Complies. In providing written advice, a practitioner may rely in good faith on the advice of another practitioner only if that advice is reasonable considering all facts and circumstances.
4. Violates. The practitioner cannot rely on the advice of a person who the practitioner knows or should know is not competent to provide the advice or who has an unresolved conflict of interest.

5. Research (1 Gradable Item)

Answer: IRC § 6695(b)

§ 6695. Other assessable penalties with respect to the preparation of tax returns for other persons

(b) Failure to sign return

Any person who is a tax return preparer with respect to any return or claim for refund, who is is required by regulations prescribed by the Secretary to sign such return or claim, and who fails to comply with such regulations with respect to such return or claim shall pay a penalty of $50 for such failure, unless it is shown that such failure is due to reasonable cause and not due to willful neglect. The maximum penalty imposed under this subsection on any person with respect to documents filed during any calendar year shall not exceed $25,000.

6. Allowable under IRS Rules (5 Gradable Items)

1. Acceptable. According to Circular 230, a CPA who knows that a client has not complied with the revenue laws of the U.S. is required to promptly inform the client of the noncompliance and must also advise the client of the consequences of the noncompliance under the Code and regulations.
2. Unacceptable. Attorneys, CPAs, and enrolled agents are bound to charge in accordance with published fee information for a reasonable period of time, but not less than 30 days from the last publication of such information (Sec. 10.30 of Circular 230).
3. Acceptable. Circular 230 provides that a CPA may not directly or indirectly make any uninvited solicitation of employment in matters relating to the Internal Revenue Service if the solicitation violates federal or state law or other applicable rule. No rules are violated; therefore, Nancy's solicitation is permitted.
4. Unacceptable. Circular 230 lists several examples of disreputable conduct for which an enrolled agent may be disbarred or suspended from practice before the Internal Revenue Service. Suggesting that he is improperly able to obtain special consideration from an Internal Revenue Service employee is disreputable conduct.
5. Unacceptable. An agent may represent conflicting interests before the IRS only if all directly interested parties expressly consent in writing after full disclosure. According to Circular 230, a conflict of interest exists if (a) the representation of one client will be directly adverse to another client or (b) there is a significant risk that the representation of one or more client(s) will be materially limited by the practitioner's responsibilities to another client, a former client or a third person, or by a personal interest of the practitioner. Joseph should determine whether a conflict of interest exists and get all appropriate consents to the representation.

Gleim Simulation Grading

Task	Correct Responses		Gradable Items		Score per Task
1	___	÷	6	=	___
2	___	÷	4	=	___
3	___	÷	5	=	___
4	___	÷	4	=	___
5 (Research)	___	÷	1	=	___
6	___	÷	5	=	___
			Total of Scores per Task		___
		÷	Total Number of Tasks		6
			Total Score		___%

STUDY UNIT TWO
CPAs AND THE LAW

(26 pages of outline)

This study unit describes an accountant's responsibility to clients and third parties under state and federal law. The **Securities Act of 1933** and the **Securities Exchange Act of 1934** are the basis of federal securities law. The focus is to whom and for what accountants have responsibility (liability). Thus, CPAs may be liable to clients and third parties based on breach of contract, negligence, fraud, or violations of securities laws. Also covered are accountants' privileged communications and access to, and retention of, working papers.

2.1 SECURITIES ACT OF 1933

1. **Overview**
   a. The purpose of the 1933 act is to regulate the initial offering of securities by requiring the filing of a registration statement with the SEC prior to sale or an offer to sell. State securities laws also apply.
   b. Each **state** has adopted its own securities laws **(blue-sky laws)**.
      1) Generally, both federal and state securities laws must be complied with. However, federal securities laws partially preempt blue-sky laws.
2. **Objectives**
   a. The following are the objectives of the 1933 act:
      1) Disclosure to potential investors of all material information
      2) Prevention of fraud
   b. The goal is to provide investors with adequate information so they can make informed investment decisions.
   c. The SEC does not judge the merits of an investment or guarantee the accuracy of the information contained in the registration statement.
      1) Registration does not insure investors against loss.
      2) SEC rules protect investors in low-cost, high-risk penny stocks. Brokers that sell penny stocks must provide potential investors with documents that explain the (high) risks of the investments and the related commission structure.

3. **Definition, Markets, and Parties**

   a. The 1933 act defines the term "security" to include almost any offering that constitutes an investment:

      Any note; stock; treasury stock; bond; debenture; evidence of indebtedness; certificate of interest or participation in any profit-sharing agreement; collateral-trust certificate; preorganization certificate or subscription; transferable share; investment contract; voting-trust certificate; certificate of deposit for a security; fractional undivided interest in oil, gas, or other mineral rights; any put, call, straddle, option, or privilege on any security or, in general, any interest or instrument commonly known as a "security," or any certificate of interest or participation in, temporary or interim certificate for receipt for, guarantee of, or warrant or right to subscribe to or purchase any of the foregoing.

      1) The test of whether something is a security requires analysis of whether
         a) A person invests in a common enterprise,
         b) With a reasonable expectation of profits,
         c) To be derived solely from the efforts of a third party, such as management.
      2) Courts have held an investment to be a security even though the investor provided some of his or her own effort.

   b. **Securities markets** may have a physical location, e.g., the New York Stock Exchange, or no physical location, e.g., the over-the-counter (OTC) market. The 1934 act defines an exchange as an organization, association, or group (incorporated or not) that is, maintains, or provides a market or facility for uniting purchasers and sellers of securities.

   c. **Every person involved** in the initial offering and sale of securities is a **party to an issuance** and is subject to the 1933 act. The act broadly classifies these persons as issuers, underwriters, or dealers.

      1) An **issuer** is the individual or the business organization initially offering a security for sale to the public (generally, to raise money).
         a) An issuer includes a controlling person, one who owns more than 10% of the company's stock.
      2) An **underwriter** is any person who participates in the original offering of securities from the issuer with the intention of distributing them.
      3) A **dealer** is any person who is engaged in the business of offering, selling, buying, dealing, or otherwise trading in securities issued by another.
         a) A dealer also may be a **broker**, a person who executes securities transactions for others.

4. **Categories of Issuers**

   a. Under the SEC's integrated disclosure system, four categories of issuers are recognized:

      1) A **nonreporting issuer** (one who need not file reports under the 1934 act) must use detailed Form S-1.
      2) An **unseasoned issuer** has reported for at least 3 consecutive years under the 1934 act. It must use Form S-1 but provides less detailed information and may include some information by reference to other 1934 act reports.
      3) A **seasoned issuer** has filed for at least 1 year and has a market capitalization of at least $75 million. It may use Form S-3 to report even less detail and may include even more information by reference.
      4) A **well-known seasoned issuer** has filed for at least 1 year and (a) has a worldwide market capitalization of at least $700 million or (b) has issued for cash in a registered offering at least $1 billion of debt or preferred stock in the past 3 years. Such an issuer also may use Form S-3.

b. An **emerging growth company** (EGC) is an issuer with annual gross revenues less than $1 billion, an amount periodically adjusted for inflation. An issuer remains an EGC until (1) its annual gross revenues exceed $1 billion (adjusted), (2) 5 years after its initial public offering, (3) it has issued more than $1 billion in nonconvertible debt, or (4) it is a large accelerated filer.

1) The financial reporting requirements (and cost) are reduced for EGCs.

5. **Registration under the 1933 Act**

a. Any offer or sale of a security to the public requires registration unless a specific exemption applies.

b. To comply with the 1933 act, an issuer of securities must prepare and publicly file

1) A registration statement
2) A prospectus

c. A **registration statement** is a complete disclosure to the SEC of all material information with respect to the issuance of the specific securities. It includes the prospectus that will be provided to each potential investor.

1) The purpose of registration is to provide adequate and accurate public disclosure of financial and other pertinent information that potential investors may use to evaluate the merits of the securities. The registration statement includes the following:

a) A description of

i) The registrant's business, property, and competition
ii) The significant provisions of the security to be offered for sale
iii) Management, compensation of directors and officers, their holdings of the registrant's securities, and material transactions with these individuals

- The registrant must disclose the compensation paid to the CEO, CFO, the other three highest-paid officers, and the directors.

iv) Material legal proceedings
v) The principal purpose for which the proceeds will be used

b) The most recent audited financial statements and management's discussion and analysis (MD&A)

c) An indication of whether the registrant's independent public accountant has changed within the past 2 fiscal years

d) The signatures of the issuer, CEO, CFO, chief accounting officer, and a majority of the directors

d. A **prospectus** must be furnished to any interested investor. Its purpose is to supply sufficient facts to make an informed investment decision. However, access is equated with delivery. Thus, actual delivery of a hard copy is not required if the prospectus was timely filed with the SEC.

e. The registration statement is **effective on the 20th day** after filing unless the SEC accelerates the effective date or requires an amendment. A new 20-day period begins after an amendment.

f. **Regulation S-X** sets forth the form and content of and requirements for the financial statements required to be filed under the Securities Act of 1933 and other registration statements and reports under the Securities and Exchange Act of 1934.

6. **Shelf Registration under the 1933 Act**
   a. Generally, the entire allotment of securities is made available for purchase on the effective date of the registration statement.
      1) An exception is a **shelf registration**. After the registration statement is filed, the securities are put on the shelf for up to 3 years until the best time for an offering is determined.
      2) A shelf registration is available only to seasoned issuers and well-known seasoned issuers.
7. **Exempt Securities under the 1933 Act**
   a. Securities issued by the following are exempt from registration:
      1) Domestic governments if used for a governmental purpose
      2) Not-for-profit organizations
      3) Domestic banks and savings and loan associations
      4) Issuers that are federally regulated common carriers
      5) A receiver or trustee in bankruptcy with prior court approval
      6) State-regulated insurers (but only their insurance policies and annuity contracts are exempt)
      7) A corporation in reorganization if approved by a court or other governmental body
      8) An issuer that exchanges them with the issuer's existing security holders if no commission or other consideration is paid
         a) Thus, stock dividends and stock splits are generally exempt.
   b. **Commercial Paper (Negotiable Instruments)**
      1) Any note, draft, or banker's acceptance issued to acquire working capital is exempt from registration if it has a maturity of not more than 9 months when issued.
         a) But an investment vehicle (e.g., a money market fund) that holds short-term commercial paper is not exempt.
8. **Exempt Transactions by Issuers under the 1933 Act**
   a. **Intrastate Offerings**
      1) Under the safe harbor provisions of Rule 147, an issue qualifies as intrastate if
         a) The issuer is organized or incorporated in the state in which the issue is made;
         b) 80% of the proceeds are to be used in that state;
         c) 80% of its assets are located there, and the issuer does at least 80% of its business (gross revenues) within that state;
         d) All the purchasers and offerees are residents of the state;
         e) No resales to nonresidents occur for at least 9 months after the initial sale by the issuer is completed; and
         f) Steps are taken to prevent interstate distribution.

b. **Regulation A** permits certain issuers to offer up to $5 million of securities in any 12-month period without full registration. It imposes no limitations on the number and nature of investors, and resale is not restricted. However, neither an issuer subject to the reporting requirements of the 1934 act immediately before the offering nor investment companies are eligible for the exemption.

1) The **JOBS Act of 2012** provides for a second tier of Regulation A offerings. In this tier, the amount sold in a 12-month period must not exceed $50 million, the securities may be offered and sold publicly, and the issuer must file audited financial statements annually and other disclosures required by the SEC.

2) The SEC integrates all registrations and exempted offerings. For example, three registrations of $2 million each would not qualify for exemption under Regulation A if issued within one 12-month period. The SEC does not integrate an offering unless it is made within 6 months before or after another offering.

3) Regulation A filings are less detailed, time consuming, and costly than full registration statements.

a) A formal registration statement and prospectus are not required.

b) An offering statement containing a notification and an offering circular must be filed with the SEC's regional office, and the 20-day waiting period must be observed. The offering circular also must be provided to offerees and purchasers of the underlying securities. Sales may be made after the SEC has approved the filing.

c) The issuer may **test the waters** by use of broadcast or written advertisements. But no oral communications with buyers are allowed until the SEC receives the advertisements. No sales are allowed until the offering statement is approved by the SEC.

c. **Regulation D** establishes three separate exemptions (Rules 504, 505, and 506) related to small issues and small issuers:

1) Certain procedural rules must generally be complied with to qualify for a Regulation D exemption. However, except for the notice to the SEC, these rules **do not apply to Rule 504 transactions**.

a) No general solicitation or advertising is permitted, for example, by placing information on a website.

b) The issuer must exercise reasonable care to ensure that the purchasers of the securities are not underwriters and that such purchasers are purchasing strictly for their own investment purposes.

c) The SEC must be notified by filing Form D within 15 days of the first offering.

d) The exemption is only for transactions in which securities are offered or sold by the issuer, not for the securities.

i) The securities are **restricted**. Resale must be after registration or under some exemption.

ii) Immediate rollover of the securities is precluded.

e) **Accredited investors** include most institutional investors and individuals that meet income or net worth thresholds (excluding the value of a person's primary residence). All other investors are nonaccredited. If the offer is to nonaccredited investors, they must be given material information about the issuer, its business, and the securities being offered prior to the sale.

2) **Rule 504** permits qualified issuers to sell up to $1 million of securities during a 12-month period to any number of purchasers. Registration is not required, and the issuer need not provide specific financial information.
   a) Nonaccredited and accredited investors may purchase the securities.
   b) General solicitation is allowed, and the securities issued are not restricted and can be freely traded, if the offering is
      i) Registered in a state that requires a publicly filed registration statement, and disclosure documents are delivered to investors, or
      ii) Sold exclusively according to state law exemptions that permit general solicitation and advertising, as long as sale is only to accredited investors.
3) **Rule 505** provides exemption from registration to all issuers other than investment companies for a limited offering of securities up to $5 million in any 12-month period.
   a) The issue may be purchased by an unlimited number of accredited investors.
   b) The issuer must reasonably believe that no more than 35 purchasers are not accredited investors.
4) **Rule 506** implements the private placement exemption from registration for "transactions by an issuer not involving any public offering." Section 4(2) provides this exemption. Rule 506, unlike Rules 504 and 505, has no ceiling amount.
   a) Rule 506 provides a safe harbor for a private placement, but noncompliance with Rule 506 does not necessarily mean that the exemption cannot be claimed.
   b) The offering may be purchased by an unlimited number of accredited investors.
   c) General solicitation and advertising are permitted if sales are to accredited investors only.
   d) No more than 35 of the purchasers are not accredited investors. But their knowledge and experience must suffice to allow them to evaluate the risks and merits of the investment.
   e) The issuer must take reasonable steps to confirm that all purchasers are accredited investors as defined by the SEC if the offering is to the general public.
   f) Generally, the issuer requires the purchaser to sign an investment letter stating that (s)he is purchasing for investment only and not for resale. For this reason, the shares are called lettered stock.

d. **Section 4(6)** exempts up to $5 million of offers and sales if made only to **accredited investors**. The number of such investors may be unlimited, and no information is required to be given to them, but general advertising and solicitation are not permitted. Moreover, (1) the SEC must be informed of sales under the exemption, (2) resale is restricted, and (3) precautions must be taken to prevent nonexempt or unregistered resales.

e. **Crowdfunding** on the Internet raises small amounts from many people through (1) brokers or (2) funding portals. Under the JOBS Act, an exemption from registration is granted to eligible, domestic, nonpublic issuers in the amount of $1 million (periodically adjusted). Investments are limited based on income and net worth, transfer of securities is limited for 1 year, and a purchaser has a right of action against certain parties for negligent communications made in the offer or sale of securities.

Exempt Transactions by Issuers

Exemption	Maximum Price	Investors	Method of Offer	Resale
Rule 147 (intrastate offerings)	No maximum	Purchasers and offerees must be state residents	General solicitation and advertising, but interstate distribution not permitted	No resales to nonresidents for at least 9 months
Regulation A (excludes issuers that report under 1934 act)	$5 million in 12-month period	No limit	Testing the waters; sales after approval of offering statement	Not restricted
Regulation D -- Rule 504 (excludes most issuers that report under 1934 act)	$1 million in 12-month period	No limit	General solicitation allowed if compliant with state law	Not restricted if compliant with state law
-- Rule 505	$5 million in 12-month period	No more than 35 purchasers who are not accredited	No general solicitation or advertising	Restricted
-- Rule 506	No maximum	No more than 35 purchasers who are not accredited. Must have the knowledge and experience to evaluate the risks and merits.	No general solicitation and advertising unless all sales are to accredited investors	Restricted
Rule 4(6)	$5 million	Only accredited but number unlimited	No general solicitation or advertising	Restricted
Crowdfunding	$1 million	No limit but amount limited by income and net worth	Funding portals on Internet	Restricted

9. **Secondary Trading Exemptions under the 1933 Act**
   a. The act generally exempts the following:
      1) Transactions by any person other than an issuer, an underwriter, or a dealer
      2) Transactions by dealers that do not involve original distributions or resales within a limited period after the effective date of a registration
      3) Unsolicited brokers' transactions that execute customer orders on an exchange or over the counter

Stop and review! You have completed the outline for this subunit. Study multiple-choice questions 1 through 6 beginning on page 69.

2.2 SECURITIES EXCHANGE ACT OF 1934

1. **Overview**
   a. The 1934 act primarily addresses secondary distribution (resale) of securities. The following are the main elements of the 1934 act:
      1) Registration of all regulated public companies with the **Securities and Exchange Commission (SEC)**
         a) The SEC is an administrative agency created by the 1934 act to enforce the federal securities laws. It has the power to (1) issue rules, (2) investigate violations, (3) conduct hearings to decide whether violations have occurred (adjudication), and (4) impose penalties.
         b) The SEC may deny, suspend, or revoke registration, or it may order a suspension of trading of the securities. These sanctions are in addition to civil and criminal liability imposed by the federal securities laws.

c) The SEC may prohibit an individual who has committed **securities fraud** from serving as an officer or director of a public company. It also may freeze extraordinary payments during an investigation of securities law violations.

d) The SEC oversees the Public Company Accounting Oversight Board (PCAOB).

e) The SEC has recognized the FASB as the standard-setter for U.S. GAAP.

f) As an administrative agency, the SEC cannot prosecute criminal cases.

2) Periodic reporting, which requires providing up-to-date statements about all business operations and matters potentially affecting the value of securities

3) Antifraud provisions

4) Insider liability for short-swing profits

2. **Registration under the 1934 Act**

a. All regulated, publicly held companies must **register with the SEC**.

1) Registration is required of all companies that

a) List securities on a national securities exchange (Section 12 of the 1934 act) or

b) Have at least 500 shareholders of equity securities and total gross assets exceeding $10 million.

2) Also required to report under the 1934 act are the following:

a) An issuer that has registered securities under the 1933 act

b) National securities exchanges

3) Charitable organizations, investment companies, and savings and loans are exempt from registration under this act.

b. Registration and reporting requirements under the 1934 act are in addition to, not a substitute for, those under the 1933 act.

c. An over-the-counter issuer may terminate its registration if (1) the holders of its registered equity securities are fewer than 300 or (2) the issuer has had fewer than 500 shareholders and less than $10 million in assets on closing day in each of the last 3 years.

d. In addition to disclosing financial statements audited by a firm registered with the PCAOB, registration requires disclosure of the following:

1) Corporate organization

2) Financial structure

3) A description of all securities

4) Names of officers, directors, underwriters, and holders of more than 10% of a nonexempt equity security

5) A description of the nature of the business

6) Financial statements

7) A description of bonus and profit-sharing arrangements

3. **Periodic Reporting**

a. Following registration, an issuer must file reports with the SEC.

1) **Annual reports** certified by the CEO and CFO are filed on **Form 10-K**. The report must be filed within 60 days of the last day of the fiscal year for large accelerated filers ($700 million or more in public float, i.e., shares held by the public and not insiders), 75 days for accelerated filers ($75 million to $700 million), and 90 days for nonaccelerated filers (less than $75 million).

a) The 10-K report contains information about the entity's (1) business activities, (2) securities, (3) stock prices (but not all price changes), (4) management-related persons (e.g., officers), (5) disagreements about accounting and disclosure, (6) audited financial statements, and (7) other matters.

2) **Quarterly reports** certified by the CEO and CFO are filed on **Form 10-Q**. They need not contain audited financial statements. But the quarterly financial information must be reviewed by an independent auditor. Form 10-Q must be filed within 40 days of the last day of the first 3 fiscal quarters by large accelerated filers and accelerated filers and within 45 days by nonaccelerated filers.

a) In addition to financial information, Form 10-Q reports changes during the quarter, for example, (1) legal proceedings, (2) changes in nature or amount of securities or indebtedness, (3) matters submitted to shareholders for a vote, (4) exhibits and reports on Form 8-K, (5) other material events not reported on Form 8-K, and (6) the anticipated effect of recently issued accounting standards on financial statements when they are adopted in a future period.

3) **Current reports** must be promptly filed on **Form 8-K**. It describes certain material events that must be disclosed within 4 calendar days. They include (a) changes in control of the registrant, (b) the acquisition or disposition of a significant amount of assets other than in the ordinary course of business, (c) bankruptcy or receivership, (d) resignation of a director, and (e) a change in the registrant's certifying accountant.

Periodic Issuer Reporting to SEC under the 1934 Act

Report	Form	Content	Timing
Annual (certified by CEO and CFO)	10-K	Audited financial statements and many other matters	60, 75, or 90 days after fiscal year end
Quarterly (certified by CEO and CFO)	10-Q	Reviewed quarterly financial information and changes during quarter	40 or 45 days after end of first 3 quarters
Current	8-K	Material events	Within 4 calendar days of event

b. Any person or group of persons who acquires beneficial ownership of more than 5% of a class of registered equity securities of certain issuers must file Schedule 13D with the SEC within 10 days after the acquisition.

c. **Proxy Solicitation under the 1934 Act**

1) **Section 14(a)** of the 1934 act makes it unlawful for any person to solicit any proxy with respect to any registered security in violation of SEC rules and regulations. A **proxy** is a power of attorney given by a shareholder to a third party authorizing the party to exercise the voting rights of the shares. Solicitation includes any request for a proxy or any request to revoke a proxy. Ten days prior to mailing a proxy statement to shareholders, the issuing company must file a copy with the SEC.

d. **Tender Offers under the 1934 Act**

1) A tender offer is a general invitation by an individual or a corporation to all shareholders of another corporation to tender their shares for a specified price. The following must file a statement (within 10 days in the case of a post-acquisition tender offer) with the SEC, the issuer, and the securities exchanges:

a) Any person or group that acquires beneficial ownership of more than 5% of a class of registered securities

b) A person or group that makes a tender offer for more than 5% of such securities
c) An issuer offering to repurchase its registered securities
d) The target of a hostile tender offer

e. **Insiders under the 1934 Act**

1) Under **Section 16** of the 1934 act, insiders required to report to the SEC are (a) directors, (b) officers, and (c) any person beneficially owning more than 10% of the stock of a corporation listed on a national stock exchange or registered with the SEC.

a) Insiders must report on **Form 3** (the initial filing), **Form 4** (changes), and **Form 5** (an annual statement) the following:

i) An ownership statement within 10 days of becoming an insider
ii) A statement by the end of the second business day following the day on which the insider engaged in a transaction in the company's equity securities
iii) An annual statement within 45 days after the company's fiscal year end

2) Under **Section 16(a)**, insiders who do not comply with SEC reporting requirements are subject to administrative and criminal penalties.

f. **Sarbanes-Oxley Act of 2002**

1) In every annual or quarterly filing with the SEC, the CEO and CFO must certify that the periodic report complies fully with the 1934 act. They also must certify that

a) To the best of their knowledge, the financial statements are free of material misstatements.
b) They are responsible for the system of internal control and have evaluated its effectiveness.
c) They have informed the audit committee and the independent auditors of all significant control deficiencies and any fraud, whether or not material.
d) Significant changes were (or were not) made in internal controls, including corrective actions.

2) Intentional violations of the above section of SOX can result in the forfeiture of

a) Any bonus or other incentive-based compensation received during the previous 12 months and
b) Any profits received from the sale of stock during the previous 12 months.

3) Issuers must report in plain English to the public on a rapid and current basis additional information about material changes in financial condition or operations.

a) The SEC determines the disclosures necessary or useful to protect investors and the public interest.

4) **Unknowingly** certifying filings that do not meet the requirements of the act can result in fines of up to $1 million and up to 10 years imprisonment.

5) **Knowingly** certifying filings that do not meet the requirements of the act can result in fines of up to $5 million and up to 20 years imprisonment.

4. **Antifraud Provisions**

a. **Insider trading** under Rule 10b-5 is the purchase or sale of **any security** by an individual who (1) has access to **material, nonpublic information**; (2) has not disclosed it before trading; and (3) has a fiduciary obligation to the issuer, the shareholders, or any other source of the information. Thus, the definition of an insider is much broader than under Section 16.

1) The following are examples of insiders for Rule 10b-5 purposes:
   a) Corporate officers
   b) Lawyers
   c) Auditors
   d) Other parties, such as tippees (recipients of information from insiders) and employees of government agencies entrusted with confidential corporate information
2) The SEC may bring a civil action against anyone violating the 1934 act by "purchasing or selling a security while in possession of material nonpublic information."
   a) Under **Section 20A**, a private suit for damages may be brought by a contemporaneous purchaser or seller of shares of the same class.

5. **Short-Swing Profits under the 1934 Act**
   a. Under **Section 16(b)** of the 1934 Act, insiders may be sued for short-swing profits on **registered equity securities** by the issuer or a shareholder suing on behalf of the corporation if the issuer does not sue within 60 days after a request.
      1) Short-swing profits are from sale and purchase (purchase and sale) of the issuer's stock within a **6-month period**. "Profit" per share is the excess of the highest sales price over the lowest purchase price during the period.
      2) Strict liability is imposed, and the insider need **not** have material, nonpublic information.

Stop and review! You have completed the outline for this subunit. Study multiple-choice questions 7 through 10 beginning on page 70.

2.3 FEDERAL STATUTORY LIABILITY OF CPAS AND OTHERS

1. **Overview**
   a. This subunit explains the liability provisions of the securities laws introduced in the previous subunits. They apply not only to accountants but also to other parties subject to the securities laws.
   b. A public accounting firm and its members are prohibited from holding any direct or material indirect financial interest in an audit client or its affiliates.
      1) Materiality is "a fact which, if it had been correctly stated or disclosed, would have deterred or tended to deter the average prudent investor from purchasing the securities in question."
   c. A statute of limitations determines the maximum amount of time after an act or incident during which legal action can be pursued.

Background

Prior to passage of the Securities Act of 1933 and the Securities Exchange Act of 1934, issuers were required to do little financial reporting. The stock market crash of 1929 and the ensuing Great Depression left many with the impression that reporting by publicly traded companies had been misleading or even fraudulent. The securities acts made two major changes: They assigned the power of accounting rule-making to the SEC and required most issuers to have their financial statements audited by independent CPAs.

The AICPA has tested CPA candidates on what the plaintiff needs to prove to win a judgment against a CPA in a suit under Section 11 of the 1933 act. Thus, candidates should **know and be able to cite Section 11 of the 1933 act.**

2. **Section 11 of the 1933 Act**

   a. An accountant who prepares or audits and certifies the financial statements included in a registration statement or prospectus is **civilly liable without proof of fault**.

   b. Any person who acquires a security issued under a registration statement or prospectus that contains a **misstatement or omission of a material fact** may sue the following:

      1) The issuer
      2) Every person who signed the registration statement
      3) Every director of the corporation or partner in the partnership issuing the security
      4) Experts who participated in preparation of the registration statement, e.g., accountants, engineers, and lawyers
      5) Every underwriter

   c. To recover under Section 11, a plaintiff must prove the following:

      1) The plaintiff acquired a security subject to registration.
      2) The plaintiff incurred a loss (damages).
      3) The registration statement contained a material misstatement or omission.

         a) But the accountant is liable only for a material misstatement or omission in a part of the statement for which (s)he was responsible.

   d. A defendant's liability extends to acquirers of a security described in the registration statement or the prospectus.

      1) The acquirer need not have given value.
      2) Privity of contract is not required.
      3) The acquirer need not prove reliance, negligence, or fraud.

EXAMPLE

Public Corp. engages Accountant to review events subsequent to the date of a certified balance sheet. The objective is to determine whether any material change has occurred that should be disclosed to prevent the balance sheet from being misleading with regard to the registration statement required for a bond issue. Accountant does not discover a material uninsured loss. Astute purchases some of the bonds. Public files for protection from creditors under the Bankruptcy Act. It defaults on payment of interest on the bonds. No contract exists between Astute and Accountant. Nevertheless, Accountant is liable to Astute for damages incurred because the registration statement did not include the material loss.

   e. If the plaintiff proves the basic elements of its case, any defendant except the issuer avoids liability by proof of **due diligence**.

      1) Due diligence means the accountant reasonably believed, at the time the registration statement became effective, that the financial statements did not contain an omission or misstatement of a material fact.

         a) The belief must be based on a reasonable investigation.

Background

In the early 1960s, BarChris was a New York company that specialized in the construction of bowling alleys. In desperate need of cash, the firm issued subordinated debentures based on inflated amounts included in a registration statement submitted to the SEC. In assigning blame for the incident, the judge found that the employee of BarChris's auditor, Peat, Marwick, Mitchell and Co., who was responsible for investigating the claims of the registration statement, had no defense based on due diligence. The judge listed multiple specific deficiencies, such as failing to read the prospectus, failing to read the minutes of the executive committee, and even failing to discover that the company was withholding checks because it did not have enough cash to cover them. The judge included a statement in the opinion that stands as a warning to anyone in the practice of auditing: "Most important of all, he was too easily satisfied with glib answers to his inquiries."

f. A successful plaintiff is entitled only to monetary damages under Section 11. They are generally measured by the plaintiff's loss, but resale is not required to prove loss.

1) The loss equals the difference between the price paid for the security and one of the following:

Action	Before Suit	After Suit
Security sold	Purchase price – Sales price	Purchase price – Greater of market value or sales price
Security not sold	Purchase price – Market value	Purchase price – Market value

2) The purpose of this measure of damages is to prevent unjust enrichment of the plaintiff.

3) If the purchaser sells the security back to the issuer, the purchaser will recover the price paid.

EXAMPLE

Reni successfully sued CPA under Section 11. Reni paid $50 per share for the stock that was the basis for the suit. The suit was brought on June 1. The market value of the stock on June 1 was $45. Reni sold the stock for $47 on June 5 before the jury reached a verdict. Reni's damages are $3 per share ($50 – $47). If Reni had not sold the stock, damages would be $5 per share ($50 – $45). If Reni had sold the stock on June 5 for $40, damages would be $5 per share ($50 – $45).

3. **Failure to Register under the 1933 Act**

a. Section 12(a)(1) imposes strict civil liability if

1) The required registration was not made;
2) A registered security was sold, but a prospectus was not delivered or was not current; or
3) An offer to sell was made before a required registration.

b. The purchaser may sue only his or her seller.

4. **Antifraud Provisions under the 1933 Act**

a. These apply to all securities, both registered and exempt.

b. Section 12(a)(2) imposes liability on any person to the immediate purchaser for material misstatements or omissions in any communication made with respect to the offer or sale of any security.

1) The purchaser may sue only his or her seller.
2) The seller's defenses under Section 12(a)(2) include proving that

a) (S)he did not know, and should not have known, about the misstatement or omission, or

b) The decline in value was not caused by the seller's misstatements.

c. Under Section 17(a), liability is imposed for fraud, material misrepresentations, and omissions in any securities sale. However, this broad provision does **not allow** the purchaser to file suit on his or her behalf.

Civil Remedies under the 1933 Act

Section	Prohibition	Plaintiffs	Defendants	Liability
11	Misstatement or omission in registration statement or prospectus	Acquirers of the covered securities	Issuer Signers Directors Experts Underwriters	Strict for issuer Negligence for others
12(a)(1)	No registration No delivery of current prospectus Sale before registration	Purchaser	Seller	Strict
12(a)(2)	Material misstatement or omission in any communication about offer or sale of any security	Purchaser	Seller	Negligence
17(a)	Fraud, material misrepresentation, omission in any securities sale	SEC enforcement (no implied private remedy)	Offerors and sellers	Civil or criminal

5. **Criminal Liability under the 1933 Act**

Background

Criminal liability under federal law has been rare for auditors, but a few cases have had a major impact. One of the most infamous was in connection with the Equity Funding scandal of the early 1970s. The fraud perpetrated by middle and upper management was so massive that the court concluded the auditors must have known about it. Three external audit personnel were convicted on criminal charges.

More recently, the old and distinguished accounting firm Arthur Andersen was convicted on a single criminal count of altering a document related to an audit of its scandal-plagued client Enron. Even though that single conviction was overturned, the firm's reputation had been so damaged by other revelations that no publicly traded company was willing to have its name associated with an Arthur Andersen audit. The firm voluntarily surrendered its licenses to practice before the SEC and has never resumed the practice of auditing.

a. Liability is based on willful violations of the act in the sale of securities.
   1) Willful violations are essentially fraud.
   2) The maximum penalty is 5 years in prison and a $10,000 fine.

6. **False or Misleading Statements under the 1934 Act**
   a. Section 18(a) of the 1934 act imposes liability for making or causing a **false or misleading statement (or omission) of a material fact** in any **filing** with the SEC under the act.
   b. A plaintiff must prove the following:
      1) A false statement about, or omission of, a material fact
      2) Reliance on the misstatement in buying or selling the security
         a) Proof that the price of the security was affected by the misstatement **(fraud-on-the-market theory)** may substitute for proof of reliance.
      3) Damages (loss)
   c. A **defense** to a suit based on Section 18(a) is to prove that the defendant acted in good faith and had **no knowledge** that the statement was false or misleading.
      1) Good faith is an absence of an intent to deceive.

The AICPA has tested CPA candidates on Section 10(b) of the Securities Exchange Act of 1934. CPA candidates should expect to see multiple-choice questions on the liability of CPAs and what a plaintiff must prove to recover damages under Section 10(b). Thus, candidates should **know and be able to cite Section 10(b) of the 1934 act.**

7. **Section 10(b) of the 1934 Act**
   a. Section 10(b) is the antifraud provision of the 1934 act.
      1) The SEC's **Rule 10b-5** states that it is illegal for any person, directly or indirectly, to use interstate commerce or a national securities exchange to defraud anyone in connection with the purchase or sale of any security, whether or not required to be registered.
         a) Rule 10b-5 most often is applied to insider trading and corporate misstatements.
         b) A person may violate Rule 10b-5 without actively participating in the purchase or sale of the security.
            i) All that is required is that the party's activity be connected with the purchase or sale.
   b. Liability is only to actual purchasers or sellers. They need not be in privity with the defendant.
   c. The SEC or a private party may sue. A **plaintiff must prove** each of the following:
      1) An oral or written misstatement or omission of a material fact or other fraud
      2) Its connection with any purchase or sale of securities
      3) The defendant's intent to deceive, manipulate, or defraud **(scienter)**
      4) Reliance on the misstatement
         a) If the plaintiff is the SEC, reliance is not required.
         b) A private plaintiff ordinarily need not prove reliance in omission cases. Indirect reliance is presumed (fraud-on-the-market theory).
      5) Loss caused by the reliance
   d. Remedies include
      1) Damages (no resale is necessary)
      2) Rescission of a securities contract
      3) Injunctions
   e. An accountant may be liable for misrepresentations contained in unaudited financial statements if (s)he knew or should have known of them.
      1) The accountant has a duty to perform a minimal investigation and not to ignore suspicious circumstances.
   f. An accountant is liable for aiding and abetting violations of the 1934 act when (s)he
      1) Is generally aware of his or her participation in an activity that, as a whole, is improper and
      2) Knowingly aids the activity. Silence may constitute aiding.
8. **Proxy Statements under the 1934 Act**
   a. Under Section 14(a), if a **proxy statement** contains a false or misleading statement of material fact, or omits such a fact, a shareholder who reasonably relies on it may sue the proxy solicitor. [Section 18(a) of the 1934 act also covers liability for misleading statements.]
9. **Tender Offers under the 1934 Act**
   a. Under Section 14(e), in a **tender offer**, it is illegal for any person to
      1) Make a misstatement of a material fact or omission of such a fact or
      2) Engage in any fraudulent or deceptive practice.

Civil Remedies under the 1934 Act

Section	Prohibition	Plaintiffs	Defendants
18(a)	Material false or misleading statement or omission in any SEC filing	Purchasers or sellers who rely and incur damages	Filers (defense is good faith or no knowledge)
14(a)	Material false or misleading proxy statement	Government Shareholders	Parties making the solicitation
14(e)	Material misstatement or omission of fact or fraud with respect to a tender offer	Government Possible private suit by target or its shareholders	Tender offeror
16(a)	Failure of insiders to comply with SEC reporting rules	Government administrative and criminal actions	Insiders (as defined in Section 16)
16(b)	Short-swing profit made by insiders on registered equity securities	Issuer Shareholder suit	Insiders (as defined in Section 16) strictly liable
Rule 10b-5	Fraud with regard to purchase or sale of any security	Government Purchaser or seller	Any person who commits fraud (but scienter must be proven)
Section 20A	Insider trading	Government Contemporaneous purchasers or sellers	Any purchaser or seller having material, nonpublic information

10. **Criminal Liability under the 1934 Act**
    a. The 1934 act imposes **criminal penalties** for willfully and knowingly making a materially false or misleading statement.
        1) For an individual, the penalty is a fine of up to $5 million or 20 years in prison.
        2) For a corporation or other entity that is not a natural person, the maximum fine is $25 million.
        3) Reckless disregard for the truth of a statement is sometimes deemed the equivalent of a willful violation.
        4) For an accountant, compliance with professional standards is not an absolute defense.
11. **Private Securities Litigation Reform Act of 1995**
    a. Among the provisions of this act are
        1) A prohibition on referral fees to be paid by an attorney to brokers, dealers, or their associates to obtain a client in any implied private action;
        2) A prohibition on the payment of legal fees to private parties seeking funds paid solely as the result of an action brought by the SEC;
        3) Modification of class action guidelines;
        4) A statute of limitations for private rights of action;
        5) Safe harbor rules for forward-looking statements; and
        6) Audit requirements for fraud detection and disclosure and proportionate liability.
            a) Audits should
                i) Provide reasonable assurance of detecting illegal acts having a direct and material effect on financial statement amounts,
                ii) Be designed to identify material related-party transactions, and
                iii) Include an evaluation as to whether a substantial doubt exists about the issuer's ability to continue as a going concern.

b) Accountants must report illegal acts to management and the audit committee unless they are clearly inconsequential.

i) Failure to act on reported material illegal acts may result in a departure from a standard report or resignation from the audit.

- In this case, the accountants should report their conclusions to the board immediately.
- The board must then, within 1 business day, notify the SEC.
- If the accountants do not receive a copy of the notice within the 1-day period, they must give the SEC a copy of their report within 1 business day.

b. Joint and several liability is imposed for a knowing violation of the securities laws. Otherwise, liability is proportionate to the defendant's percentage of responsibility for the total damages.

12. **Sarbanes-Oxley Act of 2002 (SOX)**

a. This act was a response to numerous accounting scandals. It applies to issuers of publicly traded securities subject to federal securities laws.

b. Among other things, the act regulates the public accounting profession. For this purpose, it established the **Public Company Accounting Oversight Board (PCAOB)**.

1) Violations of the Board's rules are violations of the Securities Exchange Act of 1934 and are subject to the same penalties.

2) The PCAOB

a) Registers public accounting firms;
b) Establishes or adopts by rule standards for audit reports;
c) Inspects and investigates accounting firms;
d) Conducts disciplinary proceedings;
e) Imposes sanctions; and
f) Enforces compliance with its rules, the act, professional standards, and securities laws relevant to audit reports and the obligations of accountants.

c. The **audit committee** must be directly responsible for appointing, compensating, and overseeing the work of the public accounting firm employed by the issuer. In addition, the accounting firm must report directly to the audit committee, not to management.

1) The act requires that each member of the audit committee, including at least one who is a financial expert, be an independent member of the issuer's board of directors.

a) An independent director is not affiliated with, and receives no compensation (other than for service on the board) from, the issuer.

The AICPA has heavily tested Section 404 of the Sarbanes-Oxley Act of 2002. Candidates should **know and be able to cite Section 404 of SOX**.

13. **Section 404 of SOX**
    a. Under Section 404 of the act, management must establish and document internal control procedures and include in the annual report **a report on the company's internal control over financial reporting**.
        1) This report is to include the following:
            a) A statement of management's responsibility for internal control
            b) Management's assessment of the effectiveness of internal control as of the end of the most recent fiscal year
            c) Identification of the framework used to evaluate the effectiveness of internal control (such as the report of the Committee of Sponsoring Organizations)
            d) A statement about whether significant changes in controls were made after their evaluation, including any corrective actions
            e) A statement that the external auditor has issued an attestation report on management's assessment
        2) Because of Section 404, **two audit opinions** are expressed: one on internal control and one on the financial statements.
            a) However, a corporate issuer with a market capitalization of less than $75 million is exempt from the required audit of management's assertions about control and procedures for financial reporting (Dodd-Frank Wall Street Reform and Consumer Protection Act of 2010).
        3) The auditor must evaluate whether the control structure and procedures
            a) Include records accurately and fairly reflecting the firm's transactions and
            b) Provide reasonable assurance that transactions are recorded so as to permit statements to be prepared in accordance with GAAP.
        4) The auditor's report also must **describe any material weaknesses** in the controls.
        5) The evaluation is not to be the subject of a separate engagement. It must be in conjunction with the audit of the financial statements.
    b. Auditors of issuers must not perform the following nonaudit services absent a specific PCAOB exemption or audit committee preapproval:
        1) Appraisal and other valuation services, designing and implementing financial information systems, actuarial functions, and bookkeeping if the results are subject to audit
        2) Management and human resource services
        3) Legal and other expert services not pertaining to the audit
        4) Investment banking, advisory, and broker-dealer services
        5) Internal audit outsourcing that involves financial accounting
        6) Certain tax services
    c. Audit firms may continue to provide conventional tax planning and other nonaudit services not specifically prohibited to audit clients if preapproved by the audit committee.
    d. Still another provision of the act prohibits the conflict of interest that arises when the CEO, CFO, controller, chief accounting officer, or the equivalent was employed by the company's public accounting firm within 1 year preceding the audit.

e. Auditors must retain their audit **working papers** for at least 7 years.

    1) It is a **crime** for auditors to fail to maintain all audit or review working papers for at least 5 years.

        a) If retention is for more than 5 years but fewer than 7 years, sanctions that are not criminal penalties may be imposed by the PCAOB.

f. Second-partner review and approval of audit reports is required.

    1) Furthermore, the lead audit partner and the reviewing partner must rotate off the audit every 5 years.

g. Public accounting firms must register with the PCAOB and be subject to **inspection every 3 years (1 year for large firms)**.

    1) Moreover, they must adopt quality control standards and reasonably supervise any associated person with regard to auditing and quality control standards.
    2) Registrants must file an annual report with the PCAOB that contains basic information about firm activities. They also must file a special report within 30 days of a reportable event, e.g., initiation of legal action against the firm.

h. **Auditor reports to audit committees** must include

    1) All critical accounting policies and practices to be used
    2) All material alternative treatments of financial information within GAAP discussed with management
    3) Ramifications of the use of alternative disclosures and treatments
    4) The treatment preferred by the external auditors

i. Correcting adjustments identified by the public accountants must be disclosed in an issuer's required periodic U.S. GAAP-based reports.

j. Tampering with records, e.g., altering audit working papers to impair their integrity or availability for use in an official proceeding, is a crime punishable by up to 20 years in prison.

k. The act created a **25-year felony** for defrauding shareholders of issuers. It prohibits the knowing or attempted execution of any fraud upon persons in connection with securities of issuers or the purchase or sale of such securities.

14. **Dodd-Frank Wall Street Reform and Consumer Protection Act of 2010**

a. This comprehensive legislation was enacted after the economic crisis in 2008. The act extends to, among other things, (1) the financial services industry, (2) consumer protection, (3) financial markets, (4) securities laws, (5) financial reporting and governance, and (6) broker-dealer audits.

b. The act enlarges the scope of the SEC's authority to prosecute those who **aid and abet** securities law violations.

    1) Moreover, the legal standard for those involved is now "knowing or reckless" instead of merely knowing.

c. Auditors of **broker-dealers** are subject to inspection by the PCAOB and possible sanctions.

    1) All broker-dealers must be audited by registered auditors.

d. The **Financial Stability Oversight Council** has been established to (1) identify, in advance, financial system risks; (2) comment to the SEC about accounting issues; and (3) report annually to Congress about financial market and regulatory matters.

e. **Investment advisors** with $25 million to $100 million of assets under management must register with state regulators.

    1) But an advisor required to register with at least 15 states may register with the SEC.

f. Shareholders have the right to a nonbinding vote on **compensation** for specified corporate officers at least once every 3 years.
   1) The act also requires independent compensation committee members and disclosure of independent compensation committee advisors and related fees or conflicts of interest.
   2) A public company must have a **clawback policy** defining how to recover performance-based executive compensation after a financial restatement.
   3) The SEC now has the power to give shareholders with at least 3% of the voting interests access to the corporation's **proxy** procedures.

g. The SEC may compensate **whistleblowers** who provide information other than that from an audit or investigation.
   1) Whistleblowers may sue retaliating employers.
   2) Under SOX, (a) whistleblower claims may be asserted for up to 180 days, (b) trial by jury is allowed, and (c) whistleblower rights and remedies may not be waived.

h. **Credit rating agencies** are to be examined annually by the SEC. These agencies (1) must disclose their methods, (2) are subject to investor suits, and (3) must consent to use of their ratings in **registration statements**.

i. **Over-the-counter derivatives** are regulated by the SEC and the Commodity Futures Trading Commission (CFTC).
   1) Hedge funds and private equity funds must register with the SEC.
   2) If derivatives can be cleared, the act requires that they be centrally cleared and exchange traded.
   3) The act prohibits the Federal Reserve and the Federal Deposit Insurance Corporation from assisting most insured depository institutions that participate in swap markets.

Stop and review! You have completed the outline for this subunit. Study multiple-choice questions 11 through 18 beginning on page 71.

2.4 STATE LAW LIABILITY TO CLIENTS AND THIRD PARTIES

1. **Contractual Liability**
   a. The contract between an accountant and a client is a personal service contract.
   b. Legal issues arising from contract disputes include (1) whether the elements of a contract are present, (2) the duties of the parties, (3) who may enforce the contract, (4) who is liable for breach of contract, and (5) what remedies are available for breach.

2. **Accountant's Duties**
   a. The accountant is implicitly bound by the contract to perform the engagement with **due care** (nonnegligently) and in compliance with **professional standards**.
      1) Moreover, an accountant must comply with the law and is responsible for exercising independent professional judgment.

EXAMPLE

An accountant and a client entity contract for the accountant to perform an audit for $2,500. The audit is contracted to be done within 3 months. The audit actually takes 6 months. A breach of contract has occurred.

b. An understanding should be established regarding what services the accountant is to perform for the client. An **engagement letter** puts this understanding in writing.

1) The engagement letter should describe the services agreed upon by the client and accountant, fees to be paid, and other pertinent details.
2) Although not necessary for the formation of a contract, an engagement letter may prevent contract disputes.
3) An engagement letter may provide for services or procedures beyond those required by (a) U.S. generally accepted auditing standards (GAAS), (b) standards of the Public Company Accounting Oversight Board (PCAOB) governing performance of services for public companies, (c) U.S. generally accepted accounting principles (GAAP), or (d) other applicable professional standards.

EXAMPLE

The engagement letter may provide for positive confirmation of all accounts receivable. Professional standards may, in the circumstances of the specific engagement, permit negative confirmation of a sample of accounts receivable.

The AICPA has tested CPA candidates on potential liability. A CPA can be liable for negligence, fraud, and breach of contract. CPA candidates should expect to see different types of multiple-choice questions on when a CPA is liable and how a CPA can defend against a liability claim.

3. **Contractual Liability to Third Parties**

a. An accountant potentially may be liable to third-party beneficiaries of the contract.

4. **Contractual Defenses**

a. Typical defenses to breach of contract include the following:

1) Failure of consideration
   a) What was bargained for may have (1) become worthless, (2) ceased to exist, or (3) not been performed as promised.
2) Alleged obligation not within scope of contract
3) Full or substantial performance rendered
4) Purpose of the contract contrary to law or public policy
5) Suspension or termination of performance justified because of client's breach
6) Failure of a condition precedent, an event that must occur before contractual performance is due

5. **Liability for Negligence**

a. An accountant has a duty to exercise **reasonable care and diligence**.

1) The accountant should have the degree of skill commonly possessed by other accountants in the same or similar circumstances.
2) Ordinary negligence may arise from an accountant's act or failure to act given a duty to act, for example, failing to observe inventory or confirm receivables.
3) An accountant may be liable in tort to a client for losses caused by the accountant's negligence.
   a) A **tort** is a private wrong resulting from the breach of a legal duty imposed by society.
      i) The duty is not created by contract or other private relationship.

b. A client must prove all of the elements of negligence.

1) The accountant owed the client a **duty**.
2) The accountant **breached** this duty.
3) The accountant's breach **actually and proximately caused** the client's injury.

a) Proximate cause is a chain of causation that is not interrupted by a new, independent cause. Moreover, the injury would not have occurred without the proximate cause. However, actual causation is insufficient. The injury also must have been reasonably foreseeable. Thus, the concept of proximate cause limits liability.

4) The client suffered **damages**.

c. **Negligent misrepresentation** occurs when the accountant makes a false representation of a material fact not known to be false but intended to induce reliance.

1) The plaintiff must have reasonably relied on the accountant's misrepresentation and incurred damages.

d. Gross negligence is failure to use even slight care.

1) An accountant may be liable for punitive damages if (s)he is grossly (but not ordinarily) negligent.

a) Extreme circumstances must exist for punitive damages to be awarded.

e. Auditor-accountants are not guarantors and therefore have **no general duty to discover fraud**.

1) Nevertheless, an auditor is held liable for failure to discover fraud when the auditor's negligence prevented discovery.
2) An auditor who fails to follow professional standards and does not discover fraud will probably be liable if compliance would have detected the fraud.

EXAMPLE

U.S. GAAS and PCAOB standards require an auditor to plan and perform the audit to provide **reasonable assurance** about whether the financial statements are free of material misstatement, whether caused by error or fraud. An auditor must (1) identify risks of material misstatement due to fraud; (2) assess the identified risks; and (3) respond by changing the nature, timing, and extent of audit procedures.

f. Accountants may be liable for failure to communicate to the client findings or circumstances that indicate misstatements in the accounting records or fraud.

1) They also must communicate all significant deficiencies and material weaknesses in internal control.

6. **Liability to Third Parties for Negligence**

a. The majority rule is that the accountant is liable to **foreseen** (but not necessarily individually identified) **third parties** (foreseen users and users within a foreseen class of users).

1) Foreseen third parties are those to whom the accountant intends to supply the information or knows the client intends to supply the information.

a) They also include persons who use the information in a way the accountant knows it will be used.

EXAMPLE

Smith, CPA, was engaged by Client, Inc., to audit its annual financial statements. Client's president told Smith that the financial statements would be distributed to South Bank in connection with a loan application. Smith was negligent in performing the audit. Subsequently, the financial statements were given to West Bank as well. West Bank lent Client $50,000 in reliance on the financial statements. West Bank suffered a loss on the loan. Smith is liable to West Bank because it is within a foreseen class of users, and the loan is a transaction similar to that for which the financial statements were audited.

b. In some states, the accountant is liable to all **reasonably foreseeable third parties**. They are all members of the class of persons whose reliance on the financial statements the accountant may reasonably anticipate.

EXAMPLE

Smith, CPA, is engaged to audit the annual financial statements of Client. Smith is not informed of the intended use of the statements. However, Smith knows that they are routinely distributed to lessors, suppliers, trade creditors, and lending institutions. Client uses the statements, which were negligently prepared, to obtain a lease from XYZ, Inc., a reasonably foreseeable party. Smith will be liable to XYZ because it is a member of a class of reasonably foreseeable third parties.

c. The traditional view was that an accountant was liable for **negligence** only to a plaintiff that was in **privity of contract** with the accountant or a primary beneficiary of the engagement. Typically, a third party is considered to be a primary beneficiary if the following apply:

1) The accountant is retained principally to benefit the third party.
2) The third party is identified.
3) The benefit pertains to a specific transaction. Thus, the accountant knows the particular purpose for which the third party will use and rely upon the work.

EXAMPLE

Smith, CPA, was engaged by Client, Inc., to audit Client's annual financial statements. Client told Smith that the audited financial statements were required by Bank in connection with a loan application. Bank is a primary beneficiary and may recover damages caused by the CPA's negligence.

4) A primary beneficiary is the same as an intended third-party beneficiary.

7. **Strict Liability in Tort**

a. Strict liability without fault is not a basis for recovery from an accountant.

8. **Defenses to Negligence**

a. Typical defenses to negligence include the following:

1) The alleged duty was not owed.
2) The accountant did not breach the duty.
   a) The accountant exercised reasonable care.
   b) Compliance with the relevant professional standards is evidence, but not necessarily sufficient proof, that the accountant exercised the diligence due under the circumstances.
3) The plaintiff did not suffer a loss.
4) The accountant's behavior was not the cause of the party's loss. For example, the loss may have been caused by the client's own negligence or by a third party.
5) The plaintiff is not within a class of parties to whom an accountant is potentially liable under the applicable state law.

6) The person alleging harm assumed the risk, e.g., by accepting a contract containing an effective disclaimer.
7) The statute of limitations has expired.

9. **Compliance with Professional Standards as a Defense**

a. Compliance with professional standards is a defense to malpractice lawsuits.

1) For example, U.S. GAAS and PCAOB standards prescribe rules and procedures for conducting audits.
2) U.S. GAAP prescribe rules for presentation of financial information.
3) But courts may insist on standards higher than professional standards.

10. **Contributory and Comparative Negligence**

a. Under the contributory negligence doctrine, a plaintiff who is responsible for his or her own injuries does not receive any damages from the defendant, even if the plaintiff is only 1% responsible.

1) Contributory negligence is no longer applied in most states.

b. Under the comparative negligence doctrine, a plaintiff who is responsible for his or her own injuries may recover the percentage of damages attributable to the defendant's actions.

EXAMPLE

A plaintiff proves that the defendant acted negligently. But if the plaintiff is 35% responsible for his or her own injuries, the plaintiff in a comparative negligence state may collect 65% (100% – 35%) of the damages.

1) In more than half of the states, if the court decides that the plaintiff has a certain percentage of fault, (50% or 51% depending on the state), the plaintiff cannot recover any damages from the defendant.

a) This approach is partial comparative negligence.

EXAMPLE

A plaintiff proves that the defendant acted negligently. But if the plaintiff is 65% responsible for his or her own injuries, the plaintiff in a partial comparative negligence state cannot recover any damages.

11. **Liability for Fraud**

a. Fraud is an intentional misrepresentation. An accountant is liable for losses that result from his or her commission of fraud. Punitive and compensatory damages are permitted.

EXAMPLE

An accountant is engaged to audit financial statements. To increase profits from the engagement, the accountant planned to and did omit necessary audit procedures. The accountant committed fraud.

b. A finding of fraud requires proof of the following elements:

1) The accountant made a **misrepresentation**.
2) The misrepresentation was made with **scienter**, that is, with actual or implied knowledge of fraud.
3) The misrepresentation was of a **material fact**.
4) The misrepresentation induced **reliance**.
5) Another person **justifiably relied** on the misstatement.
6) The other person suffered a **loss**.

c. The element of scienter may be satisfied by proof of **gross negligence** (i.e., a reckless disregard for the truth).

   1) The result is **constructive fraud**, that is, fraud with the scienter requirement satisfied by gross negligence.

d. Liability for fraud cannot be disclaimed.

12. **Liability to Third Parties for Fraud**

   a. Liability is to all **reasonably foreseeable users** of the work product. A foreseeable user is any person that the accountant should have reasonably foreseen would be injured by justifiable reliance on the misrepresentation.

      1) Privity is not required. Privity, in this context, means that the accountant and the plaintiff were parties to the contract that resulted in the loss.
      2) A foreseeable user has the right to sue.

13. **Defenses to Fraud**

   a. A plaintiff has the burden to prove each element of fraud. Credible evidence that the accountant can introduce to disprove one of those elements tends to negate liability.

      1) Negligence of a client is not a defense.
      2) Expiration of the statute of limitations is a defense.

Stop and review! You have completed the outline for this subunit. Study multiple-choice questions 19 through 27 beginning on page 74.

2.5 PRIVILEGED COMMUNICATION AND CONFIDENTIALITY

1. **Accountant-Client Privilege**

   a. Federal law does not recognize a broad privilege for accountant-client communications.
   b. However, a confidentiality privilege covers most tax advice provided to a current or prospective client by any individual (CPA, attorney, enrolled agent, or enrolled actuary) qualified under federal law to practice before the IRS.

      1) The privilege does not apply to criminal tax matters, private civil matters, disclosures to other federal regulatory bodies, or state and local tax matters.

   c. The privilege is available only in matters brought before the IRS or in proceedings in federal court in which the U.S. is a party.

      1) The privilege applies only to advice on legal issues.

   d. A majority of the states do not recognize a privilege for accountant-client communications.
   e. A minority of the states have statutes that grant the privilege. It is applicable in criminal and civil matters and is not limited to the subject matter of the audit.

EXAMPLE

State law provides for an accountant-client privilege. The IRS, in conducting a proper investigation, requests Accounting Firm to provide it with records on Client. The federal privilege does not apply. Firm complies, and Client sues Firm in state court. Firm asserts that federal law does not recognize the privilege and preempts state law. State court determines that, because the disclosure was without notice to Client and was made in the absence of service of legal process compelling disclosure, Firm is liable to Client for the voluntary disclosure.

   f. If the privilege exists, it belongs to the client.
   g. If any part of the privileged communication is disclosed by either the client or the accountant, the privilege is lost completely.

EXAMPLE

In the previous example, disclosure by Firm to a third party (the IRS) negates the privilege with respect to the information. The information is no longer recognized as a protected confidential communication under the law of the state. However, Firm may still be liable to Client. Given the existence of a state privilege, Firm is still liable if, in the specific case, federal law does not preempt state law. Firm has a professional duty under the AICPA *Code of Professional Conduct*. It must not disclose confidential client information without consent except, for example, to comply with an enforceable summons or subpoena.

h. Client communications with accountants retained by attorneys to aid in litigation are protected by the attorney-client privilege. This privilege is recognized in both federal and state courts.
   1) The accountant is considered the attorney's agent.

2. **Working Papers**

a. Working papers are confidential records made by an accountant while performing an engagement. Working papers may include each of the following:
   1) Plans for the engagement
   2) Documentation of the client's accounting system
   3) Results of tests performed
   4) Written representations from the client or the client's legal counsel
   5) Explanations
   6) Reconciliations

b. Working papers are the **property of the accountant**.
   1) Because they are prepared by the accountant, they provide the best evidence of the accountant's efforts in the event of a lawsuit.
   2) However, working papers may be subpoenaed by a third party for use in litigation in the numerous states that do not recognize a privilege for accountant-client communications.
   3) Absent a court order or client consent, third parties have no right of **access** to working papers.
      a) The accountant may be liable for malpractice if (s)he allows a third party, including a purchaser of his or her practice, unauthorized access to working papers.
         i) The AICPA *Code of Professional Conduct* (Rule 301) states that a member shall not disclose any confidential client information except with the specific consent of the client.
      b) If confidential accountant-client communications are privileged under state law, disclosure is not permitted except in limited circumstances, for example, when
         i) The statute allows disclosure to a state peer review board or
         ii) Federal law preempts the state law.
   4) At a minimum, an accountant who does not audit public companies should **retain** working papers until the state statute of limitations on litigation that might arise has lapsed. The limitations period varies by state and according to the type of claim.
      a) Retention of working papers ensures that the accountant will have the evidence necessary to defend against claims in a lawsuit.

Stop and review! You have completed the outline for this subunit. Study multiple-choice questions 28 through 30 on page 77.

QUESTIONS

2.1 Securities Act of 1933

1. Under the Securities Act of 1933, which of the following statements, if any, are correct regarding the purpose of registration?

I. The purpose of registration is to allow for the detection of management fraud and prevent a public offering of securities when management fraud is suspected.

II. The purpose of registration is to adequately and accurately disclose financial and other information upon which investors may determine the merits of securities.

A. I only.

B. II only.

C. Both I and II.

D. Neither I nor II.

Answer (B) is correct.

REQUIRED: The true statements, if any, about the purpose of registration under the Securities Act of 1933.

DISCUSSION: One purpose of the Securities Act of 1933 is disclosure. The act was designed to provide complete and fair disclosure to potential investors. It applies only to the initial issuance of securities. Disclosure is accomplished through the requirement that a registration statement be filed with the SEC. Once potential investors have complete disclosure, the assumption is that they can make reasonable decisions. The second purpose is prevention, not detection, of fraud through enforcement of its antifraud provisions. Thus, although the 1933 act does not provide for evaluation of the merits of securities or examination by government auditors, its civil remedies, criminal penalties, and disclosure requirements (including financial statements audited by CPAs) help prevent fraud.

2. When a common stock offering requires registration under the Securities Act of 1933,

A. The registration statement is automatically effective when filed with the SEC.

B. The issuer would act unlawfully if it were to sell the common stock without providing the investor with a prospectus.

C. The SEC will determine the investment value of the common stock before approving the offering.

D. The issuer may make sales 10 days after filing the registration statement.

Answer (B) is correct.

REQUIRED: The true statement about an offering that must be registered under the Securities Act of 1933.

DISCUSSION: If an issue is required to be registered under the Securities Act of 1933, a registration statement and a prospectus must be prepared and filed with the SEC. The prospectus contains financial material and other information about the issuer and the offering. A prospectus must be provided to any person interested in investing in the security offered.

Answer (A) is incorrect. A registration statement generally becomes effective 20 days after filing. Answer (C) is incorrect. The SEC does not determine the investment value of the security. Answer (D) is incorrect. The issuer may not sell the security until registration is effective. Registration generally becomes effective on the 20th day after filing.

3. Dee is the owner of 12% of the shares of common stock of D&M Corporation that she acquired in Year 1. She is the treasurer and a director of D&M. The corporation registered its securities in Year 2 and made a public offering pursuant to the Securities Act of 1933. If Dee decides to sell part of her holdings in Year 9, the shares

A. Would be exempt from registration because the corporation previously registered them within 3 years.

B. Must be registered regardless of the amount sold or manner in which they are sold.

C. Would be exempt from registration because she is not an issuer.

D. Must be registered if Dee sells 50% of her shares through her broker to the public.

Answer (D) is correct.

REQUIRED: The true statement as to whether a controlling person's stock sale must be registered.

DISCUSSION: In general, any offer to sell securities in interstate commerce is subject to registration unless the securities or the transaction is exempt. Most transactions are exempt because they involve sales by persons other than issuers, underwriters, or dealers, e.g., transactions by ordinary investors selling on their own account. Dee, however, is considered an issuer because she is a controlling person, that is, one who owns more than 10% of the company's stock and who has the direct or indirect ability to control the company. A sale of 6% of D&M's common stock to the public in the ordinary course of business (e.g., through a broker) would not qualify for an exemption under the Securities Act of 1933 and would be subject to SEC registration.

Answer (A) is incorrect. The previous registration is irrelevant. Answer (B) is incorrect. Under Rule 144, an insider who has held restricted securities for at least 1 year may resell without registration in any 3-month period the greater of 1% of the total shares of that class outstanding or the average weekly volume traded. Notice must be given to the SEC, adequate information about the issuer must be publicly available, and sales must be through brokers' transactions or in transactions with a market maker. Also, the sale might be exempt if no public offer is made or if certain other requirements are met. Answer (C) is incorrect. A controlling person is an issuer.

4. Which of the following requirements must be met by an issuer of securities who wants to make an offering by using shelf registration?

	Original Registration Statement Must Be Kept Updated	The Offeror Must Be a First-Time Issuer of Securities
A.	Yes	Yes
B.	Yes	No
C.	No	Yes
D.	No	No

Answer (B) is correct.

REQUIRED: The requirements for a shelf registration.

DISCUSSION: SEC Rule 415 permits shelf registration of securities. Under a shelf registration, issuers may file the registration statement prior to the actual sale. This type of registration allows issuers to leave the securities on the shelf until market conditions are favorable. Only seasoned and well-known seasoned issuers are eligible for the use of shelf registration. However, issuers are required to update the registration statement frequently to avoid stale information.

5. An offering made under the provisions of Regulation A of the Securities Act of 1933 requires that the issuer

A. File an offering circular with the SEC.

B. Sell only to accredited investors.

C. Provide investors with the prior 4 years' audited financial statements.

D. Provide investors with a proxy registration statement.

Answer (A) is correct.

REQUIRED: The requirement for a stock offering made under Regulation A.

DISCUSSION: Under Regulation A, a small public issue of securities is exempt from full registration with the SEC if certain requirements are met. Regulation A applies to issuances not exceeding $5 million if the issuer files an offering circular with the SEC, provides it to each offeree and purchaser, and observes the 20-day waiting period.

Answer (B) is incorrect. Regulation A does not restrict resale, have an investor sophistication requirement, or limit the number of buyers. Also, no disclosure is necessary if the offering is $100,000 or less. Answer (C) is incorrect. Regulation A provides an exemption from the otherwise required filing of a registration statement and prospectus. Answer (D) is incorrect. Filing proxy statements is required under the 1934 act. Regulation A provides exemption from filing requirements of the 1933 act.

6. Frey, Inc., intends to make a $2 million common stock offering under Rule 505 of Regulation D of the Securities Act of 1933. Frey

A. May sell the stock to an unlimited number of nonaccredited investors.

B. May make the offering through a general advertising.

C. Must notify the SEC within 15 days after the first sale of the offering.

D. Must provide all investors with a prospectus.

Answer (C) is correct.

REQUIRED: The true statement about a securities offering under Rule 505.

DISCUSSION: Rule 505 provides exemption from the requirements of the 1933 act to all issuers other than investment companies for sales of securities up to $5 million in any 12-month period. Under Rule 505, securities may be sold to no more than 35 nonaccredited investors and to an unlimited number of accredited investors. Rule 505 also provides that the issuer must notify the SEC within 15 days after the first offering.

Answer (A) is incorrect. Rule 505 prohibits sale to more than 35 nonaccredited investors. Answer (B) is incorrect. Exemption under Rules 505 and 506 of Regulation D is conditioned on no general solicitation. Answer (D) is incorrect. A prospectus need not be provided. However, if some investors are nonaccredited, they must be furnished with material information about the issuer, its business, and the securities being offered.

2.2 Securities Exchange Act of 1934

7. Integral Corp., with assets in excess of $4 million, has issued common and preferred stock and has 350 shareholders. Its stock is sold on the New York Stock Exchange. Under the Securities Exchange Act of 1934, Integral must be registered with the SEC because

A. It issues both common and preferred stock.

B. Its shares are listed on a national stock exchange.

C. It has more than 300 shareholders.

D. Its shares are traded in interstate commerce.

Answer (B) is correct.

REQUIRED: The basis for required registration under the Securities Exchange Act of 1934.

DISCUSSION: The Securities Exchange Act of 1934 requires all regulated, publicly held corporations to register with the SEC. Covered corporations either (1) list shares on a national securities exchange or (2) have at least 500 shareholders of equity securities and total gross assets exceeding $10 million.

Answer (A) is incorrect. Issuing preferred stock is not a sufficient condition for registering or reporting under the 1934 act. Answer (C) is incorrect. The threshold is 500 shareholders and total gross assets of $10 million or more. Answer (D) is incorrect. Shares trading in interstate commerce are insufficient to trigger registration requirements under the 1934 act.

8. Under Section 12 of the Securities Exchange Act of 1934, in addition to companies whose securities are traded on a national exchange, what class of companies is subject to the SEC's registration requirements?

A. Companies with annual revenues in excess of $5 million and 300 or more shareholders.

B. Companies with annual revenues in excess of $10 million and 500 or more shareholders.

C. Companies with assets in excess of $5 million and 300 or more shareholders.

D. Companies with assets in excess of $10 million and 500 or more shareholders.

Answer (D) is correct.

REQUIRED: The companies subject to registration requirements under Section 12 of the Securities Exchange Act of 1934.

DISCUSSION: All regulated, publicly held companies must register with the SEC. Registration is required of all companies that have at least 500 shareholders of equity securities and total gross assets exceeding $10 million.

Answer (A) is incorrect. A minimum amount of assets, not annual revenues, and more than 300 shareholders are required for registration requirements. Answer (B) is incorrect. A minimum amount of assets, not annual revenues, is required for registration requirements. Answer (C) is incorrect. The minimum amount of assets and shareholders required for registration requirements is higher than $5 million in assets and 300 or more shareholders.

9. Which of the following events must be reported to the SEC under the reporting provisions of the Securities Exchange Act of 1934?

	Tender Offers	Insider Trading	Solicitation Proxies
A.	Yes	Yes	Yes
B.	Yes	Yes	No
C.	Yes	No	Yes
D.	No	Yes	Yes

Answer (A) is correct.

REQUIRED: The events that must be reported to the SEC under the Securities Exchange Act of 1934.

DISCUSSION: The Securities Exchange Act of 1934 governs dealings in securities subsequent to their initial issuance. The act requires all regulated, publicly held companies to register with the SEC. The act requires disclosure of matters concerning tender offers, insider trading, and the solicitation of proxies.

10. Which of the following persons is **not** an insider of a corporation subject to the Securities Exchange Act of 1934 registration and reporting requirements?

A. The president.

B. A member of the board of directors.

C. A shareholder who owns 8% of the outstanding common stock and whose spouse owns 4% of the outstanding common stock.

D. An owner of 15% of the total face value of the corporation's outstanding debentures.

Answer (D) is correct.

REQUIRED: The individual not deemed an insider.

DISCUSSION: For the purposes of Section 16(b), an insider is an officer, a director, or a beneficial owner of 10% or more of any class of equity securities registered under the 1934 act. The holder of debentures (unsecured bonds) is not an insider because a debenture is a debt security, not an equity security.

Answer (A) is incorrect. An officer is an insider. Answer (B) is incorrect. A director is an insider. Answer (C) is incorrect. A 12% owner is considered an insider even though 4% of the ownership is beneficial. A shareholder is a beneficial owner if shares are owned by his or her spouse, minor children, a relative with the same residence, or a trust of which (s)he is a beneficiary.

2.3 Federal Statutory Liability of CPAs and Others

11. One of the elements necessary to recover damages if there has been a material misstatement in a registration statement filed under the Securities Act of 1933 is that the

A. Issuer and plaintiff were in privity of contract with each other.

B. Issuer failed to exercise due care in connection with the sale of the securities.

C. Plaintiff gave value for the security.

D. Plaintiff suffered a loss.

Answer (D) is correct.

REQUIRED: The element necessary to recover damages under the 1933 act.

DISCUSSION: Under Section 11, the plaintiff must prove that (s)he was an acquirer of a security covered by a registration statement, (s)he suffered a loss, and the statement misstated or omitted a material fact.

Answer (A) is incorrect. Plaintiff may have obtained the security from a party other than defendant. Answer (B) is incorrect. Neither negligence nor fraud need be proven by the plaintiff. However, any defendant except an issuer may employ the due diligence defense by proving that (s)he was not negligent and that (s)he reasonably investigated the statement and reasonably believed it to be free of material falsehoods or omissions. Answer (C) is incorrect. That the plaintiff gave value for the security need not be shown.

12. How does the Securities Act of 1933, which imposes civil liability on auditors for misrepresentations or omissions of material facts in a registration statement, expand auditors' liability to purchasers of securities beyond that of common law?

A. Purchasers only have to prove loss caused by reliance on audited financial statements.

B. Privity with purchasers is not a necessary element of proof.

C. Purchasers have to prove either fraud or gross negligence as a basis for recovery.

D. Auditors are held to a standard of care described as "professional skepticism."

Answer (B) is correct.

REQUIRED: The factor that results in expanded liability of a CPA under the Securities Act of 1933.

DISCUSSION: Under the Securities Act of 1933, a purchaser need only prove damages resulting from the purchase of securities covered by a registration statement containing a false statement or omission of a material fact in a section audited or prepared by the auditor. The auditor must then prove that (s)he was not negligent (or fraudulent), usually by showing that (s)he acted with due diligence.

To recover damages at common law based on contract or negligence, privity between the plaintiff and accountant may be required. To recover under the Securities Act of 1933, however, a purchaser of securities need not prove privity of contract with a CPA.

Answer (A) is incorrect. More must be proved under the 1933 act, e.g., material misstatement or omission. Answer (C) is incorrect. Purchasers need not prove either fraud or gross negligence to recover under the 1933 act. Answer (D) is incorrect. Such a standard does not apply at common law or under the 1933 act.

13. Burt, CPA, issued an unmodified opinion on the financial statements of Midwest Corp. These financial statements were included in Midwest's annual report, and Form 10-K was filed with the SEC. As a result of Burt's reckless disregard for GAAS, material misstatements in the financial statements were not detected. Subsequently, Davis purchased stock in Midwest in the secondary market without ever seeing Midwest's annual report or Form 10-K. Shortly thereafter, Midwest became insolvent, and the price of the stock declined drastically. Davis sued Burt for damages based on Section 10(b) and Rule 10b-5 of the Securities Exchange Act of 1934. Burt's best defense is that

A. There has been no subsequent sale for which a loss can be computed.

B. Davis did not purchase the stock as part of an initial offering.

C. Davis did not rely on the financial statements or Form 10-K.

D. Davis was not in privity with Burt.

Answer (C) is correct.

REQUIRED: The best defense of a grossly negligent accountant sued under Rule 10b-5.

DISCUSSION: The plaintiff must have relied on the misstatement or omission of a material fact with regard to the purchase or sale of a security if (s)he is to recover under Rule 10b-5. In the case of an omission, reliance is implied by materiality. Davis did not see the relevant annual report or Form 10-K and will therefore have difficulty in proving reliance.

Answer (A) is incorrect. Damages may be proven without a subsequent sale. Answer (B) is incorrect. Rule 10b-5 applies to a misstatement or an omission of a material fact in connection with any purchase or sale of a security if the wrongful act involved interstate commerce, the U.S. mail, or a national securities exchange. Answer (D) is incorrect. Privity is not required.

14. Under the Securities and Exchange Act of 1934, which of the following penalties could be assessed against a CPA who intentionally violated the provisions of Section 10(b), Rule 10b-5 of the act?

	Civil Liability for Monetary Damages	Criminal Liability for a Fine
A.	Yes	Yes
B.	Yes	No
C.	No	Yes
D.	No	No

Answer (A) is correct.

REQUIRED: The penalty(ies), if any, for an intentional violation of Section 10(b), Rule 10b-5 of the Securities and Exchange Act of 1934.

DISCUSSION: Section 10(b) of the 1934 act and SEC Rule 10b-5 are antifraud provisions. They make it unlawful for any person to employ, in connection with the purchase or sale of any security, any manipulative or deceptive device or any contrivance in contravention of SEC rules and regulations. Any buyer or seller of any security who suffers a monetary loss may bring a private civil suit to rescind the transaction or to receive monetary damages. Punitive damages are not recoverable. The 1934 act also provides for criminal sanctions for willful violations. Liability is imposed for false material statements in applications, reports, documents, registration statements, and press releases. For an individual, the penalty is a fine not to exceed $5 million, 20 years in prison, or both. An individual who proves (s)he had no knowledge of the rule or regulation will not be imprisoned. If the person is not a natural person (e.g., a corporation), the maximum fine is $25 million.

15. The antifraud provisions of Rule 10b-5 of the Securities Exchange Act of 1934

A. Apply only if the securities involved were registered under the Securities Act of 1933 or the Securities Exchange Act of 1934.

B. Require that the plaintiff show negligence on the part of the defendant in misstating facts.

C. Require that the wrongful act be accomplished through the mail, any other use of interstate commerce, or through a national securities exchange.

D. Apply only if the defendant acted with intent to defraud.

Answer (C) is correct.

REQUIRED: The element of a violation of the antifraud provisions of Rule 10b-5.

DISCUSSION: The scope of Rule 10b-5 is broad but not absolute. Rule 10b-5 applies to certain wrongful acts done in connection with the purchase or sale of any security by use of (1) any means or instrumentality of interstate commerce, (2) the mails, or (3) any facility of any national securities exchange.

Answer (A) is incorrect. Rule 10b-5 also applies to unregistered securities. Answer (B) is incorrect. Intent to deceive must be proved. Answer (D) is incorrect. An intent to deceive or manipulate suffices.

16. The Sarbanes-Oxley Act of 2002 requires management of publicly traded corporations to do all of the following **except**

A. Establish and document internal control procedures and to include in their annual reports a report on the company's internal control over financial reporting.

B. Provide a report to include a statement of management's responsibility for internal control and of management's assessment of the effectiveness of internal control as of the end of the company's most recent fiscal year.

C. Provide an identification of the framework used to evaluate the effectiveness of internal control (such as the COSO report), and a statement that the external auditor has issued an attestation report on management's assessment.

D. Provide a statement that the board approves the choice of accounting methods.

Answer (D) is correct.

REQUIRED: The false statement about management's responsibilities under the Sarbanes-Oxley Act.

DISCUSSION: The Sarbanes-Oxley Act of 2002 imposes many requirements on management, boards of directors, and auditors. Section 404 applies to internal controls and reports thereon. Section 404 requires management to establish and document internal control procedures and to include in their annual reports a report on the company's internal control over financial reporting. The report is to include (1) a statement of management's responsibility for internal control, (2) management's assessment of the effectiveness of internal control as of the end of the most recent fiscal year, (3) identification of the framework used to evaluate the effectiveness of internal control (such as the COSO report), and (4) a statement that the external auditor has issued an attestation report on management's assessment. (But PCAOB AS No. 5 requires a registered auditor merely to express an opinion, or disclaim an opinion, on internal control, not management's assessment.) Section 301 does address activities of the board, but it does not require the board to approve the choice of accounting methods and policies. Rather, it may assist in the choices of methods and policies.

17. Rules issued under the Sarbanes-Oxley Act of 2002 restrict former members of an audit engagement team from accepting employment as a chief executive officer (CEO), chief financial officer (CFO), chief accounting officer (CAO), or controller of an audit client that files reports with the Securities and Exchange Commission. How many annual audit period(s) must be completed before such employment can be accepted?

A. 1

B. 2

C. 3

D. 5

Answer (A) is correct.

REQUIRED: The time that must elapse before a member of an audit team may become a CEO, CFO, CAO, or controller of a public client.

DISCUSSION: A provision of SOX prohibits the conflict of interest that arises when the CEO, CFO, CAO, controller, or any person in an equivalent position was employed by a public client's audit firm during the 1-year period preceding the audit.

18. The Sarbanes-Oxley Act of 2002 (SOX) has strengthened auditor independence by requiring a public company to

A. Engage auditors to report in accordance with the Foreign Corrupt Practices Act (FCPA).

B. Report the nature of disagreements with former auditors.

C. Select auditors through audit committees.

D. Hire a different CPA firm from the one that performs the audit to perform the company's tax work.

Answer (C) is correct.

REQUIRED: The Sarbanes-Oxley requirement that strengthened auditor independence.

DISCUSSION: The audit committee must hire and pay the external auditors. Such affiliation inhibits management from changing auditors to gain acceptance of a questionable accounting method. Also, a successor auditor must inquire of the predecessor before accepting an engagement.

Answer (A) is incorrect. No report under the FCPA is required. Answer (B) is incorrect. Reporting the nature of disagreements with auditors is a long-time SEC requirement. Answer (D) is incorrect. The SOX does not restrict who may perform tax work. Other engagements, such as outsourcing internal auditing or certain consulting services, are limited.

2.4 State Law Liability to Clients and Third Parties

19. Which of the following penalties is usually imposed against an accountant who, in the course of performing professional services, breaches contract duties owed to a client?

A. Specific performance.

B. Punitive damages.

C. Money damages.

D. Rescission.

Answer (C) is correct.

REQUIRED: The penalty usually imposed on an accountant in breach of contract.

DISCUSSION: The accountant-client contract is a personal service contract. Recovery for breach of contract is ordinarily limited to compensatory damages, and punitive damages are rarely allowed. Thus, an accountant is usually liable for money damages.

Answer (A) is incorrect. Specific performance for a personal service contract is not granted. Answer (B) is incorrect. Punitive damages for breach of contract are rarely allowed. Answer (D) is incorrect. Rescission returns the parties to the positions they would have occupied if the contract had not been made. It would only be applicable if the breach were material, such as an unjustifiable failure to perform.

20. Sun Corp. approved a merger plan with Cord Corp. One of the determining factors in approving the merger was the financial statements of Cord that were audited by Frank & Co., CPAs. Sun had engaged Frank to audit Cord's financial statements. While performing the audit, Frank failed to discover certain irregularities that later caused Sun to suffer substantial losses. For Frank to be liable under common-law negligence, Sun, at a minimum, must prove that Frank

A. Knew of the irregularities.

B. Failed to exercise due care.

C. Was grossly negligent.

D. Acted with scienter.

Answer (B) is correct.

REQUIRED: The plaintiff's burden of proof under common-law negligence.

DISCUSSION: An accountant has a duty to a client to exercise the skill and care that an ordinarily prudent accountant would in the same circumstances. An accountant who fails to exercise due care is negligent. The CPA's best defense would be that the false statements were immaterial.

Answer (A) is incorrect. If the accountant knew of the irregularities, (s)he would be negligent (and possibly fraudulent) for failure to investigate further or to notify Sun of the irregularities. Answer (C) is incorrect. All that is needed to establish common-law negligence is proof that the accountant failed to exercise due care. Answer (D) is incorrect. Proving scienter is necessary to establish fraud but not negligence.

21. Which of the following statements is generally true regarding the liability of a CPA who negligently expresses an opinion on an audit of a client's financial statements?

A. The CPA is liable only to those third parties who are in privity of contract with the CPA.

B. The CPA is liable only to the client.

C. The CPA is liable to anyone in a class of third parties who the CPA knows will rely on the opinion.

D. The CPA is liable to all possible foreseeable users of the CPA's opinion.

Answer (C) is correct.

REQUIRED: The liability of a CPA to third parties for negligence in auditing a client's financial statements.

DISCUSSION: Nearly all American courts once followed the landmark case of *Ultramares v. Touche*. The *Ultramares* rule limits a CPA's liability to persons in privity of contract with the accountant. Under *Ultramares*, only clients and primary beneficiaries of the engagement are permitted to sue the CPA. Currently, most courts extend a CPA's liability to anyone in a class of foreseen (but not necessarily individually identified) third parties who the CPA knows will use the information.

Answer (A) is incorrect. Lack of privity is not an effective defense against foreseen users that a CPA knows will rely on his or her opinion. Answer (B) is incorrect. A CPA incurs liability to certain third parties that are foreseen. Answer (D) is incorrect. While a few courts have adopted the broader view of holding the negligent CPA liable to reasonably foreseeable third-party users, none have adopted a rule of liability for all possible users of the CPA's opinion.

22. A client suing a CPA for negligence must prove each of the following factors **except**

A. Breach of duty of care.

B. Proximate cause.

C. Reliance.

D. Injury.

Answer (C) is correct.

REQUIRED: The factor not required to be proven in a negligence lawsuit.

DISCUSSION: A client suing an accountant for the unintentional tort of negligence must establish the following elements: (1) The accountant owed the client a duty, (2) the accountant breached this duty, (3) the accountant's breach actually and proximately caused the client's injury, and (4) the client suffered damages. Reasonable reliance on a misrepresentation is an element of fraud or of negligent misrepresentation.

Answer (A) is incorrect. Breach of a duty to conform to a specific standard of conduct for the protection of the plaintiff from unreasonable risk of injury is an element of the tort of negligence. Answer (B) is incorrect. Proximate cause is an element of the tort of negligence. Thus, liability is imposed not for all consequences of a negligent act but for those with a relatively close connection. Answer (D) is incorrect. The plaintiff must prove that damage to the defendant's person or property resulted from the negligent act.

23. Under state law, which of the following statements most accurately reflects the liability of a CPA who fraudulently gives an opinion on an audit of a client's financial statements?

A. The CPA is liable only to third parties in privity of contract with the CPA.

B. The CPA is liable only to known users of the financial statements.

C. The CPA probably is liable to any person who suffered a loss as a result of the fraud.

D. The CPA probably is liable to the client even if the client was aware of the fraud and did not rely on the opinion.

Answer (C) is correct.

REQUIRED: The liability of a CPA for a fraudulent opinion.

DISCUSSION: The distinctive feature of fraud is scienter, that is, intentional misrepresentation or reckless disregard for the truth (sometimes found in gross negligence). Because fraud entails moral turpitude, the courts permit all foreseeable users of an accountant's work product to bring suit for damages proximately caused by the fraud.

Answer (A) is incorrect. Accountant liability can extend to all persons who incur loss resulting from the accountant's fraud regardless of privity. Answer (B) is incorrect. Accountant liability can extend to all persons who incur loss resulting from the accountant's fraud, not only those known to the accountant. Answer (D) is incorrect. An element of a fraud action is that the plaintiff relied justifiably on the material misstatement.

24. Which of the following facts must be proven for a plaintiff to prevail in a state-law negligent misrepresentation action?

A. The defendant made the misrepresentations with a reckless disregard for the truth.

B. The plaintiff justifiably relied on the misrepresentations.

C. The misrepresentations were in writing.

D. The misrepresentations concerned opinions.

Answer (B) is correct.

REQUIRED: The fact that must be proven to establish negligent misrepresentation.

DISCUSSION: Negligent misrepresentation occurs when the accountant makes a false representation of a material fact not known to be false but intended to induce reliance. The plaintiff must reasonably have relied on the accountant's misrepresentation and incurred damages.

Answer (A) is incorrect. Reckless disregard for the truth is an element in proving that a misrepresentation was grossly negligent. Answer (C) is incorrect. Under the negligence theory, the statements relied upon may be oral or written. A written misstatement is not necessary to prove negligent misrepresentation. Answer (D) is incorrect. Facts, not opinions, form the bases of a negligent misrepresentation case.

25. Which of the following statements, if any, are true regarding the state law elements that must be proven to support a finding of constructive fraud against a CPA?

I. The plaintiff has justifiably relied on the CPA's misrepresentation.

II. The CPA has acted in a grossly negligent manner.

A. I only.

B. II only.

C. Both I and II.

D. Neither I nor II.

Answer (C) is correct.

REQUIRED: The statements, if any, of the state law elements that must be proven to support a finding of constructive fraud.

DISCUSSION: The tort of intentional misrepresentation (fraud, deceit) consists of a material misrepresentation made with scienter and an intent to induce reliance. The misstatement also must have proximately caused damage to a plaintiff who justifiably relied upon it. Scienter exists when the defendant makes a false representation with knowledge of its falsity or with reckless disregard as to its truth. For constructive fraud, the scienter requirement is met by proof of gross negligence (reckless disregard for the truth).

26. Ford & Co., CPAs, expressed an unmodified opinion on Owens Corp.'s financial statements. Relying on these financial statements, Century Bank lent Owens $750,000. Ford was unaware that Century would receive a copy of the financial statements or that Owens would use them to obtain a loan. Owens defaulted on the loan. To succeed in a common-law fraud action against Ford, Century must prove, in addition to other elements, that Century was

A. Free from contributory negligence.

B. In privity of contract with Ford.

C. Justified in relying on the financial statements.

D. In privity of contract with Owens.

Answer (C) is correct.

REQUIRED: The element of a prima facie case of common-law fraud.

DISCUSSION: The tort of intentional misrepresentation (fraud, deceit) consists of a material misrepresentation made with scienter and an intent to induce reliance. The misstatement also must have proximately caused damage to a plaintiff who justifiably relied upon it. Scienter exists when the defendant makes a false representation with knowledge of its falsity or with reckless disregard as to its truth.

27. Which of the following elements, if present, would support a finding of constructive fraud on the part of a CPA?

A. Gross negligence in applying generally accepted auditing standards.

B. Ordinary negligence in applying generally accepted accounting principles.

C. Identified third-party users.

D. Scienter.

Answer (A) is correct.

REQUIRED: The element supporting a finding of constructive fraud on the part of a CPA.

DISCUSSION: Scienter is a prerequisite to liability for fraud. Scienter exists when the defendant makes a false representation with knowledge of its falsity or with reckless disregard as to its truth. For constructive fraud, the scienter requirement is met by proof of gross negligence (reckless disregard for the truth).

Answer (B) is incorrect. A good faith failure to comply with GAAS, PCAOB standards, other applicable auditing standards, or GAAP is evidence of negligence. To prove fraud, more is required. Answer (C) is incorrect. For fraud, a CPA may be liable to all foreseeable users of his or her work. Answer (D) is incorrect. Scienter is a necessary element of fraud. For constructive fraud, the scienter element is proven by evidence of gross negligence.

2.5 Privileged Communication and Confidentiality

28. Which of the following statements is true regarding a CPA's working papers? The working papers must be

A. Transferred to another accountant purchasing the CPA's practice even if the client has not given permission.

B. Transferred permanently to the client if demanded.

C. Turned over to any government agency that requests them.

D. Turned over pursuant to a valid federal court subpoena.

Answer (D) is correct.

REQUIRED: The true statement about working papers.

DISCUSSION: The AICPA's Conduct Rule 301, *Confidential Client Information*, does not affect a CPA's obligation to comply with a validly issued and enforceable subpoena. Because no federal accountant-client privilege exists, a federal court may subpoena working papers.

Answer (A) is incorrect. A CPA is required to obtain the client's permission before transferring his or her working papers to another CPA. This is true even if the other accountant is purchasing the CPA's firm. Answer (B) is incorrect. Working papers are the property of the CPA and ordinarily need not be transferred to the client upon request. Answer (C) is incorrect. Unless a summons or subpoena is issued, a governmental request need not be honored. Moreover, some states have provided for an accountant-client privilege.

29. Which of the following statements concerning an accountant's disclosure of confidential client data is generally true?

A. Disclosure may be made to any state agency without subpoena.

B. Disclosure may be made to any party with the consent of the client.

C. Disclosure may be made to comply with an IRS audit request.

D. Disclosure may be made to comply with generally accepted accounting principles.

Answer (B) is correct.

REQUIRED: The condition allowing disclosure of confidential client data.

DISCUSSION: Under Conduct Rule 301, an accountant may disclose any confidential client information with the specific consent of the client.

Answer (A) is incorrect. Disclosure may be made to a state agency only pursuant to a subpoena or summons or with the client's consent. Answer (C) is incorrect. Without a client's consent, an accountant may disclose confidential information to the IRS only pursuant to a subpoena or summons. Answer (D) is incorrect. Compliance with GAAP is a responsibility of clients who issue financial statements, not the accountants who report on them.

30. A CPA is permitted to disclose confidential client information without the consent of the client to

I. Another CPA who has purchased the CPA's tax practice

II. A successor CPA firm if the information concerns suspected tax return irregularities

III. A voluntary peer review board

A. I and III only.

B. II and III only.

C. II only.

D. III only.

Answer (D) is correct.

REQUIRED: The accountant's permitted disclosure(s) without the client's consent.

DISCUSSION: The AICPA *Code of Professional Conduct* (Rule 301) states that a member may not disclose any confidential client information except with the specific consent of the client. But this rule should not be understood to preclude a CPA from responding to an inquiry made by an investigative body of a state CPA society, the trial board of the AICPA, or an AICPA or state peer review body, or pursuant to a validly issued and enforceable subpoena.

2.6 PRACTICE TASK-BASED SIMULATIONS

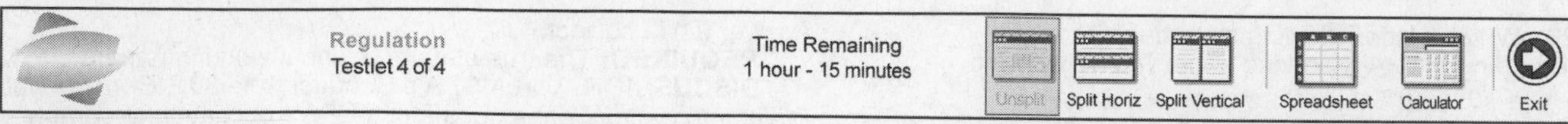

DIRECTIONS

Note: If you believe you have encountered a software malfunction, report it to the test center staff immediately.

Navigation

To navigate from task to task, use the controls at the bottom of the screen. Click on the **Next** button to advance to the next task, or the **Previous** button to go to the previous task. To go directly to any task, click on its number.

If you would like a reminder to revisit a task, or want to indicate that you are finished with it, click on the reminder flag below the task number. To clear the flag, click on it again. Reminder flags are for your use only – they do not contribute to your score.

Tabs

In this part of the examination, you will be asked to complete various tasks. Every task has one or more **Work Tabs**. Some tasks have one or more **Information Tabs**, others may have none. Every task has a **Help** tab.

If a task has **Information Tabs**, you may use the information in them to complete your responses in the **Work Tabs**.

Work tab **Information tab** **Help tab**

Work Tabs:

- **Work Tabs** are identified with a pencil icon. This is where your responses are expected.
- Each task has one or more **Work Tabs**.
- **Work Tabs** contain directions for completing the task – be sure to read these directions carefully.
- The **Work Tab** name in the example above is for illustration only – yours will differ.
- You must complete all of the **Work Tabs** in each task to receive full credit.

Information Tabs:

- The Authoritative Literature will be provided in all tasks in the AUD, FAR, and REG sections for your reference.
- Your simulation may have one or more additional **Information Tabs**. Like the Authoritative Literature tabs, **Information Tabs** do not have a pencil icon.
- If your task has additional **Information Tabs**, go through each to familiarize yourself with the task content.

Help Tab:

- The **Help Tab** provides assistance with the exam software that is used in this task. For example, if the task is to compose a memorandum, **Help** will provide information about the word processor.

The Toolbar

The toolbar at the top of the screen shows the amount of time remaining for you to complete the tasks. In addition, the following tools are available. Note that only the **Exit** button is displayed when Directions are visible - the others will appear when you begin the tasks.

Click on these buttons to split or unsplit the screen. You can split the screen vertically or horizontally.

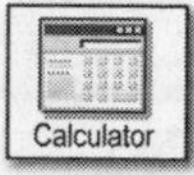

Click on this button to display the calculator; click on it again to hide the calculator. To move the calculator, click on the calculator title bar and drag the calculator to the desired location.

Click on this button to use the spreadsheet; click on it again to hide the spreadsheet. To move the spreadsheet, click on the the spreadsheet title bar and drag the spreadsheet to the desired location.

Click on this button to go on to the next part of the examination. You must complete all of the tasks to receive full credit. Once you click on **Exit** and confirm the action, you will NOT be able to return to this testlet.

= Reminder | Directions | 1 2 3 4 5 | Previous | Next

Select from the list provided the phrase that correctly matches each item below. Each choice may be used once, more than once, or not at all.

Item	***Answer***
1. Must be exercised in preparing, approving, and filing tax returns.	
2. A substitute for proof of reliance on a misstatement.	
3. A person who prepares for compensation a claim for a refund.	
4. Must include all critical accounting policies and practices to be used.	
5. Must include the treatment of financial information preferred by the external auditors.	
6. Requires audits to provide reasonable assurance of detecting illegal acts.	
7. Imposes civil liability for fraud in a new issue of securities.	
8. Accountants' nonfraud civil liability to third parties under this act requires proof of privity of contract.	
9. Prohibits any scheme to defraud.	

Choices	
A) Liability	H) Due diligence
B) Fraud-on-the-market theory	I) Nonaudit services
C) Securities Act of 1933	J) Sarbanes-Oxley Act of 2002
D) Privity	K) Section 404 of SOX
E) Rule 10b-5 of the Securities Exchange Act of 1934	L) Audit reports to audit committees
F) Private Securities Litigation Reform Act of 1995	M) Securities Exchange Act of 1934
G) Tax return preparer	

The CPA firm of Martinson, Brinks, & Sutherland, a partnership, was the auditor for Masco Corporation, a medium-sized wholesaler. Masco leased warehouse facilities and sought financing for leasehold improvements to these facilities. Masco assured its bank that the leasehold improvements would result in a more efficient and profitable operation. Based on these assurances, the bank granted Masco a line of credit.

The loan agreement required annual audited financial statements. Masco submitted its audited financial statements to the bank. They showed an operating profit of $75,000, leasehold improvements of $250,000, and net worth of $350,000. In reliance on the statements, the bank lent Masco $200,000. The audit report that accompanied the financial statements disclaimed an opinion because the cost of the leasehold improvements could not be determined from the company's records. The part of the audit report applicable to leasehold improvements reads as follows:

> Additions to fixed assets for the year were found to include principally warehouse improvements. Most of this work was done by company employees, and the costs of materials and overhead were paid by Masco. Unfortunately, complete, detailed cost records were not kept of these leasehold improvements, and no exact determination could be made of the actual cost of the improvements. The total amount capitalized is set forth in note 4.

Late in the following year, Masco went out of business, at which time it was learned that the claimed leasehold improvements were totally fictitious. The labor expenses charged as leasehold improvements proved to be operating expenses. No item of building material cost had been recorded. No independent investigation of the existence of the leasehold improvements was made by the auditors.

If the $250,000 had not been capitalized, the income statement would have reflected a substantial loss from operations, and the net worth would have been correspondingly decreased.

The bank has sustained a loss on its loan to Masco of $200,000 and now seeks to recover damages from the CPA firm.

Items 1 through 8 are questions regarding CPA liability. Select the correct answer from the list provided.

Item	***Answer***
1. What basis for liability does not apply to an accountant?	
2. What basis for liability applies to Martinson, Brinks, & Sutherland?	
3. What is the class of persons to which the bank belongs for the purpose of determining the accountant's liability for negligence?	
4. What element of fraud is not included in negligent misrepresentation?	
5. Intent is an element of fraud. What may be substituted for intent?	
6. What type of causation is an element of negligence?	
7. One characteristic of a primary beneficiary is that the accountant is retained principally for its benefit. What is another characteristic, if any, of a primary beneficiary?	
8. What is the class of persons to which a defendant is liable for fraud?	

Choices	
A) Negligence	I) Primary beneficiaries
B) Gross negligence	J) Privity of contract
C) Fraud	K) Proximate cause
D) Relationship to a specific transaction	L) Identification of the third party
E) Strict liability in tort	M) Duty to discover fraud
F) Foreseen third parties	N) Supervening cause
G) Reasonably foreseeable users	O) Scienter
H) Implied cause	P) None of the answer choices

= Reminder　Directions　1 2 3 4 5　Previous　Next

Butler Manufacturing Corp. planned to raise capital for a plant expansion by borrowing from banks and making several stock offerings. Butler engaged Weaver, CPA, to audit its December 31, Year 1, financial statements. Butler told Weaver that the financial statements would be given to certain named banks and included in the prospectuses for the stock offerings.

In performing the audit, Weaver did not confirm accounts receivable and, as a result, failed to discover a material overstatement of accounts receivable. Also, Weaver was aware of a pending class action product liability lawsuit that was not disclosed in Butler's financial statements. Despite being advised by Butler's legal counsel that Butler's potential liability under the lawsuit would result in material losses, Weaver expressed an unmodified opinion on Butler's financial statements.

In May Year 2, Union Bank, one of the named banks, relied on the financial statements and Weaver's opinion in giving Butler a $500,000 loan.

Butler raised an additional $16,450,000 through the following stock offerings, which were sold completely:

- June Year 2 – Butler made a $450,000 unregistered offering of Class B nonvoting common stock under Rule 504 of Regulation D of the Securities Act of 1933. This offering was sold over 2 years to 30 nonaccredited investors and 20 accredited investors by general solicitation. The SEC was notified 18 days after the first sale of this offering.
- September Year 2 – Butler made a $10,000,000 unregistered offering of Class A voting common stock under Rule 506 of Regulation D of the Securities Act of 1933. This offering was sold over 2 years to 200 accredited investors and 30 nonaccredited investors through a private placement. The SEC was notified 14 days after the first sale of this offering.
- November Year 2 – Butler made a $6,000,000 unregistered offering of preferred stock under Rule 505 of Regulation D of the Securities Act of 1933. This offering was sold during a 1-year period to 40 nonaccredited investors by private placement. The SEC was notified 18 days after the first sale of this offering.

Shortly after obtaining the Union loan, Butler began experiencing financial problems but was able to stay in business because of the money raised by the offerings. Butler was found liable in the product liability suit. This resulted in a judgment Butler could not pay. Butler also defaulted on the Union loan and was involuntarily petitioned into bankruptcy. This caused Union to sustain a loss and Butler's stockholders to lose their investments.

Weaver's liability extends to various infractions. Select the entity from the list provided that has jurisdiction for each infraction listed below. Each choice may be used once, more than once, or not at all.

Item	***Answer***
1. The offering did not comply with the 15-day notice requirement	
2. Failure to confirm accounts receivable	
3. Expressing an unmodified opinion on statements containing a material departure from GAAP	
4. Negligence in performing an audit	
5. Gross negligence for failure to qualify an opinion	

Choices
A) Civil Court
B) AICPA
C) SEC
D) Criminal Court
E) IRS

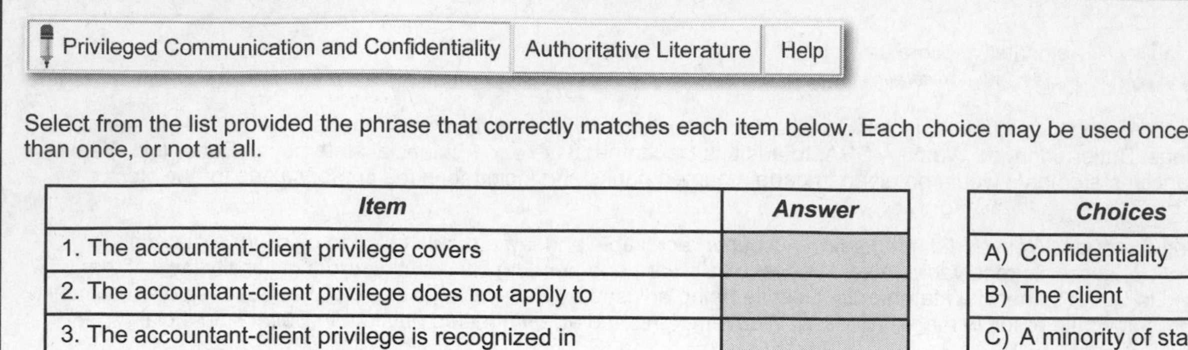

Select from the list provided the phrase that correctly matches each item below. Each choice may be used once, more than once, or not at all.

Item	Answer
1. The accountant-client privilege covers	
2. The accountant-client privilege does not apply to	
3. The accountant-client privilege is recognized in	
4. Working papers are the property of	
5. Client records are the property of	
6. An accountant who allows a third party access to working papers is violating accountant-client	
7. Working papers should be retained until expiration of	
8. Confidential client information may be released to third parties if approved by	

Choices
A) Confidentiality
B) The client
C) A minority of states
D) Divorce matters
E) Consulting services
F) Tax advice
G) Statute of limitations
H) The accountant
I) Most states
J) Criminal tax matters

Select from the list provided the phrase that correctly matches each item below. Each choice may be used once, more than once, or not at all.

Item	Answer
1. A registration that does not make the entire allotment of securities available on the registration date is called a	
2. An issuer must prepare and file a	
3. Exemptions to the 1933 act include	
4. Parties to issuance of a security include	
5. Penalties the SEC may impose include	
6. An issuer not required to file reports is a	

Choices
A) Underwriters
B) Shelf registration
C) Civil penalties
D) Prospectus
E) Seasoned issuer
F) Suspend trading
G) Short-term commercial paper
H) Nonreporting issuer

Unofficial Answers

1. Federal Statutory Liability (9 Gradable Items)

1. H) Due diligence. Due diligence must be exercised in preparing, approving, and filing returns, documents, claims for refund, and other papers relating to IRS matters.
2. B) Fraud-on-the-market theory. Proof that the price of a security was affected by a material misstatement or omission may substitute for proof of reliance.
3. G) Tax return preparer. A tax return preparer is a person who prepares for compensation, or hires a person to prepare for compensation, a substantial part of an income tax return or claim for refund.
4. L) Audit reports to audit committees. Audit reports to audit committees must include all critical accounting policies and practices to be used, treatments of financial information discussed with management, their ramifications, and the auditors' preferred treatment.
5. L) Audit reports to audit committees. Audit reports to audit committees must include all critical accounting policies and practices to be used, treatments of financial information discussed with management, their ramifications, and the auditors' preferred treatment.
6. F) Private Securities Litigation Reform Act of 1995. The Private Securities Litigation Reform Act of 1995 requires audits to provide reasonable assurance of detecting illegal acts having a direct and material effect on the financial statements.
7. C) Securities Act of 1933. Section 17 of the 1933 act imposes civil liability for aiding and abetting securities fraud in new issues of securities. However, private parties may not sue under this section.
8. C) Securities Act of 1933. Section 12 of the 1933 act requires proof of reliance, privity of contract, and that the transaction involved interstate commerce or the mails.
9. E) Rule 10b-5 of the Securities Exchange Act of 1934. Rule 10b-5 of the 1934 Act prohibits any person in connection with the purchase or sale of any security from employing any device, scheme, or artifice to defraud.

2. Bases for Liability (8 Gradable Items)

1. E) Strict liability in tort. Liability without fault is not a basis for recovery from an accountant.
2. A) Negligence. The auditors failed to exercise reasonable care and diligence. Omitting an investigation of the leasehold improvements was negligent. The accountant breached a legal duty, and the breach actually and proximately caused the defendant's damages. The auditors were not grossly negligent because the facts do not indicate that they failed to use even slight care.
3. F) Foreseen third parties. The majority rule is that the accountant is liable to foreseen (but not necessarily individually identified) third parties (foreseen users and users within a foreseen class of users). Foreseen third parties are those to whom the accountant intends to supply the information or knows the client intends to supply the information. They also include persons who use the information in a way the accountant knows it will be used. Financial statements are commonly distributed to lenders.
4. O) Scienter. Negligent misrepresentation includes all elements of fraud except scienter. Scienter is actual or implied knowledge of fraud.
5. B) Gross negligence. Gross negligence is failure to use even slight care. The element of intent required to prove fraud is satisfied by gross negligence.
6. K) Proximate cause. The plaintiff must prove that (1) the defendant breached a legal duty to the plaintiff and (2) the breach actually and proximately caused the plaintiff's damages. The concept of proximate cause limits liability to damages that are reasonably foreseeable.
7. L) Identification of the third party. A third party is considered to be a primary beneficiary if (1) the accountant is retained principally to benefit the third party, (2) the third party is identified, and (3) the benefit pertains to a specific transaction.
8. G) Reasonably foreseeable users. Liability for fraud extends to all reasonably foreseeable users of the accountant's work product.

3. CPA's Liability (5 Gradable Items)

1. C) SEC. The offerings under SEC Rules 504 and 506 did not comply with the notice requirement (15 days after the first offering). The offering under Rule 505 exceeded the $5,000,000 limit and also did not comply with the notice requirement.
2. B) AICPA. Weaver violated AICPA Conduct Rule 202, *Compliance with Standards*. Weaver did not confirm accounts receivable, a generally accepted auditing standard.
3. B) AICPA. Weaver violated AICPA Conduct Rule 203, *Accounting Principles*, by expressing an unmodified opinion on statements containing a material departure from GAAP (nonrecognition of a probable, material contingent liability).
4. A) Civil Court. Union will be successful in a common-law fraud suit against Weaver in civil court. To be successful in a lawsuit for accountant's negligence, there must be
   - Duty
   - Breach
   - Plaintiff known as intended user
   - Reliance
   - Loss
5. A) Civil Court. Weaver was grossly negligent for failing to qualify its opinion after being advised of Butler's potential material losses from the product liability lawsuit by legal counsel. Weaver will be liable if sued in civil court to anyone who relied on Weaver's opinion and suffered a loss as a result of this fraudulent omission.

4. Privileged Communication and Confidentiality (8 Gradable Items)

1. F) Tax advice. Federal law does not recognize a broad privilege for accountant-client communications. However, a confidentiality privilege covers most tax advice provided to a current or prospective client.
2. J) Criminal tax matters. The accountant-client privilege does not apply to criminal tax matters, private civil matters, disclosures to other federal regulatory bodies, or state and local tax matters.
3. C) A minority of states. A minority of states recognize the accountant-client privilege. A majority do not.
4. H) The accountant. Working papers are the property of the accountant. Absent a court order or client consent, third parties are not allowed access to working papers.
5. B) The client. Client records are the property of the client and must be returned upon request of the client.
6. A) Confidentiality. Third party access to working papers is prohibited by the confidential accountant-client provisions of the AICPA *Code of Professional Conduct*.
7. G) Statute of limitations. An accountant who does not audit public companies should retain working papers until the state statute of limitations on litigation that might arise has expired.
8. B) The client. The client always has the option to permit the release of his or her confidential information.

5. Registration Process (6 Gradable Items)

1. B) Shelf registration. The entire allotment of securities is made available for purchase on the effective date of the registration statement. An exception is a shelf registration. After the registration statement is filed, the securities are put on the shelf for up to 3 years until the best time for an offering is determined. A shelf registration is available only to seasoned issuers and well-known seasoned issuers.
2. D) Prospectus. To comply with the 1933 act, an issuer of securities must prepare and publicly file both a registration statement and a prospectus.
3. G) Short-term commercial paper. The 1933 act exempts short-term commercial paper, intrastate offerings, and secondary trading.
4. A) Underwriters. Every person involved in the initial offering and sale of securities is subject to the 1933 act. The act broadly classifies these persons as issuers, underwriters, or dealers.
5. F) Suspend trading. The SEC may deny, suspend, or revoke registration, or it may order a suspension of trading of the securities. These sanctions are in addition to civil and criminal liability imposed by federal securities laws.
6. H) Nonreporting issuer. A nonreporting issuer is not required to file reports under the 1934 act.

Gleim Simulation Grading

Task	Correct Responses		Gradable Items		Score per Task
1	____	÷	9	=	____
2	____	÷	8	=	____
3	____	÷	5	=	____
4	____	÷	8	=	____
5	____	÷	6	=	____
			Total of Scores per Task		____
		÷	Total Number of Tasks		5
			Total Score		____%

STUDY UNIT THREE
INDIVIDUAL TAXATION AND GROSS INCOME

(25 pages of outline)

This study unit begins our coverage of individual taxation. Filing status determines the amount of the standard deductions, personal exemptions, and applicable tax rates. Certain taxpayers may also be able to claim a dependency exemption. To qualify as a taxpayer's dependent, an individual must be either a qualifying child or a qualifying relative; the criteria for both are heavily tested on the CPA exam.

The following formula provides an overview of the steps to compute federal income tax liability for individual taxpayers. This study unit also presents taxable and nontaxable income items, income items for which there are no exclusions, and income items for which the Internal Revenue Code provides partial or complete exclusion from gross income.

Individual Income Tax

FORMULA

	GROSS INCOME
–	Adjustments (above the line)
=	**ADJUSTED GROSS INCOME**
–	Greater of Itemized Deductions or Standard Deduction
–	Personal Exemptions
=	**TAXABLE INCOME**
×	Tax Rate
=	**GROSS TAX** Liability
–	Credits
=	**NET TAX** Liability or Refund Receivable

As of the date of publication, the IRS had not yet released all of the 2015 tax forms. Please check www.gleim.com/taxforms for any updates.

Form **1040** Department of the Treasury—Internal Revenue Service (99)
U.S. Individual Income Tax Return **2014** OMB No. 1545-0074 IRS Use Only—Do not write or staple in this space.

For the year Jan. 1–Dec. 31, 2014, or other tax year beginning , 2014, ending , 20 See separate instructions.

Your first name and initial	Last name	Your social security number
If a joint return, spouse's first name and initial	Last name	Spouse's social security number
Home address (number and street). If you have a P.O. box, see instructions.	Apt. no.	▲ Make sure the SSN(s) above and on line 6c are correct.
City, town or post office, state, and ZIP code. If you have a foreign address, also complete spaces below (see instructions).		**Presidential Election Campaign**
Foreign country name	Foreign province/state/county / Foreign postal code	Check here if you, or your spouse if filing jointly, want $3 to go to this fund. Checking a box below will not change your tax or refund. ☐ You ☐ Spouse

Filing Status

Check only one box.

1 ☐ Single
2 ☐ Married filing jointly (even if only one had income)
3 ☐ Married filing separately. Enter spouse's SSN above and full name here. ▶
4 ☐ Head of household (with qualifying person). (See instructions.) If the qualifying person is a child but not your dependent, enter this child's name here. ▶
5 ☐ Qualifying widow(er) with dependent child

Exemptions

6a ☐ **Yourself.** If someone can claim you as a dependent, **do not** check box 6a . . . . .
b ☐ **Spouse** . . . . .

Boxes checked on 6a and 6b

c **Dependents:**

(1) First name Last name	(2) Dependent's social security number	(3) Dependent's relationship to you	(4) ✓ if child under age 17 qualifying for child tax credit (see instructions)
			☐
			☐
			☐
			☐

No. of children on 6c who:
• lived with you
• did not live with you due to divorce or separation (see instructions)

Dependents on 6c not entered above

If more than four dependents, see instructions and check here ▶ ☐

d Total number of exemptions claimed . . . . . Add numbers on lines above ▶

Income

Attach Form(s) W-2 here. Also attach Forms W-2G and 1099-R if tax was withheld.

If you did not get a W-2, see instructions.

Line	Description	Line
7	Wages, salaries, tips, etc. Attach Form(s) W-2	7
8a	**Taxable** interest. Attach Schedule B if required	8a
b	**Tax-exempt** interest. **Do not** include on line 8a . . . 8b	
9a	Ordinary dividends. Attach Schedule B if required	9a
b	Qualified dividends . . . 9b	
10	Taxable refunds, credits, or offsets of state and local income taxes	10
11	Alimony received	11
12	Business income or (loss). Attach Schedule C or C-EZ	12
13	Capital gain or (loss). Attach Schedule D if required. If not required, check here ▶ ☐	13
14	Other gains or (losses). Attach Form 4797	14
15a	IRA distributions 15a — b Taxable amount	15b
16a	Pensions and annuities 16a — b Taxable amount	16b
17	Rental real estate, royalties, partnerships, S corporations, trusts, etc. Attach Schedule E	17
18	Farm income or (loss). Attach Schedule F	18
19	Unemployment compensation	19
20a	Social security benefits 20a — b Taxable amount	20b
21	Other income. List type and amount	21
22	Combine the amounts in the far right column for lines 7 through 21. This is your **total income** ▶	22

Adjusted Gross Income

Line	Description	Line
23	Educator expenses	23
24	Certain business expenses of reservists, performing artists, and fee-basis government officials. Attach Form 2106 or 2106-EZ	24
25	Health savings account deduction. Attach Form 8889	25
26	Moving expenses. Attach Form 3903	26
27	Deductible part of self-employment tax. Attach Schedule SE	27
28	Self-employed SEP, SIMPLE, and qualified plans	28
29	Self-employed health insurance deduction	29
30	Penalty on early withdrawal of savings	30
31a	Alimony paid b Recipient's SSN ▶	31a
32	IRA deduction	32
33	Student loan interest deduction	33
34	Tuition and fees. Attach Form 8917	34
35	Domestic production activities deduction. Attach Form 8903	35
36	Add lines 23 through 35	36
37	Subtract line 36 from line 22. This is your **adjusted gross income** ▶	37

For Disclosure, Privacy Act, and Paperwork Reduction Act Notice, see separate instructions. Cat. No. 11320B Form **1040** (2014)

Form 1040 (2014) Page 2

Tax and Credits

38 Amount from line 37 (adjusted gross income) 38

39a Check if: ☐ You were born before January 2, 1950, ☐ Blind. ☐ Spouse was born before January 2, 1950, ☐ Blind. } Total boxes checked ▶ 39a

b If your spouse itemizes on a separate return or you were a dual-status alien, check here ▶ 39b ☐

Standard Deduction for—
• People who check any box on line 39a or 39b or who can be claimed as a dependent, see instructions.
• All others:
Single or Married filing separately, $6,200
Married filing jointly or Qualifying widow(er), $12,400
Head of household, $9,100

40 Itemized deductions (from Schedule A) or your standard deduction (see left margin) . . 40

41 Subtract line 40 from line 38 41

42 Exemptions. If line 38 is $152,525 or less, multiply $3,950 by the number on line 6d. Otherwise, see instructions 42

43 Taxable income. Subtract line 42 from line 41. If line 42 is more than line 41, enter -0- 43

44 Tax (see instructions). Check if any from: a ☐ Form(s) 8814 b ☐ Form 4972 c ☐ 44

45 Alternative minimum tax (see instructions). Attach Form 6251 . . . 45

46 Excess advance premium tax credit repayment. Attach Form 8962 . . . 46

47 Add lines 44, 45, and 46 . . . ▶ 47

48 Foreign tax credit. Attach Form 1116 if required . . 48

49 Credit for child and dependent care expenses. Attach Form 2441 49

50 Education credits from Form 8863, line 19 50

51 Retirement savings contributions credit. Attach Form 8880 51

52 Child tax credit. Attach Schedule 8812, if required . 52

53 Residential energy credits. Attach Form 5695 . . . 53

54 Other credits from Form: a ☐ 3800 b ☐ 8801 c ☐ 54

55 Add lines 48 through 54. These are your total credits 55

56 Subtract line 55 from line 47. If line 55 is more than line 47, enter -0- . . ▶ 56

Other Taxes

57 Self-employment tax. Attach Schedule SE 57

58 Unreported social security and Medicare tax from Form: a ☐ 4137 b ☐ 8919 . . 58

59 Additional tax on IRAs, other qualified retirement plans, etc. Attach Form 5329 if required 59

60a Household employment taxes from Schedule H 60a

b First-time homebuyer credit repayment. Attach Form 5405 if required . . . 60b

61 Health care: individual responsibility (see instructions) Full-year coverage ☐ . 61

62 Taxes from: a ☐ Form 8959 b ☐ Form 8960 c ☐ Instructions; enter code(s) 62

63 Add lines 56 through 62. This is your total tax . . . . ▶ 63

Payments

If you have a qualifying child, attach Schedule EIC.

64 Federal income tax withheld from Forms W-2 and 1099 . . 64

65 2014 estimated tax payments and amount applied from 2013 return 65

66a Earned income credit (EIC) 66a

b Nontaxable combat pay election 66b

67 Additional child tax credit. Attach Schedule 8812 . . . 67

68 American opportunity credit from Form 8863, line 8 . 68

69 Net premium tax credit. Attach Form 8962 69

70 Amount paid with request for extension to file . . . 70

71 Excess social security and tier 1 RRTA tax withheld . . . 71

72 Credit for federal tax on fuels. Attach Form 4136 . . . 72

73 Credits from Form: a ☐ 2439 b ☐ Reserved c ☐ Reserved d ☐ 73

74 Add lines 64, 65, 66a, and 67 through 73. These are your total payments . . . ▶ 74

Refund

75 If line 74 is more than line 63, subtract line 63 from line 74. This is the amount you overpaid 75

76a Amount of line 75 you want refunded to you. If Form 8888 is attached, check here ▶ ☐ 76a

Direct deposit? See instructions.

▶ b Routing number ▶ c Type: ☐ Checking ☐ Savings

▶ d Account number

77 Amount of line 75 you want applied to your 2015 estimated tax ▶ 77

Amount You Owe

78 Amount you owe. Subtract line 74 from line 63. For details on how to pay, see instructions ▶ 78

79 Estimated tax penalty (see instructions) 79

Third Party Designee

Do you want to allow another person to discuss this return with the IRS (see instructions)? ☐ Yes. Complete below. ☐ No

Designee's name ▶ Phone no. ▶ Personal identification number (PIN) ▶

Sign Here

Joint return? See instructions. Keep a copy for your records.

Under penalties of perjury, I declare that I have examined this return and accompanying schedules and statements, and to the best of my knowledge and belief, they are true, correct, and complete. Declaration of preparer (other than taxpayer) is based on all information of which preparer has any knowledge.

Your signature	Date	Your occupation	Daytime phone number
Spouse's signature. If a joint return, both must sign.	Date	Spouse's occupation	If the IRS sent you an Identity Protection PIN, enter it here (see inst.)

Paid Preparer Use Only

Print/Type preparer's name	Preparer's signature	Date	Check ☐ if self-employed	PTIN
Firm's name ▶			Firm's EIN ▶	
Firm's address ▶			Phone no.	

www.irs.gov/form1040 Form 1040 (2014)

SCHEDULE A (Form 1040)

Department of the Treasury
Internal Revenue Service (99)

Itemized Deductions

▶Information about Schedule A and its separate instructions is at *www.irs.gov/schedulea*.

▶ Attach to Form 1040.

OMB No. 1545-0074

2014

Attachment Sequence No. **07**

Name(s) shown on Form 1040 | **Your social security number**

Section	Line	Description	Box	Amount	Box	Total
Medical and Dental Expenses		**Caution.** Do not include expenses reimbursed or paid by others.				
	1	Medical and dental expenses (see instructions)	1			
	2	Enter amount from Form 1040, line 38 [2]				
	3	Multiply line 2 by 10% (.10). But if either you or your spouse was born before January 2, 1950, multiply line 2 by 7.5% (.075) instead	3			
	4	Subtract line 3 from line 1. If line 3 is more than line 1, enter -0-			4	
Taxes You Paid	5	State and local **(check only one box):**				
		a ☐ Income taxes, **or** / b ☐ General sales taxes	5			
	6	Real estate taxes (see instructions)	6			
	7	Personal property taxes	7			
	8	Other taxes. List type and amount ▶ ________	8			
	9	Add lines 5 through 8			9	
Interest You Paid	10	Home mortgage interest and points reported to you on Form 1098	10			
	11	Home mortgage interest not reported to you on Form 1098. If paid to the person from whom you bought the home, see instructions and show that person's name, identifying no., and address ▶ ________	11			
Note. Your mortgage interest deduction may be limited (see instructions).	12	Points not reported to you on Form 1098. See instructions for special rules	12			
	13	Mortgage insurance premiums (see instructions)	13			
	14	Investment interest. Attach Form 4952 if required. (See instructions.)	14			
	15	Add lines 10 through 14			15	
Gifts to Charity	16	Gifts by cash or check. If you made any gift of $250 or more, see instructions	16			
If you made a gift and got a benefit for it, see instructions.	17	Other than by cash or check. If any gift of $250 or more, see instructions. You **must** attach Form 8283 if over $500 . . .	17			
	18	Carryover from prior year	18			
	19	Add lines 16 through 18			19	
Casualty and Theft Losses	20	Casualty or theft loss(es). Attach Form 4684. (See instructions.)			20	
Job Expenses and Certain Miscellaneous Deductions	21	Unreimbursed employee expenses—job travel, union dues, job education, etc. Attach Form 2106 or 2106-EZ if required. (See instructions.) ▶ ________	21			
	22	Tax preparation fees	22			
	23	Other expenses—investment, safe deposit box, etc. List type and amount ▶ ________	23			
	24	Add lines 21 through 23	24			
	25	Enter amount from Form 1040, line 38 [25]				
	26	Multiply line 25 by 2% (.02)	26			
	27	Subtract line 26 from line 24. If line 26 is more than line 24, enter -0-			27	
Other Miscellaneous Deductions	28	Other—from list in instructions. List type and amount ▶ ________			28	
Total Itemized Deductions	29	Is Form 1040, line 38, over $152,525? ☐ **No.** Your deduction is not limited. Add the amounts in the far right column for lines 4 through 28. Also, enter this amount on Form 1040, line 40. ☐ **Yes.** Your deduction may be limited. See the Itemized Deductions Worksheet in the instructions to figure the amount to enter.			29	
	30	If you elect to itemize deductions even though they are less than your standard deduction, check here . . . . ▶ ☐				

For Paperwork Reduction Act Notice, see Form 1040 instructions. Cat. No. 17145C **Schedule A (Form 1040) 2014**

SCHEDULE B
(Form 1040A or 1040)

Department of the Treasury
Internal Revenue Service (99)

Interest and Ordinary Dividends

▶ Attach to Form 1040A or 1040.
▶ Information about Schedule B and its instructions is at *www.irs.gov/scheduleb*.

OMB No. 1545-0074
2015
Attachment Sequence No. **08**

Name(s) shown on return | **Your social security number**

Part I Interest

(See instructions on back and the instructions for Form 1040A, or Form 1040, line 8a.)

Note: If you received a Form 1099-INT, Form 1099-OID, or substitute statement from a brokerage firm, list the firm's name as the payer and enter the total interest shown on that form.

			Amount
1	List name of payer. If any interest is from a seller-financed mortgage and the buyer used the property as a personal residence, see instructions on back and list this interest first. Also, show that buyer's social security number and address ▶	1	
2	Add the amounts on line 1	2	
3	Excludable interest on series EE and I U.S. savings bonds issued after 1989. Attach Form 8815	3	
4	Subtract line 3 from line 2. Enter the result here and on Form 1040A, or Form 1040, line 8a . . . . ▶	4	

Note: If line 4 is over $1,500, you must complete Part III.

Part II Ordinary Dividends

(See instructions on back and the instructions for Form 1040A, or Form 1040, line 9a.)

Note: If you received a Form 1099-DIV or substitute statement from a brokerage firm, list the firm's name as the payer and enter the ordinary dividends shown on that form.

			Amount
5	List name of payer ▶	5	
6	Add the amounts on line 5. Enter the total here and on Form 1040A, or Form 1040, line 9a . . . . ▶	6	

Note: If line 6 is over $1,500, you must complete Part III.

Part III Foreign Accounts and Trusts

(See instructions on back.)

You must complete this part if you **(a)** had over $1,500 of taxable interest or ordinary dividends; **(b)** had a foreign account; or **(c)** received a distribution from, or were a grantor of, or a transferor to, a foreign trust.

		Yes	**No**
7a	At any time during 2015, did you have a financial interest in or signature authority over a financial account (such as a bank account, securities account, or brokerage account) located in a foreign country? See instructions		
	If "Yes," are you required to file FinCEN Form 114, Report of Foreign Bank and Financial Accounts (FBAR), to report that financial interest or signature authority? See FinCEN Form 114 and its instructions for filing requirements and exceptions to those requirements		
b	If you are required to file FinCEN Form 114, enter the name of the foreign country where the financial account is located ▶		
8	During 2015, did you receive a distribution from, or were you the grantor of, or transferor to, a foreign trust? If "Yes," you may have to file Form 3520. See instructions on back		

For Paperwork Reduction Act Notice, see your tax return instructions. Cat. No. 17146N **Schedule B (Form 1040A or 1040) 2015**

3.1 FILING STATUS

1. **Overview**
   a. The amounts of the standard deductions, personal exemptions, and applicable tax rates vary with filing status.
   b. Filing status on the last day of the year determines the filing status for the entire year.
2. **Single**
   a. An individual must file as single if (s)he neither is married nor qualifies for widow(er) or head of household status.
3. **Married Filing a Joint Return**
   a. Married individuals who file a joint return account for their items of income, deduction, and credit in the aggregate.
      1) A joint return is allowed when spouses use different accounting methods.
      2) Spouses with different tax years may not file a joint return.
   b. Two individuals are treated as legally married for the entire tax year if, on the last day of the tax year, they are
      1) Legally married and cohabiting as spouses,
      2) Legally married and living apart but not separated pursuant to a valid divorce decree or separate maintenance agreement, or
      3) Separated under a valid divorce decree that is not yet final.
   c. If a spouse dies and the surviving spouse does not remarry before the end of the tax year, a joint return may be filed.
   d. Since 2013, same-sex couples have qualified for married filing status. The related Supreme Court rulings of 2015 have little effect on federal taxes, other than an expected increase in the volume of married same-sex taxpayers filing joint returns.
4. **Married Filing a Separate Return**
   a. Each spouse accounts separately for items of income, deduction, and credit. A spouse who uses his or her own funds to pay expenses of jointly owned property is entitled to any deduction attributable to the payments.
   b. If one spouse files separately, so must the other.
5. **Qualifying Widow(er) or Surviving Spouse**
   a. The qualifying widow(er) status is available for 2 years following the year of death of the husband or wife if the following conditions are satisfied:
      1) The taxpayer did not remarry during the tax year.
      2) The widow(er) qualified (with the deceased spouse) for married filing joint return status for the tax year of the death of the spouse.
      3) A qualifying widow(er) maintains a household for the entire taxable year. Maintenance means the widow(er) furnishes more than 50% of the costs to maintain the household for the tax year.
         a) The household must be the principal place of abode of a dependent of the widow(er). The widow(er) must be entitled to claim a dependency exemption amount for the dependent.
         b) The dependent must be a son or daughter, a stepson or daughter, or an adopted child. This does not include a foster child.
      4) A widow(er) can file a joint return in the tax year of the death of the spouse. (S)he is also entitled to the full personal exemption amount for the deceased spouse.

6. **Head of Household**
   a. An individual qualifies for head of household status if (s)he satisfies conditions with respect to filing status, marital status, and household maintenance.
   b. **Filing status.** The individual may not file as a qualifying widow(er).
   c. **Marital status.** A married person does not qualify for head of household status unless the conditions below are satisfied. A married individual who lives with a dependent apart from the spouse qualifies for head of household status if, for the tax year,
      1) (S)he files separately;
      2) (S)he pays more than 50% toward maintaining the household; and
      3) For the last 6 months,
         a) The spouse is not a member of the household,
         b) The household is the principal home of a child of the individual, and
         c) The individual can claim a dependency exemption for the child.
   d. **Household maintenance.** To qualify for head of household status, an individual must maintain a household that is the principal place of abode for a qualifying individual for at least half of the tax year.
      1) To maintain a household for federal filing status purposes, an individual must furnish more than 50% of the qualifying costs of maintaining the household during the tax year.

Qualifying Costs	Nonqualifying Costs
Property tax	Clothing
Mortgage interest	Education
Rent	Medical treatment
Utilities	Life insurance
Upkeep	Transportation
Repair	Vacations
Property insurance	Services by the taxpayer
Food consumed on premises	Services by the dependent

      2) Qualifying person and time. The taxpayer must maintain a household that constitutes the principal place of abode for more than half of the taxable year for at least one qualified individual who is
         a) An unmarried son or daughter, unmarried grandchild, or unmarried stepchild, or
         b) Any other person eligible to be claimed as a dependent, except for those eligible under a multiple-support agreement.
      3) There are two special rules concerning a qualifying person.
         a) First, the taxpayer with a dependent parent qualifies even if the parent does not live with the taxpayer. Otherwise, the IRS maintains that the qualifying individual must occupy the same household (except for temporary absences).
         b) Second, if a qualifying child lives with the taxpayer, that qualifying child need not be the taxpayer's dependent.

NOTE: Nonresident aliens cannot qualify for the head of household status.

Stop and review! You have completed the outline for this subunit. Study multiple-choice questions 1 through 7 beginning on page 112.

3.2 EXEMPTIONS

The AICPA has consistently tested the rules and regulations pertaining to the personal and dependent exemptions. Take the time necessary to understand this information, as the requirements for each can easily be confused. Work through the questions in the Gleim materials to reinforce your knowledge of these topics.

1. **Personal and Dependent Exemptions**
   a. An individual's deduction for exemptions is the sum of a personal exemption amount for the individual and a spouse, along with a dependent exemption amount for each qualified dependent. The amount for each individual is $4,000 for 2015.
   b. **Personal exemptions for the spouse.** Normally, a joint return must be filed. However, a taxpayer filing as married filing separately may deduct an exemption for the spouse if the spouse has no gross income and is not a dependent of another taxpayer.
      1) If divorced or legally separated, no exemption is allowed.
      2) If a spouse dies in the current year, an exemption is allowed as long as the spouse would have qualified for an exemption on the date of death and the qualifying widow(er) does not remarry during that year.
2. **Qualified Dependent**
   a. To qualify as a dependent, the individual must be a qualifying child or a qualifying relative.
   b. To be a **qualifying child**, four tests must be met.
      1) **Relationship** – The child must be the taxpayer's son, daughter, stepson, stepdaughter, brother, sister, stepbrother, stepsister, or any descendant of any such relative.
         a) Adopted individuals and eligible foster children meet the relationship test.
      2) **Age** – The child must be under the age of 19 or a full-time student under the age of 24.
         a) To qualify as a full-time student, the dependent must be enrolled at an educational organization for at least 5 months during the tax year.
      3) **Principal Residence** – The child must have the same principal place of abode as the taxpayer for more than half of the year.
      4) **Not Self-Supporting** – The child must not have provided over half of his or her own support.
   c. To be a **qualifying relative**, four tests must be met.
      1) **Relationship or residence.** An individual must satisfy either a relationship **or** a residence requirement to qualify as a dependent.
         a) Residence. The residence requirement is satisfied for any individual who merely resides with the taxpayer for the entire tax year.

b) Relationship. The relationship requirement is satisfied by existence of an extended (by blood) or immediate (by blood, adoption, or marriage) relationship. The relationship need be present to only one of the two married persons who file a joint return. Any relationship established by marriage is not treated as ended by divorce or by death.

i) Extended relationships: grandparents and ancestors, grandchildren and descendants, uncles or aunts, nephews or nieces

ii) Immediate relationships

- Parent: natural, adoptive, stepparent, father- or mother-in-law
- Child: natural, adoptive, stepchild, son- or daughter-in-law, foster child (who lives with claimant entire tax year)
- Sibling: full or half brother or sister, adoptive brother or sister, stepbrother or sister, brother- or sister-in-law

NOTE: Cousins do not meet the relationship test. However, if they lived with the taxpayer all year, they meet the residence test.

2) **Gross taxable income** of the relative must be less than the amount of the dependency exemption ($4,000 for 2015).

a) Only income that is taxable to the relative should be included in gross income. Social security income for low income taxpayers, tax-exempt interest income, and tax-exempt scholarships are excluded.

3) **Support.** The person who may claim an individual as a dependent must provide more than 50% of the (economic) support of the individual for the year.

a) Support includes welfare benefits, Social Security benefits, and any support provided by the exemption claimant, the dependent, and any other person.

b) Only amounts provided during the calendar year qualify as support.

i) Amounts paid in arrears (i.e., payment for child support for a previous year) are not considered support for the current year.

c) Support includes money and items, or amounts spent on items, such as

i) Food, clothing, shelter, utilities
ii) Medical and dental care and insurance
iii) Education
iv) Child care, vacations, etc.

d) Excluded. Certain items (or amounts spent on them) have not been treated as support, e.g., scholarship received by a dependent, taxes, or life insurance premiums.

e) A divorced or separated individual need not meet the support test if (s)he and the (ex-)spouse meet (or have met) the following conditions:

i) Provided more than 50% of the support
ii) Had (between them) custody for more than 50% of the year
iii) Lived apart for the last half of the year
iv) Did not have a multiple support agreement in effect

NOTE: The parent having custody for more than 50% of the year is entitled to the exemption, but the exemption amount may be allocated to the noncustodial parent if there is an agreement signed by both parents and attached to the noncustodial parent's return.

f) Multiple support agreement. One person of a group that together provides more than 50% of the support of an individual may, pursuant to an agreement, be allowed the dependency exemption amount.

i) The person must be otherwise eligible to claim the exemption and must provide more than 10% of the support.

ii) No other person may provide more than 50% of the support.

iii) Each other person in the group who provides more than 10% of the support must sign a written consent filed with the return of the taxpayer who claims the exemption.

4) The individual must **not be a qualifying child** of any other taxpayer.

a) A child being adopted is eligible to be claimed as a dependent by the adopting parents if the adoption taxpayer identification number (ATIN) is assigned.

b) Both a dependent who dies before the end of the year and a child born during the year may be claimed as dependents.

d. There are special rules that apply to an individual qualifying as a dependent.

1) Ineligible dependents. If an individual meets the requirements to be classified as a dependent on another person's tax return, the individual (dependent) is not entitled to the deduction for personal exemptions for himself or herself.

2) Filing status (occasionally referred to as the joint return test). An individual does not qualify as a dependent on another's return if the individual is married and files a joint return.

a) However, such an individual can qualify as a dependent if (s)he files a joint return solely to claim a refund of withheld tax without regard to the citizenship test.

EXAMPLE

Mr. and Mrs. Kind provided more than half the support for their married daughter and son-in-law who lived with the Kinds all year. Neither the daughter nor the son-in-law is required to file a 2015 tax return. They do so only to get a refund of withheld taxes. The Kinds may claim the daughter and the son-in-law as dependents on their 2015 joint return.

3) Citizenship. To qualify as a dependent, an individual must be, for any part of the year, a U.S. citizen, resident, or national, or a Canadian or Mexican resident.

4) Taxpayer identification number. The taxpayer must provide the correct Taxpayer Identification Number (TIN) of a dependent on the income tax return.

3. **Phaseout of Personal Exemptions**

a. The amount of each exemption that an individual may claim is phased out if the individual's AGI exceeds a threshold amount. Each exemption amount ($4,000 in 2015) is reduced by 2% for each $2,500 ($1,250 MFS) by which the individual's AGI exceeds the applicable threshold amount.

b. The deduction for personal exemptions is completely phased out when the taxpayer's AGI exceeds an applicable cap threshold.

EXAMPLE

Taxpayer A and B file a joint return for this year. They are entitled to five personal exemptions (three children). Their gross amount of personal exemptions is $20,000 ($4,000 × 5). Their AGI of $314,900 exceeds the applicable threshold amount of $309,900 by $5,000. They must reduce the gross exemption amount by $800 ($5,000 ÷ $2,500 = 2; 2 × 2% = 4%; $20,000 × .04 = $800). Their allowable deduction for personal exemptions is $19,200 ($20,000 – $800).

THE DEDUCTION FOR PERSONAL EXEMPTIONS -- 2015					
Filing Status	Amount per Exemption	Threshold AGI Amount	Step Size	Phaseout Rate	AGI Cap
Married Filing Joint	$4,000	$309,900	$2,500	2%	$432,400
Surviving Spouse	4,000	309,900	2,500	2%	432,400
Head of Household	4,000	284,050	2,500	2%	406,550
Unmarried (other than above)	4,000	258,250	2,500	2%	380,750
Married Filing Separately	4,000	154,950	1,250	2%	216,200

Stop and review! You have completed the outline for this subunit. Study multiple-choice questions 8 through 11 beginning on page 113.

3.3 GROSS INCOME

1. **Overview**
   a. The Internal Revenue Code (IRC) defines gross income (GI) as all income from whatever source derived except as otherwise provided.
   b. The IRC enumerates types of income that constitute gross income. The list is not exhaustive.
      1) Compensation for services, including fees, commissions, and fringe benefits
      2) Gross income derived from business
      3) Gains derived from dealings in property
      4) Interest
      5) Rents
      6) Royalties
      7) Dividends
      8) Alimony and separate maintenance payments
      9) Annuities
      10) Income from life insurance and endowment contracts
      11) Pensions
      12) Income from discharge of indebtedness
      13) Distributive share of partnership gross income
      14) Income in respect of a decedent (income earned but not received before death)
      15) Income from an interest in an estate or trust
   c. Other types of income also constitute GI unless a statute specifically excludes them.

EXAMPLE

John receives a lump sum for signing a noncompete agreement. John should recognize the entire lump sum as ordinary income in the year received.

2. **Timing**
   a. Items are included in income based on the method of accounting used by the taxpayer.
      1) The cash method of accounting includes income when constructively received.
      2) The accrual method of accounting reports income when
         a) All events have occurred fixing the right to receive the income
         b) The amount can be determined with reasonable accuracy
      3) The accrual method of accounting is generally required when there are inventories.
      4) The hybrid method allows a business to use the cash method for the portion of the business that is not required to be on the accrual method.
      5) Income is reported when it can be estimated with reasonable accuracy. Adjustments are made in a later year for any differences between the actual amount and the previously reported amounts.
3. **Constructive Receipt**
   a. Income does not need to be in a taxpayer's possession for inclusion in GI. It is considered constructively received when the following criteria are met:
      1) Credited to his or her account
      2) Made available so that (s)he may draw upon it at any time or could draw upon it if notice of intention to withdraw had been given
      3) Control of receipt is not subject to substantial limitations or restrictions
4. **Claim-of-Right Doctrine**
   a. A taxpayer receiving income under a claim of right and without restrictions on its use is taxed on that income in the year received even though the right to retain the income is not yet fixed or the taxpayer may later be required to return it.
5. **Compensation for Services**
   a. All compensation for personal services is GI. The form of payment is irrelevant.
      1) If property is given in lieu of cash, the FMV of the property is included in GI.
      2) GI of an employee includes any amount paid by an employer for a liability (including taxes) or an expense of the employee.

EXAMPLE

Rick's employer pays his car payment in lieu of direct deposit into Rick's personal account. The amount of the payment is included in GI.

      3) Net earnings, per related schedules (C, F), etc., from self-employment are included in GI.
         a) The director of a corporation is considered self-employed, and all director and consulting fees received are included in GI.
   b. Generally, prepaid income is taxable in the year received whether the taxpayer uses the cash or the accrual method of accounting, except
      1) Prepayments for merchandise inventory are not income until the merchandise is shipped.
      2) Both service and certain non-service advanced payments are allowed a limited 1-year deferral (Rev. Proc. 2004-34).

EXAMPLE

Beth is a piano instructor. She is a calendar-year taxpayer using the accrual method of accounting. On November 2 of Year 1, she received $4,800 for a contract for 96 1-hour lessons beginning on that date. The contract provided Beth give 8 lessons in Year 1 and 48 lessons in Year 2, with the remaining lessons to be given in Year 3. Beth should report $400 on her Year 1 return and the remaining prepayment of $4,400 on her Year 2 return.

6. **Business Income**

   a. GI for a business is calculated in a manner similar to individuals.

      1) Self-employment income is reported on Schedule C, which is discussed in Study Unit 4, Subunit 1.
      2) Supplemental income is reported on Schedule E. This includes income from

         a) Rental real estate
         b) Royalties
         c) Partnerships and LLCs (from Schedule K-1)
         d) S corporations (K-1)
         e) Estates (K-1)
         f) Trusts (K-1)

7. **Investment Income**

   a. An investor in property seeks a return of the investment (capital) and GI from the investment, which may be in the form of gains, interest, rents, royalties, or dividends.
   b. A gain on disposition of investment property is generally the net increase (appreciation) in value of the property.

      1) Realization. Investment income is realized upon a taxable event such as a disposition of the property by a sale or an exchange.
      2) Amount realized is computed as follows:

         Total money received and to be received
         \+ FMV[1] of property received and to be received
         \+ Amount of liabilities transferred with the property
         – Any selling expenses
         = Amount realized

         [1]*FMV = Fair market value at time of disposition.*

      3) Gain realized is computed as follows:

         Amount realized
         – Adjusted basis
         = Gain (or loss) realized

      4) Adjusted basis (AB) indicates the amount of capital invested in the property and not yet recovered by tax benefit (i.e., depreciation). Adjusted basis generally is computed as follows:

         Basis on acquisition (e.g., cost)
         \+ Debt on property
         ± Adjustments to basis (e.g., depreciation, improvements)
         = Adjusted basis (AB)

      5) Gain recognized. All gain realized is recognized unless a statutory provision provides for its nonrecognition by way of exclusion or deferral. Recognition means the income is to be included in gross income.

c. **Interest.** All interest is GI for tax purposes unless an exclusion applies. Examples of taxable interest include

1) Merchandise premium, e.g., a toaster given to a depositor for opening an interest-bearing account
2) Imputed interest on below-market term loans

d. **Rents.** Rent is income from an investment, not from the operation of a business. Examples of GI to a lessor include

1) A bonus received for granting a lease
   a) A lessee's refundable deposit is not income to the lessor.
2) Value received to cancel or modify a lease
   a) Amounts received by a lessee to cancel a lease, however, are treated as amounts realized on disposition of an asset/property (a capital gain).
3) An amount paid by a lessee to maintain the property in lieu of rent, e.g., property tax payments
   a) The lessor may be entitled to a deduction for all or part of the amount, e.g., property tax deduction.
4) The FMV of lessee improvements made to the property in lieu of rent
   a) The cost of maintenance can be deducted by the lessee as a rental expense.
   b) The cost of capital expenditures can be capitalized and depreciated by the lessee.
   c) The FMV of lessee improvements not made in lieu of rent are excluded.
5) Prepaid rent, with no restriction as to its use, which is income when received regardless of the method of accounting
6) Rental income from a residence unless the residence is rented out for less than 15 days a year
   a) If rental income is excluded, the corresponding rental deductions are also disallowed.

e. **Royalties.** Royalties are payments to an owner by people who use some right belonging to that owner. Royalties constitute GI.

f. **Dividends.** Amounts received as dividends constitute GI.

1) Dividends are constructively received when made subject to the unqualified demand of a shareholder. If a corporation declares a dividend in December and pays such that the shareholders receive it in January, the dividend is not treated as received in December.

g. **Dividend reinvestment plans (DRP).** A DRP allows a taxpayer to use his or her dividends to buy more shares of stock in the corporation instead of receiving the dividends in cash.

1) Even though the dividends are reinvested, they are still included in GI.
2) The basis of stock received as a result of a DRP is the FMV of the stock (determined on the dividend payment date).
3) If the DRP allows a member to use the dividends to buy stock at a price less than FMV, the discount (FMV – discounted price) is GI to the member.
   a) If the DRP allows a member to use cash to purchase stock at a discounted price, the discount is included in GI.
4) Any service charge subtracted from the cash dividends before the dividends are used to buy additional stock is considered dividend income.

EXAMPLE

David is a member of a DRP. He received $500 in dividends. On that date, he purchased five shares for $100 per share (FMV = $150 per share). David must report the $500 dividend as GI and the $250 discount as GI.

8. **Alimony and Separate Maintenance Payments**
   a. Alimony and separate maintenance payments are included in the GI of the recipient (payee) and are deducted from the gross income of the payor.
   b. A payment is considered to be alimony (even if paid to a third party) when it is
      1) Paid in cash
      2) Paid pursuant to a written divorce or separation instrument
      3) Terminated at death of recipient
      4) Not designated as other than alimony (e.g., child support)
      5) Not paid to a member of the same household
      6) Not paid to a spouse with whom the taxpayer is filing a joint return
   c. Child support payments are an exclusion from the GI of the recipient and are not deductible by the payor. These payments are not alimony.
      1) If the divorce or separation instrument specifies payments of both alimony and child support and only partial payments are made, the payments are considered to be child support until this obligation is fully paid, and any excess is then treated as alimony.
      2) If the payment amount is to be reduced based on a contingency relating to a child (e.g., attaining a certain age, marrying), the amount of the reduction will be treated as child support.
   d. Property settlements are not treated as alimony.
      1) Property transferred to a spouse or former spouse incident to a divorce is treated as a transfer by gift, which is specifically excluded from GI.
         a) "Incident to a divorce" means a transfer of property within 1 year after the date the marriage ceases or a transfer of property related to the cessation of the marriage.
         b) This exclusion does not apply if the spouse or former spouse is a nonresident alien.
   e. Third party payments. Payments to a third party for the benefit of the payor's ex-spouse are considered qualified alimony payments if all other requirements are met.

9. **Annuities**
   a. Annuity payments are included in GI unless a statute provides for their exclusion. Taxpayers are permitted to recover the cost of the annuity (the price paid) tax-free.
   b. Retirees are able to recover their contributions to their pensions, often paid in the form of an annuity, tax-free. Any excess is included in GI.

10. **Life Insurance and Endowments**
    a. Proceeds received due to the death of the insured are generally excluded from GI. Interest paid on the proceeds of a policy that is retained by the insurance company is GI to the beneficiary.

11. **Discharge of Indebtedness**
    a. Discharge of indebtedness can result in GI.
    b. GI includes the cancelation of indebtedness when a debt is canceled in whole or part for consideration.
       1) If a debtor performs services to satisfy a debt, the debtor must recognize the amount of the debt as income.

c. If a creditor gratuitously cancels a debt, the amount forgiven is treated as a gift.

d. Exception: GI does not include discharges that

1) Occur in bankruptcy (except a stock for debt transfer).
2) Occur when the debtor is insolvent but not in bankruptcy.
    a) The maximum amount that can be excluded is the amount by which liabilities exceed the FMV of assets.
3) Are related to qualified farm indebtedness.
4) Are related to principal residence indebtedness. The basis of the residence is reduced by the excluded income.
5) Are related to a purchase-money debt reduction in which a seller reduces the debt and the debtor is not in bankruptcy and is not insolvent. The discharge is treated as a purchase price adjustment.

e. When a taxpayer excludes discharge of indebtedness under 1), 2), or 3) above, the taxpayer must reduce his or her tax attributes in the following order:

1) NOLs
2) General business credit
3) Capital loss carryovers
4) Basis reductions

NOTE: However, the taxpayer may first elect to decrease the basis in depreciable property.

12. **Partnerships and S Corporations**

a. A partner's share of partnership income is included in the partner's GI, whether distributed or not. An owner's pro rata share of S corporation income is also included, whether distributed or not.

13. **Decedent, Estates, and Trusts**

a. Income in respect of a decedent is included in GI.
b. Income from an interest in an estate or trust is included in GI.

The AICPA has regularly tested candidates' knowledge of what types of income constitute gross income. Both theoretical and calculation questions have covered this topic.

14. **Subpart F Income**

a. To prevent U.S. persons from deferring income recognition by shifting income to low- or no-tax jurisdictions, Subpart F provisions were enacted. In general, qualified income from controlled foreign corporations (CFC) is included in income for the U.S. shareholder. The following defines the key terms for understanding what is qualified income:

1) CFC: A foreign corporation owned more than 50% by U.S. shareholders.
2) U.S. Shareholder: A U.S. person with 10% or more voting-ownership in the CFC.
3) U.S. Person: A U.S. citizen, resident alien, domestic corporation, partnership, estate, or trust.

b. Qualified income includes a variety of sources; however, the most significant and only source covered in this review is foreign-based-company income. It consists of the following three categories:

1) Foreign-personal-holding-company (FPHC) income,
2) Foreign-based-company sales income, and
3) Foreign-based-company services income.

c. The sales income does not qualify if the item sold was manufactured or sold within the country of the CFC. The service income only qualifies if the service is performed outside the country of the CFC.

d. The provisions of Subpart F are exceedingly intricate and contain numerous general rules, special rules, definitions, exceptions, exclusions, and limitations, which require careful consideration. Only the basics required for the CPA exam are covered in this course.

Stop and review! You have completed the outline for this subunit. Study multiple-choice questions 12 through 17 beginning on page 115.

3.4 OTHER GROSS INCOME

1. **Gross Income (GI)**
   a. GI includes all nonexcluded items of income for tax purposes. Some types of GI not enumerated in Sec. 61 are specifically included by other Code sections or case law.
2. **Prizes and Awards**
   a. If the prize or award is in a form other than money, the amount of GI is the FMV of the property. The honoree may avoid inclusion by rejecting the prize or award. Some prizes and awards are excludable (e.g., transfers to charities, employee achievement).
3. **Inducements**
   a. Businesses normally transfer value (even as "gifts") in exchange for past or anticipated economic benefits. The FMV of the inducement is income to the recipient.
4. **Unemployment Benefits**
   a. Unemployment benefits received under a federal or state program are GI.
   b. Supplemental unemployment benefits from a noncontributory fund that is company financed are taxable as wages (not unemployment).
5. **Bargain Purchase**
   a. If an employer transfers property to an employee at less than its FMV, the difference may be income to the employee.
6. **Scholarships**
   a. Any amounts received as a scholarship or fellowship for room, board, or incidental expenses are GI.
7. **Treasure Trove**
   a. A treasure trove is GI for the tax year in which it is undisputedly in the taxpayer's possession.

EXAMPLE

Rich purchased an old piano for $500 last year. In the current year, Rich finds $10,000 hidden in the piano. Rich must report the $10,000 as gross income in the current year.

8. **Gambling Winnings**
   a. All gambling winnings are GI.
      1) Gambling losses, e.g., nonwinning lottery tickets, are deductible only to the extent of winnings and only as a miscellaneous itemized deduction.
      2) Gambling losses over winnings for the taxable year cannot be used as a carryover or carryback to reduce gambling income from other years.

9. **Illegal Activities**
   a. Income from illegal activities is GI.
10. **Social Security Benefits (SSB)**
    a. SSB are generally not taxable unless additional income is received. The GI inclusion is dependent upon the relation of provisional income (PI) to the base amount (BA) and the adjusted base amount (ABA).

Background

Treating Social Security benefits as other annuity benefits are treated is not practical because Social Security amounts are very difficult to predict: Taxpayers' earnings change drastically over a lifetime, and Congress occasionally readjusts benefit formulas. Congress's solution has been to tax only that portion of Social Security benefits that exceeds a base amount related to other sources of income.

b. PI = Adjusted GI (AGI) + Tax-exempt interest (excluded foreign income) + 50% of Social Security benefits.
c. Base amount (BA) means $32,000 if married filing jointly (MFJ), $0 if married filing separately and having lived with spouse at any time during the tax year (MFSLT), or $25,000 for all others.
d. Adjusted base amount (ABA) is $44,000 if MFJ, $0 if MFSLT, or $34,000 for all others.
e. If PI < BA, there is no inclusion. If PI falls between BA and ABA, up to 50% of Social Security benefits will be included. If PI > ABA, up to 85% of Social Security benefits will be included.

EXAMPLE

Mr. and Mrs. Slom, both over 65 and filing jointly, received $20,000 in Social Security benefits. Additionally, they reported $30,000 of taxable interest, $15,000 of tax-exempt interest, $18,000 in dividends, and a taxable pension of $16,000. Therefore, their AGI, excluding Social Security benefits, is $64,000 ($30,000 taxable interest + $18,000 dividends + $16,000 taxable pension payments).

- Provisional income is $89,000 [$64,000 AGI + $15,000 tax-exempt interest + 50% of SS benefits ($10,000)].
- The adjusted base amount is $44,000.
- The amount of $17,000 (85% of SS benefits) will be included in GI since it is less than 85% of the excess of PI over the ABA plus the lesser of 50% of the incremental BA ($6,000) or 50% of SS benefits.
- Calculation of included Social Security benefits is as follows:

1)	AGI, excluding SS benefits		$64,000
2)	+ Tax-exempt interest (excluded foreign income)	+	15,000
3)	= Modified AGI	=	$79,000
4)	+ 50% of SS benefits	+	10,000
5)	= Provisional income (PI)	=	$89,000
6)	– BA ($32,000, $25,000, or $0)	–	32,000
7)	= Excess PI (If < $0, then $0 inclusion)	=	$57,000
8)	– Incremental base amount ($12,000, $9,000, or $0)	–	12,000
9)	= Excess PI	=	$45,000
10)	Smaller of amount in line 7 or 8		$12,000
11)	50% of line 10		6,000
12)	Smaller of amount in line 4 or 11		6,000
13)	Multiply line 9 by 85%		38,250
14)	Add lines 12 and 13		44,250
15)	SS benefits × 85%		17,000
16)	Taxable benefits = Smaller of amount in line 14 or 15		17,000

11. **Original Issue Discount (OID)**

    a. OID is the excess, if any, of the stated redemption price at maturity over the issue price and is included in income based on the effective interest rate method of amortization.

EXAMPLE

Cathy purchases a 20-year, 7% bond at original issue for $10,000. The stated redemption price is $12,400, and interest is paid annually. The ratable monthly portion of OID is $10. Assume that the effective rate of interest is 10%. During the first year held, interest income is $1,000 ($10,000 × 10%) and interest received is $868 ($12,400 × 7%). The difference of $132 ($1,000 – $868) is included in income under the effective interest rate method. This amount increases the investor's book value from $10,000 to $10,132. The second year's interest is $1,013.20, and the discount amortization is $145.20.

12. **Reimbursed Employee Expenses**

    a. There are two types of employee reimbursement plans:

        1) Nonaccountable. Under nonaccountable plans, employee reimbursements (advances) are included in GI, and all expenses may be deducted from AGI subject to the 2% floor.

        2) Accountable. Under accountable plans, employees must submit requests for reimbursement. Only reimbursements in excess of expenses must be included in GI.

EXAMPLE

John submitted reimbursement requests to his employer for $10,500 in airfare. John was later refunded for $500 in airfare he did not use. If John does not remit the funds to his employer, John must include the $500 in GI.

13. **Reimbursements for Moving Expenses**

    a. Qualified reimbursements are excluded from GI. If the reimbursement is not for qualified moving expenses, it is included in gross income.

14. **Bartered Services or Goods**

    a. Bartered services or goods are included in GI at the fair market value of the item(s) received in exchange for the services.

Stop and review! You have completed the outline for this subunit. Study multiple-choice questions 18 through 22 beginning on page 117.

3.5 EXCLUSIONS

1. **Specifically Stated**

    a. An item of income generally constitutes GI unless a provision of the IRC specifically states that all or part of it is not treated as income.

2. **Not Specifically Stated**

    a. Certain items are not treated as income for federal income tax purposes even though no IRC section specifically excludes them. The following are examples:

        1) Unrealized income. Income must be realized before it constitutes GI. Generally, a gain is not realized until the property is sold or disposed. Mere fluctuations in market value are not treated as income for tax purposes.

        2) Return of capital. An amount invested in an asset is generally not treated as income for tax upon an otherwise taxable disposition of the asset. Receipt of payment of debt principal is return of capital and not income. The value of one's own services, however, is not treated as capital invested.

        3) Cost of goods sold. This is considered a return of capital.

4) Loans. Receipt of loan funds does not give rise to income.
5) Intra-family services. The value of services rendered by a person for himself or herself is not treated as income for tax purposes. The same applies for gratuitous services performed by one member of a family for another.
6) Use of one's own property. Income is not imputed for the economic benefit of the use of property owned by oneself.
7) Survivor benefits for public safety officers killed in the line of duty. The annuity must be a result of a governmental plan meeting certain requirements and is attributable to the officer's service as a public safety officer.

3. **Life Insurance Proceeds**

a. In general, proceeds of a life insurance policy paid by reason of the death of the insured are excluded from GI.

NOTE: The Pension Protection Act of 2006 requires benefits from "employer-owned" life insurance contracts to be included in GI to the extent they exceed premiums paid "effective for contracts issued after August 17, 2006."

b. The exclusion is allowed regardless of form of payment or recipient. Interest earned on proceeds (after death of the insured) is GI to the beneficiary.
c. The amount of each payment in excess of the death benefit prorated over the period of payment is interest income.

EXAMPLE

A $75,000 policy pays off in $6,000 installments over 15 years. The principal amount per installment, $5,000 ($75,000 ÷ 15 years), is excluded. The remaining $1,000 ($6,000 – $5,000) is taxable interest income.

d. If the owner of a policy transfers the policy to another person for consideration, the proceeds are taxable. However, amounts paid to acquire the policy and subsequent premium payments are treated as return of investment capital.
e. Any amounts received as accelerated death benefits under a life insurance contract for individuals who are either terminally ill (certified by a physician that death can be reasonably expected to result within 24 months) or chronically ill are excluded from GI.
f. Dividends paid on insurance policies are excluded from GI to the extent cumulative dividends do not exceed cumulative premiums and provided the cash value does not exceed the net investment, which it normally does not.

1) Interest on Veterans Administration insurance dividends left on deposit with the VA is excluded from GI.

4. **Annuity Contracts**

a. Taxpayers are permitted to recover the cost of the annuity (the price paid) tax-free (e.g., dividends from life insurance policy). The nontaxable portion of an annuity is calculated as follows:

1) Calculate the expected return. This is equal to the annual payment multiplied by the expected return multiple (life expectancy determined from an actuarial table).
2) The exclusion ratio is equal to the investment in the contract (or its cost) divided by the expected return.
3) The current exclusion is calculated by multiplying the exclusion ratio by the amount received during the year.

EXAMPLE

Xavier, age 56, purchased an annuity contract to provide monthly payments of $150 until his death. The annuity cost is $35,000. The annual exclusion is calculated as follows:

Annual payment	$ 1,800
Exclusion multiple	× 27.7
Expected return	$49,860

Age	Exclusion Multiple
55	28.6
56	27.7
57	26.8

Exclusion ratio $\frac{35,000}{49,860} = 70\%$

Annual exclusion = $1,260

4) A simplified method is required for retirement plan (employee) annuities with starting dates after November 18, 1996. The nontaxable portion is calculated by dividing the investment in the contract, as of the annuity starting date, by the number of anticipated monthly payments.

Age of Primary Annuitant on the Annuity Starting Date	Number of Anticipated Monthly Payments
55 and under	360
56-60	310
61-65	260
66-70	210
71 and over	160

a) If the annuity has a fixed number of payments, use that number instead.

5. **Pensions**

a. Pensions are most often paid in the form of an annuity. Therefore, the rules for pensions are similar to the rules for annuities. Employees are able to recover their cost tax-free.

b. The investment in the pension is the amount contributed by the employee in after-tax dollars.

c. Amounts withdrawn early are treated as a recovery of the employee's contributions (excluded from GI) and of the employer's contributions (included in GI).

1) After all contributions are withdrawn, additional withdrawals are fully included in GI.

d. A noncontributory plan results in all withdrawals being included in GI.

6. **Gifts**

a. A gift is a transfer for less than full or adequate consideration. The IRC excludes from the GI of the recipient the value of property acquired by gift.

1) Voluntary transfers from employer to employee are presumed to be compensation, not gifts.

7. **Prizes and Awards**

a. Certain prizes and employee achievement awards may qualify for exclusion from the employee's GI.

b. An award recipient may exclude the FMV of the prize or award if
   1) The amount received is in recognition of religious, scientific, charitable, or similar meritorious achievement;
   2) The recipient is selected without action on his or her part;
   3) The receipt of the award is not conditioned on substantial future services; and
   4) The amount is paid by the organization making the award to a tax-exempt organization (including a governmental unit) designated by the recipient.

c. A prize or award may qualify for exclusion as a scholarship.

d. Employee achievement awards may qualify for exclusion from the recipient employee's GI if they are awarded as part of a meaningful presentation for safety achievement or length of service and
   1) The awards do not exceed $400 for all nonqualified plan awards or
   2) The awards do not exceed $1,600 for all qualified plan awards.

e. A qualified plan award is an employee achievement award provided under an established written program that does not discriminate in favor of highly compensated employees.

8. **Scholarships**

a. Amounts received by an individual as scholarships or fellowships are excluded from GI to the extent that the individual is a candidate for a degree from a qualified educational institution and the amounts are used for required tuition or fees, books, supplies, or equipment (not personal expenses).

b. GI includes any amount received, e.g., as tuition reduction, in exchange for the performance of such services as teaching or research.

c. Generally, a reduction in undergraduate tuition for an employee of a qualified educational organization does not constitute GI.
   1) The exclusion is not allowed for amounts representing payments for services (e.g., research, teaching) performed by the student as a condition for receiving the qualified scholarship.

d. Student loan forgiveness
   1) Federal, state, and/or local government student loan indebtedness may be discharged if the former student engages in certain employment, e.g., in a specified location, for a specified period, or for a specified employer. Income from discharge of indebtedness is excluded.

9. **Redemption of U.S. Savings Bonds to Pay Educational Expenses**

a. If a taxpayer pays qualified higher education expenses during the year, a portion of the interest on redemption of a Series EE U.S. Savings Bond is excluded.

b. To qualify,
   1) The bond must have been issued to the taxpayer after December 31, 1989, at a discount.
   2) The taxpayer, the taxpayer's spouse, or a dependent incurs tuition and fees to attend an eligible educational institution.
   3) The taxpayer's modified AGI must not exceed a certain limit. For 2015, the exclusion is reduced when MAGI exceeds a threshold of $77,200 ($115,750 if a joint return). The amount at which the benefit is completely phased out is $92,200 ($145,750 if a joint return).
   4) The purchaser of the bonds must be the sole owner of the bonds (or joint owner with his or her spouse).
   5) The issue date of the bonds must follow the 24th birthday(s) of the owner(s).

c. The exclusion rate equals qualified expenses divided by the total of principal and interest (not to exceed 100% or 1.0).
d. The amount of qualified expenses is reduced by the total of qualified scholarships (excluded from income), employer-provided educational assistance, expenses for American Opportunity and Lifetime Learning credits, and other higher education related benefits.

10. **Interest on State and Local Government Obligations**
 a. Payments to a holder of a debt obligation incurred by a state or local governmental entity are generally exempt from federal income tax.

Background

Historically, this exemption has been extremely important to state and local governments. It allows them to offer their debt at lower interest rates, thereby lowering their cost of capital.

 b. Exclusion of interest received is allowable even if the obligation is not evidenced by a bond, is in the form of an installment purchase agreement, or is an ordinary commercial debt.
 c. These obligations must be in registered form.
 d. The exclusion applies to obligations of states, the District of Columbia, U.S. possessions, and political subdivisions of each of them.
 e. The interest on certain private activity bonds and arbitrage bonds is not excluded.
  1) Private activity bonds are bonds of which more than 10% of the proceeds are to be used in a private business and more than 10% of the principal or interest is secured or will be paid by private business property, or more than 5% or $5 million of the proceeds are to be used for private loans.
  2) Interest on private activity bonds can still be excluded if the bond is for residential rental housing developments, public facilities (such as airports or waste removal), or other qualified causes.
 f. Interest on state, local, and federal tax refunds is not excluded.

11. **Compensation for Injury or Sickness**
 a. Gross income does not include benefits specified that might be received in the form of disability pay, health or accident insurance proceeds, workers' compensation awards, or other "damages" for personal physical injury or physical sickness.
 b. Specifically excluded from GI are amounts received
  1) Under workers' compensation acts as compensation for personal injuries or sickness
  2) Under an accident and health insurance policy purchased by the taxpayer even if the benefits are a substitute for lost income
  3) By employees as reimbursement for medical care and payments for permanent injury or loss of bodily function under an employer-financed accident or health plan
   a) If the employer contributed to the coverage (employer contributions are excluded), then the amount received must be prorated into taxable and nontaxable amounts. Payments made from a qualified trust on behalf of a self-employed person are considered employer contributions.
  4) As a pension, annuity, or similar allowance for personal injuries or sickness resulting from active service in the armed forces of any country
  5) Wrongful death damages to the extent they were received due to personal injury or sickness

6) Damages received for personal injury or physical sickness
7) Payments received for emotional distress if an injury has its origin in a physical injury or sickness

c. Specifically included in GI are
   1) Compensation for slander of reputation
   2) Damages for lost profits in a business
   3) Punitive damages received
      a) If a judgment results in both actual and punitive damages, the judgment must be allocated
   4) Damages received **solely** for emotional distress

d. Interest earned on an award for personal injuries is not excluded from GI.

e. Recovery of deductions
   1) If the taxpayer incurred medical expenses in Year 1, deducted these expenses on his or her Year 1 tax return, and received reimbursement for the same medical expenses in Year 2, the reimbursement is included in gross income on the Year 2 return in an amount equal to the previous deduction.

12. **Recovery of Tax Benefit Item**

a. GI includes items received for which the taxpayer received a tax benefit in a prior year.

EXAMPLE

Taxpayer writes off bad debt in Year 1. In Year 7, the debtor pays Taxpayer the principal of the debt written off, which must be included in GI since the deduction in Year 1 reduced the tax liability.

EXAMPLE

In 2014, a taxpayer who files single elected to itemize deductions, claiming $7,000 of state income tax paid. In 2015, the state refunded $2,000. The taxpayer must include the refund in gross income for 2015 to the extent the 2014 deduction exceeded the 2014 standard deduction, which is $800 ($7,000 itemized deduction – $6,200 standard deduction for 2014).

b. Amounts recovered during the tax year that did not provide a tax benefit in the prior year are excluded.

EXAMPLE

Taxpayer pays state income tax in excess of the standard deduction and itemizes deductions. Subsequent refunds in excess of the applicable standard deduction must be included in GI. However, if Taxpayer used the standard deduction, the refund would not be included because no tax benefit was realized.

c. A similar rule applies to credits.

13. **Gain on Sale of Principal Residence**

a. A taxpayer may exclude up to $250,000 ($500,000 for married taxpayers filing jointly) of realized gain on the sale of a principal residence.

14. **Stock Dividends**

a. Generally, a stockholder does not include in GI the value of a stock dividend (or right to acquire stock) declared on its own shares unless one of the following exceptions applies:
   1) Any shareholder can elect to receive cash or other property.
   2) Some common stock shareholders receive preferred stock, while other common stock shareholders receive common stock.
   3) The distribution is of preferred stock (but a distribution of preferred stock merely to adjust conversion ratios as a result of a stock split or dividend is excluded).
   4) If a shareholder receives common stock and cash for a fractional portion of stock, then only the cash received for the fractional portion is included in GI.

15. **Foreign-Earned Income Exclusion**
    a. U.S. citizens may exclude up to $100,800 (in calendar year 2015) of foreign-earned income and a statutory housing cost allowance from GI.
    b. To qualify for exclusion, the taxpayer must either be a resident of one or more foreign countries for the entire taxable year or be present in one or more foreign countries for 330 days during a consecutive 12-month period.
    c. The $100,800 limitation must be prorated if the taxpayer is not present in (or a resident of) the foreign country for the entire year.
    d. This exclusion is in lieu of the foreign tax credit.
    e. Deductions attributed to the foreign-earned income (which is excluded) are disallowed.
16. **Lease Improvements**
    a. The value of improvements made by the real property lessee, including buildings erected, is excludable by the lessor unless the lessee provided the improvements in lieu of rent. Income realized by the lessor from the improvements subsequent to termination of the lease is included.
    b. Additionally, amounts received by a retail lessee as cash or rent reductions are not included in gross income if used for qualified construction or improvements to the retail space.
17. **Insurance Payments for Living Expenses**
    a. If an individual's principal residence is damaged by casualty or the individual is denied access by governmental authorities to the casualty, then amounts paid to reimburse for living expenses are excluded from GI. The exclusion is limited to actual living expenses incurred less the normal living expenses the taxpayer would have incurred during the period.
18. **Rental Value of Parsonage**
    a. Ministers may exclude from GI the rental value of a home or a rental allowance to the extent the allowance is used to provide a home. However, for self-employment tax purposes, income is calculated without regard to the housing allowance for nonretired ministers.
19. **Combat Zone Compensation**
    a. Military officers may exclude compensation up to an amount equal to the highest rate of basic pay at the highest pay grade that enlisted personnel may receive (plus any hostile fire or imminent danger pay).
    b. The exclusion applies only to compensation received while serving in a combat zone or while hospitalized as a result of duty in a combat zone.
    c. Military personnel below officer level are allowed the same exclusion without the cap.
    d. Amounts received in return for **foster care** are excluded.

Expect to see questions testing exclusions from gross income on your exam. You may see questions that give a list of items and ask for the amount of those items excluded from gross income.

Stop and review! You have completed the outline for this subunit. Study multiple-choice questions 23 through 30 beginning on page 118.

QUESTIONS

3.1 Filing Status

1. A husband and wife can file a joint return even if

A. The spouses have different tax years, provided that both spouses are alive at the end of the year.

B. The spouses have different accounting methods.

C. Either spouse was a nonresident alien at any time during the tax year, provided that at least one spouse makes the proper election.

D. They were divorced before the end of the tax year.

Answer (B) is correct.

REQUIRED: The condition under which a husband and wife may file a joint return.

DISCUSSION: There is no provision disallowing spouses from filing a joint return because they have different accounting methods.

Answer (A) is incorrect. The IRC disallows spouses with different tax years from filing a joint return. Answer (C) is incorrect. The IRC provides that neither spouse can be a nonresident alien during the tax year and still file a joint return, unless the nonresident alien spouse is married to a U.S. citizen or resident alien at year end and both spouses elect to have the nonresident alien treated as a resident alien. Answer (D) is incorrect. Spouses must be married on the last day of the tax year to be allowed to file a joint return.

2. Which of the following, if any, are among the requirements to enable a taxpayer to be classified as a "qualifying widow(er)"?

I. A dependent has lived with the taxpayer for 6 months.

II. The taxpayer has maintained the cost of the principal residence for 6 months.

A. I only.

B. II only.

C. Both I and II.

D. Neither I nor II.

Answer (D) is correct.

REQUIRED: The requirements, if any, to file as a qualifying widow(er).

DISCUSSION: Filing as a surviving spouse or qualifying widow(er) requires the individual's spouse to have died during one of the previous 2 tax years. In addition, the survivor must maintain a household that is the principal place of residence for a dependent child. "Maintain" means the spouse furnishes over 50% of the costs of the household for the entire year.

3. Emil Gow's wife died in Year 1. Emil did not remarry and continued to maintain a home for himself and his dependent infant child during Year 2 and Year 3, providing full support for himself and his child. For Year 1, Emil properly filed a joint return. For Year 3, Emil's filing status is

A. Single.

B. Head of household.

C. Qualifying widower.

D. Married filing joint return.

Answer (C) is correct.

REQUIRED: The filing status of a widower.

DISCUSSION: Emil qualifies as a qualifying widower whose spouse died in either of the 2 preceding tax years, who has not remarried, and who maintains a household that constitutes a principal place of abode of a dependent who is a child or stepchild of the taxpayer.

Answer (A) is incorrect. A qualifying widower status is more beneficial to Emil. Answer (B) is incorrect. A qualifying widower status is more beneficial to Emil. Answer (D) is incorrect. Emil was not married at the end of Year 3.

4. In which of the following situations may taxpayers file as married filing jointly?

A. Taxpayers who were married but lived apart during the year.

B. Taxpayers who were married but lived under a legal separation agreement at the end of the year.

C. Taxpayers who were divorced during the year.

D. Taxpayers who were legally separated but lived together for the entire year.

Answer (A) is correct.

REQUIRED: The qualifications to file married filing jointly.

DISCUSSION: Two individuals are treated as legally married for the entire tax year if, on the last day of the tax year, they are legally married and not separated pursuant to a valid divorce decree (that is final) or separate maintenance agreement. Therefore, taxpayers who were married but lived apart during the year qualify for filing status as married filing jointly.

Answer (B) is incorrect. Living under the legal separation agreement on the last day of the year disqualifies taxpayers from filing married filing jointly. Answer (C) is incorrect. A finalized divorce decree disqualifies for status of married filing jointly. Answer (D) is incorrect. Living under the legal separation agreement on the last day of the year disqualifies taxpayers from filing married filing jointly.

5. A taxpayer's spouse dies in August of the current year. Which of the following is the taxpayer's filing status for the current year?

A. Single.

B. Qualifying widow(er).

C. Head of household.

D. Married filing jointly.

Answer (D) is correct.

REQUIRED: The taxpayer's filing status for the current year.

DISCUSSION: The qualifying widow(er) status is available for 2 years following the year of death of the husband or wife; however, the surviving spouse can file a joint return in the tax year of the death of the deceased spouse. (S)he is also entitled to the full personal exemption amount for the deceased spouse.

Answer (A) is incorrect. A taxpayer cannot file as single in the year his or her spouse dies. Answer (B) is incorrect. A taxpayer cannot file as a qualifying widow(er) in the year his or her spouse dies. However, the qualifying widow(er) status is available for the 2 years following the year of death of the spouse under certain conditions. Answer (C) is incorrect. A taxpayer cannot file as head of household in the year his or her spouse dies because the taxpayer will not be considered unmarried.

6. A couple filed a joint return in prior tax years. During the current tax year, one spouse died. The couple has no dependent children. What is the filing status available to the surviving spouse for the first subsequent tax year?

A. Qualified widow(er).

B. Married filing separately.

C. Single.

D. Head of household.

Answer (C) is correct.

REQUIRED: The filing status of the surviving spouse for years subsequent to death.

DISCUSSION: For the year of death, the living spouse may choose MFJ status. Because the surviving spouse has no dependents (qualifying individuals), the only filing status available for subsequent years is single.

Answer (A) is incorrect. In order to elect to file as widow(er), the household must be the principal place of abode of a dependent of the surviving spouse. The spouse must be entitled to claim a dependency exemption amount for the dependent. Answer (B) is incorrect. Both filing statuses for married individuals require the taxpayer to be married. Married status is terminated for years subsequent to death. Answer (D) is incorrect. The surviving spouse does not have any qualifying (dependent) individuals as required for head of household status.

7. For head of household filing status, which of the following costs are considered in determining whether the taxpayer has contributed more than one-half the cost of maintaining the household?

	Food Consumed in the Home	Value of Services Rendered in the Home by the Taxpayer
A.	Yes	Yes
B.	No	No
C.	Yes	No
D.	No	Yes

Answer (C) is correct.

REQUIRED: The item(s) considered keeping up a home for head of household filing status.

DISCUSSION: The cost of maintaining a household for head of household status includes expenditures for the mutual benefit of the occupants, e.g., food consumed in the home, rent, or real estate taxes. Not included is the value of services rendered in the home by the taxpayer or the rental value of a home owned by the taxpayer.

3.2 Exemptions

8. Joe and Barb are married, but Barb refuses to sign a Year 1 joint return. On Joe's separate Year 1 return, an exemption may be claimed for Barb if

A. Barb was a full-time student for the entire Year 1 school year.

B. Barb attaches a written statement to Joe's income tax return, agreeing to be claimed as an exemption by Joe for Year 1.

C. Barb was under the age of 19.

D. Barb had no gross income and was not claimed as another person's dependent in Year 1.

Answer (D) is correct.

REQUIRED: The circumstance(s) under which a married person filing separately may claim a personal exemption for the spouse.

DISCUSSION: A taxpayer filing as married filing separately may claim an exemption for his or her spouse if that spouse has no gross income and is not a dependent of another taxpayer.

9. Al and Mary Lew are married and filed a joint 2015 income tax return in which they validly claimed the $4,000 personal exemption for their dependent 17-year-old daughter, Dora. Since Dora earned $8,600 in 2015 from a part-time job at the college she attended full-time, Dora was also required to file a 2015 income tax return. What amount was Dora entitled to claim as a personal exemption in her 2015 individual income tax return?

A. $0

B. $1,050

C. $1,550

D. $4,000

Answer (A) is correct.

REQUIRED: The personal exemption deduction allowed a dependent.

DISCUSSION: An exemption is allowed for each dependent whose gross income for the taxable year is less than the exemption amount ($4,000 in 2015) or who is a child of the taxpayer and has not attained the age of 19. No personal exemption may be taken on the return of an individual who can be claimed as a dependent on another taxpayer's return. Dora's parents are entitled to claim her as a dependent on their return. Therefore, Dora is not entitled to a personal exemption herself.

10. In 2015, Sam Dunn provided more than half the support for his wife, his father's brother, and his cousin. Sam's wife was the only relative who was a member of Sam's household. None of the relatives had any income, nor did any of them file an individual or a joint return. All of these relatives are U.S. citizens. Which of these relatives should be claimed as a dependent or dependents on Sam's 2015 joint return?

A. Only his wife.

B. Only his father's brother.

C. Only his cousin.

D. His wife, his father's brother, and his cousin.

Answer (B) is correct.

REQUIRED: The relative(s) who could be claimed as a dependent on the taxpayer's return.

DISCUSSION: The IRC lists those relatives who may be claimed as dependents if they receive over half of their support from the taxpayer. The taxpayer's uncle is included in this list, so Sam's father's brother may be claimed by him as a dependent.

Answer (A) is incorrect. Sam's wife is entitled to her own personal exemption and is not classified as a dependent. Answer (C) is incorrect. Sam's cousin only meets this test if he was a member of Sam's household for the entire year. Answer (D) is incorrect. Sam's wife is entitled to her own personal exemption and is not classified as a dependent. In addition, the IRC does not include cousins in its list of relatives, and Sam's cousin was not a member of the household.

11. Jim and Kay Ross contributed to the support of their two children, Dale and Kim, and Jim's widowed parent, Grant. For 2015, Dale, a 19-year-old, full-time college student, earned $6,150 as a bookkeeper. Kim, a 23-year-old bank teller, earned $13,650. Grant received $7,825 in dividend income and $6,825 in nontaxable Social Security benefits. Grant, Dale, and Kim are U.S. citizens and were over one-half supported by Jim and Kay. How many exemptions can Jim and Kay claim on their 2015 joint income tax return?

A. 2

B. 3

C. 4

D. 5

Answer (B) is correct.

REQUIRED: The number of exemptions that a married couple filing a joint return can claim.

DISCUSSION: On a joint return, there are two taxpayers, and an exemption is allowed for each. An exemption is also allowed for each dependent. Kim does not qualify as a dependent because she had gross income in excess of the exemption amount ($4,000 in 2015). Although a parent can also qualify as a dependent, Grant has gross income in excess of the exemption and therefore cannot be claimed. The gross income test does not apply to a person such as Dale, who is a child of the claimant, under age 24, and a full-time student. Thus, Jim and Kay can claim themselves and Dale for a total of three exemptions on their return.

3.3 Gross Income

12. Which of the following conditions must be present in a post-1984 divorce agreement for a payment to qualify as deductible alimony?

I. Payments must be in cash.
II. The payments must end at the recipient's death.

A. I only.

B. II only.

C. Both I and II.

D. Neither I nor II.

Answer (C) is correct.

REQUIRED: The conditions required in a post-1984 divorce agreement for payments to qualify as deductible alimony.

DISCUSSION: In order for payments to qualify as deductible alimony, they must meet all of the following requirements:

1) Paid in cash
2) Paid pursuant to a written divorce or separation instrument
3) Not designated as other than alimony
4) Terminated at death of recipient
5) Not paid to a member of the same household
6) Not paid to a spouse with whom the taxpayer is filing a joint return

13. Pierce Corp., an accrual-basis, calendar-year C corporation, had the following 2015 receipts:

2016 advance rental payments for a lease ending in 2017	$250,000
Lease cancelation payment from a 5-year lease tenant	100,000

Pierce had no restrictions on the use of the advance rental payments and renders no services in connection with the rental income. What amount of gross income should Pierce report on its 2015 tax return?

A. $350,000

B. $250,000

C. $100,000

D. $0

Answer (A) is correct.

REQUIRED: The amount of gross income for the current year.

DISCUSSION: Both cash- and accrual-basis taxpayers must include rental payments in gross income upon actual or constructive receipt if the taxpayer has an unrestricted claim to the amount. A lease cancelation payment is in lieu of rent and is included in income like rent. Because Pierce had no restrictions on the use of the payments, the entire amount of the payments is included in income.

Answer (B) is incorrect. A lease cancelation payment is a payment made in lieu of rent and is included in income like rent. Answer (C) is incorrect. Without restrictions on the use, prepaid rent is income when received even if the lessor uses the accrual method of accounting. Answer (D) is incorrect. Without restrictions on the use, prepaid rent is income when received, and lease cancelation payments are made in lieu of rent and are included in income like rent.

14. Chrisp, a freelance photographer, uses the cash method for business. The tax year ends on December 31. Which of the following should **not** be included in the determination of Chrisp's gross income for the current year?

A. Chrisp owns controlling shares of a closely-held corporation and is planning to delay the bonus payment from the corporation until January of the next year. Bonus was authorized on December 15 of the current year and may be drawn at any time.

B. Chrisp received a check from a client on December 28 of the current year for a family portrait produced on December 22 of the current year. The check was dated December 23 of the current year but was not deposited until January 4 of the following year.

C. A client notified Chrisp on December 27 of the current year that a check was ready. The check was not picked up until January 4 of the following year.

D. Chrisp received a dividend check on January 4 of the following year. The dividends were declared payable on December 30 of the current year.

Answer (D) is correct.

REQUIRED: The item of income actually or constructively received in the following year.

DISCUSSION: Taxpayers are required to include in gross income any item of income actually or constructively received during the tax year. If there are actual restrictions on the access to the income, then the income is not considered constructively received. Although dividends were declared on December 30, Chrisp did not have access to the income until he actually received the dividend check on January 4, requiring recognition in the following year.

Answer (A) is incorrect. The bonus authorized on December 15 was payable at any time, and Chrisp chose not to accept it until January of the next year. However, since he had access to the bonus if he wanted it, he had constructive receipt of the income and has to include it in income for the current tax year. Answer (B) is incorrect. Chrisp was in possession of the check dated for December 23. He had constructive receipt of the income and must include it in his current year tax return. Answer (C) is incorrect. The check was ready on December 27 and could have been cashed in December. Therefore, Chrisp was in constructive receipt of the income but chose not to collect it until January.

15. Darr, an employee of Source C corporation, is not a shareholder. Which of the following should be included in Darr's gross income?

A. Employer-provided medical insurance coverage under a health plan.

B. A $15,000 gift from the taxpayer's grandparents.

C. The fair market value of land that the taxpayer inherited from an uncle.

D. The dividend income on shares of stock that the taxpayer received for services rendered.

Answer (D) is correct.

REQUIRED: The item included in the gross income of an employee.

DISCUSSION: The dividend income as well as the FMV of the stock would be included in Darr's gross income. The FMV of the stock is classified as compensation.

Answer (A) is incorrect. Employer-provided medical coverage is excluded from an employee's gross income. However, any benefits (reimbursement) from the employer-provided plan in excess of expenses should be included. Answer (B) is incorrect. Gifts are excluded from gross income. Answer (C) is incorrect. Land acquired by inheritance is excluded.

16. An individual received $50,000 during the current year pursuant to a divorce decree. A check for $25,000 was identified as annual alimony, checks totaling $10,000 were identified as annual child support, and a check for $15,000 was identified as a property settlement. What amount should be included in the individual's gross income?

A. $50,000

B. $40,000

C. $25,000

D. $0

Answer (C) is correct.

REQUIRED: The amount included in an individual's gross income.

DISCUSSION: Alimony is gross income to the recipient and deductible by the payor. Alimony is payment in cash, paid pursuant to a written divorce decree, not designated as other than alimony (e.g., child support), terminated at death of recipient, not paid to a member of the same household, and not paid to a spouse with whom the taxpayer is filing a joint return. Child support and property settlement payments are not alimony. Thus, the $25,000 of alimony is included in gross income.

Answer (A) is incorrect. Child support payments are an exclusion from gross income of the recipient and are not deductible by the payor. These payments are not alimony. Property settlement payments are not treated as alimony. They are treated as a transfer by gift, which is specifically excluded from gross income. Answer (B) is incorrect. Property settlement payments are not treated as alimony. They are treated as a transfer by gift, which is specifically excluded from gross income. Answer (D) is incorrect. Alimony is gross income to the recipient and deductible by the payor. Thus, $25,000 of alimony is included in gross income.

17. Nare, an accrual-basis, calendar-year taxpayer, owns a building that was rented to Mott under a 10-year lease expiring August 31, Year 3. On January 2, Year 1, Mott paid $30,000 as consideration for canceling the lease. On November 1, Year 1, Nare leased the building to Pine under a 5-year lease. Pine paid Nare $5,000 rent for each of the 2 months of November and December, and an additional $5,000 for the last month's rent. What amount of rental income should Nare report in its Year 1 income tax return?

A. $10,000

B. $15,000

C. $40,000

D. $45,000

Answer (D) is correct.

REQUIRED: Total income for rent, prepaid rent, and lease cancelation.

DISCUSSION: Rent is income. Value received by a landlord to cancel or modify a lease is income. Prepaid rent, with no restriction as to its use, is income when received even if the lessor uses the accrual method of accounting. Nare's total income for Year 1 is $45,000 ($30,000 cancelation + $10,000 Year 1 rent + $5,000 prepaid last month rent).

Answer (A) is incorrect. Amounts paid to cancel a lease are income. In addition, prepaid rent is income in the year received even if the lessor uses the accrual method of accounting. Answer (B) is incorrect. Amounts paid to cancel a lease are income. Answer (C) is incorrect. Prepaid rent is income in the year received even if the lessor uses the accrual method of accounting.

3.4 Other Gross Income

18. In 2015, Emil Gow won $10,000 in a state lottery and spent $800 for the purchase of lottery tickets. Emil elected the standard deduction on his 2015 income tax return. The amount of lottery winnings that should be included in Emil's 2015 gross income is

A. $0

B. $2,900

C. $3,700

D. $10,000

Answer (D) is correct.

REQUIRED: The amount of state lottery winnings included in gross income.

DISCUSSION: Gambling winnings (whether legal or illegal) are included in gross income. Therefore, Emil must include the full $10,000 in gross income. Gambling losses, i.e., amounts spent on nonwinning tickets, may be deductible but only as an itemized deduction to the extent of gambling winnings.

Answer (A) is incorrect. All gambling winnings constitute gross income. Answer (B) is incorrect. If the standard deduction is claimed, itemized deductions are not allowed. In addition, the standard deduction reduces AGI, not the amount included in gross income. Answer (C) is incorrect. Although the standard deduction may reduce taxable income, it does not reduce the amount of gambling winnings included in gross income.

19. Easel Co. has elected to reimburse employees for business expenses under a nonaccountable plan. Easel does not require employees to provide proof of expenses and allows employees to keep any amount not spent. Under the plan, Mel, an Easel employee for a full year, gets $400 per month for business automobile expenses. At the end of the year, Mel informs Easel that the only business expense incurred was for business mileage of 7,965 at a rate of 57.5 cents per mile, the IRS standard mileage rate at the time of travel. Mel encloses a check for $300 to refund the overpayment to Easel. What amount should be reported in Mel's gross income for the year?

A. $0

B. $300

C. $4,580

D. $4,800

Answer (D) is correct.

REQUIRED: The gross income reported for reimbursements from a nonaccountable plan.

DISCUSSION: In a nonaccountable plan, the reimbursements are included in the employee's gross income, and all the expenses are deducted from AGI (below-the-line-deductions). These expenses are a miscellaneous itemized deduction subject to the 2% floor. Since the employee accounted to the employer and returned the excess reimbursement, this could have qualified as an "accountable plan." Under an accountable plan, the employee would include nothing in income and take no deduction. However, the company uses a nonaccountable plan, and Mel must include $4,800 ($400 × 12 months) in his gross income.

Answer (A) is incorrect. Under a nonaccountable plan, Mel must include all reimbursements in gross income ($4,800). Answer (B) is incorrect. With a nonaccountable plan, the amount included in gross income is the total reimbursement (not limited to overpayment of the reimbursement). Answer (C) is incorrect. Under a nonaccountable plan, Mel must include all reimbursements in gross income ($4,800).

20. Porter was unemployed for part of the year. Porter received $35,000 of wages, $4,000 from a state unemployment compensation plan, and $2,000 from his former employer's company-paid supplemental unemployment benefit plan. What is the amount of Porter's gross income?

A. $35,000

B. $37,000

C. $39,000

D. $41,000

Answer (D) is correct.

REQUIRED: The total amount of gross income.

DISCUSSION: Gross income is all income from whatever source derived except as otherwise provided. All compensation (wages) for personal services is gross income. Unemployment benefits received under a federal or state program are gross income. Supplemental unemployment is included in gross income as wages (not under unemployment). Porter's total gross income is $41,000 ($35,000 wages + $4,000 state unemployment + $2,000 supplemental unemployment).

Answer (A) is incorrect. Although the $35,000 he received as wages is included in gross income, so are the $4,000 of state unemployment and the $2,000 of supplemental unemployment, for a total of $41,000. Answer (B) is incorrect. Although both the $35,000 of wages and $2,000 of supplemental unemployment are included in gross income, so is the $4,000 of state unemployment. Answer (C) is incorrect. Although both the $35,000 of wages and $4,000 of state unemployment are included in gross income, so is the $2,000 of supplemental unemployment.

21. Paul Crane, age 25, is single with no dependents and had an adjusted gross income of $30,000 in 2015, exclusive of $2,000 in unemployment compensation benefits received in 2015. The amount of Crane's unemployment compensation benefits taxable for 2015 is

A. $2,000

B. $1,000

C. $500

D. $0

Answer (A) is correct.

REQUIRED: The amount of taxable unemployment compensation.

DISCUSSION: All unemployment compensation constitutes gross income. The IRC does not allow exclusion or deduction of any of it.

22. Blake, a single individual, age 67, had a 2015 adjusted gross income of $60,000 exclusive of Social Security benefits. Blake received Social Security benefits of $8,400 and interest of $1,000 on tax-exempt obligations during 2015. What amount of Social Security benefits must be included in Blake's 2015 taxable income?

A. $0

B. $4,200

C. $7,140

D. $8,400

Answer (C) is correct.

REQUIRED: The amount of Social Security benefits included in gross income.

DISCUSSION: Provisional income ($65,200) exceeded the adjusted base amount ($34,000) by $31,200. Since 85% of this excess plus 50% of Social Security benefits equals $30,720 ($26,520 + $4,200), which exceeds 85% of the total Social Security benefits ($7,140), the latter amount is included.

Answer (A) is incorrect. A portion of Social Security benefits must be included in taxable income when provisional income exceeds the base amount. Blake's provisional income exceeds the adjusted base amount; therefore, 85% of his Social Security benefits ($7,140) are included in gross income. Answer (B) is incorrect. Provisional income exceeds the adjusted base amount; therefore, 85% of his Social Security benefits ($7,140) are included in gross income. Answer (D) is incorrect. The inclusion is limited to 85% of Social Security benefits.

3.5 Exclusions

23. Sam and Ann Hoyt filed a joint federal income tax return for the calendar year 2015. Among the Hoyts' cash receipts during 2015 was the following: $6,000 first installment on a $75,000 life insurance policy payable to Ann in annual installments of $6,000 each over a 15-year period, as beneficiary of the policy on her uncle, who died in 2014. What portion of the $6,000 installment on the life insurance policy is excludable from 2015 gross income in arriving at the Hoyts' adjusted gross income?

A. $0

B. $1,000

C. $5,000

D. $6,000

Answer (C) is correct.

REQUIRED: The life insurance proceeds excluded from gross income.

DISCUSSION: Proceeds under a life insurance contract paid by reason of death of the insured are excluded from gross income. But the amount of each payment in excess of the death benefit prorated over the period of payment ($75,000 ÷ 15 years = $5,000 per year) is interest income ($6,000 – $5,000), which is included in gross income.

Answer (A) is incorrect. The portion paid by reason of death, i.e., the amount of coverage, is excluded. Answer (B) is incorrect. The amount of interest included in gross income is $1,000. Answer (D) is incorrect. Only the portion paid by reason of death, i.e., the amount of coverage, is excluded.

24. In 2015, Joan accepted and received a $10,000 award for outstanding civic achievement. Joan was selected without any action on her part, and no future services are expected of her as a condition of receiving the award. What amount should Joan include in her 2015 gross income in connection with this award?

A. $0

B. $4,000

C. $5,000

D. $10,000

Answer (D) is correct.

REQUIRED: The amount of a civic achievement award the recipient must include in gross income.

DISCUSSION: Prizes and awards made primarily in recognition of charitable, scientific, educational, etc., achievement are excluded from gross income only if the recipient was selected without any action on his or her part, is not required to render substantial future services as a condition of receiving the prize or award, and assigns it to charity. Thus, Joan cannot exclude any amount of the $10,000 award from gross income since she failed to assign it to charity.

25. Klein, a master's degree candidate at Briar University, was awarded a $12,000 scholarship from Briar in Year 1. The scholarship was used to pay Klein's Year 1 university tuition and fees. Also in Year 1, Klein received $5,000 for teaching two courses at a nearby college. What amount must be included in Klein's Year 1 gross income?

A. $0

B. $5,000

C. $12,000

D. $17,000

Answer (B) is correct.

REQUIRED: The amount of scholarship received that is includible in gross income.

DISCUSSION: Scholarships may be excluded from gross income provided a student is enrolled in a degree-seeking program and that the scholarship is used for qualified expenses such as tuition and fees. However, amounts received for services such as teaching must be included in gross income.

Answer (A) is incorrect. Klein must include the $5,000 received for teaching the two courses. Answer (C) is incorrect. Klein may exclude the $12,000 scholarship but must include the $5,000 for teaching. Answer (D) is incorrect. Klein may exclude the $12,000 scholarship.

26. Charles and Marcia are married cash-basis taxpayers. In 2015, they had interest income as follows:

- $500 interest on federal income tax refund
- $600 interest on state income tax refund
- $800 interest on federal government obligations
- $1,000 interest on state government obligations

What amount of interest income is taxable on Charles and Marcia's 2015 joint income tax return?

A. $500

B. $1,100

C. $1,900

D. $2,900

Answer (C) is correct.

REQUIRED: The amount of interest income included in gross income.

DISCUSSION: Unless otherwise excluded in another section, the IRC includes interest in gross income. The IRC excludes from gross income interest on most obligations of states or political subdivisions of a state (e.g., municipal bonds). This exclusion does not apply to the obligations of the United States (with the exception of EE bonds used for qualifying education expenses) or interest on state income tax overpayments. Interest income is taxable unless specifically excluded from gross income.

27. Clark filed Form 1040EZ for the 2014 taxable year. In July 2015, Clark received a state income tax refund of $900, plus interest of $10, for overpayment of 2014 state income tax. What amount of the state tax refund and interest is taxable in Clark's 2015 federal income tax return?

A. $0

B. $10

C. $900

D. $910

Answer (B) is correct.

REQUIRED: The amount of a recovered item that produced no tax benefit, and interest, includible in gross income.

DISCUSSION: If a taxpayer obtains a deduction for an item that reduces taxes in one year and later recovers all or a portion of the prior deduction, the recovery is included in gross income in the year it is received. To the extent the expense did not reduce federal income taxes in the earlier year, the recovery is excluded from income. A taxpayer who files Form 1040EZ may claim no deductions other than the standard deduction and one personal exemption. Thus, the state tax paid produced no tax benefit and is excluded from gross income. Interest on state income tax refunds is not excludable. It is expressly included in gross income.

Answer (A) is incorrect. The interest on the tax refund is not excludable. Answer (C) is incorrect. The state income tax paid was not deducted on the Form 1040EZ and is thus excluded from gross income. Furthermore, the interest on the tax refund is not excludable. Answer (D) is incorrect. The state income tax paid was not deducted on the Form 1040EZ and is thus excluded from gross income.

28. DAC Foundation awarded Kent $75,000 in recognition of lifelong literary achievement. Kent was not required to render future services as a condition to receive the $75,000. What condition(s) must have been met for the award to be excluded from Kent's gross income?

I. Kent was selected for the award by DAC without any action on Kent's part.

II. Pursuant to Kent's designation, DAC paid the amount of the award either to a governmental unit or to a charitable organization.

A. I only.

B. II only.

C. Both I and II.

D. Neither I nor II.

Answer (C) is correct.

REQUIRED: The conditions under which an award may be excluded from a taxpayer's gross income.

DISCUSSION: Prizes and awards made primarily in recognition of charitable, scientific, educational, etc., achievement are excluded from gross income only if the recipient was selected without any action on his or her part, is not required to render substantial future services as condition of receiving the prize or award, and assigns it to charity.

Answer (A) is incorrect. Kent must also assign the award to charity. Answer (B) is incorrect. Kent must have been selected without any action on his or her part. Answer (D) is incorrect. Prizes and awards made primarily in recognition of charitable, scientific, educational, etc., achievement are excluded from gross income only if the recipient was selected without any action on his or her part, is not required to render substantial future services as condition of receiving the prize or award, and assigns it to charity.

29. During 2015, Adler had the following cash receipts:

Wages	$18,000
Interest income from investments in municipal bonds	400
Unemployment compensation	1,500

What is the total amount that must be included in gross income on Adler's 2015 income tax return?

A. $18,000

B. $18,400

C. $19,500

D. $19,900

Answer (C) is correct.

REQUIRED: The amount included in gross income on a taxpayer's income tax return.

DISCUSSION: The IRC specifically includes wages and unemployment compensation as gross income. Furthermore, the IRC excludes from gross income interest on most obligations of states or political subdivisions of a state (e.g., municipal bonds).

Answer (A) is incorrect. Unemployment compensation is also included in gross income. Answer (B) is incorrect. Interest on state and local government obligations is specifically excluded from gross income, and unemployment compensation is included in gross income. Answer (D) is incorrect. Interest on state and local government obligations is specifically excluded from gross income.

30. Cassidy, an individual, reported the following items of income and expense during the current year:

Salary	$50,000
Alimony paid to a former spouse	10,000
Inheritance from a grandparent	25,000
Proceeds of a lawsuit for physical injuries	50,000

What is the amount of Cassidy's adjusted gross income?

A. $40,000

B. $50,000

C. $115,000

D. $125,000

Answer (A) is correct.

REQUIRED: The taxpayer's adjusted gross income, including determining which items are gross income and which items are deducted from gross income.

DISCUSSION: A taxpayer's adjusted gross income equals all gross income items, as defined by Section 61 of the Internal Revenue Code, less any available deductions from gross income, as defined by the Internal Revenue Code.

Salary	$ 50,000
Alimony Paid	(10,000)
AGI	$ 40,000

The inheritance and proceeds for physical injury are excluded from gross income.

Answer (B) is incorrect. A deduction is allowed for alimony paid to a former spouse. Answer (C) is incorrect. Inheritances are excluded from the gross income of the recipient as gifts, and proceeds of a lawsuit for physical injuries, provided they are for actual damages, are specifically excluded from gross income as compensation for injury or sickness. Answer (D) is incorrect. Only one item is includible in gross income, and a deduction is allowed for alimony paid to a former spouse.

3.6 PRACTICE TASK-BASED SIMULATIONS

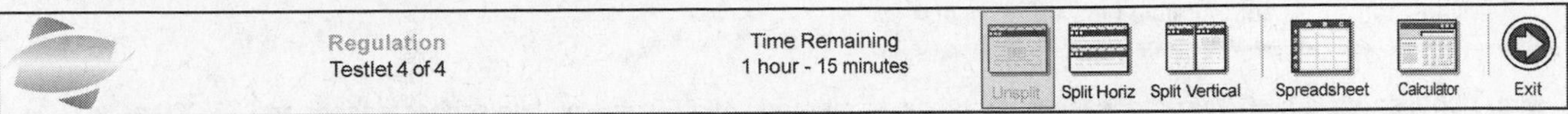

DIRECTIONS

Note: If you believe you have encountered a software malfunction, report it to the test center staff immediately.

Navigation

To navigate from task to task, use the controls at the bottom of the screen. Click on the **Next** button to advance to the next task, or the **Previous** button to go to the previous task. To go directly to any task, click on its number.

If you would like a reminder to revisit a task, or want to indicate that you are finished with it, click on the reminder flag below the task number. To clear the flag, click on it again. Reminder flags are for your use only – they do not contribute to your score.

Tabs

In this part of the examination, you will be asked to complete various tasks. Every task has one or more **Work Tabs**. Some tasks have one or more **Information Tabs**, others may have none. Every task has a **Help** tab.

If a task has **Information Tabs**, you may use the information in them to complete your responses in the **Work Tabs**.

Work tab **Information tab** **Help tab**

Work Tabs:

- **Work Tabs** are identified with a pencil icon. This is where your responses are expected.
- Each task has one or more **Work Tabs**.
- **Work Tabs** contain directions for completing the task – be sure to read these directions carefully.
- The **Work Tab** name in the example above is for illustration only – yours will differ.
- You must complete all of the **Work Tabs** in each task to receive full credit.

Information Tabs:

- The Authoritative Literature will be provided in all tasks in the AUD, FAR, and REG sections for your reference.
- Your simulation may have one or more additional **Information Tabs**. Like the Authoritative Literature tabs, **Information Tabs** do not have a pencil icon.
- If your task has additional **Information Tabs**, go through each to familiarize yourself with the task content.

Help Tab:

- The **Help Tab** provides assistance with the exam software that is used in this task. For example, if the task is to compose a memorandum, **Help** will provide information about the word processor.

The Toolbar

The toolbar at the top of the screen shows the amount of time remaining for you to complete the tasks. In addition, the following tools are available. Note that only the **Exit** button is displayed when Directions are visible - the others will appear when you begin the tasks.

Click on these buttons to split or unsplit the screen. You can split the screen vertically or horizontally.

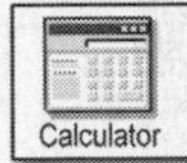

Click on this button to display the calculator; click on it again to hide the calculator. To move the calculator, click on the calculator title bar and drag the calculator to the desired location.

Click on this button to use the spreadsheet; click on it again to hide the spreadsheet. To move the spreadsheet, click on the the spreadsheet title bar and drag the spreadsheet to the desired location.

Click on this button to go on to the next part of the examination. You must complete all of the tasks to receive full credit. Once you click on **Exit** and confirm the action, you will NOT be able to return to this testlet.

Mrs. Vanessa Vick, a 40-year-old, cash-basis taxpayer, earned $45,000 as a private school teacher and $5,000 as a part-time real estate agent in 2015. Mr. Victor Vick, who died on July 1, 2015, had been permanently disabled on his job and collected state disability benefits until his death. For all of 2015 and 2016, the Vicks' residence was the principal home of both Mr. Vick's 11-year-old daughter, Victoria, and Mrs. Vick's unmarried cousin, Veranda Vascusio, who had no income in either year. During 2015, Victoria received $200 a month in survivor Social Security benefits that began on August 1, 2015, and will continue until her 18th birthday. In 2015 and 2016, Mrs. Vick provided over one-half the support for Victoria and Veranda, both of whom were U.S. citizens. Mrs. Vick did not remarry.

Select from the lists provided the proper filing status and exemption status for each of the criteria below.

Criteria	Filing Status Answer	Exemptions Answer
1. The filing status and the number of exemptions that Mrs. Vick can claim on the 2015 federal income tax return to get the most favorable tax results.		
2. The filing status and the number of exemptions that Mrs. Vick can claim on the 2016 federal income tax return to get the most favorable tax results, if she solely maintains the costs of her home.		

Filing Status	Exemptions
A) Single	E) One
B) Married Filing Joint	F) Two
C) Head of Household	G) Three
D) Qualifying Widow with dependent children	H) Four

Constructive Receipt of Income | Authoritative Literature | Help

Enter in the shaded cells the amount of income that Drake, who uses the cash method of accounting, should report on his 2015 federal income tax return for the transactions described below.

Transaction	Amount
1. A dividend check for $75 received on January 3, 2016. The dividends were declared payable on December 28, 2015.	
2. Paycheck for $800 received on December 24, 2015, but not cashed until January 4, 2016.	
3. Garnished wages for 2015 of $1,500 to pay Drake's debts.	
4. Wages of $200 paid directly to Drake's sister, at Drake's request, on November 15, 2015.	
5. A $985 payment on a sale of real property that was placed in escrow on December 15, 2015, but not received by Drake until January 10, 2016, when the transaction was closed.	

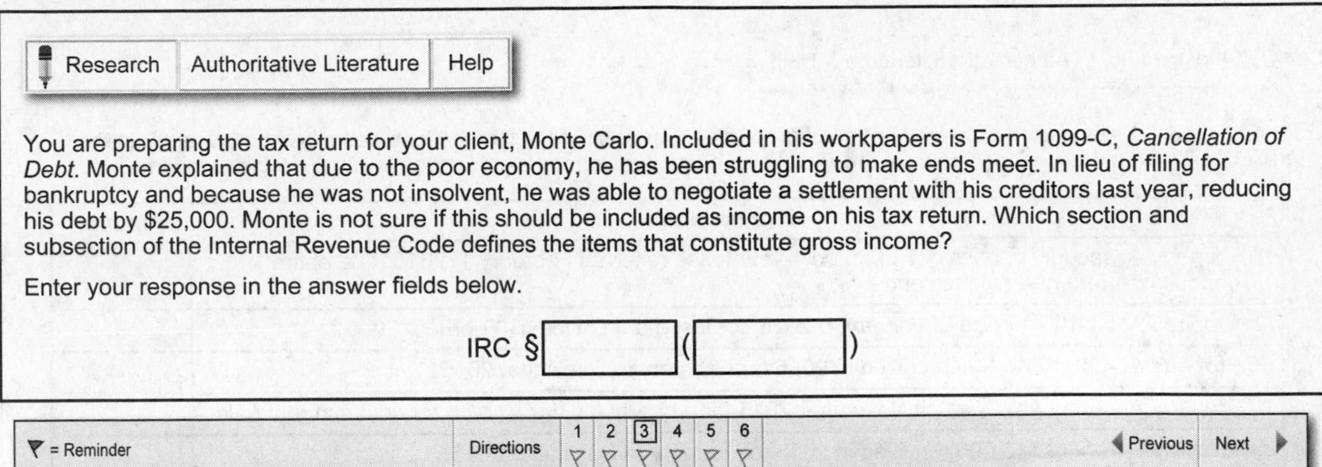

Research | Authoritative Literature | Help

You are preparing the tax return for your client, Monte Carlo. Included in his workpapers is Form 1099-C, *Cancellation of Debt*. Monte explained that due to the poor economy, he has been struggling to make ends meet. In lieu of filing for bankruptcy and because he was not insolvent, he was able to negotiate a settlement with his creditors last year, reducing his debt by $25,000. Monte is not sure if this should be included as income on his tax return. Which section and subsection of the Internal Revenue Code defines the items that constitute gross income?

Enter your response in the answer fields below.

IRC § [ ] ([ ])

= Reminder | Directions | 1 2 [3] 4 5 6 | Previous | Next

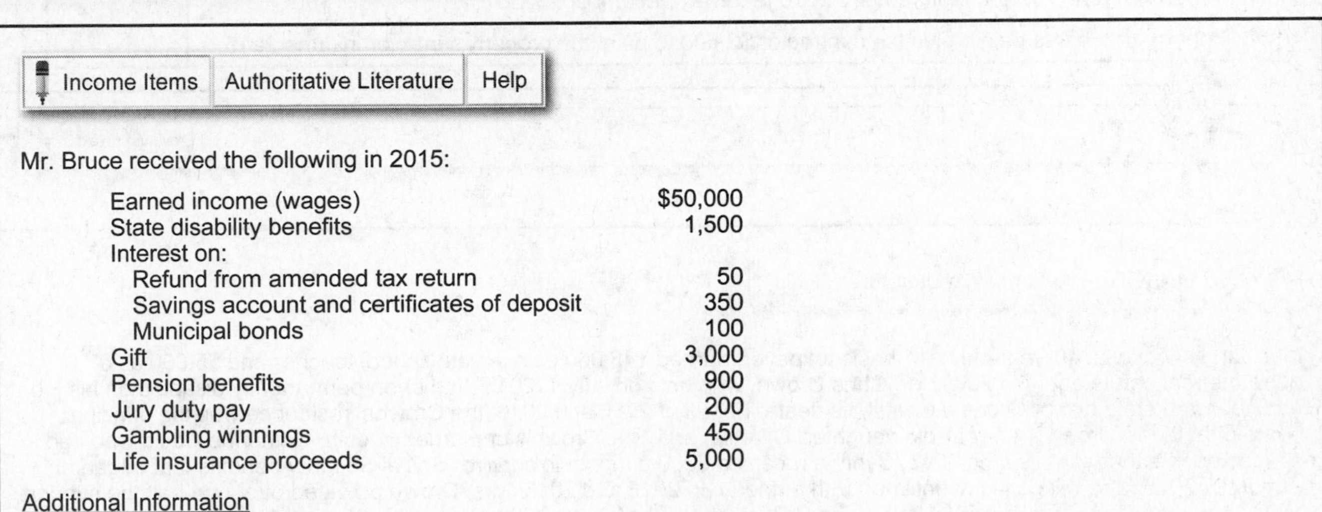

Income Items | Authoritative Literature | Help

Mr. Bruce received the following in 2015:

Earned income (wages)	$50,000
State disability benefits	1,500
Interest on:	
Refund from amended tax return	50
Savings account and certificates of deposit	350
Municipal bonds	100
Gift	3,000
Pension benefits	900
Jury duty pay	200
Gambling winnings	450
Life insurance proceeds	5,000

Additional Information

- Mrs. Bruce, who died on July 1, 2015, had been permanently disabled on her job and collected state disability payments until her death.
- Mr. Bruce received the $3,000 cash gift from his uncle.
- Mr. Bruce received the pension distributions from a qualified pension plan, paid for exclusively by his wife's employer.
- Mr. Bruce had $100 in gambling losses in 2015.
- Mr. Bruce was the beneficiary on his wife's life insurance policy. He received a lump-sum distribution.

Enter the amount that is taxable and should be included in adjusted gross income (AGI) in the shaded cells on Mr. Bruce's 2015 federal income tax return below.

Income Items	*Amount Taxable*
1. State disability benefits	
2. Interest income	
3. Pension benefits	
4. Gift	
5. Life insurance proceeds	
6. Jury duty pay	
7. Gambling winnings	

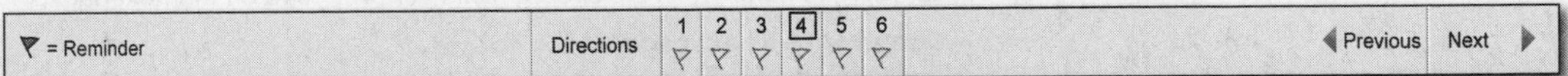

= Reminder | Directions | 1 2 3 [4] 5 6 | Previous | Next

Johnny, a cash-basis taxpayer, owns two rental properties. For each of the transactions described below, enter in the shaded cells the amount of income from the rental properties that Johnny must include in his 2015 gross income.

Transaction	Amount
1. Property A: security deposit of $1,000 on 1-year lease received February 1, 2015. The entire deposit was returned at lease end.	
2. Property A: $1,400 received February 1, 2015, for last month of lease (February 2016).	
3. Property A: rent of $15,400 received in 2015 for February to December 2015.	
4. Property A: tenant paid $350 in November 2015 for property repairs, with no reduction in rent paid.	
5. Property B: rent of $18,000 received in 2015 for January to December 2015.	
6. Property B: security deposit of $1,500 received January 1, 2015, to be used for last month's rent.	
7. Property B: rent of $1,600 for January 2016 received December 28, 2015.	
8. Property B: tenants paid a painting contractor $2,500 to paint the property's interior in June 2015.	

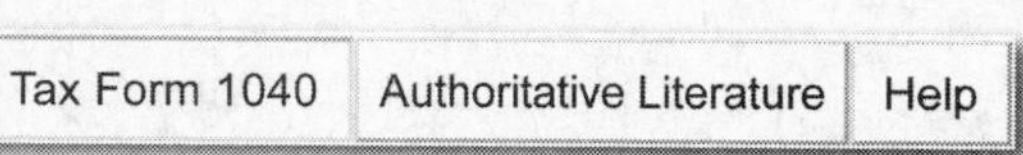

Mrs. Cindy Crown, a 40-year-old cash-basis taxpayer, earned $45,000 as a private school teacher and $5,000 as a part-time real estate agent in 2015. Mr. Chris Crown, who died on July 1, 2015, had been permanently disabled on his job and collected state disability benefits until his death. For all of 2015 and 2016, the Crowns' residence was the principal home of both Mr. Crown's 11-year-old daughter, Cynthia, and Mrs. Crown's unmarried cousin, Catherine Cook, who had no income in either year. During 2015, Cynthia received $200 a month in survivor Social Security benefits that began on August 1, 2015, and will continue until her 18th birthday. In 2015 and 2016, Mrs. Crown provided over one-half the support for Cynthia and Catherine, both of whom were U.S. citizens. Mrs. Crown did not remarry. Mr. and Mrs. Crown received the following in 2015:

Earned income (wages)	$50,000
State disability benefits	1,500
Interest on:	
Refund from amended tax return	50
Savings account and certificates of deposit	350
Municipal bonds	100
Gift	3,000
Pension benefits	900
Jury duty pay	200
Gambling winnings	450
Life insurance proceeds	5,000

Additional Information

- Mrs. Crown paid $150 in penalties for withdrawing money from her CD before it matured.
- Mrs. Crown received the $3,000 cash gift from her uncle.
- Mrs. Crown received the pension distributions from a qualified pension plan, paid for exclusively by her husband's employer.
- Mrs. Crown had $100 in gambling losses in 2015.
- Mrs. Crown was the beneficiary of the life insurance policy on her husband's life. She received a lump-sum distribution. The Crowns had paid $500 in premiums.
- Mrs. Crown also contributed $2,000 to her Roth IRA during 2015.

Using the information provided above, enter the appropriate numbers in the shaded cells in Form 1040 on the next page.

-- Continued on next page --

Tax Form 1040 | Authoritative Literature | Help -- **Continued**

Form **1040** Department of the Treasury—Internal Revenue Service
U.S. Individual Income Tax Return 201X (99) IRS Use Only—Do not write or staple in this space.

Income

Attach Form(s) W-2 here. Also attach Forms W-2G and 1099-R if tax was withheld.

If you did not get a W-2, see instructions.

Enclose, but do not attach, any payment. Also, please use **Form 1040-V.**

Line	Description		Box
7	Wages, salaries, tips, etc. Attach Form(s) W-2		7
8a	**Taxable** interest. Attach Schedule B if required		8a
b	**Tax-exempt** interest. **Do not** include on line 8a	8b	
9a	Ordinary dividends. Attach Schedule B if required		9a
b	Qualified dividends	9b	
10	Taxable refunds, credits, or offsets of state and local income taxes		10
11	Alimony received		11
12	Business income or (loss). Attach Schedule C or C-EZ		12
13	Capital gain or (loss). Attach Schedule D if required. If not required, check here ▶ ☐		13
14	Other gains or (losses). Attach Form 4797		14
15a	IRA distributions	15a — b Taxable amount	15b
16a	Pensions and annuities	16a — b Taxable amount	16b
17	Rental real estate, royalties, partnerships, S corporations, trusts, etc. Attach Schedule E		17
18	Farm income or (loss). Attach Schedule F		18
19	Unemployment compensation		19
20a	Social security benefits	20a — b Taxable amount	20b
21	Other income. List type and amount		21
22	Combine the amounts in the far right column for lines 7 through 21. This is your **total income** ▶		22

Adjusted Gross Income

Line	Description	Box	
23	Educator expenses	23	
24	Certain business expenses of reservists, performing artists, and fee-basis government officials. Attach Form 2106 or 2106-EZ	24	
25	Health savings account deduction. Attach Form 8889	25	
26	Moving expenses. Attach Form 3903	26	
27	Deductible part of self-employment tax. Attach Schedule SE	27	
28	Self-employed SEP, SIMPLE, and qualified plans	28	
29	Self-employed health insurance deduction	29	
30	Penalty on early withdrawal of savings	30	
31a	Alimony paid b Recipient's SSN ▶	31a	
32	IRA deduction	32	
33	Student loan interest deduction	33	
34	Tuition and fees. Attach Form 8917	34	
35	Domestic production activities deduction. Attach Form 8903	35	
36	Add lines 23 through 35		36
37	Subtract line 36 from line 22. This is your **adjusted gross income** ▶		37

For Disclosure, Privacy Act, and Paperwork Reduction Act Notice, see instructions. Cat. No. 11320B Form **1040** (201X)

= Reminder | Directions | 1 2 3 4 5 6 | ◀ Previous | Next ▶

Unofficial Answers

1. Filing Status (4 Gradable Items)

1. B) Married Filing Joint, H) Four. Upon the death of one spouse, the married-filing-jointly status is allowable provided that the surviving spouse does not remarry before the end of the tax year. This election is also dependent on the treatment of the executor of the spouse's estate. An individual who files a return is allowed a personal exemption amount for himself or herself, for his or her spouse, and for any other dependent who satisfies the dependent status tests. If one spouse dies during the year, an exemption is allowed provided that the surviving spouse does not remarry during the year. Veranda is a related dependent who derived over half her support from Mrs. Vick. Victoria is a residential dependent who derived over half her support from Mrs. Vick. Thus, four exemptions are available.
2. D) Qualifying Widow with dependent children, G) Three. A surviving spouse (qualifying widow) is a taxpayer whose spouse died during either of 2 preceding taxable years and who maintains his or her home as a household that is the principal place of residence of a dependent who is a child or stepchild of the taxpayer and with respect to whom the taxpayer is entitled to a dependency deduction. The individual shall be considered as maintaining a household only if over half of the cost of maintaining the household is furnished by the taxpayer. Mrs. Vick will also be allowed a personal exemption and two dependency exemptions for Veranda and Victoria.

2. Constructive Receipt of Income (5 Gradable Items)

1. $0. Taxpayers are required to include in gross income any item of income actually or constructively received during the tax year. If there are actual restrictions on the access to the income, then the income is not considered constructively received. Although dividends were declared on December 28, 2015, Drake did not have access to the income until he actually received the dividend check on January 3, 2016. Thus, he would recognize the dividend income in 2016.
2. $800. The paycheck was made available to Drake in 2015. Regardless of Drake's ability to cash or deposit the check, Drake constructively received $800 that must be reported as income on his 2015 federal income tax return.
3. $1,500. A taxpayer using the cash-basis method of accounting should include income when it is constructively received. Income, although not actually in a taxpayer's possession, is constructively received in the taxable year during which it is credited to his or her account, set apart for him or her, or otherwise made available without restriction. Drake constructively received the $1,500 in garnished wages in 2015.
4. $200. A taxpayer cannot avoid tax liability by assigning his or her income to another person. The $200 in wages paid to Drake's sister were constructively received by Drake and must be included in his 2015 gross income.
5. $0. Taxpayers are required to include in gross income any item of income actually or constructively received during the tax year. If there are actual restrictions on access to the income, then the income is not considered constructively received. Since Drake's control of the receipt of the funds in the escrow account is substantially limited until the transaction has closed, Drake has not constructively received the income until the closing of the transaction in 2016.

3. Research (1 Gradable Item)

Answer: IRC § 61(a)

§ 61. Gross income defined

(a) General definition

Except as otherwise provided in this subtitle, gross income means all income from whatever source derived, including (but not limited to) the following items:

(1) Compensation for services, including fees, commissions, fringe benefits, and similar items;
(2) Gross income derived from business;
(3) Gains derived from dealings in property;
(4) Interest;
(5) Rents;
(6) Royalties;
(7) Dividends;
(8) Alimony and separate maintenance payments;
(9) Annuities;
(10) Income from life insurance and endowment contracts;
(11) Pensions;
(12) Income from discharge of indebtedness;
(13) Distributive share of partnership gross income;
(14) Income in respect of a decedent; and
(15) Income from an interest in an estate or trust.

4. Income Items (7 Gradable Items)

1. $0. Under Section 104(c), disability benefits arising from permanent loss are not included in gross income provided the benefits are calculated with reference to the nature of the injury and not the period the employee is absent from work. Thus, if the amounts do not represent retirement pay, the disability benefits should be excluded from gross income.
2. $400. All interest is included in gross income unless expressly excluded. Interest on tax refunds, savings accounts, and certificates of deposit is included in gross income. Interest generated on qualified municipal bonds is tax-exempt.
3. $900. Because the entire cost of the pension was paid by the employer, the entire amount of the pension benefits received is included in gross income.
4. $0. Gross income does not include the value of property acquired by a gift resulting from a detached and disinterested generosity.
5. $0. Gross income does not include amounts received (whether in a single sum or otherwise) under a life insurance contract if such amounts are paid due to the death of the insured.
6. $200. Gross income includes income from any source that is not expressly excluded. Jury duty pay is included in gross income. Note: An employee can deduct jury pay surrendered to an employer who continued to pay employee's normal salary.
7. $450. Gross income includes income from any source that is not expressly excluded. Gambling winnings are included in gross income. In order to determine adjusted gross income, no deduction is allowed above the line to compensate for gambling losses because, to the extent of gambling winnings, these losses are an itemized deduction in Schedule A not subject to the 2% floor.

5. Rental Income (8 Gradable Items)

1. $0. Security deposits not intended as rent are income only if the lessor becomes entitled to them upon the the lessee's violation of the lease. Johnny would include the $1,000 in gross income for 2016.
2. $1,400. Advance rent payments must be included in income in the year received. Thus, Johnny will include the $1,400 in gross income for 2015.
3. $15,400. Both cash- and accrual-basis taxpayers must include amounts in gross income upon actual or constructive receipt if the taxpayer has an unrestricted claim to such amounts. Thus, the rent payments of $15,400 that Johnny received for Property A are included in his gross income.
4. $0. As a general rule, if a lessee pays any of the expenses of his or her lessor, such payments are additional rental income to the lessor. However, the fair market value of expenses paid that are not made in lieu of rent is not additional rental income. Johnny does not include the $350 in gross income for 2015.
5. $18,000. Both cash- and accrual-basis taxpayers must include amounts in gross income upon actual or constructive receipt if the taxpayer has an unrestricted claim to such amounts. Thus, the rent payments of $18,000 that Johnny received for Property B are included in his gross income.
6. $1,500. If a security deposit is intended as an advance rent payment, it must be included in income in the year received.
7. $1,600. Advance rent payments must be included in income in the year received. Thus, Johnny will include the $1,600 in gross income for 2015.
8. $0. The value of leasehold improvements not made in lieu of rent is excluded from the lessor's gross income.

6. Tax Form 1040 (10 Gradable Items)

Form **1040** Department of the Treasury—Internal Revenue Service **U.S. Individual Income Tax Return** **201X** (99) IRS Use Only—Do not write or staple in this space.

Income	7	Wages, salaries, tips, etc. Attach Form(s) W-2			7	50,000	[1]
	8a	**Taxable** interest. Attach Schedule B if required			8a	400	[2]
Attach Form(s) W-2 here. Also attach Forms W-2G and 1099-R if tax was withheld.	b	**Tax-exempt** interest. **Do not** include on line 8a	8b				
	9a	Ordinary dividends. Attach Schedule B if required			9a		
	b	Qualified dividends	9b				
	10	Taxable refunds, credits, or offsets of state and local income taxes			10		
	11	Alimony received			11		
	12	Business income or (loss). Attach Schedule C or C-EZ			12		
	13	Capital gain or (loss). Attach Schedule D if required. If not required, check here ▶ ☐			13	0	[3]
	14	Other gains or (losses). Attach Form 4797			14		
	15a	IRA distributions	15a		15b		
		b Taxable amount					
	16a	Pensions and annuities	16a		16b	900	[4]
		b Taxable amount					
Enclose, but do not attach, any payment. Also, please use **Form 1040-V.**	17	Rental real estate, royalties, partnerships, S corporations, trusts, etc. Attach Schedule E			17		
	18	Farm income or (loss). Attach Schedule F			18		
	19	Unemployment compensation			19		
	20a	Social security benefits	20a		20b		
		b Taxable amount					
	21	Other income. List type and amount			21	650	[5]
	22	Combine the amounts in the far right column for lines 7 through 21. This is your **total income** ▶			22	51,950	[6]
Adjusted Gross Income	23	Educator expenses	23				
	24	Certain business expenses of reservists, performing artists, and fee-basis government officials. Attach Form 2106 or 2106-EZ	24				
	25	Health savings account deduction. Attach Form 8889	25				
	26	Moving expenses. Attach Form 3903	26				
	27	Deductible part of self-employment tax. Attach Schedule SE	27				
	28	Self-employed SEP, SIMPLE, and qualified plans	28				
	29	Self-employed health insurance deduction	29				
	30	Penalty on early withdrawal of savings	30	150 [7]			
	31a	Alimony paid b Recipient's SSN ▶	31a				
	32	IRA deduction	32	0 [8]			
	33	Student loan interest deduction	33				
	34	Tuition and fees. Attach Form 8917	34				
	35	Domestic production activities deduction. Attach Form 8903	35				
	36	Add lines 23 through 35			36	150	[9]
	37	Subtract line 36 from line 22. This is your **adjusted gross income** ▶			37	51,800	[10]

Cat. No. 11320B Form **1040** (201X)

[1] $50,000. Wages for 2015 for Cindy Crown are the total of her $45,000 of private school salary and $5,000 real estate commission.

[2] $400. The $50 of interest on the tax return refund and the $350 of savings account and CD interest is taxable interest. The municipal bond interest is non-taxable.

[3] $0. Cindy Crown did not sell any capital assets during the year.

[4] $900. Pension benefits, unless specifically excluded, are fully included in the computation of gross income.

[5] $650. Jury duty pay and gambling winnings are included in gross income. Gambling losses do not offset gambling winnings. Gambling losses are deductible on Schedule A up to the amount of gambling winnings.

[6] $51,950. Total income equals the total of line 7 through line 21 ($50,000 + $400 + $0 + $900 + $650).

[7] $150. The penalty on early withdrawal from a CD is a deduction for calculating adjusted gross income.

[8] $0. Contributions to a Roth IRA are not deductible.

[9] $150. The total deductions for calculating adjusted gross income are $150.

[10] $51,800. Adjusted gross income equals total income of $51,950 less "for AGI" deductions for a total of $51,800.

Gleim Simulation Grading

Task	Correct Responses		Gradable Items		Score per Task
1	____	÷	4	=	____
2	____	÷	5	=	____
3 (Research)	____	÷	1	=	____
4	____	÷	7	=	____
5	____	÷	8	=	____
6	____	÷	10	=	____
			Total of Scores per Task		____
		÷	Total Number of Tasks		6
			Total Score		____%

STUDY UNIT FOUR
SELF-EMPLOYMENT, FARMING, AND ADJUSTMENTS

(28 pages of outline)

Gross income is reduced by deductions to compute taxable income. No amount can be deducted from gross income unless allowed by the Internal Revenue Code (IRC). Deductible business expenses apply to sole proprietorships as well as other business entities. Employers who pay wages are required to pay tax based on the employee's pay. This includes Social Security tax, Medicare tax, and Unemployment tax. Not all payments made to employees are includible in their gross income. Above-the-line deductions are deducted from gross income to arrive at adjusted gross income (AGI).

Deductions to compute taxable income are heavily tested on the CPA exam. The business expense deductions explained in this study unit are also tested in the corporate context. The CPA exam has decreased its testing of exact amounts of limits. Nevertheless, you should be familiar with limit and threshold amounts.

As of the date of publication, the IRS had not yet released all of the 2015 tax forms. Please check www.gleim.com/taxforms for any updates.

4.1 BUSINESS INCOME AND EXPENSES

1. **Self-Employment Income**
   a. A sole proprietor generally reports all self-employment income and expense on Schedule C.
   b. Gross income (GI) includes all income from a trade or business.
      1) GI from a business that sells products or commodities is

         Gross sales (receipts)
         – Cost of goods sold
         + Other GI (e.g., rentals)
         = GI from the business

      2) Cost of goods sold (COGS) is treated as a return of capital, which is not income for tax purposes. COGS for a tax year, typically, is

         Beginning inventory
         + Inventory purchased during year
         – Year-end inventory
         = COGS

      3) COGS should be determined in accordance with the accounting method consistently used by the business.

SCHEDULE C (Form 1040)

Department of the Treasury Internal Revenue Service (99)

Profit or Loss From Business

(Sole Proprietorship)

▶ Information about Schedule C and its separate instructions is at *www.irs.gov/schedulec.*

▶ Attach to Form 1040, 1040NR, or 1041; partnerships generally must file Form 1065.

OMB No. 1545-0074

2015

Attachment Sequence No. 09

Name of proprietor | **Social security number (SSN)**

A Principal business or profession, including product or service (see instructions) | **B Enter code from instructions** ▶

C Business name. If no separate business name, leave blank. | **D Employer ID number (EIN),** (see instr.)

E Business address (including suite or room no.) ▶

City, town or post office, state, and ZIP code

F Accounting method: (1) ☐ Cash (2) ☐ Accrual (3) ☐ Other (specify) ▶

G Did you "materially participate" in the operation of this business during 2015? If "No," see instructions for limit on losses ☐ Yes ☐ No

H If you started or acquired this business during 2015, check here ▶ ☐

I Did you make any payments in 2015 that would require you to file Form(s) 1099? (see instructions) ☐ Yes ☐ No

J If "Yes," did you or will you file required Forms 1099? ☐ Yes ☐ No

Part I Income

1	Gross receipts or sales. See instructions for line 1 and check the box if this income was reported to you on Form W-2 and the "Statutory employee" box on that form was checked ▶ ☐	1	
2	Returns and allowances	2	
3	Subtract line 2 from line 1	3	
4	Cost of goods sold (from line 42)	4	
5	**Gross profit.** Subtract line 4 from line 3	5	
6	Other income, including federal and state gasoline or fuel tax credit or refund (see instructions)	6	
7	**Gross income.** Add lines 5 and 6 ▶	7	

Part II Expenses. Enter expenses for business use of your home **only** on line 30.

8	Advertising	8		18	Office expense (see instructions)	18	
9	Car and truck expenses (see instructions)	9		19	Pension and profit-sharing plans	19	
10	Commissions and fees	10		20	Rent or lease (see instructions):		
11	Contract labor (see instructions)	11		a	Vehicles, machinery, and equipment	20a	
12	Depletion	12		b	Other business property	20b	
13	Depreciation and section 179 expense deduction (not included in Part III) (see instructions)	13		21	Repairs and maintenance	21	
				22	Supplies (not included in Part III)	22	
				23	Taxes and licenses	23	
				24	Travel, meals, and entertainment:		
14	Employee benefit programs (other than on line 19)	14		a	Travel	24a	
15	Insurance (other than health)	15		b	Deductible meals and entertainment (see instructions)	24b	
16	Interest:			25	Utilities	25	
a	Mortgage (paid to banks, etc.)	16a		26	Wages (less employment credits)	26	
b	Other	16b		27a	Other expenses (from line 48)	27a	
17	Legal and professional services	17		b	**Reserved for future use**	27b	

28	**Total expenses** before expenses for business use of home. Add lines 8 through 27a ▶	28	
29	Tentative profit or (loss). Subtract line 28 from line 7	29	
30	Expenses for business use of your home. Do not report these expenses elsewhere. Attach Form 8829 unless using the simplified method (see instructions). **Simplified method filers only:** enter the total square footage of: (a) your home: ________ and (b) the part of your home used for business: ________. Use the Simplified Method Worksheet in the instructions to figure the amount to enter on line 30	30	
31	**Net profit or (loss).** Subtract line 30 from line 29. • If a profit, enter on both **Form 1040, line 12** (or **Form 1040NR, line 13**) and on **Schedule SE, line 2.** (If you checked the box on line 1, see instructions). Estates and trusts, enter on **Form 1041, line 3.** • If a loss, you **must** go to line 32.	31	

32 If you have a loss, check the box that describes your investment in this activity (see instructions).

• If you checked 32a, enter the loss on both **Form 1040, line 12,** (or **Form 1040NR, line 13**) and on **Schedule SE, line 2.** (If you checked the box on line 1, see the line 31 instructions). Estates and trusts, enter on **Form 1041, line 3.**

• If you checked 32b, you **must** attach **Form 6198.** Your loss may be limited.

32a ☐ All investment is at risk.

32b ☐ Some investment is not at risk.

2. **Ordinary and Necessary Expense**
   a. A deduction from gross income is allowed for all ordinary and necessary expenses paid or incurred during a tax year in carrying on a trade or business.
   b. These deductions apply to sole proprietors as well as other business entities.
3. **Trade/Business and Expenses Defined**
   a. A trade or business is a regular and continuous activity that is entered into with the expectation of making a profit.
      1) "Regular" means the taxpayer devotes a substantial amount of business time to the activity.
   b. An activity that is not engaged in for a profit is a hobby (personal).
      1) An activity that results in a profit in any 3 of 5 consecutive tax years (2 of 7 for the breeding and racing of horses) is presumed not to be a hobby.
   c. An expense must be **both** ordinary and necessary to be deductible.
      1) "Ordinary" implies that the expense normally occurs or is likely to occur in connection with businesses similar to the one operated by the taxpayer claiming the deduction.
         a) The expenditures need not occur frequently.
      2) "Necessary" implies that an expenditure must be appropriate and helpful in developing or maintaining the trade or business.
      3) Implicit in the "ordinary and necessary" requirement is the requirement that the expenditures be reasonable.
4. **Compensation**
   a. Cash and the FMV of property paid to an employee are deductible by the employer.
5. **Rent**
   a. Advance rental payments may be deducted by the lessee only during the tax periods to which the payments apply.
   b. Generally, even a cash-method taxpayer must amortize prepaid rent expense over the period to which it applies. The exception to this rule is if the payments do not extend beyond a year.
6. **Entertainment and Meals**
   a. Entertainment includes recreation, e.g., entertaining guests at a nightclub or theater, or by vacations, trips, etc., and furnishing a hotel suite, food and beverages, or the like to a customer or a member of his or her family.
      1) Club dues for social gatherings are not deductible, e.g., country club membership dues.
      2) Dues paid to professional clubs are deductible if they are paid for business reasons and the principal purpose is professional, i.e., not for entertainment.
   b. The expense must be **directly related** or **associated with** the active conduct of a trade or business. The predominant purpose must be the furthering of the trade or business of the taxpayer incurring the expense.
      1) **"Directly related"** means that business is actually conducted during the entertainment period.
      2) **"Associated with"** means that the entertainment must occur directly before or after a business discussion.

c. There is a 50% limit to deductible amounts for meal and entertainment expenses and related expenses, such as taxes, tips, and parking fees.
   1) Transportation to and from a business meal is not limited.
   2) The IRS has denied deductions for any meal or entertainment expense over $75 for which the claimant did not provide substantiating evidence.

d. Meal expenses are not deductible if neither the taxpayer nor an employee of the taxpayer is present at the meal.

7. **Travel**

a. While away from home overnight on business, travel expenses are deductible. Travel expenses include transportation, lodging, and meal expenses in an employment-related context.

b. No deduction is allowed for
   1) Travel that is primarily personal in nature
   2) The travel expenses of the taxpayer's spouse unless
      a) There is a bona fide business purpose for the spouse's presence,
      b) The spouse is an employee, and
      c) The expenses would be otherwise deductible.
   3) Commuting between home and work
   4) Attending investment meetings
   5) Travel as a form of education

c. A new rule allows for lodging deductions when not traveling away from home (e.g., a conference or tradeshow held at a local hotel with evening events), if qualified under one of two tests or rules.
   1) The deduction is allowed if all the facts and circumstances indicate the lodging is for carrying on a taxpayer's trade or business. One factor under this test is whether the taxpayer incurs an expense because of a bona fide condition or requirement of employment imposed by the taxpayer's employer.
   2) A safe harbor rule applies if
      a) The lodging is necessary for the individual to participate fully in, or be available for, a bona fide business meeting, conference, training activity, or other business function;
      b) The lodging is for a period that does not exceed 5 calendar days and does not recur more frequently than once per calendar quarter;
      c) The employee's employer requires the employee to remain at the activity or function overnight (if the individual is an employee); and
      d) The lodging is not lavish or extravagant under the circumstances and does not provide any significant element of personal pleasure, recreation, or benefit.

8. **Foreign Travel**

a. Traveling expenses of a taxpayer who ventures outside of the United States away from home must be allocated between time spent on the trip for business and time spent for pleasure.

EXAMPLE

Scott's foreign trip is for more than a week, and he spends most of his time as a personal vacation. However, he spends some time at a business-related conference.

Only the expenses related to the conference, including lodging, local travel, etc., may be deducted.

b. No allocation is required when
   1) The trip is for no more than 1 week and
   2) A personal vacation was not the major consideration or
   3) The personal time spent on the trip is less than 25% of the total time away from home.

9. **Automobile Expenses**
   a. Actual expenses for automobile use are deductible (e.g., services, repairs, gas).
   b. Alternatively, the taxpayer may deduct the standard mileage rate ($.575 per mile for 2015), plus parking fees, tolls, etc.

10. **Taxes**
   a. Taxes paid or accrued in a trade or business are deductible.
   b. Taxes paid or accrued to purchase property are treated as part of the cost of the property.
   c. Sales tax is treated as part of the property's cost.
      1) If capitalized, the sales tax may be recoverable as depreciation.
      2) If the cost of the property is currently expensed and deductible, so is the tax.
   d. Occupational license taxes are deductible.
   e. Property tax.
      1) Tax on real and personal property is an itemized deduction for individuals.
      2) Tax on business property is a business expense (i.e., deducted on a business return, for example, Schedule C or E).
      3) Local improvements.
         a) Taxes assessed for local benefit that tend to increase the value of real property are added to the property's adjusted basis and are not currently deductible as tax expense.
   f. Income taxes.
      1) State and local taxes imposed on net income of an individual are NOT deductible on Schedule C.
         a) They are deductible as a personal, itemized deduction not subject to the 2% exclusion.
         b) They are not a business expense of a sole proprietorship.
      2) Federal income taxes generally are not deductible.
      3) Individual taxpayers may claim an itemized deduction for either general state and local sales taxes or state income taxes, but not both.
   g. Employment taxes.
      1) An employer may deduct the employer portion of FICA and FUTA taxes.
      2) An employee may not deduct FICA tax.
      3) A self-employed person is allowed a deduction for the employer's portion of the FICA taxes paid to arrive at his or her AGI. For 2015, this equals
         a) 6.2% of the first $118,500 of net self-employment income plus
         b) 1.45% of net self-employment income (no cap).
      4) The employee portion includes an additional 0.9% for high-income earnings, i.e., earnings in excess of $200,000 ($250,000 MFJ, $125,000 MFS).

11. **Insurance Expense**
    a. Trade or business insurance expense paid or incurred during the tax year is deductible.
    b. A cash-method taxpayer may not deduct a premium before it is paid.
    c. Prepaid insurance must be apportioned over the period of coverage.
12. **Bad Debts**
    a. A bad debt deduction is allowed only for a bona fide debt arising from a debtor-creditor relationship based upon a valid and enforceable obligation to pay a fixed or determinable sum of money.
    b. Worthless debt is deductible only to the extent of adjusted basis in the debt.
        1) A cash-basis taxpayer has no basis in accounts receivable and generally has no deduction for bad debts.
    c. A **business bad debt** is one incurred or acquired in connection with the taxpayer's trade or business.
        1) Partially worthless business debts may be deducted to the extent they are worthless and specifically written off.
        2) A business bad debt is treated as an ordinary loss.
    d. A **nonbusiness bad debt** is a debt other than one incurred or acquired in connection with the taxpayer's trade or business.
        1) Investments are not treated as a trade or business.
        2) A partially worthless nonbusiness bad debt is not deductible.
        3) A wholly worthless nonbusiness debt is treated as a short-term capital loss.
    e. Worthless corporate securities are not considered bad debts. They are generally treated as a capital loss.
    f. The **specific write-off method** must be used for tax purposes. The reserve method is used only for financial accounting purposes.
13. **Loan Costs**
    a. Costs of business borrowing are generally deductible.
    b. Costs of obtaining a loan, other than interest, are deductible over the period of the loan. Examples of such costs are recording fees and mortgage commissions.
    c. Interest is deductible when paid, as are payments in lieu of interest.
        1) Prepayment penalties are treated as interest and are deductible when paid.
        2) Points are treated as interest. They must be amortized.
            a) However, ordinary points on acquisition indebtedness of a principal residence may be treated as currently deductible loan costs.
            b) Points paid on refinancing must be amortized.
        3) Prepaid interest in any form must be amortized over the period of the loan.
            a) Any undeducted balance is deductible in full when the loan is paid off.
14. **Business Gifts**
    a. Expenditures for business gifts are deductible. They must be ordinary and necessary.
    b. Deduction is limited to $25 per recipient per year for excludable items.
        1) The $25 limit does not apply to incidental items costing (the giver) $4 each or less.
        2) A husband and wife are treated as one taxpayer, even if they file separate returns and have independent business relationships with the recipient.

15. **Employee Achievement Awards**
    a. Up to $400 of the cost of employee achievement awards is deductible by an employer for all nonqualified plan awards.
        1) An employee achievement award is tangible personal property awarded as part of a meaningful presentation for safety achievement or length of service.
    b. Deduction of qualified plan awards is limited to $1,600 per year.
        1) A qualified plan award is an employee achievement award provided under an established written program that does not discriminate in favor of highly compensated employees.
        2) If the average cost of all employee achievement awards is greater than $400, then it is not a qualified plan award.
16. **Start-Up and Organization Costs**
    a. Taxpayers can deduct up to $5,000 of start-up costs and $5,000 of organizational costs in the taxable year in which the business begins.
        1) Examples of start-up costs are costs incurred to prepare to enter into the trade or business, to secure suppliers and customers, and to obtain certain supplies and equipment (noncapital).
        2) Examples of organizational costs are legal and accounting fees; costs of state filings; and expenses of meetings with directors, shareholders, or partners.
        3) Any start-up or organizational costs in excess of $5,000 are capitalized and amortized proportionally over a 180-month period beginning with the month in which the active trade or business begins.
            a) These amounts are reduced, but not below zero, by the cumulative cost of the start-up costs or organizational costs that exceed $50,000.
        4) Taxpayers are not required to file a separate election statement. The taxpayer needs only to expense or capitalize the cost; from there, the election is irrevocable.
17. **Vacant Land**
    a. Interest and taxes on vacant land are deductible.
18. **Medical Reimbursement Plans**
    a. The cost of such a plan for employees is deductible by the employer.
19. **Political Contributions**
    a. Contributions to a political party or candidate and, generally, lobbying expenses are not deductible.
    b. However, expense in connection with appearances before and communications with any **local** council or similar governing body with respect to legislation of direct interest to the taxpayer is deductible.
    c. Up to $2,000 of direct cost of such activity at the state or federal level is deductible.
        1) Also, if total direct costs exceed $2,000, then this de minimis exception is entirely unavailable.
20. **Intangibles**
    a. The cost of intangibles must generally be capitalized.
    b. Amortization is allowed if the intangible has a determinable useful life.

21. **Tax-Exempt Income**
    a. An expenditure related to producing tax-exempt income is not deductible, e.g., interest on a loan used to purchase tax-exempt bonds.
22. **Public Policy**
    a. A trade or business expenditure that is ordinary, necessary, and reasonable may be nondeductible if allowing the deduction would frustrate public policy.
    b. Examples are
        1) Fines and penalties paid to the government for violation of the law
        2) Illegal bribes and kickbacks
        3) Two-thirds of damages for violation of federal antitrust law
        4) Expenses of dealers in illegal drugs (as determined at the federal level)
            a) However, adjustment to gross receipts is permitted for the cost of merchandise.
23. **Miscellaneous Ordinary and Necessary Business Expenses**
    a. Miscellaneous ordinary and necessary business expenses are deductible.
    b. Examples include costs of advertising, bank fees, depreciation, amortization, office supplies, etc.
24. **Capital Expenditures**
    a. Capital expenditures are made in acquiring or improving property that will have a useful life of longer than 1 year.
        1) For example, replacing machinery is generally a capital expenditure.
    b. If the property is a depreciable asset, the cost is recovered through depreciation.
    c. If the property is not a depreciable asset, the amount of the capital expenditure might be recovered at the time of disposition.
25. **Business Use of Home**
    a. Expenses incurred for the use of a person's home for business purposes are deductible only if strict requirements are met.
        1) The portion of the home must be used exclusively and regularly as
            a) The principal place of business for any trade or business of the taxpayer;
            b) A place of business that is used by patients, clients, or customers in the normal course of the taxpayer's trade or business; or
            c) A separate structure that is not attached to the dwelling unit that is used in the taxpayer's trade or business.
        2) If the taxpayer is an employee, the business use of the home must also be for the convenience of the employer.
    b. The exclusive-use test is strictly applied. Any personal use of the business portion of the home by anyone results in complete disallowance of the deductions. There are two exceptions to the exclusive-use test:
        1) Retail/wholesale. A retailer or wholesaler whose **sole** location of his or her business is his or her home need not meet the exclusive-use test.
            a) The ordinary and necessary business expenses allocable to an identifiable space used regularly for inventory or product sample storage by a taxpayer in the active pursuit of his or her trade or business are deductible.
        2) Day care. If the business portion of a home is used to offer qualifying day care, the exclusive-use test need not be met.

c. If the taxpayer has more than one business location, the primary factor in determining whether a home office is a taxpayer's principal place of business is the relative importance of the activities performed at each business location.

   1) If the primary location cannot be determined by the relative importance test, then the amount of time spent at each location will be used.

d. A home office qualifies as a "principal place of business" if used by the taxpayer to conduct administrative or management activities of the taxpayer's trade or business and there is no other fixed location where the taxpayer conducts such activities.

e. Deduction for business use is limited to

   1) Gross income derived from the use, minus
   2) Deductions related to the home, allowed regardless of business or personal use, e.g., interest or taxes, minus
   3) Deductions allocable to the trade or business for which the home office is used that are not home office expenses, e.g., employee compensation, minus
   4) Home office expense other than depreciation (limited to remaining gross income), minus
   5) Depreciation related to the home office (limited to remaining gross income).

EXAMPLE

Tammy has $30,000 of gross income from a business activity conducted in a home office. Of mortgage interest and property taxes allocable to the home office, $10,000 is deductible as personal expenses. Tammy has $20,000 of home office expenses and $15,000 of business deductions that are not home office expenses. Only $5,000 [$30,000 – ($10,000 + $15,000)] is deductible as home office expenses.

f. Any currently disallowed amount is deductible in succeeding years, subject to the same limitations.

g. A new, simplified option allows taxpayers to claim a deduction of $5 per square foot of home office space, up to 300 square feet, for a maximum deduction of $1,500. This option eliminates depreciation record keeping and recapture.

26. **Rental Property Income and Expense**

a. Generally, rental property activity is reported on Schedule E for individuals.

b. Expenses related to the production of rental income are generally deductible to arrive at adjusted gross income.

c. Rental property expenditures may be deducted by depreciation. Generally, a Section 179 deduction is not allowed for rental property. The exceptions to this include a deduction for leasehold improvement property (not residential), restaurant property, and retail improvement property.

d. Special rules limit deductions on the rental of a residence or a vacation home.

   1) **Minimum rental use.** The property must be rented for more than 14 days during the year for deductions to be allowable.
   2) **Minimum personal use.** The vacation-home rules apply when the taxpayer uses the residence for personal purposes for the greater of (a) more than 14 days or (b) more than 10% of the number of days for which the residence is rented.

      a) When the residence is rented for less than 15 days, the rental income does not need to be reported. Any corresponding rental expenses cannot be deducted.

e. A residence is deemed to have been used by the taxpayer for personal purposes if the home is used by
   1) The taxpayer for personal purposes, by any other person who owns an interest in the rental property, or by the relatives of either
      a) However, if the taxpayer rented or tried to rent the property for 12 or more consecutive months, the days during which (s)he used the property as a main home do not count as personal days.
   2) Any individual under a reciprocal arrangement, whether or not rent is charged
   3) Any individual, unless a fair rental is charged

f. If the taxpayer spends substantially full-time repairing or maintaining the rental property, such time does not count toward the personal use test.

g. If the property passes the minimum rental-use test but fails the minimum personal-use test, the property is considered a vacation home, and rental deductions may not exceed the gross income derived from rental activities.
   1) When deductions are limited to gross income, the order of deductions is
      a) The allocable portion of expenses deductible regardless of rental income (e.g., mortgage interest and property taxes)
      b) Deductions that do not affect basis (e.g., ordinary repairs and maintenance)
      c) Deductions that affect basis (e.g., depreciation)
   2) Expenses must be allocated between the personal use and the rental use based on the number of days of use of each.

h. If the property passes both the minimum rental-use test and the minimum personal-use test, then all deductions may be taken and a loss may occur, subject to the passive loss limits.

Minimum Use Tests

	Rental Use	Personal Use
Pass	> 14 days	≤ 14 days or < 10%
Fail	≤ 14 days	greater of > 14 days or > 10%

SCHEDULE E (Form 1040)
Department of the Treasury
Internal Revenue Service (99)

Supplemental Income and Loss

(From rental real estate, royalties, partnerships, S corporations, estates, trusts, REMICs, etc.)

▶ Attach to Form 1040, 1040NR, or Form 1041.

▶ Information about Schedule E and its separate instructions is at *www.irs.gov/schedulee*.

OMB No. 1545-0074
2015
Attachment Sequence No. **13**

Name(s) shown on return | **Your social security number**

Part I **Income or Loss From Rental Real Estate and Royalties** **Note:** If you are in the business of renting personal property, use **Schedule C** or **C-EZ** (see instructions). If you are an individual, report farm rental income or loss from **Form 4835** on page 2, line 40.

A Did you make any payments in 2015 that would require you to file Form(s) 1099? (see instructions) ☐ Yes ☐ No

B If "Yes," did you or will you file required Forms 1099? ☐ Yes ☐ No

1a	Physical address of each property (street, city, state, ZIP code)
A	
B	
C	

1b	Type of Property (from list below)	**2** For each rental real estate property listed above, report the number of fair rental and personal use days. Check the **QJV** box only if you meet the requirements to file as a qualified joint venture. See instructions.		**Fair Rental Days**	**Personal Use Days**	**QJV**
A			**A**			☐
B			**B**			☐
C			**C**			☐

Type of Property:
1 Single Family Residence 3 Vacation/Short-Term Rental 5 Land 7 Self-Rental
2 Multi-Family Residence 4 Commercial 6 Royalties 8 Other (describe)

Income:	**Properties:**	**A**	**B**	**C**
3 Rents received	**3**			
4 Royalties received	**4**			
Expenses:				
5 Advertising	**5**			
6 Auto and travel (see instructions)	**6**			
7 Cleaning and maintenance	**7**			
8 Commissions	**8**			
9 Insurance	**9**			
10 Legal and other professional fees	**10**			
11 Management fees	**11**			
12 Mortgage interest paid to banks, etc. (see instructions)	**12**			
13 Other interest	**13**			
14 Repairs	**14**			
15 Supplies	**15**			
16 Taxes	**16**			
17 Utilities	**17**			
18 Depreciation expense or depletion	**18**			
19 Other (list) ▶	**19**			
20 Total expenses. Add lines 5 through 19	**20**			
21 Subtract line 20 from line 3 (rents) and/or 4 (royalties). If result is a (loss), see instructions to find out if you must file **Form 6198**	**21**			
22 Deductible rental real estate loss after limitation, if any, on **Form 8582** (see instructions)	**22**	( )	( )	( )

23a Total of all amounts reported on line 3 for all rental properties	**23a**	
b Total of all amounts reported on line 4 for all royalty properties	**23b**	
c Total of all amounts reported on line 12 for all properties	**23c**	
d Total of all amounts reported on line 18 for all properties	**23d**	
e Total of all amounts reported on line 20 for all properties	**23e**	
24 **Income.** Add positive amounts shown on line 21. **Do not** include any losses	**24**	
25 **Losses.** Add royalty losses from line 21 and rental real estate losses from line 22. Enter total losses here	**25**	( )
26 **Total rental real estate and royalty income or (loss).** Combine lines 24 and 25. Enter the result here. If Parts II, III, IV, and line 40 on page 2 do not apply to you, also enter this amount on Form 1040, line 17, or Form 1040NR, line 18. Otherwise, include this amount in the total on line 41 on page 2	**26**	

For Paperwork Reduction Act Notice, see the separate instructions. Cat. No. 11344L **Schedule E (Form 1040) 2015**

27. **Domestic Production Activities Deduction**
   a. **Domestic production gross receipts** (DPGR) are defined by Section 199 as gross receipts that are derived from
      1) The sale, exchange, or other disposition; or any rental, lease, or licensing of
         a) Qualified production property that is manufactured, produced, grown, or extracted in the United States by the taxpayer in whole or in significant part
         b) Any qualified film produced by the taxpayer in the United States
         c) Electricity, natural gas, or potable water produced by the taxpayer in the United States
      2) Construction performed in the United States
      3) Engineering and architectural services performed in the United States for a construction project located in the United States
   b. Qualified **production property** generally includes tangible personal property, computer software, and sound recordings.
   c. Gross receipts from the sale or lease of **personal property** that is manufactured in the United States are considered DPGR.
      1) The gross receipts from the lease, rental, or license of property to a related party do not qualify as DPGR.
         a) Employees are considered related parties to an employer.
         b) All employees of a company and its subsidiaries are considered to be employed by a single employer.
   d. When determining the income attributable to **domestic activities**, a company does not include any gross receipts from nondomestic production in the calculation of DPGR.
      1) If nondomestic production gross receipts are less than 5% of the total gross receipts for the company, the company may treat all gross receipts as though they are DPGR.
   e. The deduction applies to taxpayers that perform manufacturing, production, or extraction activities in the United States.
      1) The deduction for income attributable to domestic gross income is equal to the lesser of the following:
         a) 9% of the qualified production activities income (QPAI),
            i) QPAI is calculated by taking the DPGR and subtracting the sum of the following from it:
               - The cost of goods sold attributable to DPGR;
               - Other deductions, expenses, or losses that are directly attributable to DPGR; and
               - A proper share of other deductions, expenses, or losses that are not directly allocable to DPGR or another class of income.
         b) 9% percent of the taxable income of the taxpayer, or
         c) 50% of the W-2 wages for the year allocable only to qualified production activities income instead of all wages.

Stop and review! You have completed the outline for this subunit. Study multiple-choice questions 1 through 6 beginning on page 159.

4.2 FICA AND FUTA TAXES

1. **Federal Insurance Contributions Act (FICA) -- Social Security & Medicare Tax**
   a. Employers are required to pay tax based on the employee's pay.
   b. The **employer** must pay
      1) 6.2% of the first $118,500 (2015) of wages paid for Social Security tax plus
      2) 1.45% of all wages for Medicare tax. There is no cap on this tax.
   c. The Additional Medicare Tax on earned income is a 0.9% tax on wages and net self-employment income in excess of a threshold.
      1) This additional tax applies to earned income exceeding $200,000 for single, head-of-household, or surviving spouse; $250,000 for married filing jointly; and $125,000 for married filing separately. Employers withhold an additional 0.9% for income beyond $200,000 regardless of filing status.
   d. The employer must withhold the following amounts from the **employee's** wages:
      1) Tier 1 – From $0 to $118,500; 7.65% × Employee's wages (Social Security + Medicare)
      2) Tier 2 – From $118,500 to $200,000 or $250,000; 1.45% × Employee's wages (Medicare)
      3) Tier 3 – Above $200,000 of earned income; 2.35% × Employee's wages (Medicare + Additional Medicare)
      4) Overwithholding is alleviated as a credit against the income tax if the overwithholding resulted from multiple employer withholding.
   e. Contributions made by the employee are not tax deductible by the employee, while those made by the employer are deductible by the employer.
   f. An employer must pay FICA taxes for all household employees who are paid more than $1,900 during the year 2015.
2. **Net Investment Income Tax (NIIT)**
   a. All investment income in excess of deductions allowable for such income and income from passive activities are subject to a 3.8% **net investment income tax**. This tax essentially applies FICA taxes to income that previously was not subject to the taxes.
   b. The tax is imposed on the lesser of an individual's net investment income or any excess of modified adjusted gross income (MAGI) for the tax year over a specified threshold.

Filing Status	Threshold Amount
Married filing jointly, surviving spouse	$250,000
Single, head of household	$200,000
Married filing separately	$125,000

   c. MAGI is the sum of AGI and excludable foreign earned income/housing costs after any deductions, exclusions, or credits applicable to the foreign earned income.
   d. Net investment income tax does not apply to non-resident aliens.

3. **Self-Employment Tax**

   a. The FICA tax liability is imposed on net earnings from self-employment at the employer rate plus the employee rate as follows:

      1) Tier 1 – From $0 to $118,500; 15.3% × Net self-employment income
      2) Tier 2 – From $118,500 to $200,000 or $250,000; 2.9% × Net self-employment income
      3) Tier 3 – Above $200,000 or $250,000; 3.8% × Net self-employment income

   b. NI from self-employment – (.0765 × NI from self-employment) = Net Earnings from Self-Employment.

   c. Net income from self-employment does not include the following:

      1) Rents
      2) Gain or loss from disposition of business property
      3) Capital gain or loss
      4) Nonbusiness interest
      5) Dividends
      6) Income or expenses related to personal activities
      7) Wages, salaries, or tips received as an employee

   d. A self-employed person is allowed a deduction for the employer's portion of the FICA taxes paid to arrive at his or her AGI. For 2015, this equals

      1) 6.2% of the first $118,500 of net self-employment income plus
      2) 1.45% of net self-employment income (no cap).

   e. The additional 0.9% Medicare tax is only imposed on the employee portion of self-employment tax. Therefore, it is not deductible.

      1) Individuals with wages and self-employment income calculate their liabilities in three steps:

         a) Calculate the tax on any wages in excess of the applicable threshold without regard to any withholding;
         b) Reduce the applicable threshold by the total amount of Medicare wages received, but not below zero; and
         c) Calculate the tax on any self-employment income in excess of the reduced threshold.

EXAMPLE

C, a single filer, has $130,000 in wages and $145,000 in self-employment income. C's wages are not in excess of the $200,000 threshold for single filers, so C is not liable for the surtax on these wages. Before calculating the tax on self-employment income, the $200,000 threshold for single filers is reduced by C's $130,000 in wages, resulting in a reduced self-employment threshold of $70,000. C is liable to pay the additional 0.9% tax on $75,000 of self-employment income ($145,000 – $70,000).

   f. The employee's portion of the FICA taxes is not deductible.

   g. The income inclusion for self-employment taxes differs from gross income inclusion in the case of ministers and/or clergymen.

      1) A minister may exclude the rental value of his or her home or parsonage if it is not connected with the performance of religious duties.
      2) The rental value is not excluded from the income used to compute self-employment taxes.

3) Any wages received by ministers and/or clergymen on a W-2 are not subject to Social Security but are included in self-employment income unless one of the following applies:

   a) The minister and/or clergyman is a member of a religious order and has taken a vow of poverty.
   b) The minister and/or clergyman requests and is granted an exemption from self-employment tax by the IRS.
   c) The minister and/or clergyman is subject only to the Social Security laws of a foreign country under the provisions of a Social Security agreement between the United States and that country.

4. **Federal Unemployment Taxes (FUTA)**

   a. This tax is imposed on employers. The tax is 6.0% of the first $7,000 of wages paid to each employee. The employee does not pay any portion of FUTA.
   b. If state unemployment tax is paid, a credit is available, which reduces the applicable tax rate up to 5.4%.

Stop and review! You have completed the outline for this subunit. Study multiple-choice questions 7 through 9 beginning on page 160.

4.3 EMPLOYEE BENEFITS

1. **Fringe Benefits**

   a. An employee's GI does not include the cost of any qualified fringe benefit supplied or paid for by the employer.

2. **Employee Discounts**

   a. Certain employee discounts on the selling price of qualified property or services of their employer are excluded from GI.
   b. The employee discount may not exceed

      1) The gross profit percentage normally earned on merchandise or
      2) 20% of the price offered to customers in the case of qualified services.

3. **Working Condition**

   a. Benefits provided to an employee by his or her employer are excludable if such benefits are provided as a working condition fringe benefit.

EXAMPLE

Jamaal, a pharmaceutical salesperson, spends most of his day driving to various medical facilities. He was provided a vehicle as a fringe benefit. The business use of the vehicle is not included in GI. Any personal use would be included in GI.

4. **De Minimis**

   a. The value of property or services (not cash) provided to an employee is excludable as a de minimis fringe benefit if the value is so minimal that accounting for it would be unreasonable or impracticable.
   b. The following are examples of de minimis fringe benefits. The list is not exhaustive.

      1) Occasional use of company copy machines
      2) Occasional company parties or picnics
      3) Occasional tickets to entertainment/sporting events (not season tickets)
      4) Occasional taxi fare or meal money due to overtime work
      5) Traditional noncash holiday gifts with a small FMV

NOTE: Use of an employer-provided car more than once a month for commuting and membership to a private country club or athletic facility are never excludable as de minimis fringe benefits.

c. An eating facility for employees is treated as a de minimis fringe benefit if

1) It is located on or near the business premises of the employer and
2) The facility's revenue normally equals or exceeds its operating costs.

NOTE: The excess value of the meals over the fees charged to employees is excluded from employees' income.

d. The value of an on-premises athletic facility provided by an employer is generally excluded from GI of employees.

5. **Qualified Transportation Fringe Benefits**

a. Up to $250 a month may be excluded for the value of employer-provided transit passes and transportation in an employer-provided "commuter highway vehicle."

b. Additionally, an exclusion of up to $250 per month is available for employer-provided parking.

c. Employees may use both of these exclusions.

NOTE: The parity for transit and parking benefits expired but is expected to be renewed retroactively.

6. **Moving Reimbursements**

a. Qualified moving reimbursements are excludable amounts received from an employer that would be deductible if paid by the individual.

7. **Employer-Provided Educational Assistance**

a. Up to $5,250 may be excluded by the employee for employer-provided educational assistance.

b. Excludable assistance payments may not include the cost of meals, lodging, transportation, tools, or supplies that the employee retains after the course.

8. **Employer-Provided Life Insurance**

a. Proceeds of a life insurance policy for which the employer paid the premiums may be excluded from the employee's GI.

b. The cost of group term life insurance up to a coverage amount of $50,000 is excluded from the employee's GI.

EXAMPLE

Janet, who is 40 years old, is provided with $150,000 of nondiscriminatory group term life insurance by her employer. Based on the IRS uniform premium cost table, the total annual cost of a policy of this type is $1.20 per $1,000 of coverage. Janet contributed $50 toward the policy. Janet should include $70 in GI.

Amount in excess of $50,000:	$100,000
Cost of $100,000 policy:	120
– Janet's contribution:	50
GI to Janet:	$70

c. Premiums paid by the employer for excess coverage (coverage over $50,000) are included in GI.

d. The employer must report the amount taxable to the employee on Form W-2.

e. The exclusion applies only to coverage of the employee. Payments for coverage of an employee's spouse or dependent are included as GI.

9. **Accident and Health Plans**
   a. Benefits received by an employee under an accident and health plan under which the employer paid the premiums or contributed to an independent fund are excluded from GI of the employee.
   b. The benefits must be either
      1) Payments made due to permanent injury or loss of bodily functions or
      2) Reimbursement paid to the employee for medical expenses of the employee, spouse, or dependents. Any reimbursement in excess of medical expenses is included in income.
10. **Death Benefits**
   a. All death benefits received by the beneficiaries or the estate of an employee from or on behalf of an employer are included in GI.
      1) This is for employer paid death benefits, not to be confused with death benefits of a life insurance plan provided by an employer.
11. **Dependent Care Assistance**
   a. An employee may exclude costs incurred by an employer for care of dependents who are under the age of 13 or disabled that allow the employee's gainful employment.
   b. The maximum amount of the exclusion is the lesser of
      1) $5,000 ($2,500 if married filing separately) or
      2) The lesser of the earned income for the taxable year of the employee or the employee's spouse, if married.
   c. The value of dependent care provided by an employer at an on-site facility is based on the value of services provided and not the actual cost.
12. **Meals and Lodging**
   a. The value of meals furnished to an employee by or on behalf of the employer is excluded from the employee's GI if the meals are furnished on the employer's business premises and for the employer's convenience. The exclusion does not cover meal allowances.
   b. The value of lodging is excluded from GI if the lodging is on the employer's premises, is for the convenience of the employer, and must be accepted as a condition of employment.
13. **Incentive Stock Options**
   a. An employee may not recognize income when an incentive stock option is granted or exercised depending upon certain restrictions.
   b. The employee recognizes long-term capital gain if the stock is sold 2 years or more after the option was granted and 1 year or more after the option was exercised.
      1) The employer is not allowed a deduction.
   c. Otherwise, the excess of the stock's FMV on the date of exercise over the option price is ordinary income to the employee when the stock is sold.
      1) The employer may deduct this amount.
      2) The gain realized is short-term or long-term capital gain.

d. Nonqualified stock option
   1) An employee stock option is not qualified if it does not meet numerous technical requirements to be an incentive stock option.
   2) If the option's FMV is ascertainable on the grant date,
      a) The employee has GI equal to the FMV of the option.
      b) The employer is allowed a deduction.
      c) There are no tax consequences when the option is exercised.
      d) Capital gain or loss is reported when the stock is sold.
   3) If the option's FMV is not ascertainable on the grant date,
      a) The excess of FMV over the option price is GI to the employee when the option is exercised.
      b) The employer is allowed a corresponding compensation deduction.
      c) The employee's basis in the stock is the exercise price plus the amount taken into ordinary income.

14. **Cafeteria Plans**

a. A cafeteria plan is a benefit plan under which all participants are employees, and each participant has the opportunity to select between cash and nontaxable benefits.
   1) If the participant chooses cash, such cash is GI.
   2) If qualified benefits are chosen, they are excludable to the extent permitted by the IRC.
b. The employee must choose the benefit before the tax year begins.
c. Any unused benefit is forfeited.
d. Self-employed individuals are not included.
e. Employers **may** offer participation in a cafeteria plan to an employee on the employee's first day of employment, but employers **must** offer participation after the employee completes 3 years of employment.
f. The plan cannot discriminate in favor of highly compensated employees.
g. Every employer maintaining a cafeteria plan must file an information return, reporting the number of eligible and participating employees, the total cost of the plan for the tax year, and the number of highly compensated employees.
h. Nontaxable benefits include
   1) Dependent care assistance
   2) Group term life insurance coverage up to $50,000
   3) Disability benefits
   4) Accident and health benefits
   5) Group legal services
i. Plans may not offer scholarships, educational assistance, or meals and lodging (for the convenience of the employer).
j. Deferred compensation plans other than 401(k) plans do not qualify for exclusion under a cafeteria plan.
k. Nonemployee beneficiaries (e.g., spouses) may not participate in a cafeteria plan. They might benefit, however, depending on the plan selection.

Stop and review! You have completed the outline for this subunit. Study multiple-choice questions 10 through 14 beginning on page 161.

4.4 FARM INCOME AND EXPENSES

1. **Farm Income**

   a. Income from farming activity is reported in Part I of Schedule F (Form 1040). In addition to Part I, accrual method taxpayers must use Part III for reporting income.

   b. **Gains from Sales**

      1) In general, gains from the sale of livestock, produce, and grains are reported on Schedule F.

         a) Gains from the sale of livestock used for draft (hauling), dairy, breeding, or sporting purposes generally result in capital gains and are not reported on Schedule F.

   c. **Distributions from a Cooperative**

      1) All distributions from a farm cooperative must be reported.

   d. **Payments from Agricultural Programs**

      1) Government payments for these programs are usually reported to the farmer on Form 1099-G.
      2) The amount reported on Schedule F includes direct, counter-cyclical, price support, diversion, and cost-share payments, along with payments in the form of materials or services.

   e. **Commodity Credit Corporation (CCC) Loans**

      1) Farmers may choose to treat CCC loans secured by pledged crops as taxable income in the year the loan proceeds are received.

         a) If the pledged crops are later forfeited to the CCC in full payment of the loan, any outstanding loan amount is taxable income.

   f. **Crop Insurance Proceeds**

      1) Payments received for losses to crops are income in the year received.

         a) A 1-year deferment of income is allowed if the payment was received in the year of the damage.

      2) Federal crop disaster payments are treated the same as crop insurance proceeds.

   g. **Custom Hire (Machine Work)**

      1) Payment received for contract work or custom work performed off the taxpayer's own farm for others or for the use of the taxpayer's property or machines is income regardless of the form of payment.

   h. Other income includes tax credits, bartering income, discharge of indebtedness, excess depreciation recapture, prizes, etc.

   i. **Farm Income Averaging**

      1) If a taxpayer is engaged in a farming or fishing business, (s)he may be able to average all or some of his or her current year's farm income by shifting it to the 3 prior years (base years).
      2) An individual, a partner in a partnership, or a shareholder in an S corporation may elect farm income averaging on a timely filed return (including extensions) or later if the IRS approves.
      3) The taxpayer need not have engaged in a farming business in any base year.

4) Corporations, partnerships, S corporations, estates, and trusts cannot use farm income averaging.

5) To elect farm income averaging as a tax computation method, you must file a Schedule J with your income tax return for the election year. This includes late or amended returns if the period of limitations on filing a claim for credit or refund has not expired.

SCHEDULE F (Form 1040)
Department of the Treasury Internal Revenue Service (99)

Profit or Loss From Farming

▶ Attach to Form 1040, Form 1040NR, Form 1041, Form 1065, or Form 1065-B.
▶ Information about Schedule F and its separate instructions is at *www.irs.gov/schedulef*.

OMB No. 1545-0074
2015
Attachment Sequence No. **14**

Name of proprietor | **Social security number (SSN)**

A Principal crop or activity | **B Enter code from Part IV** ▶ | C Accounting method: ☐ Cash ☐ Accrual | **D Employer ID number (EIN), (see instr)**

E Did you "materially participate" in the operation of this business during 2015? If "No," see instructions for limit on passive losses ☐ Yes ☐ No
F Did you make any payments in 2015 that would require you to file Form(s) 1099 (see instructions)? ☐ Yes ☐ No
G If "Yes," did you or will you file required Forms 1099? ☐ Yes ☐ No

Part I **Farm Income—Cash Method.** Complete Parts I and II (Accrual method. Complete Parts II and III, and Part I, line 9.)

1a	Sales of livestock and other resale items (see instructions)	1a		
b	Cost or other basis of livestock or other items reported on line 1a	1b		
c	Subtract line 1b from line 1a		1c	
2	Sales of livestock, produce, grains, and other products you raised		2	
3a	Cooperative distributions (Form(s) 1099-PATR)	3a	3b Taxable amount	3b
4a	Agricultural program payments (see instructions)	4a	4b Taxable amount	4b
5a	Commodity Credit Corporation (CCC) loans reported under election			5a
b	CCC loans forfeited	5b	5c Taxable amount	5c
6	Crop insurance proceeds and federal crop disaster payments (see instructions)			
a	Amount received in 2015	6a	6b Taxable amount	6b
c	If election to defer to 2016 is attached, check here ▶ ☐		6d Amount deferred from 2014	6d
7	Custom hire (machine work) income			7
8	Other income, including federal and state gasoline or fuel tax credit or refund (see instructions)			8
9	**Gross income.** Add amounts in the right column (lines 1c, 2, 3b, 4b, 5a, 5c, 6b, 6d, 7, and 8). If you use the accrual method, enter the amount from Part III, line 50 (see instructions) ▶			9

Part II **Farm Expenses—Cash and Accrual Method.** Do not include personal or living expenses (see instructions).

10	Car and truck expenses (see instructions). Also attach **Form 4562**	10	23	Pension and profit-sharing plans	23	
11	Chemicals	11	24	Rent or lease (see instructions):		
12	Conservation expenses (see instructions)	12	a	Vehicles, machinery, equipment	24a	
13	Custom hire (machine work)	13	b	Other (land, animals, etc.)	24b	
14	Depreciation and section 179 expense (see instructions)	14	25	Repairs and maintenance	25	
15	Employee benefit programs other than on line 23	15	26	Seeds and plants	26	
16	Feed	16	27	Storage and warehousing	27	
17	Fertilizers and lime	17	28	Supplies	28	
18	Freight and trucking	18	29	Taxes	29	
19	Gasoline, fuel, and oil	19	30	Utilities	30	
20	Insurance (other than health)	20	31	Veterinary, breeding, and medicine	31	
21	Interest:		32	Other expenses (specify):		
a	Mortgage (paid to banks, etc.)	21a	a		32a	
b	Other	21b	b		32b	
22	Labor hired (less employment credits)	22	c		32c	
			d		32d	
			e		32e	
			f		32f	

33	**Total expenses.** Add lines 10 through 32f. If line 32f is negative, see instructions ▶	33	
34	**Net farm profit or (loss).** Subtract line 33 from line 9	34	

If a profit, stop here and see instructions for where to report. If a loss, complete lines 35 and 36.

35 Did you receive an applicable subsidy in 2015? (see instructions) ☐ Yes ☐ No

36 Check the box that describes your investment in this activity and see instructions for where to report your loss.
a ☐ All investment is at risk. b ☐ Some investment is not at risk.

For Paperwork Reduction Act Notice, see the separate instructions. Cat. No. 11346H **Schedule F (Form 1040) 2015**

j. **Special Circumstances**

1) The gain from sales caused by drought, flood, or other weather-related conditions can be postponed for 4 years. If, because of the weather-related conditions, a farmer who uses the cash method of accounting sells more livestock (including poultry) than (s)he would have sold under normal business conditions, the farmer may choose to include the gain from the sale of the additional livestock in income next year instead of the current year.

a) The election applies to all livestock, whether held for resale or other purposes. It applies even if the livestock was not actually raised or sold within an area designated for federal assistance, as long as the weather-related condition forced the sale.

2. **Farm Expenses**

a. Farmers are allowed to deduct any ordinary and necessary costs of operating a farm for profit.

b. Payments or portions thereof used by a farmer for personal or living expenses do not qualify as farm expenses and are not reported on Schedule F; however, they may be deductible and reported elsewhere on Form 1040 and related schedules.

c. Generally, farming deductions are claimed in Part II of Schedule F.

d. **Part I**

1) **Cost of Sales**

a) The cost of livestock and other resale purchases are deductible as COGS on line 1d.

b) These are the only expenses reported in Part I.

e. **Part II**

1) **Car and Truck Expenses**

a) The actual expenses or standard mileage rate may be deducted.

b) If the actual expenses are used, then the amounts for depreciation and rent/lease are reported on separate lines of the return.

2) **Conservation**

a) Expenses paid to conserve soil and water, or to prevent erosion of land used for farming, may be deducted.

b) The deduction is limited to 25% of gross farm income, and the expenses must be consistent with an approved conservation plan.

3) **Custom Hire/Machine Work**

a) Expenses for equipment rental with an operator.

b) Expenses for rentals without an operator are deductible, but on a separate line of the schedule.

4) **Depreciation/Sec. 179**

a) Only allowed for farm equipment. In other words, there is no deduction for home (except for business portion), personal items, land, livestock for resale, or other inventory.

5) **Employee Benefit Programs**

a) Examples include health and pension plans.

b) Pension and profit-sharing plan expenses are reported on a separate line from other programs.

6) **Feed**
   a) In general, cash basis taxpayers can deduct prepaid livestock feed only in the year the feed is consumed.

7) **Freight/Trucking**
   a) Transportation cost associated with the purchase of livestock for resale is not freight expense. Instead the cost is added to the cost of the livestock and deducted when the livestock is sold.

8) **Insurance**
   a) Premiums for farm business insurance and employee accident and health insurance are deductible, although separately reported.
   b) Amounts credited to a reserve for self-insurance or premiums paid for lost earnings coverage due to sickness or disability are not deductible.

9) **Interest**
   a) Business mortgage interest and other business interest (e.g., investment) are deductible but are separately stated on the return.

10) **Labor Hired**
   a) Deductible amounts for farm labor include boarding cost but not the value of farm products used by farm labor.

11) **Rental/Leases**
   a) In addition to deducting machine rentals, mentioned under "Custom Hire/ Machine Work" on the previous page, land and animal rentals or leases are deductible.

12) **Repairs and Maintenance**
   a) Incidental repair and maintenance costs of farm assets are deductible.
   b) The work must not add value to or appreciably prolong the life of the asset (those costs would be capitalized and depreciated).
   c) Repairs or maintenance on the farmer's home are personal expenses and not deductible.

13) **Taxes**
   a) Deductible taxes include real estate and personal property taxes on farm business assets, FICA taxes to match employee withholding, FUTA tax, and federal highway use tax.
   b) Taxes not included on Schedule F are federal income, estate, gift, improvement (e.g., paving, sewers), personal use property (e.g., home), and sales taxes.

14) **Utilities**
   a) Deductible utilities are those for business use on the farm.
   b) Only the business percentage of charges of a second phone line (including the base rate) are deductible.
   c) The first phone line is considered 100% personal.

15) **Miscellaneous**
   a) Chemicals; fertilizers and lime; gasoline, fuel, and oil; seeds and plants; storage and warehousing; supplies; and veterinary, breeding, and medicine each have their own return line for reporting.

16) **Other Expenses**

a) Other expenses include carryover of at-risk loss; bad debts; start-up costs; business use of home; forestation costs; legal and professional fees; travel, meals, and entertainment; and reproductive period expenses.

17) Farmers must **withhold federal income, Social Security, and Medicare taxes** from the salaries and wages of farm employees.

Stop and review! You have completed the outline for this subunit. Study multiple-choice questions 15 through 20 beginning on page 163.

4.5 ABOVE-THE-LINE DEDUCTIONS

1. **Overview**

a. Above-the-line deductions are deducted from gross income to arrive at adjusted gross income (AGI).

```
Gross income - Above-the-line deductions = Adjusted gross income (AGI)
```

1) "Above-the-line deductions" is a term used in our materials, but they can also be referred to as "adjustments," "deductions to arrive at AGI," and "deductions for AGI."

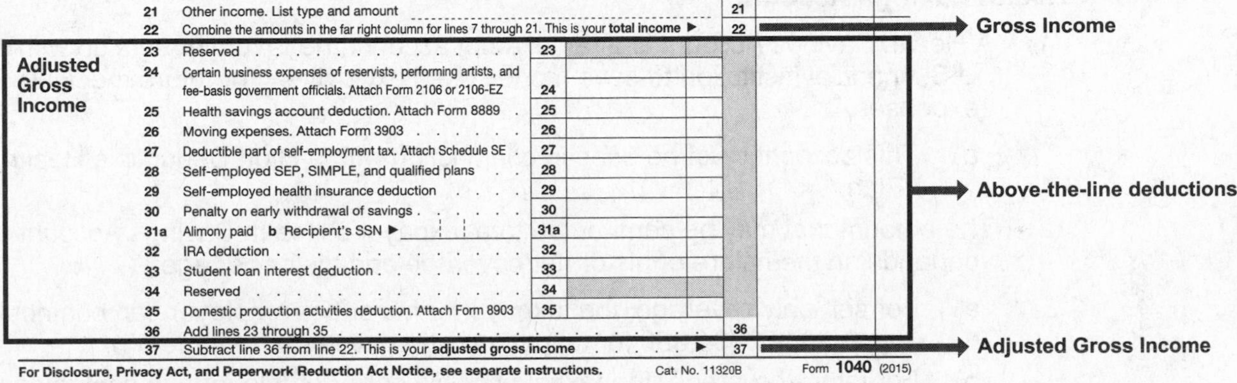

Line	Description	Box
21	Other income. List type and amount	21
22	Combine the amounts in the far right column for lines 7 through 21. This is your **total income** ▶	22
23	Reserved	23
24	Certain business expenses of reservists, performing artists, and fee-basis government officials. Attach Form 2106 or 2106-EZ	24
25	Health savings account deduction. Attach Form 8889	25
26	Moving expenses. Attach Form 3903	26
27	Deductible part of self-employment tax. Attach Schedule SE	27
28	Self-employed SEP, SIMPLE, and qualified plans	28
29	Self-employed health insurance deduction	29
30	Penalty on early withdrawal of savings	30
31a	Alimony paid **b** Recipient's SSN ▶	31a
32	IRA deduction	32
33	Student loan interest deduction	33
34	Reserved	34
35	Domestic production activities deduction. Attach Form 8903	35
36	Add lines 23 through 35	36
37	Subtract line 36 from line 22. This is your **adjusted gross income** ▶	37

For Disclosure, Privacy Act, and Paperwork Reduction Act Notice, see separate instructions. Cat. No. 11320B Form **1040** (2015)

NOTE: This section of Form 1040 is condensed to help you conceptualize the difference between Gross Income and Adjusted Gross Income. Because the deductions are above line 37, they are referred to as above-the-line.

2. **Educator Expenses**

a. In 2015, primary and secondary school educators may claim an above-the-line deduction for up to $250 annually in unreimbursed expenses paid or incurred for books and supplies used in the classroom. Each taxpayer (educator) on a joint return may deduct up to $250.

1) Books, supplies, computer equipment (including related software and services) and other equipment, and supplementary materials used in the classroom qualify for the deduction.

2) An eligible educator is an individual who, for at least 900 hours during a school year, is a kindergarten through grade 12 teacher, instructor, counselor, principal, or aide.

3) The term "school" is defined as one that provides elementary or secondary education, as determined under state law.

NOTE: This provision expired but is expected to be renewed retroactively.

3. **Health Savings Account Deduction**

   a. **Archer MSAs**

      1) Archer MSAs (previously called Medical Savings Accounts) allow individuals who are self-employed or employed by a small employer and covered by a high deductible health insurance plan to make tax-deductible contributions to pay medical expenses.
      2) The deduction for an Archer MSA is not included with other medical expenses and is not subject to the 10% (7.5% if 65 or older) limitation.
      3) The following are nontaxable:

         a) Earnings generated by the plan
         b) Distributions from an Archer MSA used to pay medical expenses
         c) Distributions made after the age of 65
         d) Distribution made upon death or disability

      4) Distributions that do not meet any criteria [under 3) above] are subject to a 15% penalty tax.
      5) Contributions are limited to a percentage of the deductible of the required high-deductible health plan (i.e., varies per health plan).
      6) An Archer MSA can be rolled into a Health Savings Account tax-free.

   b. **Health Savings Account**

      1) A Health Savings Account is a tax-exempt account the taxpayer sets up with a U.S. financial institution to save money used exclusively for future medical expenses.

         a) This account must be used in conjunction with a High Deductible Health Plan.

      2) The amount that may be contributed to a taxpayer's Health Savings Account depends on the nature of his or her coverage and his or her age.

         a) For self-only coverage, the taxpayer or his or her employer can contribute up to $3,350 ($4,350 for taxpayers who have reached age 55).
         b) For family coverage, the taxpayer or his or her employer can contribute up to $6,650 ($8,650 for taxpayers who have both reached age 55).

      3) The taxpayer must have the insurance for the whole year to contribute the full amount.

         a) For each month that (s)he did not have a High Deductible Health Plan, (s)he must reduce the amount that can be contributed by one-twelfth.

      4) Contributions to a Health Savings Account for 2015 may include contributions made until April 15, 2016.

4. **Moving Expenses**

   a. Deduction for job-related relocation
   b. Moving expenses are deductible to arrive at AGI to the extent the expenses are not reimbursed or paid for by the taxpayer's employer.

      1) If expenses exceed reimbursements, only the qualified expenses in excess of the reimbursement are deductible.
      2) If reimbursements exceed expenses, the excess is included in income.

   c. Qualifications

      1) The individual's new principal place of work is at least **50 miles farther from the former residence than was the former principal place of work**. Measurement is by the shortest possible commonly traveled route.

2) If the individual did not have a former principal place of work, the new principal place of work must be at least 50 miles from the taxpayer's former residence.
3) The individual is **employed full time in the new location during at least 39 weeks in the 12-month period immediately following the move**.
    a) If the individual is self-employed, the above 39-week requirement must be met, and full-time employment during at least 78 weeks of the 24-month period immediately following the move is required.
4) Moving expenses may be deducted in the year in which they were incurred even if the 39- or 78-week employment requirement has not yet been satisfied.
    a) If the time requirements are subsequently not met, an amended return must be filed or the amount of the deduction must be reported as gross income in the following year.

d. Direct expenses
1) Are deductible to arrive at AGI
2) Include the expenses of actually moving a taxpayer and his or her household goods and personal effects and travel (including lodging) from the former residence to the new residence
    a) Instead of actual expenses, a mileage rate of $.23 per mile in 2015 can be used for driving one's own automobile.
    b) The cost of meals en route is not deductible as a direct moving expense.
    c) Expenses incurred by members of the taxpayer's household are deductible.

e. Indirect expenses
1) Are not deductible
2) Include house hunting; temporary living expenses; and expenses related to the sale, purchase, or lease of a residence

5. **Self-Employment**

a. **Self-Employment Tax**
1) A self-employed person is allowed a deduction for the employer's portion of the FICA taxes paid to arrive at his or her AGI. The deduction for the employer's share is equal to 50% of the self-employment tax. For 2015, the deduction equals
    a) 6.2% of the first $118,500 of net self-employment income plus
    b) 1.45% of net self-employment income (no cap).
2) The 0.9% additional Medicare tax is on the employee's portion of FICA taxes. Therefore, the 0.9% tax is not deductible.

b. **Self-Employed SEP, SIMPLE, and Qualified Plans**
1) A self-employed individual can deduct specified amounts paid on his or her behalf to a qualified retirement or profit-sharing plan, such as a SEP or SIMPLE plan.
2) The most common self-employed retirement plan used is a SEP (Keogh) plan.
    a) The maximum annual deduction is limited to the lesser of 25% of the self-employed earnings or $53,000 (indexed for inflation).
    b) The annual contribution limit is the lesser of 100% of the earned income derived from the trade or business or $53,000.
    c) Self-employed earnings are reduced by the deductible part of self-employment taxes.

d) Contributions to the plan are subtracted from net earnings to calculate self-employed earnings, creating a circular computation. For convenience, a standard rate of 20% is used to calculate the allowed deduction.

EXAMPLE

Alice has business income of net self-employed earnings of $125,000 before the deductible part of self-employment taxes of $25,000. The maximum annual deduction is calculated as follows:

($125,000 – $25,000) × 20% = $20,000

3) Another option for a self-employed taxpayer is a Savings Incentive Match Plan for Employees (SIMPLE).

a) Self-employed taxpayers may make both employer contributions and elective employee contributions.

b) Employee contributions are considered deferred compensation and are limited to $12,500 in 2015.

c) An employer match of up to 3% of self-employed earnings may be deducted as an above-the-line deduction.

c. **Self-Employed Health Insurance Deduction**

1) Self-employed individuals can deduct 100% of payments made for health insurance coverage for the individual, his or her spouse, and dependents.

2) The deduction is limited to the taxpayer's earned income derived from the business for which the insurance plan was established.

6. **Penalty on Early Withdrawal of Savings**

a. Deduction is allowable for penalties from an early withdrawal of funds from certificates of deposit or other time savings accounts.

b. The deduction is taken in the year the penalty is incurred.

7. **Alimony**

a. Alimony is gross income to the recipient and deductible by the payor.
b. Alimony payments may not extend past the death of the payee spouse.
c. Child support is neither gross income to the recipient nor deductible by the payor.

8. **IRA Deduction**

a. **Individual Retirement Arrangement (IRA) Contributions**

1) For 2015, contributions are fully deductible (subject to certain qualifying rules and limitations) up to the lesser of $5,500 ($6,500 for taxpayers age 50 and over) or 100% of includible compensation.

2) To qualify for the return year, contributions must be made by the due date of the return without regard to extensions.

3) Compensation includes alimony and earned income but not pensions, annuities, or other deferred compensation distributions.

4) An additional $5,500 ($6,500 for taxpayers age 50 and over) may be contributed to the IRA for the taxpayer's nonworking spouse if a joint return is filed.

a) The combined IRA contributions by both spouses cannot exceed their combined compensation for the year.

5) If the taxpayer is an active participant in an employer-sponsored retirement plan and has earned income of over $98,000 [married filing jointly or qualifying widow(er)] in 2015 ($61,000 in 2015 for head of household or single taxpayers, and $0 for married filing separate), the IRA deduction is proportionately reduced over a phaseout range.

a) An individual is not labeled an active plan participant due to the status of that individual's spouse.
b) If an individual's spouse is an active plan participant, that individual's deductible contribution will be phased out when AGI is between $183,000 and $193,000.

6) Excessive contributions may be subject to a 6% excise tax.
7) The owner of an IRA must begin receiving distributions by April 1 of the calendar year following the later of the calendar year in which the employee attains age 70 1/2 or the calendar year in which the employee retires.
8) IRA distributions made before age 59 1/2 are subject to regulation taxation plus a 10% penalty tax. Exceptions to the penalty include distributions for
   a) Death or disability
   b) Medical expenses in excess of 10% (7.5% if 65 or older) of AGI
   c) Qualified higher education expenses
   d) The purchase of a first home (up to $10,000)

b. **Roth IRAs and Roth 401(k)s**

1) The Roth IRA is a **nondeductible** IRA.
2) Earnings on contributions are not taxed, provided they meet certain requirements to be considered a qualified distribution. To be a qualified distribution, the distribution must
   a) Satisfy the 5-year holding period.
      i) The distribution may not be made before the end of the 5-tax-year period.
      ii) The holding period begins with the tax year to which the contribution relates, not the year of contribution.

EXAMPLE

A contribution made on April 6, designated as a 2010 contribution, may be withdrawn tax-free in 2015 if it is otherwise a qualified distribution.

   b) Meet one of four other requirements. It must be
      i) Made on or after the date on which the individual attains age 59 1/2,
      ii) Made to a beneficiary or the individual's estate on or after the individual's death,
      iii) Attributed to the individual's disability, or
      iv) To pay for qualified first-time homebuyer expenses.

3) Distributions are treated as made from contributions first; thus, no portion of a distribution is treated as attributable to earnings or includible in gross income until the total of all distributions from the Roth IRA exceeds the amount of contributions.
   a) Nonqualified distributions are included in income after recovery of contribution, and they are subject to the 10% early withdrawal penalty.

EXAMPLE

John made $5,500 in contributions to his Roth IRA over the last decade. The value of John's Roth IRA is now $8,500. If the $8,500 is distributed and the distribution is qualified, John will not owe any tax or 10% penalty. If the distribution is unqualified, John will owe taxes at his marginal tax rate on the $3,000 in earnings and will owe a penalty ($300) of 10% of the earnings.

4) The overall limit for contributions to IRAs, both deductible and nondeductible, is $5,500 ($6,500 for taxpayers age 50 and over).

5) Contributions to a Roth IRA may continue past the age of 70 1/2.
6) Contributions to Roth IRAs are phased out when AGI is between $116,000 and $131,000 (between $183,000 and $193,000 for joint filers and $0 and $10,000 for married filing separate).

9. **Education**

a. **Student Loan Interest Deduction**

1) Taxpayers may deduct $2,500 of interest paid on qualified educational loans in 2015. This deduction is available for each year interest is paid.
2) The deduction is subject to income limits.
   a) The phaseout range begins when AGI exceeds $65,000 ($130,000 for joint filers) and ends at $80,000 ($160,000 for joint filers).
   b) The amount of reduction in the deduction can be calculated as follows:

$$\$2{,}500 \times \frac{(AGI - \$65{,}000)}{\$15{,}000 \text{ phaseout range}}$$

b. **Tuition and Fees**

1) Taxpayers may deduct a maximum of $4,000 of qualified higher education expenses paid by the taxpayer during the year on behalf of the taxpayer, the taxpayer's spouse, or a dependent of the taxpayer.
2) Taxpayers with AGI exceeding $65,000 ($130,000 for joint filers) will not be entitled to the full deduction.
   a) Taxpayers with an AGI between $65,000 and $80,000 ($130,000 and $160,000 for joint filers) are able to deduct $2,000
   b) Taxpayers with an AGI exceeding $80,000 ($160,000) do not receive any deduction

   NOTE: This provision has expired but is expected to be renewed. Until renewal, the 2014 amounts will be used in this Knowledge Transfer Outline.

c. **Coverdell Education Savings Accounts (CESA)**

1) Taxpayers may make **nondeductible contributions** of $2,000 per child (beneficiary) to a CESA.
2) Contributions to CESAs are phased out when AGI is between $95,000 and $110,000 (between $190,000 and $220,000 for joint filers).
3) The earnings may be distributed tax free, provided they are used for qualified education expenses.
4) This income exclusion is not available for any year in which the American Opportunity Credit or Lifetime Learning Credit is claimed.

10. **Domestic Production Activities Deduction**

a. Generally, up to 9% of income derived from qualified production activities within the U.S. may be deducted. Refer to Subunit 4.1, "Business Income and Expenses," for details.

11. **Jury Duty Pay**

a. Jury duty pay is included in gross income.
b. However, jury duty pay remitted to an employer in exchange for regular pay is an above-the-line deduction.

Stop and review! You have completed the outline for this subunit. Study multiple-choice questions 21 through 30 beginning on page 164.

QUESTIONS

4.1 Business Income and Expenses

1. On December 1, 2015, Krest, a self-employed cash-basis taxpayer, borrowed $200,000 to use in her business. The loan was to be repaid on November 30, 2016. Krest paid the entire interest amount of $24,000 on December 1, 2015. What amount of interest was deductible on Krest's 2015 income tax return?

A. $0

B. $2,000

C. $22,000

D. $24,000

Answer (B) is correct.

REQUIRED: The amount of prepaid interest deductible on Krest's tax return for the current year.

DISCUSSION: Costs of business borrowing are generally deductible, but prepaid interest in any form must be amortized over the period of the loan. Only 1 month of the loan has expired, so $2,000 [$24,000 × (1 ÷ 12)] is deductible.

Answer (A) is incorrect. The interest related to the expired portion of the loan is deductible. Answer (C) is incorrect. This is the prepaid interest that should be amortized in 2016. Answer (D) is incorrect. Only one month of interest is deductible, not the entire interest amount of $24,000.

2. Mock operates a retail business selling illegal narcotic substances. When Mock calculates business income, he may adjust for

I. Cost of merchandise

II. Business expenses other than the cost of merchandise

A. I only.

B. II only.

C. Both I and II.

D. Neither I nor II.

Answer (A) is correct.

REQUIRED: The deductible items allowed to arrive at business income.

DISCUSSION: An adjustment to gross receipts is permitted for the cost of merchandise related to the selling of illegal narcotic substances (Sec. 280E), even if the narcotics are listed in the Controlled Substances Act. However, all other business expenses related to the sales are not deductible.

Answer (B) is incorrect. Business expenses for the sale of narcotics are not deductible. Answer (C) is incorrect. An adjustment for cost of merchandise is allowed, but business expenses associated with the sale of narcotics are not deductible. Answer (D) is incorrect. An adjustment to gross receipts is permitted for the cost of merchandise related to the selling of illegal narcotic substances.

3. Phil Armonic is actively engaged in the oil business and owns numerous oil leases in the Southwest. During 2015, he made several trips to inspect oil wells on the leases. As a result of these overnight trips, he paid the following

Plane fares	$4,000
Hotels	1,000
Meals	800
Entertaining lessees	500

Of the $6,300 in expenses incurred, he can claim as deductible expenses

A. $6,300

B. $5,650

C. $5,000

D. $4,650

Answer (B) is correct.

REQUIRED: The deductible amount of expenses incurred on overnight trips.

DISCUSSION: A deduction is allowed for travel expenses while away from home in the pursuit of a trade or business. Both meal and entertainment expenses are limited to 50% of their cost. Assuming that Armonic's expenses meet the business relation requirements, his total deduction is

Plane fares	$4,000
Hotels	1,000
Meals ($800 × 50%)	400
Entertainment ($500 × 50%)	250
Total deduction	$5,650

Answer (A) is incorrect. Only part of the expenses may be deducted. Answer (C) is incorrect. Meal and entertainment expenses are deductible but limited to 50%. Answer (D) is incorrect. The cost of lodging is deductible as travel expense.

4. The following 2015 information pertains to Sam and Ann Hoyt, who filed a joint federal income tax return for the calendar year 2015:

Adjusted gross income -- $34,000
$100 contribution to a recognized political party

The Hoyts itemized their deductions. What amount of the $100 political contribution were the Hoyts entitled to claim as a credit against their 2015 tax?

A. $0

B. $25

C. $50

D. $100

Answer (A) is correct.

REQUIRED: The amount taxpayers are entitled to claim as a credit for political contributions.

DISCUSSION: Contributions to a political party or candidate are not deductible.

5. Recasto owns a second residence that is used for both personal and rental purposes. During 2015, Recasto used the second residence for 50 days and rented the residence to Louis for 200 days. Which of the following statements is true?

A. Depreciation may not be deducted on the property under any circumstances.

B. A rental loss may be deducted if rental-related expenses exceed rental income.

C. Utilities and maintenance on the property must be divided between personal and rental use.

D. All mortgage interest and taxes on the property will be deducted to determine the property's net income or loss.

Answer (C) is correct.

REQUIRED: The true statement regarding Recasto's second residence.

DISCUSSION: The expenses for rental property must be allocated between personal and rental use. Deductions are only allowed for those expenses related to the rental expense. In order to qualify to deduct these amounts, the taxpayer must pass the "Minimum Rental Use" test, which states that the property must be rented for at least 15 days to qualify as business use. In addition, if the taxpayer uses the residence for personal use more than either 14 days or 10% of the days it is rented, the deductions are further limited.

Answer (A) is incorrect. Expenses allocable to the rental use are deductible. Answer (B) is incorrect. Although the minimum rental use test was passed, the residence failed the minimum personal use test. Therefore, it cannot qualify for any passive activity loss deduction. Answer (D) is incorrect. The expenses must be allocated between personal and rental use.

6. Basic Partnership, a cash-basis, calendar-year entity, began business on February 1, 2015. Basic incurred and paid the following in 2015:

Filing fees incident to the creation of the partnership	$ 3,600
Accounting fees to prepare the representations in offering materials	12,000

Basic elected to amortize costs. What is the maximum amount that Basic may deduct on the 2015 partnership return?

A. $5,000

B. $3,300

C. $0

D. $3,600

Answer (D) is correct.

REQUIRED: The amount of organizational costs that is deductible in the current tax year.

DISCUSSION: A partnership may elect to deduct up to $5,000 of any qualified organizational expenses (in addition to $5,000 of any startup costs) it incurs in the tax year in which it begins business. The $5,000 deducted for organizational expenses must be reduced by the amount by which the expenses exceed $50,000. Any remaining balance of organizational expenditures that are not immediately deductible must be amortized over a 15-year period. Organizational costs include costs associated with the formation of the partnership. They do not include syndication fees. Thus, the filing fees are the only fees that may be deducted. The maximum amount that Basic may deduct is $3,600.

Answer (A) is incorrect. A $5,000 deduction includes the syndication fees. Answer (B) is incorrect. The figure of $3,300 is the result of amortizing the organizational costs over 11 months. Answer (C) is incorrect. The figure of $0 does not include the filing fees.

4.2 FICA and FUTA Taxes

7. Michael operates his health food store as a sole proprietorship out of a building he owns. Based on the following information regarding Year 6, compute his net self-employment income (for SE tax purposes) for Year 6.

Gross receipts	$100,000
Cost of Goods Sold	49,000
Utilities	6,000
Real estate taxes	1,000
Gain on sale of business truck	2,000
Depreciation expense	5,000
Section 179 expense	1,000
Mortgage interest on building	7,000
Contributions to Keogh retirement plan	2,000
Net operating loss (NOL) from Year 5	10,000

A. $14,000

B. $16,000

C. $24,000

D. $31,000

Answer (D) is correct.

REQUIRED: The sole proprietor's net self-employment income.

DISCUSSION: Net earnings from self employment are gross income derived from a trade or business, less allowable deductions attributable to the trade or business. Capital gains and losses and contributions to retirement plans are not considered income or expenses for self-employment purposes. In addition, net operating losses are not considered for self-employment purposes. Michael's net self-employment income is computed as follows:

Gross receipts	$100,000
Cost of goods sold	(49,000)
Utilities	(6,000)
Real estate taxes	(1,000)
Depreciation expense	(5,000)
Section 179 expense	(1,000)
Mortgage interest	(7,000)
Net self-employment income	$ 31,000

Answer (A) is incorrect. The NOL is not considered when computing self-employment income. Answer (B) is incorrect. The NOL is not considered when computing self-employment income. Answer (C) is incorrect. The gain on the sale of the business truck, contributions to the Keogh retirement plan, and the NOL are not considered when computing self-employment income.

8. The self-employment tax is

A. Fully deductible as an itemized deduction.

B. Fully deductible in determining net income from self-employment.

C. Partially deductible from gross income in arriving at adjusted gross income.

D. Not deductible.

Answer (C) is correct.

REQUIRED: The true statement concerning deductibility of the self-employment tax.

DISCUSSION: To arrive at AGI, a self-employed person is allowed a deduction for the employer's portion of the self-employment tax paid. This is an above-the-line deduction.

Answer (A) is incorrect. Only a portion of the self-employment tax may be deducted, and the deduction is above-the-line. Answer (B) is incorrect. Only a portion of the self-employment tax may be deducted to arrive at AGI. Answer (D) is incorrect. A deduction for self-employment tax is available.

9. An employee who has had Social Security tax withheld in an amount greater than the maximum for a particular year may claim

A. Such excess as either a credit or an itemized deduction, at the election of the employee, if that excess resulted from correct withholding by two or more employers.

B. Reimbursement of such excess from his employers if that excess resulted from correct withholding by two or more employers.

C. The excess as a credit against income tax, if that excess resulted from correct withholding by two or more employers.

D. The excess as a credit against income tax, if that excess was withheld by one employer.

Answer (C) is correct.

REQUIRED: The true statement about the result of Social Security tax withheld in excess of the maximum amount.

DISCUSSION: When an employee overpays the Social Security tax, proper adjustments must be made. If the overpayment cannot be adjusted, the amount must be refunded. If the overpayment resulted from correct withholding by two or more employers, the extra Social Security tax may be used to reduce income taxes.

Answer (A) is incorrect. The overpayment is not available as a deduction. Answer (B) is incorrect. It is not the employer's responsibility to refund the tax (the employer turned it over to the government). Answer (D) is incorrect. The extra Social Security tax may be used to reduce income taxes only when an employee has worked for two or more employers.

4.3 Employee Benefits

10. Under a "cafeteria plan" maintained by an employer,

A. Participation must be restricted to employees and their spouses and minor children.

B. At least 3 years of service are required before an employee can participate in the plan.

C. Participants may select their own menu of benefits.

D. Provision may be made for deferred compensation other than 401(k) plans.

Answer (C) is correct.

REQUIRED: The true statement about a cafeteria plan maintained by an employer.

DISCUSSION: A cafeteria plan is one in which the employees may choose among their fringe benefits. Participation is restricted to the employee. There is no minimum period of employment required. Benefits that do not qualify include (1) deferred compensation plans other than Sec. 401(k) plans, (2) scholarships and fellowship grants or tuition reductions, (3) educational assistance, and (4) other fringe benefits.

Answer (A) is incorrect. Spouses and other nonemployee beneficiaries may not participate in a cafeteria plan. Answer (B) is incorrect. No minimum period of employment is required. The maximum period of employment an employer may require is 3 years. Answer (D) is incorrect. Deferred compensation plans other than Sec. 401(k) plans do not qualify for exclusion under a cafeteria plan.

11. John Budd files a joint return with his wife. Budd's employer pays 100% of the cost of all employees' group term life insurance under a qualified plan. Under this plan, the maximum amount of tax-free coverage that may be provided for Budd by his employer is

A. $100,000

B. $50,000

C. $10,000

D. $5,000

Answer (B) is correct.

REQUIRED: The maximum amount of employer-paid group term life insurance cost excludable by the employee.

DISCUSSION: Benefits received from an employer are compensation for services and are included in gross income unless provided otherwise. Included in gross income is the cost of group term life insurance paid by the employer, but only to the extent that such cost exceeds the cost of $50,000 of such insurance. The plan cannot discriminate in favor of highly-compensated employees.

12. Howard, an employee of Ogden Corporation, died on June 30, 2015. During July, Ogden made employee death payments of $10,000 to his widow and $10,000 to his 15-year-old son. What amounts should be included in gross income by the widow and son in their respective tax returns for 2015?

	Widow	Son
A.	$0	$0
B.	$10,000	$10,000
C.	$5,000	$5,000
D.	$7,500	$7,500

Answer (B) is correct.

REQUIRED: The employee death benefits a widow and son should each include in gross income.

DISCUSSION: All death benefits received by the beneficiaries or the estate of an employee from or on behalf of an employer are included in gross income. Therefore, the widow and the son should each include the full $10,000 received as employee death benefits.

13. In 2011, Ross was granted an incentive stock option (ISO) by his employer as part of an executive compensation package. Ross exercised the ISO in 2013 and sold the stock in 2015 at a gain. Ross's profit was subject to the income tax for the year in which the

A. ISO was granted.

B. ISO was exercised.

C. Stock was sold.

D. Employer claimed a compensation deduction for the ISO.

Answer (C) is correct.

REQUIRED: The year in which the taxpayer's profit on an ISO is subject to the income tax.

DISCUSSION: According to the Internal Revenue Code, an employee will have no income tax consequences on the grant date or the exercise date of an incentive stock option if that employee meets two requirements. First, the employee cannot dispose of the stock within 2 years after the grant date or within 1 year after the exercise date. Second, the employee must be employed by the company on the grant date until 3 months prior to the exercise date. Since Ross meets these requirements, he is not subject to any tax on the grant or exercise dates. Ross did, however, recognize a capital gain when he sold the stock in 2015.

Answer (A) is incorrect. There are no income tax consequences on the grant date. Answer (B) is incorrect. There are no income tax consequences on the exercise date. Answer (D) is incorrect. An employer may not take a deduction for the amount of the profit on an incentive stock option.

14. Frank Clarke, an employee, was covered under a noncontributory pension plan. Frank died on April 15, 2015, at age 64 and, pursuant to the plan, his widow received monthly pension payments of $500 beginning May 1, 2015. Mrs. Clarke also received an employee death payment of $10,000 in May 2015. How much should she include in her gross income for 2015?

A. $5,000

B. $9,000

C. $10,000

D. $14,000

Answer (D) is correct.

REQUIRED: The amount of monthly pension payments and/or the amount of a lump-sum death benefit that is included in gross income.

DISCUSSION: All death benefits received by the beneficiaries or the estate of an employee from, or on behalf of, an employer are included in gross income. The pension payments must be included unless Frank made contributions to the pension plan.

4.4 Farm Income and Expenses

15. Jon, a cash-basis taxpayer, is the sole proprietor of a deer farm. Part of his farm land was transferred to the bank for partial payment of a loan. The remaining loan balance was discharged. He received the following amounts during 2015:

Deer sales	$100,000
Alimony	5,000
Debt discharge	9,000

Each of the deer had been purchased 2 years earlier for $5,000 and sold this year for $10,000. One of the deer sales was a buck that Jon had purchased and used for breeding. What amount does Jon report on Schedule F as gross income?

A. $50,000

B. $54,000

C. $109,000

D. $114,000

Answer (B) is correct.

REQUIRED: The calculated gross income for Form 1040 Schedule F.

DISCUSSION: Most farm-related income is reported in Part 1 of Form 1040 Schedule F; however, one exception to that is the reporting of capital gains. Capital assets include livestock used for breeding and are reported on Schedule D. The cost of livestock purchased for resale is calculated in to arrive at gross income. Jon's gross income includes the gain from nine deer ($100,000 ÷ $10,000 – 1 capital asset) and the debt discharge. The gross income is $54,000 ($90,000 of sales – $45,000 COGS + $9,000 debt discharge). Alimony received is reported on line 11 of Form 1040, not on Schedule F.

Answer (A) is incorrect. The deer used for breeding is a capital asset and reported on Schedule D (not Schedule F). In addition, gross income includes the $9,000 from the discharge of debt. Answer (C) is incorrect. The deer used for breeding is a capital asset and reported on Schedule D (not Schedule F). In addition, the cost of the sales is calculated in to arrive at gross income. Answer (D) is incorrect. Alimony and capital gains are reported on Form 1040 and Schedule D, respectively, and the cost of sales is calculated in arriving at gross farm income.

16. Farmer Jane received the following income during the current year:

Materials as a direct payment from agricultural program	$30,000
Insurance proceeds for crop losses last year	50,000
Rental of spare rooms attached to residence	14,400
Discharge of loan for farming property	2,500

What is Jane's gross income reported on Schedule F?

A. $30,000

B. $32,500

C. $82,500

D. $96,900

Answer (C) is correct.

REQUIRED: The calculated gross income for Form 1040 Schedule F.

DISCUSSION: Only farm-related income is reported on Schedule F. In general, any income or expenses related to Jane's personal residence is not farm related; therefore, the rental income is not farm related and not reported on Schedule F but would instead be reported on Schedule E. Farm income this year does include crop insurance proceeds since the loss was last year and deferment is only allowed for payments in the year of the damage. Payments from agricultural programs are farm income regardless of whether paid in cash, materials, or services. Discharge of indebtedness for farm assets is farm income. Jane's gross farm income is $82,500 ($30,000 + $50,000 + $2,500).

Answer (A) is incorrect. Crop insurance proceeds along with any discharge of farm indebtedness are reported on Schedule F. Answer (B) is incorrect. Crop insurance proceeds are reported on Schedule F. Answer (D) is incorrect. Only farm-related income is reported on Schedule F. Income related to the personal residence (e.g., rent) is not farm related.

17. A cash-basis farmer with gross farm income of $95,000 incurred the following expenses:

Feed for the current year	$ 5,000
Combine rental with an operator	1,500
Auger rental without an operator	50
Phone line installation	65
Farm labor	30,000

The phone installation expense is for a first line into the home of the farmer. The line is used 20% for business. The farm labor cost includes $15,000 for wages, $12,000 for boarding, and $3,000 for farm products used by the labor. What is the net farm profit?

A. $58,385

B. $58,450

C. $61,450

D. $64,885

Answer (C) is correct.

REQUIRED: The net farm profit.

DISCUSSION: Farmers may deduct any ordinary and necessary costs of operating a farm for profit. Only feed expense for the amount consumed during the current tax year may be deducted by a cash basis taxpayer. Both farm-related rentals (i.e., with or without an operator) are deductible. Farmers may only deduct the business portion of phone installations for other than the first line. Farm labor and labor boarding costs are deductible, but not the value of farm products used by farm labor. The net farm profit is $61,450 [$95,000 – $5,000 – $1,500 – $50 – ($30,000 – $3,000)].

Answer (A) is incorrect. Installation cost of a first line in a home is a personal expense, even if the farmer uses it for business. In addition, the value of farm products used by hired labor is not deductible. Answer (B) is incorrect. The value of farm products used by hired labor is not deductible. Answer (D) is incorrect. The feed and rentals are all deductible. In addition, the cost of installing the phone line (first line) and the value of farm products used by hired labor are not deductible.

18. Which of the following may use income averaging for farming?

A. Corporations.

B. Partnerships.

C. Trusts.

D. S corporation shareholder.

Answer (D) is correct.

REQUIRED: The entity or individual allowed to use income averaging for farming.

DISCUSSION: Individuals, partners, and S corporation shareholders are allowed to average all or some of his or her current year's farm income by shifting it to the 3 prior years (base years).

Answer (A) is incorrect. Neither a corporation nor its shareholders may average their farm income. Answer (B) is incorrect. A partner may use farm income averaging but not the partnership. Answer (C) is incorrect. Individuals, not trusts, may use farm income averaging.

19. During the current year, a farmer paid $20,000 for an approved conservation plan to prevent erosion of farm land. If the farmer had gross receipts of $80,000 and $20,000 in costs of livestock sold, what is the farmer's net farm profit?

A. $40,000

B. $45,000

C. $60,000

D. $80,000

Answer (B) is correct.

REQUIRED: The net farm profit (Schedule F).

DISCUSSION: Net farm profit equals gross farm income less applicable expenses. Gross farm income equals total sales less the cost of livestock sold ($60,000). The conservation cost deduction is limited to 25% of gross farm income ($15,000). The net farm profit is $45,000 ($60,000 – $15,000).

Answer (A) is incorrect. The conservation cost deduction is limited to 25% of gross farm income. Answer (C) is incorrect. The farmer is allowed a limited deduction for the cost of the conservation plan. Answer (D) is incorrect. The farmer is allowed a deduction for the cost of the livestock sold and a limited deduction for the cost of the conservation plan.

20. In June of Year 1, a farmer paid a premium of $3,000 for tornado insurance on the barn. The policy will cover a period of 3 years beginning on July 1, Year 1. During the same year, the farmer spent $5,000 to repair the barn roof and another $5,000 to repair the house roof, which were damaged by a tornado in April. The farmer has dedicated 1/5 of the house as an office for operating the farm. How much may be deducted in Year 1 for insurance and repairs/maintenance?

	Insurance	Repairs/Maintenance
A.	$1,000	$10,000
B.	$3,000	$8,000
C.	$1,000	$1,000
D.	$500	$6,000

Answer (D) is correct.

REQUIRED: The amount of the deduction for prepaid insurance premium and repairs/maintenance.

DISCUSSION: Advanced payments of insurance premiums are deductible, but only in the year to which they apply, regardless of the accounting method used. Coverage of the barn is a farm business expense. The portion of the premium that is currently deductible is $500 [$3,000 × (6 ÷ 36 months)]. The repair/maintenance expenses must be separated into business use and personal use. Only the business use expenses are deductible. The barn repair expense is 100% business, but the house repair is only 1/5 business. The repair/maintenance deduction is $6,000 [$5,000 barn + ($5,000 × 20%)].

Answer (A) is incorrect. The premiums only cover 6 months of Year 1. In addition, the repair/maintenance expense must be apportioned between business and personal. Answer (B) is incorrect. Advanced payments of insurance premiums are only deductible in the year to which they apply. Also, only 20% of the repair to the roof of the house is a business expense. Answer (C) is incorrect. The premiums only cover 6 months of Year 1. Also, 100% of the repair to the barn is deductible.

4.5 Above-the-Line Deductions

21. In 2015, a self-employed taxpayer had gross income of $57,000. The taxpayer paid self-employment tax of $8,000, health insurance of $6,000, and $5,000 of alimony. The taxpayer also contributed $2,000 to a traditional IRA. What is the taxpayer's adjusted gross income?

A. $55,000

B. $50,000

C. $46,000

D. $40,000

Answer (D) is correct.

REQUIRED: The taxpayer's AGI.

DISCUSSION: In 2015, self-employed individuals can deduct 50% of FICA taxes paid and 100% of payments made for health insurance coverage for the individual and his or her family. Alimony is gross income to the recipient and deductible by the payor. Contributions of up to $5,500 to an individual retirement account are deductible. The taxpayer's AGI is $40,000 ($57,000 GI – $4,000 SE tax paid – $6,000 health insurance – $5,000 alimony – $2,000 contribution to IRA).

Answer (A) is incorrect. Self-employment taxes and health insurance, along with alimony paid, also reduce GI to arrive at AGI. Answer (B) is incorrect. Self-employment taxes and health insurance paid also reduce GI to arrive at AGI. Answer (C) is incorrect. Self-employment health insurance paid also reduces GI to arrive at AGI.

22. Emil Gow owns a two-family house that has two identical apartments. Gow lives in one apartment and rents out the other. In 2015, the rental apartment was fully occupied, and Gow received $7,200 in rent. During the year ended December 31, 2015, Gow paid the following:

Real estate taxes	$6,400
Painting of rental apartment	800
Annual fire insurance premium	600

In 2015, depreciation for the entire house was determined to be $5,000. What amount should Gow include in his adjusted gross income for 2015?

A. $2,900

B. $800

C. $400

D. $100

Answer (C) is correct.

REQUIRED: The amount to be reported as net rental income includible in AGI.

DISCUSSION: Ordinary and necessary expenses paid or incurred during the tax year for the production of income are deductible for AGI. This includes deduction for depreciation on property held for production of income. Personal expenses are not deductible as rental expense. Insurance, taxes, and depreciation must be allocated between rental and personal expense.

Gross rental income		$7,200
Less: Rental expense		
Maintenance and repair	$ 800	
Depreciation ($5,000 × 1/2)	2,500	
Real estate tax ($6,400 × 1/2)	3,200	
Insurance ($600 × 1/2)	300	(6,800)
Net rental income		$ 400

The interest and taxes attributable to the apartment Emil occupies are deductible as an itemized deduction.

Answer (A) is incorrect. Depreciation attributable to the rental portion is deductible. Answer (B) is incorrect. All of the painting expenses attributable to the rental portion of the apartment are deductible. Answer (D) is incorrect. The personal portion of the fire insurance premium is not deductible.

23. Grey, a calendar-year taxpayer, was employed and resided in New York. On February 2, 2015, Grey was permanently transferred to Florida by his employer. Grey worked full-time for the entire year. In 2015, Grey incurred and paid the following unreimbursed expenses in relocating:

Lodging and travel expenses while moving	$1,000
Pre-move house-hunting costs	1,200
Costs of moving household furnishings and personal effects	1,800

What amount was deductible as moving expense on Grey's 2015 tax return?

A. $4,000

B. $2,800

C. $1,800

D. $1,000

Answer (B) is correct.

REQUIRED: The amount of deductible moving expenses.

DISCUSSION: Unreimbursed, direct moving expenses are eligible for an above-the-line deduction. Direct expenses include the actual moving costs and certain expenses incurred while moving, such as lodging and traveling (but not meals). Indirect expenses, such as house-hunting costs, are not deductible.

Answer (A) is incorrect. House-hunting costs and other indirect moving expenses are not deductible. Answer (C) is incorrect. Lodging and travel expenses while moving are deductible as direct moving expenses. Answer (D) is incorrect. The cost of the actual move is deductible as a direct moving expense.

24. A 33-year-old taxpayer withdrew $30,000 (pretax) from a traditional IRA. The taxpayer has a 33% effective tax rate and a 35% marginal tax rate. What is the total tax liability associated with the withdrawal?

A. $10,000

B. $10,500

C. $13,000

D. $13,500

Answer (D) is correct.

REQUIRED: The tax liability associated with an early distribution from a traditional IRA.

DISCUSSION: IRA distributions made before age 59 1/2 are subject to taxation as well as a 10% penalty. Each amount is calculated based on the distribution. No penalty is applied if it is for reason of death or disability, use of medical expenses in excess of 10% (7.5% if age 65 or older) limitation, or up to $10,000 use of purchase of a first home. None of these circumstances are applicable; therefore, tax and penalty apply to the entire $30,000. The applicable tax rate is 35% for a tax liability of $10,500 ($30,000 × 35%), which is added to the penalty of $3,000 ($30,000 × 10%), for a total of $13,500.

Answer (A) is incorrect. Early distributions from a traditional IRA must be taxed as well as penalized. Answer (B) is incorrect. In addition to the tax at a rate of 35%, a 10% penalty is also applicable. Answer (C) is incorrect. The tax rate used should be the marginal rate, not the effective rate.

25. In 2015, Barlow moved from Chicago to Miami to start a new job, incurring costs of $1,200 to move household goods and $2,500 in temporary living expenses. Barlow was not reimbursed for any of these expenses. What amount should Barlow deduct as an above-the-line deduction for moving expense?

A. $1,200

B. $2,700

C. $3,000

D. $3,700

Answer (A) is correct.

REQUIRED: The allowable moving expense deduction.

DISCUSSION: A deduction for moving expenses paid or incurred in connection with the commencement of work by the taxpayer at a new place of work is allowed. The expenses of actually moving the taxpayer, family, and household goods are deductible above-the-line. Indirect moving expenses, including house-hunting trips, temporary living expenses, and expenses related to the sale, purchase, or lease of a residence are not deductible.

Answer (B) is incorrect. Even a small percentage of indirect moving expenses is not deductible. Answer (C) is incorrect. Even a percentage of temporary living expenses is not deductible. Answer (D) is incorrect. Indirect moving expenses, including temporary living expenses, are not deductible.

26. With regard to tax recognition of alimony in connection with a 2015 divorce, which one of the following statements is true?

A. The divorced couple may be members of the same household when payments are made.

B. Payments may be made in cash or property.

C. If the payor spouse pays premiums for insurance on his life as a requirement under the divorce agreement, the premiums are alimony if the payor spouse owns the policy.

D. Payments must terminate at the death of the payee spouse.

Answer (D) is correct.

REQUIRED: The amounts deductible as alimony.

DISCUSSION: Only amounts that are required to be included as gross income of the recipient as alimony are deductible by the payor in calculating AGI. A component of the alimony definition is that the payor has no liability to make the payment for any period after the death of the payee spouse.

Answer (A) is incorrect. Alimony consists of payments when the payor and payee are not members of the same household. Answer (B) is incorrect. Alimony payments must be made in cash. Answer (C) is incorrect. The payments are not made to the payee spouse (the payor spouse owns the policy).

27. In the current year, an unmarried individual with modified adjusted gross income of $25,000 paid $1,000 interest on a qualified education loan entered into on July 1. How may the individual treat the interest for income tax purposes?

A. As a $500 deduction to arrive at AGI for the year.

B. As a $1,000 deduction to arrive at AGI for the year.

C. As a $1,000 itemized deduction.

D. As a nondeductible item of personal interest.

Answer (B) is correct.

REQUIRED: The treatment of interest paid for qualified higher education loans.

DISCUSSION: Taxpayer may deduct up to $2,500 of interest paid on qualified educational loans. The deduction is subject to income limits. The phaseout range begins when AGI exceeds $65,000 for unmarried individuals and ends at $80,000. The deduction is taken above-the-line to arrive at AGI for the year.

Answer (A) is incorrect. The reduction in the deduction does not begin until AGI exceeds $65,000. Answer (C) is incorrect. The deduction is taken above-the-line to arrive at AGI for the year. Answer (D) is incorrect. Taxpayers may take an above-the-line deduction up to $2,500 of interest paid on qualified educational loans.

28. Dale received $1,000 in 2015 for jury duty. In exchange for regular compensation from her employer during the period of jury service, Dale was required to remit the entire $1,000 to her employer in 2015. In Dale's 2015 income tax return, the $1,000 jury duty fee should be

A. Claimed in full as an itemized deduction.

B. Claimed as an itemized deduction to the extent exceeding 2% of adjusted gross income.

C. Deducted from gross income in arriving at adjusted gross income.

D. Included in taxable income without a corresponding offset against other income.

Answer (C) is correct.

REQUIRED: The deductibility of jury duty pay.

DISCUSSION: Pay for jury duty is compensation gross income. Jury duty pay remitted to an employer (in return for being paid during the duty) is deductible for AGI.

29. For 2015, Val and Pat White, both age 30, filed a joint return. Val earned $45,000 in wages and was covered by his employer's qualified pension plan. Pat was unemployed and received $6,000 in alimony payments for the first 4 months of the year before remarrying. The couple had no other income. Each contributed $5,500 to an IRA account. The allowable IRA deduction on their 2015 joint tax return is

A. $11,000

B. $5,750

C. $5,500

D. $0

Answer (A) is correct.

REQUIRED: The allowable IRA deduction for a married couple filing a joint return.

DISCUSSION: The maximum amount that any taxpayer under the age of 50 may deduct for a contribution to an IRA is limited to the lesser of $5,500 ($6,500 if qualified for a catch-up contribution) or the taxpayer's compensation gross income for the year. The limit is applied separately to each spouse who has compensation and makes a contribution to a separate IRA account. Taxable alimony is treated as compensation for this purpose. The deduction is for AGI. If one spouse is covered by an employer's retirement plan, the deduction is proportionately reduced once earned income exceeds $98,000 in 2015. Thus, Val and Pat may deduct $11,000.

Answer (B) is incorrect. The additional spousal IRA deduction of $250 previously applied when only one of the spouses had compensation or an election was made to treat one spouse as having no compensation for the year. Taxable alimony is compensation. In addition, the IRA deduction for a nonworking spouse is now $5,500. Answer (C) is incorrect. The spouse is allowed a $5,500 deduction whether or not the spouse has any earned income. Thus, each spouse may deduct $5,500 for contributions to separate IRAs. Answer (D) is incorrect. Although phasing out applies if one spouse is covered by an employer's retirement plan, phasing out does not begin until earned income exceeds $98,000 in 2015.

30. Tom and Wendy Burg, married and filing joint income tax returns, derive their entire income from the operation of their retail music store. Their 2015 adjusted gross income was $50,000. The Burgs itemized their deductions on Schedule A for 2015. The following unreimbursed cash expenditures were among those made by the Burgs during 2015:

Qualified moving expenses when new residence is 35 miles from prior residence	$650
Fee for breaking lease on prior apartment residence located 35 miles from new residence	500
Security deposit placed on apartment at new location	900

What amount should the Burgs deduct for moving expenses in their itemized deductions on Schedule A for 2015?

A. $0

B. $500

C. $900

D. $1,400

Answer (A) is correct.

REQUIRED: The taxpayer's allowable unreimbursed moving expense deduction.

DISCUSSION: Moving expenses are deductible to arrive at AGI, not on Schedule A. A moving expense deduction is allowed if the taxpayer has a new principal place of work at least 50 miles farther from the old residence than was the former principal place of work. The definition of qualified moving expenses does not include security deposits or the cost of breaking the lease on the prior apartment.

4.6 PRACTICE TASK-BASED SIMULATIONS

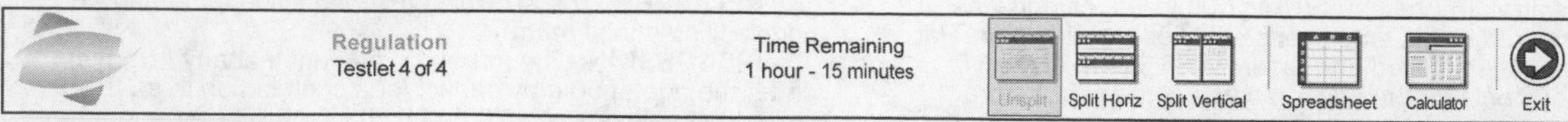

DIRECTIONS

Note: If you believe you have encountered a software malfunction, report it to the test center staff immediately.

Navigation

To navigate from task to task, use the controls at the bottom of the screen. Click on the **Next** button to advance to the next task, or the **Previous** button to go to the previous task. To go directly to any task, click on its number.

If you would like a reminder to revisit a task, or want to indicate that you are finished with it, click on the reminder flag below the task number. To clear the flag, click on it again. Reminder flags are for your use only – they do not contribute to your score.

Tabs

In this part of the examination, you will be asked to complete various tasks. Every task has one or more **Work Tabs**. Some tasks have one or more **Information Tabs**, others may have none. Every task has a **Help** tab.

If a task has **Information Tabs**, you may use the information in them to complete your responses in the **Work Tabs**.

Work tab **Information tab** **Help tab**

Work Tabs:

- **Work Tabs** are identified with a pencil icon. This is where your responses are expected.
- Each task has one or more **Work Tabs**.
- **Work Tabs** contain directions for completing the task – be sure to read these directions carefully.
- The **Work Tab** name in the example above is for illustration only – yours will differ.
- You must complete all of the **Work Tabs** in each task to receive full credit.

Information Tabs:

- The Authoritative Literature will be provided in all tasks in the AUD, FAR, and REG sections for your reference.
- Your simulation may have one or more additional **Information Tabs**. Like the Authoritative Literature tabs, **Information Tabs** do not have a pencil icon.
- If your task has additional **Information Tabs**, go through each to familiarize yourself with the task content.

Help Tab:

- The **Help Tab** provides assistance with the exam software that is used in this task. For example, if the task is to compose a memorandum, **Help** will provide information about the word processor.

The Toolbar

The toolbar at the top of the screen shows the amount of time remaining for you to complete the tasks. In addition, the following tools are available. Note that only the **Exit** button is displayed when Directions are visible - the others will appear when you begin the tasks.

Click on these buttons to split or unsplit the screen. You can split the screen vertically or horizontally.

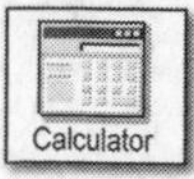

Click on this button to display the calculator; click on it again to hide the calculator. To move the calculator, click on the calculator title bar and drag the calculator to the desired location.

Click on this button to use the spreadsheet; click on it again to hide the spreadsheet. To move the spreadsheet, click on the the spreadsheet title bar and drag the spreadsheet to the desired location.

Click on this button to go on to the next part of the examination. You must complete all of the tasks to receive full credit. Once you click on **Exit** and confirm the action, you will NOT be able to return to this testlet.

= Reminder Directions 1 2 3 4 5 6 Previous Next

David, a newly licensed CPA, opened an office in 2015 as a sole practitioner engaged in the practice of public accountancy. David reports on the cash basis and has adopted the calendar year for income tax reporting purposes. David has many items for both business and personal matters that can be included in income and as deductions.

For each of David's transactions, select from the list provided the appropriate tax treatment. Each choice may be used once, more than once, or not at all.

Transaction	***Answer***
1. Fee for the biennial permit to practice as a CPA	
2. Alimony paid to his former spouse, who reports the alimony as taxable income	
3. Personal medical expenses charged on a credit card in December 2015 but not paid until January 2016	
4. Personal casualty loss sustained	
5. Insurance premiums paid on David's life	
6. Penalty paid to bank on early withdrawal of savings	
7. Interest income on mortgage loan receivable	
8. Write-offs of uncollectible accounts receivable from accounting practice	
9. Foreign income tax withheld at source on dividend received	
10. Employer's portion of self-employment tax paid with 2015 return filed in April 2016	

Choices
A) Not taxable
B) Deductible on page 1 of Form 1040 to arrive at adjusted gross income
C) Deductible in full in Schedule A -- Itemized Deductions, 100% deductible
D) Deductible in Schedule A -- subject to threshold of 10% (7.5% if 65 or older) of adjusted gross income
E) Deductible in Schedule A -- subject to threshold of 10% of adjusted gross income and threshold of $100
F) Deductible in Schedule B -- Interest and Dividend Income
G) Deductible in Schedule C -- Profit or Loss from Business
H) Deductible in Schedule D -- Capital Gains or Losses
I) Deductible in Schedule E -- Supplemental Income and Loss
J) Deductible in Form 4797 -- Sales of Business Property
K) Claimed in Form 1116 -- Foreign Tax Credit, or in Schedule A -- Itemized Deductions
L) Based on gross self-employment income
M) Based on net earnings from self-employment
N) Not deductible
O) Taxable as interest income in Schedule B -- Interest and Dividend Income
P) Taxable as other income on page 1 of Form 1040

▼ = Reminder | Directions | 1 2 3 4 5 6 | Previous | Next

During the year, Murray, a sole proprietor, paid the expenses shown in the following table. Each of the expenses is assumed to be ordinary, necessary, and substantiated while engaging in an activity for profit, unless otherwise noted. In the third column of the table, enter the amounts that are deductible as a business expense reported on Schedule C. If none of a particular business expense is a reportable business expense deduction, enter a zero for that expense in the third column.

Expense	***Amount***	***Amount Deductible on Schedule C***
1. Property taxes paid on Murray's house	$1,620.00	
2. Wages paid to Murray's employees	$15,400.00	
3. Amount paid for a dinner party thanking his customers	$350.00	
4. Contributions to the campaign of a candidate for governor	$1,000.00	
5. Interest paid on a loan used to purchase bonds issued by the state of Texas	$2,750.00	

Business Expenses | Authoritative Literature | Help

A client operates a small business organized as a C corporation. The client wants to know how certain deductible items are treated for tax purposes by a business.

The business generates sufficient income, and a full deduction of any item would not generate a net loss. For each item in the table below, select from the list provided the appropriate treatment of the deductible item for each entity. A choice may be used once, more than once, or not at all.

Item	***Allowable Deduction***
1. Business use of home	
2. Payments to owners for services rendered	
3. Payments for health insurance for owners	
4. Business meals and entertainment expenses	
5. Political contributions	
6. Business gifts	

Choices
A) 100% deductible without any limitation
B) 50% deductible without any limitation
C) 25% deductible without any limitation
D) Deductible but limited to $25 per recipient
E) 100% deductible limited to portional use
F) 100% deductible to the extent of profits without regard to this deduction
G) Not deductible

A taxpayer employing both full-time and seasonal employees must determine the appropriate amounts of FICA and FUTA taxes to pay for (or withhold from) the employees. For each situation given, calculate the correct amount to be paid or withheld based on the current year's rates.

Situation	***Amount Paid or Withheld***
1. FICA tax withheld by employer on wages of $60,000 paid to an employee.	
2. Taxpayer's employer's share of FICA for self-employment income of $120,000.	
3. FUTA tax on $5,000 of wages for seasonal employee who only worked during the third quarter of the year. No SUTA tax was paid.	
4. FUTA taxes on $6,000 of wages for seasonal employee for the first quarter of the year. No SUTA tax was paid.	
5. FUTA taxes on $60,000 of wages for full-time employee from Jan-Dec, when a 5.40% state unemployment rate was paid.	

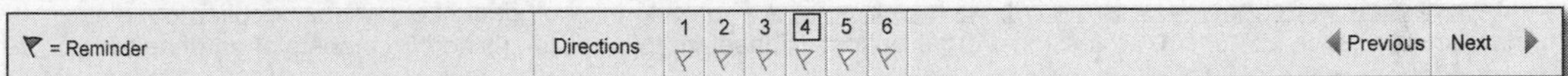

For each item in the left column, determine whether it can be an above-the-line deduction, a deduction from AGI to arrive at taxable income, or neither. Double-click on the shaded cells in the right column and select from the choice list provided.

Item	***Allowable Deduction***
1. Unreimbursed expenses incurred by an eligible educator for books and supplies used in the classroom	
2. Unreimbursed direct moving expenses incurred for qualified business-related relocation	
3. Payments for child support	
4. Alimony payments	
5. Charitable contributions made to qualified organizations	
6. Qualified medical expenses that exceed 10% of AGI	
7. Interest paid on qualified educational loans	
8. Tuition and fees paid for qualified higher education	
9. State income taxes paid	

Choices
A) Above-the-line deduction
B) Deduction from AGI to arrive at taxable income
C) Neither

= Reminder | Directions | 1 2 3 4 5 6 | Previous | Next

Research | Authoritative Literature | Help

Almost Ready, Inc., incurred $15,000 of expenditures in preparing its model car business. The expenditures include market research costs and advertising fees. Almost Ready would like to deduct these expenses on its current tax return as start-up expenditures. Which section and subsection of the Internal Revenue Code defines start-up expenditures?

Enter your response in the answer fields below.

IRC § [ ] ([ ])

= Reminder | Directions | 1 2 3 4 5 6 | Previous | Next

Unofficial Answers

1. Tax Treatment (10 Gradable Items)

1. G) Deductible in Schedule C -- Profit or Loss from Business. Professionals can deduct expenses peculiar to their profession, such as dues to professional organizations. These are to be distinguished from costs of entering the profession.
2. B) Deductible on page 1 of Form 1040 to arrive at adjusted gross income. Payments included in the recipient's income as alimony are deductible by the payor in computing adjusted gross income.
3. D) Deductible in Schedule A -- subject to threshold of 10% (7.5% if 65 or older) of adjusted gross income. A deduction for expenses paid for the medical care of the taxpayer, spouse, or dependent is allowed. It is treated as paid when charged on the credit card. The medical expenses are an itemized deduction only to the extent they exceed 7.5% of the taxpayer's adjusted gross income.
4. E) Deductible in Schedule A -- subject to threshold of 10% of adjusted gross income and threshold of $100. An itemized deduction is allowed for personal casualty losses to the extent that the loss from each casualty exceeds $100 and the aggregate of all such losses during the tax year exceeds 10% of the taxpayer's adjusted gross income.
5. N) Not deductible. Proceeds of an insurance policy paid by reason of the death of the insured are excludable. The premiums paid are a personal expense of the taxpayer, and Sec. 262(a) generally disallows deduction of personal, living, or family expenses.
6. B) Deductible on page 1 of Form 1040 to arrive at adjusted gross income. Penalties for premature withdrawal from a time savings account, certificate of deposit, or similar class of deposit may be deducted from gross income to arrive at adjusted gross income.
7. O) Taxable as interest income in Schedule B -- Interest and Dividend Income. Interest on a receivable is gross income. Interest income is reported on Schedule B.
8. N) Not deductible. David reports income on the cash basis. Therefore, the accounts receivable have not been included in income, and no deduction will arise from writing them off as uncollectible.
9. K) Claimed in Form 1116 -- Foreign Tax Credit, or in Schedule A -- Itemized Deductions. A deduction for foreign income taxes paid or accrued during the tax year is allowed. A foreign tax credit on income earned and subject to tax in a foreign country is also available. The deduction is an alternative to the credit.
10. B) Deductible on page 1 of Form 1040 to arrive at adjusted gross income. A self-employed person may deduct one-half of his or her self-employment taxes. It is treated as a trade or business expense deductible to arrive at adjusted gross income.

2. Schedule C Expenses (5 Gradable Items)

1. $0. Property taxes paid for Murray's house may be deducted by him as a personal expense on Schedule A, but they cannot be reported as a business deduction on Schedule C.
2. $15,400. Wages paid for services rendered by employees are deductible by the employer.
3. $175. Amounts paid for entertainment that is directly related to the conduct of an active trade or business are deductible. However, the deduction is limited to 50% of the actual costs incurred.
4. $0. Political contributions are not deductible unless related to appearing before or communicating with a local council with respect to legislation that would directly affect the taxpayer. A gubernatorial candidate's campaign would not qualify for this exception.
5. $0. Expenses incurred to produce tax-exempt income are not deductible. Interest income received from bonds issued by state and local governments is excluded from gross income.

3. Business Expenses (6 Gradable Items)

1. E) 100% deductible limited to portional use. The limit is based on the amount of use of the home for business activity.
2. A) 100% deductible without any limitation. There is no deduction limit for compensation paid.
3. A) 100% deductible without any limitation. Deductions for health insurance payments are not limited.
4. B) 50% deductible without limitation. Deductions for qualified business meals and entertainment expenses are limited to 50%.
5. G) Not deductible. Political contributions are not deductible.
6. D) Deductible but limited to $25 per recipient. Expenditures for business gifts are deductible but are limited to $25 per recipient.

4. FICA and FUTA Taxes (5 Gradable Items)

1. $4,590. For 2015, FICA tax withheld from an employee's wages is 6.20% of the first $118,500 for Social Security and 1.45% for Medicare ($60,000 × 7.65%).
2. $9,087. The employer's share of FICA taxes for self-employment income is 6.20% of the first $118,500 for Social Security and 1.45% for Medicare. The tax is calculated as follows: ($118,500 × 6.20%) + ($120,000 × 1.45%).
3. $300. Employers must pay FUTA tax of 6.0% of the first $7,000 of wages for 2015. The FUTA tax on this employee's wages is $300 ($5,000 × 6.0%).
4. $360. Employers must pay FUTA tax of 6.0% of the first $7,000 of wages for 2015. The FUTA tax on this employee's wages is $360 ($6,000 × 6.0%).
5. $42. FUTA tax is imposed on the first $7,000, which this particular employee would have received during the first 6 months of the year; therefore, the applicable rate was 6.0%. In addition, if state unemployment tax is paid, a credit is available, which reduces the applicable tax rate up to 5.4%. The FUTA tax for this employee is $42 [$7,000 × (6.0% - 5.4%)].

5. 1040 Deductions (9 Gradable Items)

1. Above-the-line deduction. Qualified educator expense is an adjustment to gross income to arrive at AGI (above-the-line deduction).
2. Above-the-line deduction. Moving expense for job-related relocation is an adjustment to gross income to arrive at AGI (above-the-line deduction).
3. Neither. Payments for child support are not tax deductible.
4. Above-the-line deduction. Alimony is gross income to the recipient and deductible by the payor. It is an above-the-line deduction.
5. Deduction from AGI to arrive at taxable income. Charitable contributions are itemized deductions from AGI to arrive at taxable income.
6. Deduction from AGI to arrive at taxable income. Amounts paid for qualified medical expenses that exceed 10% of AGI are deductible from AGI to arrive at taxable income.
7. Above-the-line deduction. Taxpayers may deduct up to $2,500 of interest paid on qualified educational loans in 2015. This deduction is an above-the-line deduction.
8. Above-the-line deduction. Amount paid for qualified higher education expenses is an above-the-line deduction.
9. Deduction from AGI to arrive at taxable income. Paid state income taxes are deductible from AGI as an itemized deduction, to arrive at taxable income.

6. Research (1 Gradable Item)

Answer: IRC § 195(c)

§ 195. Start-up expenditures

(c) Definitions -- For the purposes of this section --

(1) Start-up expenditures

The term "start-up expenditure" means any amount --

(A) paid or incurred in connection with --

(i) investigating the creation or acquisition of an active trade or business, or

(ii) creating an active trade or business, or

(iii) any activity engaged in for profit and for the production of income before the day on which the active trade or business begins, in anticipation of such activity becoming an active trade or business, and

(B) which, if paid or incurred in connection with the operation of an existing active trade or business [in the same field as the trade or business referred to in subparagraph (A)], would be allowable as a deduction for the taxable year in which paid or incurred.

The term "start-up expenditure" does not include any amount with respect to which a deduction is allowable under section 163(a), 164, or 174.

Gleim Simulation Grading

Task	Correct Responses		Gradable Items		Score per Task
1	____	÷	10	=	____
2	____	÷	5	=	____
3	____	÷	6	=	____
4	____	÷	5	=	____
5	____	÷	9	=	____
6 (Research)	____	÷	1	=	____
			Total of Scores per Task		____
		÷	Total Number of Tasks		6
			Total Score		____ %

STUDY UNIT FIVE
DEDUCTIONS FROM AGI, CREDITS, AMT, AND LIMITATIONS

(28 pages of outline)

Taxpayers are allowed to take certain deductions from AGI, including the greater of the standard or itemized deductions and certain tax credits. The following are common deductions tested on the CPA exam:

Adjustments to Gross Income

- Educator expenses
- Certain business expenses of reservists, performing artists, etc.
- Health savings account deduction
- Moving expenses
- Deductible part of self-employment tax
- Self-employed SEP, SIMPLE, and qualified plans
- Self-employed health insurance deduction
- Penalty on early withdrawal of savings
- Alimony paid
- IRA deduction
- Student loan interest deduction
- Tuition and fees deduction
- Domestic production activities deduction
- Jury duty repayments

Itemized Deductions

- Medical and dental expenses
- Taxes paid
- Interest paid
- Gifts to charity
- Casualty and theft losses
- Job expenses and certain miscellaneous deductions
- Unreimbursed employee expenses
- Tax preparation fees
- Other expenses (e.g., investment fees, safe deposit box, etc.)
- Other miscellaneous deductions

The basics of the alternative minimum tax (AMT), an additional income tax, are presented in Subunit 5.4. AMT has been tested more often in the corporate context and is explained further in Study Unit 8, "Corporate Tax Computations."

The CPA exam does test the method of computing income tax liability. In the past, however, candidates have generally not been required to memorize the tax rates for each bracket for each filing status. The computation questions have generally provided brackets and rates to be applied for specific questions. Nevertheless, you should be prepared to answer questions on the current rate-bracket structure (e.g., what is the highest marginal rate?).

2015 Individual Income Tax Rates and Brackets

Rate Taxable Income Filing Status	10% The First	15% From 10% Max. up to	25% From 15% Max. up to	28% From 25% Max. up to	33% From 28% Max. up to	35% From 33% Max. up to	39.6% From 35% Max. up to
Married Filing Jointly and Qualifying Widow(er)	$18,450	$74,900	$151,200	$230,450	$411,500	$464,850	$Balance
Head of Household	$13,150	$50,200	$129,600	$209,850	$411,500	$439,000	$Balance
Single	$9,225	$37,450	$90,750	$189,300	$411,500	$413,200	$Balance
Married Filing Separately	$9,225	$37,450	$75,600	$115,225	$205,750	$232,425	$Balance

As of the date of publication, the IRS had not yet released all of the 2015 tax forms. Please check www.gleim.com/taxforms for any updates.

5.1 STANDARD AND ITEMIZED DEDUCTIONS

1. **Taxable Income**
   a. Taxable income is adjusted gross income (AGI) minus either the itemized deductions or the standard deduction, and the deduction for personal exemptions.
   b. Below-the-line deductions are all the deductions that may be subtracted from AGI to arrive at taxable income.

`Taxable income = Adjusted gross income - Greater of allowable itemized deductions on Schedule A or the standard deduction - Personal exemptions`

2. **Itemized vs. Standard**
   a. The taxpayer itemizes deductions if the total amount of allowable itemized deductions, after all limits have been applied, is greater than the amount of the standard deduction. Otherwise, the taxpayer claims the standard deduction. A taxpayer must elect to itemize, or no itemized deductions will be allowed.
      1) Election is made by filing Schedule A of Form 1040.
      2) Election made in any other taxable year is not relevant.
      3) Election may be changed by filing an amended return (Form 1040X).
      4) A person who itemizes may not file either Form 1040EZ or Form 1040A.
3. **Standard Deduction Unavailable**
   a. The following taxpayers are **not allowed** the standard deduction:
      1) Persons who itemize deductions
      2) Nonresident alien individuals
      3) Individuals who file a "short period" return
      4) A married individual who files a separate return and whose spouse itemizes
      5) Partnerships, estates, and trusts
4. **Standard Deduction**

STANDARD DEDUCTION AMOUNTS -- 2015

Filing Status	Basic	Additional Age 65/Blind
Married Filing Jointly (MFJ)	$12,600	$1,250
Qualifying Widow(er)	12,600	1,250
Head of Household (HH)	9,250	1,550
Single (other than above)	6,300	1,550
Married Filing Separately (MFS)	6,300	1,250

   a. The standard deduction is the sum of the basic standard deduction and the additional standard deductions.
   b. The **basic standard deduction** amount (shown in the table above) depends on filing status and dependency status on another's return.
      1) The basic standard deduction amount of a child under age 19 or a student under age 24 who can be claimed as a dependent on another individual's income tax return is limited to the greater of either
         a) $1,050 or
         b) Earned income for the year plus $350 up to the otherwise applicable standard deduction.
            i) Earned income does not include either dividends or capital gains from the sale of stock.

c. **Additional standard deduction** amounts, indexed for inflation, appear in the table on the previous page.

1) An individual who has attained the age of 65 or is blind is entitled to the amount.
2) An individual who both has reached age 65 and is blind is entitled to twice the amount.
3) The individual is entitled to the amount if (s)he attains age 65 before the end of the tax year
    a) Even if (s)he dies before the end of the year, but
    b) Not if (s)he dies before attaining age 65 even if (s)he would have otherwise reached age 65 before year's end.
4) A person who becomes blind on or before the last day of the taxable year is entitled to the amount.
5) Once qualified, the standard deduction is allowed in full.
    a) It is not prorated if a person dies during a tax year.

Traditionally, the AICPA has heavily tested itemized deductions, mostly with questions requiring calculations. Always read the questions very carefully. A question may contain one small, easily missed detail that changes the amount of the deduction.

5. **Itemized Deductions**

a. Schedule A is the form where itemized deductions are listed.
b. Itemized deductions include

1) Medical and dental expenses
2) Taxes paid
3) Interest paid
4) Charitable contributions
5) Casualty and theft losses
6) Other miscellaneous deductions
7) Job expenses (covered in Subunit 5.2)

6. **Medical and Dental Expenses**

a. Amounts paid for qualified medical expenses that exceed 10% (7.5% if 65 or older or spouse of individual 65 or older) of AGI may be deducted.
b. To qualify for a deduction, an expense must be paid during the taxable year for the taxpayer, the taxpayer's spouse, or a dependent and must not be compensated for by insurance or otherwise during the taxable year.
c. Deductible medical expenses are amounts paid for

1) Diagnosis, cure, mitigation, treatment or prevention of disease, or for the purpose of affecting any structure or function of the body
2) Transportation primarily for and essential to medical care
3) Medical insurance
4) Qualified long-term care premiums and services

d. A medical expense deduction is not allowed for amounts paid for any activity or treatment designed merely to improve an individual's general health or sense of wellness, even if recommended by a physician.

1) Examples include participation in a health club, a stop-smoking clinic, or a weight-loss institute.

a) Such expenses may be deductible if the services are prescribed by a physician who provides a written statement that they are necessary to alleviate a physical or mental defect or illness.

SCHEDULE A (Form 1040)

Department of the Treasury Internal Revenue Service (99)

Itemized Deductions

▶ Information about Schedule A and its separate instructions is at *www.irs.gov/schedulea*.

▶ Attach to Form 1040.

OMB No. 1545-0074

2014

Attachment Sequence No. 07

Name(s) shown on Form 1040 | Your social security number

Section	Line	Description	Box	Amount	Box	Amount
Medical and Dental Expenses		**Caution.** Do not include expenses reimbursed or paid by others.				
	1	Medical and dental expenses (see instructions)	1			
	2	Enter amount from Form 1040, line 38 [2]				
	3	Multiply line 2 by 10% (.10). But if either you or your spouse was born before January 2, 1950, multiply line 2 by 7.5% (.075) instead	3			
	4	Subtract line 3 from line 1. If line 3 is more than line 1, enter -0-			4	
Taxes You Paid	5	State and local **(check only one box):** a ☐ Income taxes, **or** b ☐ General sales taxes	5			
	6	Real estate taxes (see instructions)	6			
	7	Personal property taxes	7			
	8	Other taxes. List type and amount ▶	8			
	9	Add lines 5 through 8			9	
Interest You Paid	10	Home mortgage interest and points reported to you on Form 1098	10			
Note. Your mortgage interest deduction may be limited (see instructions).	11	Home mortgage interest not reported to you on Form 1098. If paid to the person from whom you bought the home, see instructions and show that person's name, identifying no., and address ▶	11			
	12	Points not reported to you on Form 1098. See instructions for special rules	12			
	13	Mortgage insurance premiums (see instructions)	13			
	14	Investment interest. Attach Form 4952 if required. (See instructions.)	14			
	15	Add lines 10 through 14			15	
Gifts to Charity	16	Gifts by cash or check. If you made any gift of $250 or more, see instructions	16			
If you made a gift and got a benefit for it, see instructions.	17	Other than by cash or check. If any gift of $250 or more, see instructions. You **must** attach Form 8283 if over $500	17			
	18	Carryover from prior year	18			
	19	Add lines 16 through 18			19	
Casualty and Theft Losses	20	Casualty or theft loss(es). Attach Form 4684. (See instructions.)			20	
Job Expenses and Certain Miscellaneous Deductions	21	Unreimbursed employee expenses—job travel, union dues, job education, etc. Attach Form 2106 or 2106-EZ if required. (See instructions.) ▶	21			
	22	Tax preparation fees	22			
	23	Other expenses—investment, safe deposit box, etc. List type and amount ▶	23			
	24	Add lines 21 through 23	24			
	25	Enter amount from Form 1040, line 38 [25]				
	26	Multiply line 25 by 2% (.02)	26			
	27	Subtract line 26 from line 24. If line 26 is more than line 24, enter -0-			27	
Other Miscellaneous Deductions	28	Other—from list in instructions. List type and amount ▶			28	
Total Itemized Deductions	29	Is Form 1040, line 38, over $152,525? ☐ **No.** Your deduction is not limited. Add the amounts in the far right column for lines 4 through 28. Also, enter this amount on Form 1040, line 40. ☐ **Yes.** Your deduction may be limited. See the Itemized Deductions Worksheet in the instructions to figure the amount to enter.			29	
	30	If you elect to itemize deductions even though they are less than your standard deduction, check here ▶ ☐				

Itemized deductions subject to 2%-of-AGI exclusion

For Paperwork Reduction Act Notice, see Form 1040 instructions. Cat. No. 17145C Schedule A (Form 1040) 2014

e. The cost of in-patient hospital care (including meals and lodging) is deductible as a medical expense.

1) If the principal reason an individual is in an institution (e.g., nursing home, rehabilitation facility, or disability-specific school) other than a hospital is the need for and availability of the medical care furnished by the institution, the full costs of meals, lodging, and other services necessary (including special schooling) for furnishing the medical care are all deductible.

f. Only drugs that require a prescription are qualified medical expenses.

g. The following are also considered deductible medical expenses:

1) Eyeglasses
2) A guide dog
3) Wheelchair, crutches, or artificial limbs
4) Special beds
5) Air conditioning
6) Dehumidifying equipment

h. Expenditures for new building construction or for permanent improvements to existing structures may be deductible in part.

1) The excess of the cost of a permanent improvement over the increase in value of the property is a deductible medical expense.

a) Even when the cost of the capital asset is not deductible, the cost of operating and maintaining the asset may be deductible when the asset is operated primarily for medical care.

2) Construction of ramps for the disabled, installation of elevators, widening of doorways, or lowering of kitchen cabinets or equipment may each qualify.

i. Travel

1) Amounts paid for transportation essential to (and primarily for) medical care are deductible.

a) This includes the transportation cost of traveling on a doctor's order to alleviate a specific chronic ailment.

2) The taxpayer may choose between actual expenditures (e.g., taxis, air fare) or $.23 per mile for 2015 (plus the cost of tolls and parking).

3) Expenditures for lodging are deductible up to $50 per night per individual.

j. Insurance

1) Premiums paid for medical insurance that provides for reimbursement of medical care expenses are deductible.

2) Self-employed health insurance payments may be deducted as an above-the-line deduction.

7. **Taxes Paid**

a. A taxpayer who itemizes deductions is permitted to deduct the full amount of certain taxes that are paid and incurred during the taxable year, subject to the limit on aggregate itemized deductions.

b. Recovery of a tax benefit item is generally included in gross income.

1) The recovered amount is included in income to the extent total allowable itemized deductions (for the applicable year) exceed the standard deduction (for the same year).

c. Real Property

1) The owner may deduct state, local, and foreign real property taxes.
2) If real property is bought or sold during the year, the real property tax is apportioned between the buyer and the seller on the basis of the number of days each one held the property during the real property tax year (regardless of nonproration agreements between buyers and sellers).
   a) The purchaser is presumed to own the property on the date of sale.
3) Special assessments for local improvements increase the basis of the property and are not deductible.

d. Ad Valorem, Personal Property Taxes

1) These taxes are deductible, but only if the tax is
   a) Substantially in proportion to the value of the property,
   b) Imposed on an annual basis, and
   c) Actually imposed.

e. Income Taxes

1) State income taxes are deductible.
2) Foreign income taxes paid are deductible, unless the foreign tax credit is claimed.
3) Individual taxpayers may claim an itemized deduction for general state and local sales tax in lieu of state income tax.

f. The following taxes are not deductible:

1) Federal taxes on income, estates, gifts, inheritances, legacies, and successions
2) State taxes on cigarettes and tobacco, alcoholic beverages, gasoline, registration, estates, gifts, inheritances, legacies, and successions
3) Licensing fees of highway motor vehicles (if based on the weight of the vehicle)

8. **Interest Paid**

a. **Qualified Residence Interest**

1) Qualified residence interest is deductible on no more than $1 million of acquisition indebtedness ($500,000 if married filing separately) and $100,000 of home equity indebtedness (aggregate amount) ($50,000 if married filing separately).
2) It is interest paid or accrued during the tax year on acquisition or home equity indebtedness that is secured by a qualified residence.
3) A qualified residence includes the principal residence of the taxpayer and one other residence owned by the taxpayer.
4) A taxpayer who has more than two residences may select, each year, the residences used to determine the amount of qualified residence interest.
5) Acquisition indebtedness is debt incurred in acquiring, constructing, or substantially improving a qualified residence. The debt must be secured by the residence.
6) Home equity indebtedness is all debt other than acquisition debt that is secured by a qualified residence to the extent it does not exceed the fair market value of the residence reduced by any acquisition indebtedness.

7) Points paid by the borrower are prepaid interest, which is typically deductible over the term of the loan.
    a) Amounts paid as points may be deducted in the year paid if
        i) The loan is used to buy or improve a taxpayer's principal home and is secured by that home;
        ii) Payment of points is an established business practice in the area where the loan is made; and
        iii) The points paid do not exceed points generally charged in the area.
8) Points paid by the seller are a selling expense that reduces the amount realized on the sale.
    a) The purchaser can elect to deduct points on the acquisition indebtedness of a principal residence by reducing the basis.
9) Qualified mortgage insurance qualifies as home mortgage interest. The taxpayer may allocate these premiums over the shorter of the mortgage or 84 months. Though expired, the qualified mortgage insurance premium deduction is expected to be renewed for 2015. This outline and the related questions assume renewal.

b. **Investment Interest Expense**

1) The IRC allows the deduction of a limited amount of investment interest as an itemized deduction.
2) Investment interest is interest paid or incurred (on debt) to purchase or carry property held for investment.
3) Investment interest does **not** include qualified residence interest or passive activity interest.
    a) Passive activity interest is includible with passive activities and deductible within the passive loss rules.
4) Limit
    a) Investment interest may be deducted only to the extent of net investment income, which is any excess of investment income over investment expense.
    b) Investment income is
        i) Non-trade or nonbusiness income from
            - Interest
            - Dividends not subject to the capital gains tax
            - Annuities, royalties, and other gross income from property held for investment
        ii) Net gain on the disposition of property held for investment
            - A taxpayer may elect to treat all or a portion of long-term capital gains and qualified dividends as investment income.
        iii) Income treated as gross portfolio income under the PAL rules
        iv) Income from interests in activities that involve a trade or business in which the taxpayer does not materially participate, if the activity is not treated as passive activity under the PAL rules
    c) Investment income is **not**
        i) From rental real estate activity in which the taxpayer actively participates
5) Disallowed investment interest is carried forward indefinitely. It is deductible to the extent of investment income in a subsequent tax year.
6) Interest related to producing tax-exempt income is not deductible.

c. **Personal Interest Expense**

1) The general rule is that personal interest expense may **not** be deducted.
2) This includes interest on credit card debt, revolving charge accounts and lines of credit, car loans, medical fees, premiums, etc.
3) Personal interest expense does not include
   a) Interest on trade or business debt
   b) Investment interest
   c) Passive activity interest
   d) Qualified residence interest
   e) Interest on the unpaid portion of certain estate taxes
   f) Student loan interest

9. **Charitable Contributions**

a. Charitable contributions are deductible only if they are made to qualified organizations.

b. Qualified organizations can be either public charities or private foundations.

1) Generally, a public charity is one that derives more than one-third of its support from its members and the general public.

c. Donations can be made in the form of cash or noncash property.

d. Individuals may carry forward excess contributions for 5 years.

e. All rights and interest to the donation must be transferred to the qualified organization.

f. Additional donation requirements:

1) Clothing and household items donated must be in good or better condition.
   a) The exception to this rule is that a single item donation in less than good condition but still a $500 value or more is deductible with a qualified appraisal.
2) Cash or cash equivalent donations require a bank record alone or a receipt, letter, etc., from the donee regardless of the amount. The receipt, etc., must
   a) Be provided at the time of donation
   b) State the name of the organization
   c) Include the date and amount of the donation
3) Donations of $250 or more continue to require substantiation by a written receipt from the organization (the bank record alone is insufficient).
4) A qualified appraisal for real property donations is required to be attached to the tax return for property valued over $5,000.

g. If a donation is in the form of property, the amount of the donation depends upon the type of property and the type of organization that receives the property.

1) Capital gain property is property on which a long-term capital gain would be recognized if it were sold on the date of the contribution.
2) Ordinary income property is property on which ordinary income or short-term capital gain would be recognized if it were sold on the date of the contribution.

h. There are basically two types of charitable organizations: those classified as **50% limit organizations** and those classified as **non-50% limit organizations**.

1) 50% limit organizations, which encompass the majority of qualified charitable organizations, are generally public organizations. The following list represents some 50% organizations (IRS Publication 526 contains a complete, detailed list):
   a) Churches
   b) Educational organizations

c) Hospitals and certain medical research organizations
d) Organizations that are operated only to receive, hold, invest, and administer property and to make expenditures to or for the benefit of state and municipal colleges and universities
e) The United States or any state, the District of Columbia, a U.S. possession (including Puerto Rico), a political subdivision of a state or U.S. possession, or an Indian tribal government
f) Private operating foundations
g) Private nonoperating foundations that make qualifying distributions of 100% of contributions within 2 1/2 months following the year they receive the contribution

2) Non-50% limit organizations are all qualified charities that are not designated as 50% limit organizations.
a) They are generally other private organizations.

i. Charitable contribution deductions are subject to limitations.
1) The overall limitation on charitable deductions is 50% of AGI (applicable to the total of all charitable contributions during the year), but certain contributions may be individually limited to 30% or 20% of AGI, depending on the type of contribution given (refer to the next page).
2) Any donations that exceed this limitation can be carried forward and potentially deducted in the next 5 tax years.
3) Further limitations:
a) 30% limitation. This 30% limit applies to gifts to all qualified charitable organizations other than 50% limit organizations.
b) Special 30% limitation for capital gain property. A special 30% limitation applies to gifts of capital gain property given to 50% limit organizations.
i) It is only applicable if the donor elects NOT to reduce the fair market value of the donated property by the amount that would have been long-term capital gain if (s)he had sold the property.
ii) If the reduction is elected, then only the 50% limitation applies.
c) 20% limitation. This limitation applies to capital gain property donated to Non-50% limit charities. The limit is actually the lesser of 20% of AGI or 30% of AGI minus capital gain contributions to public charities.
d) In accounting for the different limitations, all donations subject to the 50% limit are considered before the donations subject to the 30% limit.
e) In carrying over excess contributions to subsequent tax years, the excess must be carried over to the appropriate limitation categories. If a contribution in the 30% category is in excess of the limit, the excess is carried over and subject to the 30% limitation in the next year.

j. The value of services provided to a charitable organization is not deductible.
1) However, out-of-pocket, unreimbursed expenses incurred in rendering the services are deductible.

k. The value of a ticket to a charitable event is a deductible contribution to the extent the purchase price exceeds the FMV of the event's admission.

l. Generally, a deduction is allowed in the year the contribution is paid, including amounts charged to a bank credit card.

m. Up to $50 per month of actual expenses incurred for maintaining a qualified student may be deducted if there is a written agreement with the sponsoring charitable organization.

Form of Property	Amount of Donation	Limitation
50% Limit Organizations (Mainly Public)		
Cash	Cash amount	50% AGI
Capital Gain Property	FMV (elect not to reduce FMV by potential long-term capital gain)	30% AGI (special limit)
• Tangible personal property unrelated to donee's purpose	Lower of FMV or AB	50% AGI
• Election to reduce property to adjusted basis	Lower of FMV or AB	50% AGI
Ordinary Income Property	Lower of FMV or AB	50% AGI
Services	Unreimbursed expenses	50% AGI
Non-50% Limit Organizations (Mainly Private)		
Cash	Cash amount	30% AGI (regular limit)
Capital Gain Property	Lower of FMV or AB	Lesser of: 20% AGI or excess of 30% AGI over contributions to public charities
Ordinary Income Property	Lower of FMV or AB	30% AGI (regular limit)
Services	Unreimbursed expenses	30% AGI (regular limit)

10. **Casualty and Theft Losses**

a. Taxpayers who itemize may deduct a limited amount for losses to nonbusiness property that arise from theft, fire, or other casualty.

b. In general, the loss amount is the lesser of the decline in FMV or the AB minus insurance reimbursements.

c. Limitation.

1) Only the amount of each loss over $100 is deductible.
2) Only the aggregate amount of all losses in excess of 10% of AGI is deductible.
3) If the loss was covered by insurance, timely filing of an insurance claim is prerequisite to deduction.

d. If the net amount of all personal casualty gains and losses after applying the $100 limit (but before the 10%-of-AGI threshold) is positive, each gain or loss is treated as a capital gain or loss.

e. If the net amount is negative, the excess over 10% of AGI is deductible as an itemized deduction.

f. The cost of appraising a casualty loss is treated as a cost to determine tax liability (a miscellaneous itemized deduction subject to the 2%-of-AGI exclusion).

g. The cost of insuring a personal asset is a nondeductible personal expense.

11. **Other Miscellaneous Deductions**

a. The following expenses are deductible as miscellaneous itemized deductions (not subject to 2% limit) and are reported on line 28, Schedule A (Form 1040):

1) Amortizable premium on taxable bonds
2) Casualty and theft losses from income-producing property
3) Federal estate tax on income in respect of a decedent
4) Gambling losses up to the amount of gambling winnings
5) Impairment-related work expenses of persons with disabilities
6) Repayments of more than $3,000 under a claim of right
7) Unrecovered investment in a pension

Stop and review! You have completed the outline for this subunit. Study multiple-choice questions 1 through 16 beginning on page 202.

5.2 JOB EXPENSES AND CERTAIN MISCELLANEOUS DEDUCTIONS

1. **Overview**
   a. These itemized deductions are subject to a 2%-of-AGI exclusion.
   b. Only that portion of the aggregate amount of these deductions that exceeds the threshold amount of 2% of AGI may be deducted from AGI.
   c. Any surplus cannot be carried forward to a succeeding year.
   d. The three categories of these itemized deductions are unreimbursed employee expenses, tax preparation fees, and other expenses.
2. **Unreimbursed Employee Expenses**
   a. Employee expenditures **not reimbursed** by the employer are itemized deductions. These expenses are deductible because services as an employee are considered trade or business.
      1) Employee travel away from home (including meals and lodging)
         a) **Travel expenses** include transportation, lodging, and meal expenses incurred in an employment-related context. To qualify for a deduction, the taxpayer must be away from his or her tax home overnight, and the purpose of the trip must be connected with the taxpayer's business.
         b) Only 50% of meals are deductible.
         c) If the employee's meal expenses are reimbursed by his or her employer and the reimbursement is not treated as compensation, the employer's deduction is limited to 50% of the expenses.
         d) If the employee's meal expenses are reimbursed by his or her employer and treated as compensation, the employee's deduction is limited to 50% of the expenses.
            i) Employers are not subject to the 50% limit to the extent they treat the reimbursement as compensation to employees.
      2) A new rule allows for lodging deductions when not traveling away from home, if qualified under one of two tests or rules.
         a) The deduction is allowed if all the facts and circumstances indicate the lodging is for carrying on a taxpayer's trade or business. One factor under this test is whether the taxpayer incurs an expense because of a bona fide condition or requirement of employment imposed by the taxpayer's employer.
         b) A safe harbor rule applies if
            i) The lodging is necessary for the individual to participate fully in, or be available for, a bona fide business meeting, conference, training activity, or other business function;
            ii) The lodging is for a period that does not exceed 5 calendar days and does not recur more frequently than once per calendar quarter;
            iii) The employee's employer requires the employee to remain at the activity or function overnight (if the individual is an employee); and
            iv) The lodging is not lavish or extravagant under the circumstances and does not provide any significant element of personal pleasure, recreation, or benefit.

3) Employee transportation expenses
   a) **Transportation expenses** include taxi fares, automobile expenses, tolls and parking fees, and airfare.
   b) These expenses are treated as travel expenses if the employee is away from home overnight. Otherwise, they are transportation expenses.
   c) Commuting costs are nondeductible.
   d) Actual automobile expenses may be used for the deduction, or the taxpayer may use the standard mileage rate.
      i) The standard mileage rate is $.575 per mile for 2015, plus parking fees and tolls.
      ii) Actual expenses must be allocated between business use and personal use of the automobile. A deduction is allowed only for the business use.
   e) Reimbursements for transportation from an employer not exceeding $.575 per mile for 2015 must be adequately substantiated by a record of time, place, and business purpose.
4) Outside salesperson expenses
5) Employee entertainment expenses
   a) **Entertainment expenses** are subject to the 50% limitation and are deductible only if they are directly related to or associated with the taxpayer's employment.
6) Employee home office expenses
7) Employee uniforms (provided they are not usable away from work)
8) Union dues and initiation fees
9) Professional dues and memberships
10) Subscriptions to business journals
11) Job-seeking expenses (in the same business)
12) Education expenses
   a) **Education expenses** may be deductible only if incurred to maintain or improve skills that are required in the taxpayer's current employment context or if incurred to meet legal requirements or employer requirements.
   b) In contrast, the expense of education to enter a trade, business, or profession or to meet the minimum education requirements is not deductible, even if state law requires the education.

3. **Tax Preparation Fees**

a. Tax preparation expenses include the following:
   1) Return preparation: manuals, legal and accounting advice, preprinted forms or tax packages, but not time spent preparing one's own return
   2) Representation in proceedings with the IRS
   3) Accountant and attorney fees to obtain a letter ruling
   4) Appraisal fees relating to the resolution of tax issues
   5) Contesting tax liability of another (if the tax liability is also personal to the taxpayer)
   6) Fees paid for filing the tax return electronically

4. **Other Expenses**

a. Other expenses include the following:

1) **Investment expenses**

a) Safe-deposit box rental fees when the box is used to store income-producing securities or investment-related documents

b) Subscriptions to investment journals

c) Investment counsel fees

d) Custodial fees on an IRA

2) Legal fees to collect alimony are cost for the collection of income deductible and subject to 2%-of-AGI floor.

3) **Hobby expenses**

a) A hobby is an activity for which profit is not a primary motive. Some hobbies, however, do generate income. Hobby expenses may be deducted, but only to the extent of the hobby's income.

b) If expenses exceed the income of a hobby, the expenses must be deducted in the following order:

i) Expenses that are deductible even if not incurred in a trade, business, or investment activity (e.g., taxes, interest)

ii) Expenses that do not reduce the tax basis of any of the hobby's assets (e.g., utilities)

iii) Expenses that reduce the tax basis of the hobby's assets (e.g., depreciation)

c) The amount of expenses that do not exceed the hobby's gross income are deductions from AGI. Items ii) and iii) above are miscellaneous itemized deductions subject to the 2%-of-AGI floor.

5. **Summary of Itemized Deductions Subject to 2%-of-AGI Exclusion**

a. Hobby expenses (other than taxes and interest)
b. Unreimbursed employee expenses
c. Tax preparation fees
d. Investment expenses

NOTE: A convenient mnemonic to help remember the itemized deductions subject to 2%-of-AGI exclusion is Harry Uses Tax Information.

6. **Summary of Employee Expenditures Subject to 2%-of-AGI Exclusion**

a. Home office expenses
b. Union dues
c. Professional dues and memberships
d. Uniforms
e. Job-seeking expenses (in the same business)
f. Entertainment expenses
g. Transportation expenses
h. Subscriptions to business journals
i. Travel expenses
j. Outside salesperson expenses
k. Education expenses

NOTE: A mnemonic to help remember the employee expenditures subject to 2%-of-AGI exclusion is Harry Usually Prefers Using Journal Entries To Show Total Operating Expenses.

7. **Overall Limitation**

   a. In 2015, married taxpayers filing a joint return with AGI that exceeds $309,900 ($284,050 if head of household, $258,250 if single, and $154,950 if married filing separately) must reduce the aggregate amount of their itemized deductions. The amount of the reduction is the lesser of 80% of otherwise allowable itemized deductions or 3% of the amount by which AGI exceeds the threshold.

   b. The overall limitation does **not** apply to deductions for the following:

      1) Medical expenses
      2) Investment interest expenses
      3) Casualty or theft losses
      4) Gambling losses (to the extent of gains)

8. **Recovery of Tax Benefits**

   a. Recovery of a tax benefit item is generally included in gross income.

   b. The recovered amount is included in income to the extent total allowable itemized deductions (for the applicable year) exceed the standard deduction (for the same year).

Stop and review! You have completed the outline for this subunit. Study multiple-choice questions 17 through 19 beginning on page 207.

5.3 TAX CREDITS

1. **Overview**

   a. Tax credits are used to achieve policy objectives, such as encouraging energy conservation or providing tax relief to low-income taxpayers. A $1 credit reduces gross tax liability by $1. Most credits are nonrefundable, meaning that once tax liability reaches zero, no more credits can be taken to produce refunds. However, there are several refundable credits, including taxes withheld and the Earned Income Credit.

2. **Nonrefundable Personal Credits**

   a. These credits include the

      1) Foreign Tax Credit
      2) Child and Dependent Care Credit
      3) Lifetime Learning Credit
      4) Retirement Savings Contribution Credit
      5) Child Tax Credit
      6) Credit for the Elderly or the Disabled
      7) General Business Credit
      8) Adoption Credit

   b. **Foreign Tax Credit.** This an alternative to deduction of the tax. The credit is equal to the lesser of

      1) Foreign taxes paid/accrued during the tax year or
      2) The portion of U.S. tax liability (before credits) attributed to all foreign-earned income.

$$FTC = U.S.\ income\ tax^{1} \times \frac{Foreign\ source\ taxable\ income^{2}}{Worldwide\ taxable\ income}$$

[1] Before the FTC
[2] Not more than worldwide TI

         a) If the credit is limited to the amount in 2) above, unused foreign tax credits will equal the difference between 1) and 2).

         b) The unused credits can be carried back for 1 year and then carried forward for 10 years.

c. **Child and Dependent Care Credit.** A taxpayer is eligible for this credit only if 1) and 2) below are satisfied.

1) Child and dependent care expenses are incurred to enable a taxpayer to maintain gainful employment.

a) The expenses may be incurred when the taxpayer is employed or actively seeking employment.

2) The taxpayer provides more than half the cost of maintaining a household for a dependent under age 13 or an incapacitated spouse or dependent.

a) Qualifying expenses include household services such as babysitting, housekeeping, and nursing. Outside services, such as day care facilities, must be in qualified facilities. Outside expenses for the care of an incapacitated spouse or dependent qualify only if the individual spends more than 8 hours a day in the taxpayer's home.

b) Total child and dependent care expenses cannot exceed the taxpayer's earned income. For married taxpayers, the income for this limitation is the smaller income of the two.

i) If one of the spouses is a full-time student at an educational institution or is unable to care for himself or herself, (s)he is considered to have earned $250 per month if there is one qualifying individual and $500 per month if there are two or more qualifying individuals.

c) Child and dependent care expenses are limited to $3,000 for one qualifying individual and $6,000 for two or more individuals.

d) The credit is equal to 35% of the child and dependent care expenses. This rate is reduced by 1% (but not below 20%) for each $2,000 (or part thereof) by which AGI exceeds $15,000. Therefore, taxpayers with AGI over $43,000 will have a credit of 20%.

d. The **Lifetime Learning Credit** is 20% of qualified tuition expenses paid by the taxpayer. The maximum credit allowed per year is $2,000 and is limited to 20% of the first $10,000 of expenses.

1) The Lifetime Learning Credit phases out for AGI between $55,000 and $65,000 for singles and between $110,000 and $130,000 on a joint return.

2) The Lifetime Learning Credit is available in years that the American Opportunity Credit is not claimed with respect to the same student.

3) The Lifetime Learning Credit is available for an unlimited number of years and can be used for both graduate- and undergraduate-level courses.

e. **Retirement Savings Contribution Credit.** Unlike most other tax topics allowing a credit or deduction, this credit is in addition to the exclusion or deduction from GI for qualified contributions. In general, a taxpayer may claim a credit for an eligible contribution to an eligible retirement plan.

1) AGI limit is $30,500 ($61,000 MFJ, $45,750 HH) in 2015.
2) The maximum credit is 50% of $2,000 contribution (i.e., $1,000).

f. **Child Tax Credit**

1) Taxpayers who have qualifying children are entitled to the Child Tax Credit of $1,000 per child.

a) **Qualifying child** is defined as the taxpayer's child, stepchild, sibling, step-sibling, or a descendant of any of these, or an eligible foster child (1) who is a U.S. citizen or resident alien, (2) for whom the taxpayer may claim a dependency exemption, and (3) who is less than 17 years old as of the close of the tax year.

b) The credit is allowed only for tax years consisting of 12 months.

2) The credit begins to phase out when modified AGI reaches $110,000 for joint filers, $55,000 for married filing separately, and $75,000 for single filers. The credit is reduced by $50 for each $1,000 of modified AGI above the thresholds.

g. **Elderly or Disabled Credit.** An individual may be eligible for this credit if (s)he was age 65 before the close of the tax year or retired before the close of the tax year due to a total and permanent disability.

1) The credit is equal to 15% multiplied by the initial base amount, which is

a) $5,000 for single filers
b) $7,500 for married filing jointly (both aged 65 or older)
c) $3,750 for married filing separately

2) The initial base amount is reduced by the following:

a) Tax-exempt Social Security benefits
b) Pension or annuity benefits excluded from gross income
c) Disability income if under 65
d) One-half the excess of AGI over

i) $7,500 for single
ii) $10,000 for married filing jointly
iii) $5,000 for married filing separately

3) A married person filing separately who lives with the spouse at any time during the year may not claim the credit.

h. **General Business Credit.** The General Business Credit (GBC) is a set of several credits commonly available to businesses. The GBC includes credits for investment, research, work opportunity, welfare-to-work, low-income housing, alternate motor vehicle and alcohol fuels, among others.

1) Overall limit. The GBC is limited to net income tax minus the greater of the tentative minimum tax or 25% of net regular tax over $25,000.

On Form 1040, the regular tax (line 44) is the tax computed on taxable income. The income tax (line 47) is the regular tax (line 44) plus the AMT (line 45) plus excess advance premium tax credit repayment (line 46). The net income tax is the income tax (line 47) minus the nonrefundable credits other than the General Business Credit. The General Business Credit will not be available when the alternative minimum tax exceeds the regular tax.

EXAMPLE

The taxpayer has a regular tax of $60,000 and a tentative minimum tax of $57,000. The taxpayer also has $10,000 of potential general business credits. Since the regular tax exceeds the tentative minimum tax, there is no alternative minimum tax. The taxpayer is allowed a General Business Credit computed as follows:

$60,000	Regular tax
(0)	Alternative minimum tax
$60,000	Income tax
(0)	Nonrefundable credits other than General Business Credit
$60,000	Net income tax
(57,000)	Greater of tentative minimum tax or 25% of net regular tax over $25,000
$ 3,000	General Business Credit

a) Net income tax is the sum of regular income tax and minimum tax liability, reduced by nonrefundable credits other than those that comprise the General Business Credit.

b) Tentative minimum tax is an amount used in computing the alternative minimum tax.

c) Net regular tax is the taxpayer's regular income tax liability (i.e., without alternative minimum tax) reduced by nonrefundable credits.

d) Excess over the limit may be allowable as a current deduction to the extent it is attributable to the Work Opportunity Tax Credit and the Alcohol Fuels Credit.

e) Any excess of the combined GBC over the limit (and not allowed as a current deduction) may be carried back 1 year and forward 20 as a credit. It is carried to the earliest year to which it could be used, then to the next, and so on.

2) **Work Opportunity Tax Credit (WOTC).** Employers may take a credit equal to 40% (reduced to 25% for employment of more than 120 hours but less than 400) of the first $6,000 paid to employees from certain targeted groups who work at least 400 hours ($10,000 for LT Family Assistance Recipients and $3,000 for Qualified Summer Youth Employees).

a) The maximum credit is $2,400 ($6,000 × 0.40) [$4,000 for LT Family Assistance Recipients ($10,000 × 0.40) and $1,200 for Qualified Summer Youth Employees ($3,000 × 0.40)].

b) The credit is not available for an individual with less than 120 hours of service performed for the employer.

c) The second-year credit allowed only for LT Family Assistance Recipients is 50% of the first $10,000. The maximum credit for both years is $9,000 ($4,000 + $5,000).

i) Qualified wages include

- Remuneration for employment
- Amount received under accident and health plans
- Contributions by employers to accident and health plans
- Educational assistance
- Dependent care expenses

3) **Research Credit.** A credit is allowed for 20% of the amount by which the taxpayer's qualified research expenditures for a tax year exceed its base-period amount. Though expired, this provision is expected to be renewed for 2015. This course, including questions, assumes renewal.

i. **Adoption Credit.** A credit is allowed for qualified adoption expenses incurred by the taxpayer.

1) Qualified adoption expenses are reasonable and necessary adoption expenses, including adoption fees, court costs, attorney fees, and other directly related expenses.

2) The maximum credit is $13,400 per qualified child, including a special-needs adoption.

a) The credit for a child with special needs is allowed regardless of the actual expenses paid or incurred in the year the adoption becomes final.

b) The amount of the credit allowable for any tax year is phased out for taxpayers with modified adjusted gross income (MAGI) in excess of $201,010 and is fully eliminated when MAGI reaches $241,010.

3) Any unused credit may be carried forward for up to 5 years and is not subject to the MAGI phaseout.

3. **Refundable Credits**

   a. A refundable credit is payable as a refund to the extent the credit amount exceeds tax otherwise due. Refundable credits include credits for the following:

      1) Taxes withheld
      2) Earned Income Credit
      3) Additional Child Tax Credit
      4) American Opportunity Credit

   b. Withholdings from employee wages for income tax are treated as refundable credit. Withholdings from wages for Social Security (FICA) tax are also refundable but only if an aggregate is withheld in excess of the maximum by two or more employers.

   c. **Earned Income Credit (EIC)**

      1) To qualify for Earned Income Tax Credit, the taxpayer and spouse (if married and filing a joint return), must meet all of the following criteria:

         a) Have a valid Social Security number
         b) Have earned income from employment, self-employment, or another source
         c) Cannot use the married filing separately filing status
         d) Must be a U.S. citizen or resident alien all year or a nonresident alien married to a U.S. citizen or resident alien and choose to file a joint return and be treated as a resident alien
         e) Cannot be the qualifying child (QC) of another person
         f) Have adjusted gross income and earned income less than the thresholds in 6) on the following page
         g) Have investment income less than $3,400 for 2015

      2) Earned income includes wages, salaries, tips, and net earnings from self-employment. Disqualified income includes interest, dividends, capital gain net income, net passive income, unemployment compensation, and any compensation that is not taxable (other than excluded combat-zone pay).

      3) An individual without a QC must have his or her principal residence in the U.S. for more than half of the tax year, be at least 25 but not over 64 years old, and not be a dependent of another.

      4) Taxpayers with one or more QCs are eligible for a higher applicable percentage and more lenient phase-out amounts. In order for a child to be a QC, three tests must be met:

         a) Relationship. The child must be related by birth or adoption or be an eligible foster child or stepchild.
         b) Residency. The taxpayer must provide the child's principal place of abode for more than half of the year.
         c) Age. The child must be under age 19 at the close of the tax year, be permanently disabled, or be a student under the age of 24.

5) Calculation of EIC. Multiply the individual's earned income by the applicable percentage.

EIC: Maximum Amounts, 2015

Type of Taxpayer	Applicable Percentage	Earned Income Amount	Maximum EIC
0 QC	7.65%	$ 6,580	$ 503
1 QC	34%	$ 9,880	$3,359
2 QC	40%	$13,870	$5,548
3 or more QC	45%	$13,870	$6,242

6) Phaseout of EIC. Decrease the maximum EIC by any phaseout, which is determined by multiplying the applicable phaseout percentage by the excess of the amount of the individual's AGI (or earned income, if greater) over the beginning amount. No EIC is available when AGI or earned income exceeds the completed phaseout amount.

EIC: Phaseout Amounts, 2015

Type of Taxpayer	Applicable Phaseout Percentage	Beginning Phaseout Amount	Beginning Phaseout Amt. for Joint Filers	Completed Phaseout Amount	Completed Phaseout Amt. for Joint Filers
0 QC	7.65%	$ 8,240	$13,760	$14,820	$20,340
1 QC	15.98%	$18,110	$23,630	$39,131	$44,651
2 QC	21.06%	$18,110	$23,630	$44,454	$49,974
3 or more QC	21.06%	$18,110	$23,630	$47,747	$53,267

d. **Additional Child Tax Credit**

1) This credit is available for certain taxpayers who get less than the full amount of the Child Tax Credit.
2) Through 2017, the credit is refundable up to the lesser of 15% of earned income in excess of $3,000, or the unclaimed portion of the nonrefundable credit. The refund is capped at the per child credit amount.

e. The **American Opportunity Credit** provides a maximum allowed credit of $2,500 per student per year for the first 4 years of post-secondary education. The credit may be used for qualified tuition and expenses.

1) The credit is computed as 100% of the first $2,000 of expenses and 25% of the second $2,000 of expenses.
2) Qualified expenses include required tuition, fees, and course materials. The credit is not allowed for room and board, activity fees, and any other fees or expenses not related to the student's academic course of instruction.
3) The credit phases out for AGI between $80,000 ($160,000 for joint filers) and $90,000 ($180,000 for joint filers). The amount of reduction in credit can be calculated as follows:

$$\text{Amount of credit allowed} \times \frac{\text{AGI} - \$80{,}000\ (\$160{,}000 \text{ for joint filers})}{\$10{,}000\ (\$20{,}000 \text{ for joint filers})}$$

4) Up to 40% of the credit is refundable.
5) The American Opportunity Credit is allowed per student while the Lifetime Learning Credit is calculated per taxpayer, without reference to the number of students.

Stop and review! You have completed the outline for this subunit. Study multiple-choice questions 20 through 23 beginning on page 208.

5.4 ALTERNATIVE MINIMUM TAX

1. The alternative minimum tax (AMT) is applied only if the tentative minimum tax exceeds the taxpayer's regular tax liability. Individuals use Form 6251 to calculate AMT. The formula below is an overview of the AMT.

AMT FORMULA

	Taxable income		
+	Tax preferences		
+	Personal exemptions		
+	Standard deduction if taxpayer does not itemize		
+/–	Certain other adjustments		
=	**Alternative minimum taxable income (AMTI)**		
–	Exemption amount	2015	25% phaseout for excess over
	Married filing jointly	$83,400	$158,900
	Single	$53,600	$119,200
	Married filing separately	$41,700	$ 79,450
=	**Alternative minimum tax base**		
×	Rate	2015	
	AMT base (married filing jointly)		
	First $185,400 ($92,700 MFS)	26%	
	Excess	28%	
=	**Tentative minimum tax**		
–	Regular income tax		
=	**Alternative minimum tax**		

2. Tax **preference** items receive favorable treatment in computing regular income tax, e.g., tax-exempt interest on private activity bonds (issued after 1986 but excluding those issued in 2009 and 2010), excess depletion, intangible, drilling cost, small business stock exclusion (purchased prior to September 28, 2010, or after December 31, 2015). (Though expired, the small business stock exclusion is expected to be extended for 2015.)
3. AMT **adjustments** represent either a limitation on itemized deductions or timing differences.
   a. Only certain itemized deductions are allowed in calculating the AMT. The following are not allowed:
      1) Miscellaneous itemized deductions
      2) State, local, and foreign income taxes
      3) Real and personal property taxes
   b. Medical expense deduction is allowed, but only for the amount that exceeds 10% of AGI as opposed to 7.5% for regular tax for those 65 or over.
   c. The standard deduction and personal exemptions are not allowed.
   d. Timing differences may permit the taxpayer to defer income temporarily or to accelerate deductions. Appropriate adjustments are made, taking into account the timing of different accounting methods.
      1) For example, the installment method is not allowed for sales of dealer property. Another example is when depreciation is taken under MACRS using the 200%-declining-balance method, and 150%-declining-balance method for AMT.
   e. Interest from refinancing in excess of the acquisition amount is not allowed (i.e., interest on loan amount qualified for regular itemized tax deduction, in excess of acquisition amount).
      1) Interest from home equity indebtedness may only be deducted if the indebtedness was incurred to acquire, construct, or substantially improve a qualified residence.

Form **6251**

Department of the Treasury
Internal Revenue Service (99)

Alternative Minimum Tax—Individuals

▶ **Information about Form 6251 and its separate instructions is at *www.irs.gov/form6251*.**
▶ **Attach to Form 1040 or Form 1040NR.**

OMB No. 1545-0074

2014

Attachment Sequence No. **32**

Name(s) shown on Form 1040 or Form 1040NR | **Your social security number**

Part I Alternative Minimum Taxable Income (See instructions for how to complete each line.)

1	If filing Schedule A (Form 1040), enter the amount from Form 1040, line 41, and go to line 2. Otherwise, enter the amount from Form 1040, line 38, and go to line 7. (If less than zero, enter as a negative amount.)	1	
2	Medical and dental. If you or your spouse was 65 or older, enter the **smaller** of Schedule A (Form 1040), line 4, **or** 2.5% (.025) of Form 1040, line 38. If zero or less, enter -0-	2	
3	Taxes from Schedule A (Form 1040), line 9	3	
4	Enter the home mortgage interest adjustment, if any, from line 6 of the worksheet in the instructions for this line	4	
5	Miscellaneous deductions from Schedule A (Form 1040), line 27	5	
6	If Form 1040, line 38, is $152,525 or less, enter -0-. Otherwise, see instructions	6	( )
7	Tax refund from Form 1040, line 10 or line 21	7	( )
8	Investment interest expense (difference between regular tax and AMT)	8	
9	Depletion (difference between regular tax and AMT)	9	
10	Net operating loss deduction from Form 1040, line 21. Enter as a positive amount	10	
11	Alternative tax net operating loss deduction	11	( )
12	Interest from specified private activity bonds exempt from the regular tax	12	
13	Qualified small business stock (7% of gain excluded under section 1202)	13	
14	Exercise of incentive stock options (excess of AMT income over regular tax income)	14	
15	Estates and trusts (amount from Schedule K-1 (Form 1041), box 12, code A)	15	
16	Electing large partnerships (amount from Schedule K-1 (Form 1065-B), box 6)	16	
17	Disposition of property (difference between AMT and regular tax gain or loss)	17	
18	Depreciation on assets placed in service after 1986 (difference between regular tax and AMT)	18	
19	Passive activities (difference between AMT and regular tax income or loss)	19	
20	Loss limitations (difference between AMT and regular tax income or loss)	20	
21	Circulation costs (difference between regular tax and AMT)	21	
22	Long-term contracts (difference between AMT and regular tax income)	22	
23	Mining costs (difference between regular tax and AMT)	23	
24	Research and experimental costs (difference between regular tax and AMT)	24	
25	Income from certain installment sales before January 1, 1987	25	( )
26	Intangible drilling costs preference	26	
27	Other adjustments, including income-based related adjustments	27	
28	**Alternative minimum taxable income.** Combine lines 1 through 27. (If married filing separately and line 28 is more than $242,450, see instructions.)	28	

Part II Alternative Minimum Tax (AMT)

29 Exemption. (If you were under age 24 at the end of 2014, see instructions.)

IF your filing status is . . .	**AND line 28 is not over . . .**	**THEN enter on line 29 . . .**
Single or head of household	$117,300	$52,800
Married filing jointly or qualifying widow(er)	156,500	82,100
Married filing separately	78,250	41,050

If line 28 is **over** the amount shown above for your filing status, see instructions. — 29

30	Subtract line 29 from line 28. If more than zero, go to line 31. If zero or less, enter -0- here and on lines 31, 33, and 35, and go to line 34	30	
31	• If you are filing Form 2555 or 2555-EZ, see instructions for the amount to enter. • If you reported capital gain distributions directly on Form 1040, line 13; you reported qualified dividends on Form 1040, line 9b; **or** you had a gain on both lines 15 and 16 of Schedule D (Form 1040) (as refigured for the AMT, if necessary), complete Part III on the back and enter the amount from line 64 here. • **All others:** If line 30 is $182,500 or less ($91,250 or less if married filing separately), multiply line 30 by 26% (.26). Otherwise, multiply line 30 by 28% (.28) and subtract $3,650 ($1,825 if married filing separately) from the result.	31	
32	Alternative minimum tax foreign tax credit (see instructions)	32	
33	Tentative minimum tax. Subtract line 32 from line 31	33	
34	Add Form 1040, line 44 (minus any tax from Form 4972), and Form 1040, line 46. Subtract from the result any foreign tax credit from Form 1040, line 48. If you used Schedule J to figure your tax on Form 1040, line 44, refigure that tax without using Schedule J before completing this line (see instructions)	34	
35	**AMT.** Subtract line 34 from line 33. If zero or less, enter -0-. Enter here and on Form 1040, line 45	35	

For Paperwork Reduction Act Notice, see your tax return instructions. Cat. No. 13600G Form **6251** (2014)

Form 6251 (2014) Page **2**

Part III **Tax Computation Using Maximum Capital Gains Rates**

Complete Part III only if you are required to do so by line 31 or by the Foreign Earned Income Tax Worksheet in the instructions.

36	Enter the amount from Form 6251, line 30. If you are filing Form 2555 or 2555-EZ, enter the amount from line 3 of the worksheet in the instructions for line 31	36	
37	Enter the amount from line 6 of the Qualified Dividends and Capital Gain Tax Worksheet in the instructions for Form 1040, line 44, or the amount from line 13 of the Schedule D Tax Worksheet in the instructions for Schedule D (Form 1040), whichever applies (as refigured for the AMT, if necessary) (see instructions). If you are filing Form 2555 or 2555-EZ, see instructions for the amount to enter	37	
38	Enter the amount from Schedule D (Form 1040), line 19 (as refigured for the AMT, if necessary) (see instructions). If you are filing Form 2555 or 2555-EZ, see instructions for the amount to enter	38	
39	If you did not complete a Schedule D Tax Worksheet for the regular tax or the AMT, enter the amount from line 37. Otherwise, add lines 37 and 38, and enter the **smaller** of that result or the amount from line 10 of the Schedule D Tax Worksheet (as refigured for the AMT, if necessary). If you are filing Form 2555 or 2555-EZ, see instructions for the amount to enter	39	
40	Enter the **smaller** of line 36 or line 39	40	
41	Subtract line 40 from line 36	41	
42	If line 41 is $182,500 or less ($91,250 or less if married filing separately), multiply line 41 by 26% (.26). Otherwise, multiply line 41 by 28% (.28) and subtract $3,650 ($1,825 if married filing separately) from the result . . . ▶	42	
43	Enter: • $73,800 if married filing jointly or qualifying widow(er), • $36,900 if single or married filing separately, or • $49,400 if head of household.	43	
44	Enter the amount from line 7 of the Qualified Dividends and Capital Gain Tax Worksheet in the instructions for Form 1040, line 44, or the amount from line 14 of the Schedule D Tax Worksheet in the instructions for Schedule D (Form 1040), whichever applies (as figured for the regular tax). If you did not complete either worksheet for the regular tax, enter the amount from Form 1040, line 43; if zero or less, enter -0-. If you are filing Form 2555 or 2555-EZ, see instructions for the amount to enter	44	
45	Subtract line 44 from line 43. If zero or less, enter -0-	45	
46	Enter the **smaller** of line 36 or line 37	46	
47	Enter the **smaller** of line 45 or line 46. This amount is taxed at 0%	47	
48	Subtract line 47 from line 46	48	
49	Enter: • $406,750 if single • $228,800 if married filing separately • $457,600 if married filing jointly or qualifying widow(er) • $432,200 if head of household	49	
50	Enter the amount from line 45	50	
51	Enter the amount from line 7 of the Qualified Dividends and Capital Gain Tax Worksheet in the instructions for Form 1040, line 44, or the amount from line 19 of the Schedule D Tax Worksheet, whichever applies (as figured for the regular tax). If you did not complete either worksheet for the regular tax, enter the amount from Form 1040, line 43; if zero or less, enter -0-. If you are filing Form 2555 or Form 2555-EZ, see instructions for the amount to enter	51	
52	Add line 50 and line 51	52	
53	Subtract line 52 from line 49. If zero or less, enter -0-	53	
54	Enter the smaller of line 48 or line 53	54	
55	Multiply line 54 by 15% (.15) . . . . ▶	55	
56	Add lines 47 and 54	56	
	If lines 56 and 36 are the same, skip lines 57 through 61 and go to line 62. Otherwise, go to line 57.		
57	Subtract line 56 from line 46	57	
58	Multiply line 57 by 20% (.20) . . . . ▶	58	
	If line 38 is zero or blank, skip lines 59 through 61 and go to line 62. Otherwise, go to line 59.		
59	Add lines 41, 56, and 57	59	
60	Subtract line 59 from line 36	60	
61	Multiply line 60 by 25% (.25) . . . . ▶	61	
62	Add lines 42, 55, 58, and 61	62	
63	If line 36 is $182,500 or less ($91,250 or less if married filing separately), multiply line 36 by 26% (.26). Otherwise, multiply line 36 by 28% (.28) and subtract $3,650 ($1,825 if married filing separately) from the result	63	
64	Enter the **smaller** of line 62 or line 63 here and on line 31. If you are filing Form 2555 or 2555-EZ, do not enter this amount on line 31. Instead, enter it on line 4 of the worksheet in the instructions for line 31 . .	64	

Form **6251** (2014)

EXAMPLE

A taxpayer over 65 with AGI of $100,000 and taxable income of $92,000 has the following return items:

- $10,500 medical expenses
- $5,000 mortgage interest paid
- $2,000 municipal bond interest received

This taxpayer's AMTI is calculated as follows:

AGI	$100,000
Exempt interest	2,000
Medical expense [$10,500 – ($100,000 × .10)]	(500)
Mortgage interest	(5,000)
AMTI	$ 96,500

Stop and review! You have completed the outline for this subunit. Study multiple-choice questions 24 through 26 on page 209.

5.5 LOSSES AND LIMITS

1. **Casualty and Theft Losses**

   a. The IRC allows deduction for losses caused by theft or casualties, whether business or personal.

   b. A casualty loss arises from a sudden, unexpected, or unusual event caused by an external force, such as fire, storm, shipwreck, earthquake, sonic boom, etc.

      1) Losses resulting from ordinary accidents are not deductible. Examples of these include dropping a vase or progressive deterioration, such as rust or insect damage.

   c. Theft includes robbery, larceny, etc. It may also include loss from extortion, blackmail, etc.

      1) Misplacing or losing items or having them confiscated by a foreign government is not considered theft.

   d. In general, the loss amount is the lesser of the decline in FMV or the AB minus insurance reimbursements.

      1) However, if business or investment property is completely lost or stolen, FMV is disregarded and AB is used to compute the loss.

   e. Reimbursement

      1) Only the amount of loss not compensated by insurance is deductible.
      2) Any excess recovered over the amount of property basis is gain.

   f. Timing

      1) A casualty loss is deductible in the tax year in which it occurs.
      2) A theft loss is deductible when it is discovered.

   g. Inventory

      1) The normal casualty and theft loss rules do not apply to inventory. The loss is accounted for by increasing COGS.

      2) Any insurance reimbursement is gross income.

   h. Business casualty losses are taken above-the-line; personal casualty losses are taken below-the-line.

2. **Disaster Areas**

   a. A taxpayer is subject to a special rule if (s)he sustains a loss from a federally declared disaster area.
   b. Disaster loss treatment is available when a personal residence is rendered unsafe due to the disaster in the area and is ordered to be relocated or demolished by the state or local government.
   c. The taxpayer has the option of deducting the loss on
      1) The return for the year in which the loss actually occurred or
      2) The preceding year's return (by filing an amended return).
   d. Revocation of the election may be made before the expiration of time for filing the return for the year of loss.
   e. A disaster loss deduction is computed the same as a casualty loss.
      1) If the disaster loss is claimed on the preceding year's return, the AGI limitation is based on the prior year's AGI.
   f. The loss is calculated on Form 4684, *Casualties and Thefts*, and carried over to Schedule A, *Itemized Deductions*.

3. **Capital Losses**

   a. Capital gain or loss realized on the sale or exchange of a capital asset is discussed in Study Unit 6, Subunit 3.
      1) An individual taxpayer may deduct net capital losses to the extent that they do not exceed the lesser of ordinary income or $3,000 ($1,500 if married filing separately).
      2) The individual may carry forward any excess capital losses indefinitely.

4. **Net Operating Loss (NOL)**

   a. A net operating loss occurs when business expenses exceed business income.
   b. The NOL is deductible when carried to a year in which there is taxable income.
      1) NOLs are first carried back for 2 years. Any remaining NOL is carried forward up to 20 years.
      2) The taxpayer can elect to forgo the carryback and start with the carryforward period.
   c. Although NOLs are typically business deductions, an individual may have an NOL.
      1) NOLs relating to casualty and theft losses for an individual may be carried back for 3 years.
      2) NOLs associated with federally declared disaster areas and incurred by a small business or a farmer may be carried back 3 years.
      3) NOLs attributable to farming business may be carried back for 5 years.
   d. Calculation
      1) Start with taxable income (a negative amount) and make the following adjustments:
         a) Add back NOLs either carried forward or back into the current tax year.
         b) Add back personal exemptions.
         c) Add back excess of nonbusiness deductions over nonbusiness income.
            i) For this purpose, nonbusiness deductions are
               - Alimony,
               - Contributions to self-employed retirement plans,
               - Loss from the sale of investment property, and
               - Either the standard deduction or all itemized deductions.

            NOTE: Business deductions include all (even personal) casualty losses.

ii) Nonbusiness income includes

- Interest,
- Dividends,
- Gain on the sale of investment property, and
- Treasure trove.

iii) Rents and wages are business income.

e. Capital Losses

1) The amount of capital loss (CL) included in the NOL of a noncorporate taxpayer is limited.

2) Before the limit is applied, the CL must be separated into business CL and nonbusiness CL.

3) Capital losses are included in the NOL only as follows:

a) Nonbusiness CL is deducted to the extent of nonbusiness capital gain (CG).

i) Any excess nonbusiness CL is not deductible.

b) If nonbusiness CG exceeds nonbusiness CL [in a) above], then such excess is applied against any excess of nonbusiness deductions over nonbusiness income.

c) If nonbusiness CG exceeds excess nonbusiness deductions [in b) above], then the excess nonbusiness CG may offset business CL.

i) Business CL may also be deducted to the extent of business CG.

EXAMPLE

For 2015, Sally realized a $30,000 net loss (sales of $200,000 less expenses of $230,000) from operating a sole proprietorship without regard to dispositions of property other than inventory. Other than this, the income tax return showed gross income of $10,000 ($4,500 of wages, $1,000 interest on personal savings, and a $4,500 long-term capital gain on business property). The excess of deductions over income was $30,300 ($10,000 gross income – $30,000 loss from business operations – $6,300 standard deduction – $4,000 personal exemption).

To compute Sally's NOL,
(1) Add back the $4,000 personal exemption amount and
(2) Add the $5,300 excess of nonbusiness deductions over nonbusiness income ($6,300 standard deduction – $1,000 interest).

Thus, Sally's NOL for the current tax year is $21,000 [$(30,300) "negative taxable income" + $4,000 + $5,300].

f. If the NOL is carried back, the taxpayer files for a tax refund, which may require a recomputation of taxable income.

g. An NOL carried forward is a deduction to arrive at AGI.

5. **At-Risk Rules**

a. The amount of a loss allowable as a deduction is limited to the amount a person has at risk in the activity.

b. A loss is the excess of deductions over gross income attributable to the activity.

c. The amount at risk and any deductible loss are calculated on Form 6198.

d. The rules apply to individuals, partners in partnerships, members in limited liability companies, shareholders of S corporations, trusts, estates, and certain closely held C corporations.

e. The rules are applied separately to each trade, business, or income-producing activity.

f. A person's amount at risk in an activity is determined at the close of the tax year.

1) A person's initial at-risk amount includes money contributed, the adjusted basis of property contributed, and borrowed amounts.

2) Recourse debt

a) A person's at-risk amount includes amounts borrowed only to the extent that, for the debt, the person has either personal liability or pledged property as security.

b) The at-risk amount does not include debt if one of the following applies:

i) Property pledged as security is used in the activity.

ii) Personal liability is protected against by insurance, guarantees, stop-loss agreements, or similar arrangements.

iii) The creditor is a person with an interest in the activity or one related to the taxpayer.

3) Nonrecourse debt is generally excluded from the amount at risk.

a) The amount at risk in the activity of holding real property includes qualified nonrecourse financing (QNRF).

b) In qualified nonrecourse financing, the taxpayer is not personally liable, but the financing is

i) Incurred in a real estate activity;

ii) Secured by the real property;

iii) Not convertible to an ownership interest; and

iv) Either from an unrelated third party, from a related party but on commercially reasonable terms, or guaranteed by a governmental entity.

g. Adjustments to an at-risk amount are made for events that vary the investors' economic risk of loss.

1) Add contributions of money and property (its AB), recourse debt increases, QNRF increase, and income from the activity.

2) Subtract distributions, liability reductions, and tax deductions allowable (at year end), but only to the extent they reduce the at-risk amount to zero.

a) If the amount at risk decreases below zero, previously allowed losses must be recaptured as income.

h. Disallowed losses are carried forward.

i. If a deduction would reduce basis in property and part or all of the deduction is disallowed by the at-risk rules, the basis is reduced anyway.

6. **Passive Activity Loss (PAL) Limitation Rules**

a. The amount of a loss attributable to a person's passive activities is allowable as a deduction or credit only against, and to the extent of, gross income or tax attributable to those passive activities (in the aggregate).

1) The excess is deductible or creditable in a future year, subject to the same limits.

b. The passive activity rules apply to individuals, estates, trusts (other than grantor trusts), personal service corporations, and closely held corporations.

1) Although passive activity rules do not apply to grantor trusts, partnerships, and S corporations directly, they do apply to the owners of these entities.

c. A passive activity is either rental activity or a trade or business in which the person does not materially participate.

1) A taxpayer materially participates in an activity during a tax year if (s)he satisfies one of the following tests:

a) Participates more than 500 hours.

b) The taxpayer's participation constitutes substantially all of the participation in the activity.

c) Participates more than 100 hours and exceeds the participation of any other individual.

d) Materially participated in the activity for any 5 years of the preceding 10 years before the year in question.

e) Materially participated in a personal service activity for any 3 years preceding the year in question.

f) Participates in the activity on a regular, continuous, and substantial basis.

d. Passive activity rules do not apply to

1) Active income/loss/credit

2) Portfolio income/loss/credit

3) Casualty and theft losses, vacation home rental, qualified home mortgage interest, business use of home, or a working interest in an oil or gas well held through an entity that does not limit the person's liability

e. Rental Real Estate

1) All rental activity is passive.

2) However, a person who actively participates in rental real estate activity is entitled to deduct up to $25,000 of losses from the passive activity from other than passive income.

3) This exception to the general PAL limitation rule applies to a person who

a) Actively participates in the activity

b) Owns 10% or more of the activity (by value) for the entire year

c) Has MAGI of less than $150,000 [phaseout begins at $100,000; shown in 4)a) below]

4) $25,000 of a tax year loss from rental real estate activities in excess of passive activity gross income is deductible against portfolio or active income.

a) The $25,000 limit is reduced by 50% of the person's MAGI (i.e., AGI without regard to PALs, Social Security benefits, and qualified retirement contributions [e.g., IRAs]) over $100,000.

b) Excess rental real estate PALs are suspended. They are treated as other PALs carried over.

5) Active participation is a less stringent requirement than material participation.

a) It is met with participation in management decisions or arranging for others to provide services (such as repairs).

b) There will not be active participation if at any time during the period there is ownership of less than 10% of the interest in the property (including the spouse's interest).

6) Real property trades or businesses

a) The passive activity loss rules do not apply to certain taxpayers who are involved in real property trades or businesses.

b) An individual may avoid passive activity loss limitation treatment on a rental real estate activity if two requirements are met:

i) More than 50% of the individual's personal services performed during the year are performed in the real property trades or businesses in which the individual materially participates.

ii) The individual performs more than 750 hours of service in the real property trades or businesses in which the individual materially participates.

c) This provision also applies to a closely held C corporation if 50% of gross receipts for the tax year are from real property trades or businesses in which the corporation materially participated.

d) Any deduction allowed under this rule is not taken into consideration in determining the taxpayer's AGI for purposes of the phaseout of the $25,000 deduction.

e) If 50% or less of the personal services performed are in real property trades or businesses, the individual will be subject to the passive activity limitation rules.

f. Suspension. A PAL not allowable in the current tax year is carried forward indefinitely and treated as a deduction in subsequent tax years.

g. PALs continue to be treated as PALs even after the activity ceases to be passive in a subsequent tax year, except that it may also be deducted against income from that activity.

h. Disposition of a Passive Activity

1) Suspended (and current-year) losses from a passive activity become deductible in full in the year the taxpayer completely disposes of all interest in the passive activity.

2) The loss is deductible first against net income or gain from the taxpayer's other passive activities. The remainder of the loss, if any, is then treated as nonpassive.

7. **Hobby Losses**

a. Hobby expenses can be deducted to the extent the hobby generates income.

Stop and review! You have completed the outline for this subunit. Study multiple-choice questions 27 through 30 on page 210.

QUESTIONS

5.1 Standard and Itemized Deductions

1. In 2015, Welch paid the following expenses:

Premiums on an insurance policy against loss of earnings due to sickness or accident	$3,000
Physical therapy after spinal surgery	2,000
Premium on an insurance policy that covers reimbursement for the cost of prescription drugs	500

In 2015, Welch recovered $1,500 of the $2,000 that she paid for physical therapy through insurance reimbursement from a group medical policy paid for by her employer. Disregarding the adjusted gross income percentage threshold, what amount could be claimed on Welch's 2015 income tax return for medical expenses?

A. $4,000

B. $3,500

C. $1,000

D. $500

Answer (C) is correct.

REQUIRED: The amount of deductible medical expenses.

DISCUSSION: Medical expenses are deductible to the extent they exceed 10% (7.5% for age 65 and over) of AGI. Medical care expenses include amounts paid for the diagnosis, cure, medication, treatment, or prevention of a disease or physical handicap or for the purpose of affecting any structure or function of the body. The term medical care also includes amounts paid for insurance covering medical care. However, the amount deductible for expenses incurred for medical care is reduced by the amount of reimbursements. The cost of insurance against loss of earnings is not deductible. Therefore, deductible medical expenses are $1,000 [($2,000 – $1,500 reimbursement) + $500].

Answer (A) is incorrect. The cost of insurance against loss of earnings is not deductible. Answer (B) is incorrect. The cost of insurance against loss of earnings is not deductible. The cost of insurance for medical care, which includes the cost of prescription drugs, is deductible. Answer (D) is incorrect. The cost of insurance covering medical expenses is deductible.

2. Poole, 45 years old and single, is in the 15% tax bracket. He had 2015 adjusted gross income of $30,000. The following information applies to Poole:

Medical expenses	$11,000
Standard deduction	6,300
Personal exemption	4,000

The relevant tax brackets are

Income	Tax
≤ $9,225	10%
$9,225 to $37,450	15%

Poole wishes to minimize his income tax. What is Poole's 2015 total income tax rounded to the nearest dollar?

A. $3,116

B. $2,494

C. $2,239

D. $1,789

Answer (C) is correct.

REQUIRED: The income tax of an unmarried individual.

DISCUSSION: Taxable income is defined as adjusted gross income minus the standard deduction (or total itemized deductions, if greater) and the deduction for personal exemptions. For a single taxpayer in 2015, the basic standard deduction is $6,300. Qualifying medical expenses in excess of 10% of AGI may be deducted as an itemized deduction. Poole's income tax is computed as follows:

Medical expenses	$11,000
Less: 10% of AGI ($30,000 × .10)	(3,000)
Allowable medical expenses	$ 8,000
Use the greater of	
Allowable itemized deductions or	$ 8,000
Standard deduction	6,300
AGI	$30,000
Itemized deductions	(8,000)
Personal exemption	(4,000)
Taxable income	$18,000
Tax Computation:	
First: $9,225 × .10	$ 923
Balance: $8,775 × .15	1,316
Income tax	$ 2,239

Answer (A) is incorrect. The AGI must be reduced by the $4,000 personal exemption and $8,000, the greater of the standard deduction or itemized deductions, before calculating the tax. Answer (B) is incorrect. The itemized deductions of $8,000 should be used because they exceed the standard deduction. The itemized deductions consist of the allowable medical expenses [$11,000 – ($30,000 × 10%)]. Answer (D) is incorrect. The medical expenses must be reduced by 10% of AGI to find the allowable itemized deductions.

3. Which of the following requirements must be met in order for a single individual to qualify for an additional standard deduction?

	Must Be Age 65 or Older or Blind	Must Support Dependent Child or Aged Parent
A.	Yes	Yes
B.	No	No
C.	Yes	No
D.	No	Yes

Answer (C) is correct.

REQUIRED: The requirement for a single individual to qualify for the additional standard deduction.

DISCUSSION: An additional standard deduction is allowed for a taxpayer if, during the year, the taxpayer is age 65 or over or blind. The respective amounts are doubled if the taxpayer is both elderly and blind. Support of a dependent is a condition of an additional personal exemption amount, not an increase to the standard deduction.

Answer (A) is incorrect. The additional standard deduction amount is not available to single individuals merely supporting a dependent child or aged parent. Answer (B) is incorrect. The additional standard deduction amount is available to individuals 65 (or over) or blind. Answer (D) is incorrect. The additional standard deduction amount is available for taxpayers who are age 65 or over or blind.

4. During 2015, Hall spent a total of $1,000 for state lottery tickets. Her lottery winnings for 2015 totaled $200. Hall's lottery transactions should be reported as follows:

	Other Income on Page 1	Schedule A -- Itemized Deductions: Subject to 2% AGI Floor	Schedule A -- Itemized Deductions: Not Subject to 2% AGI Floor
A.	$0	$0	$0
B.	$200	$0	$200
C.	$200	$200	$0
D.	$200	$0	$0

Answer (B) is correct.

REQUIRED: The correct reporting for income and deductions from lottery transactions.

DISCUSSION: Gambling losses are deductible to the extent of gambling winnings as an itemized deduction not subject to the 2%-of-AGI floor.

Answer (A) is incorrect. Hall will be allowed a deduction as he has gambling winnings. Answer (C) is incorrect. Gambling losses are deductible but not subject to the 2%-of-AGI floor. Answer (D) is incorrect. Gambling losses are deductible to the extent of gambling winnings.

5. Moore, a single taxpayer, had $50,000 in adjusted gross income for 2015. During 2015, she contributed $18,000 to her church. She had a $10,000 charitable contribution carryover from her 2014 church contribution. What was the maximum amount of properly substantiated charitable contributions that Moore could claim as an itemized deduction for 2015?

A. $10,000

B. $18,000

C. $25,000

D. $28,000

Answer (C) is correct.

REQUIRED: The amount of deductible charitable contributions.

DISCUSSION: Properly substantiated cash contributions by individuals to qualified charities are limited to 50% of the taxpayer's AGI, or $25,000 in this case. The carryover is deductible this year to the extent that the total deduction does not exceed the 50%-of-AGI limit, or $7,000 ($25,000 – $18,000).

Answer (A) is incorrect. The contribution made this year is fully deductible. The carryover is deductible to the extent that the total charitable contribution deduction does not exceed 50% of AGI. Answer (B) is incorrect. The carryover is deductible to the extent that the total charitable contribution deduction does not exceed 50% of AGI. Answer (D) is incorrect. The total charitable contribution is limited to 50% of a taxpayer's AGI.

6. The Browns borrowed $20,000, secured by their home, to pay their son's college tuition. At the time of the loan, the fair market value of their home was $400,000, and it was unencumbered by other debt. The interest on the loan qualifies as

A. Deductible personal interest.

B. Deductible qualified residence interest.

C. Nondeductible interest.

D. Investment interest expense.

Answer (B) is correct.

REQUIRED: The nature and deductibility of interest.

DISCUSSION: Qualified residence interest is deductible. It is interest paid or accrued during the tax year on home acquisition or home equity indebtedness. Home equity indebtedness is all debt other than acquisition debt that is secured by a qualified residence to the extent it does not exceed the fair market value of the residence, reduced by any acquisition indebtedness.

Answer (A) is incorrect. Personal interest is generally not deductible. Answer (C) is incorrect. The interest is deductible. Answer (D) is incorrect. It is qualified residence interest, not investment interest.

7. In 2015, Smith paid $6,000 to the tax collector of Big City for realty taxes on a two-family house owned by Smith's mother. Of this amount, $2,800 covered back taxes for 2014, and $3,200 covered 2015 taxes. Smith resides on the second floor of the house, and his mother resides on the first floor. In Smith's itemized deductions on his 2015 return, what amount was Smith entitled to claim for realty taxes?

A. $6,000

B. $3,200

C. $3,000

D. $0

Answer (D) is correct.

REQUIRED: The amount of deductible property taxes.

DISCUSSION: Taxes may be deducted only by the person on whom they are legally levied. Smith does not own the house, therefore none of the taxes paid can be deducted on his tax return and the payment is treated as a gift to Smith's mother. Smith's mother is entitled to the deduction only if she pays the taxes.

Answer (A) is incorrect. The total amount of taxes are not levied on Smith. Answer (B) is incorrect. Had Smith owned the property, the deduction would not have been limited to current taxes. Assuming he is a cash-basis taxpayer, the deductions are taken when amounts are paid. Answer (C) is incorrect. The IRC generally does not allow a deduction for paying the liability of another. It is treated as a gift.

8. In 2015, Joan Frazer's residence was totally destroyed by fire. The property had an adjusted basis and a fair market value of $130,000 before the fire. During 2015, Frazer received insurance reimbursement of $120,000 for the destruction of her home. Frazer's 2015 adjusted gross income was $70,000. Frazer had no casualty gains during the year. What amount of the fire loss was Frazer entitled to claim as an itemized deduction on her 2015 tax return?

A. $2,900

B. $3,000

C. $9,900

D. $10,000

Answer (A) is correct.

REQUIRED: The amount of the deductible casualty loss.

DISCUSSION: A personal casualty loss is limited to the amount of the loss exceeding 10% of AGI and a $100 nondeductible floor. The casualty loss is $10,000 ($130,000 FMV – $120,000 reimbursement). The itemized deduction is $2,900 ($10,000 loss – $7,000 10% of AGI limit – $100 floor).

Answer (B) is incorrect. It does not take into account the nondeductible floor. Answer (C) is incorrect. The loss can only be deducted to the extent that it exceeds 10% of AGI. Answer (D) is incorrect. It ignores the AGI limit and floor.

9. The 2015 deduction by an individual taxpayer for interest on investment indebtedness is

A. Limited to investment interest paid in 2015.

B. Limited to the taxpayer's 2015 interest income.

C. Limited to the taxpayer's 2015 net investment income.

D. Not limited.

Answer (C) is correct.

REQUIRED: The true statement concerning limits on deductibility of interest on investment indebtedness.

DISCUSSION: The deduction for interest on investment indebtedness is limited to the amount of net investment income for the taxable year. Any disallowed investment interest may be carried over and treated as investment interest paid or accrued in the succeeding taxable year.

Answer (A) is incorrect. Interest on investment indebtedness is deductible only to the extent of net investment income for the taxable year, not investment interest paid. Answer (B) is incorrect. The deduction for interest on investment indebtedness is not tied to general interest income. Answer (D) is incorrect. The deduction for interest on investment indebtedness is limited.

10. Jimet, an unmarried taxpayer, qualified to itemize 2015 deductions. Jimet's 2015 adjusted gross income was $30,000, and he made a $2,000 cash donation directly to a needy family. In 2015, Jimet also donated stock, valued at $3,000, to his church. Jimet had purchased the stock 4 months earlier for $1,500. What was the maximum amount of the charitable contribution allowable as an itemized deduction on Jimet's 2015 income tax return?

A. $0

B. $1,500

C. $2,000

D. $5,000

Answer (B) is correct.

REQUIRED: The maximum allowed charitable contribution deduction.

DISCUSSION: A deduction is allowed for contributions to a qualified organization. Therefore, no deduction is allowed for the contribution to the family. However, a deduction is available for the donation of stock in the amount of $1,500. Since the stock has not been held long term, it is ordinary income property, and the deduction is equal to the lesser of FMV or AB.

Answer (A) is incorrect. A deduction is allowed. Answer (C) is incorrect. The cash may not be deducted. Answer (D) is incorrect. Only the stock is allowed as a deduction, and the deduction amount is $1,500.

11. Alan Curtis, who is single, had an adjusted gross income of $40,000 in 2015, and he used the standard deduction in his 2015 return. During 2015, Alan contributed $300 to the building fund of State University. What amount was deductible for contributions in Alan's 2015 return?

A. $0

B. $50

C. $100

D. $300

Answer (A) is correct.

REQUIRED: The deduction for charitable contributions when the standard deduction is claimed.

DISCUSSION: Charitable contributions are allowed as an itemized deduction. Itemized deductions are an election in lieu of the standard deduction.

Answer (B) is incorrect. No deduction is allowed for charitable contributions when the standard deduction is claimed. Answer (C) is incorrect. No deduction is allowed for charitable contributions when the standard deduction is claimed. Answer (D) is incorrect. Alan would only be allowed this deduction if he chose to itemize on his tax return.

12. Smith paid the following unreimbursed medical expenses:

Dentist and eye doctor fees	$ 5,000
Contact lenses	500
Facial cosmetic surgery to improve Smith's personal appearance (surgery is unrelated to personal injury or congenital deformity)	10,000
Premium on disability insurance policy to pay him if he is injured and unable to work	2,000

What is the total amount of Smith's tax-deductible medical expenses before the adjusted gross income limitation?

A. $17,500

B. $15,500

C. $7,500

D. $5,500

Answer (D) is correct.

REQUIRED: The amount of deductible medical expenses.

DISCUSSION: Medical expenses are deductible to the extent they exceed 10% (7.5% for age 65 and over) of AGI. Medical care expenses include amounts paid for the diagnosis, cure, medication, treatment, or prevention of a disease or physical handicap or for the purpose of affecting any structure or function of the body. Therefore, $5,500 ($5,000 dentist and eye doctor fees + $500 contact lenses) qualifies for the deduction before the AGI limitation.

Answer (A) is incorrect. Cosmetic surgery is not deductible unless it corrects a congenital deformity. Furthermore, only premiums paid for medical insurance that provides for reimbursement of medical care expenses is deductible. Answer (B) is incorrect. Cosmetic surgery is not deductible unless it corrects a congenital deformity. Answer (C) is incorrect. Only premiums paid for medical insurance that provides for reimbursement of medical care expenses is deductible.

13. In the current year, Drake, a disabled taxpayer, made the following home improvements:

	Cost
Pool installation, which qualified as a medical expense and increased the value of the home by $25,000.	$100,000
Widening doorways to accommodate Drake's wheelchair. The improvement did not increase the value of his home.	10,000

For regular income tax purposes and without regard to the adjusted gross income percentage threshold limitation, what maximum amount would be allowable as a medical expense deduction in the current year?

A. $110,000

B. $85,000

C. $75,000

D. $10,000

Answer (B) is correct.

REQUIRED: The maximum allowable medical deduction.

DISCUSSION: Amounts paid for qualified medical expenses that exceed 10% (7.5% for age 65 and over) of AGI may be deducted. The deduction must be paid during the taxable year for the taxpayer, the taxpayer's spouse, or a dependent and must not be compensated for by insurance or otherwise during the taxable year. Deductible medical expenses are amounts paid for (1) diagnosis, cure, mitigation, treatment or prevention of disease, or for the purpose of affecting any structure or function of the body; (2) transportation primarily for and essential to medical care; (3) medical insurance; and (4) qualified long-term care premiums and services. Expenditures for new building construction or for permanent improvements to existing structures may also be deductible in part. The excess of the cost of a permanent improvement over the increase in value of the property is a deductible medical expense. Therefore, $75,000 ($100,000 – $25,000 increase in FMV) is deductible. Construction of handicap entrance/exit ramps, installation of elevators, or widening of doorways also qualify.

Answer (A) is incorrect. Only the excess of the cost of the pool installation over the increase in value of the property is a deductible medical expense. Answer (C) is incorrect. Widening the doorways also qualifies as a medical expense. Answer (D) is incorrect. The excess of the cost of the pool over the increase in value of the property is also deductible as a medical expense.

14. The Rites are married, file a joint income tax return, and qualify to itemize their deductions in the current year. Their adjusted gross income for the year was $55,000, and during the year they paid the following taxes:

Real estate tax on personal residence	$2,000
Ad valorem tax on personal automobile	500
Current-year state and city income taxes withheld from paycheck	1,000

What total amount of the expense should the Rites claim as an itemized deduction on their current-year joint income tax return?

A. $1,000

B. $2,500

C. $3,000

D. $3,500

Answer (D) is correct.

REQUIRED: The total amount of taxes that should be claimed as itemized deductions for the current year return.

DISCUSSION: Under the IRC, only nonbusiness related taxes may be claimed as itemized deductions. Itemized deductible taxes include taxes on real property, personal property, income (except for federal), excess profits, generation-skipping transfer (imposed on income distributions), and general sales (deductible in lieu of income taxes). Three requirements exist for claiming a deduction for personal property tax. The first is an ad valorem requirement, meaning the tax must be in proportion to the value of the property. Secondly, the tax is deductible if imposed on an annual basis. The final requirement is that the tax be imposed on personal property. All three taxes paid by the Rites are deductible as itemized deductions for a total itemized deduction of $3,500 ($2,000 + $500 + $1,000).

Answer (A) is incorrect. Although the current-year state and city income taxes withheld from their paychecks are deductible as itemized deductions ($1,000), so are the real estate tax on their personal residence and the ad valorem tax on their personal automobile. Answer (B) is incorrect. Although the real estate tax on their personal residence and the ad valorem tax on their personal automobile are deductible as itemized deductions [$2,500 ($2,000 + $500)], so is the amount withheld from their paychecks for current-year state and city income taxes. Answer (C) is incorrect. Although the real estate tax on their personal residence and current-year state and city income taxes withheld from their paychecks are deductible as itemized deductions ($2,000 + $1,000), so is the amount of ad valorem tax on their personal automobile.

15. How may taxes paid by an individual to a foreign country be treated?

A. As an itemized deduction subject to the 2% floor.

B. As a credit against federal income taxes due.

C. As an adjustment to gross income.

D. As a nondeductible.

Answer (B) is correct.

REQUIRED: The treatment of taxes paid to a foreign country.

DISCUSSION: A taxpayer may elect either a credit or an itemized deduction for taxes paid to other countries or U.S. possessions.

Answer (A) is incorrect. If treated as an itemized deduction, it is not subject to the 2% floor. Answer (C) is incorrect. The foreign tax can be treated as a credit or deduction, not an adjustment. Answer (D) is incorrect. Foreign taxes paid can be deductible.

16. In 2015, Wood's residence had an adjusted basis of $150,000, and it was destroyed by a tornado. An appraiser valued the decline in market value at $175,000. Later that same year, Wood received $130,000 from his insurance company for the property loss and did not elect to deduct the casualty loss in an earlier year. Wood's 2015 adjusted gross income was $60,000, and he did not have any casualty gains. What total amount can Wood deduct as a 2015 itemized deduction for the casualty loss, after the application of the threshold limitations?

A. $39,000

B. $38,900

C. $19,900

D. $13,900

Answer (D) is correct.

REQUIRED: The amount of casualty loss deduction.

DISCUSSION: The amount of a personal casualty loss is equal to the lesser of adjusted basis or the decline in FMV due to the casualty. Therefore, Wood's loss is equal to $150,000. Additionally, several limits apply. First, the loss must be reduced by any insurance recovery. Additionally, the loss must be reduced by $100 per casualty and is only deductible to the extent that it exceeds 10% of AGI. Therefore, Wood's deductible loss is

Adjusted basis	$150,000
Less: Insurance	(130,000)
$100 floor	(100)
10% of AGI	(6,000)
Deductible loss	$ 13,900

Answer (A) is incorrect. The deductible loss is based on the lesser of adjusted basis and FMV and must be reduced by $100. Answer (B) is incorrect. The deductible loss is based on the lesser of adjusted basis and the decline in FMV. Answer (C) is incorrect. The loss must be reduced by 10% of AGI.

5.2 Job Expenses and Certain Miscellaneous Deductions

17. Which expense, both incurred and paid in 2015, can be claimed as an itemized deduction subject to the 2%-of-AGI floor?

A. Employee's unreimbursed business car expense.

B. One-half of the self-employment tax.

C. Employee's unreimbursed moving expense.

D. Self-employed health insurance.

Answer (A) is correct.

REQUIRED: The expense that is an itemized deduction subject to the 2%-of-AGI floor.

DISCUSSION: Unreimbursed employee expenses, including car expenses, are deductible as itemized deductions subject to the 2%-of-AGI floor.

Answer (B) is incorrect. One-half of the self-employment tax is an above-the-line deduction. Answer (C) is incorrect. An employee's unreimbursed direct moving expenses are available as an above-the-line deduction. Answer (D) is incorrect. Self-employed health insurance is an above-the-line deductible expense equal to 100% of the actual amount paid during the taxable year.

18. Hall, a divorced person and custodian of her 12-year-old child, filed her 2015 federal income tax return as head of household. She submitted the following information to the CPA who prepared her 2015 return:

- The divorce agreement, executed in 2004, provides for Hall to receive $3,000 per month, of which $600 is designated as child support. After the child reaches 18, the monthly payments are to be reduced to $2,400 and are to continue until remarriage or death. However, for 2015, Hall received a total of only $5,000 from her former husband. Hall paid an attorney $2,000 in 2015 in a suit to collect the alimony owed.

The $2,000 legal fee that Hall paid to collect alimony should be treated as a(n)

A. Deduction in arriving at AGI.

B. Itemized deduction subject to the 2%-of-AGI floor.

C. Itemized deduction not subject to the 2%-of-AGI floor.

D. Nondeductible personal expense.

Answer (B) is correct.

REQUIRED: The deductible amount of a fee paid to collect alimony.

DISCUSSION: Fees to collect alimony are considered expenditures for the production of income, deductible as a miscellaneous itemized deduction subject to the 2%-of-AGI exclusion.

Answer (A) is incorrect. The fee is not listed in the IRC as a deduction for AGI. Answer (C) is incorrect. The fee is not listed as not subject to the 2%-of-AGI exclusion. Answer (D) is incorrect. The fee is treated as paid or incurred to produce income.

19. Which of the following is a miscellaneous itemized deduction subject to the 2% of adjusted gross income floor?

A. Gambling losses up to the amount of gambling winnings.

B. Medical expenses.

C. Real estate tax.

D. Employee business expenses.

Answer (D) is correct.

REQUIRED: Identify the itemized deduction subject to the 2% of AGI floor.

DISCUSSION: Miscellaneous itemized deductions are subject to a 2%-of-AGI exclusion. Only that portion of the aggregate amount of allowable second-tier itemized deductions that exceeds the threshold amount of 2% of AGI may be deducted from AGI. Any surplus cannot be carried forward to a succeeding year. The three categories of miscellaneous itemized deductions are employee expenses, tax determination expenses, and other expenses.

Answer (A) is incorrect. Gambling losses up the amount of gambling winnings are reported on Schedule A after itemized deductions subject to the 2% of AGI floor. Answer (B) is incorrect. Medical expenses are subject to a 10% (7.5% for age 65 and over) of AGI floor and not part of the deductions subject to the 2% of AGI floor. Answer (C) is incorrect. Real estate taxes are itemized deductions but are reported above those subject to the 2% of AGI floor.

5.3 Tax Credits

20. To qualify for the Child Care Credit on a joint return, at least one spouse must

	Have an Adjusted Gross Income of $15,000 or Less	Be Gainfully Employed when Related Expenses Are Incurred
A.	Yes	Yes
B.	No	No
C.	Yes	No
D.	No	Yes

Answer (B) is correct.

REQUIRED: The requirement(s) to qualify for the Child Care Credit on a joint return.

DISCUSSION: The IRC allows a nonrefundable credit to a provider of care to dependents for a limited portion of expenses necessary to enable gainful employment. The credit claimant must have qualified child care expenses when the claimant is employed or actively seeking gainful employment. The credit amount is not eliminated when AGI exceeds $15,000, only phased down from 35% to 20% in increments of 1% for each $2,000 AGI exceeds $15,000.

Answer (A) is incorrect. Qualifying expenses may be incurred when the claimant is actively seeking gainful employment, and the credit is not eliminated by reference to AGI. The credit is phased from 35% to 20%. Answer (C) is incorrect. The credit is not eliminated when AGI exceeds a cap amount. The credit is phased from 35% to 20%. Answer (D) is incorrect. Qualifying expenses may be incurred when the claimant is actively seeking gainful employment.

21. Which of the following credits is a combination of several tax credits to provide uniform rules for the current and carryback-carryover years?

A. General Business Credit.

B. Foreign Tax Credit.

C. Minimum Tax Credit.

D. Research Credit.

Answer (A) is correct.

REQUIRED: The credit that is actually a combination of several credits.

DISCUSSION: The General Business Credit is a set of several credits commonly available to businesses, including credits for investment, research, and work opportunity jobs, among others.

Answer (B) is incorrect. The Foreign Tax Credit is a specific, individual credit. Answer (C) is incorrect. The Minimum Tax Credit is a specific, individual credit. Answer (D) is incorrect. The Research Credit is a specific, individual credit.

22. Which of the following credits can result in a refund even if the individual had **no** income tax liability?

A. Foreign Tax Credit.

B. Elderly and Permanently and Totally Disabled Credit.

C. Earned Income Credit.

D. Child and Dependent Care Credit.

Answer (C) is correct.

REQUIRED: The credit that is refundable.

DISCUSSION: A refundable credit is payable as a refund to the extent the credit amount exceeds tax otherwise due. Some of the refundable credits are credits for taxes withheld, overpayments of income tax, and the Earned Income Credit.

Answer (A) is incorrect. The credit for foreign taxes paid is not refundable. Answer (B) is incorrect. The Elderly and Disabled Credit is not refundable. Answer (D) is incorrect. The Child and Dependent Care Credit is not refundable.

23. Which of the following statements about the Child and Dependent Care Credit is correct?

A. The credit is nonrefundable.

B. The child must be under the age of 18 years.

C. The child must be a direct descendant of the taxpayer.

D. The maximum credit is $600.

Answer (A) is correct.

REQUIRED: The true statement about the Child and Dependent Care Credit.

DISCUSSION: A nonrefundable tax credit is allowed for child and dependent care expenses incurred to enable the taxpayer to be gainfully employed. To qualify, the taxpayer must provide more than half the cost of maintaining a household for a dependent under age 13 or an incapacitated spouse or dependent. The maximum credit is equal to 35% of up to $3,000 of child and dependent care expenses for one qualifying individual ($6,000 for two or more individuals).

Answer (B) is incorrect. A child who is not incapacitated must be under the age of 13. Dependents who are incapacitated do not have an age restriction. Answer (C) is incorrect. Direct "descendant" is not a requirement (e.g., incapacitated spouse). Answer (D) is incorrect. The maximum credit is $1,050 ($3,000 expense limit × 35%) for one qualifying individual and $2,100 ($6,000 expense limit × 35%) for two or more qualifying individuals.

5.4 Alternative Minimum Tax

24. The alternative minimum tax (AMT) is computed as the

A. Excess of the regular tax over the tentative AMT.

B. Excess of the tentative AMT over the regular tax.

C. The tentative AMT plus the regular tax.

D. Lesser of the tentative AMT or the regular tax.

Answer (B) is correct.

REQUIRED: The correct computation of the alternative minimum tax (AMT).

DISCUSSION: The alternative minimum tax is the excess of the minimum tax over the regular tax. The AMT is payable in addition to the regular tax.

Answer (A) is incorrect. AMT is an additional tax. Answer (C) is incorrect. AMT equals tentative AMT minus regular tax. Answer (D) is incorrect. AMT equals the difference, and not the lesser, of tentative AMT and regular tax.

25. Alternative minimum tax preferences include

	Tax-Exempt Interest from Private Activity Bonds Issued during 2015	Charitable Contributions of Appreciated Capital Gain Property
A.	Yes	Yes
B.	Yes	No
C.	No	Yes
D.	No	No

Answer (B) is correct.

REQUIRED: The AMT preference items.

DISCUSSION: AMT preferences are items that are allowed relatively favorable treatment in determining regular taxable income. These preferences are added back to TI to find AMTI. Tax-exempt interest from private activity bonds is an AMT preference item. A charitable contribution of appreciated capital gain property is not an AMT preference item.

Answer (A) is incorrect. A charitable contribution of capital gain property is not an alternative minimum tax preference. Answer (C) is incorrect. Tax-exempt interest from private activity bonds is an AMT preference item, but a charitable contribution of capital property is not. Answer (D) is incorrect. Tax-exempt interest from private activity bonds is an AMT preference item.

26. In 2015, Don Mills, a single taxpayer, had $70,000 in taxable income before personal exemptions. Mills had no tax preferences. His itemized deductions were as follows:

State and local income taxes	$5,000
Home mortgage interest on loan to acquire residence	6,000
Miscellaneous deductions that exceed 2% of adjusted gross income	2,000

What amount did Mills report as alternative minimum taxable income before the AMT exemption?

A. $72,000

B. $75,000

C. $77,000

D. $83,000

Answer (C) is correct.

REQUIRED: The adjustments made to TI to reach AMTI.

DISCUSSION: The itemized deduction for state and local income taxes and miscellaneous itemized deductions exceeding the 2%-of-AGI floor are AMT adjustment items that must be added back to TI to find AMTI. Therefore, AMTI is $77,000 ($70,000 TI + $5,000 + $2,000).

Answer (A) is incorrect. The itemized deduction for state and local income taxes is an AMT adjustment item that should also be added back. Answer (B) is incorrect. The miscellaneous itemized deductions exceeding the 2%-of-AGI floor are an AMT adjustment item that should also be added back. Answer (D) is incorrect. Qualified home mortgage interest is not an AMT adjustment item.

5.5 Losses and Limits

27. Lee qualified as head of a household for 2015 tax purposes. Lee's 2015 taxable income was $100,000, exclusive of capital gains and losses. Lee had a net long-term capital loss of $8,000 in 2015. What amount of this capital loss can Lee offset against 2015 ordinary income?

A. $0

B. $3,000

C. $4,000

D. $8,000

Answer (B) is correct.

REQUIRED: The deductible amount of a net capital loss.

DISCUSSION: Capital losses offset capital gains. Excess of capital losses over capital gains (net capital loss) is deductible against ordinary income, but only up to $3,000 in the current tax year.

Answer (A) is incorrect. Lee may offset part of the capital loss. Answer (C) is incorrect. The offset is limited to $3,000. Answer (D) is incorrect. The whole amount of the loss may not be offset in the current year.

28. Don Wolf became a general partner in Gata Associates on January 1, 2015, with a 5% interest in Gata's profits, losses, and capital. Gata is a distributor of auto parts. Wolf does not materially participate in the partnership business. For the year ended December 31, 2015, Gata had an operating loss of $100,000. In addition, Gata earned interest of $20,000 on a temporary investment while awaiting delivery of equipment that is presently on order. The principal will be used to pay for this equipment. Wolf's passive loss for 2015 is

A. $0

B. $4,000

C. $5,000

D. $6,000

Answer (C) is correct.

REQUIRED: The amount treated as a passive loss.

DISCUSSION: In general, losses arising from one passive activity may be used to offset income from other passive activities but may not be used to offset active or portfolio income. Wolf's $5,000 operating loss ($100,000 × 5%) may not be used to offset his $1,000 portfolio income ($20,000 × 5%); i.e., interest and dividends are portfolio income. Therefore, his passive loss for 2015 is his $5,000 operating loss. The losses may be carried forward indefinitely or until the entire interest is disposed of.

Answer (A) is incorrect. The operating losses are passive since Wolf does not materially participate. Answer (B) is incorrect. The interest income is classified as portfolio income and is not offset by passive losses. Answer (D) is incorrect. The $1,000 interest constitutes income, not loss.

29. Which of the following statements about losses in federally declared disaster areas is **false**?

A. The taxpayer has the option of deducting the loss on the return for the year immediately preceding the year in which the disaster actually occurred.

B. If the taxpayer's home is located in a federally declared disaster area, and the state government orders that it be torn down, the taxpayer may be able to treat the loss in value as a casualty loss from a disaster.

C. Disaster area loss deductions are figured using the usual rules for casualty losses.

D. Once made, the election to deduct the loss on the prior-year return cannot be revoked.

Answer (D) is correct.

REQUIRED: The false statement about losses in federally declared disaster areas.

DISCUSSION: If a taxpayer sustains a loss from a disaster in an area subsequently designated as a federal disaster area, a special rule may help the taxpayer to cushion his or her loss. Disaster loss treatment is available with respect to a personal residence declared unsafe and ordered to be demolished by the state or local government. The taxpayer also has the option of deducting the loss on his or her return for the year in which the loss occurred or on the return for the previous year. Revocation of the election to deduct the loss on the preceding year's tax return may be made before the expiration of time for filing the return for the year of loss. The calculation of the deduction for a disaster loss follows the same rules as those for nonbusiness casualty losses.

Answer (A) is incorrect. It is a true statement about losses in federally declared disaster areas. Answer (B) is incorrect. It is a true statement about losses in federally declared disaster areas. Answer (C) is incorrect. It is a true statement about losses in federally declared disaster areas.

30. The at-risk rules

A. Limit a taxpayer's deductible losses from investment activities.

B. Limit the type of deductions in income-producing activities.

C. Apply to business and income-producing activities on a combined basis.

D. Apply at the entity level for partnerships and S corporations.

Answer (A) is correct.

REQUIRED: The correct statement concerning the at-risk rules.

DISCUSSION: The at-risk rules limit a taxpayer's deductible losses from each business and income-producing activity to the amount for which the taxpayer is at risk with respect to that activity.

Answer (B) is incorrect. The losses from each activity, not the type of deductions, are limited. Answer (C) is incorrect. The at-risk rules apply to each business and income-producing activity separately. Answer (D) is incorrect. The at-risk rules apply at the partner or shareholder level for these pass-through entities.

5.6 PRACTICE TASK-BASED SIMULATIONS

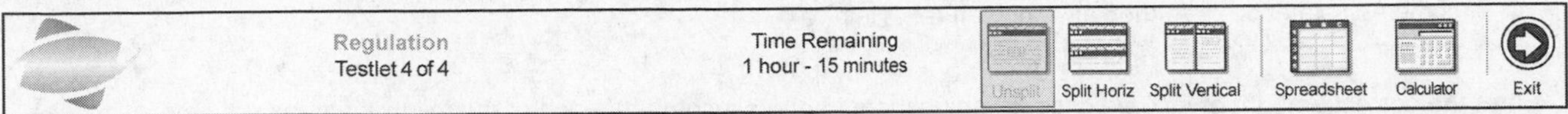

DIRECTIONS

Note: If you believe you have encountered a software malfunction, report it to the test center staff immediately.

Navigation

To navigate from task to task, use the controls at the bottom of the screen. Click on the **Next** button to advance to the next task, or the **Previous** button to go to the previous task. To go directly to any task, click on its number.

If you would like a reminder to revisit a task, or want to indicate that you are finished with it, click on the reminder flag below the task number. To clear the flag, click on it again. Reminder flags are for your use only – they do not contribute to your score.

Tabs

In this part of the examination, you will be asked to complete various tasks. Every task has one or more **Work Tabs**. Some tasks have one or more **Information Tabs**, others may have none. Every task has a **Help** tab.

If a task has **Information Tabs**, you may use the information in them to complete your responses in the **Work Tabs**.

Work tab **Information tab** **Help tab**

Work Tabs:

- **Work Tabs** are identified with a pencil icon. This is where your responses are expected.
- Each task has one or more **Work Tabs.**
- **Work Tabs** contain directions for completing the task – be sure to read these directions carefully.
- The **Work Tab** name in the example above is for illustration only – yours will differ.
- You must complete all of the **Work Tabs** in each task to receive full credit.

Information Tabs:

- The Authoritative Literature will be provided in all tasks in the AUD, FAR, and REG sections for your reference.
- Your simulation may have one or more additional **Information Tabs**. Like the Authoritative Literature tabs, **Information Tabs** do not have a pencil icon.
- If your task has additional **Information Tabs**, go through each to familiarize yourself with the task content.

Help Tab:

- The **Help Tab** provides assistance with the exam software that is used in this task. For example, if the task is to compose a memorandum, **Help** will provide information about the word processor.

The Toolbar

The toolbar at the top of the screen shows the amount of time remaining for you to complete the tasks. In addition, the following tools are available. Note that only the **Exit** button is displayed when Directions are visible - the others will appear when you begin the tasks.

Click on these buttons to split or unsplit the screen. You can split the screen vertically or horizontally.

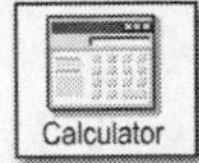

Click on this button to display the calculator; click on it again to hide the calculator. To move the calculator, click on the calculator title bar and drag the calculator to the desired location.

Click on this button to use the spreadsheet; click on it again to hide the spreadsheet. To move the spreadsheet, click on the the spreadsheet title bar and drag the spreadsheet to the desired location.

Click on this button to go on to the next part of the examination. You must complete all of the tasks to receive full credit. Once you click on **Exit** and confirm the action, you will NOT be able to return to this testlet.

= Reminder | Directions | 1 2 3 4 5 6 | Previous | Next

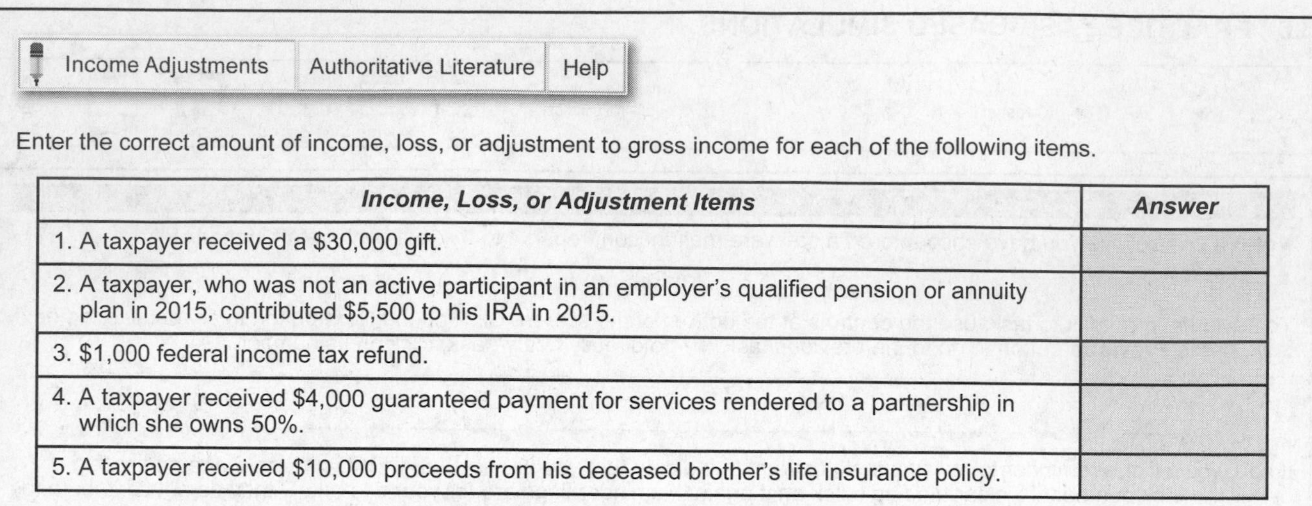

Income Adjustments | Authoritative Literature | Help

Enter the correct amount of income, loss, or adjustment to gross income for each of the following items.

Income, Loss, or Adjustment Items	Answer
1. A taxpayer received a $30,000 gift.	
2. A taxpayer, who was not an active participant in an employer's qualified pension or annuity plan in 2015, contributed $5,500 to his IRA in 2015.	
3. $1,000 federal income tax refund.	
4. A taxpayer received $4,000 guaranteed payment for services rendered to a partnership in which she owns 50%.	
5. A taxpayer received $10,000 proceeds from his deceased brother's life insurance policy.	

In each of the following situations, enter the amount of credit that may be claimed on a taxpayer's income tax return. If the value of a cell is zero or if the cell should be left blank, enter a zero (0) to receive credit for the answer.

Situation	Credit Amount
1. Taxpayer A: Single, AGI $60,000. Paid $5,000 of tuition for 5th year of college.	
2. Taxpayer B: MFJ, AGI $51,000. Contributed $5,500 to IRA account and took a $5,500 deduction for AGI.	
3. Taxpayer C: Qualifying small business. Incurs $15,000 of qualified first year wages for a LT family assistance recipient, who worked over 500 hours during the year.	
4. Taxpayer D: Qualified adoption expenditures $5,000, MAGI $100,000. Finalized the adoption of a special-needs child this year.	
5. Taxpayer E: Single, MAGI $80,000. Taxpayer has a child age 10, for whom a dependency exemption may be claimed.	
6. Taxpayer F: Single, earned income includes $3,500 wages and $3,000 unemployment compensation. Taxpayer does not have any qualifying children.	

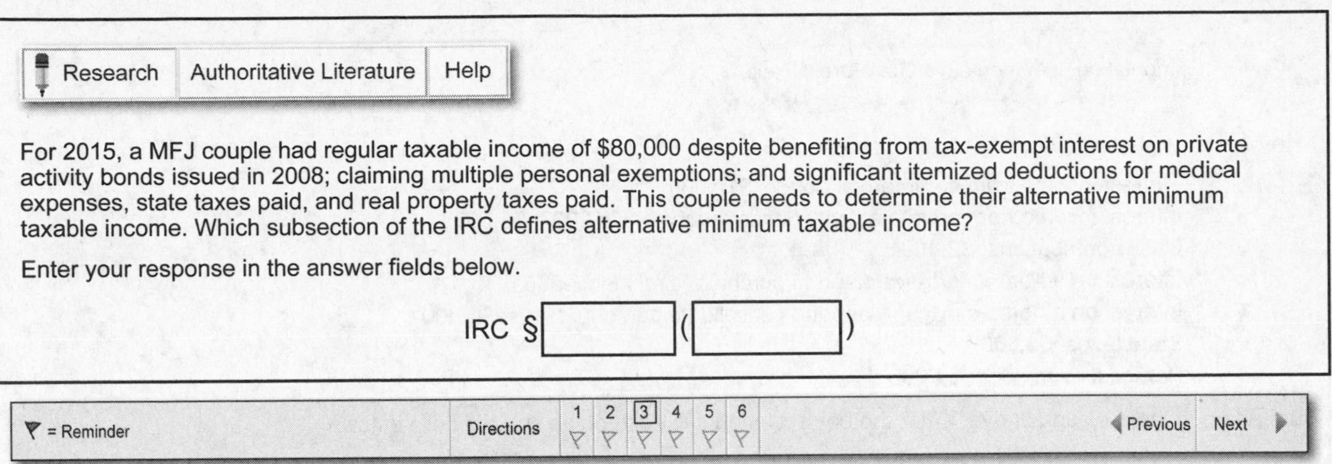

Research | Authoritative Literature | Help

For 2015, a MFJ couple had regular taxable income of $80,000 despite benefiting from tax-exempt interest on private activity bonds issued in 2008; claiming multiple personal exemptions; and significant itemized deductions for medical expenses, state taxes paid, and real property taxes paid. This couple needs to determine their alternative minimum taxable income. Which subsection of the IRC defines alternative minimum taxable income?

Enter your response in the answer fields below.

IRC § [ ] ([ ])

= Reminder | Directions | 1 2 3 4 5 6 | Previous | Next

Tax Treatment | Authoritative Literature | Help

For each of the following items, select from the list provided the appropriate tax treatment for Beth Page. A choice may be used once, more than once, or not at all.

Transaction	*Answer*
1. For 2015, Page had a $30,000 cash charitable contribution carryover from her 2014 cash donation to the American Red Cross. Page made no additional charitable contributions in 2014.	
2. During 2015, Page had investment interest expense of $1,000. This amount did not exceed her net investment income.	
3. For 2015, Page paid $1,500 to an unrelated person to care for her son while she worked.	
4. In 2015, Page paid $4,000 interest on the $60,000 acquisition mortgage of her principal residence. The mortgage is secured by Page's home. Page received a Form 1098 listing the interest she paid.	

Choices
A) Not deductible on Form 1040
B) Deductible in full on Schedule A -- Itemized Deductions
C) Deductible on Schedule A -- Itemized Deductions subject to a limitation of 50% of adjusted gross income
D) Deductible on Schedule A -- Itemized Deductions as miscellaneous deduction subject to a threshold of 2% of adjusted gross income
E) Deductible on Schedule E -- Supplemental Income and Loss
F) A credit is allowable

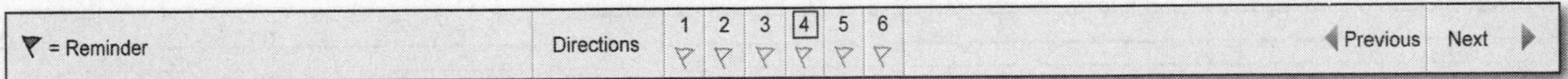

= Reminder | Directions | 1 2 3 4 5 6 | Previous | Next

Herbert, a single taxpayer, has taxable income of $80,000, which includes the following items, for the 2015 taxable year:

- Interest income from commercial bonds: $12,000
- Interest income from private activity bonds purchased in 2007: $3,500
- Cash contributions: $2,400
- Interest on a home mortgage used to purchase a residence: $5,600
- Interest on a home mortgage used to consolidate personal debts: $4,000
- State taxes: $3,600
- Personal exemption: $4,000

Based on the information above, enter the correct amount in each of the shaded cells below.

Questions	***Answer***
1. What is Herbert's regular taxable income?	
2. What is the amount of Herbert's tax preference items?	
3. What is the amount of Herbert's other adjustments?	
4. What is Herbert's alternative minimum taxable income?	

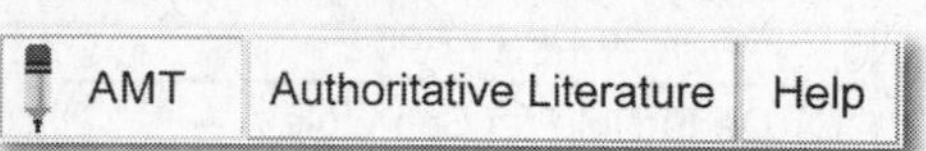

Select from the choices the best description of each item's relationship to AMT computation. Each answer choice may be used once, more than once, or not at all.

Item	***Answer***
1. Depletion in excess of adjusted basis	
2. Medical expenses that do not exceed 10% of AGI	
3. Capital gains	
4. Accelerated depreciation on property placed in service in 2004	
5. Standard deduction	

Choices
A) Other adjustment
B) Tax preference item
C) Does not require adjustment to taxable income

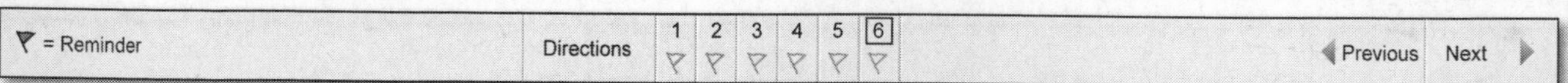

Unofficial Answers

1. Income Adjustments (5 Gradable Items)

1. $0. Gifts are not included in the gross income of the taxpayer receiving the gift.
2. $(5,500). Since the taxpayer is not an active plan participant, he may deduct $5,500 for the contribution to the IRA. Active participant's deductions may be further limited based on AGI.
3. $0. A refund of federal income tax paid is not gross income because it did not provide a tax benefit.
4. $4,000. Guaranteed payments are ordinary income to the partner receiving them. Therefore, the entire $4,000 is gross income.
5. $0. Gross income does not include amounts received (whether in a single sum or otherwise) under a life insurance contract, if such amounts are paid due to the death of the insured.

2. Tax Credits (6 Gradable Items)

1. $500. The Lifetime Learning Credit is 20% of qualified expenses and is allowed for any year the American Opportunity Credit is not taken or allowed (post 4th year). The applicable expenses are limited to $10,000. The credit phases out for a single taxpayer with AGI between $55,000 and $65,000. Taxpayer A's credit is calculated as follows: $5,000 × 20%, i.e., $1,000, reduced by 50% ($60,000 – $55,000) ÷ $10,000, i.e., $500.
2. $1,000. Despite taking the above-the-line deduction for the contribution to the IRA, Taxpayer B is still allowed a retirement savings contribution credit equal to 50% of $2,000. Taxpayer B's AGI is below the $61,000 phaseout threshold for MFJ taxpayers.
3. $4,000. Qualified employers may take the Work Opportunity Tax Credit (WOTC) equal to 40% of the first $10,000 wages paid to LT family assistance recipients who work at least 400 hours. Generally, the credit is 40% of the first $6,000 wages paid to qualifying employees.
4. $13,400. The maximum adoption credit amount of $13,400 is allowed regardless of the actual expenses paid or incurred in the year the adoption becomes final for a special-needs child.
5. $750. Taxpayers who have qualifying children are entitled to the child tax credit of $1,000 per child. Taxpayer E has one qualifying child. The credit for single taxpayers begins to phase out by $50 per $1,000 in excess of $75,000. Taxpayer E's $1,000 credit is reduced by $250: ($80,000 – $75,000) ÷ ($1,000 × $50).
6. $268. Qualified taxpayers are allowed an earned income credit based on an applicable percentage. As a single individual with no children, Taxpayer F's credit is 7.65% of the $3,500 earned income.

3. Research (1 Gradable Item)

Answer: IRC § 55(b)

§ 55. Alternative minimum tax imposed

(b) Tentative minimum tax

(2) Alternative minimum taxable income

The term "alternative minimum taxable income" means the taxable income of the taxpayer for the taxable year—

(A) determined with the adjustments provided in section 56 and section 58, and

(B) increased by the amount of the items of tax preference described in section 57.

If a taxpayer is subject to the regular tax, such taxpayer shall be subject to the tax imposed by this section (and, if the regular tax is determined by reference to an amount other than taxable income, such amount shall be treated as the taxable income of such taxpayer for purposes of the preceding sentence).

4. Tax Treatment (4 Gradable Items)

1. C) Deductible on Schedule A -- Itemized Deductions subject to a limitation of 50% of adjusted gross income. Charitable contributions are deducted on Schedule A, limited to 50% of AGI.
2. B) Deductible in full on Schedule A -- Itemized Deductions. Investment interest expense is fully deductible on Schedule A as long as it does not exceed net investment income.
3. F) A credit is allowable. A credit may be taken for dependent care.
4. B) Deductible in full on Schedule A -- Itemized Deductions. Mortgage interest is fully deductible on Schedule A.

5. AMT Computation (4 Gradable Items)

1. $80,000. As given in the facts, Herbert's taxable income is $80,000.
2. $3,500. Tax preference items include any interest income received from private activity bonds purchased after 1986 and not including those purchased in 2009 and 2010.
3. $11,600. Other adjustments represent a limitation on itemized deductions or timing differences. Certain itemized deductions, including home equity refinancing, state and local taxes, and personal exemptions, are not included when calculating AMT. The total other adjustments for Herbert would be the interest paid on the mortgage taken out to consolidate personal debts, state taxes paid, and the personal exemption ($4,000 + $3,600 + $4,000).
4. $95,100. Alternative minimum taxable income is equal to taxable income, plus any tax preference items, plus or minus any other adjustments. In this case, the other adjustments represent deductions that were taken when computing regular tax but are not allowed when computing AMT. Thus, they should be added back to taxable income ($80,000 + $3,500 + $11,600).

6. AMT (5 Gradable Items)

1. B) Tax preference item. Depletion in excess of adjusted basis receives preferential treatment when computing regular taxable income and must be added back to reach alternative minimum taxable income (AMTI).
2. A) Other adjustment. Medical expenses are deductible for AMT purposes only to the extent that they exceed 10% of AGI. Once the 7.5% treatment ends for those 65 and over, there will no longer be a difference between regular tax treatment and AMT treatment.
3. C) Does not require adjustment to taxable income. Capital gains and losses are treated the same way for regular taxable income and AMTI.
4. A) Other adjustment. Accelerated depreciation on property placed in service after 1987 receives preferential treatment when computing regular taxable income and must be added back to reach AMTI. Using MACRS creates a timing difference, which results in accelerated deductions.
5. A) Other adjustment. The standard deduction is not taken when computing AMTI.

Gleim Simulation Grading

Task	Correct Responses		Gradable Items		Score per Task
1	____	÷	5	=	____
2	____	÷	6	=	____
3 (Research)	____	÷	1	=	____
4	____	÷	4	=	____
5	____	÷	4	=	____
6	____	÷	5	=	____
			Total of Scores per Task		____
		÷	Total Number of Tasks		6
			Total Score		____ %

STUDY UNIT SIX
PROPERTY TRANSACTIONS

(28 pages of outline)

The tax treatment of property transactions is integrated with that of other transactions on the CPA exam. Visualize the following steps to analyze the income tax consequences of property transactions.

1. Determine gain or loss realized.
2. Apply related party sales rules.
3. Apply nonrecognition rules.
4. Apply Sec. 1245 and 1250 recapturing rules.
5. Characterize gains and losses under Sec. 1231.
6. Apply capital loss rules.
7. Apply other loss limits.
   a. At-risk rules
   b. Passive activity loss rules
   c. Net operating loss rules
8. Report gross income, claim deductions, and compute taxable income and tax liability in accordance with other rules. For example,
   a. Apply installment sales rules.
   b. Deduct allowable capital losses.
   c. Phase out personal exemptions with capital gains included in taxable income.
   d. Apply tax rates separately to capital gains and other income.

The sale of a business requires special attention. When more than one asset of a business is transferred in bulk (total consideration exchanged for assets in combination), including all the assets of a sole proprietorship, gain or loss must be accounted for separately for each asset transferred. Allocation among assets of consideration paid or to be paid is by agreement of parties, by relative FMV of assets, or by the residual method. Also note the following:

- Capital gain or loss might arise from assets that have no fixed or determinable useful life, such as goodwill that was not amortized (self-created goodwill) under Sec. 197 or an exclusive franchise.
- Ordinary income or loss might arise from the following assets:
  - Inventory
  - Accounts receivable
  - Covenants not to compete (all ordinary)
  - Sec. 1245 property, e.g., equipment
  - Sec. 1250 property, i.e., depreciable realty
  - Sec. 1231 property, e.g., depreciable trade or business property

6.1 BASIS

1. **Overview**

   a. When a taxpayer acquires property, his or her basis in the property is initially cost, transferred, or exchanged basis.

      1) **Cost basis** is the sum of capitalized acquisition costs.

         a) Cost basis includes the fair market value (1245 ordinary income) of property given up. If it is not determinable with reasonable certainty, use FMV of property received.

         b) A rebate to the purchaser is treated as a reduction of the purchase price. It is not included in basis nor in gross income.

      2) **Transferred basis** is computed by reference to basis in the property in the hands of another.

      3) **Exchanged basis** is computed by reference to basis in other property previously held.

         a) The basis of property converted into business use is the lesser of the FMV of the property at the conversion date or the adjusted basis at conversion.

2. **Capitalized Costs**

   a. Initial basis in purchased property is the cost of acquiring it. Only capital costs are included.

      1) Capital expenditures may be made by cash, by cash equivalent, in property, with liability, or by services.

   b. Expenditure must be capitalized if it (1) results in a betterment to the unit of property, (2) adapts the unit of property to a new or different use, or (3) results in a restoration of the unit of property.

      1) Expenditure is a betterment if it ameliorates a condition or defect that existed before acquisition of the property or arose during the production of the property; is for a material addition to the property; or increases the property's productivity, efficiency, strength, etc.

      2) Expenditure is an adaptation to a new or different use if it adapts the unit of property to a use inconsistent with the taxpayer's intended ordinary use at the time the taxpayer originally placed the property into service.

      3) Expenditure is a restoration if it

         a) Restores a basis that has been taken into account,

         b) Returns the unit of property to working order from a state of nonfunctional disrepair,

         c) Results in a rebuilding of the unit of property to a like-new condition after the end of the property's alternative depreciation system class life, or

         d) Replaces a major component or substantial structural part of the unit of property.

Common Capitalized Costs (for Sec. 1012)

Purchase Price (Stated)
NOTE: Not unstated interest
Liability to which property is subject

Closing Costs
Brokerage commissions
Pre-purchase taxes
Sales tax on purchase
Excise taxes
Title transfer taxes
Title insurance
Recording fees
Attorney fees
Document review, preparation

Miscellaneous Costs
Appraisal fees
Freight
Installation
Testing

Major Improvements
New roof
New gutters
Extending water line to property
Demolition costs and losses
New electrical wiring

EXAMPLE

If you buy a building for $20,000 cash and assume a mortgage of $80,000 on it, your basis is $100,000.

c. **Expenses not properly chargeable to a capital account.** Costs of maintaining and operating property are not added to basis.

3. **Lump-Sum Assets**

a. When more than one asset is purchased for a lump sum, the basis of each is computed pro rata by apportioning the total cost based on the relative FMV of each asset.

$$\text{Allocable cost (basis)} = \frac{\text{FMV of asset}}{\text{FMV of all assets purchased}} \times \text{Lump sum purchase price}$$

b. Alternatively, the transferor and transferee may agree in writing as to the allocation of consideration or the FMV of any assets. The agreement is binding unless the IRS deems it improper.

c. The residual method must be used for any transfers of a group of assets that constitutes a trade or business and for which the buyer's basis is determined only by the amount paid for the assets.

d. The residual method allocates purchase price for both transferor and transferee to asset categories up to FMV in the following order:

1) Cash and cash equivalents
2) Near-cash items, such as CDs, U.S. government securities, foreign currency, and other marketable securities
3) Accounts receivable, mortgages, and credit card receivables acquired in the ordinary course of business
4) Property held primarily for sale to customers in the ordinary course of a trade or business or stocks included in dealer inventory
5) Assets not listed in 1) through 4) above
6) Sec. 197 intangibles, such as patents and covenants not to compete except goodwill and going-concern value
7) Goodwill and going-concern value

NOTE: When the purchase price is lower than the aggregate FMV of the assets other than goodwill/going-concern value, the price is allocated first to the face amount of cash and then to assets 2) through 6) above, according to relative FMVs.

4. **Property for Services**

   a. The FMV of property received in exchange for services is income (compensation) to the provider when it is not subject to a substantial risk of forfeiture and not restricted as to transfer. The property acquired has a tax cost basis equal to the FMV of the property.

EXAMPLE

Jim's neighbor needs his fence painted and offers to give Jim a rare baseball card if Jim paints his fence. The baseball card has a fair market value of $500. If Jim paints the fence, he has a $500 basis in the baseball card.

   b. Sale of restricted stock to an employee is treated as gross income to the extent the FMV exceeds the price paid. This amount is included in gross income in the first taxable year in which the property is unrestricted.

5. **Gifts**

   a. The donee's basis in property acquired by gift is the donor's basis, increased for any gift tax paid attributable to appreciation. The donee's basis is increased by

$$\text{Gift tax paid} \times \left[\frac{\text{FMV (at time of gift)} - \text{Donor's basis}}{\text{FMV (at time of gift)} - \text{Annual exclusion}}\right]$$

   NOTE: The 2015 annual exclusion is $14,000.

   b. If the FMV on the date of the gift is less than the donor's basis, the donee has a dual basis for the property.

      1) Loss basis. The FMV at the date of the gift is used if the property is later transferred at a loss.
      2) Gain basis. The donor's basis is used if the property is later transferred at a gain.
      3) If the property is later transferred for more than FMV at the date of the gift but for less than the donor's basis at the date of the gift, no gain (loss) is recognized.

   c. Depreciable basis is transferred basis adjusted for gift taxes paid. If converted from personal to business use, it is the lessor FMV on the date of conversion or the transferor's adjusted basis.

EXAMPLE

Bobby received a house as a gift from his father. At the time of the gift, the house had a FMV of $80,000 and the father's adjusted basis was $100,000. If no events occurred that changed the basis and Bobby sells the house for $120,000, Bobby will have a $20,000 gain because he must use the father's adjusted basis ($100,000) at the time of the gift to figure his gain. If he sells the house for $70,000, he will have a $10,000 loss because he must use the FMV ($80,000) at the time of the gift to figure his loss.

If the sale was between $80,000 and $100,000, Bobby would not recognize a gain or a loss.

6. **Inherited Property**

   a. Basis is the FMV on the date of death or 6 months after if the executor elects the alternate valuation date for the estate tax return. The FMV basis rule also applies to the following property:

      1) Property received prior to death without full and adequate consideration (if a life estate was retained in it) or subject to a right of revocation. Reduce basis by depreciation deductions allowed the donee.
      2) One-half of community property interests.
      3) Property acquired by form of ownership, e.g., by right of survivorship, except if consideration was paid to acquire the property from a nonspouse.

7. **Uniform Capitalization Rules**

   a. Costs for construction (manufacture) of real or tangible personal property to be used in trade or business and costs of producing or acquiring property for sale to customers (retail) are capitalized.

      1) Capitalize all costs necessary to prepare it for its intended use, both direct and most allocable indirect costs, e.g., engineering, permit, material, storage, and equipment rent.

         a) Costs and losses associated with demolishing a structure are allocated to the land. The basis of any new building constructed on the land is its original cost (not FMV).

      2) Construction period interest and taxes must be capitalized as part of building cost.

      3) Indirect costs not capitalized include, among others, marketing, selling, advertising, distribution, research, experimental, Sec. 179, strike, warranty, unsuccessful bid, and deductible service costs.

   b. Uniform capitalization rules do not apply if property is acquired for resale and the company's annual gross receipts (for the past 3 years) do not exceed $10 million.

8. **Adjusted Basis**

   a. Initial basis is adjusted consistent with tax-relevant events. Adjustments include the following:

      1) Certain expenditures subsequent to acquisition are property costs, and they increase basis, e.g., legal fees to defend title or title insurance premiums.

      2) Basis must be increased for expenditures that prolong the life of the property by at least 1 year or materially increase its value. Assessments that increase the value of property should be capitalized.

         a) Examples include major improvements (e.g., new roof, addition to building, etc.) and zoning changes.

         b) Maintenance, repair, and operating costs are not capitalized.

EXAMPLE

In order to save money on their utility bills, Mr. and Mrs. Thrifty paid to replace their old roof with a new one with better insulation. The new roof materially increased the value of the house, so the cost of the roof should be added to the basis of the house.

      3) Increase to basis may result from liability to the extent it is secured by real property and applied to extend its life.

      4) Basis must be reduced by the larger of the amount of depreciation allowed or allowable (even if not claimed). Unimproved land is not depreciated.

      5) A shareholder does not recognize gain on the voluntary contribution of capital to a corporation. The shareholder's stock basis equals his or her basis in the contributed property. The corporation has a transferred basis in the property.

         a) A return of capital distribution reduces basis and becomes a capital gain when the shareholder's basis in the stock reaches zero.

      6) The basis of stock acquired in a nontaxable distribution (e.g., stock rights) is allocated a portion of the basis of the stock upon which the distribution was made.

         a) If the new shares and old shares are not identical, the basis is allocated in proportion to the FMV of the original stock and the distribution as of the date of distribution.

         b) If the new and old shares are identical (e.g., stock splits) the old basis is simply divided among the new total of shares.

c) If the FMV of the stock rights is less than 15% of the FMV of the stock upon which it was issued, the rights have a basis of zero (unless an election is made to allocate basis).

7) Basis adjustment is required for certain specific items that represent a tax benefit. Three examples follow:

a) Casualty losses reduce basis by the amount of the loss, by any amounts recovered by insurance, and by any amounts for which no tax benefit was received, e.g., $100 floor for individuals.

b) Debt discharge. Specific exclusion from gross income is allowed to certain insolvent persons for debt discharged. Taxpayers may elect to reduce basis in depreciable assets by the amount of the exclusion. If an election is not made, they must reduce certain tax attributes.

c) Credit for building rehabilitation. The full amount of the credit must be deducted from the basis.

Stop and review! You have completed the outline for this subunit. Study multiple-choice questions 1 through 5 beginning on page 244.

6.2 DEPRECIATION AND AMORTIZATION

Candidates should expect to be tested on capital cost recovery for corporations, including depreciation, Sec. 179 expense, and amortization.

1. **Accelerated Cost Recovery (ACR)**

a. Tax accounting methods of depreciation that allow a deduction in excess of a current year's decline in economic value are accelerated cost recovery methods.

b. Property subject to the allowance for depreciation is tangible property used in trade, in business, or for production of income and has a determinable, limited useful life.

c. The amount of a current depreciation deduction is computed by applying a rate to depreciable basis.

2. **General Information**

Background

Accelerated depreciation is a tax relief measure highly desired by businesses. Quickly expensing the cost of investment in plant and equipment for tax purposes allows businesses to significantly reduce their tax liability. In 1971, Congress regularized the haphazard use of accelerated depreciation by introducing the Asset Depreciation Range (ADR) system. Assets of a similar nature or use could be classed together, thereby simplifying the calculation of depreciation expense.

a. The IRS (the service) has published a list of acceptable useful life ranges by types of asset: the **asset depreciation range (ADR)**.

b. Straight-line depreciation. The annual amount allowable is the depreciable basis reduced for salvage value (SV) and divided by the useful life of the asset.

$$(\text{Basis} - \text{SV}) \div \text{Useful life}$$

c. 150% declining balance. Basis (not reduced by SV) minus previously allowable deductions, which is adjusted basis (AB), is multiplied by 150% of the straight-line rate.

$$\text{AB} \times (150\% \div \text{Useful life})$$

1) The rate is constant. It is applied to declining basis. It is generally applicable to used property with a useful life of at least 3 years and used depreciable real property.

d. 200% declining balance. The constant rate is 200% of the straight-line rate.

$$AB \times (200\% \div \text{Useful life})$$

1) It is generally allowable for property with a useful life of at least 3 years and new residential rental property.

e. Unit of Production Method

$$(\text{Basis} - SV) \times \left(\frac{\text{\# of units produced during tax year}}{\text{Estimated total of units asset will produce}}\right)$$

f. Operating Days Method

$$(\text{Basis} - SV) \times \left(\frac{\text{\# of days used during tax year}}{\text{Estimated total of days asset can be used}}\right)$$

g. Income Forecast Method

$$(\text{Basis} - SV) \times \left(\frac{\text{Income generated by the property during tax year}}{\text{Estimated total of income from the property during its useful life}}\right)$$

1) The income forecast method is limited to film, videotapes, sound recordings, copyrights, books, and patents.
2) The estimated total of income to be produced from the asset must include all income forecasted to be earned before the close of the 10th year following the tax year in which the property was placed in service.

3. **MACRS: 1987 and After**

Background

The deliberations leading up to the passage of the Tax Reform Act of 1986, including the intense discussions around reconciling the House and Senate versions, were heavily reported in the news media. One of the Act's provisions was the creation of the Modified Accelerated Cost Recovery System (MACRS).

a. The modified accelerated cost recovery system (MACRS) applies to property placed in service in 1987 or later.
   1) A switch is made to straight-line on adjusted (reduced for allowable depreciation) basis when it yields a higher amount.
   2) Real property costs are recovered using a straight-line rate on unadjusted basis.
   3) Salvage value is ignored.
   4) The 200%-declining-balance method is used for MACRS recovery periods of 3, 5, 7, and 10 years (except farm property).
   5) 150% is used for 15- and 20-year property and farm personal property.

b. Mid-year (personal property) and mid-month (real property) conventions apply.
   1) Under the mid-year convention, each asset is treated as placed into service at the midpoint of the year in which it was actually placed into service.
   2) Under the mid-month convention, each asset is treated as placed into service at the midpoint of the month in which it was actually placed into service.
   3) A mid-quarter convention applies when asset acquisition is bunched at the end of the year.
      a) Each asset is treated as placed in service at the midpoint of the quarter in which it actually was placed in service.
      b) Apply the convention to all depreciable property acquired during the tax year when the sum of the bases of all depreciable personal property placed in service during the last quarter of the year exceeds 40% of those placed in service during the entire year.

c) The first year depreciation is calculated by multiplying the full-year amount by the following percentages based on the quarter placed in service:

87.5% for the first quarter
62.5% for the second quarter
37.5% for the third quarter
12.5% for the fourth quarter

EXAMPLE

The formula for 3-year property placed in service in the third quarter is AB × (200% ÷ Useful life) × 37.5%.

c. IRS tables provide rates to be applied to the unadjusted basis (except for Sec. 179 expense) for each year of service. The rate incorporates applicable methods, applicable recovery periods, and conventions.

d. Depreciation is allowed during a disposition year.

e. Personal property is assigned a recovery period of either 3, 5, 7, 10, 15, or 20 years, according to the midpoint of the ADR class life applicable to the type of property. The half-year or mid-quarter convention is applied.

MACRS Recovery Periods (Personal Property)			
MACRS Recovery Period (# of Years)	Midpoint of ADR for Class (# of Years)	DB Rate Applicable Percent	Examples
3	4 or less	200	Special tools, e.g., for rubber manufacturing Most race horses
5	>4, <10	200	Computers, office machinery (e.g., copier) Cars, trucks R&E equipment
7	≥10, <16	200	Most machinery Office furniture and equipment Agricultural structures (single-purpose) Property without ADR midpoint & not otherwise classified
10	≥16, <20	200	Water vessels, e.g., barge Petroleum processing equipment Food & tobacco manufacturing
15	≥20, <25	150	Data communication plants, e.g., for phone Sewage treatment plants Billboards
20	≥25	150	Utilities, e.g., municipal sewers Not real property with ADR midpoint 27.5 years

f. Real property. The straight-line method and the mid-month convention apply.

1) Residential rental property. The straight-line rate is based on a 27 1/2-year recovery period.

a) It is real property with at least 80% of gross rents coming from dwelling units. Partial use by the owner is included. Transient use of more than half the units excludes the property, e.g., a motel.

2) Nonresidential real estate is assigned a 39-year recovery period.

a) It is real property that is not residential rental property.

b) It also includes real property with an ADR midpoint of less than 27 1/2 years.

3) Some realty has a recovery period less than 27 1/2 years, e.g., specified farm buildings.

4) The following three types of real property qualify for 15-year, straight-line depreciation:
   a) Qualified leasehold improvement property
   b) Qualified restaurant property
   c) Qualified retail improvement property

NOTE: Though this provision is expired, it is expected to be renewed and has been treated as though renewed in this course.

g. Alternative depreciation system (ADS). MACRS is mandatory unless ADS is required or elected. ADS utilizes a straight-line rate based on longer recovery periods. Examples of ADS recovery periods follow:

# Years	Items
5	Cars, light trucks, certain technological equipment
12	Personal property with no class life
15	Agricultural structures (single-purpose)
40	Residential rental and nonresidential real estate

1) ADS is required for each of the following:
   a) Listed property
   b) Property used, leased, or financed by tax-exempt organizations
   c) Tangible property used predominantly outside the U.S.
   d) Imported property from a country that engages in discriminatory trade practices

h. Election must be made by the due date, including extensions, for the tax return of the year in which the property was placed in service.

4. **Sec. 179 Expense**

a. A person may elect to deduct all or part of the cost of Sec. 179 property acquired during the year as an expense rather than a capital expenditure.
   1) Sec. 179 expense is treated as depreciation.
      a) It must be elected by the taxpayer.
      b) It reduces basis in the property (but not below zero) prior to computation of any other depreciation deduction allowable for the first year.
      c) It is subject to recapture under Sec. 1245 as depreciation.

b. Sec. 179 property is depreciable personal property used in the active conduct of a trade or business.
   1) Sec. 179 property must be acquired by purchase from an unrelated party.

NOTE: Specifically excluded from the Sec. 179 election are air-conditioning and heating units, property used for lodging, property used by tax-exempt organizations, and property used outside the United States.

c. For 2015, though expired, an extension of the increased limits is expected and, therefore, a deduction may be for no more than either
   1) $500,000 minus the excess of Sec. 179 costs for the year over $2 million or
   2) Taxable income from the active conduct of any trade or business during the tax year.
      a) Current-year excess over TI may be carried forward and treated as Sec. 179 cost in a subsequent year subject to the overall limitation.

d. Apply the following limits in the order presented:
   1) Pass-through entities. Apply each limit on Sec. 179 expense first at the entity level and then at the partner/shareholder level.
   2) Trusts and estates may not claim a Sec. 179 deduction.
   3) Only the business-use portion of the cost of Sec. 179 property may be expensed.
   4) Cost of Sec. 179 property does not include the basis determined by reference to other property held by the taxpayer.
   5) No more than the statutory amount may be deducted as depreciation on cars and certain luxury items. Excess over the limit may not be expensed under Sec. 179.
   6) The limit described in item c. on the previous page.

e. Recapture. Sec. 179 property need not be used to elect the deduction. The amount of allowed Sec. 179 deduction may be allocated to Sec. 179 property as desired. But if Sec. 179 property is disposed of prior to the end of the MACRS recovery period, gross income includes any
   1) Excess of Sec. 179 deduction over
   2) MACRS deductions allowable, notwithstanding Sec. 179.

   NOTE: Recapture also applies when the business use of the Sec. 179 property changes to less than 50% of total use.

5. **Bonus Depreciation**

a. A first-year depreciation (also called bonus depreciation) of 50% of the adjusted basis is allowed for qualified property. This provision is expected to be extended for 2015. The questions in this course treat the topic as being extended for 2015.
   1) This is in addition to the Section 179 deduction.
   2) Qualifying property must be new, generally have a 20-year or less recovery period, and be acquired by the taxpayer after December 31, 2007, and before January 1, 2016, and placed in service before January 1, 2016 (or before January 1, 2017, in the case of property with a longer production period and certain noncommercial aircraft). Qualifying property includes leasehold improvements.
   3) First-year depreciation of 100% was allowed for assets placed in service between September 8, 2010, and January 1, 2012.
   4) The deduction is permitted for both regular and AMT purposes.

6. **Amortization**

a. Amortization accounts for recovery of capital (e.g., intangible assets, Sec. 197) in a similar manner as straight-line depreciation. Intangible assets make up the majority of amortizable assets and are recovered over the asset's useful life or, in the case of Sec. 197 intangibles, 15 years. Other items are amortized over a period specified for that item.

b. Any start-up costs or organizational expenses after the allowed $5,000 immediate deduction are amortized over 15 years. Amortization starts with the month the active trade or business begins.

c. Costs of acquiring a lease are amortized over the lease term.
   1) Renewal options are included in the term if less than 75% of the cost is attributable to the period prior to renewal. Allocate the cost over the original and renewal term, unless the contract (reasonably) specifies otherwise.

2) Improvements by the lessee are deducted under the MACRS method.

a) For a lease entered into before September 26, 1985, the lessee could elect to recover the costs over the remaining lease term.

d. Intangibles. The cost of certain intangibles acquired (not created) in connection with the conduct of a trade or business or income-producing activity is amortized over a 15-year period, beginning with the later of the month in which the intangible is acquired or business begins.

1) Qualified intangibles do not include intangibles that result from the taxpayer's own efforts, unless in connection with the acquisition of a trade or business.

2) Qualified intangibles include the following:

a) Acquired goodwill and going-concern value

b) The work force, information base, patent, copyright, know-how, customers, suppliers, or similar items

c) Licenses, permits, or other rights granted by governmental units

d) Covenants not to compete

e) Any franchise, trademark, or trade name

3) Excluded from intangible amortization treatment are the following:

a) Interests in corporations, partnerships, trusts, estates

b) Interests in land

c) Most financial instruments and contracts

d) Leases of intangible personal property

e) Professional sports franchises

4) Loss realized on disposition of a qualified intangible is disallowed if the taxpayer retains other qualified intangibles acquired in the same (set of) transaction(s). The amount disallowed is added to the basis of the intangibles retained.

e. Reforestation costs not immediately deductible are amortized over 7 years. Amortization starts the sixth month of the year costs are incurred.

f. The cost of geological and geophysical expenses related to domestic oil and gas exploration or development are amortized over 2 years. Like reforestation cost, amortization begins on the mid-point of the year costs are paid or incurred.

g. Pollution control facility costs are amortized over 5 years, with an exception of 7 years for atmospheric facilities.

h. Research and experimentation costs have a 5-year amortization period.

7. **Depletion**

a. Depletion accounts for recovery of investment in natural resources property.

b. Only a person who has an economic interest in a (mineral) property is entitled to deductions for depletion.

1) A person has an economic interest if (s)he

a) Acquires by investment an interest in the mineral in place

b) Derives income from extraction of the mineral

c) Looks to the extracted mineral for return of capital

2) Investment need not be in cash and could be in, for example,

a) Land that ensures control over access to the mineral

b) Stationary equipment used to extract and produce the mineral

c. Cost depletion is computed as follows:

`Adjusted basis in mineral property ÷ Estimated mineral units available at year's start × Mineral units sold during year`

NOTE: The total deductions are limited to unrecovered capital investment.

1) Percentage depletion, which allows deduction in excess of capital investment, is the lower of
   a) 50% of the person's TI before depletion (100% in some cases)
   b) A percentage (specified by statute) of gross income from the property less related rents or royalties paid or incurred

Stop and review! You have completed the outline for this subunit. Study multiple-choice questions 6 through 10 beginning on page 246.

6.3 CAPITAL GAINS AND LOSSES

Background

Few topics in the tax code have been the subject of as much back-and-forth political pressure as capital gains. They are often the primary source of income for the very rich, i.e., those who do not work for wages. Thus, parties to the tax debate who maintain that upper-income taxpayers should shoulder a greater share of the national tax burden have always found capital gains an appropriate item to tax heavily, allowing wage earners some relief. Those on the other side of the debate respond that capital gains should be either lightly taxed or not at all, since new capital projects provide employment for those at all points on the economic spectrum. Because of these conflicting visions, the treatment of capital gains has undergone a dizzying number of changes over the life of the Internal Revenue Code.

1. **Capital Assets**
   a. All property is characterized as a capital asset, unless expressly excluded.
   b. The following types of property are not capital assets:
      1) Inventory (or stock in trade) -- property held primarily for sale to customers in the ordinary course of a trade or business
      2) Real or depreciable property used in a trade or business
      3) Accounts or notes receivable acquired in the ordinary course of trade or business for services rendered or for 1) or 2) above
      4) Copyrights and artistic compositions held by the person who composed them
      5) Certain U.S. government publications acquired at reduced cost
   c. Property held either for personal use or for the production of income is a capital asset, but dealer property (i.e., property held primarily for sale to customers in the ordinary course of trade or business) is not.
      1) Stocks, bonds, commodities, and the like are capital assets unless they are dealer property.
      2) Land held primarily for investment (capital asset), which is then subdivided, may be treated as converted to property held for sale in a trade or business.
   d. Goodwill is a capital asset when generated within the business. If a business sells its assets and receives more than the FMV of those assets, the remainder is considered a capital gain from the sale of goodwill.
2. **Gain (Loss) Realized and Recognized**
   a. Generally, all gains (losses) are realized on the sale or other disposition of property. This includes sales or exchanges that are required in characterizing a realized gain or loss as capital. For capital assets that become wholly worthless during the year, the sale or disposition date is considered to be the last day of the year.
      1) For real property, a sale or exchange occurs on the earlier of the date of conveyance or the date that the burdens of ownership pass to the buyer.

2) Also, liquidating distributions and losses on worthless securities are treated as sales or exchanges.
3) The transfer of a franchise is not treated as a sale or exchange of a capital asset if the transferor retains significant power, rights, or continuing interest with respect to the franchise.

b. The following formula shows computation of gain or loss realized:

	Money received (or to be received)		
+	FMV of other property received [1]		
+	Liability relief [2]		
–	Money or other property given up		
–	Selling expenses [3]		Amount realized
–	Liabilities assumed [2]	–	Adjusted basis
=	Amount realized	=	Gain (loss) realized

[1] *If FMV of other property received is not determinable with reasonable certainty, FMV of the property given up is used.*

[2] *Whether recourse or nonrecourse.*

[3] *Selling expenses are subtracted from gross receivables to yield the amount realized.*

EXAMPLE

The purchase price of a building was $400,000 ($100,000 cash + $300,000 mortgage). Two years later, improvements of $80,000 were made to the building. The building sold for $700,000 ($600,000 cash + $100,000 mortgage balance). A total of $180,000 depreciation had been taken as of the date sold. The adjusted basis is $300,000 ($400,000 original basis + $80,000 improvements – $180,000 depreciation taken). The realized gain is $400,000 ($700,000 cash and liability relief – $300,000 adjusted basis).

c. All realized gains must be recognized unless the IRC expressly provides otherwise. Conversely, no deduction is allowed for a realized loss unless the IRC expressly provides for it.

NOTE: Though personal-use property is a capital asset, and gains from such property are recognized, a loss is not deductible.

3. **Holding Period**

a. The holding period of an asset is measured in calendar months, beginning on the day after acquisition and including the disposal date.

Acquisition by or of	Holding Period -- Starts or by reference to
Sale or exchange	Acquisition [1]
Gift: for gain	Donor's acquisition
for loss	Acquisition
Inheritance	Automatic LT
Nontaxable exchanges	
Like-kind (Sec. 1031)	Include HP of exchanged asset [2]
Corporate stock (Sec. 351)	Include HP of contributed asset
Property in entity	Include transferor's HP
Partnership interest (Sec. 721)	Include HP of contributed asset [2]
Property in entity	Include transferor's HP [2]
Ordinary income property	Exchange
Involuntary conversion (Sec. 1033)	Include HP of converted asset
Residence (Sec. 1034)	Include HP of old home
Use conversion (T/B & personal)	Include period of prior use
Optioned property	Exclude option period
Securities	Trading date
Short sales (Ss)	Earlier of Ss closing or property sale date
Commodity futures	LT after 6-month HP

[1] *Always start computation using day after date of applicable acquisition.*

[2] *If capital asset or Sec. 1231 property; otherwise, the holding period starts the day after date of exchange.*

b. Long-term capital gain or loss (LTCG or LTCL) is realized from a capital asset held for more than 1 year. Short-term capital gain or loss (STCG or STCL) is realized if the asset was held 1 year or less.

c. For individuals, net capital gain (NCG) is the excess of net LTCG over net STCL. Net STCG is not included in NCG. Do not confuse it with capital gain net income.

d. Net STCG is treated as ordinary income for individuals. Net capital gain rates do not apply to net STCG.

   1) Net STCG = STCG – STCL.
   2) But net STCG may be offset by net LTCL.

4. **Taxation**

   a. For individuals, net short-term capital gain is taxed as ordinary income.

   b. For individuals, capital transactions involving **long-term holding periods** (assets held for over 12 months) are grouped by tax rates. The maximum capital gains rates are 0%, 15%, 20%, 25%, or 28%. These capital transaction groups are combined into "baskets."

      1) **15/20% Basket**

         a) The capital gains rate is **0%** if the taxpayer is in the 10% or 15% income tax brackets.

         b) The capital gains rate is **15%** if the taxpayer is in the 25%, 28%, 33%, or 35% income tax brackets.

         c) The capital gains rate is **20%** if the taxpayer is in the 39.6% tax bracket.

      2) **25% Basket**

         a) The capital gains rate is **25%** on unrecaptured Sec. 1250 gains (discussed further in Subunit 6.7).

      3) **28% Basket**

         a) The capital gains rate is **28%** on gains and losses from the sale of collectibles and gains from Sec. 1202 stock (certain small business stock).

   c. After gains and losses are classified in the appropriate baskets, losses for each long-term basket are first used to offset any gains within that basket.

   d. If a long-term basket has a net loss, the loss will be used first to offset net gain for the highest long-term rate basket, then to offset the next highest rate basket and so on.

EXAMPLE

A taxpayer realizes a $10,000 net loss in the 15/20% basket, a $5,000 net gain in the 25% basket, and an $8,000 net gain in the 28% basket. The taxpayer will first apply the net loss against the gain in the 28% basket, reducing the gain in this basket to zero. Then, the remaining $2,000 loss is applied against the gain in the 25% basket, leaving a $3,000 net capital gain in the 25% basket.

   e. A carryover of a net long-term capital loss from a prior year is used first to offset any net gain in the 28% basket, then to offset any net gain in the 25% basket, and finally to offset any net gain in the 15/20% basket. Likewise, net STCL is also used first to offset net gain for the highest long-term basket and so on.

EXAMPLE

A taxpayer has a $1,000 long-term capital loss carryover, a net short-term capital loss of $2,000, a $1,000 net gain in the 28% basket, and a $5,000 net gain in the 15/20% basket. Both losses are first applied to offset the 28% rate gain, using the $1,000 loss carryover first until completely exhausted. Since no gain exists in the 28% basket after applying the carryover, the net STCL is then applied against the next highest gain in the 15/20% basket. As a result, only a $3,000 net capital gain remains in the 15/20% basket.

f. An individual may use a net capital loss in the current year up to the lesser of $3,000 ($1,500 if MFS) or ordinary income.
   1) An individual may carry forward any excess CLs indefinitely.
   2) The carryforward is treated as a CL incurred in the subsequent year.
   3) Net STCL is treated as having been deductible in the preceding year before net LTCL.
   4) No carryover is allowed from a decedent to their estate.

g. Schedule D (Form 1040) is used to compute and summarize capital gains and/or losses on the sale or disposition of capital assets listed on Form 8949, and the summary combines the long-term gains (losses) with the short-term gains (losses). When these capital gains and losses all net to a gain, it is called capital gain net income.

h. For corporations, all capital gain is taxed at the corporation's regular tax rate.

i. A corporation may use CLs only to offset CGs each year. A corporation must carry the excess CL back 3 years and forward 5 years and characterize all carryovers as STCLs (regardless of character).

5. **Return of Capital**

a. The amount of a distribution is a dividend to the extent of earnings and profits. Dividends do not reduce the shareholder's basis in the stock.

b. A shareholder treats the amount of a distribution in excess of earnings and profits (E&P) as tax-exempt return of capital to the extent of his or her basis. A distribution in excess of basis is a capital gain.

6. **Wash Sales**

a. A current loss realized on a wash sale of securities is not recognized. A wash sale occurs when substantially the same securities are purchased within 30 days before or after being sold at a loss.
   1) The disallowed loss is added to the basis of the stock purchased in the wash sale.
   2) The holding period includes that of the originally purchased stock.
   3) Spouses are treated as one person.

EXAMPLE

Taxpayer sells 100 shares of ABC stock for $400, a loss of $200. Within 30 days, Taxpayer purchases an identical 100 shares of ABC for $500 and sells all 100 shares two months later for $900. Taxpayer recognizes no loss (i.e., $200) on first sale and only $200 gain ($900 sale price – $500 cost – $200 basis adjustment due to loss) on subsequent sale of stock.

7. **Small Business Stock**

a. Sec. 1244 stock is stock (common or preferred, voting or nonvoting) of a small business corporation held since its issuance (e.g., not acquired by gift) and issued for money or other property (not stock or securities).

b. Up to $50,000 ($100,000 if MFJ) of loss realized on disposition or worthlessness of Sec. 1244 stock is treated as an ordinary loss.
   1) The limit applies to Sec. 1244 stock held in all corporations.
   2) The limit is applied at a partner level, if applicable.
   3) The loss is considered to be from a trade or business for NOL purposes.

c. To be classified as a small business corporation, the aggregate amount of money and property received by the corporation for stock cannot exceed $1 million.
   1) Even if the contributions exceed $1 million, part of the stock (up to $1 million) may be designated by the corporation as qualifying for Sec. 1244 ordinary loss treatment.

d. If the basis of property contributed in exchange for Sec. 1244 stock exceeds its FMV, the excess is treated as capital loss before any other realized loss may be treated as ordinary.

1) Basis in the stock is equal to the property's basis in the hands of the transferor when contributed.

e. Additional investment without issuance of additional shares of Sec. 1244 stock increases original basis; however, any resulting loss must be apportioned between the qualifying Sec. 1244 stock and the nonqualifying additional capital interest.

8. **Small Business Stock Exclusion**

a. Under Section 1202, taxpayers may exclude 50% of the gain from the sale or exchange of small business stock. The stock must have been issued after August 10, 1993, and held for more than 5 years. The exclusion increases to 75% for stock acquired after February 17, 2009, and before September 28, 2010. The exclusion increases to 100% for stock acquired after September 27, 2010, and before January 1, 2016. This exclusion expired but is expected to be renewed and applicable for 2015.

Capital gains and losses has been a heavily tested topic on CPA exams, with both conceptual and calculation questions being used to test this area.

9. **Nonbusiness Bad Debt**

a. A business bad debt is deductible to arrive at AGI (above-the-line) as ordinary loss. A nonbusiness bad debt is treated as a STCL.

10. **Business Start-up Costs**

a. Capitalized amounts not yet amortized upon disposition of the business are treated as a capital loss.

11. **Short Sales**

a. Property held long-term substantially identical to property sold short (at that time) results in any loss on the short sale being treated as long-term.

12. **Casualties**

a. Casualty losses on personal-use capital assets are itemized deductions.

13. **Market Discount Bonds**

a. Gain on sale is treated as ordinary income to the extent the market discount could have accrued as interest.

$$\text{Taxable accrued market discount} = \text{Market discount} \times \frac{\text{\# of days security held}}{\text{\# of days from acquisition to maturity}}$$

EXAMPLE

John purchases a $100, 360-day bond for $90. The market discount equals $10. If John sells the bond 180 days later, he must recognize $5 (half of the discount) as ordinary income (interest).

14. **Bond Premium Treatment**

a. The bondholder may either (1) elect to amortize the premium until bond maturity and reduce the basis or (2) elect not to amortize and treat the premium as bond basis.

Stop and review! You have completed the outline for this subunit. Study multiple-choice questions 11 through 17 beginning on page 247.

6.4 RELATED PARTY SALES

1. **Limited Tax Avoidance**
   a. These rules limit tax avoidance between related parties.
   b. Gain recognized on an asset transfer to a related person in whose hands the asset is depreciable is ordinary income.
   c. Loss realized on sale or exchange of property to a related person is not deductible. The transferee takes a cost basis. There is no adding of holding periods.
      1) Gain realized on a subsequent sale to an unrelated party is recognized only to the extent it exceeds the previously disallowed loss.
         a) If the gain realized on the sale to an unrelated third party is less than the amount of disallowed loss, no gain is recognized.
      2) Loss realized on a subsequent sale to a third party is recognized, but the previously disallowed loss is not added to it.
   d. For purposes of these provisions, related parties generally include
      1) Ancestors (parents, grandparents, etc.), descendants (children, grandchildren, etc.), spouses, and siblings
      2) Trusts and beneficiaries of trusts
      3) Controlled entities (50% ownership)

      NOTE: Constructive ownership rules between family members apply.
   e. Loss on sale or exchange of property between a partnership and a person owning more than 50% of the capital or profit interests in the partnership is not deductible.

Stop and review! You have completed the outline for this subunit. Study multiple-choice questions 18 through 21 beginning on page 249.

6.5 INSTALLMENT SALES

1. **Overview**
   a. An installment sale is a disposition of property in which at least one payment is to be received after the close of the tax year of the disposition.
   b. The installment method must be used to report installment sales unless election is made not to apply the method.
2. **Excluded Dispositions**
   a. Installment sales do not apply to the following dispositions:
      1) Inventory personal property sales
      2) Revolving credit personal property sales
      3) Dealer dispositions, including dispositions of
         a) Personal property of a type regularly sold by the person on the installment plan
         b) Real property held for sale to customers in the ordinary course of trade or business
      4) Securities, generally, if publicly traded
      5) Sales on agreement to establish an irrevocable escrow account
3. **Specific Dispositions Not Excluded**
   a. Not excluded from installment sale deferral are certain sales of residential lots or timeshares subject to interest on the deferred tax and property used or produced in a farming business.

4. **Recognized Gain**

   a. The amount of realized gain to be recognized in a tax year is equal to the gross profit multiplied by the ratio of payments received in the current year divided by the total contract price.

$$\text{Realized gain} = \text{Gross profit} \times \frac{\text{Payments received in the current year}}{\text{Total contract price}}$$

   b. Recognize, as income, payments received multiplied by the gross profit ratio.

$$\text{Recognized gain} = \text{Gross profit ratio} \times \text{Payments received}$$

      1) A payment is considered paid in full if the balance is placed into an irrevocable escrow account (i.e., amounts that cannot revert to the purchaser) at a later date.

   c. The gross profit is the sales price minus selling expenses (including debt forgiveness) and adjusted basis. It includes the unrecognized gain on sale of a personal residence.

      1) The sales price is the sum of any cash received, liability relief, and installment notes from the buyer. It does not include imputed interest.
      2) Gross profit includes the unrecognized gain on sale of a personal residence.

   d. The total contract price is the sales price minus liabilities assumed by the buyer (that does not exceed the seller's basis in the property).

      1) Contract price includes the excess of liability assumed over AB and selling expenses.

         a) When the liability exceeds AB and selling expenses, the gross profit percentage is 100%.

   e. The gross profit ratio is the ratio of the gross profit to the total contract price.

$$\text{Gross profit ratio} = \frac{\text{Gross profit}}{\text{Contract price}} = \frac{\text{Selling price} - \text{Selling expense} - \text{Adjusted basis}}{\text{Amount to be collected}}$$

      1) When the selling price is reduced in a future year, the gross profit on the sale will also will be reduced. Therefore, the gross profit ratio must be recalculated for the remaining periods by using the reduced sales price and subtracting the gross profit already recognized.

5. **Repossession**

   a. The seller recognizes as gain or loss any difference between the FMV of repossessed personal property and the AB of an installment sale obligation satisfied by the repossession. If real property, recognize the lesser of

      1) Cash and other property (FMV) received in excess of gain already recognized or
      2) Gross profit in remaining installments less repossession costs.

   b. Interest is imposed on deferred tax on obligations from nondealer installment sales (of more than $150,000) outstanding at the close of the tax year. This interest is applied if the taxpayer has nondealer installment receivables of over $5 million at the close of the tax year from installment sales of over $150,000 that occurred during the year.

      1) This interest is not applied to the following:

         a) Personal-use property
         b) Residential lots and time shares
         c) Property produced or used in the farming business

6. **Disposition of Installment Obligations**
   a. Excess of the FMV over the AB of an installment obligation is generally recognized if it is transferred. FMV is generally the amount realized. If a gift, use the face amount of the obligation.
   b. Exceptions. Disposition of obligations by the following events can result in the transferee treating payments as the transferor would have:
      1) Transfers to a controlled corporation
      2) Corporate reorganizations and liquidations
      3) Contributions to capital of, or distributions from, partnerships
      4) Transfer between spouses incident to divorce
      5) Transfer upon death of the obligee
   c. The date the installment payment is received determines the capital gains rate to be applied rather than the date the asset was sold under an installment sales contract.
7. **Character**
   a. Character of gain recognized depends on the nature of the property in the transferor's hands.
   b. The full amount of Secs. 1245 and 1250 ordinary gain ("depreciation recapture") must be recognized in the year of sale, even if it is more than payments received. The gain is added to basis before further applying the installment method.
   c. An anti-avoidance rule applies to an installment sale of property to a related party. On a second disposition (by the related party transferee in the first sale), payments received must be treated as a payment received by the person who made the first (installment) sale to a related party.
      1) A second disposition by gift is included. The FMV is treated as the payment.
      2) Death of the first disposition seller or buyer does not accelerate recognition.

Stop and review! You have completed the outline for this subunit. Study multiple-choice question 22 on page 250.

6.6 NONRECOGNITION TRANSACTIONS

1. **General Rule**
   a. The general rule is to recognize all gain realized during the tax year. This topic discusses some transactions for which the IRC requires or permits exclusion or deferral of all or part of the gain realized in the current tax year.
2. **Like-Kind Exchanges**
   a. Sec. 1031 defers recognizing gain or loss to the extent that property productively used in a trade or business or held for the production of income (investment) is exchanged for property of like kind.
   b. Like-kind property is alike in nature or character but not necessarily in grade or quality.
      1) Properties are of like kind if each is within a class of like nature or character, without regard to differences in use (e.g., business or investment), improvements (e.g., bare land or house), location, or proximity.

General Asset Classes	
Office furniture, fixtures, and equipment (asset class 00.11)	Light general-purpose trucks (asset class 00.241)
Information systems (computers and peripheral equipment) (asset class 00.12)	Heavy general-purpose trucks (asset class 00.242)
Data handling equipment, except computers (asset class 00.13)	Railroad cars and locomotives, except those owned by railroad transportation companies (asset class 00.25)
Airplanes (airframes and engines), except those used in commercial or contract carrying of passengers or freight, and all helicopters (airframes and engines) (asset class 00.21)	Tractor units for use over-the-road (asset class 00.26)
Automobiles, taxis (asset class 00.22)	Trailers and trailer-mounted containers (asset class 00.27)
Buses (asset class 00.23)	Vessels, barges, tugs, and similar water transportation equipment, except those used in marine construction (asset class 00.28)
Industrial steam and electric generation and/or distribution systems (asset class 00.4)	

EXAMPLE

Taxpayer C transfers a railroad car (asset class 00.25) to D in exchange for a tractor-trailer container (asset class 00.27). The properties exchanged are not of a like class because they are within different General Asset Classes. Because each of the properties is within a General Asset Class, the properties may not be classified within a Product Class. The airplane and heavy general-purpose truck are also not of a like kind. Therefore, the exchange does not qualify for nonrecognition of gain or loss under section 1031.

2) Real property is of like kind to other real property, except foreign property.
3) Personal property and real property are not of like kind.
4) A lease of real property for 30 or more years is treated as real property.

c. The following property types do not qualify for Sec. 1031 nonrecognition:

1) Money
2) Liabilities
3) Inventory
4) Partnership interest in different partnerships, e.g., general for general
5) Securities and debt instruments, e.g., stocks, bonds

d. Boot is all nonqualified property transferred in an exchange transaction.

e. **Gain is recognized** equal to the lesser of gain realized or boot received.

1) Boot received includes cash, net liability relief, and other nonqualified property (its FMV).

a) If each party assumes a liability of the other, only the net liability given or received is treated as boot.

f. Basis. Qualified property received in a like-kind exchange has an exchanged basis adjusted for boot and gain recognized.

AB of property given
\+ Gain recognized
\+ Boot given (cash, liability incurred, other property)
– Boot received (cash, liability relief, other property)
= Basis in acquired property

g. If some qualified property is exchanged, loss realized with respect to qualified or other property is not recognized. However, excess mortgage incurred cannot be netted against cash received.

3. **Involuntary Conversions**

a. A taxpayer may elect to defer recognition of gain if property is involuntarily converted into money or property that is similar or related in service or use under Sec. 1033.

1) An involuntary conversion of property results from destruction, theft, seizure, requisition, condemnation, or the threat of imminent requisition or condemnation.

2) Sec. 1033 does not apply to any realized losses.

a) Loss from condemnation or requisition of a personal-use asset is not deductible. But certain casualty losses are deductible.

b) When loss is realized, basis is determined independently of Sec. 1033.

b. Similar or related in service or use means that the property has the qualities outlined in items 1) and 2) below:

1) For an **owner-user**, functional similarity, i.e., meets a functional use test that requires that the property

a) Have similar physical characteristics
b) Be used for the same purpose

2) For an **owner-investor**, a close relationship to the service or use the previous property had to the investor, such that the owner-investor's

a) Risks, management activities, services performed, etc., continue without substantial change.

3) Generally, if property held for investment or for productive use in a trade or business is involuntarily converted due to a **federally declared disaster**, the tangible replacement property will be deemed similar or related in service or use. Any tangible property acquired and held for productive use in a trade or business is treated as similar or related in service or use to property that was

a) Held for investment or for productive use in a trade or business and
b) Involuntarily converted as a result of a federally declared disaster.

c. Direct conversion. Proceeds of an involuntary conversion are qualified property.

1) Nonrecognition is mandatory, not elective, on direct conversion to the extent of any amount realized in the form of qualified replacement property.

2) Basis in the proceeds (property) is exchanged, i.e., equal to the basis in the converted property.

d. Indirect conversion. Acquiring control of a corporation that owns similar or related-in-service-or-use property is treated as acquiring qualified property. Control is ownership of at least 80% of the voting stock and 80% of any other stock.

1) Recognized gain is limited to any excess of any amount realized over any cost of qualified property.

e. When property is converted involuntarily into nonqualified proceeds and qualified property is purchased within the replacement period, an election may be made to defer realized gain.

1) The deferral is limited to the extent that the amount realized is reinvested in qualified replacement property.

2) Basis in the qualified replacement property is decreased by the amount of any unrecognized gain.

f. The replacement period begins on the earlier of the date of disposition or the threat of condemnation and ends 2 years after the close of the first tax year in which any part of the gain is realized.
   1) If real property used in business or held for investment (not inventory, dealer property, or personal-use property) is converted by condemnation or requisition, or threat thereof, 3 years is allowed.
   2) Construction of qualified property must be complete before the end of the replacement period for its cost to be included.

g. For real property used in business or held for investment (not inventory, dealer property, personal-use property, etc.), if conversion is by condemnation, like-kind property qualifies as replacement. This standard is less stringent.
   1) Conversion must be direct. There is no indirect ownership allowance.

h. To recap, on a Sec. 1033 involuntary conversion, realized gain is generally recognized only to the extent that any amount realized exceeds the cost of the similar or related-in-service property.
   1) The gain recognized is classified as OI under Sec. 1245 or Sec. 1250.

4. **Sale of Principal Residence**

a. Sec. 121 provides an exclusion upon the sale of a principal residence. No loss may be recognized on the sale of a personal residence.

b. A taxpayer may exclude up to $250,000 ($500,000 for married taxpayers filing jointly) of realized gain on the sale of a principal residence.

c. The individual must have owned and used the residence for an aggregate of 2 of the 5 prior years.
   1) For married taxpayers, the $500,000 exclusion is available if
      a) Either spouse meets the ownership requirement
      b) Both spouses meet the use requirement
      c) Neither spouse is ineligible for the exclusion by virtue of a sale or an exchange of a residence within the last 2 years
   2) However, if one spouse fails to meet these requirements, the other qualifying spouse is not prevented from claiming a $250,000 exclusion.

d. The exclusion may be used only once every 2 years.

e. The exclusion amount may be prorated if the use and ownership tests are not met. The exclusion is based on the ratio of months used to 24 months and is a proportion of the total exclusion.
   1) The pro rata exclusion is allowed if the sale is due to a change in the place of employment, health, or unforeseen circumstances.

f. The gain on the sale of the residence must be prorated between qualified and nonqualified use.
   1) Nonqualified use includes periods that the residence was not used as the principal residence of the taxpayer.
   2) Nonqualified use does not include use before 2009.

g. Gain must be recognized to the extent of any depreciation adjustments with respect to the rental or business use of a principal residence after May 6, 1997.

h. Basis in a new home is its cost.

5. **Sec. 1202 Qualified Small Business Stock**
   a. When a taxpayer sells or exchanges Sec. 1202 small business stock that the taxpayer has held for more than 5 years, 50% of the gain may be excluded from the taxpayer's gross income.
      1) If the small business stock qualifies for this 50% exclusion, any recognized gain from the sale or exchange of the stock is subject to a maximum capital gains rate of 28%.
   b. The general requirements for stock to be treated as Sec. 1202 qualified small business stock are as follows:
      1) The stock is received after August 10, 1993.
      2) The issuing corporation is a domestic C corporation.
      3) The seller is the original owner of the stock.
      4) The corporation's gross assets do not exceed $50 million at the time the stock was issued.
   c. If the stock is acquired after February 17, 2009, and before September 28, 2010, 75% of the gain may be excluded. The exclusion increases to 100% for stock acquired after September 27, 2010, and before January 1, 2016. This exclusion expired but is expected to be renewed and applicable for 2015.

Stop and review! You have completed the outline for this subunit. Study multiple-choice questions 23 through 26 beginning on page 250.

6.7 BUSINESS PROPERTY

Author's note: Because the concepts in this subunit are challenging, we have included four examples at the end to provide additional context. Read through the outline and be sure to pay close attention to the examples in order to see the rules in practice.

1. **Overview**
   a. Secs. 1231, 1245, and 1250 recharacterize gain or loss.

Overview of Business Property Recharacterization

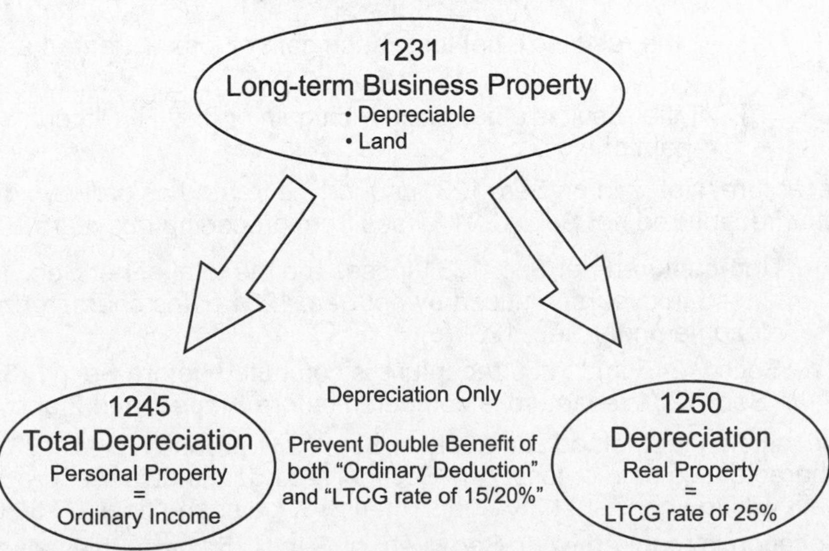

Figure 6-1

2. Sec. 1231 Property

Background

Before 1938, productive assets used in business were treated as capital property. As the Great Depression dragged on, however, it became clear that relief was needed–businesses struggling to sell their outmoded equipment found themselves subject to the limitations on recognizing capital losses. Thus, the Revenue Act of 1938 carved out an exception to capital gain-and-loss treatment for business property. By 1942, however, another change was called for, since the treatment needed during a depression was not appropriate for a wartime economy. Firms making large profits selling to the government needed lower rates on capital gains, so Sec. 117 (forerunner of the current Sec. 1231) was modified once again to provide special treatment for capital gains.

a. Section 1231 property is property held for more than 1 year and includes
   1) All real or depreciable property used in a trade or business
   2) Involuntarily converted capital assets held in connection with a trade or business or in a transaction entered into for a profit
b. Examples of Sec. 1231 property include apartment buildings, parking lots, manufacturing equipment, and involuntarily converted investment artwork.
c. Examples of property that is not Sec. 1231 property include personal-use property and inventory.
d. Sec. 1231 is beneficial to the taxpayer. When Sec. 1231 property gains exceed losses (a net Sec. 1231 gain), each gain or loss is treated as being from the sale of a long-term capital asset. However, if Sec. 1231 property losses exceed gains (a net Sec. 1231 loss), each gain or loss is considered ordinary. Sec. 1231 has a two-step test.
   1) Step 1: Determine net gain or loss from all casualties or thefts of Sec. 1231 property for the tax year. Gain or loss from involuntary conversions by other than casualty or theft is included in Step 2 but not Step 1.
      a) If the result is a net loss, each gain or loss is treated as ordinary income or loss.
      b) If the result is a net gain, each gain or loss is included in Step 2.
   2) Step 2: Determine net gain or loss from all dispositions of Sec. 1231 property for the year, including the property included in Step 1 only if Step 1 resulted in a net gain.
      a) If the result is a net loss, each gain or loss is treated as ordinary income or loss.
      b) If the result is a net gain, each gain or loss is treated as a long-term capital gain or loss.
e. Recapture. Net gain on Sec. 1231 property is treated as ordinary income to the extent of unrecaptured net Sec. 1231 losses from preceding tax years.
   1) Unrecaptured net Sec. 1231 losses are the total of net Sec. 1231 losses for the last 5 tax years, reduced by net Sec. 1231 gains characterized as ordinary income under Sec. 1231(c).
   2) Secs. 1245 and 1250 recapture is computed before Sec. 1231 recapture, but Sec. 1231 recapture is computed before Steps 1 and 2 above.
f. The installment method can apply to Sec. 1231 property. Sec. 1231 merely characterizes gain or loss. Any Section 1231 gain that is recharacterized as capital gain will first consist of 28% gain, then 25% gain, and finally, 15/20% gain.
g. Allocation is required when Sec. 1245 or Sec. 1250 property is also Sec. 1231 property and only a portion of gain recognized is Sec. 1245 or Sec. 1250 OI.
h. Sec. 1245 and 1250 only involve gains. If disposition of business property results in a loss then the loss is a 1231 loss.

3. **Sec. 1245 Ordinary Income**
   a. Sec. 1245 property generally is depreciable personal property (tangible/intangible) used in a trade or business for over 12 months.
   b. Gain on the disposition of Sec. 1245 property is ordinary income to the extent of the lesser of all depreciation taken (including amounts expensed under Sec. 179) or gain recognized.
      1) If gain realized is not recognized (like-kind exchanges, involuntary conversions, etc.), Sec. 1245 ordinary income is limited to the sum of the following:
         a) Gain recognized
         b) FMV of property acquired that is not Sec. 1245 property and is not included in computing the recognized gain
      2) The recognized gain in excess of the depreciation taken may be treated as a gain from the sale or exchange of Sec. 1231 property.
   c. Intangible amortizable personal Sec. 1245 property examples include
      1) Leaseholds of Sec. 1245 property
      2) Professional athletic contracts, e.g., baseball
      3) Patents
      4) Goodwill acquired in connection with the acquisition of a trade or business
      5) Covenants not to compete
4. **Sec. 1250 Ordinary Income**
   a. Sec. 1250 property is all depreciable real property, such as a building or its structural components.
      1) Examples of Sec. 1250 property include shopping malls, an apartment or office building, low-income housing, rented portions of residences, and escalators or elevators (placed in service after 1986).
      2) Land is not Sec. 1250 property, but leases of land are Sec. 1250 intangible properties. Certain improvements to land may be treated as land, e.g., dams and irrigation systems.
   b. Sec. 1250 property is subject to its own recapture rules. For the three items listed below, the aggregate gain recognized on the sale or disposition of Sec. 1250 property is ordinary income.
      1) The excess of accelerated depreciation taken over S-L depreciation is ordinary income to the extent of gain recognized. This applies to purchases made before 1987.
      2) For property held less than 1 year, the remaining depreciation is recaptured.

      NOTE: Partial reduction of excess depreciation is provided for under Sec. 1250 for low-income housing and rehabilitated structures.

      3) For corporations, the gain must be computed under both Sec. 1245 and 1250. If Sec. 1245 gain is larger than Sec. 1250 gain, 20% of the difference is characterized as ordinary income.
   c. If gain realized is not recognized (like-kind exchanges, involuntary conversions, etc.), Sec. 1250 ordinary income is limited to the greater of the following:
      1) Recognized gain
      2) Excess of the potential Sec. 1250 ordinary income over the FMV of Sec. 1250 property received

5. **Gift Property**
   a. Neither Sec. 1245 nor Sec. 1250 applies to a gift disposition.
   b. Any gain realized by the donee upon a subsequent taxable disposition is subject to Sec. 1245 and Sec. 1250 characterization up to the sum of
      1) Potential Sec. 1245 and Sec. 1250 OI at the time of the gift
      2) Potential Sec. 1245 and Sec. 1250 OI arising between gift and subsequent disposition
6. **Inherited Property**
   a. Neither Sec. 1245 nor Sec. 1250 applies to a disposition by bequest, devise, or intestate succession.
   b. Exceptions: Sec. 1245 and Sec. 1250 OI are recognized for a transfer at death to the extent of any income in respect of a decedent (IRD). Sec. 1245 OI potential also results from depreciation allowed to a decedent because the depreciation does not carry over to the transferee.
7. **Installment Sales**
   a. All gain realized from a disposal of recapture property in an installment sale is characterized as ordinary income (OI) by Sec. 1245 or Sec 1250.
      1) The gain must be recognized in the period of sale.
      2) Any excess gain over Sec. 1245 or Sec. 1250 OI is accounted for by the installment method.
8. **Income for Multiple Assets**
   a. Income received or accrued for more than one asset is allocated to each asset by agreement, by FMV, or by the residual method.
      1) To compute Sec. 1245 and Sec. 1250 ordinary income, an amount realized allocable to an asset must be further allocated to each use of a mixed use asset for each tax year.
9. **Sec. 351 Exchange for Stock**
   a. Generally, no gain is recognized upon an exchange of property for all the stock of a newly formed corporation.
   b. Sec. 1245 and Sec. 1250 OI is limited to any amount of gain recognized in a Sec. 351 transaction.

The topic of business property gain (loss) recharacterization often intimidates CPA candidates as they study for the exam due to the different rules applied under Secs. 1231, 1245, and 1250. Because the AICPA has tested this area relatively often, you should have a solid understanding of these rules. Take the time necessary to understand the outline and answer the multiple-choice questions to reinforce your knowledge of this area.

EXAMPLE 1

On January 17, Year 1, Relief Corp. purchased and placed into service 7-year MACRS tangible property costing $100,000. On December 21, Year 4, Relief Corp. sold the property for $105,000 (selling price 1) after taking $60,000 in MACRS depreciation deductions.

The adjusted basis of the property is $40,000 ($100,000 historical cost – $60,000 depreciation); therefore, Relief will recognize a gain of $65,000 ($105,000 selling price 1 – $40,000 adjusted basis). Since this property qualifies for Sec. 1245 recapture, the gain will be recaptured as ordinary income to the extent of the lesser of all depreciation taken or gain realized. Thus, Relief will have $60,000 of Sec. 1245 (ordinary) gain. The remaining $5,000 of gain is Sec. 1231 (capital) gain.

EXAMPLE 2

The facts from the previous example apply, except Relief sold the property for $95,000 (selling price 2).

Relief will recognize a gain of $55,000 ($95,000 selling price 2 – $40,000 adjusted basis). Since this property qualifies for Sec. 1245 recapture, the gain will be recaptured as ordinary income to the extent of the lesser of all depreciation taken or gain realized. Thus, Relief will have $55,000 of Sec. 1245 (ordinary) gain.

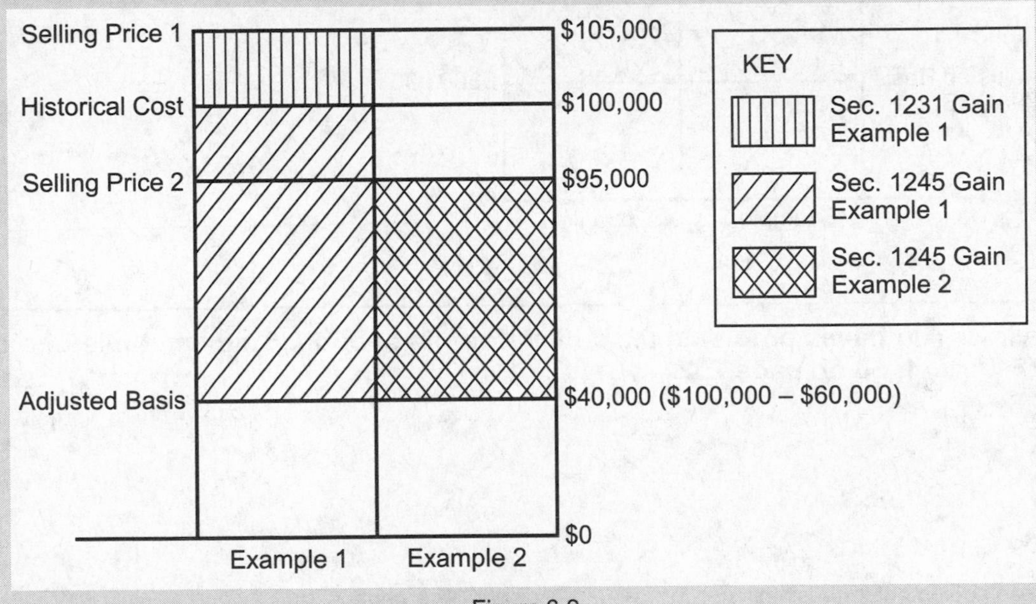

Figure 6-2

EXAMPLE 3

Martha purchased and placed into service Sec. 1250 property costing $600,000. After 5 years, the property was sold for $650,000 (selling price 1) after having taken $300,000 in MACRS depreciation deductions. Straight-line depreciation would have been $100,000.

The adjusted basis of the property is $300,000 ($600,000 historical cost – $300,000 MACRS depreciation); therefore, Martha will recognize a gain of $350,000 ($650,000 selling price 1 – $300,000 adjusted basis). Since this property is subject to Sec. 1250 recapture, the excess of accelerated depreciation taken over S-L depreciation is ordinary income to the extent of gain recognized. Thus, Martha will have $200,000 ($300,000 MACRS depreciation – $100,000 S-L depreciation) of Sec. 1250 (ordinary) gain. The remaining $150,000 ($350,000 gain recognized – $200,000 Sec. 1250 gain) is Sec. 1231 (capital) gain.

EXAMPLE 4

The facts from the previous example apply, except Martha sold the property for $400,000 (selling price 2).

Martha will recognize a gain of $100,000 ($400,000 selling price 2 – $300,000 adjusted basis). Since this property qualifies for Sec. 1250 recapture, the excess of accelerated depreciation taken over S-L depreciation is ordinary income to the extent of gain recognized, i.e., $200,000 limited to $100,000. Thus, Martha will have $100,000 of Sec. 1250 (ordinary) gain.

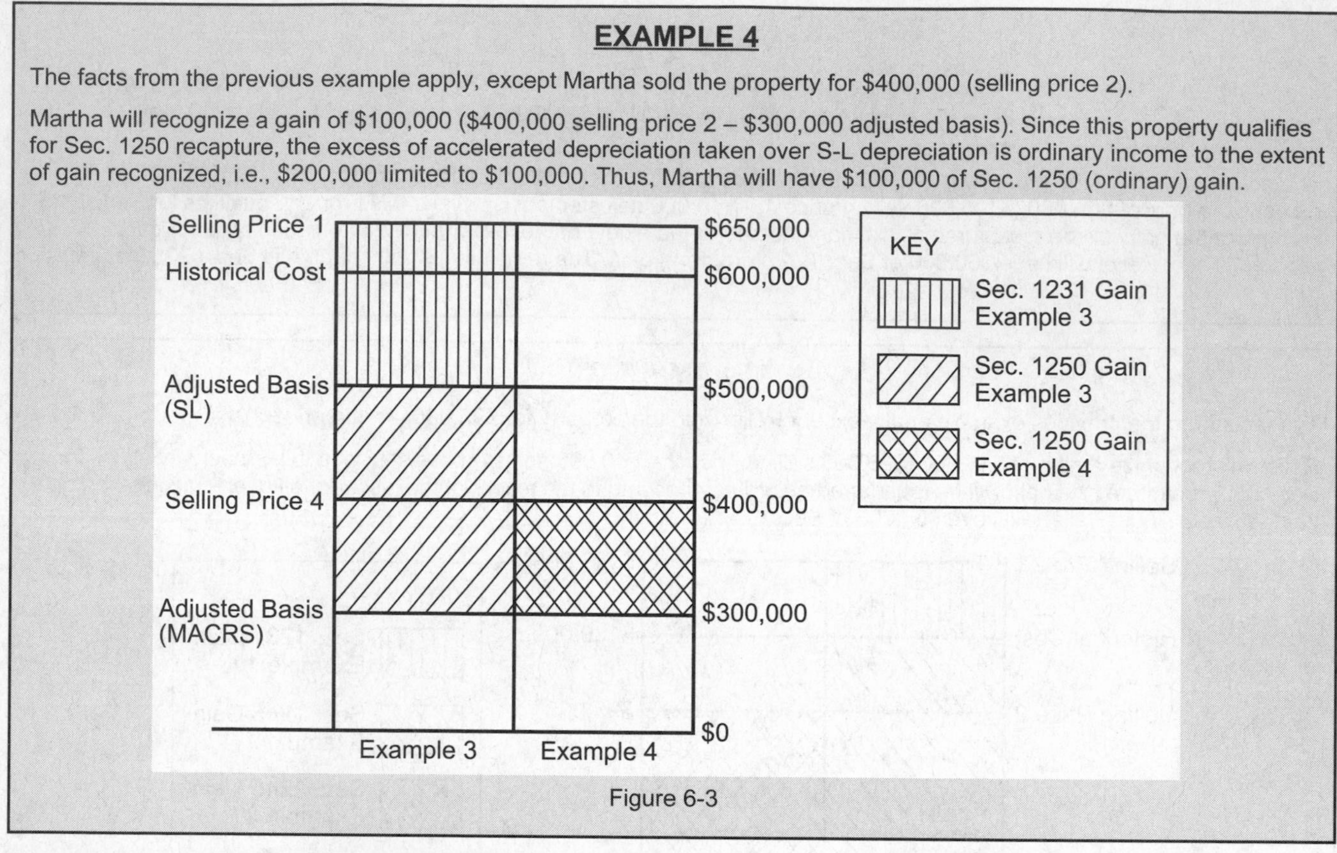

Figure 6-3

Stop and review! You have completed the outline for this subunit. Study multiple-choice questions 27 through 30 on page 252.

QUESTIONS

6.1 Basis

1. Bluff purchased equipment for business use for $35,000 and made $1,000 of improvements to the equipment. After deducting depreciation of $5,000, Bluff gave the equipment to Russett for business use. At the time the gift was made, the equipment had a fair market value of $32,000. Ignoring gift tax consequences, what is Russett's basis in the equipment?

A. $31,000
B. $32,000
C. $35,000
D. $36,000

Answer (A) is correct.

REQUIRED: The basis of an asset that was received as a gift.

DISCUSSION: According to IRS Publication 551, if the FMV of the property is equal to or greater than the donor's adjusted basis, the donee's basis is the donor's adjusted basis at the time the donee received the gift. The fair market value at the date of the gift is $32,000, while the donor's adjusted basis is $31,000 ($35,000 cost + $1,000 improvements – $5,000 depreciation). Thus, Russett's basis is equal to Bluff's adjusted basis of $31,000.

Answer (B) is incorrect. The FMV at the date of the gift is $32,000. The FMV is used only if the FMV is less than the donor's basis and the property is later sold for a loss. Answer (C) is incorrect. A basis of $35,000 ignores the $1,000 improvement that should be capitalized and the $5,000 of depreciation that reduces Bluff's adjusted basis in the equipment. Answer (D) is incorrect. A basis of $36,000 ignores the $5,000 of depreciation that reduces Bluff's adjusted basis in the equipment.

2. Fred Berk bought a plot of land with a cash payment of $40,000 and a $50,000 mortgage. In addition, Berk paid $200 for a title insurance policy. Berk's basis in this land is

A. $40,000

B. $40,200

C. $90,000

D. $90,200

Answer (D) is correct.

REQUIRED: The basis of the property acquired.

DISCUSSION: The basis of property is its cost. Cost includes cash paid and any debt to which the property is subject, regardless of whether the debt is recourse or nonrecourse. In addition, basis includes expenditures for major improvements and costs to acquire title.

Answer (A) is incorrect. Basis includes acquisition debt and costs. Answer (B) is incorrect. Basis includes acquisition debt to which the property is subject. Answer (C) is incorrect. The cost to acquire property, such as title insurance, is part of its cost basis.

3. The uniform capitalization method must be used by

I. Manufacturers of tangible personal property

II. Retailers of personal property with $2 million in average annual gross receipts for the 3 preceding years

A. I only.

B. II only.

C. Both I and II.

D. Neither I nor II.

Answer (A) is correct.

REQUIRED: The taxpayers required to use UNICAP rules.

DISCUSSION: A taxpayer that produces tangible personal property must capitalize all of the direct costs of producing the property and an allocable share of indirect costs regardless of whether the property is sold or used in the taxpayer's trade or business. A retailer that acquires property for resale must capitalize the costs unless the taxpayer's annual gross receipts for the 3 preceding years do not exceed $10 million.

4. In June of the current year, Susan's mother gave her 100 shares of a listed stock. The donor's basis for this stock, which she bought 10 years ago, was $4,000, and market value on the date of the gift was $3,000. Susan sold this stock in July of the current year for $3,500. The donor paid no gift tax. What was Susan's reportable gain or loss in the current year on the sale of the 100 shares of stock gifted to her?

A. $0

B. $500 gain.

C. $500 loss.

D. $1,000 loss.

Answer (A) is correct.

REQUIRED: The amount of gain or loss.

DISCUSSION: To compute gain, a donee's basis is the same as the donor's basis, adjusted for gift tax. For computing loss, the lower of the donor's adjusted basis or the FMV of the property is used. If the property is later transferred for more than FMV at the date of the gift but for less than the donor's basis at the date of the gift, no gain (loss) is recognized. Therefore, Susan reports neither gain nor loss.

	Gain	Loss
Amount realized	$3,500	$3,500
Less: basis	(4,000)	(3,000)
	No gain	No loss

5. Which of the following is subject to the Uniform Capitalization Rules of Code Sec. 263A?

A. Editorial costs incurred by a freelance writer.

B. Research and experimental expenditures.

C. Mine development and exploration costs.

D. Warehousing costs incurred by a manufacturing company with $12 million in annual gross receipts.

Answer (D) is correct.

REQUIRED: The uniform capitalization rules.

DISCUSSION: The uniform capitalization rules require the costs for construction (manufacture) of real or tangible personal property to be used in trade or business and costs of producing or acquiring property for sale to customers (retail) to be capitalized. The uniform capitalization rules do not apply if property is acquired for resale and the company's annual gross receipts (for the past 3 years) do not exceed $10 million. Both direct and most allocable indirect costs necessary to prepare the inventory for its intended use must be capitalized. The warehousing costs are direct costs that must be capitalized and the manufacturing company has annual gross receipts of $12 million so the exemption does not apply.

Answer (A) is incorrect. A freelance writer is not a manufacturing or acquisition activity. Answer (B) is incorrect. The research and experimental expenditures are not manufacturing or acquisition costs. Answer (C) is incorrect. Mine development and exploration costs are not manufacturing or acquisition costs.

6.2 Depreciation and Amortization

6. On August 1 of the current year, Graham purchased and placed into service an office building costing $264,000, including $30,000 for the land. What was Graham's MACRS deduction for the office building in the current year?

A. $9,600

B. $6,000

C. $3,600

D. $2,250

Answer (D) is correct.

REQUIRED: The amount of MACRS depreciation deduction.

DISCUSSION: Under MACRS, an office building is nonresidential real estate having a 39-year recovery period and is depreciated using the straight-line depreciation method. The land is not depreciable. The cost of the office building ($234,000) is divided by 39 years to yield $6,000. Because of the mid-month convention, 4.5 months of depreciation, or $2,250, is deductible in the year of purchase.

Answer (A) is incorrect. The $30,000 attributable to the land is not depreciable; nonresidential real property uses a 39-year, not a 27.5-year, recovery period; and only 4.5 months of depreciation can be expensed in the year of purchase. Answer (B) is incorrect. Only 4.5 months of depreciation can be expensed in the year of purchase. Answer (C) is incorrect. The $30,000 attributable to the land is not depreciable, and nonresidential real property uses a 39-year, not a 27.5-year, recovery period.

7. Browne, a self-employed taxpayer, had 2015 business taxable income of $435,000 prior to any expense deduction for equipment purchases. In 2015, Browne purchased and placed into service, for business use, office machinery costing $450,000. This was Browne's only 2015 capital expenditure. Browne's business establishment was not in an economically distressed area. Browne made a proper and timely expense election to deduct the maximum amount. Browne was not a member of any pass-through entity. What is Browne's deduction under the election?

A. $435,000

B. $450,000

C. $500,000

D. $2,000,000

Answer (A) is correct.

REQUIRED: The maximum amount of Sec. 179 deduction in 2015.

DISCUSSION: Tangible and depreciable personal property can be expensed by up to $500,000 in 2015, the year of acquisition. This amount is reduced when the amount of Sec. 179 property placed in service in a given year exceeds $2,000,000. Since this limit does not apply, the maximum deduction would be $500,000; however, there are other limits. Section 179(b)(3)(A) limits the deduction to taxable income derived from the active conduct of any trade or business. In this case, the maximum deduction is $435,000.

Answer (B) is incorrect. The Sec. 179 deduction is limited to taxable income. Answer (C) is incorrect. The maximum Sec. 179 deduction of $500,000 for 2015 ignores the taxable income limit. Answer (D) is incorrect. The amount of $2,000,000 is the threshold at which the deduction is reduced dollar-for-dollar, ignoring the taxable income limit in this case.

8. A taxpayer purchased and placed in service during the year a $100,000 piece of equipment. The equipment is 7-year property. The first-year depreciation for 7-year property is 14.29%. Assume that there is an allowable Sec. 179 limit in the current year of $25,000. What amount is the maximum allowable depreciation?

A. $14,290

B. $25,000

C. $35,718

D. $39,290

Answer (C) is correct.

REQUIRED: The maximum allowable depreciation.

DISCUSSION: Depreciation for an asset is first determined based upon the election of the taxpayer to take a Sec. 179 expense on the asset. However, if the taxpayer chooses to expense any of the property, the property's adjusted basis is reduced by the Sec. 179 expense in determining the applicable depreciation base. Therefore, the depreciation is calculated as follows:

Purchase price of asset	$100,000
Less: Sec. 179 expense	(25,000)
Depreciable basis	$ 75,000
Times: Depreciation rate (14.29%)	(10,718)
New Adjusted Basis of Equipment	$ 64,282

Total depreciation for the first year equals $25,000 + $10,718 = $35,718.

Answer (A) is incorrect. The Sec. 179 expense deduction may be taken and the depreciable basis of the property must be reduced by the Sec. 179 expense before applying the regular MACRS rate. Answer (B) is incorrect. The MACRS rate of 14.29% is still allowed on the equipment even if the Sec. 179 expense is made. Answer (D) is incorrect. The property's depreciable basis is reduced by the Sec. 179 expense before applying the regular MACRS rate.

9. Which of the following conditions must be satisfied for a taxpayer to expense, in the year of purchase, under Internal Revenue Code Section 179, the cost of new or used tangible depreciable personal property?

I. The property must be purchased for use in the taxpayer's active trade or business.

II. The property must be purchased from an unrelated party.

A. I only.

B. II only.

C. Both I and II.

D. Neither I nor II.

Answer (C) is correct.

REQUIRED: The conditions that must be satisfied under Sec. 179 to expense property.

DISCUSSION: In order for a property to be expensed under Sec. 179, it must be both purchased for use in the taxpayer's active trade or business as well as be purchased from an unrelated party.

Answer (A) is incorrect. The property must also be purchased from an unrelated party. Answer (B) is incorrect. The property must also be purchased for use in the taxpayer's active trade or business. Answer (D) is incorrect. At least one of the conditions must be satisfied.

10. Rock Crab, Inc., purchases the following assets during the year:

Computer	$ 3,000
Computer desk	1,000
Office furniture	4,000
Delivery van	25,000

What should be reported as the cost basis for MACRS 5-year property?

A. $3,000

B. $25,000

C. $28,000

D. $33,000

Answer (C) is correct.

REQUIRED: The cost basis for MACRS 5-year recovery property.

DISCUSSION: Under MACRS, personal property is assigned a recovery period of either 3, 5, 7, 10, 15, or 20 years, according to the midpoint of the ADR class life applicable to the type of property. Common 5-year property includes computers, office machinery (e.g., copier), cars, trucks, and R&E equipment.

The computer and delivery van are 5-year property for a total of $28,000 ($3,000 computer plus $25,000 delivery van).

Answer (A) is incorrect. The delivery van is also 5-year property under MACRS. Answer (B) is incorrect. The computer is also 5-year property under MACRS. Answer (D) is incorrect. Including the computer desk and office furniture, which are both 7-year property, results in $33,000.

6.3 Capital Gains and Losses

11. Which of the following is a capital asset?

A. Inventory held primarily for sale to customers.

B. Accounts receivable.

C. A computer system used by the taxpayer in a personal accounting business.

D. Land held as an investment.

Answer (D) is correct.

REQUIRED: The property classified as a capital asset.

DISCUSSION: All property is classified as a capital asset unless specifically excluded. Accounts receivable, inventory, and depreciable property or real estate used in a business are not capital assets. Land held as an investment, however, is a capital asset unless it is held by a dealer (the general rule and not an exception is being tested).

Answer (A) is incorrect. Inventory held primarily for sale to customers is not included in the capital assets classification. Answer (B) is incorrect. Accounts receivable are specifically excluded as capital assets. Answer (C) is incorrect. A computer system is amortized over its useful life (i.e., depreciable property used in a trade or business) and is not considered a capital asset.

12. In the current year, Susan sold an antique that she bought 6 years ago to display in her home. Susan paid $800 for the antique and sold it for $1,400. Susan chose to use the proceeds to pay a court-ordered judgment. The $600 gain that Susan realized on the sale of the antique should be treated as

A. Ordinary income.

B. Long-term capital gain.

C. An involuntary conversion.

D. A nontaxable transaction.

Answer (B) is correct.

REQUIRED: The treatment of gain on a property sale.

DISCUSSION: The antique is a capital asset. A capital asset must be held for more than 1 year for gain or loss on its sale or exchange to be treated as long-term.

Answer (A) is incorrect. The facts do not indicate that Susan held the asset as a dealer. Unless an exception applies, sale of a capital asset gives rise to capital gain or loss. Answer (C) is incorrect. How proceeds of an asset sale are used defines neither an involuntary conversion nor a capital asset. Answer (D) is incorrect. The IRC contains no provision excepting from recognition gain realized on this transaction.

13. In Year 1, Betty Lane bought 100 shares of a listed corporation's stock for $8,000. In Year 4, Betty sold this stock for $15,000. Betty had no other capital gains or losses in Year 4. How much of the Year 4 long-term capital gain should be included in Betty's Year 4 gross income?

A. $2,800

B. $3,500

C. $4,200

D. $7,000

Answer (D) is correct.

REQUIRED: The amount of long-term capital gain realized on the sale of stock.

DISCUSSION: Gain is any excess of the amount realized over adjusted basis. All $7,000 ($15,000 – $8,000) of gain realized is currently recognized unless an exception applies.

14. During the current year, all of the following events occurred: On June 1, Ben Rork sold 500 shares of Kul Corp. stock. Rork had received this stock on May 1 as a bequest from the estate of his uncle, who died on March 1. Rork's basis was determined by reference to the stock's fair market value on March 1. Rork's holding period for this stock was

A. Short-term.

B. Long-term.

C. Short-term if sold at a gain; long-term if sold at a loss.

D. Long-term if sold at a gain; short-term if sold at a loss.

Answer (B) is correct.

REQUIRED: The holding period for property acquired from a decedent.

DISCUSSION: Under Sec. 1223(11), if property acquired from a decedent is sold or otherwise disposed of by the recipient within 12 months of the decedent's death, then the property is considered to have been held for more than 12 months. Therefore, under Sec. 1223(3), it is long-term and subject to the maximum preferential tax rate of 15% (0% if the individual is in the 10% or 15% tax bracket).

15. Earl Cook, who worked as a machinist for Precision Corp., lent Precision $1,000 in Year 1. Cook did not own any of Precision's stock, and the loan was not a condition of employment. In Year 5, Precision declared bankruptcy, and Cook's note receivable from Precision became worthless. What loss can Cook claim on his Year 5 income tax return?

A. $0

B. $500 long-term capital loss.

C. $1,000 short-term capital loss.

D. $1,000 business bad debt.

Answer (C) is correct.

REQUIRED: The treatment of an uncollectible loan.

DISCUSSION: When a nonbusiness bad debt becomes worthless, the loss that results is treated as a short-term capital loss. A nonbusiness bad debt is one that arises other than in connection with a trade or business of the taxpayer.

Answer (A) is incorrect. A worthless nonbusiness bad debt is deductible. Answer (B) is incorrect. The full amount of the loss (adjusted basis) is treated as a short-term capital loss. Answer (D) is incorrect. Loans made to employers are not considered business loans unless made as a condition of employment or in order to keep employment.

16. Sand purchased 100 shares of Eastern Corp. stock for $18,000 on April 1 of the prior year. On February 1 of the current year, Sand sold 50 shares of Eastern for $7,000. Fifteen days later, Sand purchased 25 shares of Eastern for $3,750. What is the amount of Sand's recognized gain or loss?

A. $0

B. $500

C. $1,000

D. $2,000

Answer (C) is correct.

REQUIRED: The recognized gain or loss on a wash sale of stock.

DISCUSSION: A current loss realized on a wash sale of securities is not recognized. A wash sale occurs when substantially the same securities are purchased within 30 days before or after being sold at a loss. Although Sand sold 50 shares of Eastern on February 1st, they reacquire 25 more shares of Eastern less than 30 days later. Thus, the 25 shares that Sand reacquires 15 days later do not contribute to the recognized loss on February 1st. If the total realized loss on February 1st is $2,000 ($9,000 basis of shares sold – $7,000 sales price), only half is recognized because only half is not subsequently reacquired.

Answer (A) is incorrect. Sand may recognize a $1,000 loss equal to the shares of stock sold on February 1st not subsequently reacquired 15 days later. Answer (B) is incorrect. The realized loss on February 1st is related to 50 shares. If 25 shares are subsequently reacquired, half the loss must not be recognized, not 75% of it. Answer (D) is incorrect. Half of the shares sold on February 1st are reacquired within the 30-day wash sale period. Thus, the realized loss of $2,000 must be reduced by the 25 shares reacquired 15 days later.

17. On March 10, Year 6, James Rogers sold 300 shares of Red Company common stock for $4,200. Rogers had acquired the stock in Year 1 at a cost of $5,000. On April 4, Year 6, he repurchased 300 shares of Red Company common stock for $3,600 and held them until July 18, Year 6, when he sold them for $6,000. How should Rogers report the above transactions for Year 6?

A. A long-term capital loss of $800.

B. A long-term capital gain of $2,400.

C. A long-term capital gain of $1,600.

D. A long-term capital loss of $800 and a short-term capital gain of $2,400.

Answer (C) is correct.

REQUIRED: The amount and character of capital gain after stocks purchased in a wash sale are sold.

DISCUSSION: The sale of stock on March 10 was a wash sale because identical stock was repurchased within 30 days. The $800 loss realized in March will not be recognized for tax purposes. The disallowed loss is added to the basis of the stock that is subsequently purchased in April. The basis in the stock purchased in April is $4,400 ($3,600 cost + $800 disallowed loss), and a gain of $1,600 is recognized when the stock is sold for $6,000 on July 18. The gain is long-term because the holding period of stock acquired in a wash sale includes the holding period of the originally purchased stock.

6.4 Related Party Sales

18. Gibson purchased stock with a fair market value of $14,000 from Gibson's adult child for $12,000. The child's cost basis in the stock at the date of sale was $16,000. Gibson sold the same stock to an unrelated party for $18,000. What is Gibson's recognized gain from the sale?

A. $0

B. $2,000

C. $4,000

D. $6,000

Answer (B) is correct.

REQUIRED: The amount of gain recognized when stock acquired from a related party is sold to an unrelated third party.

DISCUSSION: Under Sec. 267, losses are not allowed on sales or exchanges of property between related parties. Gibson's adult child realized a $4,000 loss ($16,000 – $12,000) on the sale but may not deduct it. On the subsequent sale, Gibson realized a $6,000 gain ($18,000 sales price – $12,000 basis). However, he only recognizes a gain of $2,000 ($18,000 – $16,000) because the Sec. 267(d) disallowed loss is used to offset the subsequent gain on the sale of the property.

Answer (A) is incorrect. There is a recognized gain from the sale. Answer (C) is incorrect. The fair market value at date of related party sale is irrelevant. Answer (D) is incorrect. The realized gain is recognized to the extent it exceeds the previously disallowed loss.

Questions 19 and 20 are based on the following information. Conner purchased 300 shares of Zinco stock for $30,000 in 1997. On May 23, 2015, Conner sold all the stock to his daughter Alice for $20,000, its fair market value at the time. Conner realized no other gain or loss during 2015. On July 26, 2015, Alice sold the 300 shares of Zinco for $25,000.

19. What amount of the loss from the sale of Zinco stock can Conner deduct in 2015?

A. $0

B. $3,000

C. $5,000

D. $10,000

Answer (A) is correct.

REQUIRED: The amount of deductible loss in a related party sale.

DISCUSSION: The $10,000 realized loss ($20,000 proceeds – $30,000 basis) on the sale of the stock from father to daughter is disallowed. The daughter takes a cost basis of $20,000 in the stock as well as a new holding period. Related parties include ancestors, descendants, spouses, and siblings.

20. What was Alice's recognized gain or loss on her sale?

A. $0

B. $5,000 long-term gain.

C. $5,000 short-term loss.

D. $5,000 long-term loss.

Answer (A) is correct.

REQUIRED: The amount of gain recognized when stock acquired from a related party is sold to an unrelated third party.

DISCUSSION: The $5,000 realized gain ($25,000 proceeds – $20,000 basis) is recognized only to the extent it exceeds the previously disallowed loss of $10,000. Since the realized gain on the sale to an unrelated third party is less than the amount of disallowed loss, no gain is recognized.

21. Among which of the following related parties are losses from sales and exchanges **not** recognized for tax purposes?

A. Father-in-law and son-in-law.

B. Brother-in-law and sister-in-law.

C. Grandfather and granddaughter.

D. Ancestors, lineal descendants, and all in-laws.

Answer (C) is correct.

REQUIRED: The identification of the related party.

DISCUSSION: Losses are not allowed on sales or exchanges of property between related parties. Related parties include ancestors (grandfather), descendants (granddaughter), spouses, and siblings.

6.5 Installment Sales

22. The following data pertain to installment sales of personal property made by Fred Dale, an accrual-method taxpayer, in his retail furniture store:

Year of Sale	Installment Sales	Profit	Collections in Year 3
Year 1	$ 50,000	$15,000	$10,000
Year 2	100,000	40,000	30,000
Year 3	150,000	75,000	40,000

These sales were not under a revolving credit plan. Under the installment method, Dale should report gross profit for Year 3 of

A. $35,000

B. $75,000

C. $80,000

D. $130,000

Answer (B) is correct.

REQUIRED: The amount collected that is reported as gross profit.

DISCUSSION: The installment method is usually disallowed for dispositions of property by dealers. This includes any disposition of (1) personal property, if the person regularly sells such personal property on the installment plan, and (2) real property held by the taxpayer for sale to customers in the ordinary course of his or her trade or business. Exceptions are made for property used or produced in the trade or business of farming and, if so elected, sales of residential lots or timeshares, subject to interest payments on the deferred tax. Dale is excluded from installment sale deferral because the disposition of his property falls under "personal property of a type regularly sold by the person on the installment plan." Because he does not qualify, he must recognize all of his profit in Year 3, which is stated in the question as $75,000.

Answer (A) is incorrect. The amount of $35,000 results from subtracting the collections in Year 3 from the installment sale profits. Answer (C) is incorrect. The amount of $80,000 results from adding all the collections in Year 3. Answer (D) is incorrect. The amount of $130,000 results from adding the profits from installment sales in all 3 years.

6.6 Nonrecognition Transactions

23. A heavy-equipment dealer would like to trade some business assets in a nontaxable exchange. Which of the following exchanges would qualify as nontaxable?

A. The company jet for a large truck to be used in the corporation.

B. Investment securities for antiques to be held as investments.

C. A road grader held in inventory for another road grader.

D. A corporate office building for a vacant lot.

Answer (D) is correct.

REQUIRED: The transaction qualifying as a like-kind exchange.

DISCUSSION: Property qualifying for a like-kind treatment under IRC Sec. 1031 depends on the property's nature or character, but not necessarily in grade or quality. Real property is of like kind to other real property, except foreign property. Thus, the corporate office building and vacant lot qualify as a nontaxable exchange even though they are not used for the same purpose.

Answer (A) is incorrect. Personal properties are of like kind if they are of a like class. Airplanes (class 00.21) and trucks (class 00.24) are not of a like class. Answer (B) is incorrect. Securities and debt instruments do not qualify for Sec. 1031 nonrecognition. Thus, the investment securities disqualify the transaction as like-kind. Answer (C) is incorrect. Inventory is specifically excluded from like-kind exchange treatment.

24. Joan Reed exchanged commercial real estate that she owned for other commercial real estate plus cash of $50,000. The following additional information pertains to this transaction:

Property given up by Reed	
Fair market value	$500,000
Adjusted basis	300,000
Property received by Reed	
Fair market value	450,000

What amount of gain should be recognized in Reed's income tax return?

A. $200,000

B. $150,000

C. $50,000

D. $0

Answer (C) is correct.

REQUIRED: The recognized gain or loss on an exchange of like-kind property with boot.

DISCUSSION: Neither gain nor loss is recognized on an exchange of like-kind property held for productive use in a trade or business or for investment. When boot (cash) is received, gain or loss is recognized to the extent of the boot. Reed recognizes a $50,000 gain.

Answer (A) is incorrect. This amount is the realized gain. Answer (B) is incorrect. This amount results from subtracting the adjusted basis of the property given up from the fair market value of the property received by Reed. Answer (D) is incorrect. In a like-kind exchange, realized gain must be recognized to the extent of boot received ($50,000).

25. On October 1, 2015, Donald Anderson exchanged an apartment building, having an adjusted basis of $375,000 and subject to a mortgage of $100,000, for $25,000 cash and another apartment building with a fair market value of $550,000 and subject to a mortgage of $125,000. The property transfers were made subject to the outstanding mortgages. What amount of gain should Anderson recognize in his tax return for 2015?

A. $0

B. $25,000

C. $125,000

D. $175,000

Answer (B) is correct.

REQUIRED: The gain recognized in a like-kind exchange of properties subject to mortgages.

DISCUSSION: Anderson's realized gain is

Fair market value of building received		$ 550,000
Mortgage on old building		100,000
Cash received		25,000
Total amount realized		$ 675,000
Less: Basis of old building	$ 375,000	
Mortgage on new building	125,000	(500,000)
Realized gain (only $25,000 recognized)		$ 175,000

Under Reg. 1.1031(d)-2, excess mortgage incurred cannot be netted against cash received to reduce the amount of boot received.

Answer (A) is incorrect. The $25,000 cash boot received by Anderson is recognized gain. Answer (C) is incorrect. The mortgages are netted. Thus, Anderson is considered to have given $25,000 boot by taking the larger mortgage and not to have received another $100,000 boot. Answer (D) is incorrect. Gain realized is recognized only to the extent of boot received in a like-kind exchange.

26. Wynn, a 60-year old single individual, sold his personal residence for $450,000. Wynn had owned his residence, which had a basis of $250,000, for 6 years. Within 8 months of the sale, Wynn purchased a new residence for $400,000. What is Wynn's recognized gain from the sale of his personal residence?

A. $0

B. $50,000

C. $75,000

D. $200,000

Answer (A) is correct.

REQUIRED: The amount of recognized gain from sale of a personal residence.

DISCUSSION: Wynn will realize a $200,000 ($450,000 sales price – $250,000 adjusted basis) gain on the sale of the residence. Sec. 121, as amended by the Taxpayer Relief Act of 2000, allows an exclusion of up to $250,000 for single taxpayers on the sale of a principal residence. Therefore, Wynn's recognized gain is $0 ($200,000 realized gain – up to $250,000 exclusion).

Answer (B) is incorrect. The purchase price of the new residence does not calculate into the gain of the old residence. Answer (C) is incorrect. The amount of gain to be recognized is equal to the realized gain on the sale of the residence, $200,000, less the exclusion amount of up to $250,000. Answer (D) is incorrect. This is the amount of realized gain on the sale of Wynn's principal residence. The exclusion amount of up to $250,000 from Sec. 121 offsets this amount so that the recognized gain is $0.

6.7 Business Property

27. On January 2, Year 1, Bates Corp. purchased and placed into service 7-year MACRS tangible property costing $100,000. On December 31, Year 3, Bates sold the property for $102,000, after having taken $47,525 in MACRS depreciation deductions. What amount of the gain should Bates recapture as ordinary income?

A. $0

B. $2,000

C. $47,525

D. $49,525

Answer (C) is correct.

REQUIRED: The amount of gain recaptured as ordinary income in Sec. 1245.

DISCUSSION: Depreciable tangible property used in a trade or business is Sec. 1245 property. Sec. 1245 states that gain realized on the disposition of this property is recaptured as ordinary income to the extent of the lesser of depreciation taken or realized gain.

Answer (A) is incorrect. Sec. 1245 recaptures as ordinary income the realized gain to the extent of the depreciation taken. Answer (B) is incorrect. The amount of Sec. 1231 gain is $2,000. Answer (D) is incorrect. The realized gain is $49,525. Sec. 1245 states that realized gain up to the amount of depreciation taken is reclassified as ordinary income.

28. A taxpayer sold for $200,000 equipment that had an adjusted basis of $180,000. Through the date of the sale, the taxpayer had deducted $30,000 of depreciation. Of this amount, $17,000 was in excess of straight-line depreciation. What amount of gain would be recaptured under Section 1245, *Gain from Dispositions of Certain Depreciable Property*?

A. $13,000

B. $17,000

C. $20,000

D. $30,000

Answer (C) is correct.

REQUIRED: The amount of Sec. 1245 ordinary income recapture.

DISCUSSION: Gain on the disposition of Sec. 1245 property is ordinary income to the extent of the lesser of all depreciation taken or gain realized. The realized gain in excess of the depreciation taken may be treated as a gain from the sale or exchange of Sec. 1231 property. The $20,000 gain realized is less than the depreciation taken ($30,000).

Answer (A) is incorrect. For Sec. 1245 property, straight-line depreciation is recaptured up to the realized gain. Answer (B) is incorrect. Sec. 1245 recapture does not distinguish between straight-line and accelerated depreciation. Answer (D) is incorrect. Recapture is limited to the lesser of all depreciation taken or gain realized.

29. Platt owns land that is operated as a parking lot. A shed was erected on the lot for the related transactions with customers. With regard to capital assets and Sec. 1231 assets, how should these assets be classified?

	Land	Shed
A.	Capital	Capital
B.	Sec. 1231	Capital
C.	Capital	Sec. 1231
D.	Sec. 1231	Sec. 1231

Answer (D) is correct.

REQUIRED: The classification of property as a Sec. 1231 or capital asset.

DISCUSSION: Capital assets are any property not excluded by IRC definition. Real property used in a trade or business is excluded. Sec. 1231 property includes all real or depreciable property used in the taxpayer's trade or business and held more than 1 year.

30. Dove Corp. began operating a hardware store in the current year after constructing a building at a total cost of $100,000 on land previously acquired for $50,000. In the current year, the land had a fair market value of $60,000. Dove paid real estate taxes of $5,000 in the current year. What is the total depreciable basis of Dove's business property?

A. $100,000

B. $150,000

C. $155,000

D. $160,000

Answer (A) is correct.

REQUIRED: The depreciable basis of a company's business property.

DISCUSSION: The depreciable basis equals the total capitalized costs of the building. Land is not depreciated. Furthermore, real estate taxes are an expense and are not capitalized. Therefore, only the costs of constructing the building are capitalized and subsequently depreciated.

Answer (B) is incorrect. Land is not depreciated. Answer (C) is incorrect. Land is not depreciated, and real estate taxes are an expense. Answer (D) is incorrect. This amount includes the FMV of the land, and land is not depreciated.

6.8 PRACTICE TASK-BASED SIMULATIONS

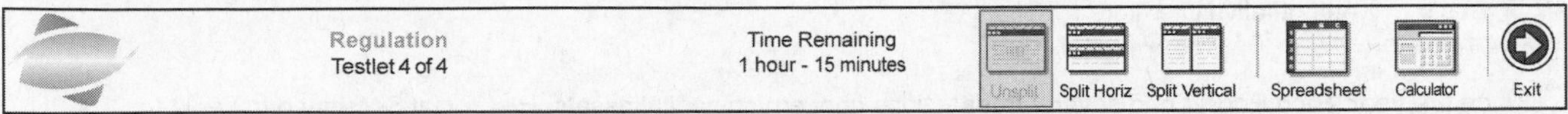

DIRECTIONS

Note: If you believe you have encountered a software malfunction, report it to the test center staff immediately.

Navigation

To navigate from task to task, use the controls at the bottom of the screen. Click on the **Next** button to advance to the next task, or the **Previous** button to go to the previous task. To go directly to any task, click on its number.

If you would like a reminder to revisit a task, or want to indicate that you are finished with it, click on the reminder flag below the task number. To clear the flag, click on it again. Reminder flags are for your use only – they do not contribute to your score.

Tabs

In this part of the examination, you will be asked to complete various tasks. Every task has one or more **Work Tabs**. Some tasks have one or more **Information Tabs**, others may have none. Every task has a **Help** tab.

If a task has **Information Tabs**, you may use the information in them to complete your responses in the **Work Tabs**.

Work tab **Information tab** **Help tab**

Work Tabs:

- **Work Tabs** are identified with a pencil icon. This is where your responses are expected.
- Each task has one or more **Work Tabs**.
- **Work Tabs** contain directions for completing the task – be sure to read these directions carefully.
- The **Work Tab** name in the example above is for illustration only – yours will differ.
- You must complete all of the **Work Tabs** in each task to receive full credit.

Information Tabs:

- The Authoritative Literature will be provided in all tasks in the AUD, FAR, and REG sections for your reference.
- Your simulation may have one or more additional **Information Tabs**. Like the Authoritative Literature tabs, **Information Tabs** do not have a pencil icon.
- If your task has additional **Information Tabs**, go through each to familiarize yourself with the task content.

Help Tab:

- The **Help Tab** provides assistance with the exam software that is used in this task. For example, if the task is to compose a memorandum, **Help** will provide information about the word processor.

The Toolbar

The toolbar at the top of the screen shows the amount of time remaining for you to complete the tasks. In addition, the following tools are available. Note that only the **Exit** button is displayed when Directions are visible - the others will appear when you begin the tasks.

Click on these buttons to split or unsplit the screen. You can split the screen vertically or horizontally.

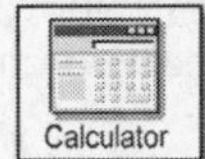

Click on this button to display the calculator; click on it again to hide the calculator. To move the calculator, click on the calculator title bar and drag the calculator to the desired location.

Click on this button to use the spreadsheet; click on it again to hide the spreadsheet. To move the spreadsheet, click on the the spreadsheet title bar and drag the spreadsheet to the desired location.

Click on this button to go on to the next part of the examination. You must complete all of the tasks to receive full credit. Once you click on **Exit** and confirm the action, you will NOT be able to return to this testlet.

= Reminder | Directions | 1 2 3 4 5 6 | Previous | Next

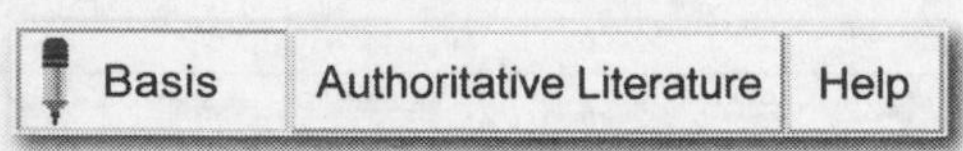

During the year, Rich Poorer had several transactions concerning capital assets. His Social Security number is 000-12-8899. His transactions are listed below.

- Rich purchased a parcel of vacant land on July 31, 2014, for $4,750 cash and a note in the amount of $10,000, which is secured by a mortgage. He paid $250 for a title insurance policy when he purchased the land.
- Rich's father gave Rich a ring on July 31, 2013, when it was appraised at $9,750. His father purchased the ring on July 31, 2003, for $5,250. No part of the ring's value exceeded the $14,000 per year exclusion from transfer tax.
- On March 31, 2015, Rich purchased a rare Ford Mustang from his friend, William Wealthy, for $12,000. Rich made a $4,000 down payment and will pay the remaining $8,000 in two payments in 2016 and 2017. William had purchased this car for personal use on July 31, 2003, for $10,000.
- On May 31, 2015, Rich purchased 100 shares of Builder, Inc., common stock for $4,500. Rich had sold 100 shares of Builder, Inc., common stock (which he acquired at a cost of $5,250 on July 31, 2003) for $4,000 on May 15, 2015.
- Rich inherited some rare silver coins when the testator died on May 31, 2015. The testator had purchased the coins for $5,000 on July 31, 2003. During 2015, the value of the coins was $9,750 on May 31, $10,250 on August 31, and $10,750 on November 30. The coins were distributed by the estate on August 31, 2015, and Rich sold them for $10,500 on September 30, 2015. The estate did not elect the alternate valuation date.

Using the information provided about Rich's property transactions, enter in the shaded cells below the amount of basis and the holding period for each item.

Item	***Answer***
1. On July 31, 2015, what is Rich's basis in the land?	
2. On July 31, 2015, what is Rich's holding period for the land?	months
3. On July 31, 2015, what is Rich's basis in the ring?	
4. On July 31, 2015, what is Rich's holding period for the ring?	months
5. On July 31, 2015, what is Rich's basis in the car?	
6. On July 31, 2015, what is Rich's holding period for the car?	months
7. On July 31, 2015, what is Rich's basis in the stock?	
8. On July 31, 2015, what is Rich's holding period for the stock?	months
9. On July 31, 2015, what is Rich's basis in the coins?	

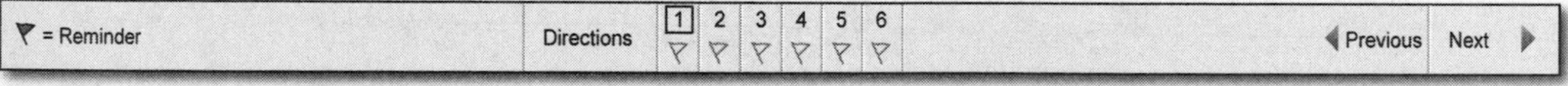

On May 31, 2015, Jack purchased a rare Chevy Camaro from his friend, Andy Affluent, for $12,000. Jack made a $4,000 down payment and will pay the remaining $8,000 in two payments in 2016 and 2017. Andy had purchased this car for personal use on August 31, 2004, for $9,000.

Fill out Form 6252 on the next page by entering numbers in the shaded cells to determine the amount of gain recognized in the current year. Enter percentages as decimals with four spaces.

-- Continued on next page --

Installment Sale | Authoritative Literature | Help | **-- Continued**

Form **6252** Department of the Treasury Internal Revenue Service

Installment Sale Income

▶ Attach to your tax return.
▶ Use a separate form for each sale or other disposition of property on the installment method.
▶ Information about Form 6252 and its instructions is at www.irs.gov/form6252.

OMB No. 1545-0228 **2015** Attachment Sequence No. **79**

Name(s) shown on return: Andrew Affluent — Identifying number: 123-45-6789

1 Description of property ▶ Chevy Camaro
2a Date acquired (mm/dd/yyyy) ▶ 08/31/2004 **b** Date sold (mm/dd/yyyy) ▶ 05/31/2015
3 Was the property sold to a related party (see instructions) after May 15, 1980? If "No," skip line 4 . . . . ☐ Yes ☐ No
4 Was the property you sold to a related party a marketable security? If "Yes," complete Part III. If "No," complete Part III for the year of sale and the 2 years after the year of sale . . . ☐ Yes ☐ No

Part I Gross Profit and Contract Price. Complete this part for the year of sale only.

Line	Description	Sub-line	Amount	Line	Amount
5	Selling price including mortgages and other debts. **Do not** include interest, whether stated or unstated			5	[1]
6	Mortgages, debts, and other liabilities the buyer assumed or took the property subject to (see instructions)	6	0		
7	Subtract line 6 from line 5	7	[2]		
8	Cost or other basis of property sold	8	[3]		
9	Depreciation allowed or allowable	9	[4]		
10	Adjusted basis. Subtract line 9 from line 8	10	[5]		
11	Commissions and other expenses of sale	11	0		
12	Income recapture from Form 4797, Part III (see instructions)	12	0		
13	Add lines 10, 11, and 12			13	[6]
14	Subtract line 13 from line 5. If zero or less, **do not** complete the rest of this form (see instructions)			14	[7]
15	If the property described on line 1 above was your main home, enter the amount of your excluded gain (see instructions). Otherwise, enter -0-			15	0
16	**Gross profit.** Subtract line 15 from line 14			16	[8]
17	Subtract line 13 from line 6. If zero or less, enter -0-			17	0
18	**Contract price.** Add line 7 and line 17			18	[9]

Part II Installment Sale Income. Complete this part for the year of sale **and** any year you receive a payment or have certain debts you must treat as a payment on installment obligations.

Line	Description	Sub-line	Amount	Line	Amount
19	Gross profit percentage (expressed as a decimal amount). Divide line 16 by line 18. For years after the year of sale, see instructions			19	[10]
20	If this is the year of sale, enter the amount from line 17. Otherwise, enter -0-			20	0
21	Payments received during year (see instructions). **Do not** include interest, whether stated or unstated			21	[11]
22	Add lines 20 and 21			22	[12]
23	Payments received in prior years (see instructions). **Do not** include interest, whether stated or unstated	23	0		
24	**Installment sale income.** Multiply line 22 by line 19			24	[13]
25	Enter the part of line 24 that is ordinary income under the recapture rules (see instructions)			25	0
26	Subtract line 25 from line 24. Enter here and on Schedule D or Form 4797 (see instructions)			26	[14]

Part III Related Party Installment Sale Income. Do not complete if you received the final payment this tax year.

27 Name, address, and taxpayer identifying number of related party

28 Did the related party resell or dispose of the property ("second disposition") during this tax year? . . . ☐ Yes ☐ No

29 **If the answer to question 28 is "Yes," complete lines 30 through 37 below unless one of the following conditions is met. Check the box that applies.**

- a ☐ The second disposition was more than 2 years after the first disposition (other than dispositions of marketable securities). If this box is checked, enter the date of disposition (mm/dd/yyyy) . . . ▶
- b ☐ The first disposition was a sale or exchange of stock to the issuing corporation.
- c ☐ The second disposition was an involuntary conversion and the threat of conversion occurred after the first disposition.
- d ☐ The second disposition occurred after the death of the original seller or buyer.
- e ☐ It can be established to the satisfaction of the IRS that tax avoidance was not a principal purpose for either of the dispositions. If this box is checked, attach an explanation (see instructions).

Line	Description	Line	Amount
30	Selling price of property sold by related party (see instructions)	30	
31	Enter contract price from line 18 for year of first sale	31	
32	Enter the **smaller** of line 30 or line 31	32	
33	Total payments received by the end of your 2014 tax year (see instructions)	33	
34	Subtract line 33 from line 32. If zero or less, enter -0-	34	
35	Multiply line 34 by the gross profit percentage on line 19 for year of first sale	35	
36	Enter the part of line 35 that is ordinary income under the recapture rules (see instructions)	36	
37	Subtract line 36 from line 35. Enter here and on Schedule D or Form 4797 (see instructions)	37	

For Paperwork Reduction Act Notice, see page 4. Cat. No. 13601R Form **6252** (2015)

▼ = Reminder | Directions | 1 [2] 3 4 5 6 | ◀ Previous | Next ▶

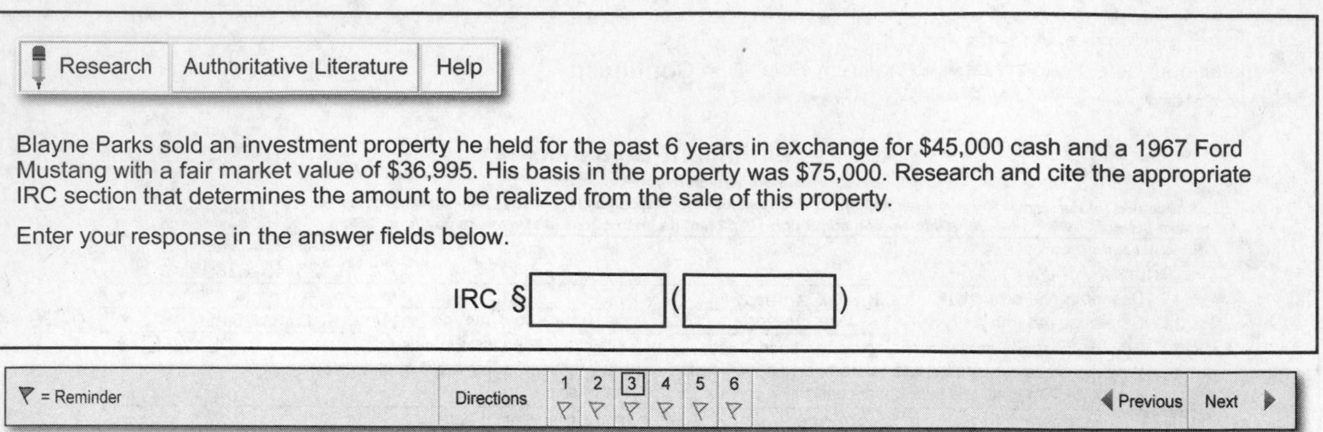
Research | Authoritative Literature | Help

Blayne Parks sold an investment property he held for the past 6 years in exchange for $45,000 cash and a 1967 Ford Mustang with a fair market value of $36,995. His basis in the property was $75,000. Research and cite the appropriate IRC section that determines the amount to be realized from the sale of this property.

Enter your response in the answer fields below.

IRC § [ ] ([ ])

= Reminder | Directions | 1 2 3 4 5 6 | Previous | Next

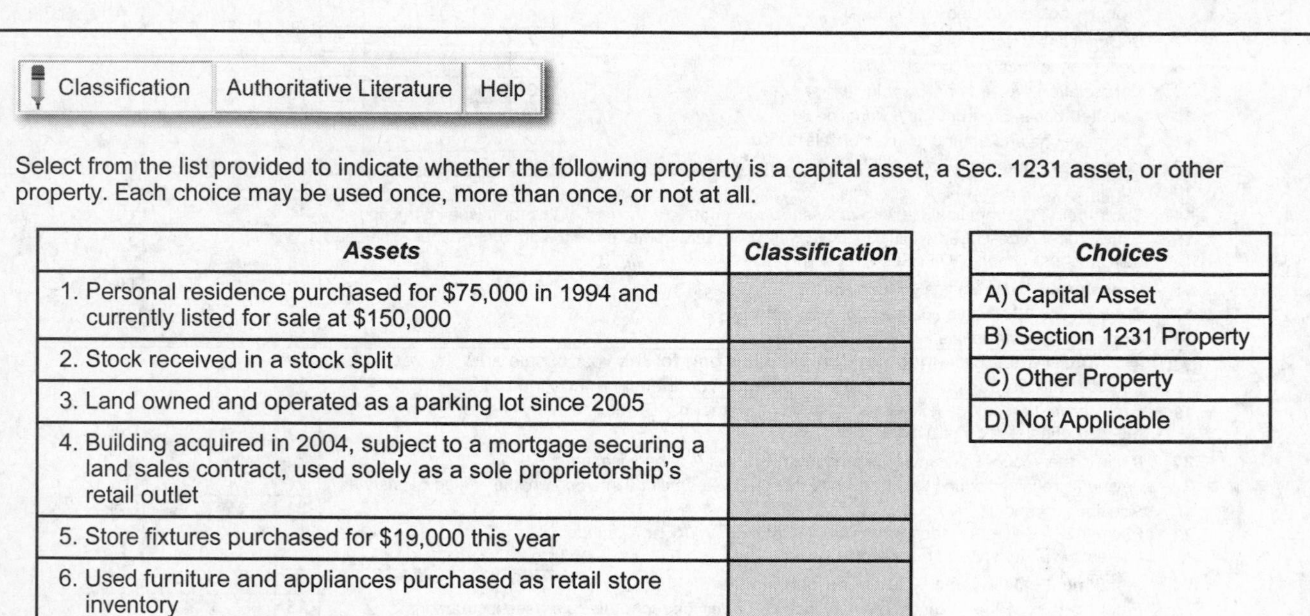
Classification | Authoritative Literature | Help

Select from the list provided to indicate whether the following property is a capital asset, a Sec. 1231 asset, or other property. Each choice may be used once, more than once, or not at all.

Assets	***Classification***
1. Personal residence purchased for $75,000 in 1994 and currently listed for sale at $150,000	
2. Stock received in a stock split	
3. Land owned and operated as a parking lot since 2005	
4. Building acquired in 2004, subject to a mortgage securing a land sales contract, used solely as a sole proprietorship's retail outlet	
5. Store fixtures purchased for $19,000 this year	
6. Used furniture and appliances purchased as retail store inventory	
7. Accounts receivable from sale of the furniture and appliances sold at retail	
8. Acquired goodwill	
9. Delivery truck acquired in exchange for parcel of land in 2007, used to deliver furniture for the store since acquisition	
10. Treasury stock	

Choices
A) Capital Asset
B) Section 1231 Property
C) Other Property
D) Not Applicable

= Reminder | Directions | 1 2 3 4 5 6 | Previous | Next

For each of the following transactions, (1) enter the amount of the gain or loss, and (2) select from the list provided the character of the gain or loss. Each choice may be used once, more than once, or not at all.

Transaction	Amount	Character
1. Sale of 1,000 shares of XYZ common stock purchased on 10/15/14 for $20,000 and sold on 2/15/15 for $23,000.		
2. Sale of 2,000 shares of ABC common stock purchased on 3/23/15 for $125,000 and sold on 12/31/15 for $139,000.		
3. Sale of van purchased on 1/25/14 for $10,000 and sold on 6/03/15 for $9,000.		
4. Sale of land purchased on 06/30/01 for $110,000 and sold on 7/04/15 for $169,000.		
5. $45,000 of insurance recovery received from a 5-year-old building that was destroyed in a fire. The building was used in a business, had a FMV of $65,000, and an adjusted basis of $50,000.		

Character Choices
A) Ordinary Income
B) Ordinary Loss
C) Short-Term Capital Gain
D) Long-Term Capital Gain
E) Short-Term Capital Loss
F) Long-Term Capital Loss

Nonrecognition Transactions | Authoritative Literature | Help

Select from the list provided to indicate whether a gain or loss would be recognized, not recognized, or partially recognized in each of the following situations. Each choice may be used once, more than once, or not at all.

Situation	Answer
1. Mr. and Mrs. Taylor realized a $115,000 loss on the sale of their principal residence. They have owned and used the residence for the past year. Due to Mr. Taylor's job, the Taylors moved and claimed this exclusion 18 months ago.	
2. A partnership exchanged 15 laptops worth $12,000 for $3,500 cash and five powerful desktop computers worth $13,000.	
3. Patrick owned an office building that was destroyed by a tornado. The building had a tax basis of $350,000, and Patrick received $425,000 from his insurance company. He used that entire amount to purchase securities as part of his new plan to retire and play the stock market.	
4. A transportation company realized a loss upon the exchange of two charter buses for eight taxis that will be rented to customers in the same fashion as the buses.	
5. A taxpayer is the original owner of stock issued by ABC Corp., a domestic C corporation, in 2004. ABC's gross assets at the time were valued at $28 million. Due to excellent growth by ABC, the taxpayer decided to sell the stock for a large gain in 2015.	
6. Larry, a best-selling author, exchanged waterfront property in Florida for a ski lodge in Aspen, Colorado, realizing a $1 million gain.	

Choices
A) Recognize gain (loss) in full
B) Do not recognize gain (loss)
C) Partially recognize gain (loss)

= Reminder | Directions | 1 2 3 4 5 6 | Previous | Next

Unofficial Answers

1. Basis (9 Gradable Items)

1. $15,000. The basis of property is generally its cost. Cost includes cash paid and any debt that the property is subject to. Basis also includes expenditures for major improvements and costs to acquire title.
2. 24 months. The character of gain on property disposition varies with the holding period. The holding period generally commences when the taxpayer acquires the property.
3. $5,250. The general rule is that the basis of property acquired by gift is the donor's adjusted basis, increased by any gift tax attributable to appreciation. Rich's father had a cost basis in the ring that was unadjusted for depreciation, and no gift tax was imposed on the transfer. Thus, Rich has a transferred basis of $5,250 in the ring.
4. 144 months. The holding period of property generally begins on the date following the date of acquisition. However, if property has the same basis in whole or in part as it had in the hands of a prior holder, the holding period of the prior holder is added (tacked on) to the present owner's holding period.
5. $12,000. Transferee takes a cost basis.
6. 4 months. Holding period on a sale or exchange commences upon acquisition.
7. $5,750. Deduction of loss realized on a wash sale is disallowed. The sale of stock on May 15 was a wash sale because identical stock was repurchased within 30 days (on May 31). The disallowed loss is added to the basis of the stock that was subsequently purchased on May 31. The basis in the stock purchased is $5,750 ($4,500 cost + $1,250 disallowed loss).
8. 144 months. The holding period of stock acquired in a wash sale includes the holding period of the originally purchased stock.
9. $9,750. The basis of property received from a decedent is generally the fair market value of the property on the date of the decedent's death. If the executor elects the alternate valuation date for the estate tax return, the basis of the assets is their fair market value 6 months after death or the date of sale or distribution, if earlier. Rich's basis in the silver on July 31, 2015, is the $9,750 fair market value on the date of death. No basis adjustment is made for estate taxes paid.

2. Installment Sale (14 Gradable Items)

See the form on the next page.

[1] $12,000. The contract price for the sale of the Camaro is $12,000. This is the total of the $4,000 down payment and two $4,000 installment payments.

[2] $12,000. Since no mortgages were assumed, the total contract price is still $12,000.

[3] $9,000. The cost basis for the Camaro is the $9,000 paid for it when it was purchased on August 31, 2004.

[4] $0. Since the Camaro was for personal use, no depreciation deductions were taken.

[5] $9,000. If no depreciation is taken, the adjusted basis is the same as the cost basis.

[6] $9,000. The sum of lines 10, 11, and 12 is $9,000 ($9,000 + $0 + $0).

[7] $3,000. Line 5 less line 13 equals $3,000 ($12,000 – $9,000).

[8] $3,000. The gross profit is the excess of the contract price over the basis in the Camaro.

[9] $12,000. The contract price is the $12,000 that Andrew will receive in total for the Camaro.

[10] 25.00%. The gross profit percentage is the gross profit divided by the contract price ($3,000 ÷ $12,000).

[11] $4,000. The $4,000 down payment is considered a payment received during the year.

[12] $4,000. The total of lines 20 and 21 is $4,000 ($4,000 + $0).

[13] $1,000. The installment sale income equals the payment received times the gross profit percentage ($4,000 × .2500).

[14] $1,000. Line 24 less line 25 equals $1,000 ($1,000 – $0).

Form **6252** | **Installment Sale Income** | OMB No. 1545-0228
Department of the Treasury Internal Revenue Service

► Attach to your tax return.
► Use a separate form for each sale or other disposition of property on the installment method.
► Information about Form 6252 and its instructions is at *www.irs.gov/form6252.*

2015 Attachment Sequence No. **79**

Name(s) shown on return: Andrew Affluent | Identifying number: 123-45-6789

1 Description of property ► Chevy Camaro
2a Date acquired (mm/dd/yyyy) ► 08/31/2004 **b** Date sold (mm/dd/yyyy) ► 05/31/2015
3 Was the property sold to a related party (see instructions) after May 14, 1980? If "No," skip line 4 . . . . ☐ Yes ☐ No
4 Was the property you sold to a related party a marketable security? If "Yes," complete Part III. If "No," complete Part III for the year of sale and the 2 years after the year of sale . . . . ☐ Yes ☐ No

Part I Gross Profit and Contract Price. Complete this part for the year of sale only.

Line	Description	Line	Amount		Line	Amount	
5	Selling price including mortgages and other debts. **Do not** include interest, whether stated or unstated				5	12,000	[1]
6	Mortgages, debts, and other liabilities the buyer assumed or took the property subject to (see instructions)	6	0				
7	Subtract line 6 from line 5	7	12,000	[2]			
8	Cost or other basis of property sold	8	9,000	[3]			
9	Depreciation allowed or allowable	9		[4]			
10	Adjusted basis. Subtract line 9 from line 8	10	9,000	[5]			
11	Commissions and other expenses of sale	11	0				
12	Income recapture from Form 4797, Part III (see instructions)	12	0				
13	Add lines 10, 11, and 12				13	9,000	[6]
14	Subtract line 13 from line 5. If zero or less, **do not** complete the rest of this form (see instructions)				14	3,000	[7]
15	If the property described on line 1 above was your main home, enter the amount of your excluded gain (see instructions). Otherwise, enter -0-				15	0	
16	**Gross profit.** Subtract line 15 from line 14				16	3,000	[8]
17	Subtract line 13 from line 6. If zero or less, enter -0-				17	0	
18	**Contract price.** Add line 7 and line 17				18	12,000	[9]

Part II Installment Sale Income. Complete this part for the year of sale **and** any year you receive a payment or have certain debts you must treat as a payment on installment obligations.

Line	Description	Line	Amount	Line	Amount	
19	Gross profit percentage (expressed as a decimal amount). Divide line 16 by line 18. For years after the year of sale, see instructions			19	.2500	[10]
20	If this is the year of sale, enter the amount from line 17. Otherwise, enter -0-			20	0	
21	Payments received during year (see instructions). **Do not** include interest, whether stated or unstated			21	4,000	[11]
22	Add lines 20 and 21			22	4,000	[12]
23	Payments received in prior years (see instructions). **Do not** include interest, whether stated or unstated	23	0			
24	**Installment sale income.** Multiply line 22 by line 19			24	1,000	[13]
25	Enter the part of line 24 that is ordinary income under the recapture rules (see instructions)			25	0	
26	Subtract line 25 from line 24. Enter here and on Schedule D or Form 4797 (see instructions)			26	1,000	[14]

Part III Related Party Installment Sale Income. Do not complete if you received the final payment this tax year.

27 Name, address, and taxpayer identifying number of related party

28 Did the related party resell or dispose of the property ("second disposition") during this tax year? . . . . ☐ Yes ☐ No

29 **If the answer to question 28 is "Yes," complete lines 30 through 37 below unless one of the following conditions is met. Check the box that applies.**

a ☐ The second disposition was more than 2 years after the first disposition (other than dispositions of marketable securities). If this box is checked, enter the date of disposition (mm/dd/yyyy) . . . . ►

b ☐ The first disposition was a sale or exchange of stock to the issuing corporation.

c ☐ The second disposition was an involuntary conversion and the threat of conversion occurred after the first disposition.

d ☐ The second disposition occurred after the death of the original seller or buyer.

e ☐ It can be established to the satisfaction of the IRS that tax avoidance was not a principal purpose for either of the dispositions. If this box is checked, attach an explanation (see instructions).

Line	Description	Line	Amount
30	Selling price of property sold by related party (see instructions)	30	
31	Enter contract price from line 18 for year of first sale	31	
32	Enter the **smaller** of line 30 or line 31	32	
33	Total payments received by the end of your 2014 tax year (see instructions)	33	
34	Subtract line 33 from line 32. If zero or less, enter -0-	34	
35	Multiply line 34 by the gross profit percentage on line 19 for year of first sale	35	
36	Enter the part of line 35 that is ordinary income under the recapture rules (see instructions)	36	
37	Subtract line 36 from line 35. Enter here and on Schedule D or Form 4797 (see instructions)	37	

For Paperwork Reduction Act Notice, see page 4. Cat. No. 13601R Form **6252** (2015)

3. Research (1 Gradable Item)

Answer: IRC § 1001(b)

§ 1001. Determination of amount of and recognition of gain or loss

(b) Amount realized

The amount realized from the sale or other disposition of property shall be the sum of any money received plus the fair market value of the property (other than money) received. In determining the amount realized–

(1) there shall not be taken into account any amount received as reimbursement for real property taxes which are treated under section 164(d) as imposed on the purchaser, and

(2) there shall be taken into account amounts representing real property taxes which are treated under section 164(d) as imposed on the taxpayer if such taxes are to be paid by the purchaser.

4. Classification (10 Gradable Items)

1. A) Capital Asset. Capital assets include all property held unless specifically excluded by the IRC. Specifically excluded are inventory, depreciable business property, real property used in a trade or business, copyrights and artistic compositions developed by the owner, accounts and notes receivable, and certain U.S. government publications acquired at reduced cost. Personal-use property, such as a residence, is a capital asset.
2. A) Capital Asset. Capital assets include all property held unless excluded by the IRC. Stock is not specifically excluded unless the stock is dealer property (held for sale to customers in the ordinary course of the taxpayer's trade or business).
3. B) Section 1231 Property. Capital assets include all property held unless excluded by the IRC. Real property used in a trade or business is specifically excluded. Sec. 1231 property includes all real or depreciable property used in the taxpayer's trade or business and held for more than 1 year.
4. B) Section 1231 Property. Capital assets include all property held unless excluded by the IRC. Real property used in a trade or business is specifically excluded. Sec. 1231 property includes all real or depreciable property used in the taxpayer's trade or business and held for more than 1 year.
5. C) Other Property. Capital assets include all property held unless excluded by the IRC. Depreciable business property, such as the store fixtures, is specifically excluded. Real or depreciable property used in the taxpayer's trade or business is Sec. 1231 property, but only if held for more than 1 year.
6. C) Other Property. Capital assets include all property held unless excluded by the IRC. Inventory is specifically excluded. Since inventory is neither "used" in a trade or business nor depreciable, it is not Sec. 1231 property.
7. C) Other Property. Capital assets include all property held unless excluded by the IRC. Sec. 1221(4) specifically excludes accounts or notes receivable acquired in the ordinary course of business from the sale of inventory. Accounts receivable are not within Sec. 1231.
8. B) Section 1231 Property. Capital assets include all property held unless excluded by Sec. 1221. Acquired goodwill, because it is amortizable, meets the definition of "depreciable" business property. Hence, it is excluded from the category of capital assets. Acquired goodwill is Sec. 1231 property because it is depreciable property used in a trade or business and held more than 1 year. Internally generated goodwill is a capital asset.
9. B) Section 1231 Property. Capital assets include all property held unless excluded by the IRC. Depreciable property used in a trade or business is specifically listed as excluded. Sec. 1231 property includes all real or depreciable property used in the taxpayer's trade or business and held more than 1 year.
10. D) Not Applicable. Treasury stock is not an asset.

5. Gains and Losses (10 Gradable Items)

1. $3,000 and C) Short-Term Capital Gain. Taxpayer realized $23,000 on the sale when he had a $20,000 cost basis in the stock. Thus, he realized and recognized a gain of $3,000. The stock was a capital asset. Gain from the sale or exchange of a capital asset held for less than 1 year is short-term capital gain.
2. $14,000 and C) Short-Term Capital Gain. Taxpayer realized $139,000 on the sale when he had a $125,000 cost basis in the stock. Thus, he realized and recognized a gain of $14,000. The stock was a capital asset. Gain from the sale or exchange of a capital asset held for less than 1 year is short-term capital gain.
3. $1,000 and F) Long-Term Capital Loss. Taxpayer realized $9,000 on the sale when he had a $10,000 cost basis in the van. Thus, he realized a loss of $1,000. The van was personal-use property, not depreciable. Thus, it was a capital asset. Loss from the sale or exchange of a capital asset held for more than 1 year is long-term capital loss.
4. $59,000 and D) Long-Term Capital Gain. The amount realized was $169,000. Vacant land is not depreciable, so its basis was the $110,000 cost. Thus, there is a $59,000 gain ($169,000 – $110,000). The vacant land is personal-use property held as a capital asset. Since the property was held for over 12 months and sold after May 5, 2003, it is included in the 15% basket.
5. $5,000 and B) Ordinary Loss. Sec. 1033 nonrecognition does not apply to losses. The amount of the casualty loss is the adjusted basis, net of amounts recovered, e.g., insurance proceeds. Thus, taxpayer recognizes a loss of $5,000 ($50,000 adjusted basis – $45,000 recovery). Sec. 1231 property is depreciable or real property used in a trade or business and held for more than 1 year, and nonpersonal capital assets held for more than 1 year and involuntarily converted. If there is a net loss for the year from involuntary conversion of property, including by fire, used in the trade or business or capital assets held long-term for investment or in connection with a trade or business, the loss is treated as an ordinary loss. If so, even if the involuntarily converted properties are otherwise Sec. 1231 property, the gains and losses are not included further in Sec. 1231 computations.

6. Nonrecognition Transactions (6 Gradable Items)

1. B) Do not recognize gain (loss). Losses on the sale of a principal residence are not recognized, regardless of whether the taxpayers are eligible to take the exclusion.
2. C) Partially recognize gain (loss). Laptop and desktop computers are in the same asset class, so this transaction qualifies for nonrecognition under Sec. 1031. When nonqualified property (also called boot) is also received in a like-kind exchange, a gain is recognized in an amount equal to the lesser of gain realized or boot received.
3. A) Recognize gain (loss) in full. Property is involuntarily converted if the conversion is the result of destruction. If the property is converted in nonqualified proceeds, such as insurance proceeds, any gain realized may be deferred as long as the proceeds are used to purchase qualified replacement property. If the proceeds are not properly reinvested, the entire gain is recognized.
4. A) Recognize gain (loss) in full. Personal properties are of a like kind if they are of a like class. Automobiles, such as taxis, are not in the same asset classes as buses. Since the assets are not of a like kind, the loss must be recognized.
5. C) Partially recognize gain (loss). When qualified small business stock that has been held for at least 5 years is sold, only 50% of the gain must be recognized in gross income. Sec. 1202 defines qualified small business stock as stock issued after August 10, 1993, by a domestic C corporation with gross assets of less than $50 million at issuance. In addition, the taxpayer selling the stock must be the original owner.
6. B) Do not recognize gain (loss). Real property is of a like kind to other real property, even if they have different uses or are located in different states. Sec. 1031 allows the taxpayer to defer recognition of the gain.

Gleim Simulation Grading

Task	Correct Responses		Gradable Items		Score per Task
1	____	÷	9	=	____
2	____	÷	14	=	____
3 (Research)	____	÷	1	=	____
4	____	÷	10	=	____
5	____	÷	10	=	____
6	____	÷	6	=	____
			Total of Scores per Task		____
		÷	Total Number of Tasks		6
			Total Score		____ %

STUDY UNIT SEVEN
CORPORATE TAXABLE INCOME

(14 pages of outline)

Corporate taxable income computations generally parallel those for individuals. Federal tax is determined by applying applicable tax rates to taxable income. Shareholders are then subject to federal income tax on distributions out of corporate earnings and profits (dividends). In addition to regular income tax, a C corporation may also be subject to the AMT (alternative minimum tax), the AET (accumulated earnings tax), and the PHC (personal holding company) tax. A corporation is required to make payments of estimated income tax and for FICA tax on wages paid.

As of the date of publication, the IRS had not yet released all of the 2015 tax forms. Please check www.gleim.com/taxforms for any updates.

7.1 DEFINITION AND ACCOUNTING

1. **General Classification**
   a. If no election is made for a newly formed domestic entity, an entity with two or more members will be classified as a partnership, and an entity with a single member will be disregarded as an entity separate from the owner. A newly formed foreign entity with limited liability will be classified as an association taxed as a corporation.
   b. Certain businesses must be classified as corporations for federal tax purposes. Among the entities treated as corporations are ones incorporated under state or federal law, associations, joint stock companies, insurance companies, certain banks, state-owned organizations, certain foreign organizations, and publicly traded partnerships.
   c. **C corporations** are corporations other than S corporations.
   d. An **S corporation** is a pass-through entity that is not subject to the regular corporate income tax. Qualified corporations that elect subchapter S status are treated similarly to partnerships.
   e. **Partnerships, trusts, and estates** are generally not treated as corporations.
   f. **Publicly traded partnerships** are ineligible entities and must generally be taxed as corporations.
   g. **Limited Liability Company (LLC).** Normally, an LLC would elect partnership status to avoid being taxed as a corporation. This election allows for limited liability of the owners while at the same time retaining the single taxation. The owners are allowed to participate in the operations of the business, and there are no restrictions on the type of owners.
   h. **Professional Association (PA).** An association of professionals, e.g., accountants, doctors, or lawyers, is treated as a corporation for tax purposes if it is both organized under a state's Professional Association Act and operated as a corporation. One individual may be a professional association.
   i. **Personal Service Corporation (PSC).** The corporate rates do not apply to PSCs. These corporations are taxed at a flat rate of 35%.
      1) A PSC's principal activity is performing personal services, substantially by employee-owners. An employee-owner owns more than 10% of the stock.

2) The IRS may allocate income, deductions, credits, exclusions, and other allowances between a PSC and its employee-owners if substantially all the PSC's services are performed for one other corporation, partnership, or entity, and the principal purpose of the PSC is tax avoidance.

j. **Personal Holding Company (PHC).** Any nonexempt closely held corporation is classified as a PHC if a significant portion of its income is passive in nature. PHCs are subject to a penalty tax on excess personal holding company income.

2. **Check-the-Box**

a. The "check-the-box" regulations apply to business entities other than trusts that are separate for federal tax purposes. The regulations allow an eligible entity to decide whether it will be taxed as a corporation or a partnership. An eligible entity is a business that is not required to be treated as a corporation under federal tax law.

3. **Single vs. Multi-Member Entities**

a. An eligible entity with a single member can elect to be taxed as a corporation or disregarded as an entity separate from its owner (sole proprietorship).

b. An eligible entity with two or more members can elect to be taxed as either a partnership or a corporation.

4. **Tax Year**

a. Generally, a corporation may elect either a calendar or fiscal tax year.

1) A PSC is required to use a calendar tax year.

a) An exception exists for a valid business purpose or a PSC that makes "minimum distributions."

2) A corporate tax return is due on or before the 15th day of the 3rd month following the close of the tax year (e.g., March 15 for a calendar year corporation).

a) A corporation that files Form 7004 and pays its estimated unpaid tax liability is allowed an extension of up to 6 months.

5. **Accounting Method**

a. No formal election is required for the accounting method of a newly incorporated C corporation. Any method allowed by the C corporation may be "elected" by using that method on their initial return. For example, a newly formed C corporation that chooses to use the accrual method must only use this method on its initial return in order to elect the method.

b. The cash method may be used only by PSCs, S corporations, certain farming corporations, and C corporations that have average annual gross receipts of no more than $5 million in the 3 preceding tax years. Tax shelters may not use the cash method. A newly incorporated C corporation makes its initial accounting method selection simply by using the chosen method on its initial return.

6. **Corporation Income Tax Formula**

	Income
–	Exclusions
=	Gross income
–	Deductions
=	Taxable income
×	Tax rate
=	Gross regular tax liability
–	Credits
=	Net regular tax liability or refund receivable
+	AMT
+	FICA taxes
+	Special taxes
=	Tax liability or refund receivable

CPA candidates should be familiar with the contents of Form 1120 (exclusion of Schedules) below.

Form **1120**
Department of the Treasury
Internal Revenue Service

U.S. Corporation Income Tax Return

For calendar year 2014 or tax year beginning ____________, 2014, ending ____________, 20 ____

▶ Information about Form 1120 and its separate instructions is at *www.irs.gov/form1120.*

OMB No. 1545-0123

2014

A Check if:
1a Consolidated return (attach Form 851) ☐
b Life/nonlife consolidated return ☐
2 Personal holding co. (attach Sch. PH) ☐
3 Personal service corp. (see instructions) ☐
4 Schedule M-3 attached ☐

TYPE OR PRINT
Name
Number, street, and room or suite no. If a P.O. box, see instructions.
City or town, state, or province, country and ZIP or foreign postal code

B Employer identification number
C Date incorporated
D Total assets (see instructions) $

E Check if: (1) ☐ Initial return (2) ☐ Final return (3) ☐ Name change (4) ☐ Address change

Income	1a	Gross receipts or sales	1a	
	b	Returns and allowances	1b	
	c	Balance. Subtract line 1b from line 1a		1c
	2	Cost of goods sold (attach Form 1125-A)		2
	3	Gross profit. Subtract line 2 from line 1c		3
	4	Dividends (Schedule C, line 19)		4
	5	Interest		5
	6	Gross rents		6
	7	Gross royalties		7
	8	Capital gain net income (attach Schedule D (Form 1120))		8
	9	Net gain or (loss) from Form 4797, Part II, line 17 (attach Form 4797)		9
	10	Other income (see instructions—attach statement)		10
	11	**Total income.** Add lines 3 through 10 ▶		11
Deductions (See instructions for limitations on deductions.)	12	Compensation of officers (see instructions—attach Form 1125-E) ▶		12
	13	Salaries and wages (less employment credits)		13
	14	Repairs and maintenance		14
	15	Bad debts		15
	16	Rents		16
	17	Taxes and licenses		17
	18	Interest		18
	19	Charitable contributions		19
	20	Depreciation from Form 4562 not claimed on Form 1125-A or elsewhere on return (attach Form 4562)		20
	21	Depletion		21
	22	Advertising		22
	23	Pension, profit-sharing, etc., plans		23
	24	Employee benefit programs		24
	25	Domestic production activities deduction (attach Form 8903)		25
	26	Other deductions (attach statement)		26
	27	**Total deductions.** Add lines 12 through 26 ▶		27
	28	Taxable income before net operating loss deduction and special deductions. Subtract line 27 from line 11		28
	29a	Net operating loss deduction (see instructions)	29a	
	b	Special deductions (Schedule C, line 20)	29b	
	c	Add lines 29a and 29b		29c
Tax, Refundable Credits, and Payments	30	**Taxable income.** Subtract line 29c from line 28 (see instructions)		30
	31	Total tax (Schedule J, Part I, line 11)		31
	32	Total payments and refundable credits (Schedule J, Part II, line 21)		32
	33	Estimated tax penalty (see instructions). Check if Form 2220 is attached ▶ ☐		33
	34	**Amount owed.** If line 32 is smaller than the total of lines 31 and 33, enter amount owed		34
	35	**Overpayment.** If line 32 is larger than the total of lines 31 and 33, enter amount overpaid		35
	36	Enter amount from line 35 you want: **Credited to 2015 estimated tax** ▶	**Refunded** ▶	36

Sign Here ▶

Under penalties of perjury, I declare that I have examined this return, including accompanying schedules and statements, and to the best of my knowledge and belief, it is true, correct, and complete. Declaration of preparer (other than taxpayer) is based on all information of which preparer has any knowledge.

Signature of officer | Date | ▶ Title

May the IRS discuss this return with the preparer shown below (see instructions)? ☐ Yes ☐ No

Paid Preparer Use Only

Print/Type preparer's name	Preparer's signature	Date	Check ☐ if self-employed	PTIN
Firm's name ▶			Firm's EIN ▶	
Firm's address ▶			Phone no.	

For Paperwork Reduction Act Notice, see separate instructions. Cat. No. 11450Q Form **1120** (2014)

Stop and review! You have completed the outline for this subunit. Study multiple-choice questions 1 through 4 on page 277.

7.2 GROSS INCOME OF A CORPORATION

1. **Scope**
   a. Gross income of a corporation, similar to individual taxation, is all income from whatever source derived unless specifically excluded.
2. **Excluded Items**
   a. **Capital contributions** are excluded from a corporation's gross income.
      1) Gifts from nonshareholder. Property other than money gifted from a nonshareholder has a zero basis. When money is contributed instead of property, it is given a basis equal to the value of the money and the basis of other property is reduced. First, reduce basis in property acquired within 1 year after the gift, then in all depreciable property, if any, and then in any remaining property, in proportion to the relative basis of any property in each of these categories.
      2) Pro rata contributions by shareholders, whether voluntary or by assessment, are not deductible by the shareholders. Instead, their individual basis in the stock is increased. The corporation may take a transferred basis in the property.
   b. **Treasury stock.** No gain or loss is recognized by a corporation on the sale or exchange of its own stock (including treasury stock).
3. **Included Items**
   a. **Life insurance income.** Proceeds received due to the death of the insured are generally excluded from gross income.
      1) If an employer purchases a policy that covers an employee and is issued after August 17, 2006, the proceeds from the policy are taxable to the extent proceeds exceed premiums paid.
      2) Proceeds received under a policy transferred for consideration (e.g., secured debt) are income to the recipient only to the extent that the proceeds exceed the consideration.
   b. **Discharge of debt.** Except in stock-for-debt exchanges, income from cancelation of a corporation's debt at less than the outstanding carrying amount is excluded to the extent the corporation is insolvent. When the exclusion applies, the following tax attributes of the corporation must be reduced (dollar for dollar) in the order listed.
      1) NOLs and NOL carryovers
      2) The general business credit
      3) Capital loss carryovers
      4) Basis in property of the corporation
      5) Foreign tax credit carryovers

      NOTE: An election to first reduce basis is available.
   c. **Bond repurchase.** A corporation's income includes the issue price of its own bond minus the repurchase price and any premium it has already recognized. Subunit 7.3 discusses repurchase at a premium.
   d. **Sinking-fund income.** Interest or other income from property (including money) in a sinking fund to satisfy an obligation is income (even if in the hands of a trustee).

e. **Unrestrained claim.** Both cash- and accrual-basis taxpayers must include in gross income, in the year of receipt, amounts actually or constructively received if the taxpayer has an unrestrained claim to the amounts (e.g., prepaid rent).

f. **Refunds.** As with individuals, a refund of state taxes deducted for a prior year is included in income for the current year, to the extent that the deduction in the prior year generated a tax benefit. If the deduction generated no tax benefit, the refund is not included.

Stop and review! You have completed the outline for this subunit. Study multiple-choice questions 5 through 8 beginning on page 278.

7.3 DEDUCTIONS OF A CORPORATION

Deductions of a corporation have been regularly tested on the CPA exam. You should be familiar with calculating both corporate book income and corporate taxable income. In a question testing corporate deductions, you may be given corporate book income, along with other information, and asked to calculate corporate taxable income.

NOTE: This subunit covers deductions with special rules. Ordinary deductions without restrictions (e.g., utilities) are not specifically addressed.

1. **Overview**
   a. Theoretically, all corporate expenditures have a business objective. Deductions from corporate gross income for ordinary and necessary business expenses are allowed. Differences from deductions for individuals are discussed below.
      1) Organizational expenditures are allowed an immediate expense and amortization of balance.
      2) Deduction is allowed for dividends received from corporations.
      3) Interest on a corporation's own debt is generally deductible.
      4) AGI and limits based on it do not apply to a corporation.
      5) Personal deductions, e.g., the standard deduction, are not allowed.
      6) Passive activity loss rules do not apply to C corporations.
2. **Organizational Expense and Start-Up Costs**
   a. Costs of organizing a corporation are properly chargeable to a capital account. They generally are not deductible as a current expense because they benefit more than one tax period.
      1) However, a corporation may elect to expense up to $5,000 of qualified organizational expenses and $5,000 of start-up costs in the taxable year in which the business begins.
         a) The amount expensed is reduced by the costs exceeding $50,000.
         b) The remaining balance is amortized over a 15-year (180-month) period beginning with the month business began.
         c) Only expenditures incurred before the end of the tax year in which the corporation commences business may be expensed (amortized). When they are paid is irrelevant.
         d) The election is irrevocable.
   b. Qualifying organizational expenditures are ones incurred incidental to formation of the corporation and are distinct from start-up costs. Examples are legal fees for drafting the charter, incorporation fees, expenses for temporary directors, and organizational meeting costs.

c. Organizational expenditures that are not qualified are costs related to the transfer of assets to the corporation or the issuance and sale of stock. Examples are printing stock certificates; professional fees for issuing stock; and costs incurred in the marketing, advertising, or promoting of stock issuances.

d. Examples of start-up costs are costs incurred to prepare to enter into the trade or business, to secure suppliers and customers, and to obtain certain supplies and equipment.

3. **Charitable Contributions**

a. A corporation's charitable contribution is deductible only if it is made to a qualified organization.

b. Deductible amounts must be paid during the tax year. An accrual method corporation may elect to deduct an amount authorized by the board during the current tax year and paid not later than 2 1/2 months after the close of the tax year.

c. A corporation may deduct the adjusted basis of inventory and other ordinary income property contributed.

d. A corporation is allowed a deduction for the donation of qualified food and book inventory.

1) The deduction is equal to basis plus one-half of the gain that would have been recognized if the asset were sold at FMV.

2) The deduction may not exceed two times the asset's basis.

e. In general, the deduction for the contribution of capital gain property is the property's FMV.

f. The property must be used in a manner related to the organization's exempt purpose. It must not be disposed of for value.

g. Deductions are limited to 10% of taxable income (TI) before any

1) Charitable contributions
2) Dividends-received deduction
3) Dividends-paid deduction
4) NOL carryback
5) Capital loss carryback

h. Excess over the TI limit is deductible during the succeeding 5 tax years.

1) No carryback is allowed.
2) Current-year contributions are deducted first.
3) FIFO treatment applies to carryforwards.

4. **Dividends-Received Deduction (DRD)**

a. A special corporate deduction for dividends received from domestic taxable corporations is allowed.

b. Amounts deductible vary with the percentage of the stock of the distributing corporation (by voting and value) owned by the recipient.

Percent of Ownership	Percent of Dividends Deductible	Limit: Percent of TI of Recipient
< 20%	70%	70%
≥ 20%, < 80%	80%	80%
≥ 80% & affiliated	100%	100%

1) Members of an affiliated group of corporations may deduct 100% of the dividends received from a member of the same affiliated group.

c. To be eligible for the DRD, a corporation must hold the stock at least 46 days during the 90-day period that begins 45 days before the stock becomes ex-dividend with respect to the dividend.

d. A corporation cannot take a DRD if it holds a short position in substantially similar or related property.

e. The DRD may be reduced when the investment company receives substantial amounts of income from sources other than dividends from domestic corporations eligible for the DRD.

f. The DRD is limited by the recipient corporation's adjusted taxable income. The TI limit amount varies with the recipient's stock ownership of the corporation.

   1) To compute the limit, use TI before any of the following:

      a) Dividends-received deduction
      b) Dividends-paid deduction
      c) NOL deduction
      d) Capital loss carryback
      e) Certain extraordinary dividend adjustments

   2) First, compute the limit with respect to 20%-and-more-owned corporate dividends.

   3) The TI limit does not apply if a current NOL exists or an NOL results from the DRD.

EXAMPLE

A corporation has taxable income of $1,000, including $10,000 in dividends received from a less-than-20%-owned domestic taxable corporation but before DRD. The DRD before applying the TI limit is $7,000 ($10,000 × 70%). Because the DRD produces an NOL, it is not limited to 70% of taxable income before the deduction ($700).

g. The DRD is allowable for dividends received from foreign corporations if the following are met:

   1) The distributing foreign corporation is at least 10% owned by the recipient domestic corporation,
   2) The foreign corporation is subject to U.S. federal income tax,
   3) The foreign corporation has income effectively connected with a trade or business in the U.S., and
   4) The foreign corporation is not a foreign personal holding company.

h. The DRD is allowable only on the portion of the dividends attributable to the effectively connected income.

i. Credit for foreign taxes deemed paid by the corporation on the dividend producing earnings and profit (E&P) may be allowable.

j. An S corporation may not claim the DRD.

k. Disqualified dividends. No deduction is allowed, or it is further restricted, for dividends received from the following:

   1) Mutual savings banks (they are like interest)
   2) Real estate investment trusts
   3) Domestic international sales corporations, generally
   4) Public utilities, on preferred stock
   5) A corporation exempt from tax during the distribution year

5. **Gifts**

   a. Distinguish gifts from charitable contributions, which are made to qualified organizations. A deduction for business gifts is allowable only to the extent of $25 per donee per year. The following are not treated as gifts for this limit:

      1) Signs or promotional materials used on the recipient's business premises
      2) An item costing less than $4 having a permanent imprint of the donor's name

6. **Compensation**

   a. Compensation, e.g., salary, wages, or bonuses, is a deductible business expense unless the services are capital in nature.

   b. Unreasonable compensation to a shareholder is generally treated as a distribution, characterized as a dividend, to the extent of earnings and profits.

   c. Compensation by an accrual taxpayer (corporation) to a cash-basis taxpayer (employee) is not deductible by the corporation until the period in which the cash-basis taxpayer receives the payment and recognizes the income.

   d. Payments made by March 15 of the succeeding year may be accrued and expensed in a prior year if related to services rendered in that prior year.

   e. Deduction is disallowed to a publicly held corporation for compensation in excess of $1 million paid in any tax year to certain employees.

      1) The limit applies to compensation paid to the chief operating officer and to the four other officers whose compensation must be reported to shareholders under the Securities Exchange Act of 1934.

         a) No amount of a "parachute payment" made to an officer, shareholder, or highly compensated person is deductible.

      2) The following forms of remuneration are not included in the $1 million limit:

         a) Income from pension plans, annuity plans, and specified employer trusts

         b) Benefits that are tax-free under the Code

         c) Commissions based on income generated by the individual performance of the employee

         d) Compensation based on performance goals

      3) The disallowance of the deduction for the compensation payment does not change the employee's reporting of the compensation for income tax purposes.

         a) The $1 million and any excess is generally compensation gross income.

         b) The salary, bonus, or other payment is not required to be treated as a dividend.

         c) Dividend reporting for compensation may be required if part or all of the compensation is unreasonable.

   f. Stock. FMV of property received for services is gross income when it is not subject to a substantial risk of forfeiture and its value can be ascertained with reasonable certainty. Deduction of the compensation is allowed when the amount is included as gross income but only if federal income tax on the compensation is withheld.

EXAMPLE

Employee purchases stock (FMV = $1,000) in Year 1 for $500. In Year 8, when its FMV is $2,000, Employee's rights in it are no longer subject to a substantial risk of forfeiture. Employee includes $1,500 in gross income in Year 8. Employer may deduct $1,500 in Year 8.

      1) Sale prior to vesting in a non-arm's-length transaction results in gross income computed from the current FMV of the property. Further, gross income is includible upon a subsequent arm's-length sale.

EXAMPLE

In the example above, Employee sold the stock to Spouse in Year 2 for $750 when its FMV was $1,500. The sale in Year 8 was by Spouse. Employee includes and Employer deducts $1,000 in Year 2 and $500 in Year 8.

   g. Education. An employer's expenditures for employee education are deductible as a business expense. An individual, in contrast, may deduct only educational expenses required to maintain or improve skills in a present position.

7. **Travel and Meals**
   a. Travel and meals are deductible business expenses. Meals bought while traveling or served on the business premises are deductible by 50% of the amount incurred.
      1) All meals served on the business premises are fully deductible if provided to more than half of the employees for the convenience of the employer.
      2) Expenses for **entertainment** that are ordinary and necessary to the business are deductible by up to 50% of the amount incurred.
   b. Limitation of deduction
      1) If the employee's meal and entertainment expenses are reimbursed by his or her employer and the reimbursement is not treated as compensation, the employer's deduction is limited to 50% of the expenses.
      2) If the employee's meal expenses are reimbursed by his or her employer and the reimbursement is treated as compensation, the employee's deduction is limited to 50% of the expenses.
         a) Employers are not subject to the 50% limit to the extent they treat the reimbursement as compensation to employees.
8. **Insuring an Employee**
   a. Reasonable amounts of expenditures to promote employee health, goodwill, and welfare are deductible. Reasonable amounts paid or incurred for employee life insurance are included.
   b. Key employee. Premiums for life insurance covering an officer or employee are not deductible if the corporation is a direct or indirect beneficiary.
   c. A deduction is denied for interest expense incurred with respect to corporate-owned life insurance policies, or endowment or annuity contracts.
9. **R&E Expenditures**
   a. Qualified research and experimental expenditures may be capitalized, amortized, or currently deducted.
      1) Generally, costs incidental to development of a model, process, or similar property are included.
      2) Not included are costs of market research, sociological research, or development of art.
      3) Purchase of equipment and land receives its regular treatment and may not be deducted immediately.
10. **Fines**
    a. Fines and penalties paid to a governmental entity are not deductible.
11. **Bad Debts**
    a. For cash-basis taxpayers, income is only recognized when actually received. Therefore, any bad debt will not be included as part of income since the cash is never received. Accrual-basis taxpayers, however, do recognize the income and are allowed a bad debt deduction.
    b. The reserve method is not allowed (except for financial institutions).
       1) A corporation must use the direct charge-off method or the nonaccrual-experience method.
       2) The nonaccrual-experience method is a procedure for not recognizing income if it is expected to be uncollectible. This is similar to treatment by cash-basis taxpayers in that the income is never recognized and therefore there is no need for a deduction.

12. **Worthless Securities**

    a. Loss incurred when a security becomes worthless is generally treated as a capital loss subject to the capital loss limitations. Loss incurred when a security of an affiliated corporation becomes worthless may be treated as an ordinary loss.

13. **Stock Redemptions**

    a. Generally, deduction of amounts paid or incurred with respect to a stock redemption or the redemption of the stock of any related person is not allowed. An exception to the general rule is the allowance for deductions for interest paid or accrued within the tax year on indebtedness.

14. **Original Issue Discount**

    a. OID is treated as deductible interest expense.
    b. Constant yield method. OID is deductible as interest, using the yield method to amortize the discount.
        1) Constant yield to maturity is computed and applied to adjusted issue price (AIP) to compute deductible interest.
        2) The OID portion does not include cash interest payments made to the holder during the period.
        3) AIP is the original issue price adjusted for OID previously taken into account.
        4) Yield to maturity is determined on the basis of compounding at the end of each (typically 6-month) accrual period.
            a) Daily portions of OID must be computed. It is the ratable daily portion of the excess of AIP multiplied by yield to maturity over cash interest payable for the bond year.

EXAMPLE

Consider a 5-year 10% bond issued on June 30, Year 1, with a \$10,000 face, a \$9,250 original issue price, and 12% yield.

Year 1 amortization of interest:

$$\$9{,}250 \text{ price} \times 12\% \text{ yield} \times \frac{6 \text{ months}}{12 \text{ months}}$$

$$= \$555 - \$500 \left(\$10{,}000 \text{ face} \times 10\% \times \frac{6 \text{ months}}{12 \text{ months}} \right) \text{cash paid}$$

$$= \$55 \text{ interest}$$

Year 2 amortization of interest:

$$(\$9{,}250 \text{ price} + \$55 \text{ interest}) \times 12\% \text{ yield}$$

$$= \$1{,}116.60 - \$1{,}000 \; (\$10{,}000 \text{ face} \times 10\%) \text{ cash paid}$$

$$= \$116.60 \text{ interest}$$

15. **Repurchase at Premium**

    a. A corporation that repurchases its own bonds may deduct as interest expense the excess of the repurchase price over the issue price.
        1) Issue price is adjusted for OID deducted.
        2) No more than the normal call premium on nonconvertible debt is allowable, unless the corporation can show that the excess is not attributed to a conversion feature.
        3) A call premium not exceeding 1 year's interest at the rate stated in the bond is considered normal.

16. **Interest Expense**
    a. Interest expense incurred on borrowings used to repurchase stock is deductible in the period in which it is paid or incurred. However, other expenses related to a stock purchase on reorganization are generally not deductible.
17. **Casualty Losses**
    a. Casualty losses are deductible. When business property is partially destroyed, the deductible amount is the lesser of the decline in FMV or the property's adjusted basis (prior to the loss).
        1) When business property is completely destroyed, the deductible amount is the property's adjusted basis (prior to the loss).
        2) Unlike individuals, there is no $100-per-loss or 10%-of-AGI floor for corporations.
18. **Taxes**
    a. State income taxes based on gross income are deductible. However, federal income taxes are not.

Stop and review! You have completed the outline for this subunit. Study multiple-choice questions 9 through 21 beginning on page 279.

7.4 LOSSES OF A CORPORATION

1. The following rules apply only for corporations, not individuals.
2. **Net Operating Loss (NOL)**
    a. An NOL is any excess of deductions over gross income.
    b. Modified deductions for some items are used in computing an NOL.
        1) An NOL carried over from other tax years is not allowed in computing a current NOL.
        2) A dividends-received deduction (DRD) may produce or increase an NOL.
            a) A corporation is entitled to disregard the limitations on a DRD when calculating an NOL. The DRD would increase the NOL.
        3) Charitable contributions are not allowed in computing a current NOL.
        4) The allowable depreciation may not create or increase an NOL.
    c. Applying NOLs as a deduction. Generally, a corporation's NOL is carried back to each of the 2 preceding tax years and forward to the 20 succeeding tax years.
        1) A corporation may elect to forgo carryback and only carry the NOL forward.
        2) The NOL must be applied to the earliest tax year to which it can be carried and used to the fullest extent possible in that year.
        3) The NOL reduces TI, but not below zero, for that year.
        4) TI for the carryover year is adjusted TI.
            a) A charitable contribution allowable in a carryback year remains deductible because the charitable contribution 10%-of-TI limit is applied before an NOL carryback.
            b) Applying an NOL as a deduction in a subsequent tax year and computing excess NOL carryover from the subsequent year are complex when the charitable contribution 10%-of-TI limit applies.

d. Carryback procedure. Carryback of an NOL results in overpayment in a prior tax year.

1) Claiming a refund requires filing an amended return (Form 1120X), which must be filed during the statute of limitations period.
2) Application for quick refund of tax as a result of an NOL carryback is permitted (Form 1139).
3) The application window is the date the loss year return is due until 12 months from the close of the tax year.

3. **Capital Gain and Loss**

a. Capital gain net income (CGNI) occurs when net short-term capital gain (net STCG) exceeds net long-term capital loss (net LTCL).
b. Net capital gains (NCGs) constitute gross income.
c. Net capital gains (net LTCG – net STCL) are currently taxed as ordinary income.

1) The 35% alternative tax on NCGs does not apply at current rates.
2) Net STCGs (STCGs – STCLs) are treated as ordinary income (OI) unless offset by LTCLs.

d. A corporation's capital losses are deductible only to the extent of capital gains, whether they are short- or long-term.

1) A net capital loss (NCL) is not deductible against OI in the tax year incurred.

NCL = Excess of CLs (ST & LT) over CG (ST & LT)

2) It cannot produce or increase an NOL.
3) When figuring a current-year net capital loss, capital losses carried from other years are not included.
4) A corporation may not carry a capital loss from, or to, a year during which it is an S corporation.

e. A corporation's NCL for a particular tax year may be carried back to each of the 3 preceding tax years and forward to the 5 succeeding tax years.

1) No election to forgo carryback is provided.
2) The NCL must be used to the extent possible in the earliest applicable tax year.
3) The oldest unused NCL is applied first.

f. The NCL is treated as an STCL in a carryover tax year. It offsets only a net capital gain before the carryover, but it may not produce or increase an NOL.

4. **Passive Activity Loss (PAL)**

a. The passive activity loss limitation rules explained in Study Unit 5, Subunit 5, apply to individuals, estates, and trusts (other than grantor trusts). Special PAL rules apply to closely held corporations and personal service corporations. Even though the PAL rules do not apply to grantor trusts, partnerships, and S corporations directly, they do apply to the owners of these entities.

Stop and review! You have completed the outline for this subunit. Study multiple-choice questions 22 through 26 beginning on page 283.

7.5 RECONCILING BOOK AND TAXABLE INCOME

Background

The divergence of tax accounting from financial accounting has received the stamp of approval of the U.S. Supreme Court. In the case *Thor Power Tool Company v. Commissioner* (1979), the Court noted that "the primary goal of financial accounting is to provide useful information to management, shareholders, creditors, and other properly interested . . . the primary goal of the income tax system is the equitable collection of revenue."

1. **Reconciliation**
   a. Corporations file federal returns using Form 1120. Reconciliation of income per books of the corporation with income per tax is reported on Schedule M-1. It addresses differences, both permanent and temporary, for general financial reporting and tax accounting. Schedule M-3 is required for corporations with total assets of $10 million or more.
2. **Temporary and Permanent Differences**
   a. Temporary differences are timing differences and occur because tax laws require the recognition of some income and expenses in a different period than that required for book purposes. These differences originate in one period and reverse or terminate in one or more subsequent periods. Accelerated depreciation is an example of a temporary difference, as tax depreciation is greater than book in the beginning.
   b. Permanent differences result from transactions that will not be offset by any corresponding differences in other periods. The tax exempt income from municipal bonds interest is an example of a permanent difference, as it will not be taxable in a later period.
3. **Calculation**
   a. To reconcile income per books with income per tax, the following adjustments are made to net income (loss) per books (similar to Schedule M-1).

	Net income (loss) per books
+	Federal income tax
+	Excess of capital losses over capital gains
+	Income subject to tax not recorded on books
+	Expenses recorded on books not deducted on the tax return
–	Income recorded on books not subject to tax
–	Deductions on this return not charged against book income (e.g., depreciation)
=	Taxable income

   b. Examples of expenses recorded on books that are not deductible include contributions in excess of 10% taxable income limitation, book depreciation expense in excess of allowable tax depreciation, disallowed travel and entertainment costs (50% of meals and entertainment expenses are nondeductible), life insurance premiums on key personnel when the corporation is the beneficiary, political contributions, and interest expense to carry tax-free interest instruments (e.g., municipal bonds).
   c. Examples of nontaxable income include prepaid rent or interest previously received and recorded for tax purposes but not earned until the current year, life insurance proceeds received on the death of key personnel, and tax-exempt interest.
4. **Schedule M-3**
   a. In an effort to increase transparency and provide the IRS with more detail about book income and tax differences, Schedule M-3 is required for large entities. The schedule shows the differences by category, dollar amount, and status as permanent or temporary. Part 1 asks certain questions about the financial statements and reconciles book net income to net income for tax purposes. Parts II and III reconcile book net income to taxable income, indicating temporary and permanent differences. Carefully review the Form 1120 Schedule M-3 on the following page.

Stop and review! You have completed the outline for this subunit. Study multiple-choice questions 27 through 30 beginning on page 284.

SCHEDULE M-3 (Form 1120)

Department of the Treasury
Internal Revenue Service

Net Income (Loss) Reconciliation for Corporations With Total Assets of $10 Million or More

▶ Attach to Form 1120 or 1120-C. ▶ Information about Schedule M-3 (Form 1120) and its separate instructions is available at *www.irs.gov/form1120*.

OMB No. 1545-0123

2014

Name of corporation (common parent, if consolidated return) | **Employer identification number**

Check applicable box(es): (1) ☐ Non-consolidated return (2) ☐ Consolidated return (Form 1120 only)

(3) ☐ Mixed 1120/L/PC group (4) ☐ Dormant subsidiaries schedule attached

Part I Financial Information and Net Income (Loss) Reconciliation (see instructions)

1a Did the corporation file SEC Form 10-K for its income statement period ending with or within this tax year?

☐ **Yes.** Skip lines 1b and 1c and complete lines 2a through 11 with respect to that SEC Form 10-K.

☐ **No.** Go to line 1b. See instructions if multiple non-tax-basis income statements are prepared.

b Did the corporation prepare a certified audited non-tax-basis income statement for that period?

☐ **Yes.** Skip line 1c and complete lines 2a through 11 with respect to that income statement.

☐ **No.** Go to line 1c.

c Did the corporation prepare a non-tax-basis income statement for that period?

☐ **Yes.** Complete lines 2a through 11 with respect to that income statement.

☐ **No.** Skip lines 2a through 3c and enter the corporation's net income (loss) per its books and records on line 4a.

2a Enter the income statement period: Beginning MM/DD/YYYY Ending MM/DD/YYYY

b Has the corporation's income statement been restated for the income statement period on line 2a?

☐ **Yes.** (If "Yes," attach an explanation and the amount of each item restated.)

☐ **No.**

c Has the corporation's income statement been restated for any of the five income statement periods preceding the period on line 2a?

☐ **Yes.** (If "Yes," attach an explanation and the amount of each item restated.)

☐ **No.**

3a Is any of the corporation's voting common stock publicly traded?

☐ **Yes.**

☐ **No.** If "No," go to line 4a.

b Enter the symbol of the corporation's primary U.S. publicly traded voting common stock . . . . ☐

c Enter the nine-digit CUSIP number of the corporation's primary publicly traded voting common stock . . . . ☐

Line	Description	Line	Amount
4a	Worldwide consolidated net income (loss) from income statement source identified in Part I, line 1 .	4a	
b	Indicate accounting standard used for line 4a (see instructions): (1) ☐ GAAP (2) ☐ IFRS (3) ☐ Statutory (4) ☐ Tax-basis (5) ☐ Other (specify) ______		
5a	Net income from nonincludible foreign entities (attach statement)	5a	( )
b	Net loss from nonincludible foreign entities (attach statement and enter as a positive amount) . . .	5b	
6a	Net income from nonincludible U.S. entities (attach statement)	6a	( )
b	Net loss from nonincludible U.S. entities (attach statement and enter as a positive amount)	6b	
7a	Net income (loss) of other includible foreign disregarded entities (attach statement)	7a	
b	Net income (loss) of other includible U.S. disregarded entities (attach statement)	7b	
c	Net income (loss) of other includible entities (attach statement)	7c	
8	Adjustment to eliminations of transactions between includible entities and nonincludible entities (attach statement)	8	
9	Adjustment to reconcile income statement period to tax year (attach statement)	9	
10a	Intercompany dividend adjustments to reconcile to line 11 (attach statement)	10a	
b	Other statutory accounting adjustments to reconcile to line 11 (attach statement)	10b	
c	Other adjustments to reconcile to amount on line 11 (attach statement)	10c	
11	**Net income (loss) per income statement of includible corporations.** Combine lines 4 through 10 .	11	

Note. Part I, line 11, must equal the amount on Part II, line 30, column (a), and Schedule M-2, line 2.

12 Enter the total amount (not just the corporation's share) of the assets and liabilities of all entities included or removed on the following lines.

	Total Assets	Total Liabilities
a Included on Part I, line 4 . . . . ▶		
b Removed on Part I, line 5 . . . . ▶		
c Removed on Part I, line 6 . . . . ▶		
d Included on Part I, line 7 . . . . ▶		

For Paperwork Reduction Act Notice, see the Instructions for Form 1120. Cat. No. 37961C **Schedule M-3 (Form 1120) 2014**

QUESTIONS

7.1 Definition and Accounting

1. In Year 1, Brun Corp. properly accrued $10,000 for an income item on the basis of a reasonable estimate. In Year 2, Brun determined that the exact amount was $12,000. Which of the following statements is true?

A. Brun is required to file an amended return to report the additional $2,000 of income.

B. Brun is required to notify the IRS within 30 days of the determination of the exact amount of the item.

C. The $2,000 difference is includible in Brun's Year 2 income tax return.

D. The $2,000 difference of income must be included when the reasonable estimate amount is determined.

Answer (C) is correct.

REQUIRED: The true statement about accrual of a reasonable estimate when the exact amount is greater than the estimate.

DISCUSSION: Under the accrual method of accounting, income is includible in gross income when all the events have occurred that fix the right to receive the income and the amount can be determined with reasonable accuracy. If an amount of income is properly accrued on the basis of a reasonable estimate and the exact amount is subsequently determined, the difference, if any, shall be taken into account for the taxable year in which such determination is made.

Answer (A) is incorrect. The excess is reported as gross income in the tax year in which the exact amount is determined, in this case, in Year 2. Answer (B) is incorrect. Notification is not necessary. Answer (D) is incorrect. The taxpayer cannot include an amount (s)he is not aware of. The additional amount of $12,000 was determined later.

2. An S corporation engaged in manufacturing has a year end of June 30. Revenue consistently has been more than $10 million under both cash and accrual basis of accounting. The stockholders would like to change the tax status of the corporation to a C corporation using the cash basis with the same year end. Which of the following statements is correct if it changes to a C corporation?

A. The year end will be December 31, using the cash basis of accounting.

B. The year end will be December 31, using the accrual basis of accounting.

C. The year end will be June 30, using the accrual basis of accounting.

D. The year end will be June 30, using the cash basis of accounting.

Answer (C) is correct.

REQUIRED: The appropriate year end for a C corporation.

DISCUSSION: C corporations that are not personal service corporations, S corporations, or small C corporations (less than an average of $5 million in revenues per year over the past 3 years) must use the accrual basis of accounting. A corporation can use a fiscal year end; June 30 is therefore allowed.

Answer (A) is incorrect. C corporations that are not personal service corporations, S corporations, or small C corporations (less than an average of $5 million in revenues per year over the past 3 years) must use the accrual basis of accounting. A corporation is not required to use a calendar year end; it can use a fiscal year end. Answer (B) is incorrect. The corporation does not need to change its tax year to a calendar year end. The C corporation can keep the fiscal year end of June 30. Answer (D) is incorrect. C corporations that are not personal service corporations or small C corporations must use the accrual basis of accounting.

3. In order to adopt a fiscal tax year on its first federal income tax return, a corporate taxpayer must

A. Maintain books and records and report income and expenses using that tax year.

B. Attach a completed Form 1128, *Application to Adopt, Change, or Retain a Tax Year*, to his or her fiscal-year-basis income tax return.

C. File a short-period return.

D. Get IRS approval.

Answer (A) is correct.

REQUIRED: The procedure that a taxpayer must follow to adopt a fiscal tax year on its first tax return.

DISCUSSION: Permission from the IRS is generally not needed to place a taxpayer's first tax year on either a calendar- or a fiscal-year basis. A taxpayer's first tax year is selected on the initial return. However, in order to adopt a fiscal year, the new taxpayer must adopt that year on the books and records before the due date for filing the return for that year (not including extensions).

Answer (B) is incorrect. A completed Form 1128, *Application to Adopt, Change, or Retain a Tax Year*, is not required to adopt a fiscal tax year on a taxpayer's first federal income tax return. Answer (C) is incorrect. A short-period tax year return is for a period of less than 12 months for taxpayers with special circumstances. Answer (D) is incorrect. IRS approval is not necessary on the initial return.

4. ABC Corporation ends its tax year on October 30. When must ABC's income tax return be filed for the year ending October 30, Year 1?

A. January 15, Year 2.

B. March 15, Year 2.

C. February 15, Year 2.

D. April 15, Year 2.

Answer (A) is correct.

REQUIRED: The proper income tax return due date for a fiscal year corporation.

DISCUSSION: A corporation must file its return on or before the 15th day of the third month following the close of the tax year. For a fiscal-year corporation with a year end of 10/30/Yr 1, the return must be filed by 1/15/Yr 2.

Answer (B) is incorrect. Calendar year corporations must file by this date. Answer (C) is incorrect. February 15, Year 2, is 1 month late. Answer (D) is incorrect. April 15, Year 2, is 3 months late.

7.2 Gross Income of a Corporation

5. On December 31, 1993, Homer Corporation issued $2 million of 50-year bonds for $2.6 million. On December 31, 2015, Homer issued new bonds with a face amount of $3 million for which it received $3.4 million. Part of the proceeds received were used to repurchase $2,320,000 of the bonds issued in 1993. No elections were made to adjust the basis of any property. Assume the straight-line method is used for premium amortization. What is the taxable income to Homer on the repurchase of the 1993 bonds?

A. $0

B. $16,000

C. $264,000

D. $336,000

Answer (B) is correct.

REQUIRED: The amount of taxable income to a corporation on the repurchase of its bonds.

DISCUSSION: If bonds are issued by a corporation and are subsequently repurchased at a price less than the issue price minus any amount of premium already recognized as income, the difference is included in income for the taxable year. Prior to 1987, a corporation could elect to exclude the income and reduce the basis of property, but this election is available in post-1986 years only in cases of bankruptcy or insolvency. The amount of income taxable to Homer is

Original issue price	$2,600,000
Less: face amount	(2,000,000)
Total premium	$ 600,000
Issue price	$2,600,000
Less: premium already recognized as income [($600,000 ÷ 50 years) × 22 years]	(264,000)
Issue price less premium already included in income	$2,336,000
Less: repurchase price	(2,320,000)
Amount included in 2015 income	$ 16,000

Answer (A) is incorrect. The difference between bonds issued by a corporation and subsequently repurchased at a price less than the issue price, minus any amount of premium already recognized as income, must be included in income for the taxable year. Answer (C) is incorrect. This amount is the premium already recognized as income. Answer (D) is incorrect. This amount is the total premium less the premium already included in income.

6. The following information pertains to treasury stock sold by Lee Corporation to an unrelated broker in the current year:

Proceeds received	$50,000
Cost	30,000
Par value	9,000

What amount of capital gain should Lee recognize in the current year on the sale of this treasury stock?

A. $0

B. $20,000

C. $21,000

D. $41,000

Answer (A) is correct.

REQUIRED: The gain a corporation should report as a result of the sale of treasury stock.

DISCUSSION: A corporation does not recognize gain or loss on the receipt of money or other property in exchange for its stock, including treasury stock. Therefore, no gain or loss is recognized by Lee as a result of the treasury stock sale.

7. For the year ended December 31, 2015, Kell Corp.'s book income, before income taxes, was $70,000. Included in the computation of this $70,000 was $10,000 of proceeds of a life insurance policy, representing a lump-sum payment in full as a result of the death of Kell's controller. Kell was the owner and beneficiary of this policy since 2005. In its income tax return for 2015, Kell should report taxable life insurance proceeds of

A. $10,000

B. $8,000

C. $5,000

D. $0

Answer (D) is correct.

REQUIRED: The extent to which proceeds of a life insurance policy constitute gross income.

DISCUSSION: For employer-owned policies issued prior to August 17, 2006, proceeds of a life insurance policy paid by reason of death of the insured are excluded by the beneficiary. Since no part of the $10,000 represents interest on proceeds retained by the insurance company, no part of it is reported as gross income.

8. Sanders Corporation issued a $1 million 10-year debenture for $1.2 million on January 1, 2008. In 2015, how much of a premium (income) must Sanders report on its 2015 income tax return from issuance of this bond?

A. $240,000

B. $200,000

C. $20,000

D. $0

Answer (C) is correct.

REQUIRED: The income reported from the issuance of a 10-year debenture.

DISCUSSION: In the case of a bond, the amount of amortizable bond premium for the taxable year shall be allowed as a deduction. The amount is amortized over the life of the bond. Thus, Sanders must report $20,000 [($1,200,000 – $1,000,000) ÷ 10].

Answer (A) is incorrect. Incorrectly amortizing the issue price over 5 years results in $240,000. Answer (B) is incorrect. The total premium is $200,000. Answer (D) is incorrect. The premium may be amortized over the life of the bond.

7.3 Deductions of a Corporation

9. Which of the following costs are amortizable organizational expenditures?

A. Professional fees to issue the corporate stock.

B. Printing costs to issue the corporate stock.

C. Legal fees for drafting the corporate charter.

D. Commissions paid by the corporation to an underwriter.

Answer (C) is correct.

REQUIRED: The costs amortizable as organizational expenditures.

DISCUSSION: A corporation may elect to amortize qualified organizational expenses over a period of not less than 180 months. Expenditures associated with the formation of the corporation, including legal fees for drafting the corporate charter, are amortizable.

10. Which of the following entities must include in gross income 100% of dividends received from unrelated taxable domestic corporations in computing regular taxable income?

	Personal Service Corporations	Personal Holding Companies
A.	Yes	Yes
B.	No	No
C.	Yes	No
D.	No	Yes

Answer (A) is correct.

REQUIRED: The corporations that must include dividends received in taxable income.

DISCUSSION: A dividend received by one from another member of a group filing a consolidated return is eliminated. The recipient adjusts its taxable income to eliminate the dividend from the group's consolidated taxable income. Otherwise, all dividends constitute gross income. Distinguish inclusion from the deduction from gross income received from taxable domestic corporations.

Answer (B) is incorrect. All corporations must include in gross income 100% of dividends received from unrelated domestic corporations. Answer (C) is incorrect. Personal service corporations are not the only entities that must include in gross income 100% of dividends received from unrelated domestic corporations. Answer (D) is incorrect. Personal holding companies are not the only entities that must include in gross income 100% of dividends received from unrelated domestic corporations.

11. For the year ended December 31, 2015, Kelly Corp. had net income per books of $300,000 before the provision for federal income taxes. Included in the net income were the following items:

Dividend income from an unaffiliated domestic taxable corporation (Taxable income limitation does not apply, and there is no portfolio indebtedness.)	$50,000
Bad debt expense (represents the increase in the allowance for doubtful accounts)	80,000

If no bad debt was written off, what is Kelly's taxable income for the year ended December 31, 2015?

A. $250,000

B. $330,000

C. $345,000

D. $380,000

Answer (C) is correct.

REQUIRED: The determination of taxable income.

DISCUSSION: First, a 70% dividends received deduction (DRD) is allowed if the corporation owns less than 20% of the distributing corporation (presumed unless the facts state otherwise). Thus, there is a $35,000 DRD ($50,000 × 70%). Second, the deductibility of bad debts is limited to the direct write-off method. The reserve method is no longer allowed except for certain financial institutions. Therefore, $80,000 must be added back to the financial net income. Thus, the taxable income for 2015 is $345,000 ($300,000 – $35,000 + $80,000).

Answer (A) is incorrect. Only 70% of the dividend income is deductible. Also, the $80,000 of bad debt expense must be added back to book income because only actual bad debt write-offs are deductible. Answer (B) is incorrect. Only 70% of the dividend income ($35,000) is deductible. Answer (D) is incorrect. Only 70% of the dividend income ($35,000) is deductible.

12. Tapper Corp., an accrual-basis, calendar-year corporation, was organized on January 2, 2015. During 2015, revenue was exclusively from sales proceeds and interest income. The following information pertains to Tapper:

Taxable income before charitable contributions for the year ended December 31, 2015	$500,000
Tapper's matching contribution to employee-designated qualified universities made during 2015	10,000
Board of directors' authorized contribution to a qualified charity (authorized December 1, 2015; made February 1, 2016)	30,000

What is the maximum allowable deduction that Tapper may take as a charitable contribution on its tax return for the year ended December 31, 2015?

A. $0

B. $10,000

C. $30,000

D. $40,000

Answer (D) is correct.

REQUIRED: The maximum deduction allowed for charitable contributions.

DISCUSSION: The total amount of charitable contributions is limited to 10% of a corporation's adjusted taxable income. Tapper is limited to a $50,000 ($500,000 × 10%) deduction. Contributions to qualifying charities are deductible in the year paid. In addition, an accrual-method corporation may deduct a contribution authorized by the board of directors during the current tax year and paid no later than 2 1/2 months after the close of the tax year. Tapper has qualifying contributions totaling $40,000, which is under the 10% limit of $50,000, so Tapper may fully deduct its qualifying contributions in 2015.

Answer (A) is incorrect. Both of the contributions are fully deductible in 2015. Answer (B) is incorrect. The contribution authorized by the board on 12/1/15 and paid on 2/1/16 is fully deductible in 2015. Answer (C) is incorrect. The contribution to qualified universities is fully deductible in 2015.

13. In 2015, Kara Corp. incurred the following expenditures in connection with the repurchase of its stock from shareholders:

Interest on borrowings used to repurchase stock	$100,000
Legal and accounting fees in connection with the repurchase	400,000

The total of the above expenditures deductible in 2015 is

A. $0

B. $100,000

C. $400,000

D. $500,000

Answer (B) is correct.

REQUIRED: The amount that a corporation may deduct for expenses related to the repurchase of its stock.

DISCUSSION: Interest expense incurred on business borrowings is deductible in the period in which it is paid or accrued. However, other expenses related to a stock repurchase or reorganization are capitalized.

Answer (A) is incorrect. Interest expense incurred on business borrowings is deductible. Answer (C) is incorrect. Amounts paid or incurred in connection with a stock redemption are not deductible. Answer (D) is incorrect. The interest is deductible, but the costs associated with the repurchase are not.

14. Placebo Corp. is an accrual-basis, calendar-year corporation. On December 13, 2015, the board of directors declared a 2%-of-profits bonus to all employees for services rendered during 2015 and notified them in writing. None of the employees own stock in Placebo. The amount represents reasonable compensation for services rendered and was paid on March 13, 2016. Placebo's bonus expense may

A. Not be deducted on Placebo's 2015 tax return because the per-share employee amount cannot be determined with reasonable accuracy at the time of the declaration of the bonus.

B. Be deducted on Placebo's 2015 tax return.

C. Be deducted on Placebo's 2016 tax return.

D. Not be deducted on Placebo's tax return because payment is a disguised dividend.

Answer (B) is correct.

REQUIRED: The treatment of bonus compensation.

DISCUSSION: Under Sec. 404, certain contributions paid by an employer are subject to being treated as deferred compensation and are deductible in the year of payment. This limitation is applicable if the deduction would otherwise be allowed under Sec. 162(a). The deduction is required in the payment year unless distributed prior to March 15. Because the present amount was paid on March 13, the time of receipt was within the allocated period of time, and the compensation can be deducted as a business expense under Sec. 162 in 2015.

Answer (A) is incorrect. This determination is not required by Sec. 404. Answer (C) is incorrect. Sec. 404 is not applicable due to the timely payment of the bonus. Answer (D) is incorrect. The facts of the problem provide that the amount of the bonus represents reasonable compensation and not a disguised dividend.

15. John Budd is the sole shareholder of Ral Corp., an accrual-basis taxpayer engaged in wholesaling operations. Ral's retained earnings at January 1, 2015, amounted to $1 million. For the year ended December 31, 2015, Ral's book income, before federal income tax, was $300,000. Included in the computation of this $300,000 were the following:

Key employee insurance premiums paid on Budd's life (Ral is the beneficiary of this policy.)	$3,000
Group term insurance premiums paid on $10,000 life insurance policies for each of Ral's four employees (The employees' spouses are the beneficiaries.)	4,000

What amount should Ral deduct for key employee and group life insurance premiums in computing taxable income for 2015?

A. $0

B. $3,000

C. $4,000

D. $7,000

Answer (C) is correct.

REQUIRED: The amount that a corporation may deduct for payment of life insurance premiums.

DISCUSSION: Ral Corp. may deduct the premiums paid for group term life insurance. However, no deduction is allowed for premiums paid for life insurance for which the corporation is the beneficiary.

Answer (A) is incorrect. Premiums paid for group term life insurance are deductible. Answer (B) is incorrect. Premiums paid for life insurance for which the corporation is the beneficiary are not deductible. Answer (D) is incorrect. The group term life premiums are deductible, but the key employee insurance premiums are not.

16. If a corporation's charitable contributions exceed the limitation for deductibility in a particular year, the excess

A. Is not deductible in any future or prior year.

B. May be carried back or forward for 1 year at the corporation's election.

C. May be carried forward to a maximum of 5 succeeding years.

D. May be carried back to the preceding year.

Answer (C) is correct.

REQUIRED: The treatment of a corporation's excess charitable contributions.

DISCUSSION: A corporation may carry unused charitable contributions forward for 5 years. Current contributions are deducted before carryovers. Carryovers are applied on a FIFO basis. Carrybacks of excess charitable contributions are not permitted.

17. Pope, a C corporation, owns 15% of Arden Corporation. Arden paid a $3,000 cash dividend to Pope. What is the amount of Pope's dividends-received deduction?

A. $3,000

B. $2,400

C. $2,100

D. $0

Answer (C) is correct.

REQUIRED: The DRD for a 15% owner.

DISCUSSION: The DRD is available only to corporations. The deduction is based on the distributee corporation's percentage ownership of the distributing corporation and may be limited to taxable income. The deduction percentage is 70% for corporations with less than 20% ownership in the distributing corporation. Pope's deduction is $2,100 ($3,000 dividend × 70%).

Answer (A) is incorrect. The deduction is limited based on Pope's ownership percentage of Arden. Pope must own 80% or more of Arden to take a 100% DRD. Answer (B) is incorrect. An 80% deduction requires 20% to 79% ownership of the distributing corporation. Answer (D) is incorrect. Corporations are allowed a deduction based on ownership. The minimum deduction is 70%.

18. The costs of organizing a corporation in 2015

A. May be deducted in full in the year in which these costs are incurred even if paid in later years.

B. May be deducted only in the year in which these costs are paid.

C. May be amortized over a period of not less than 180 months, even if these costs are capitalized on the company's books.

D. Are nondeductible capital expenditures.

Answer (C) is correct.

REQUIRED: The deductibility of a corporation's organization costs.

DISCUSSION: A corporation may elect to amortize the expenditures over a period of not less than 180 months, beginning with the month in which the corporation starts business.

19. Gero Corporation had operating income of $160,000 after deducting $10,000 for contributions to State University, but not including dividends of $2,000 received from nonaffiliated taxable domestic corporations (not from debt-financed portfolio stock). In computing the maximum allowable deduction for contributions, Gero should apply the percentage limitation to a base amount of

A. $172,000

B. $170,400

C. $170,000

D. $162,000

Answer (A) is correct.

REQUIRED: The base amount for the percentage limitation on charitable contributions.

DISCUSSION: The charitable contribution deduction is limited to 10% of a corporation's taxable income (TI) computed before the charitable contribution deduction, dividends-received deduction (not dividends income), net operating loss carryback, and capital loss carryback. Gero's base amount is $172,000 ($160,000 operating income + $10,000 contributions + $2,000 dividends).

Answer (B) is incorrect. TI for the limit is computed before the dividends-received deduction. Answer (C) is incorrect. TI for the limit includes the contributions. Answer (D) is incorrect. TI for the limit includes dividends and contributions.

20. In 2015, Pine Corporation had losses of $20,000 from operations. It received $180,000 in dividends from a 25%-owned domestic corporation. Pine's taxable income is $160,000 before the dividends-received deduction. What is the amount of Pine's dividends-received deduction?

A. $0

B. $144,000

C. $128,000

D. $180,000

Answer (C) is correct.

REQUIRED: The dividends-received deduction of a corporation.

DISCUSSION: A corporate deduction for dividends received from domestic taxable corporations is allowed. Pine Corporation may deduct 80% of dividends received from a domestic corporation in which Pine owned between 20% and 80% of the stock. This dividends-received deduction is limited to 80% of taxable income. Without regard to the limitation, Pine could deduct $144,000 ($180,000 × 80%). Pine, however, is limited to a $128,000 deduction ($160,000 taxable income × 80%). Thus, Pine's dividends-received deduction is $128,000.

Answer (A) is incorrect. Pine is entitled to a dividends-received deduction. Answer (B) is incorrect. Pine's dividends-received deduction is limited to 80% of taxable income. Answer (D) is incorrect. Pine may not deduct all of the dividends received.

21. Beta, a C corporation, reported the following items of income and expenses for the year:

Gross income	$600,000
Dividend income from a 30% owned domestic corporation	100,000
Operating expenses	400,000

What is Beta's taxable income for the year?

A. $200,000

B. $220,000

C. $230,000

D. $300,000

Answer (B) is correct.

REQUIRED: The amount of the C corporation's taxable income for the year.

DISCUSSION: Corporation income tax is calculated by subtracting deductions from gross income. Deductions from corporate gross income for ordinary and necessary business expenses are allowed. An 80% dividends received deduction (DRD) is allowed if the corporation owns between 20% and 80% of the distributing corporation. Thus, there is an $80,000 DRD ($100,000 x 80%). So, taxable income is $220,000 ($600,000 gross income + $100,000 dividend income – $400,000 operating expenses – $80,000 DRD).

Answer (A) is incorrect. Dividend income and the dividends received deduction is included in the calculation of taxable income. Answer (C) is incorrect. A 70% dividends received deduction results in $230,000. Answer (D) is incorrect. An 80% DRD is allowed if the corporation owns between 20% and 80% of the distributing corporation.

7.4 Losses of a Corporation

22. For each of the years 2012 through 2014, Geyer, Inc., a calendar-year corporation, had net income (loss) per books as follows:

2012	$ 15,000
2013	10,000
2014	(60,000)

Included in Geyer's gross revenues for 2014 were taxable dividends of $20,000 received from an unrelated 20%-owned domestic corporation. If Geyer elects to give up the carryback period, what is its NOL that may be carried forward to 2015?

A. $35,000

B. $51,000

C. $60,000

D. $76,000

Answer (D) is correct.

REQUIRED: The net operating loss (NOL) carryover.

DISCUSSION: Barring any allowable special election, an NOL may be carried back to each of the 2 preceding taxable years and forward to the 20 succeeding taxable years. The NOL must be carried to the earliest possible year, unless an election is made to give up the 2-year carryback. Because Geyer made this election, the 2014 net operating loss is a carryforward to 2015. In computing the net operating loss, the dividends received deduction (DRD) is computed without regard to the 80%-of-taxable-income limitation.

Net loss per books	$(60,000)
Allowable DRD ($20,000 × 80%)	(16,000)
NOL carryover	$(76,000)

Answer (A) is incorrect. The amount of $35,000 is merely the sum of net income (loss) per books for 2012, 2013, and 2014. Answer (B) is incorrect. The corporation elected to forgo the carryback of the NOL. Answer (C) is incorrect. In computing the NOL, the dividends-received deduction is computed without regard to the 80%-of-taxable-income limitation.

23. Baker Corp., a calendar-year C corporation, realized taxable income of $36,000 from its regular business operations for calendar-year 2015. In addition, Baker had the following capital gains and losses during 2015:

Short-term capital gain	$ 8,500
Short-term capital loss	(4,000)
Long-term capital gain	1,500
Long-term capital loss	(3,500)

Baker did not realize any other capital gains or losses since it began operations. What is Baker's total taxable income for 2015?

A. $46,000

B. $42,000

C. $40,500

D. $38,500

Answer (D) is correct.

REQUIRED: The taxable income after considering capital gains and losses.

DISCUSSION: For corporations, all capital gains (short-term and long-term) are taxed at the corporation's regular tax rate. The capital gain net income ($2,500) in addition to the business income ($36,000) results in total taxable income of $38,500.

Answer (A) is incorrect. The amount of $46,000 excludes the capital losses. Answer (B) is incorrect. The amount of $42,000 excludes the long-term capital loss. Answer (C) is incorrect. The amount of $40,500 excludes the long-term capital gains and losses.

24. For the year ended December 31, 2015, Taylor Corp. had a net operating loss of $200,000. Taxable income for the earlier years of corporate existence, computed without reference to the net operating loss, was as follows:

	Taxable Income
2010	$ 5,000
2011	10,000
2012	20,000
2013	30,000
2014	40,000

If Taylor makes no special election to waive the net operating loss carryback, what amount of net operating loss will be available to Taylor for the year ended December 31, 2016?

A. $200,000

B. $130,000

C. $110,000

D. $95,000

Answer (B) is correct.

REQUIRED: The amount of net operating loss (NOL) carryforward.

DISCUSSION: A corporation's NOL is carried back to each of the 2 preceding tax years and forward to the 20 succeeding tax years. The NOL must be applied first to the earliest qualifying tax year and used to the fullest extent possible in that year and each succeeding year. Therefore, Taylor must carry the NOL back to 2013 and offset taxable income of $30,000. This procedure is continued for 2014 and offsets another $40,000 of taxable income. The remaining NOL of $130,000 ($200,000 – $70,000) is available for the year ended December 31, 2016, and 19 years forward.

Answer (A) is incorrect. Forgoing the 2-year carryback and applying the entire NOL to the 20-year carryforward requires a special election. Answer (C) is incorrect. The NOL can only be carried back to the 2, not 3, preceding tax years. Answer (D) is incorrect. The loss may only be carried back 2 years, not 5 years.

25. A C corporation has gross receipts of $150,000, $35,000 of other income, and deductible expenses of $95,000. In addition, the corporation incurred a net long-term capital loss of $25,000 in the current year. What is the corporation's taxable income?

A. $65,000

B. $87,000

C. $90,000

D. $115,000

Answer (C) is correct.

REQUIRED: The correct calculation of corporate taxable income.

DISCUSSION: Net capital gains (NCGs) constitute gross income. However, a corporation's capital losses are deductible only to the extent of capital gains, whether they are short- or long-term. Therefore, a net capital loss is not deductible against ordinary income in the tax year incurred. The corporation has taxable income of $90,000 ($150,000 + $35,000 – $95,000).

Answer (A) is incorrect. Capital losses are deductible only to the extent of capital gains; therefore, a net capital loss is not deductible against ordinary income in the tax year incurred. Answer (B) is incorrect. Only individuals (not corporations) are allowed to deduct up to $3,000 of net capital losses in the current year. Corporations may only deduct capital losses up to the amount of capital gains. Answer (D) is incorrect. Both gross receipts and other income are additions (increases) to taxable income. In addition, there are other reductions to taxable income to consider in this problem.

26. Wonder, Inc., had 2015 taxable income of $200,000 exclusive of the following:

Gain on sale of land used in business	$25,000
Loss on sale of machinery used in business	(13,000)
Loss on sale of securities held 3 years	(4,000)
Loss on sale of securities held 3 months	(3,000)

On what amount of taxable income should Wonder compute tax?

A. $200,000

B. $202,500

C. $205,000

D. $212,000

Answer (C) is correct.

REQUIRED: The taxable income of a corporation with both capital and Sec. 1231 gains and losses.

DISCUSSION: The sale of the land and the sale of machinery used in the business are Sec. 1231 transactions, if held more than 1 year. Since the gain and loss net to a gain of $12,000, they are a long-term capital gain and loss. The capital losses on the securities are fully deductible because they do not exceed the $12,000 net Sec. 1231 gain.

Answer (A) is incorrect. Net capital gain constitutes taxable income. Answer (B) is incorrect. The Code allows no deduction for net capital gains. Answer (D) is incorrect. The net Sec. 1231 gain is treated as capital gain and is already included in taxable income.

7.5 Reconciling Book and Taxable Income

27. In the current year, Starke Corp., an accrual-basis, calendar-year corporation, reported book income of $380,000. Included in that amount was $50,000 municipal bond interest income, $170,000 for federal income tax expense, and $2,000 interest expense on the debt incurred to carry the municipal bonds. What amount should Starke's taxable income be as reconciled on Starke's Schedule M-1 of Form 1120, *U.S. Corporation Income Tax Return*?

A. $330,000

B. $500,000

C. $502,000

D. $550,000

Answer (C) is correct.

REQUIRED: The corporation's taxable income given book income and some of its components.

DISCUSSION: The municipal bond income and the related interest expenses are not considered for tax purposes. The federal tax expense is not deductible for federal income tax purposes. Therefore, the net Schedule M-1 adjustment of $122,000 ($2,000 + $170,000 – $50,000) results in taxable income of $502,000 ($380,000 + $122,000).

Answer (A) is incorrect. The $170,000 income tax expense and the $2,000 interest expense on the municipal bonds are positive adjustments to book income. Answer (B) is incorrect. Interest expense on tax-exempt investments is not deductible. Answer (D) is incorrect. The $50,000 of municipal bond interest is a negative adjustment, and $2,000 of related interest expense is a positive adjustment.

28. On January 2 of the current year, Shaw Corp., an accrual-basis, calendar-year C corporation, purchased all the assets of a sole proprietorship, including $300,000 in goodwill. Current-year federal income tax expense of $110,100 and $7,500 for annual amortization of goodwill based on a 40-year amortization period were deducted to arrive at Shaw's reported book income of $239,200. What should be the amount of Shaw's current-year taxable income, as reconciled on Shaw's Schedule M-1 of Form 1120, *U.S. Corporation Income Tax Return*?

A. $239,200

B. $329,300

C. $336,800

D. $349,300

Answer (C) is correct.

REQUIRED: The taxable income reconciled on Schedule M-1.

DISCUSSION: The capitalized costs of certain Sec. 197 intangibles, including goodwill, may be amortized over a 15-year period beginning on the date of acquisition. Therefore, the deduction for tax purposes would be $20,000 ($300,000 ÷ 15), resulting in subtracting an additional $12,500 ($20,000 – $7,500) from book net income to arrive at taxable income (M-1 adjustment). The federal income tax expense must be added to book income to arrive at taxable income. Thus, Shaw Corp.'s current-year taxable income is $336,800 ($239,200 + $110,100 – $12,500).

Answer (A) is incorrect. This figure is the amount of income per books. Answer (B) is incorrect. This figure reflects goodwill amortization of $27,500 rather than $20,000. Answer (D) is incorrect. The $349,300 does not reflect the $12,500 amortization adjustment.

29. Would the following expense items be reported on Schedule M-1 of the corporation income tax return showing the reconciliation of income per books with income per return?

	Interest Incurred on Loan to Carry U.S. Obligations	Provision for State Corporation Income Tax
A.	Yes	Yes
B.	No	No
C.	Yes	No
D.	No	Yes

Answer (B) is correct.

REQUIRED: The item reported on Schedule M-1.

DISCUSSION: Items treated differently in computing income per books and taxable income are reported and reconciled on Schedule M-1. Items treated the same for financial and tax purposes are not reported on the schedule. Both interest to carry U.S. obligations and state income tax are deducted in computing book income and taxable income.

30. In the reconciliation of income per books with income per return,

A. Only temporary differences are considered.

B. Only permanent differences are considered.

C. Both temporary and permanent differences are considered.

D. Neither temporary nor permanent differences are considered.

Answer (C) is correct.

REQUIRED: The differences included in the reconciliation of income per books with income per return.

DISCUSSION: Reconciling income per books with income per return considers both temporary differences (i.e., differences expected to be eliminated in the future, such as an accelerated method of depreciation for tax purposes and a straight-line method for financial reporting purposes) and permanent differences (i.e., differences not expected to be eliminated in the future, such as that caused by the deduction of federal income tax for financial reporting purposes).

Answer (A) is incorrect. Permanent differences must be reconciled. Answer (B) is incorrect. Temporary differences must be reconciled. Answer (D) is incorrect. Both temporary and permanent differences must be reconciled.

7.6 PRACTICE TASK-BASED SIMULATIONS

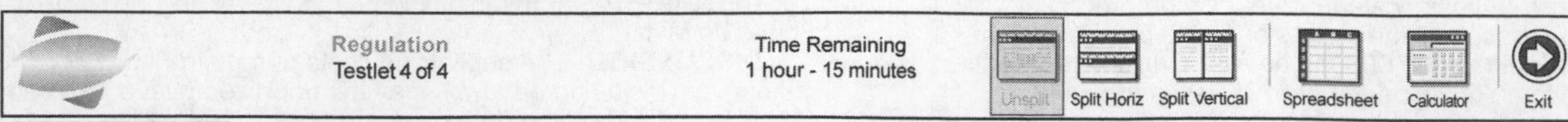

DIRECTIONS

Note: If you believe you have encountered a software malfunction, report it to the test center staff immediately.

Navigation

To navigate from task to task, use the controls at the bottom of the screen. Click on the **Next** button to advance to the next task, or the **Previous** button to go to the previous task. To go directly to any task, click on its number.

If you would like a reminder to revisit a task, or want to indicate that you are finished with it, click on the reminder flag below the task number. To clear the flag, click on it again. Reminder flags are for your use only – they do not contribute to your score.

Tabs

In this part of the examination, you will be asked to complete various tasks. Every task has one or more **Work Tabs**. Some tasks have one or more **Information Tabs**, others may have none. Every task has a **Help** tab.

If a task has **Information Tabs**, you may use the information in them to complete your responses in the **Work Tabs**.

Work tab **Information tab** **Help tab**

Work Tabs:

- **Work Tabs** are identified with a pencil icon. This is where your responses are expected.
- Each task has one or more **Work Tabs.**
- **Work Tabs** contain directions for completing the task – be sure to read these directions carefully.
- The **Work Tab** name in the example above is for illustration only – yours will differ.
- You must complete all of the **Work Tabs** in each task to receive full credit.

Information Tabs:

- The Authoritative Literature will be provided in all tasks in the AUD, FAR, and REG sections for your reference.
- Your simulation may have one or more additional **Information Tabs**. Like the Authoritative Literature tabs, **Information Tabs** do not have a pencil icon.
- If your task has additional **Information Tabs**, go through each to familiarize yourself with the task content.

Help Tab:

- The **Help Tab** provides assistance with the exam software that is used in this task. For example, if the task is to compose a memorandum, **Help** will provide information about the word processor.

The Toolbar

The toolbar at the top of the screen shows the amount of time remaining for you to complete the tasks. In addition, the following tools are available. Note that only the **Exit** button is displayed when Directions are visible - the others will appear when you begin the tasks.

Click on these buttons to split or unsplit the screen. You can split the screen vertically or horizontally.

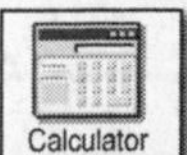

Click on this button to display the calculator; click on it again to hide the calculator. To move the calculator, click on the calculator title bar and drag the calculator to the desired location.

Click on this button to use the spreadsheet; click on it again to hide the spreadsheet. To move the spreadsheet, click on the the spreadsheet title bar and drag the spreadsheet to the desired location.

Click on this button to go on to the next part of the examination. You must complete all of the tasks to receive full credit. Once you click on **Exit** and confirm the action, you will NOT be able to return to this testlet.

= Reminder | Directions | 1 2 3 4 5 6 | Previous | Next

Select from the choices provided the effect each item below will have on a corporation's current year gross income. Each choice may be used once, more than once, or not at all.

Deduction Items	Deductibility
1. Expense for term life insurance premiums paid on policies for corporate officers. The corporation is the policy owner and beneficiary.	
2. State franchise tax expense for 2015.	
3. Charitable contributions.	
4. Dividends received from an unaffiliated taxable domestic corporation in which the corporation owns 15% of stock.	
5. Payment of penalty for delinquent taxes.	
6. Bonuses paid to nonshareholder employees.	

Choices
A) Fully deductible
B) Partially deductible
C) Nondeductible
D) Deduction may be limited by AGI

= Reminder | Directions | 1 2 3 4 5 6 | Previous | Next

Net Operating Loss | Authoritative Literature | Help

For each of the following situations, enter the correct amounts in the shaded cells below. If the value of a cell is zero or should be left blank, you must enter a (0) to receive credit for your work.

Situation	Answer
1. For the tax year ended December 31, Year 4, Kustan Co. had gross income of $300,000 and operating expenses of $500,000. Included in the operating expenses is a contribution of $7,000 made to qualifying charities. What is Kustan's net operating loss for Year 4?	
2. During Year 3, Tennis Corporation had gross income of $70,000 and operating expenses of $95,000. Tennis Co. also received dividend income of $60,000 from a domestic corporation in which Tennis is a 25% shareholder. What is Tennis Co.'s net operating loss for Year 3?	
3. For each of the following years, Gobby Corporation had net income (loss) per books as follows: • Year 1 -- $20,000 • Year 2 -- $15,000 • Year 3 -- $(65,000) What amount of NOL may be carried forward to Year 4?	
4. For Year 3, Association Corporation had taxable income of $60,000 before using any of its net operating loss from Year 2. Association's books and records reflect the following income (losses): • Year 1 -- $15,000 • Year 2 -- $(40,000) If Association does not elect to forgo the carryback period, what amount of taxable income must Association report on its Year 3 tax return?	

Federal Tax | Authoritative Literature | Help

Following is the ISAA Corp.'s condensed income statement before federal income tax for the year ended December 31, 2015:

Sales		$1,000,000
Cost of sales		(550,000)
Gross profit		$ 450,000
Operating expenses		(250,000)
Operating income		$ 200,000
Other income (loss):		
Interest	$ 8,000	
Dividends	33,180	
Net long-term capital loss	(6,400)	34,780
Income before federal income tax		**$ 234,780**

Additional Information

Interest arose from the following sources:

U.S. Treasury notes	$4,000
Municipal arbitrage bonds	1,000
Other municipal bonds	3,000
Total interest	**$8,000**

Dividends arose from the following sources:

Taxable Domestic Corporation	Date Stock Acquired	Percent Owned by ISAA	
Rest Corp.	09/01/11	10	$10,000
Son Corp. (sold 1/10/15)	12/01/14	5	10,000
SIT Corp.	07/01/09	30	8,750
Real estate investment trust	06/01/14		3,750
Mutual fund corp. (capital gains dividends)	04/01/13	0.1	400
Money market fund (interest-paying securities only)	03/01/12	0.1	280
Total dividends			**$33,180**

Operating expenses include the following:

- ISAA pledged $5,000 to charity for 2015 and paid the $5,000 in February.
- Estimate of $15,000 for bad debts. Actual bad debts for the year amounted to $10,000.
- Key employee life insurance premiums of $4,000. ISAA is the beneficiary of the policies.
- State income taxes of $12,000.
- During 2015, ISAA estimated federal income tax payments of $30,000. These payments were debited to prepaid tax expense on ISAA's books.
- ISAA declared and paid dividends of $10,000 during 2015.
- ISAA was not subject to the alternative minimum tax in 2015.
- ISAA paid its employees (nonofficers) $100,000 during the year.

Assume corporate income tax rates are as follows:

Taxable Income

Over	But Not Over	Pay	Percent on Excess	Of the Amount Over
$ 0	$ 50,000	$ 0	15	$ 0
50,000	75,000	7,500	25	50,000
75,000	100,000	13,750	34	75,000
100,000	335,000	22,250	39	100,000
335,000	10,000,000	113,900	34	335,000
10,000,000	15,000,000	3,400,000	35	10,000,000
15,000,000	18,333,333	5,150,000	38	18,333,333
18,333,333			35	

-- Continued on next page --

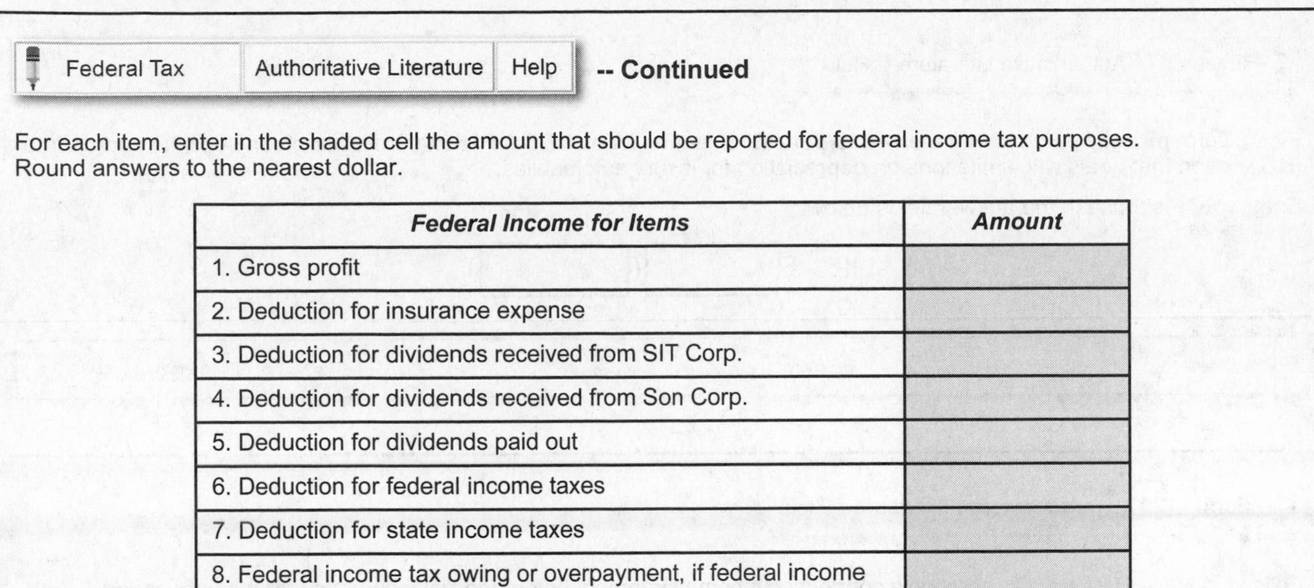

Federal Tax | Authoritative Literature | Help -- **Continued**

For each item, enter in the shaded cell the amount that should be reported for federal income tax purposes. Round answers to the nearest dollar.

Federal Income for Items	*Amount*
1. Gross profit	
2. Deduction for insurance expense	
3. Deduction for dividends received from SIT Corp.	
4. Deduction for dividends received from Son Corp.	
5. Deduction for dividends paid out	
6. Deduction for federal income taxes	
7. Deduction for state income taxes	
8. Federal income tax owing or overpayment, if federal income tax before credits was $20,000	

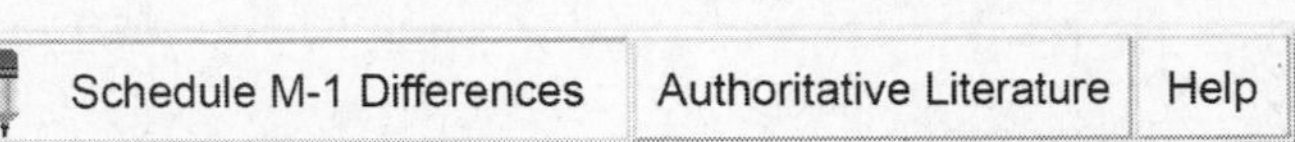

First, indicate by writing "yes" or "no" whether the following items will adjust net income per books to compute taxable income. Next, for those items that will cause an adjustment, indicate by writing "increase" or "decrease" how it will affect net income per books. Write "N/A" if there is no adjustment.

Item	*Adjustment?*	*Increase/Decrease*
1. $87,000 of straight-line depreciation on a corporation's books. Depreciation reported on their tax return was $74,000.		
2. Interest income from Treasury and commercial bonds.		
3. A corporation had $56,000 of capital losses and $63,000 of capital gains.		
4. Charitable contributions equal to $33,000. Taxable income without regard to the contributions was $299,000.		
5. Federal income tax paid.		
6. Life insurance proceeds received upon the death of key personnel. The amount received was less than the premiums paid on the insurance policy.		

Research | Authoritative Literature | Help

Plush Corp. recently purchased a Mercedes-Benz E350 sedan for its CEO for $55,000. Research and cite the appropriate IRC section that deals with limitations on depreciation for luxury automobiles.

Enter your response in the answer fields below.

IRC § [ ] ([ ])

= Reminder | Directions | 1 2 3 4 5 6 | Previous | Next

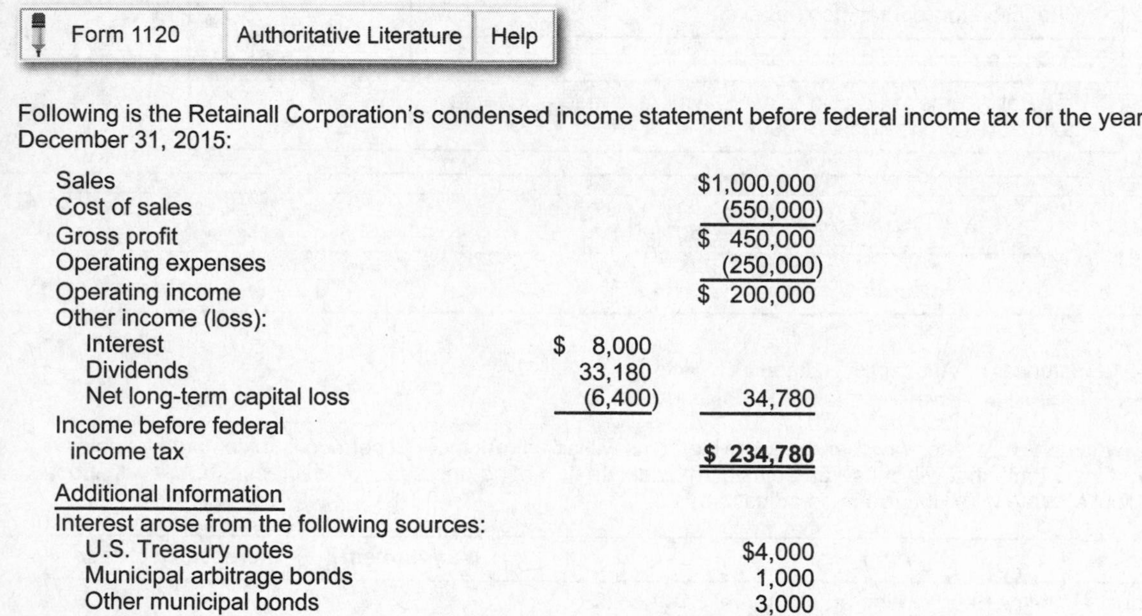

Form 1120 | Authoritative Literature | Help

Following is the Retainall Corporation's condensed income statement before federal income tax for the year ended December 31, 2015:

Sales		$1,000,000
Cost of sales		(550,000)
Gross profit		$ 450,000
Operating expenses		(250,000)
Operating income		$ 200,000
Other income (loss):		
Interest	$ 8,000	
Dividends	33,180	
Net long-term capital loss	(6,400)	34,780
Income before federal income tax		$ 234,780

Additional Information

Interest arose from the following sources:

U.S. Treasury notes	$4,000
Municipal arbitrage bonds	1,000
Other municipal bonds	3,000
Total interest	$8,000

Dividends arose from the following sources:

Taxable Domestic Corporation	Date Stock Acquired	Percent Owned by Retainall	
Blanko Corp.	09/01/11	10	$10,000
Fathers Corp. (sold 1/10/15)	12/01/14	5	10,000
Silver Corp.	07/01/09	30	8,750
Real estate investment trust	06/01/14	1	3,750
Mutual fund corp. (capital gains dividends)	04/01/13	0.1	400
Money market fund (interest-paying securities only)	03/01/12	0.1	280
Total dividends			$33,180

Operating expenses include the following:

- Retainall pledged $5,000 to charity for 2015 and paid the $5,000 in February.
- Estimate of $15,000 for bad debts. Actual bad debts for the year amounted to $10,000.
- Key employee life insurance premiums of $4,000. Retainall is the beneficiary of the policies.
- State income taxes of $12,000.
- During 2015, Retainall estimated federal income tax payments of $30,000. These payments were debited to prepaid tax expense on Retainall's books.
- Retainall declared and paid dividends of $10,000 during 2015.
- Retainall was not subject to the alternative minimum tax in 2015.
- Retainall paid its employees (nonofficers) $100,000 during the year.

-- Continued on next page --

Form 1120 | Authoritative Literature | Help -- Continued

Using the information for Retainall Corp. on the previous page, enter the appropriate amount in each of the shaded cells below.

Form **1120** Department of the Treasury Internal Revenue Service

U.S. Corporation Income Tax Return

For calendar year 2014 or tax year beginning ________________, 2014, ending ________________, 20 ______

▶ Information about Form 1120 and its separate instructions is at *www.irs.gov/form1120.*

OMB No. 1545-0123 **2014**

A Check if:	TYPE OR PRINT		
1a Consolidated return (attach Form 851) ☐		Name: Retainall Corporation	B Employer identification number: 98 7654321
b Life/nonlife consolidated return ☐		Number, street, and room or suite no. If a P.O. box, see instructions.: 12345 Ace Avenue	C Date incorporated: 1-1-01
2 Personal holding co. (attach Sch. PH) ☐		City or town, state, or province, country and ZIP or foreign postal code: Newtown, PA 35000	D Total assets (see instructions): $ 10,000,000
3 Personal service corp. (see instructions) ☐			
4 Schedule M-3 attached ☐			

E Check if: (1) ☐ Initial return (2) ☐ Final return (3) ☐ Name change (4) ☐ Address change

Income	1a	Gross receipts or sales	1a				
	b	Returns and allowances	1b				
	c	Balance. Subtract line 1b from line 1a				1c	
	2	Cost of goods sold (attach Form 1125-A)				2	
	3	Gross profit. Subtract line 2 from line 1c				3	
	4	Dividends (Schedule C, line 19)				4	
	5	Interest				5	
	6	Gross rents				6	
	7	Gross royalties				7	
	8	Capital gain net income (attach Schedule D (Form 1120))				8	
	9	Net gain or (loss) from Form 4797, Part II, line 17 (attach Form 4797)				9	
	10	Other income (see instructions—attach statement)				10	
	11	**Total income.** Add lines 3 through 10 ▶				11	
Deductions (See instructions for limitations on deductions.)	12	Compensation of officers (see instructions—attach Form 1125-E) ▶				12	
	13	Salaries and wages (less employment credits)				13	
	14	Repairs and maintenance				14	
	15	Bad debts				15	
	16	Rents				16	
	17	Taxes and licenses				17	
	18	Interest				18	
	19	Charitable contributions				19	
	20	Depreciation from Form 4562 not claimed on Form 1125-A or elsewhere on return (attach Form 4562)				20	
	21	Depletion				21	
	22	Advertising				22	
	23	Pension, profit-sharing, etc., plans				23	
	24	Employee benefit programs				24	
	25	Domestic production activities deduction (attach Form 8903)				25	
	26	Other deductions (attach statement)				26	
	27	**Total deductions.** Add lines 12 through 26 ▶				27	
	28	Taxable income before net operating loss deduction and special deductions. Subtract line 27 from line 11				28	
	29a	Net operating loss deduction (see instructions)	29a				
	b	Special deductions (Schedule C, line 20)	29b				
	c	Add lines 29a and 29b				29c	

= Reminder | Directions | 1 2 3 4 5 6 | ◀ Previous | Next ▶

Unofficial Answers

1. Deductions (6 Gradable Items)

1. C) Nondeductible. Premiums for life insurance covering an officer or employee are not deductible if the corporation is a direct or indirect beneficiary.
2. A) Fully deductible. State taxes and licenses are fully deductible for federal tax purposes.
3. D) Deduction may be limited by AGI. A C corporation's charitable deductions are limited to 10% of taxable income (TI) with some adjustments made.
4. B) Partially deductible. A corporation that owns 15% of another corporation is able to deduct 70% of dividends received.
5. C) Nondeductible. Fines and penalties paid to a governmental entity are not deductible.
6. A) Fully deductible. Compensation, e.g., salary, wages, or bonuses, is a deductible business expense unless the services are capital in nature.

2. Net Operating Loss (4 Gradable Items)

1. $193,000. A deduction for charitable expenses is not allowed in computing a current NOL; thus, this amount should be subtracted from operating expenses. Therefore, Kustan's NOL for Year 4 is $193,000 [$300,000 – ($500,000 – $7,000)].
2. $13,000. When calculating a NOL, the dividends-received deduction (DRD) is computed without regard to the 80% of taxable income limitation (i.e., $35,000 × 80% = $28,000 deduction limit). Thus, Tennis will have a DRD of $48,000 ($60,000 × 80%). Therefore, Tennis will have a NOL of $13,000 ($70,000 gross income + $60,000 dividend income – $95,000 operating expenses – $48,000 DRD).
3. $30,000. A NOL may be carried back to each of the 2 preceding taxable years and forward to the 20 succeeding taxable years. The NOL must be carried to the earliest possible year unless an election is made to give up the 2-year carryback. Since Gobby did not make this election, the $65,000 loss in Year 3 must be carried back to Year 1 and Year 2. Gobby will therefore be able to carry over a $30,000 NOL ($65,000 NOL in Year 3 – $20,000 Year 1 income – $15,000 Year 2 income) to Year 4.
4. $35,000. A NOL can be carried back 2 years and forward 20 years. The NOL must be carried back to the earliest year to which such a loss may be carried. The Year 2 NOL of $40,000 must first be carried back to offset the $15,000 of income from Year 1. This leaves a $25,000 NOL carryover, which is carried forward to reduce Year 3's $60,000 taxable income to $35,000.

3. Federal Tax (8 Gradable Items)

1. $450,000. Gross profit is gross sales minus the cost of goods sold. No code provision excludes the cost of goods sold from gross income. However, gross receipts allocable to the cost of goods sold is simply not treated as income for federal income tax purposes.
2. $0. Deduction of premiums paid on life insurance covering the life of an officer or employee is disallowed if the corporation is directly or indirectly a beneficiary.
3. $7,000. A corporation is allowed a deduction for 80% of dividends received from affiliated taxable domestic corporations of which it owns at least 20% of the stock.
4. $0. The deduction for dividends received is disallowed for dividends on stock held by the taxpayer for 45 days or less.
5. $0. A deduction for dividends paid applies to the accumulated earnings tax but not to computing taxable income for regular income tax. The dividends did not reduce income per books, so no adjustment for income per return was required. But the dividends paid do affect retained earnings.
6. $0. Federal income taxes are not deductible. Note that, because they were not deducted in computing income per books, a Schedule M-1 adjustment is not required.
7. $12,000. State income taxes are deductible.
8. $10,000. The $30,000 in payments of estimated tax are treated as a refundable credit against tax.

4. Schedule M-1 Differences (6 Gradable Items)

1. Yes and Increase. Book depreciation expense in excess of the amount allowable for tax purposes is an expense that is recorded in net income per books but is not deducted on the tax return. The excess should be added back to book income.
2. No and N/A. Tax-exempt interest earned will lead to a decrease in book income during reconciliation. However, interest from U.S. Treasury and commercial bonds is not tax-exempt.
3. No and N/A. Capital losses in excess of capital gains require an increase in net income per books. When capital gains exceed capital losses, no adjustment is necessary.
4. Yes and Increase. Corporations are only allowed to deduct charitable contributions to the extent they exceed 10% of taxable income before charitable contributions are considered. The excess is an expense that is recorded in net income per books but is not deducted on the tax return. The excess amount should be added back to book income during reconciliation.
5. Yes and Increase. Federal income tax paid is not allowed as a deduction when computing taxable income. Amounts paid for Federal income taxes should be added back to book income during reconciliation.
6. Yes and Decrease. Income that is not subject to tax causes an adjustment to net income per books during reconciliation. Life insurance proceeds are excluded from gross income as long as they do not exceed premiums and other amounts paid by the policyholder. The proceeds should be subtracted from book income during reconciliation.

5. Research (1 Gradable Item)

Answer: IRC § 280F(a)(1)(A)

§ 280F. Limitation on depreciation for luxury automobiles; limitation where certain property used for personal purposes

(a) Limitation on amount of depreciation for luxury automobiles

(1) Depreciation

(A) Limitation

(i) $2,560 for the 1st taxable year in the recovery period,

(ii) $4,100 for the 2nd taxable year in the recovery period,

(iii) $2,450 for the 3rd taxable year in the recovery period, and

(iv) $1,475 for each succeeding taxable year in the recovery period.

6. Form 1120 (12 Gradable Items)

Form **1120** Department of the Treasury Internal Revenue Service

U.S. Corporation Income Tax Return

For calendar year 2014 or tax year beginning ______, 2014, ending ______, 20 ___

▶ Information about Form 1120 and its separate instructions is at *www.irs.gov/form1120.*

OMB No. 1545-0123 **2014**

A Check if:
1a Consolidated return (attach Form 851) ☐
b Life/nonlife consolidated return ☐
2 Personal holding co. (attach Sch. PH) ☐
3 Personal service corp. (see instructions) ☐
4 Schedule M-3 attached ☐

TYPE OR PRINT

Name: Retainall Corporation
Number, street, and room or suite no. If a P.O. box, see instructions.: 12345 Ace Avenue
City or town, state, or province, country and ZIP or foreign postal code: Newtown, PA 35000

B Employer identification number: 98 7654321
C Date incorporated: 1-1-01
D Total assets (see instructions): $ 10,000,000

E Check if: (1) ☐ Initial return (2) ☐ Final return (3) ☐ Name change (4) ☐ Address change

Income	1a	Gross receipts or sales	1a	1,000,000 [1]		
	b	Returns and allowances	1b	0		
	c	Balance. Subtract line 1b from line 1a			1c	1,000,000 [2]
	2	Cost of goods sold (attach Form 1125-A)			2	550,000 [3]
	3	Gross profit. Subtract line 2 from line 1c			3	450,000 [4]
	4	Dividends (Schedule C, line 19)			4	33,180 [5]
	5	Interest			5	5,000 [6]
	6	Gross rents			6	
	7	Gross royalties			7	
	8	Capital gain net income (attach Schedule D (Form 1120))			8	
	9	Net gain or (loss) from Form 4797, Part II, line 17 (attach Form 4797)			9	
	10	Other income (see instructions—attach statement)			10	
	11	**Total income.** Add lines 3 through 10 ▶			11	488,180 [7]
Deductions (See instructions for limitations on deductions.)	12	Compensation of officers (see instructions—attach Form 1125-E) ▶			12	
	13	Salaries and wages (less employment credits)			13	100,000 [8]
	14	Repairs and maintenance			14	
	15	Bad debts			15	10,000 [9]
	16	Rents			16	
	17	Taxes and licenses			17	12,000 [10]
	18	Interest			18	
	19	Charitable contributions			19	5,000 [11]
	20	Depreciation from Form 4562 not claimed on Form 1125-A or elsewhere on return (attach Form 4562)			20	
	21	Depletion			21	
	22	Advertising			22	
	23	Pension, profit-sharing, etc., plans			23	
	24	Employee benefit programs			24	
	25	Domestic production activities deduction (attach Form 8903)			25	
	26	Other deductions (attach statement)			26	
	27	**Total deductions.** Add lines 12 through 26 ▶			27	127,000 [12]
	28	Taxable income before net operating loss deduction and special deductions. Subtract line 27 from line 11			28	
	29a	Net operating loss deduction (see instructions)	29a			
	b	Special deductions (Schedule C, line 20)	29b			
	c	Add lines 29a and 29b			29c	

[1] $1,000,000. The facts indicate that Retainall had sales of $1,000,000 for 2015.

[2] $1,000,000. Since there were no returns and allowances, the total gross receipts are still $1,000,000.

[3] $550,000. The situation indicates that Retainall has $550,000 of COGS related to its sale of inventory.

[4] $450,000. Gross profits equal sales revenue less COGS ($1,000,000 – $550,000).

[5] $33,180. The dividends received from Retainall's portfolio are fully included in gross income, and a dividends-received deduction is provided later.

[6] $5,000. The $4,000 of interest from U.S. Treasury notes is included in gross income as well as the $1,000 interest from the arbitrage bonds. The $3,000 of municipal bond interest is not taxable and is excluded from gross income.

[7] $488,180. The total income for Retainall is gross profit plus dividends and interest ($450,000 + $33,180 + $5,000).

[8] $100,000. The situation indicates that Retainall pays its nonofficer employees $100,000 in wages for 2015.

[9] $10,000. Bad debts can only be deducted when they are written off. Since Retainall only wrote off $10,000 of bad debts, only $10,000 is deductible.

[10] $12,000. State income taxes are a deductible expense of a corporation that is ordinary and necessary.

[11] $5,000. Charitable contributions that are pledged by a corporation are deductible if they are paid within 2 1/2 months after the close of the corporation's tax year. In addition, the $5,000 is not in excess of 10% limitation.

[12] $127,000. The total deductions for line 12 through line 26 equals $127,000 ($100,000 + $10,000 + $12,000 + $5,000). The dividends received deduction appears on line 29b so this amount is not considered for "total deductions."

Gleim Simulation Grading

Task	Correct Responses		Gradable Items		Score per Task
1	___	÷	6	=	___
2	___	÷	4	=	___
3	___	÷	8	=	___
4	___	÷	6	=	___
5 (Research)	___	÷	1	=	___
6	___	÷	12	=	___
			Total of Scores per Task		___
		÷	Total Number of Tasks		6
			Total Score		___ %

STUDY UNIT EIGHT
CORPORATE TAX COMPUTATIONS

(18 pages of outline)

The only credits explained in the corporate tax study unit are the foreign tax credit and the minimum tax credit. Like the alternative minimum tax, these credits also apply to individuals. The subject matter appears here because it has been tested most commonly in the corporate context. You should also review the general business credit and its limits discussed in Study Unit 5, Subunit 3, which also apply to corporations.

8.1 REGULAR INCOME TAX

1. **Tax Brackets**
   a. Sec. 11 imposes tax on the taxable income of most corporations using a multi-bracket graduated rate system.

If Taxable Income Is

Over	But Not Over	The Tax Is	Of the Amount Over
$ 0	$ 50,000	15%	$ 0
50,000	75,000	$ 7,500 + 25%	50,000
75,000	100,000	13,750 + 34%	75,000
100,000	335,000	22,250 + 39%	100,000
335,000	10,000,000	113,900 + 34%	335,000
10,000,000	15,000,000	3,400,000 + 35%	10,000,000
15,000,000	18,333,333	5,150,000 + 38%	15,000,000
18,333,333		6,416,667 + 35%	18,333,333

2. **Surtax**
   a. Two of the rate brackets include surtaxes.
   b. A surtax of 5% is charged on taxable income (TI) between $100,000 and $335,000, which eliminates the tax savings on the first $100,000 of taxable income from the benefits of 15% and 25% rates.
   c. A 3% surtax is charged on TI between $15,000,000 and $18,333,333, which recaptures the tax savings from $335,000 to $10,000,000 by phasing out the 34% rate.
3. **Top Rate**
   a. All TI of a corporation with TI over $18,333,333 is taxed at a flat rate of 35%.
   b. The alternative tax on a corporation's net capital gain (when regular rates exceed 35%) is not applicable (currently). Thus, long-term capital gain of a corporation does not receive preferred treatment. The two surtaxes apply.

c. Personal service corporations are taxed at a flat rate of 35% on all taxable income.

d. A controlled group of corporations (which is discussed in Subunit 8.4) must allocate a single application of reduced rates for lower brackets between them. Rates are applied to the aggregate TI of the group as if the group were a single corporation.

4. **Disallowed Corporate Credits**

   a. Most tax credits are allowable to corporations. However, the following are not permitted:

      1) Earned Income Credit
      2) Child and Dependent Care Credit
      3) Elderly and Disabled Credit
      4) Child Tax Credit
      5) Adoption Credit
      6) American Opportunity Credit
      7) Lifetime Learning Credit

Stop and review! You have completed the outline for this subunit. Study multiple-choice questions 1 and 2 on page 314.

8.2 FOREIGN TAX CREDIT (FTC)

1. **Election Options**

   a. A taxpayer may elect either a credit or a deduction for taxes paid to other countries or U.S. possessions.

2. **Credit Application**

   a. Generally, the FTC is applied against gross tax liability after the AMT (alternative minimum tax) but before all other credits.

3. **Other Taxes**

   a. The FTC may offset **AMT** liability. However, the FTC is not creditable against the **AET (accumulated earnings tax)** or the **PHC (personal holding company) tax**.

4. **Pass-Through Entities**

   a. Pass-through entities apportion the foreign taxes among the partners, shareholders (of an S corporation), or beneficiaries (of an estate). The individuals elect and compute a credit or deduction on their personal returns.

5. **Non-U.S. Taxpayer**

   a. For a non-U.S. taxpayer, the FTC is allowed only for foreign taxes paid on income effectively connected with conduct of a trade or business in the U.S. and against U.S. tax on the effectively connected income.

6. **Qualified Foreign Taxes**

   a. Qualified foreign taxes (QFTs) include foreign taxes on income, war profits, and excess profits.

   b. QFTs must be analogous to the U.S. income tax.

      1) They must be based on a form of net annual income, including gain.
      2) Concepts such as realization should be incorporated into the tax structure.

   c. Foreign taxes paid on foreign earned income or housing costs excluded as excessive may neither be credited nor deducted.

   d. Deemed QFT. A domestic corporation that owns at least 10% (voting) of a foreign corporation is deemed to have paid foreign taxes paid by the foreign corporation on income that it distributed to the domestic corporation as a dividend.

7. **FTC Limit**
   a. The maximum amount of tax that may be credited is computed using the following formula:

$$FTC = U.S.\ income\ tax^{1} \times \frac{Foreign\ source\ taxable\ income^{2}}{Worldwide\ taxable\ income}$$

[1]*Before the FTC*
[2]*Not more than total TI*

   b. The limit must be applied separately to nonbusiness interest income and all other income.
   c. The amount used for TI in the numerator and denominator is regular TI with adjustments. For example, an individual must add back personal exemptions.
8. **Carryover**
   a. Foreign tax paid in excess of the FTC limit may be carried back 1 year and forward 10 years in chronological order.
      1) The carryover is treated as foreign tax paid subject to the FTC limit.
      2) The carryover may not be applied in any year when a deduction for foreign taxes is taken (in lieu of the FTC).

Stop and review! You have completed the outline for this subunit. Study multiple-choice questions 3 and 4 on page 315.

8.3 CONSOLIDATED RETURNS

1. **Overview**
   a. A single federal income tax return may be filed by two or more includible corporations that are members of an affiliated group.
2. **Includible corporations** are all corporations **except** the following:
   a. Tax-exempt corporations
   b. S corporations
   c. Foreign sales corporations (FSCs)
   d. Insurance corporations
   e. REITs (real estate investment trusts)
   f. Regulated investment companies
   g. DISCs (domestic international sales corporations)
   h. Those corporations that claim Sec. 936 possessions tax credit
3. **Affiliated Groups**
   a. An affiliated group includes each corporation in a chain of corporations under the following conditions:
      1) The other group members must directly own stock in the corporation that represents both
         a) 80% or more of total voting power **and**
         b) 80% or more of total value outstanding.
      2) A parent corporation must directly own stock as outlined in 1) above (80% voting and value) of at least one includible corporation.

4. **Election**
   a. Election to file a consolidated return is made by the act of filing a consolidated return.
   b. Consent of each included corporation is required.
   c. Consolidated financial statements or IRS approval is not required to file a consolidated return.
   d. Consent of the IRS is required to terminate an election.
   e. Controlled group restrictions (mandatory rules for certain related companies) apply without regard to some of its members filing a consolidated return.
5. **Tax Year**
   a. Each subsidiary included in a consolidated return must adopt the parent's tax year.
6. **Accounting Methods**
   a. One or more members of a controlled group filing a consolidated return may use the cash method, and one or more others may use the accrual method.
7. **Consolidation**
   a. The corporations remove from taxable income (TI) items that are separately consolidated or that are treated specially. Net TI is consolidated and then adjusted for the items removed after separate consolidation.
   b. **Items that are consolidated separately** include the following:
      1) Charitable contribution deductions
      2) Dividends received and paid deductions
      3) Percentage depletion of mineral properties
      4) NOL deductions
      5) Sec. 1231 gains and losses
      6) Capital gains and losses
8. **Dividends on a Consolidated Return**
   a. A dividend distributed by one consolidated corporation to another is eliminated.
   b. The dividends-received deduction (DRD) is not allowed for such dividends.
   c. Deduction for dividends received from corporations outside the consolidating group is computed on a consolidated basis.
9. **Losses**
   a. Losses of one consolidating corporation may offset TI of another. Consolidated NOL is computed using consolidated items (aggregate of consolidating corporations' separate items) as follows:

      TI (Separate net TI)
      \+ Net capital gain
      – Sec. 1231 net loss
      – Charitable contribution deduction
      – Dividends-received deduction
      – Dividends-paid deduction
      = **Consolidated NOL**

   b. Carryover of a consolidated NOL is allowed only to a prior or subsequent year of a consolidation election. Special rules apply when members change.

10. **Intercompany Transactions**
    a. An intercompany transaction is a transaction between corporations that are members of the same consolidated group. In the consolidated tax return, any gain or loss realized on the intercompany transaction is deferred.
    b. A single-entity approach is used to resolve the deferred gain or loss.
    c. For consolidation purposes, the buyer in the intercompany transaction assumes the same basis and holding period as the selling member. The consolidated gain or loss is recognized upon the happening of an event such as
        1) The acquiring corporation claiming depreciation
        2) One of the members leaving the consolidated group
        3) Disposition of the property outside of the consolidated group
    d. The character of the recognized gain or loss is determined with reference to the consolidated group member holding the property immediately before the recognition event.

EXAMPLE

P and S are two affiliated corporations that file consolidated tax returns. P sells an asset held for investment (i.e., a capital asset) to S at a gain of $10,000. S holds the property as inventory and sells to an unrelated party at an additional gain of $5,000. Under the single-entity approach, the consolidated entity recognizes $15,000 of ordinary income upon the sale to the outside party.

    e. In certain other intercompany transactions, the income and expense items net each other out.

The AICPA has tested candidates' knowledge of the rules and regulations for filing consolidated returns. Most of the released AICPA questions test the theory and do not require calculations.

Stop and review! You have completed the outline for this subunit. Study multiple-choice questions 5 through 9 beginning on page 315.

8.4 CONTROLLED GROUPS

1. **Definition**
    a. A controlled group of corporations includes corporations with a specified degree of relationship by stock ownership.
2. **Parent-Subsidiary Controlled Group**
    a. This type of controlled group consists of
        1) Two corporations if one of the corporations owns stock that represents
            a) 80% or more of total voting power **or**
            b) 80% or more of total value outstanding of the stock of the other
        2) Any other corporation that meets the requirements in 1) above (if the two corporations discussed there and others in the group own stock in it)

EXAMPLE

Each corporation has a single class of stock. P owns 80% of S stock. P and S each owns 40% of O stock. P, S, and O each owns 30% of T stock. P, S, O, and T are a controlled group.

3. **Brother-Sister Controlled Group**
   a. Any two or more corporations are considered a brother-sister controlled group if the stock of each owned by the same five or fewer persons (only individuals, trusts, or estates)
      1) Represents either
         a) 80% or more of voting power of all classes or
         b) 80% or more of value of all classes and
      2) Represents either (counting for each person only the smallest amount owned by that person in any of the corporations)
         a) More than 50% of voting power of all classes or
         b) More than 50% of value of all classes.

EXAMPLE

Alpha, Bravo, and Charley Corporations, each with one class of stock, have the following ownership:

	80% Test			
Shareholders	Alpha	Bravo	Charley	50% Test
Mike	45%	5%	30%	5%
Sierra	30%	65%	10%	10%
Oscar	25%	30%	60%	25%
	100%	100%	100%	40%

Alpha, Bravo, and Charley passed the 80% test but not the 50% test and therefore are not a controlled brother-sister group.

4. **Rights** to acquire stock are treated as the stock would be.
5. **Constructive Ownership**
   a. Stock both actually and constructively owned is counted. Generally, a person constructively owns stock owned by a
      1) Family member [spouse (not legally separated), child, grandchild, parent, or grandparent] and
      2) Corporation, partnership, estate, or trust
         a) In which (s)he has a 5% or more interest
         b) In proportion to that interest
6. **Limit on Tax Benefits**
   a. Each of the following is an example of tax benefit items of which only one must be shared by the members of a controlled group:
      1) Tax brackets
      2) Sec. 179 expensing maximum of $500,000 (expired but expecting renewal)
      3) AMT exemption base of $40,000
      4) General business credit $25,000 offset
      5) AET $250,000 presumed deduction base

      NOTE: A controlled group generally may choose any method to allocate the amounts among themselves. By default, an item is divided equally among members.
7. **Intergroup Transactions**
   a. Anti-avoidance rules apply to transactions between members of a controlled group.
   b. Loss is not recognized when property is sold by one member of a controlled group to another.
      1) The loss may be recognized on a subsequent sale to an unrelated third party.
   c. Expenditure to a controlled group member is not deductible before being included in the income of the payee.

d. Gain on sale or exchange of property by a controlled group member to a member in whose hands the property is depreciable is treated as ordinary income.

e. The IRS is authorized to redetermine the price for property transferred between members of a controlled group.

   1) To reflect income clearly or to prevent tax evasion, the price may be redetermined to reflect an arm's-length price.
   2) Three methods to determine an arm's-length price are by reference to
      a) Comparable uncontrolled prices
      b) Resale prices
      c) Cost plus return

Stop and review! You have completed the outline for this subunit. Study multiple-choice questions 10 and 11 beginning on page 317. Note that these are questions on consolidated returns as well as controlled groups.

8.5 ALTERNATIVE MINIMUM TAX (AMT)

1. **AMT Formula**

   a. The alternative minimum tax is an income tax in addition to the regular income tax. The formula for computing AMT is illustrated within the example at the end of this subunit. The generalized structure is presented below.

   b. AMT income (AMTI) is based on taxable income (TI).

      1) AMTI is TI after amounts are added or subtracted for tax preferences, adjustments, and loss limitations.
      2) The AMT base is AMTI reduced by an exemption amount and any AMT NOL carryover.

   c. Tentative AMT is determined by first multiplying a rate times the AMT base and then subtracting the AMT foreign tax credit.

      1) For corporations, a 20% rate applies.
      2) For individuals, a two-tiered graduated rate schedule applies.
         a) A 26% rate applies to the first $185,400 ($92,700 if married filing separately) of AMTI (net of the exemption amount).
         b) A 28% rate applies to any excess.

   d. AMT is the excess tentative AMT over regular income tax.

   e. AMT must be reported and paid at the same time as regular tax liability.

   f. Estimated payments of AMT are required.

2. **Tax Preference Items**

   a. These items generate tax savings by reducing the taxpayer's taxable income. Therefore, they must be added back to taxable income when computing AMTI.

   b. Small business stock. When computing taxable income, noncorporate taxpayers may exclude up to 50% (100% for stock purchased after September 27, 2010 and before January 1, 2015) of gain realized on the sale or exchange of qualified small business stock held more than 5 years.

      1) Generally, 7% of the excluded gain is added as an AMT tax preference item. However, stock purchased between September 27, 2010, and January 1, 2015, is excluded from tax preference treatment (though provision expired post-2014, it is expected to be renewed for 2015).

c. Private activity bonds (other than those **issued** in 2009 and 2010). Add any tax-exempt interest minus expenses (including interest) attributable to earning it.
d. Percentage depletion. Add any excess of deduction claimed over adjusted basis.
e. Intangible drilling costs (IDC). Add any excess of IDC amortized over 10 years over 65% of net income from oil, gas, and geothermal properties.

3. **Adjustments**
   a. Usually, adjustments eliminate "time value" tax savings from accelerated deductions or deferral of income. An adjustment is an increase or a decrease to TI in computing AMTI.
   b. Adjustments affecting corporate and noncorporate taxpayers:
      1) Accelerated depreciation
         a) Real property. The AMT allowable amount is computed using a straight-line method, 40-year recovery period, and the mid-month convention.
         b) Personal property. Generally, the AMT allowable amount is computed using the 150%-declining-balance method and changing to the straight-line method when it yields a larger amount.
         c) Section 1250 property placed in service after December 31, 1998, does not require an adjustment, as all of it is depreciated using a straight-line method.
      2) Installment sales. The installment method is not allowed for a disposition of stock in trade in the ordinary course of business (e.g., inventory). Add any balance (+ or –) of current-year gain recognized, disregarding the installment method, minus gain recognized under the installment method.
      3) Long-term contracts. The percentage-of-completion method must be used to determine AMTI. Add any balance (+ or –) if the completed-contract or cash-basis method is normally used.
         a) The same percentage of completion must be used for AMT and regular tax.
         b) Small construction contracts require a simplified method of allocating costs in applying the percentage-of-completion method. The contract's estimated duration must be less than 2 years.
         c) No AMT adjustment is made for home construction contracts.
      4) Pollution control facilities (certified). For facilities placed in service after 1998, calculate the amortization deduction for AMT under MACRS using the straight-line method. Add any balance (+ or –).
      5) Mining exploration and development. If these expenditures were expensed for regular tax purposes, the expenditures must be capitalized and amortized over a 10-year period for AMT. Add any balance for the difference.
         a) Tax loss. If a worthless mine is abandoned, expenditures capitalized but unamortized can be deducted from AMTI.
      6) Net operating loss adjustments. To determine the NOL amount for AMT,
         a) Subtract all amounts added to TI as tax preference amounts, to the extent they increased the regular tax NOL.
         b) Tax adjustments made for the AMTI calculation must be made for the NOL calculation.
      7) Distributions from a trust or estate.

c. Adjustments affecting only noncorporate taxpayers:

1) Research and experimental expenditures. Add any balance (+ or –) of regular tax deduction claimed for the year (normally expensed), minus expenditures capitalized and amortized over 10 years (beginning in year made).
2) Circulation expenditures. Add any balance (+ or –) of regular tax deduction for the year (normally expensed), minus the expenditures capitalized and amortized over 3 years (beginning in year made).
3) Incentive stock option (ISO). Add any balance (+ or –) of the FMV of the stock when exercised, minus the amount paid for stock.

d. Adjustments affecting only corporate taxpayers:

1) ACE adjustment (covered below).

4. **ACE Adjustment**

a. A corporation must make an additional adjustment (upward or downward) to TI, the adjusted current earnings (ACE) adjustment, in computing AMTI.

1) When computing ACE for AMTI, the AMTI amount is gross of the ACE adjustment and the AMT NOL deduction.
2) ACE is not the same as earnings and profits but is based on undistributed corporate earnings.

b. Adjustments to AMTI to compute ACE include the following:

1) Organizational expenditures amortized and deducted (Sec. 248) are added.
2) The 70% dividends-received deduction attributable to < 20%-owned corporations is added.
3) Life insurance proceeds on a corporate officer are added.
4) Installment method on nondealer sales is disregarded unless interest is paid.
5) LIFO recapture must be recorded for the excess of FIFO inventory valuation over LIFO inventory valuation.
6) Depreciation is computed using the alternative depreciation system method. AMT basis is used.
   a) For corporations, this adjustment is not required for property placed in service after 1993.

c. Not requiring adjustment for ACE are the following:

1) Long-term capital gains
2) DRD of 80% or 100% of dividends received
3) Discharge of debt income excluded by Sec. 108 (state and local bonds)
4) Tax-exempt interest from state and local bonds issued in 2009 and 2010

d. Amount of ACE adjustment = (ACE – AMTI) × 75%.

1) AMTI is gross of the ACE adjustment and NOL deduction.
2) Add the ACE adjustment amount if ACE > AMTI.
3) Subtract the ACE adjustment amount if ACE < AMTI.
   a) Limit negative ACE adjustments to prior years'
      i) Aggregate positive ACE adjustments, minus
      ii) Aggregate negative ACE adjustments.

5. **AMT NOL**

a. The alternative minimum tax net operating loss (AMT NOL) is technically an adjustment to taxable income (TI). After tax preferences have been computed and added to TI and all other adjustments have been computed and made, one of the two AMT NOL adjustment steps is performed.

b. NOL year. Compute the AMT NOL. It is carried back or forward to another tax year.

   1) The AMT NOL is modified for each of the tax preferences and other adjustments for the current tax year.

c. Profit year. An AMT NOL is a final adjustment to TI in computing AMTI in a tax year in which (before reduction by part or all of unused AMT NOLs) there is AMT base.

   1) Limit: 90% of AMTI. Alternative NOL may not offset more than 90% of the AMTI (computed without the alternative NOL deduction).

6. **AMT Exemption**

   a. An exemption is allowed that reduces AMTI to produce the AMTI base.

      1) The basic exemption is phased out at $.25 for each dollar of AMTI above a threshold.
      2) All members of a controlled group must share the exemption amount.
      3) The basic exemption for a corporation is $40,000.
      4) The AMT exemption is phased out beginning when AMTI is $150,000 and is fully phased out when AMTI is $310,000.

7. **AMT FTC**

   a. Only one credit is allowed in computing AMT: the AMT foreign tax credit (FTC). The AMT FTC is the lower of

      1) The FTC or
      2) 90% of gross tentative AMT computed before any AMT NOL deduction and FTC.

8. **Minimum Tax Credit (MTC)**

   a. A credit is allowed for AMT paid in a tax year against regular tax liability in 1 or more subsequent tax years.

   b. **Individuals.** The MTC amount is the AMT that would have been computed if the only adjustments made to TI in computing AMTI were those for (tax-favored) items that result in deferral, as opposed to exclusion, of income. To compute the MTC amount, recompute the most recent year's AMT without adjustment for the following (exclusion) items and add carryover MTC:

      1) Standard deduction
      2) Personal exemptions deduction
      3) Miscellaneous itemized deductions
      4) Tax-exempt interest on private activity bonds (not necessary for bonds issued in 2009 or 2010)
      5) Qualified interest expense (qualified mortgage interest, investment interest, etc.)
      6) Charitable contributions of appreciated property
      7) Medical expenses
      8) Depletion
      9) Taxes

   c. **Corporations.** A corporation's credit for AMT is for both deferred items and exclusion items.

   d. The MTC allowable is limited to current-year gross regular tax (reduced by certain credits) minus current-year tentative minimum tax.

	Gross regular tax
–	Credits
–	Tentative minimum tax (for current year)
=	MTC maximum allowable

1) The current-year gross regular tax amount is reduced by the amount currently allowable for each of the following:
   a) Refundable credits
   b) Nonrefundable personal credits
   c) Foreign tax, drug testing, nonconventional source fuel credits
   d) General business credit

e. Any MTC amount beyond the current limit may be carried forward indefinitely.

9. **Small Corporations**

   a. Certain "small corporations" are exempt from the AMT.
      1) A corporation will initially qualify as a small corporation if it had average gross receipts of $5 million or less for the 3 years that ended with its first tax year beginning after December 31, 1996.
      2) Small corporation status is maintained as long as average gross receipts for the prior 3 years do not exceed $7.5 million.
   b. If a small corporation has average gross receipts exceeding $7.5 million, it will lose its small corporation status and will be liable for the AMT.

COMPUTATIONAL EXAMPLE

AMT COMPUTATIONS

Taxable income (for regular tax)		$200,000
Tax preference items (+)		
Excess depletion	$15,000	
Tax-exempt bonds [1]	25,000	$ 40,000
Adjustment items (+/–)		
Depreciation on machinery ($150 – $105)	$45,000	
Mining exploration costs	15,000	60,000
Gross tentative AMTI		$300,000
ACE adjustment (see computation at right)		60,000
AMT NOL deduction		(20,000)
AMTI		$340,000
Less: AMT exemption (see computation at right)		0
AMTI (the base)		$340,000
Rate for AMT		× .20
Gross tentative AMT		$ 68,000
Foreign tax credit (AMT)		0
Tentative minimum tax		$ 68,000
Less: regular tax		(62,500)
AMT		$ 5,500

ACE Adjustment

ACE		$ 400,000
Gross tentative AMTI	$300,000	
Installment sales	20,000	
Tentative AMTI net adjustments		(320,000)
Difference		$ 80,000
Times: percentage		× .75
ACE adjustment		$ 60,000

AMT Exemption

Basic exemption		$ 40,000
Less:		
AMTI	$340,000	
Threshold	(150,000)	
Excess	$190,000	
Times: percentage	× .25	
Phaseout amount		47,500
AMT exemption		$ 0

[1] No adjustment for amounts attributed to bonds issued in 2009 and 2010.

Stop and review! You have completed the outline for this subunit. Study multiple-choice questions 12 through 15 beginning on page 318.

8.6 ESTIMATED TAX

1. **Due Dates**

   a. A corporation is required to make estimated tax payments on the 15th day of the 4th, 6th, 9th, and 12th months of the tax year.
   b. Any difference between the estimated tax and actual tax is due with the return by the 15th day of the 3rd month following the end of the tax year (March 15 for calendar-year corporations).
   c. An extension of time to file the tax return does not provide an extension of time to pay the tax liability without incurring interest and/or penalty.

2. **Estimated Payments**
   a. Tax includes the regular income tax and the AMT, net of credits and payments.
   b. Each quarterly estimated tax payment required is 25% of the lesser of
      1) 100% of the prior year's tax (provided a tax liability existed and the preceding tax year was 12 months) or
      2) 100% of the current year's tax.

      NOTE: Any increase in estimated tax during the year should be reconciled and paid on the next estimated payment.
   c. A corporation with uneven income flows can make its estimated tax payments by annualizing its income.
      1) A corporation has the option of annualizing income and paying its estimated taxes accordingly.
      2) If income in later quarters is greater than in prior quarters, the estimated tax payments must be increased so that 100% of the shortfall is covered.
   d. Paying 100% of the prior year's tax is not an option for a large corporation.
      1) A large corporation may make its first quarter estimated tax payment based on the preceding year's tax liability and make up any difference in its second quarter payment.
         a) A large corporation is one with taxable income of $1 million or more during any of the 3 preceding years.
3. **Penalty**
   a. Penalty is imposed in the amount by which any required installment exceeds estimated tax paid multiplied by the federal short-term rate plus 5% (3% for individuals).
   b. The penalty accrues from the installment due date until the underpayment is paid or, if earlier, the due date for filing the tax return.
   c. The penalty is not allowed as an interest deduction.
   d. If any underpayment of estimated tax is indicated by the tax return, Form 2220 should be submitted with the return.
   e. **No** estimated tax penalty is imposed if
      1) Tax liability shown on the return for the tax year is less than $500
      2) The IRS waives all or part of the penalty for good cause
      3) An erroneous IRS notice to a large corporation is withdrawn by the IRS
4. **Refund**
   a. A corporation may obtain quick refund of estimated tax paid, but adjustment is allowed only if the overpayment is both ≥ $500 and ≥ 10% of the corporation's estimate of its tax liability.
   b. Application is filed (Form 4466) after the close of the tax year but before the return due date (without extensions).

Stop and review! You have completed the outline for this subunit. Study multiple-choice questions 16 through 19 beginning on page 319.

8.7 ACCUMULATED EARNINGS TAX (AET)

1. **Application**
   a. The accumulated earnings tax (AET) is imposed only on a corporation that, for the purpose of avoiding income tax at the shareholder level, allows earnings and profits to accumulate instead of distributing them to shareholders.
   b. A corporation is presumed to have the avoidance purpose or intent to the extent it accumulates (does not distribute) earnings beyond its (reasonable) business needs.
2. **Penalty**
   a. The tax of 20% (effective as of 2013) imposed on accumulated taxable income (ATI) is a penalty tax in addition to the regular income tax and AMT.
   b. No offsetting credit or deduction is allowed for either the corporation or its shareholders, not even upon subsequent distribution of the earnings.
   c. Excess undistributed earnings of preceding tax years are excluded from the AET base.
3. **Determination of Liability**
   a. AET liability is generally determined by the IRS only on an audit. A corporation does not file a form to compute AET with its annual income tax return.
4. **Exempt Entities**
   a. AET liability is incurred only by a corporation that unreasonably accumulates current earnings. But every corporation may incur AET, even if publicly held, unless the corporation is expressly exempt. No AET liability is incurred by the following:
      1) S corporations
      2) Tax-exempt corporations
      3) PHCs (personal holding companies)
      4) FPHCs (foreign personal holding companies)
      5) PFICs (passive foreign investment companies)
5. **Accumulated Taxable Income (ATI)**
   a. Accumulated taxable income (ATI) is the AET base. ATI is a measure of the corporation's ability to distribute dividends from current-year earnings. ATI is taxable income, net of specific adjustments, a dividends-paid deduction, and the accumulated earnings credit (AEC). Specific adjustments to TI include
      1) NOLs. Add any deduction that reduced TI.
      2) DRD. Add dividends-received deductions that reduced TI.
      3) Charitable contributions. Adjust TI by
         a) Subtracting excess over 10% of TI disallowed
         b) Adding carryover applied to reduce TI for the year
      4) Federal income tax accrued.
         a) Subtract it from TI
         b) Do not subtract AET or PHC tax
      5) Capital gains. Adjust TI by
         a) Subtracting net capital gains for the tax year
         b) Adding federal income tax on the gain
      6) Capital losses. Adjust TI by
         a) Subtracting excess of net capital losses over net capital gains
         b) Adding amounts carried back or forward to the year
         c) Adding the lesser of
            i) Accumulated E&P
            ii) Net capital gains subtracted in prior years but not yet added back to TI in prior years

6. **Dividends-Paid Deduction**

   a. A deduction from TI in computing ATI is allowed for four types of distributions attributable to E&P. Only differences with dividends deducted in computing PHC tax liability are discussed below.

      1) Dividends are distributions treated as ordinary dividend income.
      2) Throwback dividends are deductible with the appropriate election.
      3) Consent dividends are deducted.
      4) Distributions in complete liquidation are deducted (to the extent of current E&P).
      5) Preferential dividends are not allowed.

7. **Accumulated Earnings Credit (AEC)**

   a. The AEC is a deduction for ATI. Generally, the AEC is the increased amount of reasonable needs of the business during the tax year.

   b. The AEC is the greater of

      1) The general credit -- the portion of retained current E&P for reasonable needs of the business less capital gain adjustments, or
      2) The minimum floor -- the statutory amount (generally, $250,000) less accumulated E&P at the close of the preceding year. The minimum floor cannot be lower than zero.

   c. In calculating the minimum floor, the statutory amount above is lowered to $150,000 for certain service corporations whose principal function is service in such fields as health, law, engineering, or accounting.

EXAMPLE

Calendar Corp., AEC for 2015

The general credit		
Current E&P (2015)	$225,000	
Less: dividends-paid deduction	(0)	
Retained current E&P	$225,000	
Reasonable needs (given -- is covered in the next topic)		$535,000
Less: accumulated E&P (12/31/14)		(415,000)
Retained current E&P to meet reasonable needs		120,000
Less: net capital gain adjustments		
Capital gain	$ 10,000	
Less: tax on the gain	(3,400)	(6,600)
The general credit		$113,400
The minimum floor		
Statutory amount		$250,000
Less: accumulated E&P (12/31/14)		(415,000)
The minimum floor		$ 0
AEC (greater of the general credit or the minimum floor)		$113,400

8. **Reasonable Needs of the Business**

   a. AET is based on the excess of undistributed current earnings over the increase in the reasonable needs of the business.

      1) Reasonable needs of a business include only those items required to meet future needs and for which there are specific, foreseeable plans for use.

   NOTE: Most businesses are able to avoid the AET by documenting reasonable needs of the business periodically.

b. Reasonable needs might include the following:

   1) Raw materials purchase
   2) Equipment update
   3) Expansion of production facilities
   4) Retirement of business debt
   5) Redeeming stock in gross estate of a shareholder
   6) Product liability loss reserves
   7) Realistic business contingencies
   8) Acquiring a related business
   9) Investments or loans to suppliers or customers
   10) Working capital

c. The following are **not** considered reasonable needs of a business. Any of them may trigger determination of AET liability.

   1) Funding plans to

      a) Declare a stock dividend or
      b) Redeem stock of a shareholder

   2) Unrealistic business hazard protection
   3) Investment property unrelated to business activities of the corporation
   4) Loans to shareholders

Stop and review! You have completed the outline for this subunit. Study multiple-choice questions 20 through 24 beginning on page 320.

8.8 PERSONAL HOLDING COMPANY TAX

1. **Penalty**

   a. The tax of 20% (effective as of 2013) imposed on undistributed personal holding company income is a penalty in addition to regular income tax and AMT.

   b. No offsetting credit or deduction is allowed for either the corporation or its shareholders, not even upon subsequent distribution of the earnings.

2. **Self-Assessment**

   a. Self-assessment of personal holding company (PHC) tax liability is required. Schedule PH is filed with Form 1120 by a PHC. There is a 6-year statute of limitations if the schedule is not filed.

3. **Objective Tests**

   a. Every corporation that is not exempt and meets two objective tests (with respect to stock ownership distribution and the nature of its income) is a PHC subject to PHC tax.

      1) Stock ownership test. The corporation's outstanding shares are, directly or indirectly, owned 50% or more by value, by five or fewer shareholders, at any time during the last half of the year.

      2) Nature of income test. Sixty percent or more of adjusted ordinary gross income (AOGI) of the corporation is personal holding company income (PHCI).

4. **Exempt Entities**

   a. No PHC tax liability is incurred by the following:

      1) S corporations
      2) Tax-exempt corporations
      3) FPHCs (foreign personal holding companies)
      4) Banks
      5) Insurance companies

5. **Income**

   a. PHC status is limited to corporations with personal holding company income (PHCI) of at least 60% of adjusted ordinary gross income (AOGI).

   b. Ordinary gross income (OGI) is GI for regular tax adjusted for property disposition transactions.

	GI
+	Losses on property dispositions that reduced GI
=	GI for PHC tax
–	Gains on disposition of Sec. 1231 property
–	Gains on disposition of capital assets
=	OGI

   c. Adjusted ordinary gross income (AOGI) is OGI reduced by certain items related to rentals and other activities.

	OGI
–	Rental property items (only property tax interest, depreciation, rent paid)
–	Interest on tax refunds, judgments, condemnation awards
–	Interest (to a dealer) on U.S. obligations
–	Some mining property expenses
=	AOGI

      1) The following items attributable to rental property income are deducted for AOGI. Adjusted income from rents (AIR) refers to rental income net of these items:

         a) Property taxes
         b) Interest
         c) Depreciation
         d) Rent paid

      2) No deduction for other rental property expenses is made, including

         a) Maintenance
         b) Administration
         c) Other expenses

   d. Personal holding company income (PHCI) is generally passive-type income.

   e. PHCI includes the following:

      1) Interest, unless exempt from GI
      2) Dividends, i.e., taxable distributions from E&P
      3) Annuity proceeds, to the extent included in gross income
      4) Royalties (special rules apply)
      5) Rental income, unless excepted
      6) Personal services income, if conditions are met
      7) Distributions from estates or trusts

   f. AIR is PHCI only if

      1) AIR is less than 50% of AOGI.
      2) Distributions from E&P equal or exceed the amount by which PHCI, excluding rental income, is more than 10% of OGI.

      NOTE: AIR does not include rental income from leasing property to a more-than-25% shareholder.

g. Personal service income is PHCI only if
   1) It is earned by a 25%-or-more shareholder,
   2) It is from a personal services contract, and
   3) Either some person other than the corporation is entitled to perform the services, or the contract designates who will.

   NOTE: Unless the services are unique such that no one other than the 25%-or-more shareholder can perform them, the income is not PHCI.

The AICPA has tested candidates' knowledge of the personal holding company tax. Remember that one income amount, personal holding company income, is used to determine whether or not a corporation meets the nature of income test. If the corporation is a personal holding company, then another income amount, undistributed personal holding company income, is used to calculate the amount of personal holding company tax owed by the corporation. Be careful not to confuse these two amounts.

6. **Tax**

a. The PHC tax is 20% (effective as of 2013) of the undistributed personal holding company income (UPHCI) of a PHC. PHCI for determining the base, UPHCI, is not the same as PHCI for determining if a corporation is a PHC. UPHCI is taxable income, net of specific adjustments and a dividends-paid deduction. Specific adjustments include
   1) NOLs. Add any deduction that reduced TI in the present year.
      a) Subtract an NOL from the preceding tax year in full,
      b) Less any dividends-received deduction for that year.
   2) DRD. Add dividends received deducted in computing TI.
   3) Charitable contributions. Adjust TI by
      a) Subtracting excess over 10% of TI disallowed
      b) Adding carryover applied to reduce TI for the year
   4) Federal income tax accrued.
      a) Subtract this tax from TI.
      b) Do not subtract PHC tax.
   5) Capital gains. Adjust TI by
      a) Subtracting net capital gains for the year
      b) Adding federal income tax on the gain (tax – tax without NCG)
   6) Excess rental deductions. Add to TI any excess of
      a) Deductions claimed on rental property over
      b) Income from the property.

      NOTE: This adjustment does not apply if the corporation can prove that
      - The rental activity was bonafide,
      - It produced the highest obtainable rent, and
      - There was a reasonable expectation of profit or the property was necessary to conduct the business.

7. **Dividends-Paid Deduction**

a. A deduction from TI in computing UPHCI is allowed for five types of distributions attributable to E&P.
   1) Dividends. Distributions are treated as ordinary dividend income to the extent of E&P.
      a) This includes dividend income received in redemption of stock or in partial liquidation.
      b) If property other than money is distributed, its AB is used.

2) Throwback dividends. Dividends paid during the 2 1/2 months following the close of the tax year are treated as paid on the last day of the (preceding) tax year.
   a) Election is required for a PHC deduction.
   b) Limit. No more is allowed than the lesser of 20% of dividends paid for the year or UPHCI before throwback dividends.
3) Consent dividends. This type of dividend addresses a situation of current accumulated earnings with insufficient liquidity to distribute dividends.
   a) Shareholders on the last day of the tax year must consent to treat an amount as a currently taxable dividend (to them) even though no distribution was made.
   b) Only ordinary dividend income is deductible.
4) Complete liquidation. The dividends-paid deduction includes the amount of distributions within the 24 months after adopting a plan of complete liquidation to the extent of any current E&P for the tax year of the distribution minus any capital loss deduction.
5) Deficiency dividend. A corporation is allowed 90 days to pay a deficiency dividend after a determination of PHC tax liability is made.
   a) It must be paid in cash.
   b) The corporation must elect to apply it to the year of liability.
   c) Interest and penalties otherwise imposed still apply.

b. Preferential dividends are **not** allowed to be deducted. The entire amount of a distribution is considered to be preferential if
   1) The distribution is not pro rata to the shareholders or
   2) For a particular class of stock, the distribution is greater or less than the amount to which that class of stock is otherwise entitled.

c. Dividend carryover. Excess dividends paid (over UPHCI before the DPD) may be treated as a DPD for UPHCI for the following 2 tax years only.

Stop and review! You have completed the outline for this subunit. Study multiple-choice questions 25 through 30 beginning on page 322.

QUESTIONS

8.1 Regular Income Tax

1. A corporation may reduce its regular income tax by taking a tax credit for

A. Dividends-received exclusion.

B. Foreign income taxes.

C. State income taxes.

D. Accelerated depreciation.

Answer (B) is correct.
REQUIRED: The available tax credit.
DISCUSSION: A credit is available for certain foreign income taxes paid or accrued. Note that credits are more valuable than deductions since they reduce the tax on a dollar-for-dollar basis.
Answer (A) is incorrect. The dividends-received exclusion is a deduction. Answer (C) is incorrect. State income taxes are deductible but do not give rise to a tax credit. Answer (D) is incorrect. Accelerated depreciation is a tax deduction, not a tax credit.

2. Which of the following tax credits **cannot** be claimed by a corporation?

A. Foreign Tax Credit.

B. Earned Income Credit.

C. Alternative Fuel Production Credit.

D. General Business Credit.

Answer (B) is correct.
REQUIRED: The tax credit that cannot be claimed by a corporation.
DISCUSSION: Most tax credits are allowable to corporations, but certain personal credits are not permitted. They include the Earned Income Credit, the Child and Dependent Care Credit, and the Elderly and Disabled Credit.

8.2 Foreign Tax Credit (FTC)

3. Sunex Co., an accrual-basis, calendar-year domestic C corporation, is taxed on its worldwide income. In the current year, Sunex's U.S. tax liability on its domestic and foreign source income is $60,000, and no prior-year foreign income taxes have been carried forward. Which factor(s) may affect the amount of Sunex's Foreign Tax Credit available in its current-year corporate income tax return?

	Income Source	The Foreign Tax Rate
A.	Yes	Yes
B.	Yes	No
C.	No	Yes
D.	No	No

Answer (A) is correct.

REQUIRED: The factor(s) that may affect the amount of the Foreign Tax Credit.

DISCUSSION: The Foreign Income Tax Credit is equal to the lesser of the actual foreign tax paid or the Foreign Tax Credit limit. The Foreign Tax Credit limit is the proportion of the taxpayer's tentative income tax (before the Foreign Tax Credit) that the taxpayer's foreign source taxable income bears to his or her worldwide taxable income for the year.

Answer (B) is incorrect. The Foreign Income Tax Credit is equal to the lesser of the actual foreign tax paid or the Foreign Tax Credit limit. Answer (C) is incorrect. The Foreign Tax Credit limit is the proportion of the taxpayer's tentative income tax (before the Foreign Tax Credit) that the taxpayer's foreign source taxable income bears to his or her worldwide taxable income for the year. Answer (D) is incorrect. The Foreign Income Tax Credit is equal to the lesser of the actual foreign tax paid or the Foreign Tax Credit limit. The Foreign Tax Credit limit is the proportion of the taxpayer's tentative income tax (before the Foreign Tax Credit) that the taxpayer's foreign source taxable income bears to his or her worldwide taxable income for the year.

4. The following information pertains to Wald Corp.'s operations for the year ended December 31, 2015:

Worldwide taxable income	$300,000
U.S. source taxable income	180,000
U.S. income tax before Foreign Tax Credit	96,000
Foreign nonbusiness-related interest earned	30,000
Foreign income taxes paid on nonbusiness-related interest earned	12,000
Other foreign source taxable income	90,000
Foreign income taxes paid on other foreign source taxable income	27,000

What amount of Foreign Tax Credit may Wald claim for 2015?

A. $28,800

B. $36,600

C. $38,400

D. $39,000

Answer (B) is correct.

REQUIRED: The Foreign Tax Credit amount.

DISCUSSION: The Foreign Tax Credit limit is the proportion of the taxpayer's tentative U.S. income tax (before the Foreign Tax Credit) that the taxpayer's foreign taxable income bears to his or her worldwide taxable income for the year. The limit must be applied separately to nonbusiness interest income.

Nonbusiness interest income computation:

($30,000 ÷ $300,000) × $96,000 = $9,600

Other foreign source taxable income computation:

($90,000 ÷ $300,000) × $96,000 = $28,800

Foreign taxes paid on the other income is less than the limit and fully creditable. The total credit is $36,600 ($9,600 + $27,000).

Answer (A) is incorrect. Foreign taxes paid on the other income is less than the limit and fully creditable. Furthermore, foreign taxes paid on nonbusiness-related interest earned is limited. Answer (C) is incorrect. The limit must be applied separately to nonbusiness interest income and other income. Answer (D) is incorrect. Qualified foreign taxes creditable are limited to the proportion of the taxpayer's tentative U.S. income tax (before the Foreign Tax Credit) that the taxpayer's foreign taxable income bears to his or her worldwide taxable income for the year.

8.3 Consolidated Returns

5. Tech Corp. files a consolidated return with its wholly owned subsidiary, Dow Corp. During 2015, Dow paid a cash dividend of $20,000 to Tech. What amount of this dividend is taxable on the 2015 consolidated return?

A. $20,000

B. $14,000

C. $6,000

D. $0

Answer (D) is correct.

REQUIRED: The taxable amount of a dividend distributed by a wholly owned subsidiary to its parent when a consolidated return is filed.

DISCUSSION: A dividend distributed by one member of a group filing a consolidated tax return to another member of that group is eliminated. The recipient of the dividend makes an adjustment to its separate taxable income that eliminates the dividend from the affiliated group's consolidated taxable income. Note that the dividends-received deduction (DRD) does not apply to intergroup dividends of affiliated groups that file a consolidated tax return.

6. With regard to consolidated tax returns, which of the following statements is true?

A. Operating losses of one group member may be used to offset operating profits of the other members included in the consolidated return.

B. Only corporations that issue their audited financial statements on a consolidated basis may file consolidated returns.

C. Of all intercompany dividends paid by the subsidiaries to the parent, 70% are excludable from taxable income on the consolidated return.

D. The common parent must directly own 51% or more of the total voting power of all corporations included in the consolidated return.

Answer (A) is correct.

REQUIRED: The true statement regarding consolidated tax returns.

DISCUSSION: Operating losses of one group member must be used to offset current-year operating profits of other group members before a net operating loss carryback or carryforward can occur.

Answer (B) is incorrect. There is no such requirement. Answer (C) is incorrect. A dividend distributed by one member of a group filing a consolidated tax return to another member of that same group is completely eliminated. There is no dividends-received deduction. Answer (D) is incorrect. A corporation must own 80% of the total voting power and 80% of the total value of the stock in order to file a consolidated return.

7. Which of the following groups may elect to file a consolidated corporate return?

A. A brother/sister-controlled group.

B. A parent corporation and all more-than-10%-controlled partnerships.

C. A parent corporation and all more-than-50%-controlled subsidiaries.

D. Members of an affiliated group.

Answer (D) is correct.

REQUIRED: The groups includible in a consolidated corporate return.

DISCUSSION: A single federal income tax return may be filed by two or more includible corporations that are members of an affiliated group. Includible corporations are all corporations except (1) tax-exempt corporations, (2) S corporations, (3) foreign sales corporations, (4) insurance corporations, (5) REITs, (6) regulated investment companies, (7) domestic international sales corporations, and (8) corporations claiming Sec. 936 possessions tax credit. An affiliated group includes each corporation in a chain of corporations under the following conditions:

1. The other group members must directly own stock in the corporation that represents 80% or more of both total voting power and total value outstanding.
2. A parent corporation must directly own stock under the 80% rules of at least one includible corporation.

Answer (A) is incorrect. A brother/sister-controlled group possession requirement is only 50% of total combined voting stock or 50% of total value of all stock. An affiliated group requires a higher percentage. Answer (B) is incorrect. An affiliated group must meet an 80% requirement for total voting power and total value outstanding. Answer (C) is incorrect. To be a member of an affiliated group, the group members must directly own stock in the corporation representing both 80% or more of total voting power and 80% or more of total value outstanding.

8. Potter Corp. and Sly Corp. file consolidated tax returns. In January of Year 1, Potter sold land, with a basis of $60,000 and a fair value of $75,000, to Sly for $100,000. Sly sold the land in December of Year 2 for $125,000. In the consolidated group's Year 1 and Year 2 tax returns, what amount of gain should be reported for these transactions in the consolidated return?

	Year 2	Year 1
A.	$25,000	$40,000
B.	$50,000	$0
C.	$50,000	$25,000
D.	$65,000	$0

Answer (D) is correct.

REQUIRED: The amount of gain on the sale of land to be reported in the consolidated returns.

DISCUSSION: A sale or exchange of property between members of the consolidated group is a deferred intercompany transaction. In the case of nondepreciable property (e.g., land) not sold on the installment basis, the gain is not reported until the property is sold outside the group. Therefore, Potter should report no income in the consolidated return for Year 1 as a result of the sale. For Year 2, however, Potter should recognize the full amount of the $65,000 gain ($125,000 – $60,000).

Answer (A) is incorrect. The Year 1 sale is a deferred intercompany transaction between members of a consolidated group. The gain realized is reported when the property is sold outside the group. Answer (B) is incorrect. The deferred intercompany gain of $15,000 is recognized when the property is sold outside the group. Answer (C) is incorrect. The gain is reported when the property is sold outside the group.

9. Jans, an individual, owns 80% and 100% of the total value and voting power of A and B Corporations, respectively, which in turn own the following (both value and voting power):

	Ownership	
Property	A Corp.	B Corp.
C Corp.	80%	--
D Corp.	--	100%

All companies are C corporations except B Corp., which had elected S status since inception. Which of the following statements is correct with respect to the companies' ability to file a consolidated return?

A. A, C, and D may file as a group.

B. A and C may not file as a group, and B and D may not file as a group.

C. A and C may file as a group, and B and D may file as a group.

D. A and C may file as a group, but B and D may not file as a group.

Answer (D) is correct.

REQUIRED: The includible corporations for filing consolidated returns and requirements of an affiliated group.

DISCUSSION: A single federal income tax return may be filed by two or more includible corporations that are members of an affiliated group. Includible corporations are not tax-exempt corporations, S corporations, foreign sales corporations, insurance corporations, real estate investment trusts, regulated investment companies, domestic international sales corporations, or corporations that claim Sec. 936 possessions tax credit. An affiliated group includes each corporation in a chain of corporations in which the other group members directly own 80% or more of both total value and voting power, and a parent corporation must directly own stock of 80% voting and value of at least one includible corporation. All corporations qualify for consolidated treatment of returns under the 80% voting power and value outstanding rules, but because B Corp. elected S status, neither B Corp. nor D Corp. may file a consolidated return.

Answer (A) is incorrect. D Corp. is not affiliated with the A and C Corp. group. The election of S status by B Corp. breaks the chain of affiliated corporations. Answer (B) is incorrect. A and C may file as a group. An affiliated group includes each corporation in a chain of corporations in which the other member of the group directly owns stock in the corporation representing 80% of both total voting power and value outstanding. B Corp.'s election of S status disqualifies B and D from filing a consolidated return. Answer (C) is incorrect. Although A and C may file as a group, B Corp.'s election of S status disqualifies B and D from filing as a group. Corporations excluded from filing consolidated returns include tax-exempt corporations, S corporations, foreign sales corporations, insurance corporations, real estate investment trusts, regulated investment companies, domestic international sales corporations, or corporations that claim Sec. 936 possessions tax credit.

8.4 Controlled Groups

10. Consolidated returns may be filed

A. Either by parent-subsidiary corporations or by brother-sister corporations.

B. Only by corporations that formally request advance permission from the IRS.

C. Only by parent-subsidiary affiliated groups.

D. Only by corporations that issue their financial statements on a consolidated basis.

Answer (C) is correct.

REQUIRED: The requirement for corporations to file consolidated tax returns.

DISCUSSION: Corporations must be members of an affiliated group to file a consolidated tax return. An affiliated group consists of one or more chains of includible corporations that are connected through stock ownership with a common parent corporation. There is an 80% ownership requirement. Only parent-subsidiary affiliated groups will meet this requirement of having a common parent corporation.

Answer (A) is incorrect. Brother-sister corporations exist if two corporations are owned by five or fewer persons with certain stock ownership requirements. They must not have a common parent corporation; one (or more) individual(s) may own the stock. Answer (B) is incorrect. There is no requirement that formal advance permission be obtained from the IRS. Answer (D) is incorrect. Corporations are not required to issue financial statements on a consolidated basis in order to file tax returns on a consolidated basis.

11. Prin Corp., the parent corporation, and Strel Corp., both accrual-basis, calendar year C corporations, file a consolidated return. During the current year, Strel made dividend distributions to Prin as follows:

	Adjusted tax basis	FMV
Cash	4,000	4,000
Land	2,000	9,000

What amount of income should be reported in Prin and Strel's consolidated income tax return for the current year?

A. $13,000

B. $11,000

C. $6,000

D. $0

Answer (D) is correct.

REQUIRED: The amount of income to include in dividends of a consolidated entity.

DISCUSSION: Dividends paid from one member of a consolidated group to another member are eliminated. None of the dividends, whether in cash or property, are included in the consolidated income tax return for the current year. The DRD is not allowed for such dividends.

8.5 Alternative Minimum Tax (AMT)

12. If a corporation's tentative minimum tax exceeds the regular tax, the excess amount is

A. Carried back to the first preceding taxable year.

B. Carried back to the third preceding taxable year.

C. Payable in addition to the regular tax.

D. Subtracted from the regular tax.

Answer (C) is correct.

REQUIRED: The application of the alternative minimum tax.

DISCUSSION: The excess of the tentative minimum tax over the regular tax is payable in addition to the regular tax. This excess is called the alternative minimum tax and is due on the same date as the regular tax.

13. The credit for prior-year alternative minimum tax liability may be carried

A. Forward for a maximum of 5 years.

B. Back to the 3 preceding years or carried forward for a maximum of 5 years.

C. Back to the 3 preceding years.

D. Forward indefinitely.

Answer (D) is correct.

REQUIRED: The true statement regarding the AMT credit.

DISCUSSION: The minimum tax credit can be carried forward indefinitely. It may be used to offset regular tax liabilities in future years to the extent the regular tax liability exceeds the corporation's tentative minimum tax in the carryforward year.

14. Bent Corp., a calendar-year C corporation, purchased and placed into service residential real property during February 2015. No other property was placed into service during 2015. What convention must Bent use to determine the depreciation deduction for the alternative minimum tax?

A. Full-year.

B. Half-year.

C. Mid-quarter.

D. Mid-month.

Answer (D) is correct.

REQUIRED: The convention used for depreciation of residential real property for AMT.

DISCUSSION: AMT depreciation of real property is computed using a straight-line method, 40-year recovery period, and the mid-month convention.

Answer (A) is incorrect. The full-year convention does not exist. Answer (B) is incorrect. The half-year convention is the general convention for personal property. Answer (C) is incorrect. The mid-quarter convention does not apply to depreciation of real property.

15. Eastern Corp., a calendar-year corporation, was formed January 3, 2015, and on that date placed 5-year property in service. The property was depreciated under the general MACRS system. Eastern did not elect to use the straight-line method. The following information pertains to Eastern:

Eastern's 2015 taxable income	$300,000
Adjustment for the accelerated depreciation taken on 2015 5-year property	1,000
2015 tax-exempt interest from specified private activity bonds issued in 2014	5,000

What was Eastern's 2015 alternative minimum taxable income before the adjusted current earnings (ACE) adjustment?

A. $306,000

B. $305,000

C. $304,000

D. $301,000

Answer (A) is correct.

REQUIRED: The alternative minimum taxable income before the adjusted current earnings adjustment.

DISCUSSION: The accelerated portion of MACRS depreciation is considered an adjustment item. Tax-exempt interest from the private activity bonds is considered a preference item. Both items must be added back to taxable income before consideration of the ACE adjustment.

8.6 Estimated Tax

16. When computing a corporation's income tax expense for estimated income tax purposes, which of the following should be taken into account?

	Corporate Tax Credits	Alternative Minimum Tax
A.	No	No
B.	No	Yes
C.	Yes	No
D.	Yes	Yes

Answer (D) is correct.

REQUIRED: The item(s) accounted for in computing estimated tax payments required.

DISCUSSION: A corporation is required to make payments of estimated tax liability in quarterly installments. The estimated tax liability is the sum of the regular income tax, AMT, and certain other taxes, reduced by corporate tax credits.

17. Blink Corp., an accrual-basis, calendar-year corporation, carried back a net operating loss for the tax year ended December 31, Year 1. Blink's gross revenues have been under $500,000 since inception. Blink expects to have profits for the tax year ending December 31, Year 2. Which method(s) of estimated tax payment can Blink use for its quarterly payments during the Year 2 tax year to avoid underpayment of federal estimated taxes?

I. 100%-of-the-preceding-tax-year method
II. Annualized income method

A. I only.

B. Both I and II.

C. II only.

D. Neither I nor II.

Answer (C) is correct.

REQUIRED: The acceptable method(s) of estimating quarterly tax payments.

DISCUSSION: Blink Corp. qualifies as a small corporation because it has not had taxable income exceeding $1 million during any of the 3 preceding years. However, it must have shown a tax liability in the previous year in order to use the 100%-of-the-preceding-tax-year method. Since the previous year generated an NOL, this method cannot be used. The annualized income method is available in this situation.

18. Finbury Corporation's taxable income for the year ended December 31, 2014, was $2 million. For Finbury to escape the estimated tax underpayment penalty for the year ending December 31, 2015, its total 2015 estimated tax payments must equal at least

A. 100% of the 2014 tax liability.

B. 80% of the 2015 tax liability.

C. 90% of the 2015 tax liability.

D. 100% of its 2015 tax liability.

Answer (D) is correct.

REQUIRED: The minimum amount of estimated tax payments to avoid the underpayment penalty.

DISCUSSION: A large corporation will not be considered to have underpaid its income tax if it pays 100% of the tax shown on the return for the tax year. A large corporation is one having $1 million or more taxable income during any of its 3 preceding tax years. Large corporations are not able to avoid underpaying their taxes by relying on the 100% of the tax shown on the return for the preceding year exception.

19. No penalty will be imposed on a corporation for underpayment of estimated tax for a particular year if

A. The tax for that year is less than $500.

B. Estimated tax payments for the year equal at least 80% of the tax shown on the return for that year.

C. The corporation is a personal holding company.

D. The alternative minimum tax is at least $1,000.

Answer (A) is correct.

REQUIRED: The condition under which a corporation is not liable for the penalty on underpayment of estimated tax.

DISCUSSION: No estimated tax underpayment penalty is imposed on a corporation if actual tax liability shown on the return for the tax year is less than $500.

Answer (B) is incorrect. The applicable percentage is 100%. Answer (C) is incorrect. No exception exempts PHCs from the penalty. Answer (D) is incorrect. The code requires estimated tax payments of AMT.

8.7 Accumulated Earnings Tax (AET)

20. The accumulated earnings tax

A. Should be self-assessed by filing a separate schedule along with the regular tax return.

B. Applies only to closely held corporations.

C. Can be imposed on S corporations that do not regularly distribute their earnings.

D. Cannot be imposed on a corporation that has undistributed earnings and profits of less than $150,000.

Answer (D) is correct.

REQUIRED: The entities subject to, the limits on, and the procedural characteristics of the AET.

DISCUSSION: The Accumulated Earnings Credit (AEC) is deducted from taxable income (TI) to determine accumulated taxable income (ATI), the AET base. The minimum credit base is $250,000. However, the minimum credit base is $150,000 for certain service corporations. The AET base is not less than any excess of the minimum credit base ($150,000) over accumulated E&P. Thus, AET is not imposed on a corporation that has undistributed earnings and profits of less than $150,000.

Answer (A) is incorrect. AET is not self-assessed. It is assessed, if at all, on an IRS audit. Filing a separate return reporting AET is not required. Answer (B) is incorrect. AET can apply to publicly held corporations. Answer (C) is incorrect. An S corporation is expressly exempt from AET. Its shareholders are currently subject to tax on its earnings.

21. In determining whether a corporation is subject to the accumulated earnings tax, which of the following items is **not** a subtraction in arriving at accumulated taxable income?

A. Federal income tax.

B. Capital loss carryback.

C. Dividends-paid deduction.

D. Accumulated Earnings Credit.

Answer (B) is correct.

REQUIRED: The item that does not reduce ATI.

DISCUSSION: The accumulated earnings tax is applied to accumulated taxable income, which is taxable income, subject to certain adjustments. Capital loss carrybacks and carryovers are not allowed. Instead, capital losses are deductible in full in the year incurred (but must be reduced by prior net capital gain deductions).

Answer (A) is incorrect. Federal income taxes are deducted as an adjustment to taxable income. Answer (C) is incorrect. The dividends-paid deduction is subtracted from adjusted taxable income. Answer (D) is incorrect. The Accumulated Earnings Credit is subtracted from adjusted taxable income.

22. Daystar Corp., which is not a mere holding or investment company, derives its income from retail sales. Daystar had accumulated earnings and profits of $145,000 at December 31, 2014. For the year ended December 31, 2015, it had earnings and profits of $115,000 and a dividends-paid deduction of $15,000. No throwback distributions have been made. It has been determined that $20,000 of the current and accumulated earnings and profits for 2015 is required for the reasonable needs of the business. How much is the allowable Accumulated Earnings Credit at December 31, 2015?

A. $90,000

B. $105,000

C. $230,000

D. $250,000

Answer (B) is correct.

REQUIRED: The allowable Accumulated Earnings Credit.

DISCUSSION: The Accumulated Earnings Credit is the greater of (1) the difference between $250,000 and the accumulated earnings and profits at the end of the prior year or (2) the difference between current earnings and profits retained for the reasonable needs of the business (minus the long-term capital gain adjustments of the current year) and the accumulated earnings and profits at the end of the prior year.

The difference between $250,000 and Daystar's accumulated earnings and profits at the end of the prior year ($145,000) is $105,000. Since the minimum credit base is greater than the $20,000 of reasonable needs of the business, the available Accumulated Earnings Credit is $105,000. The amount of $100,000 ($115,000 current E&P – $15,000 dividends-paid deduction) will be used in 2015, and $5,000 will be available in following years.

Answer (A) is incorrect. The dividends-paid deduction is used to compute the accumulated taxable income but not the Accumulated Earnings Credit. Answer (C) is incorrect. The minimum credit base is greater than current earnings and profits retained for the reasonable needs of the business, and there is no LTCG adjustment to be made. Answer (D) is incorrect. The minimum credit base is $250,000 reduced by accumulated E&P.

23. Kari Corp., a manufacturing company, was organized on January 2, 2015. Its 2015 federal taxable income was $400,000, and its federal income tax was $100,000. What is the maximum amount of accumulated taxable income that may be subject to the accumulated earnings tax for 2015 if Kari takes only the minimum Accumulated Earnings Credit?

A. $300,000

B. $150,000

C. $50,000

D. $0

Answer (C) is correct.

REQUIRED: The maximum amount of ATI that may be subject to the accumulated earnings tax.

DISCUSSION: The accumulated earnings tax is applied to accumulated taxable income, which is taxable income subject to certain adjustments. Federal income taxes are deducted as an adjustment to taxable income.

Without showing a reason for the accumulation, the minimum Accumulated Earnings Credit is $250,000 for nonservice corporations. The credit is a negative adjustment to taxable income in computing ATI. ATI is $50,000 ($400,000 taxable income – $100,000 federal income tax – $250,000 minimum Accumulated Earnings Credit).

Answer (A) is incorrect. The Accumulated Earnings Credit is a negative adjustment to taxable income in computing ATI. Answer (B) is incorrect. The minimum Accumulated Earnings Credit is $250,000 for nonservice corporations. Answer (D) is incorrect. Some of the income is subject to the accumulated earnings tax.

24. The accumulated earnings tax can be imposed

A. On both partnerships and corporations.

B. On companies that make distributions in excess of accumulated earnings.

C. On personal holding companies.

D. Regardless of the number of shareholders in a corporation.

Answer (D) is correct.

REQUIRED: The characteristic of the accumulated earnings tax.

DISCUSSION: The accumulated earnings tax (AET) is imposed only on a corporation that, for the purpose of avoiding income tax at the shareholder level, allows earnings and profits to accumulate instead of being distributed. The AET will be imposed regardless of the number of shareholders, provided the corporation does not qualify as a personal holding company.

Answer (A) is incorrect. Partnerships, along with any other entities that are not corporations, are not subject to the AET. Answer (B) is incorrect. Distributions in excess of accumulated earnings are the opposite of accumulated earnings. ATI, the AET base, will be zero in such a case. Answer (C) is incorrect. Personal holding companies are excluded from the AET. They are subject to tax on undistributed PHC income.

8.8 Personal Holding Company Tax

25. Edge Corp. met the stock ownership requirements of a personal holding company. What sources of income must Edge consider to determine if the income requirements for a personal holding company have been met?

I. Interest earned on tax-exempt obligations

II. Dividends received from an unrelated domestic corporation

A. I only.

B. II only.

C. Both I and II.

D. Neither I nor II.

Answer (B) is correct.

REQUIRED: The items included in personal holding company income.

DISCUSSION: A personal holding company tax is assessed on the undistributed personal holding company income (PHCI) of many C corporations. This tax is self-assessed when 50% or more of the value of the corporation's shares are owned by five or fewer shareholders at any time during the last half of the fiscal year, and 60% or more of AGI is PHCI. PHCI includes taxable interest and dividends but not tax-exempt interest.

26. Zero Corp. is an investment company authorized to issue only common stock. During the last half of the current year, Edward owned 450 of the 1,000 outstanding shares of stock in Zero. Zero would **not** be subject to the personal holding company (PHC) penalty tax if the remaining 550 shares of common stock were owned by

A. An estate in which Edward is the beneficiary.

B. Edward's brother.

C. Fifty-five shareholders who are related neither to each other nor to Edward, in equal lots of 10 shares each.

D. Edward's grandmother.

Answer (C) is correct.

REQUIRED: The ownership requirements of a personal holding company.

DISCUSSION: One of the tests used to determine if a company is subject to the personal holding company (PHC) penalty tax is the stock ownership test. More than 50% of the value of the outstanding stock must be owned by five or fewer individuals at some time during the last 6 months of the tax year. However, if 10 or more unrelated taxpayers own equal shares, the ownership requirement cannot be met. Therefore, if 55 taxpayers own equal lots of 10 shares each, Zero will not be subject to the personal holding company penalty tax.

Answer (A) is incorrect. Stock owned by an estate is considered under the constructive ownership rules as being owned by its beneficiaries, pushing Zero over the 50%-ownership limit for a PHC. Answer (B) is incorrect. Ownership of stock by a brother is considered under the constructive ownership rules as being owned by Edward, pushing Zero over the 50%-ownership limit for a PHC. Answer (D) is incorrect. Ownership of stock by a grandmother is considered under the constructive ownership rules as being owned by Edward, pushing Zero over the 50%-ownership limit for a PHC.

27. Kane Corp. is a calendar-year domestic personal holding company. Which deduction(s) must Kane make from current year taxable income to determine undistributed personal holding company income prior to the dividends-paid deduction?

	Federal Income Taxes	Net Long-Term Capital Gain Less Related Federal Income Taxes
A.	Yes	Yes
B.	Yes	No
C.	No	Yes
D.	No	No

Answer (A) is correct.

REQUIRED: The determination of undistributed personal holding company income.

DISCUSSION: Undistributed personal holding company income is taxable income net of specific adjustments and the dividends-paid deduction. Federal income taxes accrued and capital gains (net of related federal taxes) are subtracted from taxable income.

28. Benson, a singer, owns 100% of the outstanding capital stock of Lund Corporation. Lund contracted with Benson, specifying that Benson was to perform personal services for Magda Productions, Inc., in consideration of which Benson was to receive $50,000 a year from Lund. Lund contracted with Magda, specifying that Benson was to perform personal services for Magda, in consideration of which Magda was to pay Lund $1 million a year. Personal holding company income will be attributable to

A. Benson only.

B. Lund only.

C. Magda only.

D. All three contracting parties.

Answer (B) is correct.

REQUIRED: The corporation to which the personal holding company income will be attributed.

DISCUSSION: Amounts received by corporations under personal service contracts involving a 25%-or-more shareholder are personal holding company income if the contract designates specifically that only the shareholder will provide the services. As such, Lund has personal service income of $1 million a year.

Answer (A) is incorrect. Benson is an individual, and personal holding company income applies only to corporations. Answer (C) is incorrect. Magda is paying the income, not receiving it. Answer (D) is incorrect. Not all parties will have personal holding company income.

29. The following information pertains to Hull, Inc., a personal holding company, for the year ended December 31, 2015:

Undistributed personal holding company income	$100,000
Dividends paid during 2015	20,000
Consent dividends reported in the 2015 individual income tax returns of the holders of Hull's common stock, but not paid by Hull to its shareholders	10,000

In computing its 2015 personal holding company tax, what amount should Hull deduct for dividends paid?

A. $0

B. $10,000

C. $20,000

D. $30,000

Answer (D) is correct.

REQUIRED: The amount and types of dividends paid deductible from TI in computing the PHC tax base.

DISCUSSION: A deduction from TI in computing UPHCI is allowed for five types of distributions attributable to E&P. The full amount of distributions treated as ordinary dividend income are deductible, as are consent dividends. A consent dividend is treated as a dividend currently taxable to the shareholders even though no distribution was made.

30. Tan Corp. calculated the following taxes for the current year:

Regular tax liability	$210,000
Tentative minimum tax	240,000
Personal holding company tax	65,000

What is Tan's total tax liability for the year?

A. $210,000

B. $240,000

C. $275,000

D. $305,000

Answer (D) is correct.

REQUIRED: The total tax liability for a corporation.

DISCUSSION: The tentative minimum tax is the total amount of tax due. If the tentative minimum tax (AMT) exceeds the regular tax, the additional amount is the alternative minimum tax, which is payable in addition to the regular tax liability. Therefore, the AMT equals $30,000 ($240,000 – $210,000) and is due in addition to the regular tax liability. Personal holding company tax is an additional tax assessed to corporations that are owned by 5 or fewer individuals and having 60% of their adjusted gross income consisting of net rent, interest, royalties, and dividends. Therefore, the total tax liability is $305,000 ($210,000 regular tax liability + $30,000 AMT + $65,000 PHC tax).

Answer (A) is incorrect. The AMT and the personal holding company tax are also included in the current year's tax liability. Answer (B) is incorrect. The personal holding company tax is also included in the current year's tax liability. Answer (C) is incorrect. The AMT is also included in the current year's tax liability.

8.9 PRACTICE TASK-BASED SIMULATIONS

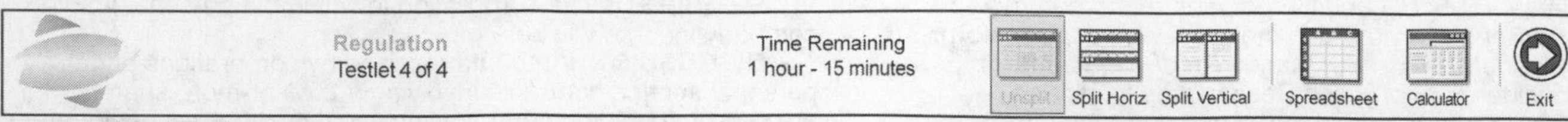

DIRECTIONS

Note: If you believe you have encountered a software malfunction, report it to the test center staff immediately.

Navigation

To navigate from task to task, use the controls at the bottom of the screen. Click on the **Next** button to advance to the next task, or the **Previous** button to go to the previous task. To go directly to any task, click on its number.

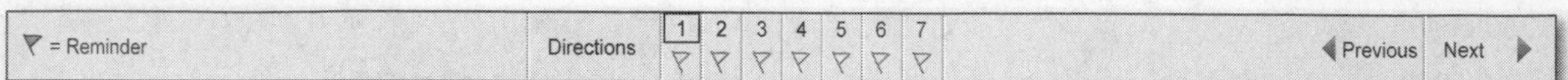

If you would like a reminder to revisit a task, or want to indicate that you are finished with it, click on the reminder flag below the task number. To clear the flag, click on it again. Reminder flags are for your use only – they do not contribute to your score.

Tabs

In this part of the examination, you will be asked to complete various tasks. Every task has one or more **Work Tabs**. Some tasks have one or more **Information Tabs**, others may have none. Every task has a **Help** tab.

If a task has **Information Tabs**, you may use the information in them to complete your responses in the **Work Tabs**.

Work tab **Information tab** **Help tab**

Work Tabs:

- **Work Tabs** are identified with a pencil icon. This is where your responses are expected.
- Each task has one or more **Work Tabs**.
- **Work Tabs** contain directions for completing the task – be sure to read these directions carefully.
- The **Work Tab** name in the example above is for illustration only – yours will differ.
- You must complete all of the **Work Tabs** in each task to receive full credit.

Information Tabs:

- The Authoritative Literature will be provided in all tasks in the AUD, FAR, and REG sections for your reference.
- Your simulation may have one or more additional **Information Tabs**. Like the Authoritative Literature tabs, **Information Tabs** do not have a pencil icon.
- If your task has additional **Information Tabs**, go through each to familiarize yourself with the task content.

Help Tab:

- The **Help Tab** provides assistance with the exam software that is used in this task. For example, if the task is to compose a memorandum, **Help** will provide information about the word processor.

The Toolbar

The toolbar at the top of the screen shows the amount of time remaining for you to complete the tasks. In addition, the following tools are available. Note that only the **Exit** button is displayed when Directions are visible - the others will appear when you begin the tasks.

Click on these buttons to split or unsplit the screen. You can split the screen vertically or horizontally.

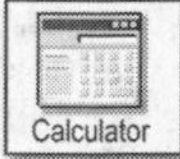

Click on this button to display the calculator; click on it again to hide the calculator. To move the calculator, click on the calculator title bar and drag the calculator to the desired location.

Click on this button to use the spreadsheet; click on it again to hide the spreadsheet. To move the spreadsheet, click on the the spreadsheet title bar and drag the spreadsheet to the desired location.

Click on this button to go on to the next part of the examination. You must complete all of the tasks to receive full credit. Once you click on **Exit** and confirm the action, you will NOT be able to return to this testlet.

= Reminder | Directions | 1 2 3 4 5 6 | Previous | Next

Comfort, Inc., is a calendar-year, accrual-basis corporation that commenced operations on January 1, 2012. Comfort is not subject to the uniform capitalization rules.

Check the appropriate box to indicate whether each corporate revenue item is fully taxable, partially taxable, or nontaxable, for regular tax purposes, on Comfort, Inc.'s 2015 federal income tax return.

Corporate Revenues	***Fully Taxable***	***Partially Taxable***	***Nontaxable***
1. Dividends from the 20%-owned domestic corporation. The taxable income limitation does not apply. Comfort does not have the ability to exercise significant influence.			
2. Recovery of an account from prior year's bad debts. Comfort uses an estimate of uncollectibles based on an aging of accounts receivable for book purposes. The account was written off for tax purposes and reduced Comfort's income tax liability.			
3. Refund of state franchise tax overpayment, previously expensed on Comfort's 2013 federal tax return, which reduced federal taxes that year.			
4. Interest income from municipal bonds purchased by Comfort in 2015 on the open market.			
5. Proceeds paid to Comfort by reason of death, under a life insurance policy that Comfort had purchased on the life of one of its vice presidents. Comfort was the beneficiary and used the proceeds to pay the premium charges for the group term insurance policy for its other employees.			

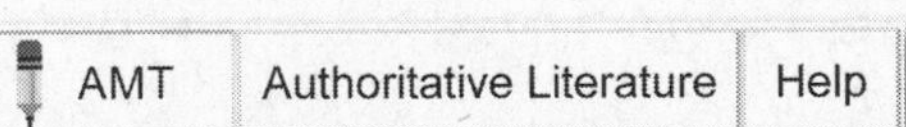

On its 2015 federal income tax return, Global Corp. reported the same amounts for regular income tax and alternative minimum tax purposes. Select from the list provided to indicate whether each item, taken separately, contributes to overstating, understating, or correctly stating Global's 2015 alternative minimum taxable income (AMTI) prior to the adjusted current earnings calculation (ACE). Each choice may be used once, more than once, or not at all.

Taxation Item	***Answer***
1. For regular tax purposes, Global Corp. deducted the maximum MACRS depreciation on 7-year personal property placed in service on January 1, 2015. Global Corp. made no Sec. 179 election to expense the property in 2015.	
2. For regular income tax purposes, Global Corp. depreciated nonresidential real property placed in service January 1, 1997, under the general MACRS depreciation system for a 39-year depreciable life.	
3. Global Corp. excluded state highway construction general obligation bond interest income earned in 2015 for regular income tax and alternative minimum tax (AMT) purposes.	

Choices
A) Overstating Global Corp.'s 2015 AMTI prior to the ACE
B) Understating Global Corp.'s 2015 AMTI prior to the ACE
C) Correctly stating Global Corp.'s 2015 AMTI prior to the ACE

= Reminder | Directions | 1 2 3 4 5 6 | Previous | Next

IRS Form 1125-A - Cost of Goods Sold | Authoritative Literature | Help

Buddy Corp. is a calendar-year, accrual-basis corporation that commenced operations on January 1, 2012. The following adjusted accounts appear on Buddy's records for the year ended December 31, 2015. Buddy is not subject to the uniform capitalization rules.

Gross sales	$2,000,000
Cost of goods sold	350,000

Additional Information

Beginning inventory was $550,000 and ending inventory was $650,000. The corporation utilizes the lower of cost or market for valuing closing inventory. It does not use LIFO and Section 263A rules do not apply. No salaries are part of inventory costs.

Given the information above, complete the shaded areas of the Schedule A - Cost of Goods Sold, for the IRS Form 1120.

Form **1125-A** (Rev. December 2012) Department of the Treasury Internal Revenue Service

Cost of Goods Sold

▶ **Attach to Form 1120, 1120-C, 1120-F, 1120S, 1065, or 1065-B.**
▶ **Information about Form 1125-A and its instructions is at *www.irs.gov/form1125a*.**

OMB No. 1545-2225

Name: Buddy Corp. | **Employer identification number**: 59-154-8855

1	Inventory at beginning of year	1	
2	Purchases	2	
3	Cost of labor	3	
4	Additional section 263A costs (attach schedule)	4	
5	Other costs (attach schedule)	5	
6	**Total.** Add lines 1 through 5	6	
7	Inventory at end of year	7	
8	**Cost of goods sold.** Subtract line 7 from line 6. Enter here and on Form 1120, page 1, line 2 or the appropriate line of your tax return (see instructions)	8	

9a Check all methods used for valuing closing inventory:
(i) ☐ Cost
(ii) ☐ Lower of cost or market
(iii) ☐ Other (Specify method used and attach explanation.) ▶

b Check if there was a writedown of subnormal goods ▶ ☐

c Check if the LIFO inventory method was adopted this tax year for any goods (if checked, attach Form 970) ▶ ☐

d If the LIFO inventory method was used for this tax year, enter amount of closing inventory computed under LIFO . . . 9d

e If property is produced or acquired for resale, do the rules of section 263A apply to the entity (see instructions)? ☐ Yes ☐ No

f Was there any change in determining quantities, cost, or valuations between opening and closing inventory? If "Yes," attach explanation ☐ Yes ☐ No

(12-2012)

= Reminder | Directions | 1 2 3 4 5 6 | ◀ Previous | Next ▶

Kimberly Corp. is a calendar-year, accrual-basis corporation that commenced operations on January 1, 2012. The following adjusted accounts appear on Kimberly's records for the year ended December 31, 2015. Kimberly is not subject to the uniform capitalization rules.

Revenues and Gains		Costs and Expenses	
Gross sales	$2,000,000	Cost of goods sold	$ 350,000
Dividends:		Salaries and wages	470,000
20%-owned domestic corporation	10,000	*Depreciation:*	
XYZ Corp.	10,000	Real property	50,000
Interest:		Personal property (3)	100,000
U.S. Treasury bonds	26,000	Bad debt (4)	10,000
Municipal bonds	25,000	State franchise tax	25,000
Insurance proceeds	40,000	Vacation expense	10,000
Gain on sale:		Interest expense (5)	16,000
Unimproved lot (1)	20,000	Life insurance premiums	20,000
XYZ stock (2)	5,000	Federal income taxes	200,000
State franchise tax refund	14,000	Entertainment expense	20,000
Total	$2,150,000	Other expenses	29,000
		Total	1,300,000
		Net income	$ 850,000

Additional Information

(1) Gain on the sale of unimproved lot -- Purchased in 2013 for use in business for $50,000; sold in 2015 for $70,000. Kimberly has never had any Sec. 1231 losses.

(2) Gain on sale of XYZ stock -- Purchased in 2013.

(3) Personal property -- The book depreciation is the same as tax depreciation for all the property that was placed in service before January 1, 2015. The book depreciation is straight line over the useful life, which is the same as class life. Company policy is to use half-year convention per books for personal property. Furniture and fixtures costing $56,000 were placed in service on January 1, 2015.

(4) Bad debt -- Represents the increase in the allowance for doubtful accounts based on an aging of accounts receivable. Actual bad debts written off were $7,000.

(5) Interest expense on

Mortgage loan	$10,000
Loan obtained to purchase municipal bonds	4,000
Line-of-credit loan	2,000

Enter in the shaded cells the amount that should be reported on Kimberly Corp.'s 2015 federal income tax return for each item below.

Reportable Item	Amount
1. What amount of interest income from the U.S. Treasury bonds is taxable?	
2. Determine the tax depreciation expense under the modified accelerated cost recovery system (MACRS) for the furniture and fixtures that were placed in service on January 1, 2015. Assume that no irrevocable depreciation election is made. Round the answer to the nearest thousand. Kimberly Corp. did not use the alternative depreciation system (ADS) or a straight-line method of depreciation. No election was made to expense part of the cost of the property.	
3. Determine the amount of bad debt to be included as an expense item.	
4. Determine Kimberly Corp.'s net long-term capital gain.	
5. What amount of interest expense is deductible?	

= Reminder | Directions | 1 2 3 4 5 6 | Previous | Next

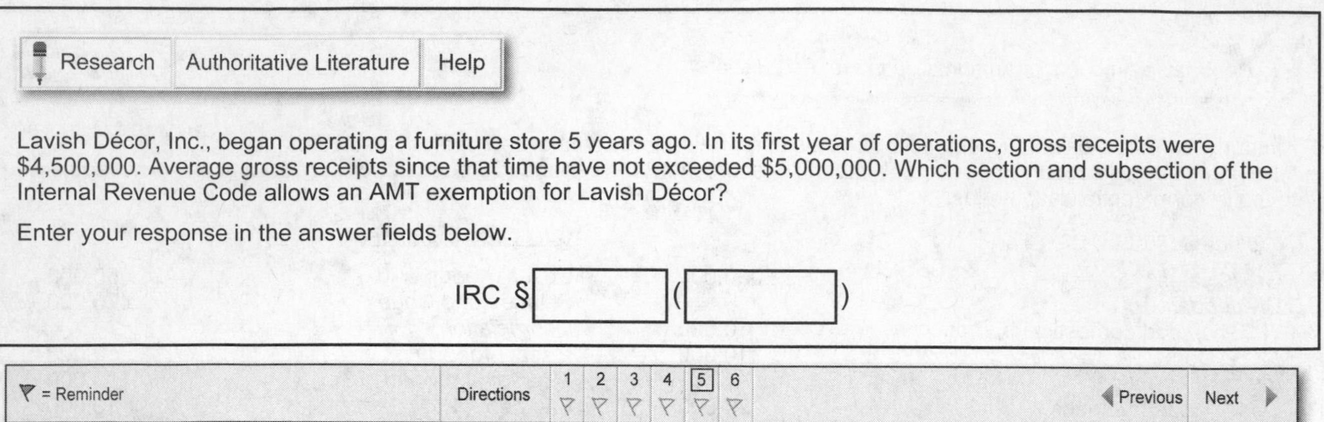

Research | Authoritative Literature | Help

Lavish Décor, Inc., began operating a furniture store 5 years ago. In its first year of operations, gross receipts were $4,500,000. Average gross receipts since that time have not exceeded $5,000,000. Which section and subsection of the Internal Revenue Code allows an AMT exemption for Lavish Décor?

Enter your response in the answer fields below.

IRC § [ ] ([ ])

= Reminder | Directions | 1 2 3 4 5 6 | Previous | Next

Green Corp. is a calendar-year, accrual-basis corporation that commenced operations on January 1, 2012. Green is not subject to the uniform capitalization rules.

Check the appropriate box to indicate whether each corporate expenditure is fully deductible, partially deductible, or nondeductible, for regular tax purposes, on Green Corp.'s 2015 federal income tax return.

Corporate Expenditures	***Fully Deductible***	***Partially Deductible***	***Nondeductible***
1. Organization expense incurred at corporate inception in 2012 to draft the corporate charter. No deduction was taken for the organization expense, either in 2012 or in any year since.			
2. Life insurance premiums paid by the corporation for its executives as part of their compensation for services rendered. The corporation is neither the direct nor the indirect beneficiary of the policy, and the amount of compensation is reasonable.			
3. Vacation pay earned by employees, which vested under a plan by December 31, 2015, and was paid February 1, 2016.			
4. State franchise tax liability that has accrued during the year and was paid on March 15, 2016.			
5. Entertainment expense to lease a luxury skybox during football season to entertain clients. The skybox lease includes tickets for each seat in the skybox for all home games played. A bona fide business discussion precedes each game. The cost of regular seats would have been one-half the amount paid.			

Unofficial Answers

1. Corporate Revenues (5 Gradable Items)

1. Partially Taxable. A corporation is allowed a deduction for 80% of dividends received from taxable domestic corporations of which it owns more than 20% but less than 80% of the stock.
2. Fully Taxable. Recovered items, such as bad debts, are excluded from income only if the prior deduction did not reduce the taxpayer's federal income tax. Thus, the amount recovered is fully taxable.
3. Fully Taxable. Items recovered, for example, previously paid taxes, are excluded from income only if the prior deductions did not reduce the taxpayer's federal income tax. Since the tax overpayment reduced federal taxes in 2013, the amount refunded is fully taxable in 2015.
4. Nontaxable. Interest on obligations of states is generally excluded from gross income unless it is interest on private activity bonds or arbitrage bonds.
5. Nontaxable. Proceeds under a life insurance contract paid by reason of death of the insured are excluded from gross income. The use that the proceeds are put to does not affect the exclusion.

2. AMT (3 Gradable Items)

1. B) Understating. Global Corp. is required to use the alternative depreciation system defined in Sec. 168(g) for AMT purposes. The personal property will have a depreciation rate of 150% rather than 200%, causing tax depreciation to be higher than AMT depreciation and resulting in an understatement of AMTI.
2. B) Understating. The class life used for nonresidential real property for AMT purposes is 40 years. The effect will be that tax depreciation will be higher than AMT depreciation, resulting in an understatement of AMTI. For Section 1250 property placed into service after 12/31/98, the tax preference has been eliminated.
3. C) Correctly Stating. This bond is excluded for both tax and AMT purposes. Therefore, Global Corp.'s AMTI is correctly stated.

3. IRS Form 1125-A - Cost of Goods Sold (6 Gradable Items)

Form **1125-A** (Rev. December 2012) Department of the Treasury Internal Revenue Service

Cost of Goods Sold

► Attach to Form 1120, 1120-C, 1120-F, 1120S, 1065, or 1065-B.
► Information about Form 1125-A and its instructions is at *www.irs.gov/form1125a.*

OMB No. 1545-2225

Name: Buddy Corp. | **Employer identification number:** 59-154-8855

1	Inventory at beginning of year	1	550,000
2	Purchases	2	450,000
3	Cost of labor	3	
4	Additional section 263A costs (attach schedule)	4	
5	Other costs (attach schedule)	5	
6	**Total.** Add lines 1 through 5	6	1,000,000
7	Inventory at end of year	7	650,000
8	**Cost of goods sold.** Subtract line 7 from line 6. Enter here and on Form 1120, page 1, line 2 or the appropriate line of your tax return (see instructions)	8	350,000

9a Check all methods used for valuing closing inventory:
(i) ☐ Cost
(ii) ☑ Lower of cost or market
(iii) ☐ Other (Specify method used and attach explanation.) ►

b Check if there was a writedown of subnormal goods ► ☐

c Check if the LIFO inventory method was adopted this tax year for any goods (if checked, attach Form 970) ► ☐

d If the LIFO inventory method was used for this tax year, enter amount of closing inventory computed under LIFO | 9d |

e If property is produced or acquired for resale, do the rules of section 263A apply to the entity (see instructions)? ☐ Yes ☐ No

f Was there any change in determining quantities, cost, or valuations between opening and closing inventory? If "Yes," attach explanation ☐ Yes ☐ No

(12-2012)

4. Reportable Amounts (5 Gradable Items)

1. $26,000. The exclusion from income of interest on obligations of a state does not apply to obligations of the U.S.

2. $8,000. Under MACRS, the recovery period for office furniture and equipment is 7 years. The 200%-declining-balance method is used for MACRS recovery periods of 3, 5, 7, and 10 years, and the half-year convention applies. The rate is 2 ÷ 7. The tax depreciation expense for the furniture and fixtures, based on the assumptions given in the question, is $8,000 [$56,000 × (2 ÷ 7) ÷ 2].

3. $7,000. Corporations that are not financial institutions must use the direct charge-off method or the nonaccrual-experience method. The reserve method is not allowed. Kimberly's deduction is the $7,000 actually written off during 2013.

4. $25,000. The unimproved lot is Sec. 1231 property since it was held for more than 1 year and used in the business. Because there are no Sec. 1231 losses, the Sec. 1231 gain on the land is treated as a capital gain. Gains on both the land and the stock are long-term capital gains, since each was held for more than 1 year. Net long-term capital gain is the excess of long-term capital gains for the taxable year over the long-term capital losses for such year, or $25,000 ($20,000 gain on sale of land + $5,000 gain on sale of stock).

5. $12,000. Generally, all expenses of a corporation are ordinary and necessary business expenses, including interest expense. Interest on debt incurred to carry tax-free obligations is not an allowable deduction. Thus, the $10,000 interest on the mortgage loan and the $2,000 interest on the line-of-credit loan are deductible.

5. Research (1 Gradable Item)

Answer: IRC § 55(e)(1)

§ 55. Alternative minimum tax imposed

(e) Exemption for small corporations

(1) In general

(A) $7,500,000 gross receipts test

The tentative minimum tax of a corporation shall be zero for any taxable year if the corporation's average annual gross receipts for all 3-taxable-year periods ending before such taxable year does not exceed $7,500,000. For purposes of the preceding sentence, only taxable years beginning after December 31, 1993, shall be taken into account.

(B) $5,000,000 gross receipts test for first 3-year period

Subparagraph (A) shall be applied by substituting "$5,000,000" for "$7,500,000" for the first 3-taxable-year period (or portion thereof) of the corporation, which is taken into account under subparagraph (A).

(C) First taxable year corporation in existence

If such taxable year is the first taxable year that such corporation is in existence, the tentative minimum tax of such corporation for such year shall be zero.

(D) Special rules

For purposes of this paragraph, the rules of paragraphs (2) and (3) of section 448 (c) shall apply.

6. Corporate Deductions (5 Gradable Items)

1. Nondeductible. Organizational expenditures are those incurred incidental to the formation of the corporation but not those connected with issuing or selling stock or with transferring assets to the corporation. The cost of drafting the corporate charter is an organization expense. A corporation can elect to amortize its organization costs over at least 180 months, starting with the month in which it begins business. The election is made by simply taking the deduction. No election statement is required for expenditures after September 2008. No election was made (no deduction was claimed for 2012 and any year thereafter), and the capitalized expense cannot be deducted until the corporation is liquidated.

2. Fully Deductible. The amounts paid are compensation income to the executives and are ordinary and necessary deductible business expenses of the corporation to the extent they are reasonable.

3. Fully Deductible. An accrual-basis taxpayer may claim a deduction when (a) all events have occurred that establish the existence of the liability, and (b) the amount of the liability can be determined with reasonable accuracy. In addition, this all-events test will not be satisfied until economic performance has occurred. Since the liability is fixed (the right to the pay is vested), the amount has been determined, and the services have already been performed, the amount is fully deductible.
4. Fully Deductible. The state franchise tax liability is an ordinary and necessary business expense deductible by the corporation. The amount is fully deductible because the liability accrued during 2015 and was paid by an accrual-basis company.
5. Partially Deductible. Assuming that the entertainment meets the requirements for the associated-with test for entertainment, the cost is a business expense. However, Section 274(l)(2) limits the deduction of a skybox lease to the sum of the face amount of non-luxury box tickets for the number of seats in the skybox. No other cost of leasing a skybox is deductible. Furthermore, the deduction for entertainment expenses is limited to 50% of the otherwise allowed expenses [Sec. 274(n)].

Gleim Simulation Grading

Task	Correct Responses		Gradable Items		Score per Task
1	___	÷	5	=	___
2	___	÷	3	=	___
3	___	÷	6	=	___
4	___	÷	5	=	___
5 (Research)	___	÷	1	=	___
6	___	÷	5	=	___
			Total of Scores per Task		___
		÷	Total Number of Tasks		6
			Total Score		___ %

STUDY UNIT NINE
CORPORATE TAX SPECIAL TOPICS

(15 pages of outline)

This study unit addresses the federal income tax aspects of utilizing the corporate structure for investments. Develop an understanding of the fundamental general rules: nonrecognition on contributions by shareholders in the control group, recognition of gain on distributions of appreciated property by the corporation, shareholder dividend treatment of distributions to the extent of earnings and profits, and nonrecognition by parties to a reorganization.

9.1 FORMATION

1. **Overview**

   a. Without Sec. 351, any gain realized on the transfer of property to a corporation in exchange for stock of the corporation would be recognized.

EXAMPLE

A taxpayer transfers property with a basis of $10,000 and an FMV of $20,000 for a corporation's stock with an FMV of $20,000. The taxpayer realizes and recognizes a $10,000 gain ($20,00 FMV – $10,000 basis).

   b. Sec. 351 requires that no gain or loss be recognized if property is transferred to a corporation by one or more persons solely in exchange for stock in the corporation and, immediately after the exchange, such person or persons control the corporation. This nonrecognition treatment is mandatory, not elective.

2. **Sec. 351**

   a. **Control** is ownership of 80% or more of the voting power of stock and 80% or more of the shares of each class of nonvoting stock of the corporation.

      1) Stock exchanged for services is not counted toward the 80%.

         a) The FMV of the stock is gross income to the shareholder.
         b) The shareholder's basis in the stock exchanged for services is its FMV.

      2) Nonqualified preferred stock is treated as boot received and is not counted as stock toward the 80%-ownership test.

b. **Solely for stock.** To the extent the shareholder receives the corporation's stock in exchange for property, nonrecognition is required. This is so even if the shareholder receives some boot (money or other property) in the exchange.

   1) Disparate value. Inequality of FMV of the stock and property exchanged is not relevant in itself.

      a) The shareholder may have gross income if the disparity represents an (unstated) additional transaction, e.g., payment of compensation, a constructive dividend.

   2) Sec. 351 may apply to an exchange after formation.
   3) Sec. 351 can apply to contributions of property even if the corporation issues no stock in the exchange, e.g., a capital contribution by a sole shareholder who receives no stock in exchange for the contribution.
   4) Sec. 351 may also apply when the corporation exchanges treasury stock.

c. **Boot.** The shareholder recognizes gain realized to the extent of money and the FMV of other property (except the stock of the corporation) received in the exchange.

   1) FMV of property given up is used if FMV of property received cannot be ascertained.
   2) Character of the gain depends on the property contributed.
   3) No loss is recognized on the receipt of boot.

d. **Liabilities.** Sec. 351 applies even if the corporation assumes the shareholder's liability or takes property subject to a liability in the exchange.

   1) The amount of the liabilities is treated as recognized gain from the sale or exchange of an asset only to the extent it exceeds the AB of all property contributed by the shareholder.
   2) If tax avoidance was a purpose or if no business purpose was present for the assumption or transfer, the full amount of gain is recognized.

e. The corporation recognizes no gain on exchange of its stock for property (including money).

   1) Treasury stock is included.
   2) The corporation recognizes gain on exchanging other property (neither money nor its stock), even with a shareholder, unless an exception applies.

3. **Basis of Shareholder in Stock**

a. A control group shareholder's basis in the stock of the corporation is the adjusted basis in contributed property adjusted for the boot received and the gain recognized.

	AB in contributed property
–	Boot received
	Money, including
	Liability relief (corporation assumes or takes subject to)
	Property received FMV (other than above and the corporation's stock)
+	Gain recognized (by shareholder)
=	Basis in stock of issuing corporation

b. All liability is treated as boot when computing stock basis.

c. Holding period is generally tacked; i.e., the holding period of the property exchanged for stock is added to the holding period of the stock.

d. Sole proprietor. If a capital asset and other assets (e.g., Sec. 1231 property) are contributed when incorporating a business, each share received in the exchange has a split holding period.

4. **Basis of Shareholder in Boot**
   a. Boot generally has a basis equal to fair market value.
5. **Basis of Corporation in Property**
   a. The corporation's initial carryover basis in property exchanged by a control group shareholder for its stock is an adjusted carryover basis.

	AB in property to shareholder
+	Gain recognized by shareholder
=	Basis in property to corporation

   b. This basis also applies when the shareholder receives nothing in return.
   c. This basis is also the corporation's initial depreciable basis in the property.
      1) Allowable depreciation is apportioned based on the number of months the corporation owned the asset.
   d. Holding period is tacked.

Stop and review! You have completed the outline for this subunit. Study multiple-choice questions 1 through 5 beginning on page 347.

9.2 CURRENT EARNINGS AND PROFITS

1. **Definition**
   a. The term "earnings and profits (E&P)" is the federal tax accounting version of financial accounting's retained earnings. Though similar in purpose, they are not the same amount. E&P determines whether corporate distributions are taxable dividends.
      1) There are two types of E&P, current and accumulated. A corporation first determines its current E&P, which is the E&P for the current year. Then any excess current E&P after making distributions is added to the accumulated E&P balance, and any distributions in excess of current E&P reduce the accumulated E&P balance.

	Current E&P
–	Distributions
=	Increase (decrease) to accumulated E&P

2. **Calculation**
   a. Calculating current E&P starts with the current-year taxable income or loss and then makes various positive and negative adjustments.
      1) The positive adjustments include some exempt income, deductions, and deferred income. Examples include interest from municipal bonds, injury compensation, life insurance proceeds, DRD, capital and NOL carryover, depreciation in excess of straight-line, income per completed contract method, and deferred income from an installment sale.
      2) The negative adjustments include some nondeductible items for taxable income and recognized deferred income. Examples include life insurance premiums, penalties, fines, municipal bond expense, excessive compensation, federal income taxes, portion of meals and entertainment, and prior-year(s) installment sales.
      3) Transactions excluded from both E&P and taxable income do not require any adjustment. Examples include unrealized gains and losses, gifts, state tax refunds, and contributions to capital.

Stop and review! You have completed the outline for this subunit. Study multiple-choice question 6 on page 349.

9.3 DISTRIBUTIONS

1. **Definition**
   a. A **distribution** is any transfer of property by a corporation to any of its shareholders with respect to the shareholder's shares in the corporation. Property is defined as money, bonds or other obligations, stock in other corporations, and other property, including receivables.

2. **Distribution Amount**

   Money
   \+ Obligations (FMV), e.g., a bond
   \+ Property (FMV), other
   – Related liabilities, recourse or not
   = Distribution amount

3. **Corporate Treatment**
   a. A corporation is required to file a Form 1099-DIV no later than February 28 of the following year for each shareholder if the corporation did any of the following at the shareholder level:
      1) Paid gross dividends of $10 or more during the calendar year
      2) Withheld any federal income taxes under the backup withholding rules
      3) Made payments of $600 or more as part of a liquidation
   b. **Corporate loss unrecognized.** No loss realized on an ordinary distribution of property (AB > FMV) may be recognized. The shareholder takes a FMV basis in the property.
      1) Loss on a sale to a more-than-50% shareholder is not recognized.
         a) Stock owned by related parties is attributed to the shareholder.
         b) The shareholder takes a FMV basis in the property.
         c) Gain realized on a subsequent taxable disposition to an unrelated party is recognized only to the extent it exceeds the previously disallowed loss.
   c. **Corporate gain recognized.** Gain realized on distributed property must be recognized by the corporation as if the property were sold to the distributee at its FMV. But no gain is recognized to the corporation on distribution of money or obligations it issues, e.g., bonds.
      1) Liabilities. FMV is conclusively presumed to be no less than liabilities related to the property subject to which the shareholder assumes or takes the property, whether with recourse or not.
      2) The character of recognized gain is determined by treating the distribution as a sale to the shareholder.
         a) Gain recognized on depreciable property in the hands of a more-than-50% shareholder distributee is ordinary income.
      3) Earnings and profits (E&P). Recognized gains increase E&P. Tax on the gain reduces E&P.

4. **Shareholder Treatment**

The CPA exam has often contained questions regarding shareholder treatment of corporate distributions. A common question format has asked for the distribution amount that is taxable as dividend income to the shareholder.

a. **Dividend.** The amount of a distribution is a dividend to the extent, first, of any current E&P and then of any accumulated E&P (AE&P).

1) When distributions during the year exceed current E&P, pro rata portions of each distribution are deemed to be from current E&P.

   a) If the current E&P balance is positive, the positive balance is computed as of the close of the taxable year, without regard to the amount of E&P at the time of the distribution.

   b) If the current E&P balance is negative, prorate the negative balance to the date of each distribution made during the year.

2) Treatment of a distribution is determined by reference to AE&P only after any current E&P have been accounted for.

   a) AE&P constitute the remaining balance of E&P from prior tax years.

   b) Deficit in AE&P never results from a distribution. It results from any aggregate excess of current E&P deficits over unused positive AE&P. Deficit in AE&P does not offset current E&P.

   c) Current E&P are added to AE&P after determining treatment of distributions.

3) Distributions > AE&P. When distributions exceed both current E&P and AE&P, allocate AE&P to distributions in their chronological order.

4) Distributions from current E&P are first allocated to preferred stock, and any excess is then allocated to common stock.

EXAMPLE

Impartial, Inc., has a zero balance in AE&P but $25,000 in current E&P. Impartial makes a distribution of $20,000 to its preferred shareholders and a distribution of $10,000 to its common shareholders. The preferred shareholders will report the $20,000 as dividend income. The common shareholders will report $5,000 as dividend income and $5,000 as a return of capital.

5) To determine E&P from taxable income, adjustments similar to those used to reconcile income per books with taxable income must be made. For example, tax-exempt interest would be added to taxable income because, although it is excluded from gross income, it represents earnings available for distribution as dividends.

   a) Gain recognized on distribution of appreciated property increases E&P.

   b) E&P are determined at the end of the tax year.

      i) They are then reduced for money and the greater of FMV or AB of other property (net of liabilities) distributed during the year.

      ii) If E&P remain for the current year, they increase a positive AE&P balance or reduce a negative AE&P balance.

6) Constructive dividends are treated the same as other dividends.

   a) Constructive dividends are undeclared distributions to shareholders.

      i) Examples include the use of corporate vehicles or money borrowed from the corporation to purchase personal items.

   b) Like other dividends, constructive dividends may not be deducted by the company, creating double taxation of that income (corporate level and shareholder level).

b. **Capital recovery.** A shareholder treats the amount of a distribution in excess of dividends as tax-exempt return of capital to the extent of his or her basis.

1) Basis in the stock is reduced (but not below zero).
2) Apportion the distribution among the shares if they have different bases.

EXAMPLE

Corporation distributes $90,000 when E&P are $60,000. Shareholder N receives $30,000 of the distribution, of which $20,000 is a dividend (2/3).

	# of Shares	Basis	Dividend	Capital Recovery	Gain
Block 1	1,000	$ 3,000	$10,000	$3,000	$2,000
Block 2	1,000	$15,000	$10,000	$5,000	0

c. **Gain on sale.** Any excess of the amount of a distribution over E&P and basis is treated as gain on the sale of the stock (e.g., the $2,000 in the example above).

1) Character of the gain is determined by the nature of the property in the hands of the shareholder (e.g., a capital asset or dealer property).

2) Loss may be recognized only if the stock becomes worthless or is redeemed.

d. **Basis in distributed property.** The shareholder's basis in property received in a nonliquidating distribution is generally its FMV at the time of the distribution.

1) The FMV is used for obligations of the distributing corporation.
2) If liabilities assumed or liabilities of property taken are

a) < FMV, then the shareholder's basis in the property is its FMV
b) > FMV and the distributee shareholder assumes personal liability, then the shareholder's basis should equal the liability

5. **Extraordinary Dividend**

a. Additional gain may be recognized by a shareholder who sells stock on which an extraordinary dividend was received.

b. An extraordinary dividend is a dividend on stock held 2 years or less that exceeds 10% (5% for preferred stock) of either the basis or the FMV of the stock.

c. Basis in the stock is reduced by the nontaxed portion of the extraordinary dividend, i.e., the amount of a DRD (dividends-received deduction).

d. If the nontaxed portion of the dividend exceeds the stock's basis, the excess is treated as a gain from the sale or exchange of such stock in the year the extraordinary dividend is received.

6. **Stock Distributions**

a. A corporation recognizes no gain or loss on distribution of its own stock. Generally, a shareholder does not include a distribution of stock or rights to acquire stock in gross income unless it is a

1) Distribution in lieu of money (treated as a dividend)
2) Disproportionate distribution
3) Distribution of preferred stock
4) Distribution of convertible preferred stock
5) Distribution of common and preferred stock, resulting in receipt of preferred stock by some shareholders and common stock by other shareholders

b. A **proportionate distribution** of stock issued by the corporation is generally not gross income to the shareholders.

1) A shareholder allocates the aggregate basis (AB) in the old stock to the old stock and new stock in proportion to the FMV of the old and new stock.

a) Basis is apportioned by relative FMV to different classes of stock if applicable.

2) The holding period of the distributed stock includes that of the old stock.
3) E&P are not altered for a tax-free stock dividend.

c. **Stock rights.** Treat a distribution of stock rights as a distribution of the stock.

1) Basis is allocated based on the FMV of the rights.

a) Basis in the stock rights is zero if their aggregate FMV is less than 15% of the FMV of the stock on which they were distributed, unless the shareholder elects to allocate.

2) Basis in the stock, if the right is exercised, is any basis allocated to the right, plus the exercise price.

3) Holding period of the stock begins on the exercise date.

4) No deduction is allowed for basis allocated to stock rights that lapse. Basis otherwise allocated remains in the underlying stock.

7. **Taxable Stock Distribution**

a. Distributions of stock described in 1) through 6) below are subject to tax. Unless otherwise stated in 1) through 6) below, the amount of a distribution subject to tax is the FMV of distributed stock or stock rights.

1) Any shareholder has an option to choose between a distribution of stock or a distribution of other property. The amount of the distribution is the greater of

a) The FMV of stock or

b) The cash or FMV of other property.

2) Some shareholders receive property, and other shareholders receive an increase in their proportionate interests.

3) Some common shareholders receive common stock; others receive preferred stock.

4) Distribution is on preferred stock.

5) Convertible preferred stock is distributed, and the effect is to change the shareholder's proportionate stock ownership.

6) Constructive stock distributions change proportionate interests resulting from, e.g., a change in conversion ratio or redemption price.

b. E&P are reduced by the FMV of stock and stock rights distributed.

c. Basis in the underlying stock does not change. Basis in the new stock or stock rights is their FMV.

d. Holding period for the new stock begins on the day after the distribution date.

e. If a distribution of a stock dividend or stock right is taxable when received, the basis is the FMV on the date of acquisition.

1) When the dividend is taxable, there is no tacking on of the holding period for the underlying stock.

2) The holding period begins the day following the acquisition date.

8. **Stock Split**

a. A stock split is not a distribution.

b. Basis in the old stock is also "split" and allocated to the new stock.

c. Holding period of the new stock includes that of the old stock.

Stop and review! You have completed the outline for this subunit. Study multiple-choice questions 7 through 13 beginning on page 349.

9.4 REDEMPTIONS

1. **Overview**
   a. Stock is redeemed when a corporation acquires its own stock from a shareholder in exchange for property, regardless of redeemed stock being canceled, retired, or held as treasury stock.
   b. A shareholder is required to treat amounts realized on a redemption (not in liquidation) either as a distribution (a corporate dividend) or as a sale of stock redeemed.
2. **Dividend or Sale Treatment**
   a. Redemptions of stock by a corporation are treated as dividends unless certain conditions are met. If any of the following conditions are met, the exchange is treated as a sale, and the gains or losses are capital gains and losses.
      1) The redemption is not essentially equivalent to a dividend.
      2) The redemption is substantially disproportionate.
      3) The distribution is in complete redemption of all of a shareholder's stock.
      4) The distribution is to a noncorporate shareholder in partial liquidation.
      5) The distribution is received by an estate.
3. **Gain Recognition**
   a. A **corporation** recognizes gain realized on a distribution
      1) As if the property distributed were sold at FMV to the distributee immediately prior to the distribution
      2) Even if stock is redeemed by the distribution
4. **Loss Recognition**
   a. No recognition of loss realized is allowed by the corporation, unless the redemption is
      1) In complete liquidation of the corporation or
      2) Of stock held by an estate (to pay death taxes).
5. **Recognition of Depreciated Property Distribution**
   a. A corporation recognizes ordinary income on the distribution of depreciated property to the extent of depreciation or amount realized, whichever is less.
6. **Shareholder Treatment**
   a. A **shareholder** treats a redemption in the same manner as a regular distribution. The amount is a dividend to the extent of E&P. Any unrecovered basis in the redeemed stock is added to the shareholder's basis in stock retained.
7. **Stock Reacquisition**
   a. The expenses incurred in connection with any reacquisition by a corporation of its own stock or the stock of a related person (50% relationship test) are not deductible. An exception exists for any cost allocable to an indebtedness and amortized over the life of the indebtedness (e.g., financial advisory costs).
8. **Sale Treatment**
   a. The shareholder treats qualifying redemptions as if the shares redeemed were sold to a third party.
   b. Gain or loss is any spread between AB of the shares and the FMV of property received.
   c. Character of gain or loss depends on the nature of the stock in the shareholder's hands.
   d. Basis in distributed property is its FMV.
   e. Holding period for the property starts the day after the redemption exchange.

f. This treatment applies only to redemptions that
   1) Terminate a shareholder's interest
   2) Are substantially disproportionate between shareholders
   3) Are not essentially equivalent to a dividend
   4) Are received by an estate
   5) Are from a shareholder, other than a corporation, in partial liquidation

g. Treatment of a redemption as a sale is determined separately for each shareholder.

9. **Termination of Interest**

a. Termination of a shareholder's interest must be complete to qualify. All the corporation's stock owned by the shareholder must be redeemed in the exchange for the property.
   1) Family attribution rules apply but may be waived if the following three requirements are met:
      a) The shareholder may not retain any interest, except as a creditor, in the corporation.
      b) The shareholder may not acquire any interest, except by bequest or inheritance, for 10 years.
      c) A written agreement must be filed with the IRS stating that the IRS will be notified if a prohibited interest is acquired.

10. **Substantially Disproportionate**

a. Substantially disproportionate means that the amount received by shareholders is not in the same proportion as their stock holdings.

b. It is tested by determining the shareholders' applicable ownership percentages (including constructive ownership) both before and after redemption.

c. A redemption is substantially disproportionate with respect to a shareholder if, immediately after the redemption, the shareholder owns
   1) Less than 50% of the voting power of outstanding stock and
   2) Less than 80% each of the interest in the
      a) Voting stock owned before the redemption
      b) Common stock owned before the redemption

11. **Equivalency to a Dividend**

a. Not essentially equivalent to a dividend means that there is a meaningful reduction in the shareholder's proportionate interest in the corporation. Reduction in voting power is generally required for a redemption.

12. **Estate**

a. An estate may treat a qualifying redemption (e.g., to pay death taxes) as a sale.
   1) Redeemed stock must be valued at more than 35% of the gross estate net of deductions allowed.
   2) Deductions allowed are administration expenses, funeral expenses, claims against the estate (including death taxes), and unpaid mortgages.

13. **Partial Liquidations**

a. Partial liquidations are one type of redemption.

14. **Constructive Ownership**

a. The (redeemed) shareholder is treated as owning shares owned by certain related parties, e.g., family members (excluding siblings and grandparents).

Stop and review! You have completed the outline for this subunit. Study multiple-choice questions 14 through 16 on page 352.

9.5 COMPLETE LIQUIDATION

1. **Defined**
   a. Under a plan of complete liquidation, a corporation redeems all of its stock in a series of distributions.
2. **Corporate Gains**
   a. A corporation recognizes any gain or loss realized on distributions in complete liquidation as if the property were sold at its FMV to the shareholder immediately before its distribution.
   b. Gain or loss is computed on an asset-by-asset basis.
   c. FMV of distributed property is treated as not less than related liabilities that the shareholder assumes or to which the property is subject.
   d. Character of amounts recognized depends on the nature of the asset in the hands of the distributing corporation, e.g., Secs. 1245 and 1250.
3. **Corporate Losses**
   a. A corporation generally recognizes any losses realized on liquidating distributions.
   b. Certain realized losses are not recognized when the distributee shareholder is related to the corporation. A more-than-50% shareholder, actually or constructively, is a typical related distributee.
      1) Applicable distributions are of assets non-pro rata or acquired within 5 years by a contribution to capital or a Sec. 351 exchange.
      2) Permanent disallowance results, even if post-contribution.
   c. Precontribution loss. The amount of a loss inherent on a contribution reduces loss recognized on distribution.
      1) Applicable dispositions are of assets a liquidating corporation distributes, sells, or exchanges that were acquired by a contribution to capital or by a Sec. 351 exchange when its AB exceeded FMV for the principal purpose of recognizing the loss on liquidation.
      2) The loss limit operates by requiring that basis for computing the amount of loss be reduced by loss inherent on contribution.
   d. Carryovers. Unused, unexpired NOLs, capital losses, and charitable contribution carryover amounts are lost.
4. **Shareholder Treatment**
   a. A shareholder treats amounts distributed in complete liquidation as realized in exchange for stock.
   b. Capital recovery to the extent of basis is permitted before recognizing gain or loss.
   c. Holding period will not include that of the liquidated corporation.
   d. Amounts realized include money and the FMV of other distributed property received.
      1) Liabilities to which property is subject reduce the amount realized.
      2) Allocation of amounts realized to each block of stock is required.

EXAMPLE

Consider a single liquidating distribution to Shareholder S on February 1, 2015, of $70 cash and a car (FMV – $25) subject to a liability of $15. S's amount realized is $80 [$70 + ($25 – $15)].

Block	Shares	Acquired	Basis	Amount Realized	Gain (Loss) Realized
A	1	5/12	$10	$20	$ 10
B	3	10/13	90	60	(30)

e. Character of recognized gain or loss depends on the nature of each block of the stock in the hands of the shareholder.

EXAMPLE

If S in the previous example held the stock for investment, S would recognize LTCG on Block A and STCL on Block B.

f. Basis in distributed property is its FMV, but only after gain or loss on its receipt has been recognized.

5. **Reporting**

   a. A corporation must file an information return (Form 966, *Corporation Dissolution or Liquidation*) reporting adoption of a plan or resolution for its dissolution, or partial or complete liquidation, within 30 days of adoption.

      1) The IRS requires a corporation to file Form 1099-DIV for each calendar year it makes partial distribution(s) of $600 or more under a plan of complete liquidation.
      2) Liquidation expenses incurred are deductible by the dissolved corporation.

Stop and review! You have completed the outline for this subunit. Study multiple-choice questions 17 through 19 on page 353.

9.6 PARTIAL LIQUIDATION

1. **Noncorporate Shareholder**

   a. A noncorporate shareholder treats a distribution as a sale to the extent it is (in redemption) in partial liquidation of the corporation.

2. **Corporate Distributor**

   a. The corporation making the distribution recognizes gain but not loss.

3. **Corporate Distributee**

   a. A corporation that receives a distribution in redemption for partial liquidation of another corporation treats the distribution as a dividend to the extent of E&P of the distributing corporation. The distributee corporation is eligible for the dividends received deduction.

4. **Contraction of the Corporation**

   a. Partial liquidation refers to contraction of the corporation. Focus is not on the shareholders but on genuine reduction in size of the corporation.
   b. Partial liquidation must be pursuant to a plan. The partial liquidation must be complete within either the tax year of plan adoption or the succeeding tax year.
   c. Pro rata distributions do not preclude partial liquidation sale treatment, and shareholders are not required to surrender stock to the corporation.
   d. Safe harbor. Noncorporate shareholders apply partial liquidation sale treatment to distributions received if the following conditions are satisfied:

      1) The distribution is attributable to the corporation ceasing to conduct a trade or business that it actively conducted for at least 5 years ending with the date of the distribution.
      2) Immediately after the distribution, the corporation continues to conduct at least one active trade or business it has conducted for 5 years.

Stop and review! You have completed the outline for this subunit. Study multiple-choice questions 20 and 21 beginning on page 353.

9.7 SUBSIDIARY LIQUIDATION

1. **Nonrecognition**
   a. Neither the parent corporation nor a controlled subsidiary recognizes gain or loss on a liquidating distribution to the parent.
2. **Control**
   a. Control means the parent owns 80% or more of both the voting power and total value of the stock of the liquidating corporation.
3. **Basis**
   a. Basis in property distributed to the parent is transferred to the parent, and basis in stock in the subsidiary disappears.
4. **Liabilities**
   a. No gain is recognized on distributions that satisfy obligations of the subsidiary to the parent.
5. **Tax Attributes**
   a. Tax attributes of the subsidiary, such as NOLs and capital losses, carry over to the parent. Holding period will include that of the subsidiary.
6. **Minority Shareholders**
   a. Complete liquidation rules apply to distributions made to shareholders other than the parent. The subsidiary recognizes gain but not losses. The shareholder recognizes gain or loss and takes FMV basis in the property.

Stop and review! You have completed the outline for this subunit. Study multiple-choice questions 22 and 23 on page 354.

9.8 REORGANIZATIONS

1. **Overview**
   a. For federal tax purposes, a qualified reorganization of one or more corporations is considered a mere change in form of investment rather than a disposition of assets. For this reason, a general rule of nonrecognition applies to qualifying reorganizations. However, gain is recognized to the extent of boot.
2. **Shareholders**
   a. In a reorganization, a shareholder recognizes no gain or loss on an exchange of stock or securities solely for stock or securities in the same or another corporation that is a party to the reorganization.
   b. Boot. Gain on nonqualifying property (generally, property other than stock or securities in a corporation that is a party to the reorganization) is recognized.
      1) Amount recognized is the lesser of gain realized or FMV of nonqualifying property.
      2) Securities received when none are surrendered are nonqualifying property.
         a) The FMV of any excess of face value received over that given up is boot.
      3) Character. The shareholder is deemed to have received only stock and then to have redeemed the stock for cash.
         a) Gain is treated as a dividend (OI) to the extent of E&P, if the exchange has the effect of a dividend distribution.
   c. Loss. No loss is recognized.
   d. Basis in stock or qualified securities received is exchanged.
      1) Basis in boot is (tax) cost.

3. **Transferor Corporation (Acquired or Purchased)**
   a. A corporation that is a party to a reorganization generally recognizes no gain or loss on exchange of property solely for stock or securities of another corporate party.
   b. Gain is recognized only on boot not distributed (by the transferee). Liability relief is not boot unless it was for a nonbusiness or tax-avoidance purpose.
   c. The transferor (acquired) corporation recognizes gain realized if it distributes property other than stock or securities of another corporate party.
      1) The amount of liability in excess of basis is treated as the FMV of the property.
      2) No loss is recognized unless distribution is to a creditor.
   d. The transferor (acquired) corporation, finally, recognizes no gain or loss on distribution (even if the distribution is to a creditor) of
      1) Stock or securities it received from a party to the reorganization
      2) Boot received, except for post-acquisition gain realized
4. **Transferee Corporation (Acquiring or Purchasing)**
   a. The transferee corporation recognizes gain only on appreciated property (but not its own stock or securities) exchanged.
   b. Basis in property acquired from the transferor is transferred, i.e., the basis of the property
      1) In the hands of the transferor corporation, plus
      2) Gain recognized by the transferor corporation.
5. **Reorganization Types**
   a. Nonrecognition treatment applies only if the change in corporate structure fits within the definition of one of the following specific reorganization types.

The CPA exam has required candidates to determine from a series of facts whether a qualified reorganization has occurred. It also has tested candidates on the basic characteristics of the types of reorganizations.

      1) Type A: Statutory merger or consolidation. Under state law, two corporations merge into one. Stock in the non-surviving corporation is canceled. In exchange, its shareholders receive stock in the surviving corporation.
         a) Merger. One of the corporations remains, while the other is no longer in existence.
         b) Consolidation. Existing corporations are combined into a newly formed corporation.
      2) Type B: Stock-for-stock. Shareholders acquire stock of a corporation solely for part or all of the voting stock of the acquiring corporation or its parent.
         a) No boot is allowed.
         b) The acquiring corporation must control the acquired corporation after the exchange; i.e., it must own 80% of the stock (voting and all other).
      3) Type C: Stock-for-assets. One corporation acquires substantially all the assets of another in exchange for its voting stock (or its parent's). The transferor (sale of assets) corporation must liquidate.
         a) Only 20% of the assets acquired may be exchanged for other than voting stock of the acquiring corporation. Limited amounts of boot are thus allowable.
         b) "Substantially all assets" means ≥ 90% of the FMV of net assets and ≥ 70% of gross assets.

4) Type D: Division
   a) A corporation transfers all or part of its assets to another in exchange for the other's stock.
   b) The transferor or its shareholders must control the transferee after the exchange. Control means owning 80% of voting power and 80% of each class of nonvoting stock.
   c) The stock or securities of the controlled corporation must be distributed to shareholders of the corporation that transferred assets to the controlled corporation.
   d) Distribution of the stock need not be pro rata among the shareholders of the corporation that transferred assets to the controlled corporation. Thus, division of the original corporation may result.
5) Type E: Recapitalization. The capital structure of the corporation is modified by exchanges of stock and securities between the corporation and its shareholders.
6) Type F: Reincorporation. Stock and securities are exchanged upon a mere change in the name, form, or place of incorporation.
7) Type G: Bankruptcy reorganization. Stock, securities, and property are exchanged pursuant to a court-supervised bankruptcy proceeding.

6. **Nonrecognition Requirements**
   a. Nonrecognition applies only to the extent each of several statutory and judicially sourced requirements are met.
      1) The reorganization must be pursuant to a plan, a copy of which is filed with the return of each participating corporation.
      2) Nonrecognition treatment applies only with respect to distributions in exchange for stock or securities of a corporation that is a party to the reorganization.
      3) Business purpose, other than tax avoidance, must be present.
      4) Owners of the reorganized enterprise(s) must retain an interest in the continuing enterprise. At least 40% continuity of equity interest by value is a benchmark.
      5) Continuity of business enterprise. The acquiring corporation must continue either operating the historic business of the acquired corporation or using a significant portion of the acquired corporation's historic business assets. Continuing a significant line of business is sufficient if there was more than one.

Stop and review! You have completed the outline for this subunit. Study multiple-choice questions 24 through 28 beginning on page 355.

9.9 PROCEDURE

1. **Return Due Date**
   a. A corporation must file a return (postmarked) no later than the 15th day of the 3rd month after the close of its tax year (March 15 for a calendar-year corporation). An automatic extension of 6 months is provided to a corporation that files Form 7004 and pays its estimated tax liability on or before the initial due date.
2. **Termination**
   a. A corporation that has no taxable income in the current year and has ceased doing business, dissolved, and retained no assets does not exist for federal tax purposes, without regard to state law. A final tax return should be filed; thereafter, no return is required.

3. **Liability Payment and Penalties**
   a. Tax liability must be paid when the return is due, disregarding extensions.
   b. Penalties are imposed for not filing or paying when and as required.
      1) Failure-to-file penalty is 5% of the tax for each month or fraction of a month the failure continues, up to a maximum of 25%.
      2) Failure-to-pay penalty is 1/2% of the tax for each month or fraction of a month the failure continues. The failure-to-file penalty is reduced by the failure-to-pay penalty if both apply.
      3) Interest is also charged on underpayments of tax and penalties.
4. **Closed Cases**
   a. Cases closed after examination will not be reopened to make adjustments unfavorable to the taxpayer except under certain circumstances. Qualifying circumstances include evidence of fraud, malfeasance, collusion, concealment, or misrepresentation of a material fact.

Stop and review! You have completed the outline for this subunit. Study multiple-choice questions 29 and 30 on page 356.

QUESTIONS

9.1 Formation

1. Ames and Roth form Homerun, a C corporation. Ames contributes several autographed baseballs to Homerun. Ames purchased the baseballs for $500, and they have a total fair market value of $1,000. Roth contributes several autographed baseball bats to Homerun. Roth purchased the bats for $5,000, and they have a fair market value of $7,000. What is Homerun's basis in the contributed bats and balls?

A. $0

B. $5,500

C. $6,000

D. $8,000

Answer (B) is correct.

REQUIRED: Basis in property contributed to a corporation.

DISCUSSION: The basis of property acquired by a corporation in connection with a Sec. 351 transaction is the same as the basis in the hands of the transferor (shareholder), increased by the amount of gain recognized by the transferor on such transfer. Since neither shareholder received any boot, no gain was recognized. Thus, the corporation's total basis in the transferred assets is the same as that in the shareholder's hands, or $5,500 ($500 + $5,000).

Answer (A) is incorrect. The basis of property acquired by a corporation in connection with a Sec. 351 transaction is the same as the basis in the hands of the transferor (shareholder), increased by the amount of gain recognized by the transferor on such transfer. Answer (C) is incorrect. The $6,000 takes a basis equal to the fair market value of Ames's contribution and the adjusted basis of Roth's contribution. The basis of property acquired by a corporation in connection with a Sec. 351 transaction is the same as the basis in the hands of the transferor (shareholder), increased by the amount of gain recognized by the transferor on such transfer. Answer (D) is incorrect. A basis of $8,000 is equal to the fair market value of each of the contributions. The basis of property acquired by a corporation in connection with a Sec. 351 transaction is the same as the basis in the hands of the transferor (shareholder), increased by the amount of gain recognized by the transferor on such transfer.

2. On July 1 of the current year, Rich, sole proprietor of Kee Nail, transferred all of Kee's assets to Merit, Inc., a new corporation, solely for a certain percentage of Merit's stock. Dee, who is not related to Rich, also bought some of Merit's stock on July 1. Merit's outstanding capital stock consisted of 1,000 shares of common stock with a par value of $100 per share. For the transfer of Kee Nail's assets to be tax-free, what is the minimum number of shares of Merit's stock that must be owned by Rich and Dee immediately after the exchange?

A. 500

B. 501

C. 800

D. 801

Answer (C) is correct.

REQUIRED: The minimum number of shares of stock that must be owned by two transferors immediately after the exchange for the transfer to be tax-free.

DISCUSSION: A transfer of assets for stock of a corporation is tax-free if the transferors are in control of the corporation immediately after the exchange. A person who transfers appreciated property will receive the benefit if another transferor transfers property and together they meet the control test. Property includes money. Control is ownership of stock possessing at least 80% of the total combined voting power of all classes of stock entitled to vote and at least 80% of the total number of shares of all other classes of stock of the corporation. At a minimum, Rich and Dee must own 800 shares (1,000 shares × 80%).

Answer (A) is incorrect. The number 500 results from multiplying the 1,000 shares of common stock by 50%. Answer (B) is incorrect. The number 501 results from a greater than 50% ownership. Transferors must own a minimum of 80% of the common shares. Answer (D) is incorrect. A total of 801 shares is greater than the 80% minimum number of shares of ownership to receive tax-free treatment.

3. In April, A and B formed X Corp. A contributed $50,000 cash, and B contributed land worth $70,000 (with an adjusted basis of $40,000). B also received $20,000 cash from the corporation. A and B each receive 50% of the corporation's stock. What is the tax basis of the land to X Corp.?

A. $40,000

B. $50,000

C. $60,000

D. $70,000

Answer (C) is correct.

REQUIRED: Tax basis of land transferred to X Corporation.

DISCUSSION: The basis of land to X corporation is the adjusted basis to B ($40,000) increased by B's recognized gain ($20,000). B's realized gain is $30,000. Recognized gain is the lesser of boot received ($20,000) and realized gain.

Answer (A) is incorrect. A $40,000 basis would be the applicable tax basis to X Corp. if B did not recognize any gain on the transfer. Answer (B) is incorrect. Neither the use of the FMV of the property nor a reduction equal to the boot received is how X Corp. calculates the basis of the land ($50,000 is the FMV of the property transferred to X Corp. reduced by the boot received by B). Answer (D) is incorrect. The inclusion of gain realized in the basis of the land is limited to the boot received by B.

4. Adams, Beck, and Carr organized Flexo Corp. with authorized voting common stock of $100,000. Adams received 10% of the capital stock in payment for the organizational services that he rendered for the benefit of the newly formed corporation. Adams did not contribute property to Flexo and was under no obligation to be paid by Beck or Carr. Beck and Carr transferred property in exchange for stock as follows:

	Adjusted Basis	Fair Market Value	Percentage of Flexo Stock Acquired
Beck	$ 5,000	$20,000	20%
Carr	60,000	70,000	70%

What amount of gain did Carr recognize from this transaction?

A. $40,000

B. $15,000

C. $10,000

D. $0

Answer (D) is correct.

REQUIRED: The gain recognized on the transfer of property to a corporation in exchange for stock.

DISCUSSION: This formation qualifies as a nonrecognition-of-gain transaction under Sec. 351. The control requirement is satisfied since Beck and Carr have ownership of at least 80% of the stock. Since Carr did not receive any boot property, (s)he will not recognize gain from this transaction.

Answer (A) is incorrect. An amount of $40,000 results from subtracting Carr's adjusted basis of $60,000 from the authorized voting common stock of $100,000. Answer (B) is incorrect. An amount of $15,000 results from subtracting Beck's adjusted basis of $5,000 from Beck's fair market value of property of $20,000. The question refers to Carr's recognized gain. Answer (C) is incorrect. An amount of $10,000 is the difference in the adjusted basis and the fair market value of the property exchanged by Carr.

5. Clark and Hunt organized Jet Corp. with authorized voting common stock of $400,000. Clark contributed $60,000 cash. Both Clark and Hunt transferred other property in exchange for Jet stock as follows:

	Other Property		
	Adjusted Basis	Fair Market Value	Percentage of Jet Stock Acquired
Clark	$ 50,000	$100,000	40%
Hunt	120,000	240,000	60%

What was Clark's basis in Jet stock?

A. $0

B. $100,000

C. $110,000

D. $160,000

Answer (C) is correct.

REQUIRED: The shareholder basis in a corporate formation.

DISCUSSION: This series of exchanges is presumed to qualify for nonrecognition treatment under Sec. 351 as the contributors, immediately after the exchange, are in control of the corporation. Therefore, Clark's basis in stock will be the value of cash transferred ($60,000) plus the adjusted basis of the other property ($50,000), or $110,000.

Answer (A) is incorrect. Clark has transferred value to the corporation. Answer (B) is incorrect. The cash transferred, plus the adjusted basis of the property, determines the stock basis. Answer (D) is incorrect. The exchange of property for stock qualifies for nonrecognition treatment.

9.2 Current Earnings and Profits

6. What is the current earnings and profits (E&P) of a corporation with taxable income of $10,000 that included the following unadjusted items:

Meals and entertainment	$ 200
Capital loss carried over from prior year	3,000

A. $7,100

B. $10,000

C. $12,800

D. $12,900

Answer (D) is correct.

REQUIRED: The current E&P of the corporation.

DISCUSSION: Current E&P is the current-year taxable income adjusted for specific items. Positive adjustments include loss carryovers, as they were negative adjustments in the year they occurred. Negative adjustments include the nondeductible portion of meals and entertainment. Corporations are allowed to deduct 50% of qualifying meals and entertainment expenses. The corporation's current E&P is $12,900 [$10,000 + $3,000 – ($200 × 50%)].

Answer (A) is incorrect. The loss carryover is a positive adjustment, and the excess portion of deductible meals and entertainment is a negative adjustment. Answer (B) is incorrect. Taxable income is only the starting point for calculating current E&P. Both positive and negative adjustments must be made in order to arrive at current E&P. Answer (C) is incorrect. Only the nondeductible portion of meals and entertainment for taxable income is adjusted for current E&P.

9.3 Distributions

7. Nyle Corp. owned 100 shares of Beta Corp. stock that it bought 16 years ago for $9 per share. This year, when the fair market value of the Beta stock was $20 per share, Nyle distributed this stock to a noncorporate shareholder. Nyle's recognized gain on this distribution was

A. $2,000

B. $1,100

C. $900

D. $0

Answer (B) is correct.

REQUIRED: The amount of gain recognized by a corporation on distribution of stock.

DISCUSSION: A corporation must recognize gain realized on distributions of property. The definition of property excludes stock, but only if issued by the corporation. Thus, Nyle Corp. must recognize gain of $1,100 ($2,000 FMV – $900 basis).

Answer (A) is incorrect. The FMV of the stock is $2,000. Answer (C) is incorrect. The basis of the stock is $900. Answer (D) is incorrect. A corporation recognizes gain or loss on distribution of stock that is not issued by the corporation.

8. Fox, the sole shareholder in Fall, a C corporation, has a tax basis of $60,000. Fall has $40,000 of accumulated positive earnings and profits at the beginning of the year and $10,000 of current positive earnings and profits for the current year. At year end, Fall distributed land with an adjusted basis of $30,000 and a fair market value (FMV) of $38,000 to Fox. The land has an outstanding mortgage of $3,000 that Fox must assume. What is Fox's tax basis in the land?

A. $38,000

B. $35,000

C. $30,000

D. $27,000

Answer (A) is correct.

REQUIRED: Shareholder basis of property received in a nonliquidating distribution.

DISCUSSION: In a nonliquidating distribution, the shareholder's basis in property received is the FMV at the date of distribution. If the shareholder also assumes a liability with the property distribution, it must be compared to the property's FMV. In the event the liability exceeds the FMV, the liability is the shareholder's basis in the property. If the liability is less, as this situation indicates ($3,000 < $38,000), the basis will remain equal to the FMV.

Answer (B) is incorrect. The property's FMV is not reduced by the liability assumed. If the liability exceeds the FMV of the property assumed, the liability is the basis. Otherwise, it does not affect basis. Answer (C) is incorrect. The shareholder's basis in the property distribution is equal to the FMV at the date of distribution, not the adjusted basis under the corporation. Answer (D) is incorrect. The beginning amount for the shareholder's basis is not the corporation's adjusted basis. The FMV at the time of distribution is the shareholder's basis. Additionally, there is no adjustment for a liability assumed by the shareholder unless the liability exceeds the FMV of the property.

9. Lincoln Corp., a calendar-year C corporation, made a nonliquidating cash distribution of $1.5 million to its shareholders with respect to its stock. At that time, Lincoln's current and accumulated earnings and profits totaled $825,000, and its total paid-in capital for tax purposes was $10 million. Lincoln had no corporate shareholders. Which of the following statements, if any, are true regarding Lincoln's cash distribution?

I. The distribution was taxable as $1.5 million in dividends to its shareholders.

II. The distribution reduced its shareholders' adjusted bases in Lincoln stock by $675,000.

A. I only.

B. II only.

C. Both I and II.

D. Neither I nor II.

Answer (B) is correct.

REQUIRED: The true statements, if any, regarding a corporation's cash distribution.

DISCUSSION: In general, any distribution of money or property made by a corporation to its shareholders with respect to their stock out of the corporation's earnings and profits is treated as a taxable dividend. The current and accumulated earnings and profits therefore determine the level of taxability. The dividend will equal $825,000. The remaining distribution of $675,000 will reduce the adjusted bases of shareholders' stock, as it is treated as a return of capital. Therefore, only Statement II is correct.

10. On January 1, Year 1, Kee Corp., a C corporation, had a $50,000 deficit in E&P. For Year 1, Kee had current E&P of $10,000 and made a $30,000 cash distribution to its shareholders. What amount of the distribution is taxable as dividend income to Kee's shareholders?

A. $30,000

B. $20,000

C. $10,000

D. $0

Answer (C) is correct.

REQUIRED: The amount of the distribution taxable as dividend income to the shareholders.

DISCUSSION: Treatment of a distribution is determined by reference to accumulated E&P only after any current E&P have been accounted for. To the extent current E&P are sufficient to cover a distribution, the distribution is treated as a taxable dividend, even if there is a deficit in the accumulated E&P. Thus, the current E&P of $10,000 results in ordinary dividend income to Kee's shareholders of $10,000.

Answer (A) is incorrect. The amount treated as ordinary dividend income cannot exceed the amount of positive current and accumulated E&P. Answer (B) is incorrect. It exceeds current and accumulated E&P. Answer (D) is incorrect. Distributions are treated as coming out of current E&P first without regard to accumulated E&P.

11. Webster, a C corporation, has $70,000 in accumulated and no current earnings and profits. Webster distributed $20,000 cash and property with an adjusted basis and fair market value of $60,000 to its shareholders. What amount should the shareholders report as dividend income?

A. $20,000

B. $60,000

C. $70,000

D. $80,000

Answer (C) is correct.

REQUIRED: Calculation of dividend income.

DISCUSSION: A corporate distribution is a dividend that must be included in the recipient's gross income to the extent it comes from current or accumulated earnings and profits (E&P). To the extent the distribution exceeds current and accumulated E&P, it is treated as a return of capital to the shareholder. The total distribution is equal to the fair market value of the items distributed, or $80,000 ($20,000 + $60,000). Since Webster had only $70,000 of E&P, the distribution will be taxed as a dividend only to that extent. The remaining $10,000 ($80,000 total distribution – $70,000) will be treated as a return of capital or capital gain.

Answer (A) is incorrect. The $20,000 ignores the property distribution of $60,000. Distributions are treated as a dividend to the extent of E&P. Because the total distribution of $80,000 ($20,000 cash + $60,000 property) exceeds E&P, the excess is treated as a return of capital or capital gains. Answer (B) is incorrect. Distributions are treated as a dividend to the extent of E&P. The $60,000 dividend income ignores the $20,000 cash distribution. Answer (D) is incorrect. The $10,000 ($80,000 total distribution – $70,000) excess over E&P is treated either as a capital recovery or a capital gain.

12. Brisk Corp. is an accrual-basis, calendar-year C corporation with one individual shareholder. At year end, Brisk had $600,000 accumulated and current earnings and profits as it prepared to make its only dividend distribution for the year to its shareholder. Brisk could distribute either cash of $200,000 or land with an adjusted tax basis of $75,000 and a fair market value of $200,000. How would the taxable incomes of both Brisk and the shareholder change if land were distributed instead of cash?

	Brisk's taxable income	Shareholder's taxable income
A.	No change	No change
B.	Increase	No change
C.	No change	Decrease
D.	Increase	Decrease

Answer (B) is correct.

REQUIRED: Effect of a property distribution on a corporation's and shareholder's taxable income.

DISCUSSION: The shareholder will include the cash or the FMV of the property in their income regardless of the two distributions. Each will also be dividend income because Brisk has sufficient E&P. Brisk's taxable income will increase, based on the gain from the property's excess FMV over its adjusted basis.

Answer (A) is incorrect. Even though the shareholder's taxable income will not change based on the cash or property distribution, Brisk's taxable income will increase as a result of the property distribution gain. Answer (C) is incorrect. Brisk's taxable income should increase as a result of the property distribution, and the shareholder's taxable income will not change if property is distributed. Answer (D) is incorrect. Brisk's taxable income will increase, yet the shareholder's taxable income will not decrease. The shareholder will include the FMV of the property in income, not the corporation's adjusted basis.

13. A corporation that has both preferred and common stock has a deficit in accumulated earnings and profits at the beginning of the year. The current earnings and profits are $25,000. The corporation makes a dividend distribution of $20,000 to the preferred shareholders and $10,000 to the common shareholders. How will the preferred and common shareholders report these distributions?

A. Preferred - $20,000 dividend income; common - $10,000 dividend income.

B. Preferred - $20,000 dividend income; common - $5,000 dividend income, $5,000 return of capital.

C. Preferred - $15,000 dividend income; common - $10,000 dividend income.

D. Preferred - $20,000 return of capital; common - $10,000 return of capital.

Answer (B) is correct.

REQUIRED: The amount and character of dividends distributed to preferred and common shareholders.

DISCUSSION: The amount of a distribution is a dividend to the extent, first, of any current E&P and, then, of any accumulated E&P. To the extent current E&P are sufficient to cover a distribution, the distribution is treated as a taxable dividend, even if there is a deficit in the accumulated E&P. The amount of a distribution in excess of dividends is treated as tax-exempt return of capital to the extent of the shareholder's basis. Distributions are first allocated to the preferred shareholders and then to the common shareholders.

Answer (A) is incorrect. Only $5,000 of the distribution to common shareholders is dividend income, while the other $5,000 is treated as a return of capital since there is no accumulated E&P remaining. Answer (C) is incorrect. There is a $20,000 distribution to the preferred shareholders, and $5,000 of the distribution to common shareholders must be treated as a return of capital. Answer (D) is incorrect. Distributions are not treated as a return of capital until there is no current and accumulated E&P remaining.

9.4 Redemptions

14. Elm Corp. is an accrual-basis, calendar-year C corporation with 100,000 shares of voting common stock issued and outstanding as of December 30, Year 1. On December 31, Year 1, Hall surrendered 2,000 shares of Elm stock to Elm in exchange for $33,000 cash. Hall had no direct or indirect interest in Elm after the stock surrender. Additional information follows:

Hall's adjusted basis in 2,000 shares of Elm on December 31, Year 1 ($8 per share)	$16,000
Elm's accumulated earnings and profits at January 1, Year 1	25,000
Elm's Year 1 net operating loss	(7,000)

What amount of income did Hall recognize from the stock surrender?

A. $33,000 dividend.

B. $25,000 dividend.

C. $18,000 capital gain.

D. $17,000 capital gain.

Answer (D) is correct.

REQUIRED: The income recognized from a stock redemption.

DISCUSSION: In the case of a stock redemption in complete liquidation of a shareholder's interest, the redemption is treated as a sale or exchange of a capital asset. Therefore, Hall's income from the redemption is a $17,000 capital gain ($33,000 – $16,000 basis).

Answer (A) is incorrect. The amount of cash exchanged for the Elm stock is $33,000. Answer (B) is incorrect. The amount of Elm's accumulated earnings and profits at January 1, Year 1, is $25,000. Answer (C) is incorrect. The difference between Elm's accumulated earnings and profits and Elm's Year 1 net operating loss is $18,000.

15. Zeb, an individual shareholder, owned 25% of Towne Corporation stock. Pursuant to a series of stock redemptions, Towne redeemed 10% of the shares of stock Zeb owned in exchange for land having a fair market value of $30,000 and an adjusted basis of $10,000. Zeb's basis for all of his Towne stock was $200,000. Zeb reported the redemption transaction as if it were a dividend. Zeb's basis in the land and his Towne stock (immediately after the redemption) is

A. Land, $30,000; stock, $200,000.

B. Land, $30,000; stock, $180,000.

C. Land, $10,000; stock, $200,000.

D. Land, $20,000; stock, $200,000.

Answer (A) is correct.

REQUIRED: The basis in land received in a redemption of stock treated as a dividend, and the basis in the stock after the redemption.

DISCUSSION: If a redemption of shares does not qualify as a sale or exchange, it is treated as a dividend. The amount of a dividend distribution is the amount of money received plus the fair market value of the property received. Zeb has a $30,000 dividend. The basis of property received in a distribution is the FMV of such property. Therefore, Zeb's basis in the land is $30,000. A dividend distribution does not affect the basis in a shareholder's stock, so Zeb's stock basis remains $200,000.

16. As an investment, Rambo Corporation owns 10% of the stock of Duntulum Corporation with a basis of $8,000 and a market value of $50,000. Rambo uses the Duntulum stock to redeem approximately 1%, or $10,000 par value, of its own outstanding stock from unrelated, noncorporate shareholders. As a result of this transaction, Rambo must report

A. $42,000 gain.

B. No gain or loss.

C. $2,000 gain.

D. $50,000 gain.

Answer (A) is correct.

REQUIRED: The gain recognized by the distributing corporation on a redemption using appreciated property.

DISCUSSION: The general rule is that a corporation does not recognize gain or loss on the distribution of property with respect to its stock. But a corporation that distributes appreciated property must recognize gain equal to the excess of the FMV of the property over its adjusted basis, as if the stock were sold to the distributee immediately before the exchange. The recognized gain is $42,000 ($50,000 – $8,000).

Answer (B) is incorrect. A corporation that distributes appreciated property must recognize gain realized. Answer (C) is incorrect. The amount of $2,000 is the difference between the $10,000 of redeemed Rambo stock and the $8,000 basis of Duntulum Corporation stock. Answer (D) is incorrect. The amount of $50,000 is the market value of the Duntulum stock owned by Rambo.

9.5 Complete Liquidation

17. Krol Corporation distributed marketable securities in redemption of its stock in a complete liquidation. On the date of distribution, these securities had a basis of $100,000 and a fair market value of $150,000. What gain does Krol have as a result of the distribution?

A. $0

B. $50,000 capital gain.

C. $50,000 Sec. 1231 gain.

D. $50,000 ordinary gain.

Answer (B) is correct.

REQUIRED: The gain to a corporation on distribution of property in redemption of its stock in a complete liquidation.

DISCUSSION: Gain or loss is recognized when a corporation distributes property as part of a complete liquidation. Krol recognizes a $50,000 gain ($150,000 FMV – $100,000 AB). It is a capital gain because the marketable securities are a capital asset.

Answer (A) is incorrect. A corporation must recognize any gain it realizes on distribution of property in redemption of its stock in a complete liquidation. Answer (C) is incorrect. The transaction results in a capital gain. Sec. 1231 property is property held for more than 1 year. It includes real or depreciable property used in a trade or business and involuntarily converted capital assets. Answer (D) is incorrect. The transaction results in a capital gain.

18. Mintee Corp., an accrual-basis, calendar-year C corporation, had no corporate shareholders when it liquidated in Year 1. In cancelation of all their Mintee stock, each Mintee shareholder received in Year 1 a liquidating distribution of $2,000 cash and land with a tax basis of $5,000 and a fair market value of $10,500. Before the distribution, each shareholder's tax basis in Mintee stock was $6,500. What amount of gain should each Mintee shareholder recognize on the liquidating distribution?

A. $0

B. $6,000

C. $6,500

D. $12,500

Answer (B) is correct.

REQUIRED: The amount of gain recognized from a complete liquidation.

DISCUSSION: The amount realized on the liquidation of a corporation is the amount of money received plus the FMV of property received. The recognized gain is the amount by which this exceeds adjusted basis of the corporation's stock. The recognized gain on this distribution is

Amount realized	$12,500
Less: Adjusted basis	(6,500)
Gain recognized	$ 6,000

Answer (A) is incorrect. A gain is recognized. Answer (C) is incorrect. The amount of $6,500 is the shareholders' original basis. Answer (D) is incorrect. The amount of $12,500 is the FMV of the distribution.

19. A corporation was completely liquidated and dissolved during the current year. The filing fees, professional fees, and other expenditures incurred in connection with the liquidation and dissolution are

A. Deductible in full by the dissolved corporation.

B. Deductible by the shareholders and not by the corporation.

C. Treated as capital losses by the corporation.

D. Not deductible by either the corporation or the shareholders.

Answer (A) is correct.

REQUIRED: The tax treatment for expenses incurred in connection with a corporate liquidation.

DISCUSSION: The filing fees, professional fees, and other liquidation-related expenses are deductible in the final tax return of the corporation.

Answer (B) is incorrect. The expense is not incurred by the shareholders. Therefore, the shareholders cannot deduct them. Answer (C) is incorrect. The expenses are deductible as trade or business expenses. Answer (D) is incorrect. The expenses are deductible by the corporation.

9.6 Partial Liquidation

20. How does a noncorporate shareholder treat the gain on a redemption of stock that qualifies as a partial liquidation of the distributing corporation?

A. Entirely as capital gain.

B. Entirely as a dividend.

C. Partly as capital gain and partly as a dividend.

D. As a tax-free transaction.

Answer (A) is correct.

REQUIRED: The treatment of a partially liquidating distribution received by a noncorporate shareholder.

DISCUSSION: A redemption made in partial liquidation of an interest held by a noncorporate shareholder is treated as a distribution in exchange for the stock, i.e., a sale. The shareholder will treat any gain on the redemption as a capital gain. The amount of the distribution is the FMV of the property.

21. On January 1, Year 1, Can Corporation distributed Sec. 1231 land with a market value of $300,000 and an adjusted basis of $205,000 under a plan of partial liquidation under the Sec. 302(b)(4) rules. The distribution was made to individual shareholder Clem, who had owned 40% of Can since it was founded. Clem's stock interest redeemed in the partial liquidation had a basis of $140,000. What are the amount and the character of gain/loss that Can should recognize on the distribution?

A. $160,000 Sec. 1231 gain.

B. $95,000 Sec. 1231 gain.

C. $95,000 capital gain.

D. $65,000 Sec. 1231 loss.

Answer (B) is correct.

REQUIRED: The amount and the character of gain or loss recognized by a corporation on distributing property in a partial liquidation.

DISCUSSION: The distribution of appreciated property in a partial liquidation requires the distributing corporation to recognize gain on the distribution as if the property had been sold to the distributee immediately before the distribution. Therefore, Can will recognize a Sec. 1231 gain of $95,000 ($300,000 – $205,000).

Answer (A) is incorrect. The FMV of the property distributed is treated as the amount realized by the corporation. Answer (C) is incorrect. The corporation is treated as having sold a Sec. 1231 asset. Answer (D) is incorrect. It is the difference between the adjusted basis of the Sec. 1231 and the basis of Clem's stock.

9.7 Subsidiary Liquidation

22. On January 1, Year 1, Pearl Corporation owned 90% of the outstanding stock of Seso Corporation. Both companies were domestic corporations. Pursuant to a plan of liquidation adopted by Seso in March Year 1, Seso distributed all of its property in September Year 1 in complete redemption of all its stock, when Seso's accumulated earnings equaled $18,000. Seso had never been insolvent. Pursuant to the liquidation, Seso transferred to Pearl a parcel of land with a basis of $10,000 and a fair market value of $40,000. How much gain must Seso recognize in Year 1 on the transfer of this land to Pearl?

A. $0

B. $18,000

C. $27,000

D. $30,000

Answer (A) is correct.

REQUIRED: The amount of gain that must be recognized by a subsidiary on the distribution of appreciated property to its parent in a complete liquidation.

DISCUSSION: A controlled corporation generally recognizes no gain or loss upon making a liquidating distribution of property to its parent corporation. The control requirement must be met: the parent corporation must own at least 80% of the voting power and 80% of the total value of the stock of the corporation being liquidated. Seso will recognize no gain on the transfer of the land to Pearl.

Answer (B) is incorrect. The amount of $18,000 is Seso's accumulated earnings. Answer (C) is incorrect. The amount of $27,000 is 90% of the difference between the adjusted basis and fair market value of the land Seso transferred to Pearl. Answer (D) is incorrect. The amount of $30,000 is the difference between the adjusted basis and fair market value of the land Seso transferred to Pearl.

23. Forrest Corp. owned 100% of both the voting stock and total value of Diamond Corp. Both corporations were C corporations. Forrest's basis in the Diamond stock was $200,000 when it received a lump sum liquidating distribution of property as a result of the redemption of all of Diamond stock. The property had an adjusted basis of $270,000 and a fair market value of $500,000. What amount of gain did Forrest recognize on the distribution?

A. $0

B. $70,000

C. $270,000

D. $500,000

Answer (A) is correct.

REQUIRED: Recognized gain of liquidating distribution to a parent corporation.

DISCUSSION: Neither the parent corporation nor a controlled subsidiary recognizes gain or loss on a liquidating distribution to the parent. Control means the parent owns 80% or more of both the voting power and total value of the stock of the liquidating corporation. Forrest Corp. controls Diamond Corp. because it owns 100% of both the voting stock and total value of Diamond Corp. Therefore, Forrest does not recognize any gain on the liquidating distribution.

Answer (B) is incorrect. The amount of $70,000 uses the AB to calculate a gain. Special rules apply to complete liquidations between parent and controlled corporations. Answer (C) is incorrect. The amount of $270,000 is the AB of the distribution; however, in a complete liquidation, the amount realized is the FMV. In addition special rules apply to complete liquidations between parent and controlled corporations. Answer (D) is incorrect. The amount of $500,000 is the realized gain (not recognized gain) in a complete liquidation between noncontrolling corporations. Special rules apply to complete liquidations between parent and controlled corporations.

9.8 Reorganizations

24. Jaxson Corp. has 200,000 shares of voting common stock issued and outstanding. King Corp. has decided to acquire 90% of Jaxson's voting common stock solely in exchange for 50% of its voting common stock and retain Jaxson as a subsidiary after the transaction. Which of the following statements is true?

A. King must acquire 100% of Jaxson stock for the transaction to be a tax-free reorganization.

B. The transaction will qualify as a tax-free reorganization.

C. King must issue at least 60% of its voting common stock for the transaction to qualify as a tax-free reorganization.

D. Jaxson must surrender assets for the transaction to qualify as a tax-free reorganization.

Answer (B) is correct.

REQUIRED: The requirements of a stock-for-stock acquisition.

DISCUSSION: A Type B, or stock-for-stock, acquisition qualifies as a tax-free reorganization if the shareholders of one company acquire the stock of the target company solely in exchange for stock of their company. The acquiring company must control at least 80% of the stock of the target company after the exchange.

Answer (A) is incorrect. Only 80% or more of the target company's stock must be acquired. Answer (C) is incorrect. There is no such requirement for a stock-for-stock reorganization. Answer (D) is incorrect. Assets need not be surrendered for qualification as a tax-free reorganization.

25. Pursuant to a plan of corporate reorganization adopted in July Year 1, Gow exchanged 500 shares of Lad Corp. common stock that he had bought in January Year 1 at a cost of $5,000 for 100 shares of Rook Corp. common stock having a FMV of $6,000. Gow's recognized gain on this exchange was

A. $1,000 long-term capital gain.

B. $1,000 short-term capital gain.

C. $1,000 ordinary income.

D. $0

Answer (D) is correct.

REQUIRED: The amount of gain recognized in a corporate reorganization.

DISCUSSION: The exchange of stock for stock in obtaining control of a corporation qualifies as a reorganization. No gain or loss is recognized in a reorganization if stock or securities are exchanged solely for stock or securities in the same corporation or in another corporation that was a party to the reorganization. For Gow, since no boot was received, no gain is recognized.

Answer (A) is incorrect. The amount of $1,000 is the difference between the $6,000 of Rook Corporation common stock and $5,000 of Lad Corporation common stock. No capital gain is recognized. Long-term capital gain occurs for capital property held longer than 1 year. Answer (B) is incorrect. The amount of $1,000 is the difference between the $6,000 of Rook Corporation common stock and $5,000 of Lad Corporation common stock. This transaction is tax-free, and no gain is recognized. Answer (C) is incorrect. The amount of $1,000 is the difference between the $6,000 of Rook Corporation common stock and $5,000 of Lad Corporation common stock. No gain is recognized because the transaction is a stock-for-stock reorganization.

26. Pursuant to a plan of reorganization adopted in Year 1, Summit Corporation exchanged 1,000 shares of its common stock and paid $40,000 cash for Hansen Corporation's assets with an adjusted basis of $200,000 (fair market value of $300,000). Hansen Corporation was liquidated shortly after the exchange, with its shareholders receiving the Summit stock and cash. The 1,000 shares of Summit common stock had a fair market value of $260,000 on the date of the exchange. What is the basis to Summit of the assets acquired in the exchange?

A. $200,000

B. $240,000

C. $260,000

D. $300,000

Answer (A) is correct.

REQUIRED: The basis to the acquiring corporation of assets received in a qualified reorganization.

DISCUSSION: Summit Corporation's exchange of 1,000 shares of common stock and $40,000 cash for the assets of Hansen Corporation is a qualified reorganization, assuming that all or substantially all of Hansen's assets are acquired and that Hansen distributes the stock, securities, and other property it receives, as well as the other property it has retained, as part of the reorganization. Since it is a qualified reorganization, Hansen, the transferor corporation, will have a realized gain of $100,000 ($300,000 received – $200,000 adjusted basis). In a qualifying reorganization, the transferor corporation recognizes no gain if the assets other than stock or securities received are distributed immediately to its shareholders or creditors.

The basis of the assets to Summit equals the transferor's adjusted basis in the assets ($200,000) increased by any gain recognized by the transferor ($0).

Answer (B) is incorrect. The amount of $240,000 results from adding the adjusted basis of Hansen Corporation's assets ($200,000) and the amount of cash ($40,000) paid for Hansen's assets. Answer (C) is incorrect. The amount of $260,000 is the fair market value of Summit's common stock. Answer (D) is incorrect. The amount of $300,000 is the fair market value of Hansen Corporation's assets.

27. Pursuant to a plan of corporate reorganization adopted in Year 1, Myra Eber exchanged 1,000 shares of Faro Corporation common stock that she had purchased for $75,000 for 1,800 shares of Judd Corporation common stock having a fair market value of $86,000. As a result of this exchange, Eber's recognized gain and her basis in the Judd stock should be

	Recognized Gain	Basis
A.	$0	$11,000
B.	$11,000	$75,000
C.	$0	$86,000
D.	$0	$75,000

Answer (D) is correct.

REQUIRED: The gain recognized on the exchange of stock and the basis in the new stock.

DISCUSSION: A shareholder does not recognize any gain or loss in a reorganization on an exchange of stock or securities in a corporation solely for stock or securities in the same or another corporation that is a party to the reorganization. Since, pursuant to a reorganization, Eber exchanged shares of Faro stock solely for shares of Judd stock, Eber will recognize no gain. Since there is no recognition of gain or loss, Eber's basis in the new stock will be the same as her basis in the stock exchanged.

Answer (A) is incorrect. In a reorganization qualifying for nonrecognition, the shareholder's basis is exchanged. Answer (B) is incorrect. Since no boot was received in a qualified reorganization, no gain was recognized. Answer (C) is incorrect. It is the basis of the stock given up in the exchange.

28. Ace Corp. and Bate Corp. combine in a qualifying reorganization and form Carr Corp., the only surviving corporation. This reorganization is tax-free to the

	Shareholders	Corporation
A.	Yes	Yes
B.	Yes	No
C.	No	Yes
D.	No	No

Answer (A) is correct.

REQUIRED: The taxability of reorganization.

DISCUSSION: This exchange represents a Type A statutory consolidation wherein neither the shareholders nor the corporations involved will recognize income, provided no boot is exchanged.

9.9 Procedure

29. A calendar-year corporation received an automatic extension of time for filing its Year 1 return by submitting an application on Form 7004. On what date is the corporation's return due?

A. September 30, Year 2.
B. September 15, Year 2.
C. August 15, Year 2.
D. March 15, Year 2.

Answer (B) is correct.

REQUIRED: The due date for the corporation's federal income tax return.

DISCUSSION: A corporation must file its return on or before the 15th day of the 3rd month following the close of the tax year. For a calendar-year-end corporation, the due date for a tax return is 3/15/Yr 2. By filing Form 7004, the corporation receives an automatic 6-month extension for filing the tax return, which moves the due date to 9/15/Yr 2. However, the corporation must pay its estimated tax liability by the original due date. The time for payment of the taxes is not extended.

30. Under which of the following circumstances would a corporation be required to file a federal income tax return?

A. The corporation has disposed of all of its assets except for a small sum of cash retained to pay state taxes to preserve its corporate charter.
B. A corporation with no assets that stops doing business and dissolves is treated as a corporation under state law for limited purposes connected with winding up its affairs.
C. The corporation has dissolved and is in bankruptcy.
D. In 2014, Corporation M ceased doing business and disposed of all of its assets. However, during all of 2015, M was in the process of suing Corporation B.

Answer (A) is correct.

REQUIRED: The corporation that is required to file a federal income tax return.

DISCUSSION: Sec. 6012(a)(2) requires every corporation subject to taxation under subtitle A of the Code to file a federal income tax return.

Answer (B) is incorrect. When a corporation with no assets that stops doing business and dissolves is treated as a corporation under state law for limited purposes connected with winding up its affairs, the corporation is considered not in existence. Answer (C) is incorrect. When the corporation has dissolved and is in bankruptcy, the corporation is considered not in existence. Answer (D) is incorrect. The corporation in this situation has ceased business and dissolved. Reg. 1.6012-2(a)(2) states that, for federal income tax purposes, a corporation is not in existence if it has ceased business and dissolved.

9.10 PRACTICE TASK-BASED SIMULATIONS

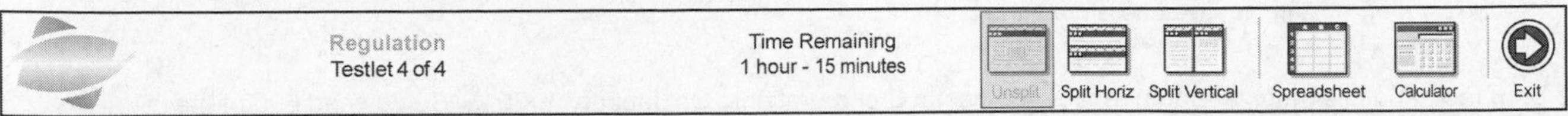

DIRECTIONS

Note: If you believe you have encountered a software malfunction, report it to the test center staff immediately.

Navigation

To navigate from task to task, use the controls at the bottom of the screen. Click on the **Next** button to advance to the next task, or the **Previous** button to go to the previous task. To go directly to any task, click on its number.

If you would like a reminder to revisit a task, or want to indicate that you are finished with it, click on the reminder flag below the task number. To clear the flag, click on it again. Reminder flags are for your use only – they do not contribute to your score.

Tabs

In this part of the examination, you will be asked to complete various tasks. Every task has one or more **Work Tabs**. Some tasks have one or more **Information Tabs**, others may have none. Every task has a **Help** tab.

If a task has **Information Tabs**, you may use the information in them to complete your responses in the **Work Tabs**.

Work tab **Information tab** **Help tab**

Work Tabs:

- **Work Tabs** are identified with a pencil icon. This is where your responses are expected.
- Each task has one or more **Work Tabs**.
- **Work Tabs** contain directions for completing the task – be sure to read these directions carefully.
- The **Work Tab** name in the example above is for illustration only – yours will differ.
- You must complete all of the **Work Tabs** in each task to receive full credit.

Information Tabs:

- The Authoritative Literature will be provided in all tasks in the AUD, FAR, and REG sections for your reference.
- Your simulation may have one or more additional **Information Tabs**. Like the Authoritative Literature tabs, **Information Tabs** do not have a pencil icon.
- If your task has additional **Information Tabs**, go through each to familiarize yourself with the task content.

Help Tab:

- The **Help Tab** provides assistance with the exam software that is used in this task. For example, if the task is to compose a memorandum, **Help** will provide information about the word processor.

The Toolbar

The toolbar at the top of the screen shows the amount of time remaining for you to complete the tasks. In addition, the following tools are available. Note that only the **Exit** button is displayed when Directions are visible - the others will appear when you begin the tasks.

Click on these buttons to split or unsplit the screen. You can split the screen vertically or horizontally.

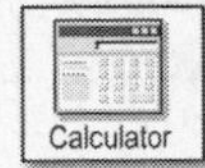

Click on this button to display the calculator; click on it again to hide the calculator. To move the calculator, click on the calculator title bar and drag the calculator to the desired location.

Click on this button to use the spreadsheet; click on it again to hide the spreadsheet. To move the spreadsheet, click on the the spreadsheet title bar and drag the spreadsheet to the desired location.

Click on this button to go on to the next part of the examination. You must complete all of the tasks to receive full credit. Once you click on **Exit** and confirm the action, you will NOT be able to return to this testlet.

= Reminder | Directions | 1 2 3 4 5 6 | Previous | Next

Liquidation | Authoritative Literature | Help

Son, Inc., and Clef, Inc., are both taxable domestic C corporations. On January 1, 2015, Son owned 800 of the outstanding shares of the only class of stock of Clef. Dawn owned the other 200 shares of Clef but owned none of the outstanding shares of Son. Son's basis in its Clef stock was $200,000, and Dawn's basis in her stock in Clef was $50,000. Clef had $10,000 of accumulated earnings and profits on January 1, 2015. On October 13, 2014, Clef contributed numerous copyrights to a tax-exempt organization. By July 4, 2015, Clef had paid all its liabilities to third parties. Clef was subsequently liquidated on August 30, 2015. In the complete liquidation, Clef distributed to Son a building and a computer, and to Dawn a concert grand piano, an electronic keyboard, and $82,000 in cash. Clef had no other assets other than an amount reserved for taxes.

Immediately before the distribution, the fair market values and Clef's adjusted bases are as follows:

Asset	FMV	Clef's Adjusted Basis
Building	$550,000	$250,000
Computer	$25,000	$30,000
Piano	$15,000	$10,000
Keyboard	$3,000	$4,000

The building was subject to a $175,000 mortgage. All of the noncash assets Clef distributed were purchased on August 30, 2011, 2 months after the corporation was formed. Clef had claimed allowable depreciation on the building using the straight-line method.

Enter either the correct amount or holding period (in number of months) for each item below.

Item	*Answer*
1. Loss recognized by Clef, Inc., on the distribution of the computer	
2. Gain recognized by Clef, Inc., on the distribution of the concert piano	
3. Son, Inc.'s basis in the building	
4. Son, Inc.'s basis in the computer	
5. Dawn's gain or loss recognized on the distribution of the piano and keyboard	
6. Dawn's holding period for the piano on December 31, 2015	
7. Dawn's holding period for the keyboard on December 31, 2015	

Redemptions | Authoritative Literature | Help

Based on the following scenarios, enter the amount of capital gain or loss that would be recognized by the shareholder for each redemption of stock. Enter losses as a negative with a leading minus sign (–), and enter zeros for blank cells (i.e., no gain or loss).

Redemptions	*Capital Gain or Loss*
1. Len, an individual shareholder, owned 15% of Elwood Corporation stock. Elwood redeemed 10% of the shares Len owned in exchange for equipment having a FMV of $40,000 and an adjusted basis of $15,000. Len's basis in all of his stock was $230,000.	
2. Jan purchased 300 shares of Weimer Brothers, Inc., 12 years ago for $40,000. Jan held all of the shares until the present time. In 2014, Weimer Brothers redeemed 100% of Jan's stock for $175,000.	
3. Henry's estate owned 15% of Aaron, Inc.'s outstanding shares. The estate bought the shares in 2009 for $65,000. This year, Aaron redeemed the stock for a building worth $90,000 and an adjusted basis of $75,000.	
4. Williams Corporation redeemed 250 shares worth $44,000 from an individual shareholder as part of a partial liquidation. The shares were originally purchased at $100 per share.	

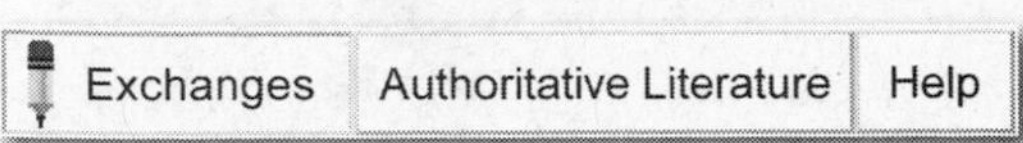

Sing, Inc., is a taxable domestic C corporation. On January 1, 2015, of its 2,000 issued and outstanding shares, 1,575 were owned by Snap, while the remaining 425 shares were owned by unrelated parties. On April 30, 2015, Snap received from Sing an additional 200 shares of Sing stock and $25,000 in cash in exchange for land worth $500,000 (subject to a $250,000 mortgage). The exchange was for a valid business purpose and not to avoid taxes. Sing had redeemed the 200 shares of stock from an unrelated party on October 31, 2013, for $200,000, and its FMV on April 30, 2015, was $1,125 per share. The stock has a $100-per-share par value. Snap purchased the land for $200,000 on October 31, 2005, as an investment and has made no improvements to it.

Enter either the correct amount or holding period (in number of months) for each item, all of which are presented in reference to the April 30, 2015, transaction.

Item	***Answer***
1. Gain recognized by Snap on April 30, 2015	
2. Snap's basis in the stock	
3. Snap's holding period for the stock on October 31, 2015	
4. Gain recognized by Sing, Inc.	
5. Sing, Inc.'s holding period for the land on October 31, 2015	
6. Sing, Inc.'s basis in the land	

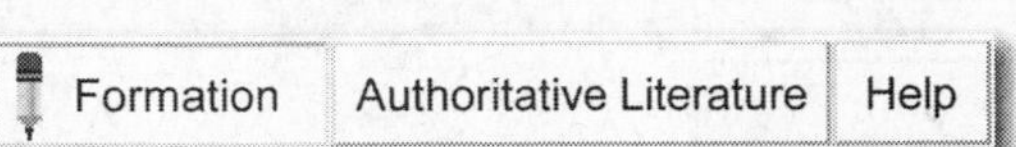

For each of the following corporate formations, (1) enter the amount of gain or loss that will be recognized by the shareholders as a whole, and (2) enter the corporation's basis in the property after the transfer.

Corporate Formation	***Gain or Loss***	***Basis***
1. David transferred equipment worth $45,000 and a basis to him of $36,000 to Heat, Inc. Heat also assumed a $60,000 loan held for business purposes related to the equipment. In exchange, David received 90% of the company's stock and $25,000 cash.		
2. John and Kelly started Back Stop, Inc., in 2015. Kelly transferred a building with a basis of $120,000 and a FMV of $150,000 for 60% of the stock. John agreed to operate the company on a day-to-day basis in exchange for his stock.		
3. Evan transferred land with a FMV of $1.9 million for 100% of the shares of his newly formed corporation. Evan's basis in the land was $2.1 million.		
4. Joaquin and Rafael joined a corporation when Joaquin transferred computers that had a FMV of $5,000 and an adjusted basis of $2,500 and Rafael transferred equipment with a $20,000 FMV and an adjusted basis to him of $18,000. In return, Joaquin received 20% of all the stock and $1,000 cash. Rafael received 80% of all of the corporation's outstanding stock and $4,000 cash.		
5. Melvin incorporated his sole proprietorship in 2015. He transferred inventory with a $93,000 basis and $112,000 FMV, and the corporation assumed an $87,000 loan held against the inventory. The loan was taken out 2 weeks before the transfer, 6 months after the inventory was purchased because Melvin knew it could provide a tax benefit.		

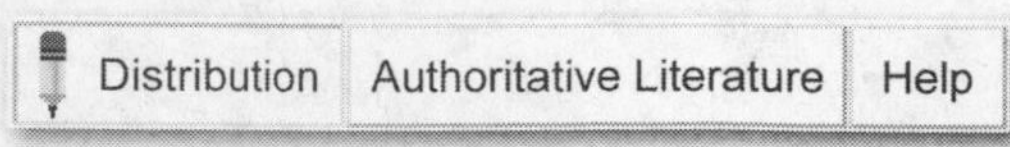

Select from the list provided the correct tax treatment of the amount received by the shareholder in each of the following distributions. Each choice may be used once, more than once, or not at all.

Distribution	***Tax Treatment***
1. In 2001, Emilio purchased stock for $60,000. In 2014, he received a return of capital of $24,000 and reduced the basis of his stock by that amount. In 2015, he received a distribution of $45,000, which reduced the basis of his stock to zero. At no time did the corporation have E&P.	
2. Energy Corp. had a deficit in accumulated earnings and profits at the beginning of 2015. Throughout the year, they had current earnings and profits of $115,000 and made a cash distribution of $135,000. The shareholders' basis in the stock was $120,000.	
3. Toby holds 100% of Vance Corp.'s stock. His basis in the stock is $80,000. Vance has $60,000 of accumulated E&P and $15,000 of current E&P. In the current year, Vance distributed $180,000 cash to Toby.	
4. Angel, Inc., had $72,000 of E&P on January 1, 2015. During 2015, Angel had current E&P of $30,000 and made a $52,000 cash distribution to its shareholders.	
5. Roger holds 30,000 shares of Murtagh, Inc.'s 300,000 shares at a basis of $120,000. Murtagh has $500,000 of accumulated E&P and $200,000 of current E&P. Murtagh distributed one stock right per share in lieu of money for each share outstanding. Each stock right is valued at $8.	

Choices
A) No dividend or capital gain
B) $70,000 dividend and $50,000 capital gain
C) $30,000 dividend and $12,000 capital gain
D) $52,000 dividend
E) $115,000 dividend
F) $25,000 dividend and $75,000 capital gain
G) $75,000 dividend and $25,000 capital gain
H) $9,000 capital gain
I) $36,000 dividend

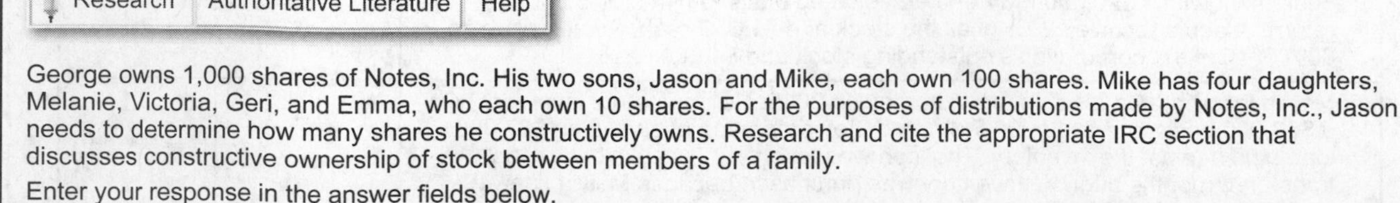

George owns 1,000 shares of Notes, Inc. His two sons, Jason and Mike, each own 100 shares. Mike has four daughters, Melanie, Victoria, Geri, and Emma, who each own 10 shares. For the purposes of distributions made by Notes, Inc., Jason needs to determine how many shares he constructively owns. Research and cite the appropriate IRC section that discusses constructive ownership of stock between members of a family.

Enter your response in the answer fields below.

IRC § [ ] ([ ])

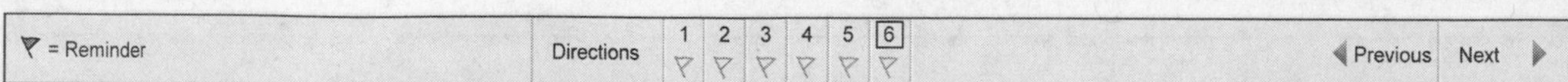

Unofficial Answers

1. Liquidation (7 Gradable Items)

1. $0. A corporation recognizes no loss in a complete liquidation on a distribution of appreciated property to a parent corporation (one that owns 80% or more of the voting power and the total value of the stock of the liquidating subsidiary).
2. $5,000. When an 80%-or-more-owned subsidiary is liquidated, the rules generally applicable to complete liquidations apply to distributions to shareholders other than the parent corporation. Thus, the liquidating corporation recognizes the $5,000 gain realized on the piano as if it were sold to Dawn at its FMV.
3. $250,000. A parent corporation's basis in property received in a distribution in complete liquidation of its 80%-or-more-owned subsidiary is the subsidiary corporation's basis in the property immediately before the distribution.
4. $30,000. A parent corporation's basis in property received in a distribution in complete liquidation of its 80%-or-more-owned subsidiary is the subsidiary corporation's basis in the property immediately before the distribution.
5. $50,000. When an 80%-or-more-owned subsidiary is completely liquidated, the rules generally applicable to complete liquidations apply to distributions to shareholders other than the parent corporation. Thus, Dawn treats the amounts distributed (the cash and the FMV of the other property) as realized in exchange for her stock. She realizes and recognizes a gain of $50,000 [$82,000 (cash) + $15,000 (piano) + $3,000 (keyboard) – $50,000 basis in her stock].
6. 4 months. Dawn's basis in the piano was not determined by reference to Clef's basis in it. Thus, her holding period began the day after she acquired the piano (September 1).
7. 4 months. Dawn's basis in the keyboard was not determined by reference to Clef's basis in it. Thus, her holding period began the day after she acquired the keyboard (September 1).

2. Redemptions (4 Gradable Items)

1. $0. This distribution meets the requirements to be treated as a dividend rather than a sale or exchange. Thus, the shareholder would have dividend income, not a capital gain.
2. $135,000. This redemption terminated the shareholder's interest, so the redemption must be treated as a sale of the stock redeemed, and the amount realized is a long-term capital gain.
3. $25,000. This redemption is received by an estate, so the redemption must be treated as a sale of the stock redeemed, and the amount realized ($90,000 – $65,000) is a long-term capital gain.
4. $19,000. This redemption is a partial liquidation by a noncorporate shareholder, so the redemption must be treated as a sale of the stock redeemed, and the $19,000 [$44,000 – ($250 × $100)] realized is a long-term capital gain.

3. Exchanges (6 Gradable Items)

1. $75,000. Snap owns 80% or more [(1,575 shares owned by Snap + 200 additional shares) ÷ (2,000 total outstanding shares + 200 additional shares) × 100] of the stock of Sing, Inc., immediately after the exchange. Thus, this is a Sec. 351 exchange. Snap recognizes realized gain to the extent of cash and the FMV of other property other than the Sing stock received, or $25,000, plus the $50,000 excess of the $250,000 liability that the property was subject to, over Snap's $200,000 adjusted basis in all property contributed.
2. $0. Snap's basis in the stock is the adjusted basis in the land contributed increased by the gain he recognized and decreased by the boot he received. The boot is the cash and the liability that the contributed property was subject to. Thus, Snap's basis in the stock is $0 [$200,000 + ($25,000 + $50,000) gain recognized – ($25,000 + $250,000)].
3. 120 months. Because Snap's basis in the stock was determined in part by reference to the basis in the contributed property, his holding period for the property includes the period for which he held the land.
4. $0. A corporation recognizes neither gain nor loss on the sale or exchange of its own stock, including treasury stock.
5. 120 months. By reference to the contributing shareholder's basis in it, Sing, Inc.'s holding period includes the period during which the shareholder held it.
6. $275,000. Sing, Inc., acquires a transferred basis in the contributed property. It is the basis of the property ($250,000) in the hands of the contributing shareholder increased by gain recognized by the shareholder on the exchange ($75,000).

4. Formation (5 Gradable Items)

1. $49,000 and $85,000. When property other than stock in the corporation (boot) is received, the shareholder must recognize realized gain to the extent of the boot received in the exchange ($25,000). In addition, the amount of the liabilities is treated as recognized gain but only to the extent it exceeds the AB of all property contributed by the shareholder, $24,000 ($60,000 liability – $36,000 AB). The corporation's basis in the property is equal to the adjusted basis in the hands of the shareholder, plus any gain recognized ($85,000 = $36,000 AB + $49,000 gain recognized).
2. $30,000 and $150,000. Stock exchanged for services is not counted toward the 80% control threshold. The FMV of the stock received in exchange for services is gross income to the shareholder. Any other shareholders involved in the transaction must recognize any gain on the transfer of property. The corporation's basis in the property is equal to the adjusted basis in the hands of the shareholder, plus any gain recognized.
3. $0 and $2.1 million. IRC Sec. 351 requires that no gain or loss be recognized if property is transferred to a corporation by an individual solely in exchange for stock and if such person is in control of the corporation immediately after the exchange. The corporation's basis in the property is equal to the adjusted basis in the hands of the shareholder, plus any gain recognized.
4. $3,000 and $23,500. When property other than stock in the corporation (boot) is received, the shareholder must recognize realized gain to the extent of the boot received in the exchange. Joaquin realized a gain of $2,500 ($5,000 FMV – $2,500 basis) but only recognizes $1,000 boot (cash). Rafael received $4,000 cash, but recognized gain is limited by realized gain of only $2,000 ($20,000 FMV – $18,000 basis). The corporation's basis in the property is equal to the adjusted basis in the hands of the shareholder, plus any gain recognized.
5. $106,000 and $199,000. If liabilities are transferred for the purpose of tax avoidance, the full amount of gain will be recognized. The corporation's basis in the property is equal to the adjusted basis in the hands of the shareholder, plus any gain recognized.

5. Distribution (5 Gradable Items)

1. H) $9,000 capital gain. Because earnings and profits (E&P) were zero, the first $60,000 distributed reduced Emilio's basis to zero. The remaining $9,000 of the distributions is a capital gain to Emilio.
2. E) $115,000 dividend. The amount of distribution is a dividend to the extent, first, of any current E&P and, then, of any accumulated E&P. To the extent current E&P are sufficient to cover a distribution, the distribution is treated as a taxable dividend, even if there is a deficit in the accumulated E&P. The excess is treated as a return of capital to the extent of the shareholder's basis.
3. G) $75,000 dividend and $25,000 capital gain. A distribution is a dividend that is included in the recipient's gross income to the extent that it is made from current and accumulated earnings and profits (E&P) of a corporation. Any additional distribution is treated by the shareholder as a nontaxable return of capital to the extent of the shareholder's basis. Once the basis has been exceeded, any additional distribution is treated as a capital gain ($180,000 distribution – $75,000 dividend – $80,000 basis).
4. D) $52,000 dividend. A distribution is a dividend that is included in the recipient's gross income to the extent that it is made from current and accumulated earnings and profits (E&P) of a corporation. Once the shareholder has received enough distributions to reduce the basis in the stock to zero, any additional distributions will be treated as a capital gain.
5. B) $70,000 dividend and $50,000 capital gain. When a shareholder receives stock rights in lieu of money, the entire amount of the distribution received by the shareholder will be treated as a taxable dividend to the extent of current and accumulated E&P. Any additional distribution will be treated as a return of capital to the extent of the shareholder's basis in the stock. If the distribution exceeds the basis, the excess will be treated as a capital gain. Since Roger holds 10% of Murtagh's stock, $70,000 will be a dividend [10% × ($500,000 + $200,000)]. Roger received $240,000 total and recognizes a $50,000 capital gain ($240,000 – $70,000 dividend – $120,000 basis).

6. Research (1 Gradable Item)

Answer: IRC § 318(a)(1)

§ 318. Constructive ownership of stock

(a)(1) Members of family

(A) In general

An individual shall be considered as owning the stock owned, directly or indirectly, by or for—

(i) his spouse (other than a spouse who is legally separated from the individual under a decree of divorce or separate maintenance) and

(ii) his children, grandchildren, and parents.

(B) Effect of adoption

For purposes of subparagraph (A)(ii), a legally adopted child of an individual shall be treated as a child of such individual by blood.

Gleim Simulation Grading

Task	Correct Responses		Gradable Items		Score per Task
1	____	÷	7	=	____
2	____	÷	4	=	____
3	____	÷	6	=	____
4	____	÷	5	=	____
5	____	÷	5	=	____
6 (Research)	____	÷	1	=	____
			Total of Scores per Task		____
		÷	Total Number of Tasks		6
			Total Score		____%

STUDY UNIT TEN
S CORPORATIONS

(13 pages of outline)

An S corporation is generally not subject to a federal tax on its income. Its items of income, loss, deduction, and credit are passed through to its shareholders on a per-day and per-share basis. Each shareholder is taxed on his or her share of the S corporation's income as it is earned. Distributions of cash or property generally are not income to its shareholders.

10.1 ELIGIBILITY AND ELECTION

1. **Overview**
   a. A corporation is treated as an S corporation only for those days for which each specific eligibility requirement is met and the required election is effective.
2. **Eligibility**
   a. Eligibility depends on the nature of the corporation, its shareholders, and its stock.
   b. An S corporation must have only one class of stock.
      1) Variation in voting rights of that one class of stock is permitted.
      2) Rights to profits and assets on liquidation must be identical.
      3) Debt may be treated as a disqualifying second class of stock.
   c. Issuance of debt does not disqualify S corporation status. A conversion feature or some other provision that would entitle the debtholder to control of the corporation is generally needed to disqualify S corporation status.
   d. The number of shareholders may not exceed 100.
      1) A husband and wife are considered a single shareholder for this purpose.
      2) Family members in a six-generation range are considered one shareholder.
      3) A nonresident alien (NRA) may not own any shares.
      4) Each shareholder must be either an individual, an estate, a single-member LLC, or a qualified trust.
         a) Certain small business trusts and tax-exempt organizations can be shareholders.
         b) Partnerships, Charitable Remainder Unitrusts, and Charitable Remainder Annuity Trusts may not be shareholders.
      5) The following is a list of qualified trusts that are allowed as shareholders of an S corporation:
         a) A trust, all of which is treated as owned by an individual who is a citizen or resident of the United States.
         b) A trust described in a) immediately before the death of the deemed owner that continues in existence after such death.
            i) This provision lasts for 2 years, beginning on the day of the deemed owner's death.

c) A trust that receives a stock transfer pursuant to the terms of a will.

i) This provision lasts for 2 years, beginning on the day of the stock transfer.

d) A trust created primarily to exercise the voting power of stock transferred to it. This does not apply to any foreign trust.

e. The corporation must be domestic and eligible.

1) Ineligible corporations include financial institutions, such as banks (that use the reserve method of accounting) and insurance companies.

f. S corporations can own C corporations or Qualified Subchapter S Subsidiaries (QSSS).

1) A QSSS is an electing domestic corporation that qualifies as an S corporation and is 100% owned by an S corporation parent.

3. **Election**

a. An eligible corporation must make the election for S corporation status.
b. All shareholders at the time the election is made must file a consent.

1) Each person who was a shareholder at any time during the part of the tax year before the election is made must also consent.
2) If any former shareholders do not consent, the election is considered made for the following year.

c. Election made within the first 2 1/2 months of the beginning of the corporation's tax year is effective from the first day of that tax year.
d. Election made after the first 2 1/2 months of the corporation's tax year will become effective on the first day of the following tax year.
e. The IRS can treat a late-filed election as timely filed if it determines that reasonable cause existed for failing to file the election in a timely manner.
f. After revocation or termination of an election, a new election cannot be effectively made for 5 years without the consent of the IRS.
g. The IRS can waive the effect of an invalid election resulting from failure to qualify as an S corporation and/or failing to obtain the necessary shareholder consents.

4. **Termination**

a. Upon the occurrence of a terminating event, an S corporation becomes a C corporation.

1) The IRS may waive termination.

a) The terminating event must be inadvertent and corrected within a reasonable time.

b. An S corporation election is terminated by any of the following:

1) An effective revocation. A majority of the shareholders (voting and nonvoting) must consent.
2) Any eligibility requirement not being satisfied on any day.
3) Passive investment income (PII) termination.

c. The termination is effective as of the date the disqualifying event, other than a PII termination, occurs.
d. **PII termination** occurs when, for 3 consecutive tax years, the corporation has both Subchapter C E&P on the last day and PII that is greater than 25% of gross receipts.

1) An S corporation does not have E&P unless it was formerly a C corporation or acquired E&P in a tax-free reorganization, e.g., a merger.

2) Gross receipts are gross receipts of the S corporation for the tax year.

   a) This amount is reduced by capital losses (other than on stock and securities) to the extent of capital gains.

3) PII consists of gross receipts from dividends, interest, royalties, rents, and annuities, reduced by

   a) Interest on accounts receivable (notes) for inventory sold in the ordinary course of trade or business

   b) Rents from a lease under which significant services are rendered to the lessee (those not customarily rendered)

4) Interest includes tax-exempt interest.
5) Termination is effective at the beginning of the following tax year.
6) Receipts from sales and exchanges of stock and securities are not considered PII.

The AICPA has used theoretical questions to test candidates' knowledge of requirements for S corporation eligibility, election, and termination.

5. **Accounting Method**

   a. An S corporation is not required to use the accrual method.
   b. Accounting method election is generally made by the S corporation.
   c. Shareholders, however, personally elect

      1) Credit or a deduction for foreign income taxes
      2) Percentage or cost depletion for oil and gas properties
      3) Treatment of mining exploration expenditures

6. **Tax Year**

   a. An S corporation generally must adopt a calendar tax year.
   b. With IRS consent, it may adopt a fiscal year, if it establishes a valid business purpose for doing so, that

      1) Does not result in deferral of income to shareholders but
      2) Coincides with a natural business year.

         a) A natural business year may end with or after the end of the peak period of a cyclical business.

   c. An S corporation that deposits the equivalent amount of the deferred tax may elect a fiscal year.

      1) A new S corporation is limited to no more than 3 months' deferral of income to its shareholders.
      2) An existing S corporation may continue to use the fiscal year previously adopted.

   d. To change its tax year other than by a Sec. 444 election, an S corporation should file Form 1128 by the 15th day of the 2nd month of the new tax year.
   e. When S status is terminated, creating a short year, nonseparately computed income is allocated on a pro rata basis unless certain exceptions apply or an election is made.

7. **Administration**

   a. The tax treatment of S corporation items of income, loss, deduction, and credit is determined at the corporate level.
   b. The S corporation files a tax return (Form 1120S).

c. Each shareholder must report a pro rata share of income and expenses on his or her personal tax return.
   1) The shareholder's reporting must be consistent with the corporate return.
      a) An exception applies if the shareholder notifies the IRS of the inconsistency.
   2) A shareholder's pro rata share of items is reported on his or her tax return for his or her tax year in which the S corporation tax year ends.

EXAMPLE

Compliance Corporation is a calendar-year S corporation. Compliance has two shareholders: Shelly, with a year end of June 30 of the current year, and Julie, with a year end of December 31 of the current year. Because Julie is a calendar-year taxpayer, she will report any current-year income from Compliance on her current-year return. Shelly, on the other hand, will report any current-year income from Compliance on her return for the following year.

d. Administrative and judicial proceedings to determine proper treatment of items are unified at the level of the S corporation.

Stop and review! You have completed the outline for this subunit. Study multiple-choice questions 1 through 8 beginning on page 377.

10.2 OPERATIONS

1. **Exempt Taxes**
   a. Provisions that govern taxation of C corporations also govern taxation of S corporations unless a specific exception applies. S corporations are expressly exempt from the following taxes:
      1) Corporate income tax
      2) AMT (alternative minimum tax)
      3) AET (accumulated earnings tax)
      4) PHC (personal holding company) tax
2. **Reported Items**
   a. The items of income, deduction (including losses), and credit of an S corporation are reported by the corporation.
   b. A shareholder computes taxable income by taking into account the pro rata share of items passed through from the S corporation. The shareholder reports his or her pro rata share in the tax year within which the tax year of the S corporation ended.

EXAMPLE

Super, Inc., an S corporation, properly reported nonseparately stated net income from operations of $100,000 for its tax year ending November 30, Year 1. Sheldon, a calendar-year taxpayer who owns 5% of the shares of Super, Inc., must include $5,000 of ordinary income in his tax return for Year 1, which is due on or before April 15, Year 2.

3. **Items Separately Stated**
   a. S corporation items of income, deduction, and credit, which could alter the tax liability of shareholders if taken into account by them on their personal returns, are required to be stated and passed through separately. Separately stated items include
      1) Sec. 1231 gains and losses
      2) Net short-term capital gains and losses
      3) Net long-term capital gains and losses
      4) Dividends
      5) Charitable contributions

6) Taxes paid to a foreign country or to a U.S. possession
7) Tax-exempt interest and related expense
8) Investment income and related expense
9) Amounts previously deducted (e.g., bad debts)
10) Real estate activities
11) Sec. 179 deduction (immediate expensing of new business equipment)
12) Credits
13) Deductions disallowed in computing S corporation income

4. **Corporate Level Items**

a. Items not required to be separately stated organizational costs (e.g., utilities and other ordinary items of income and expense) are combined at the corporate level, and a net amount of ordinary income or loss is passed through to shareholders.

5. **Amortizable Items**

a. Shareholders (who are individuals) may elect to deduct ratably the expenses incurred during the tax year for

1) Research and experimentation costs (over a 10-year period)
2) Mining exploration and development costs (over a 10-year period)
3) Increasing the circulation of a periodical (over a 3-year period)
4) Intangible drilling costs (over a 5-year period)

6. **Allocation**

a. The amount of each item that each shareholder takes into account is computed on a per-day and then a per-share basis. A shareholder's holding period does not include the date of acquisition but does include the date of disposition. All allocations are made on a per-share, per-day basis.

EXAMPLE

Axel transfers 100 shares of GNR Corp., an S Corporation, to fellow shareholder Duff on March 14. Therefore, Axel is allotted 73 days of ownership (January 1 – March 14) amounting to 20% (73 days ÷ 365 days) of each stock, or 20 shares combined. Duff will receive the other 80% (292 days ÷ 365 days) of each stock, or 80 shares combined.

1) Upon a termination of a shareholder's interest during the tax year, an election is available to allocate items according to the books and records of the corporation (its accounting methods) instead of by daily proration.

7. **IRS Reallocation**

a. Pro rata shares of S corporation items passed through may be reallocated by the IRS among shareholders who are members of the same family.

b. Distributive shares must reflect reasonable compensation for services or capital furnished to the corporation by family members.

c. The IRS may disregard a stock transfer (by gift or sale) motivated primarily by tax avoidance.

8. **Character**

a. The shareholder characterizes each item as the corporation would.

9. **Disallowed Deductions**

a. An S corporation is not allowed certain deductions.

1) These are deductions for items that must be separately stated.
2) Each shareholder may be allowed deductions for his or her pro rata share of the items passed through.

10. **Carryovers**

    a. Carryovers (e.g., NOL) between S and C corporations are permitted with limitations. This applies to corporations that change their status from C to S or from S to C.

       NOTE: Do not confuse this rule with the carryover rules for built-in gains tax explained in Subunit 10.4.

11. **Employee Fringe Benefits**

    a. A person who directly or by attribution owns more than 2% of the stock of an S corporation (voting power or amount) on any day during its tax year is not considered an employee entitled to employee benefits (i.e., they are employee-owners, not employees).
    b. The S corporation must treat an amount paid for fringe benefits as deductible compensation, and the shareholder must include the amount in gross income.
    c. This rule does not apply to pension and profit-sharing plans.
    d. This rule precludes

       1) Payments to accident and health plans
       2) Group-term life insurance coverage up to $50,000
       3) Medical reimbursement plans and disability plans
       4) Meals and lodging furnished for the convenience of the employer
       5) Cafeteria plans
       6) Qualified transportation benefits
       7) Personal use of employer-provided property or services
       8) Adoption assistance program
       9) Employment achievement award

    e. Fringe benefits available to 2% shareholders include the following:

       1) Dependent care assistance program
       2) Educational assistance program
       3) Compensation for injury and sickness
       4) No additional-cost service
       5) Qualified employee discount
       6) Working condition fringe
       7) De minimis fringe
       8) On-premises athletic facilities

    f. Accident and health insurance premiums paid by an S corporation are considered for services rendered.

       1) The premiums are deductible by the S corporation and includible in the shareholder's W-2.
       2) The premiums are excludable for Social Security and Medicare if the payments are made under a "qualified plan," such as a cafeteria plan.
       3) Qualified plans are those that treat all employees uniformly and do not give preferential treatment to key employees.

    g. The medical insurance deduction is available for 2% shareholders of S corporations for amounts paid by their corporation for health insurance on their behalf.

       1) The premiums must be included in income by the 2% shareholder.

          a) A deduction is allowed above-the-line on Form 1040 if the taxpayer has self-employment earnings at least equal to the deduction.

12. **Stock Basis**

a. An individual is considered as owning the stock directly by or for

   1) The individual's spouse (other than a legally separated spouse)
   2) The individual's children, grandchildren, and parents

b. Generally, if a shareholder purchases stock, the shareholder's original basis in the stock is its cost.

   1) If a shareholder receives stock in exchange for property, the basis is the same as the property's basis.
   2) If a shareholder lends money to the S corporation, the basis is usually the amount of the loan.
   3) If a shareholder guarantees a third-party loan to an S corporation, the loan does not increase the shareholder's basis. Two exceptions apply:

      a) The shareholder makes payments on the loan.
      b) The shareholder is the primary signer on the note, and the S corporation is the guarantor.

c. The adjusted basis of the shareholder's stock is calculated at year end with increases for the shareholder's pro rata share of the following:

   1) All income items of the S corporation, including tax-exempt income, that are separately stated
   2) Any nonseparately stated income of the S corporation
   3) The amount of the deduction for depletion (other than oil and gas) that is more than the basis of the property being depleted

EXAMPLE

The taxpayer's basis in the S corporation is $12,000 at the beginning of the year. The corporation has ordinary income of $6,000, tax-exempt interest of $2,000, and a long-term capital gain of $1,500. The taxpayer's basis will be increased by $9,500 ($6,000 + $2,000 + $1,500) to $21,500 at the end of the year.

d. The adjusted basis of the shareholder's stock must also be decreased by the shareholder's pro rata share of the following:

   1) Distributions by the S corporation that were not included in income (done before determining the allowable loss deduction)
   2) All separately stated loss and deduction items
   3) Any nonseparately stated loss of the S corporation
   4) Any expenses of the S corporation that are not deductible in figuring its taxable income or are not properly capitalized
   5) The shareholder's deduction for depletion of oil and gas property held by the S corporation to the extent it is not more than the shareholder's share of the adjusted basis of the property

EXAMPLE

The taxpayer's basis at the beginning of the year is $22,000. The taxpayer withdraws $16,000 during the year, and the corporation has an ordinary loss of $9,000. Basis in the corporation is first reduced by the $16,000 distribution to $6,000. Only $6,000 of the loss is deductible by the shareholder, limited to basis.

e. After basis in the shareholder's S corporation stock has been reduced to zero, the shareholder's basis in debt of the S corporation to that shareholder is reduced (but not below zero) by his or her share of items of loss and deduction.

   1) In a subsequent tax year, items passed through must restore the basis in the debt before basis in the stock.

2) Limit. A shareholder's share of loss and deduction items in excess of basis in the debt is not deductible.
    a) The excess is suspended and carried over indefinitely.
    b) It may be deducted in a subsequent tax year in which basis is restored to debt or to stock.

EXAMPLE

The taxpayer's basis in the corporation is made up of $19,500 stock basis and $2,500 debt basis. The stock basis is first reduced by the $16,000 distribution to $3,500. Then, the stock basis is reduced to zero by the loss passthrough. Next, the debt basis is reduced to zero by the loss passthrough, with $3,000 of the loss carried forward ($9,000 – $3,500 – $2,500).

13. **At-Risk Rules**
    a. At-risk rules are applied at the shareholder level.
        1) If the shareholder's pro rata share of passed-through losses exceeds his or her amount at risk at the close of his or her tax year, the excess is not deductible.
            a) The excess is suspended and carried forward indefinitely.
            b) It is deductible when the shareholder's amount at risk has increased.
    b. Each shareholder's at-risk amount equals, basically, the sum of the following:
        1) Money and the adjusted basis of property contributed to the corporation
        2) Amounts borrowed and lent to the corporation to the extent the shareholder has personal liability for repayment or (s)he has pledged as security for repayment property not used in the activity (of the corporation)
            a) However, it does not include other debts of the corporation to third parties, even if the repayment is guaranteed by the shareholder.
            b) The shareholder's amount at risk is increased or decreased by the shareholder's pro rata share of passed-through income and deduction (tax-exempt related also) and by distributions to the shareholder.
    c. The shareholder's basis in his or her stock and debt of the corporation is reduced (subject to prior application of the basis loss limitation), even if current deductibility of the loss is prohibited by the at-risk rules.
14. **Passive Activity Loss Rules**
    a. Current deductibility of any passive activity losses passed through is limited, at the shareholder level, to passive activity income.
        1) Passive activity includes rental activity or an activity of the corporation in which the shareholder does not materially participate.
            a) Material participation by the S corporation is not sufficient.
    b. A shareholder's amount at risk must be reduced by the full amount allowable as a current deduction after application of the at-risk rules, even if part of it must be suspended by the passive loss rules.
15. **Failure to File Penalty**
    a. The penalty is imposed in the amount of the number of persons who were shareholders during any part of the year, multiplied by $195 for each of up to 12 months (including a portion of one) that the return was late or incomplete.

Past CPA exams have contained questions asking for calculations of both a shareholder's adjusted basis in S corporation stock and a shareholder's share of net income from the S corporation.

Stop and review! You have completed the outline for this subunit. Study multiple-choice questions 9 through 23 beginning on page 379.

10.3 DISTRIBUTIONS

1. **Overview**
   a. Distributions include nonliquidating and liquidating distributions of money or other property but not of the S corporation's own stock or obligations. The amount of a particular distribution is the sum of any money plus the FMV of property distributed.
2. **Shareholder Accounts**
   a. S corporations are required to maintain records, with respect to each shareholder, referred to as
      1) Accumulated adjustments account (AAA)
      2) Other adjustments account (OAA)
      3) Previously taxed income account (PTI account)

      These records, along with the shareholder's basis in his or her stock and any Subchapter C E&P, are used to determine the shareholder's tax treatment of distributions.
   b. Distributions from an S corporation reduce the retained earnings in the following order:
      1) AAA
      2) PTI
      3) AE&P
      4) OAA
      5) Stock basis
   c. Note that AAA, OAA, and PTI records and information are needed by S corporations only for purposes of helping shareholders determine taxability of distributions when the S corporation has E&P.
   d. Subchapter C E&P. An S corporation does not have E&P unless it was formerly a C corporation or acquired E&P in a tax-free reorganization, e.g., a merger.
   e. The accumulated adjustments account (AAA) represents the current cumulative balance of the S corporation.
      1) It is calculated without regard to any net negative adjustments (excess of losses and deductions over income and gains).
      2) AAA is not affected by any transactions related to when it was a C corporation (e.g., federal income taxes).
      3) Expenditures that are not deductible by the S corporation decrease basis in stock and the AAA.
      4) Adjustment is not made to the AAA for tax-exempt income (which increases basis) or related nondeductible expenses (which reduce basis). These adjustments are made to OAA.
      5) The AAA balance can be reduced below zero. (Basis may not.)
   f. The OAA represents a cumulative balance of tax-exempt interest earned and life insurance proceeds, reduced by expenses incurred in earning it.
   g. The PTI account represents a balance of undistributed net income on which the shareholders were already taxed prior to 1983.

3. **Distributions of Property**
   a. An S corporation recognizes gain realized on the distribution of appreciated property (FMV > basis).
   b. The amount and character of the gain and its treatment are determined as if the distributed property were sold to the shareholder at its FMV.
      1) Ordinary income results if the property is depreciable in the hands of a more-than-50% shareholder.
   c. The gain is passed through pro rata to each shareholder.
      1) The shareholder's basis in his or her stock and the AAA is increased by his or her shares as if the S corporation had sold the property.
      2) The distributee (recipient) shareholder must determine the proper treatment of the distribution.

EXAMPLE

The S corporation sells an investment asset with a basis of $15,000 for $23,000. The corporation reports an $8,000 gain, which flows through to the shareholders.

   d. When loss property (basis > FMV) is distributed, no loss may be recognized by the S corporation.
      1) The loss is passed through to the shareholders and is nondeductible.
         a) Each shareholder must reduce the basis in his or her stock in the S corporation and take a FMV basis in the property distributed.
         b) The distributee (recipient) shareholder must determine the proper treatment of the distribution.
      2) Sale instead of distribution results in pass-through of loss.

EXAMPLE

The S corporation has a capital asset with a basis of $7,000 and a FMV of $5,000, which it distributes to the sole shareholder. The corporation has a nondeductible loss of $2,000. The shareholder reduces basis by $7,000 and has a $5,000 basis in the asset. If the corporation sold the asset and distributed the proceeds, the shareholder would have a $2,000 deductible loss.

   e. An S corporation is not required to recognize gain on the liquidating distributions of certain installment obligations.
      1) The shareholder treats each payment as a passed-through item.

4. **Shareholder Treatment of Distributions**
   a. Shareholder treatment of distributions from the S corporation is determined at the end of the S corporation's tax year.
      1) The AAA, OAA, bases in shareholders' stock, and basis in corporate-shareholder debt must be adjusted for the S corporation's items of income, deduction, etc., before each shareholder determines the proper treatment of his or her distributions.
   b. No E&P. Shareholder treatment of distributions is straightforward when the S corporation has no Subchapter C E&P.
      1) That portion of distributions that does not exceed the basis in the shareholder's stock is treated as tax-free return of capital.
      2) Excess over basis is treated as gain on sale of the stock.
         a) The character depends on the nature of the stock in the hands of the shareholder and his or her holding period.

c. If there are Subchapter C E&P, the distribution is first treated as return of capital (tax-free) to the extent of the shareholder's AAA balance and then to PTI (up to any basis in the shareholder's stock).

1) Excess distribution beyond AAA and PTI is dividend income to the extent of Subchapter C E&P in the corporation.
2) Excess distribution beyond Subchapter C E&P is return of capital to the extent of OAA.
3) Excess distribution beyond OAA is return of capital to the extent of any remaining basis in the stock.
4) Any excess distribution over remaining basis distributed is treated as gain from the sale of the stock.

S Corporation without Subchapter C E&P

Shareholder Distribution	Tax Result
To extent of basis in stock	Not subject to tax; reduces basis in stock
In excess of basis of stock	Taxed as capital gain

S Corporation with Subchapter C E&P

Shareholder Distribution	Tax Result
To extent of AAA	Not subject to tax; reduces AAA and basis in stock
To extent of PTI	Already taxed previously; reduces basis in stock
To extent of C corporation E&P	Taxed as a dividend; does not reduce basis in stock
To extent of OAA	Not subject to tax; reduces OAA and basis in stock
To extent of basis in stock	Not subject to tax; reduces basis in stock
In excess of basis	Taxed as capital gain

NOTE: In the above determination of shareholder treatment of distributions, any amount to be treated as tax-free return of capital reduces the shareholder's basis in his or her stock.

EXAMPLE

A single-owner S corporation has AAA of $12,000, PTI of $4,000, and E&P of $8,000. The shareholder's basis is $25,000. The first $12,000 of any distribution reduces AAA and shareholder basis by $12,000 and is nontaxable. The next $4,000 of distributions reduces PTI and shareholder basis by $4,000 and is nontaxable. The next $8,000 of distributions is classified as dividend income and reduces E&P. The next $9,000 of distributions is a tax-free reduction of basis ($25,000 – $12,000 – $4,000) and is classified as return of capital. Any distributions above $33,000 will be taxed as capital gain income.

d. An election may be made to treat distributions as coming first from Subchapter C E&P.

1) This results in ordinary dividend income to the distributee (recipient) to the extent of the E&P.
2) Any excess distribution is treated as in 4.b. on the previous page.

e. Cash distributions within a relatively short transition period subsequent to termination of an S election are treated as a return of capital to the extent of the AAA.

1) Basis in shareholder stock is reduced.

f. Form 1099-DIV is used to report any distribution that is in excess of the accumulated adjustments account and that is treated as a dividend to the extent of accumulated earnings and profits.

Stop and review! You have completed the outline for this subunit. Study multiple-choice questions 24 through 27 beginning on page 383.

10.4 SPECIAL TAXES

1. **Overview**
   a. Although S corporations are not generally subject to income tax, the following four special taxes are imposed on S corporations.
2. **Passive Investment Income (PII) Tax**
   a. An S corporation with Subchapter C E&P at the close of its tax year and more PII than 25% of its gross receipts is subject to a tax of 35% of excess net passive income.
   b. Gross receipts (GR) and PII are defined in item 4.d of Subunit 10.1.
   c. Net passive income (NPI) is PII reduced by expenses directly attributable to its production.
   d. PII tax liability is allocated to the PII items and reduces the amount of the item passed through to shareholders.
   e. S corporations are required to make estimated payments of PII tax.
3. **Built-In Gains (BIG) Tax**
   a. An S corporation that, upon conversion from C to S status, had net appreciation inherent in its assets is subject to tax of 35% on net gain recognized (up to the amount of built-in gain on conversion) during the recognition period.
   b. The recognition period normally is the 10-year period beginning on the date the S election became effective. For 2009 and 2010, the 10-year period was reduced to a 7-year period. This means if 2008 was the 7th year of S election, then the recognition period has ended for sales in 2009. Likewise, if 2009 was the 7th year, then the recognition period has ended for sales in 2010.
      1) For 2011-2014, the recognition period is reduced to 5 years for disposals by S corporations if the 5th taxable year precedes the applicable year (2011-2014).
         a) Thus, the conversion must have taken place effective 2008 for 2013 disposals.
   c. The tax liability is passed through, as a loss, pro rata to its shareholders.
      1) It reduces basis in each shareholder's stock and any AAA balance.
      2) Subchapter C E&P are not reduced by BIG tax liability.
   d. S corporations are required to make estimated payments of BIG tax.
   e. Any net operating or capital loss carryover arising in a tax year in which the S corporation was a C corporation can offset the built-in gain for the tax year.
4. **LIFO Recapture**
   a. Any excess of the FIFO inventory value over the LIFO inventory value at the close of the last tax year of C corporation status is gross income to a corporation that used the LIFO method to inventory goods.
   b. Basis of the inventory is increased by the amount on which the recapture tax is imposed.
   c. The recapture income is spread over 4 years: the last C corporation year and the first 3 years of the S corporation.

EXAMPLE

Miles, Inc., switched from a C Corporation to an S Corporation at the beginning of the current year. Miles had used the LIFO inventory valuation method during its existence as a C Corporation. Miles's inventory for the previous year was $2,750,000, and if it used the FIFO method, its inventory would be valued at $3,000,000. Therefore, for the previous year's tax return, Miles must include an additional $250,000 of gross income due to the LIFO recapture, and the tax associated with this additional gross income will be paid over four equal annual installments beginning with the previous year.

5. **General Business Credit Recapture**
   a. An S corporation remains liable for any recapture attributable to credits during C corporation tax years.

Stop and review! You have completed the outline for this subunit. Study multiple-choice questions 28 through 30 on page 385.

QUESTIONS

10.1 Eligibility and Election

1. Bristol Corp. was formed as a C corporation on January 1, 1985, and elected S corporation status on January 1, 1991. At the time of the election, Bristol had accumulated C corporation earnings and profits that have not been distributed. Bristol has had the same 25 shareholders throughout its existence. In 2015, Bristol's S election will terminate if it

A. Increases the number of shareholders to 50.

B. Adds a decedent's estate as a shareholder to the existing shareholders.

C. Takes a charitable contribution deduction.

D. Has passive investment income exceeding 90% of gross receipts in each of the 3 consecutive years ending December 31, 2015.

Answer (D) is correct.
REQUIRED: The S corporation termination event.
DISCUSSION: An S corporation's status will terminate if (1) it has C corporation earnings and profits at the close of 3 consecutive years, and (2) during those 3 years, over 25% of the gross receipts of the S corporation was due to passive investment income. First, the existence of the undistributed earnings and profits satisfies the first test. Second, with 90% passive investment income within the gross receipts, the termination is effective.
Answer (A) is incorrect. An S corporation is limited to a maximum of 100 shareholders. Answer (B) is incorrect. An estate is an eligible shareholder. Answer (C) is incorrect. A charitable contribution deduction will not terminate the election.

2. Which of the following conditions will prevent a corporation from qualifying as an S corporation?

A. The corporation has both common and preferred stock.

B. The corporation has one class of stock with different voting rights.

C. One shareholder is an estate.

D. One shareholder is a grantor trust.

Answer (A) is correct.
REQUIRED: The condition that will prevent a corporation from qualifying as an S corporation.
DISCUSSION: An S corporation may have only one class of stock.
Answer (B) is incorrect. An S corporation may have only one class of (common) stock, but shares of that class may have different voting rights. Answer (C) is incorrect. A decedent's estate may be a shareholder. Answer (D) is incorrect. A grantor trust may be a shareholder for a 2-year period following the death of a grantor.

3. Top Corp., which has been operating since 1997, has an October 31 year end, which coincides with its natural business year. On May 15, 2015, Top filed the required form to elect S corporation status. All of Top's shareholders consented to the election, and all other requirements were met. The earliest date that Top can be recognized as an S corporation is

A. November 1, 2014.

B. May 15, 2015.

C. November 1, 2015.

D. November 1, 2016.

Answer (C) is correct.
REQUIRED: The earliest date an S corporation election will be effective.
DISCUSSION: An S corporation election made within the first 2 1/2 months of the year is effective the first day of that tax year. An election made after the first 2 1/2 months of the year is effective as of the next year. Note that an S corporation may have a fiscal year that coincides with its natural business year (with IRS consent). Top Corp. filed for the S election after the first 2 1/2 months of the November 1, 2014, to October 31, 2015, fiscal year. Thus, Top will be recognized as an S corporation beginning on the first day of the following fiscal year, November 1, 2015.

4. On February 10, 2015, Ace Corp., a calendar-year corporation, elected S corporation status, and all shareholders consented to the election. There was no change in shareholders in 2015. Ace met all eligibility requirements for S status during the pre-election portion of the year. What is the earliest date on which Ace can be recognized as an S corporation?

A. February 10, 2015.

B. February 10, 2016.

C. January 1, 2016.

D. January 1, 2015.

Answer (D) is correct.

REQUIRED: The effective date of an S corporation election.

DISCUSSION: The S corporation election is effective for the current tax year if it is made on or before March 15 for calendar-year corporations, subject to certain exceptions relating to ineligibility and complete consent. Since this election was made on February 10 and no exceptions applied, the election will be effective for the entire taxable year in which it was made.

5. An S corporation has 30,000 shares of voting common stock and 20,000 shares of nonvoting common stock issued and outstanding. The S election can be revoked voluntarily with the consent of the shareholders holding, on the day of the revocation,

	Shares of Voting Stock	Shares of Nonvoting Stock
A.	0	20,000
B.	7,500	5,000
C.	10,000	16,000
D.	20,000	0

Answer (C) is correct.

REQUIRED: The number of shares required to consent to a voluntary revocation of an S election.

DISCUSSION: An S corporation election may be terminated by revocation. A revocation may be made only with the consent of shareholders who, at the time the revocation is made, hold more than one-half of the number of issued and outstanding shares of stock (including both voting and nonvoting stock) of the corporation.

6. Lindal Corporation, organized in 2015, immediately filed an election for S corporation status under the rules of Subchapter S. What is the maximum amount of passive investment income that Lindal will be allowed to earn and still qualify as an S corporation?

A. 80% of gross receipts.

B. 50% of gross receipts.

C. 20% of gross receipts.

D. No limit on passive investment income.

Answer (D) is correct.

REQUIRED: The maximum amount of passive investment income allowable to an S corporation.

DISCUSSION: There is no limit on the amount of passive investment income that a corporation can earn and still qualify as an S corporation. S corporation status is terminated if the corporation has had passive investment income in excess of 25% of gross receipts for 3 consecutive taxable years and has had Subchapter C earnings and profits at the end of each of those taxable years. Subchapter C earnings and profits are those accumulated during a taxable year for which a Subchapter S election was not in effect. Lindal filed an S election immediately after formation which prevents C corporation earnings and profits.

7. Zinco Corp. was a calendar-year S corporation. Zinco's S status terminated on April 1, 2015, when Case Corp. became a shareholder. During 2015 (365-day calendar year), Zinco had nonseparately computed income of $310,250. If no election was made by Zinco, what amount of the income, if any, was allocated to the S corporation short year for 2015?

A. $233,750

B. $155,125

C. $76,500

D. $0

Answer (C) is correct.

REQUIRED: The allocation of income to the S corporation short year.

DISCUSSION: Nonseparately computed income will be allocated on a pro rata basis unless certain exceptions apply or an election is made. Since neither of these conditions apply, the S corporation will be deemed to generate $76,500 ($310,250 × 90 ÷ 365) of income in the S corporation short year.

Answer (A) is incorrect. The figure of $233,750 is the amount allocated to the C corporation short year. Answer (B) is incorrect. Zinco's portion of the nonseparately computed income must be allocated on a pro rata basis to the S corporation short year. Answer (D) is incorrect. Some of the income should be allocated.

8. If a corporation's status as an S corporation is revoked or terminated after January 1, 2015, how many years is the corporation required to wait before making a new S election in the absence of IRS consent to an earlier election?

A. 1

B. 3

C. 5

D. 10

Answer (C) is correct.

REQUIRED: The number of years that must pass after revocation or termination of an S election before a new S election can be made.

DISCUSSION: A new S election can be made without IRS consent 5 years after revocation or termination of an S election.

Answer (A) is incorrect. The applicable period is more than 1 year. Answer (B) is incorrect. The applicable period is more than 3 years. Answer (D) is incorrect. The applicable period is less than 10 years.

10.2 Operations

9. Bern Corp., an S corporation, had an ordinary loss of $36,500 for the year ended December 31, 2015. On January 1, 2015, Meyer owned 50% of Bern's stock. Meyer held the stock for 40 days in 2015 before selling the entire 50% interest to an unrelated third party. Meyer's basis for the stock was $10,000. Meyer was a full-time employee of Bern until the stock was sold. Meyer's share of Bern's 2015 loss was

A. $0

B. $2,000

C. $10,000

D. $18,250

Answer (B) is correct.

REQUIRED: The allocable share of an S corporation item when a shareholder's interest changes during the tax year.

DISCUSSION: The amount of each S corporation item, which each shareholder takes into account, is computed on a per-day and per-share basis. The portion of the loss passed through to Meyer is

$$\$36,500 \times 50\% \times \frac{40}{365} = \$2,000$$

10. A shareholder's basis in the stock of an S corporation is increased by the shareholder's pro rata share of income from

	Tax-Exempt Interest	Taxable Interest
A.	No	No
B.	No	Yes
C.	Yes	No
D.	Yes	Yes

Answer (D) is correct.

REQUIRED: The item(s) that increase(s) a shareholder's basis in S corporation stock.

DISCUSSION: Interest income received by an S corporation, whether taxable or nontaxable, increases the basis of an S corporation shareholder's stock.

11. Graphite Corp. has been a calendar-year S corporation since its inception on January 2, 2009. On January 1, 2015, Smith and Tyler each owned 50% of the Graphite stock in which their respective bases were $12,000 and $9,000. For the year ended December 31, 2015, Graphite had $80,000 in ordinary business income and $6,000 in tax-exempt income. Graphite made a $53,000 cash distribution to each shareholder on December 31, 2015. What total amount of income from Graphite is includible in Smith's 2015 adjusted gross income?

A. $96,000

B. $93,000

C. $43,000

D. $40,000

Answer (D) is correct.

REQUIRED: The amount of income a shareholder should recognize from an S corporation.

DISCUSSION: All of an S corporation's income is taxed to the shareholders each year, whether distributed or not. Each shareholder's basis is increased by his or her share of income, including tax-exempt income. Distributions in general then reduce the shareholder's basis, and any distribution that is not in excess of basis is treated as a tax-free return of capital. Therefore, Smith will recognize $40,000 of ordinary income ($80,000 × 50% interest). The tax-exempt income is not included in a shareholder's income. The distribution does not affect Smith's gross income because it does not exceed his basis ($12,000 basis + $43,000 income).

12. Lane, Inc., an S corporation, pays single coverage health insurance premiums of $4,800 per year and family coverage premiums of $7,200 per year. Mill is a 10% shareholder-employee in Lane. On Mill's behalf, Lane pays Mill's family coverage under the health insurance plan. What amount of insurance premiums is includible in Mill's gross income?

A. $0

B. $720

C. $4,800

D. $7,200

Answer (D) is correct.

REQUIRED: The amount of insurance premiums includible in a taxpayer's gross income.

DISCUSSION: Certain fringe benefits received by shareholders owning more than 2% of the stock of an S corporation are included in the shareholder's W-2. Health insurance premiums are not a tax-free benefit to shareholders holding more than 2%.

Answer (A) is incorrect. The health insurance received by an employee-owner from an S corporation is compensation for services. Answer (B) is incorrect. The premium for family coverage is $7,200 and is not related to the level of ownership. Answer (C) is incorrect. The $4,800 health insurance premiums are not paid for Mill by Lane.

13. With regard to S corporations and their shareholders, the "at-risk" rules applicable to losses

A. Depend on the type of income reported by the S corporation.

B. Are subject to the elections made by the S corporation's shareholders.

C. Take into consideration the S corporation's ratio of debt to equity.

D. Apply at the shareholder level rather than at the corporate level.

Answer (D) is correct.

REQUIRED: The proper application of the at-risk rules to S corporations and shareholders.

DISCUSSION: The at-risk rules do not apply directly to S corporations. They apply directly to individuals as shareholders of S corporations. The at-risk rules limit a shareholder's deduction for losses and other deductions from an S corporation to the total of (1) the adjusted basis of the shareholder's stock in the S corporation and (2) the shareholder's adjusted basis of any debt owed by the S corporation to the shareholder.

Answer (A) is incorrect. The type of income does not affect the at-risk rules. Answer (B) is incorrect. Shareholder elections do not affect the at-risk rules. Answer (C) is incorrect. The debt equity ratio does not affect the at-risk rules.

14. Sandy is the sole shareholder of Swallow, an S corporation. Sandy's adjusted basis in Swallow stock is $60,000 at the beginning of the year. During the year, Swallow reports the following income items:

Ordinary income	$30,000
Tax-exempt income	5,000
Capital gains	10,000

In addition, Swallow makes a nontaxable distribution to Sandy of $20,000 during the year. What is Sandy's adjusted basis in the Swallow stock at the end of the year?

A. $60,000

B. $70,000

C. $80,000

D. $85,000

Answer (D) is correct.

REQUIRED: Shareholder's adjusted basis in the stock of an S corporation.

DISCUSSION: The adjusted basis of the shareholder's stock is figured at year end with increases for the shareholder's pro rata share of all income items, including tax-exempt income, that are separately stated and any nonseparately stated income. Also, all separately and nonseparately stated losses, distributions, and deduction items decrease the basis of the shareholder's stock on a pro rata basis. Sandy's stock basis on January 1, Year 1, is $60,000.

Original basis	$60,000
Ordinary income	30,000
Tax-exempt income	5,000
Capital gains	10,000
Nontaxable distribution	(20,000)
Adjusted basis	$85,000

Answer (A) is incorrect. A $60,000 adjusted basis ignores the effects of the income items and the nontaxable distribution. Answer (B) is incorrect. A $70,000 adjusted basis excludes the effects of the tax-exempt income and the capital gains. Answer (C) is incorrect. An $80,000 adjusted basis does not include the effects of the tax-exempt income.

15. Bow, Inc., an S corporation, has three equal shareholders. For the year ended December 31, 2015, Bow had taxable income and current earnings and profits of $300,000. Bow made cash distributions totaling $120,000 during 2015. For 2015, what amount from Bow should be included in each shareholder's gross income?

A. $140,000

B. $100,000

C. $60,000

D. $40,000

Answer (B) is correct.

REQUIRED: The gross income of a shareholder of an S corporation with current earnings that made distributions.

DISCUSSION: Each shareholder includes in his or her personal gross income his or her share of ordinary income and separately stated items of the S corporation on a per-day and per-share basis. Each shareholder's share is 1/3 of $300,000. Shareholder inclusion will be $100,000 each. Excess distributions are treated as tax-free return of capital.

16. Rap, Inc., was organized in January 2015 and immediately made an S election. Rap, Inc.'s stock is entirely owned by Howard, who contributed $40,000 to start the business. Rap reported the following results for the 2015 year:

Ordinary income	$36,000
Short-term capital loss	4,000
Charitable contributions	1,000
Tax-exempt income	1,000
Sec. 179 deduction	10,000

On April 12, 2015, Howard received a $30,000 cash distribution from the corporation. What is the adjusted basis of his stock on January 1, 2016?

A. $41,000

B. $32,000

C. $31,000

D. $10,000

Answer (B) is correct.

REQUIRED: The basis of an S corporation shareholder's stock after a distribution.

DISCUSSION: The adjusted basis of the shareholder's stock is figured at year end with increases for the shareholder's pro rata share of all income items, including tax-exempt income, that are separately stated and any nonseparately stated income. Also, all separately and nonseparately stated losses and deduction items decrease the basis of the shareholder's stock on a pro rata basis. Howard's stock basis on January 1, 2016, is $32,000.

Original basis	$40,000
Ordinary income	36,000
Tax-exempt income	1,000
Short-term capital loss	(4,000)
Charitable contributions	(1,000)
Sec. 179 deduction	(10,000)
Cash distribution	(30,000)
Adjusted basis	$32,000

Answer (A) is incorrect. The Sec. 179 deduction and charitable contributions reduce the basis. Answer (C) is incorrect. The charitable contributions reduce the basis. Answer (D) is incorrect. Other factors besides the cash distribution are considered.

17. Bobby owns 50% of Jingles, Inc., an S corporation filing tax returns on a calendar year. For tax year 2015, the corporation has an operating loss of $15,000 and separately stated tax-exempt income of $10,000. Bobby individually loans the corporation $4,000. His basis on January 1, 2015, is $2,000. What is his basis in the stock at year end 2015?

A. $1,000

B. $3,500

C. $(9,000)

D. $0

Answer (D) is correct.

REQUIRED: The S corporation shareholder's basis in stock at year end.

DISCUSSION: The IRC provides guidelines for adjustments to the basis of a shareholder's S corporation stock. The increases include items of income (including tax-exempt income) that are passed through to the shareholder, nonseparately stated (ordinary) income, and the excess of deductions for depletion over the basis of the property subject to depletion. A loan made to an S corporation also increases the shareholder's basis for the amount of the loan. The basis of Bobby's stock is decreased by the amount of loss allocable to him; however, it cannot reduce his basis below zero.

	Stock Basis	Loan Basis
Basis at January 1	$ 2,000	
Loan to corporation		$4,000
Tax-exempt interest	5,000	
Ordinary loss of S corporation	(7,000)	(500)
Basis at December 31	$ 0	$3,500

Answer (A) is incorrect. Half of the ordinary loss will reduce basis, half of the tax-exempt income will increase basis, and the personal loan will increase basis. Answer (B) is incorrect. The figure of $3,500 is the basis in the corporation, not the basis in the stock. Answer (C) is incorrect. Basis can never be negative.

18. Bob and Sally, unmarried taxpayers, each owned 50% of Lostalot, Inc., an S corporation. The corporation had a $50,000 operating loss for the tax year ending December 31, 2015. As of December 31, 2014, Bob's basis in his stock was $15,000 and Sally's was $5,000. During the 2015 tax year, Sally mortgaged her home for $25,000 and loaned the money to the corporation. Although not personally liable, Bob told her not to worry and that if anything happened, he would help pay the mortgage debt. Calculate the amount of allowable loss deduction each shareholder would be able to recognize on their individual 2015 tax returns.

A. Bob: $25,000, and Sally: $25,000.

B. Bob: $15,000, and Sally: $5,000.

C. Bob: $15,000, and Sally: $30,000.

D. Bob: $15,000, and Sally: $25,000.

Answer (D) is correct.

REQUIRED: The loss deduction that may be recognized on a shareholder's individual return.

DISCUSSION: Bob and Sally's share of the loss is $25,000 each. However, the deduction for each is limited to their basis in the S corporation. Bob's deduction is limited to his $15,000 basis in the stock. Sally's basis consists of her $5,000 stock basis and her $25,000 debt basis. Sally has enough basis to cover her share of the loss.

Answer (A) is incorrect. Bob's basis is not large enough to cover the $25,000 share of the loss. Answer (B) is incorrect. Sally's basis is larger than $5,000. Answer (C) is incorrect. Sally's share of the loss is not $30,000.

19. The Haas Corp., a calendar-year S corporation, has two equal shareholders. For the year ended December 31, 2015, Haas had taxable income and current earnings and profits of $60,000, which included $50,000 from operations and $10,000 from investment interest income. There were no other transactions that year. Each shareholder's basis in the stock of Haas will increase by

A. $50,000

B. $30,000

C. $25,000

D. $0

Answer (B) is correct.

REQUIRED: The increase in the basis of a shareholder's stock in an S corporation.

DISCUSSION: The shareholder's basis in stock of the S corporation is increased (decreased) by his or her share of separately and nonseparately stated items of income or deduction and loss. Thus, the basis in the stock of each shareholder will be increased by $30,000 [($50,000 × 50%) + ($10,000 × 50%)].

20. As of January 1, 2015, Kane owned all 100 issued shares of Manning Corp., a calendar-year S corporation. On the 41st day of 2015, Kane sold 25 of the Manning shares to Rodgers. For the year ended December 31, 2015 (a 365-day calendar year), Manning had $73,000 in nonseparately stated income and made no distributions to its shareholders. What amount of nonseparately stated income from Manning should be reported on Kane's 2015 tax return?

A. $56,800

B. $54,750

C. $16,250

D. $0

Answer (A) is correct.

REQUIRED: The shareholder's income from an S corporation when shares are transferred during the year.

DISCUSSION: Each shareholder shall include in gross income the pro rata share of the S corporation's income. The pro rata share is the taxpayer's share of the corporation's income after assigning an equal portion of the income to each day of the taxable year and then dividing that portion pro rata among the shares outstanding on each day. Therefore, each day of the year will be assigned $200 of income ($73,000 ÷ 365). Kane's share will be $56,800 [$8,200 (41 days × $200 × 100% ownership) plus $48,600 (324 days × $200 × 75% ownership)].

Answer (B) is incorrect. The figure of $54,750 applies Kane's end-of-year ownership percentage to the entire year's income instead of on a pro rata basis for the shares outstanding on each day. Answer (C) is incorrect. The figure of $16,250 is Rodgers's pro rata share. Answer (D) is incorrect. Each shareholder must include in taxable income the pro rata share of the S corporation's income.

21. Which of the following items is **not** a separately stated item for Form 1120S shareholders?

A. Charitable contributions made by the corporation.

B. Sec. 179 deduction.

C. Depreciation.

D. Tax-exempt interest.

Answer (C) is correct.

REQUIRED: The item that is not a separately stated item for Form 1120S shareholders.

DISCUSSION: An S corporation passes a pro rata share of its total income (loss) through to the individual shareholders except for items that require separate treatment by the shareholder. Charitable contributions made by the corporation, Sec. 179 deduction, and tax-exempt interest must be separately stated. Depreciation, however, is combined with other nonseparately stated income or loss.

Answer (A) is incorrect. Charitable contributions made by the corporation are separately stated for Form 1120S shareholders. Answer (B) is incorrect. A Sec. 179 deduction is an item that is separately stated for Form 1120S shareholders. Answer (D) is incorrect. Tax-exempt interest is an item that is separately stated for Form 1120S shareholders.

22. Evan, an individual, has a 40% interest in EF, an S corporation. At the beginning of the year, Evan's basis in EF was $2,000. During the year, EF distributed $100,000 and reported operating income of $200,000. What amount should Evan include in gross income?

A. $38,000

B. $40,000

C. $80,000

D. $118,000

Answer (C) is correct.

REQUIRED: The amount included in gross income from an S corporation.

DISCUSSION: An S corporation shareholder is required to take the pro rata share of items passed through into account in computing the shareholder's personal taxable income for his or her tax year within which the tax year of the S corporation ended. The S corporation had $200,000 of operating income, and Evan is a 40% shareholder. Therefore, Evan must report $80,000 ($200,000 × 40%) of income from the S corporation.

Answer (A) is incorrect. This figure is 40% of the distribution minus Evan's basis of $2,000. Answer (B) is incorrect. This figure is Evan's share of the distribution. Answer (D) is incorrect. This figure is the income of the other S corporation shareholders minus Evan's basis in the S corporation stock.

23. Tap, a calendar-year S corporation, reported the following items of income and expense in the current year:

Revenue	$44,000
Operating expenses	20,000
Long-term capital loss	6,000
Charitable contributions	1,000
Interest expense	4,000

What is the amount of Tap's ordinary income?

A. $13,000

B. $19,000

C. $20,000

D. $24,000

Answer (C) is correct.

REQUIRED: The amount of Tap's ordinary income.

DISCUSSION: The items of income, deduction, and credit of an S corporation are reported by the corporation; however, an S corporation is not allowed deductions for items that must be separately stated, which include long-term capital losses and charitable contributions. Therefore, Tap's ordinary income equals $20,000 ($44,000 revenue – $20,000 operating expenses – $4,000 interest expense).

Answer (A) is incorrect. The long-term capital loss and charitable contribution must be stated separately and are therefore not deductible by the S corporation. Answer (B) is incorrect. The charitable contribution must be stated separately and is therefore not deductible by the S corporation. Answer (D) is incorrect. The S corporation may deduct the $4,000 of interest expense.

10.3 Distributions

24. If an S corporation has no accumulated earnings and profits, the amount distributed to a shareholder

A. Must be returned to the S corporation.

B. Increases the shareholder's basis in the stock.

C. Decreases the shareholder's basis in the stock.

D. Has no effect on the shareholder's basis in the stock.

Answer (C) is correct.

REQUIRED: The true statement regarding a distribution by an S corporation that has no accumulated earnings and profits.

DISCUSSION: Distribution from an S corporation with no Subchapter C earnings and profits is treated as a tax-free return of capital to the extent of a shareholder's basis in his or her stock of the corporation, decreasing the stock's basis. Excess is treated as gain or loss on the sale of the stock.

25. Packer Corp., an accrual-basis, calendar-year S corporation, has been an S corporation since its inception. Starr was a 50% shareholder in Packer throughout the current year and had a $10,000 tax basis in Packer stock on January 1. During the current year, Packer had a $1,000 net business loss and made an $8,000 cash distribution to each shareholder. What amount of the distribution was includible in Starr's gross income?

A. $8,000

B. $7,500

C. $4,000

D. $0

Answer (D) is correct.

REQUIRED: The amount includible in Starr's income from the distribution.

DISCUSSION: Cash or property from distributions from S and C Corporations are only taxable to the recipient to the extent of the earnings and profits of the corporation. Any distribution in excess of earnings and profits reduces the basis of the stock held in the corporation until the basis is reduced to zero. Once the stock basis is reduced to zero, any further distributions are treated as a capital gain. Since Packer Corp. has a $1,000 business loss, it did not have sufficient earnings and profits to pay taxable dividends. Therefore, the cash distribution received by Starr reduces his basis in the stock of the S corporation, and he is not required to include the cash distribution in gross income.

Answer (A) is incorrect. There were no earnings and profits to pay the $8,000 cash distribution, and it is not included in gross income. Answer (B) is incorrect. The business loss is not used to offset the cash distribution received from Starr in determining the amount of gross income. Answer (C) is incorrect. Starr received an $8,000 cash distribution, and it was not included in gross income because there are not earnings and profits in the S corporation because it was not a C corporation.

26. Jenny Corporation (an S corporation) is owned entirely by Craig. At the beginning of 2015, Craig's adjusted basis in his Jenny Corporation stock was $20,000. Jenny reported ordinary income of $5,000 and a capital loss of $10,000. Craig received a cash distribution of $35,000 in November 2015. What is Craig's gain from the distribution?

A. $0

B. $10,000

C. $20,000

D. $35,000

Answer (B) is correct.

REQUIRED: The sole shareholder's gain from the distribution of an S corporation.

DISCUSSION: The basis is increased by the ordinary income to $25,000. The $35,000 distribution is taken next and, since it exceeds the basis, there is a $10,000 gain. The capital loss is nondeductible because there is no basis left after the deduction from the distribution for Craig and it is carried over.

Answer (A) is incorrect. If the distribution is greater than the basis, the excess is taxable as a sale or an exchange of property (a taxable capital gain). Answer (C) is incorrect. The distribution is taken before the deduction for the capital loss. Answer (D) is incorrect. The entire distribution is not taxable, only the difference between the distribution and the basis.

27. Beck Corp. has been a calendar-year S corporation since its inception on January 2, 2012. On January 1, 2015, Lazur and Lyle each owned 50% of the Beck stock in which their respective tax bases were $12,000 and $9,000. For the year ended December 31, 2015, Beck had $81,000 in ordinary business income and $10,000 in tax-exempt income. Beck made a $51,000 cash distribution to each shareholder on December 31, 2015. What was Lazur's tax basis in Beck after the distribution?

A. $1,500

B. $6,500

C. $52,500

D. $57,500

Answer (B) is correct.

REQUIRED: The basis of an S corporation shareholder's stock after a distribution.

DISCUSSION: The adjusted basis of the shareholder's stock is figured at year end with increases for the shareholder's pro rata share of all income items, including tax-exempt income, that are separately stated and any nonseparately stated income. Also, all separately and nonseparately stated losses and deduction items decrease the basis of the shareholder's stock on a pro rata basis. Lazur's tax basis in Beck after the distribution is $6,500.

Original basis	$ 12,000
Ordinary income ($81,000 × 50%)	40,500
Tax-exempt income ($10,000 × 50%)	5,000
Cash distribution	(51,000)
Adjusted basis	$ 6,500

Answer (A) is incorrect. The shareholder's adjusted basis includes his or her pro rata share of tax-exempt income. Answer (C) is incorrect. The shareholder's adjusted basis is increased by his or her share of tax exempt income and decreased by the amount of the cash distribution. Answer (D) is incorrect. The shareholder's adjusted basis is decreased by the amount of the cash distribution.

10.4 Special Taxes

28. Tax Corp. converted from C to S status in 2015. The net appreciation inherent in its assets is subject to a tax on net gain recognized

A. At the time of the conversion.

B. During a recognition period of 2 years.

C. With no effect on any shareholder's basis in the stock.

D. Up to the amount of built-in gain on conversion.

Answer (D) is correct.

REQUIRED: The true statement about the built-in gains tax.

DISCUSSION: An S corporation that, upon conversion from C to S status after 1986, had net appreciation inherent in its assets is subject to a tax of 35% on net gain recognized (up to the amount of built-in gain on conversion) during the recognition period.

Answer (A) is incorrect. The net appreciation inherent in its assets is subject to a tax on net gain recognized during the recognition period. Answer (B) is incorrect. The recognition period normally is a 10-year period beginning on the date the S election became effective. Answer (C) is incorrect. The tax liability is passed through, as a loss, pro rata to its shareholders, and it reduces each shareholder's basis in the stock.

29. Commerce Corp. elects S corporation status as of the beginning of Year 2015. At the time of Commerce's election, it held a machine with a basis of $20,000 and a fair market value of $30,000. In March of 2015, Commerce sells the machine for $35,000. What would be the amount subject to the built-in gains tax?

A. $0

B. $5,000

C. $10,000

D. $15,000

Answer (C) is correct.

REQUIRED: Recognized gain subject to built-in gains tax.

DISCUSSION: An S corporation that, upon conversion from C to S status after 1986, had net appreciation inherent in its assets is subject to tax of 35% on net gain recognized (up to the amount of built-in gain on conversion) during the recognition period. The recognition period normally is the 10-year period beginning on the date the S election became effective. Commerce would be subject to built-in gains tax on $10,000 ($30,000 FMV at conversion – $20,000) of the recognized gain from the transaction in March.

Answer (A) is incorrect. The inherent appreciation in the machine at the time of conversion is subject to the built-in gains tax. Answer (B) is incorrect. The amount of $5,000 is the post-conversion gain, not the inherent appreciation. Answer (D) is incorrect. Only the inherent appreciation at the time of the conversion is subject to the built-in gains tax.

30. Magic Corp., a regular C corporation, elected S corporation status at the beginning of the current calendar year. It had an asset with a basis of $40,000 and a fair market value (FMV) of $85,000 on January 1. The asset was sold during the year for $95,000. Magic's corporate tax rate was 35%. What was Magic's tax liability as a result of the sale?

A. $0

B. $3,500

C. $15,750

D. $19,250

Answer (C) is correct.

REQUIRED: The gain on a sale reported by a C corporation that elected to be a S corporation.

DISCUSSION: An S corporation that, upon conversion from C to S status, had net appreciation inherent in its assets is subject to a built-in gains tax of 35% on net gain recognized (up to the amount of built-in gain on conversion) during the recognition period. Magic had $45,000 ($85,000 FMV in January 1 – $40,000 basis) of built-in gains at the time that Magic elected to be an S corporation. The tax on the $45,000 is $15,750 ($45,000 × 35%).

Answer (A) is incorrect. A gain on the sale is recognized by Magic. Answer (B) is incorrect. The figure of $3,500 is the corporate tax on the gain that occurred after the S corporation election. Answer (D) is incorrect. The figure of $19,250 is the corporate tax on the entire gain of $55,000 ($95,000 amount realized – $40,000 basis).

10.5 PRACTICE TASK-BASED SIMULATIONS

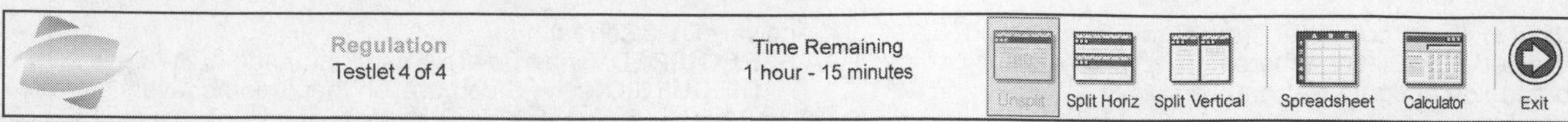

DIRECTIONS

Note: If you believe you have encountered a software malfunction, report it to the test center staff immediately.

Navigation

To navigate from task to task, use the controls at the bottom of the screen. Click on the **Next** button to advance to the next task, or the **Previous** button to go to the previous task. To go directly to any task, click on its number.

If you would like a reminder to revisit a task, or want to indicate that you are finished with it, click on the reminder flag below the task number. To clear the flag, click on it again. Reminder flags are for your use only – they do not contribute to your score.

Tabs

In this part of the examination, you will be asked to complete various tasks. Every task has one or more **Work Tabs**. Some tasks have one or more **Information Tabs**, others may have none. Every task has a **Help** tab.

If a task has **Information Tabs**, you may use the information in them to complete your responses in the **Work Tabs**.

Work tab **Information tab** **Help tab**

Work Tabs:

- **Work Tabs** are identified with a pencil icon. This is where your responses are expected.
- Each task has one or more **Work Tabs**.
- **Work Tabs** contain directions for completing the task – be sure to read these directions carefully.
- The **Work Tab** name in the example above is for illustration only – yours will differ.
- You must complete all of the **Work Tabs** in each task to receive full credit.

Information Tabs:

- The Authoritative Literature will be provided in all tasks in the AUD, FAR, and REG sections for your reference.
- Your simulation may have one or more additional **Information Tabs**. Like the Authoritative Literature tabs, **Information Tabs** do not have a pencil icon.
- If your task has additional **Information Tabs**, go through each to familiarize yourself with the task content.

Help Tab:

- The **Help Tab** provides assistance with the exam software that is used in this task. For example, if the task is to compose a memorandum, **Help** will provide information about the word processor.

The Toolbar

The toolbar at the top of the screen shows the amount of time remaining for you to complete the tasks. In addition, the following tools are available. Note that only the **Exit** button is displayed when Directions are visible - the others will appear when you begin the tasks.

Click on these buttons to split or unsplit the screen. You can split the screen vertically or horizontally.

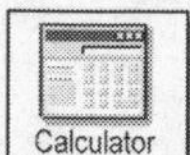

Click on this button to display the calculator; click on it again to hide the calculator. To move the calculator, click on the calculator title bar and drag the calculator to the desired location.

Click on this button to use the spreadsheet; click on it again to hide the spreadsheet. To move the spreadsheet, click on the the spreadsheet title bar and drag the spreadsheet to the desired location.

Click on this button to go on to the next part of the examination. You must complete all of the tasks to receive full credit. Once you click on **Exit** and confirm the action, you will NOT be able to return to this testlet.

= Reminder | Directions | 1 2 3 4 5 6 | Previous | Next

For each of the described situations below, enter the correct amount into the shaded cells.

Situation	*Amount*
1. Samantha's basis in S corporation stock was $100,000 before adjusting for current-year activity that includes $10,000 tax-exempt interest income, $20,000 nonseparately stated income, and $15,000 excess of depletion deduction over the basis of the property being depleted. What is Samantha's basis in her S corporation stock after considering these items?	
2. In Year 1, Lisa acquired 100% of the stock of Dance, Inc., for $25,000 cash. Dance incurred a loss of $7,800 for Year 1. On January 1, Year 2, Dance properly elected S corporation status. Its net income for Year 2 was $10,000. A dividend of $2,500 was declared and paid in Year 2. What is Lisa's basis in Dance as of December 31, Year 2?	
3. Broken Spoons, Inc., was organized in January 2015 as a properly elected S corporation. The corporation's stock is entirely owned by Hal, who contributed $40,000 to start the business. For the 2015 year, the corporation reported ordinary income of $36,000, a short-term capital loss of $4,000, and a Sec. 179 deduction of $10,000. On April 12, 2015, Hal received a $30,000 cash distribution from Broken Spoons. What is the basis of Hal's stock on January 1, 2016?	
4. Reed owns 50% of DCH, Inc., an S corporation that files tax returns on a calendar-year basis. In Year 5, DCH has an operating loss of $15,000 and separately stated tax-exempt income of $10,000. During the year, Reed individually loans the corporation $4,000. His basis on January 1, Year 5, is $2,000. What is his basis in the stock on December 31, Year 5?	

Randall, Incorporated, a calendar-year taxpayer, has been in existence for several years. Randall files an S election on January 15, 2015, to be treated as an S corporation starting in the 2015 tax year. All of Randall's five shareholders agree to the election.

For each of the following taxes, determine whether the S election exempts a corporation form the tax. Check the box to the right of the item if a corporation may still be required to pay the tax despite filing an S election.

Tax Item	*Required to Pay*
1. Corporate alternative minimum tax	
2. Passive investment income tax	
3. Personal holding company tax	
4. General business credit recapture	
5. Built-in gains tax	
6. Accumulated earnings tax	
7. Corporate income tax	
8. LIFO recapture tax	

= Reminder | Directions | 1 2 3 4 5 6 | Previous | Next

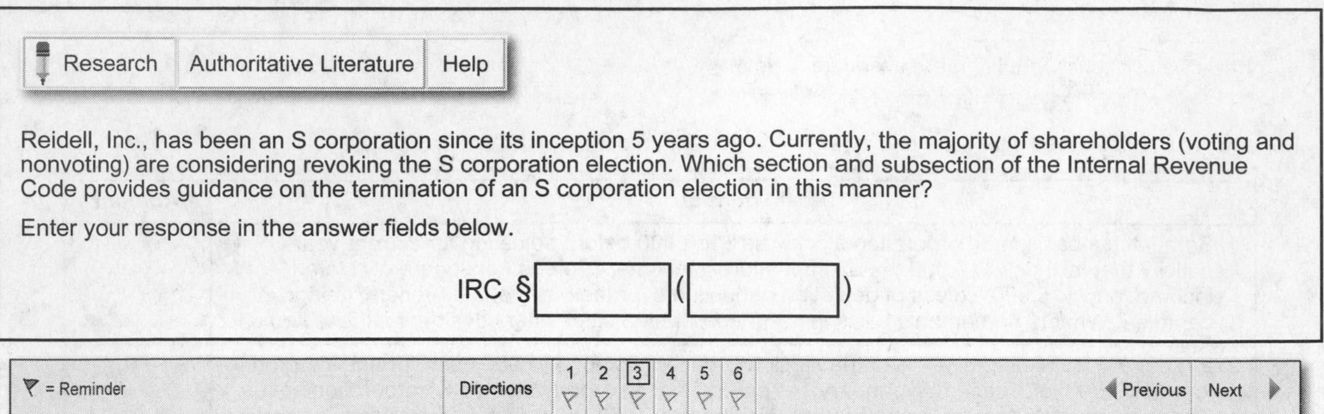

Research | Authoritative Literature | Help

Reidell, Inc., has been an S corporation since its inception 5 years ago. Currently, the majority of shareholders (voting and nonvoting) are considering revoking the S corporation election. Which section and subsection of the Internal Revenue Code provides guidance on the termination of an S corporation election in this manner?

Enter your response in the answer fields below.

IRC § [ ] ([ ])

= Reminder | Directions | 1 2 3 4 5 6 | Previous | Next

IRS Form 1120S (K-1): Danny Morales | Authoritative Literature | Help

Soar, Inc., was a C corporation until January 1, 2014, when its election to be an S corporation became effective. Among Soar's items of income, expense, loss, and credit for the current tax year were reasonable salary expense, a contribution to a qualified tax-exempt organization, interest-related expense, and a net loss on the disposal of property.

Additional Information:

Address:	6850 Parish Avenue, Gainesville, FL 32608
EIN:	59-7891234
Shareholders:	Diana Bauza, 1234 Cherry Road, Gainesville, FL 32608; 300 shares, acquired 02/01/10, SSN: 123-45-6789, Officer; (352)123-4567 Danny Morales, 4321 Maple Lane, Gainesville, FL 32608; 200 shares, acquired 02/01/10, SSN: 987-65-4321

Soar calculates its total income to be $200,000. Included in the calculation of income are the following items:

1. Rent earned from rental real estate properties	$ 50,000
2. Dividends received from qualified corporations	$ 10,000
3. Interest received from corporate bonds	$ 18,000
4. Interest earned from accounts receivable (derived in the normal course of business)	$ 12,000
5. Income earned during the ordinary course of business	$110,000

Soar also incurred the following expenses and losses throughout the year:

1. Sold equipment bought in 2012 with an adjusted basis of $30,000 for $20,000.	$(10,000)
2. Donated cash to charity	$ (5,000)
3. Sec. 179 expense taken on machinery placed into service during the current tax year	$(30,000)
4. Interest expense on investment debts	$ (6,000)
5. Expenses incurred during the ordinary course of business	$(10,000)

Soar and its two shareholders operate on a cash basis and calendar year.

Complete the IRS Form 1120S Schedule K-1 for Soar, Inc., shareholder Danny Morales on the next page. Fill in the shaded cells only.

-- Continued on next page --

IRS Form 1120S (K-1): Danny Morales | Authoritative Literature | Help -- Continued

671113

☐ Final K-1 ☐ Amended K-1 OMB No. 1545-0123

Schedule K-1 (Form 1120S) **2015**

Department of the Treasury
Internal Revenue Service

For calendar year 2015, or tax year beginning ________, 2015 ending ________, 20 ____

Shareholder's Share of Income, Deductions, Credits, etc. ▶ See back of form and separate instructions.

Part I Information About the Corporation

A Corporation's employer identification number
59-7891234

B Corporation's name, address, city, state, and ZIP code
Soar Inc.
6850 Parish Avenue
Gainesville, FL 32608

C IRS Center where corporation filed return

Part II Information About the Shareholder

D Shareholder's identifying number
987-65-4321

E Shareholder's name, address, city, state, and ZIP code
Danny Morales
4321 Maple Lane
Gainesville, FL 32608

F Shareholder's percentage of stock ownership for tax year . . . . ________ %

For IRS Use Only

Part III Shareholder's Share of Current Year Income, Deductions, Credits, and Other Items

1	Ordinary business income (loss)	13	Credits
2	Net rental real estate income (loss)		
3	Other net rental income (loss)		
4	Interest income		
5a	Ordinary dividends		
5b	Qualified dividends	14	Foreign transactions
6	Royalties		
7	Net short-term capital gain (loss)		
8a	Net long-term capital gain (loss)		
8b	Collectibles (28%) gain (loss)		
8c	Unrecaptured section 1250 gain		
9	Net section 1231 gain (loss)		
10	Other income (loss)	15	Alternative minimum tax (AMT) items
11	Section 179 deduction	16	Items affecting shareholder basis
12	Other deductions		
		17	Other information

* See attached statement for additional information.

For Paperwork Reduction Act Notice, see Instructions for Form 1120S. IRS.gov/form1120s Cat. No. 11520D **Schedule K-1 (Form 1120S) 2015**

▼ = Reminder | Directions | 1 2 3 4 5 6 | Previous | Next

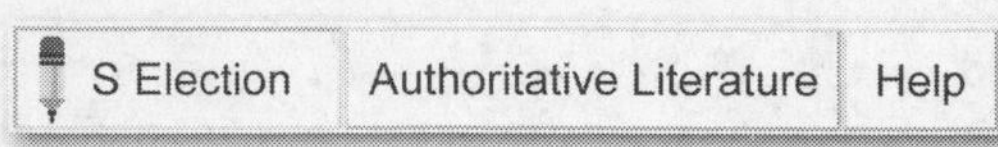

Select from the list provided the best match for each item. Each choice may be used once, more than once, or not at all. Assume that Subchapter S rules, if applicable, would require the corporation to adopt the calendar year for purposes of reporting federal income taxes.

Situation	Answer
1. Ownership of the 1,000 shares outstanding are evenly divided among 80 shareholders. The shareholders are 78 individuals, 10 of whom are married to each other, and two estates.	
2. A domestic corporation elects S status on April 15.	
3. Articles of incorporation authorize 800 shares of voting common stock, 200 shares of nonvoting preferred, and no other shares.	
4. A domestic corporation elects S status on March 3.	
5. Articles of incorporation authorize 1,000 shares of common stock and no other stock. One-fifth of the common stock has no voting rights.	

Choices
A) Permitted
B) Not permitted
C) Retroactively effective
D) Concurrently effective
E) Subsequently effective

S Corporation Distributions | Authoritative Literature | Help

For each of the distributions described in items 1 through 5, compute the proper tax amount and enter the amount(s) into the shaded cells of the proper column. Either column could have $0 for an answer.

Situation	Capital Gain	Ordinary Income
1. Distribution of $15,000 cash to a shareholder if the accumulated adjustments account balance is $5,000 and the shareholder's basis in his or her stock is $15,000. There are no Subchapter C earnings and profits.		
2. Distribution of $15,000 cash to shareholder if the accumulated adjustments account balance is $10,000. The shareholder's basis in his or her stock is $15,000. The Subchapter C earnings and profits balance is $5,000. No election to apply distributions to earnings and profits first has been made.		
3. Distribution of a computer to a shareholder when its basis to the S Corporation was $15,000 and its fair market value was $10,000. The accumulated adjustments account balance is $10,000, and the shareholder's basis in his or her stock is $10,000. There are no Subchapter C earnings and profits.		
4. Distribution of $15,000 cash to a shareholder when the accumulated adjustment account balance is $5,000 and the shareholder's basis in his or her stock is $5,000. The shareholder has made a bona fide loan (the balance is $5,000) to the corporation. There are no Subchapter C earnings and profits.		
5. Distribution of $15,000 cash to a shareholder when the accumulated adjustments account balance is $5,000 and the shareholder's basis in his or her stock is $5,000. There is $5,000 of Subchapter C earnings and profits. No election to apply distributions to earnings and profits first has been made.		

= Reminder | Directions | 1 2 3 4 5 6 | Previous | Next

Unofficial Answers

1. Basis Calculations (4 Gradable Items)

1. $145,000. The shareholder of an S corporation's stock must increase his or her basis for all items of income to the S corporation that are both separately and nonseparately stated, as well as the deduction for depletion in excess of the basis of property depleted. Therefore, all items increase Samantha's basis in her S corporation stock.
2. $32,500. Lisa's basis in Dance, Inc., without taking the dividend into account, was $35,000 ($25,000 purchase price + $10,000 income for Year 2). The $2,500 dividend reduces that basis to $32,500. The $7,800 loss from Year 1 (a C corporation year) is a carryover loss and does not affect the basis computation.
3. $32,000. The basis of the shareholder's stock is figured at year end with increases for the shareholder's pro rata share of all income items that are separately stated and any nonseparately stated income. Also, all separately and nonseparately stated losses and deduction items decrease the basis of the shareholder's stock on a pro rata basis. Hal's stock basis on January 1, 2015, is $32,000 ($40,000 original basis + $36,000 ordinary income – $4,000 short-term capital loss – $10,000 Sec. 179 deduction – $30,000 cash distribution).
4. $0. The IRC provides guidelines for adjustments to the basis of a shareholder's S corporation stock. The increases include items of income (including tax-exempt income) that are passed through to the shareholder, nonseparately stated (ordinary) income, and the excess of deductions for depletion over the basis of the property subject to depletion. A loan made to an S corporation also increases the shareholder's basis for the amount of the loan. The basis of Reed's stock is decreased by the amount of loss allocable to him; however, it cannot reduce his basis below zero.

	Stock Basis	Loan Basis
Basis at Jan. 1	$ 2,000	
Loan to corporation		$4,000
Tax-exempt interest	5,000	
Ordinary loss of S corp.	(7,000)	(500)
Basis at Dec. 31	$ 0	$3,500

2. Tax Exemptions (8 Gradable Items)

1. No. S corporations are not subject to corporate alternative minimum tax.
2. Yes. Although S corporations are not subject to income tax, four special taxes are imposed on them. Those taxes are the passive investment income tax, the built-in gains tax, the LIFO recapture tax, and the general business credit recapture.
3. No. S corporations are not subject to personal holding company tax.
4. Yes. Although S corporations are not subject to income tax, four special taxes are imposed on them. Those taxes are the passive investment income tax, the built-in gains tax, the LIFO recapture tax, and the general business credit recapture.
5. Yes. Although S corporations are not subject to income tax, four special taxes are imposed on them. Those taxes are the passive investment income tax, the built-in gains tax, the LIFO recapture tax, and the general business credit recapture.
6. No. S corporations are not subject to accumulated earnings tax.
7. No. S corporations are not subject to corporate income tax.
8. Yes. Although S corporations are not subject to income tax, four special taxes are imposed on them. Those taxes are the passive investment income tax, the built-in gains tax, the LIFO recapture tax, and the general business credit recapture.

3. Research (1 Gradable Item)

Answer: IRC § 1362(d)(1)

§ 1362. Election; revocation; termination

(d) Termination

(1) By revocation

(A) In general

An election under subsection (a) may be terminated by revocation.

(B) More than one-half of shares must consent to revocation

An election may be revoked only if shareholders holding more than one-half of the shares of stock of the corporation on the day on which the revocation is made consent to the revocation.

(C) When effective

Except as provided in subparagraph (D)–

(i) a revocation made during the taxable year and on or before the 15th day of the 3rd month thereof shall be effective on the 1st day of such taxable year, and

(ii) a revocation made during the taxable year but after such 15th day shall be effective on the 1st day of the following taxable year.

(D) Revocation may specify prospective date

If the revocation specifies a date for revocation which is on or after the day on which the revocation is made, the revocation shall be effective on and after the date so specified.

4. IRS Form 1120S (K-1): Danny Morales (10 Gradable Items)

671113

☐ Final K-1 ☐ Amended K-1 OMB No. 1545-0123

Schedule K-1 (Form 1120S) 2015
Department of the Treasury
Internal Revenue Service

For calendar year 2015, or tax year beginning ________, 2015 ending ________, 20 ____

Shareholder's Share of Income, Deductions, Credits, etc. ▶ See back of form and separate instructions.

Part I Information About the Corporation

A Corporation's employer identification number
59-7891234

B Corporation's name, address, city, state, and ZIP code
Soar Inc.
6850 Parish Avenue
Gainesville, FL 32608

C IRS Center where corporation filed return

Part II Information About the Shareholder

D Shareholder's identifying number
987-65-4321

E Shareholder's name, address, city, state, and ZIP code
Danny Morales
4321 Maple Lane
Gainesville, FL 32608

F Shareholder's percentage of stock ownership for tax year . . . . 40 % [1]

For IRS Use Only

Part III Shareholder's Share of Current Year Income, Deductions, Credits, and Other Items

No.	Item	Amount	No.	Item
1	Ordinary business income (loss)	44,800 [2]	13	Credits
2	Net rental real estate income (loss)	20,000 [3]		
3	Other net rental income (loss)	0 [4]		
4	Interest income	7,200 [5]		
5a	Ordinary dividends	0		
5b	Qualified dividends	4,000 [6]	14	Foreign transactions
6	Royalties			
7	Net short-term capital gain (loss)			
8a	Net long-term capital gain (loss)			
8b	Collectibles (28%) gain (loss)	0		
8c	Unrecaptured section 1250 gain			
9	Net section 1231 gain (loss)	(4,000) [7]		
10	Other income (loss)		15	Alternative minimum tax (AMT) items
11	Section 179 deduction	12,000 [8]	16	Items affecting shareholder basis
12	Other deductions	2,000 [9]		
		2,400 [10]		
			17	Other information

* See attached statement for additional information.

For Paperwork Reduction Act Notice, see Instructions for Form 1120S. IRS.gov/form1120s Cat. No. 11520D Schedule K-1 (Form 1120S) 2015

[1] 40%. Since Danny owns 200 out of 500 shares, he is a 40% shareholder.

[2] $44,800. Ordinary income from Soar was $110,000 during the year. Accounts receivable of $12,000 was received in the normal course of business. Soar also had $10,000 of expenses related to earning its ordinary income for the year. Therefore, Soar's net income for the year was $112,000. Danny has a 40% share of the $112,000 income for a total of $44,800.

[3] $20,000. Soar earned a total of $50,000 from rental real estate, and Danny's 40% share is $20,000.

[4] $0. The situation does not provide for any other rental activities.

[5] $7,200. Danny's share of the interest from corporate bonds is 40% of $18,000. The interest from the accounts receivable is considered earned during the normal course of business, not portfolio income. Therefore, it is excluded from interest income.

[6] $4,000. Danny's share of the qualified dividends is 40% of $10,000.

[7] $(4,000). The equipment sold during the year was the only Sec. 1231 loss incurred during the year, and Danny's share is 40% of the $10,000 loss.

[8] $12,000. Danny's share of the Sec. 179 deduction is 40% of $30,000.

[9] $2,000. Danny's share of the donation to charity is 40% of $5,000.

[10] $2,400. Danny's share of the investment interest expense is 40% of $6,000.

5. S Election (5 Gradable Items)

1. A) Permitted. The number of S corporation shareholders is limited to 100. However, a husband and wife are treated as a single shareholder for this purpose. Eligible shareholders include individuals, estates, and qualified trusts.
2. E) Subsequently effective. An S election made after the first 2 1/2 months of the corporation's tax year becomes effective the first day of the following tax year.
3. B) Not permitted. An S corporation is permitted only one class of stock. Thus, a corporation with common and preferred stock cannot be an S corporation.
4. C) Retroactively effective. An S election made within the first 2 1/2 months of the corporation's tax year is effective from the first day of that tax year.
5. A) Permitted. An S corporation may have only one class of stock. However, different voting rights among the stock of that class do not preclude S status.

6. S Corporation Distributions (10 Gradable Items)

1. $0 of capital gain and $0 of ordinary income. If an S corporation has no Subchapter C earnings and profits, distributions reduce the basis of the stock until the basis reaches zero, and further distributions are treated as gain from the sale or exchange of the stock.
2. $0 of capital gain and $5,000 of ordinary income. If an S corporation has Subchapter C earnings and profits, distributions are first made from the accumulated adjustments account (treated as nontaxable return of income already taxed to the shareholder), then made from accumulated earnings and profits (taxable dividends), and lastly treated as gain from the sale or exchange of property to the extent they are in excess of the shareholder's remaining basis in the stock.
3. $0 of capital gain and $0 of ordinary income. The amount of a distribution from an S corporation to a shareholder with respect to his or her stock is the sum of any money distributed plus the fair market value of all (other) property distributed. Thus, the amount of the distribution is $10,000. When there are no Subchapter C earnings and profits, the amount of a distribution reduces the basis of the shareholder in his or her stock until the basis is zero. Excess (there is none here) is treated as gain from the sale of the stock.
4. $10,000 of capital gain and $0 of ordinary income. If an S corporation has no Subchapter C earnings and profits, distributions reduce the basis of the stock until the basis reaches zero, and further distributions will be treated as gain from the sale or exchange of the stock. Basis in a loan to the corporation affects the amount of passed-through loss that the shareholder may deduct, but it does not directly determine the shareholder's treatment of a distribution.
5. $5,000 of capital gain and $5,000 of ordinary income. If an S corporation has Subchapter C earnings and profits, distributions are first made from the accumulated adjustments account (treated as nontaxable return of income already taxed to the shareholder), then made from accumulated earnings and profits (taxable dividends), and lastly treated as gain from the sale or exchange of property to the extent they are in excess of the shareholder's remaining basis in the stock. Note that basis is also reduced by the amount treated as distributed from the AAA but not by the amount treated as distributed from E&P.

Gleim Simulation Grading

Task	Correct Responses		Gradable Items		Score per Task
1	___	÷	4	=	___
2	___	÷	8	=	___
3 (Research)	___	÷	1	=	___
4	___	÷	10	=	___
5	___	÷	5	=	___
6	___	÷	10	=	___
			Total of Scores per Task		___
		÷	Total Number of Tasks		6
			Total Score		___ %

STUDY UNIT ELEVEN
PARTNERSHIPS AND EXEMPT ORGANIZATIONS

(22 pages of outline)

A partnership is a business organization other than a corporation, trust, estate, or qualified joint venture co-owned by two or more persons and operated for a profit. The partnership, as an untaxed flow-through entity, reports taxable income or loss and separately stated items. For the computation of personal income tax liability, each partner considers his or her distributive share of the partnership's taxable income or loss and each of the partnership's separately stated items, whether or not any distributions are made from the partnership to the partner. Federal income tax rules for partnerships are similar to those for S corporations. Nonseparately and separately stated partnership items are currently taxed to the partners, but distributions are generally received tax-free.

Certain organizations may qualify for exemption from federal income tax under Sec. 501(a). They are referred to as nonprofit organizations. Most organizations seeking recognition of exemption from federal income tax must use application forms specifically prescribed by the IRS.

11.1 PARTNERSHIP FORMATION AND TAX YEAR

1. **Overview**

   a. Realized gain or loss is not generally recognized by a partner when a partnership interest is received in exchange for property contributed to the partnership unless boot is received.

EXAMPLE

In 2015, Albert acquired a 20% interest in a partnership by contributing a parcel of land and $10,000 in cash. At the time of Albert's contribution, the land had a fair market value of $50,000, an adjusted basis to Albert of $20,000, and was subject to a mortgage of $70,000. Albert's relinquished liability is a gain. When Albert became a 20% partner, he was relieved of 80% of the mortgage debt. Thus, 80% of his $70,000 mortgage, or $56,000, is a benefit to Albert because the other partners are assuming part of the mortgage obligation. Therefore, Albert has a gain of $26,000 ($56,000 benefit – $10,000 cash – $20,000 AB of property).

	Cash contributed	$ 10,000
+	AB of property contributed	20,000
+	Any gain recognized on contributed property or services	26,000
+	Share of partnership liabilities	14,000
–	Partner's liability assumed by partnership	(70,000)
=	**Basis in partnership interest**	$ 0

2. **Contributed Property**

   a. A **partner's basis** in contributed items is exchanged for basis in the partnership interest received, adjusted for gain recognized and liabilities. The formula to calculate basis in a partnership is as follows:

	Cash contributed
+	AB of property contributed
+	Any gain recognized on contributed property or services
+	Share of partnership liabilities
–	Partner's liability assumed by partnership
=	**Basis in partnership interest**

   b. When a partner contributes **property subject to a liability**, or the partnership assumes a liability of the contributing partner, the partner is treated as receiving a distribution of money from the partnership in the amount of the liability. A distribution reduces the partner's basis in the partnership interest.

   c. Recognized gain. To the extent liabilities assumed by the partnership exceed the partner's aggregate AB in all property contributed, the partner recognizes gain.

      1) Note that a partner still bears responsibility for his or her share of the liabilities assumed by the partnership. Basis of other partners also increases by their share of assumed liability.

      2) The gain recognized may be characterized as ordinary income by Sec. 1245 and 1250.

         a) Ordinary income recapture potential in excess of the amount of gain recognized remains with the property in the hands of the partnership.

The AICPA has tested on the calculation of the initial basis of a partner's interest in a partnership. Questions have described the various items contributed by a partner and asked for the amount of the contributing partner's basis in the partnership.

3. **Contributed Services**

   a. A partner who receives a partnership interest in exchange for services recognizes compensation income equal to the FMV of the partnership interest.

      1) Gross income must be reported when an interest received is subject to neither substantial risk of forfeiture nor restrictions on transfer.

      2) The income reported is ordinary.

   b. A partner's interest has ascertainable FMV if sold shortly after receipt.

4. **Partnership's Gain**

   a. The partnership realizes neither gain nor loss when it receives contributions of money or property in exchange for partnership interests.

5. **Partnership's Basis in Contributed Property**

   a. The partnership's basis in contributed property is equal to the contributing partner's AB in the property immediately before contribution increased by any gain recognized by the partner. It is not adjusted for liabilities.

EXAMPLE

In 2015, Albert provided services to Jim's Sole Proprietorship in exchange for a 20% share of the newly created partnership. If the FMV of the assets equals $500,000 and the liabilities equal $100,000, Albert recognizes $80,000 as compensation income ($400,000 × 20%). Albert's basis in the partnership is equal to the compensation income recognized; in this case, it is $80,000.

6. **Holding Periods**

   a. The holding period (HP) of the partner's interest includes the HP of contributed capital and Sec. 1231 assets.

      1) If the interest was received in exchange for ordinary income property or services, the HP starts the day following the exchange.

      2) The partnership's HP in contributed property includes the partner's HP even if the partner recognized gain.

7. **Partner-Purchased Interest**

   a. The basis in a partnership interest purchased from a partner is its cost, which is the sum of the purchase price and the partner's share of partnership liabilities.

   b. The partnership may elect to adjust the basis in its assets by the difference between the transferee's basis in his or her partnership interest and his or her proportionate share of the partnership's adjusted basis (AB) in its assets. This is referred to as a Sec. 754 election.

      1) The difference is allocated first to Sec. 1231 property and capital assets and then to other partnership property. Finally, allocation is made to assets within each of the two classes.

         a) For upward adjustment, allocation is on the basis of relative appreciation of classes and assets. No adjustment is made to a depreciated class or asset.

         b) For downward adjustment, allocation is on the basis of relative depreciation of classes and assets. No allocation is made to an appreciated class or asset.

8. **Partners' Capital Accounts**

   a. A capital account is maintained for each partner at the partnership level.

      1) A partner's initial capital account balance is the FMV of the assets (net of liabilities) (s)he contributed to the partnership.

      2) It is separate from the partner's AB in his or her partnership interest.

9. **Partnership Tax Year**

   a. The partnership's tax year is determined with respect to the partners' tax years.

      1) Unless an exception applies, the partnership must use a required tax year. A required tax year is the first of a), b), or c) below that applies.

         a) Majority interest tax year. It is the tax year of partners owning more than 50% of partnership capital and profits if they have the same year as determined on the first day of the partnership's tax year.

         b) Principal partners' tax year. It is the same tax year of all principal partners, i.e., partners owning 5% or more of capital and profits.

         c) Least aggregate deferral tax year.

            i) Multiply each partner's ownership percentage by the number of months of income deferral for each possible partnership tax year.

            ii) Select the tax year that produces the smallest total tax deferral.

            iii) The deferral period begins with the possible partnership tax-year end date and extends to the partner's tax-year end date.

EXAMPLE

Test 12/31	Year End	Ownership	×	Months Deferred	=	Deferral
Tom Barnes	12/31	50%		0		0.0
Jerry Corp	11/30	50%		11		5.5
				Total Deferral		5.5
Test 11/30						
Tom Barnes	12/31	50%		1		0.5
Jerry Corp	11/30	50%		0		0.0
				Total Deferral		0.5

The least aggregate deferral tax year is 11/30.

2) Any time there is a change in partners or a partner changes his or her tax year, the partnership may be required to change its tax year.

b. When each partner includes his or her pro rata share of partnership income depends on both the partnership tax year and the individual's tax year.

1) If the partner's tax year coincides with the partnership's, the partner reports his or her distributive share of partnership items, including guaranteed payments, in that year.

2) If the partner's tax year does not coincide with the partnership's, the partner reports his or her distributive share of partnership items, including guaranteed payments, in the tax year in which the partnership's tax year ends.

c. A year other than one required may be adopted for a business purpose, with IRS approval. Income deferral is not a business purpose.

1) Natural business year. Accounting for a natural business year, e.g., in a seasonal line of business, can be an acceptable business purpose.

a) The business is considered seasonal if, in any 12-month period, at least 25% of annual gross receipts were received during the last 2 months of the year in each of the preceding 3 years.

2) Fiscal year. A partnership may elect a tax year that is neither the required year nor a natural business year.

a) The year elected may result in no more than 3 months' deferral (between the beginning of a tax year elected and the required tax year).

b) The partnership must pay an amount approximating the amount of additional tax that would have resulted had the election not been made.

10. **Partnership Elections**

a. **Elections** are generally made by the partnership.

1) Partnership-level election examples are accounting methods, tax year, inventory methods, start-up costs, installment sales, and depreciation methods.

2) Each partner makes certain elections for his or her distributive share, e.g., deduction (credit) for foreign tax expense of the partnership or the order of reducing tax attributes upon forgiveness of partnership debt.

Stop and review! You have completed the outline for this subunit. Study multiple-choice questions 1 through 3 beginning on page 416.

11.2 PARTNER'S TAXABLE INCOME

1. **Overview**
   a. A partner's taxable income may be affected by his or her interest in a partnership in several ways, e.g., as a result of his or her distributive share of partnership taxable income and separately stated items, from sale of his or her partnership interest, and from dealings with the partnership.
   b. Partnership taxable income is determined in the same way as for individuals, except that certain deductions are not allowed for a partnership, and other items are required to be separately stated.
2. **Separately Stated Items**
   a. Each partnership item of income, gain, deduction, loss, or credit that may vary the tax liability of any partner must be separately stated. Items that must be separately stated include the following:
      1) Ordinary income (loss)
      2) Rental activities and related expenses
      3) Guaranteed payments
      4) Interest and dividend income
      5) Royalties
      6) Net short- and long-term capital gain or loss from the sale or exchange of capital assets
      7) Sec. 1231 gain and loss
      8) Other income
         a) Portfolio income
         b) Cancelation of debt
         c) Recovery items (e.g., prior taxes, bad debts, etc.)
         d) Investment income
      9) Sec. 179 deductions
      10) Other deductions
         a) Charitable contributions
         b) Investment expense
         c) Depletion on oil and gas wells
      11) Foreign income taxes paid or accrued
      12) Tax-exempt income and related expenses
      13) Distributions
3. **Ordinary Income (Loss)**
   a. Generally, this includes taxable items of income, gain, loss, or deduction that are not separately stated.
      1) Ordinary income is different from taxable income, which is the sum of all taxable items, including the separately stated items and the partnership ordinary income or loss.
         a) Ordinary income includes such items as gross profit, administrative expenses, and employee salaries.
         b) Exception: Guaranteed payments are subtracted as expenses for computing taxable income but are separately stated as income to the recipient partner.

4. **Deductions**
   a. Certain deductions, e.g., charitable contributions, are disallowed in computing taxable income.
      1) These are items that must be separately stated by the partnership.
      2) Each partner may be entitled to his or her distributive share of these items in computing his or her personal tax liability.
5. **Partner's Distributive Share**
   a. Each partner is taxed on his or her share of partnership income whether or not it is distributed.
   b. A partner's distributive share of any partnership item is allocated by the partnership agreement as long as the allocation has economic effect and is substantial. The partnership agreement includes modifications up to the partnership return due date (without extensions).
      1) An allocation has **economic effect** by satisfying one of three tests defined by the regulations. The applicability of each test is determined in sequential order.
         a) **The Big Three Test.** Economic effect is achieved if the partnership agreement includes the following:
            i) Partners' capital accounts are properly maintained,
            ii) Liquidating distributions are made in accordance with the partners' positive capital account balances, and
            iii) Partners must restore deficit balances in their capital accounts.
         b) **The Alternate Test.** Economic effect is achieved if the partnership agreement includes items i) and ii) of the Big Three Test and contains a qualified income offset provision.
         c) **Economic Effect Equivalence.** Economic effect is achieved if the resulting allocation achieves the same result as would have been achieved under the Big Three Test without containing the provisions required by the Big Three Test.
      2) **Substantiality** is present for an allocation if there is a reasonable possibility that the allocation will affect substantially the after-tax economic position of the partners. The allocation is not substantial if it enhances the after-tax economic consequences of one partner and does not diminish the after-tax consequences of another partner.
   c. If the partnership agreement does not allocate a partnership item or lacks substantial economic effect, the item must be allocated to partners according to their interests in the partnership.
   d. **Precontribution gain or loss.** To the extent of gain not recognized on contribution of property to the partnership, gain or loss subsequently recognized on the sale or exchange of an asset must be allocated to the contributing partner.
      1) Postcontribution gain or loss is allocated among partners as distributive shares, i.e., as any other gain or loss.

EXAMPLE

Tony and Mary form a partnership as equal partners. Tony contributes cash of $100,000, and Mary contributes an asset with a basis of $80,000 and an FMV of $100,000. Two years later, the partnership sells the asset for $110,000. The $30,000 gain ($110,000 selling price – $80,000 basis) is allocated, $25,000 to Mary [$20,000 precontribution gain + (50% partnership interest × $10,000 postcontribution gain)] and $5,000 to Tony (50% partnership interest × $10,000 postcontribution gain).

2) Accounting for variation between the property's FMV and AB immediately before contribution also applies to related deductions. For example, depreciation must be apportioned and allocated.

e. **Character.** The character of distributive shares of partnership items is generally determined at the partnership level.

1) Any capital loss (FMV < AB) inherent at contribution is capital loss to the extent of any loss realized when the partnership disposes of the property. This applies for 5 years after contribution.

2) To the extent of variations between FMV and AB on contribution, partnership gain or loss on inventory and unrealized receivables is ordinary income. This taint on the inventory disappears 5 years after contribution.

f. If the size of a partner's interest in the partnership varies (e.g., by sale, purchase, exchange, liquidation) during a partnership tax year, the distributive shares of partnership items must be apportioned on a daily basis.

1) The partnership may change profit and loss ratios up to the date of the return. However, certain items (such as cash-paid interest) must be allocated based on the number of days of ownership.

2) The following items of a cash-basis partnership must be accounted for on an accrual basis but only for apportioning distributive shares: payments for services or the use of property, interest, and taxes.

6. **Adjustments to Basis**

a. The basis of a partner's interest in a partnership is adjusted each year for subsequent contributions of capital, partnership taxable income (loss), separately stated items, variations in the partner's share of partnership liabilities, and distributions from the partnership to the partner.

	Initial basis
+	Subsequent contributions to capital
+/–	Distributive share of partnership taxable income (loss)
+	Separately stated taxable and nontaxable income
–	Separately stated deductible and nondeductible expenditures
+	Increase in allocable share of partnership liabilities
–	Decrease in allocable share of partnership liabilities
–	Distributions from partnership
=	**Adjusted basis in partnership interest**

EXAMPLE

The taxpayer's ownership and basis in the partnership are 50% and $15,000, respectively, at the beginning of the year. The partnership has ordinary income of $8,000, made charitable contributions of $3,000, and made a $5,000 distribution to the taxpayer. The taxpayer's basis at the end of the year is $12,500 [$15,000 beginning basis + ($8,000 ordinary income × 50% ownership) – ($3,000 charitable contribution × 50% ownership) – $5,000 distribution].

b. Basis is adjusted for variations in a partner's allocable share of partnership liabilities during the year, e.g., by payments on principal.

1) Partner capital accounts are not adjusted for partnership liability variations.

c. Basis is not reduced below zero.

d. Basis is reduced without regard to losses suspended under passive activity loss rules and at-risk rules.

e. No adjustment to basis is made for guaranteed payments received.

7. **Loss Limits**

   a. A partnership ordinary loss is a negative balance of taxable income.

   b. Basis limit. A partner is allowed to deduct the pro rata share of the partnership's ordinary loss only to the extent of his or her basis in the partnership.

      1) Excess loss is deductible in a subsequent year in which AB is greater than zero.

   c. At-risk rules. Each partner may deduct only a partnership ordinary loss to the extent (s)he is at risk with respect to the partnership.

      1) The at-risk limits also apply at the partnership level with respect to each partnership activity.

         a) The amount of a partnership loss currently deductible (up to an amount for which the partnership bears economic risk of loss with respect to each partnership activity) is allocated to partners as a deductible distributive share.

      2) A limited partner is at risk in the partnership to the extent of contributions and his or her share of qualified nonrecourse financing, that is, the amount the partner would lose if the partnership suddenly became worthless.

   d. Passive activity losses are deductible in the current year only to the extent of gains from passive activities (in the aggregate).

      1) Partnership ordinary loss is generally passive to a partner unless the partner materially participates in the partnership activity.

Past CPA exam questions have tested candidates' knowledge of calculating a partner's share of taxable income and the partner's adjusted basis in the partnership. Also, questions have asked for the calculation of the partnership's income.

8. **Sale of a Partnership Interest**

   a. A sale or exchange of a partnership interest results in capital gain or loss, except that any gain realized attributable to unrealized receivables and inventory is ordinary income.

   b. Gain or loss realized includes the selling partner's share of partnership liabilities.

   c. LTCG results if the partner held the interest more than 1 year.

   d. Gain realized on the sale of a partnership is OI to the extent attributable to the partner's share of Sec. 751, or "hot" assets. These include unrealized receivables (URs) and inventory.

      1) URs are rights to payments to the extent not already included in income under the partnership's accounting method. The rights to payment may be for services or for goods other than capital assets.

         a) URs also include the OI potential (recapture) in Sec. 1245 and Sec. 1250 property and in franchises, trademarks, or trade names.

         b) Note that, to the extent that an accrual-method partnership has basis in an account receivable, the receivable is not unrealized.

2) "Inventory" in this context includes not only inventory held for sale but also any partnership property characterized as other than Sec. 1231 property or a capital asset in the hands of the partnership, selling partner, or a distributee partner (e.g., copyrights, accounts receivable, unrealized receivables).
   a) The "substantially appreciated" (120%) test no longer applies to sales or exchanges but still applies to distributions. The application to distributions is further explained later in item 2.c.1)b)i) in Subunit 11.5.

EXAMPLE

S sells a 25% interest (AB = $100,000) in Partnership to B for $200,000. Partnership's assets are cash ($80,000), land (FMV = $300,000, AB = $160,000), and inventory (FMV = $400,000, AB = $280,000). Of S's realized gain of $100,000, at least $30,000 is ordinary income [($400,000 – $280,000) × 25%].

9. **Liability Relief**
   a. A partner's relief from partnership liabilities is treated as a distribution of money.

EXAMPLE

Tami sold her share of a partnership for $29,000. Her basis in the partnership is $24,000, including $10,000 of liabilities. The selling price is considered to be $39,000 ($29,000 cash received plus the $10,000 relief of liabilities). Thus, her gain on the sale of the partnership interest is $15,000 ($39,000 – $24,000).

10. **Gift of a Partnership Interest**
    a. Generally, no gain is recognized upon the gift. However, if partnership liabilities allocable to the gifted interest exceed the AB of the partnership interest, the donor must recognize gain. No loss is recognized on the gift.
    b. The donee's basis in the interest is the donor's basis after adjustment for the donor's distributive share of partnership items up to the date of the gift.
    c. For purposes of computing a loss on a subsequent sale of the interest by the donee, the FMV of the interest immediately prior to the gift is used.
    d. Generally, partnership interest gifted to a related minor is attributed to others (e.g., parents).
       1) There are limits on the amount of partnership income that can be allocated to a related minor.
11. **Inheritance**
    a. The tax year of a partnership closes with respect to a partner whose entire interest in the partnership terminates, whether by death, liquidation, or otherwise.
    b. The successor has a FMV basis in the interest.
    c. The partnership tax year does not close with respect to the other partners.
12. **Family Partnerships**
    a. A family partnership is one consisting of a taxpayer and his or her spouse, ancestors, lineal descendants, or trusts for the primary benefit of any of them. Siblings are not treated as members of the taxpayer's family for these purposes.
    b. Services. A services partnership is one in which capital is not a material income-producing factor.
       1) In a family partnership, a family member is treated as a services partner only to the extent (s)he provides services that are substantial or vital to the partnership.

c. Capital. A family member is treated as a partner in a partnership in which capital is a material income-producing factor, whether the interest is acquired by gift or purchase.

1) The partnership agreement is disregarded to the extent a partner receives less than reasonable compensation for services.

EXAMPLE

R gives Son a gift of $250,000. Son contributes it in exchange for a 50% interest in a newly formed partnership with R. R&S Partnership continues what was R's sole proprietorship. The reasonable value of R's services the following tax year is $75,000. Of R&S's gross income of $125,000, $75,000 must be allocated to R for his services. Son's distributive share attributable to his capital interest is no more than $25,000 [($125,000 – 75,000) × 50%].

2) This rule applies to all, not just family members.

d. Spouses filing a joint return may elect out of partnership treatment by choosing to be a qualified joint venture.

1) The only members of the joint venture must be the spouses, and both must materially participate and make the election.
2) Each spouse will be treated as a sole proprietor, allowing both to receive Social Security benefits.

13. **Reporting Requirements**

a. A partnership, as a conduit, is not subject to federal income tax. But it must report information including partnership items of income, loss, deduction, and credit to the IRS.
b. A partnership is required to file an initial return for the first year in which it receives income or incurs expenditures treated as deductions for federal income tax purposes.
c. Form 1065 is used for the partnership's information return.
d. Any partnership item that may vary tax liability of any partner is separately stated on Schedule K.
e. A Schedule K-1 is prepared for each partner and contains the partner's distributive share of partnership income and separately stated items to be reported on the partner's tax return.
f. A partnership return is due (postmark date) on or before the 15th day of the 4th month following the close of the partnership's tax year (April 15th for calendar-year partnerships).
g. Signature by any partner is evidence that the partner was authorized to sign the return. Only one partner is required to sign the return.
h. Inadequate filing. Penalty is imposed in the amount of the number of persons who were partners at any time during the year, multiplied by $195 for each of up to 12 months (including a portion of one) that the return was late or incomplete.
i. Each partner must report his or her share of items consistently with their treatment on the partnership return unless

1) The partner identifies inconsistency on a filed statement, or
2) The partnership has no more than 10 partners, and no estate or nonresident alien is a partner.

14. **Partnership Tax Administration**

a. The IRC provides for designation of a tax matters partner (TMP), e.g., the general partner holding the largest partnership interest.
b. When the IRS enters into a settlement agreement with any partner, it must offer consistent settlement terms to any other partner who so requests.

c. Each partner is bound to a settlement agreement entered into between the IRS and the TMP unless the partner files notice otherwise.

d. Small partnerships. Consistent and binding settlements do not apply to a small partnership, i.e., one that has no more than 10 partners, each being a natural person or an estate.

Stop and review! You have completed the outline for this subunit. Study multiple-choice questions 4 through 7 beginning on page 417.

11.3 PARTNERS DEALING WITH OWN PARTNERSHIP

1. **Overview**

   a. The Code recognizes that a partner can engage in property, services, and loan transactions with the partnership in a capacity other than as a partner, i.e., as an independent, outside third party. The tax result, in general, is as if the transaction took place between two unrelated persons after arm's-length negotiations.

2. **Customary Partner Services**

   a. When a partner performs services for the partnership that are customarily performed by a partner, the partner's return is generally his or her share of profits of the partnership business.

      1) It is gross income, not as compensation, but as a distributive share of partnership income.

      2) The value of the services is not deductible by the partnership.

3. **Guaranteed Payments**

   a. A guaranteed payment (GP) is a payment to a partner for services rendered or capital used that is determined without regard to the income of the partnership.

      1) It is used to distinguish payments that are a function of partnership income and payments connected with partners acting in a nonpartner capacity.

   b. Services. The services must be a customary function of a partner. They are normal activities of a partner in conducting partnership business.

   c. Use of capital. The payment may be stated to be interest on the partner's capital account or to be rent on contributed property.

   d. Fixed amount stated. If the partnership agreement provides for a GP in a fixed amount, e.g., annual salary amount, the GP amount is the stated amount.

   e. Stated minimum amount. The partnership agreement may allocate a share of partnership income to the partner. Any excess over the partner's pro rata share is considered GP.

   GP = Stated minimum amount - Partner's share of partnership income

   f. For purposes of determining the partner's gross income, the GP is treated as if made to a nonpartner.

      1) The partner separately states the GP from any distributive share.

      2) The payment is ordinary income to the partner.

      3) The payment is reported in the tax year in which the partnership makes the GP.

      4) Receipt of a GP does not directly affect the partner's AB in his or her partnership interest.

g. For purposes of determining deductibility by the partnership, a GP is treated as if made to a nonpartner.

   1) The payment is deductible if it would have been deductible if made to a nonpartner.
   2) Usually, deductible GPs are for a general business expenditure that need not be separately stated.
   3) Investment interest expense is an exception. It should be separately stated even if it is GP and even if it is deductible by a partner.

   NOTE: If the GP exceeds the partnership's ordinary income, the resulting ordinary loss is allocated among the partners (including the partner who receives the GP).

h. For all other purposes, the GP is treated as if made to a partner in his or her capacity as a partner. A partner is not an employee of the partnership. Partnership contributions to a self-employment retirement plan are not deductible by the partnership.

4. **Nonpartner Capacity**

   a. Payments to a partner without regard to income of the partnership for property or for services not customarily performed by a partner are generally treated as if the transaction took place between two unrelated persons after arm's-length negotiations.
   b. Loans. Interest paid to a partner on a (true) loan is all gross income to the partner and a deductible partnership item.
   c. Services. Payments to the partner for services rendered (of a nature not normally performed by a partner) to or for the partnership are gross income to the partner and generally an ordinary deductible expense of the partnership.
   d. Property. A partner acting as a nonpartner (independent third party, outsider) can sell (or exchange) property to (or with) the partnership, and vice-versa. Gain or loss on the transaction is recognized, unless an exception applies.

EXAMPLE

Partnership sells land to Partner. Partnership recognizes loss. The loss is a partnership item allocable to partners as distributive shares. Partner takes a cost basis in the property.

   e. Character and loss limit rules

      1) Applicability. These character and loss limit rules apply to any transaction between the partnership and either
         a) A partner who owns more than 50% of the partnership or
         b) Another partnership, if more than 50% of the capital or profits interest of each is owned by the same persons.
      2) Character. Any gain recognized is OI if the property is held as other than a capital asset by the acquiring partner or partnership.

EXAMPLE

Dora has held a capital asset for several years. The asset has a basis of $16,000 and an FMV of $24,000. She sells the asset to a partnership in which she is more than a 50% owner. The partnership will hold the property as a depreciable asset. Her gain of $8,000 ($24,000 – $16,000) will be ordinary income since she sold a capital asset to a more than 50% owned partnership that is not a capital asset to the partnership. If the partnership were to hold the asset as a capital asset, her gain would be capital gain.

3) Loss limit. No deduction is allowed for realized losses.
   a) The acquiring party has a cost basis.
   b) A subsequent taxable disposition event results in gain recognition limited to the previously unrecognized gain.
   c) Expenditures are deductible when, and not before, the amount is includible in gross income by the payee even if the payor is an accrual-method taxpayer.

f. Distribution for contribution. When a partner contributes property to a partnership and immediately receives a distribution, the transaction is essentially a sale.
   1) Gain realized is recognized to the extent the contributed property is deemed purchased by the other partners.

EXAMPLE

P and Q contributed land with FMVs of $250,000 and $500,000, respectively, each in exchange for a 50% interest in PQ Partnership. PQ mortgaged the land for $550,000 and distributed $250,000 of the proceeds to Q. Q recognizes any gain realized on 50% of the land she contributed. Fifty percent of the AB in the land is included in Q's basis in her partnership interest.

Stop and review! You have completed the outline for this subunit. Study multiple-choice questions 8 through 10 beginning on page 418.

11.4 TREATMENT OF PARTNERSHIP LIABILITIES

1. **Overview**
   a. A partner's share of partnership liabilities affects the partner's basis in his or her partnership interest and can result in increased gain being recognized by the partner. Any increase in a partner's share of liabilities of the partnership increases the partner's basis. The opposite is true for a decrease in partnership liabilities.
2. **Recourse Liabilities**
   a. A liability is a recourse liability if the creditor has a claim against the partnership or any partner for payment if the partnership defaults.
   b. Partners generally share recourse liabilities based on their ratio for sharing losses.
      1) However, regulations allocate a recourse liability to the partner(s) who would be liable for it if, at the time, all partnership debts were due, all partnership assets (including cash) had zero value, and hypothetical liquidation occurred.
      2) A partner who pays more than his or her proportionate share of a partnership debt that becomes uncollectible is permitted to take a bad debt deduction equal to the amount in excess of that partner's share of the debt.
   c. A limited partner cannot share in recourse debt in excess of any of his or her obligations to make additional contributions to the partnership and any additional amount(s) (s)he would actually lose if the partnership could not pay its debt.
3. **Nonrecourse Liabilities**
   a. The creditor has no claim against the partnership or any partners. At most, the creditor has a claim against a particular secured item of partnership property.
   b. All partners share in nonrecourse liabilities based on their ratio for sharing profits.

Stop and review! You have completed the outline for this subunit. Study multiple-choice questions 11 and 12 beginning on page 419.

11.5 DISTRIBUTION OF PARTNERSHIP ASSETS

1. **Overview**

   a. A distribution is a transfer of value from the partnership to a partner in reference to his or her interest in the partnership.

      1) A distribution may be in the form of money, liability relief, or other property.
      2) A draw is a distribution.

2. **Current Distributions**

   a. A current (or operating) distribution reduces the partner's basis in the partnership interest.

      1) A decrease in a partner's allocable share of partnership liabilities is treated as a distribution of money.

   b. Money distributions. The partnership recognizes no gain.

      1) A partner recognizes gain only to the extent the distribution exceeds the AB in the partnership interest immediately before the distribution.
      2) Gain recognized is capital gain.
      3) Basis in the interest is decreased, but not below zero.
      4) Loss is not recognized.

   c. Property Distributions

      1) Partnership. Generally, no gain or loss is recognized by the partnership when it distributes property, including money. Sec. 1245 and Sec. 1250 do not trigger recognition on the distribution.

         a) Precontribution gain or loss. If property is distributed to a noncontributing partner within 7 years of contribution, the partnership recognizes gain or loss realized to the extent of any unrealized gain or loss, respectively, that existed at the contribution date.

            i) Allocate this recognized gain (loss) to the contributing partner.
            ii) The contributing partner's basis in his or her partnership interest is increased.
            iii) Basis in the property is also increased.
            iv) The distributee has a transferred basis.

         b) Disproportionate distributions of unrealized receivables or substantially appreciated inventory (SAI) result in gain recognition.

            i) Inventory is considered substantially appreciated if its FMV exceeds 120% of the partnership's adjusted basis. Gains from such distributions are taxed as ordinary income.

      2) Partner. The distributee partner generally recognizes gain only to the extent that money (including liability relief) exceeds his or her AB in his or her interest.

   d. The partner's basis in the distributed property is the partnership's AB in the property immediately before distribution, but it is limited to the distributee's AB in his or her partnership interest minus any money received in the distribution.

   e. When the above limit applies, allocate basis

      1) First to unrealized receivables and inventory, up to partnership AB in them, and
      2) Second to other (noncash) property.

f. If the available basis is too small, the decrease (partnership basis in assets – basis in partnership interest) is allocated to the assets. The decrease is allocated by the following steps:

1) Assign each asset its partnership basis.
2) Calculate the decrease amount.
3) Allocate the decrease first to any assets that have declined in value.
4) Allocate any remaining decrease to the assets based on relative adjusted basis at this point in the calculation.

EXAMPLE

Karen has a $6,000 basis in the BK partnership immediately before receiving a current distribution (there is no remaining precontribution gain). The distribution consists of $5,000 cash, a computer with a FMV of $1,500 and a $4,000 basis to the partnership, and a desk with a FMV of $500 and a $1,500 basis to the partnership. Karen's basis in the distributed property is determined as follows:

Beginning basis in partnership interest	$6,000
Less: Money received	(5,000)
Remaining basis to allocate	$1,000

			Computer	**Desk**
Step 1 -- Allocate partnership basis to each asset		Partnership basis in assets	$ 4,000	$ 1,500
Step 2 -- Calculate decrease				
Total partnership basis	$ 5,500			
Basis to allocate	(1,000)			
Decrease amount	$ 4,500			
Step 3 -- Allocate decrease to assets with a decline in FMV		Decline in FMV	(2,500)	(1,000)
		Relative adjusted basis	$ 1,500	$ 500
Step 4 -- Allocate remaining decrease of $1,000 ($4,500 – $2,500 – $1,000) based on relative adjusted basis		Remaining decrease	(750)*	(250)*
		Karen's basis in distributed property	$ 750	$ 250

* $750 = (1,500 ÷ 2,000) × $1,000
$250 = (500 ÷ 2,000) × $1,000

g. The partner's holding period in the distributed property includes that of the partnership.

h. The partner's basis in his or her ownership interest in the partnership is reduced by the amount of money and the AB of property received in the distribution.

3. **Disproportionate Distributions**

a. Gain is recognized on a distribution of property that is disproportionate with respect to unrealized receivables (URs) or substantially appreciated inventory (SAI).

b. The distribution will be recharacterized as if the URs or SAI were distributed.

4. **Liquidating Distributions**

a. Distributions liquidating the entire interest of a partner may be due to partnership termination and/or the retirement or death of the partner. Sale to the partnership of a partner's entire interest is treated as a liquidating distribution.

b. Payments to a retired partner that are determined by partnership income are treated as a distributive share of partnership income, regardless of the period over which they are paid. The income is characterized at the partnership level.

c. Amounts received from the partnership in liquidation of a partnership interest are generally treated the same as other (nonliquidating) distributions.

   1) Gain is recognized to the extent money distributed exceeds the liquidating partner's AB in the partnership interest immediately before the distribution.

      a) Decrease of the partner's share of partnership liabilities is treated as a distribution of money.

      b) The gain is capital gain. However, precontribution gain or disproportionate distribution of SAI or URs could result in ordinary income.

   2) The liquidating partner is treated as a partner for tax purposes until all payments in complete liquidation have been made.

d. Loss. A loss is realized when money and the FMV of property distributed are less than the AB of the partnership interest.

   1) No loss is recognized if any property other than money, URs, and inventory is distributed in liquidation of the interest.

   2) Loss recognized is limited to any excess of the AB in the partnership interest over the sum of money and the AB in the URs and inventory.

   3) Loss recognized is characterized as if from sale of a capital asset.

EXAMPLE

Amber has a basis in the partnership of $17,000. In complete liquidation of her interest, she received $11,000 in cash and receivables with a basis of $0. Amber will report a capital loss of $6,000 ($17,000 – $11,000 – $0) from the liquidation. The basis of the receivables will be $0 to her. If she had received a capital asset instead of the receivables, she would not qualify to take a loss, and the capital asset would have a basis to her of $6,000 ($17,000 – $11,000).

e. The distributee's basis in (noncash) property received in a distribution in liquidation is any excess of his or her AB in the partnership interest immediately before distribution over any amount of money received.

   1) If the total partnership basis of assets distributed exceeds the partner's basis in the partnership interest, allocate the decrease in the same manner as for current distributions.

   2) For liquidating distributions only, if the basis in the partnership interest exceeds the total partnership basis of distributed assets, allocate the increase by the following steps:

      a) Determine amount of basis to be allocated.

	Beginning basis
–	Money received
–	Unrealized receivables and inventory
=	**Basis to allocate**

      b) Allocate any appreciation to each asset.

      c) Allocate any remaining basis (basis to allocate – appreciation of distributed assets) to the assets based on FMV prior to the distribution.

f. The distributee's holding period in the distributed property includes that of the partnership.

g. Gain on the sale of URs distributed by the partnership is OI.

   1) Gain or loss realized on inventory distributed depends on the nature of the property in the distributee's hands.

   2) If the distributee sells or exchanges the inventory 5 years or more after distribution, capital gain treatment may be available.

Be prepared to answer questions regarding basis and gain (loss) calculations resulting from both current and liquidating distributions of partnership assets.

Stop and review! You have completed the outline for this subunit. Study multiple-choice questions 13 through 17 beginning on page 420.

11.6 TERMINATION OF PARTNERSHIP

1. **Overview**
   a. A partnership terminates for federal tax purposes only when operations of the partnership cease or 50% or more of the total partnership interests are sold or exchanged within any 12-month period.
   b. Sale or exchange termination is treated as a distribution of assets immediately followed by the contribution of those assets to a new partnership.
   c. The tax year of a partnership closes with respect to a partner whose entire interest in the partnership terminates by death, liquidation, or other means.
      1) A deceased partner's allocable share of partnership items up to the date of death will be taxed to the decedent on his or her final return.
      2) Any items allocated after the date of death will be the responsibility of the successor in interest.
2. **Merger**
   a. The merging partnership's tax year is used if the partners of the merged firms own more than 50% of the resulting partnership. Otherwise, a new tax year is started.
3. **Split**
   a. The old partnership's tax year continues; however, if partners owned less than 50% of the original partnership, a new tax year should be started.

EXAMPLE

On January 1 of the current year, the partners' interests in the capital, profits, and losses of Ripple Partnership were

	Percent of Capital, Profits, and Losses
Pebble	20%
Rock	35%
Stone	45%

On February 8, Rock sold his entire interest to an unrelated party. Pebble sold his 20% interest in Ripple to a different unrelated party on December 24. Assuming no other transactions took place in the current year, Ripple Partnership terminated for tax purposes as of December 24 because 50% or more of the total partnership interest in capital and profits had been sold within a 12-month period.

EXAMPLE

Tin-Pan-Alley-Cat Partnership is in the manufacturing and wholesaling business. Tin owns a 40% interest in the capital and profits of the partnership, while each of the other partners owns a 20% interest. All of the partners are calendar-year taxpayers. On November 3 of the current year, a decision is made to separate the manufacturing business from the wholesaling business, and two new partnerships are formed. Tin-Pan Partnership takes over the manufacturing business, and Alley-Cat Partnership takes over the wholesaling business. For tax purposes, Tin-Pan is considered to be a continuation of the Tin-Pan-Alley-Cat Partnership because Tin-Pan owned more than 50% of the original partnership. Alley-Cat Partnership will start a new tax year.

Stop and review! You have completed the outline for this subunit. Study multiple-choice questions 18 and 19 on page 422.

11.7 ELECTING LARGE PARTNERSHIPS

1. **Overview**
   a. Large partnerships meeting certain requirements may now elect to use simplified reporting requirements. An electing large partnership combines most items of partnership income, deduction, credit, and loss at the partnership level and passes through net amounts to the partners.
2. **Number of Partners**
   a. An electing large partnership is any partnership with 100 or more nonservice partners during the preceding tax year. Service partnerships and commodity trading partnerships may not make this election.
3. **Sale of Interests**
   a. An electing large partnership will not terminate if 50% or more of its interests are sold or exchanged in a 12-month period.
4. **Separately Stated Items**
   a. Separately stated items include
      1) Net income or loss from passive loss limitation activities
      2) Net income or loss from other activities (e.g., portfolio income)
      3) Net capital gain or loss for portfolio items and passive activity (netting of the gains and losses occurs at the partnership level)
      4) Tax-exempt interest
      5) Net AMT adjustments
      6) General credits
      7) Low-income housing credit
      8) Rehabilitation credit
      9) Foreign income taxes (deduction or credit)
5. **Deductions and Credits Generally Combined at Partnership Level**
   a. An electing large partnership generally does not separately report deductions to partners.
      1) Miscellaneous itemized deductions are generally combined and reduced at the partnership level.
         a) Instead of applying the 2% floor to each deduction, 70% of the total of these deductions is disallowed at the partnership level.
      2) Income and expenses from passive activities are combined to determine net income or loss.
      3) The deduction for charitable contributions is determined at the partnership level and deducted subject to a 10%-of-taxable-income limitation in determining partnership income.

6. **Capital Gains and Losses**
   a. For electing large partnerships, netting of capital gains and losses occurs at the partnership level.
      1) Each partner separately takes into account the partner's distributive shares of net capital gain or loss for each passive activity and for portfolio and active business items.
      2) Net capital gain or loss that is taken into account by a partner is treated as LTCG or LTCL.
      3) Any excess net STCG over net LTCL will be consolidated with the partnership's other taxable income and not separately reported.

Stop and review! You have completed the outline for this subunit. Study multiple-choice questions 20 through 22 beginning on page 422.

11.8 EXEMPT ORGANIZATIONS

1. **Exempt Status**
   a. Exempt status generally depends on the nature and purpose of an organization.
      1) An organization is tax-exempt only if it is of a class specifically described by the IRC as one on which exemption is conferred.
      2) It may be organized as a corporation, trust, foundation, fund, community chest, society, etc.
      3) An organization operated for the primary purpose of carrying on a trade or business for profit is generally not tax-exempt.
   b. Examples of organization types that may be exempt are religious or apostolic organizations, political organizations, social clubs, athletic clubs, fraternal beneficiary associations, chambers of commerce, real estate boards, labor organizations, civic welfare associations, and certain domestic and foreign corporations.
   c. Organizations that foster national or international amateur sports competition may be exempt if they do not provide athletic facilities or equipment.
   d. Fraternal beneficiary associations that operate under the lodge system and provide payment of life, sick, accident, or other benefits to members and their dependents are an exempt class.
   e. Social clubs organized for pleasure, recreation, and other nonprofitable purposes, substantially all of the activities of which are for such purposes, are an exempt class.
      1) No part of net earnings may inure to the benefit of any private shareholder.
      2) Exempt status is lost if 35% or more of its receipts are from sources other than membership fees, dues, and assessments.
   f. **Prohibited Transactions**
      1) Certain employee trusts lose exempt status if they engage in prohibited transactions, e.g., lending without adequate security or reasonable interest, or paying unreasonable compensation for personal services.
   g. **Religious, Charitable, Scientific, Educational, Literary**
      1) Organizations formed and operated exclusively for religious, charitable, scientific, educational, literary, or similar purposes are a broad class of exempt organizations.
      2) No part of net earnings may inure to the benefit of any private shareholder or individual.
      3) No substantial part of its activities may attempt to influence legislation or a political candidacy (e.g., Political Action Committees).

4) In general, if a substantial part of the activities of an organization consists of attempting to influence legislation, the organization will lose its exempt status. However, most organizations can elect to replace the substantial part of activities test with a lobbying expenditure limit.
5) If an election for a tax year is in effect for an organization and that organization exceeds the lobbying expenditure limits, an excise tax of 25% will be imposed on the excess amount.
6) Exempt status will be lost if the organization directly participates in a political campaign.

h. **Private Foundations**

1) Each domestic or foreign exempt organization is a private foundation unless, generally, it receives more than a third of its support (annually) from its members and the general public. In this case, the private foundation status terminates, and the organization becomes a public charity.
2) Exempt status of a private foundation is subject to statutory restrictions, notification requirements, and excise taxes.
3) A charitable, religious, or scientific organization is presumed to be a private foundation unless it either
    a) Is a church or has annual gross receipts under $5,000 or
    b) Notifies the IRS that it is not a private foundation (on Form 1023) within 15 months from the end of the month in which it was organized.

i. **Feeder Organization**

1) An organization must independently qualify for exempt status. It is not enough that all of its profits are paid to exempt organizations.

j. **Homeowners' Association**

1) It is treated as a tax-exempt organization.
2) A homeowners' association is one organized for acquisition, construction, management, maintenance, etc., of residential real estate or condominiums. A cooperative housing corporation is excluded.
3) A condominium management association, to be treated as a tax-exempt housing association, must file a separate election for each tax year by the return due date of the applicable year.

2. **Requirements for Exemption**

a. An organization, other than an employee's qualified pension or profit-sharing trust, must apply in writing to its IRS district director for a ruling or a determination that it is tax-exempt.

1) To establish its exemption, an organization must file a **written application** with the key director for the district in which the principal place of business or principal office of the organization is located.
    a) Religious, charitable, scientific, educational, etc., organizations (public charities) use Form 1023. Form 1024 is used by most others.
    b) If filed within the 15-month period, retroactive treatment is available.

b. **Annual Information Return**

1) Exempt organizations are generally required to file annual information returns on or before the 15th day of the 5th month following the close of the taxable year.
2) Exempt status may be denied or revoked for failure to file.
3) The organization reports all gross income, receipts, and disbursements.
   a) The amount of contributions received is reported.
   b) All substantial contributions are identified.
4) Those exempted from the requirement include a(n)
   a) Church or church-affiliated organization
   b) Exclusively religious activity or any religious order
   c) Organization (other than a private foundation) having annual gross receipts that are not more than $50,000
   d) Stock bonus, pension, or profit-sharing trust that qualified under Sec. 401
5) Private foundations are required to file annual information returns on Form 990 or Form 990-PF, regardless of the amounts of their gross receipts.
6) Organizations with under $50,000 in gross receipts that do not have to file an annual notice will be required to file a Form 990-N.
   a) The form is due by the 15th day of the 5th month following the close of the tax year.
   b) The form requires the organization to provide the name and mailing address of the organization, any other names used, a web address (if one exists), the name and address of the principal officer, and a statement confirming the organization's annual gross receipts are $50,000 or less.
   c) Failure to file the annual report for 3 years in a row will subject the organization to loss of its exempt status, requiring the organization to reapply for recognition.
7) A central or parent organization may file Form 990, *Return of Organizations Exempt from Income Tax*, for two or more local organizations that are not private foundations. However, this return is in addition to the central or parent organization's separate annual return if it must file one.
   a) Form 990-EZ is a shortened version of Form 990. It is designed for use by small exempt organizations and nonexempt charitable trusts. An organization may file Form 990-EZ instead of Form 990 if it meets both of the following requirements:
      i) Its gross receipts during the year were less than $200,000.
      ii) Its total assets at the end of the year were less than $500,000.

3. **Unrelated Business Income Tax**

a. Tax-exempt organizations are generally subject to tax on income from unrelated business income (UBI).

b. An unrelated business is a trade or business activity regularly carried on for the production of income (even if a loss results) that is not substantially related to performance of the exempt purpose or function, i.e., that does not contribute more than insubstantial benefits to the exempt purposes.

c. Certain qualified sponsorship payments received by an exempt organization have not been subject to unrelated business income tax.
   1) A qualified sponsorship payment is one from which the payor does not expect any substantial return or benefit other than the use or acknowledgment of the payor's name or logo.
   2) The payor may not receive a substantial return.

d. Exempt organizations subject to tax on UBI are required to comply with the Code provisions regarding installment payments of estimated income tax by corporations [Sec. 6655(g)(3)].

e. An unrelated business income (UBI) tax return (Form 990-T) is required of an exempt organization with at least $1,000 of gross income used in computing the UBI tax for the tax year [Reg. 1.6012-2(e)].

4. **Charitable Deduction**

a. Solicitations for contributions or other payments by tax-exempt organizations must include a statement if payments to that organization are not deductible as charitable contributions for federal income tax purposes. Donations to the following organizations are tax deductible:
   1) Corporations organized under an Act of Congress
   2) All 501(c)(3) organizations except those testing for public safety
   3) Cemetery companies
   4) Cooperative hospital service organizations
   5) Cooperative service organizations of operating educational organizations
   6) Child-care organizations

Stop and review! You have completed the outline for this subunit. Study multiple-choice questions 23 through 30 beginning on page 423.

QUESTIONS

11.1 Partnership Formation and Tax Year

1. Strom acquired a 25% interest in Ace Partnership by contributing land having an adjusted basis of $16,000 and a fair market value of $50,000. The land was subject to a $24,000 mortgage, which was assumed by Ace. No other liabilities existed at the time of the contribution. What was Strom's basis in Ace?

A. $0

B. $16,000

C. $26,000

D. $32,000

Answer (A) is correct.

REQUIRED: The partner's basis in a partnership after a contribution of property with a liability in excess of basis.

DISCUSSION: A partner's basis in a partnership equals the adjusted basis of the property contributed plus the partner's share of all partnership liabilities minus any liability of the partner assumed by the partnership. A liability assumed by the partnership is treated as a distribution to the partner. The basis of this partnership interest is the basis of the contributed land ($16,000) reduced by the liability assumed by the partnership ($24,000) and increased by the partner's share of partnership liabilities ($6,000 = $24,000 × .25) and recognized gain on contributed property ($2,000). Thus, the basis will be $0.

Answer (B) is incorrect. The amount of $16,000 is the basis of the contributed property, which must be reduced by the liability assumed by the partnership and increased by the partner's share of partnership liabilities and recognized gain on contributed property. Answer (C) is incorrect. The amount of $26,000 is the FMV of the land reduced by the liability. The basis of the land, not the FMV, should be used to determine the partner's basis. Additionally, the partner's basis should be increased by his or her share of partnership liabilities and recognized gain on contributed property. Answer (D) is incorrect. The amount of $32,000 results from using the FMV of the land rather than the adjusted basis.

2. The holding period of a partnership interest acquired in exchange for a contributed capital asset begins on the date

A. The partner is admitted to the partnership.

B. The partner transfers the asset to the partnership.

C. The partner's holding period of the capital asset began.

D. The partner is first credited with the proportionate share of partnership capital.

Answer (C) is correct.

REQUIRED: The partner's holding period for a partnership interest acquired in exchange for a contributed capital asset.

DISCUSSION: The holding period of the partner's interest includes the holding period of contributed capital and Sec. 1231 assets. The holding period on an interest acquired in exchange for money, ordinary income property, or services begins the day after the exchange.

3. Nolan designed Timber Partnership's new building. Nolan received an interest in the partnership for the services. Nolan's normal billing for these services would be $80,000, and the fair market value of the partnership interest Nolan received is $120,000. What amount of income should Nolan report?

A. $0

B. $40,000

C. $80,000

D. $120,000

Answer (D) is correct.

REQUIRED: The recognized income from services in exchange for interest in a partnership.

DISCUSSION: A partner who receives a partnership interest in exchange for services recognizes compensation income equal to the FMV of the partnership interest. Gross income must be reported when an interest received is subject to neither substantial risk of forfeiture nor restrictions on transfer. The income reported is ordinary.

Answer (A) is incorrect. Income includes compensation for services. This is not a nonrecognition transaction. Answer (B) is incorrect. The value of service performed is also considered income. Answer (C) is incorrect. Income from services exchanged for partnership interest is not valued based on normal billing.

11.2 Partner's Taxable Income

4. On January 2, 2015, Arch and Bean contribute cash equally to form the JK Partnership. Arch and Bean share profits and losses in a ratio of 75% to 25%, respectively. For 2015, the partnership's ordinary income was $40,000. A distribution of $5,000 was made to Arch during 2015. What is Arch's share of taxable income for 2015?

A. $5,000

B. $10,000

C. $20,000

D. $30,000

Answer (D) is correct.

REQUIRED: The partner's share of partnership taxable income.

DISCUSSION: Arch's 75% share of the partnership's $40,000 ordinary income, or $30,000, is Arch's share of taxable income for 2015 even if not distributed. Distributions are received free of tax by the partner, provided (s)he has adequate basis in the partnership, i.e., at least as much basis as the distribution. A partner's basis is increased by his or her share of partnership income and decreased by distributions.

Answer (A) is incorrect. The amount of $5,000 is the distribution to the partner. The partner is taxed on his or her distributive share of partnership taxable income. Answer (B) is incorrect. Arch's profit share is 75%, not 25%. Answer (C) is incorrect. Arch's profit share is 75%, not 50%.

5. Molloy contributed $40,000 in cash in exchange for a one-third interest in the RST Partnership. In the first year of partnership operations, RST had taxable income of $60,000. In addition, Molloy received a $5,000 distribution of cash and, at the end of the partnership year, had a one-third share in the $18,000 of partnership recourse liabilities. What was Molloy's basis in RST at year end?

A. $55,000

B. $61,000

C. $71,000

D. $101,000

Answer (B) is correct.

REQUIRED: The taxpayer's adjusted basis in partnership.

DISCUSSION: A partner's initial basis in the partnership interest received is equal to any cash contribution made. The basis of a partner's interest in a partnership is adjusted up for allocable share of partnership taxable income and increases in the partner's share of partnership liabilities and adjusted down for distributions from the partnership to the partner. Molloy's basis at year end is $61,000 ($40,000 initial basis + $20,000 taxable income – $5,000 distribution + $6,000 liability assumed).

Answer (A) is incorrect. Basis is adjusted for a partner's share of assumed liability. Answer (C) is incorrect. Basis is adjusted down for distributions made during the year. Answer (D) is incorrect. Taxable income of the partnership is allocated to each partner according to the partner's share of interest in the partnership.

6. Evan, a 25% partner in Vista Partnership, received a $20,000 guaranteed payment in 2015 for deductible services rendered to the partnership. Guaranteed payments were not made to any other partner. Vista's 2015 partnership income consisted of

Net business income before guaranteed payments	$80,000
Net long-term capital gains	10,000

What amount of income should Evan report from Vista Partnership on her 2015 tax return?

A. $37,500

B. $27,500

C. $22,500

D. $20,000

Answer (A) is correct.

REQUIRED: The amount of partner income.

DISCUSSION: A partner will report the ownership portion of the partnership income. Partnership income is the balance of the taxable income of a partnership that is not required to be separately stated. Capital gains and losses are generally segregated from ordinary net income and carried into the income of the individual partners. Any guaranteed payment (GP), while deductible for the partnership, is included in gross income of the receiving partner. Reportable income is calculated as follows:

Business income pre-GP	$80,000	
Less: GP	(20,000)	
Reportable partnership income	$60,000	
25% interest		$15,000
Guaranteed payment		20,000
25% capital gain		2,500
Total		$37,500

Answer (B) is incorrect. The amount of $27,500 results from not deducting the guaranteed payment from net business income and adding only 25% of the guaranteed payment in the income calculation. Answer (C) is incorrect. The amount of $22,500 ignores the partner's share of partnership ordinary income. Answer (D) is incorrect. The amount of $20,000 ignores the business income and net capital gains.

7. At the beginning of 2015, Paul owned a 25% interest in Associates Partnership. During the year, a new partner was admitted, and Paul's interest was reduced to 20%. The partnership liabilities at January 1, 2015, were $150,000 but decreased to $100,000 at December 31, 2015. Paul's and the other partners' capital accounts are in proportion to their respective interests. Disregarding any income, loss, or drawings for 2015, the basis of Paul's partnership interest at December 31, 2015, compared to the basis of his interest at January 1, 2015, was

A. Decreased by $37,500.

B. Increased by $20,000.

C. Decreased by $17,500.

D. Decreased by $5,000.

Answer (C) is correct.

REQUIRED: The change in basis of a partner's interest in the partnership.

DISCUSSION: A decrease in a partner's share of partnership liabilities is treated as a distribution of money to the partner. At the beginning of the year, Paul's 25% share of the $150,000 of partnership liabilities was $37,500. At the end of the year, Paul's 20% share of the $100,000 of partnership liabilities was $20,000. Thus, Paul's share of partnership liabilities decreased by $17,500 ($37,500 – $20,000), and his basis was reduced by the same amount.

Answer (A) is incorrect. The beginning balance of Paul's share of partnership liabilities is $37,500. Answer (B) is incorrect. The ending balance of Paul's share of partnership liabilities is $20,000. Answer (D) is incorrect. A decrease in $5,000 only uses the $100,000 ending amount for partnership liabilities for calculating partner basis.

11.3 Partners Dealing with Own Partnership

8. Sara is a member of a four-person, equal partnership. Sara is unrelated to the other partners. In 2015, Sara sold 100 shares of a listed stock to the partnership for the stock's fair market value of $20,000. Sara's basis for this stock, which was purchased in 2004, was $14,000. Sara's recognized gain on the sale of this stock was

A. $0

B. $1,500

C. $4,500

D. $6,000

Answer (D) is correct.

REQUIRED: The partner's recognized gain on the sale of stock to the partnership.

DISCUSSION: When a partner engages in a transaction with the partnership not in a capacity as a partner, the transaction is considered to occur between the partnership and a nonpartner. Sara recognizes a $6,000 long-term capital gain ($20,000 proceeds less $14,000 AB). If Sara had owned more than 50% of the capital or profit interest of the partnership, a gain could still have been recognized, but a loss on a sale to the partnership would not.

Answer (A) is incorrect. Sara is treated as having sold the stock to an independent third party, and the full amount of realized gain is recognized. Answer (B) is incorrect. The full amount of realized gain is recognized. Answer (C) is incorrect. When a partner engages in a transaction with the partnership not in a capacity as a partner, the transaction is considered to occur between the partnership and a nonpartner.

9. Freeman, a single individual, reported the following income in the current year:

Guaranteed payment from services rendered to a partnership	$50,000
Ordinary income from an S corporation	$20,000

What amount of Freeman's income is subject to self-employment tax?

A. $0

B. $20,000

C. $50,000

D. $70,000

Answer (C) is correct.

REQUIRED: The amount of income subject to self-employment tax.

DISCUSSION: Amounts received as guaranteed payments from services rendered to a partnership are subject to self-employment tax [Reg Sec. 1.707-1(c)]. The amount is deemed to be similar to a salary to the partner. Ordinary income from an S corporation is simply considered a distribution that passes through to the shareholders and is therefore not subject to the self-employment tax. Therefore, Freeman's income subject to self-employment tax is $50,000.

Answer (A) is incorrect. The guaranteed payment is subject to the tax. Answer (B) is incorrect. The S corporation ordinary income is not subject to the self-employment tax, while the guaranteed payment is. Answer (D) is incorrect. The ordinary income is not subject to the tax.

10. Peterson has a one-third interest in the Spano Partnership. During 2015, Peterson received a $16,000 guaranteed payment, which was deductible by the partnership, for services rendered to Spano. Spano reported a 2015 operating loss of $70,000 before the guaranteed payment. What, if any, are the net effects of the guaranteed payment?

I. The guaranteed payment increases Peterson's tax basis in Spano by $16,000.

II. The guaranteed payment increases Peterson's ordinary income by $16,000.

A. I only.

B. II only.

C. Both I and II.

D. Neither I nor II.

Answer (B) is correct.

REQUIRED: The income from a partnership to be reported by a partner who receives a guaranteed payment.

DISCUSSION: For purposes of determining the partner's gross income, the guaranteed payment (GP) is treated as made to a nonpartner. The partner separately states the GP from any distributive share. The payment is ordinary income to the partner.

Answer (A) is incorrect. Receipt of the GP does not directly affect Peterson's tax basis in his partnership interest. Answer (C) is incorrect. The payment is ordinary income to the partner. Answer (D) is incorrect. For purposes of determining the partner's gross income, the guaranteed payment is treated as made to a nonpartner. The partner separately states the GP from any distributive share. The payment is ordinary income to the partner.

11.4 Treatment of Partnership Liabilities

11. A $100,000 increase in partnership liabilities is treated in which of the following ways?

A. Increases each partner's basis in the partnership by $100,000.

B. Increases the partners' bases only if the liability is nonrecourse.

C. Increases each partner's basis in proportion to their ownership.

D. Does not change any partner's basis in the partnership regardless of whether the liabilities are recourse or nonrecourse.

Answer (C) is correct.

REQUIRED: The correct treatment of an increase in partnership liabilities.

DISCUSSION: A partner's share of a partnership liability is treated as if the partner contributed an equivalent amount of money to the partnership. The deemed contribution increases the partner's basis in his or her partnership interest. Normally, general partners share liabilities based on their ratio for sharing economic losses (recourse liability).

Answer (A) is incorrect. Each partner's share increases based on his or her ratio for sharing economic losses (recourse liability) or partnership profits (nonrecourse liability). Answer (B) is incorrect. A recourse liability also increases a partner's share, but does so based on his or her ratio for sharing losses. Answer (D) is incorrect. The increase in partnership liabilities does affect the partner's basis in his or her partnership interest.

12. On January 4, 2015, Smith and White contributed $4,000 and $6,000 in cash, respectively, and formed the Macro General Partnership. The partnership agreement allocated profits and losses 40% to Smith and 60% to White. In 2015, Macro purchased property from an unrelated seller for $10,000 cash and a $40,000 mortgage note that was the general liability of the partnership. Macro's liability

A. Increases Smith's partnership basis by $16,000.

B. Increases Smith's partnership basis by $20,000.

C. Increases Smith's partnership basis by $24,000.

D. Has no effect on Smith's partnership basis.

Answer (A) is correct.

REQUIRED: The effect of an increase in liability on a partner's basis.

DISCUSSION: A partner's share of a partnership liability is treated as if the partner contributed an equivalent amount of money to the partnership. The deemed contribution increases the partner's basis in the partnership interest. Smith's partnership basis will increase by $16,000 ($40,000 × 40%). The cash payment (exchange) for the property has a net zero effect on partner basis.

11.5 Distribution of Partnership Assets

13. Baker is a partner in BDT with a partnership basis of $60,000. BDT made a liquidating distribution of land with an adjusted basis of $75,000 and a fair market value of $40,000 to Baker. What amount of gain or loss should Baker report?

A. $35,000 loss.

B. $20,000 loss.

C. $0

D. $15,000 gain.

Answer (C) is correct.

REQUIRED: The partner's gain or loss from a liquidating distribution.

DISCUSSION: A partner recognizes gain only to the extent a money distribution exceeds the AB in the partnership interest immediately before the distribution. In the case of capital property distributions, there is no gain or loss; instead, the partner's basis in the property is adjusted for any variance between the partner's partnership basis and the partnership's AB in the property distributed. Therefore, Baker has a $0 gain (loss).

Answer (A) is incorrect. The amount of $35,000 represents a loss by the partnership; however, no gain or loss is recognized by the partnership when it distributes property, including money. Answer (B) is incorrect. A gain can only be recognized when cash is distributed. Losses are never recognized. In addition, the value of distributed property is determined by the partnership's adjusted basis (not the FMV). Answer (D) is incorrect. Gains are only recognized when cash in excess of partnership interest is distributed (not property).

14. Owen's tax basis in Regal Partnership was $18,000 at the time Owen received a nonliquidating distribution of $3,000 cash and land with an adjusted basis of $7,000 to Regal and a fair market value of $9,000. Regal did not have unrealized receivables, appreciated inventory, or properties that had been contributed by its partners. Disregarding any income, loss, or any other partnership distribution for the year, what was Owen's tax basis in Regal after the distribution?

A. $9,000

B. $8,000

C. $7,000

D. $6,000

Answer (B) is correct.

REQUIRED: The basis of distributive property in the partnership.

DISCUSSION: A current distribution reduces the partner's basis in the partnership. The partner's basis in his or her ownership interest in the partnership is reduced by the amount of money and the adjusted basis of property received in the distribution. Therefore, Owen's basis in Regal is

Basis of the partnership interest	$18,000
Less: cash received	(3,000)
Less: the adjusted basis of the property received	(7,000)
Basis in the partnership	$ 8,000

Answer (A) is incorrect. Owen's basis in the partnership is reduced by the cash received and the adjusted basis (not the FMV) of property received. Answer (C) is incorrect. The amount of $7,000 is the adjusted basis of the land, not the partnership. Answer (D) is incorrect. Owen's basis in the partnership is reduced by the adjusted basis (not the FMV) of the property received.

Questions 15 and 16 are based on the following information. The adjusted basis of Jody's partnership interest was $50,000 immediately before Jody received a current distribution of $20,000 cash and property with an adjusted basis to the partnership of $40,000 and a fair market value of $35,000.

15. What amount of taxable gain must Jody report as a result of this distribution?

A. $0

B. $5,000

C. $10,000

D. $20,000

Answer (A) is correct.

REQUIRED: The gain or loss recognized on a distribution with no Sec. 751 assets.

DISCUSSION: Gain is recognized by a partner on a distribution only to the extent that money distributed exceeds the partner's adjusted basis in the partnership interest immediately before the distribution. Gain would be capital. Since Jody's $50,000 adjusted basis in his partnership interest exceeds the $20,000 cash distributed, Jody recognizes no gain.

Answer (B) is incorrect. The amount of $20,000 is less than Jody's AB in the partnership interest immediately before the distribution. Answer (C) is incorrect. The money distributed is less than Jody's AB in the partnership interest immediately before the distribution. Answer (D) is incorrect. No gain is recognized when the money distributed is less than Jody's AB in the partnership interest immediately before the distribution.

16. What is Jody's basis in the distributed property?

A. $0

B. $30,000

C. $35,000

D. $40,000

Answer (B) is correct.

REQUIRED: The partner's basis in the distributed property.

DISCUSSION: The basis of property distributed to a partner (not in liquidation of his or her interest) is the property's AB to the partnership immediately before the distribution. It cannot exceed the AB of the partner's interest in the partnership less any money received in the same distribution.

Basis of partnership interest	$50,000
Less: cash received	(20,000)
Basis in distributed property	$30,000

Answer (A) is incorrect. The basis in the property is the AB to the partnership immediately before the distribution. Answer (C) is incorrect. The basis is limited to the AB of the partner's interest reduced by any money received in the same distribution, not the fair market value. Answer (D) is incorrect. The basis is limited to the AB of the partner's interest reduced by any money received in the same distribution.

17. Fern received $30,000 in cash and an automobile with an adjusted basis and market value of $20,000 in a proportionate liquidating distribution from EF Partnership. Fern's basis in the partnership interest was $60,000 before the distribution. What is Fern's basis in the automobile received in the liquidation?

A. $0

B. $10,000

C. $20,000

D. $30,000

Answer (D) is correct.

REQUIRED: The distributee's basis in noncash property from liquidating distribution.

DISCUSSION: The distributee's basis in (noncash) property received in a distribution in liquidation is any excess of his or her AB in the partnership interest immediately before distribution over any amount of money received. Therefore, Fern's basis in the automobile is $30,000 ($60,000 basis – $30,000 cash received in distribution).

Answer (A) is incorrect. The cash distributed was only $30,000 and not $60,000 (i.e., equal to Fern's basis in the partnership interest). Answer (B) is incorrect. The amount of $10,000 would be the basis if the distribution included $50,000 in cash. In addition, the basis in the automobile is not equal to the difference between the cash received and the value of the automobile nor the difference between the distribution and the basis in the partnership interest. Answer (C) is incorrect. Carryover basis of capital assets from the partnership is adjusted for any difference in the total distribution and the partner's basis in the partnership interest.

11.6 Termination of Partnership

18. On January 3, 2015, the partners' interests in the capital, profits, and losses of Able Partnership were

	Percent of Capital, Profits, and Losses
Dean	25%
Poe	30%
Ritt	45%

On February 4, 2015, Poe sold her entire interest to an unrelated party. Dean sold his 25% interest in Able to another unrelated party on December 20, 2015. No other transactions took place in 2015. For tax purposes, which of the following statements is true with respect to Able?

A. Able terminated as of February 4, 2015.

B. Able terminated as of December 20, 2015.

C. Able terminated as of December 31, 2015.

D. Able did not terminate.

Answer (B) is correct.

REQUIRED: The result when two partners sell their interests.

DISCUSSION: A partnership terminates for tax purposes only if (1) no part of any business, financial operation, or venture of the partnership continues to be carried on by its partners in a partnership, or (2) within a 12-month period, there is a sale or exchange of 50% or more of the total interest in partnership capital and profits. On December 20, 2015, the partnership ceased to operate as a partnership because over 50% of the partnership interest was sold.

Answer (A) is incorrect. At that time, only 30% of the partnership interest had been sold. Answer (C) is incorrect. The partnership terminates on the date when 50% of the partnership has been sold during any 12-month period, not at the year ending such sales. Answer (D) is incorrect. A partnership terminates when 50% or more of the partnership interests are sold within a 12-month period.

19. Curry's sale of her partnership interest causes a partnership termination. The partnership's business and financial operations are continued by the other members. What, if any, are the effects of the termination?

I. There is a deemed distribution of assets to the remaining partners and the purchaser.

II. There is a hypothetical recontribution of assets to a new partnership.

A. I only.

B. II only.

C. Both I and II.

D. Neither I nor II.

Answer (C) is correct.

REQUIRED: The effects, if any, of the termination.

DISCUSSION: Distributions liquidating the entire interest of a partner occur upon termination. Gain may result, and the partners will have constructively contributed the distributed assets back to the partnership at a stepped-up basis.

Answer (A) is incorrect. There is a second consequence in that a hypothetical recontribution of assets to a new partnership also occurs. Answer (B) is incorrect. A deemed distribution of assets to the remaining partners and the purchaser also occurs. Answer (D) is incorrect. There is at least one effect as a result of the termination.

11.7 Electing Large Partnerships

20. All of the following items are separately reportable items for electing large partnerships **except**

A. Tax-exempt interest.

B. Taxable income or loss from passive loss limitation activities.

C. Sec. 1231 gains and losses.

D. Net capital gain or loss.

Answer (C) is correct.

REQUIRED: The item that is not separately stated for electing large partnerships.

DISCUSSION: Since 2000, to simplify reporting of partnership income, the number of items that must be separately reported to partners by an electing large partnership has been reduced. The taxable income of an electing large partnership considers Sec. 1231 gains and losses. Net Sec. 1231 gain is considered long-term capital gain, while net Sec. 1231 loss is considered ordinary and is consolidated with other partnership ordinary income.

Answer (A) is incorrect. Tax-exempt interest is separately stated for electing large partnerships. Answer (B) is incorrect. Taxable income or loss from passive loss limitation activities is separately stated for electing large partnerships. Answer (D) is incorrect. Net capital gain or loss is separately stated for electing large partnerships.

21. For an electing large partnership, charitable contributions are

A. Separately reported to the partners.

B. Allowed as a deduction at the partnership level without limitation.

C. Allowed as a deduction at the partnership level, subject to a 10%-of-partnership-taxable-income limitation.

D. Allowed as a deduction at the partnership level, subject to a 50%-of-partnership-taxable-income limitation.

Answer (C) is correct.

REQUIRED: The treatment of charitable contribution deductions in electing large partnerships.

DISCUSSION: An electing large partnership does not separately state its charitable contributions to its partners. Instead, the Sec. 170 charitable contribution deduction is allowed at the partnership level in determining partnership taxable income, subject to a 10%-of-taxable-income limitation, similar to the limitation applicable to corporate donors.

Answer (A) is incorrect. Charitable contributions are not separately stated in an electing large partnership. Answer (B) is incorrect. Charitable contribution deductions are subject to a limitation. Answer (D) is incorrect. The deduction limitation is not 50%.

22. For electing large partnerships, combining capital gains and losses

A. Occurs completely at the partner level.

B. Occurs at both the partnership level and at the partner level for all capital gains and losses.

C. Occurs at the partnership level, except net capital gain or loss for passive activities and other activities are each separately stated.

D. Occurs at the partnership level, with passive activities and other activities being reported together at the partnership level and all other capital gains and losses being separately stated.

Answer (C) is correct.

REQUIRED: The treatment of capital gains and losses in electing large partnerships.

DISCUSSION: For electing large partnerships, netting of capital gains and losses occurs at the partnership level. Each partner separately takes into account the partner's distributive shares of net capital gain or loss for each passive activity and for portfolio and active business items. Net capital gain or loss that is taken into account by a partner is treated as long-term capital gain or long-term capital loss. Any excess net short-term capital gain over net long-term capital loss will be consolidated with the partnership's other taxable income and will not be separately reported.

Answer (A) is incorrect. The combination occurs at the partnership level. Answer (B) is incorrect. The combination occurs only at the partnership level. Answer (D) is incorrect. Passive activities and other activities are separately stated, and all other capital gains and losses are reported together at the partnership level.

11.8 Exempt Organizations

23. Which of the following is **not** an exempt organization?

A. American Society for Prevention of Cruelty to Animals.

B. Red Cross.

C. State-chartered credit unions.

D. Privately owned nursing home.

Answer (D) is correct.

REQUIRED: The organization that does not qualify as exempt.

DISCUSSION: Exempt status generally depends on the nature and purpose of an organization. Among the types of organizations that may qualify as exempt are corporations, trusts, foundations, funds, community funds, etc. A more complete list can be found in Sec. 501(c) along with the permitted stated purposes and requirements.

Answer (A) is incorrect. The American Society for Prevention of Cruelty to Animals is an exempt organization according to Sec. 501(c). Answer (B) is incorrect. The Red Cross is an exempt organization according to Sec. 501(c). Answer (C) is incorrect. State-chartered credit unions are exempt organizations.

24. Of the organizations listed below, which organization could **not** receive approval for tax-exempt status under Internal Revenue Code Sec. 501(c)(3)?

A. A local chapter of the Salvation Army.

B. A partnership for scientific research.

C. A college alumni association.

D. A local boys club.

Answer (B) is correct.

REQUIRED: The organization that is not tax-exempt under Sec. 501(c)(3).

DISCUSSION: Organizations formed and operated exclusively for religious, charitable, scientific, educational, literary, or similar purposes are a broad class of exempt organizations. No part of the net earnings may accrue to the benefit of any private shareholder or individual.

Answer (A) is incorrect. The Salvation Army operates exclusively for charitable purposes with no part of net earnings accrued for the benefit of a private shareholder or individual. Answer (C) is incorrect. A college alumni association does not accrue any part of its net earnings for the benefit of an individual. Answer (D) is incorrect. A boys club operates exclusively for charitable purposes with no part of net earnings accrued for the benefit of a private shareholder or individual.

25. Which of the following is **not** an organization exempt from federal income taxes under Subchapter F of the Internal Revenue Code (Sec. 501 et seq.)?

A. Civic leagues or organizations operated exclusively for the promotion of social welfare.

B. Fraternal benefit societies.

C. Labor, agricultural, or horticultural organizations.

D. Blue Cross and Blue Shield organizations.

Answer (D) is correct.

REQUIRED: The organization that is not tax-exempt under Sec. 501.

DISCUSSION: Tax-exempt status is available to various classes of nonprofit organizations under Sec. 501(a). Sec. 501(c)(2) through (25) lists several organizations that may qualify for tax-exempt status, including civic leagues; fraternal benefit societies; and labor, agricultural, or horticultural organizations. Blue Cross and Blue Shield organizations are health insurance companies, not qualifying organizations.

26. Which of the following statements is true with respect to tax-exempt organizations?

A. A foundation may qualify for exemption from federal income tax if it is organized for the prevention of cruelty to animals.

B. A partnership may qualify as an organization exempt from federal income tax if it is organized and operated exclusively for one or more of the purposes found in Sec. 501(c)(3).

C. An individual can qualify as an organization exempt from federal income tax.

D. In order to qualify as an exempt organization, the organization must be a corporation.

Answer (A) is correct.

REQUIRED: The true statement with respect to tax-exempt organizations.

DISCUSSION: Exempt status generally depends on the nature and purpose of an organization. Among the types of organizations that may qualify as exempt are corporations, trusts, foundations, funds, community funds, etc. A more complete list can be found in Sec. 501(c) along with the permitted stated purposes and requirements.

Answer (B) is incorrect. A partnership is, by definition, a for-profit association. Also, a partnership is not listed as a type of organization that may qualify for exempt status in Sec. 501(c) or (d). Answer (C) is incorrect. An individual is not an organization described in Sec. 501(c) or (d) that may qualify for exempt status. Answer (D) is incorrect. Other types of organizations listed in Sec. 501(c) or (d) may also qualify.

27. Which of the following organizations exempt from federal income tax under Sec. 501(a) must file an annual information return on Form 990 or Form 990-PF?

A. An organization, other than a private foundation, having gross receipts in each year that normally are not more than $50,000.

B. A school below college level, affiliated with a church or operated by a religious order, that is not an integrated auxiliary of a church.

C. A private foundation exempt under Sec. 501(c)(3) of the Internal Revenue Code.

D. A stock bonus, pension, or profit-sharing trust that qualifies under Sec. 401 of the Internal Revenue Code.

Answer (C) is correct.

REQUIRED: The organization that is required to file an annual information return.

DISCUSSION: Most exempt organizations are required to file various returns and reports at some time during or following the close of their accounting periods. Private foundations are required to file annual information returns on Form 990 or Form 990-PF, regardless of the amounts of their gross receipts.

28. An incorporated exempt organization subject to tax on its current-year unrelated business income (UBI)

A. Must make estimated tax payments if its tax can reasonably be expected to be $100 or more.

B. Must comply with the Code provisions regarding installment payments of estimated income tax by corporations.

C. Must pay at least 70% of the tax due as shown on the return when filed, with the balance of tax payable in the following quarter.

D. May defer payment of tax for up to 9 months following the due date of the return.

Answer (B) is correct.

REQUIRED: The timing of payment obligations with respect to UBI tax.

DISCUSSION: Exempt organizations subject to tax on UBI are required to comply with the Code provisions regarding installment payments of estimated income tax by corporations [Sec. 6655(g)(3)].

Answer (A) is incorrect. Like a corporation, quarterly payments of estimated tax are required of an exempt organization that expects estimated tax on UBI to equal or exceed $500 for the tax year. Answer (C) is incorrect. Tax on UBI is due in full when the UBI return and annual information return are due. Answer (D) is incorrect. Tax on UBI is due in full when the UBI return and annual information return are due.

29. Which of the following organizations exempt from federal income tax must generally file an annual information report?

A. An organization, other than a private foundation, with annual gross receipts that normally are not more than $50,000.

B. A private foundation.

C. A church.

D. A religious order.

Answer (B) is correct.

REQUIRED: The organization that must file an annual information return.

DISCUSSION: Most organizations exempt from tax under Sec. 501(a) must file annual information returns on Form 990, *Return of Organization Exempt from Income Tax*. Those excepted from the requirement are

1. A church or church-affiliated organization
2. An exclusively religious activity or religious order
3. An organization (other than a private foundation) having annual gross receipts that are not more than $50,000
4. A stock bonus, pension, or profit-sharing trust that qualified under Sec. 401
5. A Keogh plan whose total assets are less than $100,000

Answer (A) is incorrect. Such an organization is specifically exempt from filing annual information returns. Answer (C) is incorrect. A church is specifically exempt from filing annual information returns. Answer (D) is incorrect. A religious order is specifically exempt from filing annual information returns.

30. Which transaction will **not** always cause an employee trust to lose exempt status?

A. Compensating an employee for personal services.

B. Lending at below market rates.

C. Lending without security.

D. Lending with some, but not adequate, security.

Answer (A) is correct.

REQUIRED: The permissible transaction for an exempt employee trust.

DISCUSSION: Certain employee trusts lose exempt status if they engage in prohibited transactions, e.g., lending without adequate security or reasonable interest, or paying unreasonable compensation for personal services./ Reasonable compensation is permissible.

Answer (B) is incorrect. Lending without reasonable interest is a prohibited transaction and will cause the trust to lose exempt status. Answer (C) is incorrect. Lending without adequate security is a prohibited transaction. Answer (D) is incorrect. Lending without adequate security will cause a trust to lose exempt status.

11.9 PRACTICE TASK-BASED SIMULATIONS

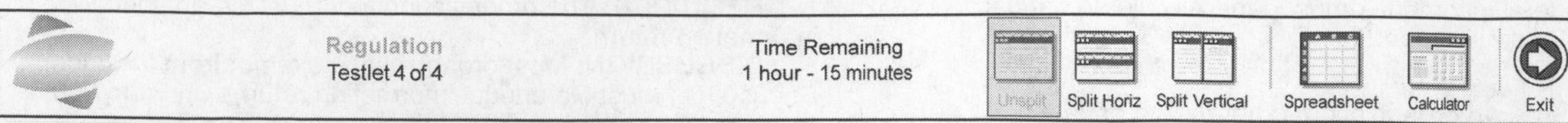

DIRECTIONS

Note: If you believe you have encountered a software malfunction, report it to the test center staff immediately.

Navigation

To navigate from task to task, use the controls at the bottom of the screen. Click on the **Next** button to advance to the next task, or the **Previous** button to go to the previous task. To go directly to any task, click on its number.

If you would like a reminder to revisit a task, or want to indicate that you are finished with it, click on the reminder flag below the task number. To clear the flag, click on it again. Reminder flags are for your use only – they do not contribute to your score.

Tabs

In this part of the examination, you will be asked to complete various tasks. Every task has one or more **Work Tabs**. Some tasks have one or more **Information Tabs**, others may have none. Every task has a **Help** tab.

If a task has **Information Tabs**, you may use the information in them to complete your responses in the **Work Tabs**.

Work tab **Information tab** **Help tab**

Work Tabs:

- **Work Tabs** are identified with a pencil icon. This is where your responses are expected.
- Each task has one or more **Work Tabs**.
- **Work Tabs** contain directions for completing the task – be sure to read these directions carefully.
- The **Work Tab** name in the example above is for illustration only – yours will differ.
- You must complete all of the **Work Tabs** in each task to receive full credit.

Information Tabs:

- The Authoritative Literature will be provided in all tasks in the AUD, FAR, and REG sections for your reference.
- Your simulation may have one or more additional **Information Tabs**. Like the Authoritative Literature tabs, **Information Tabs** do not have a pencil icon.
- If your task has additional **Information Tabs**, go through each to familiarize yourself with the task content.

Help Tab:

- The **Help Tab** provides assistance with the exam software that is used in this task. For example, if the task is to compose a memorandum, **Help** will provide information about the word processor.

The Toolbar

The toolbar at the top of the screen shows the amount of time remaining for you to complete the tasks. In addition, the following tools are available. Note that only the **Exit** button is displayed when Directions are visible - the others will appear when you begin the tasks.

Click on these buttons to split or unsplit the screen. You can split the screen vertically or horizontally.

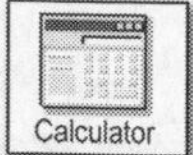

Click on this button to display the calculator; click on it again to hide the calculator. To move the calculator, click on the calculator title bar and drag the calculator to the desired location.

Click on this button to use the spreadsheet; click on it again to hide the spreadsheet. To move the spreadsheet, click on the the spreadsheet title bar and drag the spreadsheet to the desired location.

Click on this button to go on to the next part of the examination. You must complete all of the tasks to receive full credit. Once you click on **Exit** and confirm the action, you will NOT be able to return to this testlet.

= Reminder | Directions | 1 2 3 4 5 6 | Previous | Next

Partnership Formation | Authoritative Literature | Help

For each scenario, enter the amount of the contributing partner's basis in the partnership interest.

Scenario	Partner's Basis
1. Mel transferred property used in a sole proprietorship to the HIJ partnership in exchange for a one-fourth interest. The property had an original cost of $60,000, an adjusted tax basis to Mel of $40,000, and a fair market value of $55,000. The partnership has no liabilities.	
2. Katie received a 20% capital interest in Cruise Associates, a partnership, in return for services rendered, plus a contribution of assets with a basis to Katie of $100,000 and a fair market value of $125,000. The fair market value of Katie's 20% interest was $155,000.	
3. Bob acquired a 40% interest in House Partnership by contributing property with an adjusted basis of $88,000 and a fair market value of $121,000, subject to a mortgage of $55,000.	
4. Charlene contributed land with a $15,000 basis and an $18,000 FMV to the REG Partnership in 2014. In 2015, the land was distributed to Jackie, another partner in the partnership. At the time of the distribution, the land had a $20,000 fair market value, and Jackie had a $30,000 basis for her partnership interest.	

= Reminder | Directions | 1 2 3 4 5 6 | Previous | Next

Partner's Income | Authoritative Literature | Help

For each of the following situations, determine the amount of income that the partner should report as income from the partnership or the amount of capital gain or loss the partner should recognize.

Situation	Income
1. Jasper is a partner in Goldmine Partnership. For the year ended December 31, 2015, Jasper's share of partnership income was $60,000, which included long-term capital gains of $9,000, Sec. 1231 loss of $4,500, $500 of dividends, and $14,000 of interest paid to partners for use of capital. Determine Jasper's ordinary income allocation.	
2. Bridgette has 60% interest in Overton partnership. Bridgette is unrelated to the other partners. In 2015, Bridgette sold 2,500 shares of a listed stock to Overton for the stock's fair market value of $75,000. Bridgette's basis for this stock, which was purchased in 2004, was $86,000.	
3. Andrew has 25% interest in the profit and losses of Power Partnership. Power's ordinary income is $120,000 after a $15,000 deduction for a guaranteed payment made to Andrew for services rendered. None of the $120,000 ordinary income was distributed to the partners.	
4. Alfred sold 40% of his business to his daughter, Clara. The resulting partnership had an operating income of $90,000. Capital is a material income-producing factor. Alfred performed services worth $54,000, which is reasonable compensation, and Clara performed no services. Determine the income that Clara should report.	
5. Courtney owns a 70% interest in Razzle Partnership and an 85% interest in Dazzle Partnership. In August 2015, Dazzle sold land to Razzle for $2.3 million. The land had a basis to Dazzle of $2.5 million. In September 2015, Razzle sold the land to an unrelated individual for $3 million. Determine the gain that Razzle should recognize.	

= Reminder | Directions | 1 2 3 4 5 6 | Previous | Next

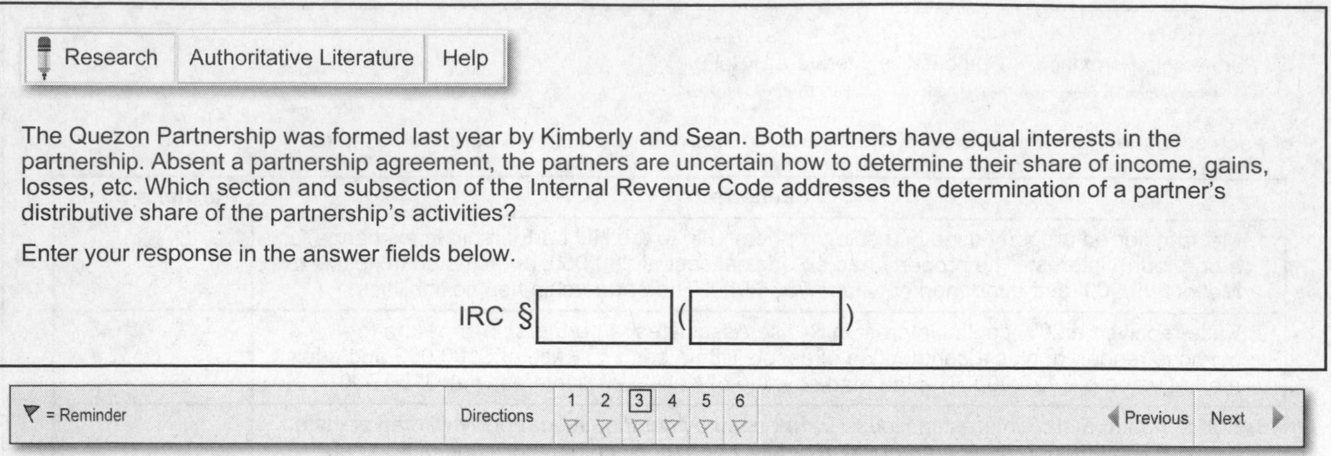

The Quezon Partnership was formed last year by Kimberly and Sean. Both partners have equal interests in the partnership. Absent a partnership agreement, the partners are uncertain how to determine their share of income, gains, losses, etc. Which section and subsection of the Internal Revenue Code addresses the determination of a partner's distributive share of the partnership's activities?

Enter your response in the answer fields below.

IRC § [ ] ([ ])

Rachel, Susan, and Trisha formed the RST partnership on January 1, 2011, and properly adopted a calendar tax year. The partnership elected to use the cash receipts and disbursements method of accounting. Among RST's items of income, expense, loss, and credit for its 2015 tax year were a guaranteed payment to Susan for services rendered, expenses attributable to investment income, and a long-term capital loss. RST had no other capital gains or losses during the tax year. Susan, a domestic partner, has a $7,000 basis in the RST partnership immediately before receiving a current distribution. The distribution consists of $6,000 cash, a computer with a FMV of $2,500 and a $5,000 basis to the partnership, and a desk with a FMV of $1,500 and a $2,500 basis to the partnership.

In addition, RST has the following items in its current-year financial statements:

1) RST received $15,000 in prepaid rent from a tenant leasing one of RST's offices.
2) RST also earned $16,000 of tax-exempt interest during the year. RST incurred $6,000 in interest expense on a loan used to purchase the tax-exempt bonds.
3) One of RST's key partners died during the year, and RST received $30,000 in life insurance proceeds, which was included in book income.
4) RST spent $8,000 on meals and entertainment to attract new clients. Business was discussed at each meeting.
5) RST purchased a new machine during the year to assist in operations. RST elected to immediately expense $39,000 of the machine under code section 179. RST uses the same depreciation method for book and tax purposes for the machine.
6) During the year, Trisha contributed an additional $10,000 cash to the partnership. No property was contributed.
7) Trisha also received $20,000 in a guaranteed payment during the year.
8) Net income recorded on the books for financial accounting purposes for the year was $100,000. The partners' combined capital accounts at the beginning of the year totaled $50,000.

Based on the facts above, enter in the shaded cells Susan's basis in the distributed property.

Calculation Items	***Computer***	***Desk***
Partnership basis in assets		
Decline in FMV		
Relative adjusted basis		
Remaining decrease to be allocated		
Susan's basis in distributed property		

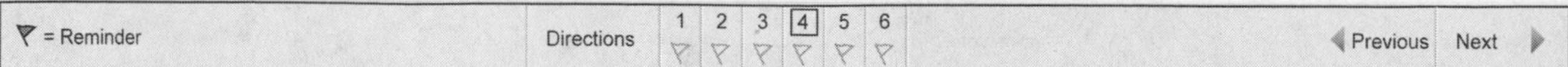

Schedules M-1 and M-2 | Authoritative Literature | Help

Based on the facts below, complete Schedules M-1 and M-2.

Fort, Linda, and Yolanda formed the FLY partnership on January 1, 2011, and properly adopted a calendar tax year. The partnership elected to use the cash receipts and disbursements method of accounting. Among FLY's items of income, expense, loss, and credit for its 2015 tax year were a guaranteed payment to Linda for services rendered, expenses attributable to investment income, and a long-term capital loss. FLY had no other capital gains or losses during the tax year. Linda, a domestic partner, has a $7,000 basis in the FLY partnership immediately before receiving a current distribution. The distribution consists of $6,000 cash, a computer with a FMV of $2,500 and a $5,000 basis to the partnership, and a desk with a FMV of $1,500 and a $2,500 basis to the partnership.

In addition, FLY has the following items in its current-year financial statements:

1) FLY received $15,000 in prepaid rent from a tenant leasing one of FLY's offices.
2) FLY also earned $16,000 of tax-exempt interest during the year. FLY incurred $6,000 in interest expense on a loan used to purchase the tax-exempt bonds.
3) One of FLY's key partners died during the year, and FLY received $30,000 in life insurance proceeds, which was included in book income.
4) FLY spent $8,000 on meals and entertainment to attract new clients. Business was discussed at each meeting.
5) FLY purchased a new machine during the year to assist in operations. FLY elected to immediately expense $39,000 of the machine under code section 179. FLY uses the same depreciation method for book and tax purposes for the machine.
6) During the year, Yolanda contributed an additional $10,000 cash to the partnership. No property was contributed.
7) Yolanda also received $20,000 in a guaranteed payment during the year.
8) Net income recorded on the books for financial accounting purposes for the year was $100,000. The partners' combined capital accounts at the beginning of the year totaled $50,000.

Schedule M-1 **Reconciliation of Income (Loss) per Books With Income (Loss) per Return**

Note. Schedule M-3 may be required instead of Schedule M-1 (see instructions).

1	Net income (loss) per books	[1]	6	Income recorded on books this year not included on Schedule K, lines 1 through 11 (itemize):	
2	Income included on Schedule K, lines 1, 2, 3c, 5, 6a, 7, 8, 9a, 10, and 11, not recorded on books this year (itemize):	[2]	a	Tax-exempt interest $	[6]
3	Guaranteed payments (other than health insurance)	[3]	7	Deductions included on Schedule K, lines 1 through 13d, and 16l, not charged against book income this year (itemize):	
4	Expenses recorded on books this year not included on Schedule K, lines 1 through 13d, and 16l (itemize):		a	Depreciation $	[7]
a	Depreciation $		8	Add lines 6 and 7	[8]
b	Travel and entertainment $	[4]	9	Income (loss) (Analysis of Net Income (Loss), line 1). Subtract line 8 from line 5 .	[9]
5	Add lines 1 through 4	[5]			

Schedule M-2 **Analysis of Partners' Capital Accounts**

1	Balance at beginning of year . . .	[10]	6	Distributions: **a** Cash	[15]
2	Capital contributed: **a** Cash . . .	[11]		**b** Property	[16]
	b Property . .	[12]	7	Other decreases (itemize):	
3	Net income (loss) per books	[13]			
4	Other increases (itemize):		8	Add lines 6 and 7	[17]
5	Add lines 1 through 4	[14]	9	Balance at end of year. Subtract line 8 from line 5	[18]

Form 1065 (201X)

= Reminder | Directions | 1 2 3 4 5 6 | Previous | Next

This type of question will be presented in a spreadsheet response format that requires you to fill in the correct response in the shaded cells provided. For each of the following situations, enter in the shaded cell the partner's basis in the distributed (noncash) property.

Distribution	*Partner's Basis*
1. Quentin's adjusted basis in his Wagon Partnership interest is $63,000. During the year, Quentin received a nonliquidating distribution of $30,000 plus equipment with an adjusted basis of $20,000 to Wagon and a FMV of $25,000.	
2. Duane had an adjusted basis in his Peach Partnership interest of $80,000 on July 13, 2015. On that date, Duane received a liquidating distribution of land with an AB to Peach of $25,000 and a FMV of $35,000 and equipment with an AB to Peach of $35,000 and a FMV of $50,000. Determine the basis of the equipment only.	
3. Melissa's adjusted basis in her Statesboro Partnership interest was $32,000 when she received a nonliquidating distribution of $13,000 cash and property with an AB to Statesboro of $25,000 and a FMV of $28,000.	
4. Lucy has a $50,000 basis in the her Diamond partnership interest. She received a liquidating distribution of $10,000 cash and land with a FMV of $43,000 and a basis of $38,000.	
5. Houlihan's Partnership distributed land with a FMV of $900,000 and an adjusted basis to the partnership of $825,000 to Bruce in a nonliquidating distribution. Bruce's basis in the partnership interest was $750,000.	
6. Mary Ann's adjusted basis in Coconut Associates was $300,000 immediately before she received a distribution in complete liquidation of Coconut. She received $125,000 in cash and and equipment with an AB to Coconut of $150,000 and a FMV of $200,000.	

= Reminder | Directions | 1 2 3 4 5 6 | Previous | Next

Unofficial Answers

1. Partnership Formation (4 Gradable Items)

1. $40,000. A partner's basis in contributed items is exchanged for basis in the partnership interest received, adjusted for gain recognized and liabilities. No gain was recognized by Mel, and no liability was assumed by either party.
2. $130,000. A partner's basis in a partnership is his or her adjusted basis in the property contributed plus income recognized by the partner for receiving the interest in exchange for services. The value of a partnership interest received as compensation for services is income to the partner (FMV of the interest received). The fair market value of the services provided is $30,000 ($155,000 FMV of the interest – $125,000 FMV of assets contributed).
3. $55,000. The basis of an interest in a partnership acquired by the contribution of property is the adjusted basis of such property to the contributing partner. A decrease in a partner's individual liabilities, by reason of the assumption by the partnership of such liabilities, is treated as a distribution of money to the partner, which in turn reduces the basis of the partner's interest (but not below zero). The partner was relieved of 60% of the $55,000 liability, or $33,000. Basis equals $88,000 AB minus $33,000 liability relief.
4. $18,000. For property contributed to a partnership after June 8, 1997, that had a deferred precontribution gain or loss, the contributing partner (Charlene) must recognize the precontribution gain ($3,000 = $18,000 FMV – $15,000 basis) or loss when the property is distributed to any other partner within 7 years of its contribution. The precontribution gain or loss that is recognized equals the remaining precontribution gain or loss that would have been allocated to the contributing partner if the property had instead been sold for its fair market value on the contribution date ($3,000 = $18,000 FMV – $15,000 basis). The recognized gain is added to the contributing partner's (Charlene's) basis in the partnership interest ($3,000 gain + $15,000 basis).

2. Partner's Income (5 Gradable Items)

1. $55,000. A partner's ordinary income is the portion of taxable income not required to be stated separately. The interest paid to partners is an ordinary deduction. Book income may be adjusted to ordinary income by subtracting out all items of income and adding back all deduction and loss items, which must be separately stated ($60,000 book income – $9,000 LTCG + $4,500 Sec. 1231 – $500 dividend = $55,000 ordinary income).
2. $0. The partner owns more than 50% of the partnership. Thus, the loss on the sale of the property is disallowed because the partner and the partnership involved are related parties.
3. $45,000. The partner must report his 25% share of partnership taxable income, $30,000 ($120,000 × 25%), as well as the guaranteed payment ($15,000) he received, as compensation income.
4. $14,400. Guaranteed payments are payments to a partner for services or for the use of capital that are determined without regard to the income of the partnership. Guaranteed payments are deductible by the partnership. After deducting the payment, the partnership's remaining income is split among the partners based on their ownership percentage [($90,000 – $54,000) × 40%].
5. $500,000. If a taxpayer purchases property from a related party who sustained a loss ($2.3 million – $2.5 million = $200,000 loss) on the transaction but was not allowed a deduction for the loss due to the related party rules, any gain realized by the taxpayer on a subsequent sale of the property is recognized only to the extent that the gain exceeds the amount of the previously disallowed loss ($700,000 gain – $200,000 loss).

3. Research (1 Gradable Item)

Answer: IRC § 704(b)

§ 704. Partner's distributive share

(b) Determination of distributive share

A partner's distributive share of income, gain, loss, deduction, or credit (or item thereof) shall be determined in accordance with the partner's interest in the partnership (determined by taking into account all facts and circumstances), if—

(1) the partnership agreement does not provide as to the partner's distributive share of income, gain, loss, deduction, or credit (or item thereof); or

(2) the allocation to a partner under the agreement of income, gain, loss, deduction, or credit (or item thereof) does not have substantial economic effect.

4. Property Basis (10 Gradable Items)

Beginning basis in partnership interests	$ 7,000
Less: Money received	(6,000)
Remaining basis to allocate	$ 1,000

			Computer	Desk
Step 1 -- Allocate partnership basis to each asset.		Partnership basis in assets	$ 5,000 [1]	$ 2,500 [2]
Step 2 -- Calculate decrease.				
Total partnership basis	$ 7,500			
Basis to allocate	(1,000)			
Decrease amount	$ 6,500			
Step 3 -- Allocate decrease to assets with a decline in FMV.		Decline in FMV	(2,500) [3]	(1,000) [4]
		Relative adjusted basis	2,500 [5]	1,500 [6]
Step 4 -- Allocate remaining decrease of $3,000 ($6,500 – $2,500 – $1,000) based on relative adjusted basis.		Remaining decrease	(1,875)* [7]	(1,125)* [8]
		Susan's basis in distributed property	$ 625 [9]	$ 375 [10]

* 1,875 = (2,500 ÷ 4,000) × 3,000
1,125 = (1,500 ÷ 4,000) × 3,000

5. Schedules M-1 and M-2 (18 Gradable Items)

Schedule M-1 **Reconciliation of Income (Loss) per Books With Income (Loss) per Return**
Note. Schedule M-3 may be required instead of Schedule M-1 (see instructions).

1	Net income (loss) per books	100,000 [1]	6	Income recorded on books this year not included on Schedule K, lines 1 through 11 (itemize):	
2	Income included on Schedule K, lines 1, 2, 3c, 5, 6a, 7, 8, 9a, 10, and 11, not recorded on books this year (itemize): prepaid rent	15,000 [2]	a	Tax-exempt interest $ 16,000 insurance proceeds $30,000	$46,000 [6]
3	Guaranteed payments (other than health insurance)	20,000 [3]	7	Deductions included on Schedule K, lines 1 through 13d, and 16l, not charged against book income this year (itemize):	
4	Expenses recorded on books this year not included on Schedule K, lines 1 through 13d, and 16l (itemize):		a	Depreciation $ Sec. 179 expense $39,000	39,000 [7]
a	Depreciation $				
b	Travel and entertainment $ 4,000 interest expense $6,000	10,000 [4]	8	Add lines 6 and 7	85,000 [8]
5	Add lines 1 through 4	145,000 [5]	9	Income (loss) (Analysis of Net Income (Loss), line 1). Subtract line 8 from line 5 .	60,000 [9]

Schedule M-2 **Analysis of Partners' Capital Accounts**

1	Balance at beginning of year . . .	$50,000 [10]	6	Distributions: a Cash	6,000 [15]
2	Capital contributed: a Cash . . .	10,000 [11]		b Property	7,500 [16]
	b Property . .	0 [12]	7	Other decreases (itemize):	
3	Net income (loss) per books	100,000 [13]			
4	Other increases (itemize):				
			8	Add lines 6 and 7	13,500 [17]
5	Add lines 1 through 4	160,000 [14]	9	Balance at end of year. Subtract line 8 from line 5	146,500 [18]

Form **1065** (201X)

[1] $100,000. Net income per books is provided in the situation.

[2] $15,000. Prepaid rent was considered income for tax purposes but not for financial accounting. Therefore, prepaid rent must be added back to reconcile book to tax income.

[3] $20,000. The $20,000 guaranteed payment to Yolanda was provided in the situation.

[4] $10,000. The entire $8,000 of meals and entertainment expenses was deductible for financial accounting purposes. However, for tax purposes, only 50% of meals and entertainment expenses are deductible. Therefore, you must add back 50% of the $8,000 that is not deductible for tax purposes. In addition, the $6,000 in interest expense to purchase tax-exempt bonds is not deductible for tax purposes but is deductible for book purposes. It also must be added back to reconcile book to tax income.

[5] $145,000. The total of lines 1 through 4 equals $145,000 ($100,000 + $15,000 + $20,000 + $10,000).

[6] $46,000. The $16,000 of tax-exempt interest was included in arriving at book income; however, it is not deductible for tax purposes. Therefore, it will have to be deducted to reconcile book to tax income. The $30,000 of life insurance proceeds was included in income for book purposes but is not income for tax purposes. Therefore, it also must be subtracted to reconcile book to tax income.

[7] $39,000. The Sec. 179 expense of $39,000 taken this year is deductible for tax purposes but not for book purposes. Therefore, it will have to be subtracted to reconcile book to tax income.

[8] $85,000. The total of lines 6 and 7 is $85,000 ($46,000 + $39,000).

[9] $60,000. Line 5 less line 8 equals $60,000 ($145,000 – $85,000).

[10] $50,000. The partners' total capital account balances are provided in the situation.

[11] $10,000. Yolanda contributed $10,000 cash to the partnership.

[12] $0. The situation states that no property was contributed to the partnership.

[13] $100,000. The net income per books is given as $100,000.

[14] $160,000. The total of lines 1, 2, and 3 is $160,000 ($50,000 + $10,000 + $0 + $100,000).

[15] $6,000. Linda received a $6,000 cash distribution from the partnership during the year.

[16] $7,500. The adjusted basis of the property distributed to Linda was $2,500 for the desk and $5,000 for the computer.

[17] $13,500. The total of lines 6 and 7 is $13,500 ($6,000 + $7,500).

[18] $146,500. Line 5 less line 8 equals $146,500 ($160,000 – $13,500).

6. Partnership Distributions (6 Gradable Items)

1. $20,000. Distributed property has a basis to the partner that is equal to the property's adjusted basis (AB) to the partnership immediately before such distribution if it does not exceed the AB of the partner's interest in the partnership less any money received in the same distribution. The nonliquidating distribution reduces the partner's basis in the partnership interest to $30,000, which is still greater than the property's AB to the partnership.
2. $47,000. When a liquidation occurs and the partner's basis in the partnership exceeds the partnership's basis in the distributed assets, the excess must be allocated among the distributed assets. Equipment is first assigned its AB of $35,000. After both properties are assigned their AB, the remaining appreciation is $20,000. That amount is allocated based on the proportionate appreciation of both properties ($15,000 increase in FMV of equipment over $25,000 total increase in FMV times $20,000).
3. $19,000. The basis of property distributed to a partner is generally the property's AB to the partnership immediately before the distribution. However, the partner's basis in the property is limited to his or her basis in the partnership interest less any money received in the same distribution.
4. $40,000. Amounts received from the partnership in liquidation of a partnership interest are generally treated the same as other distributions. The partner's basis in noncash property is any excess of his or her AB in the partnership interest immediately before distribution over any amount of money received.
5. $750,000. The partner's basis in property distributed in a nonliquidating distribution is equal to the AB of the property in the hands of the partnership immediately before the distribution. However, the partner's basis in the property is limited to his or her basis in the partnership interest before the distribution.
6. $175,000. In a liquidating distribution, a partner's basis for his or her partnership interest is reduced by the amount of money received. Any remaining basis is then allocated to other property received.

Gleim Simulation Grading

Task	Correct Responses		Gradable Items		Score per Task
1	___	÷	4	=	___
2	___	÷	5	=	___
3 (Research)	___	÷	1	=	___
4	___	÷	10	=	___
5	___	÷	18	=	___
6	___	÷	6	=	___
			Total of Scores per Task		___
		÷	Total Number of Tasks		6
			Total Score		___ %

STUDY UNIT TWELVE
ESTATES, TRUSTS, AND WEALTH TRANSFER TAXES

(16 pages of outline)

This study unit addresses two different kinds of tax: income taxes and transfer taxes. Estates and trusts are legal entities defined by the assets they hold. These assets produce income. The entities are subject to tax on that income. This is referred to as fiduciary income taxation (Subunit 12.1). The formula for computing this fiduciary tax is the individual income tax formula presented earlier in Study Unit 3, modified for the distribution deduction and other special rules. Furthermore, the beneficiaries of these fiduciary entities, rather than the fiduciary, are personally subject to income tax on certain fiduciary income (Subunit 12.2).

In contrast, the gift and estate taxes (Subunits 12.3 and 12.4) are not income taxes. They are taxes on the transfer of assets from one person to another. Relatively few exclusions and deductions apply, and unified transfer tax rates and an applicable credit amount, or ACA, (formerly referred to as the unified credit) apply against all transfers. The donor or estate, not the recipient, must generally pay the tax. Finally, the generation-skipping transfer tax (Subunit 12.5) limits avoidance of gift and estate taxes.

12.1 INCOME TAXATION

1. **Principal vs. Income**
   a. Tax is imposed on taxable income (TI) of trusts and estates, not on items treated as fiduciary principal.
   b. State law defines **principal** and **income** of a trust or estate for federal income tax purposes.
      1) Many states have adopted the Revised Uniform Principal and Income Act, some with modifications.
         a) The act and state laws provide that trust instrument designations of fiduciary principal and interest components control.
         b) The act and state law also provide default designations.
   c. Generally, principal is property held eventually to be delivered to the remainderman (the person who inherits or is entitled to inherit the property).
      1) Change in form of principal is not taxable income.
      2) Income is return on, or for use of, the principal.
      3) It is held for or distributed to the income beneficiary.
   d. Principal is also referred to as the corpus or res.

Allocation of Fiduciary Receipts and Disbursements

Principal	Income
Receipts	
Consideration for property, e.g., Gain on sale	Business income
Replacement property	Insurance proceeds for lost profits
Nontaxable stock dividends	Interest
Stock splits	Rents
Stock rights	Dividends (taxable)
Liquidating dividends	Extraordinary dividends
Depletion allowance (90%), e.g., Royalties	Taxable stock dividends
	Royalties (10%)
Disbursements	
Principal payments on debt	Business (ord. & nec.) expenses, e.g., Interest expense
Capital expenditures	Production of income expenses, e.g.,
Major repairs	Maintenance/repair
Modifications	Insurance
Fiduciary fees	Rent collection fee
Tax on principal items, e.g., Capital gains	Tax on fiduciary income
	Depreciation

2. **Tax Rates**

   a. Tax is imposed on taxable income of a trust or estate at the following rates for 2015:

Fiduciary Taxable Income Brackets	Applicable Rate
$ 0 - $2,500	15%
> 2,500 - 5,900	25% (+ $375.00)
> 5,900 - 9,050	28% (+ $1,225.00)
> 9,050 - 12,300	33% (+ $2,107.00)
> 12,300	39.6% (+ $3,179.50)

3. **Simple Trust**

   a. A simple trust is formed under an instrument having the following characteristics:

      1) Requires current distribution of all its income
      2) Requires no distribution of the res (i.e., principal)
      3) Provides for no charitable contributions by the trust

4. **Complex Trust**

   a. A complex trust is any trust other than a simple trust. A complex trust can

      1) Accumulate income,
      2) Provide for charitable contributions, and
      3) Distribute amounts other than income.

5. **Grantor Trust**

   a. A grantor trust is any trust to the extent the grantor is the effective beneficiary.

      1) The income attributable to a trust principal that is treated as owned by the grantor is taxed to the grantor.

      2) The trust is disregarded.

         a) A trust is considered a grantor trust when the grantor has greater than 5% reversionary interest.

         b) A grantor is treated as the owner of a trust in which the income may be distributed or accumulated for the grantor's spouse.

c) The grantor is also taxed on income from a trust in which the income may be applied for the benefit of the grantor. Use of income for the support of a dependent is considered the application of income for the benefit of the grantor. The income that may be applied for the support of a dependent is not taxable to the grantor if it is not actually used.

6. **Application of Rules**

a. The rules for classifying trusts are applied on a year-to-year basis.

7. **Filing Requirement**

a. An estate with GI greater than or equal to $600 is required to file a tax return. A trust is required to file a return if it has either any taxable income or more than $600 of gross income.

1) The trustee, executor, or administrator must file the return no later than the 15th day of the 4th month after the close of the entity's tax year.

2) Form 1041, *U.S. Income Tax Return for Estates and Trusts*, must be used with its own tax rate schedule.

3) If a domestic estate has a beneficiary who is a nonresident alien, the representative must file a return regardless of income.

4) Estate GI includes the gain from the sale of property (not gross proceeds).

8. **Income Tax Formula**

a. TI of a trust or an estate is computed similarly to that of an individual.

b. Gross income is computed as for individuals. Capital gain is charged to principal.

c. Life insurance proceeds are generally includible in the value of the gross estate but are not considered income of the estate.

d. Income in respect of a decedent is also taxed as income if it is received by the estate.

e. Capital gains are taxed to the estate; then the gain must be added to the principal of the estate.

f. AGI does apply to fiduciaries for purposes of computing deduction limits.

1) The standard deduction is not allowed.

g. Deductions. They generally follow those allowable to an individual. Trustee fees, or administrator fees, and tax return preparation fees are deductible in full.

1) Administration expenses are deductible in full, if not deducted on the estate tax return. The amount of trustee fees deductible is not limited to the excess over 2% of AGI.

2) Depreciation. In default of a trust instrument designation, the act charges depreciation to income.

a) Depreciation is allocated based on the same proportions as income from the estate is allocated.

i) EXCEPTION: The estate instrument may contain provisions apportioning the deduction.

b) Trusts. The trust may deduct depreciation only to the extent a reserve is required or permitted under the trust instrument or local law, and income is set aside for the reserve and actually remains in the trust.

i) Any part of the deduction in excess of the trust income set aside for the reserve is then allocated between the parties according to the instrument.

ii) If the instrument is silent, depreciation is allocated in the same proportion as income.

3) Fiduciary NOLs are computed without regard to charitable contributions or distribution deductions. Carryover by the fiduciary is permitted.
   a) Pass-through for deduction on personal returns of beneficiaries is allowed only in the year the fiduciary terminates.
   b) Pass-through NOLs and capital loss carryovers are used to calculate the beneficiary's AGI and taxable income.
   c) Estates can claim a deduction for a NOL.
      i) The NOL is calculated in a similar manner as an individual's NOL deduction.
      ii) The estate cannot deduct any distributions to beneficiaries or charitable contributions in arriving at the NOL or NOL carryover.
   d) An unused NOL in the final year of the estate may carry over to the beneficiaries succeeding to the property of the estate.
4) A fiduciary may deduct a capital loss to the extent of capital gains plus $3,000. Carryover is permitted for individuals and estates; however, no carryover is allowed from a decedent's final return to his or her estate or beneficiary.
5) Miscellaneous itemized deductions are subject to the 2%-of-AGI floor.
6) Charitable contributions are deductible only if the governing instrument authorizes them. Deduction is not subject to limits based on AGI.
7) Expenses attributable to tax-exempt income are not deductible.
8) Personal exemption. A deduction is allowable but not for the year the trust or estate terminates. The amount of the deduction is
   a) $600 for an estate
   b) $300 for a simple trust
   c) $100 for a complex trust

h. Credits. Gross regular tax of a fiduciary is offset by most of the same credits available to individuals. Certain "personal" credits are unavailable. A fiduciary, for example, has no dependents.

i. Losses from a passive activity owned by the estate or trust cannot be used to offset portfolio (interest, dividends, royalties, annuities, etc.) income of the estate or trust in determining taxable income.

9. **Distribution Deduction**

a. The deduction for distributions allocates taxable income of a trust or estate (gross of distributions) between the fiduciary and its beneficiaries.

b. Simple trust. The deduction is the lesser of the amount of the distributions (required) or distributable net income (DNI) (computed without including exempt income).
   1) Generally, DNI is current net accounting income of the fiduciary reduced by any amounts allocated to principal.

c. Estates and complex trusts. The deduction is the lesser of DNI or distributions.
   1) The amount distributed is the lesser of the FMV of the property or the basis of the property in the hands of the beneficiary.
   2) The trustee(s) of a complex trust may elect to treat distributions made during the first 65 days of the (trust's) tax year as if they were made on the last day of the preceding tax year.
   3) Specific bequests distributed or credited to a beneficiary in no more than three installments are not included as amounts distributed.
   4) The fiduciary recognizes no gain on distribution of property, unless an estate executor so elects.

5) A beneficiary's basis in distributed property is transferred, with adjustments for any gain recognized to the fiduciary. Every $1 of value distributed is treated as if (first) from any current DNI.

a) The instrument might allocate the $1 to current income, accumulated income, or principal.

b) Principal (after DNI) is distributed tax-free.

10. **Distributable Net Income**

a. Distributable net income (DNI) is the maximum deductible at the fiduciary level for distributions and the maximum taxable at the beneficiary level. It is taxable income of the fiduciary (trust or estate), adjusted by the following items:

Taxable Income (TI) of fiduciary (before the distribution deduction)
\+ Personal exemption deduction ($600 estate, $300 simple trust, $100 complex trust)
\+ Tax-exempt interest minus any related expenses
\+ Capital losses allocated to principal
– Capital gains allocated to principal
– Taxable stock dividends allocated to principal
– Extraordinary dividends allocated to principal
= **Distributable net income**

b. No adjustment to fiduciary TI is made for the following:

1) Dividends, other than those in a. above.
2) NOL deductions.
3) Depreciation, if a reserve is established and all income is not distributable.
4) Certain expenditures charged to principal, such as trustee fees. They do reduce income taxable to the beneficiary.

11. **Income in Respect of a Decedent**

a. Income in respect of a decedent (IRD) is all amounts to which a decedent was entitled as gross income but that were not includible in computing taxable income on the final return. The decedent had a right to receive it prior to death; e.g., salary was earned or a sale contract was entered into.

b. Not includible on the final income tax return of a cash-method (CM) taxpayer are amounts not received. Not includible on the final income tax return of an accrual-method (AM) taxpayer are amounts not properly accrued. Examples follow:

Not IRD	IRD
Salary earned and accrued by AM taxpayer	Salary earned prior to but not received before death of a CM taxpayer
Collection of A/R by AM taxpayer	Collection of A/R by CM taxpayer
Gain on sale of property received before death	Gain on sale of property by CM taxpayer, not received before death
Rent received before death	Rent accrued but not received by CM taxpayer before death
Interest on installment debt accrued after death	Interest on installment debt accrued by CM taxpayer before death
Installment contract income recognized before death	Installment income recognized after death on contract entered into before death

c. IRD is reported by the person receiving the income.

1) The cash method applies to income once designated IRD.
2) IRD received by a trust or estate is fiduciary income.

d. A right to receive IRD has a transferred basis. The basis is not stepped-up to FMV on the date of death, as is generally the case for property acquired from a decedent.

EXAMPLE

Mrs. Hart had earned 2 weeks' salary of $2,000 that had not been paid when she died. As a cash-method taxpayer, her basis in the right to receive the $2,000 was $0. When her estate received the income, it had $2,000 of ordinary income because its basis in the right to receive it was also $0. Note that the $2,000 is not reported on Mrs. Hart's final return.

e. IRD has the same character it would have had in the hands of the decedent.

f. IRD is taxable as income to the recipient and is includible in the gross estate. Double taxation is mitigated by deductions.

1) Deductions in respect of a decedent. Expenses accrued before death, but not deductible on the final return because the decedent used the cash method, are deductible when paid if otherwise deductible.

a) They are deductible on a fiduciary income tax return.

b) They are also deductible on the estate tax return.

2) Deduction for estate tax. Estate taxes attributable to IRD included in the gross estate are deductible on the fiduciary income tax return.

a) Administrative expenses and debts of a decedent are deductible on the estate tax return (Form 706). Some of them may also be deductible on the estate's income tax return (Form 1041).

i) Double deductions are disallowed.

ii) The right to deduct the expenses on Form 706 must be waived in order to claim them on Form 1041.

b) Deduction is allowed for any excess of the federal estate tax over the amount of the federal estate tax if the IRD had been excluded from the gross estate

12. **Net Investment Income Tax**

a. Estates and Trusts are required to pay a 3.8% net investment income tax on the lesser of

1) Undistributed net investment income for the tax year or

2) Any excess Fiduciary Taxable Income over the amount at which the highest tax bracket for estates and trusts begins for the tax year ($12,300 for 2015).

b. Undistributed net investment income is net investment income reduced by distributions of net investment income to beneficiaries and deductions for amounts of net investment income paid or permanently set aside for a charitable purpose.

13. **Tax Year**

a. An estate may adopt any tax year ending within 12 months after death. Most trusts must adopt a calendar tax year. Tax-exempt and wholly charitable trusts may qualify to use a fiscal tax year. A beneficiary includes his or her share of trust income in his or her return for his or her tax year in which the trust's tax year ends, without regard to when distributions are made.

14. **Accounting Method**

a. Any permissible accounting method may be adopted.

15. **AMT**

    a. The alternative minimum tax applies to trusts and estates. It is determined in the same manner as for individuals.

16. **Estimated Payments**

    a. Trusts and estates are required to remit payments of estimated tax. The required amount and due dates of installments are determined in the same manner as for individuals. An estate is not required to pay estimated tax for its first 2 tax years. A trustee may elect to treat any portion of an estimated tax payment by the estate as made by the beneficiary. The amount would also be treated as paid or credited to the beneficiary on the last day of the tax year.

Stop and review! You have completed the outline for this subunit. Study multiple-choice questions 1 through 10 beginning on page 450.

12.2 BENEFICIARY'S TAXABLE INCOME

1. **Simple Trust**

    a. A beneficiary of a simple trust is taxed on the lower of the two amounts listed below.

        1) Trust income required to be distributed (even if not distributed)
        2) The beneficiary's proportionate share of the trust's DNI

EXAMPLE

The Triangle Trust reported DNI of $80,000 for the year. If the trustee is required to distribute $60,000 to Neil and $40,000 to Dave each year, then Neil includes $48,000 in GI [$80,000 DNI × ($60,000 Neil's required distribution ÷ $100,000 total required distribution)] and Dave includes $32,000 in GI [$80,000 DNI × ($40,000 Dave's required distribution ÷ $100,000 total required distribution)].

2. **Estates and Complex Trusts**

    a. A beneficiary of an estate or complex trust is taxed on amounts of fiduciary income required to be distributed plus additional amounts distributed to the beneficiary. However, the taxable amount is limited to the beneficiary's share of DNI.

3. **Character**

    a. The character of the income in the hands of the beneficiary is the same as in the hands of the trust or estate.

EXAMPLE

A simple trust distributes all its $10,000 income to its sole beneficiary. Its DNI is also $10,000. Included in the trust income was $1,000 of tax-exempt income. The beneficiary treats $1,000 of the income from the trust as tax-exempt interest and excludes it from his or her personal gross income.

4. **Schedule K-1 (Form 1041)**

    a. Schedule K-1 is used to report the beneficiary's share of income deductions and credits from a trust or an estate.

Stop and review! You have completed the outline for this subunit. Study multiple-choice questions 11 through 15 beginning on page 453.

12.3 GIFT TAX

1. **Definition of Gift Tax**

   a. The gift tax is a tax of the transfer imposed on the donor. The table below presents the basic tax formula modified for the gift tax.

	GIFT AMOUNT
	FMV on date of gift, for
	All gifts in the calendar year
–	Exclusions
	Annual exclusion
	$14,000 per donee
	Gift splitting between spouses
	Paid on behalf of another for
	Medical care
	Education tuition
–	Deductions
	Marital
	Charitable
=	TAXABLE GIFTS FOR CURRENT YEAR
+	Taxable gifts for prior years
=	TAXABLE GIFTS TO DATE
×	Tax Rate
=	TENTATIVE GIFT TAX
–	(Prior year's gifts × current tax rates)
–	Applicable credit amount
=	GIFT TAX LIABILITY

2. **Amount of Gift**

   a. Any excess of FMV of transferred property over the FMV of consideration for it is a gift.

	FMV of transferred property: given
–	FMV of consideration (property, money, etc.): received
	Gift amount

   b. A gift is complete when the giver has given over dominion and control such that (s)he is without legal power to change its disposition.

EXAMPLE

R opens a joint bank account with A, I, and H, with R the only depositor to the account. R, A, I, and H may each withdraw money. A gift is complete only when A, I, or H withdraws money.

   c. Gifts completed when the donor is alive (inter vivos gifts) are the only ones subject to gift tax. Transfers made in trust are included.

   d. Property passing by will or inheritance is not included.

   e. To the extent credit is extended with less than sufficient stated interest, the Code imputes that interest is charged. If the parties are related, the lender is treated as having made a gift of the imputed interest to the borrower.

      1) Gift loans are excluded if the aggregate outstanding principal is not more than $10,000.

   f. Basis in a gift is basis in the hands of the donor plus gift tax attributable to appreciation.

EXAMPLE

Thomas made a gift to his daughter of a piece of land with a FMV of $94,000. The land had a basis to Thomas of $60,000. He paid a taxable gift of $80,000 ($94,000 FMV – $14,000 annual exclusion) and a gift tax of $32,000 ($80,000 × 40%). The basis of the land to the daughter is carryover basis of $60,000 plus the gift tax attributable to the appreciation.

$$\$60{,}000 + \frac{\$34{,}000 \text{ increase in value}}{\$80{,}000 \text{ taxable gift}} \times \$32{,}000 = \$73{,}600$$

The AICPA has historically tested candidates' knowledge on the various aspects of gift tax, specifically the annual exclusion, gift splitting, medical or tuition costs, and marital deductions.

3. **Annual Exclusion**
   a. The first $14,000 of gifts of present interest to each donee is excluded from taxable gift amounts. The annual exclusion is indexed to reflect inflation.
   b. The $14,000 exclusion applies only to gifts of present interests.
   c. A present interest in property includes an unrestricted right to the immediate possession or enjoyment of property or the income from property (such as a life estate or a term for years). Gifts of future interests in property (such as remainders or reversions) do not qualify for the annual exclusion.

EXAMPLE

Edward sets up a trust with the income going to his daughter for her life and the remainder to his granddaughter. Edward has made a gift of a present interest to his daughter and a future interest to his granddaughter.

4. **Gift Splitting**
   a. Each spouse may treat each gift made to any third person as made one-half by the donor and one-half by the donor's spouse.
   b. They must be married at the time of the gift.
   c. They must make a proper election and signify their consent on the gift tax return.
   d. Each spouse may exclude $14,000 annually of gifts to each donee allowing for a combined gift of $28,000.
5. **Medical or Tuition Costs**
   a. Excluded from taxable gifts are amounts paid on behalf of another individual as tuition to an educational organization or for medical care.
   b. The payment must be made directly to the third party, i.e., the medical provider or the educational organization.
   c. Amounts paid for room, board, and books are not excluded.
6. **Marital Deduction**
   a. The amount of a gift transfer to a spouse is deducted in computing taxable gifts. Donor and donee must be married at the time of the gift, and the donee must be a U.S. citizen.
   b. The deduction may not exceed the amount includible as taxable gifts.
   c. Otherwise, the amount of the deduction is not limited.

EXAMPLE

Sid Smith gave his wife, Mary, a diamond ring valued at $20,000 and cash gifts of $30,000 during 2015. Sid is entitled to a $14,000 exclusion with respect to the gifts to Mary. The marital deduction allows Sid to exclude an additional $36,000 ($20,000 + $30,000 – $14,000).

7. **Charitable Deduction**
   a. The FMV of property donated to a qualified charitable organization is deductible. Like the marital deduction, the amount of the deduction is the amount of the gift reduced by the $14,000 exclusion with respect to the donee.
8. **Spousal Support**
   a. Transfers that represent support are not gifts.
9. **Political Contributions**
   a. Political contributions are not subject to gift tax.
10. **Computing the Gift Tax**
    a. Tentative tax is the sum of taxable gifts to each person for the current year and for each preceding year times the rate. Taxable gifts to a person is the total of gift amounts (FMV) in excess of exclusions and the marital and charitable deductions for a calendar year.
    b. The unified transfer tax rates are used.
       1) Current-year applicable rates are applied to both current and preceding years' taxable gifts.
       2) The rate is 18% for taxable gifts up to $10,000.
       3) The rates increase in small steps (e.g., 2%, 3%) over numerous brackets.
       4) The maximum rate is 40% on cumulative gifts in excess of $1 million in 2015.
    c. The tentative gift tax is reduced by the product of prior years' taxable gifts and the current-year rates.
    d. Applicable credit amount (ACA). Tentative tax may also be reduced by any ACA. The ACA is a base amount ($2,117,800 in 2015) reduced by amounts allowable as credits for all preceding tax years. This excludes the first $5.43 million of taxable gifts.

```
Gift tax liability for a current year =
Tentative tax - (Prior-year gifts × Current rates) - ACA
```

11. **Gift Tax Return**
    a. A donor is required to file a gift tax return, Form 709, for any gift(s), unless all gifts are excluded under the annual $14,000 exclusion, the exclusion for medical or tuition payments, or the deduction for qualified transfers to the donor's spouse.
       1) Gift splitting does not excuse the donor from the requirement to file.
    b. A gift tax return is due on the 15th of April following the calendar year in which a gift was made. But a gift tax return for a year of death is due no later than the estate tax return due date.
    c. A United States donee must report information on gifts from foreign persons if the aggregate of such gifts from all foreign persons exceeds $14,000.

Stop and review! You have completed the outline for this subunit. Study multiple-choice questions 16 through 21 beginning on page 454.

12.4 ESTATE TAX

1. Components of the Gross Estate

a. The estate tax is an excise tax imposed on the transfer of the taxable estate of every decedent who was a U.S. citizen or resident.

ESTATE TAX Formula

	GROSS ESTATE
–	Deductions
	Expenses, claims, taxes
	Casualty and theft losses
	Charitable bequests
	Marital deduction
=	TAXABLE ESTATE
+	Taxable gifts made after 1976
=	TOTAL TAXABLE TRANSFERS
×	Tax rate
=	TENTATIVE ESTATE TAX
–	Gift taxes paid on post-1976 gifts
–	Applicable credit amount
–	Other credits
=	ESTATE TAX LIABILITY

b. A decedent's **gross estate (GE)** includes the FMV of all property, real or personal, tangible or intangible, wherever situated, to the extent the decedent owned a beneficial interest at the time of death.

   1) Special tax avoidance rules are established for U.S. citizens or residents who surrender their U.S. citizenship or long-term residency.

c. Included are items such as cash, personal residence and effects, securities, other investments (e.g., real estate, collector items), other personal assets such as notes and claims (e.g., dividends declared prior to death if the record date had passed), and business interests (e.g., in a sole proprietorship, partnership interest).

d. Liabilities of the decedent generally do not affect the amount of the GE, unless the estate actually pays them.

e. The GE includes the value of the surviving spouse's interest in property as dower or curtesy.

   1) Dower and curtesy are common-law rights recognized in some states, usually in modified form.

      a) Dower entitles a surviving wife to a portion of lands her husband owned and possessed during their marriage.

      b) Curtesy entitles a surviving husband to a life estate in all of his wife's land if they had children.

f. The GE includes the full value of property held as joint tenants with the right of survivorship, except to the extent of any part shown to have originally belonged to the other person and for which adequate and full consideration was not provided by the decedent (i.e., the other tenant provided consideration).

   1) The GE includes 50% of property held as joint tenants by spouses or as tenants by the entirety regardless of the amount of consideration provided by each spouse.

g. The value of property interests over which the decedent had a general power of appointment (POA) are included in the GE. A POA is a power exercisable in favor of the decedent, his or her estate, his or her creditors, or the creditors of his or her estate.

h. Bonds, notes, bills, and certificates of indebtedness of the federal, state, and local governments are included in the GE, even if interest on them is exempt from income tax.

i. Gifts within 3 years of death. The gifts made prior to death are not included in the GE of a decedent.

   1) The GE does include gift taxes paid on gifts within 3 years before death.

j. The GE includes insurance proceeds on the decedent's life in certain situations.

   1) The insurance proceeds are payable to or for the estate (including if payable to the executor).
   2) The decedent had any incident of ownership in the policy at death, e.g.,
      a) Right to change beneficiaries
      b) Right to terminate the policy
   3) The proceeds of insurance policies given to others by the decedent within 3 years of death are included in the estate. This is an exception to the "gifts within 3 years of death rules."
   4) The proceeds included in the estate, listed in item c. on the previous page, are allocated proportionately if the premiums are partially paid by the insured and periodically paid by someone else.

EXAMPLE

Twenty years before her death, Joanna bought a $200,000 term insurance policy. One year before her death, she irrevocably transferred the policy and all incidents of ownership to a trust that paid the last year's premiums. Joanna's GE includes $190,000 of proceeds since Joanna paid 95% of the premiums.

k. Annuities and survivor benefits including interest. The GE includes the value of any annuity receivable by a beneficiary by reason of surviving the decedent if either of the following statements applies:

   1) The annuity was payable to the decedent.
   2) The decedent had the right to receive the annuity or payment
      a) Either alone or in conjunction with another.
      b) For his or her life or for any period not ascertainable without reference to his or her death, or for any period that does not end before his or her death.

l. Medical insurance reimbursements due the decedent at death are treated as property in which the decedent had an interest.

m. Inter vivos transfers. The GE includes assets transferred during life in which the decedent retained, at death, any of the following interests:

   1) A life estate, an income interest, possession or enjoyment of assets, or the right to designate who will enjoy the property
   2) A 5% or greater reversionary interest if possession was conditioned on surviving the decedent
   3) The power to alter, amend, revoke, or terminate the transfer
   4) An interest in a qualified terminable interest property (QTIP) trust

2. **Valuing the Gross Estate**

   a. Value is the FMV of the property unless a special valuation rule is used.

      1) Real property is usually valued at its highest and best use.
      2) A transfer of interests in a corporation or partnership to a family member is subject to estate tax-freeze rules.
         a) Generally, the retained interest is valued at zero.

b. The executor may elect to value the estate at either the date of death or the alternate valuation date. An alternate valuation date election is irrevocable.

   1) The election can be made only if it results in a reduction in both the value of the gross estate and the sum of the federal estate tax and the generation-skipping transfer tax (reduced by allowable credits).
   2) The alternate valuation date is 6 months after the decedent's death.

      a) Assets sold or distributed before then are valued on the date of sale or distribution.
      b) Assets, the value of which is affected by mere lapse of time, are valued as of the date of the decedent's death, but adjustment is made for value change from other than mere lapse of time.

         i) Examples of such assets are patents, life estates, reversions, and remainders.
         ii) The value of such assets is based on years.
         iii) Changes due to time value of money are treated as from more than mere lapse of time.

3. **Deductions from the Gross Estate**

a. Deductions from the GE in computing the taxable estate (TE) include those with respect to expenses, claims, and taxes.

NOTE: A deductible amount is allowed against gross income on the decedent's final income tax return only if the right to deduct them from the GE is waived.

b. Expenses for selling property of an estate are deductible if the sale is necessary to

   1) Pay the decedent's debts
   2) Pay expenses of administration
   3) Pay taxes
   4) Preserve the estate
   5) Effect distribution

c. Administration and funeral expenses are deductible.

d. Claims against the estate (including debts of the decedent) are deductible.

   1) Medical expenses paid within 1 year of death may be deducted on either the estate tax return or the final income tax return (not both).

e. Unpaid mortgages on property are deductible if the value of the decedent's interest is included in the GE.

f. A limited amount of state death taxes is deductible. Federal estate taxes and income tax paid on income earned and received after the decedent's death are not deductible.

g. Casualty or theft losses incurred during the settlement of the estate are deductible, if not deducted in the estate's income tax return.

h. Charitable contributions. Bequests to qualified charitable organizations are deductible.

   1) The entire interest of the decedent in the underlying property must generally be donated.
   2) Trust interests may enable deductible transfer of partial interests in underlying property.
   3) An inter vivos contribution (vs. a bequest) may result in exclusion from the GE and a current deduction for regular taxable income.

i. Marital transfers. Outright transfers to a surviving spouse are deductible from the GE, to the extent that the interest is included in the gross estate.

4. **Computing the Estate Tax and Credits**

   a. The estate tax is imposed on the sum of the TE plus gifts subject to the gift tax. However, it is reduced by gift taxes payable on those gifts and by the ACA.

      1) TE is the GE reduced by deductions.
      2) Tentative tax is the product of total taxable transfers and the applicable rate.
      3) Total taxable transfers are the sum of the TE plus taxable gifts after 1976 (valued at FMV on the date of the gifts).

   b. Applicable rates are the unified transfer tax rates. Current-year applicable rates are applied to both current and preceding years' taxable gifts. The following information is for 2015:

      1) The rate is 18% for taxable gifts up to $10,000.
      2) The rates increase in small steps (e.g., 2%, 3%) over numerous brackets.
      3) The maximum rate is 40% on cumulative gifts in excess of $1,000,000.

   c. The tentative estate tax is reduced by the credit for gift taxes payable on post-1976 gifts, based on current rates.

   d. Tentative estate tax reduced by gift taxes paid, the ACA, and other credit is the net estate tax.

   e. The ACA is a base amount ($2,117,800 in 2015), not reduced by amounts allowable as credits for gift tax for all preceding tax years.

      1) The ACA offsets the estate tax liability that would be imposed on a taxable estate of up to $5.43 million computed at current rates.
      2) Any unused amount by a deceased spouse may be used by the surviving spouse in addition to the surviving spouse's own exclusion amount. Under this portability election, the surviving spouse could potentially have an available exclusion amount of $10.86 million.

EXAMPLE

The deceased spouse only used $3.43 million of the allowed exclusion. The surviving spouse is allowed a $7.43 million exclusion ($5.43 million surviving spouse original amount + $2 million unused by the deceased spouse).

   f. Credit is allowable for death taxes paid to foreign governments.

   g. Credit is allowable on gift tax paid on gifts included in the gross estate.

   h. Prior transfers. Credit is allowed for taxes paid on transfers by or from a person who died within 10 years before, or 2 years after, the decedent's death.

      1) Amounts creditable are the lesser of the following:
         a) Estate tax paid by the (prior) transferor
         b) Amount by which the assets increase the estate tax
      2) Adjustment is made to the credit for transfers more than 2 years prior to the decedent's death.

5. **Estate Tax Return**

   a. The executor is required to file Form 706, *United States Estate Tax Return*, if the gross estate exceeds a threshold.

      1) The threshold is $5.43 million in 2015.
      2) Adjusted taxable gifts made by the decedent during his or her lifetime reduce the threshold.

   b. The estate tax return is due within 9 months after the date of the decedent's death.

      1) An extension of up to 6 months may be granted.

   c. Time for payment may be extended up to 1 year past the due date. For reasonable cause, the time for payment may be extended up to 10 years.

d. Estate tax is charged to estate property.

   1) If the tax on part of the estate distributed is paid out of other estate property, equitable contribution from the distributee beneficiary is recoverable.
   2) The executor is ultimately liable for payment of the taxes.

      a) If there is more than one executor, each must verify and sign the return.

e. An estate that includes a substantial interest in a closely held business may be allowed to delay payment of part of the estate tax, if that interest exceeds 35% of the gross estate.

   1) A closely held business includes the following, if carrying on a trade or business:

      a) A corporation, if it has 45 or fewer shareholders or if 20% or more in value of the voting stock is included in the gross estate
      b) A partnership, if it has 45 or fewer partners or if 20% or more of the capital interests in the partnership is included in the gross estate

Stop and review! You have completed the outline for this subunit. Study multiple-choice questions 22 through 28 beginning on page 456.

12.5 GENERATION-SKIPPING TRANSFER TAX (GSTT)

1. **Overview**

   a. The GSTT is imposed separately and in addition to gift and estate taxes on transfers directly or in trust for the sole benefit of a person at least two generations younger than the transferor. GSTT is generally imposed on each generation-skipping transfer (GST). A GST is a direct skip, a taxable distribution, or a taxable termination.

2. **Direct Skip**

   a. A direct skip is a transfer of an interest in property, subject to estate tax or gift tax, to a skip person. The transferor is liable for the tax.
   b. A **skip person** is either a natural person assigned to a generation that is two or more generations below the transferor or a trust, all interests of which are held by skip persons.
   c. In the case of related persons, a skip person is identified by reference to the family tree.

      1) For example, a grandchild is two generations below the grandparent.

   d. In the case of nonrelated persons, a skip person is identified by reference to age differences.

      1) For example, an individual born between 37 1/2 years and 62 1/2 years after the transferor is two generations below the transferor.

3. **Taxable Distribution**

   a. A taxable distribution is a distribution from a trust to a skip person of income or principal, other than a distribution that is a direct skip or taxable termination. The transferee is liable for the tax.

4. **Taxable Termination**

   a. A taxable termination is a termination of an interest in property held in trust. A taxable termination has not occurred if, immediately after the termination, a nonskip person has an interest in the property or if distributions are not permitted to be made to a skip person at any time following the termination.

      1) Termination may be by lapse of time, release of power, death, or otherwise.
      2) The trustee is liable to pay the tax.

5. **GSTT vs. Estate Tax**
   a. The GSTT approximates the maximum federal estate tax that would have applied to the transfer on the date of the transfer.
6. **Exemption**
   a. Each individual is allowed a $5.43 million exemption in 2015 that (s)he, or his or her executor, may allocate to GST property. The exemption is indexed for inflation. Gift splitting applies to GSTTs; $10.86 million is allocable.
7. **Inter Vivos**
   a. Inter vivos gifts are exempt from the GSTT if they are not subject to gift tax due to the $14,000 annual exclusion or the medical/tuition exclusion.

Stop and review! You have completed the outline for this subunit. Study multiple-choice questions 29 and 30 on page 458.

QUESTIONS

<u>**12.1 Income Taxation**</u>

1. Which of the following is allowed in the calculation of the taxable income of a simple trust?

A. Exemption.

B. Standard deduction.

C. Brokerage commission for purchase of tax-exempt bonds.

D. Charitable contribution.

Answer (A) is correct.

REQUIRED: Allowable reduction of income item for simple trust.

DISCUSSION: Taxable income of a trust is computed similarly to that of an individual; however, there are some significant differences. Expenses for tax-exempt income (e.g., bonds) are not deductible for individuals or trusts. A standard deduction is allowed for individuals but not trusts. In addition, simple trusts are not allowed to make charitable contributions but are allowed a $300 exemption.

Answer (B) is incorrect. Standard deductions are only available for individuals. Answer (C) is incorrect. Tax-exempt income is excluded from taxable income; therefore, expenses for such income are disallowed deductions. Answer (D) is incorrect. One of the characteristics of simple trusts is that they do not provide charitable contributions.

2. With regard to estimated income tax, estates

A. Must make quarterly estimated tax payments starting no later than the second quarter following the one in which the estate was established.

B. Are exempt from paying estimated tax during the estate's first 2 taxable years.

C. Must make quarterly estimated tax payments only if the estate's income is required to be distributed currently.

D. Are not required to make payments of estimated tax.

Answer (B) is correct.

REQUIRED: The true statement concerning estimated tax payments for estates.

DISCUSSION: Estates are required to make estimated payments of income tax except during the first 2 tax years of existence. No estimated payments are required during the estate's first 2 tax years.

Answer (A) is incorrect. Estates need not make estimated tax payments for the first 2 years of existence. Answer (C) is incorrect. Estimated tax payments are required after the first 2 years regardless of the required distribution of income. Answer (D) is incorrect. Estates are required to make payments of estimated tax after the first 2 years of existence.

3. Which of the following fiduciary entities are required to use the calendar year as their taxable period for income tax purposes?

	Estates	Trusts (Except Those that Are Tax-Exempt)
A.	Yes	Yes
B.	No	No
C.	Yes	No
D.	No	Yes

Answer (D) is correct.

REQUIRED: The tax year of estates and trusts.

DISCUSSION: An estate may adopt either a calendar tax year or any fiscal year ending not more than 12 months after death. All trusts, other than tax-exempt and wholly charitable trusts, must use a calendar tax year.

4. For income tax purposes, the estate's initial taxable period for a decedent who died on October 24

A. May be either a calendar year, or a fiscal year beginning on the date of the decedent's death.

B. Must be a fiscal year beginning on the date of the decedent's death.

C. May be either a calendar year, or a fiscal year beginning on October 1 of the year of the decedent's death.

D. Must be a calendar year beginning on January 1 of the year of the decedent's death.

Answer (A) is correct.

REQUIRED: The estate's initial taxable period.

DISCUSSION: An estate as a legal entity comes into existence upon the death of an individual. The estate may choose a taxable year ending within 12 months after the date of the decedent's death. The taxable year may be either a calendar year or fiscal year.

Answer (B) is incorrect. The estate may choose a calendar year. Answer (C) is incorrect. The legal existence of an estate commences on the date of death of an individual and therefore the tax year begins on such date. Answer (D) is incorrect. The taxable year may be either a calendar year or fiscal year beginning on the date of commencement of legal existence of the estate.

5. Ordinary and necessary administration expenses paid by the fiduciary of an estate are deductible

A. Only on the fiduciary income tax return (Form 1041) and never on the federal estate tax return (Form 706).

B. Only on the federal estate tax return and never on the fiduciary income tax return.

C. On the fiduciary income tax return only if the estate tax deduction is waived for these expenses.

D. On both the fiduciary income tax return and the estate tax return by adding a tax computed on the proportionate rates attributable to both returns.

Answer (C) is correct.

REQUIRED: The deductibility of administration expenses.

DISCUSSION: Administration expenses (and debts of a decedent) are deductible on the estate tax return, and some may also qualify as deductions for income tax purposes on the estate's income tax return. Double deductions are disallowed. A waiver of the right to deduct them on Form 706 is required in order to claim them on Form 1041.

Answer (A) is incorrect. Administration expenses are deductible on Form 706. Answer (B) is incorrect. Administration expenses are deductible on Form 1041. Answer (D) is incorrect. Administration expenses are not deductible in full on both Form 706 and Form 1041.

6. The charitable contribution deduction on an estate's fiduciary income tax return is allowable

A. If the decedent died intestate.

B. To the extent of the same adjusted gross income limitation as that on an individual income tax return.

C. Only if the decedent's will specifically provides for the contribution.

D. Subject to the 2% threshold on miscellaneous itemized deductions.

Answer (C) is correct.

REQUIRED: The charitable contributions deductible on estate's fiduciary income tax return.

DISCUSSION: Charitable contributions to a qualified organization are deductible only to the extent the will specifically provides for the contribution.

Answer (A) is incorrect. A charitable contribution is not deductible unless the will provides for the contribution. Answer (B) is incorrect. AGI limitations do not apply. Answer (D) is incorrect. The 2% threshold does not apply.

7. Raff died in 2014, leaving her entire estate to her only child. Raff's will gave full discretion to the estate's executor with regard to distributions of income. For 2015, the estate's distributable net income was $15,000, of which $9,000 was paid to the beneficiary; no income was tax-exempt. What amount can be claimed on the estate's 2015 fiduciary income tax return for the distributions deduction?

A. $0

B. $6,000

C. $9,000

D. $15,000

Answer (C) is correct.

REQUIRED: The amount deductible on a fiduciary income tax return for distributions.

DISCUSSION: The deduction for distributions is the lesser of the amount of distributions and distributable net income (DNI). DNI is net accounting income for the tax year reduced by net amounts allocated to principal. A beneficiary is subject to tax on his or her share of DNI. The income is characterized at the fiduciary level.

8. Ross, a calendar-year, cash-basis taxpayer who died in June 2015, was entitled to receive a $10,000 accounting fee that had not been collected before the date of death. The executor of Ross's estate collected the full $10,000 in July 2015. This $10,000 should appear in

A. Only the decedent's final individual income tax return.

B. Only the estate's fiduciary income tax return.

C. Only the estate tax return.

D. Both the fiduciary income tax return and the estate tax return.

Answer (D) is correct.

REQUIRED: The correct treatment of income earned before death but not received until after death.

DISCUSSION: Income that a decedent had a right to receive prior to death but that was not includible on his or her final income tax return is income in respect of a decedent. The $10,000 is properly includible in the estate's (fiduciary) income tax return because Ross was a cash-basis taxpayer and would not properly include income not yet received at the time of death in his final return. Since the money was owed to Ross (he had a right to receive it), it is an asset of the estate and must be included on the estate tax return also.

Answer (A) is incorrect. Ross was a cash-basis taxpayer and would not properly include income not received at the time of death. Answer (B) is incorrect. The $10,000 is an asset of the estate and must also be included on the estate tax return. Answer (C) is incorrect. It must also be included in the fiduciary income tax return.

Questions 9 and 10 are based on the following information. Lyon, a cash-basis taxpayer, died on January 15, Year 1. In Year 1, the estate executor made the required periodic distribution of $9,000 from estate income to Lyon's sole heir.

Year 1 Estate Income:

$20,000	Taxable interest
10,000	Net long-term capital gains allocable to corpus

Year 1 Estate Disbursements:

$ 5,000	Administrative expenses attributable to taxable income

9. For the Year 1 calendar year, what was the Lyon estate's distributable net income (DNI)?

A. $15,000

B. $20,000

C. $25,000

D. $30,000

Answer (A) is correct.

REQUIRED: The distributable net income for an estate.

DISCUSSION: Distributable net income (DNI) for this estate is found by subtracting the administrative expenses attributable to the taxable income from the taxable interest income, or $15,000 ($20,000 – $5,000). Capital gains allocable to the corpus do not affect DNI.

10. Lyon's executor does not intend to file an extension request for the estate fiduciary income tax return. By what date must the executor file the Form 1041, *U.S. Fiduciary Income Tax Return*, for the estate's Year 1 calendar year?

A. Thursday, March 15, Year 2.

B. Monday, April 16, Year 2.

C. Friday, June 15, Year 2.

D. Monday, September 17, Year 2.

Answer (B) is correct.

REQUIRED: The required date for filing Form 1041.

DISCUSSION: Form 1041, the estate fiduciary income tax return, must be filed on or before the 15th day of the 4th month after the end of the estate's taxable year if an extension request is not filed. An estate may adopt any tax year beginning within 12 months after the death of the decedent. If the 15th day of the 4th month following the close of the taxable year falls on a weekend or holiday, then the return must be filed the day after the weekend or holiday. From the choices given, it is evident that April 15, Year 2, is a Sunday; therefore, the return is due the following day (Monday, April 16, Year 2).

12.2 Beneficiary's Taxable Income

11. The Simone Trust reported distributable net income of $120,000 for the current year. The trustee is required to distribute $60,000 to Kent and $90,000 to Lind each year. If the trustee distributes these amounts, what amount is includible in Lind's gross income?

A. $0

B. $60,000

C. $72,000

D. $90,000

Answer (C) is correct.

REQUIRED: Distribution includible in Lind's gross income.

DISCUSSION: Distributable net income (DNI) is the maximum amount of the distribution on which beneficiaries can be taxed. The trust reports DNI of $120,000 and is required to distribute $150,000 ($60,000 to Kent and $90,000 to Lind). Thus, the distribution each beneficiary receives must be prorated to determine his or her share of the distribution includible in gross income. Lind receives 60% of the distribution ($90,000 ÷ $150,000). As a result, she reports $72,000 of the $120,000 DNI.

Answer (A) is incorrect. Beneficiaries of a trust must include distributions to the extent of distributable net income. Answer (B) is incorrect. Only half of the distributable net income equals $60,000. Lind must include an amount equal to her share of total distributions, or 60% ($90,000 Lind's distribution ÷ $150,000 total distribution). Answer (D) is incorrect. The amount of distribution includible in a beneficiary's gross income is limited to the trust's distributable net income. Lind is not the only beneficiary, and her includible distribution must be determined relative to all distributions.

12. Gardner, a U.S. citizen and the sole income beneficiary of a simple trust, is entitled to receive current distributions of the trust income. During the year, the trust reported:

Interest income from corporate bonds	$5,000
Fiduciary fees allocable to income	750
Net long-term capital gain allocable to corpus	2,000

What amount of the trust income is includible in Gardner's gross income?

A. $7,000

B. $5,000

C. $4,250

D. $0

Answer (C) is correct.

REQUIRED: The amount of trust income included in Gardner's gross income.

DISCUSSION: A simple trust is formed under an instrument having the following characteristics:

1. Requires current distribution of all its income
2. Requires no distribution of the principal
3. Provides for no charitable contribution by the trust

Trust income is taxed to the beneficiary of the trust whether distributed or not. Income related to the disposition of corpus is not taxable to the beneficiary because it is not earned income. The fees paid to the fiduciary are deductible from the trust income. Therefore, the trust income equals $5,000 of interest income less $750 of fiduciary fees for a total of $4,250.

Answer (A) is incorrect. The long-term capital gain allocable to the corpus is not taxable to Gardner and the fiduciary fees are deductible. Answer (B) is incorrect. The $750 of fiduciary fees are deductible in arriving at gross income for Gardner. Answer (D) is incorrect. The income of a simple trust is taxable whether or not it is distributed to Gardner.

13. A distribution to an estate's sole beneficiary for the 2015 calendar year equaled $15,000, the amount currently required to be distributed by the will. The estate's 2015 records were as follows:

<u>Estate income</u>

$40,000 Taxable interest

<u>Estate disbursements</u>

$34,000 Expenses attributable to taxable interest

What amount of the distribution was taxable to the beneficiary?

A. $40,000

B. $15,000

C. $6,000

D. $0

Answer (C) is correct.

REQUIRED: The amount of taxable distribution.

DISCUSSION: The beneficiary of an estate must include in gross income the amount of distributions from the estate limited to the amount of distributable net income. The remaining distribution is treated as corpus. In this situation, distributable net income is $6,000 ($40,000 – $34,000).

Answer (A) is incorrect. The gross income is $40,000. Answer (B) is incorrect. The $15,000 distribution exceeds distributable net income. Answer (D) is incorrect. Distributable net income is $6,000, and the distribution is $15,000.

14. Bob Jones is sole beneficiary of a trust requiring that all income, but no corpus, be distributed currently. The trust's distributable net income for 2015 was $20,000, of which $4,000 is a long-term capital gain allocated to income and $2,500 is interest on tax-exempt municipal bonds. Jones received a $15,000 distribution on December 20, 2015, and the remaining $5,000 on January 10, 2016. Assuming Jones has no other income for 2015, his adjusted gross income should be

A. $20,000

B. $17,500

C. $15,000

D. $13,500

Answer (B) is correct.

REQUIRED: The adjusted gross income of the sole beneficiary of a simple trust.

DISCUSSION: The beneficiary of a simple trust (one that is required to distribute all income currently) must include in gross income the amount of fiduciary income of the trust (whether distributed or not), limited to the amount of distributable net income. The amount included in a beneficiary's gross income retains the same character as in the hands of the trust.

Although Jones only received $15,000 in 2015, all of the distributable net income (which is the same as fiduciary income in this case) must be included in his gross income in 2015. Since the income retains the same character in the hands of the beneficiary as in the hands of the trust, Bob is entitled to exclude the $2,500 of interest on municipal bonds. Therefore, Bob's adjusted gross income is $17,500 ($20,000 distributable net income – $2,500 tax-exempt interest).

Answer (A) is incorrect. Bob is entitled to exclude the $2,500 of interest on municipal bonds. Answer (C) is incorrect. Beneficiary gross income includes income of the trust (whether distributed or not) up to DNI. Answer (D) is incorrect. The LTCG is includible in that it is allocated to income.

15. For income tax purposes, all estates

A. Must adopt a calendar year, except for existing estates with fiscal years that ended in 2015.

B. May adopt a calendar year or any fiscal year.

C. Must adopt a calendar year regardless of the year the estate was established.

D. Must use the same tax year as that of its principal beneficiary.

Answer (B) is correct.

REQUIRED: The tax year required of estates.

DISCUSSION: An estate is a new taxable entity and may choose a tax year ending within 12 months after the date of the decedent's death.

Answer (A) is incorrect. There is no requirement for an estate to adopt the calendar year. Answer (C) is incorrect. An estate is not required to use a calendar year, but this rule would apply to most trusts. Answer (D) is incorrect. There is no provision for an estate to use the tax year of its principal beneficiary.

12.3 Gift Tax

16. Which of the following payments would require the donor to file a gift tax return?

A. $30,000 to a university for a spouse's tuition.

B. $40,000 to a university for a cousin's room and board.

C. $50,000 to a hospital for a parent's medical expenses.

D. $80,000 to a physician for a friend's surgery.

Answer (B) is correct.

REQUIRED: Payment requiring a gift tax return.

DISCUSSION: Although tuition is an amount excluded as a taxable gift, room and board does not qualify. It must be reported on the gift tax return.

Answer (A) is incorrect. A payment for tuition to a medical organization may be excluded from gift tax assuming it is paid directly to the third party. Answer (C) is incorrect. Medical expenses are excluded as taxable gifts pending payment directly to the third party providing the medical care. Answer (D) is incorrect. Excluded from taxable gifts are amounts paid on behalf of another individual for medical care. The payment must be directly to the medical provider.

17. Ralph created a joint bank account for himself and his friend's son, Dave. There is a gift to Dave when

A. Ralph creates the account.

B. Ralph dies.

C. Dave draws on the account for his own benefit.

D. Dave is notified by Ralph that the account has been created.

Answer (C) is correct.

REQUIRED: The event that completes the gift.

DISCUSSION: A gift is complete when the donor has so parted with dominion and control as to leave him or her no power to change its disposition. Ralph made an indirect transfer of the money to Dave by opening the bank account. Only once Dave withdraws the money will Ralph lose all dominion and control over the property so that the action will complete the gift.

Answer (A) is incorrect. When Ralph opens the account, he can still withdraw the money so that it is not a completed gift. Answer (B) is incorrect. When Ralph dies, there may be no transfer to Dave, or there may be a devise but not a gift because a gift only occurs during a donor's lifetime. Answer (D) is incorrect. Notice has no effect here since Dave must draw on the account for a completed gift.

18. During 2015, Blake transferred a corporate bond with a face amount and fair market value of $20,000 to a trust for the benefit of her 16-year-old child. Annual interest on this bond is $2,000, which is to be accumulated in the trust and distributed to the child on reaching the age of 21. The bond is then to be distributed to the donor or her successor-in-interest in liquidation of the trust. Present value of the total interest to be received by the child is $8,710. The amount of the gift that is excludable from taxable gifts is

A. $20,000

B. $12,000

C. $8,710

D. $0

Answer (D) is correct.

REQUIRED: The excludable amount of a gift transferred in trust with income on principal to be accumulated.

DISCUSSION: Up to $14,000 of the FMV of a gift of present interest to a donee is excludable each year. A present interest is an unrestricted right to the immediate use, possession, or enjoyment of property or the income from property (such as a life estate or interest). The donee has no present interest in the transferred property, so none of its present value is excludable by the donor/trustor.

Answer (A) is incorrect. The fair market value of the bond is $20,000. Answer (B) is incorrect. The amount of $12,000 is 50% of the bond's fair market value plus one year's interest. Answer (C) is incorrect. The present value of the total amount of interest is $8,710.

19. During the current year, Mann, an unmarried U.S. citizen, made a $7,000 cash gift to an only child and also paid $28,000 in tuition expenses directly to a grandchild's university on the grandchild's behalf. Mann made no other lifetime transfers. Assume that the gift tax annual exclusion is $14,000. For gift tax purposes, what was Mann's taxable gift?

A. $35,000

B. $28,000

C. $21,000

D. $0

Answer (D) is correct.

REQUIRED: The amount of taxable gift.

DISCUSSION: The $28,000 of tuition expenses that are paid directly to the university qualify for exclusion from gift tax. The remaining $7,000 gift is offset by the $14,000 annual exclusion, resulting in a $0 taxable gift.

Answer (A) is incorrect. The $7,000 cash gift is less than the annual exclusion of $14,000; thus, it is not taxable. Tuition expenses that are directly paid to the university qualify for exclusion from gift tax. Answer (B) is incorrect. The $28,000 of tuition expenses that are directly paid to the university qualify for exclusion from gift tax. Answer (C) is incorrect. The $21,000 is calculated as $35,000 taxable gifts less the $14,000 annual exclusion. The $28,000 of tuition expenses that are directly paid to the university qualify for exclusion from gift tax. Thus, the annual exclusion amount would be used to offset the $7,000 cash gift.

20. George and Suzanne have been married for 40 years. Suzanne inherited $1,000,000 from her mother. Assume that the annual gift-tax exclusion is $14,000. What amount of the $1,000,000 can Suzanne give to George without incurring a gift-tax liability?

A. $14,000

B. $28,000

C. $500,000

D. $1,000,000

Answer (D) is correct.

REQUIRED: The amount a spouse can transfer to another spouse without incurring gift tax.

DISCUSSION: There is an unlimited marital deduction for taxable gift transfers made between spouses. George and Suzanne qualify because they were married at the time of the transfer and are both U.S. citizens. Therefore, all $1,000,000 is excluded from gift tax.

Answer (A) is incorrect. The annual exclusion is equal to $14,000. There is an unlimited marital deduction for taxable gift transfers made between spouses. George and Suzanne qualify because they were married at the time of the transfer and are both U.S. citizens. Therefore, all $1,000,000 is excluded from gift tax. Answer (B) is incorrect. The annual exclusion allowed for couples under gift splitting is equal to $28,000. There is an unlimited marital deduction for taxable gift transfers made between spouses. George and Suzanne qualify because they were married at the time of the transfer and are both U.S. citizens. Therefore, all $1,000,000 is excluded from gift tax. Answer (C) is incorrect. One-half of the total taxable gift is equal to $500,000. There is an unlimited marital deduction for taxable gift transfers made between spouses. George and Suzanne qualify because they were married at the time of the transfer and are both U.S. citizens. Therefore, all $1,000,000 is excluded from gift tax.

21. Don and Linda Grant, U.S. citizens, were married for the entire 2015 calendar year. In 2015, Don gave a $66,000 cash gift to his sister. The Grants made no other gifts in 2015. They each signed a timely election to treat the $66,000 gift as one made by each spouse. Disregarding the unified credit and estate tax consequences, what amount of the 2015 gift is taxable to the Grants for gift tax purposes?

A. $0

B. $38,000

C. $52,000

D. $66,000

Answer (B) is correct.

REQUIRED: The taxable gifts after the gift-splitting election is made.

DISCUSSION: Each spouse may treat each gift made to any third person as made one-half by the donor and one-half by the donor's spouse. Because the Grants made the gift-splitting election, each will be treated as if (s)he made a $33,000 gift to the donee. Since the gift was of a present interest, a $14,000 exclusion is available for each donor. Therefore, after a total of $28,000 in exclusions, the taxable gift will be $19,000 for each donor for a total of $38,000.

Answer (A) is incorrect. A portion of this gift is taxable. Answer (C) is incorrect. The Grants made the gift-splitting election, so each is entitled to the $14,000 exclusion. Answer (D) is incorrect. Each taxpayer is entitled to a $14,000 gift exclusion.

12.4 Estate Tax

22. Under which of the following circumstances is trust property with an independent trustee includible in the grantor's gross estate?

A. The trust is revocable.

B. The trust is established for a minor.

C. The trustee has the power to distribute trust income.

D. The income beneficiary disclaims the property, which then passes to the remainderman, the grantor's friend.

Answer (A) is correct.

REQUIRED: Property includible in a grantor's gross estate.

DISCUSSION: Any beneficial interest held by the decedent at the time of death is included in the gross estate. Retaining a right to revoke the property will cause the property's inclusion in the gross estate.

Answer (B) is incorrect. Once the trust is outside the influence of the grantor, it is no longer a beneficial interest. Thus, no inclusion in the gross estate is necessary. Answer (C) is incorrect. Retaining the power to distribute trust income by the grantor will not cause the property to be included in the gross estate. Answer (D) is incorrect. No beneficial interest remained with the decedent at the time of death. Thus, no inclusion is necessary in the grantor's gross estate.

23. Fred and Amy Kehl, both U.S. citizens, are married. All of their real and personal property is owned by them as tenants by the entirety or as joint tenants with right of survivorship. The gross estate of the first spouse to die

A. Includes 50% of the value of all property owned by the couple, regardless of which spouse furnished the original consideration.

B. Includes only the property that had been acquired with the funds of the deceased spouse.

C. Is governed by the federal statutory provisions relating to jointly held property, rather than by the decedent's interest in community property vested by state law if the Kehls reside in a community property state.

D. Includes one-third of the value of all real estate owned by the Kehls, as the dower right in the case of the wife or curtesy right in the case of the husband.

Answer (A) is correct.

REQUIRED: The survivorship rights includible in the gross estate of a decedent spouse.

DISCUSSION: Generally, the gross estate includes the full value of property held as tenants by the entirety or as joint tenants with the right of survivorship. However, if spouses held the property, the gross estate of the first to die includes only half the value of such property.

Answer (B) is incorrect. The portion of consideration paid for the property by the surviving tenant does not affect the gross estate amount when the property was held by spouses. Answer (C) is incorrect. The amount included in the gross estate when spouses held property jointly is designated by the IRC. Answer (D) is incorrect. The full value of a surviving spouse's dower or curtesy interest is included in the gross estate of a decedent spouse. Furthermore, the question does not address dower or curtesy.

24. Bell, a cash-basis, calendar-year taxpayer, died on June 1, 2014. In 2014, prior to her death, Bell incurred $2,000 in medical expenses. The executor of the estate paid the medical expenses, which were a claim against the estate, on July 1, 2014. If the executor files the appropriate waiver, the medical expenses are deductible on

A. The estate tax return.

B. Bell's final income tax return.

C. The estate income tax return.

D. The executor's income tax return.

Answer (B) is correct.

REQUIRED: The return on which a decedent's medical expenses are deductible.

DISCUSSION: The executor's waiver precludes a deduction on the estate tax return. Medical expenses incurred but not paid prior to Bell's death are deductible on her final income tax return. Although the expenses were not paid prior to Bell's death, any medical expenses attributed to a decedent should be deducted on the decedent's final income tax return if they were paid within 1 year after the date of death.

25. Alan Curtis, a U.S. citizen, died on March 1, 2014, leaving an adjusted gross estate with a fair market value of $1.4 million at the date of death. Under the terms of Alan's will, $375,000 was bequeathed outright to his widow, free of all estate and inheritance taxes. The remainder of Alan's estate was left to his mother. Alan made no taxable gifts during his lifetime. In computing the taxable estate, the executor of Alan's estate should claim a marital deduction of

A. $250,000

B. $375,000

C. $700,000

D. $1,025,000

Answer (B) is correct.

REQUIRED: The amount of the marital deduction.

DISCUSSION: A marital deduction for the value of any interest in property that passes from the decedent to the surviving spouse (which is not a terminable interest) is allowed, but only to the extent that the interest is included in the gross estate. The outright bequest of $375,000 is includible and deductible in full.

Answer (A) is incorrect. The full $375,000 of the outright transfer by bequest is deductible. Answer (C) is incorrect. The marital deduction is for the amount that passes or passed to the surviving spouse, not an amount that might have passed had intestate succession law applied. Answer (D) is incorrect. The marital deduction is an amount subtracted from the gross estate, not the estate net of the deduction.

26. In 2015, what amount of a decedent's taxable estate is effectively tax-free if the maximum applicable credit amount is taken?

A. $0

B. $14,000

C. $2,117,800

D. $5,430,000

Answer (D) is correct.

REQUIRED: The amount of a decedent's taxable estate that is effectively tax-free.

DISCUSSION: The $2,117,800 ACA for 2015 offsets the estate tax liability that would be imposed on a taxable estate of $5.43 million computed at current tax rates.

Answer (A) is incorrect. Some of the taxable estate will be effectively tax-free. Answer (B) is incorrect. Although $14,000 is the annual amount of gifts excluded per donee, it does not directly affect the tax-free portion of a decedent's estate. Answer (C) is incorrect. This amount is the ACA that offsets the estate tax liability that would be imposed on a taxable estate of $5.43 million.

27. Under the unified rate schedule,

A. Lifetime taxable gifts are taxed on a noncumulative basis.

B. Transfers at death are taxed on a noncumulative basis.

C. Lifetime taxable gifts and transfers at death are taxed on a cumulative basis.

D. The gift tax rates are 5% higher than the estate tax rates.

Answer (C) is correct.

REQUIRED: The applicability of unified transfer tax rates.

DISCUSSION: The same (unified transfer) tax rates are applied to both the inter vivos gift tax base and the estate tax base cumulatively. Gross estate tax is based on both the taxable estate and taxable inter vivos gifts. Tax paid at current-year rates on inter vivos gifts is then credited.

Answer (A) is incorrect. Lifetime taxable gifts are taxed on a cumulative basis. Answer (B) is incorrect. Transfers at death are taxed on a cumulative basis. Answer (D) is incorrect. The same rates apply to compute both gift and estate tax.

28. Daven inherited property from a parent. The property had an adjusted basis to the parent of $1,600,000. It was valued at $2,000,000 at the date of death and valued at $1,800,000 6 months after the date of death. The executor elected the alternative valuation date. What is Daven's basis in the property?

A. $0
B. $1,600,000
C. $1,800,000
D. $2,000,000

Answer (C) is correct.

REQUIRED: The basis in inherited property.

DISCUSSION: The value of the gross estate is the FMV of the property unless a special valuation rule is used. Real property is usually valued at its highest and best use. The executor may elect to use the alternative valuation date instead of the date of death. The election may only be made if it results in a reduction in both the value of the gross estate and the sum of federal estate tax that would be owed. Since the alternate valuation date results in a FMV of $1,800,000, that is the basis that Daven takes in the property inherited.

Answer (A) is incorrect. The basis of the property in the hands of the beneficiary is the FMV on the date of death or the alternate valuation date if elected. Answer (B) is incorrect. The parent's adjusted basis in the property does not determine the basis in the hands of the beneficiary. Answer (D) is incorrect. The election to use the alternate valuation date is irrevocable, and it results in a lower valuation for the estate.

12.5 Generation-Skipping Transfer Tax (GSTT)

29. The generation-skipping transfer tax is imposed

A. Instead of the gift tax.
B. Instead of the estate tax.
C. As a separate tax in addition to the gift and estate taxes.
D. On transfers of future interest to beneficiaries who are more than one generation above the donor's generation.

Answer (C) is correct.

REQUIRED: The applicability of the GSTT.

DISCUSSION: The generation-skipping transfer tax (GSTT) is imposed, as a separate tax in addition to the gift and estate taxes, on generation-skipping transfers, which are any taxable distributions or terminations with respect to a generation-skipping trust or direct skips.

Answer (A) is incorrect. The GSTT is a separate tax in addition to the gift tax. Answer (B) is incorrect. The GSTT is a separate tax from the estate tax. Answer (D) is incorrect. The GSTT prevents tax avoidance by transferring property directly to a person more than one generation below the donee.

30. Victor and Dawn both retired this year at the age of 65. Victor has decided to give his 16-year-old grandson Peter a cash gift to buy a new car. Dawn is unrelated to Peter, but she has also decided to give him a gift to help him pay for car insurance. Peter is a skip person for generation-skipping tax purposes with respect to the gift from

	Victor	Dawn
A.	No	No
B.	Yes	No
C.	No	Yes
D.	Yes	Yes

Answer (D) is correct.

REQUIRED: A recipient qualifying as a skip person for generation-skipping tax purposes with respect to the gifts from a grandparent and unrelated older donor.

DISCUSSION: Peter is a skip person with respect to the gift from Victor because Peter is two generations below Victor, a related person. Peter is also a skip person with respect to the gift from Dawn. Dawn is unrelated to Peter, but the 49-year age difference between them falls within the 37 1/2-year-to-62 1/2-year range that constitutes two generations.

12.6 PRACTICE TASK-BASED SIMULATIONS

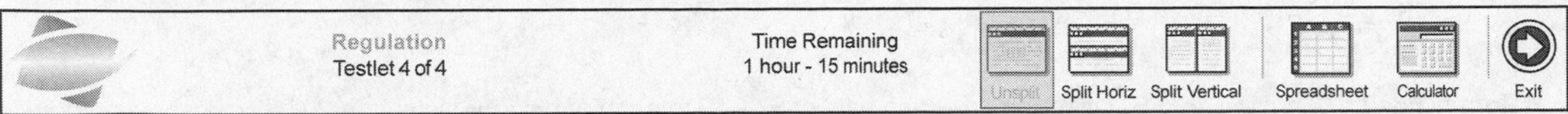

DIRECTIONS

Note: If you believe you have encountered a software malfunction, report it to the test center staff immediately.

Navigation

To navigate from task to task, use the controls at the bottom of the screen. Click on the **Next** button to advance to the next task, or the **Previous** button to go to the previous task. To go directly to any task, click on its number.

If you would like a reminder to revisit a task, or want to indicate that you are finished with it, click on the reminder flag below the task number. To clear the flag, click on it again. Reminder flags are for your use only – they do not contribute to your score.

Tabs

In this part of the examination, you will be asked to complete various tasks. Every task has one or more **Work Tabs**. Some tasks have one or more **Information Tabs**, others may have none. Every task has a **Help** tab.

If a task has **Information Tabs**, you may use the information in them to complete your responses in the **Work Tabs**.

Work tab **Information tab** **Help tab**

Work Tabs:

- **Work Tabs** are identified with a pencil icon. This is where your responses are expected.
- Each task has one or more **Work Tabs**.
- **Work Tabs** contain directions for completing the task – be sure to read these directions carefully.
- The **Work Tab** name in the example above is for illustration only – yours will differ.
- You must complete all of the **Work Tabs** in each task to receive full credit.

Information Tabs:

- The Authoritative Literature will be provided in all tasks in the AUD, FAR, and REG sections for your reference.
- Your simulation may have one or more additional **Information Tabs**. Like the Authoritative Literature tabs, **Information Tabs** do not have a pencil icon.
- If your task has additional **Information Tabs**, go through each to familiarize yourself with the task content.

Help Tab:

- The **Help Tab** provides assistance with the exam software that is used in this task. For example, if the task is to compose a memorandum, **Help** will provide information about the word processor.

The Toolbar

The toolbar at the top of the screen shows the amount of time remaining for you to complete the tasks. In addition, the following tools are available. Note that only the **Exit** button is displayed when Directions are visible - the others will appear when you begin the tasks.

Click on these buttons to split or unsplit the screen. You can split the screen vertically or horizontally.

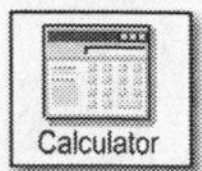

Click on this button to display the calculator; click on it again to hide the calculator. To move the calculator, click on the calculator title bar and drag the calculator to the desired location.

Click on this button to use the spreadsheet; click on it again to hide the spreadsheet. To move the spreadsheet, click on the the spreadsheet title bar and drag the spreadsheet to the desired location.

Click on this button to go on to the next part of the examination. You must complete all of the tasks to receive full credit. Once you click on **Exit** and confirm the action, you will NOT be able to return to this testlet.

= Reminder | Directions | 1 2 3 4 5 6 | Previous | Next

Gross Estate	Authoritative Literature	Help

Before his death, Remsen, a U.S. citizen, made cash gifts of $7,000 to each of his four sisters. In 2015, Remsen also paid $2,000 in tuition directly to his grandchild's university on the grandchild's behalf. Remsen made no other lifetime transfers. Remsen died on January 9, 2015, and was survived by his wife and only child, both of whom were U.S. citizens. The Remsens did not live in a community property state. At his death, Remsen owned the following:

Cash	$650,000
Marketable securities (fair market value)	900,000
Life insurance policy with Remsen's wife named as the beneficiary (fair market value)	500,000

Under the provisions of Remsen's will, the net cash, after payment of executor's fees and medical and funeral expenses, was bequeathed to Remsen's son. The marketable securities were bequeathed to Remsen's spouse. During 2015, Remsen's estate paid the following:

Executor's fees to distribute the decedent's property (deducted on the fiduciary tax return)	$15,000
Decedent's funeral expenses	25,000

The estate's executor extended the time to file the estate tax return. On January 3, 2016, the estate's executor paid the decedent's outstanding medical expense for 2015 of $10,000 and filed the extended estate tax return.

Based on the information above, select from the list provided the correct treatment for each item. Each choice may be used once, more than once, or not at all.

Tax Treatment	*Answer*
1. What is the estate tax treatment of the $7,000 cash gift to each sister?	
2. What is the estate tax treatment of the life insurance proceeds?	
3. What is the estate tax treatment of the marketable securities?	
4. What is the estate tax treatment of the $2,000 tuition payment?	
5. What is the estate tax treatment of the $650,000 cash?	

Choices
A) Fully includible in Remsen's gross estate
B) Partially includible in Remsen's gross estate
C) Not includible in Remsen's gross estate

Before his death, Aaron, a U.S. citizen, made cash gifts of $7,000 to each of his four sisters. In 2015, Aaron also paid $2,000 in tuition directly to his grandchild's university on the grandchild's behalf. Aaron made no other lifetime transfers. Aaron died on January 9, 2015, and was survived by his wife and only child, both of whom were U.S. citizens. They did not live in a community property state. At his death, Aaron owned the following:

Cash	$650,000
Marketable securities (fair market value)	900,000
Life insurance policy with Aaron's wife named as the beneficiary (fair market value)	500,000

Under the provisions of Aaron's will, the net cash, after payment of executor's fees and medical and funeral expenses, was bequeathed to Aaron's son. The marketable securities were bequeathed to Aaron's spouse. During 2015, Aaron's estate paid the following:

Executor's fees to distribute the decedent's property (deducted on the fiduciary tax return)	$15,000
Decedent's funeral expenses	25,000

The estate's executor extended the time to file the estate tax return. On January 3, 2016, the estate's executor paid the decedent's outstanding medical expense for 2015 of $10,000 and filed the extended estate tax return.

Based on the information above, select from the list provided the correct treatment for each item. Each choice may be used once, more than once, or not at all.

Tax Treatment	***Answer***
1. What is the estate tax treatment of the executor's fees?	
2. What is the estate tax treatment of the cash bequest to Aaron's son?	
3. What is the estate tax treatment of the life insurance proceeds paid to Aaron's spouse?	
4. What is the estate tax treatment of the funeral expenses?	
5. What is the estate tax treatment of the $10,000 medical expense incurred before the decedent's death and paid by the executor on January 3, 2016?	

Choices
A) Deductible from Aaron's gross estate to arrive at Aaron's taxable estate
B) Deductible on Aaron's 2015 individual income tax return
C) Deductible on either Aaron's estate tax return or Aaron's 2015 individual income tax return
D) Not deductible on either Aaron's estate tax return or Aaron's 2015 individual income tax return

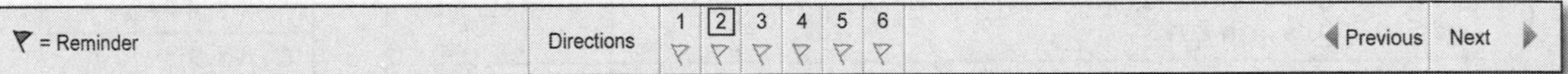

The maximum amount of the deduction of a trust or estate for distributions is its distributable net income (DNI). DNI is also the maximum amount of income of a trust or estate that the beneficiaries include in computing taxable income on their personal returns. DNI is computed by making certain adjustments to the taxable income of the trust or estate.

Check the box for the appropriate adjustment to be made to determine the DNI of each of the fiduciary's taxable income items below.

Item	*Added*	*Subtracted*	*No Adjustment*
1. Tax-exempt interest of $700			
2. Gain of $10,000 on sale of vacant land purchased as an investment by a complex trust			
3. A deduction for a net operating loss carried forward from the trust's preceding tax year			
4. Loss of $1,000 on sale of jewelry in the gross estate			
5. Extraordinary dividend of cash allocated to principal by state law when the trust instrument is silent			

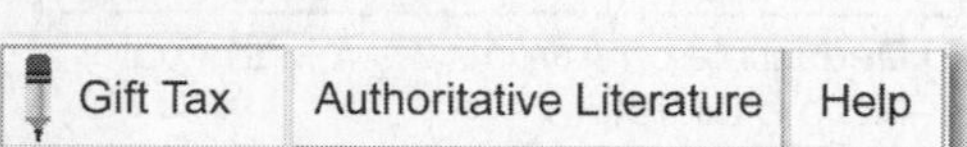

Select from the list provided to indicate whether each transaction, event, or variable described below will result in an increase or a decrease of federal gift tax liability for 2015, or if it will result in no change.

Each choice may be used once, more than once, or not at all.

Transaction, Event, or Factor	*Effect on Gift Tax Liability*
1. Kyle's $23,000 payment to State College on August 25, 2015, to pay for his nephew's tuition	
2. Linda's gift to her husband of a gold watch with a FMV of $25,000 and $40,000 cash in 2015	
3. Brandy's taxable gifts of $5.43 million during 2014, if she made a $37,000 cash gift to her friend Mary on October 13, 2015	
4. Corey's receipt of a sports car worth $85,000 as a gift from his girlfriend on June 20, 2015	
5. Zach's gift of $8,000 cash to his friend on July 31, 2015, after having already given her a $22,000 cash gift on June 12, 2015, if Zach is a calendar-year taxpayer and had given gifts totaling $5.5 million in 2014	

Choices
A) Increase gift tax liability
B) Decrease gift tax liability
C) No change in gift tax liability

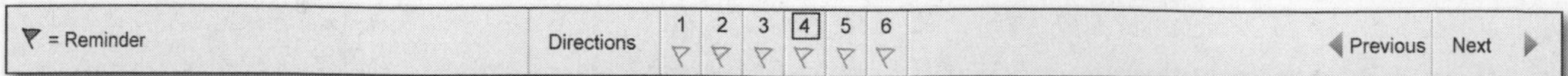

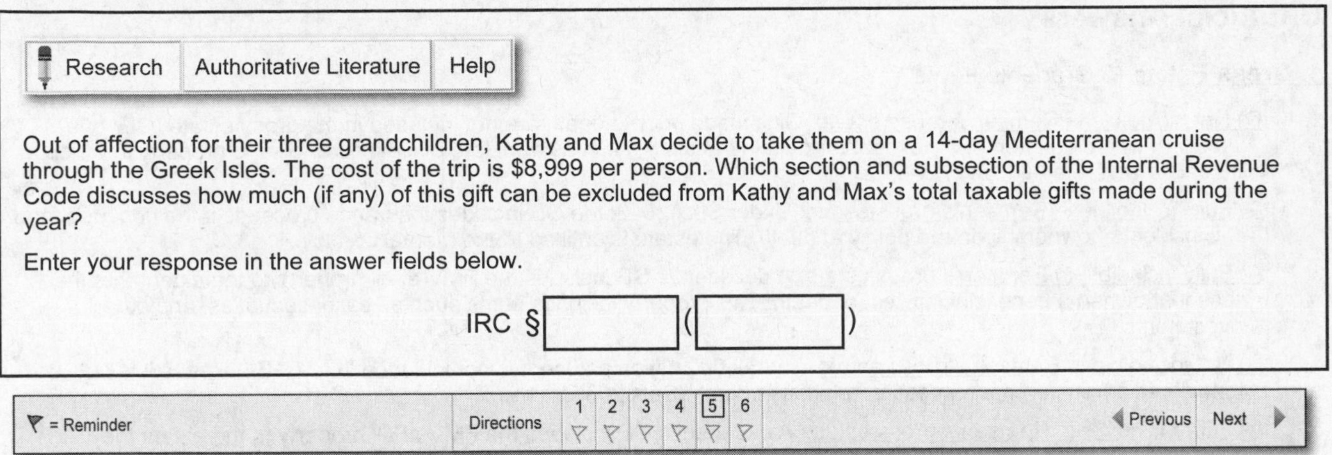

Research | Authoritative Literature | Help

Out of affection for their three grandchildren, Kathy and Max decide to take them on a 14-day Mediterranean cruise through the Greek Isles. The cost of the trip is $8,999 per person. Which section and subsection of the Internal Revenue Code discusses how much (if any) of this gift can be excluded from Kathy and Max's total taxable gifts made during the year?

Enter your response in the answer fields below.

IRC § [ ] ([ ])

Principal vs. Income | Authoritative Literature | Help

Indicate by checking the appropriate box whether each receipt or disbursement below should be allocated to principal or income of the fiduciary.

Receipt or Disbursement	***Principal***	***Income***
1. Interest on a loan that was used to purchase a shopping center that a trust would lease to retail stores		
2. Rent payments received from tenants of a shopping center owned by a trust		
3. Tax paid on the gain recognized upon an estate's sale of equipment		
4. Amounts paid to convert a shopping center owned by an estate into a series of warehouses		
5. Payment of the remaining balance of a loan used to purchase a shopping center		
6. Tax paid on the income of an estate		

Unofficial Answers

1. Gross Estate (5 Gradable Items)

1. C) Not includible in Remsen's gross estate. Gifts made prior to death are not included in the gross estate (GE) of a decedent who died after 1981, except for certain transfers, such as transfers of life insurance and property in which a life estate was retained (Sec. 2035).
2. A) Fully includible in Remsen's gross estate. Under Sec. 2042, the GE includes insurance proceeds if the decedent had any incident of ownership in the policy at death. The estate is entitled to the marital deduction.
3. A) Fully includible in Remsen's gross estate. A decedent's GE includes the FMV of all property to the extent that the decedent owned a beneficial interest at death. This property includes items such as cash, securities, and other investments.
4. C) Not includible in Remsen's gross estate. The $2,000 tuition payment is not included in the GE because it is not considered a transfer made in contemplation of death (Sec. 2035).
5. A) Fully includible in Remsen's gross estate. A decedent's GE includes the FMV of all property to the extent the decedent owned a beneficial interest at death. This property includes items such as cash, securities, and other investments.

2. Deductibility (5 Gradable Items)

1. D) Not deductible on either Aaron's estate tax return or Aaron's 2015 individual income tax return. The executor fee represents an administration fee that could be deductible on the estate tax return, but the expense has already been deducted on the fiduciary tax return. The executor fees can be deducted on either the estate tax return or on the fiduciary tax return, but not both. Thus, the fees are not deductible here.
2. D) Not deductible on either Aaron's estate tax return or Aaron's 2015 individual income tax return. The cash bequest does not qualify as a deduction from the estate tax return or the individual income tax return.
3. A) Deductible from Aaron's gross estate to arrive at Aaron's taxable estate. The proceeds are deductible as a marital deduction because they were included in the GE, they passed to the recipient spouse in a qualifying manner, and the interest is not a nondeductible terminable interest.
4. A) Deductible from Aaron's gross estate to arrive at Aaron's taxable estate. Funeral expenses are deductible from the GE to arrive at the taxable estate.
5. C) Deductible on either Aaron's estate tax return or Aaron's 2015 individual income tax return. Medical expenses paid within 1 year of death may be deducted on either the estate tax return or the final income tax return (but not both).

3. Distributable Net Income (5 Gradable Items)

1. Added. Tax-exempt interest represents distributable net income even though it was excluded from taxable income. It must be added, net of any related expenses, to taxable income in determining DNI.
2. Subtracted. Capital gain allocable to principal is subtracted from taxable income to arrive at DNI.
3. No Adjustment. A net operating loss is generally allocated to income rather than principal. It results in lower taxable income and lower DNI. Thus, no adjustment is made.
4. Added. Capital losses allocable to principal are added to taxable income when determining DNI.
5. Subtracted. An extraordinary dividend represents return of part of the cost of the stock itself. Unless allocated to income, the amount is excluded from DNI even though it constitutes gross income. Thus, the amount must be subtracted from taxable income to arrive at DNI.

4. Gift Tax (5 Gradable Items)

1. C) No change in gift tax liability. Gift tax liability is computed on the amount of taxable gifts attributable to the taxpayer in the current year. Payments of tuition on behalf of another individual are excluded from taxable gifts.
2. C) No change in gift tax liability. Gifts made to a spouse are not considered taxable gifts.
3. A) Increase gift tax liability. The applicable credit amount (ACA) is applied to the first $2,117,800 of gift tax liability (first $5.43 million of taxable gifts). Once that limit has been passed, additional taxable gifts made will increase the gift tax liability.
4. C) No change in gift tax liability. Gift tax is imposed on the donor, not the recipient of a gift.
5. A) Increase gift tax liability. The applicable credit amount (ACA) is applied to the first $2,117,800 of gift tax liability (first $5.43 million of taxable gifts). Once that limit has been passed, additional taxable gifts made will increase the gift tax liability. The balance of ACA that is available for a given year is reduced by any amount of the credit that was applied in previous years.

5. Research (1 Gradable Item)

Answer: IRC § 2503(b)

§ 2503. Taxable gifts

(b) Exclusions from gifts

(1) In general

In the case of gifts (other than gifts of future interests in property) made to any person by the donor during the calendar year, the first $10,000 of such gifts to such person shall not, for purposes of subsection (a), be included in the total amount of gifts made during such year. Where there has been a transfer to any person of a present interest in property, the possibility that such interest may be diminished by the exercise of a power shall be disregarded in applying this subsection, if no part of such interest will at any time pass to any other person.

(2) Inflation adjustment

In the case of gifts made in a calendar year after 1998, the $10,000 amount contained in paragraph (1) shall be increased by an amount equal to—

(A) $10,000, multiplied by

(B) the cost-of-living adjustment determined under section 1(f)(3) for such calendar year by substituting "calendar year 1997" for "calendar year 1992" in subparagraph (B) thereof.

If any amount as adjusted under the preceding sentence is not a multiple of $1,000, such amount shall be rounded to the next lowest multiple of $1,000.

6. Principal vs. Income (6 Gradable Items)

1. Income. Interest expense is a disbursement allocated to income.
2. Income. Rent payments are receipts allocated to income.
3. Principal. Tax paid on a principal item is a disbursement allocated to principal.
4. Principal. Capital expenditures are disbursements allocated to principal.
5. Principal. Principal payments on debt is a disbursement allocated to principal.
6. Income. Tax paid on fiduciary income is a disbursement allocated to income.

Gleim Simulation Grading

Task	Correct Responses		Gradable Items		Score per Task
1	____	÷	5	=	____
2	____	÷	5	=	____
3	____	÷	5	=	____
4	____	÷	5	=	____
5 (Research)	____	÷	1	=	____
6	____	÷	6	=	____
			Total of Scores per Task		____
		÷	Total Number of Tasks		6
			Total Score		____%

STUDY UNIT THIRTEEN
FEDERAL TAX LEGISLATION, PROCEDURES, PLANNING, AND ACCOUNTING

(26 pages of outline)

This study unit provides an understanding of federal tax legislation, tax procedures, tax planning, accounting, and the tax implications of operating in multiple jurisdictions.

Federal tax legislation is the legislative process by which tax law is established. Understanding this process provides a basis for understanding tax authority and conducting tax research. The other two sources of tax law are the judicial process and administrative law.

Tax procedures cover the processes for (1) determining a need to file a tax return, (2) collecting tax through estimated payments, (3) claiming refunds of taxes paid, and (4) assessing or collecting a deficiency in payment.

Tax planning is a continuous process of analyzing options available for a business or individual that will lower income taxes, but it is done in a way that maintains the overall objective of maximizing income. Planning options include timing of income, shifting of income, and conversion of income property. A critical aspect of tax planning is distinguishing between tax avoidance and tax evasion.

Explanation of the timing of inclusions, exclusions, and deductions is integrated into the discussion of accounting methods in the fourth subunit of this study unit. Taxpayers who operate or otherwise have a presence in more than one tax jurisdiction are subject to tax laws that are distinct for each jurisdiction.

13.1 TAX LEGISLATION

Background

The U.S. Constitution, in Article I, Section 8, grants Congress the power to lay and collect taxes. However, Section 9 states that a direct tax cannot be levied unless it is proportional to population. Since this depends on the outcome of a census, the early federal government would have found such a tax unwieldy and simply relied on tariffs (duties on imported goods) for most of its revenue.

The first tax imposed on the incomes of the citizens was levied from 1862 until 1872 to raise the huge amounts of money needed to carry on the Civil War. Some observers claimed that this directly violated the prohibition against direct taxes that are based on something other than proportional population.

In order to clear up the Constitutional issue once and for all, supporters of the income tax managed to get the Sixteenth Amendment ratified in 1913: "The Congress shall have power to lay and collect taxes on incomes, from whatever source derived, without apportionment among the several States, and without regard to any census or enumeration." Just over 7 months after ratification of this amendment, Congress enacted the Revenue Act of 1913.

The code received its most drastic overhaul in 1954 and its most recent in 1986. The current designation of the tax code is IRC 1986.

1. **Legislative Process**
   a. The Constitution lays forth the process for passage of legislative tax law. It states, "All Bills for raising Revenue shall originate in the House of Representatives; but the Senate may propose or concur with Amendments as on other Bills. Every Bill which shall have passed the House of Representatives and the Senate, shall, before it become a Law, be presented to the President of the United States: If he approve he shall sign it . . ."
   b. The general legislative process is illustrated in the following flowchart (the solid bold lines indicate the path of the revised legislation):

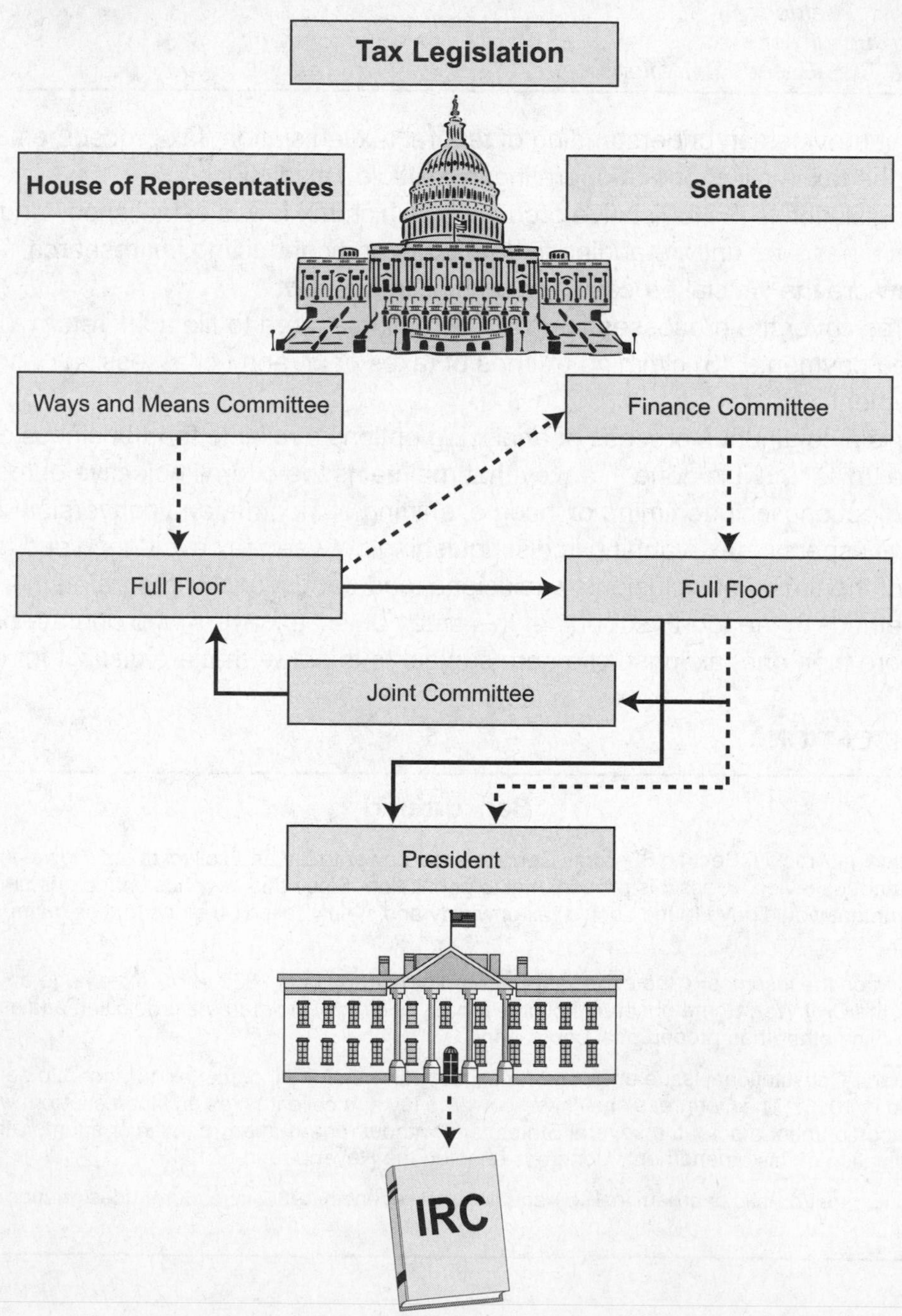

Figure 13-1

c. Tax bills are reviewed in the House Ways and Means Committee before being considered by the full House. The House version is referred to the Senate Finance Committee before being considered by the full Senate. If the Senate approves the House version as is, the bill is next presented to the President. However, the Senate often revises the House version, which requires a review by a joint House/Senate committee (this is illustrated by the solid lines in the image on the previous page). The joint committee version then returns to the House for approval, followed by the Senate, before reaching the President.

d. If signed by the President or if Congress overrides a presidential veto by a 2/3 majority vote, the bill becomes law (IRC); otherwise, the bill (generally) dies.

2. **Tax Authority**

a. Authoritative tax law consists of legislative law, administrative law, and judicial law.

Tax Authority Hierarchy

U.S. Constitution		
IRC	U.S. Supreme Court	
Treasury Regulation	Appellate Court Opinion	
U.S. Tax, District, and Federal Claims Court Opinion		
Revenue Ruling	Revenue Procedure	
Private Letter Ruling	T.A.M.	Other

Figure 13-2

b. Conflicting authority. When there are conflicting sources of tax law within the same tier of the hierarchy, the most recent rule or law takes precedence.

3. **Legislative Law**

a. Legislative law, which comes from Congress, is authorized by the Constitution and consists of the IRC and committee reports.

b. ***The Internal Revenue Code* of 1986** is the primary source of Federal tax law. It imposes income, estate, gift, employment, miscellaneous excise taxes, and provisions controlling the administration of Federal taxation. The Code is found at Title 26 of the United States Code (U.S.C.). The United States Code consists of 50 titles.

c. ***Committee Reports*** are useful tools in determining Congressional intent behind certain tax laws and helping examiners apply the law properly.

4. **Administrative Law**

a. Administrative tax law is promulgated by the Treasury department, of which the IRS is a part, and includes regulations, rules, and procedures.

b. IRC Sec. 7805(a) grants general authority to the Secretary of the Treasury to "prescribe all needful rules and regulations for the enforcement" of the Code. All regulations are written by the Office of the Chief Counsel, IRS, and approved by the Secretary of the Treasury.

1) Regulations are issued as **interpretations** of specific Code sections and are organized in a sequential system consistent with the Code.

a) Every regulation is prefixed by a number that designates the area of taxation referred to by the regulation.

2) Treasury Regulations are authorized by law. Nevertheless, courts are not bound to follow such administrative interpretations to the extent they conflict with the Code.

a) The IRS is generally bound by regulations; the courts are not.

3) The Supreme Court has stated that "Treasury Regulations must be sustained unless unreasonable and plainly inconsistent with the revenue statutes."

4) Regulations can be proposed, temporary, or final.

a) **Proposed regulations** are issued to elicit comments from the public. Public hearings are held if written requests are made.

i) Proposed regulations might be used as somewhat of an authority for taking a tax position, but the regulations themselves do not state this and must be considered as a weak authority at best.

b) **Temporary regulations** provide guidance to the IRS, tax practitioners, and the public until final regulations are issued. Temporary regulations have the same force and effect of law as final regulations until the final regulations are issued. Public hearings are not held on temporary regulations unless written requests are made. Temporary regulations

i) Can be used as somewhat of an authority
ii) May remain effective for a maximum of 3 years
iii) Must be issued concurrently as proposed regulations

c) **Final regulations** are adopted after public comment on the proposed versions has been evaluated by the Treasury.

i) When a proposed regulation becomes final or an existing regulation is amended, the document that describes the finalization or amendment is referred to as a Treasury Decision (TD).

ii) Some Code sections do not have final Treasury Regulations.

EXAMPLE

Sec. 385 was enacted in 1969 to provide guidance on whether a debt issue is considered stock or debt for tax purposes. Various versions of the proposed regulations have been issued and withdrawn. No final regulations have ever been issued.

5) The IRS is bound by the regulations. The courts are not.

a) If both temporary and proposed regulations have been issued on the same Code section and the text of both are similar, taxpayers' positions should be based on the temporary regulations because they can be cited as an authority for proposing an adjustment.

b) When no temporary or final regulations have been issued, taxpayers may use a proposed regulation to support a position. The taxpayer should indicate that the proposed regulation is the best interpretation of the Code section available.

c. A **revenue ruling** is an official interpretation of Internal Revenue law as applied to a given set of facts and is issued by the Internal Revenue Service.

1) Revenue rulings are published in Internal Revenue Bulletins (and later the Cumulative Bulletin) to inform and advise taxpayers, the IRS, and others on substantive tax issues.

2) Publication of revenue rulings is intended to promote uniform application of tax laws by IRS employees and to reduce the number of letter ruling requests.

3) Revenue rulings may be cited as precedent and relied upon when resolving disputes, but they do not have the force and effect of regulations.

a) A revenue ruling is not binding on a court.

d. A **revenue procedure** is an official IRS statement that prescribes procedures that affect the rights or duties of either a particular group of taxpayers or all taxpayers.

1) Revenue procedures primarily address administrative and procedural matters, e.g., in what format and to whom should a letter ruling request be submitted.

2) Revenue procedures do not have the force and effect of law, but they may be cited as precedent.

e. The **Internal Revenue Bulletin (IRB)** is the authoritative instrument of the Commissioner of Internal Revenue for announcing official IRS rulings and procedures and for publishing Treasury Decisions, Executive Orders, Tax Conventions, legislation, court decisions, and other items of general interest. It is published on a weekly basis by the Government Printing Office.

f. Rulings do not have the force and effect of Treasury Department Regulations, but they may be used as precedent. In applying published rulings, the effects of subsequent legislation, regulations, court decisions, rulings, and procedures must be considered. Caution is urged against reaching the same conclusion in other cases, unless the facts and circumstances are substantially the same.

g. IRS **Publications** explain the law in plain language for taxpayers and their advisors. They typically highlight changes in the law, provide examples illustrating Service positions, and include worksheets. Publications are not binding on the Service and do not necessarily cover all positions for a given issue. While a good source of general information, publications should not be cited to sustain a position.

h. **Private Letter Rulings and Technical Advice Memoranda**

1) A *Private Letter Ruling* (PLR) represents the conclusion of the Service for an individual taxpayer. The application of a private letter ruling is confined to the specific case for which it was issued, unless the issue involved was specifically covered by statute, regulations, ruling, opinion, or decision published in the Internal Revenue Bulletin.

2) Technical Advice Memoranda (TAMs) are requested by IRS area offices after a return has been filed, often in conjunction with an ongoing examination. TAMs are binding on the Service in relation to the taxpayer who is the subject of the ruling.

3) A private letter ruling to a taxpayer or a technical advice memorandum to an area director, which relates to a particular case, should not be applied or relied upon as a precedent in the disposition of other cases. However, they provide insight with regard to the Service's position on the law and serve as a guide.

4) Existing private letter rulings and memoranda [including Confidential Unpublished Rulings (CUR), Advisory Memoranda (AM), and General Counsel Memoranda (GCM)] may not be used as precedents in the disposition of other cases but may be used as a guide with other research material in formulating an area office position on an issue.

5) Whenever an area office finds that a CUR, AM, or GCM represents the sole precedent or guide for determining the disposition of an issue and cannot to its own satisfaction find justification in the Code, regulations, or published rulings to support the indicated position, technical advice should be requested from the Headquarters Office.

6) **Technical Advice** should be requested where taxpayers or their representatives take the position that the basis for the proposed action is not supported by statute, regulations, or published positions of the Service. If it is believed that the position of the Service should be published, the request for technical advice will contain a statement to that effect. Instructions for requesting technical advice from the Headquarters Office are contained in the second revenue procedure issued each year. Questions regarding the procedures should be addressed to the functional contacts listed in the revenue procedure.

7) **General Counsel Memoranda (GCM)** are legal memoranda from the Office of Chief Counsel prepared in connection with the review of certain proposed rulings (Rev. Ruls., PLRs, TCMs). They contain legal analyses of substantive issues and can be helpful in understanding the reasoning behind a particular ruling and the Service's response to similar issues in the future.

8) **Technical Memoranda (TM)** function as transmittal documents for Treasury Decisions or Notices of Proposed Rule Making (NPRMs). They generally summarize or explain proposed or adopted regulations, provide background information, state the issues involved, and identify any controversial legal or policy questions. Technical Memoranda are helpful in tracing the history and rationale behind a regulation or regulation proposal.

5. **Judicial Law**

a. Judicial law originates from the federal court system and is primarily comprised of court opinions.

b. The court system is comprised of

1) U.S. Tax Court
2) U.S. District Courts
3) U.S. Court of Federal Claims
4) Circuit Courts of Appeal
5) U.S. Supreme Court

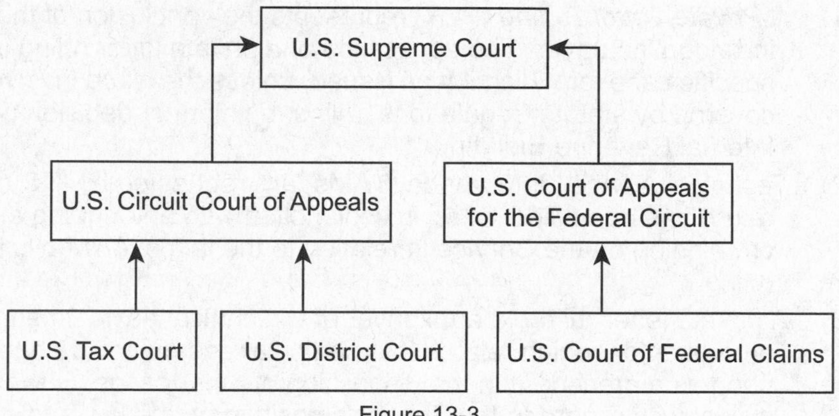

Figure 13-3

c. **Tax Court**

1) Decisions of the Tax Court are issued as either regular decisions or memorandum decisions.

a) Regular decisions establish precedent either through a new tax matter or unique facts and circumstances for a tax matter that has been previously settled.

b) A Tax Court memorandum decision is a report of a Tax Court decision thought to be of little value as a precedent because the issue has been decided one or more times before.

d. Cases from the U.S. Tax Court and the District Courts are appealed to the appropriate U.S. Circuit Court of Appeals. Cases from the U.S. Court of Federal Claims are appealed to the U.S. Court of Appeals for the Federal Circuit.

e. **U.S. Supreme Court**

1) The U.S. Supreme Court can exercise its discretionary authority to review decisions of the courts of appeals and other federal courts.

2) An appellant in an appropriate case may petition the Supreme Court to hear an appeal from the lower court's decision. A writ of certiorari is an order by the Supreme Court to send the case up for its consideration. The court's certiorari jurisdiction is purely discretionary. A denial of a petition for a writ of certiorari by the Supreme Court expresses no opinion on the merits of the case.

3) If the Court determines that various lower courts are deciding a tax issue in an inconsistent manner, it may pronounce a decision and resolve the contradiction.

6. **Tax Research**
   a. Tax research is the process of gathering situational facts, applying the most appropriate tax authorities, and clearly communicating the findings to the taxpayer/client or other interested parties. It involves analysis of information and drawing conclusions that will hold up before the IRS or the courts.
   b. Although the specific format of the **communication** will depend upon the audience (e.g., level of technical comprehension of tax law or related topics), the medium of presentation (e.g., written, oral), and other issues, the general organized format should include the following:
      - Review of relevant facts
      - Individual listing of specific issues
      - Citation of authorities
      - Solutions/Conclusions for each issue
      1) Good written communication is clear, correct, concise, consistent, constructive, coherent, and complete. As with other business writing, less is often best. Compounded sentences should be avoided. The communication should make the point and avoid repeating.

Stop and review! You have completed the outline for this subunit. Study multiple-choice questions 1 through 12 beginning on page 492.

13.2 TAX PROCEDURES

1. **Tax Prepayments and Penalties for Individuals**
   a. The IRC is structured to obtain at least 90% of the final tax through **withholding** and **estimated tax** payments. Individuals who earn income not subject to withholding must pay estimated tax on that income in quarterly installments.
      1) For a calendar-year taxpayer, the installments are due by April 15, June 15, and September 15 of the current year and January 15 of the following year. Dates are adjusted for weekends and holidays.
      2) Each of the following is treated as prepayment of tax:
         a) Overpayment of tax in a prior tax year, which has not been refunded
            i) An individual may so elect on the prior year's tax return.
            ii) It is applied to the first required installment due.
         b) Amounts withheld (by an employer) from wages
            i) The aggregate amount is treated as if equal parts were paid on each due date, unless the individual establishes the actual payment dates.
         c) Direct payment by the individual (or another on his or her behalf)
            i) It is applied to the first estimated tax payment due.
         d) Excess FICA withheld when an employee has two or more employers during a tax year who withheld (in the aggregate) more than the ceiling on FICA taxes
      3) Each installment must be 25% of the least of the following amounts:
         a) 100% [110% for taxpayers whose prior year's AGI exceeds $150,000 ($75,000 for married filing separately)] of the prior year's tax (if a return was filed)
         b) 90% of the current year's tax
         c) 90% of the annualized current year's tax (applies when income is uneven)
      4) Tax refers to the sum of the regular tax, AMT, self-employment tax, and household employee tax.

b. A penalty is imposed if, by the quarterly payment date, the total of estimated tax payments and income tax withheld is less than 25% of the required minimum payment for the year.

1) The penalty is determined each quarter.
2) The penalty is the federal short-term rate plus 3% times the underpayment.
3) The penalty is not allowed as an interest deduction.

c. The penalty will not be imposed if any of the following apply:

1) Actual tax liability shown on the return for the tax year (after reduction for amounts withheld by employers) is less than $1,000.
2) No tax liability was incurred in the prior tax year.
3) The IRS waives it for reasonable cause shown.

d. Any tax liability must be paid by the original due date of the return. An automatic extension for filing the return does not extend time for payment. Interest will be charged from the original due date.

1) A penalty of 5% per month up to 25% of unpaid liability is assessed for failure to file a return. The minimum penalty is the lesser of $135 or 100% of tax due.
2) A penalty of .5% per month up to 25% of unpaid liability is assessed for failure to pay tax.
3) In general, a failure-to-pay penalty is imposed from the due date for taxes (other than the estimated taxes) shown on the return. The penalty is .5% per month of the tax not paid, up to 25%. A failure-to-pay penalty may offset a failure-to-file penalty. When an extension to file is timely requested, a failure-to-pay penalty may be avoided by paying an estimate of unpaid tax in conjunction with the extension request, if the payment is not less than 90% of the actual tax liability due and the balance is paid when the return is filed. Exceptions and adjustments to these rules do apply in unique situations.

2. **Filing Requirements**

a. An individual must file a federal income tax return if gross income is above a threshold, net earnings from self-employment is $400 or more, or (s)he is a dependent with more gross income than the standard deduction or with unearned income over $1,050.

NOTE: In contrast to individuals, corporations (including S corps) must file an income tax return regardless of gross income.

1) The gross income threshold amount generally is the sum of the standard deduction, excluding any amount for being blind, and personal exemption amounts, excluding dependency exemptions.
2) Net unearned income of a dependent child is taxed to the dependent at the parent's marginal rate. This is referred to as the "Kiddie Tax." Net unearned income is unearned income minus the sum of

a) $1,050 (first $1,050 clause) and
b) The greater of (1) $1,050 of the standard deduction or $1,050 of itemized deductions or (2) the amount of allowable deductions that are directly connected with the production of unearned income.

NOTE: A dependent is allowed at least $2,100 ($1,050 + $1,050) reduction in unearned income.

Historically, exam questions have provided the applicable standard deduction amount for dependents with unearned income, eliminating the need to memorize the specific amount. However, you should have a general idea of the amount, and you need to be well practiced in calculating the amount taxable at the parent's rate.

3. **Due Dates and Related Extensions**

   a. **Individual** tax returns must be filed (postmarked) no later than the 15th day of the **4th** month following the close of the tax year. This is April 15 for calendar-year taxpayers.

      1) An automatic **6-month** extension is available by filing Form 4868. This extends the deadline to October 15 for calendar-year taxpayers.

      2) The extension does not grant any additional time to pay taxes due.

   b. **Corporate** tax returns, including for S corporations must be filed (postmarked) no later than the 15th day of the **3rd** month following the close of the tax year. This is March 15 for calendar-year taxpayers.

      1) An automatic **6-month** extension is available by filing Form 7004. This extends the deadline to September 15 for calendar-year taxpayers.

      2) The extension does not grant any additional time to pay taxes due.

   c. **Partnership and trust** tax returns must be filed (postmarked) no later than the 15th day of the **4th** month following the close of the tax year. This is April 15 for calendar-year taxpayers.

      1) An automatic **5-month** extension is available by filing Form 7004. This extends the deadline to September 15 for calendar-year taxpayers.

   d. **Exempt organizations** are generally required to file annual information returns by the 15th day of the **5th** month following the close of the taxable year.

      1) Form 8868 can be filed to request both an automatic **3-month** extension and an additional 3-month extension if needed.

   e. **Estate** tax returns are due within 9 months after the date of the decedent's death.

      1) An extension of up to 6 months may be granted by filing Form 4768.

   f. If the 15th day falls on a Saturday, Sunday, or legal holiday, the due date is extended until the next business day.

4. **Disclosure of Tax Positions**

   a. A taxpayer's accuracy-related penalty due to disregard of rules and regulations, or substantial understatement of income tax, may be avoided if the return position is adequately disclosed and has a reasonable basis. Generally, the penalty is equal to 20% of the underpayment. The penalty is not figured on any part of an underpayment on which the fraud penalty is charged.

      1) Disregard of the rules and regulations includes any careless, reckless, or intentional disregard.

      2) Substantial understatement of income tax occurs when the understatement is more than the larger of 10% of the correct tax or $5,000. In addition to adequate disclosure and a reasonable basis, the amount of the understatement may be reduced to the extent the understatement is due to substantial authority.

      3) Whether there is substantial authority for the tax treatment of an item depends on the facts and circumstances. Some of the items that may be considered are court opinions, Treasury regulations, revenue rulings, revenue procedures, and notices and announcements issued by the IRS and published in the IRB that involve the same or similar circumstances as the taxpayer's.

      4) To adequately disclose the relevant facts about the tax treatment of an item, use Form 8275, *Disclosure Statement*. There must also be a reasonable basis for the taxpayer's treatment of the item. Form 8275-R, *Regulation Disclosure Statement*, is used to disclose items or positions contrary to regulations.

5) Adequate disclosure has no affect on items attributable to tax shelters.
6) Showing a reasonable cause also includes showing actions were taken in good faith.
7) The reasonable basis is a significantly higher standard than the not frivolous standard applied to preparers for the same penalty.

5. **Recordkeeping**

a. Books of account or records sufficient to establish the amount of gross income, deductions, credit, or other matters required to substantiate any tax or information return must be kept.

1) Records must be maintained as long as the contents may be material in administration of any internal revenue law.
2) Employers are required to keep records on employment taxes until at least 4 years after the due date of the return or payment of the tax.

6. **Claims for Refund**

a. A claim for refund of federal income tax overpaid for the current tax year is made by filing a return (Form 1040). A refund claim for a prior year is made by filing an amended return (Form 1040X). Form 843 is used to claim a refund of any other tax.

b. Application for a tentative carryback adjustment to get a quick refund for carryback of a net operating loss, corporate net capital loss, or general business credit is made on Form 1045 (individuals) or Form 1139 (corporations).

c. A claim for refund must be made within the **statute of limitations** period for refunds. A claim must be filed by the later of 3 years from filing the return or 2 years after the tax was paid.

1) An early return is treated as filed on the due date.
2) If the claim relates to worthless securities or bad debts, the period of limitation is 7 years from the date prescribed for filing the return for the year with respect to which the claim is made.
3) If a taxpayer does not file a return, a refund must be claimed within 2 years from the time the tax was paid. Tax deducted and withheld at the source during any calendar year is deemed paid by the recipient of the income on the 15th day of the 4th month following the close of his or her tax year.

7. **Assessment of Deficiency**

a. A deficiency is any excess of tax imposed over the sum of amounts shown on the return plus amounts previously assessed (reduced by rebates). Assessment of tax is made by recording the liability of the taxpayer in the office of the Secretary of the Treasury. The following flowchart is provided to illustrate the process.

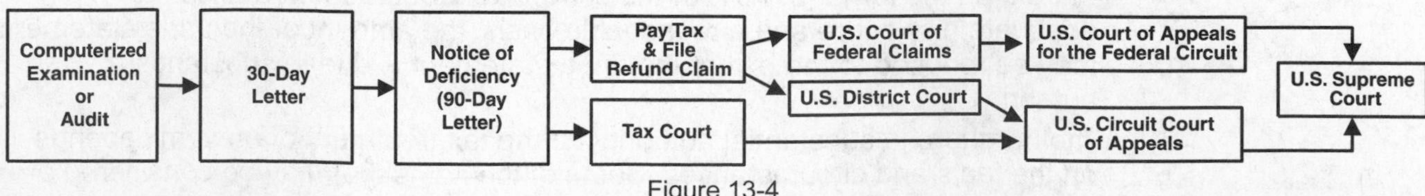

Figure 13-4

b. Computerized examination or audit of a return may result in an IRS examiner proposing an addition to tax. A letter stating the proposal is sent to the taxpayer. It is referred to as a **30-day letter**.

c. If consensus is not reached with the examiner in a conference with his or her supervisor or from an administrative appeal, a **notice of deficiency (ND)** is mailed to the taxpayer, but no sooner than 30 days after a 30-day letter.

   1) A notice of deficiency is referred to as a 90-day letter.
   2) A notice of deficiency is a prerequisite to assessment.
   3) However, immediate assessment, i.e., without a notice of deficiency, is allowed for the following:

      a) Tax shown on a return filed by a taxpayer
      b) Mathematical and clerical errors in a return
      c) Overstatement of credits
      d) Tax for which assessment is waived

d. A taxpayer may institute a proceeding in the U.S. Tax Court within the 90 days following mailing of the ND (150 days if the taxpayer lives outside the U.S.). The ND is a prerequisite to a U.S. Tax Court proceeding.

   1) Payment of the deficiency is not required. Payment after the ND is mailed does not deprive the U.S. Tax Court of jurisdiction.

e. If a petition is not filed with the U.S. Tax Court, taxes may be assessed 90 days after the ND is mailed.

   1) Filing the petition suspends the 90-day period.

f. Partial or full payment of a deficiency prior to mailing of the ND deprives the Tax Court of jurisdiction. After full payment of any deficiency balance, the taxpayer may file a claim for refund and, if it is denied by the IRS, may institute a refund proceeding in a U.S. district court or the U.S. Court of Federal Claims.

   1) A jury is available only in a U.S. district court. One or more judges decide all issues in the U.S. Tax Court and the U.S. Court of Federal Claims.

g. Authority to assess tax liability is limited by statute to specific periods.

   1) The general **statute of limitations** (S/L) for assessment of a deficiency is 3 years from the later of the date the return was due or the date it was filed.

      a) A return filed before the due date is treated as filed on the due date.
      b) The IRS generally has 10 years following the assessment to begin collection of tax by levy or a court proceeding.

   2) The S/L is 6 years if there is omission of items of more than 25% of gross income stated in the return. Gross income includes gross receipts before deduction for cost of goods sold. Only items completely omitted are counted.
   3) Failure to file. The S/L period does not commence before a return is filed.

      a) When no return has been filed, the assessment period is unlimited.

   4) Fraud. Attempting to evade tax results in an unlimited assessment period. Fraud cannot be cured by filing a correct amended return.
   5) The S/L period begins to run when a return filed late is received by the IRS.
   6) Extension. The S/L period may be extended by an agreement between the taxpayer and the IRS entered into before the S/L expires.

      a) Each time an extension has been requested (or after expiration if there has been a levy), the IRS must notify the taxpayer that the taxpayer may refuse to extend the period of limitations or may limit the extension to particular issues or to a particular period of time.

h. Mitigation of the statute of limitations. In certain circumstances, the statute of limitations may unjustly penalize the taxpayer or the government for a given return position.

EXAMPLE

The taxpayer reports an item of income in 2013. Later, the IRS asserts that this item should be reported in 2015. Since each year's assessment stands alone, the payment in 2013 does not impact the liabilities for 2015. Therefore, without the mitigation provisions outlined below, the taxpayer would have to pay twice for the same income item.

1) The mitigation provisions are limited to **income tax**, not gift, etc., when the following circumstances are met:
   a) There is a "determination" for a tax year concerning the treatment of an item of income (i.e., Tax Court decision);
   b) On the date of determination, correction of the error must be barred (i.e., statute of limitations);
   c) There must be a condition necessary for adjustment, i.e., double income (deduction); and
   d) In the proceeding of determination, the successful party must have taken a position inconsistent with the position in the closed year.

The statute of limitations, both for a taxpayer claiming a refund and for the IRS assessing a deficiency, is a consistently tested topic on the exam.

Stop and review! You have completed the outline for this subunit. Study multiple-choice questions 13 through 18 beginning on page 495.

13.3 TAX PLANNING

Background

Reduction of tax may always be important but should not be the deciding factor behind every financial action. The goal of maximizing "after-tax" wealth is not always the same as minimizing taxes. The role of tax planning is to assist individuals and businesses in reaching maximization of after-tax wealth in the most tax-efficient way possible.

1. Tax planning is the consideration of tax implications for individual or business decisions, usually with the intent of minimizing, or at least reducing, the tax liability. It includes, among other things, considering alternative treatments, projecting the tax consequences, and determining the role of taxes in decision making.
   a. The three most basic and common types of tax planning are (1) timing of income recognition, (2) shifting of income among taxpayers and jurisdictions, and (3) conversion of income among high- and low-rate activities.
2. **Timing**
   a. The timing technique accelerates or defers recognition of income and/or deductions. The advice most often heard is to defer income and accelerate deductions. This results in the lowest tax liability for the current year. However, in a year in which the taxpayer's rates are lower than the rates will be the following year, it is advisable to do just the opposite.

b. The following items should be considered when evaluating the use of timing techniques:
   1) Time value of money (e.g., can the taxpayer make a higher return on income realized and reinvested this year than the taxpayer can save in taxes by deferring the income to a future date by not selling the capital asset until later?)
   2) Future (or likelihood of proposed) tax law (i.e., will it stay the same or change?)
   3) Individual circumstances of the taxpayer (i.e., a strategy good for one is not necessarily the best strategy for another).

EXAMPLE

An accrual basis corporation has low cash flow at the end of Year 1 but will have cash on hand to pay a considerably large charitable donation by March 15, Year 2. Because the corporation has projected a lower marginal tax rate in Year 2, the board should authorize the donation for Year 1 and elect to make the payment by March 15, Year 2. Claiming the deduction in Year 1 will create a higher tax savings than it will in Year 2.

c. A taxpayer typically has more control over the recognition of some types of income (e.g., sale of capital gain property) than a taxpayer has over other types (e.g., salaries).

3. **Shifting**
   a. The basics of income shifting typically relate to moving income and therefore the accompanying tax liability from one family member to another who is subject to a lower marginal rate, or moving income between entities and their owner(s). However, tax planning also involves shifting income from one tax jurisdiction to another with different marginal tax rates.
   b. Three key terms when discussing shifting income are "assignment of income doctrine," "related party transaction," and "arm's-length transaction." An arm's-length transaction occurs when the involved parties act independently, regardless of any relation between the parties. The purpose of these transactions is to guarantee that all parties act in their own self-interest and not for the common good of all the parties involved to the detriment of the IRS.
   c. Other rules that may limit or otherwise make income shifting difficult include the "Kiddie" tax rules and gift/wealth transfer rules.
   d. Successful shifting of income among family members or entities depends on determining the following:
      1) Income/assets available for shifting
      2) Best strategy for realizing the shift
      3) Best recipient of income/asset within the family or entity

EXAMPLE

Parents with a 33% marginal rate want to invest some of their savings and minimize the overall tax liability on the family. One way these parents can accomplish this goal is to have their adult children, who have only a 15% marginal rate, purchase a rental home and borrow the money from the parents at the lowest allowable rate (i.e., applicable federal rate). This strategy will result in the rental income being taxed at only 15% instead of the higher 33% of the parents and at the lowest cost possible (due to the low rate). The parents have also shifted income to the adult children without being subject to gift tax limits, etc.

   e. In the case of shifting income among tax jurisdictions, the jurisdictions among which the income is moved could be city, county, or state jurisdictions within the U.S. In addition, shifting of income also could involve moving the income from U.S. jurisdiction to that of another nation.

f. In the case of multiple nations claiming the right to tax an individual or business, credit (subject to specific laws and treaties) will usually be given by each country for tax paid to the other. This helps to avoid double taxation and encourages international business.

EXAMPLE

A player for the National Basketball Association is drawing near to the end of his original/rookie contract in Ohio. He has offers from franchises in Ohio, New York, Illinois, Florida, and California and wishes to minimize his overall tax liability in his next contract. All other issues being equal, the player would accept the offer from the franchise in Florida. By doing so, the player would be shifting his income from a state (Ohio) with a state income tax to the only state of those making offers with no state income tax. Though the federal income tax would go unchanged, the player's overall tax liability would be reduced.

4. **Conversion**

a. Converting income from a less favorable category to a more favorable one can be achieved in various ways. Favorable conversions include converting ordinary income property into capital gain property. The opposite applies for losses.

EXAMPLE

A taxpayer wants to convert $10,000 FMV of inventory with a basis of $3,000 to capital gain property. The taxpayer will accomplish the goal by transferring the inventory to a controlled corporation for stock (the FMV would be $10,000). The taxpayer's basis in the stock is $3,000; therefore, selling the stock will result in a $7,000 capital gain for the taxpayer.

If the taxpayer simply sells the inventory (i.e., no conversion), the $7,000 gain will be ordinary.

b. Even better than converting property from a high tax rate to a low rate is converting it to nontaxable property. Examples of this include the following:

1) Employee benefits, e.g., employer-paid medical reimbursement
2) Investing in municipal bonds (i.e., nontaxable investment interest)
3) Convert nondeductible personal expense to a business expense

c. Some conversions involve a comparative analysis of minimization of current taxes to minimization of future taxes.

EXAMPLE

Contributions to an individual retirement account are deductible (subject to limitations) in the year made; however, tax applies to 100% of the withdrawals. So there is a current tax savings or deferral. On the other hand, contributions to a Roth IRA are currently taxed; however, the withdrawals are tax-exempt, including any increase in the investment over the years. This results in tax avoidance.

5. **Avoidance vs. Evasion**

Background

In a 1947 case, Judge Learned Hand stated, "Over and over again courts have said that there is nothing sinister in so arranging one's affairs as to keep taxes as low as possible. Everybody does so, rich or poor; and all do right, for nobody owes any public duty to pay more than the law demands: taxes are enforced extractions, not voluntary contributions. To demand more in the name of morals is mere cant."

a. Tax avoidance is the minimization of tax liability through legal arrangements and transactions. The goal of a business is to maximize profits, and tax avoidance is a key element in obtaining this goal. Avoidance maneuvers take place prior to incurring a tax liability.

b. Tax evasion takes place once a tax liability has already been incurred (i.e., taxable actions have been completed). A key distinction between avoidance and evasion is taxpayer "intent." A taxpayer's intent is called into question when one of the "badges" of fraud is identified. These indicators include understatement of income, improper allocation of income, claiming of fictitious deductions, questionable conduct of the taxpayer, and accounting irregularities.

c. Concerning fraud, IRC §7201 reads as follows: "Any person who willfully attempts in any manner to evade or defeat any tax imposed by this title or the payment thereof shall, in addition to other penalties provided by law, be guilty of a felony and, upon conviction thereof, shall be fined not more than $100,000 ($500,000 in the case of a corporation), or imprisoned not more than five years, or both, together with the costs of prosecution."

Stop and review! You have completed the outline for this subunit. Study multiple-choice questions 19 through 21 beginning on page 496.

13.4 ACCOUNTING METHODS

1. **Tax Year**

   a. The accounting method determines the tax year in which an item is includible or deductible in computing taxable income. The method must clearly reflect income.

   b. Federal income tax is imposed on taxable income measured for a taxable period, usually annual.

      1) A person's tax year is the annual accounting period used to keep the person's books and records. A calendar or fiscal tax year is adopted in a person's first tax year. A calendar year is the 12-month period ending on December 31. A fiscal year is any 12-month period ending on the last day of a month.

      2) A 52- or 53-week tax year is also allowed.

      3) A short tax year is allowed for a business not in existence for an entire year (365 or 366 days), e.g., the start-up year or the year at dissolution.

         a) In calculating the tax for a short tax year, the income must first be annualized. Then the tax on the annualized income is calculated, and the final step is to determine the short tax year portion of tax.

$$\text{Annualized income} = \text{Short tax year income} \times \frac{\text{12 months}}{\text{Short tax year months}}$$

Calculate tax:

$$\text{Short tax year tax} = \text{Annualized income tax} \times \frac{\text{Short tax year months}}{\text{12 months}}$$

      4) Change of tax year generally requires IRS consent. A short tax year return is then required.

2. **Accounting Method**

   a. A person must use the method of accounting regularly used to compute income in keeping books and records. The **cash method** and the **accrual method** are the most common. Specific provisions of the Internal Revenue Code (IRC) may override and require specific treatment of certain items.

      1) Change in accounting methods generally requires consent of the IRS, including change in either the overall system of accounting for gross income or deductions, or treatment of any material item used in the system.

2) IRS consent is not required for the following changes:
   a) Adopting LIFO inventory valuation
   b) Switching from declining-balance depreciation to straight-line
   c) Making an adjustment in useful life of certain assets
   d) Correcting an error in computing tax
   e) Changing from the accrual method to the installment method of reporting income

3. **Cash Method**

a. A cash-method taxpayer accounts for income when one of the following occurs:
   1) Cash is actually received
   2) A cash equivalent is actually received
   3) Cash or its equivalent is constructively received

b. Cash equivalent. At the time a person receives noncash forms of income, such as property or services, the fair market value is included in gross income. This applies even if the property or service can be currently converted into cash at an amount lower than face value.
   1) A cash equivalent is property that is readily convertible into cash and typically has a maturity of 3 months or less. Cash equivalents are so near to maturity that the risk of loss due to a change in value is immaterial. The following are considered cash equivalents:
      a) Checks, valued at face
      b) Property, e.g., land, transferable at current FMV
      c) Promissory notes, valued at FMV
   2) If the value of property received cannot be determined, the value of what was given in exchange for it is treated as the amount of income received.

EXAMPLE

A CPA performs various services for a start-up company in exchange for stock options. If the value of the stock options cannot be determined, the value of the services performed is included in income.

   3) If both the property received and the property given are impossible to value, e.g., an unsecured promise to pay from a person with unknown creditworthiness, the transaction is treated as open, and the consideration is not viewed as income until its value can be ascertained.

c. Constructive receipt. Under the doctrine of constructive receipt, an item is included in gross income when a person has an unqualified right to immediate possession.
   1) A person constructively receives income in the tax year during which it is credited to his or her account, set apart for him or her, or otherwise made available so that (s)he may draw upon it at any time.
      a) It is more than a billing or an offer, or mere promise, to pay.
      b) It includes ability to use on demand, as with escrowed funds subject to a person's order.
      c) Deferring deposit of a check does not defer income. However, dishonor retroactively negates the income.
   2) Income is not constructively received if the taxpayer's control of its receipt is subject to substantial restrictions or limitations, e.g., a valid deferred compensation agreement.

EXAMPLE

John is awarded a $10,000 bonus in 2015. If only half of the bonus is payable in 2015 with the other half paid at the end of 2016, contingent upon John completing another year of service for his employer, only $5,000 is taxable in 2015.

d. Receipt or constructive **receipt by an agent** is imputed to the principal.

e. Economic benefit. The courts have interpreted the definition of gross income to include any economic or financial benefit conferred on an employee as compensation. This economic benefit theory is applied by the IRS in situations in which an employee or independent contractor receives a transfer of property that confers an economic benefit that is equivalent to cash.

EXAMPLE

The fair rental value of a car that a dealership provides for the personal use of its president is gross income.

1) The economic benefit theory applies even when the taxpayer cannot choose to take the equivalent value of the income in cash.

f. Dividends are constructively received when made subject to the unqualified demand of a shareholder.

1) If a corporation declares a dividend in December and pays such that the shareholders receive it in January, the dividend is not treated as received in December.

g. Bonds. When a bond is sold between interest payment dates, the interest accrued up to the sale date is added to the selling price of the bond. The seller includes the accrued interest in gross income.

h. **Prepaid rent** is gross income when received.

1) Security deposits are not considered income.
2) Tenant improvements, in lieu of rent, are included.
3) Lease cancelations are included.
4) Advance rental payments must be deducted by the payee during the tax periods to which the payments apply.

i. Tips. An employee who receives $20 or more in tips a month working for any employer must report the tips to the employer by the 10th day of the following month. The tips are gross income when reported.

j. Deductions. A cash-method taxpayer deducts expenditures when actually paid, except for prepaid rent.

1) A promise to pay, without more, is not payment.
2) A check represents payment when delivered or sent.
3) A third-party (e.g., bank) credit card charge transaction represents current payment with loan proceeds. A second-party (e.g., store) credit card charge transaction is not paid until the charge is paid off.
4) Bad debt. Adjusted basis in accounts receivable is deductible when the debt becomes worthless. Since a cash-method taxpayer usually has no basis in accounts receivable, (s)he may not deduct bad debts.
5) **Interest on a loan** issued at discount, or unstated (imputed) interest, is deductible pro rata over the life of the loan.
6) A person who uses the cash method to report gross income must use the cash method to report expenses.

4. **Accrual Method**

a. An accrual-method taxpayer accounts for income in the period it is actually earned.

b. The accrual method is required of certain persons and for certain transactions.

1) If the accrual method is used to report expenses, it must be used to report income items.

2) A taxpayer that maintains inventory must use the accrual method with regard to purchases and sales.

a) Exceptions to this inventory rule include

i) **Qualifying taxpayers** who satisfy the gross receipts test for each test year.

- The average annual gross receipts (consisting of the test year and the preceding 2 years) for each test year must be $1 million or less.

ii) **Qualifying small business taxpayers** who satisfy the gross receipts test for each test year (i.e., tax year ending on or after December 31, 2000).

- The average annual gross receipts must be $10 million or less.
- The taxpayer must not be a corporation (other than an S corp) or a partnership with a corporate partner.
- The principal business activity cannot be mining, manufacturing, wholesale trade, retail trade, or information industries.

3) Generally, C corporations, partnerships with a C corporation as a partner, and tax shelters must use the accrual method.

a) Tax shelters include any arrangement for which the principal purpose is avoidance of tax, any syndicates, and any enterprise in which the interests must be registered as a security.

b) Exceptions to the general rule allow the following taxpayers to use the cash method if the entity is not a tax shelter:

i) Qualified personal service corporations

ii) Entities that meet the gross receipts test by having $5 million or less average gross receipts in the 3 preceding years

iii) Farming or tree-raising businesses

c. Income is included when all the events have occurred that fix the right to receive it and the amount can be determined with reasonable accuracy.

1) A right is not fixed if it is contingent on a future event.

2) The all-events test is satisfied when goods shipped on consignment are sold.

3) Only in rare and unusual circumstances, in which neither the FMV received nor the FMV given can be ascertained, will the IRS respect holding a transaction open once the right to receive income is fixed. In those circumstances, income is accrued upon receipt.

a) Proceeds from settlement of a lawsuit are determinable in amount with reasonable accuracy when received.

d. Prepaid income must generally be included in income when received.

1) Prepaid rent is includible in gross income in the year received. This rule applies to both cash-method and accrual-method taxpayers.

2) Prepaid income for services may be accrued over the period for which the services are to be performed, but only if it does not extend beyond the end of the next tax year.

a) If the taxpayer does not complete the performance within that period, the prepaid income is included in the year following receipt.

3) Merchandise sales. The right to income is fixed when it is earned, e.g., when goods are shipped.

a) Prepayments for goods must be included when reported for accounting purposes if reported earlier than when earned.

e. Deductions. Expenses are generally deductible in the period in which they accrue.

1) The accrual-method taxpayer may claim an allowable deduction when both of the following requirements are met:

a) All events have occurred that establish the fact of the liability, including that economic performance has occurred.

b) The amount can be determined with reasonable accuracy.

2) To the extent the amount of a liability is disputed, the test is not met. But any portion of a (still) contested amount that is paid is deductible.

3) Economic performance occurs as services are performed or as property is provided or used.

4) Under current case law, reserves for contingent liabilities (such as product warranties) are not determinable in amount with reasonable accuracy.

5) Accrued vacation pay is generally deductible when paid.

6) Deduction of an amount payable to a related party is allowed only when includible in gross income of the related party.

The accounting rules for income and deduction items under both the cash and accrual methods have often been tested. The AICPA has used questions that have focused on the timing of the inclusions of various income and expense items under each method.

5. **Hybrid Methods**

a. Any combination of permissible accounting methods may be employed if the combination clearly reflects income and is consistently used.

b. If inventory is used, the accrual method must be used for purchases and sales. The cash method may be used for other receipts and expenses if income is clearly reflected.

c. A person may use different methods for separate businesses.

6. **Inventory**

a. Gross income includes receipts reduced by cost of goods sold (COGS), whether purchased or manufactured.

1) The inventory method used must clearly reflect income.

2) Regulations require the particular treatment of certain items or an alternative acceptable treatment.

b. Additionally, the inventory method used must conform to generally accepted accounting principles of the trade or business.

c. Inventory may be valued at cost or at the lower of cost or FMV.

NOTE: Since 2008, taxpayers using a rolling-average method for financial accounting purposes have been allowed to use the same method for tax purposes if the related safe harbor rules are satisfied.

d. Purchased merchandise. Cost is invoice price reduced by trade discounts and increased by handling charges such as freight.

```
Cost = Purchase price - Trade discounts + Handling charges
```

1) Cash discounts may instead be treated as income.
2) Taxpayers with average annual gross receipts over $10 million for the 3 preceding tax years must allocate purchasing costs (e.g., administrative, warehousing) between COGS and inventory.

e. Produced merchandise. The full absorption costing method must be used.

1) Direct costs of material and labor are included in inventory.
2) Overhead for manufacturing is also included, e.g., costs for
   a) Plant administration
   b) Plant maintenance, e.g., rent, utilities, insurance
   c) Support costs, e.g., payroll, warehousing
3) Nonmanufacturing costs, e.g., marketing, need not be included in inventory, but interest must be included in inventory on property that is real or requires more than 2 years of production (1 year if it costs more than $1 million).

f. Standard methods. Any of the following methods may be used to determine inventory costs: specific identification, average cost, FIFO, and LIFO.

g. FIFO assumes that the first items acquired are the first items sold. Ending inventory contains the most recently acquired items.

h. LIFO assumes that the latest items acquired are the first items sold. If LIFO is used, inventory must be valued at cost. In a period of rising prices, LIFO results in a higher cost of goods sold than FIFO. Because COGS is higher, net income (NI) is lower, resulting in lower current tax liability.

1) LIFO may only be used for tax purposes if it is used for financial reporting.

7. **Long-Term Contracts**

a. A long-term contract is a contract completed in a tax year subsequent to the one in which it was entered into for building, construction, installation, or manufacturing. Long-term manufacturing contracts are for items that normally require more than 12 months to complete or that are unique and not usually inventory items.

1) A trade or business of a taxpayer must use the same method for each of its long-term contracts.
2) Long-term contract rules apply to direct costs and allocable portions of labor, material, and overhead costs.
3) Costs of the following do not need to be allocated to a specific contract:
   a) Unaccepted bids
   b) Marketing
   c) Research and development (if not restricted to the specific contract)

b. Completed-contract method. Receipts and expenditures are accounted for (reported) in the tax year in which the contract is completed. The method is allowed only for

1) Home construction projects or
2) Small businesses (average annual gross receipts not greater than $10 million for the 3 preceding tax years) for construction contracts expected to take not greater than 2 years to complete.

c. **Percentage-of-completion method.** The taxpayer reports as income that portion of the total contract price that represents the percentage of total work completed in the year. It may be measured by the ratio of costs for the tax year to total expected costs.

Formula:

Contract price	$ XX
Minus: total estimated cost **of contract**[1]	(XX)
Estimated total gross profit	$ XX
Times: Percent completed[2]	XX
Gross profit recognized to date	$ XX
Minus: gross profit recognized in prior periods	(XX)
Gross profit recognized in current period	$ XX

[1] Cost incurred to date plus remaining estimated cost **to complete**

[2] $\frac{\text{Total cost to date}}{\text{Total estimated cost of contract}}$

1) When the contract is complete, the taxpayer must pay interest on any additional tax that would have been incurred if actual total costs had been used instead of expected costs.
2) The taxpayer may elect not to apply the above rule if the cumulative taxable income or loss using estimated costs is within 10% of the cumulative taxable income or loss using actual costs.

8. **Installment Method**

a. The installment method is required for installment sales by both cash-method and accrual-method taxpayers, unless an election is made not to apply the method.
   1) An installment sale is a disposition of property in which at least one payment is received after the year of sale.
   2) The method applies only to gains.
   3) A loss on an installment sale is fully recognized in the year realized (unless recognition would be deferred even if the sale was not an installment sale).

b. The installment sales method is generally not applied to the following sales:
   1) Inventory personal property sales
   2) Revolving credit personal property sales
   3) Dealer dispositions
   4) Securities, generally, if publicly traded
   5) Sales by manufacturers of tangible personal property

c. Installment sale income is determined as follows:
   1) Calculate **gross profit**:

      $$\text{Contract price} - \text{Cost of goods sold}$$

   2) Calculate **gross profit percentage**:

      $$\frac{\text{Gross profit}}{\text{Contract price}}$$

   3) Calculate current-year **installment sale income**:

      $$\text{Current-year receipts} \times \text{Gross profit percentage}$$

d. The full amount of any depreciation recapture must be recognized in the year of sale, regardless of the payments received.

Stop and review! You have completed the outline for this subunit. Study multiple-choice questions 22 through 26 beginning on page 497.

13.5 MULTIPLE JURISDICTIONS

1. **Multijurisdictional Issues for State Taxes**
   a. A tax jurisdiction is a geographic area with its own distinct set of tax rules and regulations, e.g., a municipality, county, state, or country. When a taxable transaction has occurred across multiple jurisdictions, authoritative guidance must be established in order to reconcile or override the distinct sets of tax rules that may apply.
      1) The foreign tax credit presented in Study Unit 5, Subunit 3, is an example of a multijurisdictional issue.

   b. This subunit explains two of the longest-standing rules for interstate taxation: Public Law (PL) 86-272 and the Uniform Division of Income for Tax Purposes Act (UDITPA). Although the applicable taxes are state (not federal) taxes, these rules are tested as federal taxation by the AICPA because they are established at the federal level.

2. **Public Law 86-272**
   a. Before a state can tax a nonresident (e.g., a resident of another state), a minimum presence in the taxing state by the nonresident must be established. Sufficient presence to tax the nonresident is **nexus**.

   b. Public Law 86-272 limits the state's ability to tax the net income of nonresidents by establishing the following nexus rules:
      1) Nexus is not established if
         a) Activity is limited to solicitation of orders for tangible personal property,
         b) The orders are sent out of state for approval or rejection, and
         c) The orders are filled by shipment or delivery from a point outside the state if approved.

   c. The Multistate Tax Commission's (MTC's) "Statement of Information Concerning Practices of Multistate Tax Commission and Signatory States Under Public Law 86-272" lists the following as **protected in-state activities** (i.e., they will not establish nexus):
      1) Soliciting orders for sales by any type of advertising
      2) Soliciting of orders by an in-state resident with only an "in-home" office
      3) Carrying free samples and promotional materials for display or distribution
      4) Furnishing display racks and advising customers of the products without charge
      5) Providing automobiles for conducting protected activities
      6) Passing orders, inquiries, and complaints on to the home office
      7) Missionary sales activities
         a) For example, a manufacturer's solicitation of retailers to buy the manufacturer's goods from the manufacturer's wholesale customers
      8) Coordinating shipment/delivery and providing related information without charge
      9) Checking customers' inventories (e.g, re-order, but not quality control)
      10) Maintaining a sample/display room at one location for less than 14 days during the tax year
      11) Recruiting, training, and evaluating sales personnel
      12) Mediating customer complaints solely for ingratiating the sales personnel with the customer and facilitating order request
      13) Owning, leasing, using, or maintaining personal property for use in the employee's "in-home" office or automobile that is solely limited to the conducting of protected activities

d. The MTC's statement lists the following as **unprotected in-state activities** (i.e., they create nexus):

1) Making repairs to or performing maintenance or service on the property sold or to be sold
2) Collecting on accounts
3) Investigating creditworthiness
4) Installing a product at or after shipment or delivery
5) Conducting training courses, seminars, or lectures for non-soliciting personnel
6) Providing technical assistance or service for purposes other than the facilitation of the solicitation of orders
    a) For example, engineering assistance or design service
7) Investigating, handling, or otherwise assisting in resolving customer complaints, other than mediating direct customer complaints with the sole purpose of ingratiating the sales personnel with the customer
8) Approving or accepting orders
9) Repossessing property
10) Securing deposits on sales
11) Picking up or replacing damaged or returned property
12) Hiring, training, or supervising personnel (other than personnel involved only in solicitation)
13) Using agency stock checks or any other instrument or process by which sales are made within the home state by sales personnel
14) Maintaining a sample or display room at any one location in excess of 14 days during the tax year
15) Carrying samples for sale, exchange, or distribution in any manner for consideration or other value
16) Owning, leasing, using, or maintaining any of the following facilities or property in-state:
    a) Repair shop
    b) Parts department
    c) Office other than "in-home" office
    d) Warehouse
    e) Meeting place for directors, officers, or employees
    f) Stocks of goods other than samples
    g) Telephone-answering service publicly attributed to the company/representative
    h) Mobile stores
    i) Real property or fixtures to real property of any kind
17) Consigning stock of goods or other tangible personal property for sale
18) Maintaining, by the employee or other representative, an office or place of business of any kind other than a qualified "in-home" office

NOTE: Generally, telephone or other public listings indicating company/employee contact at a specific location creates nexus; however, normal distribution of business cards/stationery does not create nexus.

19) Entering into or disposing of a franchise or licensing agreement or transferring related tangible personal property
20) Conducting any activity not listed as protected that is not entirely ancillary to requests for orders, even if such activity helps to increase purchases

3. **The Uniform Division of Income for Tax Purposes Act (UDITPA)**

   a. The UDITPA was drafted by the National Conference of Commissioners on Uniform State Laws and is recommended for enactment in all states. Each state decides whether or not to adopt the act.

   b. Once nexus is established, net income must be accurately allocated or apportioned among the various jurisdictions. The UDITPA provides a uniform method for allocating and apportioning a business's income. The rules for the business's nonbusiness income are different than those for the business's business income.

   c. Nonbusiness income is all income other than business income. It is allocated, not apportioned. Specific rules apply to nonbusiness income from rents, royalties, capital gains, interest, dividends, patents, and copyrights as follows:

Property Type		Allocation based on:
Net Rents & Royalties	Real	Location of property
	Tangible Personal	Proportional use[1] or commercial domicile[2]
Capital Gains & Losses	Real	Location of property
	Tangible Personal	Location of property[3] or commercial domicile[4]
	Intangible Personal	Commercial domicile
Interest & Dividends		Commercial domicile
Patent & Copyright Royalties		Proportional use[1] or commercial domicile[2]

[1] Proportional use within the taxing state

[2] The taxpayer's commercial domicile (i.e., home state) if the taxpayer is not organized or taxed in the state the property is used

[3] Location of property at time of sale

[4] The taxpayer's commercial domicile if the taxpayer is not taxed in the state the property is located at time of sale

   d. Apportionment of business income to the taxing state is determined by the following equation:

$$\frac{\text{Property factor + Payroll factor + Sales factor}}{3}$$

NOTE: Some states only use the sales (gross receipts) factor.

1) The property factor determines the in-state use of real and tangible personal business property.

$$\frac{\text{Avg. value of in-state real and tangible personal property used}}{\text{Avg. value of all real and tangible personal property used}}$$

   a) Property owned by the taxpayer is valued at its original cost, not the AB (i.e., no depreciation reduction).

   b) Property rented by the taxpayer is valued at eight times the net annual rental rate (rate paid minus rate received from sub-rentals).

2) The payroll factor uses amounts determined by the accounting methods of the business so that accruals are treated as paid.

$$\frac{\text{In-state compensation paid}}{\text{Total compensation paid}}$$

   a) Payroll attributed to management or maintenance or otherwise allocable to nonbusiness property should be excluded from the formula.

3) The sales factor is only for business income. Capital gains are nonbusiness income and are allocated, not apportioned.

$$\frac{\texttt{In-state sales}}{\texttt{Total sales}}$$

a) Sales means net sales after discounts and returns.

b) Sales shipped to a state with no taxation of the taxpayer (i.e., no nexus), may be thrown back and taxed by the shipped-from state. If neither state taxes the taxpayer, the state in which the order was taken may be apportioned the sale.

e. If the allocation and apportionment provisions do not fairly represent the taxpayer's in-state activity, the taxpayer may request or the state may require (1) separate accounting (typically costly and difficult to carry out), (2) the exclusion of any one or more factors, (3) the inclusion of one or more additional factors, or (4) the employment of any other method to equitably allocate and apportion the income.

4. **Multijurisdictional Issues for Multinational Transactions**

a. U.S. taxpayers (individuals or business entities) are subject to tax on world-wide income. This may result in the income being subject to double-taxation. In an effort to mitigate double-taxation, various allowances have been made (e.g., foreign earned income exclusion, foreign tax credit). These allowances, to varying degrees, give up U.S. jurisdiction over foreign income.

1) Nonresident aliens are usually only subject to U.S. income tax on U.S. source income. The following table shows the general rules for determining U.S. source income of nonresident aliens:

General Rules for Income Source

Item of Income	Factor Determining Source
Salaries, wages, other compensation	Where services performed
Business Income: Personal services Sale of inventory – purchased Sale of inventory – produced	 Where services performed Where sold Where produced (Allocation may be necessary)
Interest	Residence of payer
Dividends	Whether a U.S. or foreign corporation*
Rents	Location of property
Royalties: Natural resources Patents, copyrights, etc.	Location of property Where property is used
Sale of real property	Location of property
Sale of personal property	Generally seller's tax home
Pension distributions attributable to contributions	Where services were performed that earned the pension
Investment earnings on pension contributions	Location of pension trust
Sale of natural resources	Allocation based on fair market value of product at export terminal
Scholarships Fellowships	Generally, the residence of the payer

*Exceptions include:

a) Part of a dividend paid by a foreign corporation is U.S. source if at least 25% of the corporation's gross income for the preceding 3 tax years before the year in which the dividends are declared is effectively connected with a U.S. trade or business.

b. U.S. tax law attempts to reclaim some of the loss income due to the surrendering of jurisdiction, especially when the taxpayer's accounting practices are perceived as simply a means to avoid U.S. tax law. Generally, the rules attempt to capture the income when the income is repatriated to the U.S. taxpayer. Controlled foreign corporation (CFC) and subpart F income were covered in item 14. of Study Unit 3, Subunit 3.

c. Transfer pricing is an accounting practice used to avoid proper tax treatment. Transfer pricing reallocates items of income and deduction among entities under common control. Reallocation of the income and deduction results in minimizing the U.S. tax of foreign corporations' U.S. affiliates. Since the foreign parent corporations do not normally do business in the U.S., their income is free from U.S. tax. To prevent evasion, the IRS reallocates items affecting taxable income as if the transactions were conducted in an arm's-length transaction between uncontrolled parties.

Stop and review! You have completed the outline for this subunit. Study multiple-choice questions 27 through 29 on page 499.

QUESTIONS

13.1 Tax Legislation

1. Which of the following statements with respect to regulations is **false**?

A. All regulations are written by the Office of the Chief Counsel, IRS, and approved by the Secretary of Treasury.

B. Public hearings are not held on temporary regulations without a written request.

C. Although IRS employees are bound by the regulations, the courts are not.

D. Public hearings are not held on proposed regulations.

Answer (D) is correct.

REQUIRED: The false statement regarding classes of regulations.

DISCUSSION: The purpose of proposed regulations is to give the public an opportunity to be heard before the regulations are promulgated in their final form. Public hearings are held if written requests for a hearing are made.

2. Which of the following is the primary source of Federal Tax Law?

A. The Internal Revenue Code of 1913.

B. Treasury Regulations.

C. The Internal Revenue Code of 1986.

D. The Internal Revenue Bulletin.

Answer (C) is correct.

REQUIRED: The primary source of Federal Tax Law.

DISCUSSION: The Internal Revenue Code of 1986 is the primary source of Federal Tax Law. It imposes income, estate, gift, employment, and miscellaneous excise taxes and provisions controlling the administration of Federal taxation. The Code is found at Title 26 of the United States Code.

Answer (A) is incorrect. The Internal Revenue Code (IRC) of 1913 was the first IRC to implement a federal income tax and is superseded by the 1986 Code. Answer (B) is incorrect. Treasury Regulations are administrative pronouncements that interpret and illustrate the rules contained in the Internal Revenue Code. They are a secondary source of Federal Tax Law. Answer (D) is incorrect. The Internal Revenue Bulletin is an instrument used to publish treasury decisions, executive orders, tax conventions, legislation, court decisions, and other items of general interest.

3. Which of the following is **not** one of the three classes of Treasury Regulations?

A. Temporary.

B. Judicial.

C. Final.

D. Proposed.

Answer (B) is correct.

REQUIRED: The answer that is not a class of Treasury Regulations.

DISCUSSION: The three classes of Treasury Regulations are temporary, final, and proposed regulations. Judicial is not a class of Treasury Regulations.

4. Tax legislation is first referred to which Senate committee once it is approved by the House?

A. Joint committee on taxation.

B. Budget committee.

C. Appropriations.

D. Finance.

Answer (D) is correct.

REQUIRED: The Senate committee to whom approved House tax bills are referred to.

DISCUSSION: Tax bills are reviewed in the House Ways and Means Committee before being considered by the full House. The House version is referred to the Senate Finance Committee before being considered by the full Senate. If the Senate approves the House version as is, the bill is next presented to the President. However, the Senate often revises the House version, which requires a review by a joint House/Senate committee. The joint committee version then returns to the House for approval, followed by the Senate, before reaching the President.

Answer (A) is incorrect. A bill will not reach the joint committee on taxation until after the Senate has made revisions. Answer (B) is incorrect. The budget committee does not prepare legislation. Answer (C) is incorrect. The appropriations committee oversees the spending/allocation of Treasury funds, as guided by the limits regulated by the budget committee.

5. Where do all bills for raising revenue originate?

A. House of Representatives.

B. Senate.

C. Finance Committee.

D. Supreme Court.

Answer (A) is correct.

REQUIRED: The origin of all revenue bills.

DISCUSSION: Section 7 of Article 1 of the Constitution lays forth the process for passage of legislative tax law. It states "All Bills for raising Revenue shall originate in the House of Representatives; but the Senate may propose or concur with Amendments as on other Bills . . ."

Answer (B) is incorrect. The Senate may propose or concur with amendments to tax bills but does not originate the bills. Answer (C) is incorrect. A tax bill is referred to the finance committee after it is approved by the House of Representatives. Answer (D) is incorrect. The Supreme Court does not participate in the origination of legislation.

6. When a revenue ruling conflicts with a revenue procedure, which of the two tax authorities has precedence?

A. Revenue ruling.

B. The one established first.

C. Revenue procedure.

D. The most recently established.

Answer (D) is correct.

REQUIRED: The tax authority with precedence when there is a conflict.

DISCUSSION: When there are conflicting sources of tax law within the same tier of the hierarchy (as is the case with revenue rulings and procedures), the most recent rule/law takes precedence.

Answer (A) is incorrect. Revenue rulings are in the same hierarchical tier as revenue procedures. Answer (B) is incorrect. More recent tax law within the same hierarchical tier has precedence. Answer (C) is incorrect. Revenue procedures are in the same hierarchical tier as revenue rulings.

7. Which of the following are useful tools in determining Congressional intent behind certain tax laws and helping examiners apply the law properly?

A. Committee reports.

B. Treasury regulations.

C. Revenue rulings.

D. Revenue procedures.

Answer (A) is correct.

REQUIRED: The useful tools in determining Congressional intent.

DISCUSSION: Congressional Committee Reports reflect Congress' intent behind certain tax laws and help examiners apply the law properly.

Answer (B) is incorrect. Treasury regulations are prescribed by the Secretary of the Treasury. All regulations are written by the Office of the Chief Counsel, IRS, and approved by the Secretary of the Treasury. They are not the product of Congress. Answer (C) is incorrect. Revenue rulings are official interpretations of Internal Revenue law as applied to a given set of facts, and issued by the IRS. They are not the product of Congress. Answer (D) is incorrect. Revenue procedures are official IRS statements that prescribe procedures that affect the rights or duties of either a particular group of taxpayers or all taxpayers. They are not the product of Congress.

8. In order to show that a tax preparer's application of tax law was in line with the intent of the tax law, the preparer should cite which of the following types of authoritative sources to make the most convincing case?

A. IRS publication.

B. Technical advice memorandum of another, similar case.

C. Committee report.

D. Delegation order.

Answer (C) is correct.

REQUIRED: The authoritative source for determining the intent behind certain tax law.

DISCUSSION: Committee reports are useful tools in determining Congressional intent behind certain tax laws and helping examiners apply the law properly. The committee reports are very high authority to which the courts are bound.

Answer (A) is incorrect. Publications do an excellent job of plainly explaining the law; however, they are not binding on the IRS or courts. Answer (B) is incorrect. TAMs are binding on the IRS only in relation to the taxpayer who is the subject of the ruling. Answer (D) is incorrect. Delegation orders are not authoritative sources for tax research. They simply delegate authority to perform tasks/make decisions to specified IRS employees.

9. Which of the following statements with respect to revenue rulings and revenue procedures is **false**?

A. Revenue procedures are official statements of procedures that either affect the rights or duties of taxpayers or other members of the public or should be a matter of public knowledge.

B. The purpose of revenue rulings is to promote uniform application of the tax laws.

C. Taxpayers cannot appeal adverse return examination decisions based on revenue rulings and revenue procedures to the courts.

D. IRS employees must follow revenue rulings and revenue procedures.

Answer (C) is correct.

REQUIRED: The false statement regarding revenue rulings and revenue procedures.

DISCUSSION: Revenue rulings and revenue procedures do not have the force and effect of regulations but are published to provide precedents to be used in the disposition of other cases. While taxpayers may rely on the rulings and procedures, they can also appeal adverse return examination decisions based on those rulings to the Tax Court or other federal courts.

10. Which of the following statements best describes the applicability of a constitutionally valid Internal Revenue Code section on the various courts?

A. Only the Supreme Court is not bound to follow the Code section. All other courts are bound to the Code section.

B. Only the Tax Court is bound to the Code section. All other courts may waiver from the Code section.

C. District, claims, and appellate courts are bound by the Code section. The Supreme and Tax Courts are not bound by it.

D. All courts are bound by the Code section.

Answer (D) is correct.

REQUIRED: The statement that best describes the relationship between the Internal Revenue Code and the courts.

DISCUSSION: The Internal Revenue Code is the body of tax statutes enacted by Congress as the law of federal taxation. Because it is federal law, it is binding on all federal courts.

Answer (A) is incorrect. The Supreme Court is bound to a constitutionally valid Code section. Answer (B) is incorrect. All courts are bound by a constitutionally valid Code section. Answer (C) is incorrect. All courts must follow a constitutionally valid Code section.

11. To research whether the Internal Revenue Service has announced an opinion on a Tax Court decision, refer to which of the following references for the original announcement?

A. Circular 230.

B. Federal Register.

C. Internal Revenue Bulletin.

D. Tax Court Reports.

Answer (C) is correct.

REQUIRED: The reference that contains the original announcement of an IRS opinion on a Tax Court decision.

DISCUSSION: The Internal Revenue Bulletin is published weekly and includes Treasury decisions, statutes, committee reports, U.S. Supreme Court decisions affecting the IRS, lists of the acquiescences and nonacquiescences of the IRS to decisions of the courts, and administrative rulings.

Answer (A) is incorrect. Circular 230 does not contain the original announcement of an IRS opinion on a Tax Court decision. Answer (B) is incorrect. The Federal Register does not contain the original announcement of an IRS opinion on a Tax Court decision. Answer (D) is incorrect. Tax Court Reports do not contain the original announcement of an IRS opinion on a Tax Court decision.

12. The Commissioner of Internal Revenue will **not** publicly announce acquiescence or nonacquiescence to the adverse regular decisions of which of the following courts?

A. United States Tax Court.

B. United States district court.

C. United States Supreme Court.

D. United States Court of Federal Claims.

Answer (C) is correct.

REQUIRED: The court to whose adverse regular decisions the commissioner will not publicly announce acquiescence or nonacquiescence.

DISCUSSION: The commissioner may announce his or her acquiescence or nonacquiescence with regard to the regular, reported decisions of the courts other than the Supreme Court. Acquiescence is the commissioner's public endorsement of a court decision. In some cases, only specific issues are acquiesced, or the agreement may be in result only.

13.2 Tax Procedures

13. A taxpayer understated the tax liability by $10,000. The total tax liability was $50,000. No disclosure of the return position was made by the taxpayer; however, the basis for the position is reasonable. How much of an accuracy-related penalty will the taxpayer be assessed?

A. $0

B. $1,000

C. $2,000

D. $10,000

Answer (C) is correct.

REQUIRED: The amount of an accuracy-related penalty.

DISCUSSION: A taxpayer's accuracy-related penalty due to disregard of rules and regulations, or substantial understatement of income tax, may be avoided if the return position is adequately disclosed and has a reasonable basis. Generally, the penalty is equal to 20% of the underpayment. Substantial understatement of income tax occurs when the understatement is more than the larger of 10% of the correct tax ($5,000 is 10% of the correct tax) or $5,000. This taxpayer failed to adequately disclose the return position. The penalty is $2,000 ($10,000 understatement × 20%).

Answer (A) is incorrect. Because the taxpayer substantially understated the liability and failed to adequately disclose the return position, an accuracy-related penalty is due. Answer (B) is incorrect. The penalty is greater than 10%. Answer (D) is incorrect. The penalty is less than 100% of the understatement.

14. Chris, age 5, has $3,500 of interest income and no earned income this year. Assume the current applicable standard deduction is $1,050, how much of Chris's income will be taxed at Chris's parents' maximum tax rate?

A. $0

B. $1,400

C. $2,450

D. $3,500

Answer (B) is correct.

REQUIRED: The dependent's unearned income subject to parents' marginal rate.

DISCUSSION: Net unearned income of a dependent child is taxed to the dependent at the parents' marginal rate. Net unearned income is unearned income minus the sum of

1. $1,050 (first $1,050 clause)
2. Greater of (a) $1,050 of the standard deduction or $1,050 of itemized deductions or (b) the amount of allowable deductions directly connected with the production of unearned income
3. Chris's net unearned income is $1,400 [$3,500 unearned income – ($1,050 + $1,050 std. ded.)]

Answer (A) is incorrect. Chris's net unearned income will be taxed at the parents' marginal rate. Answer (C) is incorrect. Chris's unearned income is reduced by an additional $1,050 of the standard deduction, to arrive at the net unearned income. Answer (D) is incorrect. Only Chris's net unearned income will be taxed at the parents' marginal rate.

15. Keen, a calendar-year taxpayer, reported gross income of $100,000 on his 2015 income tax return. Inadvertently omitted from gross income was a $20,000 commission that should have been included in 2015. Keen filed his 2015 return on March 17, 2016. To collect the tax on the $20,000 omission, the Internal Revenue Service must assert a notice of deficiency no later than

A. March 17, 2019.

B. April 15, 2019.

C. March 17, 2022.

D. April 15, 2022.

Answer (B) is correct.

REQUIRED: The statute of limitations on assessment of a deficiency.

DISCUSSION: The general statute of limitations for assessment of a deficiency is 3 years from the date the return was filed or due. An income tax return filed before the due date for the return is treated as if filed on the due date for statute of limitations purposes. Since Keen's return was due April 15, 2016, the statute of limitations will expire 3 years from that date.

Answer (A) is incorrect. An income tax return filed before the due date for the return is treated as if filed on the due date. Answer (C) is incorrect. A 6-year statute applies only when income items that would increase stated gross income by more than 25% are omitted. Answer (D) is incorrect. A 6-year statute applies only when income items that would increase stated gross income by more than 25% are omitted.

16. A taxpayer filed his income tax return after the due date but neglected to file an extension form. The return indicated a tax liability of $50,000 and taxes withheld of $45,000. On what amount is the penalties for late filing and late payment computed?

A. $0

B. $5,000

C. $45,000

D. $50,000

Answer (B) is correct.

REQUIRED: The amount used to assess late filing and late payment penalties.

DISCUSSION: When an income tax return is filed later than its due date and no extension has been filed, the IRS may assess a penalty on the taxpayer. The penalty is assessed only on the outstanding taxes due. The taxpayer therefore receives credit for the $45,000 in withholding taxes and the penalty is only assessed on the difference, $5,000 [Sec. 6651(b)].

Answer (A) is incorrect. The net tax due is used to assess the penalty. Answer (C) is incorrect. Only the net tax still due, not the tax already remitted, is used to assess the penalty. Answer (D) is incorrect. The taxpayer receives a credit for the taxes withheld.

17. A claim for refund of erroneously paid income taxes, filed by an individual before the statute of limitations expires, must be submitted on Form

A. 1139.

B. 1045.

C. 1040X.

D. 843.

Answer (C) is correct.

REQUIRED: The required form for submitting a claim for refund of individual income taxes.

DISCUSSION: A claim for refund of previously paid income taxes is made by filing an amended return on Form 1040X within the appropriate statute of limitations period.

Answer (A) is incorrect. Application for a tentative carryback adjustment to get a quick refund for carryback of a net operating loss, corporate net capital loss, and general business credit may be made on Form 1139 for corporations. Answer (B) is incorrect. Form 1045 is used to apply for a quick refund on a carryback for individuals. Answer (D) is incorrect. Form 843 is used to file a claim for refund of taxes paid other than income taxes.

18. Krete, an unmarried taxpayer with income exclusively from wages, filed her initial income tax return for the 2015 calendar year. By December 31, 2015, Krete's employer had withheld $16,000 in federal income taxes, and Krete had made no estimated tax payments. On April 15, 2016, Krete timely filed an extension request to file her individual tax return and paid $300 of additional taxes. Krete's 2015 income tax liability was $16,500 when she timely filed her return on April 30, 2016, and paid the remaining income tax liability balance. What amount is subject to the penalty for the underpayment of estimated taxes?

A. $0

B. $200

C. $500

D. $16,500

Answer (A) is correct.

REQUIRED: The amount subject to penalty for underpayment of estimated taxes.

DISCUSSION: No amount is subject to the penalty for the underpayment of estimated taxes. The amount withheld from wages by Krete's employer, $16,000, is treated as if an equal part was paid on each due date. Each of these installments meets the 25% of 90% of the current year's tax threshold.

Answer (B) is incorrect. This amount results from subtracting the $300 taxes paid from the additional $500 income tax liability computed on the return ($16,500 – $16,000). Answer (C) is incorrect. This amount is the additional $500 income tax liability computed on the filed return. Answer (D) is incorrect. This figure is the entire amount of income tax liability computed on the filed return.

13.3 Tax Planning

19. Company A, a U.S. company, deducted costs from research and development of a product in the U.S., then licensed rights to the product to a foreign subsidiary in a lower tax jurisdiction. The subsidiary then manufactured the product and sold each unit back to Company A (the parent company). This is an example of which tax planning technique?

A. Timing of income/deductions.

B. Shifting of income.

C. Conversion of income property.

D. Deferral of income.

Answer (B) is correct.

REQUIRED: The tax planning technique exemplified in the question.

DISCUSSION: In addition to moving income among related parties, shifting of income also involves moving income from one tax jurisdiction to another with a lower tax rate. By deducting all of the R&D expenses in the U.S. and licensing the rights to a foreign subsidiary, Company A minimized their U.S. taxable income and shifted profits to a foreign tax jurisdiction with a lower tax rate.

Answer (A) is incorrect. Timing of income deals with the recognition period of income, not the jurisdiction. Answer (C) is incorrect. Conversion of income property relates to the change in the type of income property, resulting in a different tax liability, not the jurisdiction. Answer (D) is incorrect. Deferral of income is an element of timing of income/deductions and is not exemplified in the question.

20. Electing MACRS depreciation (accelerating the depreciation deduction) over straight-line depreciation is an example of which tax planning technique?

A. Conversion.

B. Shifting.

C. Timing.

D. Assignment.

Answer (C) is correct.

REQUIRED: The tax planning technique exemplified by electing a depreciation method.

DISCUSSION: The three most basic and common types of tax planning are

1. Timing of income recognition,
2. Shifting of income among taxpayers and jurisdictions, and
3. Conversion of income among high and low rate activities.

The timing technique accelerates or defers recognition of income and/or deductions. Because election of depreciation methods accelerate or defer the depreciation deduction, it is a timing strategy.

Answer (A) is incorrect. Converting of income involves changing the type/class of income producing property. Electing a depreciation method does not change the income property but does change the period of income recognition. Answer (B) is incorrect. Shifting of income involves a change in ownership of the income or change in the tax jurisdiction of the income. Electing a depreciation method does not change the ownership or jurisdiction of income but does change the period of income recognition. Answer (D) is incorrect. Assignment of income is an element of income shifting and is not related to the effects of electing a depreciation method.

21. Which of the following falls under the tax planning strategy of income shifting?

A. Hiring a new employee in order to increase business expenses and decrease net income.

B. Hiring a family member in order to increase business expenses and increase family global net income.

C. Shifting income from one spouse to the other on a joint return.

D. Filing a separate return in lieu of a joint return.

Answer (B) is correct.

REQUIRED: The scenario that falls under income shifting.

DISCUSSION: Income shifting typically relates to moving income and therefore the accompanying tax liability from one family member to another who is subject to a lower marginal rate or moving income between entities and their owner(s). When a taxpayer hires a family member subject to a lower marginal rate (typically one of the taxpayer's children), the taxpayer, in essence, shifts income, reducing the overall (i.e., global) family tax liability.

Answer (A) is incorrect. Hiring a new employee is income shifting when it involves a non-arms-length transaction and increases overall (global) family income. Answer (C) is incorrect. Shifting income from one spouse to the other on a joint return has a net zero effect on the overall (global) family income. Answer (D) is incorrect. Filing a separate return in lieu of a joint return may or may not reduce a couples tax liability, but that act alone does not "shift" either spouse's income to another individual.

13.4 Accounting Methods

22. Aviary Corp. sold a building for $600,000. Aviary received a down payment of $120,000, as well as annual principal payments of $120,000 for each of the subsequent 4 years. Aviary purchased the building for $500,000 and claimed depreciation of $80,000. What amount of gain should Aviary report in the year of sale using the installment method?

A. $180,000

B. $120,000

C. $54,000

D. $36,000

Answer (D) is correct.

REQUIRED: The amount of gain reported under the installment method.

DISCUSSION: Under the installment method, the gain recognized is equal to the proceeds received in the current year multiplied by the gross profit percentage. The gross profit percentage is the gross profit divided by the sales price. The gross profit of $180,000 is the sales price less the AB. The AB of the asset is the $500,000 initial cost reduced by the $80,000 depreciation, or $420,000. Thus, the gross profit percentage is equal to 30% ($180,000 gross profit ÷ $600,000 sales price). The only installment received this period is the down payment of $120,000, which is multiplied by the gross profit percentage (30%) for a reported gain of $36,000 currently.

Answer (A) is incorrect. The entire gross profit is not reported in the current period under the installment method. Answer (B) is incorrect. The entire $120,000 down payment should not be reported as a gain in the current period. The reported gain must consider the gross profit percentage, which is multiplied by the current proceeds. Answer (C) is incorrect. Multiplying the gross profit percentage by the gross profit equals $54,000; however, the gain reported in the current period is the gross profit percentages multiplied by the installments received currently.

23. A taxpayer is **not** required to obtain the permission of the Commissioner of Internal Revenue to change from the

A. LIFO method to the FIFO method of valuing inventories.

B. Units-of-production method to the straight-line method of computing depreciation.

C. Cash basis to the accrual basis of reporting income.

D. Accrual method to the installment method of reporting income.

Answer (D) is correct.

REQUIRED: The change that does not require the permission of the IRS.

DISCUSSION: The general rule is that to change an accounting method the taxpayer must obtain the permission of the IRS. In general, the installment method of reporting income may be used by a taxpayer without the permission of the IRS.

Answer (A) is incorrect. A change from LIFO to FIFO requires permission from the IRS. A change from FIFO to LIFO does not require permission. Answer (B) is incorrect. A change from units-of-production to straight-line depreciation requires permission from the IRS. Answer (C) is incorrect. A change from the cash basis to the accrual basis requires permission from the IRS.

24. A cash-basis taxpayer should report gross income

A. Only for the year in which income is actually received in cash.

B. Only for the year in which income is actually received whether in cash or in property.

C. For the year in which income is either actually or constructively received in cash only.

D. For the year in which income is either actually or constructively received, whether in cash or in property.

Answer (D) is correct.

REQUIRED: The time for a cash-basis taxpayer to report gross income.

DISCUSSION: A cash-basis taxpayer should report gross income for the year in which income is either actually or constructively received in cash or property. Constructive receipt is when the payment is made available to the taxpayer or when the taxpayer has economic benefit of the funds.

Answer (A) is incorrect. Gross income is reported by a cash-basis taxpayer when actually or constructively received in cash. Answer (B) is incorrect. Gross income is reported by a cash-basis taxpayer when actually or constructively received in cash or property. Answer (C) is incorrect. Gross income is not limited to cash.

25. During Year 3, Scott charged $4,000 on his credit card for his dependent son's medical expenses. Payment to the credit card company had not been made by the time Scott filed his income tax return in Year 4. However, in Year 3, Scott paid a physician $2,800 for the medical expenses of his wife, who died in Year 1. Disregarding the adjusted gross income percentage threshold, what amount could Scott claim in his Year 3 income tax return for medical expenses?

A. $0

B. $2,800

C. $4,000

D. $6,800

Answer (D) is correct.

REQUIRED: The tax year in which medical expense is deductible.

DISCUSSION: Generally, only qualified medical expenses paid during the year on behalf of the taxpayer, his or her spouse, or a dependent are deductible. Charging to a third-party credit card is treated as a current payment. Thus, Scott is treated as having paid $6,800 of deductible medical expense in Year 3.

Answer (A) is incorrect. Qualified medical expenses paid during the year are deductible. Answer (B) is incorrect. Charging to a third-party credit card is treated as current payment. Answer (C) is incorrect. A taxpayer may deduct medical expense for his or her spouse paid during the year.

26. Soma Corp. had $600,000 in compensation expense for book purposes in Year 1. Included in this amount was a $50,000 accrual for Year 1 nonshareholder bonuses. Soma paid the actual Year 1 bonus of $60,000 on March 1, Year 2. In its Year 1 tax return, what amount should Soma deduct as compensation expense?

A. $600,000

B. $610,000

C. $550,000

D. $540,000

Answer (B) is correct.

REQUIRED: The amount of compensation expense deductible when paid.

DISCUSSION: A deduction is allowed for all ordinary and necessary business expenses paid or incurred during the taxable year, including a reasonable allowance for salaries or other compensation for personal services actually rendered. Because the bonuses were compensation to unrelated parties, Soma accrues and deducts $50,000 of them in Year 1 and an additional $10,000 in Year 1 because the payment in Year 2 was attributable to the Year 1 tax year of an accrual-method taxpayer.

Answer (A) is incorrect. The additional $10,000, although paid in Year 2, was attributable to services rendered in a prior tax year to an accrual-method taxpayer. Answer (C) is incorrect. The amount of $550,000 results from subtracting the accrued nonshareholder bonuses from compensation expense.
Answer (D) is incorrect. The amount of $540,000 results from subtracting the actual Year 1 bonuses paid in Year 2 from compensation expense.

13.5 Multiple Jurisdictions

27. What is the general term for a single geographic area that has its own distinct set of tax rules and regulations?

A. Municipality.

B. Interstate commerce.

C. Tax jurisdiction.

D. Multijurisdictional.

Answer (C) is correct.

REQUIRED: The general term for an area with its own tax rules.

DISCUSSION: A tax jurisdiction is a geographic area that has its own distinct set of tax rules and regulations. Specific examples of tax jurisdictions include a municipality, county, state, or country.

Answer (A) is incorrect. A municipality is a specific example of a tax jurisdiction. Answer (B) is incorrect. Interstate commerce is commercial activity involving multiple states, each with its own distinct set of tax rules and regulations. A state is a specific example of a tax jurisdiction. Answer (D) is incorrect. Multijurisdictional describes issues involving more than one jurisdiction.

28. Under Public Law 86-272, which activity does **not** establish nexus?

A. Solicitation of orders is approved out-of-state, and delivery is made from an in-state location.

B. Solicitation of orders is approved in-state, and delivery is made from an out-of-state location.

C. Solicitation of orders is approved in-state, and delivery is made from an in-state location.

D. Solicitation of orders is approved out-of-state, and delivery is made from an out-of-state location.

Answer (D) is correct.

REQUIRED: The rules for establishing nexus.

DISCUSSION: Public Law 86-272 limits a state's ability to tax the net income of nonresidents by establishing nexus rules. Nexus is not established if the activity is limited to solicitation of orders for tangible personal property; the orders are sent out of state for approval or rejection and, if approved, the orders are filled by shipment or delivery from a point outside the state. Solicitation of orders approved out of state and delivery made from an out-of-state location is a situation that fulfills all three requirements.

Answer (A) is incorrect. Approved orders must be filled by shipment or delivery from a point outside the state. Answer (B) is incorrect. The orders must be sent out of state for approval or rejection. Answer (C) is incorrect. The orders must be sent out of state for approval or rejection, and approved orders must be filled by shipment or delivery from a point outside the state.

29. In accordance with the UDITPA, which of the following is correct for allocating interest and dividends?

A. Allocate based on the location of the property.

B. Allocate based on the commercial domicile of the taxpayer.

C. Allocate based on proportional use within the taxing state.

D. Not allocated, but apportioned with other business income.

Answer (B) is correct.

REQUIRED: The correct statement regarding allocation of interest and dividends.

DISCUSSION: Nonbusiness income means all income other than business income. It is allocated, not apportioned. Specific rules apply to nonbusiness income from rents, royalties, capital gains, interest, dividends, patents, and copyrights. Interest and dividends are allocated based on the taxpayer's commercial domicile; i.e., they are taxed by the company's "home state."

Answer (A) is incorrect. There is no physical location for interest and dividends. Answer (C) is incorrect. Proportional use applies to tangible personal property. Interest and dividends do not have physical characteristics to be used in any particular location. Answer (D) is incorrect. The UDITPA specifically classifies interest and dividends as nonbusiness property and subject to allocation.

13.6 PRACTICE TASK-BASED SIMULATIONS

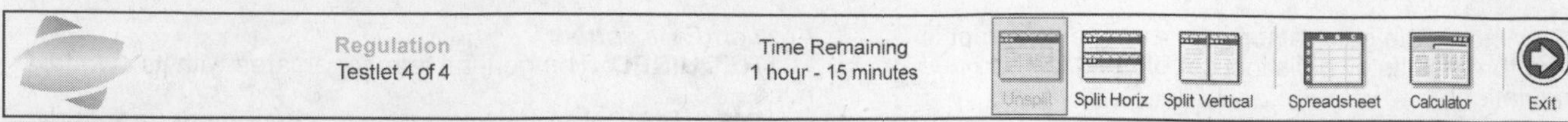

DIRECTIONS

Note: If you believe you have encountered a software malfunction, report it to the test center staff immediately.

Navigation

To navigate from task to task, use the controls at the bottom of the screen. Click on the **Next** button to advance to the next task, or the **Previous** button to go to the previous task. To go directly to any task, click on its number.

If you would like a reminder to revisit a task, or want to indicate that you are finished with it, click on the reminder flag below the task number. To clear the flag, click on it again. Reminder flags are for your use only – they do not contribute to your score.

Tabs

In this part of the examination, you will be asked to complete various tasks. Every task has one or more **Work Tabs**. Some tasks have one or more **Information Tabs**, others may have none. Every task has a **Help** tab.

If a task has **Information Tabs**, you may use the information in them to complete your responses in the **Work Tabs**.

Work tab **Information tab** **Help tab**

Work Tabs:

- **Work Tabs** are identified with a pencil icon. This is where your responses are expected.
- Each task has one or more **Work Tabs.**
- **Work Tabs** contain directions for completing the task – be sure to read these directions carefully.
- The **Work Tab** name in the example above is for illustration only – yours will differ.
- You must complete all of the **Work Tabs** in each task to receive full credit.

Information Tabs:

- The Authoritative Literature will be provided in all tasks in the AUD, FAR, and REG sections for your reference.
- Your simulation may have one or more additional **Information Tabs**. Like the Authoritative Literature tabs, **Information Tabs** do not have a pencil icon.
- If your task has additional **Information Tabs**, go through each to familiarize yourself with the task content.

Help Tab:

- The **Help Tab** provides assistance with the exam software that is used in this task. For example, if the task is to compose a memorandum, **Help** will provide information about the word processor.

The Toolbar

The toolbar at the top of the screen shows the amount of time remaining for you to complete the tasks. In addition, the following tools are available. Note that only the **Exit** button is displayed when Directions are visible - the others will appear when you begin the tasks.

Click on these buttons to split or unsplit the screen. You can split the screen vertically or horizontally.

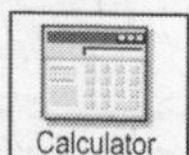

Click on this button to display the calculator; click on it again to hide the calculator. To move the calculator, click on the calculator title bar and drag the calculator to the desired location.

Click on this button to use the spreadsheet; click on it again to hide the spreadsheet. To move the spreadsheet, click on the the spreadsheet title bar and drag the spreadsheet to the desired location.

Click on this button to go on to the next part of the examination. You must complete all of the tasks to receive full credit. Once you click on **Exit** and confirm the action, you will NOT be able to return to this testlet.

= Reminder | Directions | 1 2 3 4 5 6 | Previous | Next

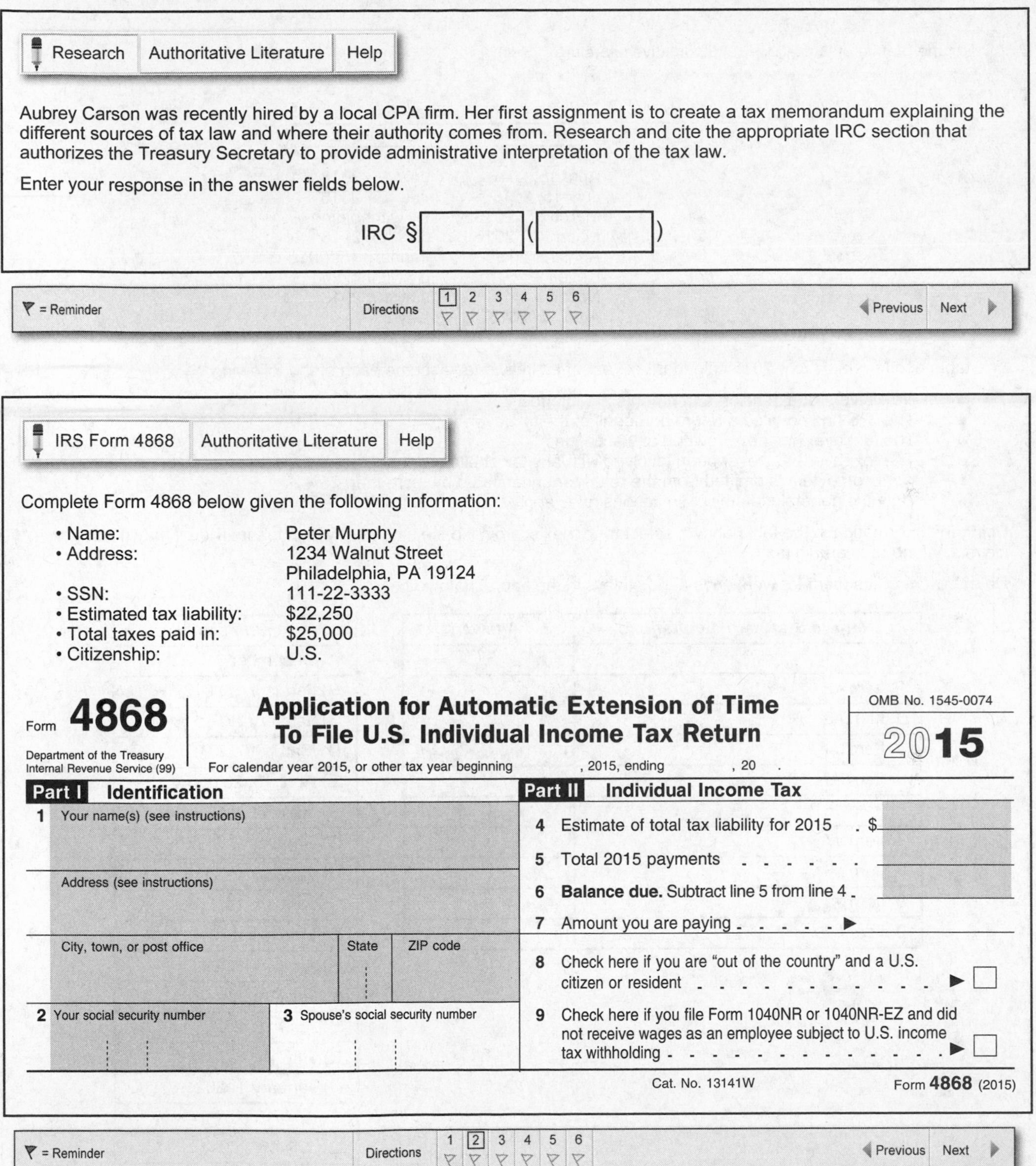

Research | Authoritative Literature | Help

Aubrey Carson was recently hired by a local CPA firm. Her first assignment is to create a tax memorandum explaining the different sources of tax law and where their authority comes from. Research and cite the appropriate IRC section that authorizes the Treasury Secretary to provide administrative interpretation of the tax law.

Enter your response in the answer fields below.

IRC § [ ] ([ ])

= Reminder | Directions | 1 | 2 | 3 | 4 | 5 | 6 | Previous | Next

IRS Form 4868 | Authoritative Literature | Help

Complete Form 4868 below given the following information:

- Name: Peter Murphy
- Address: 1234 Walnut Street
  Philadelphia, PA 19124
- SSN: 111-22-3333
- Estimated tax liability: $22,250
- Total taxes paid in: $25,000
- Citizenship: U.S.

Form **4868**

Department of the Treasury
Internal Revenue Service (99)

Application for Automatic Extension of Time To File U.S. Individual Income Tax Return

For calendar year 2015, or other tax year beginning , 2015, ending , 20 .

OMB No. 1545-0074

2015

Part I Identification

1 Your name(s) (see instructions)

Address (see instructions)

City, town, or post office | State | ZIP code

2 Your social security number

3 Spouse's social security number

Part II Individual Income Tax

4 Estimate of total tax liability for 2015 . $

5 Total 2015 payments . . . .

6 **Balance due.** Subtract line 5 from line 4 .

7 Amount you are paying . . . . . . ►

8 Check here if you are "out of the country" and a U.S. citizen or resident . . . . ► ☐

9 Check here if you file Form 1040NR or 1040NR-EZ and did not receive wages as an employee subject to U.S. income tax withholding . . . . ► ☐

Cat. No. 13141W Form **4868** (2015)

= Reminder | Directions | 1 | 2 | 3 | 4 | 5 | 6 | Previous | Next

Item Number	Circumstances	
	Filed Return	Paid Tax
1	April 15, 2016	July 15, 2016
2	April 15, 2016	July 15, 2018
3	July 15, 2016	July 15, 2016
4	March 15, 2016	By withholding
5	March 15, 2016	July 15, 2018
6	April 15, 2017	January 15, 2016
7	Never	By withholding
8	Never	July 15, 2018
9	April 15, 2018	Never
10	Never	Never

The table above relates to a 2015 calendar tax year of an individual. Assume each of the following:

- No waivers or extension agreements are in effect.
- The IRS has not filed a return on behalf of the taxpayer.
- The taxpayer has never owned any securities.
- The taxpayer has never been involved with any tax shelter.
- No income item is omitted from the return or understated by more than 25%.
- Only the general statutes of limitations rules apply.

Using the information in the table above, select from the list provided the time after which the individual may no longer claim a refund of overpaid tax.

Dates ignore adjustment for weekends and holidays in the appropriate years.

Refund Statute of Limitations	*Answer*
1. Item #1	
2. Item #2	
3. Item #3	
4. Item #4	
5. Item #5	
6. Item #6	
7. Item #7	
8. Item #8	
9. Item #9	
10. Item #10	

Choices
A) December 31, 2017
B) January 1, 2018
C) January 15, 2018
D) March 15, 2018
E) April 15, 2018
F) July 15, 2018
G) December 31, 2018
H) January 1, 2019
I) January 15, 2019
J) March 15, 2019
K) April 15, 2019
L) July 15, 2019
M) April 15, 2020
N) July 15, 2020
O) January 1, 2021
P) April 15, 2021
Q) July 15, 2021
R) January 1, 2025
S) Never
T) Not determinable

= Reminder   Directions   1 2 3 4 5 6   Previous   Next

Item Number	Circumstances	
	Filed Return	Paid Tax
1	April 15, 2016	July 15, 2016
2	April 15, 2016	July 15, 2018
3	July 15, 2016	July 15, 2016
4	March 15, 2016	By withholding
5	March 15, 2016	July 15, 2017
6	April 15, 2017	January 15, 2016
7	Never	By withholding
8	Never	July 15, 2018
9	April 15, 2018	Never
10	Never	Never

The table above relates to a 2015 calendar tax year of an individual. Assume each of the following:

- No waivers or extension agreements are in effect.
- The IRS has not filed a return on behalf of the taxpayer.
- The taxpayer has never owned any securities.
- The taxpayer has never been involved with any tax shelter.
- No income item is omitted from the return or understated by more than 25%.
- Only the general statutes of limitations rules apply.

Using the information in the table above, select from the list provided the time after which the IRS may no longer assess additional tax due.

Dates ignore adjustment for weekends and holidays in the appropriate years.

Assessment Statute of Limitations	***Answer***
1. Item #1	
2. Item #2	
3. Item #3	
4. Item #4	
5. Item #5	
6. Item #6	
7. Item #7	
8. Item #8	
9. Item #9	
10. Item #10	

Choices
A) December 31, 2017
B) January 1, 2018
C) January 15, 2018
D) March 15, 2018
E) April 15, 2018
F) July 15, 2018
G) December 31, 2018
H) January 1, 2019
I) January 15, 2019
J) March 15, 2019
K) April 15, 2019
L) July 15, 2019
M) April 15, 2020
N) July 15, 2020
O) January 1, 2021
P) April 15, 2021
Q) July 15, 2021
R) January 1, 2025
S) Never
T) Not determinable

Select from the list provided the date, court, or form that best matches each statement. Each choice may be used once, more than once, or not at all.

Dates ignore adjustment for weekends and holidays in the appropriate years.

Statement	Answer
1. The date the second installment of estimated tax is required during 2015 from an individual with a calendar tax year.	
2. An individual's claim for refund was disallowed after an IRS appeals hearing. In which court can (s)he pursue the claim?	
3. The date an individual who adopts a calendar tax year and files Form 4868 must file an income tax return for 2015.	
4. The form used by an individual to claim a quick refund for a net operating loss carryback.	
5. The date an individual who adopts a calendar tax year and files a Form 4868 must pay income tax due for 2015.	

Choices
A) April 15, 2016
B) April 15, 2015
C) June 15, 2016
D) October 15, 2016
E) U.S. Court of Federal Claims
F) U.S. Tax Court
G) Form 1040X
H) Form 1045

Select from the list provided the most appropriate tax planning techniques for each item. Each choice may be used once, more than once, or not at all.

Item	Answer
1. Completed-contract method	
2. Gifting	
3. Moving IRA funds to a Roth IRA account	
4. Purchase of municipal bonds	
5. Assignment of income	
6. Hiring a family member	
7. Carryback	
8. Employer reimbursement of employee medical expenses	
9. Electing S corp status	
10. Contributing property to a partnership	

Choices
A) Timing of income
B) Shifting of income
C) Conversion of income

Unofficial Answers

1. Research (1 Gradable Item)

Answer: IRC § 7805(a)

§ 7805. Rules and regulations

(a) Authorization

Except where such authority is expressly given by this title to any person other than an officer or employee of the Treasury Department, the Secretary shall prescribe all needful rules and regulations for the enforcement of this title, including all rules and regulations as may be necessary by reason of any alteration of law in relation to internal revenue.

2. IRS Form 4868 (9 Gradable Items)

Form **4868** — **Application for Automatic Extension of Time To File U.S. Individual Income Tax Return** — OMB No. 1545-0074 — **2015**

Department of the Treasury Internal Revenue Service (99) — For calendar year 2015, or other tax year beginning , 2015, ending , 20 .

Part I Identification			**Part II Individual Income Tax**	
1 Your name(s) (see instructions): Peter Murphy [1]			4 Estimate of total tax liability for 2015	$ 22,250 [7]
			5 Total 2015 payments	25,000 [8]
Address (see instructions): 1234 Walnut street [2]			6 **Balance due.** Subtract line 5 from line 4	0 [9]
			7 Amount you are paying ▶	
City, town, or post office: Philadelphia [3]	State [4]: PA	ZIP code: 19124 [5]	8 Check here if you are "out of the country" and a U.S. citizen or resident ▶ ☐	
2 Your social security number: 111 22 3333 [6]	3 Spouse's social security number		9 Check here if you file Form 1040NR or 1040NR-EZ and did not receive wages as an employee subject to U.S. income tax withholding ▶ ☐	

Cat. No. 13141W — Form **4868** (2015)

3. Refund Statute of Limitations (10 Gradable Items)

1. K) April 15, 2019. A claim for refund may be made within the time limits specified in the statute of limitations on refunds. A refund may be paid until the later of 3 years from the time the return was filed or 2 years from the time the tax was paid. Therefore, the refund claim must be filed by April 15, 2019.
2. N) July 15, 2020. April 15, 2019, is 3 years after the return was filed. July 15, 2020, is 2 years after the tax was paid. A refund claim must be filed by the later date, i.e., July 15, 2020.
3. L) July 15, 2019. July 15, 2019, is 3 years after the return was filed. July 15, 2018, is 2 years after the tax was paid. A refund claim must be filed by the later date, i.e., July 15, 2019. An extension of time to file a return does not extend the payment due date.
4. K) April 15, 2019. Taxes deducted and withheld at the source during any calendar year are deemed paid by the recipient of the income on the 15th day of the 4th month following the close of his or her tax year. A return filed before the due date is treated as having been filed on the last day prescribed for its filing. The return of an individual taxpayer is due on the 15th day of the 4th month following the close of his or her tax year. Therefore, the return is treated as filed and the tax is treated as paid on April 15, 2016, and a claim for refund must be filed by April 15, 2019.
5. N) July 15, 2020. A return filed before the due date is treated as having been filed on the due date. The return of an individual taxpayer is due on the 15th day of the 4th month following the close of his or her tax year. April 15, 2019, is 3 years after the return was deemed filed. July 15, 2020, is 2 years after the tax was paid. A refund claim must be filed by the later date, i.e., July 15, 2020.
6. M) April 15, 2020. In the case of a return filed after its due date, the actual date of filing governs. Three years after filing (April 15, 2020) is later than 2 years after the tax was paid and is the date by which a refund must be claimed. The fourth quarterly installment of estimated tax for an individual's 2015 tax year is due January 15, 2016, and the payment is treated as made on the 15th day of the 4th month following the close of his or her tax year.

7. E) April 15, 2018. A refund must be claimed by the later of 3 years after the return was filed or 2 years after the tax was paid. If a taxpayer does not file a return, a refund must be claimed within 2 years from the time the tax was paid. Tax deducted and withheld at the source during any calendar year is deemed paid by the recipient of the income on the 15th day of the 4th month following the close of his or her tax year. Therefore, a claim must be filed within 2 years following April 15, 2016.

8. N) July 15, 2020. A refund must be claimed by the later of 3 years after the return was filed or 2 years after the tax was paid. If a taxpayer does not file a return, a refund must be claimed within 2 years from the time the tax was paid. A refund claim must be filed by July 15, 2020.

9. P) April 15, 2021. A refund must be claimed by the later of 3 years after the return was filed or 2 years after the tax was paid. If tax was never paid for the tax year, the only basis for a refund claim would be a refundable credit such as the earned income credit. The earned income credit is treated as an overpayment of tax, which would be deemed paid on the 15th day of the 4th month following the close of the tax year. Three years after the date of filing (April 15, 2021) is later than 2 years after the date of the deemed payment (April 15, 2018) and is the last day to claim a refund.

10. E) April 15, 2018. A refund must be claimed by the later of 3 years after the return was filed or 2 years after the tax was paid. If tax was never paid for the tax year, the only basis for a refund claim would be a refundable credit such as the earned income credit. The earned income credit is treated as an overpayment of tax, which would be deemed paid on the 15th day of the 4th month following the close of the tax year. If a taxpayer does not file a return, a refund must be claimed within 2 years from the time the tax was paid. Thus, a refund claim would have to be filed by April 15, 2018.

4. Assessment Statute of Limitations (10 Gradable Items)

1. K) April 15, 2019. The statute of limitations for assessment of a deficiency is 3 years from the date the return was filed or due.

2. K) April 15, 2019. The statute of limitations for assessment of a deficiency is 3 years from the date the return was filed or due.

3. L) July 15, 2019. A deficiency may be assessed until 3 years after the return is filed, even if it is filed after the due date.

4. K) April 15, 2019. A deficiency may be assessed until 3 years after a return is filed. A return filed before the last day prescribed for filing is deemed to have been filed on the due date. Thus, the IRS may assess a deficiency on or before April 15, 2019.

5. K) April 15, 2019. A deficiency may be assessed until 3 years after a return is filed. A return filed before the last day prescribed for filing is deemed to have been filed on the due date. Thus, the IRS may assess a deficiency on or before April 15, 2019.

6. M) April 15, 2020. A deficiency may be assessed until 3 years after the return is filed, even if it is filed after the due date. April 15, 2020, is 3 years after the return was filed.

7. S) Never. A deficiency may be assessed until 3 years after a return is filed. If a return is not filed, the statute of limitations period never begins and therefore never ends.

8. S) Never. When no return has been filed, assessment proceedings may be commenced at any time.

9. P) April 15, 2021. A deficiency may be assessed until 3 years after the return is filed even if it is filed after the due date. April 15, 2021, is 3 years after the return was filed.

10. S) Never. When no return has been filed, assessment proceedings may be commenced at any time. Note that the IRS is authorized to complete and file a return on behalf of a taxpayer who fails to file.

5. Tax Procedures (5 Gradable Items)

1. C) June 15, 2015. Individuals who earn income not subject to withholding must pay estimated tax on that income in quarterly installments. For 2015, the installments are due April 15, June 15, September 15, and January 15, 2016. (Dates are adjusted for weekends and holidays.)

2. E) U.S. Court of Federal Claims. A notice of a tax deficiency is prerequisite to U.S. Tax Court jurisdiction. The forums available to seek refund of overpaid tax are the U.S. district courts and the U.S. Court of Federal Claims.

3. D) October 15, 2016. An individual income tax return must be filed (postmarked) by the 15th day of the 4th month following the close of the tax year. An automatic 6-month extension is granted to an individual who files Form 4868 on or before the initial due date.

4. H) Form 1045. A claim for refund of previously paid income taxes is made by filing an amended return on Form 1040X. However, application for a tentative carryback adjustment to get a quick refund for carryback of a net operating loss, corporate net capital loss, or general business credit is made on Form 1045 (individuals) or Form 1139 (corporations).

5. A) April 15, 2016. Payment of tax is due on the date prescribed for filing the return. The automatic extension to file granted an individual who files Form 4868 on or before the initial due date does not also extend the payment due date.

6. Tax Planning (10 Gradable Items)

1. A) Timing of income. The completed-contract method recognizes receipts and expenditures in the tax year in which the contract is completed. This moves the income and expenses from an earlier tax period (when received/expended) to a later one.
2. B) Shifting of income. In general, gifts shift income from one taxpayer to another without creating a tax liability for the recipient.
3. C) Conversion of income. Converting a traditional IRA to a Roth IRA converts the investment earnings from taxable (on distribution) income to exempt income.
4. C) Conversion of income. Purchasing municipal bonds converts taxable income to exempt income. This can be done directly by reinvesting current year taxable income in municipal bonds and indirectly by investing in municipal bonds as opposed to other taxable bond investment options.
5. B) Shifting of income. Assignment of income is a principle related to shifting of income from one taxpayer to another. The taxpayer who earned the income "assigns" another individual to receive the income without it passing through the possession of the taxpayer who earned the income.
6. B) Shifting of Income. Hiring of family members is a shifting technique to reduce the taxable income of e.g., the parents in a high marginal tax bracket, and increase the taxable income of the child with a lower marginal rate.
7. A) Timing of income. When a taxpayer carries back or forward losses into a different tax period, the taxpayer has changed the time of recognition for that loss. To the extent allowed, the taxpayer carries a loss to the year providing the greatest advantage.
8. C) Conversion of income. By reimbursing an employee's medical expenses, the employer in essence converts taxable income (had the employer simply paid the employee additional compensation) into exempt income.
9. B) Shifting of income. C corporation income is subject to taxation as corporate income and again when distributed to the shareholders as a capital gain. Electing S corp status eliminates this double taxation of the same income by shifting all the tax liability to the income distributed to the shareholders.
10. A) Timing of income. When property is contributed to a partnership in exchange for partnership interest, the contributing partner has deferred recognition of gain to a future date when the partnership sells the contributed property.

Gleim Simulation Grading

Task	Correct Responses		Gradable Items		Score per Task
1 (Research)	____	÷	1	=	____
2	____	÷	9	=	____
3	____	÷	10	=	____
4	____	÷	10	=	____
5	____	÷	5	=	____
6	____	÷	10	=	____
			Total of Scores per Task		____
		÷	Total Number of Tasks		6
			Total Score		____%

STUDY UNIT FOURTEEN
NONCORPORATE BUSINESS ENTITIES

(17 pages of outline)

This study unit addresses certain basic business structures. The most basic and common structure is the **sole proprietorship**. It consists of one individual who may be engaged in any kind of business. A sole proprietorship is ordinarily a small enterprise. Because it is not distinct from its owner, it is not a separate legal entity.

A **partnership** is an association of two or more persons carrying on a business as co-owners for profit. Unlike a sole proprietorship, a partnership often is treated as an entity distinct from its owners. For example, the Uniform Commercial Code (UCC) and bankruptcy law adopt the separate entity view. However, a partnership also is a form of agency involving the individual partners. This study unit covers (1) the form of partnership that may be created without statutory formalities (the **general partnership**), (2) partnerships created only by statute, and (3) the limited liability company (a hybrid of the corporation and the partnership).

14.1 SOLE PROPRIETORSHIPS

1. **Formation**
    a. Of all business structures, the sole proprietorship is the easiest and cheapest to create. It is formed at the will of the proprietor.
    b. Most filing, registration, and attorneys' fees are avoided.
        1) An advantage is that a sole proprietorship ordinarily can do business in any state without having to file, register, or otherwise qualify to do business in that state.
        2) The Internet allows a sole proprietorship to conduct business nationally or even internationally.
    c. Formation is subject to only a few legal requirements, for example, local zoning and licensing laws. States rarely require licensing.
        1) However, a proprietor doing business under a **fictitious name** is usually required to make a d/b/a or "doing business as" filing under state law. This kind of statute also applies to partnerships.
2. **Capitalization**
    a. A major weakness of a sole proprietorship is that it cannot raise equity capital other than the personal resources of the proprietor.
3. **Profits and Losses**
    a. The proprietor has the advantage of receiving all profits. (S)he has the disadvantage of **unlimited personal liability** for all losses and debts.
    b. The personal assets of the proprietor are therefore at risk.

4. **Taxation**
   a. The proprietor and the proprietorship are not distinct entities, so the income or loss of the business is reported by the proprietor.
   b. The proprietor receives the tax benefits of all business deductions and losses.
   c. Other tax advantages include the need to file only one return and the avoidance of the double taxation of corporate earnings.
5. **Powers of the Proprietor**
   a. The sole proprietorship is the most flexible business structure. The proprietor makes all management decisions without answering to other executives, directors, or owners. Thus, control and accountability are completely centralized.
      1) A disadvantage is that a sole proprietorship may lack the expertise and the checks and balances on decision making found in more complex structures.
6. **Termination**
   a. The duration of the sole proprietorship is at the proprietor's discretion.
   b. The interest of the proprietor may be transferred during his or her life, but the sole proprietorship is then dissolved.
      1) An advantage of a sole proprietorship is that a change in control occurs only with the proprietor's consent.
   c. The sole proprietorship is automatically terminated upon the proprietor's death.
   d. Accordingly, lack of continuity of existence is a disadvantage of this structure.

Stop and review! You have completed the outline for this subunit. Study multiple-choice questions 1 and 2 on page 526.

14.2 GENERAL PARTNERSHIPS

1. **Overview**

Background

In the U.S., partnership law has been codified in the Uniform Partnership Act of 1914 (UPA) and updated in the Revised Uniform Partnership Act (RUPA) approved by the National Conference of Commissioners on Uniform State Laws in 1994. The revised act was amended in 1997 to include provisions for limited liability partnerships (LLPs). These changes conform the law of partnership to modern business practice while retaining many features of the original act.

   a. The general partnership is the oldest, simplest, and most common business structure other than the sole proprietorship.
   b. The **Revised Uniform Partnership Act (RUPA)** defines a **partnership** as "an association of two or more persons to carry on as co-owners a business for profit."
      1) A business is any trade, occupation, or profession.
   c. The RUPA states that a partnership is an entity **distinct** from its partners. A partnership as an entity separate from its owners (partners) because
      1) The assets of a partnership are treated as those of the business unit.
      2) Title to real property may be acquired in the partnership name.
      3) Each partner is a fiduciary of the partnership.
      4) Each partner is an agent of the partnership.
      5) The partnership may sue and be sued in its own name.
         a) Thus, a legal action against the partnership does not apply to a partner who is not named as a separate defendant.

d. A partnership is **not** distinct from its partners because
   1) A partnership lacks continuity of existence.
      a) Its duration is limited by, for example, the will of the partners.
   2) No person can become a partner without consent of all the partners.
      a) A transferee of a partnership interest, unlike a transferee of shares in a corporation, does not become an owner.
   3) Debts of a partnership are ultimately the personal debts of the partners.
   4) A partnership is not subject to regular federal income tax.

e. Partners may by **contract** establish the relationships among themselves and between themselves and the partnership.
   1) The law recognizes the supremacy of the partnership agreement in most situations.
      a) Accordingly, the RUPA consists mostly of default rules that govern matters not addressed by the partnership agreement.
   2) Nevertheless, the **partnership agreement** cannot do the following:
      a) Unreasonably restrict access to books and records
      b) Eliminate the duty of loyalty or the obligation of good faith and fair dealing
      c) Unreasonably reduce the duty of care
      d) Vary the power to dissociate
      e) Waive or vary the right to seek court expulsion of another partner
      f) Vary the law applying to a limited liability partnership
      g) Vary the right to dissolution and winding up
      h) Restrict third-party rights

2. **Formation**

a. An advantage of the general partnership is that it can exist without any formalities. No filings are required, and a partnership may be created by a written or oral agreement.
   1) If the partnership exists for a definite period exceeding 1 year, the statute of frauds requires the partnership agreement to be in writing.
   2) Fictitious name statutes have been enacted in most states to protect creditors.
      a) Registration permits creditors to discover the persons liable for the entity's debts.

b. To form a partnership, the co-owners must **intend**
   1) To form a partnership and
   2) To **make a profit** even if no profit is earned.
      a) Thus, not-for-profit entities are not partnerships.

c. If the elements of a partnership are present, it is formed even if the parties do not intend to be partners.

EXAMPLE

Jim is doing business as Harvin Shoes, a sole proprietorship. In the past year, Jim has regularly joined with Stewart in the marketing of sport accessories. Jim and Stewart have formed a partnership if they divide profits equally.

d. A **partnership by estoppel** may be recognized when an actual partnership does not exist. The duties and liabilities of a partner sometimes may be imposed on a nonpartner (a purported partner).

1) A **purported partner** has represented that (s)he is a partner or has consented to such a representation. Moreover, the purported partner is assumed to be an agent of persons who have consented to the representation.

2) A third party who has reasonably relied on the representation and suffered harm as a result may assert the existence of a partnership. The purported partner then is prevented (estopped) from denying the existence of a partnership.

EXAMPLE

Lawyer A falsely represented to Client that Lawyer A and Lawyer B were partners. Client, in reasonable reliance on this statement, sought legal services from Lawyer B. Because these services were performed without due care, Client suffered harm. Lawyer A (as well as Lawyer B) is liable as a partner despite the absence of an actual partnership.

3. **Capitalization**

a. A general partnership is advantageous relative to a sole proprietorship because two or more persons may contribute cash, property, or services to the business.

1) However, a general partnership cannot raise equity by selling shares.

4. **Profits, Losses, and Distributions**

a. Unless the partners agree otherwise in the partnership agreement, the RUPA provides that partners share profits and losses equally.

1) Also, unless otherwise agreed, each partner must contribute in proportion to his or her share of the profits toward any losses of the partnership.

2) A major disadvantage of a general partnership is that each partner has **unlimited personal liability** for all losses and debts of the business.

b. A partner also has the right to distributions. A distribution is a transfer of partnership property from the partnership to a partner. A distribution may take various forms:

1) A share of profits

2) Compensation for services

3) Reimbursement for payments made, and indemnification for liabilities incurred, in the ordinary course of business or to preserve the business or its property

4) Reimbursement for advances (loans) in excess of agreed capital contributions

a) The payments made and liabilities incurred are loans that accrue interest.

c. Unless otherwise agreed, the right to compensation for services is generally a right to receive a share of the profits, not to be paid for services.

5. **Partnership Interest**

a. A partner's **transferable interest** consists of a partner's share of partnership profits and losses and the right to receive distributions.

1) Partners may transfer (assign) their interests without (a) the loss of their rights, duties, and liabilities as partner or (b) the dissolution of the partnership.

a) The assignee is entitled only to the profits the assignor would normally receive and does not automatically become a partner.

b) The assignee does not have the right to participate in the management of the partnership.

2) The ability to transfer the financial interest but not ownership status is a disadvantage of a partnership.

a) For example, a partner cannot, during his or her life or through inheritance, transfer ownership to a family member.

3) Partners, their creditors, and heirs have no interest in **specific partnership property**. Thus, a partner's interest in specific partnership property is neither assignable to, nor subject to attachment by, the partner's individual creditors.
   a) Property is partnership property when acquired with partnership assets even if it is in the name of a partner with no indication of the existence of a partnership.
   b) Property acquired without use of partnership assets in the name of a partner, with no indication of the person's capacity as a partner or of the existence of a partnership, is presumed to be **separate property**, even if used for partnership purposes.
4) When a partner dies, his or her partnership interest is personal property that may be **inherited** according to a valid will. Heirs of the partnership interest are assignees, not partners.
   a) The estate does not become a partner.
   b) The death of a partner does not dissolve the partnership.
      i) The remaining partners may choose to continue the partnership.
   c) The estate is responsible for the partner's allocated share of any partnership liabilities.
5) A judgment creditor of a partner may attach the partner's transferable interest only by securing a **charging order** (a lien on the interest) from a court.

The AICPA often tests sharing of profits, losses, and distributions in partnerships. Candidates should understand that sharing generally is determined by the default rule in the RUPA only when the partners have no relevant agreement.

6. **Taxation**
   a. A principal advantage of a partnership is that it is not a taxable entity. However, it must file an annual informational return on Form 1065.
   b. The partnership's profit or loss is passed through to the partners, who report their shares of that profit or loss on their personal income tax returns.
7. **Rights of Partners**
   a. The rights, powers, and duties of partners are largely defined by the **law of agency**.
      1) However, partners may agree to limit their rights.
   b. Each partner has a right to **equal participation in management** of the partnership.
      1) The general rule for ordinary matters is majority rule.
      2) A unanimous vote is required to (a) amend a partnership agreement, (b) admit a new partner, and (c) determine other nonroutine matters.
      3) Different classes of partners may be formed with different management rights.
      4) A disadvantage of a partnership is that a deadlock may develop when partners have equal management rights.
      5) Partnership agreements commonly restrict management rights to a few partners or even one partner.
   c. A partner's right of **access to partnership information** is the right to inspect and copy the partnership books and records.
      1) A reasonable demand for other partnership information also must be honored.
   d. The right to **use or possess partnership property** may be exercised only on behalf of the partnership.

e. The right to **choose associates** means that no partner may be forced to accept any person as a partner. A person becomes a partner only with the consent of all partners.

   1) When a partner transfers his or her interest, the transferee is entitled only to receive the share of profits and losses and the right to distributions allocated to the interest acquired.

8. **Powers of Partners**

   a. The powers granted to each partner are governed by law and by the specific terms of the partnership agreement.

      1) Each partner has consented to being both a principal and an agent of the partnership.

         a) Thus, a general partnership is bound by a contract made by a partner acting within the scope of his or her actual or apparent authority.

   b. A partner has **actual or apparent authority** to act as an **agent** of the partnership in any legal transaction that is normal for the partnership or for a similar partnership. Thus, a partner is in a fiduciary position, one requiring a high standard of ethical conduct.

      1) The partnership is bound even if the partner had no actual authority in the matter unless the third party knew or had received notice of the lack of actual authority.
      2) However, if a partner acts without actual or apparent authority, neither the partnership nor the other partners are bound by the act unless the other partners ratify the transaction.
      3) The RUPA provides for filing a **statement of partnership authority** that may give notice of limitations on the authority of a partner.

9. **Duties of Partners**

   a. Duties imposed upon partners include the **fiduciary** duties of loyalty and care. The duty of **loyalty** is limited to

      1) Not competing with the partnership,
      2) Not dealing with the partnership in the conduct or winding up of the partnership business as (or for) a party with an adverse interest, and
      3) Not exploiting a partnership opportunity or secretly using partnership assets for personal gain.

   b. The duty of **care** in the conduct or winding up of the partnership business is not to engage in (1) knowing violations of the law, (2) intentional wrongdoing, (3) gross negligence, or (4) reckless behavior.
   c. A partner also has an obligation of **good faith and fair dealing**.

      1) A partner must be honest in fact and meet reasonable (objective) standards of fair dealing.

   d. However, no duty is violated solely because a partner acts in his or her own interest. For example, a partner may lend money to, or otherwise do business with, the partnership on the same basis as a nonpartner.

10. **Liabilities of Partners**

   a. Partners are **jointly and severally liable** for any partnership obligation, including the torts committed by another partner who acted within the ordinary course of the partnership business or with the authorization of the other partners.

      1) Thus, partners are individually liable for the full amount of a partnership obligation and also liable as a group. Joint and several liability allows either joint suits or separate actions (and separate judgments) at the plaintiff's option.

b. A partner may obligate the partnership and partners by contract when (1) specifically authorized by the partnership agreement, (2) apparently carrying on partnership business in the usual manner, or (3) acting with the actual or implicit consent of the other partners.

   1) When partners agree to limit the authority of a partner to act for the partnership, a third party who has no notice of the limitation is not bound.

c. Admission into an existing partnership results in liability for partnership obligations.

   1) However, a new partner is liable for **preadmission** obligations of the partnership only to the extent of his or her investment.

d. A **withdrawing** partner remains liable for debts of the partnership incurred before withdrawal unless the creditors contractually agree otherwise.

   1) Termination of the partnership also does not discharge any partner's obligations to third parties.

11. **Termination**

The AICPA has tested candidates' knowledge of how general partnerships terminate, especially the effects of a partner's death on the partnership and the rights of the deceased partner's heirs.

a. The partners may limit the duration of the partnership to a definite term or the completion of a specific undertaking.

   1) The partnership also may be **at will**. A partnership at will is **not** limited to "a definite term or the completion of a specific undertaking."

b. The RUPA provides for dissociation, dissolution, winding up (also known as liquidation), and termination.

c. **Dissociation** is the legal effect of a partner's ceasing to be associated in carrying on the business of the partnership. A partner has the power (but not necessarily the right) to dissociate at any time, subject to payment of damages if the dissociation is wrongful.

   1) The partner's management rights (except with regard to winding up) terminate.
   2) After dissociation, the business either continues after purchase of the dissociated partner's interest, or dissolution begins.
   3) Dissociation results from the following:
      a) Notice to the partnership of a partner's express will to withdraw
      b) An event specified in the agreement
      c) Expulsion of a partner under the terms of the partnership agreement
      d) Expulsion by a unanimous vote of the other partners
      e) A court order
      f) Incapacity
      g) Death
      h) Insolvency
      i) Distribution by a trust or estate of its entire transferable interest
   4) The partnership is not necessarily dissolved by dissociation unless it occurs by **express will** of the partner in a partnership at will.
   5) A **statement of dissociation** may be filed by the partnership or a dissociated partner. It is deemed to provide notice of dissociation 90 days after filing.
      a) Such notice terminates the partner's apparent authority and his or her liability for the partnership's post-dissociation obligations.

b) Without this statement or other notice, the dissociated partner has apparent authority for 2 years to bind the partnership to contracts with third parties who reasonably believe the person is a partner.

c) A dissociated partner remains liable to creditors for predissociation obligations even if the other partners agreed to assume the debts.

d) A dissociated partner also may be liable on post-dissociation contracts for up to 2 years if third parties reasonably believe that (s)he is still a partner.

6) If the business is not wound up, the partnership must purchase the dissociated partner's interest.

a) The price is determined based on a hypothetical sale of the partnership at the dissociation date.

7) The dissociation provision supports the entity theory by increasing the continuity of partnerships.

d. **Dissolution and winding up** occur only after certain events. But dissolution may occur without winding up.

1) In a partnership at will, dissolution results from, among other things, notice of a partner's express will to withdraw.

a) Dissolution also may be by **operation of law**, e.g., because of an event that makes the partnership's business illegal.

b) Moreover, a **court** may order dissolution, e.g., because the economic purpose of the partnership cannot be achieved.

2) The actual authority of a partner to act on behalf of the partnership terminates upon dissolution except as necessary to wind up partnership affairs.

3) Apparent authority of a partner may continue to exist throughout the winding up process unless notice of the dissolution has been communicated to the other party to the transaction.

4) The fiduciary duties of the partners also remain in effect with the exception of the duty not to compete, which ceases to exist after dissolution.

5) A **statement of dissolution** may be filed by any partner who has not wrongfully dissociated.

a) It is deemed to provide notice to nonpartners 90 days after the filing regarding dissolution and the limitation of the partners' authority.

e. A partnership may **continue after dissolution** if certain requirements are met.

1) After dissolution and before winding up, all parties (including any dissociating partner who has not wrongfully dissociated) may waive the right to winding up and termination.

a) In this case, the partnership continues its business as if dissolution had not occurred.

f. **Winding up** is the administrative process of settling partnership affairs, including the use of partnership assets and any required contributions by partners to pay creditors.

1) The RUPA states that the person winding up may do the following:

a) Continue the business as a going concern for a reasonable time
b) Take judicial actions
c) Settle and close the business
d) Dispose of and transfer property
e) Discharge liabilities
f) Distribute assets
g) Settle disputes by mediation or arbitration
h) Perform other necessary acts

2) **Creditors** are paid in full before any distributions are made to partners. However, partners who are creditors share equally with nonpartner creditors under the RUPA.
   a) In practice, because partner-creditors also are liable for all partnership debts, partnership creditors are **paid first**.
3) After payment of creditors, any surplus is paid in cash to the partners.
   a) A partner has no right to a distribution **in kind (of noncash assets)** and need not accept a distribution in kind.
4) To settle partnership accounts with positive (credit) balances, each partner receives a distribution equal to the amount in his or her account. Thus, no distinction is made between distributions of capital and of profits.
   a) Profits and losses from liquidation of assets are increases (credits) and decreases (debits), respectively.
   b) Prior credits to an account include contributions made and the partner's share of profits.
   c) Prior debits include distributions received and the share of losses.
5) If a partner's account has a negative (debit) balance, the partner is liable to contribute the amount of the balance.
   a) If a partner does not make a required contribution, the other partners must pay the difference in the same proportion in which they share losses.
   b) A partner making an excess contribution may recover the excess from the other partners.
   c) Moreover, the creditors may enforce the obligation of the partners to contribute to the partnership if a partner does not pay his or her share of the losses.
6) One effect of these rules is that the priority rules for unsecured partnership creditors and individual partners' unsecured creditors are consistent with the federal Bankruptcy Code. Thus, **unsecured partnership creditors** have priority in **partnership** assets. But, regarding any amounts that cannot be recovered from the partnership assets, they have the same priority in the **partners'** assets as the partners' creditors.
   a) A personal creditor of a personally insolvent partner must obtain a lien on the partner's transferable interest in the partnership.

12. **Limited Liability Partnership (LLP)**

a. An LLP is a favorable form of organization for professionals who have not incorporated. In many states, this form is restricted to use by professionals.
   1) An LLP must file a form with the secretary of state and maintain professional liability insurance.
   2) All partners are general partners who have limited liability. Thus, no one is personally liable for partnership obligations except to the extent of the LLP's assets. But a partner remains personally liable for his or her own professional malpractice.
      a) Partners ordinarily are not liable for negligent acts committed by another partner.
      b) A partner who is an immediate supervisor is liable for any negligent acts committed within the scope of employment by an employee (or another partner).
   3) Most CPA and law firms are organized as LLPs because state laws, in general, do not allow professionals limited liability for their actions. However, they do allow professionals the ability to shield their partners from liability.

13. **Joint Ventures**

   a. A joint venture is an easily formed business structure common in international commerce. It is an association to accomplish a specific business purpose or objective and is often organized for a single transaction.

      1) A joint venture is treated as a partnership in most cases.
      2) The rights and duties of joint venturers are generally governed by the RUPA.
      3) A disadvantage of the joint venture is that it lacks continuity of existence.

         a) Moreover, the interests in the entity are not readily transferable.

Stop and review! You have completed the outline for this subunit. Study multiple-choice questions 3 through 16 beginning on page 526.

14.3 LIMITED PARTNERSHIPS

1. **Limited Partnership**

   a. A limited partnership is a partnership formed by two or more persons under a state statute. Most statutes are based on the **Revised Uniform Limited Partnership Act (RULPA)**. A limited partnership has one or more general partners and one or more limited partners.

      1) **Person** includes natural person, partnership, limited partnership, trust, estate, association, or corporation.
      2) A **general partner** assumes management of the partnership and has full personal liability for debts of the partnership.

         a) A general partner may be another partnership or a corporation if its articles of incorporation as amended permit.
         b) A person can be both a general partner and a limited partner with the rights and liabilities of each.

      3) A **limited partner** is an investor who makes a contribution of cash or other property to the partnership in exchange for an interest in the partnership.

         a) A limited partner is not active in management of the partnership.

   b. **Formation**

      1) A written certificate of limited partnership must be filed as a public record with the secretary of state of the state in which it is organized. The certificate gives potential creditors notice of the limited liability of the limited partners. If a certificate is not filed, the organization is treated as an ordinary business partnership.

         a) The certificate must contain the following:

            i) Name of the limited partnership
            ii) Address of the office of its agent for service of process
            iii) Name and address of its agent for service of process
            iv) Name and business address of each general partner
            v) Latest date upon which the limited partnership is to dissolve
            vi) Other matters the general partners include in the certificate

         b) The certificate must be signed by all general partners.
         c) Amendments also must be filed.

      2) To do business in any other state, registration as a foreign limited partnership with the secretary of state of that state is required.

c. **Operation**

1) The operation of a limited partnership, including its financial structure, capitalization, profit and loss allocation, and distributions, is similar to that of a general partnership.
2) One exception is that, without a contrary agreement, profits and losses are shared on the basis of the fair values of contributions.

d. **Partner Rights and Liabilities**

1) A **general partner** in a limited partnership has
   a) Unlimited liability for partnership liabilities,
   b) Full management powers,
   c) A share in both profits and losses, and
   d) The same rights and powers and the same liabilities as a partner in a general partnership.
2) A **limited partner** has the right to
   a) Propose and vote on partnership affairs that do not directly control partnership operations, e.g., admission of a new general partner.
   b) Withdraw from the partnership upon 6 months' notice or according to the partnership agreement.
      i) The limited partner's right of withdrawal of his or her capital contribution is restricted. It may be withdrawn (a) upon the dissolution of the partnership, (b) at the date specified in the certificate, (c) upon 6 months' notice in writing to all the members, or (d) with the consent of all the members. But all creditors must be paid, or sufficient assets must be available for creditors.
      ii) A limited partner may not withdraw his or her capital contribution if the effect is to impair creditors' rights.
   c) Do business with the partnership, e.g., make a loan to it.
   d) Inspect and copy the partnership records, including tax returns.
   e) Receive other partnership information (if just and reasonable).
   f) File a derivative action on behalf of the partnership.
   g) Assign the limited partnership interest.
   h) Apply for dissolution of the partnership.
   i) Obtain an accounting.
3) A limited partner is liable for partnership liabilities only to the extent of his or her capital contribution. (S)he has no right to participate in control of the business.
   a) Control refers to participation in the day-to-day management decisions of the partnership.
   b) A limited partner may incur personal liability by knowingly permitting his or her name to be used as part of the partnership name and held out as a participant in management. Personal liability is only to persons who reasonably believe the limited partner is a general partner.

e. **Termination**

1) A limited partnership is dissolved and wound up before termination. A limited partnership can be dissolved upon any of the following events:
   a) The time or event specified in the limited partnership agreement occurs.
   b) All the partners agree, in writing, to dissolve.

c) An event of withdrawal of a general partner occurs, e.g., death, bankruptcy, incapacity, or removal. The following are exceptions:

i) The written terms of the agreement provide that the business may be carried on by the remaining general partners (if any).

ii) If no general partner remains, the limited partners agree in writing within 90 days to continue the business and appoint one or more new general partners.

d) The limited partnership is dissolved by court order.

2) The limited partnership is not dissolved by the bankruptcy, incapacity, or death of a limited partner.

a) The personal representative of the estate of a deceased limited partner does not become a substituted limited partner. However, (s)he has the rights and liabilities of a limited partner for the purpose of settling the estate.

3) After dissolution, winding up is done by a general partner who has not caused the dissolution. If no general partner exists to conduct the winding up, it may be performed by the limited partners or by some person designated by a court.

4) Remaining assets, if any, are distributed as follows:

a) To creditors, including creditors who are partners

b) To present partners and former partners for distributions previously due to them and unpaid, except as otherwise provided in the limited partnership agreement

c) To the partners as a return of their contributions, except as otherwise provided in the limited partnership agreement

d) To the partners according to the terms of the limited partnership agreement (to the extent of any remaining assets)

5) Notice of dissolution must be given to every party affected.

6) The final distribution terminates the limited partnership.

2. **Limited Liability Limited Partnership (LLLP)**

a. An LLLP is a limited partnership in which all partners are general partners who have limited liability. Thus, partners are personally liable for partnership obligations only to the extent of the partnership's assets. But partners remain personally liable for their own professional malpractice.

1) Partners ordinarily are not liable for negligent acts committed by another partner.

2) A partner who is an immediate supervisor is liable for any negligent acts committed within the scope of employment by an employee (or another partner).

3) Some states have enacted LLLP statutes.

4) Other states permit formation of an LLLP without a specific statute. The RULPA provides that a general partner in a limited partnership has the same liability as a general partner in a general partnership. Thus, in states that permit an LLLP (a form of limited partnership) to register under the statute governing an LLP (a form of general partnership), the limitation of liability under the LLP statute extends to the general partner of the LLLP.

Stop and review! You have completed the outline for this subunit. Study multiple-choice questions 17 through 25 beginning on page 531.

14.4 LIMITED LIABILITY COMPANIES (LLCs)

1. **Overview**
   a. An LLC is a noncorporate hybrid business structure that combines the limited liability of the corporation with the tax advantages of the general partnership.
   b. The uniform act is the **Uniform Limited Liability Company Act (ULLCA)**. However, the ULLCA has not been adopted by a majority of jurisdictions, and state laws vary. Thus, business law textbooks emphasize the common aspects of state laws and the ULLCA.
   c. Like a corporation, a limited partnership, and an LLP, an LLC is a legal entity separate from its owners.
      1) An LLC may (a) enter into contracts, (b) sue, (c) be sued, (d) own property in its own name, (e) engage in other transactions in property, (f) make donations, (g) be a general or limited partner, and (h) appoint agents.
   d. Like a partnership, the LLC may have owner management, a limited duration, and restricted transfer of interests.
2. **Formation**
   a. An LLC can be formed only under a state statute.
      1) An LLC generally may be formed for any lawful purpose.
      2) An LLC is formed by one or more persons when articles of organization are filed with the appropriate secretary of state (or the equivalent). Thus, formation is more difficult than for a sole proprietorship or a general partnership.
         a) State laws vary as to when the LLC begins its legal existence, e.g., when the articles are (1) accepted by the state or (2) officially approved.
   b. The **name** of the LLC must indicate by words or abbreviations that it is an LLC. It should be distinct from the names of other businesses in the state.
   c. The **articles of organization** should state the LLC's name. It also should
      1) Include certain basic information, such as the names and addresses of organizers, the initial agent for service of process, and initial managers;
      2) Provide for existence for a specified term or at-will;
      3) Indicate whether management will be by owners or managers; and
      4) State whether one or more members will be liable for the LLC's obligations.
   d. The members' **operating agreement** ordinarily is not legally required and may be oral. It may address such matters as the following:
      1) Capitalization
      2) Sharing of profits and losses
      3) Amendment of the operating agreement
      4) Management arrangements
      5) Voting rights
         a) Without a contrary agreement, some statutes give members equal rights and some rights proportionate to their financial interests.
      6) Members' rights, including to distributions and access to records
      7) Transfer of members' interests
      8) The circumstances causing dissolution
      9) Admission and withdrawal of members
      10) Death of a member
         a) Without a contrary agreement, many states dissolve an LLC upon the death of a member.

e. The LLC must at all times maintain a registered **agent** for service of process and a registered **office** in the state.
   1) These requirements are the same as for limited partnerships and corporations.
f. The **duration** of LLCs generally is not perpetual. An LLC ordinarily dissolves after a statutory period or when a member's interest is terminated.
   1) Most state laws and LLC operating agreements permit the remaining members to continue the business after a member withdraws or the member's interest is otherwise terminated.

3. **Capitalization**
   a. Funding of an LLC is from members' **contributions**. Without an agreement to the contrary, it may consist of tangible and intangible property and services, including obligations to contribute cash or property or to perform services.
      1) The advantages of limited liability and avoidance of double taxation may attract member-investors.
   b. Another advantage is that an LLC's members may be partnerships, corporations, and nonresident aliens.
      1) An S corporation does not offer these benefits.
      2) Moreover, unlike an S corporation, an LLC (a) has no limit on the number of members, (b) can make disproportionate allocations and distributions, and (c) can distribute appreciated property without incurring a taxable gain.
      3) A member of an LLC can contribute appreciated property in exchange for a membership interest without recognizing a taxable gain.
   c. A disadvantage is that LLC interests may be considered securities. Thus, they may be subject to federal and state regulation.
4. **Profits, Losses, and Distributions**
   a. Without a contrary agreement, statutes often provide for profits and losses to be shared based on the values of members' contributions. But the ULLCA provides for sharing equally.
      1) A member is not automatically entitled to compensation, except for winding up.
   b. Without a contrary agreement, distributions upon liquidation of the LLC or dissociation of a member ordinarily are based on the values of members' contributions. A right to distributions does not exist until a member gives notice of withdrawal from the entity.
      1) In some states, the operating agreement is allowed to prohibit withdrawal.
5. **LLC Interest**
   a. A member can transfer (assign) his or her distributional interest, which is essentially the member's portion of the net assets of the LLC. This interest is **personal property**.
      1) The member has no right in specific property of the LLC.
      2) The transfer may be involuntary, for example, by an order obtained by a creditor from a court to charge the member's interest in the LLC (profits and other distributions).
      3) The transfer also may be through the estate of a deceased member.
      4) A transferee does not become a member without consent of all members or a provision in their agreement.

6. **Taxation**
   a. Members may elect to be taxed as partners, and single-member LLCs (called "disregarded entities" for tax purposes) are taxed as sole proprietorships.
   b. Taxation as a corporation may be advantageous if reinvestment in the LLC is desired, and corporate rates are lower than personal rates.
   c. Thus, an LLC has the advantage of being a pass-through entity or a taxable entity at the discretion of the member(s).
      1) But a publicly traded LLC is a taxable entity.
7. **Rights of Members and Managers**
   a. An LLC is deemed to be member-managed unless the articles of organization provide otherwise.
   b. Under the ULLCA, in a **member-managed LLC**, all members have a right to participate, and most business matters are decided by the majority.
   c. In a **manager-managed LLC**, each manager, who need not be a member, has equal rights, and most business matters are decided by the manager or by a majority of the managers.
   d. The ULLCA further provides that, in any LLC, members must **unanimously** agree about some matters, for example,
      1) Amending the operating agreement or the articles,
      2) Dissolution requirements,
      3) Waiver of the right to have the business wound up,
      4) Merger, and
      5) Admission of new members.
   e. Members have the right to inspect books and records and to be informed about the business.
8. **Powers of Members and Managers**
   a. If the articles vest management of the LLC in elected managers, they are agents of the LLC. Any one manager may have the statutory authority to bind the LLC.
      1) In a manager-managed LLC, members are not agents.
      2) Most state statutes require unanimous consent to transfer management.
   b. If the articles vest management in its members, they are agents. Thus, it may be possible, depending on the statute, for any one member to incur indebtedness or otherwise contractually bind the LLC.
   c. The fiduciary duties of care and loyalty (and possibly those of good faith and fair dealing) are imposed on those who manage LLCs.
   d. Persons who conduct business as an LLC when statutory requirements for its formation have not been met do not have limited liability and are jointly and severally liable as partners.
9. **Duties of Members and Managers**
   a. Managers are selected or removed by a majority vote of the members and are fiduciaries regarding the LLC and the members. They have duties of loyalty, care, and good faith.
      1) The members in a member-managed LLC have the same duties.

10. **Liability of Members and Managers**

    a. Like the shareholders of a corporation, but unlike the partner-managers of a limited partnership, the owners of an LLC who participate in management have limited liability.

        1) A great advantage of an LLC is that the creditors of the entity ordinarily have **no claim on the personal assets** of the members or managers.

    b. However, the members or managers remain liable for their guarantees of LLC debt or for personal misconduct (e.g., negligence or criminal behavior). Moreover, misuse of the LLC form (e.g., to commit fraud or mislead others about who is conducting the business) may cause a court to "pierce the corporate veil."

    c. Federal and state laws also may provide other means of reaching personal assets. For example, the IRS may proceed against an individual for a fraudulent transfer or nonpayment of trust fund taxes, and a state may hold individuals liable for not providing workers' compensation insurance.

11. **Termination**

    a. Generally, subject to the LLC's solvency, a member is entitled to a return of his or her capital contribution upon dissolution or other specified event. But a member is liable to the LLC for a deficiency in the agreed contribution. A member also is liable for a return that violates the operating agreement or the LLC statute.

    b. An LLC is dissolved upon

        1) Expiration of a specified time period or occurrence of a specified event.
        2) Consent of a number or percentage of members provided in their agreement.
        3) Judicial determination of the following:

            a) Frustration of purpose
            b) Impracticability of continuing because of a member's conduct
            c) Impracticability of continuing under the articles and operating agreement
            d) Inappropriate behavior of controlling members or managers
            e) The equitability of liquidation

    c. Dissolution requires a public filing.

    d. **Dissociation** occurs when a member no longer is associated with the LLC. Under the ULLCA and in about half the states, it does not result in automatic dissolution.

    e. Liquidation results in payment of proceeds in the following order:

        1) Creditors
        2) Unpaid distributions to members
        3) Members' capital contributions
        4) Remaining amounts to members as agreed or in the same ratio as distributions

12. Summary of Noncorporate Business Entities

	Formation	Capitalization	Operation	Liability	Transferability	Taxation	Termination
Sole Proprietorship	No formalities. Formed at will of proprietor.	Only personal resources of propriety.	All decisions made by proprietor.	Unlimited personal liability for all losses and debts.	Interest may be transferred during proprietor's life. Proprietorship is then dissolved.	Only sole proprietor taxed	At proprietor's discretion, transfer of interest, and death of proprietor.
General Partnership	No formalities. No filings. Formed based on written or oral agreement.	Resources of partners.	Each partner has right to equal participation in management. Can restrict management rights to one or more partners.	Partners are jointly and severally liable for any partnership obligation.	Partner may transfer financial interest without loss of rights, duties, and liabilities as partner.	Tax reporting entity only. Partners subject to tax.	Dissociation followed by dissolution and winding up.
Limited Partnership	Formalities. Must file written certificate of limited partnership with state.	Resources of general and limited partners.	General partner has full management powers. Limited partner has no management powers.	General partner has unlimited liability for partnership liabilities. Limited partner liable only to extent of capital contribution.	General partner may transfer financial interest without loss of rights, duties, and liabilities as partner. Limited partner may assign interest.	Tax reporting entity only. Partners subject to tax.	Dissolved by death, bankruptcy, incapacity, etc., of a general partner.
Limited Liability Partnership	Formalities. Must file with Secretary of State and maintain professional liability insurance.	Resources of partners.	Favorable form of organization for professionals (e.g., lawyers, CPAs, etc.) All partners are general partners with limited liability.	Not personally liable for partnership obligations except to extent of LLP's assets. Partners remain personally liable for their own malpractice.	Partner may transfer financial interest without loss of rights, duties, and liabilities as partner.	Tax reporting entity only. Partners subject to tax.	Dissociation followed by dissolution and winding up.
Limited Liability Company	Formalities. Must file articles of organization with Secretary of State.	Contributions of members. Issuance of multiple classes of stock.	Unless provided otherwise, all members have equal rights to participate in management.	Owners who participate in management have limited liability.	A member can transfer his or her distributional interest. This interest is personal property.	May elect flow through taxation or be taxed as an entity.	Dissolution followed by liquidation.

Stop and review! You have completed the outline for this subunit. Study multiple-choice questions 26 through 30 beginning on page 533.

QUESTIONS

14.1 Sole Proprietorships

1. The formation of a sole proprietorship

A. Requires registration with the federal government's Small Business Administration.

B. Requires a formal "doing business as" filing under state law if the proprietor will be conducting business under a fictitious name.

C. Requires formal registration in each state the proprietor plans to do business in.

D. Is not as easy and inexpensive to form as an S corporation.

Answer (B) is correct.

REQUIRED: The characteristic of the formation of a sole proprietorship.

DISCUSSION: A proprietor doing business under a fictitious name is usually required to make a d/b/a or "doing business as" filing under state law. Otherwise, the formation of a sole proprietorship is subject to few legal requirements, such as local zoning and licensing. In this respect, the sole proprietorship is the easiest and least expensive to create of all the business organizations.

Answer (A) is incorrect. The Small Business Administration (SBA) is a source of loans for sole proprietorships. No formal registration is required with the SBA. Answer (C) is incorrect. A sole proprietorship may conduct business in any state without having to file, register, or otherwise qualify to do business in that state. Answer (D) is incorrect. Of all business organizations, the sole proprietorship is the easiest and least expensive to create.

2. Bob decides to start a bicycle repair shop. He is the sole owner and raises additional capital by borrowing from a local bank. Which of the following may become at risk if Bob defaults on the repayment of the loan?

	Assets of the Bicycle Repair Shop	Bob's Equity Capital Invested	Bob's Personal Assets
A.	No	No	No
B.	Yes	No	No
C.	Yes	Yes	No
D.	Yes	Yes	Yes

Answer (D) is correct.

REQUIRED: The assets at risk if a sole proprietor defaults on the repayment of the loan.

DISCUSSION: Proprietors have unlimited personal liability for all losses and debts. All of Bob's assets related to the bicycle repair shop and even his personal assets may be at risk. Depending on the extent of the defaulting loan, the bank may claim rights against all of Bob's assets.

Answer (A) is incorrect. The assets of the bicycle repair shop and Bob's equity capital invested and personal assets may be at risk. Answer (B) is incorrect. Bob's equity capital invested and personal assets also may be at risk. Answer (C) is incorrect. Bob's personal assets may be at risk.

14.2 General Partnerships

3. Eller, Fort, and Owens do business as Venture Associates, a general partnership. Trent Corp. brought a breach of contract suit against Venture and Eller individually. Trent won the suit and filed a judgment against both Venture and Eller. Venture then entered bankruptcy. Under the RUPA, Trent will generally be able to collect the judgment in full from

A. Partnership assets but not partner personal assets.

B. The personal assets of Eller, Fort, and Owens.

C. Eller's personal assets only after partnership assets are exhausted.

D. Eller's personal assets.

Answer (D) is correct.

REQUIRED: The assets from which a judgment against a partnership and a specific partner may be collected.

DISCUSSION: The RUPA provides that partners are jointly and severally liable for all obligations of the partnership, including those arising out of a contract. The keys to the question are that (1) Trent sued both the partnership and one partner, (2) that partner can be held individually liable for the entire amount of a partnership obligation (joint and several liability), and (3) only parties who are judgment debtors can be held liable. Because Trent won the lawsuit against Venture and Eller, either Venture or Eller or both are liable for the judgment amount. Thus, the collection of the judgment will come from the partnership, Eller, or both. In this scenario, the partnership is in bankruptcy. When a plaintiff wins a judgment against a defendant in bankruptcy, the plaintiff typically collects very little, if any, of the judgment. Accordingly, Trent's judgment against the partnership will be subordinated to the claims of secured creditors and creditors with priority. As a result, Trent will likely seek to recover the full judgment from Eller's personal assets, given that Eller was a co-defendant in the lawsuit. Furthermore, because Venture is in bankruptcy, the RUPA provides that Trent need not seek a writ of execution against (compel collection of the judgment amount from) Venture before proceeding against Eller's personal assets.

Answer (A) is incorrect. Trent may collect in full from Eller. Answer (B) is incorrect. Fort and Owens must be judgment debtors to be held liable by Trent. Answer (C) is incorrect. Trent need not exhaust the partnership assets. Venture is in bankruptcy.

4. When parties intend to create a partnership that will be recognized under the Revised Uniform Partnership Act, they must agree to

	Conduct a Business for Profit	Share Gross Receipts from a Business
A.	Yes	Yes
B.	Yes	No
C.	No	Yes
D.	No	No

Answer (B) is correct.

REQUIRED: The item(s), if any, that must be agreed to when parties intend to create a partnership under the RUPA.

DISCUSSION: A partnership is an association of two or more persons conducting a business, which they co-own, for profit. Thus, partners must objectively intend that their business make a profit, even if no profit is earned. Each of the parties must be a co-owner; i.e., they share profits and losses of the venture and management authority (unless they agree otherwise).

Answer (A) is incorrect. The partnership agreement may specify that gross receipts are not shared. Answer (C) is incorrect. Partners must intend that their business make a profit, but partners do not have to agree to share gross receipts. Answer (D) is incorrect. Partners must intend that their business make a profit.

5. Dawn was properly admitted as a partner in the ABC Partnership after purchasing Jim's partnership interest. Jim immediately withdrew. The partnership agreement states that the partnership will continue on the withdrawal or admission of a partner. Unless the partners otherwise agree,

A. Dawn's personal liability for existing partnership debts will be limited to Dawn's interest in partnership property.

B. Jim will automatically be released from personal liability for partnership debts incurred before Dawn's admission.

C. Jim will be permitted to recover from the other partners the full amount that Jim paid on account of partnership debts incurred before Dawn's admission.

D. Dawn will be subjected to unlimited personal liability for partnership debts incurred before being admitted.

Answer (A) is correct.

REQUIRED: The effect on partnership liabilities of admitting a new partner.

DISCUSSION: As a new partner, Dawn's liability for previously existing partnership debts is limited to the amount of her capital contribution, which is Dawn's interest in partnership property.

Answer (B) is incorrect. Absent a novation, a withdrawing partner remains liable for debts incurred prior to withdrawal. Answer (C) is incorrect. Jim is liable for his share of debts incurred while he was a partner and would only be permitted to recover amounts he paid in excess of his share. Answer (D) is incorrect. Dawn's liability is limited to her capital contribution.

6. Gillie, Taft, and Dall are partners in an architectural firm. The partnership agreement is silent about the payment of salaries and the division of profits and losses. Gillie works full-time in the firm, and Taft and Dall each work half-time. Taft invested $120,000 in the firm, and Gillie and Dall invested $60,000 each. Dall is responsible for bringing in 50% of the business, and Gillie and Taft 25% each. How should profits of $120,000 for the year be divided?

	Gillie	Taft	Dall
A.	$60,000	$30,000	$30,000
B.	$40,000	$40,000	$40,000
C.	$30,000	$60,000	$30,000
D.	$30,000	$30,000	$60,000

Answer (B) is correct.

REQUIRED: The division of partnership profits when the partnership agreement is silent about salaries and the division of profits and losses.

DISCUSSION: Partners are not entitled to compensation for their actions, skill, and time applied on behalf of the partnership, except when such an arrangement is explicitly provided for in the partnership agreement. The partnership agreement is silent on this point, so salaries are not paid to the partners. Profits and losses may be divided among the partners according to any formula stipulated in the partnership agreement. In the absence of such a stipulation, partners share equally in the profits. Thus, each partner will receive $40,000.

7. Under the Revised Uniform Partnership Act, which of the following statements, if any, are correct regarding the effect of the assignment of an interest in a general partnership?

I. The assignee is personally responsible for the assigning partner's share of past and future partnership debts.

II. The assignee is entitled to the assigning partner's interest in partnership profits and surplus on dissolution of the partnership.

A. I only.

B. II only.

C. Both I and II.

D. Neither I nor II.

Answer (B) is correct.

REQUIRED: The true statement(s), if any, about assignment of an interest in a general partnership.

DISCUSSION: A partner's transferable interest consists of a partner's share of partnership profits and losses and the right to receive distributions. Partners may sell or otherwise transfer (assign) their interests to the partnership, another partner, or a third party without loss of the rights and duties of a partner (except the interest transferred). Moreover, unless all the other partners agree to accept the assignee as a new partner, the assignee does not become a partner in the firm. Without partnership status, the assignee has no obligation for partnership debts.

Answer (A) is incorrect. Without partnership status, the assignee has no obligation for partnership debts. Answer (C) is incorrect. Without partnership status, the assignee has no obligation for partnership debts. Answer (D) is incorrect. The assignee is entitled to the assigning partner's interest in partnership profits and surplus on dissolution of the partnership.

8. Cobb, Inc., a partner in TLC Partnership, assigns its partnership interest to Bean, who is not made a partner. After the assignment, Bean may assert the rights to

I. Participation in the management of TLC
II. Cobb's share of TLC's partnership profits

A. I only.

B. II only.

C. I and II.

D. Neither I nor II.

Answer (B) is correct.

REQUIRED: The right(s), if any, of an assignee of a partnership interest.

DISCUSSION: Partnership rights may be assigned without the dissolution of the partnership. The assignee is entitled only to the profits the assignor would normally receive. The assignee does not automatically become a partner and would not have the right to participate in managing the business or to inspect the books and records of the partnership. The assigning partner remains a partner with all the duties and other rights of a partner.

9. Leslie, Kelly, and Blair wanted to form a business. Which of the following business entities does **not** require the filing of organization documents with the state?

A. Limited partnership.

B. Joint venture.

C. Limited liability company.

D. Subchapter S corporation.

Answer (B) is correct.

REQUIRED: The entity created without a statutory filing.

DISCUSSION: A joint venture is an association to accomplish a specific business purpose. It is easily formed and is often organized for a single transaction. No statute requires a filing to create a joint venture.

Answer (A) is incorrect. A limited partnership is required by the RULPA to file a written certificate of limited partnership as a public record with the appropriate secretary of state. Answer (C) is incorrect. A limited liability company must file written articles of organization. Answer (D) is incorrect. A subchapter S corporation must file articles of incorporation with the state.

10. In a general partnership, which of the following acts must be approved by all the partners?

A. Dissolution of the partnership.

B. Admission of a partner.

C. Authorization of a partnership capital expenditure.

D. Conveyance of real property owned by the partnership.

Answer (B) is correct.

REQUIRED: The act that requires partner approval.

DISCUSSION: The right to choose associates means that no partner may be forced to accept any person as a partner. The RUPA states, "A person may become a partner only with the consent of all of the partners." When a partner transfers his or her interest to another, the purchaser or other transferee is entitled only to receive the share of profits and losses and the right to distributions allocated to the interest (s)he has acquired.

Answer (A) is incorrect. The dissolution of the partnership may result from notice of any partner's express will to withdraw. Answer (C) is incorrect. A partner's status grants at least apparent authority to act as an agent of the partnership in any legal transaction that is apparently for "carrying on in the ordinary course the partnership business or business of the kind carried on by the partnership" (business that is normal for the partnership or for a similar partnership). Answer (D) is incorrect. Subject to a filed statement of authority, property in the name of the partnership may be transferred by any partner in the partnership name.

11. What is a possible disadvantage of forming an LLP as opposed to remaining a general partnership?

A. Creation and continuation require compliance with statutory provisions.

B. Partners are subject to a broad personal liability shield.

C. LLPs are pass-through entities.

D. Termination of an LLP involves the same process as in a general partnership.

Answer (A) is correct.

REQUIRED: The possible disadvantage of forming an LLP.

DISCUSSION: A disadvantage of the LLP is that its creation and continuation require compliance with statutory provisions. Thus, becoming an LLP is more complicated because the partners must amend the partnership agreement and file a statement of qualification with the secretary of state.

Answer (B) is incorrect. The personal liability shield is an advantage of the formation of an LLP. Answer (C) is incorrect. Avoiding the double taxation of the corporate entity is an advantage of an LLP. Answer (D) is incorrect. The simple dissolution and winding up of a general partnership should be viewed as an advantage of the LLP formation.

12. The apparent authority of a partner to bind the partnership in dealing with third parties

A. Will be effectively limited by a formal resolution of the partners of which third parties are unaware.

B. Will be effectively limited by the filing of a statement of partnership authority.

C. Would permit a partner to submit a claim against the partnership to arbitration.

D. Must be derived from the express powers and purposes contained in the partnership agreement.

Answer (B) is correct.

REQUIRED: The true statement about the apparent authority of a partner.

DISCUSSION: Each partner in a general partnership is an agent of the partnership. The partners may not limit partnership liability to third parties by agreement among the partners alone. But apparent authority is effectively limited to the extent a third party knows of limitations imposed on a partner's authority. The RUPA provides for filing of a statement of authority that may give notice of limitations on the authority of a partner.

Answer (A) is incorrect. The scope of apparent authority is limited by the filing of a statement of authority in accordance with RUPA. Answer (C) is incorrect. The scope of apparent authority is limited to "carrying on in the ordinary course the partnership business or business of the kind carried on by the partnership." Thus, actual authority most likely is required to bind the partnership to arbitration. Answer (D) is incorrect. Apparent authority is derived from words or actions of the principal (the partnership) that reasonably induce a third party to rely on the agent's (partner's) authority. The partnership is bound even if the partner had no actual authority in the matter unless the third party knew or had received notification of the lack of actual authority.

13. Wind, who has been a partner in the PLW general partnership for 4 years, decides to withdraw from the partnership despite a written partnership agreement that states, "No partner may withdraw for a period of 5 years." Under the Revised Uniform Partnership Act (RUPA), what is the result of Wind's withdrawal?

A. Wind's withdrawal causes a dissolution of the partnership by operation of law.

B. Wind's withdrawal has no bearing on the continued operation of the partnership by the remaining partners.

C. Wind's withdrawal is not effective until Wind obtains a court-ordered decree of dissolution.

D. Wind's withdrawal causes dissociation from the partnership despite being in violation of the partnership agreement.

Answer (D) is correct.

REQUIRED: The result of an early withdrawal from a partnership.

DISCUSSION: Under the RUPA, a partnership is considered an entity substantially separate from its partners. A partner has the power (if not the right) to dissociate at any time. However, if the partner wrongfully dissociates from the partnership, (s)he is liable for any resulting damages to the other partners. After dissociation, the business either continues after purchase of the dissociated partner's interest or dissolution begins.

Answer (A) is incorrect. A partnership is not dissolved by operation of law under RUPA when a partner withdraws. Such a dissolution results from such events as the illegality of the business and certain judicial determinations. Answer (B) is incorrect. Wind will remain liable to creditors for predissociation obligations and any post-dissociation contracts for up to 2 years unless (s)he files a statement of dissociation. Answer (C) is incorrect. A court-ordered decree is not needed for the withdrawal to be effective. The partner may withdraw by notice to the partnership of an express will to withdraw.

14. X, Y, and Z have capital balances of $30,000, $15,000, and $5,000, respectively, in the XYZ Partnership. The general partnership agreement is silent as to the manner in which partnership losses are to be allocated but does provide that partnership profits are to be allocated as follows: 40% to X, 25% to Y, and 35% to Z. The partners have decided to dissolve and liquidate the partnership. After paying all creditors, the amount available for distribution will be $20,000. X, Y, and Z are individually solvent. Z will

A. Receive $7,000.

B. Receive $12,000.

C. Personally have to contribute an additional $5,500.

D. Personally have to contribute an additional $5,000.

Answer (C) is correct.

REQUIRED: The distribution of partnership assets after dissolution and liquidation.

DISCUSSION: Upon termination, a partnership must first pay all creditors, including partners who are creditors, and then distribute the remaining assets to the partners. In this case, $20,000 is available for distribution. However, the total of capital contributions is $50,000, and a $30,000 ($50,000 capital contributions – $20,000 available for distribution) loss must be allocated among the partners. When the partnership agreement does not specify otherwise, losses are allocated in the same ratio as profits. Thus, Z is properly allocated 35% of the loss, or $10,500 ($30,000 × 35%). Z's capital contribution of $5,000 is less than Z's share of the loss. Thus, Z must contribute an additional $5,500 to the partnership.

Answer (A) is incorrect. It allocates 35% of the amount available for distribution without regard to the capital contributions of the partners. Answer (B) is incorrect. If partnership assets are insufficient to return any partner's capital contribution, each partner is obligated to contribute cash to enable it. Answer (D) is incorrect. The obligation to contribute cash to permit return of capital is allocated to partners in the same proportion as is a partnership loss.

15. Under the RUPA, in which of the following situations will a partner in an LLP most likely be personally liable?

A. The managing partner in the Texas office when individuals in the New York office engaged in fraudulent activities.

B. The managing partner in the New York office when an employee in the office who was supervised by another partner engaged in fraudulent activities.

C. The partner who personally incurs an obligation in the conduct of partnership business.

D. A nonmanaging partner in an office where another partner committed negligence.

Answer (C) is correct.

REQUIRED: The situation in which a partner in an LLP is liable.

DISCUSSION: A partner who personally incurs an obligation in the conduct of partnership business is fully liable. The shield is provided only for liability that is imputed simply because a partner is a partner, not for liability directly incurred by the partner.

Answer (A) is incorrect. The managing partner in the Texas office has nothing to do with fraudulent activities in the New York office. Answer (B) is incorrect. Unlike the limitation in a limited partnership, the liability shield in an LLP protects the partners who manage the business. Answer (D) is incorrect. Under the RUPA, the liability shield extends to any obligation of the LLP.

16. A limited liability partnership (LLP)

A. Starts as a corporation.

B. Is typically adopted by providers of professional services.

C. Is ordinarily treated as a legal entity to the same extent as a corporation.

D. Offers a liability shield only for professional malpractice.

Answer (B) is correct.

REQUIRED: The true statement about an LLP.

DISCUSSION: An LLP is a general partnership that has been changed to LLP status in accordance with state law. The LLP is a business structure that is often adopted by providers of professional services (e.g., attorneys, CPAs, and physicians) and family enterprises.

Answer (A) is incorrect. An LLP is typically a general partnership that has been changed to LLP status in accordance with state law. Answer (C) is incorrect. An LLP is ordinarily treated as a legal entity to the same extent as a general partnership. Answer (D) is incorrect. Early statutes provided the limitation on personal liability only for professional malpractice, but most states have now enacted LLP legislation that provides for a broad personal liability shield.

14.3 Limited Partnerships

17. The XYZ Limited Partnership has two general partners: Smith and Jones. A provision in the partnership agreement allows the removal of a general partner by a majority vote of the limited partners. The limited partners vote to remove Jones as a general partner. Which of the following statements is true?

A. The limited partners are now liable to third parties for partnership obligations.

B. Limited partners may vote to remove a general partner without losing their status as limited partners.

C. By voting to remove a general partner, the limited partners are presumed to exercise control of the business.

D. Limited partners may participate in management decisions without limitation if this right is provided for in the limited partnership agreement.

Answer (B) is correct.

REQUIRED: The effect on the status of limited partners of voting for removal of a general partner.

DISCUSSION: A limited partner is not liable to third parties for partnership obligations if the limited partner does not take part in the control of the business. The RULPA lists several activities in which a limited partner may engage without being considered in the control of the business, among them, voting on the removal of a general partner. Excessive involvement in the management of the business may constitute taking part in the control of the business. The result is liability to those parties who have knowledge of the limited partner's participation in control or, if the limited partner is exercising the powers of a general partner, to all third parties.

Answer (A) is incorrect. Voting on the removal of a general partner is allowed by the RULPA. Answer (C) is incorrect. Voting to remove a general partner is an activity listed in the RULPA as not constituting taking part in the control of the business. Answer (D) is incorrect. Excessive involvement in the management of the business may constitute taking part in the control of the business. The result is liability to those parties who have knowledge of the limited partner's participation in control or, if the limited partner is exercising the powers of a general partner, to all third parties.

18. Marshall formed a limited partnership for the purpose of engaging in the export-import business. Marshall obtained additional working capital from Franklin and Lee by selling them each a limited partnership interest. Under these circumstances, the limited partnership

A. Will usually be treated as a taxable entity for federal income tax purposes.

B. Will lose its status as a limited partnership if it has more than one general partner.

C. Can limit the liability of all partners.

D. Can exist as such only if it is formed under the authority of a state statute.

Answer (D) is correct.

REQUIRED: The true statement regarding a limited partnership.

DISCUSSION: The limited partnership is not available as a form of business organization under the common law. An organization purporting to be a limited partnership but formed in a state with no statutory authority for such a form of business organization will very likely be treated as a general partnership.

Answer (A) is incorrect. A partnership is not a taxable entity for federal income tax purposes. Partnerships are required to file informational returns only. Answer (B) is incorrect. A limited partnership may have more than one general partner. The minimum is at least one limited and one general partner. Answer (C) is incorrect. At least one general partner must have unlimited personal liability.

19. Stanley Kowalski is a well-known retired movie personality who purchased a limited partnership interest in Terrific Movie Productions upon its initial syndication. Which of the following is true?

A. If Stanley permits his name to be used in connection with the business and is held out as a participant in the management of the venture, he will be liable as a general partner.

B. The sale of these limited partnership interests is not subject to SEC registration.

C. This limited partnership may be formed with the same informality as a general partnership.

D. The general partners are prohibited from also owning limited partnership interests.

Answer (A) is correct.

REQUIRED: The true statement about a limited partnership.

DISCUSSION: A limited partner who permits his or her name to be used in the name of the partnership or in connection with the business is liable to creditors who give credit without actual knowledge that (s)he is not a general partner. Such a limited partner forfeits limited liability because the use of his or her name may lead unsuspecting creditors to believe that (s)he is a general partner with unlimited liability.

Answer (B) is incorrect. Limited partnership interests are considered to be securities and must be registered with the SEC unless an exemption applies. Answer (C) is incorrect. A limited partnership can be formed only under a statute permitting the formation and existence of limited partnerships. Such statutes require many formalities. Answer (D) is incorrect. A general partner also may be a limited partner.

20. A valid limited partnership

A. Cannot be treated as an “association” for federal income tax purposes.

B. May have an unlimited number of partners.

C. Is exempt from all Securities and Exchange Commission regulations.

D. Must designate in its certificate the name, address, and capital contribution of each general partner and each limited partner.

Answer (B) is correct.

REQUIRED: The true statement regarding a valid limited partnership.

DISCUSSION: A valid limited partnership has no maximum limit on the number of partners (limited or general). The only requirement is that it have at least one limited and one general partner. In contrast, S corporations currently have a limit of 100 shareholders.

Answer (A) is incorrect. A partnership will be treated as an association (and taxed as a corporation) if it has more corporate than partnership attributes. Answer (C) is incorrect. A limited partnership interest is considered a security and generally subject to SEC regulations. Answer (D) is incorrect. Under the RULPA, the name and business address of each general partner (but not the other information) must be included in the certificate.

21. Which of the following rights would a limited partner **not** be entitled to assert?

A. To have a formal accounting of partnership affairs whenever the circumstances render it just and reasonable.

B. To have the same rights as a general partner to a dissolution and winding up of the partnership.

C. To have reasonable access to the partnership books and to inspect and copy them.

D. To be elected as a general partner by a majority vote of the limited partners in number and amount.

Answer (D) is correct.

REQUIRED: The right that a limited partner is not entitled to assert.

DISCUSSION: A new general partner may be admitted to a limited partnership only with the specific written consent of each and every partner (both limited and general). The limited partners therefore do not have the power to admit new general partners, and unanimous consent is needed unless the partnership agreement provides otherwise.

Answer (A) is incorrect. A limited partner is entitled to an accounting if the circumstances are reasonable. Answer (B) is incorrect. A limited partner has the same rights as a general partner in winding up a partnership. Answer (C) is incorrect. A limited partner has a reasonable right to access books and records.

22. A limited partner’s capital contribution to the limited partnership

A. Results in the limited partner having an intangible personal property right.

B. Can be withdrawn at the limited partner’s option at any time prior to the filing of a petition in bankruptcy against the limited partnership.

C. Can only consist of cash or marketable securities.

D. Must be indicated in the limited partnership’s certificate.

Answer (A) is correct.

REQUIRED: The true statement regarding a limited partner’s capital contribution.

DISCUSSION: The limited partner’s interest is an investment in the entity as a whole. The interest is personal property. It constitutes an intangible because the limited partner has no right to specific partnership property.

Answer (B) is incorrect. A limited partner’s right of withdrawal of his or her capital contribution is restricted. It may be withdrawn upon the dissolution of the partnership, at the date specified in the certificate, upon 6 months’ notice in writing to all the members, or with the consent of all the members but only if all creditors are paid or sufficient assets are available for creditors. Answer (C) is incorrect. A limited partner’s capital contribution may consist of cash, other property, or services. Answer (D) is incorrect. A limited partner’s contribution need not be described in the certificate.

23. Absent any contrary provisions in the agreement, under which of the following circumstances will a limited partnership be dissolved?

A. A limited partner dies and his or her estate is insolvent.

B. A personal creditor of a general partner obtains a judgment against the general partner’s interest in the limited partnership.

C. A general partner retires and all the remaining general partners do not consent to continue.

D. A limited partner assigns his or her partnership interest to an outsider and the purchaser becomes a substituted limited partner.

Answer (C) is correct.

REQUIRED: The circumstance in which a limited partnership is dissolved.

DISCUSSION: Retirement of a general partner generally dissolves a limited partnership or a general partnership. However, dissolution can be avoided if the business is continued by the remaining general partners either with the consent of all partners or pursuant to a stipulation in the partnership agreement.

Answer (A) is incorrect. The death of a limited partner, regardless of the solvency of the estate, does not dissolve the partnership. Answer (B) is incorrect. A judgment against the interest of a general partner is similar to an assignment of that interest, which does not dissolve the partnership. Answer (D) is incorrect. The assignment of a limited partnership interest does not dissolve the partnership. It makes no difference whether the assignee becomes a substituted limited partner.

24. Ms. Wall is a limited partner of the Amalgamated Limited Partnership. She is insolvent, and her debts exceed her assets by $28,000. Goldsmith, one of Wall's largest creditors, is resorting to legal process to obtain the payment of Wall's debt to him. Goldsmith has obtained a charging order against Wall's limited partnership interest for the unsatisfied amount of the debt. As a result of Goldsmith's action, which of the following will happen?

A. The partnership will be dissolved.

B. Wall's partnership interest must be redeemed with partnership property.

C. Goldsmith automatically becomes a substituted limited partner.

D. Goldsmith becomes in effect an assignee of Wall's partnership interest.

Answer (D) is correct.

REQUIRED: The result when a creditor obtains a charging order against an insolvent limited partner's interest.

DISCUSSION: A charging order is a court order that has the effect of an involuntary assignment of the limited partner's interest to the judgment-creditor (or an independent third party called a receiver). The limited partner's interest may be temporarily assigned until the profits distributed pay off the debt, or it may be permanently assigned using its fair value to pay off the debt.

Answer (A) is incorrect. A limited partnership is not dissolved by the bankruptcy of a limited partner or by assignment of his or her interest. Answer (B) is incorrect. Wall's partnership interest is not required to be redeemed. Answer (C) is incorrect. An assignee of a limited partnership interest does not become a substituted limited partner unless the assignor gives the assignee that right pursuant to the limited partnership agreement, or all the members of the partnership agree.

25. Wichita Properties is a limited partnership created in accordance with the provisions of the Uniform Limited Partnership Act. The partners have voted to dissolve and settle the partnership's accounts. Which of the following will be the last to be paid?

A. General partners for unpaid distributions.

B. Limited partners in respect to capital.

C. Limited and general partners in respect to their undistributed profits.

D. General partners in respect to capital.

Answer (C) is correct.

REQUIRED: The lowest priority of distribution upon liquidation of a limited partnership.

DISCUSSION: Under the RULPA, limited and general partners are treated equally. Unless the partnership agreement provides otherwise, assets are distributed as follows:

1) Creditors (including all partner-creditors)
2) Partners for unpaid distributions (i.e., declared but not paid)
3) Partners for the return of their contributions
4) Partners for remaining assets (i.e., undistributed profits) in the proportions in which they share distributions

14.4 Limited Liability Companies (LLCs)

26. Which of the following is a legal entity separate from its owners?

A. Limited partnership.

B. LLP.

C. LLC.

D. All of the answers are correct.

Answer (D) is correct.

REQUIRED: The entities that are legally separate from their owners.

DISCUSSION: Limited partnerships, LLPs, and LLCs are legally separate from their owners. Such an entity may enter into contracts, sue, be sued, and own property in its own name.

Answer (A) is incorrect. A limited partnership is allowed to be legally separate from its owners. Answer (B) is incorrect. An LLP is allowed to be legally separate from its owners. Answer (C) is incorrect. An LLC is allowed to be legally separate from its owners.

27. In the absence of a member agreement, how are profits and losses shared by members of an LLC formed under the Uniform Limited Liability Company Act (ULLCA)?

A. In proportion to their capital contributions.

B. Equally.

C. In proportion to their voting power.

D. In proportion to their partnership interests.

Answer (B) is correct.

REQUIRED: The distribution of profits and losses by an LLC formed under the ULLCA.

DISCUSSION: In the absence of a contrary agreement, profits and losses are shared equally in an LLC formed under the ULLCA. A member is not automatically entitled to compensation, except when winding up the enterprise.

28. The owners of a limited liability company are known as which of the following?

A. Partners.

B. Members.

C. Stockholders.

D. Shareholders.

Answer (B) is correct.

REQUIRED: The owners of a limited liability company.

DISCUSSION: An LLC combines the limited liability of the corporation with the tax advantages of the general partnership. Like a corporation, a limited partnership, and an LLP, an LLC is a legal entity separate from its owner-investors (called members) that can be created only under state law.

Answer (A) is incorrect. Partners are the owners of a partnership. Answer (C) is incorrect. Stockholders (also called shareholders) are the owners of a corporation. Answer (D) is incorrect. Shareholders (also called stockholders) are the owners of a corporation.

29. Which of the following parties generally has the most management rights?

A. Minority shareholder in a corporation listed on a national stock exchange.

B. Limited partner in a general partnership.

C. Member of a limited liability company.

D. Limited partner in a limited partnership.

Answer (C) is correct.

REQUIRED: The party that generally has the most management rights.

DISCUSSION: In a member-managed LLC, all members have a right to participate, and most business matters are decided by the majority. In a manager-managed LLC, each manager has equal rights, but managers are selected or removed by a majority vote of the members. An LLC is deemed to be member-managed unless the articles of organization state otherwise.

Answer (A) is incorrect. A minority shareholder in a public corporation generally has little or no management rights. Answer (B) is incorrect. A general partnership has no limited partners. Answer (D) is incorrect. In a limited partnership, a limited partner has no authority to participate in management and control of the business.

30. Which of the following is **least** likely to dissolve an LLC?

A. Expiration of a certain time period specified in the operating agreement.

B. Judicial determination of the equitability of liquidation.

C. Dissociation by any member.

D. Death of a member as outlined in the articles of organization.

Answer (C) is correct.

REQUIRED: The dissolution of an LLC.

DISCUSSION: The consent of the number or percentage of members specified in their operating agreement, not necessarily unanimous consent, dissolves an LLC. An LLC also will be dissolved upon expiration of a specified time period, death of a member as mentioned in the articles of organization, and judicial determination of the equitability of liquidation. However, mere dissociation of a member, absent a provision in the operating agreement, does not generally result in dissolution of the LLC.

Answer (A) is incorrect. An LLC will be dissolved by the expiration of a specified time period. Answer (B) is incorrect. An LLC will be dissolved by a judicial determination of the equitability of liquidation. Answer (D) is incorrect. Death of a member as outlined in its articles will result in dissolution. If the articles of organization provide for a member's death to dissolve an LLC, that will be sufficient.

14.5 PRACTICE TASK-BASED SIMULATIONS

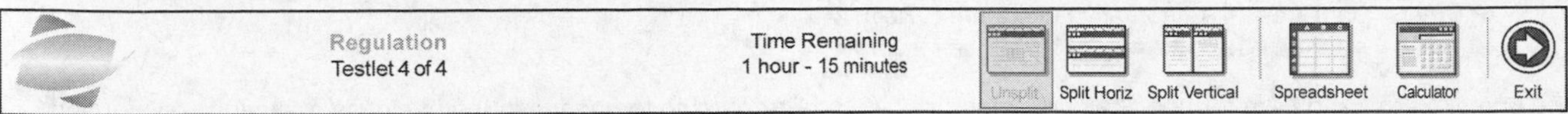

DIRECTIONS

Note: If you believe you have encountered a software malfunction, report it to the test center staff immediately.

Navigation

To navigate from task to task, use the controls at the bottom of the screen. Click on the **Next** button to advance to the next task, or the **Previous** button to go to the previous task. To go directly to any task, click on its number.

If you would like a reminder to revisit a task, or want to indicate that you are finished with it, click on the reminder flag below the task number. To clear the flag, click on it again. Reminder flags are for your use only – they do not contribute to your score.

Tabs

In this part of the examination, you will be asked to complete various tasks. Every task has one or more **Work Tabs**. Some tasks have one or more **Information Tabs**, others may have none. Every task has a **Help** tab.

If a task has **Information Tabs**, you may use the information in them to complete your responses in the **Work Tabs**.

Work tab **Information tab** **Help tab**

Work Tabs:

- **Work Tabs** are identified with a pencil icon. This is where your responses are expected.
- Each task has one or more **Work Tabs**.
- **Work Tabs** contain directions for completing the task – be sure to read these directions carefully.
- The **Work Tab** name in the example above is for illustration only – yours will differ.
- You must complete all of the **Work Tabs** in each task to receive full credit.

Information Tabs:

- The Authoritative Literature will be provided in all tasks in the AUD, FAR, and REG sections for your reference.
- Your simulation may have one or more additional **Information Tabs**. Like the Authoritative Literature tabs, **Information Tabs** do not have a pencil icon.
- If your task has additional **Information Tabs**, go through each to familiarize yourself with the task content.

Help Tab:

- The **Help Tab** provides assistance with the exam software that is used in this task. For example, if the task is to compose a memorandum, **Help** will provide information about the word processor.

The Toolbar

The toolbar at the top of the screen shows the amount of time remaining for you to complete the tasks. In addition, the following tools are available. Note that only the **Exit** button is displayed when Directions are visible - the others will appear when you begin the tasks.

Click on these buttons to split or unsplit the screen. You can split the screen vertically or horizontally.

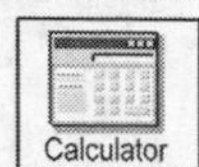

Click on this button to display the calculator; click on it again to hide the calculator. To move the calculator, click on the calculator title bar and drag the calculator to the desired location.

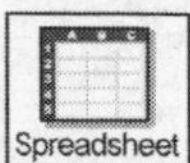

Click on this button to use the spreadsheet; click on it again to hide the spreadsheet. To move the spreadsheet, click on the the spreadsheet title bar and drag the spreadsheet to the desired location.

Click on this button to go on to the next part of the examination. You must complete all of the tasks to receive full credit. Once you click on **Exit** and confirm the action, you will NOT be able to return to this testlet.

= Reminder | Directions | 1 2 3 4 5 6 | Previous | Next

Gennie, Gerry, and Lem formed Sterling Properties Limited Partnership to engage in the business of buying, selling, and managing real estate. Gennie and Gerry were general partners. Lem was a limited partner entitled to 50% of all profits. Gennie, Gerry, and Lem agreed that Gerry's personal liability be limited to 25% of each partnership liability.

Within a few months of Sterling's formation, it became apparent to Lem that Gennie and Gerry's inexperience was likely to result in financial disaster for the partnership. Thus, Lem became more involved in day-to-day management decisions. Lem met with prospective buyers and sellers of properties, assisted in negotiating partnership loans with its various lenders, and took an active role in dealing with personnel problems. Things continued to deteriorate for Sterling, and the partners began blaming each other for the partnership's problems.

Finally, Gennie could no longer deal with the situation and withdrew from the partnership. Gerry reminded Gennie that the Sterling partnership agreement specifically prohibited withdrawal by a general partner without the consent of all the other partners. Gennie advised Gerry and Lem that she would take no part in any further partnership undertaking and would not be responsible for partnership debts incurred after this withdrawal.

With Sterling on the verge of collapse, the following situations have occurred:

- Anchor Bank, which made a loan to the partnership prior to Gennie's withdrawal, is suing Sterling and each partner individually, including Gennie, because the loan is in default. Lem denied any liability based on his limited partner status. Gennie denies liability based on her withdrawal.
- Gerry sued Gennie for withdrawing from the partnership and is uncertain about the effect of her withdrawal on the partnership.
- Lem assigned his partnership interest to Larry, who wants to become a substitute limited partner.
- Gerry, after all the above occurs, assigns his partnership interest to Garth. Larry consents to Garth's admission as a new partner, and Garth and Larry release Gerry from all prior or future partnership obligations.

Select from the list the level of liability that best describes each person's liability for the Anchor Bank loan. Each choice may be used once, more than once, or not at all.

Person	***Liability***
1. Sterling Properties	
2. Gennie	
3. Gerry	
4. Garth	
5. Lem	
6. Larry	

Choices
A) No Liability
B) A share of partnership capital
C) Partnership capital
D) Distribution to which the assignor is entitled
E) The partner's partnership interest
F) 25% of the obligation
G) Partnership property
H) The net assets of the partnership
I) The partner's net personal assets

Tiny, Slim, and Skinny are all general partners of JeansForYou. Tiny contributed $50,000, Slim contributed $30,000, and Skinny contributed $20,000. For each of the following situations, determine the amount of profit (loss) that will be allocated to Tiny, Slim, and Skinny.

Situation	*Tiny*	*Slim*	*Skinny*
1. JeansForYou had a net profit of $30,000.			
2. JeansForYou had a net profit of $60,000, and the partners have decided to allocate profits in the ratio of their financial contributions.			
3. JeansForYou had a net loss of $90,000.			
4. JeansForYou had a net loss of $120,000. The partnership agreement stated that profits are to be allocated equally but that losses should be allocated based on partner contributions.			

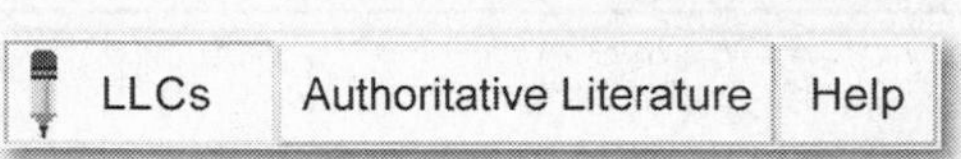

Indicate whether each statement below applies to a limited liability company (LLC) by checking the appropriate box:

Statement	*Yes*	*No*
1. An entity that has the liability of a corporation and the tax advantages of a partnership.		
2. An entity that requires a written operating agreement.		
3. An entity that must have two or more members.		
4. According to state statutes, an entity that must share profits and losses equally, absent a contrary agreement.		
5. An entity that may have multiple classes of stock.		
6. An interest in this entity may be regulated under the Securities Act of 1933 and the Securities Exchange Act of 1934.		

Teresa intends to enter into a partnership with three of her business associates. She is uncertain as to the advantages and disadvantages of becoming a limited partner or a general partner. Select from the list provided which status has the stated right or duty in each situation. Each choice may be used once, more than once, or not at all.

Right or Duty	Answer
1. Participation in the daily management of the partnership.	
2. Liability for all debts incurred on behalf of or by the partnership.	
3. The ability to assign the partnership interest.	
4. An increase in liability if a court dissolves the partnership.	
5. An increase in liability if a general partner becomes bankrupt and cannot pay amounts owed to the partnership.	

Choices
A) Limited
B) General
C) Neither limited nor general
D) Both limited and general

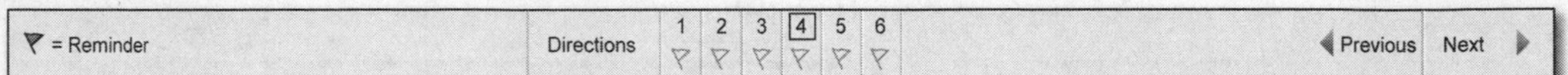

For each of the following situations, select from the list provided the effect on the business entity. Each choice may be used once, more than once, or not at all.

Situation	Answer
1. Shaun, the owner of Puppy Palace (a sole proprietorship), transferred his interest in Puppy Palace to Deborah.	
2. THF is a partnership owned by Tiffany, Heather, and Frannie. After 3 years, Frannie no longer wanted to work with Tiffany, so Frannie sold her interest in the partnership to Tiffany and Heather.	
3. Hotels LLC, was formed to sell vacant hotels to people visiting Rancho Cucomongo during its world-famous "Parade Month." Unfortunately, the governor of Rancho Cucomongo recently passed legislation that canceled "Parade Month" indefinitely.	
4. GSL is a limited partner. During their 5th year of operation, Larry, one of the limited partners, declared bankruptcy.	
5. On December 10, the sole owner of Kitty Castle, passed away.	
6. After 10 years of success, K&W partnership is done and began the process of settling partnership affairs.	

List
A) Dissociation
B) Dissolution
C) Winding Up
D) Termination
E) No effect

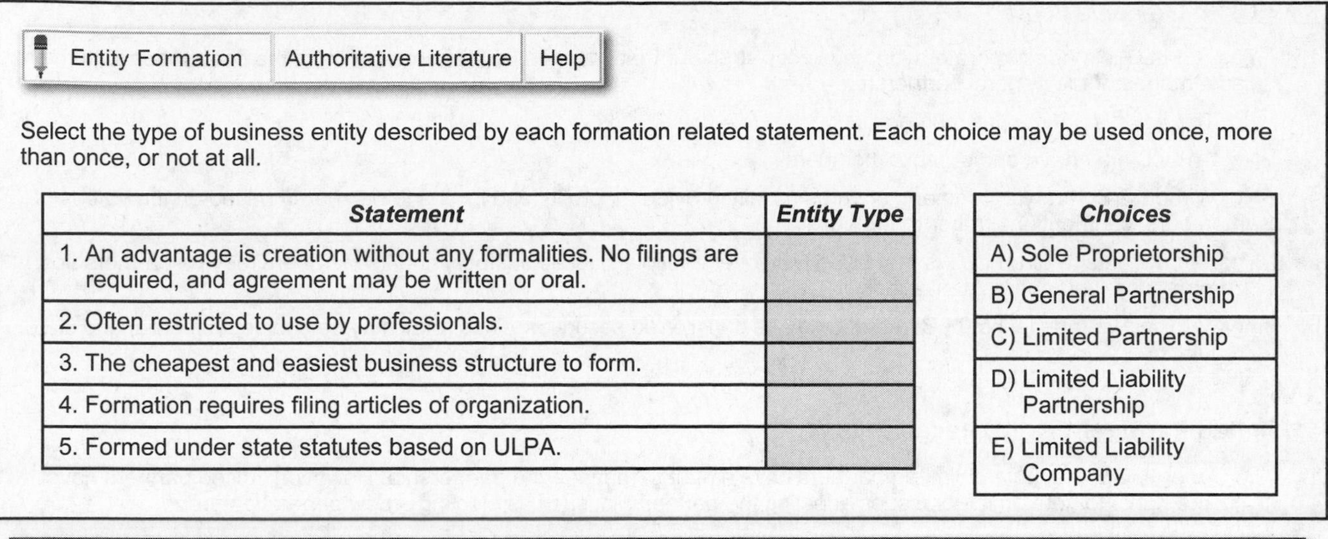

Entity Formation | Authoritative Literature | Help

Select the type of business entity described by each formation related statement. Each choice may be used once, more than once, or not at all.

Statement	Entity Type
1. An advantage is creation without any formalities. No filings are required, and agreement may be written or oral.	
2. Often restricted to use by professionals.	
3. The cheapest and easiest business structure to form.	
4. Formation requires filing articles of organization.	
5. Formed under state statutes based on ULPA.	

Choices
A) Sole Proprietorship
B) General Partnership
C) Limited Partnership
D) Limited Liability Partnership
E) Limited Liability Company

Unofficial Answers

1. Partners' Liabilities (6 Gradable Items)

1. H) The net assets of the partnership. A partnership is liable for the full amount of its obligations.
2. I) The partner's net personal assets. A general partner has unlimited liability for partnership liabilities. Thus, a creditor of the partnership has a claim against the general partner's personal assets for the partnership obligation. Withdrawal from the partnership does not nullify liability for partnership obligations incurred prior to withdrawal.
3. I) The partner's net personal assets. An agreement between partners limiting or allocating partnership liabilities does not limit the amount of each partner's liability to the partnership's creditors. Assignment of the general partnership interest does not relieve the general partner from liability for partnership obligations incurred before the assignment.
4. D) Distribution to which the assignor is entitled. Under the RULPA, Gerry's assignment of his partnership interest terminated his status as a partner. However, except as provided in the partnership agreement, an assignment does not confer on the assignee the status of a general or limited partner. Thus, Garth is a mere assignee who is entitled only to the distribution to which the assignor is entitled.
5. I) The partner's net personal assets. The limited partner's liability to a partnership creditor is generally limited to the value of his or her interest in the partnership. However, Lem has taken part in the control of the business. Thus, Lem will be treated as a general partner with unlimited liability despite assigning the partnership interest.
6. D) Distribution to which the assignor is entitled. Larry is a mere assignee of Lem's interest. Larry is therefore entitled only to the distribution to which the assignor is entitled.

2. Allocation of Profits (4 Gradable Items)

1. $10,000; $10,000; $10,000. The right to share profits, unless otherwise agreed, allows each partner to have an equal share regardless of differences in contributions. Because no other agreement is mentioned, each partner receives $10,000 of the profits ($30,000 ÷ 3 partners).
2. $30,000; $18,000; $12,000. The profits are allocated according to the ratio of their financial contributions. Therefore, Tiny receives $30,000 {$60,000 × [$50,000 ÷ ($50,000 + $30,000 + $20,000)]}, Slim receives $18,000 {$60,000 × [$30,000 ÷ ($50,000 + $30,000 + $20,000)]}, and Skinny receives $12,000 {$60,000 × [$20,000 ÷ ($50,000 + $30,000 + $20,000)]}.
3. ($30,000); ($30,000); ($30,000). Unless otherwise agreed, each partner must contribute in proportion to his or her share of the profits toward any losses of the partnership. Thus, because no other agreement is mentioned, each partner receives $30,000 of loss ($90,000 ÷ 3 partners).
4. ($60,000); ($36,000); ($24,000). The losses are allocated according to the ratio of their financial contributions. Thus, Tiny receives $60,000 of loss {$120,000 × [$50,000 ÷ ($50,000 + $30,000 + $20,000)]}, Slim receives $36,000 of loss {$120,000 × [$30,000 ÷ ($50,000 + $30,000 + $20,000)]}, and Skinny receives $24,000 of loss {$120,000 × [$20,000 ÷ ($50,000 + $30,000 + $20,000)]}.

3. LLCs (6 Gradable Items)

1. Yes. An LLC is a noncorporate hybrid business structure that combines the limited liability of the corporation with the tax advantages of the general partnership.
2. No. The agreement may also be oral.
3. No. An LLC may have one or more members
4. No. Without a contrary agreement, statutes usually provide for profits and losses to be shared based on the values of members' contributions rather than equally.
5. Yes. An advantage of an LLC is that LLCs may offer multiple classes of stock, and its members may be partnerships, corporations, and nonresident aliens.
6. Yes. A disadvantage is that LLC interest may be considered securities. Thus, they may be subject to federal and state regulation.

4. Limited Partnerships (5 Gradable Items)

1. B) General. General but not limited partners have a right to manage the partnership. However, limited partners have limited rights to vote on major issues affecting the partnership, such as electing a new general partner.
2. B) General. General partners, whether of a general partnership or a limited partnership, are personally liable for all debts of the partnership. Limited partners have limited liability.
3. D) Both limited and general. General and limited partners have the ability to assign their partnership interests to anyone. But the assignee does not thereby become a partner.
4. A) Limited. If a court finds that a limited partnership has not met the statutory requirements, the limited partners may become jointly and severally liable for all debts. But a general partner's liability for all partnership debts is not increased by a judicial or other dissolution of the partnership.
5. B) General. General partners, whether of a general partnership or limited partnership, are personally liable for all debts of the partnership. Limited partners have limited liability.

5. Termination (6 Gradable Items)

1. B) Dissolution. The interest of the proprietor may be transferred during his or her life, but the sole proprietorship is then dissolved.
2. A) Dissociation. Dissociation results from Frannie's notice to the partnership that she wants to withdraw. After dissociation, the business either continues after purchase of the dissociated partner's interest or dissolution begins.
3. B) Dissolution. An LLC will be dissolved upon judicial determination of frustration of purpose. Since the LLC was formed to sell hotels during Parade Month, the cancellation of Parade Month would constitute a frustration of purpose and the LLC will be dissolved.
4. E) No effect. The limited partnership is not dissolved by the bankruptcy, incapacity, or death of a limited partner.
5. D) Termination. The sole proprietorship is automatically terminated upon the proprietor's death.
6. C) Winding Up. Winding up is the administrative process of settling partnership affairs, including the use of partnership assets and any required contributions by partners to pay creditors.

6. Entity Formation (5 Gradable Items)

1. B) General Partnership. An advantage of the general partnership is that it can be created without any formalities. No filings are required, and the existence of the partnership may arise from a written or oral agreement.
2. D) Limited Liability Partnership. An LLP is a favorable form of organization for professionals who have not incorporated. In many states, this form is restricted to use by professionals.
3. A) Sole Proprietorship. Of all business structures, the sole proprietorship is the easiest and cheapest to create. It is formed at the will of the proprietor.
4. E) Limited Liability Company. An LLC can be formed only under a state statute, and for any lawful purpose. An LLC is formed by one or more persons who file articles of organization with the appropriate secretary of state.
5. C) Limited Partnership. A limited partnership is a partnership formed by two or more persons under a state statute. Most statutes are based on the Revised Uniform Limited Partnership Act (RULPA).

Gleim Simulation Grading

Task	Correct Responses		Gradable Items		Score per Task
1	____	÷	6	=	____
2	____	÷	4	=	____
3	____	÷	6	=	____
4	____	÷	5	=	____
5	____	÷	6	=	____
6	____	÷	5	=	____
			Total of Scores per Task		____
		÷	Total Number of Tasks		6
			Total Score		____%

STUDY UNIT FIFTEEN
CORPORATIONS

(20 pages of outline)

The basic forms of multiple-owner business structures are the partnership and the **corporation**. The corporation is the dominant form of business in the United States. The characteristic that distinguishes a corporation from all other business organizations is that, for all purposes, it is a **separate legal entity**. Unlike a sole proprietorship or a general partnership, its rights and obligations are separate from those of its owners or managers.

15.1 FORMATION

Background

In almost all cases, corporations are created under state law. Although state laws vary considerably, they are influenced by the **Model Business Corporation Act (MBCA)**, a statement of modern corporate law issued by the American Bar Association. Its purpose is to provide legislators, lawyers, and legal commissions with a basis for drafting and amending state incorporation laws. The MBCA has been amended frequently, and some of its provisions have been adopted to some degree by every state. The **Revised Model Business Corporation Act of 1984 (RMBCA)** applies to publicly held and closely held corporations. This outline is based on the RMBCA.

1. **Overview**
   a. Unlike a sole proprietorship or a general partnership, a corporation is a legal entity created under authority of a **state statute** to carry out the purposes permitted by that statute and the articles of incorporation.
      1) The corporation ordinarily is treated as a **legal person** with rights and obligations separate from its owners and managers.
   b. Corporations are governed by **shareholders** (owners) who elect a board of directors and approve fundamental changes in the corporate structure.
      1) **Directors** establish corporate policies and elect or appoint corporate **officers** who carry out the policies in the day-to-day management of the organization.
   c. A **private corporation** is organized to earn profits for its owners (for-profit corporation) or for charitable, educational, social, religious, or philanthropic purposes (not-for-profit corporation).
      1) The two most common types of private corporation are a close corporation and a publicly held corporation.
         a) A **close corporation** (or closely held corporation) has four primary characteristics:
            i) It is owned by a relatively small number of shareholders.
            ii) It does not sell its stock to the public.
            iii) The officers and directors commonly own all the stock in the corporation.
            iv) The shareholders are active in the management and control of the corporation.

b) A **publicly held corporation** sells its stock to the public, generally on a nationally recognized stock exchange. Its share price quotations are regularly published.

i) Shares of stock in the corporation are units of property interests in the net assets of the entity (including an interest in its profits).

d. A **public corporation** is organized for public purposes related to the administration of government, e.g., an incorporated municipality, and it may be funded by local taxes.

1) It is formed by specific legislation that defines its purpose and powers.

e. A corporation is **domestic** in the state in which it is organized, i.e., where its articles of incorporation are filed. It cannot be required to incorporate in any other state.

f. A corporation is **foreign** in every other state. A **certificate of authority** is required to **do business** within the borders of another state.

1) A corporation organized in another country is an **alien corporation**. It must obtain a certificate to do business from each host state.

g. An **S corporation's** shareholders have elected under federal law to be taxed similarly to a partnership. Thus, it usually does not pay income tax. (A **C corporation** is an entity subject to the corporate income tax.)

1) The shareholders report their proportionate shares of the entity's income, losses, deductions, and credits, regardless of whether they have received distributions.
2) S corporation status is terminated when one of the following eligibility requirements is not met:

a) The corporation may have only one class of stock.
b) The number of shareholders is limited to 100.
c) The corporation must be incorporated in the U.S.
d) An S corporation should not have excessive net passive investment income.
e) Shareholders are limited to individuals, estates, qualified trusts, banks, and certain tax-exempt entities (e.g., certain charities).
f) Nonresident aliens may not own shares.

h. **Professional corporations** (professional service associations) give accountants, lawyers, and other professionals the benefits of incorporation. Statutes typically restrict stock ownership to specific professionals licensed within that state.

2. **Preincorporation Contracts**

a. A **promoter** arranges for formation of the corporation. (S)he provides for the financing of the corporation and for compliance with any relevant securities law.

1) The promoter also may procure necessary personnel, services, assets, licenses, equipment, leases, etc.

b. **Prior to incorporation**, the promoter enters into ordinary and necessary contracts required for initial operation.

1) Promoters generally are personally liable on their contracts.
2) The corporation is not liable because a promoter cannot be an agent of a nonexistent entity. Prior to formation, a corporation cannot be a principal because it has no capacity to enter into contracts or employ agents.
3) A preincorporation contract made by promoters in the name of a corporation and on its behalf may bind the corporation if permitted by statute.

c. A corporation may **not ratify** a preincorporation contract because no principal existed at the time of contracting. However, **adoption** by the corporation is a legal substitute for ratification. It is acceptance of the assignment of rights and delegation of duties.

   1) Adoption may be implied from accepting the benefits of a contract.

d. If the promoter, the third party, and the corporation enter into a **novation** substituting the corporation for the promoter, only the corporation is liable and the promoter is released.

e. The promoter secures potential investors using **stock subscription agreements**. Each subscriber agrees to purchase a certain amount of stock at a specified price, payable at an agreed future time.

   1) It reflects an intent that the investor become a shareholder at the time of contracting.
   2) A **preincorporation subscription agreement** is irrevocable for 6 months, unless otherwise provided in the agreement, or all subscribers consent to revocation. Furthermore, many statutes provide that it be written.

3. **Incorporation**

a. Incorporation may be in any state. **Articles of incorporation** must be filed with the secretary of state or another designated official.

   1) A corporation may incorporate in one state but have its principal place of business or conduct its business operations in another state or states.

b. **Incorporators** sign the articles. Only one incorporator is required, and it may be a corporation or other entity.

c. Under the RMBCA, the articles must include the following:

   1) Corporation's name (must differ from the name of any corporation authorized to do business in the state)
   2) Number of authorized shares of stock
   3) Street address of the corporation's initial registered office
   4) Name of the registered agent at that office
   5) Name and address of each incorporator

d. The articles also may contain **optional provisions** (e.g., purpose and powers of the corporation, internal management, or any subject required or allowed to be addressed in the bylaws).

   1) Moreover, some subjects must be addressed only in the articles (e.g., limitation of directors' liability for breach of the duty of care, cumulative voting, supermajority voting, or preemptive rights).

e. The **date existence commences** is when the articles are filed with the secretary of state. In some states, issuance of a **certificate of incorporation** commences existence.

f. After filing, the incorporators elect the members of the **initial board of directors** if they have not been named in the articles. They also may adopt bylaws. The incorporators then resign.

g. The board of directors holds an **organizational meeting** to take all steps needed to complete the organizational structure. The new board

   1) Adopts **bylaws** if they were not adopted by the incorporators.

      a) Bylaws govern the internal structure and operation of the corporation. They may contain any provision for managing the business and regulating the entity's affairs that does not conflict with the law or the articles.
      b) Initial bylaws are adopted by the incorporators or the board.

2) Elects officers, typically a president, a treasurer, and a secretary.
3) Considers other transactions appropriate for furthering the business purposes of the corporation, such as
   a) Adopting or rejecting preincorporation contracts of the promoters,
   b) Adopting the form of certificate representing shares of stock,
   c) Accepting or rejecting stock subscriptions, and
   d) Complying with requirements for doing business in other states.

4. **Defective Incorporation**
   a. A corporation incorporated in strict compliance with the applicable state statute is a **de jure corporation**.
   b. A **de facto** corporation is recognized given
      1) A statute under which the business could have incorporated,
      2) A good-faith but unsuccessful attempt to comply with it, and
      3) Objective evidence that indicates an actual or attempted exercise of corporate powers.
   c. The RMBCA establishes a **conclusive presumption** that, when the articles have been filed, the corporation exists even if the filing was defective.
   d. An organization that is neither a de jure nor a de facto corporation may be treated as a **corporation by estoppel** in a suit by a third party. Thus, the organization is prevented (estopped) from denying corporate status if
      1) The organization has represented itself as a corporation,
      2) The third party reasonably relies on that representation and materially alters its position,
      3) The third party's conduct is fair and equitable, and
      4) Injustice can be avoided only by treating the business as a corporation.

EXAMPLE

The XYZ Company, an organization that is neither a de jure nor a de facto corporation, holds itself out to the public as a corporation. XYZ purchases an airplane from Sky Corporation but fails to pay for it. When Sky sues XYZ for payment, XYZ is estopped from asserting as a defense that it is not a valid corporation.

Stop and review! You have completed the outline for this subunit. Study multiple-choice questions 1 through 5 beginning on page 562.

15.2 OPERATION, FINANCING, AND DISTRIBUTIONS

1. **Corporate Powers**
   a. Authority for corporate action derives from the state incorporation **statute** or **the articles of incorporation**. The RMBCA grants a corporation broad authority to exercise the "same powers as an individual to do all things necessary or convenient to carry out its business and affairs."
   b. Thus, the corporation may engage in any lawful business unless a more limited purpose is stated in the articles. The powers include the right to
      1) Sue, be sued, and defend in the corporate name.
      2) Exist perpetually.
      3) Acquire real or personal property, or any legal or equitable interest, wherever located.

4) Elect directors, appoint officers and agents, hire employees, set their compensation, and lend them money or credit. Accordingly, a corporation may be liable for the conduct of agents.
   a) Under the doctrine of **respondeat superior**, or "let the master answer," a principal (e.g., a corporation) may be liable for an agent's **torts** (civil wrongs not resulting from contracts). But the wrongs must be committed within the scope of the agency.
   b) A corporation also may be liable for **crimes** involving (1) violations of statutes imposing strict liability or (2) actions of the board or executives.
5) Operate within or outside the state of incorporation.
6) Engage in any transactions involving interests in, or obligations of, any other entity.
7) Make contracts, give guarantees, incur liabilities, issue debt (whether or not convertible or containing options), or give security interests.
8) Be a partner, promoter, manager, or associate of another entity.
9) Lend money, invest funds, and hold collateral.
10) Make and amend bylaws.
11) Dispose of all or part of its property by any proper means.
12) Make donations for public welfare, charitable, scientific, or educational purposes.
13) Pay pensions and establish profit-sharing and other benefit or incentive plans.
14) Transact any lawful business in aid of governmental policy.
15) Acquire the corporation's own shares.
16) Do any lawful act in the furtherance of the business of the corporation.

c. These powers are either **inherent** or **statutory**.
d. Under the doctrine of **ultra vires**, a corporation may not act beyond its inherent powers or those provided in the articles and statutes.
   1) However, with certain exceptions, "the validity of corporate action may not be challenged on the ground that the corporation lacks or lacked power to act" (RMBCA).
   2) Articles authorizing **any lawful business transaction** are common.
e. **Express powers** are specifically granted by the articles of incorporation.
f. **Implied powers** are necessary and appropriate to carry out express powers.

2. **Piercing the Corporate Veil**

a. Courts disregard the corporate form when it is used merely to (1) commit wrongdoing, (2) shield its shareholders from liability for fraud, or (3) otherwise circumvent the law. Shareholders are then personally liable for corporate acts (as are general partners in a partnership).
b. A court might disregard a corporate entity if it finds
   1) The corporation is merely the alter ego of a shareholder, for example, if
      a) Assets of the corporation and the shareholder(s) are commingled or
      b) The corporation was established for a sham purpose.
   2) Two or more entities are related corporations (such as a parent and its subsidiary or corporations that are under common control) and in practice do not maintain sufficiently independent existence.
   3) A corporation is inadequately capitalized to carry on its intended business.

EXAMPLE

Jennifer organizes a corporation with capital of only $500, intending to buy goods (inventory) worth $1,000,000 on credit. Jennifer expects to pay for the goods from profits generated from sales. If the business is not successful, she expects not to be liable because the purchase was made in the corporation's name. The corporation is undercapitalized, and creditors may be successful in petitioning a court to pierce the corporate veil. If the creditors are successful, Jennifer could be personally liable for the debt.

3. **State Jurisdiction**
   a. Most states have **long-arm statutes** that permit exercise of **personal jurisdiction** (authority) over a foreign corporation, e.g., to require registration with the state or to allow **service of process** (giving valid notice to a defendant corporation) in another state.
      1) These statutes base personal jurisdiction on certain acts within the state:
         a) Commission of a tort,
         b) Owning property if it is the subject of the suit,
         c) Entering into a contract, or
         d) Doing business if it is the subject of the suit.
      2) The U.S. Supreme Court permits long-arm jurisdiction if the defendant has minimum contacts with the state such that exercise of that jurisdiction does not offend notions of fair play and substantial justice.
   b. **Minimum contacts** consist of activities that are not isolated and that
      1) Are purposefully directed towards the state, e.g., advertising on radio stations heard within the state and intended to generate product demand in the state, or
      2) Place a product in interstate commerce with an expectation or intent that it will ultimately be used in the state.

EXAMPLE

A citizen of Long-Arm State was injured when a van operated by an employee of Intrastate, Inc., struck her in a crosswalk while she was vacationing in Remote State. Intrastate's only business is providing landscape services in Remote State. It has no contacts with Long-Arm State. Intrastate, Inc., has no reasonable expectation of being, and would be surprised to be, forced to litigate in Long-Arm State (and then have a judgment enforced in Remote State under the Full Faith and Credit Clause of the U.S. Constitution). Long-Arm State may not exercise jurisdiction over Intrastate, Inc., consistent with federal due process constraints.

4. **Financing**
   a. **Debt** financing increases the corporation's **risk** because it must be repaid at fixed times even if the entity is not profitable. However, dividends on equity securities are discretionary. The following are advantages of debt:
      1) Debt usually provides no voting rights and does not dilute shareholder **control**.
      2) Upon liquidation, debt holders receive no more than their claims.
      3) Interest on debt is **tax deductible**. Dividends on equity securities are not.
   b. **Equity** financing in the form of common stock transfers ownership interests. But an equity interest does not confer title to any specific property of the corporation. Moreover, shareholders are not creditors.
      1) Creditors have **priority** in corporate assets in bankruptcy or liquidation. A surplus is distributed to the shareholders.
         a) Shareholders have greater potential risks and rewards than creditors.
      2) Most statutes require that the **articles** specify the number of **authorized shares** and the **classes of stock**.
         a) Authorized capital stock cannot be changed without amending the articles.
         b) The board may issue any or none of the authorized shares.

3) **Consideration for shares,** subject to securities regulation, may be cash, property (tangible or intangible), or services rendered.

a) **Watered stock** is stock not issued for adequate consideration. A person who purchases stock from a corporation is liable for any excess of par value over the price paid for it.

b) The directors' determination of **adequacy** is conclusive.

4) Another form of financing related to common equity is the entity's **retained earnings**. According to finance theory, the costs of capital of retained earnings and common stock are the same.

c. Classes of Stock

1) Common Stock

a) The most widely used classes of stock are common and preferred. Common shareholders are entitled to receive **liquidating distributions** only after all other claims have been satisfied, including those of preferred shareholders.

b) Common shareholders are not entitled to **dividends**.

i) A corporation may choose not to declare dividends. Among the reasons are insufficient retained earnings to meet a legal requirement or the need to use cash for some other purpose.

c) State statutes typically permit different classes of common stock with different rights or privileges, e.g., class A common with voting rights and class B common with no voting rights.

d) If only one class of stock is issued, it is treated as common, and each shareholder must be treated equally.

e) Common shareholders elect directors to the board.

2) Preferred Stock

a) Preferred shareholders have the right to receive (1) dividends at a specified rate (before common shareholders may receive any) and (2) distributions before common shareholders (but after creditors) upon liquidation. But they tend not to have voting rights or to receive the same capital gains as the common shareholders.

3) Treasury Stock

a) Treasury stock is the entity's own stock that has been reacquired.

b) Treasury stock reduces the shares outstanding, not the shares authorized.

c) Dividends are not paid on treasury stock.

5. **Distributions**

a. The board determines the time and amount of dividends and other distributions. A distribution (including a redemption) is a transfer of money or other property (but not the corporation's own shares) or an incurrence of debt to or for shareholders in respect of their shares.

b. Profitability is not a legal condition of a distribution, but a distribution is prohibited if, as a result,

1) The corporation cannot pay its debts as they become due in the ordinary course of business, or

2) Total assets would be less than the sum of liabilities and liquidation preferences.

c. Some states require that distributions be paid out of earned surplus and not stated capital. However, the RMBCA and many states have abolished the concepts of stated capital and surplus because they provide no protection to investors.

1) **Stated capital** is the par value of par-value stock (or the stated value of no-par stock).

2) **Capital surplus** is the excess of contributed capital over par or stated value.

a) Many states allow payment from capital surplus if approved by the shareholders or in accordance with the bylaws.

3) **Earned surplus** is retained earnings.

4) If a statute requires a stated (legal) capital, the amount received for no-par stock is allocated to stated capital and capital surplus at the board's discretion.

d. **Directors** who approve a distribution that violates the applicable state test have abused their discretion. They are jointly and severally liable to the corporation.

1) **Shareholders** generally must repay a distribution only if they know it is illegal.

6. **Dividends**

a. Dividends are returns on capital paid in cash, stock, stock rights, or other property (a dividend in kind).

1) Normally, a **preferred shareholder** is entitled to a fixed amount that must be paid **before** amounts are received by the **common shareholders**.

a) If the preferred stock is **cumulative**, any dividends not paid in preceding years (dividends in arrears) are carried over and must be paid before the common shareholders may receive anything.

2) **Liquidating dividends** are a return of, not a return on, a shareholder's capital.

b. The **declaration date** is the date the directors approve a distribution in the form of a dividend. Once declared, payment is a **legal obligation** of the corporation.

1) The directors fix a **record date**. The registered holder on the record date is sent the payment on the payment date.

EXAMPLE

The directors of ABC Corp. declare a dividend on June 1, payable to the shareholders of record as of July 1, with payment to be made August 1.

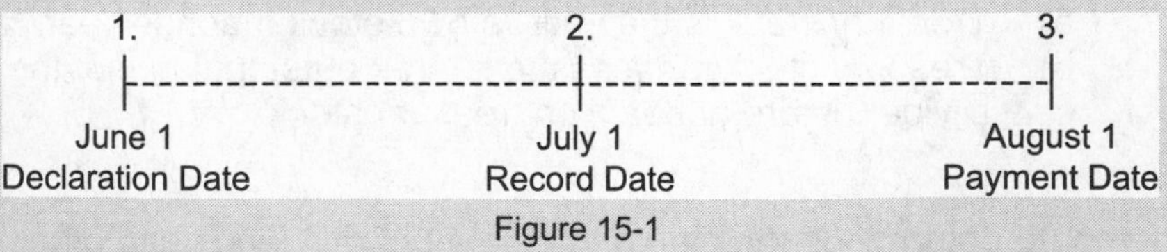

Figure 15-1

c. A **stock dividend** is payable in the stock of the corporation as a percentage of the shares outstanding. The corporation generally issues new stock for this purpose.

1) Stock dividends do not increase the equity of each shareholder because they are distributed in proportion to the shares already owned.

2) When a stock dividend is declared, the corporation transfers the legally required amount from earned surplus (retained earnings) to stated capital (common stock). Total equity is not changed.

EXAMPLE

An entity's board of directors declared a 10% dividend on the 45,000 shares of its common stock outstanding ($1 par). The stock was trading for $15 per share.

Date of declaration:		
Retained earnings [(45,000 shares × 10%) × $15 market price]	$67,500	
Common stock dividend distributable [(45,000 shares × 10%) × $1]		$ 4,500
Additional paid-in capital -- common (difference)		63,000
Date of distribution:		
Common stock dividend distributable	$ 4,500	
Common stock		$ 4,500

d. A **stock split** is an issuance of shares for the purpose of reducing the unit value of each share. Accordingly, the par or stated value, if any, also is reduced. A stock split does not increase a shareholder's proportionate ownership. It merely increases the number of shares outstanding.

   1) A stock split is not a distribution.

EXAMPLE

In the example above, the board of directors instead declared a 2-for-1 common stock split. There are currently 5,000 shares in treasury stock. The laws of the state of incorporation protect treasury stock from dilution. Thus, the entity reduces the stated value of its common stock to $0.50 per share and issues 100,000 new shares, 90,000 issued to shareholders ($45,000 × 2) and 10,000 to the treasury (5,000 × 2). Total equity remains unchanged.

100,000 shares × $0.50 (new) = 50,000 × $1 (old)

Stop and review! You have completed the outline for this subunit. Study multiple-choice questions 6 through 10 beginning on page 564.

15.3 SHAREHOLDERS' RIGHTS

1. **Shareholders**

   a. A shareholder is an owner but has no direct rights.

   b. The shareholders' primary participation is by **meeting annually and electing directors** by a **plurality** of the votes cast by the shares entitled to vote at a meeting at which a quorum is present.

      1) Shareholders must approve **fundamental corporate changes**, including

         a) Mergers and share exchanges other than short-form mergers. (Short-form mergers are described in Subunit 15.5.)

         b) Disposition of substantially all assets, leaving the corporation with **no significant continuing business activity**.

         c) Dissolutions.

      2) Shareholders may amend or repeal **bylaws**.

2. **Shareholder Meetings**

   a. Generally, shareholders may act only at a meeting.

   b. **Annual meetings** are required and must be held at a time fixed in the bylaws. The purpose is to elect new directors and to conduct necessary business.

      1) **Notice** of any meeting must be in writing, and defective notice or lack of notice voids action taken at the meeting.

c. A **quorum** must be represented in person or by proxy to conduct business. The RMBCA's default definition of a quorum for a **voting group** is a majority of the group's shares entitled to be cast.

d. **Special meetings**, e.g., to approve a merger, require written notice and a description of purpose.

1) The meeting may be called by the board, the owner(s) of at least 10% of the issued and outstanding common stock, or any other persons authorized in the articles.

e. The RMBCA permits shareholders to **act without a meeting** if all shareholders entitled to vote consent in writing to the action.

3. **Voting Rights**

a. The **articles** may provide for more or less than one vote per share. A **supermajority** also may be required.

1) Usually, each shareholder is entitled to one vote per share owned for each new director to be elected.

b. To alter the sometimes harsh effect of straight voting, some states permit **cumulative voting**. Cumulative voting enables minority shareholders to obtain representation on the board in proportion to the number of shares they own.

1) Under cumulative voting, a shareholder may allocate to any one or more candidates the following number of votes:

Number of Directors to Be Elected	×	Number of Votes to Which Shareholder is Entitled

EXAMPLE

Y Corporation is electing five directors to its board. Mary, a shareholder owning 200 of the 1,000 voting shares, can elect at least one director under cumulative voting.

- Five directors to be elected × 200 voting shares = 1,000.
- Mary casts all 1,000 of her votes for the one director of her choice instead of splitting her vote among all five directorships.
- No matter how the other 4,000 votes [5 × (1,000 – 200)] are allocated, the total cast for Mary's candidate must be at least the fifth highest.

c. The RMBCA permits different voting rights for different **classes of shares**. For example, each class may have the right to elect one director.

1) Thus, even a closely held corporation may have two or more classes of common shares with different voting rights.

EXAMPLE

XYZ Corporation is a small, closely held corporation with four shareholders, each of whom owns 25 shares. Straight voting would not permit a shareholder to elect himself or herself as director. However, the articles of incorporation designate four classes of shares, each with the right to elect one director, and each shareholder owns all the shares of one of the classes. Thus, each shareholder can elect himself or herself to the board.

d. The RMBCA specifically permits a **voting agreement**, a signed contract in which shareholders specify how they will vote their shares.

1) It is specifically enforceable. The party who breaches the contract may be legally compelled to vote the shares as agreed rather than pay damages.

e. Shareholders may transfer their shares to one or more voting trustees in exchange for **voting trust** certificates. The trust shares are registered in the trustee's name, and the trust is **irrevocable** for the stated period.
   1) The term of a voting trust is initially limited to **10 years**.
   2) Holders of the certificates are entitled to corporate distributions.
   3) A voting trust permits the trustees, such as creditors of a corporation in reorganization, to exercise concentrated voting power.

f. A **proxy** is an appointment by a shareholder for someone else to vote on his or her behalf. Usually, a proxy must be in writing or in an authorized electronic transmission. It is **revocable** at any time, e.g., by signing a later proxy.
   1) A proxy is irrevocable if it is **coupled with an interest**, e.g., if the shares are collateral for a loan.
   2) A **general proxy** permits a holder to vote on all corporate proposals other than fundamental corporate changes. A **limited proxy** permits a holder to vote only on matters specified in the proxy.
   3) A **proxy statement** is sent to a shareholder whose proxy is being solicited. Its content is regulated by the SEC. It must contain a full and accurate statement of the facts relevant to the issues to be voted on.

4. **Shareholder Agreements**

a. The RMBCA permits shareholders to change, by **unanimous** agreement, (1) the exercise of the corporate powers; (2) the management of the business and affairs of the corporation; or (3) the relationship among the shareholders, the directors, and the corporation. This flexibility may allow a close corporation to function more nearly as a partnership without loss of corporate status.
   1) A valid shareholder agreement may (a) treat the entity as a partnership or (b) dispense with traditional formalities (e.g., a board of directors). The RMBCA states that such an agreement is not, by itself, a basis for holding shareholders personally liable for corporate obligations (i.e., for piercing the corporate veil).

b. A shareholder agreement set forth in the articles, bylaws, or a separate signed agreement is not contrary to public policy.

c. A limitation on the powers or discretion of the board relieves the directors of liability and imposes it on the person(s) to whom such authority is transferred.

d. The agreement becomes ineffective when the entity's shares are publicly traded.

5. **Preemptive Rights**

a. These are important to owners of a closely held corporation. They give a shareholder an option to subscribe to a new issuance of shares in proportion to the current interest in the corporation. Thus, they limit dilution of equity.

b. Preemptive rights may not exist unless they are specifically reserved in the articles.

c. Preemptive rights do not apply to stock issued
   1) As an incentive to officers, directors, or employees.
   2) In satisfaction of conversion or option rights.
   3) For something other than money.
   4) Within 6 months of incorporation if the shares were authorized in the articles.

6. **Inspection Rights**

a. Under the RMBCA, shareholders and their agents have a fundamental **right to inspect** books and records that may not be limited by the articles or bylaws.

b. Inspection must be at the corporation's principal office during regular business hours. The shareholders must give 5 business days' written notice that states the purpose of the demand and the records to be inspected.

c. Inspection must be in good faith and for a **proper purpose**, involving, for example,

1) Corporate financial condition.
2) The propriety of dividends.
3) Mismanagement of the corporation.
4) The names and addresses of other shareholders.
5) Election of directors.
6) A shareholder suit.

d. An **improper purpose** is one that does not relate to the shareholder's interest in the corporation. Improper purposes include

1) Harassment of management.
2) Discovery of trade secrets.
3) Gaining a competitive advantage.
4) Development of a mailing list for sale or similar use.

e. Courts have permitted a shareholder to obtain a copy of a shareholder list, even when the only purpose was to engage in a takeover battle.

f. Shareholders have an unconditional right to inspect certain records, such as the articles, bylaws, minutes of shareholder meetings, and the annual report.

7. **Dissenters' (Appraisal) Rights**

a. Shareholders who disagree with fundamental corporate changes may be paid the **fair value** of their stock in cash.

b. A shareholder asserting dissenters' (appraisal) rights must make a **written demand** before the vote that the corporation purchase his or her stock if the action is approved.

c. Under the RMBCA, dissenters' rights arise from the following:

1) A disposition of assets that leaves the corporation without a significant continuing business activity.
2) Certain mergers and share exchanges. Dissenters' rights are especially important in the event of a short-form merger because shareholders are not given notice of the merger.
3) Any other action taken by shareholder vote to the extent such a right is provided in the articles, bylaws, or a board resolution.
4) An amendment to the articles that **materially and adversely** affects shareholder rights.

d. Under federal securities law, a dissident shareholder may require the corporation to furnish a list of shareholders. The dissident may then mail proxy materials to those shareholders if (s)he pays the cost of the mailing.

8. **Shareholder Suits**

a. **Direct suits** by shareholders are on their own behalf, either individually or as members of a class. For example, an individual shareholder may sue a corporation to (1) require payment of properly declared dividends, (2) recover improper dividends, (3) obtain a remedy for management's breach of duty, or (4) compel dissolution.

1) A shareholder also may enforce his or her preemptive, inspection, voting, or other rights.

b. A **shareholder derivative suit** is to recover for wrongs done to the corporation. The action is for the benefit of the corporation, and any recovery belongs to it, not to the shareholder. The corporation is the true plaintiff.

1) A shareholder must first demand that the corporation bring suit unless it is obvious the demand is futile, e.g., when the action is against the directors.

a) A shareholder cannot file a derivative suit until 90 days after the demand (unless notice of rejection has been given or irreparable harm will be done to the corporation).

2) Most states require that the shareholder prove the following:

a) (S)he owned shares at the time of wrongdoing.
b) A written demand was made on the directors.
c) The directors refused to sue.
d) The refusal was in bad faith.

9. **Shareholder Liability**

a. Shareholders are not personally liable for acts or debts of the corporation except by reason of their own acts. Thus, a shareholder's liability is limited to his or her capital contribution with certain exceptions, for example, if the corporate veil is pierced, or the corporation was defectively formed.

b. Under a **stock subscription agreement**, the subscriber is liable to the corporation for any unpaid installment balance, even if the corporation becomes insolvent or declares bankruptcy.

c. If authorized stock has a **stated value** and is originally sold for less, the purchaser is liable to the corporation for the deficiency.

1) A person who subsequently purchases the stock is subject to liability if (s)he knows the stock was issued for less than par or stated value.

d. A dividend paid when the corporation is **insolvent** is always **illegal**. State law also may require that dividends be paid only from designated accounts, that is, from retained earnings, current net profits, or any surplus. Moreover, a dividend may be illegal if it causes insolvency.

Stop and review! You have completed the outline for this subunit. Study multiple-choice questions 11 through 15 beginning on page 565.

15.4 DIRECTORS' AND OFFICERS' AUTHORITY, DUTIES, AND LIABILITY

1. **Composition of the Board**

a. Each state has a specific requirement with respect to the **number of directors** elected to sit on the board. Many states require a minimum of three. Under the RMBCA, a minimum of one director is usually required. However, the RMBCA permits a corporation to dispense with a board by unanimous shareholder agreement.

EXAMPLE

X Corp. has only one shareholder. It is incorporated in a state where the incorporation statute requires at least three directors, unless there are fewer than three shareholders, in which case the number of directors may equal the number of shareholders. X Corp. is permitted by statute to have one director.

b. A director ordinarily need not be a shareholder, be a resident of the state of incorporation, or meet an age requirement.

c. The **initial board** is usually appointed by the incorporators or named in the articles, and this board serves until the first meeting of the shareholders.

1) Subsequent directors are elected by the shareholders at the annual meeting.

d. Most publicly held corporations have two types of directors. **Inside directors** are officers and full-time employees. **Outside directors** may be unaffiliated with the corporation except for stock ownership.

e. Generally, a director serves a 1-year term and is elected by a **plurality** (not a majority) of shareholder votes.

f. In most states, shareholders may by a majority vote remove, **with or without cause**, any director or the entire board.

g. Statutes usually permit the **board to remove a director** for cause who has been declared insane or convicted of a felony, subject to shareholder review.

2. **Authority of the Board**

a. Although directors formulate overall corporate policy, they are **neither trustees nor agents** of the corporation. A director cannot act individually.

b. The board establishes and implements corporate policy, including the following:

1) Selection and removal of officers
2) Decisions about capital structure, including price of shares
3) Adding, amending, or repealing bylaws (unless shareholders have this power)
4) Initiation of fundamental changes
5) Dividends, including whether and when to declare them
6) Setting of management compensation (including directors)

c. The board may act only at a **formal meeting** or by duly executed **written consent** if authorized by state statute, unless contrary to the articles or bylaws.

1) Formal meetings are held at fixed intervals established in the bylaws.
2) **Special meetings** may be held after proper notice has been given to all directors.

d. Directors have power to bind the corporation only when **acting as a board**.

e. Actions taken by a board are expressed in **formal resolutions** adopted by a majority of the board during a meeting at which a quorum is present.

1) Generally, a **quorum** consists of a majority of board members. A director is not allowed to vote by proxy.

f. If permitted by the articles or bylaws, a board may delegate authority to **committees** composed of its members or corporate officers.

1) Committees may exercise broad **powers** consistent with the limits of the resolutions by which they were established. However, they may not take extraordinary actions.
2) Every public corporation must have an **audit committee** consisting of independent directors.

g. Directors have the **right to inspect** corporate books and records so they can perform their duties.

3. **Directors' Fiduciary Duty**

a. Directors have a **fiduciary relationship** with the corporation. They can be held personally liable for failure to be informed of matters internal to, and external but relevant to, the corporation.

b. Directors and officers owe a **fiduciary duty** to the corporation to (1) act in its best interests, (2) be loyal, (3) use due diligence in carrying out their responsibilities, and (4) disclose conflicts of interest. **Controlling or majority shareholders** owe similar duties.

   1) For example, courts often protect the interests of **minority shareholders** by

      a) Ordering the payment of dividends that were withheld in bad faith or
      b) Compelling a seller of a controlling block of shares to distribute ratably among all shareholders any **control premium** paid in excess of the fair value of the stock.

c. A **director's duty of care** is tested objectively.

   1) The RMBCA requires that a director discharge his or her duties

      a) In good faith,
      b) In a manner (s)he reasonably believes to be in the best interests of the corporation, and
      c) With the care that a person in a similar position would reasonably believe appropriate under similar circumstances.

   2) **Reliance on others.** In exercising reasonable care, a director may rely on information, reports, opinions, and statements prepared or presented by persons whom the director **reasonably believes** to be competent in the matters presented.

      a) A director also may rely on the specialized knowledge of lawyers, accountants, investment bankers, and board committees.

   3) Directors are expected to be **informed** about pertinent corporate information when giving advice. To exercise the required care, a director must

      a) Attend meetings of the board.
      b) Analyze corporate financial statements.
      c) Review pertinent legal opinions.
      d) Become knowledgeable about the available relevant information.

d. Directors owe a **duty of loyalty** to the corporation. For example, serving on the board of a competitor may violate this duty.

   1) **Conflicting interest transactions.** To protect the corporation against self-dealing, a director is required to make **full disclosure** of any financial interest (s)he may have in any transaction to which both the director and the corporation may be a party.

      a) A transaction is not improper merely on the grounds of a director's conflict of interest. If the transaction (1) is fair to the corporation or (2) has been approved by a majority of informed, disinterested directors or shareholders, it is not voidable and does not result in sanctions.

         i) An issuer generally may not make **personal loans** to its directors and officers.

   2) Directors may not usurp any **corporate opportunity**. A director must give the corporation the right of first refusal.

EXAMPLE

Skip, a director of The Fishing Corp., learns in his corporate capacity that a state-of-the-art, deep-sea hydroplane fishing vessel is available for a bargain price. The purchase of this unique hydroplane may be a business opportunity from which the corporation could benefit. If Skip purchases the hydroplane for himself without giving the corporation the right of first refusal, he is usurping a corporate opportunity.

3) Directors who approve **unlawful distributions** are personally liable for excess distributions if they fail to comply with the duty of care. However, they are entitled to (a) contribution from other liable directors and (b) recoupment from shareholders who knowingly received unlawful distributions.

4. **Officers**

a. Officers are elected or appointed by the board and generally serve at the will of the board. However, the board may not remove without cause an officer elected or employed by the shareholders.

b. Typically, statutes set a minimum number of officers, not a maximum. Under the RMBCA, the corporation has the officers stated in the bylaws or appointed by the board. They need not be shareholders. One officer must be delegated responsibility for

1) Preparing the minutes of directors' meetings.
2) Authenticating records of the corporation.

c. The usual officers are a president, vice president, secretary, and treasurer. One person ordinarily may hold more than one office. Moreover, an officer may serve as a director.

d. The officers are **agents** of the corporation.

1) They have **express authority** conferred by the bylaws or the board.
2) They have **implied authority** to do things that are reasonably necessary to accomplish their express duties.
3) Courts have held that official titles confer limited **inherent authority** on officers.

e. Officers, like directors, owe **fiduciary duties** to the corporation.

1) Officers are subject to the same duties of care and loyalty as directors.
2) According to the RMBCA, corporations may indemnify officers for liability incurred in a suit by shareholders, unless inconsistent with public policy, as provided by the articles, bylaws, board, or contract.

f. The SEC requires issuers to provide detailed disclosures about **executive compensation** paid to the CEO, CFO, and the next three highest-paid officers.

1) It also requires recognition of the **costs of equity awards** over the periods when employees must provide services.

5. **Liability and the Business Judgment Rule**

a. Courts avoid substituting their business judgment for that of **officers or directors**.

b. The rule protects an officer or a director from **personal liability** for honest mistakes of judgment if (s)he

1) Acted in good faith;
2) Was not motivated by fraud, conflict of interest, or illegality; and
3) Was not grossly negligent.

c. To avoid personal liability, directors and officers must

1) Make informed decisions (educate themselves about the issues),
2) Be free from conflicts of interest, and
3) Have a rational basis to support their position.

d. Some decisions apply to management's opposition to **tender offers**. These offers to shareholders are made by a third party to buy their stock at a price above the market price. Directors may be liable to shareholders, i.e., the business judgment rule may not apply, if

1) The directors oppose a tender offer without careful study or
2) Their actions indicate that they are opposing it to preserve their jobs.

e. Most states permit corporations to **indemnify** directors and officers for expenses of litigation involving business judgments, subject to some exceptions.

1) The RMBCA permits the **articles** to limit the liability of directors to the corporation or shareholders. However, the limitation applies only to **money damages**. The articles may not limit liability for the following:

a) Intentional infliction of harm on the corporation
b) Intentional criminal conduct
c) Unlawful distributions
d) Receipt of financial benefits to which a director is not entitled

2) Usually, an officer or director who is liable to the corporation because of **negligent** performance is not entitled to indemnification as a matter of public policy.

a) However, a **court** may order indemnification of an officer or director of a corporation (even though found negligent) if the court determines (s)he is fairly and reasonably entitled to it in view of all the relevant circumstances.

The fiduciary duty and duties of care and loyalty owed to the corporation by corporate directors and officers have been recently scrutinized due to the wave of improper practices used by large corporations that led to major scandals. You may see questions covering these topics on your exam.

Stop and review! You have completed the outline for this subunit. Study multiple-choice questions 16 through 21 beginning on page 567.

15.5 MERGERS AND TERMINATION

1. **Mergers**

a. A **merger** combines the assets of two or more corporations. One corporation is absorbed by another and ceases to exist.

1) The surviving corporation succeeds to the rights, duties, liabilities, and assets of the merged corporation.

b. In a **consolidation**, a new corporation is formed, and the two or more consolidating corporations cease operating as separate entities. Otherwise, the requirements and effects of the combination are similar to those for a merger.

c. The shareholders of a merged corporation may receive stock or other securities issued by the surviving corporation.

1) Stock of the merged (acquired) corporation is canceled.

d. A merger requires the approval of each board and of shareholders entitled to vote for each corporation. Shareholder approval must be given at a **special meeting** by a majority vote unless a statute or the articles require a supermajority.

1) Shareholders of each corporation must be provided a copy of the **plan of merger**.
2) Shareholders of **each corporation** have appraisal rights.
3) The sale of substantially all of the corporation's assets outside the regular course of business requires the approval of shareholders.
4) Under the RMBCA, no shareholder approval is required if a corporation that owns at least 90% of a subsidiary merges with the subsidiary using a **short-form merger**.

a) The parent must give 10 days' notice to the subsidiary's shareholders, and they must be given an appraisal remedy (payment of the fair value of shares + interest).

e. The purchase of substantially all of the assets of another corporation or an acquisition of another corporation's stock that allows the acquirer a controlling interest does not imply a merger. Although the acquirer must prepare consolidated financial statements, the acquiree is legally a separate entity.

   1) This transaction is a policy decision that creates **no fundamental corporate change**. Thus, shareholder approval is not necessary.

2. **Share Exchanges**

   a. The RMBCA provisions for share exchanges are similar to those for mergers.

      1) A share exchange occurs when one corporation acquires all of the shares of one or more classes or series of shares of another in exchange for shares, securities, cash, other property, etc.
      2) A share exchange maintains the separate corporate existence of both entities.
      3) Only the shareholders of the acquiree have **dissenters' rights**.

3. **Tender Offers**

   a. An acquirer may bypass board approval of a business combination by extending a tender offer of cash or shares, usually at a higher than market price, directly to shareholders to purchase a certain number of the outstanding shares.
   b. Managements of target corporations have implemented diverse strategies to counter hostile tender offers. The following are examples of antitakeover strategies:

      1) **Issuing stock.** The target significantly increases its outstanding stock.
      2) **Self-tender.** The target borrows to tender an offer to repurchase its shares.
      3) **Legal action.** A target may challenge one or more aspects of a tender offer. A resulting delay increases the costs of the raider and enables further defensive action.

4. **Dissolution**

   a. A corporation that has issued stock and commenced business may be **voluntarily dissolved** by

      1) Unanimous written consent of all shareholders or
      2) Majority shareholder vote at a special meeting called for the purpose if the directors have adopted a resolution of dissolution.

   b. The corporation files **articles of dissolution** with the secretary of state petitioning the state to dissolve the corporation. A dissolution is effective when filed.
   c. The secretary of state may proceed administratively to dissolve **involuntarily** a corporation that fails to file its annual report, pay its franchise tax, or appoint or maintain a resident agent.

      1) Written notice is sent to the corporation to correct the default.

   d. Under the RMBCA, shareholders may seek a **judicial dissolution** when a deadlock of the board is harmful to the corporation, or the directors' actions are contrary to the best interests of the corporation.

5. **Liquidation**

   a. After dissolution, the corporate business must be wound up and liquidated.
   b. The **directors** have a duty to "discharge or make reasonable provision" for **claims**. They then must distribute assets to shareholders.
   c. Directors are not liable to claimants for claims barred or satisfied if they have complied with the RMBCA's statutory procedures for

      1) Giving notice to known claimants,
      2) Publishing notice of dissolution,
      3) Requesting that other claimants present their claims, and

4) Obtaining appropriate judicial determinations, for example, of the amount of collateral needed for payment of claims.

Stop and review! You have completed the outline for this subunit. Study multiple-choice questions 22 through 26 beginning on page 569.

15.6 ADVANTAGES AND DISADVANTAGES OF CORPORATIONS

1. **Advantages**
   a. **Limited liability.** A shareholder owns a property interest in the underlying net assets of the corporation and is entitled to share in its profits. However, a shareholder's exposure to corporate liabilities is limited to his or her investment.
   b. **Separation of ownership from management.** Shareholders have no inherent right to participate in management. They elect a board that sets policy and appoints officers to conduct operations. A shareholder may be an officer or a director.
   c. **Free transferability of interests.** Without contractual or legal restriction, shares may be freely transferred, e.g., by sale, gift, pledge, or inheritance.
      1) A shareholder has no interest in specific property. (S)he owns a proportional, intangible property interest in the entire corporation.
   d. **Perpetual life.** A corporation has perpetual existence unless the articles provide for a shorter life, or it is dissolved by the state. Death, withdrawal, or addition of a shareholder, director, or officer does not end its existence.
   e. **Ease of raising capital.** A corporation raises capital (to start or expand the business) by selling stock or issuing bonds.
   f. **Constitutional rights.** A corporation is a **person** for most purposes under the **U.S. Constitution**. Thus, it has the right to equal protection, due process, freedom from unreasonable searches and seizures, and freedom of speech. It also has the right to make nearly unlimited contributions of money for political purposes.
      1) However, commercial speech (e.g., advertising) is given less protection than that provided to the same speech by natural persons.
      2) Moreover, a corporation does **not** have a right against **self-incrimination** in criminal cases.
   g. **Transfers of property to a controlled corporation.** A transfer of assets for stock of any corporation is **tax-free** if the transferors are in control of the corporation immediately after the exchange. A person who transfers appreciated property receives the benefit if another transferor transfers property and together they meet the control test. Property includes money.
      1) **Control** is ownership of stock with at least 80% of the
         a) Total combined voting power of all classes of stock entitled to vote and
         b) Total number of shares of all other classes of stock of the corporation.
2. **Disadvantages**
   a. Reduced individual control of the business
   b. Payment of taxes on corporate income and payment by the shareholders of taxes on distributions received from the corporation (unless the entity qualifies for and elects S corporation status)
   c. Substantial costs of meeting the requirements of corporate formation and operation
   d. Hostile takeover of a publicly traded corporation
   e. Transfer of unrestricted shares in a close corporation to unknown parties
   f. An inability of a minority shareholder in a close corporation to liquidate his or her interest or to influence the conduct of the business
   g. Becoming subject to state and federal regulation of securities transactions through reporting and registration requirements

3. Summary of Corporate Entities

	Formation	Capitalization	Operation	Liability	Transferability	Taxation	Termination
S corporation	Formalities. Files articles of incorporation with state. Elects S corporation status.	Members and shareholders (number of shareholders may not exceed 100).	Shareholder-elected board appoints officers to manage daily operations.	Shareholders generally are liable only to the extent of their investment.	Shareholders generally may transfer their interests to qualifying shareholders.	Flow through taxation on a per-day and per-share basis.	Upon occurrence of terminating event, S corporation becomes a C corporation.
Corporation	Formalities. Files articles of incorporation with state.	May sell common and preferred stock. May issue debt.	Shareholder-elected board appoints officers to manage daily operations.	Shareholders generally are liable only to the extent of their investment.	Shareholders generally are free to transfer their interests.	Income taxed at corporate level. Shareholders pay tax on dividends received.	Perpetual existence. Death, bankruptcy, or withdrawal of shareholder does not terminate corporation.

Stop and review! You have completed the outline for this subunit. Study multiple-choice questions 27 through 29 beginning on page 570.

QUESTIONS

15.1 Formation

1. Which of the following statements is true with respect to the general structure of a corporation?

A. The corporation is treated as a legal person with rights and obligations jointly shared with its owners and managers.

B. Shareholders establish corporate policies and elect or appoint corporate officers.

C. Corporations are governed by shareholders (owners) who elect a board of directors and approve fundamental changes in the corporate structure.

D. The board of directors is responsible for carrying out the corporate policies in the day-to-day management of the organizations.

Answer (C) is correct.

REQUIRED: The general structure of a corporation.

DISCUSSION: A corporation is an entity formed under state law that is treated as a legal person with rights and obligations separate from its owners. Shareholders hold the voting power of a corporation. This power gives them the ability to elect a board of directors and to approve fundamental changes in the corporate structure. Thus, the shareholders have the power to govern the corporation.

Answer (A) is incorrect. A corporation is a legal entity with rights and obligations separate from its owners and managers. Answer (B) is incorrect. Directors hold the power to establish corporate policies and elect or appoint corporate officers, not shareholders. Answer (D) is incorrect. Corporate officers are responsible for carrying out the policies in the day-to-day management of the organization.

2. Case Corp. is incorporated in State A. Under the Revised Model Business Corporation Act, which of the following activities engaged in by Case requires that Case obtain a certificate of authority to do business in State B?

A. Maintaining bank accounts in State B.

B. Collecting corporate debts in State B.

C. Hiring employees who are residents of State B.

D. Maintaining an office in State B to conduct intrastate business.

Answer (D) is correct.

REQUIRED: The interstate business activity that requires a certificate of authority.

DISCUSSION: A state may exercise authority over a foreign corporation if the corporation has at least minimum contacts with the state. The minimum contacts consist of activities that (1) are not isolated and (2) either are purposefully directed toward the state or place a product in the stream of interstate commerce with an expectation or intent that it will be used in the state. Maintaining an office in State B to conduct intrastate business creates minimum contacts with State B under this test.

Answer (A) is incorrect. Maintaining bank accounts in State B is an isolated activity that does not meet the minimum contacts test. Answer (B) is incorrect. The collection of debts in State B does not by itself constitute minimum contacts in State B. For example, the debts may not have arisen from activities that involved State B. Answer (C) is incorrect. Hiring employees who reside in State B is not an activity that is purposefully directed toward the state or that places a product in interstate commerce with the expectation or intent that it will be used in the state.

3. May Phillips was the principal promoter of the Waterloo Corporation, a corporation that was to have been incorporated not later than July 31. Phillips obtained written subscriptions for a total of $1.4 million of common stock from 17 individuals. She hired herself as the chief executive officer of Waterloo at $200,000 for 5 years and leased three floors of office space from Downtown Office Space, Inc. The contract with Downtown was made in the name of the corporation. Phillips had indicated orally that the corporation would be coming into existence shortly. The corporation did not come into existence, through no fault of Phillips. Which of the following is true?

A. The subscribers have a recognized right to sue for and recover damages.

B. Phillips is personally liable on the lease with Downtown.

C. Phillips has the right to recover the fair value of her services rendered to the proposed corporation.

D. The subscribers were not bound by their subscriptions until the corporation came into existence.

Answer (B) is correct.

REQUIRED: The true statement about the preincorporation activity of a corporation that did not come into existence.

DISCUSSION: A promoter is personally liable on contracts entered into on behalf of nonexistent corporations, unless such liability is excluded or performance is conditioned on adoption by the corporation. Thus, Phillips is personally liable on the lease.

Answer (A) is incorrect. The subscribers have no right to recover damages if Phillips was not at fault. They have a right to a refund of their subscriptions. Answer (C) is incorrect. A promoter has no right to compensation for services unless the corporation comes into existence and so agrees. The same is generally true of preincorporation expenses. Answer (D) is incorrect. Under the RMBCA, the subscribers are bound to their subscriptions for 6 months.

4. An organization that is neither a de jure nor a de facto corporation has attempted to exercise corporate powers. It may be treated as a corporation if

I. The other party demonstrates fair and equitable conduct.

II. Injustice can be avoided only by treating the business as a corporation.

III. A good-faith but unsuccessful effort to comply with the incorporation statute has been made.

A. I only.

B. I and II only.

C. II and III only.

D. I, II, and III.

Answer (B) is correct.

REQUIRED: The condition(s) that must be met for an organization that is not a de jure or de facto corporation to be treated as a corporation.

DISCUSSION: As a defendant in a suit, an organization that is neither a de jure nor a de facto corporation may be treated as a corporation by estoppel if certain conditions are met: (1) The organization has represented itself as a corporation, (2) the representation is followed by reasonable reliance and material alteration of position by the other party based on that representation, (3) the other party demonstrates fair and equitable conduct, and (4) injustice can be avoided only by treating the business as a corporation. In contrast, a de facto corporation is recognized given (1) a statute under which the business could have incorporated, (2) a good-faith but unsuccessful attempt to comply with it, and (3) an actual or attempted exercise of corporate powers.

Answer (A) is incorrect. For the organization to be treated as a corporation, it must be proven that injustice can be avoided only by treating the business as a corporation. Answer (C) is incorrect. For the organization to be treated as a corporation, it must be proven that injustice can be avoided only by treating the business as a corporation and that the other party's conduct was fair and equitable. If a good-faith but unsuccessful effort to comply with the incorporation statute has been made, a de facto corporation may exist. Answer (D) is incorrect. If a good-faith but unsuccessful effort to comply with the incorporation statute has been made, a de facto corporation may exist.

5. Boyle, as a promoter of Delaney Corp., signed a 9-month contract with Austin, a CPA. Prior to the incorporation, Austin rendered accounting services pursuant to the contract. After rendering accounting services for an additional period of 6 months pursuant to the contract, Austin was discharged without cause by the board of directors of Delaney. Absent agreements to the contrary, who will be liable to Austin for breach of contract?

A. Both Boyle and Delaney.

B. Boyle only.

C. Delaney only.

D. Neither Boyle nor Delaney.

Answer (A) is correct.

REQUIRED: The liability of a corporation and a promoter on a preincorporation agreement.

DISCUSSION: A promoter who contracts for a nonexistent corporation is personally liable on such contracts. Delaney is also liable because it impliedly adopted the contract by accepting Austin's performance.

Answer (B) is incorrect. The corporation impliedly adopted the contract by accepting its benefits. Answer (C) is incorrect. A promoter is generally liable on preincorporation contracts. Answer (D) is incorrect. Boyle was not released and a novation did not occur. Delaney adopted the contract by implication.

15.2 Operation, Financing, and Distributions

6. What is the doctrine under which a corporation is made liable for the torts of its employees, committed within the scope of their employment?

A. Respondeat superior.

B. Ultra vires.

C. Estoppel.

D. Ratification.

Answer (A) is correct.

REQUIRED: The doctrine making a corporation liable for the torts of its employees.

DISCUSSION: Respondeat superior, or "let the master answer," is the doctrine that is the basis for a principal's liability for an agent's torts (civil wrongs not arising from a breach of contract, e.g., negligence). For this doctrine to apply, the wrongs must be committed within the scope of the agency.

Answer (B) is incorrect. The doctrine of ultra vires prohibits actions beyond powers inherent in the corporation's existence, the articles of incorporation, and the incorporation statutes. Answer (C) is incorrect. A corporation by estoppel arises when an entity that is neither a de jure nor a de facto corporation is treated as a corporation in a suit by a third party. Thus, the entity will be prevented (estopped) from denying corporate status if (1) the organization has represented itself as a corporation, (2) the representation is followed by reasonable reliance and material alteration of position by a third party based on that representation, (3) the third party demonstrates fair and equitable conduct, and (4) injustice can be avoided only by treating the business as a corporation. Answer (D) is incorrect. Ratification is the act of accepting and giving legal effect to an obligation that was not previously enforceable against the ratifying party. For example, a principal may ratify a contract entered into by an agent with no authority. In the corporate context, a newly formed corporation cannot ratify a preincorporation contract because no principal existed at the time of contracting. However, the new entity may adopt such a contract.

7. Which of the following acts is most likely to cause a court to pierce the corporate veil?

A. Failure to designate a registered agent in the articles of incorporation (Charter).

B. Retention of excess capital.

C. Failure to conduct a significant portion of business in the chartering state.

D. Using corporate assets for the owner's personal purposes.

Answer (D) is correct.

REQUIRED: The act most likely to cause a court to pierce the corporate veil.

DISCUSSION: Typically, the corporate veil is pierced when a court finds that the corporation is merely the alter ego of a shareholder, for example, when (1) it is undercapitalized, (2) the assets of the corporation and the shareholders are commingled, (3) corporate formalities are ignored, or (4) the corporation is established for a sham purpose.

Answer (A) is incorrect. Failure to designate a registered agent in the articles of incorporation (Charter) while otherwise complying with the formalities of incorporation results in a de facto corporation. Answer (B) is incorrect. Thin capitalization is a basis for piercing the veil. Answer (C) is incorrect. The portion of business conducted in a state does not affect the validity of incorporation.

8. Which of the following statements is correct regarding both debt and common shares of a corporation?

A. Common shares represent an ownership interest in the corporation, but debt holders do not have an ownership interest.

B. Common shareholders and debt holders have an ownership interest in the corporation.

C. Common shares typically have a fixed maturity date, but debt does not.

D. Common shares have a higher priority on liquidation than debt.

Answer (A) is correct.

REQUIRED: The true statement about debt and common shares.

DISCUSSION: Common shares are equity securities. Thus, they are ownership interests. In contrast, debt holders do not have ownership interests. Rather, debt holders have claims on the corporation's assets. In the event of a liquidation, the debt holders' claims must be satisfied before any distribution to common shareholders.

Answer (B) is incorrect. Debt holders do not have an ownership interest in the corporation. Answer (C) is incorrect. Debt securities typically have a fixed maturity date, but common shares do not. Answer (D) is incorrect. In the event of bankruptcy or liquidation, creditors, including bondholders, have first claim on corporate assets.

9. Under modern statutes, the two general prerequisites to the declaration of a dividend are

I. Corporate solvency in the equity and bankruptcy senses

II. A resolution by the directors to declare a dividend.

A. I only.

B. II only.

C. Both I and II.

D. Neither I nor II.

Answer (C) is correct.

REQUIRED: The general prerequisites to the declaration of a dividend.

DISCUSSION: The board has discretion to determine the time and amount of dividends and other distributions. However, two general prerequisites are used to determine whether the board is likely to distribute dividends. Those prerequisites are corporate profitability or solvency and a resolution by the directors to declare a dividend.

10. Which of the following statements is correct regarding the declaration of a stock dividend by a corporation having only one class of par value stock?

A. A stock dividend has the same legal and practical significance as a stock split.

B. A stock dividend increases a stockholder's proportionate share of corporate ownership.

C. A stock dividend causes a decrease in the assets of the corporation.

D. A stock dividend is a corporation's ratable distribution of additional shares of stock to its stockholders.

Answer (D) is correct.

REQUIRED: The true statement about the declaration of a stock dividend.

DISCUSSION: A stock dividend is payable in the stock of the dividend-paying corporation. New stock generally is issued for this purpose. A stockholder's equity in the corporation is not increased because a stock dividend does not increase the recipient's proportional ownership of the corporation.

Answer (A) is incorrect. The practical significance of a stock split is to reduce the unit value of each share. Answer (B) is incorrect. A stock dividend is distributed in proportion to shares already owned and has no effect on a stockholder's equity. Answer (C) is incorrect. A stock dividend causes a transfer from retained earnings to stated capital, not from an asset account to stated capital.

15.3 Shareholders' Rights

11. All of the following are legal rights of shareholders in U.S. publicly traded companies **except** the right to

A. Vote on major mergers and acquisitions.

B. Receive dividends if declared.

C. Vote on charter and bylaw changes.

D. Vote on major management changes.

Answer (D) is correct.

REQUIRED: The item not a basic legal right of shareholders in publicly traded corporations.

DISCUSSION: A corporation is owned by shareholders who elect a board of directors to manage the company. The board of directors then hires managers to supervise operations. Shareholders do not vote on major management changes because the powers of the board include selection and removal of officers and the setting of management compensation. Shareholders do have the right to vote on fundamental corporate changes, e.g., mergers and acquisitions, any changes in the corporate charter and bylaws, and dissolution.

Answer (A) is incorrect. Shareholders in publicly traded U.S. corporations have the right to vote on fundamental corporate changes. Answer (B) is incorrect. Shareholders have the right to receive declared dividends. Answer (C) is incorrect. Shareholders have the right to vote on charter and bylaw changes.

12. A shareholder's fundamental right to inspect books and records of a corporation will be properly denied if the purpose of the inspection is to

A. Commence a shareholder's derivative suit.

B. Obtain shareholder names for a retail mailing list.

C. Solicit shareholders to vote for a change in the board of directors.

D. Investigate possible management misconduct.

Answer (B) is correct.

REQUIRED: The improper purpose of shareholder inspection of corporate books and records.

DISCUSSION: The fundamental right of a shareholder to inspect the corporation's books and records may be exercised only in good faith for a proper purpose. A proper purpose relates to the shareholder's interest in the corporation, not his or her personal interests, and is not contrary to the corporation's interests. Obtaining a shareholder mailing list is not in itself improper unless it is to further the shareholder's personal interests.

13. A corporate shareholder is entitled to which of the following rights?

A. Elect officers.

B. Receive annual dividends.

C. Approve dissolution.

D. Prevent corporate borrowing.

Answer (C) is correct.

REQUIRED: The right of a shareholder.

DISCUSSION: Shareholders do not have the right to manage the corporation or its business. Shareholder participation in policy and management is through exercising the right to elect directors. Shareholders also have the right to approve charter amendments, disposition of all or substantially all of the corporation's assets, mergers and consolidations, and dissolutions.

Answer (A) is incorrect. The board elects officers. Answer (B) is incorrect. A shareholder does not have a general right to receive dividends. The board determines dividend policy. Answer (D) is incorrect. Determining capital structure and whether the corporation should borrow are policy and management determinations to be made according to the board's business judgment.

14. Hughes and Brody start a business as a close corporation. Hughes owns 51 of the 100 shares of stock issued by the firm and Brody owns 49. One year later, the corporation decides to sell another 200 shares. Which of the following types of rights would give Hughes and Brody a preference over other purchasers to buy shares to maintain control of the firm?

A. Shareholder derivative rights.

B. Preemptive rights.

C. Cumulative voting rights.

D. Inspection rights.

Answer (B) is correct.

REQUIRED: The right providing a purchase preference.

DISCUSSION: Preemptive rights are important to owners of a close corporation. They are options to subscribe to a new issuance in proportion to the shareholder's current interest. Thus, they limit dilution of equity.

Answer (A) is incorrect. A shareholder may file a derivative suit to recover for wrongs done to the corporation. The action is for the benefit of the corporation. It is the true plaintiff. Answer (C) is incorrect. Cumulative voting entitles shareholders either to give one candidate as many votes as the number of directors to be elected, multiplied by the number of shares owned, or to distribute that number of votes among as many candidates as (s)he wishes. Answer (D) is incorrect. Shareholders have a fundamental right to inspect the corporation's books and records.

15. For what purpose will a shareholder of a publicly held corporation be permitted to file a shareholder derivative suit in the name of the corporation?

A. To compel payment of a properly declared dividend.

B. To enforce a right to inspect corporate records.

C. To compel dissolution of the corporation.

D. To recover damages from corporate management for an ultra vires management act.

Answer (D) is correct.

REQUIRED: The basis for a shareholder derivative suit.

DISCUSSION: A derivative suit is a cause of action brought by one or more shareholders on behalf of the corporation to enforce a right belonging to the corporation. Shareholders may bring such an action when the board of directors refuses to act on the corporation's behalf. Generally, the shareholder must show (1) (s)he owned stock at the time of the wrongdoing, (2) (s)he made a demand to the corporation to bring suit or take other appropriate action, and (3) a bad-faith refusal of the board of directors to pursue the corporation's interest. The recovery, if any, belongs to the corporation. An action to recover damages from corporate management for an ultra vires act is an example of a derivative suit. An ultra vires act is one beyond the limits of the corporate purposes defined in the articles of incorporation.

Answer (A) is incorrect. Shareholders must sue directly on their own behalf to compel payment of a properly declared dividend. Answer (B) is incorrect. Shareholders must sue directly on their own behalf to enforce a right to inspect corporate records. Answer (C) is incorrect. Shareholders must sue directly on their own behalf to compel dissolution of the corporation.

15.4 Directors' and Officers' Authority, Duties, and Liability

16. Which of the following corporate actions is subject to shareholder approval?

A. Election of officers.

B. Removal of officers.

C. Declaration of cash dividends.

D. Removal of directors.

Answer (D) is correct.

REQUIRED: The action that must be approved by the shareholders.

DISCUSSION: A corporation is governed by shareholders (owners) who elect the directors on the corporation's board and who approve fundamental changes in the corporate structure. Directors establish corporate policies and elect or appoint corporate officers who carry out the policies in the day-to-day management of the organization. In most states, the shareholders may by a majority vote remove, with or without cause, any director or the entire board.

Answer (A) is incorrect. The officers are elected by the directors. Answer (B) is incorrect. Officers are removed by the directors. Answer (C) is incorrect. The board of directors has the discretion to determine the nature, time, and amount of dividends and other distributions.

17. Which of the following actions is required to ensure the validity of a contract between a corporation and a director of the corporation?

A. An independent appraiser must render to the board of directors a fairness opinion on the contract.

B. The director must disclose the interest to the independent members of the board and refrain from voting.

C. The shareholders must review and ratify the contract.

D. The director must resign from the board of directors.

Answer (B) is correct.

REQUIRED: The action to ensure the validity of a contract between a corporation and a director.

DISCUSSION: To protect the corporation against self-dealing, a director is required to make full disclosure of any financial interest (s)he may have in any transaction to which both the director and the corporation may be a party. Under modern corporate law, a transaction is not voidable merely on the grounds of a director's conflict of interest if the transaction is fair to the corporation or has been approved by a majority of (1) informed, disinterested qualified directors or (2) holders of qualified shares. This rule applies even if the director was counted for the quorum and voted to approve the transaction. A qualified director does not have (1) a conflict of interest regarding the transaction or (2) a special relationship (familial, professional, financial, etc.) with another director who has a conflict of interest. Shares are qualified if they are not controlled by a person with (1) a conflict of interest or (2) a close relationship with someone who has a conflict. Thus, the director who contracts with the corporation cannot provide the vote that approves the contract.

Answer (A) is incorrect. No such requirement exists. However, shareholders who disagree with fundamental corporate changes have appraisal rights to receive the fair value of their shares. Answer (C) is incorrect. Shareholder ratification is unnecessary. However, if the transaction is fair, approval by shareholders prevents it from being voided. Furthermore, unanimous shareholder approval may release the director from liability even if the transaction is unfair. Answer (D) is incorrect. Resignation is not required. Self-dealing transactions are permissible in many cases.

18. Seymore was recently invited to become a director of Buckley Industries, Inc. If Seymore accepts and becomes a director, Seymore, along with the other directors, will **not** be personally liable for

A. Lack of reasonable care.

B. Honest errors of judgment.

C. Declaration of a dividend that the directors know will impair legal capital.

D. Diversion of corporate opportunities to themselves.

Answer (B) is correct.

REQUIRED: The action for which a director is not personally liable.

DISCUSSION: The directors of a corporation owe a fiduciary duty to the corporation and the shareholders. They also are expected to exercise reasonable business judgment. The law does recognize human fallibility and allows for directors to be safe from liability for honest mistakes of judgment.

Answer (A) is incorrect. Directors must discharge their duties with the care that a person in a similar position would reasonably believe appropriate under similar circumstances. Answer (C) is incorrect. Directors are prohibited from declaring dividends that would violate a state statute establishing a minimum legal capital. Answer (D) is incorrect. Directors may not exploit opportunities presented to them in their capacity as directors without first offering those opportunities to the corporation.

19. Knox, president of Quick Corp., contracted with Tine Office Supplies, Inc., to supply Quick's stationery on customary terms and at a cost less than that charged by any other supplier. Knox later informed Quick's board of directors that Knox was a majority shareholder in Tine. Quick's contract with Tine is

A. Void because of Knox's self-dealing.

B. Void because the disclosure was made after execution of the contract.

C. Valid because of Knox's full disclosure.

D. Valid because the contract is fair to Quick.

Answer (D) is correct.

REQUIRED: The enforceability of a contract entered into by a corporate officer with an interest in the contract.

DISCUSSION: An officer, like a director, owes fiduciary duties of care and loyalty to the corporation and its shareholders. Knox was required to disclose fully the financial interest in the transaction to which the corporation was a party. But a transaction approved by a majority of informed, disinterested directors or shareholders or that is fair to the corporation is valid, notwithstanding a conflict of interest.

Answer (A) is incorrect. Self-dealing does not render a transaction voidable if it is fair to the corporation. Answer (B) is incorrect. Nondisclosure does not render a transaction voidable if it is fair to the corporation. Answer (C) is incorrect. Full disclosure merely forms a basis for approval by a majority of informed, disinterested directors or shareholders.

20. The business judgment rule is a rule that immunizes corporate

A. Management from liability for actions that result in corporate losses or damages if the actions are undertaken in good faith but are not within the power of the corporation or the authority of management to make.

B. Management from liability for actions that result in corporate losses or damages if the actions are undertaken in good faith and are within both the power of the corporation and the authority of management to make.

C. Shareholders from liability for actions that result in corporate losses or damages if the actions are undertaken in good faith and are within both the power of the corporation and the authority of shareholders to make.

D. Shareholders from liability for actions that result in corporate losses or damages if the actions are undertaken in good faith but are not within the power of the corporation or the authority of shareholders to make.

Answer (B) is correct.

REQUIRED: The nature of the business judgment rule.

DISCUSSION: Courts avoid substituting their business judgment for that of the corporation's officers or directors. The rule protects an officer or a director from personal liability for honest mistakes of judgment if (s)he (1) acted in good faith; (2) was not motivated by fraud, conflict of interest, or illegality; and (3) was not grossly negligent. To avoid personal liability, directors and officers must (1) make informed decisions (educate themselves about the issues), (2) be free from conflicts of interest, and (3) have a rational basis to support their position.

Answer (A) is incorrect. The doctrine of ultra vires states that a corporation may not act beyond the powers inherent in the corporate existence or provided in the articles of incorporation and the incorporation statutes. However, ultra vires has been largely eliminated as a defense. Articles of incorporation authorizing any lawful business transaction are now common. Answer (C) is incorrect. The business judgment rule protects those who manage the corporation, not shareholders unless they also manage the corporation. Answer (D) is incorrect. The business judgment rule protects those who manage the corporation, not shareholders unless they also manage the corporation.

21. Under the Revised Model Business Corporation Act (RMBCA), which of the following statements is true regarding corporate officers of a public corporation?

A. An officer may not simultaneously serve as a director.

B. A corporation may be authorized to indemnify its officers for liability incurred in a suit by shareholders.

C. Shareholders always have the right to elect a corporation's officers.

D. An officer of a corporation is required to own at least one share of the corporation's stock.

Answer (B) is correct.

REQUIRED: The true statement about corporate officers of a public corporation.

DISCUSSION: According to the RMBCA, corporations may indemnify their officers for liability incurred in a suit by shareholders, except when inconsistent with public policy, to the extent provided by the articles of incorporation, bylaws, actions of the board, or contract.

Answer (A) is incorrect. An individual may serve as both a director and an officer. Answer (C) is incorrect. A corporation's officers are appointed by the board of directors, not by shareholders. Answer (D) is incorrect. An officer of a corporation need not be a shareholder.

15.5 Mergers and Termination

22. Under the Revised Model Business Corporation Act (RMBCA), following what type of corporate acquisition does the acquiring corporation automatically become liable for all obligations of the acquired corporation?

A. A leveraged buyout of assets.

B. An acquisition of stock for debt securities.

C. A cash tender offer.

D. A merger.

Answer (D) is correct.

REQUIRED: The corporate acquisition in which the acquirer automatically becomes liable for all obligations of the acquired corporation.

DISCUSSION: Under the RMBCA, when a merger becomes effective, (1) the entity designated in the plan of merger as the survivor comes into existence, (2) every entity merged ceases to exist separately, (3) the property and contract rights of the merged entities are vested in the survivor, and (4) the liabilities of the merged entities also are vested in the survivor.

Answer (A) is incorrect. A debt-financed purchase of assets or stock does not inherently impose liability on the acquirer for the other entity's obligations. The assets essentially are security for the debt incurred in the purchase. However, the acquirer might subsequently merge with the acquiree, in which case it would become liable. Answer (B) is incorrect. A debt-financed purchase of assets or stock does not inherently impose liability on the acquirer for the other entity's obligations. The assets essentially are security for the debt incurred in the purchase. However, the acquirer might subsequently merge with the acquiree, in which case it would become liable. Answer (C) is incorrect. Acquiring another entity's shares with a cash tender offer does not automatically vest the liabilities of the acquiree in the acquirer. However, the offer might include an undertaking to assume those liabilities.

23. Generally, a merger of two corporations requires

A. That a special meeting notice and a copy of the merger plan be given to all shareholders of both corporations.

B. Unanimous approval of the merger plan by the shareholders of both corporations.

C. Unanimous approval of the merger plan by the boards of both corporations.

D. That all liabilities owed by the absorbed corporation be paid before the merger.

Answer (A) is correct.

REQUIRED: The prerequisite to a merger.

DISCUSSION: A corporation is merged into another when shareholders of the target corporation receive cash or shares of the surviving corporation in exchange for their target corporation shares. The target shares are canceled, and it ceases to exist. State law generally requires approval by a majority of the board and of shares of each corporation. A special shareholder meeting notice (purpose is stated) and a copy of the merger plan must be provided to shareholders of each corporation to enable informed voting.

Answer (B) is incorrect. Unless a state statute or the charter imposes a supermajority requirement, majority approval is generally required. Answer (C) is incorrect. Unless a state statute or the charter imposes a supermajority requirement, majority approval is generally required. Answer (D) is incorrect. Rights and liabilities of the absorbed company generally become those of the surviving corporation.

24. Acorn Corp. wants to acquire the entire business of Trend Corp. Which of the following methods of business combination will best satisfy Acorn's objectives without requiring the approval of the shareholders of either corporation?

A. A merger of Trend into Acorn, whereby Trend shareholders receive cash or Acorn shares.

B. A sale of all the assets of Trend, outside the regular course of business, to Acorn, for cash.

C. An acquisition of all the shares of Trend through a compulsory share exchange for Acorn shares.

D. A cash tender offer, whereby Acorn acquires at least 90% of Trend's shares, followed by a short-form merger of Trend into Acorn.

Answer (D) is correct.

REQUIRED: The acquisition method that does not require shareholder approval.

DISCUSSION: A merger, consolidation, or purchase of substantially all of a corporation's assets requires approval of the board of directors of the corporation whose shares or assets are acquired. An acquiring corporation may bypass shareholder approval by using a short-form merger. No shareholder approval is required if a corporation that owns at least 90% of a subsidiary merger with the subsidiary using a short-form merger.

Answer (A) is incorrect. A merger requires the approval of shareholders. Answer (B) is incorrect. A sale of all assets outside the regular course of business requires the approval of shareholders. Answer (C) is incorrect. A compulsory share exchange requires the approval of shareholders.

25. Which of the following actions may be taken by a corporation's board of directors without shareholder approval?

A. Purchasing substantially all of the assets of another corporation.

B. Selling substantially all of the corporation's assets.

C. Dissolving the corporation.

D. Amending the articles of incorporation.

Answer (A) is correct.

REQUIRED: The action by a corporation's board not requiring shareholder approval.

DISCUSSION: The board of directors directly controls a corporation by establishing overall corporate policy and overseeing its implementation. In exercising their powers, board members must maintain high standards of care and loyalty but need not obtain shareholder approval except for fundamental corporate changes. Purchasing substantially all of the assets (or stock) of another corporation is a policy decision properly made by the board of directors, not a fundamental change. It does not require shareholder approval in the absence of a bylaw or special provision in the articles of incorporation.

Answer (B) is incorrect. Selling substantially all of the corporation's assets is considered a fundamental change and therefore must be voted on and approved by the shareholders. Fundamental changes are usually initiated by resolution of the board of directors urging the shareholders to approve the change. Answer (C) is incorrect. Dissolving the corporation is considered a fundamental change and therefore must be voted on and approved by the shareholders. Fundamental changes are usually initiated by resolution of the board of directors urging the shareholders to approve the change. Answer (D) is incorrect. Amending the articles of incorporation is considered a fundamental change and therefore must be voted on and approved by the shareholders. Fundamental changes are usually initiated by resolution of the board of directors urging the shareholders to approve the change.

26. Which of the following must take place before a corporation may be voluntarily dissolved?

A. Passage by the board of directors of a resolution to dissolve.

B. Approval by the officers of a resolution to dissolve.

C. Amendment of the certificate of incorporation.

D. Unanimous vote of the shareholders.

Answer (A) is correct.

REQUIRED: The act usually a precondition to voluntary dissolution.

DISCUSSION: If a corporation has issued stock and commenced business, its voluntary dissolution requires board approval of a dissolution resolution, shareholder vote of approval, and filing of articles of dissolution with the secretary of state. This filing serves to dissolve the corporation on its effective date. Voluntary dissolution without a board resolution is permitted upon unanimous written consent of the shareholders.

Answer (B) is incorrect. A corporation may voluntarily dissolve without approval by its officers. Answer (C) is incorrect. Filing articles of dissolution, not an amendment of the charter, is required. Answer (D) is incorrect. A majority of shares is usually sufficient to approve a board-approved dissolution resolution.

15.6 Advantages and Disadvantages of Corporations

27. Which of the following statements best describes an advantage of the corporate form of doing business?

A. Day-to-day management is strictly the responsibility of the directors.

B. Ownership is contractually restricted and is not transferable.

C. The operation of the business may continue indefinitely.

D. The business is free from state regulation.

Answer (C) is correct.

REQUIRED: The advantage of the corporate form.

DISCUSSION: A corporation has perpetual existence unless it is given a shorter life under the articles of incorporation or is dissolved by the state. Death, withdrawal, or addition of a shareholder, director, or officer does not terminate its existence.

Answer (A) is incorrect. Officers run day-to-day operations. Answer (B) is incorrect. Absent a specific contractual restriction, shares are freely transferable, e.g., by gift, sale, pledge, or inheritance. Answer (D) is incorrect. A corporation can be created only under state law.

28. In which type of business entity is the entire ownership interest most freely transferable?

A. General partnership.

B. Limited partnership.

C. Corporation.

D. Limited liability company.

Answer (C) is correct.

REQUIRED: The business entity in which the entire ownership interest is most freely transferable.

DISCUSSION: Simply acquiring a corporation's stock gives an individual an ownership interest. Shares can be freely bought and sold, usually without any restriction.

Answer (A) is incorrect. An ownership interest in a general partnership is not easily transferable. An interest can be assigned, but an assignee does not have the rights of a general partner. Moreover, the other partners must approve the admission of a new partner. Answer (B) is incorrect. An ownership interest in a limited partnership is not easily transferable. The partnership may impose restraints on assignability, for example, to qualify for an exemption from registration under federal securities law. Answer (D) is incorrect. An ownership interest in a limited liability company is not easily transferable. A transferee does not become a member absent consent of all members or a provision in their agreement.

29. In which type of business organization are income taxes always required to be paid by the entity on profits earned as well as by the owners upon distribution thereof?

A. General partnership.

B. Limited liability company.

C. C corporation.

D. S corporation.

Answer (C) is correct.

REQUIRED: The business organization in which income taxes always are paid by the entity on its profits.

DISCUSSION: A C corporation is an entity subject to the corporate income tax. Any corporation that is not an S corporation is a C corporation. An S corporation is a closely held corporation that has made an election under federal law to be taxed similarly to a partnership. Thus, an S corporation does not usually pay corporate income tax.

Answer (A) is incorrect. A general partnership is a pass-through entity that files an informational return. It avoids the double taxation to which a C corporation is subject. Answer (B) is incorrect. An LLC's members may elect to be taxed as partners, and single-member LLCs may be taxed as sole proprietorships. Also, taxation as a corporation is an option. It may be advantageous if reinvestment in the LLC is desired and corporate rates are lower than personal rates. Answer (D) is incorrect. An S corporation is a closely held corporation that has made an election under federal law to be taxed similarly to a partnership. Hence, it does not usually pay income tax.

15.7 PRACTICE TASK-BASED SIMULATIONS

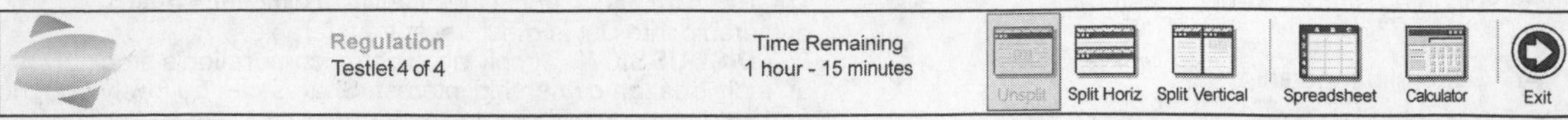

DIRECTIONS

Note: If you believe you have encountered a software malfunction, report it to the test center staff immediately.

Navigation

To navigate from task to task, use the controls at the bottom of the screen. Click on the **Next** button to advance to the next task, or the **Previous** button to go to the previous task. To go directly to any task, click on its number.

If you would like a reminder to revisit a task, or want to indicate that you are finished with it, click on the reminder flag below the task number. To clear the flag, click on it again. Reminder flags are for your use only – they do not contribute to your score.

Tabs

In this part of the examination, you will be asked to complete various tasks. Every task has one or more **Work Tabs**. Some tasks have one or more **Information Tabs**, others may have none. Every task has a **Help** tab.

If a task has **Information Tabs**, you may use the information in them to complete your responses in the **Work Tabs**.

Work tab **Information tab** **Help tab**

Work Tabs:

- **Work Tabs** are identified with a pencil icon. This is where your responses are expected.
- Each task has one or more **Work Tabs**.
- **Work Tabs** contain directions for completing the task – be sure to read these directions carefully.
- The **Work Tab** name in the example above is for illustration only – yours will differ.
- You must complete all of the **Work Tabs** in each task to receive full credit.

Information Tabs:

- The Authoritative Literature will be provided in all tasks in the AUD, FAR, and REG sections for your reference.
- Your simulation may have one or more additional **Information Tabs**. Like the Authoritative Literature tabs, **Information Tabs** do not have a pencil icon.
- If your task has additional **Information Tabs**, go through each to familiarize yourself with the task content.

Help Tab:

- The **Help Tab** provides assistance with the exam software that is used in this task. For example, if the task is to compose a memorandum, **Help** will provide information about the word processor.

The Toolbar

The toolbar at the top of the screen shows the amount of time remaining for you to complete the tasks. In addition, the following tools are available. Note that only the **Exit** button is displayed when Directions are visible - the others will appear when you begin the tasks.

Click on these buttons to split or unsplit the screen. You can split the screen vertically or horizontally.

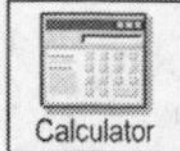

Click on this button to display the calculator; click on it again to hide the calculator. To move the calculator, click on the calculator title bar and drag the calculator to the desired location.

Click on this button to use the spreadsheet; click on it again to hide the spreadsheet. To move the spreadsheet, click on the the spreadsheet title bar and drag the spreadsheet to the desired location.

Click on this button to go on to the next part of the examination. You must complete all of the tasks to receive full credit. Once you click on **Exit** and confirm the action, you will NOT be able to return to this testlet.

= Reminder | Directions | 1 2 3 4 5 | Previous | Next

During your examination of the financial statements of Wyatt Associates, Inc., for the fiscal year ended June 30, Year 1, you discovered the following facts relating to a transaction with Flinko Corporation. The transaction occurred during April Year 1.

Flinko, one of Wyatt's major competitors, was insolvent in the equity sense because it could not meet the claims of its current creditors. Wyatt offered to purchase all of Flinko's assets, including furniture, fixtures, equipment, materials, supplies, inventory, and any and all other assets owned by Flinko. Wyatt's offering letter stated a price equal to 105% of the total of all outstanding claims of Flinko's creditors. Bob, Flinko's CEO, then offered to purchase Wyatt, which Wyatt's board immediately rejected. Bob decided to sign Wyatt's original offer.

Select from the list the appropriate ending to each statement below. Each choice may be used once, more than once, or not at all.

Statement	***Answer***
1. Wyatt's letter to Flinko is considered	
2. Flinko's offer letter to Wyatt is considered	
3. Wyatt's form of acquisition is considered	

Choices
A) A contractual offer.
B) A merger.
C) A consolidation agreement.
D) A counteroffer.
E) A self tender.
F) A consolidation.
G) An acquisition of substantially all assets.
H) A tender offer.

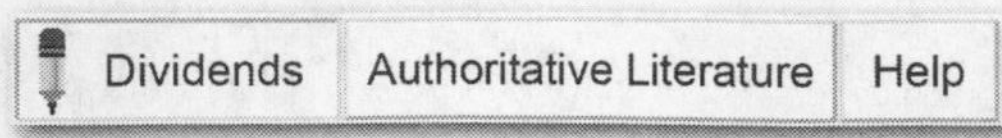

On May 12, Year 15, West purchased 6% of Ace Corp.'s outstanding $3 cumulative preferred stock and 7% of Ace's outstanding common stock. These are the only two classes of stock authorized by Ace's charter. Both classes of stock are traded on a national stock exchange. Ace uses the calendar year for financial reporting purposes.

Complete each statement by selecting from the list provided the appropriate action for each party. Each choice may be used once, more than once, or not at all.

Statement	*Answer*
1. West will	
2. Ace should	

During Year 15 and Year 16, Ace neither declared dividends nor recorded dividends in arrears as a liability on its books. On February 8, Year 17, West, a 10% shareholder, sent a written demand to examine Ace's books and records to determine Ace's financial condition. Ace has refused to permit West to examine its books and records.

Complete each statement by selecting from the list provided the appropriate action for each party following Ace's refusal. Each choice may be used once, more than once, or not at all.

Statement	*Answer*
3. Regarding the dividends, West will	
4. West is entitled to	
5. Ace is required to	

Choices
A) Be treated as a general creditor to the extent of the dividends in arrears
B) Receive nothing
C) Pierce the corporate veil because the directors violated their duty of care
D) Receive dividends immediately
E) Examine Ace's books and records
F) Record dividends in arrears
G) Disclose dividends in arrears in notes to financial statements
H) Pay dividends
I) None of the above

Bulldog Corporation produces mechanical widgets. Its profits have decreased for each of the past 10 years. Tiger, Inc., produces electrical widgets. Its profits have increased for the past 5 years, but the CEO sees an opportunity to increase its market share by combining with Bulldog.

Select from the list provided the best descriptive term for each of the following actions. Each choice may be used once, more than once, or not at all.

Action	Answer
1. Tiger's CEO sends a letter offering to purchase substantially all of Bulldog Corporation's assets.	
2. After receiving Tiger's offer, Bulldog offers to purchase Tiger's assets.	
3. Bulldog Corporation and Tiger, Inc., combine to form Bull Tiger, Inc.	
4. Tiger, Inc., offers to purchase all of Bulldog Corporation's shares.	
5. Tiger, Inc., acquires all of the shares of Bulldog Corporation and combines their operations. Bulldog, not Tiger, ceases to exist.	

Choices
A) Tender offer
B) Reverse tender
C) Contractual offer
D) Appraisal rights
E) Poison pill
F) Contractual counteroffer
G) Consolidation
H) Merger

Frost, Glen, and Bradley own 50%, 40%, and 10%, respectively, of the authorized and issued voting common stock of Xeon Corp. They had a written shareholders' agreement that provided they would vote for each other as directors of the corporation.

At the initial shareholders' meeting, Frost, Glen, Bradley, and three others were elected to a six-person board of directors. The board elected Frost as president of the corporation, Glen as secretary, and Bradley as vice president. Frost and Glen were given 2-year contracts with annual salaries of $50,000. Bradley was given a 2-year contract for $10,000 per year.

At the end of its first year of operation, Xeon was in financial difficulty. Bradley disagreed with the way Frost and Glen were running the business.

At the annual meeting, a new board of directors was elected. Bradley was excluded because Frost and Glen did not vote for Bradley. Without cause, the new board fired Bradley as vice president even though 12 months remained on Bradley's contract.

Despite the corporation's financial difficulties, the new board, relying on the assurances of Frost and Glen and based on fraudulent documentation provided by Frost and Glen, declared and paid a $200,000 dividend. Payment of the dividend caused the corporation to become insolvent.

Check the appropriate box to show who should generally prevail in the following cases.

Case	Plaintiff	Defendant
1. Bradley sued Frost and Glen to compel them to follow the written shareholders' agreement and reelect Bradley to the board.		
2. Bradley sued the corporation to be reinstated as an officer of the corporation.		
3. Bradley sued the corporation for breach of the employment contract.		
4. Bradley sued the board for declaring and paying an unlawful dividend and demanded its repayment to the corporation.		
5. Bradley sued Frost and Glen on behalf of the corporation for violating their duty of care.		

= Reminder | Directions | 1 2 3 4 5 | Previous | Next

Corporate Operation | Authoritative Literature | Help

In Year 1, Amber Corp., a closely held corporation, was formed by Adams, Frank, and Berg as incorporators and shareholders. Adams, Frank, and Berg executed a written voting agreement providing that they would vote for each other as directors and officers. In Year 5, stock in the corporation was offered to the public. This resulted in an additional 300 shareholders. After the offering, Adams holds 25%, Frank holds 15%, and Berg holds 15% of all issued and outstanding stock. Adams, Frank, and Berg have been directors and officers of the corporation since its formation. Regular meetings of the board of directors and annual shareholders meetings have been held.

Items 1 through 6 refer to the formation of Amber Corp. and the rights and duties of its shareholders, directors, and officers. For each item, indicate whether A), B), or C) is correct.

Statement	***Answer***
1. A) Amber Corp. must be formed under a state's general corporation statute. B) Amber Corp.'s articles of incorporation must include the names of all shareholders. C) Amber Corp. must include its corporate bylaws in the incorporation documents filed with the state.	
2. Amber Corp.'s initial bylaws ordinarily would be adopted by its A) Shareholders. B) Officers. C) Directors.	
3. Amber Corp.'s directors are elected by its A) Officers. B) Outgoing directors. C) Shareholders.	
4. Amber Corp.'s officers ordinarily are elected by its A) Shareholders. B) Directors. C) Outgoing officers.	
5. Amber Corp.'s day-to-day business ordinarily is operated by its A) Directors. B) Shareholders. C) Officers.	
6. A) Adams, Frank, and Berg must be elected as directors because they own 55% of the issued and outstanding stock. B) Adams, Frank, and Berg must always be elected as officers because they own 55% of the issued and outstanding stock. C) Adams, Frank, and Berg must always vote for each other as directors because they have a voting agreement.	

Unofficial Answers

1. Purchase Offers (3 Gradable Items)

1. A) A contractual offer. Wyatt made a simple contract offer to buy the assets of Flinko. No tender offer was made to Flinko's shareholders.
2. D) A counteroffer. Flinko rejected Wyatt's offer and made a counteroffer. Accordingly, Flinko could not then accept Wyatt's offer. Varying the terms of Wyatt's offer operated as a rejection.
3. G) An acquisition of substantially all assets. A merger is the combination of all the assets of two or more corporations. In a merger, one corporation is absorbed by another corporation and ceases to exist. An acquisition of substantially all assets does not necessarily end the seller's corporate existence.

2. Dividends (5 Gradable Items)

1. Receive nothing. If dividends were declared and paid for Year 15, they would have been declared at the end of the calendar year and paid soon after. West has only just purchased the cumulative preferred stock and common stock. Thus, West is not yet entitled to receive dividends.
2. None of the above. Ace does not need to take any of the listed actions for the sale of its cumulative preferred stock and common stock. Ace does not need to record or disclose any information about dividends because the purchaser has only just acquired the shares and is not yet entitled to dividends.
3. Receive nothing. West's assertion that Ace should have recorded the dividends in arrears for Year 15 and Year 16 is incorrect. A holder of cumulative preferred stock is entitled to receive all dividends in arrears plus any dividends for the current year before any dividends may be distributed to the shareholders of common stock. However, a preferred shareholder is not a creditor of the corporation until a dividend is declared. Ace did not declare dividends or record a liability, so West does not receive, and is not currently owed, anything. The dividends in arrears are a liability after dividends are declared.
4. Examine Ace's books and records. West's assertion that West is entitled to examine Ace's books and records is correct. A shareholder, upon written demand, is entitled to examine, at reasonable times, the books and records of the corporation if the examination is for a proper purpose (in good faith). If the corporation refuses to permit the examination, the shareholder may obtain a court order compelling access to the books and records.
5. Disclose dividends in arrears in notes to financial statements. Given that Ace has neither declared dividends nor recorded dividends as a liability, the dividends in arrears must be disclosed in the notes to the financial statements. Once the dividends have been declared, dividends are recorded in the following order: dividends in arrears, dividends for the current year to preferred shareholders, and dividends for the current year to the common shareholders. If the declared dividends suffice only to pay dividends in arrears and dividends for the current year to preferred shareholders, common shareholders do not receive dividends for the year.

3. Business Combinations (5 Gradable Items)

1. C) Contractual offer. Tiger has offered to enter into a contract with Bulldog to acquire its assets. No tender offer was made because the offer was not made to Bulldog's shareholders to buy their shares.
2. F) Contractual counteroffer. Bulldog's offer to buy Tiger's assets varied the terms of Tiger's offer. Thus, it acted as a rejection and counteroffer. A reverse tender is made when the target corporation (Bulldog Corporation) makes an offer to acquire the shares of the tender offeror (Tiger, Inc.).
3. G) Consolidation. A consolidation occurs when a new corporation is formed and the two or more consolidating corporations cease operating as separate entities.
4. A) Tender offer. A tender offer is made directly to the shareholders of a corporation to purchase their shares. Its advantage is that it permits a business combination without the approval of the board of the target entity.
5. H) Merger. A merger combines the assets of two or more corporations. One corporation is absorbed by another and ceases to exist. In a consolidation, a new corporation is formed, and the two or more consolidating corporations cease operating as separate entities.

4. Misconduct by Owners (5 Gradable Items)

1. Plaintiff. Bradley will be successful in the suit against Frost and Glen for failing to vote Bradley to the board of directors. The shareholders have the right to elect the directors of a corporation. They also have the right to agree among themselves about how they will vote. Thus, the voting provision of the shareholders' agreement among Bradley, Frost, and Glen is enforceable.
2. Defendant. Bradley will be unsuccessful in attempting to be reinstated as vice president. A corporation's board oversees the operations of the business, which includes appointing officers and, at its discretion, dismissing officers with or without cause.
3. Plaintiff. Bradley will be successful in collecting damages for the breach of the employment contract absent breach of the contract by Bradley or another excuse for nonperformance by the corporation.
4. Defendant. The board will prevail. It relied on the assurances and information supplied by Frost and Glen as corporate officers and is protected by the business judgment rule. Thus, only Frost and Glen will be personally liable.
5. Plaintiff. Bradley will be successful in holding Frost and Glen personally liable to the corporation for declaring and paying the dividend. Payment of a dividend that threatens a corporation's solvency is unlawful. Ordinarily, directors who approve such a dividend are personally liable for its repayment to the corporation.

5. Corporate Operation (6 Gradable Items)

1. A) Amber Corp. must be formed under a state's general corporation statute. Corporations are legal entities that must be formally created under a state's general corporation statute. The articles of incorporation must include the names and addresses of the incorporators but not the shareholders. The bylaws are adopted after the company is already incorporated and are not filed.
2. C) Directors. The board of directors holds an organizational meeting to adopt the bylaws that govern the internal management of the corporation. The power to alter, amend, or repeal the bylaws is vested in the board of directors unless this power is specifically reserved to the shareholders in the charter.
3. C) Shareholders. Shareholders participate indirectly in corporate policy by electing all directors and approving all fundamental corporate changes. However, the initial board of directors is usually elected by the incorporators and serves until the first meeting of shareholders.
4. B) Directors. The board of directors establishes and implements overall corporate policy and is responsible for appointing the corporate officers.
5. C) Officers. The corporate officers are responsible for the day-to-day operations of the business. Typically, officers elected include president, treasurer, and secretary, although the number of officers is not limited. Each officer is an agent of the corporation and has the express and implied authority to perform the duties of the office.
6. C) Adams, Frank, and Berg must always vote for each other as directors because they have a voting agreement. A voting agreement in which shareholders contract as to how they will vote their shares is specifically allowable by the RMBCA and is enforceable. Without an enforceable voting agreement or voting trust, the majority shareholders are not required to be elected to the board or as officers.

Gleim Simulation Grading

Task	Correct Responses		Gradable Items		Score per Task
1	____	÷	3	=	____
2	____	÷	5	=	____
3	____	÷	5	=	____
4	____	÷	5	=	____
5	____	÷	6	=	____
			Total of Scores per Task		____
		÷	Total Number of Tasks		5
			Total Score		____ %

STUDY UNIT SIXTEEN
AGENCY AND REGULATION

(25 pages of outline)

The first four subunits cover the law of agency, which relates to the rights and duties of the principal, the agent, and third parties. The emphasis is on (1) the formation and termination of an agency, (2) the duties of the agent to the principal and third parties, (3) the duties of the principal to the agent and third parties, (4) the agent's actual and apparent authority, and (5) the significance of whether the agency is disclosed.

The remaining subunits relate to regulation. Government regulation is an extremely broad subject. The content specification outline mentions federal laws and regulations for antitrust, copyrights, patents, money laundering, labor, employment, and ERISA.

16.1 FORMATION OF AN AGENCY

1. **Overview**
   a. An agency is an **express or implied consensual relationship** formed when two parties agree that one (the agent) will represent the other (the principal) in dealing with third parties.
      1) The **agent** has authority to act on behalf of the principal and is subject to the principal's control.
      2) The **principal** must intend for the agent to act on the principal's behalf. This intent is measured by the standard of a **reasonable person**.

EXAMPLE

Bud overheard Harold say, "I wish I had a boat." Bud went to Boatworld and told the salesperson that, acting as Harold's agent, he wanted to buy a boat. An agency was not formed.

   b. The agent must agree to act on the principal's behalf as a **fiduciary**.
   c. The agency must have a **legal purpose**.
      1) Agencies formed for an illegal purpose are terminated by operation of law.
   d. The principal must have the legal capacity to perform the act assigned to the agent.
      1) A contract entered into by an agent with a third party on behalf of an incompetent principal is generally voidable by the principal.
      2) An incompetent agent, such as a minor, can bind a competent principal because the agent's act is deemed to be the act of the principal.
   e. Personal acts, such as executing a will, may not be delegated.

2. **Formation**

   a. The basic rule is that an oral agreement is sufficient to form an agency even if the agent enters into contracts that must be in writing under the statute of frauds.

      1) Some states require the agency to be **in writing** only if the contract involves a **sale of land**.
      2) Others require an agency for any contract within the statute of frauds (e.g., a contract that cannot be **completed in 1 year**) to be in writing.

   b. An agency may be **implied in law** without intent to form the relationship.

      1) A person may be held liable as a principal for the act of another person even though (s)he did not intend to grant any authority. For example, a court may determine that an agent acted properly outside of his or her delegated authority in an emergency when unable to contact the principal.

   c. **Agency by Estoppel**

      1) This condition may arise if

         a) A person presents himself or herself as an agent,
         b) The alleged principal knows (or should know) of the representation and fails to make an effective denial, and
         c) A third party detrimentally relies on the existence of this presumed agency.

      2) The principal is prevented from asserting the nonexistence of an agency after a third party has taken some action in reasonable reliance on its existence.

   d. A **power of attorney** is a formal written appointment of an agent signed by the principal.

      1) A general power of attorney authorizes the agent to do anything that may be necessary to transact the principal's legal affairs.
      2) A special power of attorney grants authority for only specific transactions.
      3) A durable power of attorney is effective during a period of incapacity of the principal.

         a) This power of attorney must be expressly conferred in writing before the principal becomes incapacitated.

      4) Both general and special powers of attorney end upon incapacity of the principal.
      5) All powers of attorney end upon the **death** of the principal.

   e. An agency may be formed by **ratification** of another's acts.

   f. An agency relationship need not be contractual.

      1) If the agency does arise by contract, each element of a contract must be present. (Contracts are covered in Study Unit 17.)

3. **Types of Agents**

   a. **General agents** are authorized to perform all acts relevant to the purpose for which they are engaged.

   b. **Universal agents** are authorized to conduct all of the principal's business that the principal may legally delegate.

   c. **Special agents** are engaged for a particular transaction and are authorized to perform specific activities subject to specific instructions.

   d. A **del credere agent** guarantees the obligations of a third party to the principal.

      1) The obligation of a del credere agent is based on the promise to answer for the debt of another. A person making this promise is a surety.

e. In an **agency coupled with an interest**, the agent has a specific, current, beneficial interest in the subject matter of the agency.

1) This form of agency is irrevocable by the principal.
2) The agent's interest in the subject matter is not exercised for the benefit of the principal.

EXAMPLE

A stockbroker working on commission does not have an agency coupled with an interest. Receipt of a commission depends on whether the shareholder receives a benefit from the sale of the stock. The interest need not be an ownership or security interest in the stock itself.

Stop and review! You have completed the outline for this subunit. Study multiple-choice questions 1 through 4 on page 604.

16.2 AGENT'S AUTHORITY AND DUTIES

The CPA exam has tested candidates' knowledge of an agent's actual and apparent authority. Candidates need to remember that the principal is liable on contracts made by an agent who has actual, apparent, or emergency authority.

1. **Authority**

a. An agency involves mutual understanding that the agent will act on behalf of the principal under the principal's direction and control. The agent can legally bind the principal only when the agent has authority to do so.

b. **Actual Authority**

1) Actual authority is conveyed to the agent by the principal's words or conduct. The agent receives the right and power to bind the principal to third parties.
2) **Express actual authority** results from written or spoken words communicated by the principal to the agent.
3) **Implied actual authority** is incidental authority inferred from words or conduct directed to the agent by the principal.

a) It also may be inferred from custom and usage of the business or the agent's position relative to the purposes of the agency.
b) Express authority to achieve a result necessarily carries the implied authority to use reasonable means to accomplish the expressly authorized action.
c) Actual authority ceases when an agency terminates by act of the parties or operation of law.
d) Secret limitations on actual authority create apparent authority.

c. **Apparent Authority**

1) Apparent authority is granted by words or conduct of the principal directed to a third party that reasonably induces the third party to infer that the agent has actual authority.

a) It gives the agent the power, but not necessarily the right, to bind the principal to third parties.

2) Apparent authority is not based on the words or actions of the agent, and it cannot exist if the principal is undisclosed (the third party is unaware of any agency). It is based on justifiable reliance on the conduct of the principal.
   a) The third party's knowledge that the agent lacks actual authority precludes the existence of apparent authority.
3) Apparent authority may continue after termination of the agency until the third party receives notice.
4) Apparent authority ceases when the agency is automatically terminated by operation of law.

d. **Emergency authority** may be granted by a court when prompt action is needed.
   1) An agent's delegated authority may be extended if the public interest is served.

Authority of an Agent
• Actual 1) Express 2) Implied
• Apparent
• Emergency

2. **Subagents**
   a. Generally, an agent does not have the power to delegate authority or to appoint a subagent unless the principal intends to grant it.
   b. Evidence that the principal intends that the agent be permitted to delegate authority may include any of the following:
      1) An express authorization
      2) The character of the business
      3) Usage or trade
      4) Prior conduct of the principal and agent
   c. If the agent makes an unauthorized appointment of a subagent, the subagent cannot bind the principal.
   d. If the agent is authorized to appoint a subagent, the subagent
      1) Is an agent of both the principal and the agent,
      2) Binds the principal as if (s)he were the agent, and
      3) Owes a fiduciary duty to the principal and the agent.
3. **Duties to the Principal**
   a. **Types of Duties**
      1) Most agencies are formed by contract. The parties must perform according to the terms of the agreement.
      2) However, an agent has duties beyond contractual obligations. They arise by operation of law unless the parties agree otherwise.
   b. **Fiduciary Duty**
      1) The agent must act with utmost loyalty and good faith solely in the principal's interest.
      2) The agent must not do the following:
         a) Compete with the principal
         b) Buy from himself or herself for the principal without permission
         c) Make secret profits on transactions entered into for the principal
         d) Represent the principal if (s)he has a conflict of interest
         e) Misappropriate the principal's property
         f) Disclose or use confidential information obtained during the agency

3) The principal may consent to representation with full knowledge of all material facts.

c. **Duty of Obedience**

1) The agent must follow lawful explicit instructions of the principal.
2) If the instructions are not clear, the agent must act in good faith and in a reasonable manner considering the circumstances.
3) If an emergency arises and the agent cannot reach the principal, the agent may deviate from instructions to the extent that is appropriate.

d. **Duty of Care and Diligence**

1) The agent must use the care and skill of a reasonable person in like circumstances and his or her own special skills or knowledge.
2) The agent must avoid injury to the interests of the principal.

e. **Duty of Notification**

1) The agent must use reasonable efforts to notify the principal of all information (s)he has that
   a) Is relevant to the subject matter of the agency and
   b) (S)he knows or should know will be imputed to the principal.
2) A person receives notice by actual knowledge of a fact, having reason to know of its existence, or receiving formal notice.
   a) Thus, notice to an agent authorized to receive it is notice to the principal.
   b) Moreover, knowledge of an agent is assumed to be known by the principal if it is important to an authorized transaction.

EXAMPLE

Allan is Peter's agent for the sale of art. Allan falsely and intentionally overstates the value of a painting to a buyer. Peter is assumed to have knowledge of the fraud.

f. **Duty to Account**

1) The agent must
   a) Account for money or property received or expended on behalf of the principal.
   b) Not commingle his or her money or property with that of the principal.

Agent's Duties to the Principal
• Contractual Duties
• Fiduciary Duties 1) Loyalty and good faith 2) Duty not to compete 3) Duty not to engage in self-dealing 4) No secret profits 5) Avoidance of conflicts of interest 6) No misappropriation 7) Protection of confidential information
• Duty of Obedience
• Duty of Care and Diligence
• Duty of Notification
• Duty to Account

4. **Agent's Breach of Duty**
   a. The agent is liable to the principal for losses resulting from the agent's breach of a duty.
   b. Transactions between the principal and the agent may be voidable by the principal.
   c. A constructive trust in favor of the principal is imposed on profits obtained by the agent as a result of breaching the fiduciary duty.
      1) The agent, in effect, holds the profits in trust for the benefit of the principal.
      2) The principal recovers the profits by suing the agent.
   d. If the principal is sued for the agent's negligence or the agent ignores the principal's instructions, the principal has a right to indemnification from the agent.
5. **Contractual Liability to Third Parties**
   a. The agent may assume liability on any contract by
      1) Making the contract in his or her own name,
      2) Being a party to the contract with the principal, or
      3) Guaranteeing the principal's performance.

Stop and review! You have completed the outline for this subunit. Study multiple-choice questions 5 through 8 beginning on page 605.

16.3 PRINCIPAL'S DUTIES AND LIABILITIES

1. **Duties to the Agent -- Financial**
   a. The principal has a duty to **compensate** the agent for services unless the agent agrees to act gratuitously. This duty includes keeping accurate records of payments made to the agent.
      1) The reasonable value of the agent's services is implied without an expressly stated compensation.
   b. The principal has a duty to **reimburse** the agent for authorized payments made or expenses incurred by the agent on behalf of the principal.
   c. The principal has a duty to **indemnify** the agent. The indemnity is for losses suffered or expenses incurred while the agent acted
      1) As instructed in a legal transaction or
      2) In a transaction that the agent did not know to be wrongful.
   d. The principal owes no fiduciary duty to the agent.
2. **Duties to the Agent -- Occupational**
   a. The principal has a duty **not to impair** the agent's performance.
   b. The principal is not relieved of the **general duty of care** owed to the agent because a principal-agent relationship exists.
   c. The principal has a duty to **disclose known risks** involved in the task for which the agent is engaged and of which the agent is unaware.
   d. The principal has a duty to provide an agent who is an employee with reasonably **safe working conditions**.
3. **Agent's Remedies**
   a. The agent's remedies for a principal's breach of a duty include
      1) Terminating the agency relationship,
      2) Counterclaiming if the principal sues,
      3) Demanding an accounting, and
      4) Filing a civil action seeking normal tort and contract remedies.

Principal's Duties to the Agent
• Financial 1) Compensation 2) Reimbursement 3) Indemnification
• Occupational 1) Nonimpairment of agent's performance 2) General duty of care 3) Disclosure of known risks 4) Provision of reasonably safe working conditions

4. **Contractual Liability to Third Parties**
   a. If the agent has authority, either actual or apparent, the principal is liable on contracts entered into with a third party by the agent.
   b. Whether the principal is disclosed, partially disclosed, or undisclosed also determines his or her contractual liability.
      1) **Disclosed principal.** The third party knows the agent is acting for a principal and knows the identity of the principal.
      2) **Partially disclosed principal.** The third party knows the agent is acting for a principal but does not know the identity of the principal.
         a) The liability of the agent and a partially disclosed principal is **joint and several**. The third party may sue either or both and collect any amount from either until the judgment is satisfied.
      3) **Undisclosed principal.** The third party is unaware of any agency and believes that (s)he is dealing directly with a principal.
         a) Actual authority is unaffected. However, by definition, apparent authority does not exist.
         b) The third party may sue the agent of an undisclosed principal and vice versa.
            i) The third party intended to deal only with the agent, and the agent is a party to the contract.
         c) The undisclosed principal generally may sue or be sued on the contract except when it would be unfair or unjust to the other party. But the undisclosed principal may not be able to enforce a contract that
            i) Requires that credit be extended by the third party,
            ii) Involves unique personal services of the agent,
            iii) Involves nondelegable duties, or
            iv) Is a negotiable instrument signed by the agent with no indication of his or her status.

EXAMPLE

If the agent issues a check to a third party on behalf of an undisclosed principal, the third party cannot enforce the check against the principal. The principal has not endorsed it.

         d) Under traditional rules, if the undisclosed principal is discovered, the third party must elect whether to hold the principal or the agent liable for performance.

e) If the agent acts without actual authority, the undisclosed principal generally is not liable to the third party.

i) The undisclosed principal may ratify a contract formed beyond the scope of the agent's actual authority by accepting the benefits of the contract or other affirmative conduct.

ii) The third party has no right to ratification.

f) Whether the principal is disclosed does not affect the duties of the principal and agent to each other.

Contractual Liabilities

Principal	Agent's Authority	Principal's Liability to Third Party	Principal's Duty to Reimburse Agent	Principal's Right to Indemnity from Agent	Agent Liable to Third Party
Disclosed	Actual	Yes	Yes	No	No
	Apparent	Yes	No*	Yes*	No
	No Authority	No	No	No	Yes
Partially Disclosed	Actual	Yes	Yes	No	Yes
	Apparent	Yes	No*	Yes*	Yes
	No Authority	No	No	No	Yes
Undisclosed	Actual	Yes	Yes	No	Yes
	Apparent	N/A	N/A	N/A	N/A
	No Authority	No	No	No	Yes

* The agent has exceeded actual authority, and the principal has not ratified the actions of the agent. If the principal ratifies the actions of the agent, the principal has a duty to reimburse the agent but not the right to indemnity.

5. **Ratification**

a. Ratification is a voluntary election after an unauthorized act purportedly done on one's behalf to treat it as authorized.

1) Notice to a third party is not needed for ratification.

b. The principal must be aware of all material facts when assenting to the agent's act. The agent need not have performed his or her fiduciary duty or duty of due care.

c. Ratification may be either express or implied. It may be inferred from the principal's words or conduct that reasonably indicates intent to ratify.

EXAMPLE

Tony contracted to purchase 500 pounds of fish from Greg on behalf of Teresa's restaurant. Teresa did not know Tony or Greg and was unaware of the transaction. When the fish arrived, Teresa accepted the shipment. Her ratification of the transaction may be inferred.

d. Ratification is all-or-nothing. The principal may not ratify part of a transaction.

e. Ratification is irrevocable.

f. Ratification relates back to the time of the act. The act is treated as if it had been authorized at the time it was performed.

g. An agent has no liability to the third party after ratification.

1) If a principal does not ratify, the agent also is liable to the third party for breach of the implied warranty of authority.

h. An **undisclosed principal** may not be able to ratify certain contracts involving (1) personal services, (2) credit extended by the third party, or (3) nondelegable duties.

1) If the agent's unauthorized act is purportedly for an identified principal, only that person may ratify it.

a) Thus, the agent cannot substitute another principal if the identified principal does not ratify it.

i. Ratification is binding on a third party who did not withdraw from the contract before ratification, if the circumstances did not change substantially.

j. The principal must have the capacity to contract at the time of the unauthorized act and at the time of ratification.

6. **Tort Liability**

a. A principal may be liable in tort because of a personal act or the agent's wrongful act that results in harm to a third party.

1) The liability of the principal is greater when the agent is an employee rather than an independent contractor.

b. **Direct liability** results from the principal's own negligent or reckless action or failure to act in conducting business through agents if the principal does the following:

1) Negligently selects an agent
2) Fails to give proper orders or make proper regulations
3) Fails to employ the proper person or machinery given risk of harm
4) Fails to supervise the agent
5) Allows wrongful conduct by others on or with his or her property

c. **Vicarious liability** results from the actions of the agent for which the principal may be liable.

1) This liability is based upon the doctrine of **respondeat superior** (Latin for "let the master reply"). It prevents individuals from avoiding liability for a tort by hiring an agent to perform the act.

2) Vicarious liability arises when the agent

a) Committed a tort, whether or not intentional.
b) Was not authorized by the principal to perform the act.
c) Was an employee of the principal.
d) Performed an act within the scope of employment.

i) The agent's conduct must be of the kind (s)he was hired to perform.
ii) The conduct must be substantially within the time and space limits authorized by the principal.
iii) The agent must have intended to serve the principal.
iv) The act involves no more than a slight deviation from doing the principal's business in the authorized or most direct way.

3) A principal may be vicariously liable for a material misrepresentation by an agent, including one by an independent contractor.

a) This misrepresentation must be within the scope of actual or apparent authority. It may be (1) fraudulent, (2) negligent, or (3) innocent but with all the elements of fraud except wrongful intent (scienter).

EXAMPLE

Mary Lou hired John, a real estate broker, as an independent contractor to market her 15-year-old home. John told Michelle that the home was only 5 years old. Michelle bought the home. Both Mary Lou and John are liable for any harm suffered by Michelle as a result of the misrepresentation. Moreover, Mary Lou is entitled to be indemnified by John if she must pay damages to Michelle for John's misrepresentation.

d. Any agreement between a principal and agent limiting the principal's liability has no effect on the liability of the principal to third parties.

7. **Criminal Liability**
   a. A principal is liable for his or her own criminal conduct.
   b. A principal is generally not liable for a crime committed by the agent but may be held criminally liable for a crime of the agent if
      1) The principal approves or directs the crime,
      2) The principal participates or assists in the crime, or
      3) Violation of a regulatory statute constituted the crime.
8. **Agent's Legal Status**
   a. An agent ordinarily is either an employee or an independent contractor.
      1) A principal-employer has actual right of control over the physical efforts of an employee.
      2) An independent contractor is responsible only for the finished product.
   b. **Employees**
      1) The following are relevant considerations for determining whether an agent is an employee:
         a) The parties' agreement about the degree of control by the principal.
         b) The extent of supervision by the principal. A right of inspection at the end of work is consistent with independent contractor status.
         c) Whether the agent provides services exclusively for the principal.
         d) The relationship between the nature of the principal's business and the occupation and work of the agent.
         e) The specialization required for the task.
         f) How the agent is paid, whether at the end of all work or periodically per unit of time.
         g) Which party provides the agent's place of work, tools, and supplies.
         h) The duration of the relationship.
   c. **Independent Contractors**
      1) The principal is generally not liable for the torts of the independent contractor.
      2) However, such liability may result from a principal's own negligence.
      3) The principal also may be subject to strict liability.
         a) This liability of a principal is generally not vicarious.
         b) Some duties may not be delegated as a matter of law or public policy.
         c) Persons engaging in ultrahazardous activity have strict liability. Contracting out ultrahazardous activities is not a shield against liability.
      4) The principal is liable for representations made on behalf of the principal that are actually or apparently authorized or ratified by the principal.

Stop and review! You have completed the outline for this subunit. Study multiple-choice questions 9 through 12 beginning on page 606.

16.4 TERMINATION OF AN AGENCY

1. **Termination by the Parties**
   a. An agency is based on the mutual consent of the parties. Thus, it may be terminated by either party or both even if the termination breaches a contract between principal and agent.
   b. A principal may revoke a grant of authority at any time.
      1) **Revocation** may be implicit or explicit
   c. An agent may renounce the grant of authority by giving notice to the principal.
   d. If termination breaches a contract, the nonbreaching party has remedies provided by contract law.
   e. An agency terminates when the period lapses.
2. **Automatic Termination by Operation of Law**
   a. A principal's act of filing a petition in **bankruptcy** terminates an existing agency.
   b. A judicial declaration of **incompetence** of the principal or the agent terminates the agency.
   c. **Death** of either the principal or the agent terminates the agency.
   d. The **illegality** of duties to be performed by an agent automatically ends the agency.

EXAMPLE

An agency has been formed in which the agent is expected to sell the principal's real estate. If the agent fails to obtain a real estate license, the agency is void. An unlicensed agent cannot legally sell real estate for the principal.

      1) Furthermore, a change of law that makes an authorized act illegal terminates the agency.
   e. **Destruction** of the subject matter of the agency makes fulfilling the purpose of the agency impossible and terminates the agency.
   f. The agent's **violation** of a **fiduciary duty** terminates the agency. However, apparent authority does not terminate without actual or constructive notice.
      1) An agent's actual authority may be terminated if the agent obtains an interest in the subject matter of the agency.
      2) The agent's duty of loyalty is breached when that interest is both
         a) Adverse to the principal's own interest in it and
         b) Obtained without the knowledge and consent of the principal.
   g. A **change in circumstances** (such as a dramatic change in the value of a property) may be so significant that a reasonable person would infer that the agency is terminated.
      1) The agency might be revived upon a return to the initial circumstances.
      2) If the agent knows that the principal is aware of the change, and the principal does not give new directions, the agency may not terminate.
      3) If the agent has reasonable doubts as to how or whether the principal wants the agent to act, the agent may act reasonably. That is, the agency is not terminated.

Termination of an Agency
• By the Parties 1) Mutual consent 2) Principal's revocation of authority 3) Agent's renunciation of authority 4) Lapse of the period of the agency
• By Operation of Law 1) Bankruptcy 2) Death or judicially declared incompetence of a party 3) Illegality of agent's duties 4) Destruction of subject matter 5) Agent's breach of a fiduciary duty 6) Change in circumstances

3. **Agency Coupled with an Interest**
   a. An agency coupled with an interest may be terminated
      1) According to the terms of the agreement,
      2) By surrender of the authority by the agent, or
      3) Upon destruction of the subject matter of the agency.
   b. An agency coupled with an interest generally is not terminated by
      1) Revocation by the principal,
      2) Death of the principal, or
      3) Loss of legal capacity of the principal.
4. **Effect of Termination on Authority**
   a. **Actual authority** of the agent to act for the principal ceases upon termination, whether by act of the parties or by operation of law.
   b. **Apparent authority** of the agent continues to exist until the third party receives notice of the termination if the termination is by an act of the parties.
      1) Actual notice to the third party is required if the third party has already dealt with the agent.
      2) Constructive notice is generally sufficient for other third parties.
         a) The requirement is satisfied by a message posted in a trade journal or in a paper of general circulation where the agent operated.
   c. Most but not all terminations by operation of law terminate apparent authority.
      1) Notice to third parties is not usually necessary when the termination is by operation of law.
      2) According to the American Law Institute's *Restatement of the Law Third Agency*, apparent authority ends only when it is **not reasonable** to believe the agent has actual authority. Under this rule, the death of the principal does not automatically end apparent authority.
   d. If the authorization of the agent was in writing, the revocation of authorization also must be written.

Stop and review! You have completed the outline for this subunit. Study multiple-choice questions 13 through 15 beginning on page 607.

16.5 ANTITRUST LAW

1. **Overview**

    a. Antitrust law is intended to encourage competition by ensuring that markets are driven by customer demand. Markets should not be hindered by conspiracies among competitors or intentional monopolies. Thus, competition controls private economic power. Its purpose is to promote the following:

    1) Efficient allocation of resources (resulting in lower prices)
    2) Greater choice by consumers
    3) Greater business opportunities
    4) Fairness in economic behavior
    5) Avoidance of concentrated political power resulting from economic power

2. **Sherman Act of 1890**

Background

The Sherman Act was named after Ohio Republican Senator John Sherman, brother of the Civil War general William T. Sherman. The bill had almost no resistance in Congress. It passed the Senate 51-1 and the House 242-0.

a. **Section 1** makes illegal every contract, combination, or conspiracy in **restraint of trade** in interstate or foreign commerce. It applies to acts of two or more parties.

1) Thus, the parties must intend to act as a group for their actions to violate Section 1. Thus, actions must be **concerted** to violate the rule. However, no express agreement is required.

    a) By itself, **conscious parallelism** (similar behavior by independent competitors) is not a violation.

2) Restraints may be horizontal or vertical.

    a) A horizontal restraint involves collaboration among competitors at the same functional level in the chain of distribution, e.g., two manufacturers, wholesalers, or retailers.

        i) Examples are price fixing, division of markets, and group boycotts.

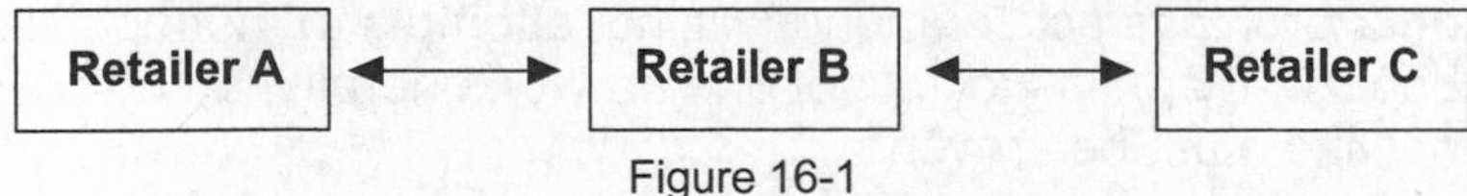

Figure 16-1

    b) A vertical restraint is imposed by parties that are not in direct competition at the same functional level of distribution.

        i) Examples are (a) resale price maintenance; (b) tying arrangements; (c) exclusive dealing agreements; and (d) customer, territorial, and location restrictions.

3) The **rule of reason** is applied. Normally, only unreasonable restraints are illegal. A court considers many factors and balances the anticompetitive and procompetitive effects of the restraint. For example,

    a) A covenant not to compete is enforceable if it is for a reasonable time and a reasonable area.
    b) Vertical territorial limitations between a seller and its distributors and retailers are acceptable if their effect on competition is not unreasonable.

b. Some arrangements among competitors are deemed to be unreasonable without inquiry as to harm or excuse. They are **illegal per se**. A plaintiff need not prove a limit on competition, and the court need not perform an economic analysis. These per-se violations may include the following:

   1) **Price fixing** is agreeing to any price.

      a) The prohibition applies to all horizontal agreements to set maximum or minimum prices. It also applies to agreements having an indirect effect on prices, for example, to eliminate interest-free, short-term credit.

      b) But resale price maintenance agreements (vertical restraints) are evaluated under the rule of reason.

   2) **Division of markets** is agreeing where, to whom, or what to sell, that is, dividing markets by product, customer, or geographic region.

   3) **Group boycotts** are agreements, also called concerted refusals to deal, not to sell to or buy from a third party.

      a) The per-se standard applies to **horizontal** group boycotts if the parties have market power, for example, those intended to eliminate a competitor. But **vertical** group boycotts are subject to the rule of reason.

   4) **Tying arrangements** condition the sale of one item on the purchase of a second item from the seller.

      a) For example, requiring a purchaser of replacement parts (the tying product) to use the seller's repair service (the tied product) limits the freedom of choice of buyers and may exclude competitors.

      b) A tying arrangement exists when a seller exploits its economic power in a market (tying product) to expand its market share of sales of another product (tied product).

      c) Tying arrangements are evaluated under the Sherman Act and the Clayton Act. They are considered illegal per se when (1) the seller has considerable economic power in the tying product and (2) a not-insubstantial amount of interstate commerce in the tied product is affected.

c. **Section 2** prohibits acts of monopolizing, attempts to monopolize, or conspiracies to monopolize. It applies to acts of one party. Generally, an objective intent to monopolize must be proven.

   1) **Monopoly** is the power to control prices or exclude competition.

      a) Monopolization is not illegal unless obtained abusively or unfairly. Thus, acquisition of power through superior products or skill, or having it thrust upon one, is not a violation.

      b) Thus, an **act of monopolization** requires (1) possession of monopoly power in the relevant market and (2) either the unfair attainment of such power or the intent to unlawfully exercise such power once lawfully obtained.

      c) The separate felonies of **attempt to monopolize** and **conspiracy to monopolize** do not require proof of monopoly power.

   2) For determining monopoly power, the relevant market consists of (a) the relevant product market and (b) the relevant geographic market.

d. Noncompliance with Section 1 or Section 2 is a crime punishable by fines and imprisonment. A corporation may be fined up to $100,000,000 per violation.

   1) Moreover, an injured party may recover treble damages (three times the actual harm) in a civil suit.

3. **Clayton Act of 1914**

   a. **Mergers or acquisitions of assets or stock** are prohibited if the effect may be to **substantially lessen competition** or **create a monopoly**. The act allows the Justice Department to prevent mergers. A lessening of competition occurs when, for example, reciprocal buying reduces the probability that other firms will enter the market.

      1) A **horizontal merger** (between competitors) is most closely examined by the Justice Department because it has the greatest tendency to lessen competition. The Federal Trade Commission and the Justice Department have jointly issued **Horizontal Merger Guidelines**. They describe the analytical process used to determine whether a horizontal merger should be challenged. The five factors traditionally considered are whether

         a) The merger will significantly increase market concentration,
         b) The merger will result in adverse competitive effects,
         c) Market entry would deter or counteract any adverse competitive effects,
         d) Any efficiency gained could be reasonably achieved by other means, and
         e) Either party to the merger would be likely to fail without the merger.

      2) A **vertical merger** (between supplier and purchaser) also may lessen competition if each controls a substantial part of the relevant market. Thus, the extent of concentration in the customer or supplier market is evaluated.

      3) A **pure conglomerate merger** involves different industries or different areas of business. It is the least likely to lessen competition unless the resulting company is so large that its size alone affects competition.

   b. The most important defense available under Section 7 of the Clayton Act is the **failing company** doctrine. It applies when (1) the acquiree is in failing condition, (2) the possibility of reorganization is extremely low, and (3) no other acquirer would have a less anticompetitive effect.

   c. The Clayton Act also prohibits the following:

      1) **Tying or tie-in sales**, that is, sales in which a buyer must take another product to buy the first product

      2) **Exclusive dealing**, a seller's requirement that a buyer purchase only the seller's products and not the products of the seller's competitors

         a) However, an exclusive dealing arrangement between a franchisor and a franchisee is legal if it is necessary to ensure product quality.

      3) **Reciprocal dealing**, a seller's use of its purchasing power to require another company to buy its products

      4) **Price discrimination** among different buyers

      5) **Interlocking directorates** (Section 8)

         a) A person may not serve as a director of two or more competing corporations when

            i) The entities are engaged in interstate or foreign commerce;

            ii) Each corporation's combined capital, surplus, and undivided profits exceeds the annually adjusted threshold (currently $31,084,000);

            iii) The elimination of competition by agreement between the entities would amount to a violation of any antitrust law; and

            iv) No grace period or de minimis exception applies.

         b) Moreover, competitive sales of (1) either firm must be less than $3,108,400, (2) either firm must be less than 2% of its total sales, or (3) each firm must be less than 4% of its total sales.

   d. The Sherman Act, not the Clayton Act, provides for criminal penalties. However, the Clayton Act provides for recovery of treble damages.

4. **Robinson-Patman Act of 1936**

   a. This act amended the Clayton Act with respect to price discrimination. Price discrimination involving commodities of like grade and quality is illegal if the effect is to lessen competition substantially or create a monopoly.

      1) Price discrimination is prohibited with respect to both buyers and sellers.

         a) Both buyer and seller can be found guilty of discrimination.

      2) Competition is presumed to have been harmed when price discrimination involves competing buyers from the same seller.

      3) Price differentiation is allowed to (a) meet lawful competition, (b) respond to changing conditions affecting the market or marketability of the product, or (c) pass on cost savings.

         a) Functional discounts to persons performing legitimate marketing functions (e.g., wholesalers) are allowed if they are reasonably related to the supplier's savings or the wholesaler's costs.

      4) Rebates, commissions, discounts, etc., to special customers are prohibited.

      5) The act does not apply to export sales or to purely intrastate sales.

      6) A violation may be found even if the price is reasonable and the discrimination is unintentional.

      7) Criminal sanctions are limited, but treble damages are recoverable.

5. **Federal Trade Commission Act of 1914**

   a. This statute prohibits unfair methods of competition, and unfair or deceptive acts, in or affecting interstate commerce.

   b. It created the Federal Trade Commission (FTC) to enforce its provisions and determine what is unfair competition or a deceptive act. But private enforcement actions are not allowed.

      1) The basic objectives of the FTC are to initiate antitrust actions and to protect the consumer public. However, the Justice Department, not the FTC, has authority to pursue criminal sanctions.

      2) The FTC also has broad authority to enforce the other antitrust laws in conjunction with the antitrust division of the U.S. Justice Department.

6. **Remedies and Sanctions**

   a. The Justice Department and the FTC are the primary but not sole enforcers of antitrust laws. Some remedies and sanctions for antitrust violations include the following:

      1) Court injunctions, forfeitures (seizures of property transported in interstate commerce), and forced divestitures may result from actions by either the public or the government.

      2) Cease and desist orders may be issued by the FTC.

      3) Treble (triple) damages may be recovered by private parties.

      4) Criminal penalties, including fines and prison sentences, may be imposed by the government.

7. **Examples of Antitrust Exemptions**

   a. Intrastate commerce

   b. Regulated utilities

   c. Reasonable noncompetition clauses involving the following:

      1) Buyers and sellers of businesses
      2) Partners in a partnership
      3) Purchasers of technology or equipment

d. Patents and copyrights
    1) A patent is a grant made by a government to an inventor. This grant provides the inventor with monopoly rights to use the invention.
    2) A copyright offers protection for original works of authorship.
e. Financial institutions
f. Labor unions
g. Transport industries
h. Major league baseball
i. Failing companies

The AICPA has tested the various antitrust statutes. Exam questions have asked for the requirements of specific acts as well as antitrust law in general.

Stop and review! You have completed the outline for this subunit. Study multiple-choice questions 16 through 19 beginning on page 608.

16.6 EMPLOYMENT LAW

1. **Federal Insurance Contributions Act (FICA)**
    a. FICA provides programs for disabled employees and families of retired, disabled, and deceased workers, including, in some cases, divorced spouses. Employers and employees contribute under this program.
    b. Employers must contribute (pay tax) based on the employee's pay.
    c. The employer must generally pay **6.20%** of the first **$118,800** of wages paid for 2015 (an estimated $118,800 for 2016) plus **1.45%** of all wages for the Medicare portion. The employer generally must withhold the same amounts from the employee's wages.
        1) Employers are responsible for withholding an additional 0.9% of an individual's wages paid in excess of $200,000 as Additional Medicare Tax ($250,000 married filing jointly or SS; $125,000 married filing separately).
        2) No employer match exists for Additional Medicare Tax.
    d. A **net investment income tax (NIIT)** of 3.8% is imposed. The tax subjects investment income to the same Medicare tax treatment as wages above the applicable threshold amounts.
    e. **Wages** are all forms of consideration paid for employment, including cash and the cash value of compensation in any medium other than cash. They include (1) wages and salaries, (2) commissions (including contingent fees), (3) bonuses, (4) productivity awards, (5) tips, (6) vacation and sick pay, (7) severance allowances, and (8) fringe benefits.
        1) Wages exclude (a) payments for moving expenses to the extent that it is reasonable to believe a corresponding deduction is allowable and (b) medical care reimbursements under a self-insured plan.
    f. **Group term life insurance** payments for retirees are treated as wages to the extent they constitute gross income and are for periods during which retirees no longer have employee status.
    g. The employer must **withhold FICA tax** from an employee's wages. The employee's contribution (tax) must be withheld upon each payment of wages, up to the maximum bases and at the same rates.

h. Contributions made by the employee are **not tax deductible** by the employee. Those made by the employer are deductible by the employer.
i. **Self-employed persons** are required to report their own taxable income and pay FICA taxes. FICA is calculated based on net income.

2. **Federal Unemployment Tax Act (FUTA)**
   a. FUTA provides for a system of temporary financial assistance for unemployed workers.
   b. FUTA tax is imposed on employers who
      1) Employ one or more covered individuals for some portion of a day in each of the 20 weeks in the current or preceding calendar year, or
      2) Pay $1,500 or more in wages in any calendar quarter of the current or preceding calendar year.
   c. The FUTA tax is **6.0%** of the **first $7,000** of wages paid annually to each employee.
      1) The employee does not pay any part of the FUTA tax.
      2) The employer pays the FUTA tax to the IRS.
         a) FUTA tax is a deductible business expense of the employer.
   d. A credit against FUTA tax liability is provided to an employer who pays state unemployment tax.
      1) The credit cannot exceed 5.4% of the first $7,000 of wages.
      2) The amount paid to a state usually depends on the employer's past experience regarding the frequency and amount of unemployment claims.
   e. **Benefits** are determined on a state-to-state basis. Thus, the state fixes the amount and duration of compensation. To collect unemployment compensation, the worker ordinarily must
      1) Have been employed and laid off without fault;
      2) Have filed a claim for the benefits; and
      3) Be able, available, and willing to work but not be able to find employment.
   f. A state may refuse benefits to employees who
      1) Have voluntarily quit work without good cause,
      2) Have been discharged for good cause (misconduct), or
      3) Refuse to actively seek or accept suitable work.

3. **Workers' Compensation**
   a. **State laws** establish programs to reimburse employees for losses sustained due to work-related injuries.
   b. Statutes allow the injured employee to recover on the basis of strict liability, thus eliminating the need to prove the employer's negligence.
      1) Employee negligence, including disobeying an employer safety rule, does not prevent recovery.
      2) The only requirement is that the employee be injured and that the injury **arise out of, and in the course of, his or her employment**. Travel to and from work or lunch is generally not within the course and scope of employment.
      3) The employer's traditional defenses of contributory or comparative negligence and assumption of the risk are eliminated.
      4) The negligence of another employee also is not a defense of the employer.
   c. Employers can purchase insurance, act as self-insurers, or pay into a state fund. Payments made for workers' compensation are deductible by the employer.
   d. Most employers are required to participate in workers' compensation programs. However, certain states exempt employers with fewer than a stated number of employees.

e. Independent contractors and casual, agricultural, or domestic employees are not eligible for workers' compensation.
f. Recovery under the statute is the employee's exclusive remedy against the employer.
g. However, if a third party causes the injury, the injured employee may bring suit in tort against the third party. A portion of any recovery is used to reimburse the employer or its insurer for workers' compensation payments.
h. Amounts awarded under typical workers' compensation laws may be for (1) wage loss, (2) medical costs and devices, (3) loss of body members, and (4) death. Only a portion of wage-earning capacity is usually awarded.

4. **Occupational Safety and Health Act**
   a. The purpose of the federal act is to develop safety standards, prevent injuries, and promote job safety. The act does not preempt state regulation.
   b. The **Occupational Safety and Health Administration (OSHA)** of the Department of Labor is authorized to develop detailed health and safety standards and to enforce them. It investigates employee complaints and conducts inspections, and it has developed procedures to encourage compliance.
   c. The act requires employers to provide employees with a **workplace free from recognized hazards** that are likely to cause death or serious physical harm. It does not require a risk-free workplace.
   d. Employers must (1) keep detailed records of job-related injuries, (2) post annual summaries of the records, and (3) report serious accidents to OSHA.
   e. The act prohibits any employer from discharging or discriminating against any employee who exercises his or her rights under the act, e.g., revealing violations or refusing in good faith to work when at risk of death or great bodily harm.
   f. OSHA may assess civil penalties that depend on (1) the seriousness of the violation, (2) whether it was willful, and (3) whether it was a repeat offense. These fines are in addition to potential criminal liability. However, the act is not a basis for an injured employee to recover civil damages.
   g. Any employer who commits a willful violation resulting in death to an employee may incur a fine, imprisonment, or both.
   h. Employees also must comply with OSHA standards.

5. **Employment Discrimination**
   a. Employment discrimination is employer behavior that penalizes certain individuals because of personal traits that bear no relation to job performance.
   b. The federal **Civil Rights Act of 1964** applies to all employers or labor unions that have 15 or more employees or members. Title VII forbids discrimination in employment on the basis of **race, color, religion, sex, or national origin**.
      1) Title VII's prohibition of **sex discrimination** applies to discrimination against both men and women, including sexual harassment and pregnancy discrimination but not sexual preference.
      2) Defenses to violations of Title VII include the following:
         a) A bona fide seniority or merit system
         b) A system based on quality or quantity of production
         c) A professionally developed ability test
         d) A bona fide occupational qualification (BFOQ) in a disparate impact case
         e) National security reasons
      3) Title VII is enforced through lawsuits by both private individuals and by the **Equal Employment Opportunity Commission (EEOC)**. A successful plaintiff suing under Title VII may obtain back pay, lost wages, and attorney's fees.

c. The federal **Age Discrimination in Employment Act (ADEA)** is intended to prohibit age discrimination. The act protects individuals who are 40 years of age or older.
   1) No intent to discriminate must be proven.
   2) The act prohibits mandatory retirement of most classes of employees under 70 but not managerial employees.
   3) Employers who have at least 20 employees must comply with the ADEA.
   4) An employer can (a) discharge or otherwise penalize an individual for good cause and (b) use reasonable factors (other than age) in making employment decisions. The ADEA also allows age criteria in bona fide employee benefit plans, bona fide seniority systems, and a bona fide occupational qualification defense.
   5) ADEA remedies include (a) unpaid back wages and other benefits arising from the discrimination; (b) an additional equal award for liquidated damages if the employer's conduct was willful; (c) attorney's fees; and (d) equitable relief, which may include hiring, reinstatement, and promotion.
      a) But most courts do not provide awards for punitive damages, pain and suffering, early retirement, etc.

d. **Discrimination Based on Disability**
   1) The federal **Americans with Disabilities Act (ADA)** provides protection from employment discrimination with respect to hiring, promotion, compensation and other conditions of employment, and termination.
      a) It is also intended to make public services, accommodations, and telecommunications more accessible.

e. The federal **Fair Labor Standards Act (FLSA)** establishes a federal minimum wage, requires extra pay for overtime work, and regulates the employment of children.
   1) The FLSA applies to an employer with at least $500,000 in sales or that is engaged in interstate commerce.
   2) The FLSA's key provisions entitle an employee covered by the act to
      a) A specified minimum wage subject to amendment,
      b) At least the **minimum wage** per hour for the **40 hours in a work week**, and
      c) **150%** of his or her regular rate for all hours worked **in excess of 40 per week**.
   3) An employer may use an hourly, weekly, or monthly basis of pay for a covered employee if the other requirements are met.
   4) The minimum wage and overtime provisions **do not apply to exempt employees**, including (a) executive, administrative, and professional personnel; (b) outside salespersons; (c) certain employees of retail businesses; (d) some agricultural workers; (e) some commercial fishing workers; (f) child actors; (g) full-time college students; and (h) certain individuals with impaired capacity.
   5) Certain employees are exempt from the overtime but not the minimum wage provisions, including (a) air carrier and railroad employees, (b) sailors on American vessels, (c) taxi drivers, (d) certain employees of motor carriers, and (e) certain local delivery employees.
   6) The FLSA also prohibits oppressive **child labor**.
      a) The basic minimum age for employment is 16. At this age, children may be employed in any nonhazardous work.
      b) Employment of 14- and 15-year-olds is limited to certain occupations, such as sales and clerical work, and is subject to hour limitations.

c) Persons under 18 are not permitted to be employed in occupations that are declared hazardous by the Secretary of Labor.

d) Legal exceptions also permit employment of children (1) in agriculture outside of school hours, (2) under age 16 by their parents, and (3) for newspaper delivery.

7) The federal **Equal Pay Act** amended the FLSA. It prohibits an employer from discriminating among employees on the **basis of sex** by paying unequal wages for the same work.

a) The act permits wage differences based on seniority, merit, or quality or quantity of work, including the piece-rate method.

b) Unlike the FLSA, the act covers executive, administrative, professional, and state and local government employees.

6. **Employee Benefit Plans**

a. The **Employee Retirement Income Security Act (ERISA)** applies to employers that voluntarily provide benefit plans for their employees.

1) Plans may be **contributory** (employers and employees contribute) or **noncontributory** (only employers contribute).

2) Contributions made by employees must vest immediately.

3) Contributions made by employers must be completely nonvested for up to 5 years and fully vested thereafter or gradually vested over a maximum of 7 years.

4) The act establishes recordkeeping and disclosure requirements.

5) Employees are not entitled to make investment decisions.

6) Participation in the Pension Benefit Guaranty Corporation is mandatory and provides for payment of some benefits when underfunded plans default.

b. The federal **Consolidated Omnibus Budget Reconciliation Act (COBRA)** amended ERISA. An employee, spouse, and other beneficiaries must be notified and offered the opportunity to continue their **group health insurance**, including dental and visual benefits, for 18 months after termination (or loss of coverage due to certain events) at the employee's expense.

1) Employers of 20 or more workers are required to comply with COBRA.

2) Federal government agencies and religious entities are exempt from COBRA.

3) Employees with disabilities are eligible to continue coverage for 29 months.

4) Coverage may be discontinued if (a) the employee was terminated for gross misconduct, (b) the employer ceases to provide group coverage, (c) the premium is not paid, (d) the employee obtains group coverage from a new (or spouse's) employer, or (e) the employee becomes eligible for Medicare.

c. The federal **Family and Medical Leave Act (FMLA)** entitles an eligible employee to 12 work weeks of leave without pay and without loss of employment. Leave is provided for (1) the birth of a child; (2) a serious health condition; or (3) the care of a spouse, son, daughter, or parent who has a serious health condition.

7. **Labor Union Law**

a. The **National Labor Relations Act (NLRA)** extends legal protection to the unionizing efforts of employees and encourages their collective bargaining. Many employees are exempt from the NLRA, for example, (1) government employees, (2) not-for-profit hospital workers, (3) those subject to the Railway Labor Act, (4) managerial employees, (5) independent contractors, (6) agricultural employees, and (7) domestic workers.

b. The NLRA established the **National Labor Relations Board (NLRB)**, an independent administrative agency. Its main functions are to oversee union representation elections and to investigate (and prosecute) charges of unfair labor practices.

1) **Section 8** of the NLRA is its most important. This section declared it an **unfair labor practice** for an employer to

a) Interfere with employees' rights to form, join, and assist labor unions and other concerted activities for mutual aid or protection;

b) Interfere with formation or administration of a union;

c) Discriminate against employees (a term that includes applicants in hiring or granting of tenure) because of union membership;

d) Discriminate against employees because they have filed charges or given testimony under the NLRA; and

e) Refuse to **bargain collectively** and in good faith with any duly designated representative of the employees about wages, hours, and conditions of employment, including sick pay and vacation pay. Thus, an employer must bargain about employee benefits.

c. Employees generally have a **right to strike**. However, a court may issue an injunction against a strike or a lockout by an employer if the parties have agreed to a no-strike clause in the collective bargaining agreement.

d. The **Labor Management Relations Act (LMRA)**, also called the **Taft-Hartley Act**, curtailed the power of unions as exhibited by crippling nationwide strikes. The act also established the Federal Mediation and Conciliation Service to assist in the settlement of labor disputes.

8. **Other Employment Issues**

a. Laws at the state and federal levels protect employees when they report employer misconduct. An example is the federal **Whistleblower Protection Act**.

Stop and review! You have completed the outline for this subunit. Study multiple-choice questions 20 through 25 beginning on page 610.

16.7 INTELLECTUAL PROPERTY LAW

1. **Patents**

a. A patent is a right conferred upon application to and approval by the federal government (U.S. Patent and Trademark Office) for the exclusive use of an invention. It must (1) be for a patentable subject, (2) have utility, and (3) be novel and not obvious to a knowledgeable person.

b. The right is given for a nonrenewable period, but an effective extension can often be provided by obtaining a new patent that involves slight modifications of the old.

1) A **utility patent** (the most common category) has a legal life ending 20 years after the date it was granted.

2) A **design patent** (not an invention) has a duration of 14 years.

3) **Business methods** also may be patented.

c. Subsequent to the grant of a patent, its owner may need to bring or defend a suit for **patent infringement**.

1) The government does not prosecute such cases but merely provides a forum (federal courts) in which the owner may assert its rights.

2. **Copyrights**

a. The federal Copyright Act provides broad rights to intellectual property consisting of "original works of authorship in any tangible medium of expression, now known or later developed."

   1) An **author's copyright** is for life plus 70 years.
   2) A **publisher's copyright** is for the earlier of the expiration of (a) 95 years from publication or (b) 120 years from creation.

b. The Copyright Act is based on specific authority granted in the Constitution.

c. Among the works protected are (1) literary, musical, and dramatic works; (2) sound recordings; (3) motion pictures and other audiovisual works; and (4) computer software.

d. The copyright holder has **exclusive rights** to reproduce, distribute, perform, display, and prepare derivative works from copyrighted material.

e. **Limited exceptions** are allowed for library or archive reproduction and **fair use** for purposes of comment, criticism, news coverage, teaching, scholarship, or research.

f. The Copyright Act does not protect ideas, processes, discoveries, principles, etc.

g. A copyright provides automatic protection when it is in tangible form.

   1) Registration with the federal **Copyright Office** is necessary only to give a copyright owner standing to sue in federal court for infringement.
   2) Furthermore, a notice of copyright is not required to be placed on the work.

Stop and review! You have completed the outline for this subunit. Study multiple-choice questions 26 and 27 on page 611.

16.8 VARIOUS LAW TOPICS

1. **Consumer Credit Protection**

a. The federal **Consumer Credit Protection Act (CCPA)** regulates extensions of credit involving goods, services, or land obtained for personal, family, household, or agricultural purposes.

   1) The CCPA includes the following:

      a) Truth-in-Lending Act
      b) Fair Credit Reporting Act
      c) Equal Credit Opportunity Act
      d) Fair Debt Collection Practices Act
      e) Fair Credit Billing Act

   2) Consumer credit protection provides for the following:

      a) Access to the consumer credit market by both creditors and consumers
      b) Full disclosure of information to the consumer
      c) Regulation of contract terms
      d) Fair reporting of credit information about consumers
      e) Creditors' remedies

2. **Truth-in-Lending Act (TILA)**

a. The act requires **disclosure** by creditors of the **terms and conditions of consumer credit**.

b. The act also prevents a creditor from baiting customers by advertising credit terms that it does not generally make available.

c. The TILA was amended by the **Credit Card Fraud Act**. It limits a **holder's liability** for unauthorized use of a credit card to a maximum of **$50**.

 1) A person who loses his or her credit card will avoid all liability for any unauthorized charges if notice is given to the issuer before any charges are made.

d. A person who has a problem with property or services purchased with a credit card has the right not to pay the amount due. But (s)he must first attempt in good faith to return the goods or give the merchant a chance to cure the problem.

e. The monthly credit card bill must disclose how long it will take to pay off the balance if only minimum payments are made. It also must state how much must be paid each month to pay off the balance in 3 years.

3. **Fair Credit Reporting Act (FCRA)**

 a. This act requires consumer credit reporting agencies to adopt reasonable procedures to maintain the confidentiality, accuracy, and relevance of their records.

4. **Equal Credit Opportunity Act (ECOA)**

 a. The act prohibits discrimination in any aspect of a consumer credit transaction. Protected categories include (1) sex, (2) marital status, (3) race, (4) color, (5) age, (6) religion, (7) national origin, (8) receipt of welfare, or (9) good-faith exercise of rights under the CCPA.

 b. The lender must consider all income disclosed by an applicant, but its sources generally are not to be considered.

  1) The lender may consider the likelihood of receiving alimony and child support. But the lender must tell the applicant that (s)he does not need to disclose them unless (s)he relies on them for credit.

 c. Lack of assets or income is an allowable reason for denying credit.

 d. A married woman may not be prevented from obtaining credit separately, and asking about marital status is prohibited.

  1) Credit should be reported in the names of both spouses.

5. **Fair Debt Collection Practices Act (FDCPA)**

 a. The act prohibits abusive, deceptive, and unfair debt collection practices of some debt collection agencies.

  1) The act applies to entities, including attorneys, that collect consumer debts for others but **not** to banks and businesses that collect their own accounts.

  2) The debts must involve (a) money, (b) property, (c) insurance, or (d) services obtained by a consumer and used for personal, family, or household purposes.

  3) A collector generally may not do the following:

   a) Use harassing or intimidating practices or abusive language
   b) Use false or misleading tactics
   c) Contact the consumer at work if the employer objects or at unusual or inconvenient times
   d) Contact the consumer at all if the debtor is represented by an attorney
   e) Contact third parties other than a spouse, parent, or financial advisor expressly about the account unless specifically authorized by a court

  4) The collector may not contact the consumer-debtor about the account after receiving a written refusal to pay except to notify the consumer of possible ramifications of nonpayment. Moreover, a debt collector may not deposit a postdated check prior to its effective date.

 b. The act permits civil actions by debtors.

  1) A collector may be liable for up to $1,000 without proof of damages for violations.

6. **Fair Credit Billing Act**
   a. The act gives the consumer a method of correcting errors on bills and bringing disputed charges to the attention of the creditor. The creditor is required to inform the customer of his or her rights with each billing statement.
      1) A creditor is not obligated to investigate the records until the customer makes an inquiry. The correction must be made within 90 days afterward.
7. **Dodd-Frank Wall Street Reform and Consumer Protection Act of 2010**
   a. The act created the Bureau of Consumer Financial Protection (BCFP), an independent entity. Its purposes include
      1) Providing consumers with timely and understandable information;
      2) Protecting consumers from unfair, deceptive, abusive, or discriminatory practices;
      3) Promoting fair competition; and
      4) Ensuring that consumer financial markets operate transparently and efficiently.
   b. The BCFP regulates
      1) Large banks and credit unions,
      2) Mortgage lenders,
      3) Private student loan companies,
      4) Payday lenders,
      5) Other nonbank lenders not previously regulated, and
      6) Sellers of financial products and services to consumers.
   c. The BCFP
      1) Provides education programs,
      2) Investigates consumer complaints,
      3) Publishes information on financial product markets and risks to consumers,
      4) Supervises compliance by persons who offer or provide a consumer financial product or service,
      5) Issues rules on consumer financial products or services, and
      6) Enforces existing laws and regulations and monitors consumer lending and investment.
8. **Money Laundering**
   a. Money laundering consists of making the profits from criminal acts appear to have been obtained from legitimate sources.
   b. **Bank Secrecy Act (BSA)**
      1) This act requires banks to file a **currency transaction report (CTR)** for any cash transactions exceeding $10,000.
      2) Banks are also required to file a **suspicious activity report (SAR)** for any unusual activity that may indicate violations.
   c. **Money Laundering Control Act (MLCA)**
      1) The MLCA made money laundering a federal crime.
      2) This act prohibits the structuring of transactions to avoid CTR filings.
   d. Violations of these acts are subject to criminal and civil penalties.
      1) Criminal penalties include up to 20 years in a federal prison or fines up to $500,000 or twice the value of the property involved.
      2) Civil penalties include forfeiture on any property traceable to the proceeds of the criminal activity.

Stop and review! You have completed the outline for this subunit. Study multiple-choice questions 28 through 30 on page 612.

QUESTIONS

16.1 Formation of an Agency

1. Forming an agency relationship requires that

A. The agreement between the principal and agent be supported by consideration.

B. The principal and agent not be minors.

C. Both the principal and agent consent to the agency.

D. The agent's authority be limited to the express grant of authority in the agency agreement.

Answer (C) is correct.

REQUIRED: The requirement to form an agency relationship.

DISCUSSION: Agency is an express or implied consensual relationship. Both the principal and agent must manifest consent to the grant of authority. The purpose and subject matter of the agency must be legal. The principal must have legal capacity to perform the act authorized.

Answer (A) is incorrect. Consideration is not required to form an agency relationship. Answer (B) is incorrect. An agent need not have legal capacity to enter into a contract to be able to bind a principal on the contract. Answer (D) is incorrect. An agent's authority can extend to more than acts specifically expressed in the agreement. For example, a universal agent is authorized to conduct all business that the principal may legally delegate.

2. Which of the following actions requires an agent for a corporation to have a written agency agreement?

A. Purchasing office supplies for the principal's business.

B. Purchasing an interest in undeveloped land for the principal.

C. Hiring an independent general contractor to renovate the principal's office building.

D. Retaining an attorney to collect a business debt owed to the principal.

Answer (B) is correct.

REQUIRED: The action requiring a written agency agreement.

DISCUSSION: Oral agreement usually suffices to form an agency, but purchase of land is subject to the statute of frauds. An agency relationship must be in writing if the object of the agency is subject to the statute of frauds.

Answer (A) is incorrect. Purchasing office supplies does not require any formality and is not subject to the requirement of a writing. Answer (C) is incorrect. An independent contractor may be an agent, but the object of the agency, office renovations, is not subject to the formality of a writing. Answer (D) is incorrect. A written agreement is not required. The object of the agency, collecting a debt, does not require a writing.

3. Jim entered into an oral agency agreement with Sally in which he authorized Sally to sell his interest in a parcel of real estate, Blueacre. Within 7 days, Sally sold Blueacre to Dan, signing the real estate contract on behalf of Jim. Dan failed to record the real estate contract within a reasonable time. Which of the following is true?

A. Dan may enforce the real estate contract against Jim because it satisfied the statute of frauds.

B. Dan may enforce the real estate contract against Jim because Sally signed the contract as Jim's agent.

C. The real estate contract is unenforceable against Jim because Sally's authority to sell Blueacre was oral.

D. The real estate contract is unenforceable against Jim because Dan failed to record the contract within a reasonable time.

Answer (C) is correct.

REQUIRED: The true statement about an oral agency to sell realty.

DISCUSSION: If the contract is within the statute of frauds, the agent's authority must be in writing if the principal is to be bound. The contract is therefore voidable at Jim's option. It was required by the statute of frauds to be written, and Sally's agency was oral. In most other situations, the agent's authority may be oral.

Answer (A) is incorrect. The contract operates only as an offer. The agency was oral. Answer (B) is incorrect. The contract operates only as an offer. The agency was oral. Answer (D) is incorrect. If Jim and Dan had entered into a binding agreement, it would be effective without recording. Compliance with the recording statute is necessary to protect against parties not privy to the contract.

4. Noll gives Carr a written power of attorney. Which of the following statements is true regarding this power of attorney?

A. It must be signed by both Noll and Carr.

B. It must be for a definite period of time.

C. It may continue in existence after Noll's death.

D. It may limit Carr's authority to specific transactions.

Answer (D) is correct.

REQUIRED: The true statement about a power of attorney.

DISCUSSION: A power of attorney is a written authorization for the agent to act on behalf of the principal. It can be general, or it can grant the agent restricted authority, such as for specific transactions.

Answer (A) is incorrect. A power of attorney is a delegation of authority and need only be signed by the principal. Answer (B) is incorrect. To be effective, a written power of attorney need not be for a definite period of time. Answer (C) is incorrect. In the absence of a special statute, the death of a principal terminates an agency relationship.

16.2 Agent's Authority and Duties

5. Ace engages Butler to manage Ace's retail business. Butler has **no** implied authority to

A. Purchase inventory for Ace's business.

B. Sell Ace's business fixtures.

C. Pay Ace's business debts.

D. Hire or discharge Ace's business employees.

Answer (B) is correct.

REQUIRED: The agent's implied authority.

DISCUSSION: An agent's actual authority is conveyed by communication to the agent from the principal. It is not feasible to state expressly each act an agent is authorized to perform. Thus, an agent may have express and implied actual authority. Implied actual authority is for acts reasonably necessary to execute express authority. Selling the business fixtures is not necessary to manage a retail business.

Answer (A) is incorrect. Buying inventory is an act necessary to execute the express authorization to manage the store. Answer (C) is incorrect. Paying business debts is an act necessary to execute the express authorization to manage the store. Answer (D) is incorrect. Hiring or discharging employees is an act necessary to execute the express authorization to manage the store.

6. Bo Borg is the vice president of purchasing for Crater Corp. He has authority to enter into purchase contracts on behalf of Crater, provided that the price under a contract does not exceed $2 million. Dent, who is the president of Crater, is required to approve any contract that exceeds $2 million. Borg entered into a $2.5 million purchase contract with Shady Corp. without Dent's approval. Shady was unaware that Borg exceeded his authority. Neither party substantially changed its position in reliance on the contract. What is the most likely result of this transaction?

A. Crater will be bound because of Borg's apparent authority.

B. Crater will not be bound because Borg exceeded his authority.

C. Crater will only be bound up to $2 million, the amount of Borg's authority.

D. Crater may avoid the contract because Shady has not relied on the contract to its detriment.

Answer (A) is correct.

REQUIRED: The most likely result when an agent exceeds his or her authority.

DISCUSSION: Apparent authority exists when a third party has reason to believe that an agent has the authority to enter into contracts of the nature involved based upon a principal's representations. Secret limitations placed on the agent's normal authority create apparent authority. In this case, it was reasonable for Shady to believe that Borg had the authority to enter into the contract, given Borg's position in the company as vice president of purchasing. That Dent secretly limited Borg's authority has no effect, and Crater Corp. can be held liable under the contract.

Answer (B) is incorrect. An agent with apparent authority has the power to bind a principal even if the agent exceeds his express authority. Answer (C) is incorrect. A principal is liable to the extent of an agent's apparent authority, not an agent's express authority. Answer (D) is incorrect. Reliance is irrelevant when the parties are bound to the contract.

7. Which act, if committed by an agent, will cause a principal to be liable to a third party?

A. A negligent act committed by an independent contractor in performance of the contract that results in injury to a third party.

B. An intentional tort committed by an employee outside the scope of employment that results in injury to a third party.

C. An employee's failure to notify the employer of a dangerous condition that results in injury to a third party.

D. A negligent act committed by an employee outside the scope of employment that results in injury to a third party.

Answer (C) is correct.

REQUIRED: The act of an agent causing a principal to be liable to a third party.

DISCUSSION: An agent, such as an employee, has a duty to give notice to the principal of all information relevant to the agency. Thus, an agent's knowledge of a relevant, dangerous condition is assumed to be known by the principal. The principal is then liable to an injured third party to the same extent as if the principal had actual knowledge of the condition.

Answer (A) is incorrect. A nonnegligent principal generally is not liable for the negligence of an independent contractor. Answer (B) is incorrect. The principal is not liable for intentional torts outside the scope of employment. Answer (D) is incorrect. The principal is not liable for negligent acts outside the scope of employment.

8. North, Inc., hired Sutter as a purchasing agent. North gave Sutter written authorization to purchase, without limit, electronic appliances. Later, Sutter was told not to purchase more than 300 of each appliance. Sutter contracted with Orr Corp. to purchase 500 tape recorders. Orr had been shown Sutter's written authorization. Which of the following statements is true?

A. Sutter will be liable to Orr because Sutter's actual authority was exceeded.

B. Sutter will not be liable to reimburse North if North is liable to Orr.

C. North will be liable to Orr because of Sutter's actual and apparent authority.

D. North will not be liable to Orr because Sutter's actual authority was exceeded.

Answer (C) is correct.

REQUIRED: The true statement about liability for a contract beyond the agent's actual authority.

DISCUSSION: A principal is liable on contracts made by an agent who has actual or apparent authority. Sutter had apparent authority to make the contract because of the principal's communication (letter) shown to the third party. Moreover, the third party's rights against the principal are not limited by the secret limits placed on actual authority. Sutter had actual authority to buy up to 300 units and apparent authority to buy the rest.

Answer (A) is incorrect. The agent is not liable to the third party. The agent had apparent authority to buy all 500 tape recorders. Answer (B) is incorrect. The agent is liable to the principal for acting beyond actual authority. Answer (D) is incorrect. The principal is liable for acts of the agent within actual or apparent authority.

16.3 Principal's Duties and Liabilities

9. Which of the following statements, if any, represent a principal's duty to an agent who works on a commission basis?

I. The principal is required to maintain pertinent records, account to the agent, and pay the agent according to the terms of their agreement.

II. The principal is required to reimburse the agent for all authorized expenses incurred unless the agreement calls for the agent to pay expenses out of the commission.

A. I only.

B. II only.

C. Both I and II.

D. Neither I nor II.

Answer (C) is correct.

REQUIRED: The duties, if any, owed by a principal to an agent who works on commission.

DISCUSSION: Most agencies are governed by contract, and fundamental duties are set forth in the agreement. The fundamental duties in an agency agreement may be express or implied. Two implied fundamental duties of a principal to an agent are to compensate the agent for his or her services and to indemnify or reimburse the agent for authorized expenses incurred on behalf of the principal. Any renunciation of these duties requires an express agreement.

10. Neal, an employee of Jordan, was delivering merchandise to a customer. On the way, Neal's negligence caused a traffic accident that resulted in damages to a third party's automobile. Who is liable to the third party?

	Neal	Jordan
A.	No	No
B.	Yes	Yes
C.	Yes	No
D.	No	Yes

Answer (B) is correct.

REQUIRED: The liability of the employer and employee for the employee's negligence.

DISCUSSION: A principal is strictly liable for a tort committed by an agent within the scope of the agent's employment (vicarious liability). This liability is without regard to the fault of the principal. Vicarious liability does not apply when the agent is an independent contractor. A person is liable for his or her own negligent acts even if acting as an agent of another.

Answer (A) is incorrect. Agent status is not a shield to liability for one's own negligence, and an employer is vicariously liable for his or her employees' acts. Answer (C) is incorrect. An employer is vicariously liable for employees' acts. This rule reflects the doctrine of respondeat superior. Answer (D) is incorrect. Agent status is not a shield to liability for a person's own negligence.

11. Generally, a disclosed principal will be liable to third parties for its agent's unauthorized misrepresentations if the agent is an

	Employee	Independent Contractor
A.	Yes	Yes
B.	Yes	No
C.	No	Yes
D.	No	No

Answer (A) is correct.

REQUIRED: The type(s) of agents, if any, for whose unauthorized misrepresentations the principal is liable.

DISCUSSION: The principal is liable for torts involving misrepresentations regardless of whether the agent is an employee or an independent contractor. The agent's misrepresentation must be (1) fraudulent, (2) negligent, or (3) innocent but material and with all of the elements of fraud except intent. A tort involving misrepresentation is an an example of vicarious liability. An example of tortious misrepresentation by an agent-independent contractor is the sale by a homeowner through a real estate broker who made a material misrepresentation to make the sale. But the principal generally is not liable for the tortious acts of an independent contractor that involve physical acts.

12. An agent will usually be liable under a contract made with a third party when the agent is acting on behalf of a

	Disclosed Principal	Undisclosed Principal
A.	Yes	Yes
B.	Yes	No
C.	No	Yes
D.	No	No

Answer (C) is correct.

REQUIRED: The liability of an agent to a third party when the principal is disclosed and undisclosed.

DISCUSSION: When a principal is undisclosed, the third party believes (s)he is dealing directly with the agent. Thus, under general contract law, an agent is liable to the third party because the third party intended to deal only with the agent. An agent who discloses the principal and acts within actual or apparent authority ordinarily binds only the principal.

16.4 Termination of an Agency

13. Bolt Corp. dismissed Ace as its general sales agent and notified all of Ace's known customers by letter. Young Corp., a retail outlet located outside of Ace's previously assigned sales territory, had never dealt with Ace. Young knew of Ace as a result of various business contacts. After his dismissal, Ace sold Young goods to be delivered by Bolt and received from Young a cash deposit for 20% of the purchase price. It was not unusual for an agent in Ace's previous position to receive cash deposits. In an action by Young against Bolt on the sales contract, Young will

A. Lose because Ace lacked any implied authority to make the contract.

B. Lose because Ace lacked any express authority to make the contract.

C. Win because Bolt's notice was inadequate to terminate Ace's apparent authority.

D. Win because a principal is an insurer of an agent's acts.

Answer (C) is correct.

REQUIRED: The outcome of a suit by a third party against a principal whose agent had no actual authority.

DISCUSSION: When a principal discharges an agent, (s)he must give actual notice of the discharge to those the agent had previously dealt with and constructive notice to others who might have known of the agency. Ace continued to have apparent authority because of Bolt's failure to give constructive notice by publication in a newspaper of general circulation in the place where the agency activities occurred. Publication in trade journals of the termination would have provided such notice and effectively terminated Ace's apparent authority.

Answer (A) is incorrect. Young will win. Ace had apparent, although not actual (express or implied), authority. Answer (B) is incorrect. Ace's lack of express authority did not preclude the existence of apparent authority. Answer (D) is incorrect. A principal is not an insurer of an agent's acts. A principal is only liable when an agent acts with actual or apparent authority.

14. The apparent authority of a general agent for a disclosed principal will terminate without notice to third parties when the

A. Principal dismisses the agent.

B. Principal or agent dies.

C. Purpose of the agency relationship has been fulfilled.

D. Time period set forth in the agency agreement has expired.

Answer (B) is correct.

REQUIRED: The occurrence automatically terminating a general agent's apparent authority.

DISCUSSION: Without a special rule, an agency and the agent's power to bind the principal terminate instantly upon the death of the principal because the principal must exist at the time the agent acts.

Answer (A) is incorrect. When an agent is dismissed, existing customers must be given actual notice. Other persons must be given constructive notice to terminate apparent authority. Answer (C) is incorrect. Fulfillment of the purpose of the agency does not terminate apparent authority. Answer (D) is incorrect. The expiration of the agency does not terminate apparent authority.

15. Pell is the principal and Astor is the agent in an agency coupled with an interest. In the absence of a contractual provision relating to the duration of the agency, who has the right to terminate the agency before the interest has expired?

	Pell	Astor
A.	Yes	Yes
B.	No	Yes
C.	No	No
D.	Yes	No

Answer (B) is correct.

REQUIRED: The person with the right to terminate an agency coupled with an interest.

DISCUSSION: An agency coupled with an interest is one in which the agent has a specific, current, beneficial interest in property that is the subject matter of the agency. A principal does not have the right or power to terminate an agency coupled with an interest. In any agency, the agent may terminate at any time without liability if no specific period for the agency has been established.

16.5 Antitrust Law

16. Long Corp. entered into agreements with its retailers whereby they agreed not to sell Long batteries beneath the minimum prices determined by Long. The agreement did not preclude the retailers from selling competing brands of batteries. The agreement is

A. Legal because the retailers are permitted to sell the competing brands at any price they choose.

B. Legal if the batteries are sold under Long's exclusive trademark.

C. An exception to the price-fixing provision of the Sherman Act.

D. Illegal per se.

Answer (C) is correct.

REQUIRED: The legality of an agreement between the manufacturer and retailer establishing minimum prices.

DISCUSSION: According to a decision of the Supreme Court, an agreement between a manufacturer and its retailers establishing minimum prices is evaluated under the rule of reason. It is not illegal per se under antitrust law. Resale price maintenance, whether of maximum or minimum prices, is a form of vertical price fixing (as opposed to horizontal price fixing by competitors). It may be struck down only if an extensive economic analysis indicates that the anticompetitive effects outweigh the procompetitive effects.

Answer (A) is incorrect. The issue is whether the agreement to maintain minimum resale prices is valid. Answer (B) is incorrect. Whether the batteries are trademarked is irrelevant. Answer (D) is incorrect. The Supreme Court has determined that maintenance of neither maximum nor minimum resale prices is a per-se violation of the Sherman Act.

17. Each of Sunrise Corp.'s distributors has a defined geographic area in which it has the exclusive right to sell, but only to franchised retailers. Franchised retailers are authorized to sell Sunrise's products only within specified locations. This marketing arrangement will be

A. Judged under the rule of reason whether or not title passes.

B. Illegal per se if title passes to the distributor or retailer but judged under the rule of reason if title does not pass (as under an agency or consignment).

C. Illegal per se whether or not title passes.

D. Illegal per se if title does not pass but judged under the rule of reason if title passes.

Answer (A) is correct.

REQUIRED: The legality of restrictions on distributors' sales to nonfranchised retailers.

DISCUSSION: Vertical territorial limitations between a manufacturer and its distributors and retailers are no longer condemned as per-se violations. They are examined under the rule of reason to determine whether they have an unreasonable effect on competition. Under prior law, vertical restraints were not permissible after title passed.

Answer (B) is incorrect. Under current law, a marketing arrangement based on assignment to distributors of defined geographic areas is not illegal per se regardless of whether title has passed. Answer (C) is incorrect. The restrictions on resale do not depend on passage of title. They will be examined under the rule of reason. Answer (D) is incorrect. Passage of title is not the determining factor.

18. The Duplex Corporation has been charged by the U.S. Justice Department with an "attempt to monopolize" the industry in which it does business. In defending itself against such a charge, Duplex will prevail if it can establish that

A. It had no intent to monopolize its industry.

B. Its percentage share of the relevant market was less than 50%.

C. Its activities do not constitute an unreasonable restraint of trade.

D. It does not have monopoly power.

Answer (A) is correct.

REQUIRED: The valid defense to "an attempt to monopolize" charge.

DISCUSSION: The Sherman Act prohibits contracts, combinations, or conspiracies in restraint of trade in addition to the formation of monopolies and attempts to monopolize. Because the Sherman Act provides for criminal sanctions, the Justice Department must prove that the defendant specifically intended the illegal act of an "attempt to monopolize." If a defendant can show no intent to monopolize, the government will not prevail.

Answer (B) is incorrect. No set percentage of the relevant market need be proven as an element of an attempt to monopolize. Answer (C) is incorrect. The rule-of-reason defense does not apply to a charge of an attempt to monopolize. Answer (D) is incorrect. Actual monopoly power is not an element of an attempt to monopolize.

19. If a defendant is charged with an unfair method of competition under the Federal Trade Commission Act,

A. The FTC may prevail even if the conduct alleged to be illegal did not violate either the Sherman or Clayton Act.

B. Criminal sanctions can generally be imposed against a defendant even though the defendant has not violated an FTC order to cease and desist.

C. There can be no violation of the act unless one or more of the specifically enumerated unfair methods of competition are established.

D. The complaint must be based upon the purchase or sale of goods, wares, or commodities in interstate commerce.

Answer (A) is correct.

REQUIRED: The true statement about the FTC's power.

DISCUSSION: The Federal Trade Commission Act authorized the Federal Trade Commission (FTC) to enforce all of the antitrust laws. The FTC also has broad authority to prevent unfair methods of competition and unfair or deceptive acts or practices.

Answer (B) is incorrect. The FTC does not have power to impose criminal sanctions. Criminal cases must be prosecuted by the U.S. Justice Department. Answer (C) is incorrect. The FTC has broad authority with respect to unfair methods of competition; they are not necessarily enumerated. Answer (D) is incorrect. The FTC has power over unfair methods of competition and deceptive acts or practices that extend to commerce in general, not just the sale of goods or commodities.

16.6 Employment Law

20. Under the Federal Insurance Contributions Act (FICA), which of the following acts will cause an employer to be liable for penalties?

	Failure to Supply Taxpayer Identification Numbers	Failure to Make Timely FICA Deposits
A.	Yes	Yes
B.	Yes	No
C.	No	Yes
D.	No	No

Answer (A) is correct.

REQUIRED: The acts for which an employer is liable.

DISCUSSION: An employer subject to FICA taxes must file quarterly returns and deposit appropriate amounts on a monthly or semiweekly basis with an authorized depository institution. For example, a monthly depositor must deposit each month's taxes on or before the 15th day of the following month. Failure to deposit appropriate amounts results in penalties. Penalties are also imposed on persons who file returns and other documents without supplying taxpayer identification numbers.

21. Under which of the following conditions is an on-site inspection of a workplace by an investigator from the Occupational Safety and Health Administration (OSHA) permissible?

A. Only if OSHA obtains a search warrant after showing probable cause.

B. Only if the inspection is conducted after working hours.

C. At the request of employees.

D. After OSHA provides the employer with at least 24 hours notice of the prospective inspection.

Answer (C) is correct.

REQUIRED: The requirement for an OSHA inspection.

DISCUSSION: Employees may request in writing that OSHA investigate for unsafe working conditions within an organization. OSHA is not required to notify the employer prior to inspection in most cases.

Answer (A) is incorrect. OSHA is required to obtain a search warrant to conduct an on-site inspection. However, the search warrant may be issued by showing (1) probable cause that conditions on the premises violate the law, or (2) the search is in accordance with reasonable legislative or administrative standards (e.g., searches are made randomly or periodically). Answer (B) is incorrect. An inspection by OSHA may occur at any time the agency chooses to audit the company in question. Answer (D) is incorrect. OSHA is not required to give an employer 24-hour notice prior to conducting its investigation except in limited circumstances.

22. Under the provisions of the Americans with Disabilities Act, in which of the following areas is a person with a disability protected from discrimination?

	Public Transportation	Privately Operated Public Accommodations
A.	Yes	Yes
B.	Yes	No
C.	No	Yes
D.	No	No

Answer (A) is correct.

REQUIRED: The areas, if any, in which persons with disabilities are protected.

DISCUSSION: The Americans with Disabilities Act prohibits discrimination with respect to employment and access to public accommodations. Employers and those who operate private and public accommodations are required to make reasonable changes to accommodate persons with disabilities by eliminating discriminatory policies and practices.

23. The Fair Labor Standards Act as amended

A. Applies to all employers whether or not engaged in interstate commerce.

B. Requires that double time be paid to any employee working in excess of 8 hours in a given day.

C. Prohibits discrimination based upon the sex of the employee.

D. Requires all employees doing the same job to receive an equal rate of pay.

Answer (C) is correct.

REQUIRED: The true statement concerning the Fair Labor Standards Act (FLSA).

DISCUSSION: The FLSA regulates the relationship between an employer and employees by providing for minimum wages, overtime, and prohibition of child labor. Also, the equal pay provision prohibits discrimination on the basis of sex. It requires equal pay for equal work.

Answer (A) is incorrect. The FLSA applies only to employers engaged in interstate commerce, the constitutional limit on federal jurisdiction over commerce. Answer (B) is incorrect. The general overtime requirement is to pay at least time-and-one-half the regular rate for all hours worked over 40 per week. Answer (D) is incorrect. The act does not require all employees doing the same job to receive an equal rate of pay but permits differentials on the basis of seniority, merit, quality, or quantity.

24. Under the Employee Retirement Income Security Act of 1974 (ERISA), which of the following areas of private employer pension plans, if any, are regulated?

	Employee Vesting	Plan Funding
A.	Yes	Yes
B.	Yes	No
C.	No	Yes
D.	No	No

Answer (A) is correct.

REQUIRED: The areas, if any, of private employer pension plans regulated by ERISA.

DISCUSSION: ERISA does not require establishment of pension plans or set benefits. Instead, ERISA regulates private pension plans to protect employees' rights to benefit payments. It imposes fiduciary duties on fund managers as well as recordkeeping, reporting, and disclosure requirements. In general, the vesting rules require that employee contributions vest immediately and that employer contributions vest after 5 years of employment.

25. Which of the following employee benefits, if any, are exempt from the provisions of the National Labor Relations Act?

	Sick Pay	Vacation Pay
A.	Yes	Yes
B.	Yes	No
C.	No	Yes
D.	No	No

Answer (D) is correct.

REQUIRED: The benefits exempt from the provisions of the NLRA.

DISCUSSION: The NLRA gave employees the right to organize unions and to bargain collectively. It also defined certain unfair labor practices by employers. Employers are required to negotiate and bargain in good faith with regard to wages, hours, and other terms and conditions of employment. The NLRA does not exempt either sick pay or vacation pay from collective bargaining.

16.7 Intellectual Property Law

26. Under the Patent Act, which of the following is true?

A. A stand-alone computer program may be copyrighted but not patented.

B. The duration of a new patent is 20 years. It may be renewed.

C. A genetically engineered bacterium is not protected.

D. The only requirement for a process, machine, manufacture, or composition of matter to be patentable is novelty (not in conflict with an existing patent).

Answer (A) is correct.

REQUIRED: The true statement about federal patent law.

DISCUSSION: A single computer program can be copyrighted but not patented. Methods of calculation, fundamental truths, principles, laws of nature, ideas, and the like are not patentable. However, a process that includes a computer program is patentable.

Answer (B) is incorrect. Under current law, the right to a utility patent lasts for a nonrenewable term of 20 years from the date the patent application is filed. Upon expiration, the invention enters the public domain. Answer (C) is incorrect. Such a bacterium is human-produced (not naturally occurring) and therefore patentable. Answer (D) is incorrect. Any new and useful process, machine, manufacture, or composition of matter, or any new and useful improvement thereof may be patented. But it must have utility and be nonobvious as well as novel.

27. M.A. Genius invented, manufactures, and distributes a flashlight needing no batteries if used in direct sunlight. Genius did not apply for a patent. Novelco bought one at a retail store, analyzed and copied it, and now sells an identical product under its own name. Which of the following is true?

A. Genius can enjoin Novelco's activities on the basis of a trade secret violation.

B. Genius can enjoin Novelco's activities because it clearly meets the novelty, utility, and nonobviousness criteria.

C. If Novelco continues to make and sell the solar flashlights, it will have to pay Genius a royalty.

D. Novelco has not violated any legal duty owed to Genius.

Answer (D) is correct.

REQUIRED: The legal effect of the use of an unpatented invention by a person who is not the inventor.

DISCUSSION: Society's interest in free competition is so strong that copying a competitor's product is lawful unless a trademark, trade secret, patent, or copyright is infringed. If a product is not protected by a patent, competitors can use information gained through reverse engineering.

Answer (A) is incorrect. Trade secrets receive only limited protection. If a competitor can discover a secret through independent means not involving a misappropriation, the owner has no protection against duplication. Answer (B) is incorrect. Patentability gives no protection unless a patent is obtained. Answer (C) is incorrect. Genius cannot claim a royalty without an exclusive right to the product.

16.8 Various Law Topics

28. The federal Consumer Credit Protection Act (CCPA) protects a credit cardholder from loss by

A. Restricting the interest rate charged by the credit card company.

B. Limiting the cardholder's liability for unauthorized use.

C. Requiring credit card companies to issue cards to qualified persons.

D. Allowing the cardholder to defer payment of the balance due on the card.

Answer (B) is correct.

REQUIRED: The protection provided by the CCPA to a credit cardholder.

DISCUSSION: The act regulates credit for personal, household, or agricultural purposes. Title 1 is the Truth-in-Lending Act (TILA). It requires disclosure by creditors before credit is extended and regulates credit cards. It serves as an antifraud act by limiting the holder's liability for unauthorized use of the card to (1) $50 or (2) the amount of money, property, labor, or services obtained by unauthorized use before the card issuer is notified, whichever is lower.

Answer (A) is incorrect. State usury law regulates interest charges. Answer (C) is incorrect. Federal law pertaining to credit card fraud does not require card companies to issue cards. Answer (D) is incorrect. Federal law pertaining to credit card fraud does not allow a cardholder to defer payment of the balance due on a card.

29. Under the federal Fair Debt Collection Practices Act (FDCPA), to which of the following would a collection service using improper debt collection practices be subject?

A. Abolishment of the debt.

B. Reduction of the debt.

C. Civil lawsuit for damages for violating the act.

D. Criminal prosecution for violating the act.

Answer (C) is correct.

REQUIRED: The debtor's remedy under the FDCPA.

DISCUSSION: Debtors may pursue civil actions, e.g., class action suits, against collection agencies that engage in abusive, deceptive, and unfair debt collection practices.

Answer (A) is incorrect. The FDCPA prevents abusive, deceptive, and unfair debt collection practices. The act does not provide for abolishment of the debt. Answer (B) is incorrect. The FDCPA does not provide for reduction of the debt. Answer (D) is incorrect. The FDCPA does not provide for criminal penalties.

30. The federal Fair Debt Collection Practices Act (FDCPA) prohibits a debt collector from engaging in unfair practices. Under the act, a debt collector generally can be prevented from

A. Contacting a third party to ascertain a debtor's location.

B. Continuing to collect a debt.

C. Communicating with a debtor who is represented by an attorney.

D. Commencing a lawsuit to collect a debt.

Answer (C) is correct.

REQUIRED: The practice prohibited by the FDCPA.

DISCUSSION: Under the FDCPA, a debt collector (but not a creditor unless it misrepresents itself as a debt collector) generally may not (1) use harassing or intimidating practices; (2) use abusive language; (3) use false or misleading tactics; (4) contact the consumer at work if the employer objects; (5) contact the consumer at unusual or inconvenient times; (6) contact the consumer at all if the debtor is represented by an attorney; and (7), unless specifically authorized by a court, contact third parties other than a spouse, parent, or financial advisor expressly about the account.

Answer (A) is incorrect. The prohibition is against contacting most third parties about payment without court authorization. Answer (B) is incorrect. The FDCPA limits the tactics that may be employed by a debt collector but does not prevent all debt collection activities. Answer (D) is incorrect. The FDCPA does not impair the ability of a creditor to assign its right to sue to enforce the contract with the debtor.

16.9 PRACTICE TASK-BASED SIMULATIONS

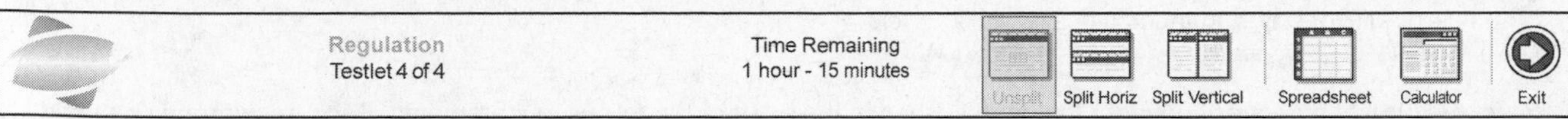

DIRECTIONS

Note: If you believe you have encountered a software malfunction, report it to the test center staff immediately.

Navigation

To navigate from task to task, use the controls at the bottom of the screen. Click on the **Next** button to advance to the next task, or the **Previous** button to go to the previous task. To go directly to any task, click on its number.

If you would like a reminder to revisit a task, or want to indicate that you are finished with it, click on the reminder flag below the task number. To clear the flag, click on it again. Reminder flags are for your use only – they do not contribute to your score.

Tabs

In this part of the examination, you will be asked to complete various tasks. Every task has one or more **Work Tabs**. Some tasks have one or more **Information Tabs**, others may have none. Every task has a **Help** tab.

If a task has **Information Tabs**, you may use the information in them to complete your responses in the **Work Tabs**.

Work tab **Information tab** **Help tab**

Work Tabs:

- **Work Tabs** are identified with a pencil icon. This is where your responses are expected.
- Each task has one or more **Work Tabs**.
- **Work Tabs** contain directions for completing the task – be sure to read these directions carefully.
- The **Work Tab** name in the example above is for illustration only – yours will differ.
- You must complete all of the **Work Tabs** in each task to receive full credit.

Information Tabs:

- The Authoritative Literature will be provided in all tasks in the AUD, FAR, and REG sections for your reference.
- Your simulation may have one or more additional **Information Tabs**. Like the Authoritative Literature tabs, **Information Tabs** do not have a pencil icon.
- If your task has additional **Information Tabs**, go through each to familiarize yourself with the task content.

Help Tab:

- The **Help Tab** provides assistance with the exam software that is used in this task. For example, if the task is to compose a memorandum, **Help** will provide information about the word processor.

The Toolbar

The toolbar at the top of the screen shows the amount of time remaining for you to complete the tasks. In addition, the following tools are available. Note that only the **Exit** button is displayed when Directions are visible - the others will appear when you begin the tasks.

Click on these buttons to split or unsplit the screen. You can split the screen vertically or horizontally.

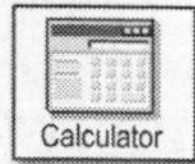

Click on this button to display the calculator; click on it again to hide the calculator. To move the calculator, click on the calculator title bar and drag the calculator to the desired location.

Click on this button to use the spreadsheet; click on it again to hide the spreadsheet. To move the spreadsheet, click on the the spreadsheet title bar and drag the spreadsheet to the desired location.

Click on this button to go on to the next part of the examination. You must complete all of the tasks to receive full credit. Once you click on **Exit** and confirm the action, you will NOT be able to return to this testlet.

Select the type of patent or copyright that is described in the each of the following statements. Each answer may be used once, more than once, or not at all.

Statement	Patent
1. Sarah Curtis designed a system for a manufacturing plant 20 years ago. Sarah informed the plant that the system design was protected for another 75 years.	
2. ABC Chemicals produced a new chemical compound. The compound is protected for another 18 years.	
3. Woodworks, Inc., created a new ornamental design to be applied to its chairs and bookshelves. Woodworks has 7 years left of protection.	
4. Sonia Curtis designed a system for a manufacturing plant 20 years ago. Sarah was just informed that her protection has expired.	
5. Joe Newman wrote a popular love story 1 year before his death. Joe's protection ceased on the day of his death.	

Choices
A) Utility patent
B) Design patent
C) Author's patent
D) Publisher's copyright
E) None of the above

Indicate whether each statement below applies to the Clayton Act of 1914 or the Federal Trade Commission Act of 1914 by selecting yes or no.

Statement	Clayton Act of 1914	Federal Trade Commission Act of 1914
1. Exclusive dealing is prohibited even if needed to protect product quality.		
2. This act established the enforcement body whose objectives are to initiate antitrust actions and protect the consumer public.		
3. Rebates to special customers are prohibited.		
4. The "failing company doctrine" may be used as a defense.		
5. This act prohibits tie-in sales.		
6. This act provides for the recovery or enforcement of treble damages.		

Exotic Pets, Inc., hired Peterson to be the manager of one of its stores. Exotic sells many kinds of animals. Peterson was given written authority by Exotic to operate the store, including the right to buy inventory. Peterson was told that any inventory purchase exceeding $2,000 required the approval of Exotic's general manager.

On June 1, Year 1, Peterson contracted with Creatures Corp. to buy snakes for $3,100. Peterson had regularly done business with Creatures on Exotic's behalf in the past and, on several occasions, had bought $1,000 to $1,750 worth of snakes from Creatures. Creatures was unaware of the limitations on Peterson's authority to buy inventory.

Peterson occasionally would buy for Exotic a certain breed of dog from Premier Breeders, Inc., which was owned by Peterson's friend. All purchases were for less than $2,000. Whenever Exotic bought dogs from Premier, Premier paid Peterson 5% of the purchase price as an incentive to do more business with Premier. Exotic's management was unaware of these payments to Peterson.

On June 20, Year 1, Mathews went to the Exotic store managed by Peterson to buy a ferret. Peterson allowed Mathews to handle one of the ferrets. Peterson knew that this particular ferret had previously bitten one of the store's clerks. Mathews was bitten by the ferret and seriously injured.

On July 23, Year 1, Peterson bought paint and brushes for $30 from Handy Hardware. Peterson charged the purchase to Exotic's account at Handy. Peterson intended to use the paint and brushes to repaint the pet showroom. Exotic's management had never specifically discussed with Peterson whether Peterson had the authority to charge purchases at Handy. Although Exotic paid the Handy bill, Exotic's president believes Peterson is obligated to reimburse Exotic for the charges.

On August 1, Year 1, Exotic's president learned of the Creatures contract and advised Creatures that Exotic would neither accept delivery of the snakes nor pay for them because Peterson did not have the authority to enter into the contract.

Exotic's president has also learned about the incentive payments Premier made to Peterson.

Peterson has duties to Exotic that are beyond contractual obligations. For each of the following, check "Yes" if the duty is required of Peterson and "No" if the duty is not required of Peterson.

Duty	***Yes***	***No***
1. Deviate from instructions if an emergency arises		
2. Notify Exotic of all known, relevant information		
3. Compete with Exotic		
4. Use special skills or knowledge Peterson possesses		
5. Represent Exotic even if Peterson has a conflict of interest		
6. Commingle money or personal property with that of Exotic		
7. Keep profits on transactions entered into for Exotic		
8. Follow lawful explicit instructions from Exotic		
9. Act solely in Exotic's interest		
10. Perform only duties expressed in the agency agreement		

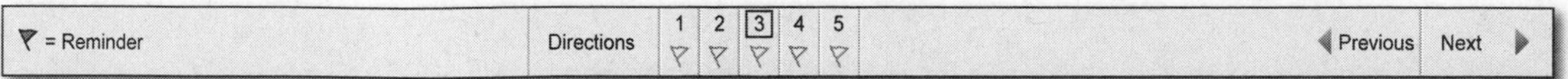

Agency: Authority and Liability | Authoritative Literature | Help

Prime Cars, Inc., buys and sells used automobiles. Occasionally, Prime has its salespeople purchase used cars from third parties without disclosing that the salesperson is in fact buying for Prime's used car inventory. Prime's management believes better prices can be negotiated using this procedure.

One of Prime's salespeople, Parker, entered into a contract with Hallow in accordance with instructions from Prime's sales manager. The car was to be delivered 1 week later.

While driving back to Prime's place of business after entering into the contract with Hallow, Parker was involved in an automobile accident with another vehicle. As a result of the accident, Hallow learned that Parker was an agent of Prime. The collision resulting from Parker's negligence injured Mathews, the driver of the other car involved in the accident.

Prime terminated Parker's employment because of the accident. Prime also refused to perform the contract entered into by Parker with Hallow. Following Prime's general business practices, Prime published an advertisement in several trade journals that gave notice that Parker was no longer employed by Prime.

Shortly thereafter, Parker approached one of Prime's competitors, Bagley Autos, Inc., and contracted to sell Bagley several used cars in Prime's inventory. Bagley's sales manager, who frequently purchased cars out of Prime's inventory from Parker, paid 25% of the total price to Parker, with the balance to be paid 10 days later when the cars were to be delivered. Bagley's sales manager was unaware of Parker's termination. Prime refused to deliver the cars to Bagley or to repay Bagley's down payment, which Prime never received from Parker.

Mathews sued both Parker and Prime for the injuries sustained in the automobile accident.

Bagley sued Prime for failing to deliver the cars or return the down payment paid to Parker.

Select from the list provided the appropriate phrase to complete each statement. Each choice may be used once, more than once, or not at all.

Situation	***Answer***
1. Hallow's claim against Prime will be based upon	
2. Hallow's claim against Parker will be based upon	
3. Mathews's claim against Prime will be based upon	
4. Mathews's claim against Parker will be based upon	
5. In the lawsuit involving Bagley and Prime, Prime's defense is	
6. In the lawsuit involving Bagley and Prime, Bagley's argument is	

Choices
A) Express actual authority
B) Implied actual authority
C) Apparent authority
D) No authority
E) Scope of employment
F) Negligence
G) Vicarious liability
H) None of the choices

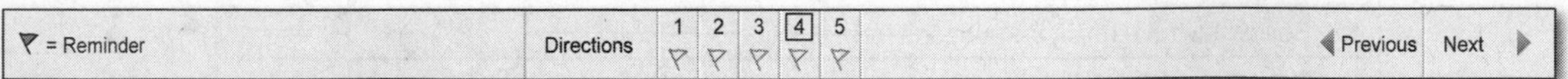

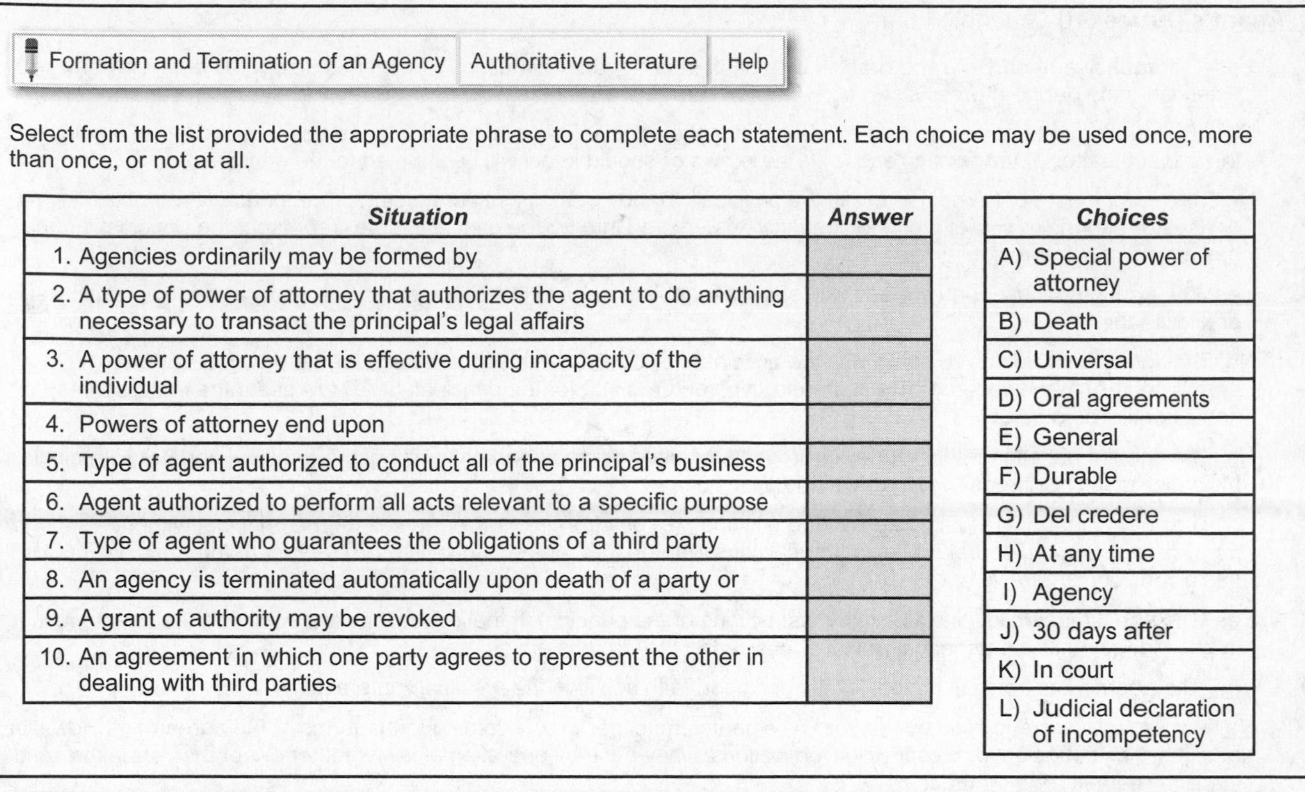

Situation	Answer
1. Agencies ordinarily may be formed by	
2. A type of power of attorney that authorizes the agent to do anything necessary to transact the principal's legal affairs	
3. A power of attorney that is effective during incapacity of the individual	
4. Powers of attorney end upon	
5. Type of agent authorized to conduct all of the principal's business	
6. Agent authorized to perform all acts relevant to a specific purpose	
7. Type of agent who guarantees the obligations of a third party	
8. An agency is terminated automatically upon death of a party or	
9. A grant of authority may be revoked	
10. An agreement in which one party agrees to represent the other in dealing with third parties	

Choices
A) Special power of attorney
B) Death
C) Universal
D) Oral agreements
E) General
F) Durable
G) Del credere
H) At any time
I) Agency
J) 30 days after
K) In court
L) Judicial declaration of incompetency

Unofficial Answers

1. Intellectual Property (5 Gradable Items)

1. E) None of the above. The duration of a utility patent is 20 years. Business processes qualify for patents.
2. A) Utility patent. Utility patents can be used for chemical compounds and last for 20 years.
3. B) Design patent. Ornamental designs qualify for design patents. Design patents have a life of 14 years.
4. A) Utility patent. Business processes qualify for utility patents and are protected for 20 years.
5. E) None of the above. Literary creations qualify for author copyrights and last for life plus 70 years.

2. Antitrust Law (6 Gradable Items)

1. No, No. The Clayton Act prohibits exclusive dealing, which occurs when a seller requires a buyer to purchase only the seller's products and not the products of the seller's competitors. But it does not prohibit an arrangement between a franchisor and a franchisee if it is necessary to ensure product quality. The FTC Act of 1914 does not apply to exclusive dealing.
2. No, Yes. The FTC Act of 1914 created the FTC. The basic objectives of the FTC are to initiate antitrust actions and to protect the consumer public. However, the Justice Department, not the FTC, has authority to pursue criminal sanctions. The Clayton Act did not establish an enforcement body.
3. No, No. The Robinson-Patman Act of 1936, not the Clayton or FTC Acts, prohibits rebates, commissions, discounts, etc., to special customers.
4. Yes, No. The most important defense available under Section 7 of the Clayton Act is the failing company doctrine. It applies when (1) the acquiree is in failing condition, (2) the possibility of reorganization is extremely low, and (3) no other acquirer would have a less anticompetitive effect.
5. Yes, No. The Clayton Act prohibits tying or tie-in sales, that is, sales in which a buyer must take another product to buy the first product. Other prohibitions include exclusive dealing, reciprocal dealing, price discrimination, and interlocking directorates.
6. Yes, Yes. The Clayton Act provides for recovery of treble damages. The FTC Act created the FTC, which enforces remedies and sanctions for antitrust violations, including recovery of treble damages by private parties.

3. Agent's Duties (10 Gradable Items)

1. Yes. Emergency authority may be granted by a court in emergency situations. An agent's delegated authority may be extended if the public interest is served.
2. Yes. The agent must use reasonable efforts to notify the principal of all information (s)he possesses that (a) is relevant to the subject matter of the agency and (b) (s)he knows or should know will be imputed to the principal.
3. No. The agent must not (a) compete with the principal, (b) buy from himself or herself for the principal without permission, (c) make secret profits on transactions entered into for the principal, or (d) represent the principal if (s)he has a conflict of interest.
4. Yes. The agent must use the care and skill of a reasonable person in like circumstances and his or her own special skills or knowledge.
5. No. The agent must not (a) compete with the principal, (b) buy from himself or herself for the principal without permission, (c) make secret profits on transactions entered into for the principal, or (d) represent the principal if (s)he has a conflict of interest.
6. No. The agent must account for money or property received or expended on behalf of the principal and not commingle his or her money or property with that of the principal.
7. No. The agent must not (a) compete with the principal, (b) buy from himself or herself for the principal without permission, (c) make secret profits on transactions entered into for the principal, or (d) represent the principal if (s)he has a conflict of interest.
8. Yes. The agent must follow lawful explicit instructions of the principal. If the instructions are not clear, the agent must act in good faith and in a reasonable manner considering the circumstances.
9. Yes. The agent must act with utmost loyalty and good faith solely in the principal's interest.
10. No. Most agencies are formed by contract. The parties must perform according to the terms of the agreement. However, an agent has duties beyond contractual obligations. They arise by operation of law whether or not they are expressed in the agreement or a contract exists.

4. Agency: Authority and Liability (6 Gradable Items)

1. A) Express actual authority. Parker acted with express actual authority in accordance with instructions from Prime's sales manager. Thus, Prime is liable to Hallow.
2. H) None of the choices. Parker is liable to Hallow. Agents acting on behalf of nondisclosed principals are liable to third parties on the contracts they enter into with such third parties on behalf of the principal. The third party intended to deal only with the agent, and the agent is a party to the contract.
3. G) Vicarious liability. Direct liability results from the principal's own negligent or reckless action or failure to act in conducting business through agents. Vicarious liability results from the actions of the agent for which the principal may be found liable. Vicarious liability arises when (1) the agent's act was a tort, whether or not intentional; (2) the agent's act was not authorized by the principal; (3) the agent was an employee of the principal; and (4) the act was within the agent's scope of employment.
4. F) Negligence. Parker is liable to Mathews because all persons are liable for their own negligence.
5. D) No authority. Parker's actual authority to enter into contracts on Prime's behalf ceased on termination of employment by Prime. Prime also will argue that the trade journal announcement was effective to terminate Parker's apparent authority in relation to Bagley. However, Prime was obligated to give actual notice to Bagley that Parker was no longer employed given their prior dealings.
6. C) Apparent authority. Parker's actual authority to enter into contracts on Prime's behalf ceased on termination of employment by Prime. Parker, however, continued to have apparent authority to bind Prime because (1) Parker was acting ostensibly within the scope of authority as evidenced by past transactions with Bagley, and (2) Bagley did not receive actual notice of Parker's termination that was required given their prior dealings.

<u>5. Formation and Termination of an Agency</u> (10 Gradable Items)

1. <u>D) Oral agreements.</u> Agencies ordinarily may be formed by oral agreements. However, some states may require a writing in particular cases, e.g., contracts for sale of land.
2. <u>E) General.</u> A general power of attorney authorizes the agent to do anything that may be necessary to transact the principal's legal affairs.
3. <u>F) Durable.</u> A durable power of attorney is effective during a period of incapacity of the principal. This power of attorney must be expressly conferred in writing before the principal becomes incapacitated.
4. <u>B) Death.</u> All powers of attorney end upon the death of a principal.
5. <u>C) Universal.</u> Universal agents are authorized to conduct all of the principal's business that the principal may legally delegate.
6. <u>E) General.</u> General agents are authorized to perform all acts relevant to the purpose for which they are engaged.
7. <u>G) Del credere.</u> A del credere agent guarantees the obligations of a third party to the principal. The obligation of a del credere agent is based on the promise to answer for the debt of another. A person making this promise is a surety.
8. <u>L) Judicial declaration of incompetency.</u> A judicial declaration of incompetence of the principal or the agent terminates the agency.
9. <u>H) At any time.</u> A principal may revoke a grant of authority at any time. Revocation may be implicit or explicit.
10. <u>I) Agency.</u> An agency is an express or implied consensual relationship formed when two parties agree that one, the agent, will represent the other, the principal, in dealing with third parties.

Gleim Simulation Grading

Task	Correct Responses		Gradable Items		Score per Task
1	____	÷	5	=	____
2	____	÷	6	=	____
3	____	÷	10	=	____
4	____	÷	6	=	____
5	____	÷	10	=	____
			Total of Scores per Task		____
		÷	Total Number of Tasks		5
			Total Score		____ %

STUDY UNIT SEVENTEEN
CONTRACTS

(26 pages of outline)

This study unit covers the general concepts of contract law, and Study Unit 18 applies specifically to contracts for sales of goods. A contract is not the physical thing, e.g., the written document, but a relationship that exists between the parties to the contract. The law recognizes that a contract has been formed when the elements of a contract (mutual assent, consideration, capacity, and legality) are met. A contract creates legal obligations or duties between parties. Once a valid, enforceable contract is formed, the law provides for remedies if an obligation in a contract is breached.

17.1 CLASSIFICATION OF CONTRACTS

1. **Express and Implied Contracts**
   a. The terms of an **express contract** are stated, either in writing or orally.
   b. The terms of an **implied contract** are wholly or partially inferred from conduct and circumstances but not from written or spoken words.
      1) A contract is **implied in fact** when the facts indicate a contract was formed.

EXAMPLE

Kelly makes an appointment with a hairdresser. Kelly keeps the appointment and permits the hairdresser to cut her hair. Kelly has promised through her actions to pay for the haircut. A court will infer from Kelly's conduct that a duty to pay was understood and agreed to.

2. **Unilateral and Bilateral Contracts**
   a. In a unilateral contract, only one party makes a promise. The other party is an actor, not a promisor. If (s)he performs a defined action (an acceptance), the promisor is obligated to keep the promise.

EXAMPLE

Amy tells Bill, "I'll pay you $10 to polish my car." This offer is for a unilateral contract. Amy (the promisor) expects Bill (the actor) to accept by the act of polishing her car, not by making a return promise.

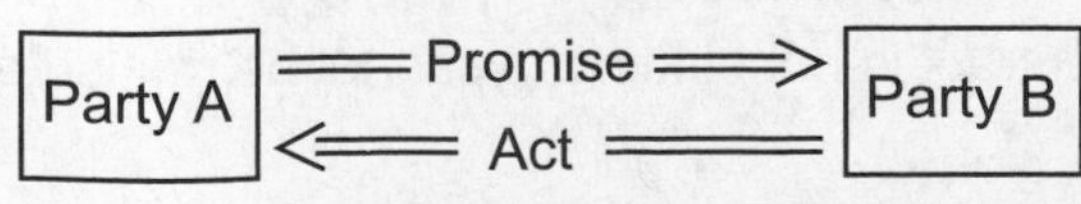

Figure 17-1

b. In a bilateral contract, both parties make promises.

EXAMPLE

Amanda tells Bob that she will provide him lodging in September if he agrees to pay her $200. This is an offer for a bilateral contract. If Bob accepts and promises to pay the $200, a bilateral contract is formed.

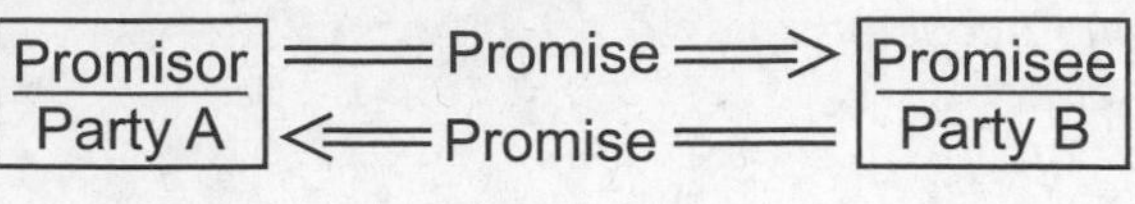

Figure 17-2

3. **Executory and Executed Contracts**

a. An executory contract is not yet fully performed. If any duty remains to be performed, the contract is executory.

EXAMPLE

Al says to Brian, "I'll pay you $10,000,000 to play football for me next season." Brian agrees, creating an executory bilateral contract. It is executory because neither party has yet performed.

If Al pays Brian the $10,000,000 and Brian refuses to play, the contract is partially executed.

b. An executed contract has been fully performed by all parties.

EXAMPLE

If Brian plays football for Al the entire season and Al pays Brian $10,000,000, the contract is fully executed.

Contract	Fully Performed
Executory	No
Executed	Yes

4. **Valid, Unenforceable, Voidable, and Void Contracts**

a. A valid contract has all the elements of a contract, and the law provides a remedy. A valid contract is legally binding on both parties.

b. An unenforceable contract has all the elements of a contract. However, the law will not enforce the contract because the contract does not comply with another legal requirement.

EXAMPLE

Amber enters into an oral contract to sell land to Brittany. To be enforceable, a contract for the sale of land must be in writing. By law, all real estate contracts must be in writing to be enforceable.

c. A party may either enforce or nullify a voidable contract.

EXAMPLE

Amber was induced to enter into a contract by Brittany's intentional deception (i.e., fraud). Amber has a choice and can either enforce the contract or elect to void the contract and collect damages for any loss sustained due to fraud.

d. A void contract is a legal nullity.

1) A void contract is not binding. It cannot be ratified and made enforceable by the parties.

EXAMPLE

An agreement requiring the commission of a crime is void. It is not recognizable as a contract, and there is no remedy provided by law.

Agreement	All Contract Elements	Law Provides a Remedy
Valid Contract	Yes	Yes
Unenforceable Contract	Yes	No
Voidable Contract	Yes	Yes, if not voided
Void Contract	No	No

Stop and review! You have completed the outline for this subunit. Study multiple-choice questions 1 and 2 on page 647.

17.2 MUTUAL ASSENT (OFFER AND ACCEPTANCE)

1. **Offer**
   a. A contract is formed when a party accepts an offer.
      1) An offer is a statement or other communication by which the offeror grants the offeree the power to accept and form an agreement.
   b. An offer must
      1) Be communicated to an offeree,
      2) Be in a communication authorized by the offeror,
      3) Indicate an objective intent to enter into a contract, and
      4) Be sufficiently definite and certain.
   c. No specific manner of communication of the offer is required. For example, nonverbal communication may be appropriate.
   d. To be legally binding, an offer must **indicate an intent to enter into a contract**.
      1) Whether an offer has been made is determined by whether a reasonable person would assume that an offer has been made (objective standard).
      2) Invitations to negotiate and preliminary negotiations do not constitute an offer. The language of commitment should be distinguished from phrases such as
         a) "Are you interested in . . . ?"
         b) "I'll probably take . . ."
      3) Advertisements usually are not offers but invitations to submit offers.
         a) However, an advertisement may be an offer if it uses clear, definite, and explicit language that leaves nothing open for negotiation.
   e. Generally, a contract must be reasonably definite as to all material terms and must set forth clearly all rights and duties of the parties.
      1) Essential terms generally include the following:
         a) **Names** of the parties
         b) **Subject matter** involved
         c) **Price and quantity**
         d) **Time and place** of performance
      2) If any term besides quantity is missing, it may be supplied by the court.

3) If a contract does not specify the time of performance, courts generally decide that performance within a reasonable time was intended.
4) The law has traditionally required definiteness regarding the price term in a contract (e.g., a court will not supply the price of real estate).

f. **Option Contracts.** An option contract results in an **irrevocable offer**.

1) In an option, the offeree exchanges something of value for the offeror's promise to hold the offer open for a specified period.

2. **Termination of Offer**

a. After termination, the ability to accept the offer no longer exists.

b. **Lapse of time.** An offer may be worded so as to terminate after a specified period or on a specified date. Unless otherwise terminated, the offer remains open for the specified time.

1) If no time is stated in the offer, the offer will terminate after a reasonable period.

c. **Death or incompetency** of either the offeror or the offeree generally terminates the power of acceptance, whether or not the other party had notice.

1) Incompetence is a lack of legally required qualifications or physical or psychological fitness to bind oneself to agreements.
2) Death or incompetency generally does not terminate an existing contract, including an offer contained in a valid option contract. The offeree has already given consideration.

d. **Destruction** or loss of the specific subject matter terminates an offer.

e. **Illegality** of a proposed contract or performance terminates the offer.

f. **Revocation.** The offeror may revoke an offer at any time prior to acceptance.

1) Revocation must be communicated to the offeree prior to the offeree's acceptance.

a) Revocation is effective when received by the offeree.

2) Notice may be communicated by any reasonable means, either directly or indirectly.

a) For example, an offeree may receive indirect notice of revocation by learning that the subject matter has been sold to another party.
b) The offeree's knowledge that a third party has offered to buy the subject matter of the offer is not a revocation.

3) An offer stating it will remain open may be terminated by giving the offeree notice that it has been revoked, unless it is an option contract.

g. **Rejection** terminates the offer. It implies an intent not to accept the offer. It may be expressed or implied by words or conduct.

1) Rejection is **effective when received** by the offeror.
2) A **counteroffer** is effective as a simultaneous rejection of an offer and a new offer from the original offeree.

a) In contrast, a mere inquiry about terms is tentative and does not indicate intent to reject the offer.

EXAMPLE

The statement "Would you consider shipping by air instead of by truck?" is not a counteroffer. It indicates no intent to reject or accept the offer.

3) If an offer states that acceptance is effective on receipt, rejection following receipt has no effect.

3. **Acceptance**

   a. The offeree has an exclusive power of acceptance, but the offeror may expressly limit what constitutes acceptance.

   b. An acceptance must relate to the terms of the offer and be positive, unequivocal, and unconditional. The acceptance may not vary the offer in any way.

      1) This principle is the **mirror image rule**.
      2) If a **conditional acceptance** requires the offeror's agreement to additional or different terms, it is a **counteroffer**, not an acceptance.

   c. Acceptance **must be communicated** to the offeror by any words and actions that a reasonable person would understand as an acceptance.

      1) A **unilateral** contract may be accepted by performance instead of by making a reciprocal promise.
      2) Taking possession of or exercising control over something may constitute acceptance.
      3) **Silence** accompanied by the appropriate circumstances from which an intent to accept may be inferred is acceptance.

         a) However, an offeror generally cannot require the offeree to respond to avoid being contractually bound.

   d. If an offeror specifies a medium of acceptance, it must be used.

      1) However, if the offer states nothing about the medium of acceptance, the offeree is implicitly authorized to accept by any reasonable medium (e.g., one that is used by the offeror, customary in similar transactions, or appropriate in the specific circumstances).
      2) Generally, acceptance by an unauthorized mode is effective upon receipt by the offeror, assuming the offer has not expired or been revoked.

   e. If the offer specifies a **time for acceptance**, the acceptance must be communicated within that time.

   f. The offeror may waive compliance with particular terms of an offer regarding acceptance. Thus, a deficient or late acceptance may be a new offer that the original offeror chooses to accept.

The AICPA has consistently tested candidates on the mailbox rule, including when an offeror attempts revocation after an acceptance has been dispatched.

4. **Mailbox Rule**

   a. Under the mailbox rule, acceptance is effectively communicated to the offeror at the **moment of dispatch** if (1) the offeree has used an authorized medium of acceptance and (2) the offer is still open.

EXAMPLE

An offer is sent by mail. It does not specify a particular medium for acceptance. A letter of acceptance is deposited in the mail. If it was properly addressed and had proper postage affixed, the acceptance is effective even if it never reaches the offeror.

      1) Under the mailbox rule, once acceptance has been dispatched, it is effective even if the offeror attempts revocation while the acceptance is in transit.

         a) If an offeree sends an acceptance **following prior dispatch of a rejection**, the acceptance is effective only if (and when) received by the offeror before receipt of the rejection.

2) The mailbox rule does not apply to an acceptance of an offer held open under an option contract.
3) An offeror negates the mailbox rule by making acceptance effective only upon receipt.

EXAMPLE

The offeror mailed a revocation on July 15, Year 1. It arrived on July 17, after the offeree had mailed an acceptance on July 16. The revocation is invalid because the acceptance was in transit before the offeree had notice of the revocation. This outcome is avoided if the offeror explicitly states that the "acceptance must be received to be effective." The first item received by the offeror controls whether a contract is formed.

5. **Mutual Assent**

	Revocation of Offer	Rejection of Offer	Acceptance of Offer
Effective	1. Upon receipt by offeree 2. Lapse of reasonable time or specified period 3. Death or incompetency of offeror or offeree 4. Illegality of contract or performance 5. Destruction (loss) of the subject matter	Upon receipt of rejection or counteroffer	1. Upon receipt 2. Under mailbox rule, upon dispatch 3. Mailbox rule negated by statement that acceptance is effective upon receipt
Implicitly effective	Offeree is aware of sale of subject matter	Offeree allows an offer to lapse	Offeree's reasonable action indicating acceptance
Ineffective	1. After offeror receives acceptance 2. Offeree party to option contract	After offeror receives acceptance	1. Offeror receives after deadline 2. Offeree sends counteroffer 3. Acceptance is not mirror image of offer 4. Acceptance is not communicated to offeror

Stop and review! You have completed the outline for this subunit. Study multiple-choice questions 3 and 4 beginning on page 647.

17.3 CONSIDERATION

1. **Definition**

a. Consideration is something of value given in a bargained-for exchange. Consideration can be viewed as the central core of the contract. It is the promise, action, or forbearance that parties agree to.

EXAMPLE

Amanda tells Bob that she will provide him lodging in September if he agrees to pay her $200. Amanda's consideration is the promise of an obligatory future action. Bob's consideration is the act of paying $200. Both parties have provided consideration that was not legally required of them before the contract was created.

b. Two elements must be present to satisfy the consideration requirement:

1) Legal sufficiency
2) A bargained-for exchange (mutuality of consideration)

c. The consideration provided by one party (the promisee) to support the enforceability of the other party's (the promisor's) promise may be (1) a bargained-for legal detriment to the promisee or (2) a legal benefit to the promisor. Consideration is always in the form of a promise, act, or forbearance.

2. **Legal Sufficiency**

   a. For a contract to be enforceable, consideration must be legally sufficient. Consideration is legally sufficient to render a promise enforceable if the promisee incurs a legal detriment or if the promisor incurs a legal benefit.

      1) To incur a legal detriment, the promisee must

         a) Do something (s)he is not legally obligated to do or
         b) Not do something (s)he has a legal right to do.

      2) Almost any legal detriment is legally sufficient. Parity of value is not required.
      3) In a **bilateral contract**, one promise is consideration for the other.
      4) Consideration may be legally sufficient without a simultaneous exchange and despite the form of the consideration.
      5) An agreement stating that a promise was made in consideration of an amount that was neither bargained for by the promisor nor paid by the promisee may be deemed insufficient.

   b. An illusory promise is insufficient. A promise is illusory if its terms impose no actual obligation on the promisor.

3. **Bargained-for Exchange**

   a. Both parties must receive something of legal value in exchange for incurring a legal detriment.

      1) A bargained-for exchange distinguishes a contract from a gift.

   b. Nominal consideration. Something almost devoid of value generally is not sufficient (e.g., a symbolic payment of $1 is not consideration).

4. **Items Not Sufficient Consideration**

   a. **Past consideration** is not sufficient consideration.

      1) Past acts cannot be bargained for. They have already happened, and the acting party cannot effectively promise to incur any legal detriment.

EXAMPLE

Father said to Daughter, "If you graduate, I promise to pay you $10,000 at the end of next month." If Daughter had already graduated at the time of the promise, Father is not obligated. Daughter incurred no legal detriment to support his promise.

      2) Accordingly, the law generally requires that modification of a contract be supported by new, bargained-for consideration.

   b. **Moral consideration.** Promises made out of a sense of honor or moral obligation are not enforceable if they lack the bargain element.

   c. **Pre-existing legal duty.** Consideration does not exist if

      1) An existing duty was imposed by law, or
      2) A person is already under contract to render a specified performance.

EXAMPLE

A contractor tells a homeowner that, unless she pays him an extra $500, he will leave her roof half repaired. The contractor has a pre-existing duty to repair the entire roof.

   d. **Part payment of an undisputed debt** is not consideration for a promise by the creditor to accept the part payment in full satisfaction of the debt.

      1) A promise to pay part of a **disputed** debt is consideration for the creditor's forgiveness of the remainder. But the dispute must be in good faith.

5. **Substitutes for Consideration**

   a. An arrangement may lack consideration but be enforceable on the basis of promissory estoppel or quasi-contract.

   b. **Promissory estoppel** applies when

      1) A promise is given that the promisor should reasonably expect to induce action or forbearance by the promisee,
      2) The promise induces the action or forbearance, and
      3) Injustice can be avoided only by enforcing the promise.

EXAMPLE

John pledged $5 million to University. In reliance on the pledge, University began construction of a new building. If John retracts the pledge, a court will most likely enforce the promise. University has acted upon John's promise and likely incurred a significant debt.

   c. The parties to a **quasi-contract** (contract implied in law) make no promises and reach no agreement. However, one of the parties is substantially benefited at the expense of the other party, and no adequate legal remedy is available.

      1) To avoid unjust enrichment, the party providing the benefit is entitled to the reasonable value (not the contract price) of the services rendered or property delivered.

   d. A new promise to pay a legal obligation barred by law is enforceable without consideration if other requirements are met, such as a writing.

      1) Examples are debts not collectible because of (a) the expiration of the statute of limitations, (b) a discharge in bankruptcy (discussed in Study Unit 20), and (c) the voidability of the obligation.

Insufficient Consideration	Substitutes for Consideration
Illusory promise	Promissory estoppel
Nominal consideration	Quasi-contract
Past consideration	Modification of contract for sale of goods
Moral consideration	
Pre-existing legal duty	Firm offer in a sale of goods
Part payment of undisputed debt	Promise to pay legal obligation barred by law

EXAMPLE

A doctor came upon an unconscious person on the sidewalk and rendered medical treatment. To avoid unjust enrichment, the patient must pay the doctor a reasonable fee even though the aid was unsolicited and no contract existed.

Stop and review! You have completed the outline for this subunit. Study multiple-choice questions 5 and 6 on page 648.

17.4 CAPACITY

1. **Overview**

   a. Parties to a contract are required to have the legal capacity to form a contract. Minors, persons lacking mental capacity, and intoxicated persons do not have full legal capacity.

2. **Minors**
   a. A minor may **disaffirm** his or her contract. Thus, the contract is **voidable** by the minor, not void.
      1) However, the minor is liable until disaffirmance. Moreover, a minor is always liable based on a quasi-contract for the reasonable value, not the contract price, of **necessaries** (e.g., food, shelter, and clothing).
      2) According to the majority rule, disaffirmance is allowed even if the minor misrepresented his or her age.
      3) A party contracting with a minor is bound to the contract.
   b. Power to disaffirm continues until a reasonable time after the minor reaches the age of majority.
      1) Any unequivocal act that indicates an intent to disaffirm is sufficient.
      2) When the contract has been partially or wholly executed, the minor must, if possible, return any consideration received from the other party.
      3) A minor may disaffirm even if (s)he cannot return the consideration.
   c. A contract entered into by a minor may be **ratified** by the minor after (s)he has reached the age of majority.
      1) Ratification may be either explicit or implied.
      2) Ratification dates back to the beginning of the contract and is for all of its terms.
      3) A contract is ratified if the minor retains the consideration for an unreasonable time after (s)he reaches majority.
         a) New consideration is not needed.
         b) Ratification may result from accepting benefits incidental to ownership, such as rents, dividends, or interest.
         c) Selling the property constitutes ratification by the minor.
3. **Persons Lacking Mental Capacity**
   a. A person lacking mental capacity is unable to understand the nature and consequences of his or her acts.
      1) If a person was judicially determined to be insane or otherwise incompetent **before** contract formation, the contract is **void** and cannot be ratified.
      2) Judicial determination of incompetence **after** the formation of a contract renders the contract merely **voidable**.
4. **Intoxicated Persons**
   a. If mental capacity is lacking due to voluntary or involuntary intoxication, the contract is **voidable** at the option of the intoxicated person.
      1) It must be proven that the intoxicated person's reason and judgment were impaired to such an extent that (s)he did not understand the legal consequences of his or her actions.

Background

If a party apparently intends to form a contract, the courts may find that the contract is enforceable even if one of the parties later claims to have been intoxicated. In *Lucy v. Zehmer*, a 1954 Virginia case, the defendant, Zehmer, claimed it should have been obvious that he was too drunk to form a contract and that he and Lucy were just exchanging big talk when they discussed the sale of the Ferguson Farm in a restaurant one night. Lucy maintained that after negotiating for 40 minutes and even signing a contract for the purpose of selling the farm, any reasonable person would assume that Zehmer had been negotiating in earnest. The appeals court concurred that Zehmer was not too drunk to understand what he was doing, that he had given every outward sign of intending to sell the property, and that the contract was valid.

Stop and review! You have completed the outline for this subunit. Study multiple-choice questions 7 and 8 on page 649.

17.5 LEGALITY

1. **Overview**

   a. Contracts are unenforceable if they are inconsistent with the U.S. Constitution, violate a statute or other rule of law, or are against public policy.

      1) A promise to commit a tort or to induce the commission of a tort is void on grounds of public policy.
      2) Agreements to commit criminal acts are void.
      3) Agreements not to press criminal charges are not enforceable. They interfere with the state's duty to protect society by prosecuting criminals.

2. **Effects of Illegality**

   a. Courts ordinarily will not assist either party to an illegal agreement. The court will leave the parties as it finds them.

   b. An illegal term may taint the whole agreement, rendering it void.

      1) If an agreement is divisible, most courts will enforce the legal portion.

   c. An agreement containing an illegal portion may have been partially performed.

      1) If the illegal portion has not yet been performed, the party who has rendered performance can withdraw from the bargain and recover the performance or its value.

   d. If one of the parties is less at fault than the other, (s)he may be allowed to recover payments made or property transferred.

   e. An agreement that appears to be legal may nonetheless be illegal due to facts and circumstances of which one party is unaware.

      1) The innocent party may sue for damages.

3. **Statutory Violations**

   a. An agreement that cannot be performed without violating a statute is void.

   b. Commission of some illegal act during the performance of a contract does not render the contract itself illegal.

      1) If the formation of the contract violated no law, and the contract can be performed without violating the law, the contract is enforceable.

   c. A party who agrees to supply goods or services while unaware that the thing supplied will be used for an unlawful purpose can enforce the agreement.

      1) However, a person who intends to accomplish an unlawful purpose may not enforce a contract made for that purpose.

4. **Licensing Statutes**

   a. Licensing statutes require a person to obtain a license to carry on a designated trade or business. Violators are subject to a fine, imprisonment, or both.

   b. The statute itself may provide that an unlicensed person is not entitled to recover for services rendered.

   c. If a licensing statute is **regulatory**, a person cannot recover for services unless (s)he holds the required license, regardless of whether the statute so states.

      1) A regulatory statute is one enacted for the protection of the public against unqualified or incompetent persons.
      2) A **revenue** collection statute is enacted merely to collect revenue, such as by requiring a vendor's license. Recovery on the contract is possible, but a fine may be payable.

5. **Contracts in Restraint of Trade**
   a. Contracts in restraint of trade restrict competition or otherwise interfere with the normal flow of goods or services.
   b. A typical restraint is a **covenant not to compete**. It is an agreement not to engage in a particular trade, profession, or business. This restraint may be valid if
      1) The purpose of the restraint is to protect a related property interest of the promisee and
      2) The restraint is no more extensive in scope and duration than is reasonably necessary to protect that property or legitimate business interest.
   c. An **employment contract** may include a covenant not to compete during or after the period of employment. It may prohibit the employee from
      1) Setting up a business in competition with the former employer,
      2) Entering the employment of a competitor, or
      3) Revealing the former employer's trade secrets (a nondisclosure agreement).
6. **Contracts of Adhesion**
   a. A contract of adhesion is one formed between parties with a great disparity of bargaining power.
      1) The weaker party's only choice is to accept the terms imposed by the stronger party or to forgo the transaction entirely (examples are rental agreements and insurance contracts).
      2) Most such contracts are upheld.
7. **Unconscionability**
   a. If one party to a contract has an excessive degree of economic power over another, the courts may find that a contract is unenforceable. Unconscionability relates to unscrupulous or unreasonable activity. The contract lacks fundamental fairness. If a contract or one of its terms is unconscionable when the contract is made, a court may
      1) Refuse to enforce the contract,
      2) Enforce the remainder of the contract without the unconscionable term, or
      3) Limit the application of the term to avoid an unconscionable result.
   b. Unconscionability may be **procedural** (an unfair negotiating process or procedural irregularity) or **substantive** (excessively unfair terms).

Background

In *Williams v. Walker-Thomas Furniture*, a 1965 District of Columbia case, the defendant company included in its contracts for sales on credit a provision that no item was considered paid for until all items were paid for. If the customer defaulted on his or her most recent purchase, (s)he was deemed to have defaulted on all purchases, and the store repossessed every item. The court found that this raised "serious questions of sharp practice and irresponsible business dealings" and refused to enforce the contracts.

8. **Exculpatory Clauses**
   a. Exculpatory clauses are contractual terms that excuse one party from liability for injury or damage caused by his or her acts.
      1) Generally, courts do not enforce a term that excuses a party's criminal conduct, intentional torts, or gross negligence.
   b. If the parties have approximately equal bargaining power, the courts are more likely to uphold an exculpatory clause.
      1) If one party has a decidedly weaker position, the contract may be held invalid as contrary to public policy.

Stop and review! You have completed the outline for this subunit. Study multiple-choice questions 9 and 10 beginning on page 649.

17.6 LACK OF GENUINE ASSENT

1. **Overview**
   a. A contract may be voidable or void if the assent of one of the parties was not genuine. Many contract defenses are based on lack of assent.
2. **Fraud**
   a. The following are the **elements of fraud**:
      1) A false representation (or concealment) of a material fact
      2) Intent to misrepresent (scienter)
      3) Intent to induce reliance
      4) Justifiable reliance by the innocent party on the misrepresentation
      5) Damage (loss) suffered by the innocent party
   b. Fraud requires an actual or implied **misrepresentation of a fact**. Misrepresentation may be expressly spoken or written words, but it can be implied from conduct.
      1) A statement of opinion is not usually subject to a claim of fraud. A fact is objective and verifiable, but an opinion is generally subject to debate.
      2) When a purchaser relies on a purported expert's opinion, the innocent party may be entitled to rescission or reformation of the contract.
      3) Statements of probabilities and predictions of future business results do not usually result in fraud.
      4) Misrepresentations of law traditionally did not entitle a party to void a contract because they were regarded as statements of opinion. But the modern trend is to treat them as statements of fact or opinion depending on the circumstances. For example, a representation that a law has been amended is factual. A representation of the legal consequences of certain events is an opinion.
   c. The misrepresentation must be material. It must concern a factor important in inducing the party to enter into the contract.
   d. **Constructive fraud** arises from gross negligence.
      1) A misrepresentation may be made with a willful and reckless disregard for its truth or falsity rather than with actual intent to deceive (scienter).
   e. **Fraud in the inducement** occurs even when the defrauded party is aware of entering into a contract and intends to do so.
      1) However, (s)he is deceived about a fact material to the contract (e.g., the nature of the goods or services).
      2) Thus, the contract is **voidable**.
   f. **Fraud in the execution** (also known as fraud in the factum) occurs when the signature of a party is obtained by a fraudulent misrepresentation that directly relates to the signing of a contract.
      1) The purported contract is **void**.
   g. The deceived party must have a justifiable reason for relying on the misrepresentation.
   h. Usually, neither party to a contract has a duty to disclose facts. However, a duty to disclose exists in the following circumstances:
      1) The parties have a fiduciary relationship.
      2) A material fact is known by one party, and the other could not reasonably discover it.
      3) A person misstates an important fact. The person must correct the misstatement as soon as (s)he learns of it.

i. For a tort claim based on fraud, injury must have been caused by the misrepresentation.
   1) The injured party may ask for damages or for rescission of the entire contract.
   2) Rescission returns the parties to the positions they would have occupied if the contract had not been made.

3. **Negligent Misrepresentation**
   a. Negligent misrepresentation is a false representation of a material fact intended to be reasonably relied upon.
      1) It may be oral, written, or implied from conduct.
      2) The party that makes the misrepresentation has **no knowledge** of its falsity but has acted **without due care**.
   b. Remedies are rescission (the right to void the contract) and damages (reliance and consequential damages).

4. **Innocent Misrepresentation**
   a. Innocent misrepresentation is a false representation of a material fact that is intended to be relied upon and that is reasonably relied on.
      1) The party that makes the misrepresentation has **no knowledge** of its falsity but has acted **with due care**.
      2) Remedies are rescission and damages (reliance damages only).

5. **Mistake**
   a. A mistake is an unintended act, omission, or error that arises in the formation of a contract.
   b. Mistakes of fact have legal significance. Mistakes in judgment of value or quality, whether mutual or unilateral, do not.
   c. A **mutual mistake** occurs when both parties to a contract are mistaken about the same material fact. A mutual mistake of material fact is (1) a basis for rescission or (2) a sufficient defense for failure to perform the contract.

EXAMPLE

Katie has a truck she uses for her gardening business. Curt approaches Katie and tells her that he would like to buy her truck. Katie agrees to sell. Curt accepts her price and pays Katie. However, without the knowledge of either party, the truck was actually destroyed in a fire a few hours before their contract was formed. Given that neither party was aware that the subject matter of the agreement had been destroyed, a mutual mistake has occurred, and rescission is available to either party.

   d. A **unilateral mistake** occurs when only one party to a contract acts on the basis of a mistaken belief or assumption. The party is generally not relieved of the contractual obligation. However, the remedy of rescission is available when
      1) The other party knew or should have known of the mistake;
      2) Enforcement would result in extreme hardship constituting injustice;
      3) The error was due to a mathematical mistake or omission of items in computing the cost of the contract; or
      4) The mistake was due to fraud, duress, or undue influence.

6. **Duress**

   a. One form of duress occurs when one party, by means of an **improper threat** that instills fear in a second party, leaves the second party with no reasonable alternative.

      1) The improper threat must have sufficient coercive effect so that it actually induces the particular person to agree to the contract.
      2) A contract entered into under this form of duress is **voidable** by the innocent party.
      3) Economic duress may arise when one party exerts extreme economic pressure that leaves the threatened party with no reasonable alternative but to comply.

         a) Economic duress may be created by threats of economic harm if the buyer does not accept the seller's terms.
         b) Merely taking advantage of another's financial difficulty is not duress.

      4) A threat of criminal prosecution is ordinarily improper. Although a person has a legal right to report a crime to the police, (s)he may not do so for private gain.

         a) A threat of a civil suit is not improper unless it is made in bad faith, that is, when such an action has no legal basis.

   b. The second form of duress is **physical compulsion** that includes threats of personal violence.

      1) It renders the contract **void**.

7. **Undue Influence**

   a. Undue influence occurs when a dominant party wrongly exploits a confidential relationship to persuade a second party to enter into an unfavorable contract.

      1) A contract is **voidable** as a result of undue influence.

   b. A fiduciary relationship, such as between a trusted lawyer, physician, or guardian and a weaker party, most often gives rise to a claim of undue influence in contract formation.

      1) However, a fiduciary relationship is not essential. A case may arise in the context of emotionally involved parties.

Contract Defense	Effect on Contract
Fraud in the execution	Void
Fraud in the inducement	Voidable
Negligent misrepresentation	Voidable
Innocent misrepresentation	Voidable
Mutual mistake of fact	Voidable
Unilateral mistake of fact	Generally none
Duress -- physical force	Void
Duress -- improper threat	Voidable
Undue influence	Voidable

Stop and review! You have completed the outline for this subunit. Study multiple-choice questions 11 through 13 beginning on page 650.

17.7 STATUTE OF FRAUDS

Background

The original Statute of Frauds was passed by the British Parliament in 1677. Jurisdictions in this country have adopted and then amended it through the years. The Statute of Frauds was passed to require that certain kinds of contracts be executed in a manner providing tangible evidence of a party's agreement to its terms. Since 1677, the phrase "statute of frauds" has come to mean any law or rule requiring a type of contract to be in writing and signed (authenticated) by the party to be bound.

1. **Contracts within the Statute**
   a. The statute of frauds requires certain kinds of contracts to be in writing and signed by the parties against whom enforcement is sought.
   b. **Agreements made in contemplation of marriage.** A promise to marry must be made in consideration for some promise other than mutual promises to marry.
   c. **Agreements that cannot be performed within 1 year of the making of the contract.** If performance is possible within 1 year, the agreement is not covered by the statute of frauds.
      1) The day the contract is made is excluded, and the 1-year period expires at the close of the contract's express termination date.

EXAMPLE

John orally contracts to maintain Mary's truck for as long as she owns it. The contract may be performed within 1 year if Mary decides to sell the truck within that time. Thus, the agreement is not required to be in writing. If John had contracted to maintain Mary's truck for the next 4 years, the contract would be unenforceable without a writing.

   d. **Agreements for the sale of an interest in land.** An interest may be a long-term lease (more than 1 year), mortgage, easement, option, life tenancy, future interest, full ownership, or other interest.
   e. **Agreements of an executor or an administrator.** A promise of an executor or administrator of an estate to pay a debt of the decedent out of the executor's or administrator's own funds must be in writing.
   f. **Agreements for the sale of goods for $500 or more.** An agreement for the sale of goods for $500 or more is not enforceable without a writing sufficient to indicate that a contract for sale has been made between the parties.
   g. **Agreements to answer for the debt of another.** A suretyship agreement must be in writing if the promise is secondary.
      1) **Main purpose rule.** A promise is secondary if its main purpose is to benefit the debtor.

EXAMPLE

Parent cosigns an educational loan for Child as a favor given based on familial affection. Parent receives no economic benefit from the guarantee. Accordingly, the promise is secondary and must be in writing.

      2) A promise is **primary** if its main purpose is to benefit the promisor (the surety, i.e., the party who agrees to pay if the debtor defaults).

EXAMPLE

Company A agrees to buy inventory from Company B. B offers a favorable price if A will guarantee payment of a debt that B owes to supplier. This promise is primary because its main purpose is to obtain an economic advantage for A, not to benefit B. A primary promise is enforceable even if it is not in writing.

      3) An oral promise made to the **debtor** is not within the statute of frauds.

Background

The traditional statute of frauds contained a provision requiring any contract for the sale of investment securities to be in writing. The increasing use of electronic networks to conduct securities transactions rendered this requirement meaningless. Thus, Article 8 of the UCC specifically states that the statute of frauds does not apply to such exchanges.

2. **The Required Writing**
   a. A written memorandum complies with the statute if it contains the following:
      1) A reasonably certain description of the parties and the subject matter
      2) The essential terms and conditions of the contract
      3) A description of the consideration (no minimum or adequate amount is required)
      4) The signatures of the parties to be charged
   b. No particular form is required. The writing may be in the form of a letter, a receipt, an invoice, a check, or an entry in a diary.
      1) The memorandum need not be completed at the time the contract is made.
   c. The agreement may consist of several writings if
      1) One is signed and
      2) The facts and circumstances clearly indicate that they all relate to the same transaction.
3. **Alternatives to the Writing Requirement**
   a. The statute does not apply when both parties to an oral contract have fully performed.
      1) An oral agreement to rescind a completely unperformed (executory) written contract is generally valid, even if the contract is one required by the statute of frauds to be in writing.
   b. When only one party has fully performed, lack of written evidence of the agreement generally does not preclude enforcement.
      1) Because only the party sought to be held liable must sign, the contract may not be enforceable against the other party.
      2) An oral acceptance of a written offer signed by the offeror is binding only on the offeror if the contract is within the statute of frauds.
   c. **Equitable estoppel.** If (1) one party to a contract has misrepresented (or concealed) a material fact, and (2) the other party has relied on the misrepresentation to his or her detriment, the party who made the misrepresentation may not rely on the statute as a defense.
   d. **Part performance.** An oral contract for the sale of land may be enforced when the contract has been partially performed.
      1) The purchaser must have taken action that is clearly based on the oral agreement and reasonably relied on the agreement to his or her substantial detriment.
         a) Mere payment of a deposit is not part performance.
      2) In most states, the party seeking to enforce the oral contract must have done at least two of the following:
         a) Paid part or all of the price
         b) Taken possession
         c) Made valuable improvements
      3) If part performance is established, a court may grant specific performance and force the transfer of the land.

Stop and review! You have completed the outline for this subunit. Study multiple-choice questions 14 through 16 beginning on page 651.

17.8 PAROL EVIDENCE RULE

The AICPA often tests whether the parol evidence rule applies to terms in a contract.

1. **Definition**
   a. Parol evidence is oral evidence.
   b. The parol evidence rule prohibits admission of oral evidence when a writing is intended to be the final and complete expression of the agreement of the parties. The terms of such a contract cannot be contradicted or varied by evidence of
      1) Any prior understanding (oral or written) or
      2) An oral understanding reached at the same time as the final writing.
   c. A writing apparently complete on its face is assumed to be completely integrated at the time of its making. It is the exclusive statement of all the terms of the agreement.
      1) A partially integrated agreement may not be contradicted but may be supplemented with consistent additional items of prior negotiations or agreements, whether written or oral.
2. **Exceptions**
   a. Parol evidence is admissible to prove or explain the following:
      1) Circumstances that make the written agreement void, voidable, or unenforceable. Examples are
         a) Lack of capacity to make a contract,
         b) Fraud,
         c) Mistake,
         d) Illegality,
         e) Duress,
         f) Undue influence, and
         g) Failure of a condition precedent.
      2) The meaning of ambiguous terms in the contract, such as
         a) Custom and usage not inconsistent with the agreement or
         b) Typographical or obvious drafting errors that clearly do not represent the intention of the parties.
      3) A subsequent modification or rescission.
      4) The existence of any separate, distinct agreement between the parties.
         a) It must be reasonable to assume that the parties intended to enter into a collateral agreement, one related to but not part of the integrated contract.
   b. An oral agreement that the contract will not be effective until a condition is satisfied relates to the validity of the whole contract. It does not contradict or vary the terms of the agreement.
   c. The parol evidence rule does not apply to statements after the contract was signed.

Stop and review! You have completed the outline for this subunit. Study multiple-choice questions 17 and 18 on page 652.

17.9 PERFORMANCE, DISCHARGE, AND BREACH

1. **Discharge by Performance**
   a. **Strict performance.** A party discharges his or her contractual obligations by performing according to the terms of the contract.
      1) **Part performance** is generally insufficient to discharge contractual duties.
         a) However, the parties may agree to accept less than full performance.
      2) If a contract does not specify a time for performance, it is due within a reasonable time after the contract is made.
   b. **Substantial performance** is a somewhat lesser standard of performance. It applies when duties are difficult to perform without some deviation from perfection.
      1) An immaterial breach of contract may accompany substantial performance.

EXAMPLE

A contractor has just completed a mansion. Upon inspection, the homeowner finds that cheap water fixtures were used throughout the house even though she explicitly required an expensive brand. Accordingly, she refuses to pay for or accept the home, attempting to void the contract. Because the breach is immaterial in relation to the value of the total contract, the homeowner must pay for and accept the house. The contractor must pay damages for the repair or replacement of the fixtures.

      2) A party who in good faith completes the job in substantial compliance with the contract has discharged his or her duties and can enforce the contract and collect the contract price.
      3) The doctrine is not applied if the party has intentionally committed this immaterial breach.
      4) The doctrine also does not apply if the party has only partially, rather than substantially, performed. Whether substantial performance has been rendered is determined from facts such as the following:
         a) To what extent has the injured party received benefits?
         b) Is the breaching party close to complete performance?
         c) How willful is the breach?
         d) How great is the certainty of completion?
   c. **Good faith** is expected of the parties in performing contractual promises.
      1) A party has a duty to act in good faith to fulfill a condition to the extent to which (s)he is able, for example, to obtain financing.
      2) A party has a duty not to prevent the other party from performing.
2. **Discharge by Agreement**
   a. The parties may end the contract by agreement without performance.
   b. **Mutual rescission** occurs when the parties to a contract agree to cancel it.
   c. **Accord and satisfaction.** Parties to a contract may make a new contract in which the prior and the new contracts are to be discharged by performance of the new contract.
      1) The new agreement is called an accord. The performance of this agreement is called a satisfaction.

EXAMPLE

A general contractor and a homeowner contract for the construction of a deck on the back of the homeowner's house. The contract specifies that the deck is to be constructed of pine, and the homeowner will pay the contractor $5,000. As construction is nearing completion, the homeowner discovers that pine has not been used in the construction of the deck and addresses this issue with the contractor. Both parties agree that the price of the deck construction will be lowered to $4,000 in light of the contractor's mistake. After the construction is completed, and the homeowner pays the contractor $4,000, neither party will be able to sue successfully for the inferior wood or decreased payment. The accord and satisfaction bars this legal action.

d. In a **composition with creditors**, the participating creditors agree to extend time for payment, take lesser sums in satisfaction of the debts owed, or accept some other plan of financial adjustment.

   1) Under general contract law, the original debts will not be discharged until the debtor has performed the new obligations.
   2) The consideration for the promise of one creditor to accept less than the amount due is found in the similar promises of the other creditors.

e. **Modification** of an existing contract's term(s) traditionally requires new consideration.

   1) However, the Restatement of Contracts does not require consideration if the change is fair given new facts. Also, modifications involving a sale of goods do not require consideration. This is discussed further in Study Unit 18.

f. A **substituted contract** is an agreement among all parties that cancels an existing contract. The new contract is supported by new consideration, which may include a promise made by a new party.

   1) A **novation** is a special form of substituted contract that replaces a party to the prior contract with another who was not originally a party. It completely releases the replaced party.
   2) For example, a real estate mortgagor (the landowner-borrower) generally may sell or otherwise transfer the property. However, absent agreement to the contrary, the mortgagor may not delegate his or her performance under the mortgage unless specifically released by the lender-mortgagee (a novation).
   3) A transfer of real property is **subject to the mortgage** when the buyer pays the seller his or her equity but is not personally liable on the existing mortgage loan.
   4) If a buyer **assumes the mortgage**, the buyer pays the mortgagor the value of the property minus the debt secured by the mortgage. The buyer also **promises** that (s)he will pay the balance of the original debt.

      a) The mortgagor is a **surety**. If the buyer defaults, the mortgagor can be held liable.

g. **Release.** One party relieves another of performance obligations without restoration to all parties' original positions. Releases are commonly used if the liability is contingent or disputed.

h. A **waiver** is an intentional and voluntary surrender of a known right and may be express or inferred from the circumstances.

3. **Discharge by Operation of Law**

a. Some contractual obligations are discharged by law, regardless of the will of the parties.

b. When one party to a contract obtains a judgment against the other for breach, the duty to perform is **merged** in the judgment and thereby discharged.

c. **Illegality.** The nonperformance of a contractual duty may be excused if, after formation, the contract becomes objectively impossible to perform (e.g., the law changes, making the contract illegal).

d. **Impossibility** is an exception to the general rule of strict performance.

   1) Circumstances must have changed so completely since the contract was formed that the parties could not reasonably have anticipated and expressly provided for the change (e.g., an essential party to the contract dies, an essential item or commodity has been destroyed, or an intervening change of law has rendered performance illegal).

2) The impossibility must be **objective** in the sense that no one could perform the duty or duties.

a) A promise to supply a commodity is not impossible to perform when a substitute supply is available.

3) If performance is partially impossible, discharge is partial.

e. **Commercial impracticability** results from an unforeseen and unjust hardship. It is a less rigid doctrine than the impossibility exception.

1) Impracticability results from occurrence of an event if its nonoccurence was a basic assumption of the contract.

a) Common events creating commercial impracticability include shortages caused by war, crop failures, or labor strikes.

2) It permits discharge when a party's performance is no longer feasible for reasons not his or her fault.

3) A fundamental issue is whether the promisor expressly or impliedly assumed the risk of such an event.

f. The doctrine of **frustration of purpose** permits discharge of parties even though performance is still possible. Frustration occurs when a contract becomes valueless, that is, when its purpose has been destroyed by an intervening event that was not reasonably foreseeable.

4. **Conditions**

a. A condition is an act, an event, or a set of facts that creates, limits, or extinguishes an absolute contractual duty to perform.

1) Failure of a condition does not subject either party to liability. However, the existence of a condition in a contract does not render it nonbinding.

b. Conditions may be classified based on their timing.

1) A condition **precedent** is an event that must occur before performance is due.

2) A **concurrent** condition must occur or be performed simultaneously.

3) A condition **subsequent** is an event that terminates an existing duty and a right to compensation for breach of contract.

c. Conditions also may be classified as express or implied.

1) An **express** condition is explicitly stated, usually preceded by such terms as "on condition that" or "subject to."

2) An **implied** condition is not expressly stated in the contract.

a) **Implied-in-fact** conditions are understood by both parties to be part of the agreement.

b) **Implied-in-law** conditions are imposed by law to promote fairness.

Conditions
Timing • Precedent • Concurrent • Subsequent Express Implied • In-fact • In-law

5. **Breach of Contract**

   a. A breach of contract is a failure of a party to perform a duty imposed by a contract.

   b. A **material breach** is an unjustified failure to perform obligations arising from a contract, such that one party is deprived of what (s)he bargained for.

      1) A material breach discharges the nonbreaching party from any obligation to perform under the contract and entitles that party to seek remedies.

   c. A **nonmaterial breach** does not deprive the nonbreaching party of the benefit of the bargain and does not discharge that party. However, the nonbreaching party may sue for damages.

      1) A breach generally is considered nonmaterial if the injured party receives substantially all of the benefits reasonably anticipated.

   d. An **anticipatory breach** occurs when one party repudiates the contract.

      1) It is an express or implied indication that (s)he has no intention to perform the contract prior to the time set for performance.

      2) Most courts allow the aggrieved party to suspend his or her own performance and

         a) Await a change of mind by the breaching party,
         b) Act to find a substitute performance, or
         c) Immediately sue for damages.

   e. A **statute of limitations** designates a period after which litigation may not be commenced. The period of limitations varies from state to state and by the type of action.

      1) The statutory period begins from the later of the date of the breach or the date when it should reasonably have been discovered.

      2) The duties to perform are not discharged. However, the ability of a party to sue successfully for nonperformance will no longer exist after the period has expired.

Stop and review! You have completed the outline for this subunit. Study multiple-choice questions 19 through 21 on page 653.

17.10 REMEDIES

1. **Overview**

   a. Legal remedies for breach of contract are primarily to compensate the other party in money for any effect of the breach on an interest in the contract. The following are interests in a contract:

      1) An **expectation** interest is the expected benefit of the contract.

      2) A **reliance** interest is the interest that arises from action in reliance on the other party's duty to perform.

      3) A **restitution** interest arises when a party has an interest in recovering the value of the benefit that his or her performance conferred on the other party.

         a) This interest exists even if a valid contract was not formed.

         b) Restitution is available to prevent unjust enrichment, correct an erroneous payment, or permit recovery of deposits advanced on a contract.

2. **Damages**

   a. A judgment awarding an amount of money to compensate for damages is the most common judicial remedy for breach of contract.

      1) **Nominal** damages are awarded when a breach is proven but the nonbreaching party cannot prove any actual damages. The usual amount is $1.00.
      2) **Compensatory** damages, also called actual or general damages, are incurred from the wrongful conduct of the breaching party. Such damages are intended to place the injured party in as good a position as if the breaching party had (a) **not** breached and (b) performed as the plaintiff reasonably expected. The following are measures of compensatory damages:

         a) **Expectation** damages compensate for the loss of the expectancy interest or benefit of the bargain.
         b) **Incidental** damages result directly from the breach.
         c) **Consequential** damages are foreseeable to a reasonable person at the time the contract was entered into.

            i) They are awarded in addition to the standard measure of damages.

      3) **Reliance** damages may be awarded when expectation damages are too speculative. They compensate for loss incurred in reliance on the other's performance. Thus, they are intended to put the injured party in as good a position as if the contract had **not** been formed.
      4) **Punitive** damages are intended to punish an individual and set an example for others.

         a) A court only awards punitive damages when the breach is malicious, willful, or physically injurious to the nonbreaching party.

      5) **Liquidated** (undisputed) damages are agreed to be paid in advance of any actual breach. A liquidated damages clause is enforceable if all of the following apply:

         a) The clause is not intended as a penalty.
         b) It reasonably forecasts the probable loss due to the breach.
         c) The loss is difficult to calculate.

   b. **Mitigation.** An injured party is required to take reasonable steps to mitigate damages (s)he may sustain. The nonbreaching party must

      1) Not accumulate losses after notice of breach,
      2) Not incur further costs or expenditures, and
      3) Make reasonable efforts to limit losses by obtaining a substitute.

3. **Other Remedies**

   a. **Specific performance.** A nonbreaching party may ask a court to order the other party to perform the action specified in the contract.

      1) Specific performance is rarely granted and only under the following conditions:

         a) No other remedy is adequate.

            i) Monetary damages are not available or are not adequate.
            ii) The subject matter of the contract is unique. For example, each parcel of land is deemed to be unique, so damages rarely are adequate.

         b) Irreparable injury will result if specific performance is not granted.

      2) A contract for personal services is not specifically enforceable.

b. **Rescission** cancels a contract and returns the parties to the positions they would have occupied if the contract had not been made.

1) Rescission results from mutual consent, conduct of the parties, or a court order. Rescission is an appropriate remedy in the following situations:

a) A material breach
b) Negligent misrepresentation
c) Innocent misrepresentation
d) A mutual mistake in contract formation
e) A unilateral mistake in contract formation

c. **Reformation.** When parties to a contract have imperfectly expressed their understanding in a written agreement, reformation allows the contract to be rewritten to reflect the parties' true intention.

d. **Quasi-contract** is outlined in Subunit 17.3.

Stop and review! You have completed the outline for this subunit. Study multiple-choice questions 22 through 24 on page 654.

17.11 CONTRACT BENEFICIARIES

1. **Third-Party Beneficiaries**

a. In a third-party beneficiary contract, at least one of the performances is intended for the direct benefit of a person not a party to the contract. This person is an **intended beneficiary**.

EXAMPLE

Able enters into a valid contract with Baker, who promises to render some performance to Carr.

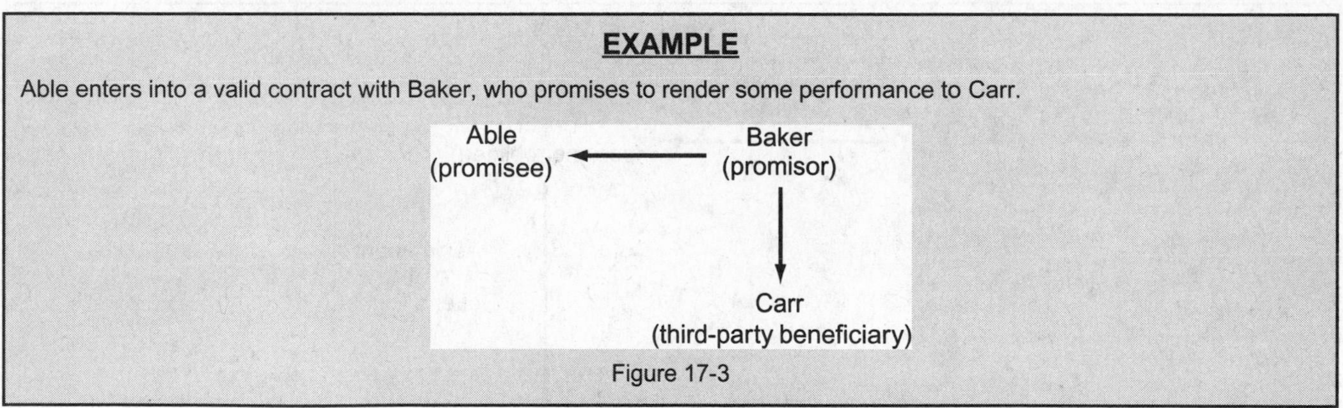

Figure 17-3

1) If a promisee's main purpose is to discharge a debt (s)he owes to a third party, the third party is a **creditor beneficiary**.

a) If the contract in the example above is breached, the creditor (Carr) may sue the promisor (Baker) as a third-party beneficiary. But the creditor also may sue the original debtor (Able).

2) If a promisee's main purpose is to confer a benefit on a third party as a gift, the third party is a **donee beneficiary**.

a) A typical donee beneficiary is the beneficiary of life insurance.

b. An **incidental beneficiary** is a nonparty who might derive a benefit if the contract is performed but whom the parties did not intend to benefit directly.

1) Because an incidental beneficiary is not an intended beneficiary, (s)he has no right to sue on the contract.

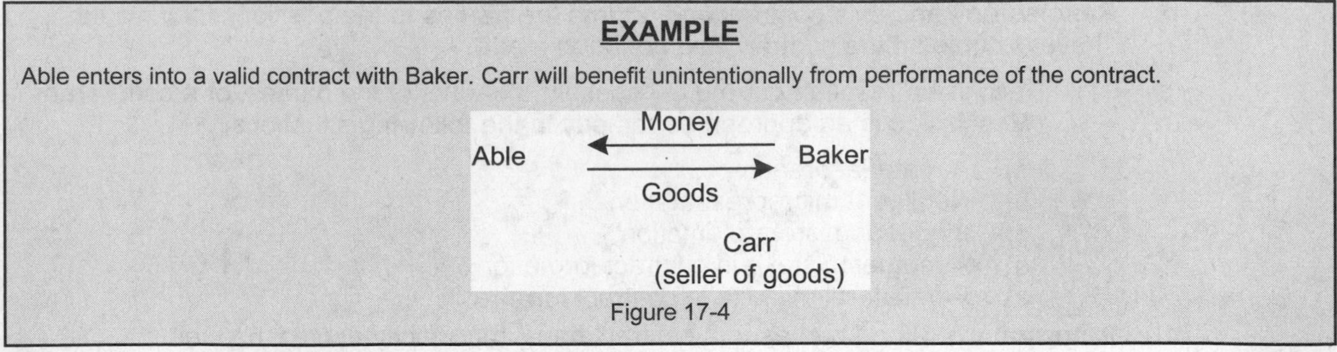

Figure 17-4

c. A third party's rights are derivative. They are the same as the promisee's.
   1) The promisor may assert any defense against the beneficiary that the promisor could have asserted against the promisee.

Stop and review! You have completed the outline for this subunit. Study multiple-choice questions 25 through 27 on page 655.

17.12 ASSIGNMENT AND DELEGATION

1. **Assignment of Rights**
   a. A party to a contract **may transfer his or her rights** under the contract to a third person.

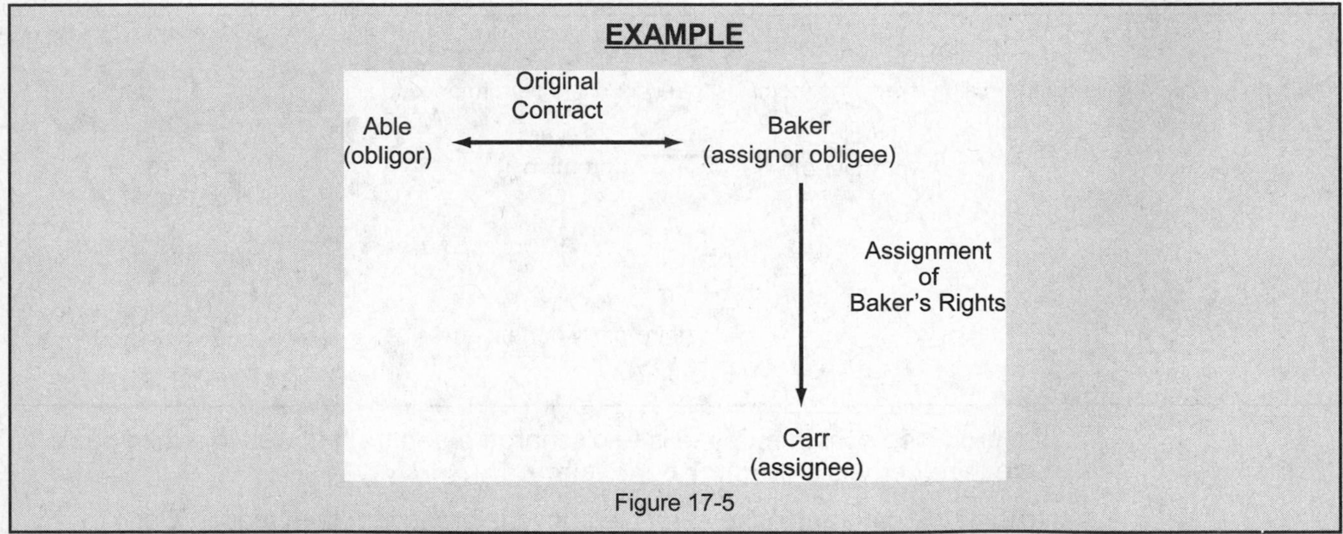

Figure 17-5

      1) The assignment may be gratuitous (without consideration).
      2) The obligee's rights are to performance by the obligor.
      3) The party making the assignment is the assignor and the person to whom the assignment is made is the assignee.
   b. When rights under a contract are assigned unconditionally, the rights of the assignor are extinguished.

c. **Contract rights are generally assignable without consent.**

1) An attempted assignment of a contract right is not effective if the contract expressly states that it is not assignable. Nevertheless, the following are assignable despite an agreement not to assign:

a) A right to receive money
b) Negotiable instruments
c) The right to receive damages for breach of contract or for payment of an account owed in a contract for the sale of goods

2) A tenant generally has the **right to assign or sublease** the premises without the consent of the landlord. The right may be restricted by the lease agreement.

a) An **assignment** transfers the lessee's interest for the **entire unexpired term** of the original lease.
b) A **sublease** is a **partial transfer** of the tenant's rights.
c) A lease term that prohibits assignment alone does not prohibit subleasing and vice versa.

d. A right cannot be assigned without consent if the assignment would result in a material increase or alteration of the duties or risks of the obligor (e.g., insurance policies).

1) Assignments of personal services contracts without consent may be invalid.

e. A contract entered into in reliance by one party on the character or creditworthiness of the other party cannot be assigned without consent.

f. **Notice of assignment.** Between assignor and assignee, assignment is effective when made, even if no notice of assignment has been communicated to the obligor.

1) Performance that the obligor renders to the assignor before receiving notification discharges the obligor's original contract obligation to the extent of the performance.

a) The assignor is deemed to be a trustee for the assignee of amounts received from the obligor after the assignment.

2) If the assignee does not give proper notice, (s)he cannot sue the obligor and force a repeat performance but would instead have to sue the assignor.

a) After notice of the assignment is given, the assignee has the additional option of suing the obligor.

EXAMPLE

Jayhawk Corp. has $70,000 of outstanding accounts receivable. On March 10, Jayhawk assigned a $30,000 account receivable due from Tiger, one of Jayhawk's customers, to Clemons Bank for value. On March 30, Tiger paid Jayhawk the $30,000. On April 5, Clemons notified Tiger of the March 10 assignment from Jayhawk to Clemons. Clemons is entitled to collect $30,000 from Jayhawk only.

g. **Revocability of Assignments**

1) An assignment given for consideration is irrevocable.

2) A gratuitous assignment is usually revocable by the assignor. The following are means of revocation:

a) Notice of revocation communicated by the assignor to the assignee or obligor
b) Assignor's receipt of performance directly from the obligor
c) Assignor's subsequent assignment of the same right to another assignee
d) Bankruptcy of the assignor
e) Death or insanity of the assignor

h. **Assignor's Warranties**

1) Unless the assignment is with recourse, the assignor does not warrant that the obligor will perform.

2) However, if assignment is for consideration, the assignor makes the following three implied warranties:

a) (S)he will do nothing to affect or impair the value of the assignment and has no knowledge of any fact that would;

b) The right assigned exists and is not subject to any limitations or defense against the assignor, except any that are stated or apparent; and

c) Any writing given or shown to the assignee as evidence of the right is genuine.

i. If an assignee releases the obligor, the assignor also is released.

j. **Assignee's rights.** The assignee of a contract acquires all the rights possessed by the assignor and no more. Thus, the assignee stands in the shoes of the assignor.

2. **Delegation of Duties**

a. A contract involves rights and duties.

1) Delegation means that a person under a duty of performance authorizes another person to render the required performance.

EXAMPLE

Able and Baker have a contract under which Able delegates his duties to Carr. Able is the delegator (obligor), Carr is the delegatee, and Baker is the obligee.

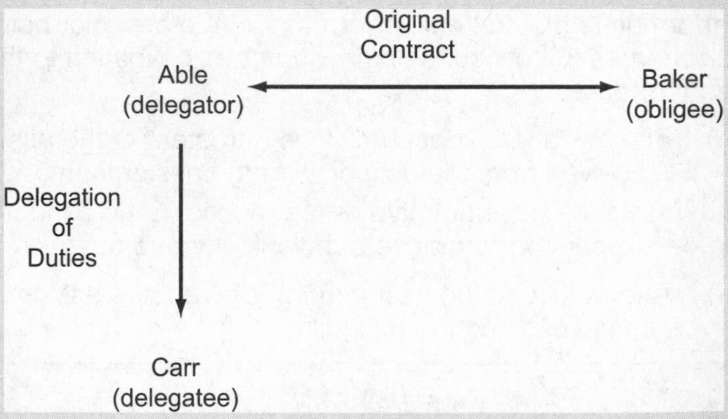

Figure 17-6

b. A delegator may delegate performance of his or her duties under a contract if the delegatee's performance will be substantially similar to the delegator's (e.g., paying money, manufacturing ordinary goods, building according to a set of plans and specifications, or delivering standard merchandise).

c. General language, such as "I hereby assign the contract," effects a delegation of duties as well as an assignment of rights.

3. **Liability after Delegation**

a. Delegation of duties does not relieve the obligor of obligations under the contract, even if notice is given to the obligee (unless the contract provides otherwise).

1) The obligee may sue the delegatee, the obligor, or both in the event of a breach.

Stop and review! You have completed the outline for this subunit. Study multiple-choice questions 28 through 30 on page 656.

QUESTIONS

17.1 Classification of Contracts

1. When a client accepts the services of an accountant without an agreement concerning payment, the result is

A. An implied-in-fact contract.

B. An implied-in-law contract.

C. An express contract.

D. No contract.

Answer (A) is correct.

REQUIRED: The type of contract formed when a client accepts an accountant's services.

DISCUSSION: Enforceable contracts may be formed without an express agreement of terms if the facts of the situation indicate (imply) an objective intent of both parties to contract. Objective intent means the apparent intent of an ordinary, reasonable person and not the actual (subjective) intent. When a client accepts the services of an accountant, there is an implied agreement to pay for them. Because the facts indicate a contract was formed, it is an implied-in-fact contract.

Answer (B) is incorrect. A contract implied in law prevents unjust enrichment of one party when the facts do not indicate both parties intended to form a contract. Answer (C) is incorrect. An express contract is one in which the terms (such as payment) are specifically agreed upon. Answer (D) is incorrect. A contract implied in fact was formed.

2. Which of the following represents the basic distinction between a bilateral contract and a unilateral contract?

A. Specific performance is available if the contract is unilateral but not if it is bilateral.

B. Only one promise is involved if the contract is unilateral, but two are involved if it is bilateral.

C. The statute of frauds applies to a bilateral contract but not to a unilateral contract.

D. Rights under a bilateral contract are assignable, whereas rights under a unilateral contract are not assignable.

Answer (B) is correct.

REQUIRED: The basic distinction between a unilateral and a bilateral contract.

DISCUSSION: In a bilateral contract, the promise of one party to perform is consideration for the promise of the other. In a unilateral contract, one party makes a promise in exchange for the other party's act, instead of in exchange for a promise from the other party (as in a bilateral contract). Thus, a unilateral contract involves only one promise, but a bilateral contract involves two promises.

Answer (A) is incorrect. The availability of specific performance is not affected by the distinction between unilateral and bilateral contracts. They may apply to either a unilateral or bilateral contract. Answer (C) is incorrect. The applicability of the statute of frauds is not affected by the distinction between unilateral and bilateral contracts. They may apply to either a unilateral or bilateral contract. Answer (D) is incorrect. The assignability of rights is not affected by the distinction between unilateral and bilateral contracts. They may apply to either a unilateral or bilateral contract.

17.2 Mutual Assent (Offer and Acceptance)

3. On September 10, Harrin, Inc., a new car dealer, placed a newspaper advertisement stating that Harrin would sell 10 cars at its showroom for a special discount only on September 12, 13, and 14. On September 12, King called Harrin and expressed an interest in buying one of the advertised cars. King was told that five of the cars had been sold and that King should come to the showroom as soon as possible. On September 13, Harrin made a televised announcement that the sale would end at 10:00 p.m. that night. King went to Harrin's showroom on September 14 and demanded the right to buy a car at the special discount. Harrin had sold the 10 cars and refused King's demand. King sued Harrin for breach of contract. Harrin's best defense to King's suit would be that Harrin's

A. Offer was unenforceable.

B. Advertisement was not an offer.

C. Television announcement revoked the offer.

D. Offer had not been accepted.

Answer (B) is correct.

REQUIRED: The legal effect of a newspaper advertisement quoting sales prices.

DISCUSSION: Newspaper advertisements that merely cite prices on items in stock are invitations to negotiate, not offers. In rare instances, an advertisement may be so definite and indicate such clear intent that it constitutes an offer and not a solicitation of offers, e.g., a promise to give one mink stole for $1 to the first person requesting it on April 5.

Answer (A) is incorrect. If an offer had existed, and King's telephone call was an acceptance, the resulting agreement would have been enforceable. Answer (C) is incorrect. No offer existed that could have been revoked. Answer (D) is incorrect. If the newspaper advertisement constituted an offer, King might argue that the offer was accepted on September 12.

4. Ann Mayer wrote Tom Jackson and offered to sell Jackson a building for $200,000. The offer stated it would expire 30 days from July 1. Mayer changed her mind and does not wish to be bound by the offer. If a legal dispute arises between the parties regarding whether there has been a valid acceptance of the offer, which of the following is true?

A. The offer cannot be legally withdrawn for the stated period of time.

B. The offer will not expire prior to the 30 days even if Mayer sells the property to a third person and notifies Jackson.

C. If Jackson phoned Mayer on August 1 and unequivocally accepted the offer, a contract would be formed, provided Jackson had no notice of withdrawal of the offer.

D. If Jackson categorically rejects the offer on July 10, Jackson cannot validly accept within the remaining stated period of time.

Answer (D) is correct.

REQUIRED: The true statement about termination of an offer.

DISCUSSION: Rejection of an offer terminates it. An offeree cannot accept an offer after rejection is effective. An attempted acceptance after rejection is a new offer.

Answer (A) is incorrect. The offer may be legally withdrawn at any time prior to acceptance, even though it states it will be held open for a specified period. An offer for sale of a building is not a firm offer under the UCC because it is not for a sale of goods. Answer (B) is incorrect. Notice to the offeree of sale of the property to a third person has the effect of terminating the offer. Answer (C) is incorrect. Acceptance on August 1 would be ineffective. The time provided for acceptance expires on July 31.

17.3 Consideration

5. For there to be consideration for a contract, there must be

A. A bargained-for detriment to the promisor(ee) or a benefit to the promisee(or).

B. A manifestation of mutual assent.

C. Genuineness of assent.

D. Substantially equal economic benefits to both parties.

Answer (A) is correct.

REQUIRED: The element that is necessary for consideration.

DISCUSSION: The consideration provided by one party (the promisee) to support the enforceability of the other party's (the promisor's) promise may be a bargained-for legal detriment to the promisee or a legal benefit to the promisor. Consideration is always in the form of a promise, act, or forbearance.

Answer (B) is incorrect. A manifestation of assent is an element of a contract distinct from consideration. Answer (C) is incorrect. Genuineness of assent is a contractual element distinct from consideration. Answer (D) is incorrect. Courts rarely question adequacy or equality of consideration.

6. In which of the following situations does the first promise serve as valid consideration for the second promise?

A. A police officer's promise to catch a thief for a victim's promise to pay a reward.

B. A builder's promise to complete a contract for a purchaser's promise to extend the time for completion.

C. A debtor's promise to pay $500 for a creditor's promise to forgive the balance of a $600 liquidated debt.

D. A debtor's promise to pay $500 for a creditor's promise to forgive the balance of a $600 disputed debt.

Answer (D) is correct.

REQUIRED: The promise that serves as valid consideration.

DISCUSSION: A promise unsupported by consideration is unenforceable. Consideration must be legally sufficient and provided in a bargained-for exchange. Legal sufficiency is found in the promisee's incurrence of a legal detriment or the promisor's receipt of a legal benefit. The debtor's promise to pay part of a disputed liability incorporates legally sufficient consideration: the legal detriment of forgoing the remainder of the disputed debt.

Answer (A) is incorrect. A pre-existing legal duty does not constitute consideration. Answer (B) is incorrect. The builder's promise was consideration for a past contract. The builder already had a contractual duty to perform it. Answer (C) is incorrect. The debtor's promise to pay a liquidated (undisputed) debt was to perform a pre-existing obligation.

17.4 Capacity

7. On May 25, Farnsworth sold Jordan, a minor, a used computer. On June 1, Jordan reached the age of majority. On June 10, Farnsworth wanted to rescind the sale. Farnsworth offered to return Jordan's money and demanded that Jordan return the computer. Jordan refused, claiming that a binding contract existed. Jordan's refusal is

A. Not justified because Farnsworth is not bound by the contract unless Jordan specifically ratifies the contract after reaching the age of majority.

B. Not justified because Farnsworth does not have to perform under the contract if Jordan has a right to disaffirm the contract.

C. Justified because Jordan and Farnsworth are bound by the contract as of the date Jordan reached the age of majority.

D. Justified because Farnsworth must perform under the contract regardless of Jordan's minority.

Answer (D) is correct.

REQUIRED: The enforceability of a contract made with a minor.

DISCUSSION: A minor can make a contract. However, the minor's contract is voidable by the minor, not void. The minor may disaffirm it until a reasonable time after reaching the age of majority. Until disaffirmance by the minor, the other party is bound to the agreement.

Answer (A) is incorrect. Farnsworth is bound by the contract. Only the minor can disaffirm it. Moreover, the minor may become bound without ratification. Passage of a reasonable time after reaching the age of majority without disaffirmance suffices to bind the minor. Answer (B) is incorrect. Farnsworth must perform under the contract regardless of whether the minor has the right to disaffirm the contract. Answer (C) is incorrect. The minor may disaffirm the contract until a reasonable time after reaching the age of majority.

8. Green was adjudicated incompetent by a court having proper jurisdiction. Which of the following statements is true regarding contracts subsequently entered into by Green?

A. All contracts are voidable.

B. All contracts are valid.

C. All contracts are void.

D. All contracts are enforceable.

Answer (C) is correct.

REQUIRED: The consequence of an adjudication of mental incompetence.

DISCUSSION: An incompetent person is one whose mental capacity is such that (s)he is unable to understand the nature and consequences of his or her acts. If a person is adjudicated insane or otherwise incompetent before a contract is entered into, the contract is void and cannot be ratified (even after the person is later adjudged competent).

17.5 Legality

9. West, an Indiana real estate broker, misrepresented to Zimmer that West was licensed in Kansas under the Kansas statute that regulates real estate brokers and requires all brokers to be licensed. Zimmer signed a contract agreeing to pay West a 5% commission for selling Zimmer's home in Kansas. West did not sign the contract. West sold Zimmer's home. If West sued Zimmer for nonpayment of commission, Zimmer would be

A. Liable to West only for the value of services rendered.

B. Liable to West for the full commission.

C. Not liable to West for any amount because West did not sign the contract.

D. Not liable to West for any amount because West violated the Kansas licensing requirements.

Answer (D) is correct.

REQUIRED: The recovery for services rendered in violation of a regulatory statute.

DISCUSSION: A person who performs services without obtaining a statutorily required license may recover only if the statute is solely a revenue measure. If the legislative intent was to protect the public from incompetent work by unqualified persons, the statute is regulatory and the contract is unenforceable, even if the defendant was benefited and the work performed was satisfactory.

Answer (A) is incorrect. A court will not give any remedy to a party who violates a regulatory statute. West will not recover in quasi-contract although Zimmer was unjustly enriched. Answer (B) is incorrect. A violator of a regulatory statute is not permitted any recovery. Answer (C) is incorrect. The contract is not subject to the statute of frauds. (It is not a contract to sell real property.) If it were, failure of West to sign would not relieve Zimmer of liability.

10. Phil Fairbanks was approached by Nickle Corporation to write the history of Nickle for $15,000. The president of Nickle told Fairbanks the job was his if he would agree to cleverly defame Nickle's leading competitor, Mogul Corporation, using sly innuendo and clever distortion of the facts. Fairbanks wrote the history. It turned out that the Mogul passages were neither sly nor clever, although they were defamatory, and Mogul obtained a judgment against Nickle. Fairbanks is seeking to collect the final $5,000 installment of the contract. Nickle refuses to pay and seeks to recover the $10,000 it has paid. In the event of a lawsuit,

A. Fairbanks will recover $5,000.

B. The court will deny relief to either Fairbanks or Nickle.

C. Nickle will recover $10,000.

D. Fairbanks will recover in quantum meruit for the value of his services.

Answer (B) is correct.

REQUIRED: The outcome of a suit based on an agreement to commit defamation.

DISCUSSION: A promise to commit a tort or to induce a tort is unenforceable on public policy grounds. The general principle is that neither party to an illegal bargain can use the judicial process to compel performance, obtain damages, or recover performance or its value.

17.6 Lack of Genuine Assent

11. The intent, or scienter, element necessary to establish a cause of action for fraud will be met if the plaintiff can show that the

A. Defendant made a misrepresentation with a reckless disregard for the truth.

B. Defendant made a false representation of fact.

C. Plaintiff actually relied on the defendant's misrepresentation.

D. Plaintiff justifiably relied on the defendant's misrepresentation.

Answer (A) is correct.

REQUIRED: The proof of intent to defraud.

DISCUSSION: The essence of fraud is that one party intentionally deceives to take advantage of another. The scienter, or intent, element of a fraud action is satisfied if the defendant knew of the falsity of a representation, or (s)he made it with reckless disregard for whether it was true. The defendant must have intended that the other party rely on the representation.

12. On April 6, Apple entered into a signed contract with Bean, by which Apple was to sell Bean an antique automobile, having a fair market value of $150,000, for $75,000. Apple believed the auto was worth only $75,000. Unknown to either party, the auto had been destroyed by fire on April 4. If Bean sues Apple for breach of contract, Apple's best defense is

A. Unconscionability.

B. Risk of loss borne by Bean.

C. Lack of adequate consideration.

D. Mutual mistake.

Answer (D) is correct.

REQUIRED: The result when the parties do not know that the subject matter has been destroyed.

DISCUSSION: A mistake of material fact made by both parties is grounds for rescission or is a sufficient defense in an action on the contract. Existence of the subject matter of the contract is a material fact. The parties generally are assumed to accept the risks concerning future events. Thus, a mistake about future facts is ordinarily not a basis for relief.

Answer (A) is incorrect. An agreement is unconscionable if it is so unfair as to be oppressive, but the facts do not suggest that Bean took unfair advantage of Apple. Answer (B) is incorrect. The seller initially has the risk of loss. No event occurred that transferred the risk to Bean. Answer (C) is incorrect. Courts seldom inquire into the adequacy or value of consideration.

13. A building subcontractor submitted a bid for construction of a portion of a high-rise office building. The bid contained material computational errors. The general contractor accepted the bid with knowledge of the errors. Which of the following statements best represents the subcontractor's liability?

A. Not liable because the contractor knew of the errors.

B. Not liable because the errors were a result of gross negligence.

C. Liable because the errors were unilateral.

D. Liable because the errors were material.

Answer (A) is correct.

REQUIRED: The effect of a material unilateral mistake.

DISCUSSION: Generally, a unilateral mistake in fact does not invalidate a contract except in limited circumstances. In this case, the subcontractor is not liable because the mistake was an obvious mathematical error and the general contractor was aware of the mistake and was not acting in good faith. The contract is voidable at the subcontractor's option.

Answer (B) is incorrect. The subcontractor would be liable under the contract if the error were the result of gross negligence. Answer (C) is incorrect. The other contracting party knew of the mistake and was acting unfairly. Answer (D) is incorrect. Only if the unilateral mistake was material to formation would it be voidable by the mistaken party in limited circumstances.

17.7 Statute of Frauds

14. Which of the following statements is true with regard to the statute of frauds?

A. All contracts involving consideration of $500 or more must be in writing.

B. The written contract must be signed by all parties.

C. The statute of frauds applies to contracts that can be fully performed within 1 year from the date they are made.

D. The contract terms may be stated in more than one document.

Answer (D) is correct.

REQUIRED: The true statement about the statute of frauds.

DISCUSSION: If a contract is within the statute of frauds, it is not enforceable at law unless requirements of the statute are satisfied. There must be a sufficient written memorandum of the contract. It may be stated in more than one document if evidence shows they are all related. One of them must be signed by the party against whom enforcement is sought.

Answer (A) is incorrect. Under the UCC, contracts for the sale of goods for $500 or more must be in writing. All contracts for $500 or more are not within the general statute of frauds. Answer (B) is incorrect. A party who signs a sufficient writing may be bound to performance, even if the other parties do not sign. Answer (C) is incorrect. The statute of frauds applies to a contract that cannot be performed within a year of its making.

15. Kram sent Fargo, a real estate broker, a signed offer to sell a specified parcel of land to Fargo for $250,000. Kram, an engineer, had inherited the land. On the same day that Kram's letter was received, Fargo telephoned Kram and accepted the offer. Which of the following statements is correct under the statute of frauds?

A. No contract could be formed because Fargo's acceptance was oral.

B. No contract could be formed because Kram's letter was signed only by Kram.

C. A contract was formed and would be enforceable against both Kram and Fargo.

D. A contract was formed but would be enforceable only against Kram.

Answer (D) is correct.

REQUIRED: The true statement under the statute of frauds about oral acceptance of a written offer to sell real property.

DISCUSSION: An agreement to sell an interest in real property is within the statute of frauds. An agreement that meets the criteria for the formation of an oral contract (offer and acceptance, consideration, mutual assent, capacity of the parties, and legality) but is within the statute of frauds is enforceable only against a party who signs a written memorandum of the offer. Fargo's oral acceptance bound Kram but not Fargo.

Answer (A) is incorrect. A contract was formed, but it is enforceable only against the party who signed the writing. The statute of frauds addresses the enforceability of a contract, not its formation. Answer (B) is incorrect. The statute of frauds only requires the signature of the party to be charged. No writing needs to be signed by Fargo. Answer (C) is incorrect. Under the statute of frauds, a contract is generally not enforceable against a party who did not sign a writing.

16. Carson agreed orally to repair Ivey's rare book for $450. Before the work was started, Ivey asked Carson to perform additional repairs to the book and agreed to increase the contract price to $650. After Carson completed the work, Ivey refused to pay and Carson sued. Ivey's defense was based on the statute of frauds. What total amount will Carson recover?

A. $0

B. $200

C. $450

D. $650

Answer (D) is correct.

REQUIRED: The amount of recovery at law for breach of an oral contract for services.

DISCUSSION: Oral contracts are enforceable. But if a contract is within the statute of frauds, it cannot be enforced at law against a party who did not sign a writing that sufficiently evidences the contract. A services contract is not subject to the statute unless it cannot be performed within a year of its making. (The oral modification is enforceable because new consideration was given.)

Answer (A) is incorrect. The contract is not subject to the statute of frauds. Answer (B) is incorrect. This amount is the difference between the initial contract price and the amended price. Answer (C) is incorrect. The recovery is not limited to the original contract price.

17.8 Parol Evidence Rule

17. Two individuals signed a written contract that was intended to be their entire agreement. The parol evidence rule will prevent the admission of evidence that is offered to

A. Prove the existence of a contemporaneous oral agreement that modifies the contract.

B. Prove the existence of a subsequent oral agreement that modifies the contract.

C. Explain the meaning of an ambiguity in the written contract.

D. Establish that fraud had been committed in formation of the contract.

Answer (A) is correct.

REQUIRED: The applicability of the parol evidence rule.

DISCUSSION: The parol evidence rule excludes any prior agreement or an oral agreement made at the time of the final writing that would tend to vary or contradict the terms of a written agreement intended to be complete. If the parties meant their written agreement to be entire, only terms incorporated directly or by reference are part of the contract as it existed at the time it was set forth in writing and signed.

Answer (B) is incorrect. Evidence of a later agreement does not modify the contract as it existed at the time it was made. Answer (C) is incorrect. Evidence to clarify an ambiguity is admissible. Answer (D) is incorrect. Evidence to prove fraud is admissible.

18. Dunne and Cook signed a contract requiring Cook to rebind 500 of Dunne's books at 80¢ per book. Later, Dunne requested, in good faith, that the price be reduced to 70¢ per book. Cook agreed orally to reduce the price to 70¢. Under the circumstances, the oral agreement is

A. Enforceable, but proof of it is inadmissible into evidence.

B. Enforceable, and proof of it is admissible into evidence.

C. Unenforceable because Dunne failed to give consideration, but proof of it is otherwise admissible into evidence.

D. Unenforceable due to the statute of frauds, and proof of it is inadmissible into evidence.

Answer (C) is correct.

REQUIRED: The enforceability of an oral modification and admissibility of evidence of it.

DISCUSSION: The parol evidence rule does not bar evidence of the oral modification because it excludes any prior agreement or an oral agreement made at the time of the final writing that would tend to vary or contradict the terms of a written agreement intended to be complete. But the consideration requirement of an enforceable contract also applies to an agreement to modify a contract. Dunne provided no new consideration bargained for in exchange for the modification.

Answer (A) is incorrect. The modification was not supported by consideration. Answer (B) is incorrect. No consideration supported the modification, and the oral statements are admissible because they were subsequent to contract formation. Answer (D) is incorrect. Neither the underlying contract nor the contract as modified is subject to the statute. The oral statements were made subsequent to contract formation.

17.9 Performance, Discharge, and Breach

19. Castle borrowed $5,000 from Nelson and executed and delivered to Nelson a promissory note for $5,000 due on April 30. On April 1, Castle offered, and Nelson accepted, $4,000 in full satisfaction of the note. On May 15, Nelson demanded that Castle pay the $1,000 balance on the note. Castle refused. If Nelson sues for the $1,000 balance, Castle will

A. Win because the acceptance by Nelson of the $4,000 constituted an accord and satisfaction.

B. Win because the debt was unliquidated.

C. Lose because the amount of the note was not in dispute.

D. Lose because no consideration was given to Nelson in exchange for accepting only $4,000.

Answer (A) is correct.

REQUIRED: The right to the balance of an undisputed debt when tender of a lesser amount is accepted in full satisfaction.

DISCUSSION: An accord is a new contract between the same parties that discharges the prior and new contracts by performance of the obligation in the new contract. Performance is the satisfaction.

Answer (B) is incorrect. A debt is unliquidated only if its amount is genuinely disputed. Answer (C) is incorrect. A creditor who accepts tender of less than the full amount of an undisputed debt in full satisfaction generally has the right to claim the balance. But when the accepted offer was to pay a lesser amount earlier than was required, acceptance discharges the entire debt. Answer (D) is incorrect. Payment before it was due was a legal detriment that constituted legally sufficient consideration.

20. Dell owed Stark $9,000. As the result of an unrelated transaction, Stark owed Ball that same amount. The three parties signed an agreement that Dell would pay Ball instead of Stark, and Stark would be discharged from all liability. The agreement among the parties is

A. A novation.

B. An executed accord and satisfaction.

C. Voidable at Ball's option.

D. Unenforceable for lack of consideration.

Answer (A) is correct.

REQUIRED: The true statement about an agreement to discharge a debtor from liability.

DISCUSSION: A novation is a contract to discharge an existing contract by substituting a new contract or new debtor. Substitution of a new promisor (Dell) for the old (Stark) is a novation.

Answer (B) is incorrect. By an accord, a promisee agrees to accept a substituted performance by the promisor. Performance of the accord (execution of the contract) is the satisfaction. Answer (C) is incorrect. No basis for voidability is apparent. Answer (D) is incorrect. The promise by Dell to pay Stark's debt is consideration for Ball's discharge of Stark.

21. On May 25, Year 1, Smith contracted with Jackson to repair Smith's cabin cruiser. The work was to begin on May 31, Year 1. On May 26, Year 1, the boat, while docked at Smith's pier, was destroyed by arson. Which of the following statements is true with regard to the contract?

A. Smith would not be liable to Jackson because of mutual mistake.

B. Smith would be liable to Jackson for the profit Jackson would have made under the contract.

C. Jackson would not be liable to Smith because performance by the parties would be impossible.

D. Jackson would be liable to repair another boat owned by Smith.

Answer (C) is correct.

REQUIRED: The parties' liability when the subject matter of a contract is destroyed.

DISCUSSION: Nonperformance is excused when circumstances change so completely that performance is objectively impossible because no one could perform the duty. Impossibility occurs when the subject matter of, or an item or commodity essential to, the contract is destroyed. The impossibility must arise after and could not have been reasonably contemplated at contract formation.

Answer (A) is incorrect. Mutual mistake is present at, not after, contract formation. It would apply if, without the knowledge of the parties, the boat were destroyed before formation. Answer (B) is incorrect. To the extent the doctrine of impossibility applies, performance by both parties is excused, and the contract is canceled. Answer (D) is incorrect. Under the doctrine of impossibility, duties are discharged, not substituted. But performance of a promise to supply a commodity is not impossible when an alternative supply is available.

17.10 Remedies

22. Amex Construction Co. contracted to build a warehouse for White Corp. The construction specifications required Amex to use Ace lighting fixtures. Inadvertently, Amex installed Perfection lighting fixtures, which are of slightly lesser quality than Ace fixtures but, in all other respects, meet White's needs. Which of the following statements is true?

A. White's recovery will be limited to monetary damages because Amex's breach of the construction contract was not material.

B. White will not be able to recover any damages from Amex because the breach was inadvertent.

C. Amex did not breach the construction contract because the Perfection fixtures were substantially as good as the Ace fixtures.

D. Amex must install Ace fixtures or White will not be obligated to accept the warehouse.

Answer (A) is correct.

REQUIRED: The true statement regarding failure to strictly perform a construction contract.

DISCUSSION: If a good-faith performance is only marginally deficient, the party has substantially performed and is entitled to receive the contract price minus damages. The doctrine does not apply when the substantially performing party has not acted in good faith.

Answer (B) is incorrect. Damages are recoverable for any breach of contract. Answer (C) is incorrect. The contract was breached. Answer (D) is incorrect. A party that substantially performs a construction contract is liable for damages but may enforce the contract.

23. In June, Mullin, a general contractor, contracted with a town to renovate the town square. The town council wanted the project done quickly, and the parties placed a clause in the contract that for each day the project extended beyond 90 working days, Mullin would forfeit $100 of the contract price. In August, Mullin took a 3-week vacation. The project was completed in October, 120 working days after it was begun. What type of damages may the town recover from Mullin?

A. Punitive damages because taking a vacation in the middle of the project was irresponsible.

B. Compensatory damages because of the delay in completing the project.

C. Liquidated damages because of the clause in the contract.

D. No damages because Mullin completed performance.

Answer (C) is correct.

REQUIRED: The damages, if any, that may be collected given a contract clause providing for penalties for late performance.

DISCUSSION: By a liquidated damages clause, the parties to a contract agree in advance to the damages to be paid in the event of a breach. A liquidated damages clause is enforceable if all of the following apply: (1) It is not intended as a penalty, (2) it reasonably forecasts the probable loss due to the breach, and (3) the loss is difficult to calculate.

Answer (A) is incorrect. Punitive damages are intended to punish a wrongdoer and to set an example for others. It is extremely rare for a court to award punitive damages in a contract suit. It might if a breach is malicious, willful, or physically injurious to the nonbreaching party, e.g., willful and malicious refusal to pay valid medical claims of an insured. Answer (B) is incorrect. Compensatory damages (also called actual damages or general damages) are damages incurred from the wrongful conduct of the breaching party. The usual measure of compensatory damages is the amount of money necessary to compensate the nonbreaching party for the breach. Answer (D) is incorrect. Mullin breached the clause in the contract requiring completion within 90 days.

24. For which of the following contracts will a court generally grant the remedy of specific performance?

A. A contract for the sale of a patent.

B. A contract of employment.

C. A contract for the sale of fungible goods.

D. A contract for the sale of stock that is traded on a national stock exchange.

Answer (A) is correct.

REQUIRED: The contract for which a court will generally grant specific performance.

DISCUSSION: Specific performance is granted when no other remedy is adequate, and irreparable injury will result if it is not granted. Thus, monetary damages are not available or are not adequate, and the subject matter of the contract is unique, e.g., a rare painting or land. A patent meets the requirements for specific performance because it is unique. In addition, monetary damages are not adequate because no reliable method exists for determining how much money the purchaser would have earned from the use of the patent.

Answer (B) is incorrect. Specific performance of a service contract is never granted. Answer (C) is incorrect. Fungible goods are not unique. Answer (D) is incorrect. Monetary damages are adequate for stock traded on a national exchange.

17.11 Contract Beneficiaries

25. Ferco, Inc., claims to be a creditor beneficiary of a contract between Bell and Allied Industries, Inc. Allied is indebted to Ferco. The contract between Bell and Allied provides that Bell is to purchase certain goods from Allied and pay the purchase price directly to Ferco until Allied's obligation is satisfied. Without justification, Bell failed to pay Ferco and Ferco sued Bell. Ferco will

A. Not prevail, because Ferco lacked privity of contract with either Bell or Allied.

B. Not prevail, because Ferco did not give any consideration to Bell.

C. Prevail, because Ferco was an intended beneficiary of the contract.

D. Prevail, provided Ferco was aware of the contract between Bell and Allied at the time the contract was entered into.

Answer (C) is correct.

REQUIRED: The rights of a creditor who is a payee of a contract between the payor and the debtor.

DISCUSSION: A creditor beneficiary has standing to enforce a contract to which (s)he is a third party. Because the intent of the promisee (Allied) in entering into the contract with Bell was specifically to have return performance (payment) to discharge the debt to a third party (Ferco), the third party is a creditor beneficiary.

Answer (A) is incorrect. Ferco was an intended beneficiary of the contract. Answer (B) is incorrect. An intended beneficiary may enforce a contract enforceable between the parties. An essential element of the contract was consideration, but not from Ferco. Answer (D) is incorrect. Creditor awareness is not sufficient. The parties to the contract must have intended direct benefit to the third party.

26. Union Bank lent $200,000 to Wagner. Union required Wagner to obtain a life insurance policy naming Union as beneficiary. While the loan was outstanding, Wagner stopped paying the premiums on the policy. Union paid the premiums, adding the amounts paid to Wagner's loan. Wagner died, and the insurance company refused to pay the policy proceeds to Union. Union may

A. Recover the policy proceeds because it is a creditor beneficiary.

B. Recover the policy proceeds because it is a donee beneficiary.

C. Not recover the policy proceeds because it is not in privity of contract with the insurance company.

D. Not recover the policy proceeds because it is only an incidental beneficiary.

Answer (A) is correct.

REQUIRED: The rights of a creditor named the beneficiary of a life insurance policy on the debtor.

DISCUSSION: Life insurance policies designating a creditor as beneficiary are common. The parties to the contract (insured and insurer) intend it to benefit the third party directly by discharging a liability if the insured dies. The intended creditor beneficiary is entitled to the proceeds.

Answer (B) is incorrect. The purpose of the insurance contract was not to confer a gift on the creditor. Answer (C) is incorrect. An assignee or a third-party beneficiary may be entitled to performance of a contract. Answer (D) is incorrect. The contract was intended to confer a benefit directly on the creditor.

27. Rice contracted with Locke to build an oil refinery for Locke. The contract provided that Rice was to use United pipe fittings. Rice did not do so. United learned of the contract and, anticipating the order, manufactured additional fittings. United sued Locke and Rice. United is

A. Entitled to recover only from Rice because Rice breached the contract.

B. Entitled to recover from either Locke or Rice because it detrimentally relied on the contract.

C. Not entitled to recover because it is a donee beneficiary.

D. Not entitled to recover because it is an incidental beneficiary.

Answer (D) is correct.

REQUIRED: The status of a manufacturer regarding a construction contract stipulating the use of its product.

DISCUSSION: A person who is neither a primary contracting party nor an intended third-party beneficiary has no right to sue on a contract. United is a mere incidental beneficiary, a person who may have been indirectly affected by the agreement but was not intended to be directly benefited.

Answer (A) is incorrect. United was not an intended beneficiary. Answer (B) is incorrect. United's reliance is irrelevant. It is merely an incidental beneficiary. Answer (C) is incorrect. A person is a donee beneficiary if the promisor's performance was intended as a gift to that person.

17.12 Assignment and Delegation

28. Moss entered into a contract to purchase certain real property from Shinn. Which of the following statements is **false**?

A. If Shinn fails to perform the contract, Moss can obtain specific performance.

B. The contract is nonassignable as a matter of law.

C. The statute of frauds applies to the contract.

D. Any amendment to the contract must be agreed to by both Moss and Shinn.

Answer (B) is correct.

REQUIRED: The legal effect and assignability of a valid real estate contract.

DISCUSSION: Contracts are generally assignable. Assignment is ineffective if a risk or duty of a party to the contract is materially increased, or an exception otherwise applies.

Answer (A) is incorrect. Each parcel of real property is considered unique. Thus, monetary damages are deemed an inadequate remedy for the buyer. (S)he may seek specific performance. Answer (C) is incorrect. A contract for the purchase and sale of real property is within the statute of frauds. Answer (D) is incorrect. To be enforceable, contract amendments must be agreed to by both parties.

29. Sisk is a tenant of Met Co. and has 2 years remaining on a 6-year lease executed by Sisk and Met. The lease prohibits subletting but is silent as to Sisk's right to assign the lease. Sisk assigned the lease to Kern Corp., which assumed all of Sisk's obligations under the lease. Met objects to the assignment. Which of the following statements is true?

A. The assignment to Kern is voidable at Met's option.

B. Sisk would have been relieved from liability on the lease with Met if Sisk obtained Met's consent to the assignment.

C. Sisk will remain liable to Met for the rent provided for in the lease.

D. With respect to the rent provided for in the lease, Kern is liable to Sisk but not to Met.

Answer (C) is correct.

REQUIRED: The rights and duties of a lessor and lessee under a lease prohibiting subletting but not assignments.

DISCUSSION: Absent a restriction against assignments in the lease, the lessee will retain the right to assign his or her interest. The prohibition against subletting does not prohibit assignments. Sisk will remain liable to Met for the rent until such time as Met agrees to a novation or a release and allows Kern to assume all of Sisk's legal obligations to Met.

Answer (A) is incorrect. The lease does not specifically limit Sisk's right of assignment. Thus, Met does not have the option to void the assignment. Answer (B) is incorrect. Only a novation would relieve Sisk from his or her lease liability. Met's consent to the assignment would not be equivalent to a novation. Answer (D) is incorrect. After an assignment, the assignee is in privity of estate with the original landlord. Thus, Kern is liable to Met for the rent provided for in the original lease. If Kern does not pay and Met recovers the rent from Sisk, Sisk will be able to seek reimbursement from Kern.

30. One of the criteria for a valid assignment of a sales contract to a third party is that the assignment must

A. Be supported by adequate consideration from the assignee.

B. Be in writing and signed by the assignor.

C. Not materially increase the other party's risk or duty.

D. Not be revocable by the assignor.

Answer (C) is correct.

REQUIRED: The requirement for a valid assignment of a sales contract.

DISCUSSION: Unless agreed otherwise, most contract rights can be assigned. However, a contract right cannot be assigned if it would materially increase the risk or duty of the other party. If an assignment would materially increase the risk or duty sustained by the other party, the assignment is invalid.

Answer (A) is incorrect. Adequate consideration is not a required element of a valid assignment. Gratuitous assignments are permissible. Answer (B) is incorrect. Generally, no writing is required for an assignment of contract rights to be valid. However, the statute of frauds requires a writing in certain situations. Answer (D) is incorrect. A gratuitous assignment is generally revocable by the assignor.

17.13 PRACTICE TASK-BASED SIMULATIONS

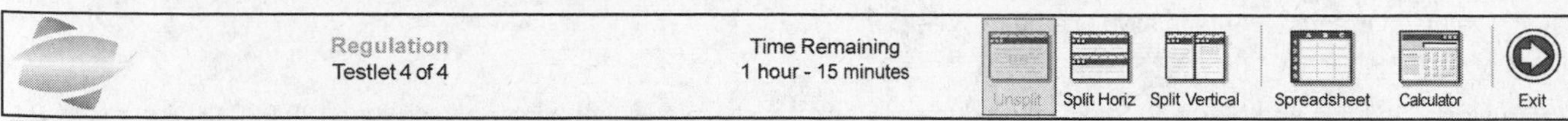

DIRECTIONS

Note: If you believe you have encountered a software malfunction, report it to the test center staff immediately.

Navigation

To navigate from task to task, use the controls at the bottom of the screen. Click on the **Next** button to advance to the next task, or the **Previous** button to go to the previous task. To go directly to any task, click on its number.

If you would like a reminder to revisit a task or want to indicate that you are finished with it, click on the reminder flag below the task number. To clear the flag, click on it again. Reminder flags are for your use only – they do not contribute to your score.

Tabs

In this part of the examination, you will be asked to complete various tasks. Every task has one or more **Work Tabs**. Some tasks have one or more **Information Tabs**, others may have none. Every task has a **Help** tab.

If a task has **Information Tabs**, you may use the information in them to complete your responses in the **Work Tabs**.

Work tab **Information tab** **Help tab**

Work Tabs:

- **Work Tabs** are identified with a pencil icon. This is where your responses are expected.
- Each task has one or more **Work Tabs**.
- **Work Tabs** contain directions for completing the task – be sure to read these directions carefully.
- The **Work Tab** name in the example above is for illustration only – yours will differ.
- You must complete all of the **Work Tabs** in each task to receive full credit.

Information Tabs:

- The Authoritative Literature will be provided in all tasks in the AUD, FAR, and REG sections for your reference.
- Your simulation may have one or more additional **Information Tabs**. Like the Authoritative Literature tabs, **Information Tabs** do not have a pencil icon.
- If your task has additional **Information Tabs**, go through each to familiarize yourself with the task content.

Help Tab:

- The **Help Tab** provides assistance with the exam software that is used in this task. For example, if the task is to compose a memorandum, **Help** will provide information about the word processor.

The Toolbar

The toolbar at the top of the screen shows the amount of time remaining for you to complete the tasks. In addition, the following tools are available. Note that only the **Exit** button is displayed when Directions are visible - the others will appear when you begin the tasks.

Click on these buttons to split or unsplit the screen. You can split the screen vertically or horizontally.

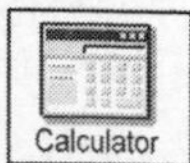

Click on this button to display the calculator; click on it again to hide the calculator. To move the calculator, click on the calculator title bar and drag the calculator to the desired location.

Click on this button to use the spreadsheet; click on it again to hide the spreadsheet. To move the spreadsheet, click on the the spreadsheet title bar and drag the spreadsheet to the desired location.

Click on this button to go on to the next part of the examination. You must complete all of the tasks to receive full credit. Once you click on **Exit** and confirm the action, you will NOT be able to return to this testlet.

= Reminder Directions 1 2 3 4 5 Previous Next

In a signed letter dated March 2, Stake offered to sell Packer a specific vacant parcel of land for $100,000. Stake had inherited the land, along with several apartment buildings in the immediate vicinity. Packer received the offer on March 4. The offer required acceptance by March 10 and required Packer to have the property surveyed by a licensed surveyor so that the exact legal description of the property could be determined.

On March 6, Packer sent Stake a counteroffer of $75,000. All other terms and conditions of the offer were unchanged. Stake received Packer's counteroffer on March 8 and, on that day, telephoned Packer and accepted it. On learning that a survey of the vacant parcel would cost about $1,000, Packer telephoned Stake on March 11 requesting that they share the survey cost equally. During this conversation, Stake agreed to Packer's proposal. Later, Stake did not share the cost.

During the course of the negotiations leading up to the March communications between Stake and Packer, Stake expressed concern to Packer that a buyer of the land might build apartment units that would compete with those owned by Stake in the immediate vicinity. Packer assured Stake that Packer intended to use the land for a small shopping center. Because of these assurances, Stake was willing to sell the land to Packer. Contrary to what Packer told Stake, Packer had already contracted with Rolf for Rolf to build a 48-unit apartment development on the vacant land to be purchased from Stake.

During the last week of March, Stake learned that the land to be sold to Packer had a fair value of $200,000. Also, Stake learned that Packer intended to build apartments on the land.

Select from the list provided the best reason each statement is correct or incorrect. Each reason may be used once, more than once, or not at all.

Statement	Answer
1. Packer can sue Stake for not equally sharing the survey costs.	
2. The contract based on Packer's March 6 counteroffer was not enforceable against Stake.	
3. Packer's assurance entitled Stake to rescind the contract.	
4. Stake's estimate of the fair value of the land entitles Stake to rescind the contract.	
5. Rolf can sue Packer.	

Choices
A) Adequacy of consideration not element of a contract
B) Breach of contract
C) Fraud in the execution
D) Fraud in the inducement
E) Modification of contract requires no consideration
F) Modification of contract requires consideration
G) Scienter
H) Writing signed by both parties
I) Writing signed by party to be held liable

On December 15, Blake Corp. telephoned Reach Consultants, Inc., and offered to hire Reach to design a security system for Blake's research department. The work will require 2 years to complete. Blake offered to pay a fee of $100,000 but stated that the offer must be accepted in writing, and the acceptance must be received by Blake no later than December 20.

On December 20, Reach faxed a written acceptance to Blake. Blake's offices were closed on December 20, and Reach's fax was not seen until December 21.

Reach's acceptance contained the following language:

> "We accept your $1,000,000 offer. Weaver has been assigned $5,000 of the fee as payment for sums owed Weaver by Reach. Payment of this amount should be made directly to Weaver."

On December 22, Blake sent a signed memo to Reach rejecting Reach's December 20 fax but offering to hire Reach for a $75,000 fee. Reach telephoned Blake on December 23 and orally accepted Blake's December 22 offer.

Items 1 through 6 relate to whether a contractual relationship exists between Blake and Reach. Select from the list provided the best reason each statement is correct or incorrect. Each reason may be used once, more than once, or not at all.

Statement	Answer
1. Blake's December 15 offer had to be in writing to be a legitimate offer.	
2. Reach's December 20 fax was an improper method of acceptance.	
3. Reach's December 20 fax was effective when sent.	
4. Reach's acceptance was invalid because it was received after December 20.	
5. Blake's receipt of Reach's acceptance by fax created a voidable contract.	
6. Reach's December 20 fax was a counteroffer.	

Choices
A) Lack of consideration
B) Mailbox rule
C) Mirror image rule
D) Mistake
E) Rejection and counteroffer
F) Specified method of acceptance
G) Specified time of delivery
H) Statute of frauds

Contractual Obligations | Authoritative Literature | Help

On April 1, Sam Stieb signed and mailed to Bold Corp. an offer to sell Bold a parcel of land for $175,000. On April 5, Bold called Stieb and requested that Stieb keep the offer open until June 1, by which time Bold would be able to determine whether financing for the purchase was available. That same day, Stieb signed and mailed a letter indicating that he would hold the offer open until June 1 if Bold mailed Stieb $100 by April 20.

On April 17, Stieb sent Bold a signed letter revoking his offers dated April 1 and April 5. Bold received that letter on April 19. However, Bold had already mailed on April 18 its acceptance of Stieb's offer of April 5 along with a check for $100. Stieb received the check and letter of acceptance on April 20.

On May 25, Bold executed and delivered the original contract of April 1 to Stieb without any variation of the original terms.

Stieb does not wish to sell the land to Bold because he has received another offer for $200,000.

Items 1 through 5 are based on the facts above. Select from the list provided the best reason each item is correct or incorrect. Each reason may be used once, more than once, or not at all.

Statement	***Answer***
1. When Stieb accepted Bold's request to keep the offer open until June 1, an option contract was formed.	
2. Bold's purported acceptance mailed on April 18 was by an authorized means.	
3. Bold could simply have bound Stieb to a contract to sell on April 5 by accepting Stieb's offer of April 1 subject to obtaining financing within 30 days (provided Bold made a good-faith effort to obtain it).	
4. An option contract was formed on April 18.	
5. Stieb entered into a contract to sell the land on May 25.	

Choices
A) Acceptance by any reasonable means
B) Acceptance cuts off power to revoke
C) Conditional acceptance a rejection
D) Lack of consideration
E) Mailbox rule
F) Option contract formed
G) Solicitation of an offer not an acceptance
H) Statute of frauds

On March 1, West signed a 2-year lease with Abco Real Estate, Inc., for warehouse space. The lease required that West repair and maintain the warehouse. On April 14, West orally asked Abco to paint the warehouse. Despite the lease provision requiring West to repair and maintain the warehouse, Abco agreed to do so by April 30. On April 29, Abco advised West that Abco had decided not to paint the warehouse. West demanded that Abco paint the warehouse under the April 14 agreement. Abco refused.

West Corp. is involved in another dispute. On September 16, West's president orally offered to hire Dodd Consultants, Inc., to do computer consulting for West. The offer provided for a 3-year contract at $5,000 per month. West agreed that Dodd could have until September 30 to decide whether to accept the offer. If Dodd chose to accept the offer, West's offer was silent on the method of acceptance.

On September 27, Dodd sent West a letter accepting the offer. West received the letter on October 2. On September 28, West's president decided that West's accounting staff could handle West's computer problems and notified Dodd by telephone that the offer was withdrawn. Dodd argued that West had no right to revoke its offer and that Dodd had already accepted the offer by mail.

Select from the list provided the best reason each statement is correct. Each choice may be used once, more than once, or not at all.

Statement	***Answer***
1. The March 1 agreement is binding.	
2. Abco's April 14 agreement to paint the warehouse is not binding.	
3. A court would allow evidence relating to the April 14 agreement.	
4. Dodd's acceptance was effective on September 27.	
5. Dodd argued that West could not revoke the offer before September 30, and a court ruled against Dodd.	
6. A court found the agreement between West and Dodd was not enforceable.	

Choices
A) Rejection of offer
B) Mailbox rule
C) Consideration
D) Lack of consideration
E) Parol evidence rule
F) Statute of frauds
G) Promissory estoppel
H) Usury law
I) Scienter

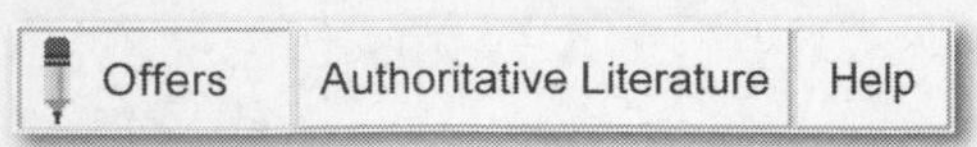

Lennox & Associates, CPAs, is hired by Chic Art Gallery to prepare its tax return. James is the owner of Chic Art Gallery. As such, he constantly enters into contracts with museums, private dealers, and individuals to buy and sell art.

Indicate whether each situation is or is not an offer by selecting the appropriate choice from the list provided. Each choice may be used once, more than once, or not at all.

Situation	*Answer*
1. James just received a new piece of art and advertises it in the local newspaper. The advertisement states only that the piece is for sale and that interested buyers should visit the gallery.	
2. The price tag on a sculpture in the gallery is $400.	
3. A potential buyer whom James has worked with before tells James she wants to buy a certain sculpture for $1,200 in 1 week but that the offer will expire in 2 days.	
4. A visitor to the gallery asks how much James wants for an original painting. James says, "I'll probably take $1,500."	
5. James approaches a visitor to the gallery and asks whether she is interested in purchasing an antique chair that has just arrived in the store.	
6. James calls an Italian art dealer and offers to buy a specific painting for $6,500. James states that he would like the painting delivered to Chic Gallery on November 10.	

Choices
Offer
Not an offer

Unofficial Answers

1. Statute of Frauds (5 Gradable Items)

1. F) Modification of contract requires consideration. The original agreement was intended for Packer to pay for the survey costs. The modification of the agreement between the parties lacked consideration. Under general contract law, agreements modifying existing contracts require consideration to be binding.

2. I) Writing signed by party to be held liable. The contract between Stake and Packer involves real estate. Thus, the statute of frauds requirements must be satisfied. The statute of frauds requires that a writing be signed by the party against whom enforcement is sought. The counteroffer is unenforceable against Stake because Stake did not sign it. As a result, Stake is not obligated to sell the land to Packer under the terms of the counteroffer.

3. D) Fraud in the inducement. Packer committed fraud in the inducement by assuring Stake that the vacant parcel would be used for a shopping center. This assurance was part of the basis for the bargain. In fact, Packer intended to use the land to construct apartment units that would be in direct competition with those owned by Stake. Stake would not have sold the land to Packer had Packer's actual intentions been known. Thus, the elements of fraud are present:

   - A false representation of a material fact
   - Packer's knowledge of the falsity
   - Intention to deceive
   - Justifiable reliance on the misrepresentation

4. A) Adequacy of consideration not element of a contract. Generally, mistakes as to adequacy of consideration or fairness of a bargain are insufficient grounds to entitle the aggrieved party to rescind a contract.

5. B) Breach of contract. Because Packer does not own the land, Packer cannot perform. Thus, Rolf can sue Packer for breach of contract.

<u>2. Contractual Relationship</u> (6 Gradable Items)

1. <u>H) Statute of frauds.</u> The statute of frauds applies to certain types of contracts, not to offers. If an oral offer is made to enter into a contract that is within the statute, the parties will be protected after an acceptance by the requirement that a writing be signed by the party to be bound. This contract must be in writing. An agreement not performable within a year is covered by the statute.
2. <u>F) Specified method of acceptance.</u> The fax complied with the method of acceptance specified by Blake. A signed fax is a valid writing that, in this case, meets the deadline.
3. <u>E) Rejection and counteroffer.</u> The purported acceptance was not effective when sent or received. It was a counteroffer under the mirror image rule because it changed terms of the offer.
4. <u>G) Specified time of delivery.</u> Reach's purported acceptance was timely because it met the condition of delivery to Blake's office by December 20.
5. <u>C) Mirror image rule.</u> Blake's receipt of Reach's fax did not create any type of contract. The fax did not mirror the terms of Blake's offer. It was a rejection and a counteroffer.
6. <u>E) Rejection and counteroffer.</u> Reach's oral acceptance apparently was within the terms of Blake's new offer made on December 22. The original offer by Blake does not apply because it was effectively rejected by the December 20 fax. The fax was in effect a rejection and counteroffer.

<u>3. Contractual Obligations</u> (5 Gradable Items)

1. <u>G) Solicitation of an offer not an acceptance.</u> Bold's request was a solicitation of an offer. Stieb's letter on April 1 was an offer to sell land. Stieb's letter on April 5 was an offer to form a contract to keep the April 1 offer open.
2. <u>A) Acceptance by any reasonable means.</u> Unless the terms of an offer require acceptance by a specified means, the offeree is implicitly authorized to accept by any reasonable means, including the one used by the offeror.
3. <u>C) Conditional acceptance a rejection.</u> Conditional acceptance is rejection of the offer. Rejection is effective when received, and it terminates the offer. Conditional acceptance is also a counteroffer effective upon receipt.
4. <u>B) Acceptance cuts off power to revoke.</u> Stieb's letters revoking his offers would have been effective when received by Bold on April 19. However, Bold's acceptance operated as an exercise of the power of acceptance, forming a contract, when it was dispatched on April 18. Revocation of an offer cannot be effective after the power of acceptance of the offer has been exercised.
5. <u>F) Option contract formed.</u> An option contract was in effect until June 1 because of Bold's April 18 acceptance. When Bold exercised the power of acceptance under the option contract, Stieb's offer of April 1 ripened into a contract.

<u>4. Contract Formation</u> (6 Gradable Items)

1. <u>F) Statute of frauds.</u> The statute of frauds requires certain kinds of contracts to be in writing and signed by the parties against whom enforcement is sought. A contract for the sale of an interest in land is one of the types of contracts that is required to be in writing by the statute of frauds. An interest in land may be a long-term lease (more than 1 year), mortgage, easement, option, life tenancy, future interest, full ownership, or other interest. Thus, a 2-year lease agreement for warehouse space is required to be in writing to be enforceable.
2. <u>D) Lack of consideration.</u> The April 14 agreement was intended to modify the existing lease between the parties. Under general contract law, agreements modifying existing contracts require consideration to be binding. Abco did not receive any consideration in exchange for its promise to paint the warehouse. Thus, the agreement is not enforceable against Abco.
3. <u>E) Parol evidence rule.</u> The parol evidence rule allows the admission of proof of a later oral agreement that modifies an existing written contract.
4. <u>B) Mailbox rule.</u> Under the mailbox rule, acceptance by the offeree (Dodd) is effectively communicated to the Offeror (West) at the moment of dispatch if the offeree has used an authorized medium of acceptance and the offer is still open. Under the mailbox rule, once acceptance has been dispatched, it is effective even if the offeror attempts revocation while the acceptance is in transit. A letter sent by mail is considered an acceptable mode of communication if the offer is silent on medium of acceptance.
5. <u>D) Lack of consideration.</u> Offers can be revoked at any time before acceptance unless the offeror receives consideration to keep the offer open. West did not receive any consideration from Dodd in exchange for its promise to keep the offer open until September 30. Thus, West effectively revoked its offer during the September 28 telephone conversation.
6. <u>F) Statute of frauds.</u> The term of the agreement was for 3 years. The statute of frauds requires that contracts that cannot be performed within 1 year from the date made be in writing. Because this was an oral contract for a period of 3 years, it is not under the statute of frauds. Dodd's attempted acceptance of the offer is not such a writing because it was not signed by West and could not be enforceable against West.

5. Offers (6 Gradable Items)

1. Not an offer. Advertisements, circulars, and catalogs are usually not offers but are invitations to submit offers. However, an advertisement can constitute an offer if it uses clear, definite, and explicit language that leaves nothing open for negotiation. In this case, the ad does not contain clear or definite language, so it is merely an invitation to submit offers.
2. Not an offer. A price tag in a store is considered a quotation or an invitation, not an offer.
3. Offer. The buyer is indicating a clear intent to enter a contract with James. An offer need not take any particular form. However, it must be communicated to an offeree, be in a communication authorized by the offeror, indicate an objective intent to enter a contract, and be sufficiently definite and certain. A reasonable person would assume that the buyer has given the power of acceptance to James.
4. Not an offer. Invitations to negotiate and preliminary negotiations do not constitute an offer. Language of commitment differs from phrases such as "Are you interested in . . ." or "I'll probably take . . ." These phrases do not indicate intent to enter a contract.
5. Not an offer. Invitations to negotiate and preliminary negotiations do not constitute an offer. Language of commitment differs from phrases such as "Are you interested in . . ." or "I'll probably take . . ." These phrases do not indicate intent to enter a contract.
6. Offer. James is indicating a clear intent to enter a contract with the art dealer. An offer need not take any particular form. However, it must be communicated to an offeree, be in a communication authorized by the offeror, indicate an objective intent to enter a contract, and be sufficiently definite and certain. A reasonable person would assume that James has given the power of acceptance to the art dealer.

Gleim Simulation Grading

Task	Correct Responses		Gradable Items		Score per Task
1	____	÷	5	=	____
2	____	÷	6	=	____
3	____	÷	5	=	____
4	____	÷	6	=	____
5	____	÷	6	=	____
			Total of Scores per Task		____
		÷	Total Number of Tasks		5
			Total Score		____ %

STUDY UNIT EIGHTEEN
SALES AND SECURED TRANSACTIONS

(34 pages of outline)

UCC **Article 2**, *Sales*, applies to **contracts for the sale of goods**. The general law of contracts (covered in Study Unit 17) also applies to sales of goods except to the extent Article 2 states different rules. Thus, with certain modifications, the elements of a contract must be present in a sale of goods: (1) mutual assent (offer and acceptance), (2) consideration, (3) legality, and (4) capacity of the parties. Under Article 2, disputes are resolved in favor of finding an enforceable contract when a reasonable basis for enforcement exists. For example, if the parties have left open certain terms, the rules in Article 2 fill the gaps in the contract. It also (1) provides warranties and other bases of recovery in products liability cases, (2) addresses performance obligations, (3) determines when title and risk of loss are transferred from the seller to the buyer, and (4) describes the defenses and remedies available in suits for breach of contract.

UCC **Article 9**, *Secured Transactions*, covers various debtor-creditor transactions. To protect against the risk of nonpayment of a debt, a promisee, seller, or lender may require the debtor to enter into a security agreement. A **security agreement** gives the creditor an interest in specific personal property owned by the debtor. If the debtor defaults, a valid **security interest** allows the creditor to (1) repossess the collateral, (2) sell it at a reasonably conducted public or private sale, and (3) apply the sale proceeds to the debt. The topics emphasized in this study unit are (1) **attachment** of a security interest to the collateral; (2) **perfection** of a security interest; (3) the rules for determining **priority** among debtors, creditors, and third parties (including the exceptions to the general rules); and (4) the **remedies** after default.

18.1 FORMATION OF A CONTRACT

1. **Overview**
   a. **Sale.** A contract for the sale of goods transfers ownership of goods from the seller to the buyer for consideration (a price).
   b. Property is the set of legally recognized and enforceable rights in one or more items.
      1) **Personal property** generally includes rights in movable tangible (physical) and intangible items.
      2) **Real property** includes rights with respect to land and attached items, which include the following:
         a) The surface of the land

b) Items attached to the land, e.g., trees, structures, and **fixtures** (personal property attached to the land and structures)

i) Whether an item is a fixture is determined primarily by the **intent** of the annexor at the time of attachment. Intent is objectively tested and may be inferred from facts such as (a) the nature of the item, (b) its manner of attachment, (c) its use, and (d) any injury to the land by its removal.

c) Materials below the surface, e.g., minerals, oil, and water

d) The airspace necessary for use and enjoyment of the surface

e) A **fee simple** (or fee simple absolute), which is the most extensive possessory interest in land

c. **Goods.** Article 2 applies only to sales of goods, a form of personal property.

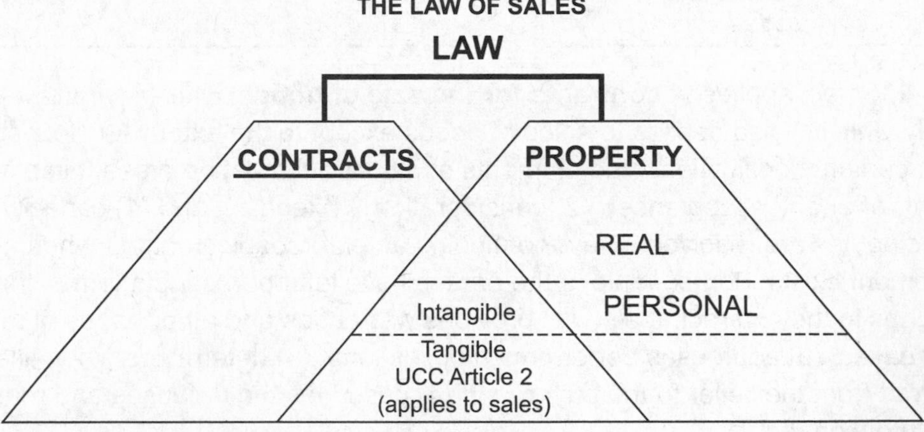

Figure 18-1

d. **Merchants.** Article 2 applies to all sales of goods between all buyers and sellers regardless of the price. Special standards apply to transactions involving merchants. Merchants

1) Are dealers in goods of the kind involved in the sales contract;
2) Represent themselves, by their occupation, as having specific knowledge or skill regarding the goods involved in the transactions; or
3) May be treated as having such knowledge or skill because they **employ** intermediaries (other merchants) who, by their occupation, represent themselves as having such knowledge or skill.

EXAMPLE

Marilyn hires Green, an expert in faux jewelry who has been working for a large and successful company, to set up, manage, and operate Marilyn's Jewelry Co. The company will make direct mail order sales to the general public and will wholesale the same products to trinket retail stores in malls throughout the country. For purposes of the UCC, Marilyn is a merchant in faux jewelry.

e. **Good faith.** The obligations of good faith, diligence, reasonableness, and care are imposed upon the parties to every contract subject to the UCC.

1) These obligations may not be disclaimed by agreement.
2) Merchants also must observe reasonable commercial standards of fair dealing in the trade.

EXAMPLE

In a contract involving the sale of goods, Pan and Nan agree that Pan (seller) will set the price term. Pan must establish the price in good faith. In most instances, good faith would require that the price be set at fair market value.

f. **Unconscionability.** A court may examine a contract for the sale of goods to determine whether it is so one-sided as to be shockingly unfair.

2. **Firm Offer**

   a. An offer by a **merchant** seller that includes assurances that it will be held open cannot be revoked for a stated period or a reasonable amount of time. However, the duration cannot be more than 3 months.

   b. The offer must be in writing and signed by the merchant offeror.

      1) If the offeree supplies the form, the firm offer term must be signed separately.

   c. Consideration is not necessary.

   d. An example of a firm offer is a rain check. It is a writing issued by a merchant when the supply of a sale item is insufficient.

      1) It offers the item at the advertised price, but no period of effectiveness need be stated.

3. **Acceptance**

   a. Unless otherwise indicated, an offer invites acceptance in any manner and by any medium reasonable under the circumstances.

      1) If the offeror indicates that a particular medium of acceptance must be used, only the indicated medium is authorized.

EXAMPLE

Big Corp. writes Small Corp. offering to sell $1 million worth of computers (goods). The offer states that Big will keep the offer open for 20 days from the date of the letter. Before the 20th day arrives, Small sends Big an acceptance by registered letter. Because this medium of acceptance is commercially reasonable under the circumstances, the acceptance is probably valid. Acceptance is effective upon delivery to the post office.

   b. The beginning of performance by the offeree may be an appropriate method of acceptance.

      1) But the offeree must notify the offeror within a reasonable time that performance has begun. Otherwise, the offeror may treat the offer as having expired prior to acceptance.

EXAMPLE

Rob (offeror) sends a fax to Lisa (offeree) requesting that Lisa begin manufacturing and shipping goods immediately. Lisa begins the requested performance but does not inform Rob. Thus, Rob may acquire goods from another source without liability to Lisa even if Lisa has begun performance.

   c. If the offer does not require a particular manner or medium for acceptance, acceptance may be by either (1) a prompt promise to ship or (2) prompt shipment of the goods to the buyer.

      1) If the seller ships **nonconforming goods**, the shipment is both an acceptance and a breach.

EXAMPLE

Steven orders 1,000 orange and blue sweatshirts from Victor. Victor ships 1,000 garnet and gold sweatshirts but does not notify him that the goods are offered only as an accommodation. Victor's shipment is both an acceptance of the offer and a breach of the resulting contract. Steven may reject the shipment and sue for damages.

2) If the seller notifies the buyer within a reasonable time that a nonconforming shipment is offered only as an **accommodation**, no breach occurs.

a) No contract has been formed, and the shipment is a counteroffer.

EXAMPLE

In the example on the previous page, assume that, before the goods arrive, Victor notifies Steven that the garnet and gold sweatshirts were sent as an accommodation. The shipment is a counteroffer. If Steven accepts delivery, a contract for the purchase and sale of garnet and gold sweatshirts is formed.

4. **Open Terms**

a. Under general contract law, the terms of a contract are required to be **definite and complete**.

1) The UCC has modified this strict approach. Thus, a contract for the sale of goods may be made in any manner sufficient to show agreement, including actions of the parties that recognize its existence.

b. Leaving open one or more terms does not prevent formation of a contract. But (1) the parties must have intended to enter into a contract, and (2) a reasonably certain basis must exist for granting a remedy.

c. If the **quantity term** is left open, the general rule is that a court may have no basis to grant a remedy. Thus, a contract may not have been formed.

1) A contract is not too indefinite because it measures the quantity by the seller's **output** or the buyer's **requirements** that occur in good faith.

a) The amount should not be unreasonably different from (1) a stated estimate or (2), given no estimate, any normal or comparable prior amount.

d. If the parties have not agreed on **price**, the court will determine a reasonable price at the time of delivery.

1) If either the buyer or the seller is to determine price, it should be a price fixed in good faith.

2) The price determined is generally the market price.

e. When parties do not specify payment or credit terms, payment is due at the time and place at which the buyer is to receive the goods.

f. When delivery terms are not specified, the buyer normally takes delivery at the seller's place of business (or home if no place of business exists).

1) Otherwise, delivery is at the place where both parties know the goods are located at the time of sale.

g. If the time for shipment or delivery is not clearly specified, it is a reasonable time.

The AICPA often tests candidates' knowledge regarding open terms in a contract for the sale of goods. The UCC enforces a contract when a reasonable basis for enforcement exists. Thus, the UCC differs from general contract law, which requires the terms of a contract to be definite and complete.

5. **Different or Additional Terms**

a. Article 2 does not apply the **mirror image rule** covered in Study Unit 17, Subunit 2. If the offeree's overall response indicates a definite acceptance, a contract is formed.

1) Acceptance may be expressly conditional upon agreement to additional or different terms.

a) In this case, a counteroffer (and rejection) is made. No contract exists unless the original offeror agrees to the counteroffer.

2) If the seller or the buyer is a **nonmerchant**, additional or different terms in an acceptance are mere proposals. The modifying terms do not become part of the contract unless the offeror agrees.

EXAMPLE

Tammy offers to sell a boat and trailer to Nan for $2,000. Nan replies, "I accept and want you to put new tires on the boat trailer." She has indicated a definite expression of acceptance, forming a contract. Her acceptance suggests an added term modifying the offer. Because Tammy is not a merchant, the additional term is merely a proposal. Tammy is not legally obligated to comply.

3) Between **merchants**, the additional or different terms automatically become part of the contract unless
   a) The terms materially alter the original contract,
   b) The offer expressly limits acceptance to the terms of the offer, or
   c) The offeror promptly objects to the modified terms.
4) The diagram below illustrates the battle of the forms (the offeror's and the offeree's):

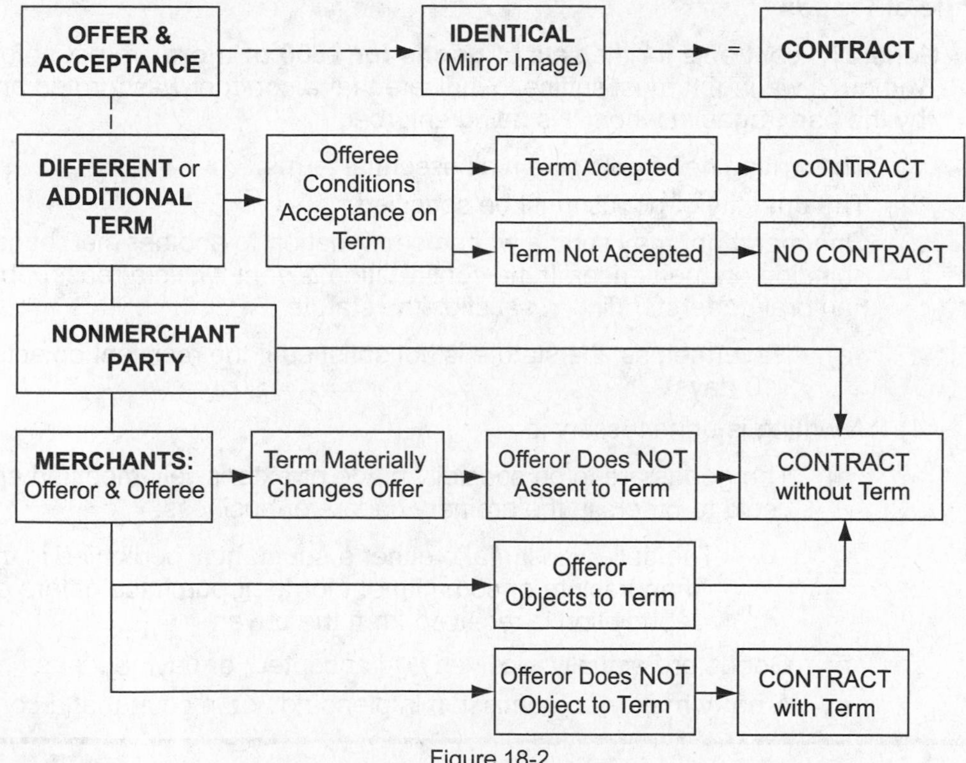

Figure 18-2

6. **Modifications**
   a. An agreement modifying a contract does not need consideration to be binding.
   b. If a written agreement signed by the parties excludes oral modification, the contract can be modified (or rescinded) only by written agreement.
   c. If any modification brings the contract within the **statute of frauds**, the modification must be in writing to be enforceable.

7. **Parol Evidence**

Background

"Parol" means oral or verbal. It is derived from the same Greek root as the word "parable." Another form of the word is parole, by which a prisoner gives his or her word that (s)he will refrain from certain conduct if released.

a. A writing intended by the parties to be a final expression of their agreement cannot be contradicted by
   1) Evidence of any prior agreement or
   2) An oral agreement made at the same time as the final writing.
b. The final expression of the agreement may be explained or supplemented by the following:
   1) Course of dealing (prior conduct between the parties)
   2) Usage of trade (a regular practice or method)
   3) Course of performance (past performance accepted without objection)
   4) Consistent additional terms (unless a court finds the writing to be complete)

8. **Statute of Frauds**

a. Generally, contracts for the **sale of goods for $500 or more** are not enforceable without a writing. It must suffice to indicate that a contract was formed and be signed by the party against whom it is being enforced
   1) The writing need not contain all essential terms.
   2) The quantity of goods must be specified.
   3) One merchant may send a written confirmation to another merchant that is binding on the sender. If the confirmation is sent within a reasonable time after an oral understanding, it satisfies the statute.
      a) Nevertheless, the statute is not satisfied if the recipient objects within 10 days.
   4) A writing is unnecessary if
      a) The goods are to be specially made or extensively modified and cannot be sold to others in the ordinary course of business.
         i) The seller must make either a substantial beginning in their manufacture or commitment for their purchase before a notice of repudiation is received from the buyer.
      b) Goods are actually received and accepted, or payment has been made.
      c) A party makes an admission in pleadings or in court that a contract exists.

Exam questions have asked for the circumstances in which a written contract is unnecessary under the statute of frauds.

9. **Auctions**

a. An auction sale is assumed to be **with reserve** unless the goods are explicitly put up without reserve. An auctioneer may withdraw an auction with reserve at any time until (s)he announces completion of the sale. An auction **without reserve** may be withdrawn only if no bid is made within a reasonable time.
   1) A bid is an offer and may be revoked at any time before acceptance by the auctioneer. No prior bid is revived by the revocation.

2) When a bid is made during the auctioneer's act of acceptance (e.g., while the hammer is falling), the auctioneer may reopen the bidding or declare the goods sold.

Stop and review! You have completed the outline for this subunit. Study multiple-choice questions 1 through 5 beginning on page 699.

18.2 PERFORMANCE

1. **General Contract Obligations**
   a. The **seller** must transfer and deliver the goods.
   b. The **buyer** must accept and pay the price in accordance with the contract.
   c. A **tender** is (1) an unconditional offer to perform (2) with a current ability to do so. If it is unjustifiably refused, the refusing party is in default, and the tendering party has remedies for breach of contract.
2. **Perfect Tender Rule**
   a. If the goods and the seller's tender of delivery fail in any way to conform to the contract, the buyer may reject the goods or the tender.
   b. This rule is subject to the seller's rights, e.g., the right to **cure** (correct the nonconformity).
      1) After rejection, the seller may notify the buyer of an intent to cure. If the seller then delivers conforming goods within the time allowed by the contract, no breach occurs.
   c. The seller's duty is to put and hold conforming goods at the buyer's disposition for a time sufficient for the buyer to take possession.
      1) The seller must give reasonable notice to enable the buyer to take delivery.
   d. **Shipment contract.** The seller must
      1) Place the goods in the care of the designated (or a reasonable) carrier and make a reasonable contract for their transportation to the buyer,
      2) Obtain and tender in due form any documents necessary to enable the buyer to take possession, and
      3) Promptly notify the buyer.
   e. **Destination contract.** The seller must transport the goods at its own risk and expense to the destination and duly tender them. This involves
      1) Putting and holding conforming goods at the buyer's disposal at a reasonable hour and for a reasonable time
      2) Providing reasonable notice to the buyer
   f. If the delivery term is **FOB** (free on board) a particular point, the tender of delivery must be made at the FOB point.
      1) "Delivery to be FOB the place of shipment" indicates a shipment contract.
      2) "Delivery to be FOB the place of destination" indicates a destination contract.
   g. Goods may be in the possession of a bailee and are to be delivered without moving them.
      1) The seller must (a) tender a negotiable document of title to the goods or (b) obtain the bailee's acknowledgment of the buyer's right to the goods.
      2) However, a tender of a (a) nonnegotiable document of title or (b) written direction to the bailee to deliver the goods to the buyer is a sufficient tender if the buyer does not object.

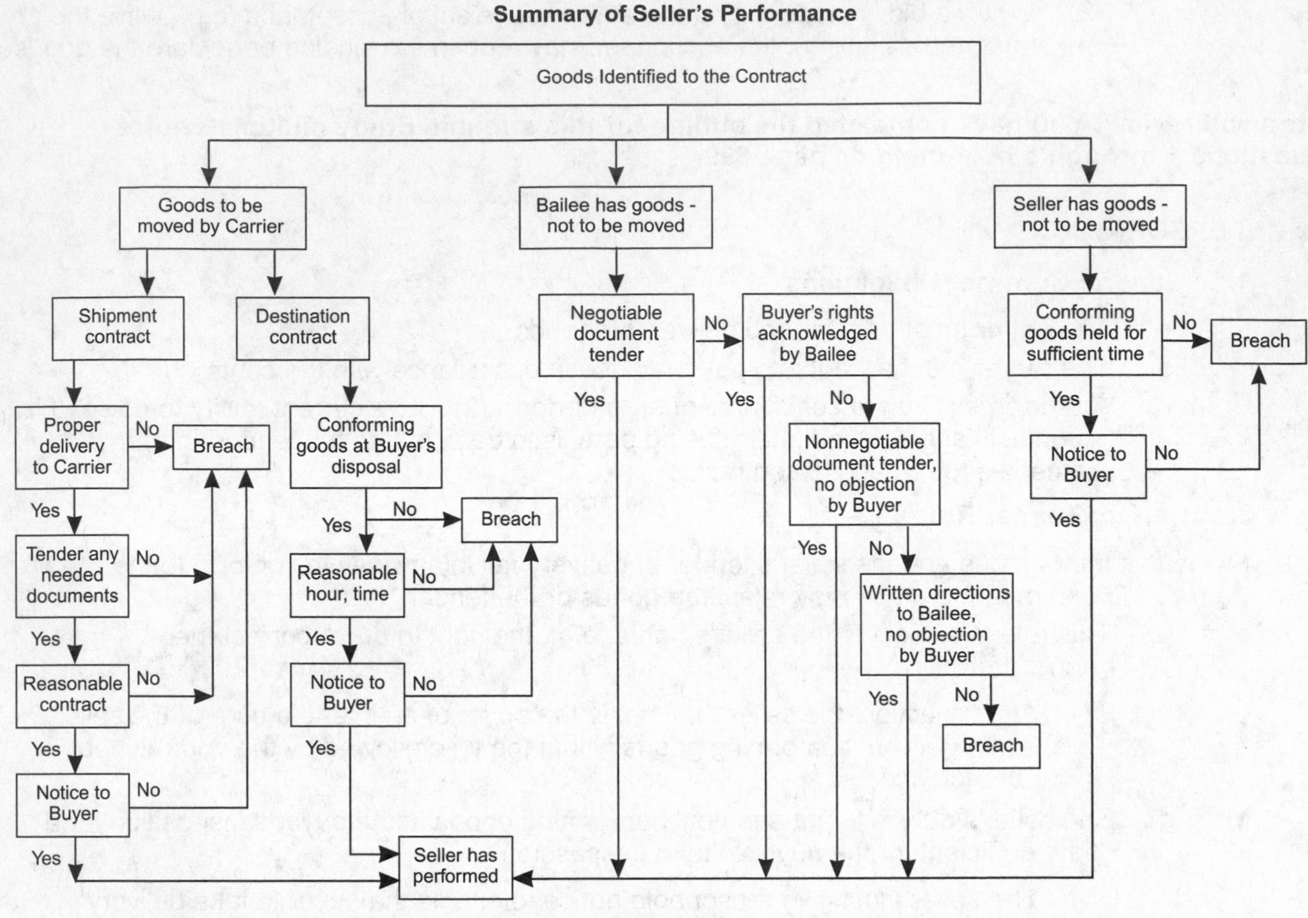

Figure 18-3

3. **Buyer's Rights and Duties**

a. After a proper tender of conforming goods, the buyer must (1) accept them and (2) pay the price. These obligations are usually subject to a right to inspect.

1) Without an agreement to the contrary, the buyer must

a) Provide facilities reasonably suited for receipt of the goods and
b) Pay at the time and place of receipt.

b. The buyer has a **right to inspect the goods** at any reasonable time and place and in any reasonable manner before payment or acceptance, unless agreed to otherwise.

1) If the buyer fails to inspect the goods within a reasonable time after receipt, (s)he loses his or her right to inspect.
2) Generally, if the contract provides for (a) payment against documents of title (a documentary sale is customary in shipment contracts) or (b) delivery **COD** (collect on delivery), the buyer has no right of inspection before payment. In these circumstances, payment is not acceptance.

EXAMPLE

Buyer Co. in New Mexico and Seller Co. in Florida contract for the sale of goods to be shipped to New Mexico. The contract provides for payment against an order bill of lading. Thus, Buyer must pay when the bank or other seller's agent in New Mexico notifies it that the bill of lading is ready, and it does not have a right of inspection prior to payment. Under these facts, the buyer is required to pay first and inspect later.

a) When payment is due before inspection, a defect in the goods does not excuse nonpayment unless the defect is obvious or the transaction is fraudulent.

b) The seller has no general duty to allow inspection before payment.

3) The buyer may reject nonconforming goods when tender is not perfect. The buyer may (a) keep them and sue for damages or (b) reject them and either cancel the contract or sue for damages.

a) The buyer's right to reject (or revoke acceptance) is subject to the seller's right to cure the nonconformity.

4) A buyer who accepts goods and later discovers their nonconformity may **revoke acceptance** if they are substantially nonconforming.

a) Acceptance must have been reasonably induced by the difficulty of detection.

Summary of Buyer's Performance [B = Buyer; S = Seller]

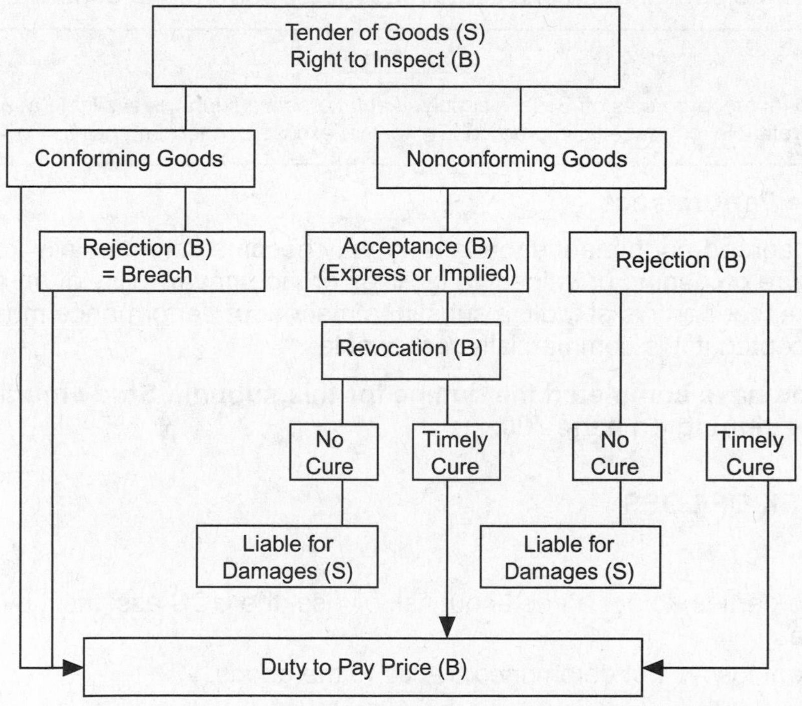

Figure 18-4

c. **Acceptance** by the buyer precludes the buyer from exercising the right of rejection.

1) The buyer can accept the delivered goods in one of three ways.

a) The buyer can expressly accept the shipment.

b) The buyer has had a reasonable opportunity to inspect the goods and has failed to reject them within a reasonable period.

c) The buyer accepts the goods by performing any act inconsistent with the rights of the true owner (seller), for example, reselling or using them.

2) The legal effect of acceptance is that the buyer must pay the contract price.

3) A buyer who accepts a defective tender is barred from receiving any remedy, **unless** the seller is notified of the defect within a reasonable time after it has been or should have been discovered.

d. In noncarrier cases, a sale is assumed to be for cash, and the price is due at tender.

4. **Commercial Impracticability**
   a. Commercial impracticability excuses nonperformance. Performance must be rendered impracticable (not feasible, although not impossible) by a subsequent event not reasonably foreseeable by the parties at the time of contracting.
   b. A seller's duty to perform is excused by failure of presupposed conditions. Breach does not occur if
      1) Performance as agreed has been made impracticable by the occurrence of a contingency, the nonoccurence of which was a **basic assumption** of the contract, or
      2) The seller complies in good faith with governmental regulations.
   c. An unexpected circumstance must arise subsequent to formation of the contract.
   d. The risk of the unexpected occurrence must not already have been allocated by the parties or by custom in the marketplace.
   e. Hardship or increase in costs alone is not sufficient. Objectively, current circumstances must be such that no one could reasonably perform the contract.

EXAMPLE

An unforeseen international embargo cuts off Seller's supply. If an alternative supply is available at a cost that will merely render performance unprofitable, commercial impracticability will not excuse nonperformance.

5. **Substitute Performance**
   a. The agreed-upon manner of delivery may become commercially impracticable due to failure of loading or unloading facilities or the unavailability of an acceptable carrier. If neither party is at fault, a substitute manner of performance must be tendered and accepted if it is commercially reasonable.

Stop and review! You have completed the outline for this subunit. Study multiple-choice questions 6 and 7 beginning on page 700.

18.3 TITLE AND RISK OF LOSS

1. **Overview**
   a. If the parties do not agree about risk of loss, the UCC assigns it by means of practical rules.
   b. Risk of loss is not determined by title to the goods.
   c. Without a breach of contract, and if no carrier or bailee is involved, risk of loss passes to the buyer when
      1) (S)he takes **physical possession** of the goods from a **merchant**.

EXAMPLE

Merchant seller sells goods to Buyer, who must take delivery at Merchant's place of business. Risk of loss does not pass to Buyer until (s)he actually picks up the goods.

      2) A **nonmerchant** seller places the goods at the buyer's disposal (a **tender of delivery**).

EXAMPLE

Seller, a nonmerchant, sells goods to Buyer, and the parties agree that the goods will be picked up by Buyer at 3:00 p.m. on Wednesday at a specified place. Seller has goods ready for Buyer at that time and place, but Buyer does not arrive. The goods are destroyed at 4:30 p.m. that day. Risk of loss passed to Buyer because Seller tendered delivery at 3:00 p.m. when (s)he had the goods ready for pick-up by Buyer.

d. If the buyer has a **right to reject** the goods because they do not conform to the contract, the risk of loss does not pass to the buyer until

1) The nonconformity is cured (i.e., corrected) or
2) The buyer accepts the goods despite the nonconformity.

EXAMPLE

Buyer orders gold kazoos from Seller in Orlando, FOB Orlando. Seller ships silver kazoos, giving Buyer a right to reject. The kazoos are destroyed in transit. The risk of loss was on Seller. If gold kazoos had been shipped, the risk of loss would have been on Buyer.

e. If the buyer **rightfully revokes acceptance**, the risk of an uninsured loss is treated as having rested on the seller from the origination of the contract.

EXAMPLE

Boat Co. accepted delivery of a shipment of life vests from Seller. Boat discovered a hidden defect in the vests and rightfully revoked acceptance. Boat then notified Seller and waited for instructions. But before any action could be taken, the vests were destroyed through no fault of Boat. Boat's insurance covers only 30% ($30,000) of the fair value of the vests ($100,000). Seller bears the remaining loss of $70,000.

f. After the seller has **identified conforming goods to the contract**, the buyer may breach the contract before the risk of loss has passed. An uninsured loss within a commercially reasonable time after the seller learns of the breach falls on the buyer.

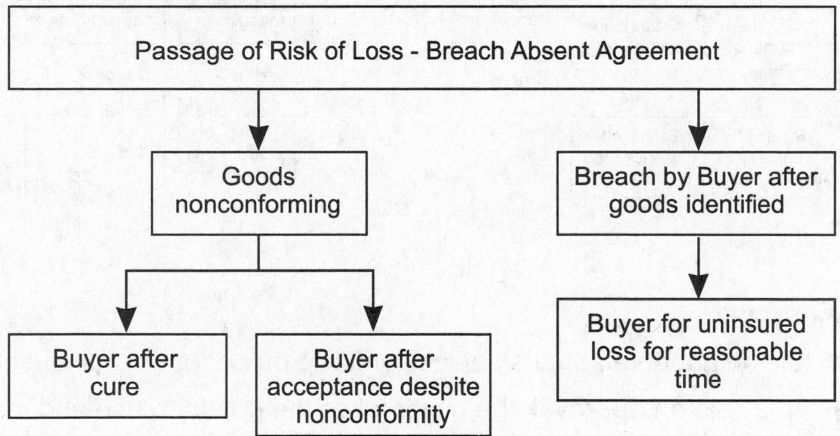

Figure 18-5

2. **Use of Carrier**

a. If a carrier is involved, the shipping terms control.

1) In a **destination** contract, the risk of loss passes to the buyer when the goods have reached the destination and are tendered to (not accepted by) the buyer.

EXAMPLE

Seller in Tampa sells 10,000 tons of beans to Buyer in Denver FOB Denver. Risk of loss during shipment is on Seller. If the goods are damaged during shipment, the loss falls on Seller.

2) In a **shipment** contract, the risk of loss passes to the buyer when the seller delivers the goods to the carrier.

EXAMPLE

Seller in Tampa sells 10,000 tons of beans to Buyer in Denver FOB Tampa. The contract authorizes shipment by carrier but does not require Seller to tender them in Denver. Risk of loss passes to Buyer when the goods are placed in possession of the carrier. If the goods are damaged in shipping, the loss falls on Buyer.

3. **Use of Warehouser**
   a. If goods are held by a warehouser or other person temporarily entrusted with their possession (a **bailee**) and are not to be shipped, risk passes after
      1) The buyer's receipt of a negotiable document of title covering the goods. (Negotiable documents are covered in Study Unit 19.)
      2) The tender to the buyer of a nonnegotiable document covering the goods.
   b. If no document of title is involved, risk passes after
      1) The bailee's acknowledgment of the buyer's right to the goods.
      2) The seller's tender to the buyer of a written direction to the bailee to deliver the goods to the buyer.

Summary of Passage of Risk of Loss

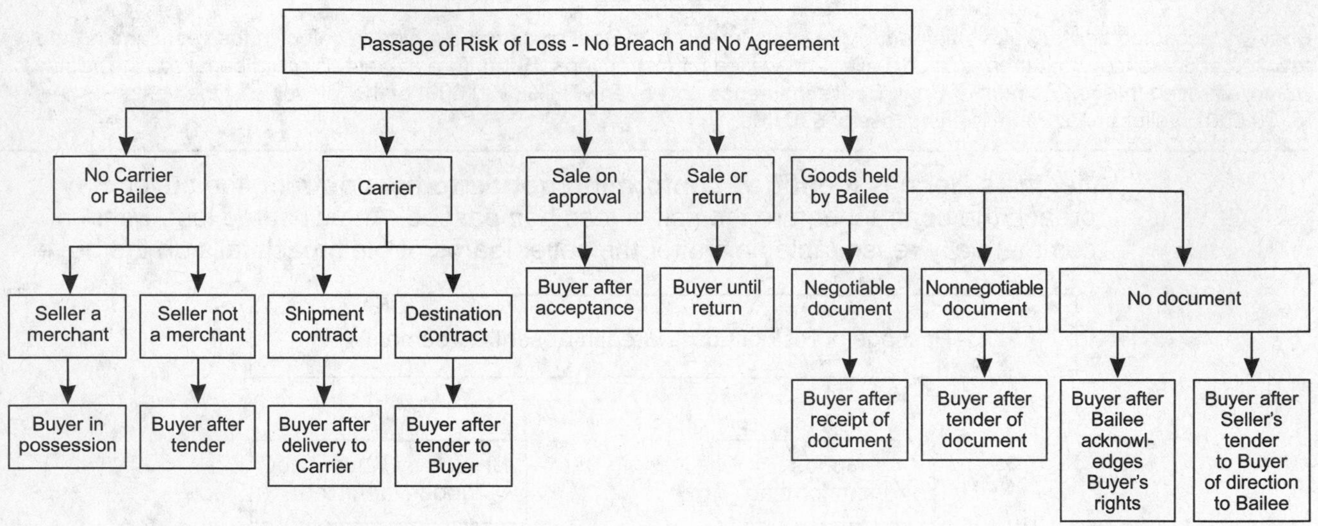

Figure 18-6

4. **Sale on Approval**
   a. In a sale on approval, the risk of loss and title do not pass until the buyer accepts.
      1) In a sale on approval, the buyer takes the goods to use and may return them even if they conform to the contract.
      2) If the buyer decides not to take the goods, the seller has the risk of loss for the return.
5. **Sale or Return**
   a. A sale or return contract is treated as an ordinary sale.
      1) The buyer takes the goods to resell them but may return those unsold.
      2) If the goods are returned, the buyer bears the expense and risk of loss while they are in transit.

6. **Identification**

a. Before title to goods can pass, the goods must exist and be identified to the contract. Identification is designation of specific goods as the subject matter of the contract.

b. If the parties do not agree upon the time and manner of identification of existing goods to the contract, the time of identification is determined as follows:

1) Identification of already identified goods occurs when the contract is made.

2) When the contract is for **future goods**, identification occurs when the goods are designated by the seller or the buyer.

a) Future goods are not yet both existing and identified.

EXAMPLE

Jean and Ellen contract for the sale of widgets when Jean has a barn filled with identical widgets. Until identification, the contract is one for the sale of future goods. Identification does not occur until either Jean or Ellen designates a quantity of the fungible widgets to which the contract refers. Until identification occurs, title cannot pass to Ellen.

3) If goods are **fungible** (one unit is the equivalent of any other), identification occurs when the contract is made. An undivided share in an identified **bulk** of fungible goods is sufficiently identified to the contract to be sold even if the quantity of the bulk is not determined.

When Goods Identified

	Already Identified	Future Goods	Fungible Goods
Contract made	✓		✓
Goods designated		✓	

7. **Passage of Title**

a. Unless the parties explicitly agree, the following rules apply:

1) Title passes to the buyer at the time and place at which the seller completes performance of physical delivery.

2) Under a destination contract, title passes when delivery is tendered there.

3) Under a shipment contract, title passes when the goods are delivered to the carrier.

4) Delivery without moving the goods may occur, for example, when a warehouser is in possession.

a) If the seller is to deliver a document of title to the goods, title passes at the time and place of delivery of the document.

b) If the goods already are identified at the time of contracting, and no documents are to be delivered, title passes at the time and place of contracting.

b. The guidance regarding passage of title is illustrated below:

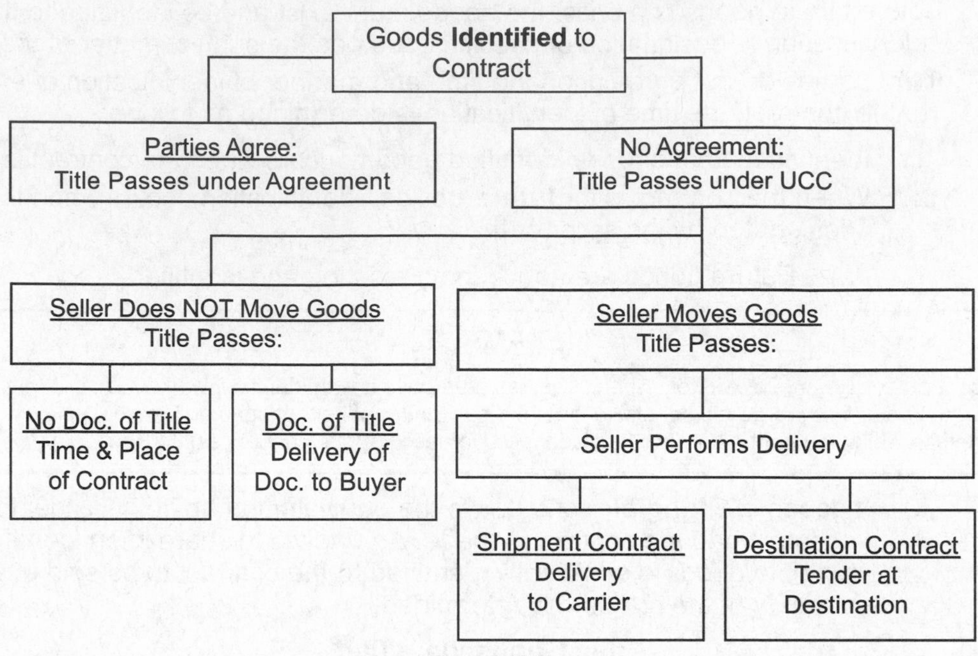

Figure 18-7

c. Reservation of a security interest has no effect on passage of title.

d. Title passes back to the **seller** by operation law as a result of the buyer's

1) Rejection or other refusal to receive or retain the goods, whether or not justified, or
2) Justified revocation of acceptance.

8. **Sales by Nonowners**

a. A purchaser receives the title that the seller has power to transfer.

b. If the seller is a **thief**, the seller's title is void. Thus, the buyer acquires no title. The actual owner can reclaim the goods from the buyer.

c. A seller has voidable title if the goods were obtained by **fraud**. A voidable title becomes valid when the goods are sold to a good-faith purchaser for value.

EXAMPLE

Jim sells a boat to Ted, who pays for the boat by check. The check is dishonored because of insufficient funds. Jim has the right to rescind the contract and recover the boat from Ted. If Ted already has resold the boat to Scott, and if Scott was a good-faith purchaser for value, Jim cannot recover the boat from Scott. Jim still has a right of action against Ted for the purchase price, but Scott retains title to the boat.

d. Any **entrusting** of goods to a merchant who deals in goods of that kind gives the merchant power to transfer all rights of the entruster to a buyer in the ordinary course of business.

EXAMPLE

Candace leaves her watch with a jeweler for repair. The jeweler sells (deals in) both new and used watches. The jeweler sells the watch to Eileen, a customer, who does not know that the jeweler has no right to sell the watch. Eileen receives good title against Candace's claim of ownership. But the good-faith purchaser (Eileen) has only those rights held by the person entrusting the goods. Thus, if a thief of the watch had entrusted it to the jeweler, Eileen would have good title against the entruster (thief). However, she would not have good title against Candace, who neither entrusted the watch to the thief nor authorized the thief to entrust the watch to the jeweler.

9. **Insurable Interest**
   a. A person has an insurable interest in the subject matter if (s)he will receive an economic benefit from its preservation or suffer economic loss from its destruction.
      1) A buyer has an insurable interest in identified goods even if (s)he has neither title nor risk of loss.
      2) A seller has an insurable interest if (s)he has title or a security interest. (Security interests are covered in Subunit 18.7.)

Stop and review! You have completed the outline for this subunit. Study multiple-choice questions 8 through 12 beginning on page 701.

18.4 WARRANTIES

1. **Types of Warranties**
   a. A warranty is an assurance by one party of the existence of a fact upon which the other party may rely.
   b. **Express warranties** are any statements of fact or promises made by any seller to the buyer that become part of their agreement. They include any description of the goods, sample, or model. The express warranty may be oral or written.
      1) To become part of the agreement, the communication must be made when the buyer could have relied upon it when (s)he entered into the contract.
      2) A statement relating to the value of the goods or a statement of the seller's opinion is not an express warranty.

EXAMPLE

Sporty is browsing at the Copter Co. She is a new pilot and is considering purchasing a particular helicopter but is concerned about its safety. Bud, the owner, tells Sporty, "Don't worry. All of our aircraft are nearly indestructible and cannot crash under any circumstances." Sporty purchases the helicopter. Subsequently, the aircraft crashes. Sporty sues Bud for breach of express warranty. Bud claims that it was not a warranty because he did not use language such as "guarantee" or "warranty" and was merely puffing. Bud will probably lose. As long as a seller makes the affirmation of fact or promise relating to the goods that becomes part of the basis of the bargain, the seller is expressly warranting the goods. It is not relevant that Bud did not intend to guarantee the goods.

   c. An **implied warranty of merchantability** arises by operation of law and need not be written. This warranty is implied in every sale by a **merchant** who deals in goods of the kind sold. The buyer need not be a merchant.
      1) The issue is whether the goods are fit for the ordinary purposes for which such goods are used.
   d. An **implied warranty of fitness for a particular purpose** also arises by operation of law. This warranty is implied whenever any seller knows
      1) The particular purpose for which the goods are to be used and
      2) That the buyer is relying on the seller to select suitable goods.

EXAMPLE

KBW is interested in climbing a mountain. KBW goes to a sporting goods store and purchases rope, hooks, pins, and maps. She tells the sales associate, "I need climbing shoes as well," and the sales associate recommends the Bumps. KBW purchases them. In fact, the Bumps are great for basketball but are useless and dangerous for mountain climbing. The Bumps shred on KBW's first outing under normal use. KBW sues for breach of warranty of fitness for a particular purpose. The store defends on the grounds that KBW never specifically said the shoes were for mountaineering. KBW will win because the store had reason to know that (1) the goods were to be used for a particular purpose (mountain climbing), and (2) the buyer would rely on the seller's skill and judgment in selecting suitable goods.

e. All sellers make the **warranty of title**. It states that

   1) The title is good,
   2) Its transfer is rightful, and
   3) The goods are free of liens and other encumbrances not known by the buyer.

f. Unless agreed otherwise, a merchant seller warrants that the goods are free of rightful claims based on infringement (unauthorized use, e.g., of a patented device).

EXAMPLE

Bo purchases a piano from Ben for cash. Two months later, Abe repossesses the piano from Bo. Abe proves that (1) he has a security interest in the piano, and (2) Ben is in default. Bo demands his money back from Ben. Bo can recover because the seller of goods warrants that they are delivered free from any security interest or other lien of which the buyer has no knowledge.

2. Disclaimer of Warranties

a. For all practical purposes, it is impossible for a seller to disclaim an **express** warranty.

b. **Implied** warranties are disclaimed by (1) the use of certain language, for example, "**as is**" or "**with all faults**;" (2) the buyer's examination; or (3) the course of dealing, course of performance, or usage of trade.

   1) Without such circumstances,

      a) The disclaimer of the implied warranty of merchantability must use the word **merchantability**, which must be conspicuous if made in a writing.

      b) The disclaimer of the implied warranty of fitness must be written and conspicuous.

c. The warranty of title and the warranty against **infringement** may be disclaimed only by specific language or by the buyer's knowledge of circumstances relating to title.

   1) A general disclaimer of warranty is ineffective.

d. A court may refuse to enforce a disclaimer on the grounds that it is unconscionable. For example, a disclaimer of liability for personal injury is not permitted.

Warranties

Type	Warrantor	Warranty	Disclaimer
Express	Any seller	Affirmation, promise, description, sample	Almost impossible
Implied -- merchantability	Merchant seller	Fit for ordinary uses	Use of word "merchantability." Conspicuous if written. Or use of "As is," etc.; buyer's examination; or course of dealing, etc.
Implied -- fitness for particular purpose	Any seller	Buyer's particular purpose	Written and conspicuous. Or use of "As is," etc.; buyer's examination; or course of dealing, etc.
Title	Any seller	Good title Rightful transfer Free from encumbrances unknown to buyer	Specific language or buyer's knowledge of circumstances relating to title
Against infringement	Merchant seller	No rightful claim of infringement	Specific language or buyer's knowledge of circumstances relating to title

Stop and review! You have completed the outline for this subunit. Study multiple-choice questions 13 through 15 beginning on page 702.

18.5 PRODUCTS LIABILITY

1. **Overview**
   a. A manufacturer or seller of a product is liable if a defective product is placed in the market and causes injury. The liability may be based on negligence (a tort) or on a warranty (a contract theory), or the liability may be strict.
      1) Users who are injured through no fault of their own and because of a defect in a product may recover from the manufacturer, wholesaler, or retailer.
2. **Negligence**
   a. The principal ways in which a manufacturer-seller may be liable are (1) negligent design, (2) manufacturing flaw, (3) failure to inspect, and (4) failure to warn.
   b. Wholesalers and retailers must inspect for defects if they have reason to believe a product is likely to be defective, e.g., because a seal was broken or complaints were received.
3. **Warranties**
   a. Generally, a plaintiff is entitled to damages upon proof that
      1) An express or implied warranty exists,
      2) The product does not conform to the warranty, and
      3) The plaintiff suffered harm as a result of the breach of warranty.
   b. Proof that the seller was at fault is not necessary.
4. **Strict Liability**
   a. This theory extends the implied warranty of merchantability by removing most defenses and reducing the elements that the plaintiff must prove.
      1) A defective product does not meet reasonable expectations as to its safety.
      2) The defects covered by strict liability are manufacturing defects and design defects.
      3) The plaintiff need not prove (a) negligence, (b) fraud, (c) reliance on statements of the seller or manufacturer, (d) notice of a defect given by the injured party, or (e) privity of contract.
         a) Moreover, the seller may not assert the defense that its acts were consistent with industry custom.
   b. A seller is liable in tort to a plaintiff who proves each of the following elements of strict products liability:
      1) The seller was in the business of selling the product.
      2) The product was defective when sold.
      3) The defect made the product unreasonably dangerous.
      4) The unreasonably dangerous condition was the legal cause of physical harm or property damage.
         a) Commercial losses (e.g., lost profits) are not recoverable.
      5) At the time the plaintiff was injured, the product was not substantially changed from the condition in which it was sold.

EXAMPLE

Purchaser informed Storekeeper that she wanted to buy a reconditioned paper shredder for use in her business. The reconditioned shredder had been manufactured by Power Shredder Company. The week after the shredder was purchased, Employee, who works for Purchaser, was injured while shredding paper when the shaft holding the shredder blade came loose after a bearing gave way. Employee asserts a claim based on strict liability in tort against Power Shredder. Employee will probably not recover because the shredder did not reach the user in substantially the same condition as when it was manufactured. Power Shredder should not be held strictly liable for selling a product containing a defect that made it unreasonably dangerous if the defect did not exist when the defendant sold the product.

c. The strict liability doctrine applies to any defendant-seller in the chain of distribution.

d. Defenses to strict product liability include (1) product misuse, (2) assumption of risk, (3) commonly known danger (such as using firearms), or (4) knowledgeable user.

Stop and review! You have completed the outline for this subunit. Study multiple-choice questions 16 and 17 on page 703.

18.6 REMEDIES

1. **Overview**

   a. The objective of a remedy is neither to penalize the breaching party nor to enrich the nonbreaching party. The UCC attempts to place the injured party in approximately the same position (s)he would have occupied if no breach of contract had occurred.

2. **Remedies of the Buyer or Seller**

   a. A party has a right to demand written assurances if (s)he has a reasonable basis for believing that performance will **not** be tendered. Until receipt of adequate assurance, the party may suspend further performance if commercially reasonable.

      1) If adequate assurance is not provided within a reasonable period (not over 30 days), the party may treat the contract as repudiated.

EXAMPLE

Seller hears a false rumor that Buyer is in financial difficulty. Seller reasonably believes the rumor. Seller may demand assurances and withhold any unpaid-for goods. Buyer sends an audited financial statement showing good financial condition. The statement is adequate assurance, and Seller must resume performance.

   b. A party has **rights after anticipatory repudiation** of a performance not yet due.

      1) If the loss will substantially impair the value of the contract, the injured party may

         a) Await performance for a commercially reasonable time;
         b) Resort to any remedy for breach, including immediate suit; or
         c) Suspend performance.

      2) The repudiating party's words, actions, or conduct must be clear.

      3) A repudiating party may, at any time before his or her next performance is due, retract repudiation unless the other party has

         a) Canceled,
         b) Materially changed his or her position in reliance on the repudiation, or
         c) Otherwise indicated that (s)he considers the repudiation final.

EXAMPLE

During March Year 1, BigCo contracts to sell 1,000 earth-moving machines to Roadbuilders Corp., delivery to be April 1, Year 2. Early in Year 2, BigCo's employees' union calls a strike. On February 15, Year 2, BigCo notifies Roadbuilders in writing, unequivocally, that it repudiates the contract for April 1 delivery. Roadbuilders simply waits and does not change its position. On March 15, BigCo notifies Roadbuilders that it retracts its repudiation. The retraction is effective.

c. The parties may **modify the contract** to limit the available remedies or provide an exclusive remedy.
   1) Substantial freedom of contract is permitted. However, any remedy must not be unconscionable or fail to accomplish its essential purpose.

d. The parties may agree to **liquidated damages**, an amount that must be a reasonable forecast of damages for breach. Such a clause must reflect (1) anticipated losses, (2) the difficulties of proof of loss, and (3) the inconvenience of obtaining another remedy.
   1) The provision usually sets a ceiling on the defaulting party's liability.
   2) If the provision is not a good-faith estimate of probable damages, it will be treated as a penalty and declared void.
   3) If a seller has properly withheld delivery of goods, the buyer may receive a refund of amounts paid minus any liquidated damages. If damages are unliquidated (not specified in the contract), the seller may retain 20% of the value of the total contract price or $500, whichever is less.
   4) The buyer's right of restitution is subject to offset to the extent the seller establishes either
      a) A right to damages other than liquidated damages or
      b) Benefits received by the buyer directly or indirectly under the contract.

e. Under the **statute of limitations**, except for a breach of warranty, one party may sue another for breach only if suit is filed within 4 years after breach. The parties may reduce (but not extend) the period, but not to less than 1 year.
   1) A plaintiff must notify the defendant within a reasonable time of the breach or be barred from any remedy.
   2) A breach of warranty occurs and establishes a cause of action when the seller tenders delivery of the goods.
      a) When discovery of breach is deferred, the statute begins to run when the breach is or should have been discovered. For example, if a heating system is installed in the summer, discovery of a defect would likely be delayed until winter.

f. The innocent party may **rescind the contract** because of fraud in its formation.
   1) A party who rescinds must return the consideration received from the other party.
   2) But rescission does not bar a claim for damages or any other remedy.
   3) The elements of fraud must be present.

3. **Seller's Breach of Contract**

a. The seller breaches by
   1) Repudiating (renouncing) all or part of the contract,
   2) Making a nonconforming tender of delivery, and
   3) Failing to deliver conforming goods.

b. The **buyer's rights** after a seller's **nonconforming tender** include accepting or rejecting the whole. The buyer also may accept any commercial unit(s) and reject the rest. Furthermore, the buyer may resort to any of the following remedies:
   1) A buyer who (a) rightfully rejects nonconforming goods or (b) justifiably revokes acceptance has a **right to cover**.
      a) To cover means to purchase substitute goods in the marketplace.
      b) Cover is not mandatory. The buyer may choose between cover and damages.

c) The buyer must act reasonably and in good faith. (S)he may recover any excess of the cover price over the contract price, minus any savings on expenses, and damages.

d) If reasonable efforts to cover have failed or are likely to fail, the buyer may have a right to obtain possession of goods wrongly withheld. However, the goods must have been identified to the contract.

2) The buyer's basic remedy when (s)he rejects the goods or justifiably revokes acceptance, or the seller fails to deliver, is to **sue for monetary damages**.

a) Damages ordinarily are the excess of market price over contract price.

b) The buyer may choose to measure damages by the difference between the contract price and the amount (s)he actually must pay.

c) The buyer is entitled to **incidental** damages. They are expenses reasonably related to the breach.

d) The buyer may be entitled to **consequential** damages (e.g., lost profits). Recovery of these damages is allowed if the seller knew or had reason to know, at the time of contracting, of the buyer's general or particular needs.

EXAMPLE

Digit agrees to sell Macro a software package for use during the upcoming tax season. Digit knows that (1) Macro intends to earn $150,000 by using this software package and (2) it is not readily available elsewhere. Digit telephones Macro in February telling her that she plans to keep the software and use it for herself during the entire tax season. Macro is unable to find replacement software. Macro may be entitled to consequential damages because Digit knew of special circumstances that made Macro unable to mitigate in the event of breach. Digit may be liable to Macro for her lost profits.

e) The UCC normally does **not** allow recovery of **punitive** damages.

3) A buyer may recover goods from an **insolvent seller** if

a) The goods have been identified to the contract,

b) The seller became insolvent within 10 days of receipt of the first payment, and

c) Tender of any unpaid portion of the price is made and kept open.

4) If the goods are unique and monetary damages are not an adequate remedy, a court may order **specific performance**.

a) The commercial feasibility of replacement determines whether the remedy is available to a buyer (but not a seller).

EXAMPLE

Cotton Co. contracts to buy all cotton planted, produced, and ginned by Farmers Co-op during the annual season at $.30/lb. The market price of cotton rises to $.80/lb. Farmers Co-op attempts to avoid performance of the contract when most of the U.S. cotton crop for the season has already been sold. Cotton Co. seeks and obtains from a court an order of good faith specific performance.

4. **Buyer's Breach of Contract**

a. The buyer's basic duty is to accept and pay for goods in accordance with the contract. The **seller's remedies** when a buyer breaches include the following:

1) A seller may **withhold delivery of goods** when the buyer

a) Is insolvent (unless the buyer pays cash, including payment for prior deliveries)

b) Fails to make a payment due on or before delivery

c) Wrongfully rejects, or revokes acceptance of, the goods

d) Repudiates the contract

2) A seller may **identify conforming goods to the contract** when a buyer breaches or repudiates a contract while the seller is still in possession.
   a) When the goods are unfinished at the time of breach, the seller must exercise reasonable commercial judgment to mitigate the loss and obtain maximum value for the unfinished goods. The seller may
      i) Stop work and resell the goods for scrap or salvage value or
      ii) Complete manufacture and wholly identify the goods to the contract.
3) A seller may recover goods in transit (in the possession of a carrier or other bailee) when (s)he discovers the buyer to be insolvent.
4) A seller may **recover goods from an insolvent buyer** when the buyer has received goods on credit and is insolvent. Demand must be made within 10 days after the buyer's receipt of the goods.
   a) No time limit applies if a misrepresentation of solvency was made in writing to the seller within 3 months prior to the delivery of the goods.
   b) The seller's right to reclaim is subject to the rights of a good-faith purchaser or other buyer in the ordinary course of business.
5) A seller may **resell the goods** when (s)he (a) possesses or controls the goods at the time of breach or (b) duly reacquires the goods in transit.
   a) The resale must be in good faith and commercially reasonable.
   b) The seller can recover any deficiency between the sales price and the contract price, plus damages resulting from breach, minus any savings.
   c) Perishable goods must be sold as rapidly as possible to mitigate damages.
   d) A good-faith purchaser takes free of any rights of the original buyer.
6) A seller may **recover the price plus incidental damages** but only under specific circumstances.
   a) The buyer accepted the goods and has not revoked acceptance,
   b) Risk of loss passed to the buyer before conforming goods were lost or damaged, or
   c) The buyer breached after the goods were identified to the contract and the seller is unable to resell the goods.
      i) If a seller is unable to resell, the goods must be held for the buyer.
      ii) The net proceeds from the sale must be credited to the buyer.
7) A seller may seek damages for **wrongful repudiation** or **nonacceptance**. The seller also may resell the goods.
8) A seller may **cancel the sales contract** if the buyer
   a) Wrongfully rejects, or revokes acceptance of, conforming goods duly delivered;
   b) Fails to make proper payment; or
   c) Repudiates the contract in whole or in part.
9) A clause providing that a seller may **accelerate payment or performance at will** when (s)he judges himself or herself insecure means it can be exercised only if the seller, in good faith, believes payment or performance is impaired (UCC 1-208).

Stop and review! You have completed the outline for this subunit. Study multiple-choice questions 18 through 21 beginning on page 703.

18.7 ATTACHMENT OF SECURITY INTERESTS

1. **Nature of Collateral**
   a. The application of Article 9 often depends on the nature of the **personal property** serving as collateral.
   b. **Goods** are **tangible** personal property consisting of fixtures and all things movable at the time a security interest attaches.
      1) Goods do not include semi-intangible and intangible items defined in this section. Goods also do not include money or unextracted minerals.
   c. The following are goods:
      1) **Consumer goods** are used for personal, family, or household purposes, for example, a refrigerator purchased for the home.
      2) **Inventory** includes goods to be held for sale or lease or to be provided under a contract for service.

EXAMPLE

Don's Wholesale buys milk from farmers and sells it to restaurants. The milk is Don's inventory.

      3) **Farm products** are (a) crops, (b) livestock, (c) supplies, and (d) unprocessed products of crops or livestock.

EXAMPLES

Milk in the possession of a dairy farmer is a farm product.

Sap that has been boiled into maple syrup is a farm product because boiling is so closely related to harvesting the sap. But once the syrup is bottled for resale, it becomes inventory.

      4) **Equipment** consists of goods that are not consumer goods, inventory, or farm products. For example, a refrigerator purchased for use in a state-owned laboratory is equipment.
   d. **Semi-intangible collateral** is represented by an indispensable writing.
      1) **Instruments** include negotiable instruments. Examples are checks, other drafts, promissory notes, or bonds. Instruments are covered in Study Unit 19.
      2) **Documents** include documents of title and receipts, e.g., bills of lading (issued by a carrier as evidence of receipt of goods for shipment) and warehouse receipts (issued by a warehouser as evidence of deposit of goods for storage). Documents are covered in Study Unit 19.
      3) **Tangible chattel paper** consists of a writing(s) providing evidence of (a) a monetary obligation (e.g., a promissory note) and (b) a security interest (e.g., a security agreement) in specific goods.

EXAMPLE

User buys a computer on credit from Supplier, signs a promissory note for the unpaid balance of the price, and gives Supplier a security interest in the machine. Supplier, to maintain its cash flow, borrows money from Bank and uses the sales contract as collateral to secure the loan. The sales contract is chattel paper. It is evidence of (1) an obligation (of User) to pay money (to Supplier) and (2) a security interest in goods.

      4) **Investment property** includes securities (a) whether or not certificated (represented by a stock certificate) and (b) whether held directly (e.g., stock registered on the books of a corporation) or indirectly (e.g., most publicly traded stock) by the debtor.
      5) **Deposit accounts** are certificates of deposit, savings, or checking accounts in a bank.

e. **Proceeds** include all items received upon disposition of collateral. Proceeds consist of any collateral that has changed in form.

EXAMPLE

A rancher obtains credit and grants the creditor a security interest in the wool from her sheep (tangible collateral in the form of a farm product). If the rancher exchanges the wool for a truck or cash, the truck or cash constitutes proceeds for the wool.

2. **Security Agreements**

   a. A security agreement is a contract between the debtor and the secured party. It grants the secured party a security interest in the collateral. The debtor generally must agree to the creation of a security interest.

      1) For secured transactions purposes, a **debtor** is a person with an interest in the collateral that is not a security interest or other lien. This person need not be accountable for payment or performance of the obligation.

      2) Most **secured parties** are persons in whose favor a security interest exists under a security agreement.

   b. A security agreement may include the following optional items:

      1) An **after-acquired property clause** creates an interest in most types of personal property to be acquired in the future. Such a clause is important to a lender that finances inventory.

         a) The clause provides for a **floating** lien that will attach (float) to specified property that the debtor may acquire in the future.

         b) The interest attaches as soon as the debtor acquires an interest in the property.

EXAMPLE

A typical after-acquired property clause might apply to "all inventory now owned or hereafter acquired by the debtor."

         c) A security interest will float to **consumer goods** under the clause only if the debtor acquires rights in the goods not more than 10 days after the secured party gives value.

      2) A **future advances clause** extends the security agreement to future liabilities of the debtor to the secured party, for example, under a continuing line of credit.

EXAMPLE

Bank lends David $50,000 to purchase manufacturing equipment. David gives Bank a security interest in the equipment. A future advances clause provides that repayment of any funds lent by Bank to David in the future will be secured by the original equipment.

      3) An **acceleration of payment clause** provides for the full amount of the debt to be due immediately upon default or within a specified period if a default is not cured.

3. **Security Interest**

   a. Under UCC Article 9, a security interest is an interest in personal property or fixtures that secures payment or performance of an obligation.

      1) **Fixtures** are goods that are so closely related to real property (buildings or land) that they are considered part of the real property. An example is a central heating system.

4. **Purchase Money Security Interest (PMSI)**
   a. A PMSI results when
      1) A person obtains credit (borrows money),
      2) The credit is used to acquire (purchase) property, and
      3) That property serves as collateral to secure the obligation to satisfy the debt (repay the money borrowed).

EXAMPLE

John purchases an office copier from We-R-Copies. One week later, John borrows $10,000 from Bank, Inc., and gives Bank a security interest in all his office equipment. Bank's security interest in the copier is **not** a PMSI.

EXAMPLE

Jan starts her own business. Jan borrows $10,000 from Bank, Inc., to purchase office equipment. She gives Bank a security interest in the equipment she intends to purchase. The next day, Jan purchases a desk. Bank's security interest in the desk is a PMSI.

EXAMPLE

Caitlin purchased a computer on credit from Hardware Heaven. She also purchased in the same transaction additional software that she planned to install in the computer. Thus, Hardware Heaven (a seller that financed the purchase) has a PMSI in the computer and the software.

5. **Attachment**
   a. Attachment of a security interest in collateral occurs when it is enforceable against the debtor, barring an explicit agreement otherwise.
   b. It is **enforceable** against the debtor when the following have occurred:
      1) The debtor has authenticated a security agreement that describes the collateral. **Authentication** means signing (manually or electronically) or otherwise confirming that the identified person intends to accept the record of the agreement.
         a) However, one of the following may substitute for authentication if it is in accordance with the security agreement:
            i) The secured party has **possession** of the collateral (but not a certificated security);
            ii) The secured party has **control** of collateral in the form of deposit accounts, electronic chattel paper, or investment property; or
            iii) The collateral is a registered certificated security **delivered** to the secured party.
      2) **Value** has been given by the secured party.
      3) The debtor has **rights** in the collateral or the power to transfer such rights.
   c. Attachment of a security interest in collateral gives rights to proceeds.

AICPA questions test candidates' knowledge about if and when a security interest would be attached in different situations.

Stop and review! You have completed the outline for this subunit. Study multiple-choice questions 22 and 23 on page 705.

18.8 PERFECTION OF SECURITY INTERESTS

1. **Overview**
   a. Perfection gives the secured party priority over most third parties who subsequently may claim an interest in the collateral. Examples are buyers from the debtor, creditors of the debtor, or a trustee in bankruptcy.
      1) Perfection gives priority over most unperfected interests and subsequent secured interests.
      2) Perfection is **not** required to enforce the secured party's rights against the debtor.
   b. Perfection of a security interest occurs only after
      1) It has attached and
      2) Other requirements have been satisfied that relate to the particular collateral.
   c. Depending on the nature of the collateral, security interests are perfected in various ways:
      1) By filing a financing statement
      2) By possession or control of the collateral
      3) By delivery of a registered certificated security
      4) Automatically (but in certain cases for a brief period only)
2. **Perfection by Filing a Financing Statement**
   a. Filing is required to perfect a security interest in the absence of a specific exception. The debtor's location controls the place of filing.
      1) Security interests in most forms of collateral may be perfected by filing.
   b. The financing statement is **sufficient** if it contains
      1) The name of the debtor (but not a trade name only),
      2) The name of the secured party, and
      3) An indication of the covered collateral.
         a) For example, a **fixture filing** must (1) indicate that it covers fixtures, (2) be filed in the real property records, and (3) describe the real property.

EXAMPLES

Mr. Zero is the sole proprietor of Z Club. Mr. Zero borrowed money from Bank and gave a security interest in the pool tables in Z Club. Bank should file the financing statement under Zero.

XYZ Partnership owns Dave's Plumbing. XYZ borrowed money from Bank and conveyed a security interest in its fleet of trucks. Bank should file the financing statement under XYZ Partnership, not Dave's Plumbing.

   c. A financing statement that contains minor errors or omissions is effective unless they are seriously misleading.
   d. However, a filing does **not** occur if a filing office refuses to accept it, e.g., because of the omission of the address of the debtor or the secured party.
      1) A financing statement that is sufficient but is not filed gives no notice. Thus, to prevent a rightful rejection, a filer should meet other applicable statutory requirements.
      2) Nevertheless, if the filing office accepts a financing without such information, the filing is fully effective.
   e. A financing statement may be filed before a security agreement is reached or a security interest attaches.

f. A filed financing statement is effective for 5 years. A **continuation statement** extending perfection for 5 years may be filed during the last 6 months of this period.

g. If a debtor moves out of the state where the security interest is perfected, it is perfected for 4 months automatically. For the security interest to remain perfected, a financing statement must be filed in the state of the debtor's new location.

3. **Perfection by Possession**

a. An example is a pawnbroker's loan of money and receipt of personal property as collateral. A security interest may be perfected by possession of the following:

1) Goods
2) Negotiable documents
3) Tangible chattel paper
4) Instruments

a) Possession is optimal for negotiable instruments because a prior perfected security interest is defeated by a holder in due course. (This topic is covered in Study Unit 19.) Also, the 20-day limit for automatic attachment described in 5.c. on the next page does not apply.

5) Money

a) Possession is the only way to perfect as security interest in money other than identifiable cash proceeds.

b. If attachment occurs when the secured party takes possession of the collateral according to the debtor's security agreement, perfection and attachment are **simultaneous**.

EXAMPLE

John owns a boat. John arranged to borrow $10,000 from Julie for 30 days and to provide Julie a security interest in the boat on June 1. On June 2, John surrendered possession of the boat to Julie, and Julie gave John $10,000. Attachment occurred on June 2 because on that date John had rights in the collateral, Julie had given value, and Julie was in possession of the collateral. Perfection occurred simultaneously with attachment because Julie had possession of the boat when attachment occurred.

1) Generally, the security interest becomes unperfected when possession ceases unless the secured party files a financing statement while in possession of the collateral.

4. **Perfection by Control**

a. Control perfects a security interest in, among other things, investment property, electronic chattel paper, and deposit accounts. Perfection ends when the secured party no longer has control.

1) For example, a secured party has control over a deposit account (e.g., a savings or checking account) if the secured party is the bank in which the account is maintained.

5. **Automatic Perfection**

   a. In some cases, perfection is automatic upon attachment.

   b. A **PMSI in consumer goods** ordinarily is automatically perfected without filing or possession.

      1) A PMSI generally results when a lender or a seller provides the purchase price of goods to the debtor and takes a security interest in the collateral purchased.

EXAMPLES

Fast Finance Co. lent Lori $1,000 to purchase a couch for use in her home and took a security interest in the couch. Lori used the $1,000 to purchase a couch. Fast's security interest is a purchase money security interest and is perfected without filing a financing statement or taking possession of the couch.

Fast Finance Co. lent Factory, Inc., $1,000 to purchase a forklift and took a security interest in the forklift. Factory purchased a forklift with the $1,000. Fast's purchase money security interest is not automatically perfected because the forklift is equipment, not consumer goods.

   c. With respect to security interests in **instruments, certificated securities, or negotiable documents**,

      1) Perfection is automatic for the 20-day period after attachment to the extent that new value is given to obtain the security interest under an authenticated security agreement.
      2) The security interest becomes unperfected at the end of 20 days unless the secured party perfects by other means.

6. **Goods in Possession of a Bailee**

   a. A **bailment** results when a person (bailor) transfers possession (not title) of personal property to a second person (bailee). At the end of the bailment, the bailee must return or otherwise account for the property.

EXAMPLE

In a field warehousing arrangement, the secured party hires a field warehouser to take possession of the inventory on the debtor's property. The field warehouser rents space from the debtor. The inventory is released to the debtor as needed for sale.

   b. If the bailee has issued a **negotiable document** covering the goods, a security interest in the goods is perfected by perfecting a security interest in the document.

      1) Any other security interest in the goods is subordinate to that interest while the bailee holds the goods.

   c. If the bailee has issued a **nonnegotiable document**, a security interest in the goods is perfected by

      1) Issuance of a document in the secured party's name,
      2) Notice to the bailee of the secured party's interest, or
      3) Filing.

7. **Temporary Release of Collateral**

   a. In some cases, a secured party may relinquish possession to the debtor for 20 days without filing while retaining a perfected security interest.

   b. The purpose of the release in the case of (1) goods held by a bailee that has not issued a negotiable document or (2) a negotiable document must be for (a) the sale or exchange of the goods or (b) activities preliminary to sale or exchange.

   c. The purpose of the release in the case of (1) an instrument or (2) a certificated security must be for the sale, exchange, or collection; registration of transfer; etc.

Perfection of a Security Interest

	Collateral									
Means of Perfection	Consumer Goods	Other Goods	Instruments	Negotiable Documents	Goods Covered by Non-negotiable Documents	Investment Property	Tangible Chattel Paper	Electronic Chattel Paper	Deposit Accounts	Money
Filing	✓	✓	✓	✓	✓ [3]	✓	✓	✓		
Possession	✓	✓	✓	✓			✓			✓
Control						✓		✓	✓	
Automatic	✓ (PMSI)		✓ (20 days) [2]	✓ (20 days) [2]		✓ (20 days) [2] (certificated)				
Temporary release of collateral (20 days)		✓ [1]	✓	✓		✓ (certificated)				

[1] Goods held by a bailee (no negotiable document).

[2] Resulting from new value given.

[3] Item 6.c. on the previous page explains the means of perfection.

8. **Proceeds**

   a. A security interest generally continues in collateral after its sale or other disposition. Moreover, a security interest attaches to **identifiable** proceeds.

      1) This interest is perfected if the security interest in the collateral was perfected.

      2) A perfected security interest in proceeds becomes unperfected on the 21st day after attachment. Nevertheless, perfection continues if the proceeds are identifiable amounts of cash or in certain other cases.

   b. Proceeds are paid in the following order:

      1) Reasonable expenses incurred by the sale

      2) Certain buyers of goods

         a) Buyer in the ordinary course of business

         b) Buyer of consumer goods from a consumer under certain circumstances

      3) Balance of debt owed to primary secured creditor

      4) The debt owed any creditor with a subordinate security interest in the collateral

   c. Once all interests have been paid, the debtor receives any surplus.

Stop and review! You have completed the outline for this subunit. Study multiple-choice questions 24 through 26 beginning on page 705.

18.9 PRIORITIES

Questions about the priority of security interests may be complicated due to the number of parties involved, differing dates when the interests were perfected, and variation in the methods of perfection. The AICPA has selected questions that have tested candidates' knowledge of these nuances.

Hierarchy of Rights or Priorities among Conflicting Interests in Collateral
(Priority, in descending order)

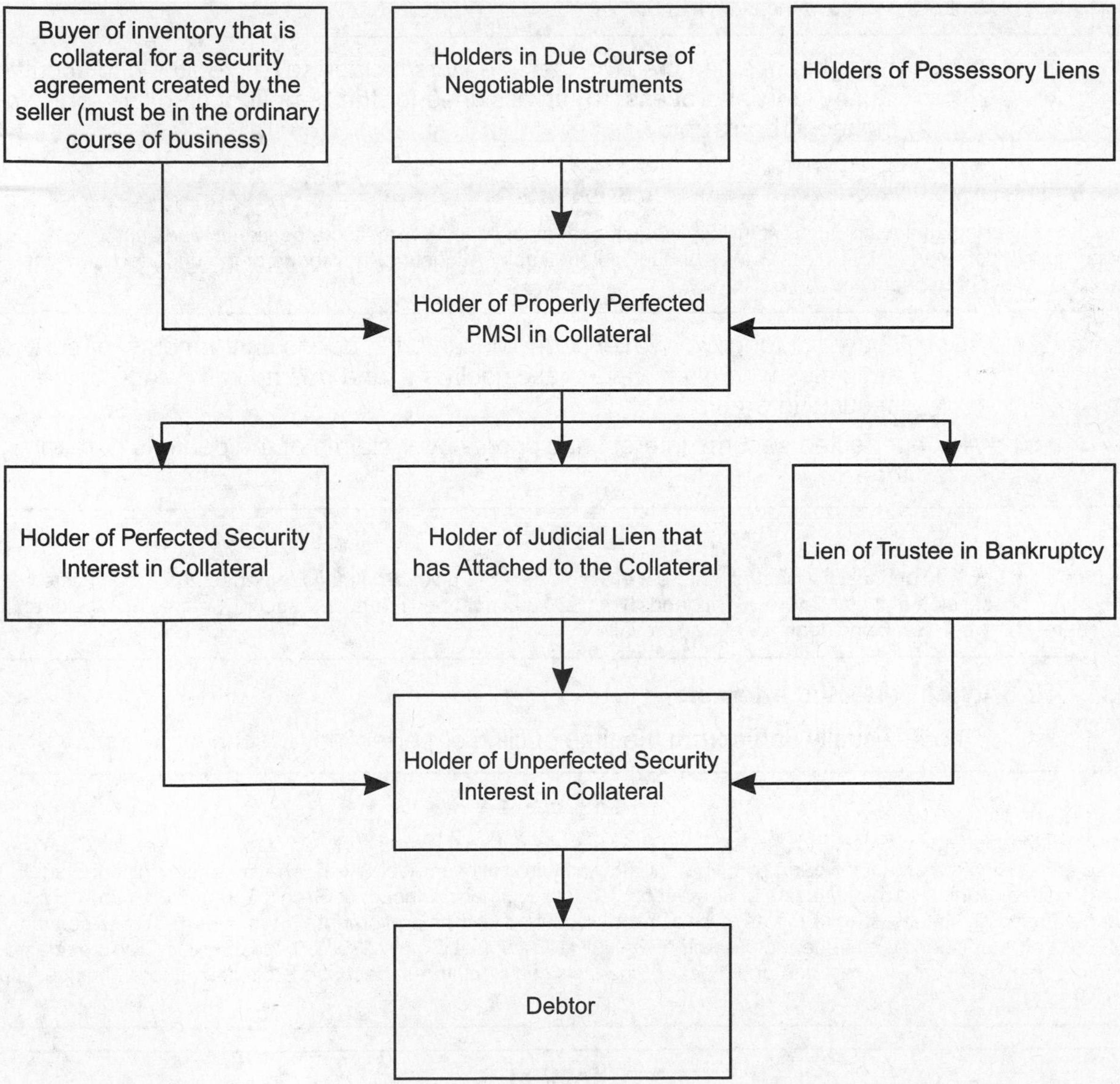

Buyer of inventory that is collateral for a security agreement created by the seller (must be in the ordinary course of business)

Holders in Due Course of Negotiable Instruments

Holders of Possessory Liens

Holder of Properly Perfected PMSI in Collateral

Holder of Perfected Security Interest in Collateral

Holder of Judicial Lien that has Attached to the Collateral

Lien of Trustee in Bankruptcy

Holder of Unperfected Security Interest in Collateral

Debtor

Figure 18-8

1. **Overview**
   a. The protection provided by a security interest varies with its priority.
   b. One general rule is that, if unperfected security interests conflict, the first to attach or become effective has priority.
   c. A second general rule is that, if continuously perfected security interests conflict, priority depends upon the order of filing or perfection with respect to the collateral.

2. **Priority of Unperfected Interests**

   a. An unperfected security interest is subordinate to, among others, the following:

      1) A perfected security interest in the same collateral.

EXAMPLE

On June 1, Bank lent Tom $20,000 and took a security interest in Tom's equipment. Bank did not file a financing statement or take possession of the equipment. On July 15, Finance Co. lent Tom $30,000 and took a security interest in the same equipment. Finance Co. properly filed a financing statement. On August 1, Tom filed for bankruptcy. Finance Co.'s security interest is perfected and has priority over Bank's unperfected security interest and over claims of Tom's other unsecured creditors (to the extent of the value of the equipment).

      2) The rights of a lien creditor. Lien creditors include (a) a creditor who acquires a lien by judicial process, (b) an assignee for the benefit of creditors, or (c) a trustee in bankruptcy.

EXAMPLE

Bank has an unperfected security interest in Tom's equipment as of June 1. Tom files a petition in bankruptcy on August 1. The bankruptcy trustee has priority over Bank's security interest as of August 1. Knowledge of the unperfected claim by the trustee is not relevant to priority.

      3) A buyer of tangible chattel paper, documents, goods, instruments, or certificated securities who gives value, takes delivery, and has no knowledge of the security interest.

   b. An unperfected security interest has priority over claims of the debtor's general creditors.

EXAMPLE

Bank lends Tom $15,000 and takes a security interest in Tom's fleet of trucks. Bank fails to perfect the security interest by filing or taking possession of the collateral. John lends Tom $20,000 but does not take a security interest in collateral. In a priority contest between Bank and John, Bank will prevail.

3. **Priority of Perfected Interests**

   a. Priority usually dates from the time of filing or perfection, whichever is first.

EXAMPLE

Bank agreed to lend Gran's Place, Inc., up to $50,000 as needed during the next year. On January 2, Year 1, Gran's executed a financing statement covering all owned or after-acquired kitchen equipment. The statement included a future advances clause. Bank filed the financing statement on January 3. Finance, Inc., lent Gran's $10,000 on March 1. Gran's executed a financing statement covering all owned or after-acquired kitchen equipment. Finance perfected its security interest by filing the financing statement on March 9. On July 1, Bank lent Gran's $30,000. On July 31, Gran's declared bankruptcy. Bank's security interest has priority over Finance's security interest because Bank filed before Finance filed or perfected.

EXAMPLE

If Bank's financing statement had been filed on July 1, Finance's security interest would have priority over Bank's security interest. Finance's priority would date from March 9 and Bank's from July 1.

   b. Without filing or perfection in a subsequent period, priority no longer dates from the time of filing or perfection. Thus, the filing or perfection must be continuous.

EXAMPLE

In the first example under 3. above, assuming no bankruptcy, Bank's filed financing statement will lapse on January 3, Year 6. On January 4, Year 6, assuming no filing of a continuation statement, Finance has a perfected security interest and Bank has an unperfected security interest.

c. If the security agreement contains a future advances clause, the perfected security interest ordinarily has the same priority for future advances as for the first advance.

4. **Buyers of Goods**

a. Generally, a perfected security interest in goods is effective against subsequent purchasers. However, certain third parties may acquire the collateral (goods) free of the security interest, even though the interest has been perfected.

1) A buyer in the **ordinary course of business** is not subject to any security interest given by his or her seller to another. The buyer's knowledge of the security interest is irrelevant unless (s)he knows that the purchase violates that interest.

EXAMPLE

Family Grocery purchased frozen yogurt from Wholesaler. Wholesaler had given a security interest in its inventory to Freezers, Inc. Freezers had properly perfected the security interest. The president of Wholesaler disclosed the security interest to Family's president before selling the yogurt. If Wholesaler defaults on its obligation to Freezers, Freezers cannot exercise its rights as a secured party against Family.

2) A buyer of **consumer goods from a consumer** is not subject to a security interest if (s)he buys (a) without knowledge of the security interest, (b) for value, (c) for consumer purposes, and (d) before the secured party files.

EXAMPLE

Sam bought a dining table from Tables, Inc., on credit. Tables took a purchase money security interest in the dining table. Several months later, Sam paid 50% of the purchase price to Tables. Sam then sold the table to Don. Don, unaware of Tables' security interest, paid $200 for the table and placed it in his dining room. Tables' security interest is unenforceable against Don. However, if Tables had filed a financing statement before Don purchased the table, Tables' security interest would be enforceable against Don.

5. **PMSIs**

a. A PMSI in **consumer goods** is automatically perfected.

b. A secured party with a PMSI who files before or within 20 days after the debtor receives delivery of the collateral ordinarily has priority over the rights of a buyer, lessee, or lien creditor that arose after the PMSI attached.

c. A perfected PMSI in goods (other than inventory) has priority over a conflicting security interest in the goods if the PMSI is perfected within 20 days after the debtor takes possession. This priority is recognized even if the conflicting interest was perfected first. Moreover, it ordinarily extends to a perfected security interest in the identifiable proceeds of goods.

EXAMPLE

On January 2, Bank lent Luke $50,000 and took a security interest in Luke's currently owned and after-acquired equipment. On June 2, Equip Corp. sold Luke equipment on credit and took a PMSI in the equipment. On June 19, Equip perfected the PMSI. Equip has priority over Bank.

d. A perfected PMSI in **inventory** has priority over a conflicting security interest if (1) the PMSI is perfected when the debtor takes possession, (2) an authenticated notice is sent to the other secured party, (3) the notice is received within 5 years before the debtor takes possession, and (4) the notice describes the collateral and states that the sender has or expects to have a PMSI in the debtor's inventory.

EXAMPLE

Bank is secured by Gavin's inventory. The security agreement contains an after-acquired property clause. Bank's security interest was perfected by filing. Subsequently, Expansion, Inc., began supplying Gavin with a new line of inventory. Expansion sold the inventory to Gavin on credit and retained a PMSI. Expansion filed a financing statement covering the collateral on June 1. Gavin took possession of the new products on June 23. On July 1, Expansion disclosed the PMSI in a letter to Bank. Expansion will not have priority over Bank with respect to the security interest in the new inventory in Gavin's possession because notice was given to Bank after Gavin took possession. If Expansion had notified Bank of the PMSI prior to June 23, however, Expansion's claim to the new inventory would have had priority over Bank's.

1) The notice requirement applies only if (a) the PMSI is perfected and (b) the other secured party filed prior to perfection of the PMSI.
2) A perfected PMSI in inventory extends to identifiable cash proceeds received no later than the time of delivery to a buyer.

EXAMPLE

Bank has a perfected PMSI in Mandy's car inventory. Sam buys a car from Mandy and pays with a check. Bank's perfected PMSI floats to the check as identifiable cash proceeds.

3) When perfected PMSIs in goods conflict, the PMSI securing all or part of the price of the collateral has priority over a PMSI securing an obligation incurred to obtain rights in the collateral.

6. **Liens Arising by Operation of Law**
   a. The holder of the lien typically has provided services or materials with respect to the goods in the ordinary course of business and has possession of the goods.
      1) With possession, the lien has priority over a perfected security interest.
      2) Without possession, the lien is subordinate to a perfected security interest.
      3) Knowledge of a security interest by a lienholder has no effect on priority.

EXAMPLE

Wendy borrows $5,000 from Bank to purchase a car and conveys a security interest in the car to Bank. Bank perfects the security interest. A week later she takes the car to Best Body Shop for a new paint job. Best Body Shop knew of Bank's security interest. When Best Body finishes the job, Wendy has insufficient money to pay. Best retains possession of the car. Wendy defaults on payment to the bank. Bank sues Best, demanding delivery of the car. Best alleges its lien, based upon common law, has priority over Bank's perfected security interest. Best's lien is not granted by statute. The court holds that Best's lien has priority. Best's awareness of Bank's interest is irrelevant.

Stop and review! You have completed the outline for this subunit. Study multiple-choice questions 27 and 28 beginning on page 706.

18.10 RIGHTS AND DUTIES OF DEBTORS, CREDITORS, AND THIRD PARTIES

1. **Possession or Control of Collateral**
   a. The secured party in possession of collateral is a bailee. (S)he must use reasonable care at all times to preserve the collateral, for example, in the case of instruments or chattel paper, by taking steps to preserve rights against prior parties.
      1) The secured party also must keep the collateral identifiable, although interchangeable collateral, such as grain, may be commingled.
   b. The bailee is strictly liable if it makes unauthorized use of the property or misdelivers it.
   c. If the secured party has possession, the debtor bears the cost of reasonable expenses incurred for preservation, use, or custody of the collateral, e.g., insurance and taxes.
   d. A secured party with possession or control may
      1) Keep any proceeds from the collateral, other than money or funds, as additional security.
      2) Create a security interest in the collateral.

e. A secured party with control of collateral has a duty to surrender control if no secured obligation is outstanding and no further commitment to give value exists. This action must be taken within 10 days after receipt of an authenticated demand by the debtor.

2. **Duty of Confirmation**

a. A secured party generally must comply with the duty of confirming, at the debtor's request, the unpaid amount of the debt. Compliance ordinarily should be within 14 days after receipt.

3. **Default**

a. Default occurs when the debtor fails to fulfill obligations under the security agreement. Typical events constituting default are (1) lack of current payments, (2) removal of or failure to insure the collateral, and (3) bankruptcy or insolvency of the debtor.

b. The secured party has three options if the debtor defaults: (1) Sue the debtor for the amount due, (2) peaceably take possession and dispose of the collateral, or (3) accept (retain) the collateral.

4. **Repossession**

a. Upon the debtor's default, the secured party may resort to self-help repossession or repossession by judicial action.

1) Self-help repossession is taking possession of the collateral without judicial action. It must be peaceable.

2) Repossession by judicial action generally requires obtaining a judicial order or judgment against the debtor.

b. After repossession, the secured party may dispose of the collateral by public or private proceedings.

1) Reasonable authenticated notice of the disposition must be given to the debtor and other appropriate parties.

EXAMPLE

Leo, with a loan from Local Bank, purchases a van and a boat. He signs, with respect to each, a promissory note for half the loan amount and a security agreement. He thereby conveys to Bank a security interest in both the van and the boat, each securing payment when due of half the remaining amount on the loan. Leo defaults on payments to Bank. Bank takes lawful possession of both van and boat. Bank sends proper written notice to Leo that the van will be sold at auction 4 weeks after date of notice. Both boat and van are sold at auction. Bank sues Leo for a deficiency in the net proceeds. With regard to the half of the amount secured by the van, the court awards a judgment for the deficiency. Because no reasonable notice was given of the sale of the boat, Bank is not entitled to a deficiency judgment for the part of the loan it secured.

2) Notice to the debtor is not required if the collateral is of a type normally sold on a recognized market, perishable, or likely to decline quickly in value.

3) All aspects of the disposition must be commercially reasonable, including the time, place, manner, method, and terms.

4) A transferee for value in good faith (a) takes the collateral free of the security interest under which the disposition took place, (b) takes free of security interests in the collateral subordinate to that interest, and (c) receives all the debtor's rights in the collateral.

5) The secured party may buy the collateral at any public disposition. If the collateral is of a type customarily sold in a recognized market or is the subject of widely distributed price quotations, the secured party may buy it at private disposition.

6) The proceeds of collection or enforcement are applied in the following order:

a) Payment of reasonable expenses of collection or enforcement

b) Satisfaction of the debt owed to the secured party under whose security interest the collection or enforcement is made

c) Satisfaction of the debts owed to subordinate secured parties

d) Payment of any surplus to the debtor

7) If the disposition is commercially reasonable but the proceeds are insufficient, the obligor is liable for any deficiency.

8) The underlying transaction may be a sale of accounts, chattel paper, promissory notes, and certain other items. In these cases, the debtor has no right to a surplus or an obligation for a deficiency.

5. **Acceptance of the Collateral**

a. Acceptance of the collateral (strict foreclosure) may be an alternative to disposition.

b. The secured party keeps the collateral in satisfaction of the debt.

c. The secured party must send an authenticated notice to other claimants.

d. The debtor must consent to the acceptance.

e. Acceptance of collateral in partial satisfaction of the obligation is not allowed if the collateral is consumer goods.

f. Disposition is required if the amount paid is at least (1) 60% of the cash price in the case of a PMSI in consumer goods or (2) 60% of the principal amount of the secured obligation in the case of a non-PMSI in consumer goods.

1) The secured party must dispose of collateral within 90 days of taking possession of it. But the debtor and all secondary obligors may agree to a longer period in an authenticated agreement.

g. Acceptance of collateral is not allowed and the collateral must be disposed of if the debtor or any party to whom notice is required to be sent objects.

6. **The Debtor's Remedies**

a. The debtor may redeem his or her interest in the collateral at any time before

1) The debt is satisfied by acceptance of the collateral,
2) The collateral has been collected,
3) The collateral is disposed of, or
4) A contract for the disposition of the collateral is entered into.

b. Failure by the secured party to comply with Article 9 provides the debtor with a right to damages for the resulting losses.

1) In the case of consumer goods, the debtor may recover an amount not less than the greater of

a) The credit service charge plus 10% of the principal of the debt or
b) The time-price differential plus 10% of the cash price.

EXAMPLE

The cash price of a chain saw is $800. If the chain saw is financed for 36 months, the payments total $1,200. The time-price differential is $400 ($1,200 – $800). Under 6.b.1)b), the debtor could recover an amount not less than $400 plus 10% of $800, for a total of $480. Under 6.b.1)a), the recovery would be an amount not less than $80 plus any credit service charges.

2) If a deficiency or surplus is put in issue in a legal proceeding and the secured party's compliance with provisions for collection, enforcement, disposition, or acceptance also is put in issue, the liability of a debtor or secondary obligor may be limited or eliminated.

a) For example, this result may follow because the proceeds of a disposition were significantly less than the proceeds of a complying disposition.

Stop and review! You have completed the outline for this subunit. Study multiple-choice questions 29 and 30 on page 707.

QUESTIONS

18.1 Formation of a Contract

1. Which of the following factors help determine whether an item of personal property has become a fixture?

	Manner of Affixation	Value of the Item	Intent of the Annexor
A.	Yes	Yes	Yes
B.	Yes	Yes	No
C.	Yes	No	Yes
D.	No	Yes	Yes

Answer (C) is correct.

REQUIRED: The factor(s) considered when determining whether personal property has become a fixture.

DISCUSSION: An item of personal property becomes a fixture if it is so closely connected to real property that it becomes part of the real property. Whether an item of personal property becomes a fixture is dependent upon the intention of the annexor. To determine the objective intent of the annexor, it is necessary to consider the manner in which the item is affixed to the real property.

2. With regard to a contract governed by Article 2 of the UCC, which one of the following statements is true?

A. Merchants and nonmerchants are treated alike.

B. The contract may involve the sale of any type of personal property.

C. The obligations of the parties to the contract must be performed in good faith.

D. The contract must involve the sale of goods for a price of $500 or more.

Answer (C) is correct.

REQUIRED: The true statement about contracts governed by UCC Article 2.

DISCUSSION: Good faith means honesty in fact. UCC 1-203 states, "Every contract or duty within this act imposes an obligation of good faith in its performance or enforcement."

Answer (A) is incorrect. Article 2 applies to both merchants and nonmerchants, but special rules are provided for certain aspects of transactions between or with merchants. Answer (B) is incorrect. Article 2 applies to sales of goods. Goods do not include such items of personal property as accounts, documents of title, instruments, money, investment securities, copyrights, and patents. Answer (D) is incorrect. No dollar amount is required to bring a sale of goods within Article 2.

3. On October 1, Baker, a wholesaler, sent Clark, a retailer, a written, signed offer to sell 200 pinking shears at $9 each. The terms were FOB Baker's warehouse, net 30, late payment subject to a 15% per annum interest charge. The offer indicated that it must be accepted no later than October 10, that acceptance would be effective upon receipt, and that the terms were not to be varied by the offeree. Clark sent a telegram, which arrived on October 6, and accepted the offer expressly subject to a change of the payment terms to 2/10, net/30. Baker phoned Clark on October 7 to reject the change of payment terms. On the phone, Clark then indicated it would accept the October 1 offer in all respects and expected delivery within 10 days. Baker did not accept Clark's oral acceptance of the original offer. Which of the following is true?

A. Baker's original offer is a firm offer, hence irrevocable.

B. There is no contract. Clark's modifications effectively rejected the October 1 offer, and Baker never accepted either of Clark's proposals.

C. Clark actually created a contract on October 6. The modifications were merely proposals and did not preclude acceptance.

D. The statute of frauds would preclude the formation of a contract in any event.

Answer (B) is correct.

REQUIRED: The true statement about the effect of conditioning an acceptance upon assent to a different term.

DISCUSSION: Because the purported acceptance by telegram was expressly conditional upon assent to the different payment terms, it was not effective as an acceptance. It operated as a rejection of the offer and a counteroffer. The effect of the counteroffer was to terminate the original offer. Thus, Clark's subsequent unconditional acceptance on October 7 of the original offer was ineffective. The rejection and counteroffer had previously been communicated to the offeror.

Answer (A) is incorrect. Even though it was made by a merchant in writing, the offer did not state that it was irrevocable. Answer (C) is incorrect. An additional or different term is usually deemed a proposal for addition to the contract, but between merchants it becomes an addition to the contract unless the offer expressly limits acceptance to its terms, the additional term materially alters the offer, or notice of objection has already been given or is given within a reasonable time. Clark's payment term failed all three tests. Moreover, the expression of acceptance was conditional and thus not effective as an acceptance. Answer (D) is incorrect. Baker's offer was written and signed. An effective oral acceptance by Clark would have permitted enforcement against Baker.

4. Under the UCC Sales Article, which of the following conditions most likely will prevent the formation of an enforceable sale of goods contract?

A. Open price.

B. Open delivery.

C. Open quantity.

D. Open acceptance.

Answer (D) is correct.

REQUIRED: The condition that will prevent the formation of an enforceable sale of goods contract.

DISCUSSION: The UCC favors open terms. One or more terms left open does not prevent the formation of a contract if (1) it appears the parties intended to make a contract and (2) there is a reasonably certain basis for granting a remedy. An offer is deemed to invite acceptance in any manner and by any medium reasonable under the circumstances. However, the term "open acceptance" is not used by the UCC Sales Article. Also, prior to acceptance, no contract can be formed.

Answer (A) is incorrect. An open price term does not prevent formation of a contract. The price is deemed to be a reasonable one (usually the market price). Answer (B) is incorrect. An open delivery term does not prevent formation of a contract. The delivery point is normally deemed to be the seller's place of business. Answer (C) is incorrect. If the quantity term is left open, a court may have no basis to grant a remedy. Thus, a contract may not have been formed. However, circumstances may remedy this defect. For example, a requirement or output term in a contract may provide a reasonably certain basis for a remedy.

5. Mayker, Inc., and Oylco contracted for Oylco to be the exclusive provider of Mayker's fuel oil for 3 months. The stated price was subject to increases of up to a total of 10% if the market price increased. The market price rose 25%, and Mayker tripled its normal order. Oylco seeks to avoid performance. Oylco's best argument in support of its position is that

A. There was no meeting of the minds.

B. The contract was unconscionable.

C. The quantity was not definite and certain enough.

D. Mayker ordered amounts of oil unreasonably greater than its normal requirements.

Answer (D) is correct.

REQUIRED: The best argument for avoiding performance on a requirements contract.

DISCUSSION: Requirements and output contracts are often unenforceable under common law because they are too indefinite. They are permitted, provided the parties act in good faith and demand or tender reasonable quantities. Absent stated estimates, normal or otherwise comparable prior requirements or output will provide the standard of reasonableness. No estimates were made. Thus, if Mayker's requirements are excessive, it will have violated its duties, and Oylco may be able to avoid performance.

Answer (A) is incorrect. Under the UCC, an agreement that one party will supply the other's requirements for a specified period within a given price range suggests a meeting of the minds (formation of a contract). Hence, Oylco's best argument is breach, not failure to reach an agreement. Answer (B) is incorrect. The difference between 10% and 25% above contract price is not so oppressive and unfair as to render the contract unconscionable. Answer (C) is incorrect. The contract does not fail for indefiniteness if the parties act in good faith and demand or tender reasonable quantities.

18.2 Performance

6. Smith contracted in writing to sell Peters a used personal computer for $600. The contract did not specifically address the time for payment, place of delivery, or Peters's right to inspect the computer. Which of the following statements is true?

A. Smith is obligated to deliver the computer to Peters's home.

B. Peters is entitled to inspect the computer before paying for it.

C. Peters may not pay for the computer using a personal check unless Smith agrees.

D. Smith is not entitled to payment until 30 days after Peters receives the computer.

Answer (B) is correct.

REQUIRED: The true statement about a contract with terms left open.

DISCUSSION: A contract for the sale of goods is enforceable if missing terms can be supplied. The buyer has a right to inspect the goods before payment unless contract terms waive the right, e.g., when delivery is COD or payment is against documents of title (a documentary sale).

Answer (A) is incorrect. Unless otherwise agreed, tender is generally due at the seller's place of business. Answer (C) is incorrect. Tender of payment by check is sufficient unless the seller demands legal tender (currency) and gives the buyer a reasonable amount of time to obtain it. Answer (D) is incorrect. Unless otherwise agreed, the price is due upon tender of delivery.

7. Rowe Corp. purchased goods from Stair Co. that were shipped COD. Under the Sales Article of the UCC, which of the following rights does Rowe have?

A. The right to inspect the goods before paying.

B. The right to possession of the goods before paying.

C. The right to reject nonconforming goods.

D. The right to delay payment for a reasonable period of time.

Answer (C) is correct.

REQUIRED: The right of a buyer of goods shipped COD.

DISCUSSION: The seller has an obligation to deliver goods that conform to the contract. The perfect tender rule allows the buyer an absolute right to reject nonconforming goods. When goods are shipped COD, payment is not considered to be an acceptance.

Answer (A) is incorrect. When goods are shipped COD, the buyer does not have the right to inspect the goods before payment. Answer (B) is incorrect. When goods are shipped COD, the buyer does not have the right to take possession before payment. Answer (D) is incorrect. When goods are shipped COD, the buyer does not have the right to tender payment at a later time.

18.3 Title and Risk of Loss

8. Under the Sales Article of the UCC, which of the following factors is most important in determining who bears the risk of loss in a sale of goods contract?

A. The method of shipping the goods.

B. The contract's shipping terms.

C. Title to the goods.

D. The manner in which the goods were lost.

Answer (B) is correct.

REQUIRED: The most important factor in determining who has the risk of loss.

DISCUSSION: The agreement as to risk of loss may be express. It also may be implicit from trade usage, course of dealing, or course of performance. If the parties do not have an agreement about risk of loss but a carrier is involved, the shipping terms control. In a destination contract, risk of loss passes to the buyer when the goods have reached the destination and are tendered to the buyer. In a shipment contract, risk of loss passes to the buyer when the seller delivers the goods to the carrier.

Answer (A) is incorrect. The type of carrier is irrelevant. Answer (C) is incorrect. The UCC never assigns risk of loss based on the location of the title. Answer (D) is incorrect. The manner in which the goods were lost by the carrier is irrelevant.

9. On Monday, Wolfe paid Aston Co., a furniture retailer, $500 for a table. On Thursday, Aston notified Wolfe that the table was ready to be picked up. On Saturday, while Aston was still in possession of the table, it was destroyed in a fire. Who bears the loss of the table?

A. Wolfe, because Wolfe had title to the table at the time of loss.

B. Aston, unless Wolfe is a merchant.

C. Wolfe, unless Aston breached the contract.

D. Aston, because Wolfe had not yet taken possession of the table.

Answer (D) is correct.

REQUIRED: The true statement about risk of loss given that the seller was a merchant.

DISCUSSION: If (1) the parties have no agreement as to risk of loss, (2) no carrier is involved, and (3) the goods are not in the possession of a bailee, the risk of loss passes to the buyer on his or her receipt of the goods if the seller is a merchant. Otherwise, the risk passes to the buyer on tender of delivery (UCC 2-509). Because Aston is a merchant (a person engaged in selling goods of the kind), risk did not pass to Wolfe on tender of delivery.

Answer (A) is incorrect. The UCC never assigns risk of loss to goods on the basis of title. Answer (B) is incorrect. The seller's, not the buyer's, status is relevant. Answer (C) is incorrect. Risk of loss would not have passed prior to receipt by Wolfe.

10. Under the Sales Article of the UCC, when a contract for the sale of goods stipulates that the seller ship the goods by common carrier, "FOB purchaser's loading dock," which of the parties bears the risk of loss during shipment?

A. The purchaser, because risk of loss passes when the goods are delivered to the carrier.

B. The purchaser, because title to the goods passes at the time of shipment.

C. The seller, because risk of loss passes only when the goods reach the purchaser's loading dock.

D. The seller, because risk of loss remains with the seller until the goods are accepted by the purchaser.

Answer (C) is correct.

REQUIRED: The party that bears the risk of loss during shipment of goods FOB purchaser's loading dock.

DISCUSSION: The parties to a contract for the sale of goods may agree who will have the risk of loss. In the absence of an express agreement, the intent with respect to risk is determined by shipping and delivery terms. The shipping term FOB purchaser's place of business indicates a destination contract. The seller bears the risk of loss until the goods reach the buyer's loading dock.

Answer (A) is incorrect. The shipping term FOB purchaser's loading dock is a destination contract. It requires the seller to bear the risk of loss until the goods are tendered at destination. Answer (B) is incorrect. When title passes does not determine who has risk of loss during transit. Answer (D) is incorrect. The tender (not acceptance) of delivery of conforming goods passes risk from the seller to the buyer in a destination contract.

11. Under the Sales Article of the UCC, unless a contract provides otherwise, before title to goods can pass from a seller to a buyer, the goods must be

A. Tendered to the buyer.

B. Identified to the contract.

C. Accepted by the buyer.

D. Paid for.

Answer (B) is correct.

REQUIRED: The prerequisite for passage of title to goods.

DISCUSSION: In every contract for the sale of goods, a seller has a duty to pass title to the buyer in exchange for the price. An express or explicit understanding between the buyer and the seller will determine when title passes. Before title can pass, two conditions must be satisfied: (1) The goods must be in existence, and (2) they must be identified to the contract. Identification is the method for designating the specific goods as the subject matter of the sales contract. It marks the time at which the buyer obtains an insurable interest. A contract to sell goods not existing and identified is subject to Article 2 as a contract to sell future goods.

12. On May 2, Lace Corp., an appliance wholesaler, offered to sell appliances worth $3,000 to Parco, Inc., a household appliances retailer. The offer was signed by Lace's president and provided that it would not be withdrawn before June 1. It also included the shipping terms: "FOB -- Parco's warehouse." Parco accepted Lace's offer. If Lace inadvertently ships the wrong appliances to Parco and Parco rejects them 2 days after receipt, title to the goods will

A. Pass to Parco when they are identified to the contract.

B. Pass to Parco when they are shipped.

C. Remain with Parco until the goods are returned to Lace.

D. Revest to Lace when they are rejected by Parco.

Answer (D) is correct.

REQUIRED: The true statement about passage of title when a seller ships nonconforming goods.

DISCUSSION: Title revests in the seller after (1) a rejection or other refusal by the buyer to receive or retain the goods, whether or not justified, or (2) a justified revocation of acceptance. Such revesting occurs by operation of law.

Answer (A) is incorrect. If the goods are to be moved, title generally passes when the seller completes its delivery obligation. Identification designates the goods. Answer (B) is incorrect. Title revested to Lace. Answer (C) is incorrect. Title did pass, but it revested to the seller upon rejection.

18.4 Warranties

13. Under the Sales Article of the UCC, most goods sold by merchants are covered by certain warranties. An example of an express warranty is a warranty of

A. Usage of trade.

B. Fitness for a particular purpose.

C. Merchantability.

D. Conformity of goods to the sample.

Answer (D) is correct.

REQUIRED: The example of an express warranty by a merchant in a sale of goods transaction.

DISCUSSION: Any statement of fact or promise made by a seller to the buyer that (1) relates to the goods and (2) becomes part of the basis of the bargain creates an express warranty that the goods will conform to the statement or promise. Express warranties also may be created by description, model, or sample. A sample that is made part of the basis of the bargain creates an express warranty that the goods will conform to the sample.

14. Thorn purchased a used entertainment system from Sound Corp. The sales contract stated that the entertainment system was being sold "as is." Under the Sales Article of the UCC, which of the following statements is(are) correct regarding the seller's warranty of title and against infringement?

I. Including the term "as is" in the sales contract is adequate communication that the seller is conveying the entertainment system without warranty of title and against infringement.

II. The seller's warranty of title and against infringement may be disclaimed at any time after the contract is formed.

A. I only.

B. II only.

C. Both I and II.

D. Neither I nor II.

Answer (D) is correct.

REQUIRED: The true statement(s), if any, about the warranty of title and against infringement.

DISCUSSION: Unless agreed otherwise, all sellers warrant that (1) the title is good, (2) its transfer is rightful, and (3) the goods are free of liens and other encumbrances not known by the buyer. The warranty of title may be disclaimed only by specific language or by the buyer's knowledge of circumstances relating to title. A general disclaimer (e.g., "as is") is ineffective. It may be disclaimed by any seller orally or in writing, but this must be done before the contract is formed.

Answer (A) is incorrect. Including the term "as is" in the sales contract is ineffective communication to disclaim the warranty of title and against infringement. Answer (B) is incorrect. The seller's warranty of title and against infringement must be disclaimed before the contract is formed. Answer (C) is incorrect. Including the term "as is" in the sales contract is ineffective communication to disclaim the warranty of title and against infringement, and the seller's warranty of title and against infringement must be disclaimed before the contract is formed.

15. Which of the following conditions must be met for an implied warranty of fitness for a particular purpose to arise in connection with a sale of goods?

I. The warranty must be in writing.

II. The seller must know that the buyer was relying on the seller in selecting the goods.

A. I only.

B. II only.

C. Both I and II.

D. Neither I nor II.

Answer (B) is correct.

REQUIRED: The requirement for a warranty of fitness to be implied.

DISCUSSION: A warranty of fitness for a particular purpose is implied (unless excluded or modified) when the seller has reason to know (1) the particular purpose for which the goods will be used and (2) that the buyer is relying on the seller's skill or judgment to choose the goods (UCC 2-315).

18.5 Products Liability

16. To establish a cause of action based on strict liability in tort for personal injuries that result from the use of a defective product, one of the elements the injured party must prove is that the seller

A. Was aware of the defect in the product.

B. Sold the product to the injured party.

C. Failed to exercise due care.

D. Sold the product in a defective condition.

Answer (D) is correct.

REQUIRED: The element of an action based on strict liability in tort.

DISCUSSION: In a strict liability suit against a seller of a product, a plaintiff who has suffered physical harm or property damage must prove (1) the product was defective, (2) the defect rendered it unreasonably dangerous, (3) the dangerous condition caused the harm, (4) the seller was engaged in the business of selling the product, and (5) the product reached the user without substantial change from the condition in which it was sold.

Answer (A) is incorrect. The seller need not have been aware of the defect. Answer (B) is incorrect. The seller need not have sold the product to the injured party (privity is not required). Answer (C) is incorrect. The seller need not have been negligent, i.e., failed to exercise due care.

17. Larch Corp. manufactured and sold Oak a stove. The sale documents included a disclaimer of warranty for personal injury. The stove was defective. It exploded, causing serious injuries to Oak's spouse. Larch was notified 1 week after the explosion. Under the UCC Sales Article, which of the following statements concerning Larch's liability for personal injury to Oak's spouse is true?

A. Larch cannot be liable because of a lack of privity with Oak's spouse.

B. Larch will not be liable because of a failure to give proper notice.

C. Larch will be liable because the disclaimer was not a disclaimer of all liability.

D. Larch will be liable because liability for personal injury cannot be disclaimed.

Answer (D) is correct.

REQUIRED: The true statement about liability for personal injury under the UCC Sales Article.

DISCUSSION: The warranty provisions were not intended to enlarge or restrict legal remedies for personal injuries. Strict liability for an unreasonably dangerous product may be viewed as the implied warranty of merchantability stripped of the contract defenses of notice of defect, privity, and disclaimer. Thus, strict liability for personal injury caused by a defective product cannot be disclaimed.

Answer (A) is incorrect. The most restrictive option under the UCC allows a member of the purchaser's family to sue for physical injury. Answer (B) is incorrect. Oak gave reasonable notice by informing Larch of the injury within 1 week of its occurrence. Answer (C) is incorrect. Even if a disclaimer of the warranty of merchantability met all technical requirements, disclaimer of liability for personal injury is presumed to be unconscionable. Furthermore, strict liability for personal injury caused by a defective product cannot be disclaimed.

18.6 Remedies

18. Unless the parties have otherwise agreed, an action for the breach of a contract within the UCC Sales Article must be commenced within

A. Four years after the cause of action has accrued.

B. Six years after the cause of action has accrued.

C. Four years after the effective date of the contract.

D. Six years after the effective date of the contract.

Answer (A) is correct.

REQUIRED: The time within which an action for the breach of a contract within the UCC Sales Article must be commenced.

DISCUSSION: Under UCC 2-725, a 4-year statute of limitations applies to cases involving sales of goods. The parties, however, may reduce (but not extend) the period for suit, but not to less than 1 year. The limitations period generally begins to run when the cause of action has accrued.

Answer (B) is incorrect. The applicable period is 4 years. Answer (C) is incorrect. The limitations period begins when the cause of action has accrued (generally when the breach occurs). Answer (D) is incorrect. An action for the breach of a contract must be commenced within 4 years after the cause of action has accrued.

19. Bush Hardware ordered 300 Ram hammers from Ajax Hardware. Ajax accepted the order in writing. On the final date allowed for delivery, Ajax discovered it did not have enough Ram hammers to fill the order. Instead, Ajax sent 300 Strong hammers. Ajax stated on the invoice that the shipment was sent only as an accommodation. Which of the following statements is true?

A. Ajax's note of accommodation cancels the contract between Bush and Ajax.

B. Bush's order can be accepted only by Ajax's shipment of the goods ordered.

C. Ajax's shipment of Strong hammers is a breach of contract.

D. Ajax's shipment of Strong hammers is a counteroffer, and no contract exists between Bush and Ajax.

Answer (C) is correct.

REQUIRED: The true statement about the shipment of goods solely as an accommodation.

DISCUSSION: Shipment of a brand different from that stipulated in the contract was a breach of the contract (UCC 2-601). Bush may (1) accept the goods despite their nonconformity, (2) rightfully reject them, or (3) resort to any of the buyer's other remedies under the UCC. UCC 2-206 and 2-508, allowing accommodation shipments and the ability to cure, respectively, are not applicable. Notice of acceptance was sent, and a cure must be made within the time for performance in most cases.

Answer (A) is incorrect. The breaching party cannot cancel the contract. Only a mutual rescission or the promised performance will discharge the seller's obligation unless the nonconforming goods are accepted. Answer (B) is incorrect. Bush's order constituted an offer to enter into either a bilateral or unilateral contract. It could be accepted either by a prompt promise to ship or by a prompt shipment, respectively. Answer (D) is incorrect. The shipment was not a counteroffer. The acceptance had already created a contract.

20. Cara Fabricating Co. and Taso Corp. agreed orally that Taso would custom manufacture a compressor for Cara at a price of $120,000. After Taso completed the work at a cost of $90,000, Cara notified Taso that the compressor was no longer needed. Taso is holding the compressor and has requested payment from Cara. Taso has been unable to resell the compressor for any price. Taso incurred storage fees of $2,000. If Cara refused to pay Taso and Taso sues Cara, the most Taso will be entitled to recover is

A. $92,000

B. $105,000

C. $120,000

D. $122,000

Answer (D) is correct.

REQUIRED: The seller's recovery after a buyer's refusal to pay for specially made goods.

DISCUSSION: A seller may recover the contract price ($120,000) and any incidental damages ($2,000) if circumstances reasonably indicate that an effort at resale would be unsuccessful (UCC 2-709). Because the machine was made to order and not adaptable to others' use, Taso should be successful in recovering the price. After recovery of the price, seller would be holding the machine for buyer.

21. Under the Sales Article of the UCC, the remedies available to a seller when a buyer breaches a contract for the sale of goods may include

	The Right to Resell Goods Identified to the Contract	The Right to Stop a Carrier from Delivering the Goods
A.	Yes	Yes
B.	Yes	No
C.	No	Yes
D.	No	No

Answer (A) is correct.

REQUIRED: The remedies available to a seller when a buyer breaches a contract for the sale of goods.

DISCUSSION: A buyer may breach or repudiate a sales contract while the seller is still in possession of the goods. The seller then can identify to the contract the conforming goods that are still in his or her possession or control. The seller can do so even if the goods were not identified at the time of the breach (UCC 2-704). The seller can resell the goods, holding the buyer liable for any loss. The seller also may recover goods in transit. The seller may stop delivery of goods in the possession of a carrier or other bailee if a buyer breaches or repudiates a sales contract (UCC 2-705). The right to stop delivery can be exercised only for a truckload, planeload, carload, or larger freight shipment unless the buyer is insolvent.

18.7 Attachment of Security Interests

22. Under the UCC Secured Transactions Article, which of the following after-acquired property may be covered by a debtor's security agreement with a secured lender?

	Inventory	Equipment
A.	Yes	Yes
B.	Yes	No
C.	No	Yes
D.	No	No

Answer (A) is correct.

REQUIRED: The scope of an after-acquired property clause.

DISCUSSION: A security agreement may provide for a security interest in after-acquired property. The security interest does not attach to consumer goods, unless the debtor acquires rights in them within 10 days after the secured party gives value. The security interest in after-acquired property also does not attach to a commercial tort claim. An after-acquired property clause can apply to both inventory and equipment.

23. Under the Secured Transactions Article of the UCC, which of the following requirements is necessary to have a security interest attach?

	Debtor Has Rights in the Collateral	Proper Filing of a Security Agreement	Value Given by the Creditor
A.	Yes	Yes	Yes
B.	Yes	Yes	No
C.	Yes	No	Yes
D.	No	Yes	Yes

Answer (C) is correct.

REQUIRED: The conditions for attachment.

DISCUSSION: Attachment occurs when the security interest is enforceable against the debtor with regard to the collateral, barring an express agreement postponing attachment. The security interest is enforceable against the debtor and third parties when (1) value has been given by the secured party, (2) the debtor has rights in the collateral or can transfer them to the secured party, and (3) the debtor has authenticated a security agreement describing the collateral. An alternative to the debtor-authentication requirement is that one of the following has occurred in accordance with the security agreement: (1) The collateral (if not a certificated security) is in the secured party's possession; (2) the secured party controls certain collateral (investment property, deposit accounts, chattel paper, or letter-of-credit rights); or (3) the collateral is a registered certificated security delivered to the secured party (UCC 9-203). Filing is relevant to perfection, not attachment.

18.8 Perfection of Security Interests

24. Perfection of a security interest permits the secured party to protect its rights by

A. Avoiding the need to file a financing statement.

B. Preventing another creditor from obtaining a security interest in the same collateral.

C. Establishing priority over the claims of most subsequent secured creditors.

D. Denying the debtor the right to possess the collateral.

Answer (C) is correct.

REQUIRED: The true statement about perfection of a security interest.

DISCUSSION: Unless perfection is by attachment, to establish priority over a previous unperfected creditor or a subsequent secured creditor, a secured party must give notice by perfecting its security interest. The methods of perfection are (1) filing a financing statement, (2) taking possession or delivery of the collateral, or (3) obtaining control of the collateral. The steps taken will depend upon the nature of the collateral.

Answer (A) is incorrect. Filing a financing statement is required to perfect an interest in certain types of collateral, such as the debtor's inventory not in the possession of the secured party. Answer (B) is incorrect. Perfection of a security interest does not bar other creditors from obtaining a security interest in the same collateral. Answer (D) is incorrect. Possession is one means of perfecting a security interest, but the parties ordinarily expect the debtor to maintain possession.

25. A secured creditor wants to file a financing statement to perfect its security interest. Under the UCC Secured Transactions Article, which of the following must be included in the financing statement?

A. An indication of the collateral.

B. An after-acquired property provision.

C. The creditor's signature.

D. The collateral's location.

Answer (A) is correct.

REQUIRED: The item that must be included in the financing statement to perfect a security interest.

DISCUSSION: To be effective, the financing statement must (1) include the name of the debtor on the public organic record, (2) include the name of the secured party or representative, and (3) indicate the collateral covered.

26. Burn Manufacturing borrowed $500,000 from Howard Finance Co., secured by Burn's current and future inventory, accounts receivable, and its proceeds. Burn's representative authenticated a sufficient security agreement that described the collateral. The security agreement was filed in the appropriate state office. Burn subsequently defaulted on the repayment of the loan, and Howard attempted to enforce its security interest. Burn contended that Howard's security interest was unenforceable. In addition, Green, who subsequently gave credit to Burn without knowledge of Howard's security interest and filed a financing statement but did not have a purchase money security interest (PMSI) in inventory, is also attempting to defeat Howard's alleged security interest. The security interest in question is valid with respect to

A. Both Burn and Green.

B. Neither Burn nor Green.

C. Burn but not Green.

D. Green but not Burn.

Answer (A) is correct.

REQUIRED: The true statement about the validity of a security interest in inventory, both current and after-acquired, and accounts receivable.

DISCUSSION: Before attachment of the security interest, the creditor gave value, the debtor had rights in the collateral, and the debtor authenticated a sufficient security agreement. Thus, attachment has occurred, and the security interest is enforceable between the debtor (Burn) and the secured party (Howard). Because Howard's security interest was perfected by filing a financing statement, Green is assumed to have notice of Howard's security interest. Howard's claim has priority over Green's because Howard filed and perfected before Green. However, if Green had perfected a PMSI in inventory and met the notice requirements, Green would have priority.

18.9 Priorities

27. On June 15, Harper purchased equipment for $100,000 from Imperial Corp. for use in its manufacturing process. Harper paid for the equipment with funds borrowed from Eastern Bank. Harper gave Eastern an authenticated security agreement covering Harper's existing and after-acquired equipment. On June 21, Harper was petitioned involuntarily into bankruptcy under Chapter 7 of the Federal Bankruptcy Code. A bankruptcy trustee was appointed. On June 23, Eastern duly filed a sufficient financing statement. Which of the parties will have a superior security interest in the equipment?

A. The trustee in bankruptcy, because the filing of the financing statement after the commencement of the bankruptcy case would be deemed a preferential transfer.

B. The trustee in bankruptcy, because the trustee became a lien creditor before Eastern perfected its security interest.

C. Eastern, because it had a perfected purchase money security interest without having to file a financing statement.

D. Eastern, because it perfected its security interest within the permissible time limits.

Answer (D) is correct.

REQUIRED: The party with a superior security interest in equipment after bankruptcy.

DISCUSSION: The equipment is purchase money collateral that secures the purchase money obligation arising from the lender's giving value to permit the debtor to obtain rights in the collateral. Hence, Eastern Bank has a PMSI. A PMSI in goods other than inventory or livestock has priority over a perfected conflicting security interest in the same collateral if it is perfected at the time the debtor receives possession of the collateral or within 20 days thereafter. Even in bankruptcy proceedings, a secured creditor with a perfected security interest may pursue its remedy against the particular property. Thus, Eastern Bank's perfected PMSI in the equipment is superior (it is not inventory). However, the trustee in bankruptcy has the status of a hypothetical lien creditor and can defeat a nonperfected security interest in the equipment.

Answer (A) is incorrect. Filing is not a transfer. It perfects the PMSI. Answer (B) is incorrect. Eastern could perfect its PMSI and retain its priority in the equipment by filing for up to 20 days after the debtor received possession. Answer (C) is incorrect. Filing was required for perfection, even though it could be done up to 20 days after the debtor received possession of the collateral.

28. Under the UCC Secured Transactions Article, what is the order of priority for the following security interests in store equipment?

I. Security interest perfected by filing on April 15.

II. Security interest attached on April 1.

III. Purchase money security interest attached April 11 and perfected by filing on April 20.

A. I, III, II.

B. II, I, III.

C. III, I, II.

D. III, II, I.

Answer (C) is correct.

REQUIRED: The order of priority for the security interests in equipment.

DISCUSSION: The basic rule is that conflicting security interests in the same collateral will rank in priority according to the time of filing or perfection. If a purchase money security interest (PMSI) in goods (e.g., equipment) other than inventory or livestock is perfected when the debtor receives possession of the collateral, or within 20 days afterward, the PMSI has priority over a conflicting security interest even if it was perfected first. The reasonable assumption is that the debtor took possession between April 11 (when the security interest attached) and April 20 (when perfection occurred). Furthermore, a perfected security interest generally has priority over a security interest that has attached but is not perfected.

18.10 Rights and Duties of Debtors, Creditors, and Third Parties

29. Under the UCC Secured Transactions Article, if a debtor is in default under a payment obligation secured by goods, the secured party has the right to

	Reduce the Claim to a Judgment	Sell the Goods and Apply the Proceeds toward the Obligations Secured	Peacefully Repossess the Goods without Judicial Process
A.	Yes	Yes	No
B.	Yes	No	Yes
C.	No	Yes	Yes
D.	Yes	Yes	Yes

Answer (D) is correct.

REQUIRED: The rights of a secured party when a debtor defaults on a payment obligation.

DISCUSSION: After default by a debtor, a secured party essentially may choose among three remedies. The secured party may (1) sue the debtor for the amount owed (reduce the claim to judgment); (2) peaceably take possession of (foreclose on) the collateral, with or without judicial process, and dispose of it in a commercially reasonable manner that includes applying the proceeds to the costs of disposition and to the obligations secured; and (3) accept (retain) the collateral in full or partial satisfaction of the obligations secured if certain conditions, for example, consent of the debtor, are met. These remedies are cumulative and allow the creditor, if unsuccessful by one method, to pursue another remedy. They also may be exercised simultaneously.

30. Under the UCC Secured Transactions Article, which of the following statements is most likely true concerning the disposition of collateral by a secured creditor after a debtor's default?

A. A good-faith transferee for value and without knowledge of any defects in the sale takes free of any subordinate liens or security interests.

B. The debtor may not redeem the collateral after the default.

C. Secured creditors with subordinate claims retain the right to redeem the collateral after the collateral is sold to a third party.

D. The collateral may only be disposed of at a public sale.

Answer (A) is correct.

REQUIRED: The statement most likely to be true concerning disposition of collateral.

DISCUSSION: When a secured party disposes of collateral after default, (1) the transferee for value receives all of the debtor's rights in the collateral, (2) the security interest under which the disposition occurs is discharged, and (3) subordinate security interests or liens are discharged unless a specific statute provides for a lien that is not dischargeable in this manner. As long as the transferee acts in good faith, (s)he will receive the property free of the foregoing interests even if the secured party does not comply with the requirements for the sale under Article 9 or any judicial proceeding.

Answer (B) is incorrect. The debtor may always redeem his or her interest in the collateral after default and before the secured party (1) collects the collateral (e.g., from account debtors); (2) disposes of, or enters into a contract for disposition of, the collateral; or (3) accepts collateral in full or partial satisfaction of the obligations secured. Answer (C) is incorrect. A good-faith transferee for value takes the property free of any subordinate security interests or liens unless a specific statute provides for a lien that is not dischargeable in this manner. Answer (D) is incorrect. Disposition sales may be either public or private.

18.11 PRACTICE TASK-BASED SIMULATIONS

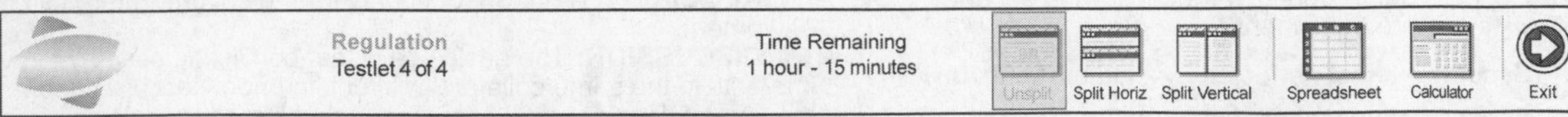

DIRECTIONS

Note: If you believe you have encountered a software malfunction, report it to the test center staff immediately.

Navigation

To navigate from task to task, use the controls at the bottom of the screen. Click on the **Next** button to advance to the next task, or the **Previous** button to go to the previous task. To go directly to any task, click on its number.

If you would like a reminder to revisit a task, or want to indicate that you are finished with it, click on the reminder flag below the task number. To clear the flag, click on it again. Reminder flags are for your use only – they do not contribute to your score.

Tabs

In this part of the examination, you will be asked to complete various tasks. Every task has one or more **Work Tabs**. Some tasks have one or more **Information Tabs**, others may have none. Every task has a **Help** tab.

If a task has **Information Tabs**, you may use the information in them to complete your responses in the **Work Tabs**.

Work tab **Information tab** **Help tab**

Work Tabs:

- **Work Tabs** are identified with a pencil icon. This is where your responses are expected.
- Each task has one or more **Work Tabs**.
- **Work Tabs** contain directions for completing the task – be sure to read these directions carefully.
- The **Work Tab** name in the example above is for illustration only – yours will differ.
- You must complete all of the **Work Tabs** in each task to receive full credit.

Information Tabs:

- The Authoritative Literature will be provided in all tasks in the AUD, FAR, and REG sections for your reference.
- Your simulation may have one or more additional **Information Tabs**. Like the Authoritative Literature tabs, **Information Tabs** do not have a pencil icon.
- If your task has additional **Information Tabs**, go through each to familiarize yourself with the task content.

Help Tab:

- The **Help Tab** provides assistance with the exam software that is used in this task. For example, if the task is to compose a memorandum, **Help** will provide information about the word processor.

The Toolbar

The toolbar at the top of the screen shows the amount of time remaining for you to complete the tasks. In addition, the following tools are available. Note that only the **Exit** button is displayed when Directions are visible - the others will appear when you begin the tasks.

Click on these buttons to split or unsplit the screen. You can split the screen vertically or horizontally.

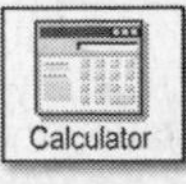

Click on this button to display the calculator; click on it again to hide the calculator. To move the calculator, click on the calculator title bar and drag the calculator to the desired location.

Click on this button to use the spreadsheet; click on it again to hide the spreadsheet. To move the spreadsheet, click on the the spreadsheet title bar and drag the spreadsheet to the desired location.

Click on this button to go on to the next part of the examination. You must complete all of the tasks to receive full credit. Once you click on **Exit** and confirm the action, you will NOT be able to return to this testlet.

= Reminder Directions 1 2 3 4 5 Previous Next

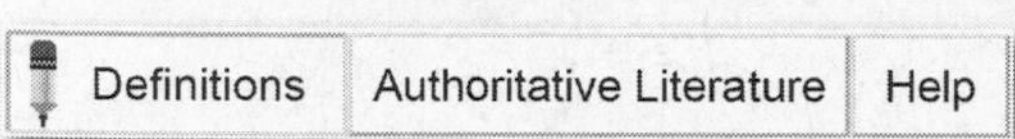

Select the best match from the list provided for each item below. Each choice may be used once, more than once, or not at all.

Item	Answer
1. Collateral that has changed in form	
2. A contract between the debtor and the secured party	
3. Includes securities entitlements	
4. Especially important to inventory financing	
5. Includes checks	
6. Includes tangible things movable when attachment occurs	
7. Consignor's interest in consigned goods	
8. A person to whom accounts have been sold	
9. Includes software	
10. Gives rights to proceeds	

Choices
A) Purchase-money security interest in inventory
B) Attachment
C) Secured party
D) Goods
E) Proceeds
F) Investment property
G) Instruments
H) After-acquired property clause
I) Security agreement
J) Future advances clause
K) Documents of title
L) General intangibles
M) Debtor
N) Security interest

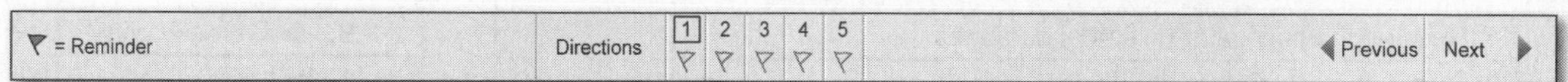

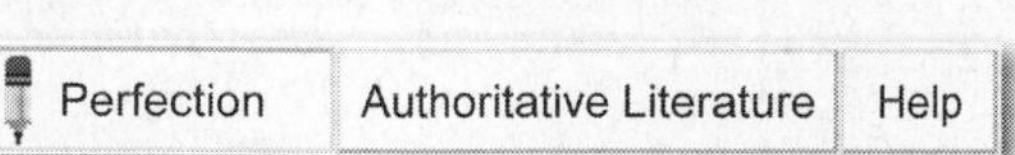

Select from the list provided the best match for each item below. Each choice may be used once, more than once, or not at all.

Statement	Answer
1. Required method in the absence of a specific exception.	
2. May occur before a security agreement is reached.	
3. Method other than filing for goods other than consumer goods.	
4. Simplest method for investment property for more than 20 days.	
5. Simplest method for purchase money security interest in most goods sold to consumers.	
6. Method when relinquishing possession of investments.	
7. Method for a registered certificated security.	
8. Perfection for a maximum of 5 years from the date of attachment.	

Choices
A) Automatic for 20 days without filing
B) Automatic upon attachment
C) Control
D) Delivery
E) Filing before attachment
F) Filing
G) Possession

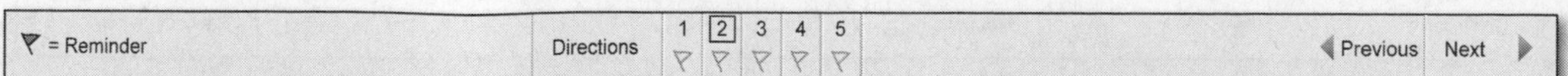

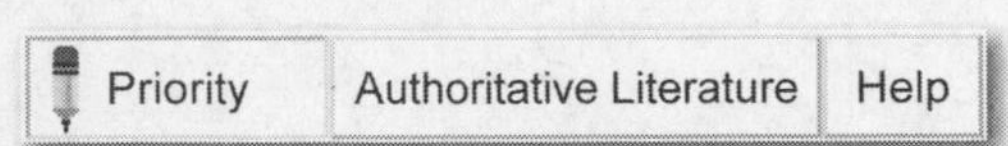

Rank the following interests in goods (other than inventory or livestock) from highest priority to lowest priority by entering a letter from A) to E). [A) is the highest priority.]

Interest	Rank
1. Security interest attached October 3	
2. General creditor	
3. Security interest perfected by filing on October 10	
4. Purchase money security interest attached October 10 and perfected by filing October 25	
5. Security interest attached on October 4 and perfected by filing on October 11	

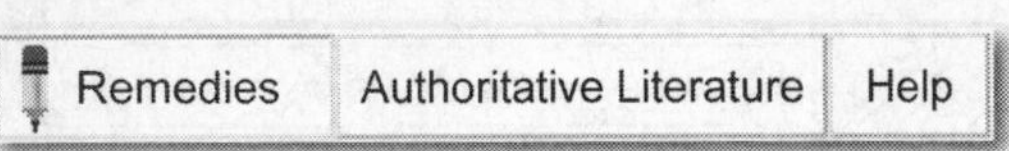

For each of the following, indicate by selecting from the list provided whether the remedy is available to the buyer, the seller, or both the buyer and the seller. Each choice may be used once, more than once, or not at all.

Remedy	Answer
1. Recover the price plus incidental damages	
2. Cancel the sales contract	
3. Modify the contract	
4. Recover goods from insolvent buyer	
5. Right to demand assurances	
6. Rescind the contract	
7. Cover	
8. Withhold delivery of goods	
9. Recover goods in transit	
10. Seek specific performance	
11. Liquidate damages	
12. Resell the goods	
13. Identify goods to the contract	
14. Sue within the statute of limitations	
15. Recover goods from an insolvent seller	
16. Seek damages for wrongful repudiation or nonacceptance	
17. Assert rights after anticipatory repudiation	

Choices
I) Buyer's remedy only
II) Seller's remedy only
III) Both buyer's and seller's remedy

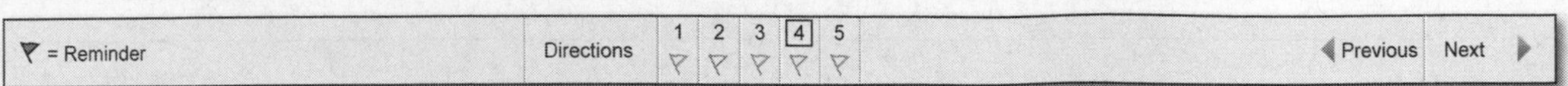

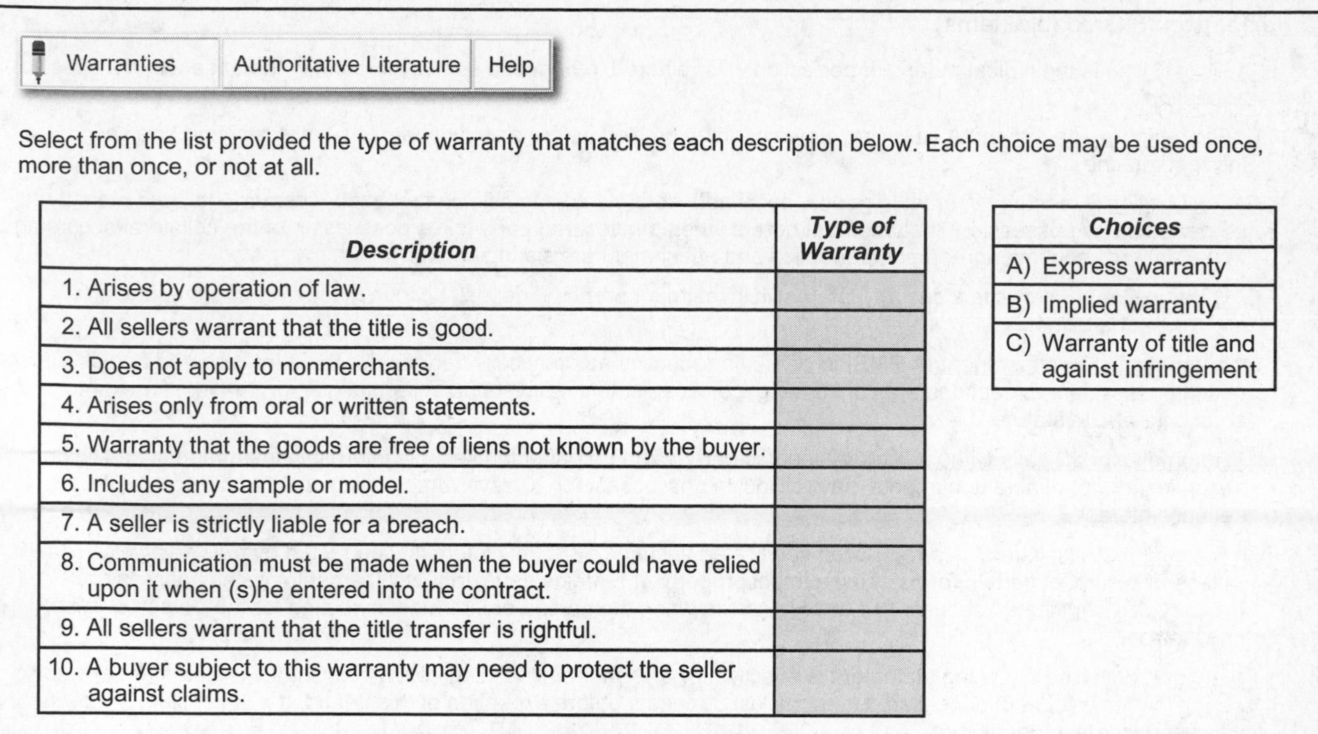

Warranties | Authoritative Literature | Help

Select from the list provided the type of warranty that matches each description below. Each choice may be used once, more than once, or not at all.

Description	Type of Warranty
1. Arises by operation of law.	
2. All sellers warrant that the title is good.	
3. Does not apply to nonmerchants.	
4. Arises only from oral or written statements.	
5. Warranty that the goods are free of liens not known by the buyer.	
6. Includes any sample or model.	
7. A seller is strictly liable for a breach.	
8. Communication must be made when the buyer could have relied upon it when (s)he entered into the contract.	
9. All sellers warrant that the title transfer is rightful.	
10. A buyer subject to this warranty may need to protect the seller against claims.	

Choices
A) Express warranty
B) Implied warranty
C) Warranty of title and against infringement

Unofficial Answers

1. Definitions (10 Gradable Items)

1. E) Proceeds. Proceeds constitute collateral that has changed in form. Proceeds include (a) what is obtained from the disposition of collateral (e.g., by sale, lease, license, or exchange), (b) collections on or distributions on account of collateral, (c) rights based on collateral, (d) claims arising from losses on collateral (e.g., from defects, damage, or nonconformity), and (e) insurance payable on the collateral. Cash proceeds include money, checks, deposit accounts, etc.
2. I) Security agreement. A security agreement is a contract between the debtor and the secured party. It grants the secured party a security interest in the collateral. The debtor generally must agree to the creation of a security interest.
3. F) Investment property. Investment property includes securities (a) whether or not certificated and (b) whether held directly (e.g., stock registered on the books of a corporation) or indirectly (e.g., most publicly traded stock) by the debtor.
4. H) After-acquired property clause. An after-acquired property clause conveys an interest in most types of personal property to be acquired in the future. Such a clause is important to a lender that finances inventory.
5. G) Instruments. Instruments include (a) negotiable instruments or (b) any writing evidencing the right to receive money that is transferred by delivery with any necessary endorsement or assignment in the ordinary course of business. Examples are checks, other drafts, promissory notes, or bonds.
6. D) Goods. Goods are fixtures and all things movable at the time a security interest attaches. Goods do not include semi-intangible and intangible items. Goods also do not include money or unextracted minerals.
7. A) Purchase-money security interest in inventory. The consignor's security interest in consigned goods is a PMSI in inventory. However, mere reservation of title in a consignment or lease is not a security interest. The arrangement must be intended as security.
8. C) Secured party. The following are secured parties: (a) a person in whose favor a security interest exists under a security agreement; (b) a person to whom accounts, chattel paper, payment intangibles, or promissory notes have been sold; (c) the holder of an agricultural lien; (d) a consignor; and (e) certain other parties.
9. L) General intangibles. General intangibles include any personal property other than goods, instruments, documents, chattel paper, investment property, deposit accounts, letters of credit, letter-of-credit rights, accounts, commercial tort claims, money, and unextracted minerals. The term includes payment intangibles and software.
10. B) Attachment. Attachment of a security interest in collateral occurs when it is enforceable against the debtor, barring an explicit agreement otherwise. Attachment of a security interest in collateral gives rights to proceeds.

2. Perfection (8 Gradable Items)

1. F) Filing. Filing is the typical means of perfection. It is required to perfect a security interest in the absence of a specific exception.
2. E) Filing before attachment. A financing statement may be filed before a security agreement is reached or a security interest attaches.
3. G) Possession. A security interest in goods, negotiable documents, tangible chattel paper, instruments, and money may be perfected by possession. If attachment occurs when the secured party takes possession of the collateral according to the debtor's security agreement, perfection and attachment are simultaneous.
4. C) Control. Control perfects a security interest in investment property, deposit accounts, letter-of-credit rights, and electronic chattel paper.
5. B) Automatic upon attachment. A PMSI in consumer goods is automatically perfected without the secured party's filing or taking possession. Exceptions are consumer goods subject to certain statutes, regulations, or treaties, for example, a certificate-of-title statute.
6. A) Automatic for 20 days without filing. A secured party having a perfected security interest in instruments, certificated securities, or negotiable documents may relinquish possession for 20 days without filing while retaining a perfected security interest.
7. D) Delivery. If the collateral is a registered certificated security, a security interest is perfected by delivery, which is a means of control of certain forms of investment property. It remains perfected until the debtor gains possession. Delivery of a certificated security to a person occurs when the person or intermediary acting for the person obtains possession.
8. F) Filing. A duly filed financing statement is effective for 5 years from the filing date. A continuation statement extending perfection for 5 years may be filed during the last 6 months before expiration of this period. If it is not filed, the security interest becomes unperfected.

3. Priority (5 Gradable Items)

1. D). An unperfected security interest has priority over the interests of general creditors but does not have priority over a perfected interest.
2. E). Any security interest, perfected or not, has priority over the interest of a general creditor.
3. B). An interest in goods (other than inventory or livestock) perfected before a purchase money security interest does not have priority over the purchase money security interest. This interest was perfected on October 10. Thus, it has priority over the interest perfected on October 11, the unperfected interest, and the interest of the general creditor.
4. A). A purchase money security interest in goods (other than inventory or livestock) that is perfected when the debtor receives possession of the collateral, or within 20 days afterward, has priority over a conflicting security interest even if it was perfected first.
5. C). An interest in goods (other than inventory or livestock) perfected before a purchase money security interest does not have priority over the purchase money security interest. This interest was perfected on October 11, so it does not have priority over the interest perfected on October 10. It has priority over the unperfected interest and the interest of a general creditor.

4. Remedies (17 Gradable Items)

1. II) Seller's remedy only. An unpaid seller can sue to recover the purchase price plus incidental damages, but only under specific circumstances: (a) the buyer accepted the goods and has not revoked acceptance, (b) risk or loss passed to the buyer before conforming goods were lost or damaged, or (c) the buyer breached after the goods were identified to the contract and the seller is unable to resell the goods.
2. II) Seller's remedy only. A seller can cancel if the buyer (a) wrongfully rejects or revokes acceptance of conforming goods duly delivered, (b) fails to make proper payment, or (c) repudiates the contract in whole or in part. The buyer is not discharged. (S)he is considered to be in breach.
3. III) Both buyer's and seller's remedy. The parties may (a) limit the remedies available to either buyer or seller or (b) provide for an exclusive remedy for either or neither party. Substantial freedom of contract is permitted. However, any remedy must not be unconscionable or fail to accomplish its essential purpose.
4. II) Seller's remedy only. When a seller discovers that the buyer has received goods on credit and is insolvent, (s)he may recover the goods. Demand must be made within 10 days after the buyer's receipt of the goods.
5. III) Both buyer's and seller's remedy. If a party has a reasonable basis for believing that performance will not be tendered, (s)he may demand adequate assurance of performance in writing. Until (s)he receives such assurance, the party may suspend further performance if suspension is commercially reasonable.
6. III) Both buyer's and seller's remedy. Fraud in the formation of a contract renders it voidable by the innocent party. A party who rescinds must return the consideration received from the other party. But rescission does not bar a claim for damages or any other remedy.
7. I) Buyer's remedy only. A buyer who rightfully rejects nonconforming goods or justifiably revokes acceptance has a right to cover. To cover means to purchase substitute goods in the marketplace.
8. II) Seller's remedy only. A seller may withhold delivery when the buyer (a) is insolvent, (b) fails to make a payment due on or before delivery, (c) wrongfully rejects the goods, (d) wrongfully revokes acceptance, or (e) repudiates the contract.
9. II) Seller's remedy only. The seller may stop delivery of goods in the possession of a carrier or other bailee when (s)he discovers the buyer to be insolvent.
10. I) Buyer's remedy only. If the goods are unique and monetary damages are not an adequate remedy, a court may order specific performance. Specific performance is available whenever the subject matter of the sales contract is unique or "in other proper circumstances."
11. III) Both buyer's and seller's remedy. The parties may set an amount in the contract that they agree to be a reasonable estimate of the damages for breach. Such a clause must be reasonable in light of (a) the anticipated losses, (b) the difficulties of proof of loss, and (c) the inconvenience of otherwise obtaining a remedy. To be enforceable, the liquidated damages amount must constitute a reasonable forecast of the damages likely to result from the breach.
12. II) Seller's remedy only. When a seller (a) possesses or controls the goods at the time of the buyer's breach or (b) duly reacquires the goods in transit, the seller has the right to resell.
13. II) Seller's remedy only. A buyer may breach or repudiate a sales contract while the seller is still in possession. In this case, the seller can identify to the contract the conforming goods that are still in his or her possession or control. The seller can do so even if the goods were not identified at the time of the breach.
14. III) Both buyer's and seller's remedy. Except for a breach of warranty, one party to a contract for the sale of goods may sue another party for breach only if the legal action is started within 4 years after breach. The parties may reduce the period, but not to less than 1 year. The parties may not extend the period.
15. I) Buyer's remedy only. A buyer may recover the goods if (a) the goods have been identified to the contract, (b) the seller became insolvent within 10 days of receipt of the first installment of the price, and (c) tender of any unpaid portion of the price is made and kept open.
16. II) Seller's remedy only. The seller may seek damages for wrongful repudiation or nonacceptance. The seller has the option to seek damages equal to the difference between the (a) the market price of the goods at the time and place of tender and (b) the unpaid contract price. The seller also may recover any incidental damages.
17. III) Both buyer's and seller's remedy. Either party, through words, actions, or circumstances, may repudiate the contract with respect to a performance not yet due. If the loss will substantially impair the value of the contract, the injured party may (a) await performance for a commercially reasonable time, (b) resort to any remedy for breach even though (s)he has also urged the other party to perform (e.g., the injured party may sue at once), or (c) suspend performance.

5. Warranties (10 Gradable Items)

1. B) Implied warranty. The implied warranties of merchantability and fitness for a particular purpose arise by operation of law.
2. C) Warranty of title and against infringement. Unless agreed otherwise, all sellers warrant that (a) the title is good, (b) its transfer is rightful, and (c) the goods are free of liens and other encumbrances not known by the buyer.
3. B) Implied warranty. An implied warranty of merchantability arises by operation of law. Thus, it is not written. This warranty is implied in every sale by a merchant who deals in goods of the kind sold. It does not apply to nonmerchants, and the buyer need not be a merchant.
4. A) Express warranty. Express warranties are any statements of fact or promise made by a merchant or nonmerchant seller to the buyer that become part of the bargain. The express warranty may be oral or written.
5. C) Warranty of title and against infringement. Unless agreed otherwise, all sellers warrant that (a) the title is good, (b) its transfer is rightful, and (c) the goods are free of liens and other encumbrances not known by the buyer.
6. A) Express warranty. Express warranties are any statements of fact or promise made by a merchant or nonmerchant seller to the buyer that become part of the bargain. They include any sample, model, or description of the goods.
7. B) Implied warranty. In a suit for breach of implied warranty, it is necessary to prove only that (a) the implied warranty existed, (b) the warranty was breached, and (c) breach was the proximate cause of the damage sustained. Thus, a seller is strictly liable for a breach of an implied warranty. Implied warranties are not based on principles of negligence.
8. A) Express warranty. To become part of the bargain, the communication must be made at such time as the buyer could have relied upon it when (s)he entered into the contract. It is not necessary for the buyer to prove that (s)he actually did rely or that the seller intended to make a warranty.
9. C) Warranty of title and against infringement. Unless agreed otherwise, all sellers warrant that (a) the title is good, (b) its transfer is rightful, and (c) the goods are free of liens and other encumbrances not known by the buyer.
10. C) Warranty of title and against infringement. A merchant-seller warrants against patent infringement and similar claims. However, a buyer who provides specifications must protect a manufacturer-seller against infringement claims.

Gleim Simulation Grading

Task	Correct Responses		Gradable Items		Score per Task
1	____	÷	10	=	____
2	____	÷	8	=	____
3	____	÷	5	=	____
4	____	÷	17	=	____
5	____	÷	10	=	____
			Total of Scores per Task		____
		÷	Total Number of Tasks		5
			Total Score		____ %

STUDY UNIT NINETEEN
NEGOTIABLE INSTRUMENTS AND DOCUMENTS

(22 pages of outline)

UCC Article 3 covers negotiable instruments. These contracts are used extensively in business as a **substitute for money** and to extend credit. Thus, they may be repeatedly negotiated. Important topics include (1) the requirements of negotiability, (2) identifying the parties to an instrument, (3) transfer of an instrument by assignment or negotiation, (4) effects of the types of endorsement, (5) the contract or warranty liability of primary and secondary parties, and (6) the **holder in due course (HDC)** concept. This study unit also discusses documents of title.

19.1 TYPES OF NEGOTIABLE INSTRUMENTS

1. **Overview**
   a. Negotiable instruments are written contracts and a form of property. They are (1) notes (including certificates of deposit) or (2) drafts (including checks).
   b. An instrument may be within the definition of a note and a draft. This ambiguity does not defeat negotiability. The person entitled to enforce the instrument may treat it as either.
2. **Promissory Notes**
   a. A promissory note contains a **promise**. The maker (1) promises unconditionally (2) to pay a fixed amount of money (3) to the order of the payee or to bearer (4) on demand or at a definite time.

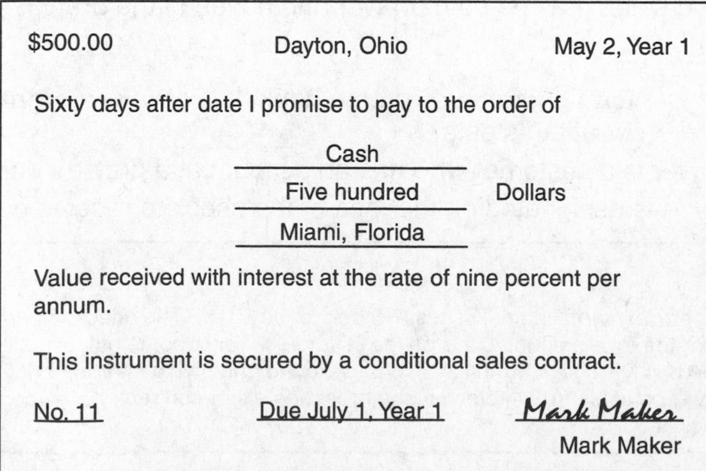

$500.00 Dayton, Ohio May 2, Year 1

Sixty days after date I promise to pay to the order of

Cash

Five hundred Dollars

Miami, Florida

Value received with interest at the rate of nine percent per annum.

This instrument is secured by a conditional sales contract.

No. 11 Due July 1, Year 1 Mark Maker

Mark Maker

Figure 19-1

      1) The **maker** signs or is identified in a note as a person undertaking to pay.

   b. A **certificate of deposit (CD)** is a form of promissory note issued by a bank. It acknowledges receipt of money with an unconditional promise to repay. It typically bears interest.

3. **Drafts**

   a. A draft contains an **order**. It is (1) an unconditional written order (2) by one person, the drawer, (3) to another person, the drawee, (4) to pay a fixed amount of money (5) to a third person, either to an identified person (the payee) or to bearer.

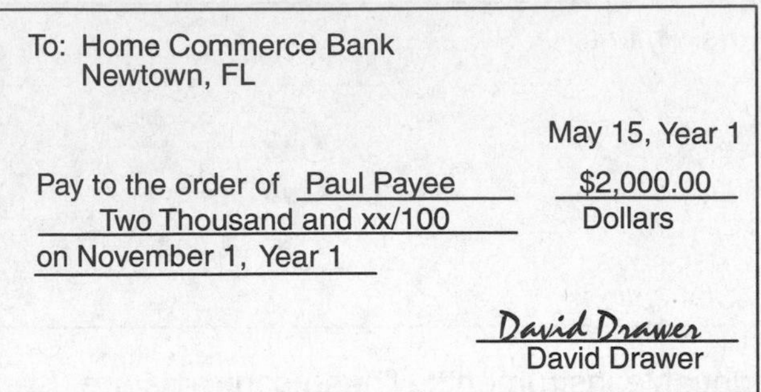

To: Home Commerce Bank
Newtown, FL

May 15, Year 1

Pay to the order of Paul Payee $2,000.00
Two Thousand and xx/100 Dollars
on November 1, Year 1

David Drawer
David Drawer

Figure 19-2

   b. The **drawer** signs or is identified in a draft as a person ordering payment.
   c. The **drawee** is the person ordered to make payment. The drawee must be obligated to the drawer either by agreement or through a debtor-creditor relationship.
   d. Drafts are usually classified as one of the following:
      1) A time draft is payable at a definite time in the future.
      2) A sight draft is payable on demand (upon presentation to the drawee).
   e. The payee usually presents a time draft to the drawee for **acceptance** (agreement to pay) before the instrument's due date.
      1) Once accepted, the time draft is returned by the drawee-acceptor to the payee, who holds it until its due date.
   f. A **trade acceptance** is a time draft used by sellers as a means to extend credit to buyers of their goods.
      1) The seller draws a draft ordering the buyer to pay money to the seller (or a third party) at some time in the future.
      2) The seller presents the draft to the buyer, and the buyer accepts it, becoming liable on the instrument.
      3) The seller may be both drawer and payee of the draft.

4. **Checks**

   a. A check is a form of draft drawn on a bank. It is always a **sight draft** that is payable on demand on or after its date.
   b. The drawer is a customer who has an account at a drawee bank.
   c. The payee is designated on the face of the check to receive payment.

EXAMPLE

Kathy purchases a computer from Triptotech and issues a check for payment. The check is part of a formal contract. Kathy, as drawer (signer), is liable for the face amount to the payee (Triptotech) or to some other holder, such as a business where Triptotech might have cashed Kathy's check. Kathy is also party to the underlying informal contract for the purchase and sale of the computer. Kathy will be liable to Triptotech if she breaches either contract. Kathy could breach both contracts by stopping payment of the check.

   d. A **postdated** check is a **time draft**. It bears a date later than the date on which the check is issued.
      1) A postdated check is payable on or after the indicated date.

e. A **certified** check has been accepted by the drawee bank, even if the funds in the drawer's account are insufficient.

1) The check is presented to the payor bank by either the drawer or the payee.
2) Certification makes the check more equivalent to money.

f. A **cashier's** check is drawn by a bank on itself. The bank is both drawer and drawee. It is often obtained by a remitter, a person not a party to the instrument who purchases it from the issuer, usually to pay a debt to the identified payee.

g. The following illustrates the processing of a typical check:

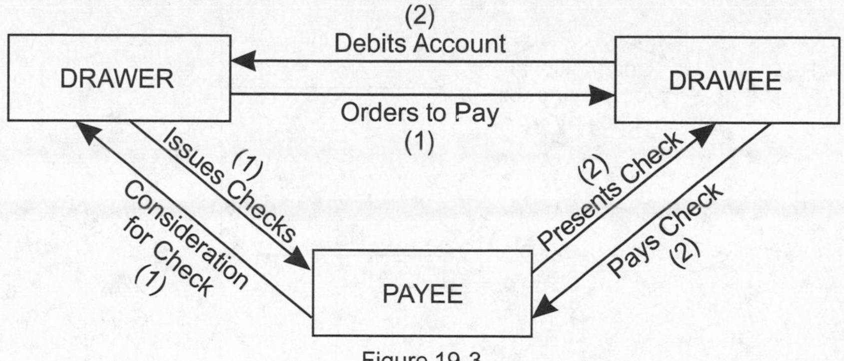

Figure 19-3

Stop and review! You have completed the outline for this subunit. Study multiple-choice questions 1 through 3 beginning on page 736.

19.2 NEGOTIABILITY

1. Definitions

a. **Transfer** of an instrument is a delivery (a voluntary transfer of possession) by a nonissuer for the purpose of giving the recipient the right to enforce the instrument.

b. **Negotiation** is a special transfer that may allow the transferee to take the instrument free of personal defenses. It is a transfer of possession of an instrument, whether voluntary or involuntary, by a person not the issuer. The transferee becomes its **holder** as a result.

1) Negotiation cannot occur unless the document is in negotiable form. Moreover, negotiation requires transfer of the entire instrument.

2. Elements of Negotiability

a. Negotiability is a matter of form. If an instrument is drafted and issued in a specified manner, it is negotiable, even if it contains additional language or uses wording different from that in the UCC. Otherwise, it is nonnegotiable. To be negotiable, an instrument must

1) Be written and signed by the maker or drawer,
2) Contain an unconditional promise or order to pay a fixed amount of money,
3) Be payable to order or bearer,
4) Be payable on demand or at a definite time, and
5) Not state any other undertaking or instruction.

b. A negotiable instrument is presumed to have been issued for consideration. Thus, no consideration need be stated on the instrument.

The AICPA has heavily tested the elements of negotiability. Be able to determine whether an instrument is negotiable given the presented facts about the instrument in the question.

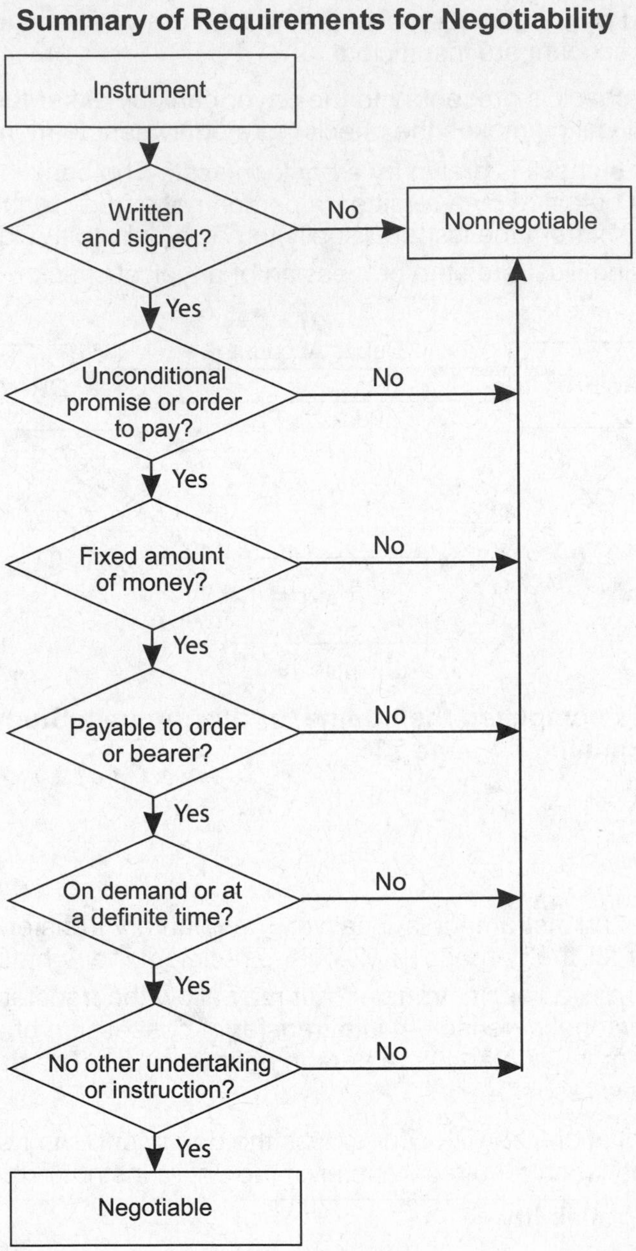

Summary of Requirements for Negotiability

Instrument

Written and signed? — No → Nonnegotiable

Yes

Unconditional promise or order to pay? — No → Nonnegotiable

Yes

Fixed amount of money? — No → Nonnegotiable

Yes

Payable to order or bearer? — No → Nonnegotiable

Yes

On demand or at a definite time? — No → Nonnegotiable

Yes

No other undertaking or instruction? — No → Nonnegotiable

Yes

Negotiable

Figure 19-4

3. **Signed Writing**
   a. A negotiable instrument must be in writing and signed by (1) the maker (a note or CD), (2) the drawer (a draft or a check), or (3) an authorized representative.

4. **Unconditional Promise or Order to Pay**
   a. A promise is "a written undertaking signed by the person undertaking to pay." It is not simply an acknowledgment of an obligation.
      1) The word "promise" need not be used.
   b. An order is "a written instruction to pay signed by the person giving the instruction." It is not a mere request.
   c. A promise or order must not state
      1) An express condition to payment,
      2) That it is subject to or governed by another writing, or
      3) That rights or obligations related to it are contained in another writing.

5. **Fixed Amount of Money**
   a. A negotiable instrument must state a promise or order to pay a fixed amount of money with or without interest or other charges described in the promise or order.
   b. Interest is not payable unless it is provided for in the instrument.
   c. Prepayment provisions and default penalties are allowed.
6. **Payable on Demand or at a Definite Time**
   a. A promise or an order that does not state any time of payment is payable on demand.
      1) Instruments payable on demand include those payable at the will of the holder. Examples are instruments "payable on demand," "payable at sight," or "payable at presentation."
      2) By definition, a check is payable on demand.
   b. A promise or an order is payable at a definite time if it is payable
      1) After passage of a definite period of time after sight or acceptance or
      2) At a fixed date or dates (or at a time or times) readily determinable at the time the promise or order is issued. This date or time may be subject to rights of
         a) Prepayment;
         b) Acceleration; or
         c) Extension at the option of the holder, maker, or acceptor.
   c. An instrument may be predated, postdated, or undated. The date of an undated instrument is the date of issue or when it first comes into the possession of a holder.
7. **Payable to Order or Bearer**
   a. Order or bearer words clearly indicate that the parties intend that the instrument be capable of circulating in commerce as a money substitute.
   b. A person identified on an **order instrument** can designate the payee.
      1) An order instrument is payable to
         a) The order of an identified person ("Payable to the order of P. Cruz") or
         b) An identified person or order ("Pay to P. Cruz or order").
      2) The initial payee should be determinable with reasonable certainty based on the intent of the person signing as (or for) the issuer.
      3) An order instrument allows the maker or drawer to transfer it to a specific person. That person can transfer the instrument to whomever (s)he wishes.
      4) The following language renders the instrument nonnegotiable:
         a) "Payable to P. Cruz"
         b) "Pay to P. Cruz only"
   c. A **bearer instrument** does not designate a specific payee. The maker or drawer agrees to pay anyone who presents the instrument for payment.

EXAMPLE

An instrument payable "to M. Cruz, the bearer" is not payable to the bearer.

      1) A promise or an order is payable to bearer if it
         a) Does not state a payee.
         b) Indicates that it is not payable to an identified person.
         c) Is payable to cash or to the order of cash.
         d) States that it is payable to bearer or to the order of bearer.
         e) Indicates that the person in possession is entitled to payment.

2) For example, an instrument made payable as follows is bearer paper:

a) Pay bearer
b) Pay to the order of bearer
c) Pay to the order of P. Cruz or bearer
d) Pay any person presenting
e) Pay $500

8. **No Other Undertaking or Instruction**

a. The person promising or ordering payment ordinarily does not promise to do or require the doing of any other act.

Stop and review! You have completed the outline for this subunit. Study multiple-choice questions 4 through 9 beginning on page 737.

19.3 ENDORSEMENTS

1. **Overview**

a. An endorsement is a signature that negotiates the instrument, restricts payment, or incurs endorser's liability.

1) Endorsement is required to negotiate an order instrument.
2) Endorsements are usually written on the back of the instrument itself.
3) The placement of any endorsement and the relative liability of endorsers are presumed to be according to the order in which their signatures appear.
4) A forged endorsement ordinarily is ineffective to negotiate an instrument payable to an identified person. Thus, no transferee can be a holder.
5) The signature of a person as maker, drawer, or acceptor is **not** an endorsement.

2. **Types of Endorsements**

a. A **blank endorsement** is an endorsement by the holder that is not a special endorsement. Thus, it identifies no particular payee. It may consist of merely the signature of the endorser.

1) A check payable to the order of Paula Payee is endorsed in blank when she writes only her name on the back of the check.
2) An order instrument endorsed in blank becomes payable to **bearer**.

EXAMPLE

If Will endorses a check payable to him in blank and then loses it on the street, Terry may find it and sell it to Watson for value without endorsing it. This constitutes a negotiation because Terry has delivered a bearer instrument that was an order instrument until it was endorsed in blank.

3) Below is an illustration of a blank endorsement on the back of a check:

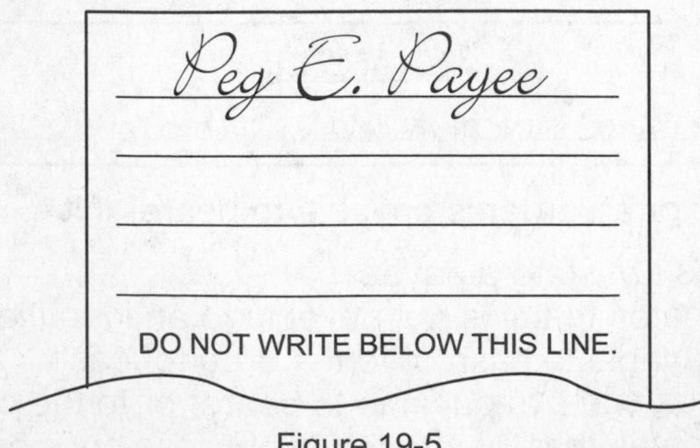

Figure 19-5

b. A **special endorsement** by a holder identifies the person to whom the instrument, whether payable to an identified person or to order, is payable.

1) For example, if Grace Smith is the payee of a check, she may specially endorse it with "Pay to Hilda Holder" or "Pay to the order of Hilda Holder" when she negotiates it to Holder.

Pay to Hilda Holder
Grace Smith

Figure 19-6

2) A specially endorsed instrument becomes payable to the order of the special endorsee and requires his or her endorsement for further negotiation.
3) Words of negotiability are **not** required in an endorsement.
4) A holder may convert a blank endorsement consisting only of a signature into a special endorsement by writing above the signature words identifying the payee. For example, if Blanche Dorser is the payee, she may endorse the instrument in blank and negotiate it to Heidi Holden. Holden may protect herself by converting the blank endorsement to a special endorsement as in the illustration below.

Pay to Heidi Holden
Blanche Dorser

Figure 19-7

5) The **last** endorsement determines whether the instrument is order or bearer paper.

c. A **restrictive endorsement** may restrict or further limit the negotiation of the instrument. However, it cannot prevent further transfer or negotiation.

1) The following are examples:
   a) Conditional endorsements
   b) Endorsements prohibiting further transfer or negotiation
   c) Endorsements for deposit or collection
   d) Endorsements to a fiduciary

d. A **conditional endorsement** purports to make the rights of the endorsee subject to the happening or nonhappening of a specified event.

Pay to endorsee, provided that she completes painting my house at 100 Safe Street by July Year 1
Emma Endorser

Figure 19-8

1) The maker, drawee, or subsequent endorser is obligated to pay when the instrument is due without regard to whether the condition has been satisfied.
   a) Thus, in the example above, endorsee (or a later holder) can obtain payment without painting the house.
   b) Endorser still may have rights against endorsee (e.g., for breach of contract) if the condition is not satisfied. But those rights would exist without the condition.

e. An **endorsement prohibiting further transfer or negotiation** does not do so.

Pay Paula Payee ONLY

Figure 19-9

f. An **endorsement for deposit or collection** forces the instrument into the banking system for deposit or collection.

1) The following are examples:

a) For Deposit Only
b) For Collection
c) Pay Any Bank

2) This endorsement limits negotiation consistent with the endorsement. It gives notice to the following that they must comply with the endorsement:

a) All nonbanking persons
b) The depositary bank (the first bank to receive an item for payment unless it is presented for immediate payment over the counter)
c) A bank that makes immediate payment over the counter

g. A **qualified endorsement** disclaims or limits contractual liability on the instrument.

1) The notation without recourse often is used.

Pay to Paula Payee without recourse *Mark Maker*

Figure 19-10

2) A qualified endorser does **not** undertake **secondary** payment liability, that is, to pay if the primarily liable party does not.

a) A qualified endorser may incur **warranty** liability.

3) Qualified endorsement does not prevent further negotiation of the instrument but may lessen its marketability.

4) A transfer of an order instrument for value gives the transferee the **specifically enforceable** right to an **unqualified** endorsement.

a) An unqualified endorsement usually guarantees payment of the instrument if the primarily liable party does not pay.

h. An **anomalous endorsement** is made by a person who is not the holder. It has no effect on negotiability. Moreover, a signature is an endorsement unless the circumstances unambiguously indicate otherwise.

1) An **accommodation** endorser signs for the benefit of another party.

a) An anomalous endorsement or a signature with words indicating suretyship provides notice that the instrument has been signed for accommodation.

i. The following table illustrates various endorsements of a negotiable instrument:

Endorsement	Blank or Special	Endorser's Liability	Further Negotiation Restricted	Transferee's Interest Restricted
John Doe	Blank	Unqualified	No	No
Without recourse, John Doe	Blank	Qualified	No	No
For deposit only John Doe	Blank	Unqualified	No	Yes
Pay Joanne Smith John Doe	Special	Unqualified	No	No
Pay Joanne Smith if she sings at party John Doe	Special	Unqualified	No	No[1]
Pay Dot Sims in Trust for Joanne Smith John Doe	Special	Unqualified	No	Yes

[1] This conditional endorsement is an illusory restriction. The endorsee (Joanne Smith) can obtain payment without satisfying the condition (UCC 3-206).

CPA exam questions testing endorsements have presented different endorsements on the same instrument. Required answers covered such topics as the classification of each endorsement and the type of negotiable instrument (i.e., bearer or order paper) resulting from a particular endorsement.

Stop and review! You have completed the outline for this subunit. Study multiple-choice questions 10 through 14 beginning on page 739.

19.4 HOLDERS IN DUE COURSE

1. **Holder**
   a. A holder is a person in possession of a negotiable instrument that is payable to (1) bearer or (2) an identified person if the identified person is the person in possession.
      1) A person becomes a holder if the instrument is (a) issued to the person or (b) negotiated to the person.
      2) A holder need not have given value, taken in good faith, or been unaware of defects in the instrument or of claims to it.
   b. If an instrument is payable to **bearer**, it is negotiated by **transfer of possession**.
   c. If an instrument is payable to an **identified person** (an order instrument), it is negotiated by (1) **transfer of possession** and (2) **endorsement** by the holder.
      1) If a holder does not endorse an order instrument, a mere transfer occurs. The transfer is an **assignment** of the transferor's rights.
         a) The transferee is merely an assignee and is subject to both real and personal defenses.
      2) A transfer of an order instrument for value gives the transferee the **specifically enforceable** right to an unqualified endorsement.
         a) But the parties may agree specifically that the transaction is an assignment.

3) The following flow chart illustrates negotiation:

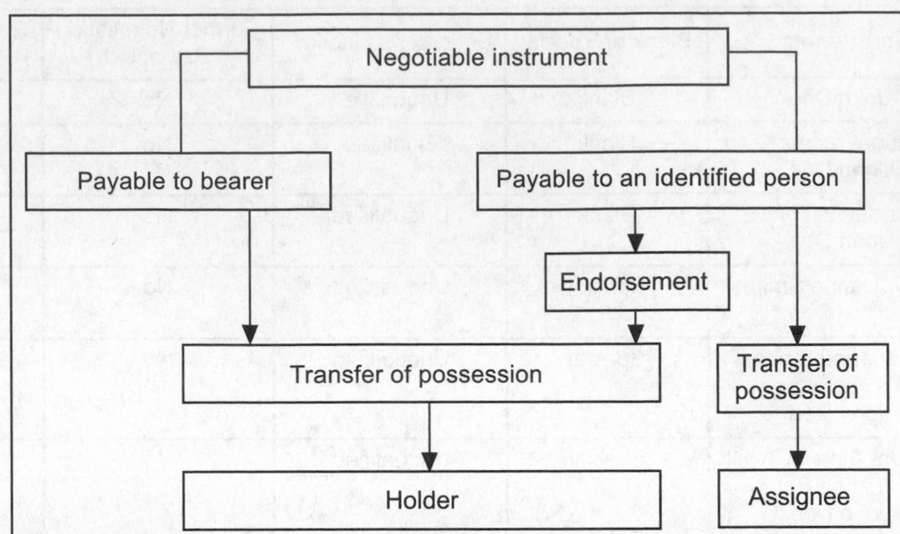

Figure 19-11

2. **Holder in Due Course (HDC)**

a. Negotiable instruments cannot effectively substitute for money unless collection is reasonably certain. Reasonable certainty is not possible unless most parties to whom negotiable instruments are negotiated are free of most claims and defenses assertible against prior parties.

1) Thus, the most significant aspect of negotiability is the status of the HDC.

b. A holder becomes an HDC to the extent the holder takes the instrument

1) In good faith,
2) For value, and
3) Without notice of the following:

a) Dishonor of the instrument or that it is overdue
b) An alteration or an unauthorized signature
c) Any defense or claim

The HDC requirements are frequently tested on the CPA exam. Questions may present a situation containing numerous facts and ask whether the holder is an HDC.

3. **Good Faith**

a. A holder must take the instrument in good faith to qualify as an HDC.

b. The good-faith requirement applies only to the holder.

c. Good faith is a subjective (honesty in fact) and an objective (observance of reasonable commercial standards of fair dealing) determination.

d. A person may take an instrument under circumstances that clearly establish existence of a defense to the instrument. An example is purchase at a very deep discount.

1) However, purchase at a reasonable discount is normal and not indicative of bad faith.

4. **Value**
   a. An HDC must have given value for the instrument.
   b. A person who receives an instrument as a gift or an inheritance is not an HDC.
   c. Value is not the same as consideration. For example, an unperformed contractual promise is not value. A holder gives value in the following ways:
      1) To the extent that (a) a promise has been performed or (b) a security interest in or lien on the instrument (other than one obtained judicially) is acquired
         a) If the promise that is consideration for the instrument is partially performed, the holder may assert rights as an HDC based on the following formula:

$$\text{Amount payable under the instrument} \times \frac{\text{Value of part performance}}{\text{Value of full performance}}$$

      2) By taking an instrument in payment of, or as security for, a pre-existing claim against any person

EXAMPLE

Tom owes Merry $1,000 on a past-due account. He transferred a negotiable instrument to Merry in payment of the account. Merry qualifies as a holder for value. She also would qualify if the instrument is reserved as collateral for an existing debt whether the debt is due or not.

      3) By issuing or transferring a negotiable instrument
      4) By incurring an irrevocable obligation to a third party

5. **No Notice of Facts Preventing HDC Status**
   a. To qualify as an HDC, a holder must not have notice that the instrument is overdue.
   b. Whether an instrument is overdue depends on whether it is a time or demand instrument.
      1) A **demand instrument** is overdue at the earliest of
         a) The day after demand for payment.
         b) In the case of a check, 90 days after its date.
         c) In the case of a noncheck, when it has been outstanding for a period after its date that is unreasonable in the circumstances.
      2) An instrument **payable at a definite time** is overdue
         a) Upon default on an installment payment of principal.
         b) The day after the due date if the instrument is not payable in installments.
         c) The day after an accelerated due date for principal.
      3) An instrument is not overdue because of a default on payment of interest unless the due date for principal has been accelerated.
   c. A holder becomes an HDC if the instrument, when issued or negotiated to the holder, does not have some apparent irregularity calling into question its authenticity, for example, forgery, alteration, or incompleteness.

EXAMPLE

Kelly signs and issues a check to Bonnie but leaves the space for the amount of payment blank. Bonnie knows that Kelly intended to fill in the space for payment in the amount of $500. Bonnie informs Manuel and, without filling in the amount, negotiates the check to Manuel for $500. Manuel may not enjoy HDC status if a court finds that this omission rendered the instrument so incomplete as to call into question its authenticity.

6. **The Shelter Principle**

   a. A person who does not qualify as an HDC but receives title through an HDC can acquire the rights and privileges of an HDC.

   b. Transfer of an instrument gives a transferee who is not an HDC any right of the transferor to enforce the instrument. This includes any right as an HDC. Thus, the transferee is an assignee of the HDC-transferor and is sheltered from personal defenses.

      1) However, a transferee who was a party to fraud or illegality affecting the instrument cannot acquire the rights of an HDC (that is, launder his or her status) by later acquiring the instrument from an HDC.

      2) Merely being aware of fraud or illegality affecting the instrument will not prevent a transferee from acquiring the rights of an HDC.

EXAMPLE

Newt fraudulently induces Mary to execute and deliver a note to him. He then negotiates the note to Bill, who qualifies as an HDC. Bill makes a gift of the note to Bruce, who sells it to Ken, who is aware of the fraud. Ken sells it to Mike after maturity. Mike is not an HDC because he was aware that the note was overdue. Bruce (who did not give value) and Ken (who did not take in good faith) were not HDCs when they owned the instrument. Nevertheless, Bruce, Ken, and Mike have the rights of an HDC. They have Bill's rights and are free of personal defenses. Mary's defense was cut off by Bill's status as an HDC.

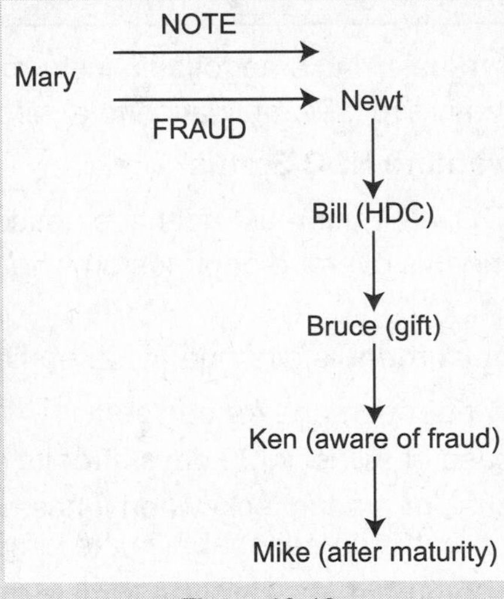

Figure 19-12

7. **The FTC Rule**

   a. Consumer groups objected to the shelter principle. It does not permit a maker or a drawer of an instrument to assert a legitimate defense after the payee transfers a negotiable instrument for value to a third person.

   b. Thus, the FTC requires a seller or a lessor of consumer goods or services to include in a consumer credit contract the following prominently printed notice that effectively prevents a transferee from having HDC status:

NOTICE
ANY HOLDER OF THIS CONSUMER CREDIT CONTRACT
IS SUBJECT TO ALL CLAIMS AND DEFENSES
WHICH THE DEBTOR COULD ASSERT AGAINST
THE SELLER OF GOODS OR SERVICES OBTAINED
PURSUANT HERETO
OR WITH THE PROCEEDS HEREOF.
RECOVERY HEREUNDER BY THE DEBTOR
SHALL NOT EXCEED AMOUNTS
PAID BY THE DEBTOR HEREUNDER.

Summary of the **Status and Rights of an Assignee, Holder, and HDC**

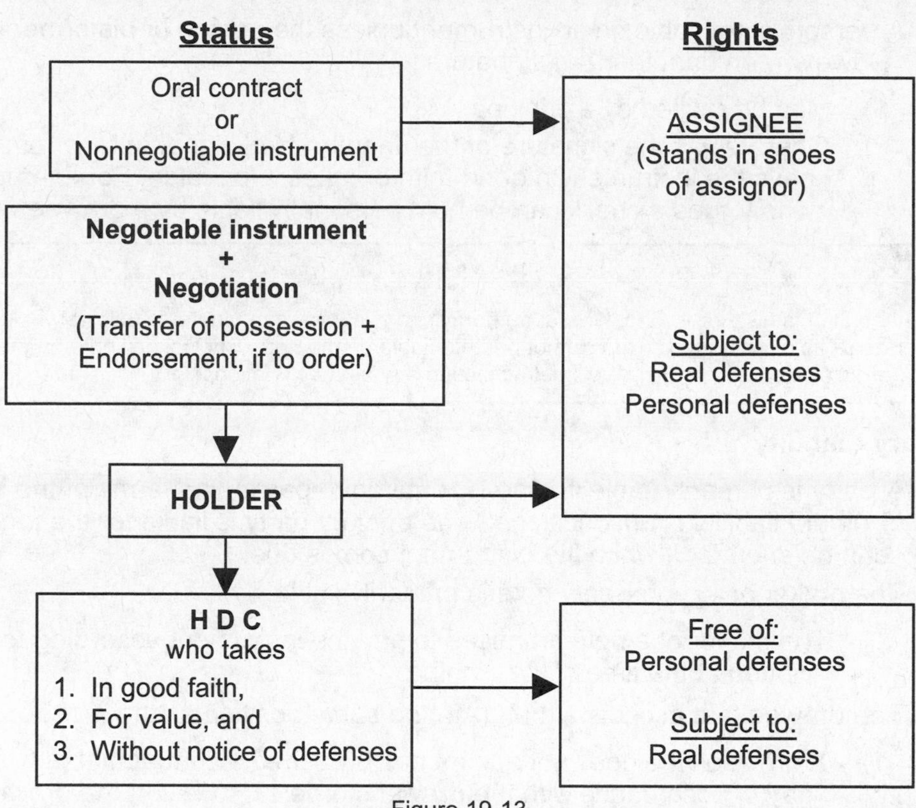

Figure 19-13

Stop and review! You have completed the outline for this subunit. Study multiple-choice questions 15 through 19 beginning on page 741.

19.5 LIABILITY AND DEFENSES

1. **Contractual Liability**
   a. Signers of a negotiable instrument, except qualified endorsers, have primary or secondary contractual liability for its face amount (including interest).
   b. A person who (1) issues a check, (2) accepts a draft in which (s)he is named as drawee, or (3) signs a promissory note is contractually liable for the face amount.
      1) When a person endorses a check to cash it, the endorsement, if unqualified, makes the endorser contractually liable. This liability extends to the endorsee and any other transferee for the face amount if the drawee (usually the drawer's bank) does not pay.
   c. Any person who signs a negotiable instrument is liable on it.
2. **Agents**
   a. The authorized signature of an agent acts as the signature of the principal and binds the principal on the instrument.
   b. The agent's authority and the principal's liability are otherwise determined by agency law. Thus, the principal is liable if the agent is authorized whether or not the principal's name is on the instrument.

3. **Unauthorized Signature**
   a. A person is not liable on an instrument unless the person or his or her agent signed it. However, an unauthorized signature
      1) May be ratified by a principal.
      2) Operates as the signature of the unauthorized signer in favor of a person who pays the instrument in good faith or takes it for value. For example, a person who forges a check can be held personally liable by a drawee who pays it.

EXAMPLE

Rob is the principal and Dan is his agent. Dan, without authority, signs a promissory note as follows: "Rob, by Dan, agent." Because Rob's "signature" is unauthorized, Rob cannot be held liable on the note. But Dan is liable on the instrument. Dan is liable even if he merely signs the note "Rob," without indicating any agency relationship.

4. **Primary Liability**
   a. A party is primarily liable if (s)he is required to pay by the terms of the instrument itself. Primary liability is unconditional. The primary party is liable for the face amount and can be sued for it when the instrument comes due.
   b. The maker of a promissory note is primarily liable.
      1) The maker of a note promises to pay the instrument according to the terms as written at the time of the signing.
   c. The drawee that accepts a draft is in the same position as the maker of a note.
      1) A drawee who does not accept has breached a contractual duty to the drawer to pay in accordance with the drawer's orders. However, the drawee owes no duty to either the payee or any holder.
      2) The issuer of a draft that is both drawer and drawee also is a primary party.
         a) An example is a bank that issues a cashier's check.

EXAMPLE

Buyer purchases goods from Seller for $5,000. The goods are to be shipped July 15. Buyer gives Seller a draft drawn on a finance company for $2,000 payable to Seller on July 15. The finance company is not liable on the draft given to Seller. It will not become liable until acceptance.

      3) **A draft has no primarily liable party until accepted by the drawee.**
5. **Secondary Liability**
   a. A party is secondarily liable when an obligation to pay arises only if the party with primary liability fails to pay. Accordingly, drawers and endorsers have secondary liability.
   b. A **drawer** is not liable unless the drawee refuses to pay. If the drawee dishonors an unaccepted draft, the drawer must pay according to its terms when it was issued.
      1) After acceptance by a bank (certification), the drawer is discharged regardless of when or by whom acceptance is obtained. If acceptance is by a party other than a bank, the drawer's liability after acceptance is that of an endorser.
      2) Acceptance of a draft by a bank after endorsement discharges the endorser.
      3) If the acceptance varies the terms of the draft, the holder may refuse and treat the instrument as dishonored. If the holder agrees, the obligation of any drawer or endorser who does not expressly agree is discharged.
      4) A drawer may disclaim liability by drawing without recourse unless the draft is a check.

c. An **endorser** is not liable unless the drawee, maker, or, possibly, other endorsers do not pay.
   1) An unqualified endorser is liable to a subsequent endorser or a party entitled to enforce the instrument even if the endorsement was not necessary.
   2) Endorsers are usually liable in the order in which they endorse.
   3) An endorser may avoid liability by a qualified endorsement.

6. **Warranty Liability**
   a. Because a negotiable instrument is property, sellers and other transferors have warranty liability. This liability is in addition to any contract liability based on a party's signature.
      1) Breach of warranty may occur whenever a person transfers or presents for payment an instrument (the property) that is defective in some respect, e.g., as a result of a forged signature.
      2) Any person who transfers an instrument and receives consideration makes certain warranties to the immediate transferee. If the transfer is by endorsement, the same warranties also are made to any subsequent transferee who takes in good faith.
      3) The following are the transfer warranties:
         a) The warrantor is entitled to enforce the instrument.
         b) All signatures are authentic and authorized.
         c) The instrument has not been altered.
         d) No defense or claim of any party is good against the warrantor.
         e) The warrantor has no knowledge of insolvency proceedings against the maker, drawer of an unaccepted draft, or acceptor.
   b. Warranty liability may be the only remedy for a wronged person. The following have warranty liability without contractual liability:
      1) A qualified endorser (without recourse)
      2) A person who negotiates an instrument without endorsing it
      3) An endorser who has been discharged because of the holder's unexcused delay in making presentment
   c. Transfer warranties cannot be disclaimed with respect to checks.

7. **Collection**
   a. The holder of an instrument, including an HDC, must proceed through these formal steps to collect on a negotiable instrument: (1) presentment, (2) dishonor, and (3) notice of dishonor to parties secondarily liable (unless waived or excused).

8. **Presentment**
   a. Presentment is a **demand for payment or acceptance** made by a person entitled to enforce the instrument to a maker, drawee, or other party obliged to pay or to a bank.
   b. Presentment may be by any commercially reasonable means, e.g., in person, by mail, through a clearinghouse or a collecting bank, or electronically.
   c. An endorser's liability (but not a guarantor's) is discharged if a check is not presented for payment (or given to a depositary bank for collection) within 30 days after the day of the endorsement.
   d. Lack of a necessary endorsement justifies return of the instrument without dishonor.

9. **Dishonor**
   a. Dishonoring an instrument (refusal to pay) triggers **secondary liability** on the instrument. Thus, a person entitled to enforce the instrument may proceed directly against a secondary party.
   b. Unaccepted drafts that are ordinary checks are usually dishonored by being returned or by timely notice of dishonor.
10. **Notice of Dishonor**
   a. Adequate notice must be given to all prior endorsers (but not guarantors), or they are discharged. However, the drawer of an unaccepted draft need not be notified.
   b. Notice of dishonor can be given by anyone in any commercially reasonable manner. For example, a party who may be required to pay may benefit from giving notice to other parties who also may be liable.
   c. Generally, notice must be given within 30 days after the day of dishonor.
11. **Real Defenses**
   a. Defenses to liability can bar collection from persons who would otherwise be primarily or secondarily liable on the instrument. Real defenses can be asserted even **against an HDC**.
   b. An instrument may be void (not merely voidable) under state law because it has been executed in connection with criminal or other illegal conduct. The defense of **illegality** is absolute against both an ordinary holder and an HDC.
   c. An instrument signed under **extreme duress** (rendering the instrument void under state law) is unenforceable by any holder or HDC.
      1) Ordinary duress making the instrument merely voidable is a personal defense.
   d. **Fraud in the execution** is committed against the signer when (s)he is induced to sign without knowledge and a reasonable opportunity to learn of the true character and essential terms of the instrument.
      1) Fraud in the execution (a real defense) differs from fraud in the inducement (a personal defense).
   e. If a party signs another's name on an instrument without permission (an **unauthorized signature** or forgery), the second party is not liable, even to an HDC. However, full liability is imposed against the forger in favor of someone who, in good faith, pays the instrument or takes it for value.
      1) If the unauthorized signature is of an endorsement, negotiation ordinarily cannot occur. No such transferee can be a holder or an HDC.
      2) However, if the forgery is of a drawer's or maker's signature, the instrument is negotiable. A transferee then may qualify as a holder or an HDC because the signature is effective as that of the unauthorized signer.
   f. **Alteration** is any unauthorized change in an instrument that modifies the obligation of a party. It is also any unauthorized addition of words or numbers.
      1) A fraudulent alteration discharges a party whose obligation is affected unless the party assents or is precluded from asserting the alteration.
      2) However, the instrument may be enforced according to its original terms by (a) a drawee or payor bank paying the instrument or (b) a person taking for value, in good faith, and without notice of the alteration.
         a) Moreover, such parties may enforce the instrument as completed if it has been altered by an unauthorized completion of an incomplete instrument.

g. **Lack of legal capacity** that renders an instrument void under state law is unenforceable by any holder or HDC.

h. **Minority** or **infancy** is a real defense only to the extent that state law recognizes it as a defense to a simple contract.

i. A **discharge in bankruptcy** is an absolute defense on any instrument regardless of the status of the holder.

   1) The purpose of bankruptcy is to settle an insolvent party's debts.

j. A **discharge of any party**. The holder may have notice of the discharge of any prior party, other than in an insolvency proceeding, when (s)he takes the instrument. In this case, even an HDC is barred from collecting on the instrument from the discharged party.

k. **Negligence** may substantially contribute to a forged signature or an alteration. A negligent person (e.g., a drawer or maker) is precluded from asserting real defenses against a person who, in good faith, pays the instrument or takes it for value or collection.

   1) Thus, these defenses are effectively changed from real to personal defenses. However, if the person asserting the preclusion is also negligent, the loss is allocated.

12. **Personal Defenses**

   a. An HDC takes a negotiable instrument free of personal defenses even if his or her transferor was not an HDC. Many traditional contract defenses are personal defenses. They are effective against anyone (1) **not** an HDC or (2) a holder through an HDC.

13. The following table summarizes defenses to performance of obligations on negotiable instruments:

Real Defenses (Effective against Holder and HDC)	**Personal Defenses – Examples** (Ineffective against HDC)
Illegality rendering the obligation void	Fraud in the inducement
Fraud in the execution	Unauthorized completion
Unauthorized signature	Failure of a condition
Fraudulent alteration	Lack or failure of consideration
Extreme duress rendering the obligation void	Theft of the instrument
Legal incapacity rendering the obligation void	Restrictive endorsement violated
Minority or infancy to the extent it is a defense to a simple contract	Payment without obtaining surrender of the instrument
Discharge in insolvency proceedings	Breach of contract or warranty
Any other discharge of which the holder has notice	Other contract defenses

Real and personal defenses have been tested in relation to whether the defenses presented in the question can be asserted against an HDC.

Stop and review! You have completed the outline for this subunit. Study multiple-choice questions 20 through 25 beginning on page 742.

19.6 DISCHARGE

1. **Overview**
   a. A party may be discharged, in whole or in part, from liability by acts or agreements with other parties that would discharge a simple contract for the payment of money.
   b. The UCC provides many ways in which a party may be discharged from liability on an instrument. However, a discharge is not effective against a person acquiring the rights of an HDC without notice of the discharge.
2. **Methods of Discharge**
   a. **Payment.** A party who pays the amount of the instrument to a person entitled to enforce the instrument is completely discharged.
      1) If a secondary party makes payment, (s)he is likewise discharged. Other parties who may be liable to the party making payment are not discharged.

EXAMPLE

Alex executes a promissory note to Baker. Baker endorses the note to Cara, who in turn endorses it to Danny. If Alex pays Danny, all parties are discharged. If Baker pays Danny, Baker and Cara are discharged, but Alex remains liable. If Cara pays Danny, she is discharged, but Alex and Baker remain liable.

      2) Partial payment discharges only to the extent of the payment.
   b. **Tender.** A party who tenders (offers) payment of an amount due to a person entitled to enforce the instrument is discharged. But the discharge is only to the extent of subsequent liability for interest on the amount tendered.
   c. **Cancelation.** A person entitled to enforce the instrument may discharge a party by a voluntary act. The act may include (1) surrender of the instrument to the party; (2) destruction, mutilation, or cancelation of the instrument; (3) striking out the party's signature; or (4) adding words to the instrument.
      1) However, striking out an endorsement has no effect on the rights of a party derived from the endorsement.
   d. **Renunciation.** A person entitled to enforce the instrument may agree not to sue or otherwise renounce rights against a party by a signed writing.
   e. **Reacquisition** is any transfer to a former holder, who may then cancel any intervening endorsements. If the instrument is thereby made payable to the reacquirer or to the bearer, the reacquirer may negotiate it.
      1) A canceled endorsement discharges that endorser, and the discharge is effective against any subsequent holder.
   f. Discharge by cancelation or renunciation does not discharge the obligation of an endorser or accommodation party with a right of recourse against the discharged party.

EXAMPLE

Able executed a promissory note to Baker and pledged a yacht as collateral. Baker negotiated the note to Carr by an unqualified endorsement and delivery. Carr allowed Able to sell the yacht. Carr has impaired the security. Baker is discharged to the extent of the collateral.

   g. **Other methods of discharge** are
      1) Fraudulent alteration,
      2) Certification of a check,
      3) Impairment of collateral,
      4) Impairment of recourse, and
      5) Unexcused delay in presentment or notice of dishonor.

Stop and review! You have completed the outline for this subunit. Study multiple-choice questions 26 and 27 on page 745.

19.7 DOCUMENTS OF TITLE

1. **Overview**
   a. A **document of title** is a record (tangible or electronic) that permits **transfer** of the ownership of goods that are in storage or transit. The person in possession of a tangible document or in control of an electronic document is entitled to receive, hold, and dispose of the document and the goods it covers.
      1) With certain exceptions, the same requirements apply to tangible and electronic documents.
   b. Documents of title generally are issued by professionals in the business of storing or delivering goods, i.e., warehousers and common carriers, respectively.
   c. A document of title has three functions:
      1) It is a **receipt** for goods.
      2) It is a **contract** between a **bailor** (one who entrusts personal property to another) and a **bailee** (one who receives such property to hold in trust). This agreement is for the storage or transport of goods.
      3) It is **evidence of title** to the goods.
2. **Negotiability**
   a. A document of title is **negotiable** only if it states that the goods are to be delivered to (1) the bearer or (2) the order of a named person. Any other document of title is **nonnegotiable**.
      1) A **bearer** is a person in (a) control of a negotiable electronic document or (b) possession of a negotiable tangible document payable to bearer or endorsed in blank.
         a) **Control** means that a system for recording transfers of electronic documents reliably establishes one person at a given time as the person to which the document has been issued or transferred. Thus, **delivery** is by voluntary transfer of
            i) Possession of a tangible document or
            ii) Control of an electronic document.
   b. Negotiable documents of title and negotiable instruments are **negotiated** similarly.
      1) Tangible documents in order form are negotiated by endorsement and delivery.
         a) Endorsement is **not** required for an electronic document.
      2) Bearer documents are negotiated by delivery alone.
      3) A blank endorsement (signature only) of an order document converts it to a bearer document.
      4) A special endorsement, e.g., endorsement to a specified person, of a bearer document converts it to an order document.
         a) Conditional or qualified endorsements do not apply to documents of title.
      5) A forged endorsement does not result in negotiation. Forgery is a real defense.

6) An endorser of a tangible document is **not** liable for any default by a bailee or a prior endorser.

Negotiability of Documents of Title

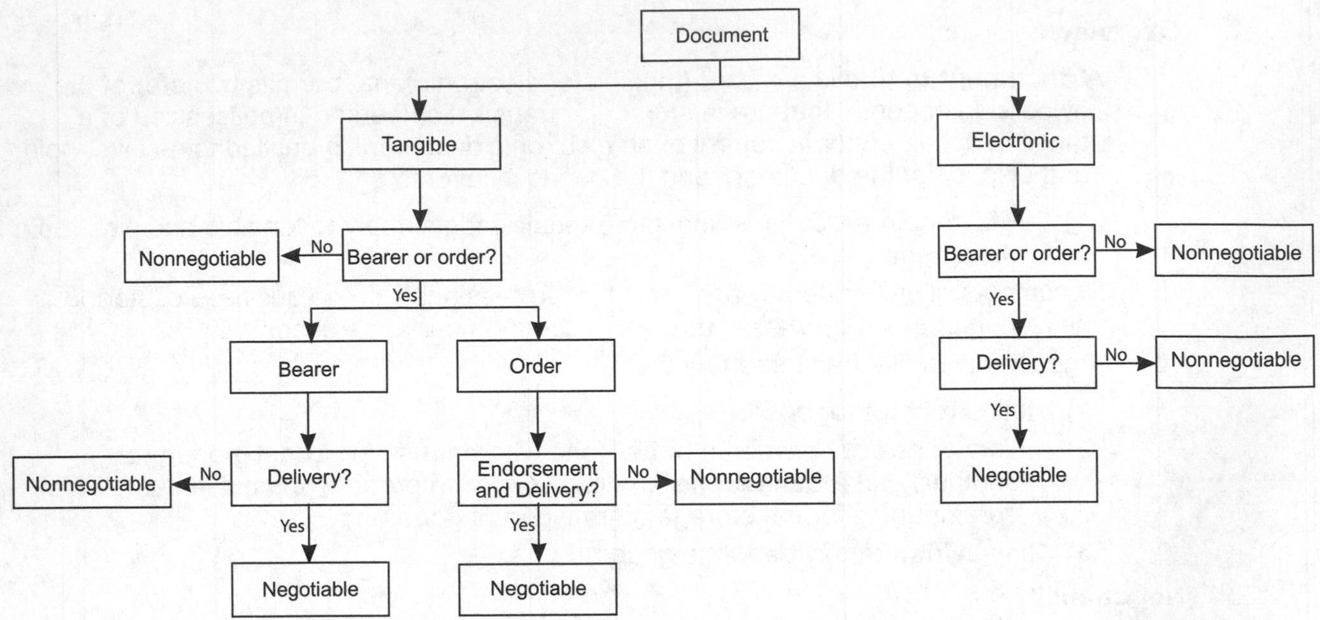

Figure 19-14

c. If the **document is negotiable**, the goods must be delivered to the holder of the document (or his or her agent or assignee).

1) A **holder** is the person in possession of a tangible document if the goods are deliverable to (a) bearer or (b) the order of the person in possession.

a) A holder is the person in control of an electronic document.

d. If the **document is nonnegotiable**, the goods usually must be delivered to the person named in the document.

1) The person requesting the goods is not required to present the document itself to obtain the goods if (s)he can prove that (s)he is (a) the bailor or (b) an assignee of the rights of the bailor.

2) Carriers and warehousers have absolute liability for misdelivery.

3. **Holder by Due Negotiation**

a. A person who takes a negotiable document of title by due negotiation is in a position similar to that of a holder in due course of a negotiable instrument.

b. A negotiable document of title is duly negotiated to a holder who purchases it

1) In good faith,
2) For value,
3) Without notice of any defense against or claim to it,
4) In the regular course of business or financing, and
5) Not in settlement or payment of a money obligation.

c. A holder by due negotiation acquires **title to the document and the goods**.

d. Furthermore, a holder by due negotiation takes the document and the goods free of claims and defenses raised by either the bailee or third parties. However, two exceptions exist:

1) The bailee is entitled to compensation for transportation or storage charges, which are usually specified in the document.

2) The holder will not be entitled to the goods when the bailor had no authority to deliver the goods to the bailee, carrier, or warehouser.
   a) A document of title issued to a bailor who was a **thief** of the goods does not represent title to the goods.
   b) But a thief can negotiate a bearer document or an order document that was endorsed in blank. A subsequent holder who takes by due negotiation then acquires rights superior to the original bailor's.

e. A transferee of any document is an **assignee** if the document has been delivered but not duly negotiated. The transferee acquires the title and rights that his or her transferor had or had actual authority to convey.

4. **Warehouse Receipts**

a. A warehouse receipt is issued by a warehouser to the person who **deposits goods for storage**. The depositor is the bailor, and the warehouser is the bailee.

b. A warehouse receipt need not be in any special form. However, it must include
   1) The location of the warehouse,
   2) The date of issue and a unique identifier,
   3) A description of the goods,
   4) The person (bearer, a specified person, or a specified person's order) to whom the goods are to be delivered,
   5) The warehouser's signature, and
   6) Certain other information.

c. With respect to the goods, a warehouser must exercise the same care that a reasonable person would under like circumstances.
   1) The warehouser is liable only for those damages caused by ordinary negligence or lack of due care.
   2) A warehouser may contractually limit its liability. The limitation does not apply if the warehouser converts the goods to its own use.

d. A warehouser must keep goods covered by each receipt separate.
   1) However, different lots of fungible goods may be commingled.

e. A warehouser has a lien on the goods enforceable by public or private sale.

5. **Bills of Lading**

a. A bill of lading is **evidence of the receipt of goods for shipment** issued by a person engaged in the business of transporting goods. The carrier is a bailee of the goods. The person delivering the goods to the carrier is the shipper and also the bailor.

b. A carrier has a lien on the goods enforceable by public or private sale. The lien extends to proceeds of the goods if the carrier has them.

c. Common carriers are special bailees and are subject to **strict liability** for losses occurring while goods are in transit. However, common carriers are not liable for damage or losses caused by
   1) An act of God,
   2) The fault of the shipper,
   3) An act of a public enemy,
   4) An act of public authority, or
   5) The inherent nature of the goods.

d. A carrier may limit its liability by contract and notation on the bill of lading. But this limit does not apply if the carrier converts the goods to its own use.

6. **Warranties**
   a. A transferor of a document of title who has negotiated or delivered it for value warrants to the immediate purchaser that
      1) The document is genuine.
      2) (S)he has no knowledge of any fact that impairs the document's worth or validity.
      3) The delivery or negotiation is rightful and fully effective with respect to the title to the document and the goods it represents.

Stop and review! You have completed the outline for this subunit. Study multiple-choice questions 28 through 30 on page 746.

QUESTIONS

<u>19.1 Types of Negotiable Instruments</u>

1. Given the following information:

> To: Middlesex National Bank
> Nassau, N.Y.
> September 15, Year 1
>
> Pay to the order of Robert Silver $4,000.00
>
> Four Thousand and xx/100 Dollars
>
> on October 1, Year 1
>
> *Lynn Dexter*
>
> Lynn Dexter

The above instrument is a

A. Draft.

B. Postdated check.

C. Trade acceptance.

D. Promissory note.

Answer (A) is correct.

REQUIRED: The type of instrument.

DISCUSSION: A draft is any three-party instrument in which one person (the drawer) orders a second person (the drawee) to pay a third person (the payee). With this instrument, Lynn Dexter is ordering Middlesex National Bank to pay Robert Silver. The instrument is a time draft because it is payable at a definite time in the future.

Answer (B) is incorrect. A check is a type of sight draft for which a bank is ordered to make the payment on demand. However, this instrument is dated September 15, Year 1, but is not payable on demand until October 1, Year 1. Thus, it is a time draft that is predated, not postdated. The check would be postdated if it had been issued prior to September 15, Year 1, and did not state a payment date. Answer (C) is incorrect. A trade acceptance is a special form of draft. The seller is both the drawer and the payee of the draft. Answer (D) is incorrect. A promissory note is a two-party instrument in which one party promises to pay another party a fixed amount of money.

2. Under the Negotiable Instruments Article of the UCC, which of the following documents would be considered an order to pay?

I. Draft
II. Certificate of deposit

A. I only.

B. II only.

C. Both I and II.

D. Neither I nor II.

Answer (A) is correct.

REQUIRED: The instrument(s) considered payable on order.

DISCUSSION: A draft is an unconditional written order by one person, the drawer, to another person, the drawee (the bank), to pay a third party on demand or at some definite time. Thus, a draft is an order instrument. A CD is a form of promissory note. It is a two-party instrument containing a promise.

3. A trade acceptance usually

A. Is an order to deliver goods to a named person.

B. Provides that the drawer is also the payee.

C. Is not regarded as a negotiable instrument under the UCC.

D. Must be made payable "to the order of" a named person.

Answer (B) is correct.

REQUIRED: The true statement about trade acceptance.

DISCUSSION: A trade acceptance is a special form of negotiable instrument. It is a time draft used by sellers as a way to extend credit to buyers of their goods. The seller draws a draft ordering the buyer to pay the seller at some time in the future. The seller is thus both drawer and payee of a trade acceptance.

Answer (A) is incorrect. A trade acceptance is a form of negotiable instrument and must be payable in money. Answer (C) is incorrect. Trade acceptances are a type of draft and as such are recognized as negotiable instruments under the UCC. Answer (D) is incorrect. A trade acceptance may be payable to order or to bearer.

19.2 Negotiability

4. There are several legally significant differences between a negotiable instrument and a contract right, and the transfer of each. Which of the following statements is true?

A. A negotiable instrument is deemed prima facie to have been issued for consideration, but a contract is not.

B. The transferee of a negotiable instrument and the assignee of a contract right take free of most defenses.

C. Neither can be transferred without a signed writing or by a transfer of possession.

D. The statute of frauds rules apply to both.

Answer (A) is correct.

REQUIRED: The true statement comparing negotiable instruments and contract rights.

DISCUSSION: A negotiable instrument is presumed to have been issued for consideration, but no such assumption is made regarding a contract. One must prove consideration to enforce a contract right, not a negotiable instrument.

Answer (B) is incorrect. The transferee of a negotiable instrument (who is not a holder in due course or a holder through an HDC) and the assignee of a contract right both take subject to all defenses the third party has against the assignor. Answer (C) is incorrect. A contract right can be transferred orally and without transfer of possession. A negotiable instrument requires an endorsement and transfer of possession if it is order paper or transfer of possession alone if it is bearer paper. Answer (D) is incorrect. The statute of frauds applies only to certain contracts. But an instrument must be in writing to be negotiable.

5. Shark holds the following:

> May 19, Year 1
>
> I promise to pay to the order of A.B. Shark $1,000 (One thousand and one hundred dollars) with interest thereon at the rate of 12% per annum
>
> *T. T. Tile*
> T. T. Tile
>
> I personally guaranty payment by T.T. Tile.
>
> *Abner Jones*
> Abner Jones

The instrument is

A. Nonnegotiable even though it is payable on demand.

B. Nonnegotiable because the numeric amount differs from the written amount.

C. Negotiable even though a payment date is not specified.

D. Negotiable because of Abner's guaranty.

Answer (C) is correct.

REQUIRED: The negotiability of the promissory note.

DISCUSSION: To be negotiable, an instrument must promise or order payment of money on demand or at a definite time. If a payment date is not specified, the UCC treats the instrument as payable on demand and negotiable as such. Moreover, the issue date is not required to appear on the face of the instrument.

Answer (A) is incorrect. The note is a writing signed by the maker. It contains an unconditional promise to pay a fixed amount of money to order. It is treated as payable on demand. Answer (B) is incorrect. Different numeric and written amounts do not defeat negotiability. Handwritten terms prevail over typewritten and printed terms, and words prevail over numbers. Answer (D) is incorrect. Although an unconditional promise is a prerequisite to negotiability of a note, providing a guaranty or security does not preclude negotiability.

6. An instrument reads as follows:

$10,000	Ludlow, Vermont	February 1, Year 1

I promise to pay to the order of Custer Corp. $10,000 within 10 days after the sale of my two-carat diamond ring. I pledge the sale proceeds to secure my obligation hereunder.

R. Harris
R. Harris

Which of the following statements correctly describes the above instrument?

A. The instrument is nonnegotiable because it is not payable at a definite time.

B. The instrument is nonnegotiable because it is secured by the proceeds of the ring's sale.

C. The instrument is a negotiable promissory note.

D. The instrument is a negotiable sight draft payable on demand.

Answer (A) is correct.

REQUIRED: The statement that describes the instrument.

DISCUSSION: The instrument is a signed writing promising to pay a fixed amount of money to the order of an identified person. An amount of money is fixed if it is possible to compute the amount from the face of the instrument. But the obligation to pay and its timing depend on an uncertain event. The promise is thus conditional, not unconditional as required for negotiability. A "definite time" is not limited to one particular date. An instrument payable on or before a stated date is payable on demand until that date and is payable at a fixed date subsequently (if not yet paid).

Answer (B) is incorrect. Existence of security does not condition the obligation to pay or affect the note's negotiability. Answer (C) is incorrect. The promise is conditioned upon the sale of the ring. Answer (D) is incorrect. A draft contains an order by the drawer to the drawee to pay a third person.

7. A secured promissory note would be nonnegotiable if it provided that

A. Additional collateral must be tendered if there is a decline in market value of the original collateral.

B. The maker waives a trial by jury upon default.

C. The maker is entitled to a 5% discount if the note is prepaid.

D. It is subject to the terms of the mortgage given by the maker to the payee.

Answer (D) is correct.

REQUIRED: The provision that defeats negotiability of a promissory note.

DISCUSSION: A negotiable instrument must include an unconditional promise or order to pay. When a promise or order is subject to or governed by the provisions of another writing, it is conditional. A conditional instrument is nonnegotiable because the rights of a holder cannot be ascertained with reasonable certainty from the face of it (within its four corners). A note that is subject to the terms of a mortgage violates this requirement and is rendered nonnegotiable.

Answer (A) is incorrect. A negotiable instrument may include a promise to maintain or protect collateral. Answer (B) is incorrect. Waiver of a benefit for the advantage or protection of the obligor does not affect negotiability. Answer (C) is incorrect. The requirement of a fixed amount of money does not preclude a provision for specified prepayment discounts.

8. Under the Negotiable Instruments Article of the UCC, which of the following instruments meets the negotiability requirement of being payable on demand or at a definite time?

A. A promissory note payable 1 year after a person's marriage.

B. A promissory note payable June 30, Year 1, whose holder can extend the time of payment until the following June 30 if the holder wishes.

C. A promissory note payable June 30, Year 1, whose maturity can be extended by the maker for a reasonable time.

D. An undated promissory note payable 1 month after date.

Answer (B) is correct.

REQUIRED: The instrument that is payable on demand or at a definite time.

DISCUSSION: A promissory note is an unconditional written promise between two parties for one to pay the other a fixed amount of money on demand or at some defined future date. An extension clause does not defeat negotiability if the instrument is payable at a fixed date and is subject to extension at the holder's option.

Answer (A) is incorrect. A person's marriage is not a definite time. Answer (C) is incorrect. The period of extension must be for a further definite time if the maker or acceptor has the option to extend the maturity date. Answer (D) is incorrect. If the instrument is payable on elapse of a definite period, the promissory note must be dated, or the definite period must begin after sight or acceptance.

9. The following instrument is in the possession of Bill North:

> On May 30, Year 1, I promise to pay Bill North, the bearer of this document, $3,800.
>
> *Joseph Peppers*
> Joseph Peppers
>
> Re: Auto Purchase Contract

This instrument is

A. Nonnegotiable because it is undated.

B. Nonnegotiable because it is not payable to order or bearer.

C. Negotiable even though it refers to the contract out of which it arose.

D. Negotiable because it is payable at a definite time.

Answer (B) is correct.

REQUIRED: The negotiability of the instrument.

DISCUSSION: The instrument is a nonnegotiable note because it is not payable to order or bearer. It is payable only to Bill North and refers to him specifically as bearer on its face.

Answer (A) is incorrect. An issue date is not necessary for negotiability. Answer (C) is incorrect. The instrument is nonnegotiable. It is not payable to order or to bearer. Reference to a separate agreement would impair negotiability only if the obligation were governed by or made subject to the other agreement. Answer (D) is incorrect. More is required for negotiability than an instrument being payable at a definite time or on demand.

19.3 Endorsements

10. Ed Johnson lost a check that he had received for professional services rendered. The instrument on its face was payable to Johnson's order. He had endorsed it on the back by signing his name and printing "for deposit only" above his name. Assuming the check is found by Amy, which of the following is true?

A. A nonbank party who purchases the instrument converts it unless the amount paid is received by the endorser or applied consistently with the endorsement.

B. The endorsement is a blank endorsement, and a holder in due course who cashed it for Amy would prevail.

C. The endorsement prevents further transfer or negotiation by anyone.

D. If Amy simply signs her name beneath Johnson's endorsement, the instrument becomes bearer paper, and a holder in due course would take free of the restriction.

Answer (A) is correct.

REQUIRED: The correct statement regarding the effect of an endorsement "for deposit only."

DISCUSSION: A restrictive endorsement "for deposit only" puts the burden on most subsequent transferees to comply with the endorsement or to be certain that the endorsement has already been complied with. Thus, a nonbank purchaser transferee of Johnson's check is required to act consistently with the endorsement; i.e., (s)he must deposit the check only in Johnson's bank account.

Answer (B) is incorrect. "For deposit only" is a restrictive endorsement (not a blank endorsement), and most subsequent transferees must comply with it. Answer (C) is incorrect. The endorsement merely restricts payment. It does not prevent transfer or negotiation (an endorsement attempting to do so is not effective). Answer (D) is incorrect. The restrictive endorsement prevents the instrument from being changed directly into bearer paper. Furthermore, a subsequent transferee could not qualify as a holder in due course if the restriction had not been complied with.

11. Under the Negotiable Instruments Article of the UCC, when an instrument is endorsed "Pay to Dee Doe" and signed "Faye Maye," which of the following statements, if any, is(are) true?

	Payment of the Instrument Is Guaranteed	The Instrument Can Be Further Negotiated
A.	Yes	Yes
B.	Yes	No
C.	No	Yes
D.	No	No

Answer (A) is correct.

REQUIRED: The true statement(s) about the effect of an endorsement of a negotiable instrument.

DISCUSSION: When the holder of a negotiable instrument, Faye Maye, wrote the words "pay to Dee Doe" on the instrument, the result was an unqualified special endorsement. The effect upon transfer of possession is that Doe may further negotiate by endorsement and transfer of possession. The unqualified endorsement by Maye results in secondary contract liability on her part if the primary party defaults and proper notice is given.

12. Jen Day received a check originally made payable to the order of one of her customers, Al Pine. The following endorsement was written on the back of the check:

Al Pine, without recourse, for collection only

The endorsement on this check is classified as

A. Blank, unqualified, and nonrestrictive.

B. Blank, qualified, and restrictive.

C. Special, unqualified, and restrictive.

D. Special, qualified, and nonrestrictive.

Answer (B) is correct.

REQUIRED: The classification of an endorsement without recourse, for collection only.

DISCUSSION: A blank endorsement specifies no particular endorsee. A special endorsement would have specified the person to whom or to whose order the instrument was payable. An endorsement is restrictive if it includes the words "for collection," "for deposit," or like terms signifying a purpose of having the instrument collected by a bank for the endorser or a particular account. The endorsement "without recourse" is qualified. It disclaims contract liability but does not eliminate warranty liability.

Answer (A) is incorrect. An endorsement bearing the notation "without recourse" is qualified. Answer (C) is incorrect. A blank endorsement specifies no particular endorsee, and an endorsement bearing the notation "without recourse" is qualified. Answer (D) is incorrect. The endorsement is blank and restrictive.

13. Under the Negotiable Instruments Article of the UCC, which of the following statements best describes the effect of a person endorsing a check "without recourse"?

A. The person has no liability to prior endorsers.

B. The person makes no promise or guarantee of payment on dishonor.

C. The person gives no warranty protection to later transferees.

D. The person converts the check into order paper.

Answer (B) is correct.

REQUIRED: The effect of a qualified endorsement.

DISCUSSION: An endorser may disclaim or limit contractual liability by using a qualified endorsement. The statement "without recourse" disclaims liability for payment of the instrument to all later transferees. The qualified endorser does not accept any liability if the instrument is not paid by the primary party. A qualified endorsement has no effect on the instrument's negotiability. However, unless otherwise agreed, a transferee for value who does not become a holder because of lack of the transferor's endorsement has a specifically enforceable right to an unqualified endorsement.

Answer (A) is incorrect. Any endorser of a negotiable instrument has no liability to prior endorsers. Answer (C) is incorrect. A qualified endorser makes the usual transfer warranties. Answer (D) is incorrect. A qualified endorsement alone does not affect whether the check is order or bearer paper.

14. One of the requirements to qualify as a holder of a negotiable bearer check is that the transferee must

A. Receive the check that was originally made payable to bearer.

B. Take the check in good faith.

C. Give value for the check.

D. Have possession of the check.

Answer (D) is correct.

REQUIRED: The requirement to qualify as a holder of a negotiable bearer check.

DISCUSSION: A person who acquires a negotiable instrument absent negotiation is a mere transferee or possessor of the instrument. Negotiable bearer paper is negotiated by mere transfer of possession. The current holder of negotiable bearer paper is by definition a person in possession.

Answer (A) is incorrect. A check would be negotiable bearer paper if it were originally made payable to order and subsequently endorsed in blank. Answer (B) is incorrect. The good faith requirement for holder-in-due-course status is not necessary to holder status. Answer (C) is incorrect. Giving value for the check is not required for status as a holder.

19.4 Holders in Due Course

15. Under the Negotiable Instruments Article of the UCC, which of the following circumstances would prevent a person from becoming a holder in due course of an instrument?

A. The person was notified that payment was refused.

B. The person was notified that one of the prior endorsers was discharged.

C. The note was collateral for a loan.

D. The note was purchased at a discount.

Answer (A) is correct.

REQUIRED: The circumstance preventing a person from becoming a holder in due course.

DISCUSSION: A holder can become a holder in due course (HDC) only if the transferee was unaware the instrument had been dishonored. Thus, if the transferee has notice that payment was refused when the instrument was presented for payment, the holder cannot be an HDC.

Answer (B) is incorrect. The transferee may be an HDC regardless of notice of the discharge of a prior endorser if (s)he meets the requirements of good faith, no notice of claims or defenses, payment of value, etc. Answer (C) is incorrect. A transferee may be an HDC with respect to any negotiable instrument if the person has no notice of a claim to it. Accordingly, if the transferee had no notice the note was collateral for a loan, as a good-faith purchaser, (s)he takes the note as an HDC. Answer (D) is incorrect. A transferee may become an HDC if (s)he gives value. The amount or adequacy of the consideration given is irrelevant. However, a very deep discount may be indicative of a defense to the instrument.

16. Silver Corp. sold 20 tons of steel to River Corp. with payment to be by River's check. The price of steel was fluctuating daily. Silver requested that the amount of River's check be left blank so that Silver could fill in the current market price. River complied with Silver's request. Within 2 days, Silver received River's check. Although the market price of 20 tons of steel at the time Silver received River's check was $80,000, Silver filled in the check for $100,000 and negotiated it to Hatch Corp. Hatch took the check in good faith, without notice of Silver's act or any other defense, and in payment of an existing obligation. River will

A. Not be liable to Hatch, because the check was materially altered by Silver.

B. Not be liable to Hatch, because Hatch failed to give value when it acquired the check from Silver.

C. Be liable to Hatch for $100,000.

D. Be liable to Hatch, but only for $80,000.

Answer (C) is correct.

REQUIRED: The effect of an unauthorized completion of a check on the drawer's liability to an HDC.

DISCUSSION: Hatch took the instrument (1) for value (in this situation, the antecedent debt), (2) in good faith, and (3) without notice of an alteration (e.g., an unauthorized completion). An alteration means an unauthorized change in or addition to the instrument. Although Silver's alteration was apparently fraudulent, Hatch may enforce the instrument according to its terms as completed. Accordingly, River is liable to Hatch, who apparently qualifies as an HDC, for the amount of the check as completed.

Answer (A) is incorrect. When an incomplete instrument has been improperly completed, a subsequent HDC may enforce it as completed. Answer (B) is incorrect. A holder takes for value when (s)he takes in payment of an existing obligation. Answer (D) is incorrect. When an incomplete instrument has been improperly completed, a subsequent HDC may enforce it as completed.

17. Bond fraudulently induced Teal to make a note payable to Wilk, to whom Bond was indebted. Bond delivered the note to Wilk. Wilk negotiated the instrument to Smith, who purchased it with knowledge of the fraud after it was overdue. If Wilk qualifies as a holder in due course, which of the following statements is true?

A. Smith has the standing of a holder in due course through Wilk.

B. Teal can successfully assert the defense of fraud in the inducement against Smith.

C. Smith personally qualifies as a holder in due course.

D. Teal can successfully assert the defense of fraud in the inducement against Wilk.

Answer (A) is correct.

REQUIRED: The effect of a holder's knowledge of fraud when (s)he has taken from an HDC.

DISCUSSION: A person who takes through a holder in due course (HDC) acquires the rights of an HDC unless the transferee was a party to any fraud or illegality affecting the instrument. This rule is the "shelter principle." Smith was not a party to the fraud. Thus, Smith can assert the rights of Wilk, the HDC.

Answer (B) is incorrect. Smith is an assignee of Wilk's rights as an HDC. Thus, Smith is not subject to personal defense (e.g., fraud in the inducement) because they are ineffective against Smith's transferor (an HDC). Answer (C) is incorrect. Smith knew of the fraud and thus cannot be an HDC. Answer (D) is incorrect. Wilk is an HDC. Fraud in the inducement is a personal defense and therefore ineffective against an HDC.

18. A $5,000 promissory note payable to the order of Neptune is discounted to Bane by blank endorsement for $4,000. King steals the note from Bane and sells it to Ott, who promises to pay King $4,500. After paying King $3,000, Ott learns that King stole the note. Ott makes no further payment to King. Ott is

A. A holder in due course to the extent of $5,000.

B. An ordinary holder to the extent of $4,500.

C. A holder in due course to the extent of $3,333.

D. An ordinary holder to the extent of $0.

Answer (C) is correct.

REQUIRED: The status of a holder after receiving notice of a defense prior to full payment.

DISCUSSION: A holder in due course (HDC) is a holder of an instrument that does not appear to be of questionable authenticity when issued or negotiated to the holder. Moreover, the holder must have taken the instrument (1) for value; (2) in good faith; and (3) without notice of certain facts that may preclude HDC status. An unsecured, executory promise to pay is not considered value given for a negotiable instrument. Prior to receiving notice of a defense against the instrument, Ott gave value equal to $3,000. Under UCC 3-302, if the promise of performance that is consideration for the instrument is partially performed, the holder may assert rights as an HDC only to the fraction of the amount payable under the instrument equal to the value of the partial performance divided by the value of the promised performance. Thus, Ott is entitled to $3,333 [$5,000 × ($3,000 ÷ $4,500)].

Answer (A) is incorrect. Ott is an HDC only with respect to the value given prior to notice of a defense. Answer (B) is incorrect. Negotiability is determined by the face of the instrument. Blank endorsement rendered it bearer paper. Mere transfer of possession to Ott constituted negotiation. Ott meets the criteria of an HDC to the extent of the value given. Answer (D) is incorrect. Negotiability is determined by the face of the instrument. Blank endorsement rendered it bearer paper. Mere transfer of possession to Ott constituted negotiation. Ott is an HDC to the extent of value given.

19. Dart induces Shorr by fraud to make a promissory note payable to Dart. Dart negotiates the note for value to Best, who was aware of the fraud. Best negotiates the note to Case, a holder in due course. Subsequently, Best repurchases the note from Case. Which of the following statements is true?

A. Best acquires rights as a holder in due course.

B. Best becomes a holder in due course upon taking the note from Dart.

C. Because of the fraud by Dart, the note is nonnegotiable.

D. Best's knowledge of Dart's fraud is immaterial in determining Best's status as a holder in due course.

Answer (A) is correct.

REQUIRED: The effect of a prior holder's knowledge of fraud when (s)he has taken from a holder in due course.

DISCUSSION: A person who takes through a holder in due course acquires the rights of a holder in due course unless the transferee engaged in any fraud or illegality affecting the instrument. Best was a prior holder with notice of a defense and therefore cannot be a holder in due course. However, the shelter principle permits Best to assert the rights of Case, the holder in due course, because Best did not engage in fraud or illegality affecting the instrument.

19.5 Liability and Defenses

20. To the extent that a holder of a negotiable promissory note is a holder in due course, the holder takes the note free of which of the following defenses?

A. Minority of the maker if it is a defense to enforcement of a simple contract.

B. Forgery of the maker's signature.

C. Discharge of the maker in bankruptcy.

D. Nonperformance of a condition precedent.

Answer (D) is correct.

REQUIRED: The defense ineffective against a holder in due course.

DISCUSSION: A holder in due course (HDC) is subject to real defenses. Real defenses include (1) infancy to the extent that it is a defense to a simple contract; (2) incapacity, duress, or illegality that makes the obligation void and not merely voidable; (3) fraud in the execution; and (4) discharge in insolvency proceedings. Alteration and unauthorized signature also may be real defenses. Traditional contract defenses, such as nonperformance of a condition precedent, are usually personal defenses. They are not valid against an HDC.

Answer (A) is incorrect. Minority of the maker is a real defense effective against an HDC. Answer (B) is incorrect. Forgery is a real defense. Answer (C) is incorrect. Discharge in bankruptcy is a real defense.

21. A maker of a note will have a real defense against a holder in due course as a result of any of the following conditions **except**

A. Discharge in bankruptcy.

B. Forgery.

C. Fraud in the execution.

D. Lack of consideration.

Answer (D) is correct.

REQUIRED: The defense ineffective against a holder in due course.

DISCUSSION: A holder in due course (HDC) is subject to real defenses. Real defenses include (1) infancy to the extent that it is a defense to a simple contract; (2) incapacity, extreme duress, or illegality that makes the obligation void; (3) fraud in the execution; and (4) discharge in insolvency proceedings. Alteration and unauthorized signature also may be real defenses. Traditional contract defenses, such as lack of consideration, are usually personal defenses and thus are not valid against an HDC. Fraud in the inducement, ordinary duress, and wrongful completion are other examples of personal defenses.

Answer (A) is incorrect. Discharge in bankruptcy is a real defense and is effective against an HDC. Answer (B) is incorrect. Forgery is a real defense and is effective against an HDC. Answer (C) is incorrect. Fraud in the execution is a real defense and is effective against an HDC.

22. Wilson drew a sight draft on Jimmy Foxx (a customer who owed Wilson money on an open account), payable to the order of Burton, one of Wilson's creditors. Burton presented it to Foxx. After examining the draft as to its authenticity and checking the amount against outstanding debts to Wilson, Foxx wrote on its face, "Accepted--payable in 10 days" and signed it. When Burton returned at the end of 10 days, Foxx told him he could not pay and was hard-pressed for cash. Burton did not notify Wilson of these facts. Two days later, when Burton again presented the instrument for payment, Burton was told that Foxx's creditors had filed a petition in bankruptcy that morning. Which of the following statements is true?

A. The instrument in question is a type of demand promissory note.

B. Wilson had primary liability on the draft at its inception.

C. Foxx was secondarily liable on the draft at its inception.

D. Foxx assumed primary liability at the time of acceptance.

Answer (D) is correct.

REQUIRED: The true statement about a sight draft that has been accepted and then dishonored by the drawee.

DISCUSSION: A sight draft is essentially a demand draft payable upon presentment to the drawee. A draft has no primarily liable party until acceptance by the drawee. Upon acceptance, Foxx assumed primary liability. However, the claim must be filed in the bankruptcy proceeding.

Answer (A) is incorrect. The instrument is a type of draft (i.e., a three-party instrument), not a type of note. Answer (B) is incorrect. Wilson had secondary liability as drawer, given that the acceptor was not a bank. Answer (C) is incorrect. Foxx had no liability on the instrument until he accepted it.

23. Robb, a minor, executed a promissory note payable to bearer and delivered it to Dodsen in payment for a stereo system. Dodsen negotiated the note for value to Mellon by transfer of possession alone and without endorsement. Mellon endorsed the note in blank and negotiated it to Bloom for value. Bloom's demand for payment was refused by Robb because the note was executed when Robb was a minor. Bloom gave prompt notice of Robb's default to Dodsen and Mellon. No holder of the note was aware of Robb's minority. Which of the following parties will be liable to Bloom?

	Dodsen	Mellon
A.	Yes	Yes
B.	Yes	No
C.	No	No
D.	No	Yes

Answer (D) is correct.

REQUIRED: The true statement about liability of parties to a promissory note executed by a minor.

DISCUSSION: Any person who signs a negotiable instrument is liable on it. A party is primarily liable if (s)he is required to pay by the terms of the instrument itself. Unqualified endorsers are secondarily liable. They are liable if (1) the party with primary liability fails to honor the instrument, and (2) the holder gives timely notice of dishonor (assuming presentment and notice of dishonor are not excused). Hence, Mellon is liable to Bloom as an endorser. Dodsen is not liable to Bloom, a subsequent transferee. A person who does not endorse an instrument is generally not liable on it (except to the immediate transferee). However, a person who transfers a negotiable instrument without endorsement, but for consideration, makes certain warranties to the immediate transferee. One such warranty is that the instrument is not subject to a defense that can be asserted against the warrantor. If minority is a defense to a simple contract, it is a defense effective even against an HDC. Thus, Dodsen breached a transfer warranty made to Mellon.

24. Jim Bass is in possession of a negotiable promissory note made payable "to bearer." Bass acquired the note from Mary Frank for value. The maker of the note was Fred Jackson. The following endorsements appear on the back of the note:

> *Sam Peters*
> Pay Jim Bass
> *Mary Frank*
> *Jim Bass*
> (without recourse)

Bass presented the note to Jackson, who refused to pay it because he was financially unable to do so. Which of the following statements is true?

A. Peters is not secondarily liable on the note because his endorsement was unnecessary for negotiation.

B. Peters is not secondarily liable to Bass.

C. If the instrument is silent about dishonor, Frank will probably not be liable to Bass unless Bass gives notice to Frank of Jackson's refusal to pay within 30 days following dishonor.

D. Bass would have a secondary liability to Peters and Frank if he had not qualified his endorsement.

Answer (C) is correct.

REQUIRED: The true statement about the liability of endorsers of a negotiable instrument.

DISCUSSION: Unqualified endorsers of an instrument are secondarily liable on the instrument. They are obligated to pay if the primarily liable party fails to do so. This liability is contingent on the holder's timely notice of dishonor unless (1) notice is excused by the terms of the instrument, or (2) the party whose obligation is being enforced waived notice. Bass must give Frank notice of Jackson's dishonor to hold Frank to her secondary liability as endorser of the instrument. If the instrument was not taken for collection by a collecting bank, notice must be given within 30 days following the day of dishonor.

Answer (A) is incorrect. All unqualified endorsers, whether or not their endorsements were necessary for negotiation, are secondarily liable on an instrument. Answer (B) is incorrect. An unqualified endorser is liable to (1) a subsequent endorser who paid the instrument or (2) a person entitled to enforce the instrument (e.g., Bass). Answer (D) is incorrect. The obligation of an endorser is owed to (1) a subsequent endorser who paid the instrument or (2) a person entitled to enforce the instrument, not to a previous endorser.

25. Ball borrowed $10,000 from Link. Ball, unable to repay the debt on its due date, fraudulently induced Park to purchase a piece of worthless costume jewelry for $10,000. Ball had Park write a check for that amount naming Link as the payee. Ball gave the check to Link in satisfaction of the debt Ball owed Link. Unaware of Ball's fraud, Link cashed the check. When Park discovered Ball's fraud, Park demanded that Link repay the $10,000. Under the Negotiable Instruments Article of the UCC, will Link be required to repay Park?

A. No, because Link is a holder in due course of the check.

B. No, because Link is the payee of the check and has no obligation on the check once it is cashed.

C. Yes, because Link is subject to Park's defense of fraud in the inducement.

D. Yes, because Link, as the payee of the check, takes it subject to all claims.

Answer (A) is correct.

REQUIRED: The liability of a payee of a check who was unaware that the drawer had been fraudulently induced to issue the instrument.

DISCUSSION: A holder in due course (HDC) is a holder of an instrument that does not appear to be of questionable authenticity when issued or negotiated to the holder. Moreover, the holder must have taken the instrument (1) for value; (2) in good faith; and (3) without notice of facts that may preclude HDC status, e.g., a claim or defense. Link is an HDC. Link gave value (satisfaction of Ball's debt) and had no notice of a defense on the instrument assertible by Park (the drawer of the check). Fraud in the inducement is a type of defense (a personal defense) that could be asserted by Park against Ball but not an HDC.

Answer (B) is incorrect. Link would be liable if (s)he (1) were not an HDC or (2) did not have the rights of an HDC. Answer (C) is incorrect. Link would be subject to real defenses, e.g., fraud in the execution, not the personal defense of fraud in the inducement. Answer (D) is incorrect. An HDC has no notice of claims to the instrument. (S)he takes free of claims not based on a real defense.

19.6 Discharge

26.

Pay to Ann Tyler
Paul Tyler
Ann Tyler
Mary Thomas
~~*Betty Ash*~~
Pay George Green only
Susan Town

Susan Town, on receiving this instrument, struck Betty Ash's endorsement. Under the Negotiable Instruments Article of the UCC, which of the endorsers of this instrument will be completely discharged from secondary liability to later endorsers of the instrument?

A. Ann Tyler.

B. Mary Thomas.

C. Betty Ash.

D. Susan Town.

Answer (C) is correct.

REQUIRED: The effect on liability after an endorsement is canceled.

DISCUSSION: Betty Ash is discharged from liability on the instrument. Susan Town, as a person presumably entitled to enforce the instrument, may discharge the obligation of a party by striking out that party's signature. However, discharge of an endorser does not discharge the obligation of an endorser or accommodation party with a right of recourse against the discharged party.

27. A check has the following endorsements on the back:

Paul Folk
without recourse
George Hopkins
payment guaranteed
Ann Quarry
collection guaranteed
Rachel Ott

Which condition occurring subsequent to the endorsements will discharge all endorsers?

A. Lack of notice of dishonor.

B. Late presentment.

C. Insolvency of the maker.

D. Certification of the check.

Answer (D) is correct.

REQUIRED: The condition that discharges all the endorsers of a check.

DISCUSSION: Certification is an unconditional promise by a bank to pay (an acceptance of liability). Prior to certification, a drawee bank is not liable on a check. But once the drawee bank certifies a check, the drawer and all prior endorsers are discharged. Moreover, by his qualified endorsement, Paul Folk is not liable on the instrument.

Answer (A) is incorrect. Unless excused, lack of notice of dishonor impairs a right of recourse and discharges secondarily liable endorsers. But the guarantors are primarily liable and are not discharged. Answer (B) is incorrect. Unless excused, late presentment discharges secondarily liable endorsers but not guarantors. Answer (C) is incorrect. Insolvency of the maker discharges nobody. A discharge in bankruptcy proceedings, however, effects discharge only of that person from liability on the instrument.

19.7 Documents of Title

28. The procedure necessary to negotiate a document of title depends principally on whether the document is

A. An order document or a bearer document.

B. A document issued by a bailee or a consignee.

C. A receipt for goods stored or goods already shipped.

D. A bill of lading or a warehouse receipt.

Answer (A) is correct.

REQUIRED: The factor most affecting the negotiation of a document of title.

DISCUSSION: The negotiation of a document of title principally depends on whether the document is an order document or a bearer document. A tangible order document must be endorsed and delivered to be properly negotiated. But delivery suffices to complete the negotiation of a bearer document or an electronic document.

Answer (B) is incorrect. The person issuing the document is irrelevant to the negotiation of a document of title. Answer (C) is incorrect. Whether the document is a receipt for goods stored or goods already shipped is irrelevant. Answer (D) is incorrect. Bills of lading and warehouse receipts are both documents of title, and negotiation requires the same procedures for both.

29. Klep stole several negotiable warehouse receipts, which were deliverable to the order of Apple from the premises of Store Co. Klep endorsed Store's name on the instruments and transferred them to Margo Wholesalers, a bona fide purchaser for value. As between Store and Margo,

A. Store will prevail because the warehouser must be notified before negotiation is effective.

B. Store will prevail because Klep's endorsement prevents negotiation.

C. Margo will prevail because it has taken a negotiable warehouse receipt as a bona fide purchaser for value.

D. Margo will prevail because the warehouse receipt was converted to a bearer instrument by Klep's endorsement.

Answer (B) is correct.

REQUIRED: The effect of a forged endorsement on a document of title.

DISCUSSION: Due negotiation means that a negotiable document of title is negotiated to a holder who purchases it (1) in good faith, (2) for value, (3) without notice of any defense against or claim to it, (4) in the regular course of business or financing, and (5) not in settlement or payment of a money obligation. A holder to whom a negotiable document of title has been duly negotiated acquires title to the document. However, negotiation of a tangible document requires an endorsement as well as delivery if the document is issued to the order of a named person. Klep's forgery of Store's endorsement does not constitute negotiation. It provides Store a real defense against Margo even though Margo was a bona fide purchaser for value.

Answer (A) is incorrect. Negotiation does not require notification of the warehouser. Answer (C) is incorrect. The warehouse receipt was not duly negotiated. Answer (D) is incorrect. A forged endorsement does not convert a warehouse receipt into a bearer instrument.

30. Which of the following is **not** a warranty made by the seller of a negotiable warehouse receipt to the purchaser of the document?

A. The document transfer is fully effective with respect to the goods it represents.

B. The warehouser will honor the document.

C. The seller has no knowledge of any facts that would impair the document's validity.

D. The document is genuine.

Answer (B) is correct.

REQUIRED: The warranty not made by the seller of a negotiable warehouse receipt.

DISCUSSION: The seller of a negotiable warehouse receipt does not guarantee that the warehouser will honor the document.

19.8 PRACTICE TASK-BASED SIMULATIONS

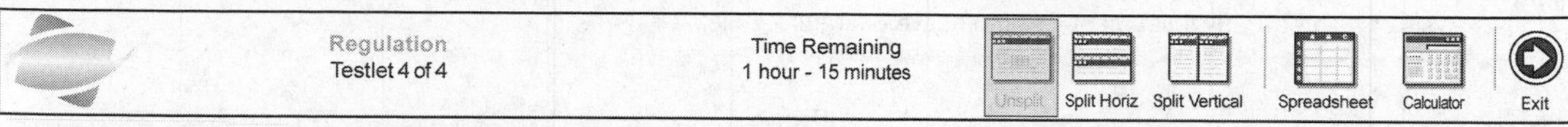

DIRECTIONS

Note: If you believe you have encountered a software malfunction, report it to the test center staff immediately.

Navigation

To navigate from task to task, use the controls at the bottom of the screen. Click on the **Next** button to advance to the next task, or the **Previous** button to go to the previous task. To go directly to any task, click on its number.

If you would like a reminder to revisit a task, or want to indicate that you are finished with it, click on the reminder flag below the task number. To clear the flag, click on it again. Reminder flags are for your use only – they do not contribute to your score.

Tabs

In this part of the examination, you will be asked to complete various tasks. Every task has one or more **Work Tabs**. Some tasks have one or more **Information Tabs**, others may have none. Every task has a **Help** tab.

If a task has **Information Tabs**, you may use the information in them to complete your responses in the **Work Tabs**.

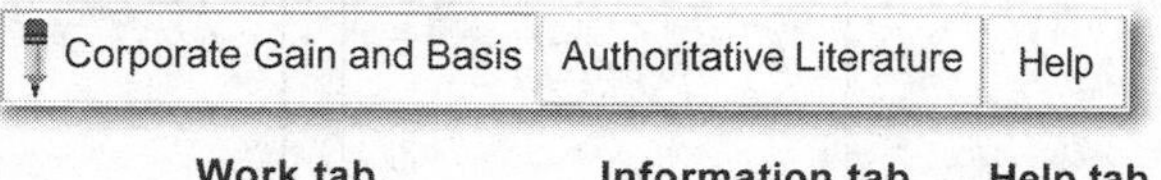

Work tab **Information tab** **Help tab**

Work Tabs:

- **Work Tabs** are identified with a pencil icon. This is where your responses are expected.
- Each task has one or more **Work Tabs**.
- **Work Tabs** contain directions for completing the task – be sure to read these directions carefully.
- The **Work Tab** name in the example above is for illustration only – yours will differ.
- You must complete all of the **Work Tabs** in each task to receive full credit.

Information Tabs:

- The Authoritative Literature will be provided in all tasks in the AUD, FAR, and REG sections for your reference.
- Your simulation may have one or more additional **Information Tabs**. Like the Authoritative Literature tabs, **Information Tabs** do not have a pencil icon.
- If your task has additional **Information Tabs**, go through each to familiarize yourself with the task content.

Help Tab:

- The **Help Tab** provides assistance with the exam software that is used in this task. For example, if the task is to compose a memorandum, **Help** will provide information about the word processor.

The Toolbar

The toolbar at the top of the screen shows the amount of time remaining for you to complete the tasks. In addition, the following tools are available. Note that only the **Exit** button is displayed when Directions are visible - the others will appear when you begin the tasks.

Click on these buttons to split or unsplit the screen. You can split the screen vertically or horizontally.

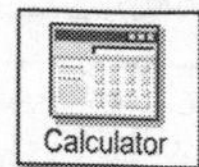

Click on this button to display the calculator; click on it again to hide the calculator. To move the calculator, click on the calculator title bar and drag the calculator to the desired location.

Click on this button to use the spreadsheet; click on it again to hide the spreadsheet. To move the spreadsheet, click on the the spreadsheet title bar and drag the spreadsheet to the desired location.

Click on this button to go on to the next part of the examination. You must complete all of the tasks to receive full credit. Once you click on **Exit** and confirm the action, you will NOT be able to return to this testlet.

= Reminder | Directions | 1 2 3 4 5 | Previous | Next

Analysis of a Three-Party Instrument | Authoritative Literature | Help

Front

April 5, Year 1

To: Pure Bank
Upton, VT

Pay to the order of M. West $1,500.00
One Thousand Five Hundred and 00/100 Dollars
on May 1, Year 1

W. Fields
W. Fields

Back

M. West

Pay to C. Larr

T. Keetin

C. Larr
without recourse

Items 1 through 8 relate to the instrument above. Select from the list provided the best match for each statement. Each choice may be used once, more than once, or not at all.

Statement	Answer
1. The instrument is a (type of instrument).	
2. The instrument is (negotiability).	
3. West's endorsement makes the instrument (type of instrument).	
4. Keetin's endorsement makes the instrument (type of instrument).	
5. Larr's endorsement makes the instrument (type of instrument).	
6. West's endorsement is considered (type of endorsement).	
7. Keetin's endorsement is considered (type of endorsement).	
8. Larr's endorsement is considered (type of endorsement).	

Choices
A) Bearer paper
B) Blank
C) Check
D) Draft
E) Negotiable
F) Nonnegotiable
G) Note
H) Order paper
I) Qualified
J) Special

▼ = Reminder | Directions | 1 2 3 4 5 | ◀ Previous | Next ▶

Negotiable Instrument Definitions | Authoritative Literature | Help

Items 1 through 7 are descriptive phrases or statements associated with terms commonly used in negotiable instruments dealings. Select from the list provided the term that is most appropriately associated with each phrase or statement. Each answer may be used only once. The abbreviation HDC will be used to refer to holder in due course.

Statement	Term
1. Demand for payment when a triggering event occurs before the stated due date.	
2. Payable to the order of the designated endorsee and requiring his or her endorsement for further negotiation.	
3. Permits a person who is not an HDC to exercise the rights of an HDC.	
4. A person in possession of negotiable bearer paper.	
5. One who has primary liability after endorsement to add his or her credit to that of a maker.	
6. Defense effective against an HDC.	
7. An ineffective attempt to restrict further negotiation of an instrument.	

Choices
A) Holder
B) Restrictive endorsement
C) Accommodation party
D) Presentment
E) Check
F) Guarantor
G) Signature
H) Bearer paper
I) Shelter principle
J) Forged signature
K) Acceleration
L) Specially endorsed instrument
M) Promise
N) Discharge in bankruptcy
O) Unauthorized completion

= Reminder | Directions | 1 2 3 4 5 | Previous | Next

Analysis of a Two-Party Instrument | Authoritative Literature | Help

During an audit of Trent Realty Corp.'s financial statements, Clark, CPA, reviewed the following instrument:

> $300,000 Belle, MD
> September 15, Year 1
>
> For value received, ten years after date, I promise to pay to the order of Dart Finance Co. Three Hundred Thousand and 00/100 dollars with interest at 9% per annum compounded annually until fully paid. This instrument arises out of the sale of land located in MD.
>
> It is further agreed that
>
> 1. I will pay all costs of collection including reasonable attorney fees.
> 2. I may prepay the amount outstanding on any anniversary date of this instrument.
>
> *G. Evans*
> G. Evans

The following transactions relate to the instrument:

1. On March 15, Year 2, Dart endorsed the instrument in blank and sold it to Morton for $275,000.
2. On July 10, Year 2, Evans informed Morton that Dart had fraudulently induced Evans to sign the instrument.
3. On August 15, Year 2, Trent, who knew of Evans's claim against Dart, purchased the instrument from Morton for $50,000. Morton did not endorse the instrument.

Select from the list provided the correct answer for each statement. Each choice may be used once, more than once, or not at all.

Statement	Answer
1. The instrument is a (type of instrument).	
2. The instrument is (negotiability).	
3. Morton is considered a (type of ownership).	
4. Trent is considered a (type of ownership).	
5. Trent could recover on the instrument from [liable party(ies)].	

Choices
A) Draft
B) Promissory note
C) Security agreement
D) Holder
E) Holder in due course
F) Holder with rights of a holder in due course under the shelter provision
G) Negotiable
H) Nonnegotiable
I) Evans, Morton, and Dart
J) Morton and Dart
K) Only Dart

On September 30, Year 1, Dayton Blasting Company purchased 25 cases of blasting caps from Whitten Blasting Cap Company. In this connection, it gave Whitten the following instrument:

> September 30, Year 1
>
> Dayton Blasting Company hereby promises to pay Whitten Blasting Cap Company Six Hundred Fifty Dollars ($650.00) on December 1, Year 1, plus interest at 6% per annum from date.
>
> Dayton Blasting Company
> By Malcolm Smalley, President

Whitten promptly transferred the above instrument to Vincent Luck for $600. James Whitten, president of Whitten, endorsed the instrument on the back as follows: "Pay to the order of Vincent Luck," signed Whitten Blasting Cap Company per James Whitten, President.

Approximately half of the blasting caps were defective, and Dayton refused to pay on the instrument. Dayton returned the defective cases and used the balance.

Select from the list provided the best match for each of the items below. Each choice may be used once, more than once, or not at all.

Item	Answer
1. Vincent Luck	
2. Dayton Blasting Company	
3. Whitten Blasting Cap Company	
4. Malcolm Smalley	
5. The instrument above	

Choices
A) Draft
B) Drawer
C) Drawee
D) Order instrument
E) Bearer instrument
F) Promissory note
G) Holder in due course
H) Assignee
I) Payee
J) Maker
K) None of the above

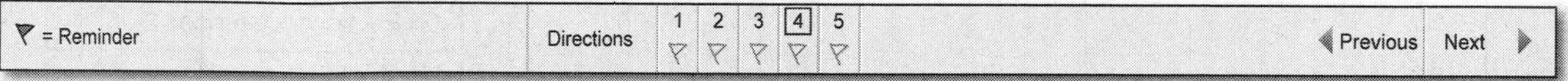

Dishonor of Note | Authoritative Literature | Help

On February 15, Year 1, P.D. Stone obtained the following instrument from Astor Co. for $1,000. Stone was aware that Helco, Inc., disputed liability under the instrument because of an alleged breach by Astor of the referenced computer purchase agreement. On March 1, Year 1, Willard Bank obtained the instrument from Stone for $3,900. Willard had no knowledge that Helco disputed liability under the instrument.

> February 12, Year 1
>
> Helco, Inc. promises to pay to Astor Co. or bearer the sum of $4,900 (four thousand nine hundred and 00/100 dollars) on March 12, Year 1 (maker may elect to extend due date to March 31, Year 1), with interest thereon at the rate of 12% per annum
>
> HELCO, INC.
>
> By: *A. J. Help*
> A. J. Help, President
>
> Reference: Computer purchase agreement dated February 12, Year 1

The reverse side of the instrument is endorsed as follows:

> Pay to the order of Willard Bank, without recourse
>
> *P. D. Stone*
> P. D. Stone

Willard Bank demanded payment from Helco, and Helco refused to pay the instrument because of Astor's breach of the computer purchase agreement. Select from the list provided the best answer to each question below. Each choice may be used once, more than once, or not at all.

Statement	Answer
1. What is Willard Bank's status regarding the instrument?	
2. Helco is asserting what type of defense?	
3. Who is primarily or secondarily liable to Willard Bank?	
4. What is the nature of the instrument?	
5. What is the nature of Stone's endorsement?	

Choices
A) Draft and order paper
B) Helco
C) Holder in due course
D) Holder with rights of a holder in due course
E) Holder
F) Note and bearer paper
G) Personal defenses
H) Qualified endorsement
I) Real defenses
J) Special endorsement
K) Stone

= Reminder | Directions | 1 2 3 4 5 | Previous | Next

Unofficial Answers

1. Analysis of a Three-Party Instrument (8 Gradable Items)

1. D) Draft. The instrument is a time draft. It is a three-party instrument containing an unconditional written order by one person, the drawer, to another person, the drawee, ordering him or her to pay a fixed amount of money to a third party, either a named payee or bearer. The instrument is not a check because it is not payable on demand.
2. E) Negotiable. The instrument is negotiable. To be negotiable, a draft must (a) be in writing, (b) be signed by the drawer, (c) contain an unconditional order to pay a fixed amount of money, (d) be payable on demand or at a definite time, (e) be payable to order or bearer, and (f) not state any undertaking or instruction in addition to the payment of money.
3. A) Bearer paper. The endorsement by West changed the instrument from an order instrument to a bearer instrument. An instrument payable to an identified person will become payable to the bearer if it is endorsed in blank. West's endorsement was an endorsement in blank because it did not identify a specific person as payee.
4. H) Order paper. Following Keetin's endorsement, the instrument became order paper. An order instrument is a promise or an order not payable to bearer but payable to the order of an identified person or to an identified person or order. For further negotiation, the instrument must be endorsed by C. Larr.
5. A) Bearer paper. The instrument, following Larr's endorsement, is bearer paper. An instrument payable to an identified person becomes payable to bearer if it is endorsed in blank. A blank endorsement consists merely of the signature of the endorser or his or her authorized agent and specifies no particular person.
6. B) Blank. West's endorsement is a blank endorsement because it does not identify a person as payee. It consists merely of the signature of West.
7. J) Special. Keetin's endorsement specifies "Pay to C. Larr" and therefore is a special endorsement. A special endorsement identifies a person to whom the instrument is payable.
8. I) Qualified. Larr's endorsement is a qualified endorsement. A qualified endorsement is used by an endorser to disclaim or limit contractual liability. It does not affect negotiability but may affect marketability.

2. Negotiable Instrument Definitions (7 Gradable Items)

1. K) Acceleration. An acceleration clause does not preclude negotiability. An acceleration clause allows the payee or other holder of a time instrument to demand payment of the entire amount, with interest, before the stated due date if a triggering event occurs, e.g., a default in payment.
2. L) Specially endorsed instrument. A special endorsement, e.g., "Pay to Michael Tal," specifically designates the person to whom the instrument is payable. The instrument is then payable to the order of the special endorsee.
3. I) Shelter principle. A person who does not qualify as an HDC but who is a transferee from an HDC acquires the rights and privileges of the HDC. The transferee is sheltered from personal defenses as if (s)he were an HDC. However, exceptions exist, e.g., if the holder was a party to fraud.
4. A) Holder. A holder is a person to whom a negotiable instrument has been issued or negotiated. Negotiation of order paper requires endorsement by the holder and transfer of possession. Bearer paper is negotiated merely by transferring possession of the instrument.
5. C) Accommodation party. An accommodation party is one who signs (endorses) an instrument for the purpose of lending his or her name (credit) to another party to the instrument. A person who signs to accommodate a maker, drawer, or acceptor is primarily liable on the instrument.
6. N) Discharge in bankruptcy. A person with a real defense is not liable, even to an HDC. The person's discharge in bankruptcy is a real defense.
7. B) Restrictive endorsement. A restrictive endorsement attempts to restrict further negotiation of the instrument. An endorsement prohibiting further transfer, e.g., "Pay Sam Gamgee Only," is one type of restrictive endorsement. The instrument remains negotiable without regard to the purported restriction.

3. Analysis of a Two-Party Instrument (5 Gradable Items)

1. B) Promissory note. The instrument is a promissory note. A promissory note is a written promise between two parties. It is an unconditional, signed promise from one party, the maker, to pay a fixed amount of money to a second party, the payee. G. Evans is the maker, and Dart is the payee.
2. G) Negotiable. The instrument is negotiable. To be negotiable, a note must (a) be in writing, (b) be signed by the maker, (c) contain an unconditional promise to pay a fixed amount of money, (d) be payable on demand or at a definite time, (e) be payable to order or bearer, and (f) not state any other undertaking or instruction in addition to the payment of money. The instrument meets each of these requirements, so it is negotiable.
3. E) Holder in due course. Morton is a holder in due course (HDC). An HDC has rights superior to those of prior parties and transferors. To be an HDC, one must be a holder of a negotiable instrument that does not bear apparent evidence of forgery or alteration or is not otherwise so irregular or incomplete as to make its authenticity questionable. The instrument must be taken (a) for value; (b) in good faith; and (c) without notice of certain facts that may preclude HDC status. If Morton met each requirement at the time of acquiring the instrument, Morton is an HDC.
4. F) Holder with rights of a holder in due course under the shelter provision. Under the shelter provision of the UCC, a person who does not qualify as an HDC may have the same rights if such person acquired the instrument from or through a prior party who was an HDC. Trent, who knew of the claim against Dart, is entitled to the advantage of the shelter provision and effectively has the rights of Morton, who was an HDC.
5. I) Evans, Morton, and Dart. Evans, the maker, and Dart, an endorser, are liable to Trent on the instrument assuming timely presentment for payment and timely notice to the endorsers after default. Morton's endorsement was not necessary to negotiate the instrument because it was bearer paper after Dart's blank endorsement. However, Morton has warranty liability to Trent. Moreover, no real defenses are stated, and personal defenses cannot be asserted against a holder through an HDC.

4. Transferred Instrument (5 Gradable Items)

1. H) Assignee. Vincent Luck is an assignee of the contract rights evidenced by the instrument. He is not a holder in due course because the instrument does not contain the words of negotiability, i.e., pay to order or bearer.
2. J) Maker. Dayton Blasting Company is the maker of the note. The maker is the person who signs or is identified in the note as the payor.
3. I) Payee. Whitten Blasting Cap Company is the person to which payment is promised.
4. K) None of the above. Smalley signed as a representative of the maker.
5. F) Promissory note. This instrument is a note because it contains a promise.

5. Dishonor of Note (5 Gradable Items)

1. C) Holder in due course. Although Stone was a mere holder because of awareness of Helco's assertion of nonliability, a taker from a holder can be an HDC. Willard had no notice of the alleged breach and meets all other requirements for HDC status.
2. G) Personal defenses. Personal defenses, such as traditional contract defenses (e.g., a breach of contract), are ineffective against an HDC.
3. B) Helco. Helco is primarily liable because it is the maker of the note. Helco has no defense effective against an HDC. Willard meets the requirements of an HDC even though its transferor (Stone) did not. Stone is not primarily liable because Stone is not the maker of the note. Stone has no secondary liability because Stone is a qualified endorser.
4. F) Note and bearer paper. This instrument is a note because it contains a promise. It is bearer paper because it is payable to an identified person or bearer.
5. H) Qualified endorsement. An endorsement without recourse (qualified endorsement) by a previous bearer does not of itself prevent the current bearer from being a holder in due course. Such an endorsement is not notice of a claim or that the instrument is overdue, dishonored, etc.

Gleim Simulation Grading

Task	Correct Responses		Gradable Items		Score per Task
1	____	÷	8	=	____
2	____	÷	7	=	____
3	____	÷	5	=	____
4	____	÷	5	=	____
5	____	÷	5	=	____
			Total of Scores per Task		____
		÷	Total Number of Tasks		5
			Total Score		____ %

STUDY UNIT TWENTY
DEBTOR-CREDITOR RELATIONSHIPS

(27 pages of outline)

This study unit covers issues related to debtor-creditor relationships. The first two subunits review the rights and duties of debtors and creditors under general contract law. Solutions to the conflict between debtor relief and creditor protection may be formal (bankruptcy) or informal. The next three subunits review federal bankruptcy law, including bankruptcy proceedings under Chapters 7, 11, and 13 of the Bankruptcy Code. The sixth subunit outlines the rights and duties of sureties.

20.1 LIENS AND ENFORCEMENT METHODS

1. **Overview**
   a. A **lien** is a legal claim on property, either real or personal, as security for payment or performance of a debt or obligation.
   b. The relative priority of liens usually is in the **order of their acquisition**.
      1) Certain liens attach only when possession is obtained and exist only as long as it is retained (e.g., artisan's liens).
      2) Concurrent liens attach simultaneously and have equal rank in distribution.
      3) A government has the power to establish the priorities of liens. It may give a statutory lien (e.g., a tax lien) priority over other liens or exempt certain property from collection by creditors.
   c. This subunit describes the most common procedures for enforcing liens.
2. **Statutory Liens**
   a. A statutory lien attaches when a party adds value to another party's property by agreement. The authority for statutory liens is based on state law.
      1) Many such liens are based on the right of one person to retain possession of the property of another until the owner pays for the goods or services. However, certain statutory liens are nonpossessory.
      2) Statutory liens include (a) artisan's liens, (b) mechanic's liens, (c) bailee's liens, and (d) tax liens.
   b. An **artisan's lien** is held by a repairer or improver of personal property, such as an automobile or computer, who retains possession of the property until paid.
      1) The work or improvement must be performed subject to an express or implied agreement for cash payment.
   c. **Mechanic's liens** (including **materialman's liens**) are liens against the real property benefited. Thus, they are not possessory.
      1) The liens secure unpaid debts from contracts for materials or services to improve specific real property. For example, a mechanic's lien may be held by the builder of a house or by someone who has merely remodeled a room in a house.

2) The holder of a mechanic's lien normally files a document (a notice of lien) that identifies the property within 60 to 120 days after work is complete.

3) Attachment of the lien to the property dates back to when the first work is done or materials are supplied.

d. A **bailee's lien** is granted to a common carrier (e.g., trucker, airline, or railroad) or warehouser to whom the debtor has entrusted goods. This possessory lien secures payment of shipment or storage charges.

1) The goods must be covered by a document of title.

e. A **tax lien** secures payment of taxes owed to a governmental entity. For example, it may be imposed on specific land on which the landowner has not paid the real property taxes. Moreover, a federal tax lien may be placed on all property of a delinquent tax payer. Only federal statutes, not state statutes, may exempt debtor assets from federal tax liens.

EXAMPLE

State **homestead exemption acts** may shield a debtor's equity in his or her home from most liens. Mortgage liens and tax liens are not exempted.

1) Artisan's and mechanic's liens have priority over all other security interests in property unless a statute expressly provides otherwise.

2) A properly recorded real estate mortgage has priority over a mechanic's lien that attaches after the mortgage is recorded.

3. **Enforcement of a Statutory Lien**

a. A statutory lien is enforceable only as to items to which liens may legally attach.

1) Statutes may allow the lienholder to foreclose the lien judicially and sell the property if the owner does not pay the debt.

a) The lienholder must give notice to the owner prior to foreclosure and sale.

b) Sale proceeds are used to pay the costs of foreclosure and sale and to satisfy the debt. Any remaining proceeds are paid to the former owner.

2) The statutory remedy is generally exclusive. For example, federal law exempts Social Security benefits from garnishment.

4. **Judicial Liens**

a. A judicial lien is acquired by judgment, seizure (levy), or another judicial process.

1) A court, after a civil proceeding, may issue a monetary judgment for one of the parties, e.g., the plaintiff. That party is a judgment creditor.

2) If the other party fails to pay, the judgment creditor may petition the court to issue a **writ of execution**. This order authorizes the sheriff to seize and sell specific nonexempt property of the judgment debtor to satisfy the judgment.

3) **Attachment**, a prejudgment remedy, is the seizure of a defendant's nonexempt property under judicial authorization and placement of it in the custody of the court. Attachment is intended to secure satisfaction of a pending judgment.

a) **Replevin** is a prejudgment remedy intended to secure property already subject to a lien or a right of repossession.

EXAMPLE

A lender seeks repossession of an automobile after the debtor's default. The lender obtains a writ of replevin by filing an affidavit and posting a bond. The sheriff then seizes (replevies) the property and turns it over to the lender pending resolution of legal proceedings.

b) **Garnishment** is a prejudgment or postjudgment collection remedy. It is directed against a third party (the garnishee) who holds property, or is a debtor, of the defendant. For example, wages or bank accounts may be garnished.

5. **Termination of Liens**

a. A lien is discharged by payment or tender of payment.

1) **Tender** is an offer to pay combined with a present ability to pay. It also discharges liability for further interest or damages. It does **not** discharge the debt.

2) A debtor may owe separate debts to one creditor. If the debtor makes a **partial** payment, the creditor may apply the payment to whichever debt (s)he chooses. But the debtor may instruct otherwise.

b. A lien is effective only as long as the property exists.

c. A lien dependent on possession terminates if the lienholder voluntarily and unconditionally surrenders possession or control of the property.

1) If the surrender is subject to an agreement that the property will be returned, the lien does not terminate. However, if a third party obtains rights to the property before it is returned, the lien terminates.

d. A lien may be terminated by waiver (i.e., a voluntary surrender of a right).

6. **Foreclosure on a Real Estate Mortgage by Judicial Sale**

a. The right to foreclose results from the debtor's default. Foreclosure is an action by the **mortgagee-lender** (or assignee) to (1) take the property from the **mortgagor-debtor**, (2) sell it to pay the debt, and (3) end the mortgagor's rights in the property.

b. To foreclose, the mortgagee must initiate a **judicial proceeding** to secure an order of sale. The sheriff or other officer of the court then conducts a sale by auction as specified by state statute.

c. The sale is confirmed by court order following a hearing.

d. The debt then is satisfied with **proceeds** of the sale.

1) A **purchase money mortgage** (PMM) is entitled to preference over other claims or liens. It is granted by a purchaser to secure payment of the purchase price. The money or credit is provided to purchase the property.

a) The mortgage must be granted at the same time that the deed is delivered.

2) An owner of property subject to a mortgage can grant a **second mortgage** (and others) on the same property to secure a debt.

a) After default and foreclosure, the first mortgage has priority. It is satisfied in full out of sale proceeds before any payment is made to another mortgagee.

3) If the proceeds are less than the sum of the debt costs and interest, the mortgagor is liable for the deficiency unless released by the mortgagee.

a) A state may restrict a deficiency to the excess of the debt over the **fair value**.

b) In a state with an **antideficiency** statute, a purchase money mortgagor is not liable for a deficiency.

4) **Surplus** proceeds belong to the mortgagor.

e. The mortgagee may buy the property at the sale.

f. The mortgagor has an **equitable right of redemption**. Prior to foreclosure, (s)he may regain rights by paying the mortgage debt plus interest and costs.

   1) The equity of redemption cannot be relinquished by agreement. Any such attempt is considered void as against public policy.
   2) Redemption might be accomplished by refinancing.

g. The mortgagor also may have a **statutory right of redemption**. The mortgagor may repurchase the property after the foreclosure sale for the statutorily specified period (not exceeding 1 year) by payment of the auction sale price.

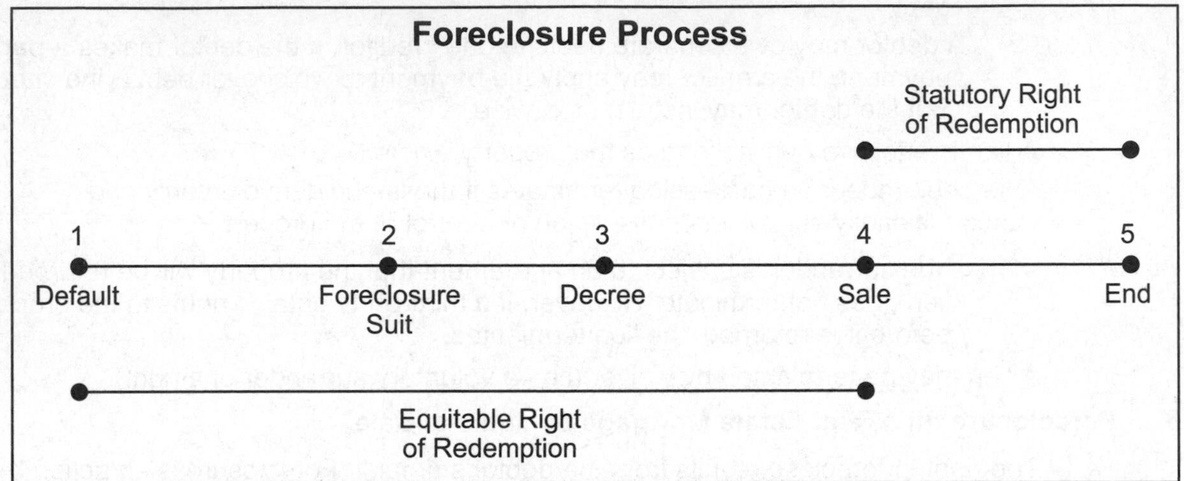

Figure 20-1

h. The **purchaser** at a judicial sale takes the property free of any claim.

i. **Foreclosure by sale** is an alternative allowed in a majority of states. The mortgagee may sell the property at public auction without resorting to the legal system.

   1) The mortgage agreement must permit this procedure, and the sale must comply with strict statutory requirements.

Stop and review! You have completed the outline for this subunit. Study multiple-choice questions 1 through 3 beginning on page 783.

20.2 COLLECTIVE REMEDIES UNDER STATE LAW

1. **Composition**

   a. A composition with creditors is a contract in which the debtor agrees to pay the creditors some fraction of the amount owed in full satisfaction of their claims. The **mutual** promises made among the creditors provide consideration.

      1) The agreement does not affect the rights of a nonconsenting creditor.
      2) The original debts are not discharged until the debtor has performed the new obligations.
      3) In an **extension** agreement, the debtor agrees to pay the full amount of all debts over a longer period.

   b. **Liquidation** of a **disputed** claim is an agreement by a debtor and creditor about the amount.

   c. No receiver is appointed. A receiver is appointed by a court to preserve property that is the subject of litigation.

2. **Assignment**
   a. A general assignment for the benefit of creditors is a **voluntary** transfer by the debtor of title to all of his or her assets to a third party (the assignee or trustee).
   b. The trustee named by the debtor (1) receives the debtor's property, (2) converts it to cash, and (3) distributes the cash to the creditors in exchange for their promises to release the debtor.
   c. Assignment is similar to a composition. However, the consent of creditors is **not** required.
   d. The assignee has **legal title** to the debtor's property.
      1) The debtor must act in good faith.
      2) Retention of any benefit from the property most likely is a fraudulent conveyance.
      3) If otherwise valid, the assignment is effective unless the creditors file an involuntary bankruptcy petition.
      4) The debtor cannot revoke the assignment, and creditors cannot use judicial process to seize the property.
      5) The assignment discharges only debts paid in full.
   e. Another possibility is to transfer the debtor's business to a creditor's committee that has full management authority.
3. **Fraudulent Transfers**
   a. Any transfer of property made with the intent to delay, hinder, or defraud creditors is voidable by the transferor's creditors. Badges of fraud are factors indicating fraudulent conveyances. They include
      1) The debtor's retention of possession or a beneficial interest,
      2) A transfer of substantially all assets,
      3) A transfer in secret,
      4) A transfer to a family member or insider,
      5) A transfer for inadequate consideration,
      6) A transfer in anticipation of legal action or financial problems,
      7) Removal or concealment of assets, and
      8) Insolvency at the time of (or shortly after) the transfer.

Stop and review! You have completed the outline for this subunit. Study multiple-choice questions 4 through 6 beginning on page 784.

20.3 BANKRUPTCY ADMINISTRATION

1. The **U.S. Constitution** (Article I) gives Congress the exclusive power to establish "uniform Laws on the subject of Bankruptcies throughout the United States." The federal statute is the Bankruptcy Reform Act of 1978.
   a. Notable amendments have been made by the Bankruptcy Reform Act of 1994 and the Bankruptcy Abuse Prevention and Consumer Protection Act of 2005.
2. **The Bankruptcy Code**
   a. Bankruptcy is a formal way of resolving the conflict between creditor rights and debtor relief. The objectives are to ensure that (1) debtor assets are fairly distributed to creditors, and (2) the debtor is given a fresh start.

b. This outline covers the specific proceedings under the following chapters of the Code, with an emphasis on Chapters 7, 11, and 13.

1) Chapter 7: Liquidation
2) Chapter 9: Adjustment of Debts of a Municipality
3) Chapter 11: Reorganization
4) Chapter 12: Adjustment of Debts of a Family Farmer or Fisherman with Regular Annual Income
5) Chapter 13: Adjustment of Debts of an Individual with Regular Income
6) Chapter 15: Ancillary and Other Cross-Border Cases

c. Chapters 1, 3, and 5 state guidance for the listed proceedings, e.g., for (1) case administration and (2) debtors, creditors, and the bankruptcy estate.

d. The following summarizes the eligibility for filing under Chapters 7, 11, and 13:

TYPES OF BANKRUPTCY	ELIGIBLE	INELIGIBLE
Chapter 7 Liquidation (voluntary or involuntary)	Individuals (subject to disqualification by the means test) Partnerships Corporations	Municipalities (eligible under Ch. 9) Railroads Insurers Banks Credit unions S&Ls
Chapter 11 Reorganization (voluntary or involuntary)	Railroads Most persons that may be debtors under Chapter 7	Shareholders Commodities and stockbrokers Insurers Banks Credit unions S&Ls
Chapter 13 Adjustment of debts of an individual (voluntary only)	Individuals	Nonindividuals Individuals without regular income

3. **Administration of Proceedings**

a. Each federal judicial district has its own bankruptcy court. A case is heard by a judge after the **filing of a petition** specifying the applicable chapter.

1) The result is an estate consisting of the debtor's property (a) at the time of filing or (b) that becomes subject to the proceeding. It is a separate legal entity.
2) Insolvency or any prior filing is **not** a requirement for filing a petition.

b. The filing of any petition operates as an **automatic stay** of most civil actions against the debtor or his or her property until the court acts. However, it does not terminate security interests or liens. The following are activities **not** stayed:

1) Alimony and child support collection
2) Criminal proceedings
3) Issuance of a notice of tax deficiency

c. **Core proceedings** are conducted by the bankruptcy judge. They resolve issues most directly related to reorganization or discharge, such as

1) Allowing creditor claims,
2) Determining the relative priority of creditor claims,
3) Confirming a plan of reorganization, and
4) Granting a discharge.

d. **Noncore proceedings** are resolved in state or other federal courts but may affect rights of the creditors or debtor. They involve property rights, personal injury claims, divorce, etc.

4. **Automatic Stay**

   a. A secured creditor may ask the court to recognize the priority of the existing security interest and allow foreclosure.

   b. The stay may be terminated because of serial filings suggestive of bad faith or abuse. If a Chapter 7, 11, or 13 case is filed within a year after dismissal of another case, the stay generally terminates after 30 days. However, the stay continues in effect if the new filing is shown to be in good faith.

      1) After a third filing within 1 year, the stay will not go into effect unless good faith is shown.

5. **Voluntary Proceedings**

   a. Most petitions are voluntary. Any person eligible to be a **debtor** under a chapter may file under it. No minimum debt or number of creditors is required.

      1) A voluntary petition results in an **automatic order for relief**. In the order, the court assumes exclusive authority over the case. The mandatory creditors' meeting is held within a reasonable time after the order.

6. **Involuntary Proceedings**

   a. An involuntary petition may be filed only under Chapter 7 or Chapter 11 against an eligible debtor. The number or timing of involuntary petitions is not limited.

      1) An involuntary petition cannot be filed against the following:

         a) Farmers
         b) Banks
         c) Insurers
         d) Nonprofit corporations
         e) Railroads
         f) Persons who owe less than $15,325

      2) If the debtor has **12 or more** different creditors, any 3 or more who together hold unsecured claims of at least $15,325 may file an involuntary petition.

      3) If the debtor has **fewer than 12** creditors, any 1 or more who alone or together have unsecured claims of at least $15,325 may file an involuntary petition.

         a) Any creditors who are the debtor's employees or are insiders, e.g., officers or directors of a corporation, relatives, or a partner, are **not** counted.

      4) Filing an involuntary petition results in an automatic stay but does **not** result in an automatic order for relief. However, if the debtor does not oppose the petition, the court will enter an order for relief.

      5) If the debtor opposes the petition, the court must hold a hearing, and the petitioner must post a bond to compensate a debtor if the case is dismissed.

         a) The court orders relief on behalf of the creditors if it finds that either of two **statutory grounds** for involuntary bankruptcy exists.

            i) The debtor is not paying undisputed debts as they become due.

            ii) Within 120 days before the filing of the petition, a custodian, assignee, or general receiver took possession of all or most of the debtor's property to enforce a lien against the property.

         b) If the case is dismissed, the creditors may have to pay the debtor's costs, attorney's fees, and damages caused when the trustee took possession of the debtor's property.

            i) A petitioner who acted in bad faith may have to pay damages for harm to the debtor's reputation.

7. **Debtor Rights and Duties**

   a. The debtor may continue to use, acquire, and dispose of his or her property until the court orders otherwise. The debtor also may incur new debts and operate a business.

      1) If necessary, the court may order the appointment of a **temporary** trustee to preserve the debtor's assets.

   b. A debtor must comply with various requirements. These include

      1) Attending and submitting to all court-scheduled examinations,
      2) Testifying if called as a witness in a hearing,
      3) Informing the trustee in writing of the location of all real property in which the debtor has an interest, and
      4) Receiving credit counseling.

8. **Trustees**

   a. Within a reasonable time after the order for relief, an **interim** trustee generally is appointed. The trustee in bankruptcy (1) represents the debtor's estate, (2) investigates the financial affairs of the debtor, and (3) holds the first meeting of creditors.

      1) A trustee is required in Chapter 7, 12, and 13 cases. A trustee is not required in a Chapter 9, 11, or 15 case, but the court may order the appointment of an interim trustee who then may be elected by the creditors as the permanent trustee.
      2) Under Chapter 7, the permanent trustee is elected by qualified creditors at their required meeting.
      3) Under all other chapters, the trustee, if any, is appointed.
      4) **Creditor committees** may be required or permitted. They facilitate communication among the debtor, the trustee, and the creditors.

   b. The following are among the powers of the trustee:

      1) Collecting and accounting for property
      2) Performing investigations
      3) Setting aside fraudulent conveyances and certain other property transfers
      4) Accepting or rejecting unperformed contracts or unexpired leases
      5) Operating the debtor's business
      6) Selling, using, or leasing estate property
      7) Investing estate money
      8) Hiring professionals
         a) A qualified trustee may perform professional services for reasonable compensation with court approval.
         b) Service as a trustee impairs a CPA's independence regarding the debtor.
      9) Filing reports
      10) Objecting to creditor claims
      11) Objecting to a discharge in a proper case
      12) Distributing assets and closing the estate

Be prepared to answer bankruptcy questions. The AICPA has tested this topic often. Exam questions have tested the details of bankruptcy law, such as the number of creditors and dollar amounts involved in filing an involuntary bankruptcy petition against a debtor.

Stop and review! You have completed the outline for this subunit. Study multiple-choice questions 7 through 13 beginning on page 785.

20.4 BANKRUPTCY LIQUIDATIONS

1. **Chapter 7**
   a. Chapter 7 uses a liquidation approach by converting a debtor's nonexempt assets into cash. It is distributed in conformity with the Code. An honest debtor then is discharged from most of the remaining debts.
   b. Eligible parties are most debtors, including individuals, partnerships, and corporations. But Chapter 7 is not available to, among others, the following:
      1) Municipalities
      2) Railroads
      3) Insurers
      4) Banks, savings and loan associations, and credit unions
2. **Abuse by an Individual Debtor**
   a. Abuse by an individual debtor with primarily consumer debts (for example, credit card debt) results in dismissal or conversion to a Chapter 13 case. Abuse is found when (1) the debtor does not pass the **means test** (if it results in a presumption of abuse), or (2) **general grounds** exist for the finding (bad faith or that all the circumstances indicate abuse).
   b. If the **debtor's income** exceeds the state median income, any interested party may seek dismissal for abuse. Otherwise, only the judge and certain administrators may move to dismiss (and then only on general grounds of abuse).
      1) The debtor's income for this purpose equals current monthly income (CMI) times 12.
   c. The **means test** determines the debtor's ability to repay general unsecured claims.
      1) Current monthly income (CMI) is a 6-month average of all income received by the debtor (and spouse if the case is joint). However, Social Security and certain other items are excluded.
      2) Presumed deductions from CMI are allowed for support and payment of higher priority debt, for example, (a) living expenses for which allowances are specified by the IRS, (b) actual expenses recognized by the IRS, and (c) secured debt coming due within 5 years.
      3) The debtor's **CMI after deductions** creates a **presumption of abuse** if it is at least
         a) $207.92 ($12,475 ÷ 60 months) regardless of the amount of general unsecured debt.
         b) $124.58 ($7,475 ÷ 60 months) if it suffices to pay at least 25% of general unsecured debt over 5 years.
            i) If CMI after deductions is less than $124.58, no presumption of abuse arises.

EXAMPLE

If CMI after deductions is $150, abuse is presumed if general unsecured debt is no more than $36,000.

($150 CMI after deductions × 60 months) ÷ 25% = $36,000

      4) The presumption of abuse may be overcome by proof of special circumstances.

3. **Debtor's Estate**

   a. The estate consists of all the debtor's nonexempt interests in property at the beginning of the case.

      1) The estate **excludes** the following:

         a) Earnings of the debtor for services after the beginning of a Chapter 7 case (but not a Chapter 11 or 13 case)
         b) Contributions to employee retirement plans
         c) Contributions made more than 365 days prior to filing to educational retirement accounts and state tuition programs
         d) Most property acquired after the filing of the petition, including gifts

      2) The estate **includes** the following:

         a) All nonexempt property currently held (wherever located)
         b) Community property
         c) Property the trustee recovers from third parties
         d) Proceeds and profits from the property of the estate
         e) Interests in property to which the debtor becomes entitled within 180 days after filing, such as

            i) Life insurance payments
            ii) Divorce settlements
            iii) Amounts received upon the death of another person, whether or not through a will

         f) Interests in property acquired by the estate after the filing of the petition

      3) Subject to court approval, the trustee may choose whether to assume an unexpired lease.

         a) The trustee has 60 days after the order for relief to assume a lease.

4. **Exempt Assets**

   a. Exempt assets are basic necessities for a fresh start (e.g., rights to receive Social Security, disability benefits, alimony, and child support). Only individual debtors, not corporations, are eligible for exemptions.

   b. **States** are permitted to require their citizens to accept the exemptions of property defined by state law. If a state has not rejected the federal exemptions, the debtor has a choice.

      1) The state homestead exemption may be decreased by the value of an addition to the homestead during the 10 years before filing. This rule applies if the added value resulted from a disposition by the debtor of nonexempt property that operated as a fraud on creditors.

   c. **Federal Exemptions**

      1) Up to $22,975 in equity in the debtor's residence and burial plot
      2) An interest in a motor vehicle up to a value of $3,675
      3) An interest up to a value of $575 in any item of household goods and furnishings, clothing, appliances, books, animals, crops, or musical instruments, with a total limited to $12,250
      4) An interest in jewelry up to a value of $1,550
      5) Any other property worth up to $1,225, plus any unused part of the $22,975 exemption in c.1) above, up to an amount of $11,500
      6) An interest in tools of the debtor's trade up to a total value of $2,300
      7) Any unmatured life insurance contract owned by the debtor

8) Certain interests in accrued dividends or interest under life insurance contracts owned by the debtor not exceeding $12,250
9) Professionally prescribed health aids
10) The right to receive Social Security, certain welfare benefits, veterans' benefits, disability benefits, alimony and support, and certain pension benefits
11) The right to receive certain personal injury and other awards up to $22,975
12) Unemployment compensation
13) The ability to void certain judicial liens, e.g., on exempt property
14) Regardless of which exemptions (federal or state) apply, amounts in tax exempt retirement accounts (but the amount in IRAs is capped at $1,245,475)

5. **Powers of the Trustee**

a. To collect the property that belongs in the estate, the trustee can (1) exercise the rights and (2) assert any defenses of the **debtor**. The trustee also can exercise the rights that would be held by an actual creditor who has obtained a **judicial lien** on the property of the debtor through legal proceedings.

1) However, no such actual creditor needs to exist. Thus, the trustee is a hypothetical (ideal) lien creditor, one with the greatest power allowed under state law.

a) For example, the trustee has priority over a secured creditor whose security interest is unperfected.

2) The trustee does **not** have the right to void **statutory liens** against the debtor's property that were effective before filing.

a) But certain statutory liens on real property (e.g., mechanic's liens) are voidable. These are liens that are not effective until the petition is filed or the time when the debtor becomes insolvent.

3) The trustee also may void liens that are not enforceable against a **good-faith purchaser for value (GFP)** on the date of the filing. A GFP is a purchaser who (a) acted honestly, (b) gave value, and (c) had no notice of an adverse claim.

4) Accordingly, the trustee can void any transfer of property or debt incurred by the debtor that could be defeated by a (a) judicial lien creditor, (b) judgment creditor, or (c) GFP.

a) Thus, the trustee can exercise the same rights as

i) The debtor,
ii) Any actual creditors, and
iii) The hypothetical creditors or purchasers listed above.

b. The trustee can **void preferential transfers**. The transfer may be (1) a voluntary property transfer, (2) a voluntary creation of a lien (a mortgage or a security interest), or (3) the involuntary creation of a lien (e.g., a creditor's judgment lien).

1) A voidable preferential transfer is one made

a) To or for the benefit of a creditor,
b) For or on account of an antecedent (pre-existing) debt,
c) During the debtor's insolvency,
d) Within 90 days prior to filing the petition, and
e) For the purpose of entitling the creditor to receive a larger portion of its claim than otherwise would be received under a distribution in bankruptcy.

2) Property purchased by an innocent third party from a preferential transferee cannot be recovered. But the preferential transferor may be liable for its value.

3) Other transfers **not** voidable as preferences include the following:

   a) Payments of accounts payable paid in the ordinary course of the debtor's and transferee's business or financial affairs
   b) If the debtor is an individual, payment of up to $600 on a consumer debt within 90 days preceding the filing of the petition
   c) If an individual's debts are primarily nonconsumer debts, any transfer worth less than $6,225
   d) Asset transfers for new value, such as materials acquired for cash or borrowed money received in exchange for a security interest

EXAMPLE

A purchase money security interest (PMSI) (one that enables the debtor to acquire the property) is not a voidable preference because new value is received. However, the PMSI must be perfected within 30 days after the debtor takes possession of the property.

   e) Bona fide transfers for domestic support obligations

EXAMPLE

On August 1, Hall filed a voluntary petition under Chapter 7 of the Federal Bankruptcy Code. Hall's assets are sufficient to pay general creditors 40% of their claims. The following transactions occurred before the filing:

- On May 15, Hall gave a mortgage on Hall's home to National Bank to secure payment of a loan National had given Hall 2 years earlier. When the loan was made, Hall's sibling was a National employee.
- On June 1, Hall purchased a boat from Olsen for $10,000 cash.
- On July 1, Hall paid off an outstanding credit card balance of $500. The original debt was $2,500.

The National mortgage was preferential because the mortgage was given to secure an antecedent debt. The payment to Olsen was not preferential because the payment was a contemporaneous exchange for new value. The credit card payment made by Hall on July 1 was not preferential because the payment was for a consumer debt of less than $600.

4) The trustee has the power to void **preferential liens**, including judgment liens and other liens obtained by any judicial proceeding. These liens arise in the circumstances described for preferential transfers.
5) The trustee may void preferential transfers and grants of security interests to **insiders** if made within 1 year before the filing of the petition.

   a) The debtor must have been insolvent at the time of the transfer or grant.
   b) Insiders are related parties, including the following:

      i) Relatives
      ii) Partners and partnerships
      iii) Corporate directors and officers
      iv) Controlling shareholders
      v) A corporation controlled by the debtor

c. The trustee can **void fraudulent transfers**.

1) A property transfer is voidable if it was made within 2 years prior to filing with actual **intent** to hinder, delay, or defraud creditors.
2) A trustee also may void a transfer or obligation for which the debtor received less than reasonably equivalent consideration if the debtor

   a) Was insolvent or was made insolvent by the transfer,
   b) Was operating a business with an unreasonably small capital, or
   c) Expected to incur debts that (s)he could not repay.

EXAMPLE

Burton's business was faltering, and the creditors were demanding immediate payment. Burton's brother had recently set up a new corporation for real estate investments. With the intent to save some of her assets, Burton transferred them to the new corporation with an understanding that Burton would receive stock after resolution of her financial problems. Five months later, Burton filed for bankruptcy. Without regard to whether the new corporation had knowledge of Burton's fraud or insolvency, the trustee can recover the assets because Burton transferred them with intent to defraud creditors within 2 years of bankruptcy.

6. **Claims**
   a. The distribution process commences with creditors' filing of proofs of claim.
      1) A proof of claim must be filed within 90 days after the first meeting of creditors.
      2) Only unsecured creditors are required to file.
      3) Upon filing, the claim is deemed valid and allowable.
         a) But if an interested party such as a creditor or the trustee objects, the bankruptcy court must decide whether to allow the claim.
         b) If a debtor has a defense to an alleged debt (e.g., fraud or failure of consideration), the claim will not be allowed.
         c) Claims are disallowed if they
            i) Are for unearned interest,
            ii) Can be offset by a claim against the creditor, or
            iii) Exceed the reasonable value of services performed by an insider or attorney.
7. **Rights of Creditors**
   a. The creditors involved in the distribution of the debtor's estate are (1) secured creditors, (2) priority creditors (unsecured), and (3) general creditors (other unsecured creditors).
   b. **Secured creditors' rights** cannot be defeated by the trustee.
      1) They are paid in full if the collateral is sufficient.
      2) To the extent of any deficiency, the secured creditor is a general creditor.
      3) A perfected property tax lien on the debtor's property is satisfied before support obligations.
      4) Between secured creditors with interests in the same collateral, the first perfected interest has priority.
   c. **Priority creditors** are unsecured creditors that are paid after the secured creditors. They have priority over the claims of general creditors.
      1) Members of a higher class of priority creditors are paid in full before members of a lower class receive anything. If the assets are insufficient to pay all claims in a given class, the claimants in the class share pro rata.
      2) The classes of priority claims listed in order of payment are as follows:
         a) Domestic support obligations to a spouse, former spouse, or child have priority over those assigned or owed directly to a government.
         b) Claims for administrative expenses and expenses incurred in preserving and collecting the estate.
         c) Claims of tradespeople (gap creditors) who extend unsecured credit in the ordinary course of business after the filing of an involuntary petition but before the earlier of the appointment of a trustee or the entry of the order for relief.

d) Wages (compensation) up to $12,475 owed to employees earned within 180 days prior to the earlier of (1) filing or (2) cessation of the debtor's business.

e) Certain contributions owed to the debtor's employee benefit plans resulting from employee services performed within 180 days prior to the earlier of (1) filing or (2) cessation of the debtor's business.

f) Claims of grain or fish producers up to $6,150 each for grain or fish deposited with the debtor but not paid for or returned.

g) Claims of consumers for the return of up to $2,775 each in deposits.

h) Certain income and other taxes owed to governmental entities.

i) Death and injury claims arising from operation of a motor vehicle or vessel by a legally intoxicated person.

d. If any money remains after payments to secured creditors and priority creditors, the general creditors are paid.

1) General creditors are unsecured creditors that are not priority creditors.
2) Higher-ranking claims are paid in full before lower-ranking claims receive anything. The rankings under this final set of priorities are as follows:

a) Allowed unsecured claims for which creditors filed proofs of claim in time or had acceptable excuses for filing late

b) Allowed unsecured claims for which proofs of claim were filed late and without acceptable excuse

c) Interest on claims already paid for the period between the filing of the petition and the date of payment of the claims

8. **Discharge**

a. Individual debtors under Chapter 7 may receive a discharge from most debts that remain unpaid after distribution of the debtor's estate.

1) A discharge means the debtor is free from further liability on certain debts.
2) The court generally grants a discharge in a Chapter 7 proceeding.
3) Corporations and partnerships cannot receive a Chapter 7 discharge.
4) Most debtors are eligible for a discharge only once every 8 years.

b. The following acts, failures to act, or circumstances of the debtor are grounds for **denial of a general discharge**:

1) Fraudulently transferring or concealing (a) property within 1 year preceding the filing of the bankruptcy petition or (b) the property of the estate after filing
2) Unjustifiably concealing or destroying business records or failing to keep adequate business records
3) Making a false oath, a fraudulent account, or a false claim in connection with the case
4) Failing to explain satisfactorily any loss or deficiency of assets
5) Refusing to testify or to obey lawful orders of the court
6) Filing a written waiver of discharge approved by the court
7) Giving or receiving a bribe in connection with the case
8) Committing within 1 year before filing any of these acts in a case involving an insider
9) Being subject to a proceeding that may limit the homestead exemption
10) Failing to complete a personal financial management course

EXAMPLE

On June 9, Amy Aker transferred property she owned to her son. The property was collateral for Aker's obligation to Simon. Aker transferred the property with the intent to defraud Simon. On July 7, Aker filed a voluntary bankruptcy petition. Because Aker transferred the property with the intent to defraud Simon within 1 year of filing the petition for relief, she will be denied a general discharge.

c. Certain debts are not covered by a Chapter 7 discharge. They remain binding on the debtor but do not prevent a general discharge. **Nondischargeable debts** include

1) Most taxes, including federal income tax coming due within 3 years prior to bankruptcy.
2) Debts incurred on the basis of materially false financial statements if (a) they were issued with the intent to deceive and (b) the creditor reasonably relied on them.
3) Debts not included in required filings in time to permit a creditor without notice of the case to make a timely filing of a proof of claim.
4) Debts resulting from fraud (including securities fraud), misrepresentation, embezzlement, larceny, or breach of fiduciary duty.
5) Debts resulting from alimony, maintenance, or child support awards.
6) Debts resulting from willful and malicious injury to another person or conversion of that person's property.
7) Debts resulting from certain educational loans made, funded, or guaranteed by a governmental unit.
8) Governmental fines and penalties, except those relating to dischargeable taxes.
9) Debts resulting from liability for operating a motor vehicle while legally intoxicated.
10) Credit card debts greater than $650 owed to a single creditor by an individual debtor for luxury goods or services incurred on or within 90 days prior to filing.
11) Credit card debts for cash advances aggregating more than $925 under an open-end credit plan obtained by an individual debtor within 70 days prior to filing.
12) Nondischarged debts from a prior bankruptcy.
13) Certain debts incurred as a result of committing securities fraud.

9. **Dismissal**

a. If a Chapter 7 case is dismissed, the debtor is not discharged.

1) Dismissal may result from, among other things, the debtor's
   a) Unreasonable delay.
   b) Failure to pay fees.
   c) Failure to provide (1) creditor's lists, (2) financial statements, (3) tax returns, (4) evidence of payment by an employer, and (5) the certificate from a credit counselor.
   d) Lack of good faith.
   e) Failure to complete a course in personal financial management.
2) If the debtor is an individual whose debts are mostly consumer debts, the court may dismiss if a discharge would result in a substantial abuse of Chapter 7.

10. **Reaffirmation**

    a. A debtor must receive extensive disclosures and sign a statement disclosing his or her income, expenses, and amounts available to pay the debt. (S)he then may enter into a reaffirmation agreement to perform an obligation to be discharged.

        1) To be legally enforceable, such an agreement must

            a) Be entered into prior to the discharge (in bankruptcy),
            b) Be in writing and filed with the court, and
            c) Conspicuously state the debtor's right to rescind until the later of the discharge or 60 days after the agreement is filed with the court.

        2) If the debtor does not have an attorney, the court must conduct a hearing to approve the agreement. If the debtor has an attorney, the attorney must file an affidavit stating that (a) the debtor has been advised of the legal effect of reaffirmation, (b) the debtor voluntarily and knowingly entered into the agreement, and (c) it creates no undue hardship.

11. **Revocation of a Discharge**

    a. A discharge previously granted may be revoked within 1 year if the trustee or a creditor proves that (1) the discharge was obtained fraudulently, (2) the debtor knowingly and fraudulently retained property of the estate, or (3) the debtor failed to obey a court order.

Stop and review! You have completed the outline for this subunit. Study multiple-choice questions 14 through 20 beginning on page 787.

20.5 REORGANIZATIONS AND ADJUSTMENTS

1. **Chapter 11 Plans**

    a. Partnerships, corporations, railroads, and debtors qualified for relief under Chapter 7 (except stock or commodity brokers) are eligible for a **reorganization**. This procedure allows for (1) a debtor (including a business) to restructure its finances, (2) the business to continue, and (3) the creditors to be paid.

    b. A case is commenced by filing a petition requesting an order for relief.

        1) Petitions may be **voluntary or involuntary**.
        2) A petition results in a suspension of creditors' actions.
        3) An involuntary petition must meet the Chapter 7 tests.
        4) Insolvency is not a condition precedent to a voluntary petition.

    c. An individual or company seeking protection under Chapter 11 generally is permitted to operate its own business as a **debtor-in-possession**. A trustee is not required.

        1) A debtor-in-possession has the same rights and duties as a trustee.
        2) The court may order the appointment of a trustee if such action is in the best interests of the parties. The creditors may elect the trustee.
        3) A court may appoint an examiner to investigate fraud, misconduct, or mismanagement if all of the following apply:

            a) Appointment is requested by an interested party.
            b) It is in the interests of creditors or equity security holders.
            c) The debtor's fixed, undisputed, unsecured debts exceed $5 million.

d. A **committee of unsecured creditors** is appointed as soon as feasible after an order for relief has been granted. The committee generally consists of persons holding the seven largest unsecured claims. Its functions include the following:

   1) Consulting with the debtor-in-possession or the trustee
   2) Requesting appointment of a trustee
   3) Independently investigating the debtor's affairs
   4) Participating in formulating the plan of reorganization
   5) Employing professionals to perform services

e. A **plan of reorganization** must be prepared and filed.

   1) The debtor has the exclusive right to file a plan during the 120 days after the order for relief and may file a plan at any time. If the creditors or shareholders do not approve the plan within 180 days, any party may file. Moreover, any party may file if a trustee has been appointed.

f. A reorganization plan must divide creditors' claims and shareholders' interests into classes. Claims in each class must be treated equally.

   1) A class is **impaired** unless the plan leaves its legal, equitable, and contractual rights unaltered.

g. **Confirmation** by the court makes the plan binding on the debtor, creditors, equity security holders, and others. Confirmation may occur after acceptance or by cramdown.

   1) **Acceptance** by a class of claims requires the holders of more than 50% of the claims representing at least two-thirds of the dollar totals to approve the plan. A class of equity interests accepts the plan if the holders of at least two-thirds of the voting interests in dollar amount approve.

      a) To avoid a cramdown, the plan must be accepted by each class unless it is not adversely affected by the plan.
      b) The court may not confirm a plan not in the creditors' best interests.
      c) A spouse or child whose claims will not be paid in cash may block the plan.

   2) Confirmation over the objection of one or more classes is a **cramdown**. The requirements are

      a) Acceptance by at least one impaired class, not including acceptance of the plan by any insider;
      b) A finding that the plan is fair; and
      c) A finding that the plan does not discriminate unfairly against any creditors.

   3) The plan also must be confirmed (approved and put into operation) by the bankruptcy court. The court must confirm the plan if

      a) It is proposed in good faith,
      b) It provides for full payment of administrative expenses,
      c) Each class has accepted the plan or is unimpaired, and
      d) Each member of an impaired class has (1) accepted the plan or (2) will receive at least the amount (s)he would have received under Chapter 7.

   4) Generally, an entity is discharged from debts that occurred prior to confirmation if they are not protected by the plan.

h. **Consumer cases** under Chapter 11 are relatively similar to those under Chapter 13. Thus, (1) property of the estate includes after-acquired property, (2) discharge occurs only after plan completion, (3) plan funding is from future earnings, and (4) a 5-year minimum contribution of disposable income is required.

i. After confirmation, the plan is implemented, and assets are distributed accordingly.

j. After the debtor has made all payments required under the plan, the court must grant the debtor a discharge of all debts covered by the plan.

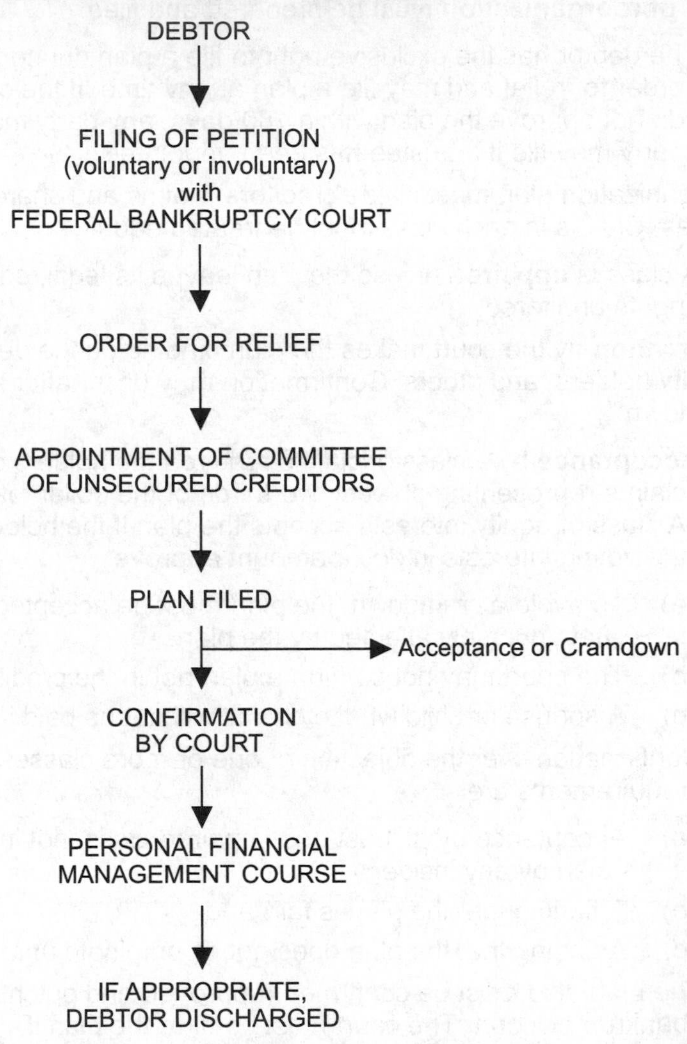

Figure 20-2

2. **Chapter 13 Plans**

   a. Chapter 13 provides for **adjustment of debts of an individual**. Its focus is on payment from future income. Thus, it may be preferable to liquidation because the debtor often is able to retain more assets.

      1) The debtor must have regular income and owe unsecured debts of less than $383,175 and secured debts of less than $1,149,525.
      2) Sole proprietorships also are eligible if the debt limitations are met.

   b. A proceeding may be initiated only by the debtor's filing of a **voluntary petition**.
   c. A trustee is appointed.
   d. The plan requires the approval of the bankruptcy judge only. The plan must meet the following requirements to be confirmed:

      1) The plan is proposed in good faith and complies with the Code.
      2) The debtor can comply with the plan.
      3) Required amounts have been paid.
      4) The value of property to be distributed on each unsecured claim equals at least the Chapter 7 amount.
      5) With regard to each secured claim,

         a) The holder has accepted the plan;
         b) The holder retains the lien on the collateral, the value of the distributed property is not less than the claim, and the plan provides for adequate payments to protect the holder from any loss in the collateral's fair value; or
         c) The debtor surrenders possession of the collateral to the holder.

   e. The debtor generally proposes either a composition or an extension plan. A **composition** plan allows the debtor to pay less than 100% of claims on a pro rata basis for each class of claims.

      1) An **extension** plan extends the payment period but does not reduce the debt.

   f. The court must hold a confirmation hearing.
   g. For the protection of creditors, the court may dismiss the proceeding or convert it into a Chapter 7 proceeding after a request by an interested party, including the debtor.
   h. After a debtor completes all or substantially all payments under the plan, the court grants a discharge of most debts. With few exceptions, the nondischargeable debts are the same as under Chapter 7.
   i. The Chapter 13 discharge upon completion of the plan bars another discharge in a Chapter 13 case for a 2-year period.

      1) If the prior discharge was in a Chapter 7 or 11 case, a 4-year period applies.

   j. A hardship discharge is available if (1) the debtor's failure is due to circumstances for which (s)he is not justly accountable, (2) creditors have received what they would have been paid under Chapter 7, and (3) modification of the plan is not feasible.

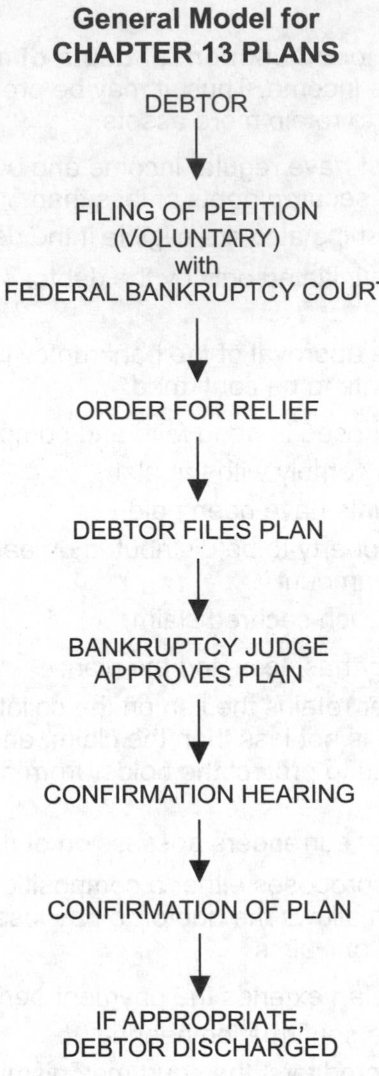

Figure 20-3

3. **Chapter 12 Plans**

   a. Chapter 12 applies to **family farmers** or **family fishermen**. A debtor proposes a plan to make payments to creditors over 3 to 5 years.

      1) The plan must provide for payments over 3 years unless the court approves a longer period for cause. Plans extended for cause must (a) propose to pay 100% of domestic support claims (child support and alimony) if any exist and (b) include all of the debtor's disposable income. A plan cannot provide for payments over more than 5 years.

   b. Chapter 12 eliminates many barriers to reorganization under Chapter 11 or 13. For example, Chapter 12 is more efficient and less expensive than Chapter 11, which is better suited to large corporate reorganizations. Also, Chapter 13 may not be advantageous because it is designed for wage earners who have smaller debts.

      1) Only a family farmer (fisherman) with **regular annual income** may file a petition. The purpose is to ensure that the debtor's annual income is sufficiently stable and regular to permit the debtor to make payments. But Chapter 12 allows for situations in which income is seasonal.

      2) Relief is voluntary, and only the debtor may file a petition.

c. Family farmers (fishermen) may be
   1) An individual or individual and spouse or
   2) A corporation or partnership.

d. An individual (and spouse) must meet the following criteria at the filing date:
   1) The individual (and spouse) must be engaged in a farming operation or a commercial fishing operation.
   2) The total debts (secured and unsecured) of the operation must not exceed $4,031,575 (if farming) or $1,868,200 (if fishing).
   3) For a family farmer, (fisherman) at least 50% (80%) of the total fixed debts (exclusive of debt for a home) must be related to the operation.
   4) More than 50% of the gross income of the individual (and spouse) for the preceding tax year (or, for family farmers only, each of the 2nd and 3rd prior tax years) must have come from the operation.

e. For a **corporation or partnership** to be an eligible debtor, it must meet the following criteria at the date of the filing:
   1) More than 50% of the outstanding stock or equity must be owned by one family (or one family and relatives).
   2) The family (and relatives) must conduct the operation.
   3) More than 80% of the value of the assets must be related to the operation.
   4) The total indebtedness must not exceed $4,031,575 (if farming) or $1,868,200 (if fishing).
   5) At least 50% (farming) or 80% (fishing) of the total fixed debts (exclusive of debt for a home occupied by a shareholder) must be related to the operation.
   6) Corporate stock cannot be publicly traded.

f. A case begins by **filing a petition** with the bankruptcy court in the area where (1) the individual lives, or (2) the corporation or partnership has its principal place of business or principal assets.
   1) Unless the court orders otherwise, the debtor also must file
      a) Schedules of assets and liabilities,
      b) A schedule of current income and expenditures,
      c) A schedule of executory contracts and unexpired leases, and
      d) A statement of financial affairs.
   2) Spouses may file a joint petition or individual petitions.
   3) The debtor must compile the following information:
      a) A list of all creditors and the amounts and nature of their claims;
      b) The source, amount, and frequency of the debtor's income;
      c) A list of all of the debtor's property; and
      d) A detailed list of the debtor's monthly farming (fishing) and living expenses.
   4) Married individuals must gather this information for each spouse.

g. When a petition is filed, an impartial **trustee** is appointed to administer the case. As under Chapter 13, the trustee evaluates the case and serves as a disbursing agent, collecting payments from the debtor and making distributions to creditors.

h. Filing the petition **automatically stays** most collection actions against the debtor or the debtor's property. The stay is by operation of law and requires no judicial action. As long as the stay is in effect, creditors generally cannot initiate or continue collection efforts (including phone calls). The bankruptcy clerk notifies all creditors whose names and addresses are provided by the debtor.
   1) A special automatic stay provision protects co-debtors. Unless the bankruptcy court authorizes otherwise, a creditor may not seek to collect a **consumer debt** from any individual who is liable to the debtor.

i. After the petition is filed, the trustee holds a **meeting of creditors**. During the meeting, the debtor answers questions under oath. The debtor must attend the meeting and answer questions about financial matters and the repayment plan. If spouses have filed jointly, both must attend.

j. After the meeting of creditors, the debtor, the trustee, and interested creditors attend a **hearing on confirmation** of the debtor's repayment plan.

   1) Payments to **secured creditors** can sometimes continue longer than 3 to 5 years. For example, if the debtor's underlying debt obligation was scheduled to be paid over more than 5 years (e.g., an equipment loan or a mortgage), the debtor may be able to pay the loan over the original repayment schedule as long as any arrearage is made up during the period of the plan.

4. **Chapter 9 Plans**

   a. Chapter 9 provides a financially-distressed **municipality** with protection from its creditors while it negotiates a plan for adjusting its debts.

   b. Reorganization is accomplished by (1) extending debt maturities, (2) reducing principal or interest, or (3) refinancing by obtaining a new loan.

   c. Chapter 9 differs significantly from other Chapters. It does **not** provide for liquidation of assets and distribution of the proceeds to creditors. Such action violates the Constitution and the reservation to the states of sovereignty over their internal affairs. Due to this severe limitation, the bankruptcy court is not as active in managing a municipal case as it is in corporate reorganizations under Chapter 11. Its functions are limited to (1) approving the petition (if the debtor is eligible), (2) confirming a plan of debt adjustment, and (3) ensuring implementation of the plan.

      1) However, the municipality may consent to the court's jurisdiction in many of the traditional areas of court oversight in bankruptcy. Thus, it obtains the protection of court orders and eliminates the need for multiple forums to decide issues.

5. **Chapter 15 Plans**

   a. Chapter 15 applies to insolvency cases involving debtors, assets, claimants, and other parties of interest from **more than one country**.

   b. The objectives of the statute are to

      1) Promote cooperation between U.S. courts and parties of interest and the courts and other competent authorities of foreign countries involved in cross-border insolvency cases;
      2) Establish greater legal certainty for trade and investment;
      3) Provide for the fair and efficient administration of cross-border insolvencies that protects the interests of all creditors and other interested entities, including the debtor;
      4) Protect and maximize of the value of the debtor's assets; and
      5) Facilitate the rescue of financially troubled businesses, thereby protecting investment and preserving employment.

   c. A Chapter 15 case is ancillary to a primary proceeding brought in another country, typically the debtor's home country. An alternative for the debtor or a creditor is to commence a full Chapter 7 or Chapter 11 case in the U.S. if the assets there are sufficiently complex. In addition, a U.S. court may authorize a trustee or other entity to act in a foreign country on behalf of a U.S. bankruptcy estate.

Background

Many dollar amounts in the Bankruptcy Code are adjusted for inflation every 3 years. The next adjustment is effective on April 1, 2016. Thus, the new amounts will be tested in the fourth quarter of 2016. Gleim will make available an update of the dollar amounts in time to allow preparation by candidates taking the CPA exam in or after October 2016.

Stop and review! You have completed the outline for this subunit. Study multiple-choice questions 21 through 24 beginning on page 789.

20.6 SURETIES

The AICPA has tested candidates' knowledge of the rights, duties, and liabilities of the various parties under a suretyship contract.

1. **Definitions**
   a. Suretyship involves at least three parties: the debtor, the creditor, and the surety.
   b. The person who actually receives the money or the credit is the debtor, principal, principal debtor, or obligor.
   c. The creditor (obligee) is the person who has permitted the debtor to receive goods, services, money, or other value without having fully paid the price.
   d. A **surety** is a legal person **contractually liable for another's debt or default**.
   e. Cosureties are two or more persons obligated to pay the same debt if the debtor defaults.
   f. Essentially the same rules apply whether or not a surety is compensated.
2. **Overview**
   a. The surety's promise is security for the payment of a debt or the performance of a duty if the debtor or obligor fails to make payment or otherwise perform.
      1) If a debtor owes more than one debt to a creditor, (s)he may give instructions about the application of a payment. The creditor must comply.
      2) Without instructions, the creditor may apply the payment as (s)he chooses.
   b. Some states still recognize a technical distinction between a surety and a guarantor. A surety is primarily liable for the debtor's obligation. Upon default, the creditor may proceed first against the surety.
      1) A **guarantor** is secondarily liable. Upon default, the creditor must proceed first against the principal debtor and obtain a judgment that is returned unsatisfied. Only then may the creditor proceed against the guarantor.
   c. An absolute surety is a guarantor of payment and is primarily liable upon the debt's maturity.
   d. A conditional guarantor of collection is not liable until the creditor has sued the debtor and is unable to collect the judgment.
   e. In the remainder of this outline, references to suretyship also include guaranty contracts.
3. **Formation of Suretyship Contract**
   a. Suretyship arises by express contract at the request of either the debtor or the creditor.
      1) The elements of a contract, including legal capacity and sufficient consideration, must be present.
         a) Separate consideration is required unless the surety's promise is made at the same time that the creditor provides consideration to the debtor.

EXAMPLE

Mom is engaged as surety to a note signed by Son. The surety contract is between Mom and Lender (not Son). The legally sufficient consideration received by Mom is the legal benefit of Lender's promise to continue dealing with Son.

2) The **statute of frauds** requires that a contract to answer for the debt of another be written and signed by the surety.
   a) A writing is needed to enforce a secondary promise, which is a promise to pay a debt or perform a contract only if the principal debtor fails to pay.
   b) The statute of frauds does not apply when the promise is original (primary).

EXAMPLE

If a buyer directs the seller to ship goods to a third person and agrees to pay $300 for them, the promise is original, and the promisor does not undertake to answer for the debt of another.

   c) If the **main purpose** of a promise to answer for the debt of another is to secure some new economic benefit, the promise may be enforced even if it is oral.

EXAMPLE

X is an essential supplier to Z. If Z guarantees X's debts to protect its supply of a vital component, the suretyship promise is not covered by the statute of frauds.

4. **Creditor's Duty to Disclose**
   a. A creditor must communicate to the surety, prior to formation of the contract, information about significant risk to the surety.
      1) The duty exists only if the creditor has reason to believe that the surety does not know the facts, and the creditor has reasonable opportunity to communicate them.
      2) The creditor should disclose what (s)he knows about the debtor if the surety inquires.
   b. A surety may not void the surety contract on the basis of misconduct of the debtor that induced the surety to enter into the surety agreement. The surety contract is between the surety and the **creditor**, not the debtor.
   c. The creditor may notify the surety when the debtor defaults but is not required to do so.
5. **Rights of a Surety**
   a. If required to perform, the surety has rights of reimbursement, subrogation, and exoneration against the principal debtor. The surety has no right to compel the creditor to proceed legally against the debtor or the collateral.
   b. **Reimbursement** is the right to sue the debtor for amounts (s)he paid to the creditor.
      1) The surety may enforce a security interest the creditor acquired in collateral.
      2) The surety is not entitled to reimbursement of amounts paid after receiving notice of a valid defense of the debtor to the payment.
      3) If the debtor has received a discharge in bankruptcy as to the creditor's claim, the surety's claim for reimbursement is barred.
   c. The right of **subrogation** entitles the surety to enforce the debt against the debtor. After payment to the creditor, the surety acquires the following legal rights of the creditor:
      1) Rights in collateral provided by the debtor
      2) Rights against other parties indebted on the same obligation
      3) Rights against cosureties
      4) Priority in bankruptcy
   d. **Exoneration** is the right of a surety to request that a court compel a capable but reluctant debtor to pay the debt before the creditor collects from the surety.

6. **Cosurety's Right of Contribution**
   a. A cosurety who pays more than the share (s)he agreed to pay is entitled to contribution from the other cosureties.
      1) Each cosurety is liable for the agreed-to proportionate part of a loss.
      2) A cosurety's contributive share is computed based on the following formula:

$$\frac{\text{Maximum liability of the cosurety}}{\text{Sum of maximum liabilities of cosureties}} \times \text{Default amount}$$

EXAMPLE

PD borrowed $100,000 from C. CS1 agreed to act as surety for up to $100,000. CS2 agreed to act as surety for up to $50,000. PD defaulted when the principal owed was $90,000. C recovered the full $90,000 from CS1. The cosureties' contributive shares are computed as follows:

CS1: $100,000 ÷ ($100,000 + $50,000) = (2 ÷ 3) × $90,000 = $60,000
CS2: $50,000 ÷ ($100,000 + $50,000) = (1 ÷ 3) × $90,000 = $30,000

CS1 has a right to a $30,000 contribution from CS2.

      3) Cosureties, like sureties, have rights of subrogation and exoneration.
      4) A cosurety's relative interest in collateral is in the proportion used to compute his or her contributive share.
      5) However, without a contrary agreement, cosureties are jointly and severally liable. Each is liable for the entire amount of loss caused by the debtor's default.

7. **Discharge of a Surety**
   a. The discharge of a surety's liability is governed by the contract.
   b. A surety is **discharged by performance** of his or her obligations (i.e., those of the principal debtor). Who renders the performance is irrelevant.
      1) Partial payment discharges a surety to the extent of the payment.
      2) If a note, bond, or draft is accepted as payment, the surety is discharged.
      3) A creditor's refusal to accept tender by the principal debtor or a surety discharges the surety.
      4) Death of a surety does not necessarily terminate liability, particularly if terms of the surety agreement bind the surety's heirs and representatives.
      5) Death or insolvency of the the debtor does not discharge the surety.
   c. An agreement between the creditor and the debtor extending time of payment discharges a surety to the extent of any loss to the surety.
      1) This agreement also extends the time for performance by the debtor of duties owed to the surety unless the agreement preserves the surety's right of recourse.
   d. The creditor's **release of the debtor** may discharge the surety unless the creditor
      1) Reserves his or her rights against the surety, and
      2) The instrument states that (a) the creditor retains rights against the surety and (b) the surety's rights against the debtor also are retained.
   e. **Modification** of the debtor-creditor contract, without consent of the surety, also may discharge the surety.
      1) However, discharge is complete only if the modification constitutes a substituted contract, or the risks of loss imposed on the surety differ fundamentally from those resulting from the original contract.
      2) Otherwise, the surety guarantees the modified contract except to the extent of actual loss caused by the modification to the surety.

f. The creditor's **impairment of collateral**, for example, by returning it to the debtor or failing to maintain a perfected security interest in it, discharges the surety to the extent of the value of the lost collateral.

g. **Rescission** or **revocation** of the principal contract releases the surety from any further liability but not from liability already incurred.

h. **Release by the creditor of a surety** releases the cosureties to the extent they cannot obtain contribution from the released surety. If a surety is released, the total liability of the cosureties equals the total liabilities of all sureties prior to the release reduced by the portion for which the released surety would have been responsible.

   1) The cosureties are not released if (a) they consent to the underlying release or (b) the creditor expressly reserves rights against them. The preservation of rights puts the released surety on notice that the release is effective only between the creditor and the released surety. Thus, the right of contribution held by the other sureties against the released surety is not impaired, and their obligations are not reduced.

EXAMPLE

If, in the previous example, C released CS1 without consent of CS2 and without reserving rights against CS2, CS2 can no longer obtain the contribution of $60,000 from CS1, and CS2 is released to that extent. Thus, CS2's liability to C is limited to $30,000.

8. **Defenses of a Surety**

   a. A surety has three kinds of defenses.

      1) Defenses based on the **suretyship contract** include the following:

         a) A valid contract of suretyship never existed.
         b) A valid contract existed, but the surety exercised a right to void it, e.g., for failure to comply with the statute of frauds or because of his or her incapacity.
         c) The creditor obtained the surety's promise by means of fraud or duress.
         d) The surety performed the contract by performing the debtor's promise.
         e) The surety tendered performance of the suretyship contract.
         f) An intended cosurety did not sign the suretyship contract.

      2) The surety may assert certain **debtor's defenses** against the creditor.

         a) But the following personal defenses of a debtor are not available to the surety:

            i) The debtor's incapacity due to infancy or mental incompetence
            ii) Discharge of the debtor's obligation in bankruptcy
            iii) A debtor's claim against the creditor for set-off

EXAMPLE

A debtor may have a claim against its creditor. The debtor could offset what it is owed against what it owes. The surety on the obligation owed to the creditor by the debtor cannot.

         b) It is **not** a defense that an insolvent debtor induced the creditor and surety to enter into a contract.

c) Defenses available to the debtor and surety include the following:
   i) Forgery of the debtor's signature on an instrument
   ii) Fraudulent or material alteration of the contractual document or other fraud by the creditor, including the creditor's failure to disclose known fraud by the debtor
   iii) Lack of a valid creditor-debtor contract (except in the case of the debtor's incapacity)
   iv) Illegality or impracticability of performing the creditor-debtor contract
   v) Performance by the debtor
   vi) The creditor's refusal to accept tender of performance by debtor or surety

3) **Special surety defenses** include the following:
   a) The creditor's release of the debtor unless the creditor reserves his or her rights against the surety
   b) Modification of the debtor-creditor contract without consent by the surety
   c) The creditor's impairment of collateral

Stop and review! You have completed the outline for this subunit. Study multiple-choice questions 25 through 30 beginning on page 791.

QUESTIONS

20.1 Liens and Enforcement Methods

1. Which of the following liens generally require(s) the lienholder to give notice of legal action before selling the debtor's property to satisfy the debt?

	Mechanic's Lien	Artisan's Lien
A.	Yes	Yes
B.	Yes	No
C.	No	Yes
D.	No	No

Answer (A) is correct.

REQUIRED: The lien(s), if any, requiring notice before sale of the debtor's property.

DISCUSSION: A mechanic's lien is a statutory lien against realty that secures an unpaid debt arising from a contract for labor, materials, or services to improve the property. An artisan's lien arises in favor of a repairer or improver of personal property who retains possession of the property until paid. Failure to pay the debt permits the lienholder to foreclose on the property and sell it. Statutes require notice to the owner prior to foreclosure and sale.

2. If a mortgagor defaults in the payment of a purchase money mortgage, and the mortgagee forecloses, the mortgagor may do any of the following except

A. Obtain any excess monies resulting from a judicial sale after payment of the mortgagee.

B. Remain in possession of the property after a foreclosure sale if the equity in the property exceeds the balance due on the mortgage.

C. Refinance the mortgage with another lender and repay the original mortgage.

D. Assert the equitable right of redemption by paying the mortgage.

Answer (B) is correct.

REQUIRED: The right not held by a defaulting mortgagor.

DISCUSSION: Most states recognize the mortgage as a security interest. The mortgagor-debtor signs a promissory note for the sum borrowed from the mortgagee-creditor. (S)he also signs a mortgage document representing the right of the mortgagee to seek judicial foreclosure of the mortgage and sale of the property upon default. The purchaser will receive a right to possession after the sale (or, in some states, after the redemption period elapses).

Answer (A) is incorrect. The mortgagor has an equity in the process equal to any amount left after payment of the debt, interest, and costs. Answer (C) is incorrect. Redemption might be accomplished by refinancing. Answer (D) is incorrect. A defaulting mortgagor has an equitable right to redeem the property before the foreclosure proceedings are complete by payment of the debt, interest, and costs. In many states, the mortgagor also has a statutory right of redemption after foreclosure.

3. Sklar Corp. owns a factory that has a fair market value of $90,000. Dall Bank holds an $80,000 first mortgage, and Rice Finance holds a $20,000 second mortgage on the factory. Sklar has discontinued payments to Dall and Rice, who have foreclosed on their mortgages. If the factory is properly sold to Bond at a judicial sale for $90,000, after expenses,

A. Rice will receive $10,000 out of the proceeds.

B. Dall will receive $77,500 out of the proceeds.

C. Bond will take the factory subject to the unsatisfied portion of any mortgage.

D. Rice has a right of redemption after the judicial sale.

Answer (A) is correct.

REQUIRED: The true statement about the effects of a judicial sale.

DISCUSSION: A first mortgage holder has priority upon foreclosure and must be paid in full prior to payment of a subsequent mortgage holder. Thus, Dall Bank will receive the first $80,000 of the proceeds, and Rice will receive the remaining $10,000. Rice will be an unsecured creditor for the remaining $10,000 of its debt.

Answer (B) is incorrect. Dall will receive payment in full before the second mortgage holder is paid anything. The proceeds are not prorated. Answer (C) is incorrect. The purchaser at the judicial sale will take the property free of any claim. Answer (D) is incorrect. The mortgagor (Sklar), not a mortgagee, has a statutory right of redemption after the sale.

20.2 Collective Remedies under State Law

4. A client has joined other creditors of the Martin Construction Company in a composition agreement seeking to avoid the necessity of a bankruptcy proceeding against Martin. Which statement describes the composition agreement?

A. It provides a temporary delay, not to exceed 6 months, insofar as the debtor's obligation to repay the debts included in the composition.

B. It does not discharge any of the debts included until performance by the debtor has taken place.

C. It provides for the appointment of a receiver to take over and operate the debtor's business.

D. It must be approved by all creditors.

Answer (B) is correct.

REQUIRED: The description of a composition among creditors.

DISCUSSION: A composition with creditors is a common-law contractual undertaking between the debtor and the creditors. The participating creditors agree to (1) extend time for payments, (2) take lesser sums in satisfaction of the debts owed, or (3) accept some other plan of financial adjustment. Under general contract law, the original debts will not be discharged until the debtor has performed the new obligations.

Answer (A) is incorrect. Although a composition may involve an extension of time, it is not limited to 6 months. Furthermore, the more common composition is to take lesser sums in satisfaction. Answer (C) is incorrect. Only a court appoints a receiver. A composition is a contractual agreement not involving judicial intervention. Answer (D) is incorrect. A composition need not be approved by all creditors but is binding only upon those participating.

5. Fran Di, doing business as Di Fashions, is hopelessly insolvent. As a means of staving off her aggressive creditors and avoiding bankruptcy, Di has decided to make a general assignment for the benefit of her creditors. Consequently, she transferred all her nonexempt property to a trustee for equitable distribution to her creditors. What are the legal consequences of Di's actions?

A. A debtor may not make an assignment for the benefit of creditors if she has been adjudicated a bankrupt and discharged within the preceding 8 years.

B. All creditors must participate in the assignment and distribution of property if a majority in number and amount participate.

C. Upon distribution of all her assigned property to the participating creditors, she is discharged from all liability.

D. She may be petitioned into bankruptcy by her creditors.

Answer (D) is correct.

REQUIRED: The legal consequences of an assignment for the benefit of creditors.

DISCUSSION: An involuntary petition by the creditors will be upheld even if contested by the debtor if the debtor is not paying his or her debts as they come due or if, during the preceding 120 days before the filing of the petition, a custodian (trustee, receiver, etc.) was appointed or permitted to take possession of the debtor's property. For this reason, Di may not be able to avoid bankruptcy.

Answer (A) is incorrect. An assignment for the benefit of creditors under state law is not an official proceeding and is not subject to federal bankruptcy rules. Answer (B) is incorrect. All creditors need not participate in the assignment, and distribution would not discharge any nonassenting creditors' claims. Answer (C) is incorrect. Distribution of assigned property to the participating creditors does not discharge the debtor from liability to the nonparticipants.

6. A debtor may attempt to conceal or transfer property to prevent a creditor from satisfying a judgment. Which of the following actions will be considered an indication of fraudulent conveyance?

	Debtor Remaining in Possession after Conveyance	Secret Conveyance	Debtor Retains an Equitable Benefit in the Property Conveyed
A.	Yes	Yes	Yes
B.	No	Yes	Yes
C.	Yes	Yes	No
D.	Yes	No	Yes

Answer (A) is correct.

REQUIRED: The indications of fraudulent conveyance.

DISCUSSION: Any transfer of property that is made with the purpose and intent to delay, hinder, or defraud creditors is voidable by the transferor's creditors. Courts recognize factors that indicate fraudulent conveyances. These factors are known as badges of fraud. They include (1) the debtor's retention of possession or a beneficial interest, (2) a transfer of substantially all assets, (3) a transfer in secret, (4) a transfer to a family member or insider, (5) a transfer for inadequate consideration, (6) a transfer in anticipation of legal action or financial problems, (7) removal or concealment of assets, and (8) insolvency at the time of or shortly after the transfer.

20.3 Bankruptcy Administration

7. To file for bankruptcy under Chapter 7 of the Federal Bankruptcy Code, an individual must

A. Have debts of any amount.

B. Be insolvent.

C. Be indebted to more than three creditors.

D. Have debts in excess of $15,325.

Answer (A) is correct.

REQUIRED: The requirement to file for protection under Chapter 7 of the Bankruptcy Code.

DISCUSSION: Under Chapter 7, generally, a debtor's nonexempt assets are converted into cash, the cash is distributed among creditors, and the debtor is discharged from most remaining obligations. Any person with a debt, if eligible under Chapter 7, may file a petition.

Answer (B) is incorrect. Insolvency is not required to file a voluntary petition. It is only necessary that the person have a legal obligation. Answer (C) is incorrect. Number-of-creditors thresholds apply only to involuntary petitions filed by creditors. Answer (D) is incorrect. Amount-of-debt thresholds apply only to involuntary petitions.

8. Green owes the following amounts to unsecured creditors: Rice, $5,700; Zwick, $4,800; Young, $15,800; and Zinc, $4,900. Green has not paid any creditor since January 1, Year 1. On May 1, Year 1, Green's sole asset, a cabin cruiser, was seized by Xeno Marine Co., the holder of a perfected security interest in the boat. On July 1, Year 1, Rice, Zwick, and Zinc involuntarily petitioned Green into bankruptcy under Chapter 7 of the Federal Bankruptcy Code. If Green opposes the involuntary petition, the petition will be

A. Upheld because the three filing creditors are owed more than $15,325.

B. Upheld because one creditor is owed more than $15,325.

C. Dismissed because there are fewer than 12 creditors.

D. Dismissed because the boat was seized more than 90 days before the filing.

Answer (A) is correct.

REQUIRED: The status of an involuntary petition under Chapter 7.

DISCUSSION: If the debtor has fewer than 12 creditors, any 1 or more creditors who alone or together have unsecured claims of $15,325 or more can file an involuntary petition. If the debtor has 12 or more creditors, any 3 or more who together hold unsecured claims of at least $15,325 can file an involuntary petition.

Answer (B) is incorrect. Young did not join in filing the petition. Answer (C) is incorrect. A debtor with fewer than 12 creditors may be involuntarily petitioned into bankruptcy by one or more creditors who alone or together are owed more than $15,325. Answer (D) is incorrect. A challenged involuntary petition is not dismissed if the debtor is generally not paying his or her bills as they become due or, within 120 days before filing, a custodian or receiver took possession of all or most of the debtor's property to enforce a lien against the property.

9. A party involuntarily petitioned into bankruptcy under Chapter 7 of the Federal Bankruptcy Code who succeeds in having the petition dismissed could recover

	Court Costs and Attorney's Fees	Compensatory Damages	Punitive Damages
A.	Yes	Yes	Yes
B.	Yes	Yes	No
C.	No	Yes	Yes
D.	Yes	No	No

Answer (A) is correct.

REQUIRED: The recovery allowed a debtor whose involuntary bankruptcy was dismissed.

DISCUSSION: A debtor who successfully contests an involuntary bankruptcy petition could recover his or her costs, including reasonable attorney's fees. The court may require the petitioner to pay damages if (s)he is found to have acted in bad faith. A petitioner whose conduct is malicious or otherwise egregious also may be required to pay punitive damages.

10. Which of the following statements is true with respect to a voluntary bankruptcy proceeding under the liquidation provisions of the Bankruptcy Code?

A. The debtor must be insolvent.

B. The liabilities of the debtor must total $15,325 or more.

C. It may be properly commenced and maintained by any person who is insolvent.

D. The filing of the bankruptcy petition constitutes an order for relief.

Answer (D) is correct.

REQUIRED: The true statement about a voluntary bankruptcy proceeding.

DISCUSSION: The voluntary bankruptcy petition is a formal request by the debtor to the court for an order for relief. Under the liquidation provisions, an order for relief is automatically given to the debtor upon the filing of the petition.

Answer (A) is incorrect. Insolvency is not required. A statement that the debtor has debts is all that is needed. Answer (B) is incorrect. In a voluntary bankruptcy proceeding, there is no minimum amount of debtor liabilities. Answer (C) is incorrect. The courts have discretion not to grant relief that would constitute a substantial abuse of the bankruptcy laws. Also, certain entities, e.g., banks, are not eligible for voluntary bankruptcy.

Questions 11 through 13 are based on the following information.

On May 1, Dart, Inc., a closely held corporation, was petitioned involuntarily into bankruptcy under the liquidation provisions of Chapter 7 of the Federal Bankruptcy Code. Dart contested the petition.

Dart has not been paying its business debts as they become due, has defaulted on its mortgage loan payments, and owes back taxes to the IRS. The total cash value of Dart's bankruptcy estate after the sale of all assets and payment of administration expenses is $100,000.

A listing of Dart's creditors is presented in the next column.

- Fracon Bank is owed $75,000 principal and accrued interest on a mortgage loan secured by Dart's real property. The property was valued at and sold, in bankruptcy, for $71,000.
- The IRS has a $12,000 recorded judgment for unpaid corporate income tax.
- JOG Office Supplies has an unsecured claim of $3,000 that was timely filed.
- Nanstar Electric Co. has an unsecured claim of $1,200 that was not timely filed.
- Decoy Publications has a claim of $15,000, of which $2,000 is secured by Dart's inventory that was valued and sold, in bankruptcy, for $2,000. The claim was timely filed.

11. Assuming the IRS does **not** join in the filing of the involuntary petition against Dart, which of the following must file?

I. JOG Office Supplies
II. Nanstar Electric Co.
III. Decoy Publications
IV. Fracon Bank

A. I, II, III, and IV.

B. II and III only.

C. I and II only.

D. III only.

Answer (D) is correct.

REQUIRED: The creditor(s) required to join in the filing of an involuntary petition.

DISCUSSION: Under Chapter 7, if a debtor has fewer than 12 creditors, an involuntary bankruptcy petition may be filed by any 1 or more creditors who alone or together have $15,325 or more of unsecured claims (in excess of security interests). Decoy must file to meet the statutory requirement because it has $13,000 ($15,000 – $2,000 secured) of unsecured debt. JOG ($3,000) or Fracon ($75,000 – $71,000 = $4,000) must join in the petition to meet the $15,325 minimum requirement. Given that the IRS does not file, Decoy is an indispensable party.

12. Which of the following statements accurately describes the result of Dart's opposing the petition?

A. Dart will win because the petition should have been filed under Chapter 11.

B. Dart will win because there are not more than 12 creditors.

C. Dart will lose because it is not paying its debts as they become due.

D. Dart will lose because of its debt to the IRS.

Answer (C) is correct.

REQUIRED: The result of the debtor's opposing the petition.

DISCUSSION: The two grounds for filing an involuntary petition for bankruptcy under Chapter 7 are (1) the debtor is not paying its bills on time, or (2) a custodian, assignee, or general receiver took possession of all or most of the debtor's property to enforce a lien against the property within 120 days of the filing of the petition. Because Dart was not paying its bills when they became due, Dart will lose.

Answer (A) is incorrect. The involuntary petition could have been filed under Chapters 7 or 11. One of the statutory grounds for involuntary bankruptcy is met because Dart is not paying its bills on time. Answer (B) is incorrect. A debtor having fewer than 12 creditors may be petitioned into bankruptcy by any 1 or more creditors having alone or together at least $15,325 unsecured claims. Answer (D) is incorrect. IRS claims will not allow the petitioner(s) to win even though the IRS claims against Dart cannot be discharged.

13. Which of the following events will follow the filing of an unopposed Chapter 7 involuntary petition against Dart?

	A Trustee Will Be Appointed	A Stay against Creditor Collection Proceedings Will Go into Effect
A.	Yes	Yes
B.	Yes	No
C.	No	Yes
D.	No	No

Answer (A) is correct.

REQUIRED: The event(s) following the filing of an involuntary petition.

DISCUSSION: When an involuntary petition in bankruptcy is filed, the court issues an order of relief if the petition is unopposed. Otherwise, a hearing is conducted. If the judge finds that one of the statutory criteria is satisfied, (s)he also will issue an order for relief. The effect of the filing is to suspend almost all legal action and collection activities against the debtor. An interim trustee is appointed to manage the bankruptcy estate's assets. The interim trustee serves until replaced by a permanent trustee elected by the creditors.

20.4 Bankruptcy Liquidations

14. Which asset is included in a debtor's bankruptcy estate in a liquidation proceeding?

A. Proceeds from a life insurance policy received 90 days after the petition was filed.

B. An inheritance received 270 days after the petition was filed.

C. Property from a divorce settlement received 365 days after the petition was filed.

D. Wages earned by the debtor after the petition was filed.

Answer (A) is correct.

REQUIRED: The asset included in a debtor's bankruptcy estate.

DISCUSSION: Most assets in which the debtor has a legal or equitable interest at the date the proceedings began is included in the estate. Other property may be added to the estate. For example, it includes property acquired by the debtor within 180 days after filing the petition if the property was acquired (1) by inheritance, (2) as proceeds of a life insurance policy, or (3) from a property settlement in a divorce case.

15. A person who voluntarily filed for bankruptcy and received a discharge under Chapter 7 of the Federal Bankruptcy Code

A. May obtain another voluntary discharge in bankruptcy under Chapter 7 after 5 years have elapsed from the date of the prior filing.

B. Will receive a discharge of all debts owed.

C. Is precluded from owning or operating a similar business for 2 years.

D. Must surrender for distribution to the creditors any amount received as an inheritance within 180 days after filing the petition.

Answer (D) is correct.

REQUIRED: The true statement about a discharge under Chapter 7.

DISCUSSION: The bankruptcy estate available for distribution to creditors includes all the debtor's nonexempt legal and equitable interests in property on the date of filing. It includes proceeds and profits from that estate. Certain property acquired after filing is also included: inheritances, property settlements (divorce), and life insurance proceeds to which the debtor becomes entitled within 180 days after filing.

Answer (A) is incorrect. Discharge is barred if there was a Chapter 7 discharge within the 8 years preceding filing the petition. Answer (B) is incorrect. Certain debts are nondischargeable. Answer (C) is incorrect. There is no such requirement.

Questions 16 and 17 are based on the following information. On February 28, Year 1, Master, Inc., had total assets with a fair value of $1.2 million and total liabilities of $990,000. On January 15, Year 1, Master made a monthly installment note payment to Acme Distributors Corp., a creditor holding a properly perfected security interest in equipment having a fair value greater than the balance due on the note. On June 15, Year 1, Master voluntarily filed a petition in bankruptcy under the liquidation provisions of Chapter 7 of the Federal Bankruptcy Code. One year later, the equipment was sold for less than the balance due on the note to Acme.

16. If Master's voluntary petition is filed properly,

A. Master will be entitled to conduct its business as a debtor-in-possession unless the U.S. Trustee appoints a trustee.

B. A trustee must be appointed by the creditors.

C. Lawsuits by Master's creditors will be stayed by the Federal Bankruptcy Code.

D. The unsecured creditors must elect a creditors' committee of 3 to 11 members to consult with the trustee.

Answer (C) is correct.

REQUIRED: The effect of properly filing a petition under Chapter 7 of the Bankruptcy Act.

DISCUSSION: If a voluntary petition has been properly completed, sworn to, and signed by the debtor, it functions as an automatic order for relief. One effect is to stay most legal proceedings and other activities of creditors seeking to collect from the debtor. Secured creditors' actions are also stayed. The court may decide a creditor is entitled to relief from the automatic stay on the grounds that it does afford the creditor adequate protection.

Answer (A) is incorrect. The U.S. Trustee appoints an interim trustee. But, with court approval, the debtor may file a bond and reacquire property under the trustee's control. Answer (B) is incorrect. Under Chapter 7, the U.S. Trustee appoints an interim trustee. The creditors may then elect a permanent trustee. Otherwise, the interim trustee continues as trustee. Answer (D) is incorrect. The creditors may, but do not have a legal duty to, elect such a committee.

17. Which of the following statements correctly describes Acme's distribution from Master's bankruptcy estate?

A. Acme will receive the total amount it is owed even if the proceeds from the sale of the collateral were less than the balance owed by Master.

B. Acme will have the same priority as unsecured general creditors to the extent that the proceeds from the sale of its collateral are insufficient to satisfy the amount owed by Master.

C. The total proceeds from the sale of the collateral will be paid to Acme even if they are less than the balance owed by Master, provided there is sufficient cash to pay all administrative costs associated with the bankruptcy.

D. Acme will receive only the proceeds from the sale of the collateral in full satisfaction of the debt owed by Master.

Answer (B) is correct.

REQUIRED: The portion of a bankruptcy estate distributable to a secured creditor.

DISCUSSION: Under the Bankruptcy Code, to the extent a creditor's claim is secured, it must be satisfied in full before distribution is made on any other claims. But the secured creditor is treated the same as a general unsecured creditor to the extent its claim exceeds the value of the collateral. Note that the collateral is part of the estate. The secured creditor is entitled to the security interest as opposed to the property itself.

Answer (A) is incorrect. Acme is treated as a general unsecured creditor with respect to any portion of its claim that exceeds the value of the collateral. Answer (C) is incorrect. The security interest must be satisfied to the extent of the security before priority claims are paid. Answer (D) is incorrect. Acme may receive an amount in addition to the proceeds of the collateral but only in its capacity as an unsecured creditor.

18. Which of the following transfers by a debtor, within 90 days of filing for bankruptcy, could be set aside as a preferential payment?

A. Making a gift to charity.

B. Paying a business utility bill.

C. Borrowing money from a bank secured by giving a mortgage on business property.

D. Prepaying an installment loan on inventory.

Answer (D) is correct.

REQUIRED: The reason for the status of a transfer as preferential or nonpreferential.

DISCUSSION: A preferential transfer is one made for the benefit of a creditor within 90 days prior to filing the petition and on account of an antecedent (pre-existing) debt. The transfer must have been made when the debtor was insolvent and must have resulted in the creditor receiving a larger portion of its claim than it otherwise would have received as a distribution in the bankruptcy proceeding. A prepayment is on account of an existing debt and is therefore a voidable preference.

Answer (A) is incorrect. A gift to a charity is not on account of an antecedent (pre-existing) debt. Answer (B) is incorrect. Payment of accounts payable in the ordinary course of the debtor's business is not a voidable preference. Answer (C) is incorrect. A contemporaneous exchange between the debtor and another, even a creditor, for new value may not be set aside. The transfer of a security interest enables the debtor to acquire the new property.

19. Which of the following claims will be paid first in the distribution of a bankruptcy estate under the liquidation provisions of Chapter 7 of the Bankruptcy Code if the petition was filed July 15, Year 1?

A. A secured debt properly perfected on March 20, Year 1.

B. Inventory purchased and delivered August 1, Year 1.

C. Employee wages due April 30, Year 1.

D. A federal tax lien filed June 30, Year 1.

Answer (A) is correct.

REQUIRED: The claim that will be paid first.

DISCUSSION: The Bankruptcy Code classifies creditors into several categories according to the priority of their claims against the debtor. It states that secured creditors' claims will be satisfied in full to the extent of the value of the security before unsecured creditors' claims will be considered. To the extent the security is insufficient, the secured creditor becomes an unsecured creditor. The tax lien, even if a security interest, would have lower priority than the secured debt perfected earlier.

Answer (B) is incorrect. A secured claim has priority over the inventory purchase before unsecured claims are satisfied. Answer (C) is incorrect. The secured claim has priority over employee wages. Answer (D) is incorrect. Even if the federal tax lien is a secured claim, the first perfected of two security interests has priority.

20. By signing a reaffirmation agreement on April 15, Year 1, a debtor agreed to pay certain debts that would be discharged in bankruptcy. On June 20, Year 1, the debtor's attorney filed the reaffirmation agreement and an affidavit with the court indicating that the debtor understood the consequences of the reaffirmation agreement. The debtor obtained a discharge on August 25, Year 1. The reaffirmation agreement would be enforceable only if it was

A. Made after discharge.

B. Approved by the bankruptcy court.

C. Not for a household purpose debt.

D. Not rescinded before discharge.

Answer (D) is correct.

REQUIRED: The enforceable reaffirmation of debt.

DISCUSSION: To be enforceable, a reaffirmation agreement must conspicuously state the debtor's right of rescission. The debtor has the right to rescind the reaffirmation until the later of the discharge or 60 days after the agreement is filed with the court.

Answer (A) is incorrect. To be legally enforceable, the reaffirmation agreement must be entered into prior to the general discharge in bankruptcy. Answer (B) is incorrect. Court approval is required if the debtor has no attorney. In the alternative, the reaffirmation agreement may be accompanied by an affidavit filed by the debtor's attorney that the debtor voluntarily and knowingly entered into the agreement and it caused no undue hardship. Answer (C) is incorrect. Almost any debt, including one incurred for household purposes, may be reaffirmed.

20.5 Reorganizations and Adjustments

21. Under Chapter 11 of the Federal Bankruptcy Code, which of the following would **not** be eligible for reorganization?

A. Retail sole proprietorship.

B. Advertising partnership.

C. CPA professional corporation.

D. Savings and loan corporation.

Answer (D) is correct.

REQUIRED: The entity ineligible for Chapter 11 reorganization.

DISCUSSION: Reorganization under Chapter 11 of the Bankruptcy Code is available only for eligible debtors. These include partnerships and corporations, railroads, and any person that may be a debtor under Chapter 7 (but not stock or commodity brokers). Ineligible debtors under Chapter 7 include municipalities, insurance companies, banks, credit unions, and savings and loan associations.

22. Under Chapter 11 of the Federal Bankruptcy Code, which of the following actions is necessary before the court may confirm a reorganization plan?

A. Provision for full payment of administration expenses.

B. Acceptance of the plan by all classes of claimants.

C. Preparation of a contingent plan of liquidation.

D. Appointment of a trustee.

Answer (A) is correct.

REQUIRED: The prerequisite to court confirmation of a reorganization plan.

DISCUSSION: The debtor generally has the exclusive right to file a reorganization plan during the 120 days after the order of relief. To be effective, the plan must be confirmed by the bankruptcy court. The plan must provide for full payment of administration expenses.

Answer (B) is incorrect. A plan that is fair and equitable may be confirmed without approval of all classes of creditors (a cramdown plan). Answer (C) is incorrect. Chapter 11 enables restructuring instead of liquidation. A contingent plan of liquidation is not required. Answer (D) is incorrect. The court has discretion to order appointment of a trustee when there is evidence of dishonesty or mismanagement or if such action is in the best interests of the parties. But normally the debtor remains in possession of his or her assets and continues to operate the business.

23. Terri Hall, CPA, is an unsecured creditor of Tree Co. for $16,000. Tree has a total of 10 creditors, all of whom are unsecured. Tree has not paid any of the creditors for 3 months. Under Chapter 11 of the federal Bankruptcy Code, which of the following statements is true?

A. Hall and two other unsecured creditors must join in the involuntary petition in bankruptcy.

B. Hall may file an involuntary petition in bankruptcy against Tree.

C. Tree may not be petitioned involuntarily into bankruptcy under the provisions of Chapter 11.

D. Tree may not be petitioned involuntarily into bankruptcy because it has fewer than 12 unsecured creditors.

Answer (B) is correct.

REQUIRED: The requirements under Chapter 11 for involuntary bankruptcy.

DISCUSSION: An involuntary bankruptcy proceeding can be commenced only under Chapter 7 and Chapter 11 against an eligible debtor. If the debtor has 12 or more different creditors, any 3 or more creditors who together hold unsecured claims of at least $15,325 can file an involuntary petition. If the debtor has fewer than 12 creditors, any 1 or more creditors who alone or together have unsecured claims of at least $15,325 can file an involuntary petition. Accordingly, Hall may file an involuntary petition in bankruptcy against Tree because she holds an unsecured claim of $16,000.

Answer (A) is incorrect. Hall has at least $15,325 in unsecured claims against Tree and can file the involuntary petition against Tree without the other creditors. Answer (C) is incorrect. Involuntary bankruptcy proceedings may be brought in Chapter 7 and 11 bankruptcy. Answer (D) is incorrect. Hall has at least $15,325 in unsecured claims against Tree and can file the involuntary petition even if she is the sole creditor.

24. Under the reorganization provisions of Chapter 11 of the Federal Bankruptcy Code, after a reorganization plan is confirmed and a final decree closing the proceedings entered, which of the following events usually occurs?

A. A reorganized corporate debtor will be liquidated.

B. A reorganized corporate debtor will be discharged from all debts except as otherwise provided in the plan and applicable law.

C. A trustee will continue to operate the debtor's business.

D. A reorganized individual debtor will not be allowed to continue in the same business.

Answer (B) is correct.

REQUIRED: The status of a debtor after completing a Chapter 11 reorganization.

DISCUSSION: At the conclusion of Chapter 11 proceedings, a corporate debtor is discharged from most debts of the business. Exceptions include debts that are provided for in the plan of reorganization approved by the creditors and certain nondischargeable debts.

Answer (A) is incorrect. A Chapter 11 reorganization allows the debtor's finances to be restructured, not liquidated. Answer (C) is incorrect. A trustee is usually not appointed to run the debtor's business. The court may, however, order the appointment of a trustee for cause or if such action is in the best interests of the parties. Answer (D) is incorrect. A reorganized individual debtor may continue in the same business without any restrictions.

20.6 Sureties

25. A party contracts to guarantee the collection of the debts of another. As a result of the guaranty, which of the following statements is true?

A. The creditor may proceed against the guarantor without attempting to collect from the debtor.

B. The guaranty must be in writing.

C. The guarantor may use any defenses available to the debtor.

D. The creditor must be notified of the debtor's default by the guarantor.

Answer (B) is correct.

REQUIRED: The true statement about a guaranty of collection.

DISCUSSION: A person who guarantees payment without qualification must pay upon default. A guarantor of collection guarantees the debt on condition that the creditor first use ordinary legal means to collect. Surety and guaranty arrangements that are collateral promises are within the statute of frauds and must be in writing.

Answer (A) is incorrect. A guarantor of collection is not liable until the creditor exercises due diligence in enforcing its remedies against the debtor. Answer (C) is incorrect. A guarantor may not use defenses that are personal to the debtor, e.g., infancy. Answer (D) is incorrect. The creditor ordinarily notifies the guarantor of the debtor's default.

26. Which of the following defenses would a surety be able to assert successfully to limit the surety's liability to a creditor?

A. A discharge in bankruptcy of the principal debtor.

B. A personal defense the principal debtor has against the creditor.

C. The incapacity of the surety.

D. The incapacity of the principal debtor.

Answer (C) is correct.

REQUIRED: The defense a surety could assert to limit his or her liability to a creditor.

DISCUSSION: The surety may assert a defense personal to the surety to limit his or her liability to a creditor. The surety may use the defense of incapacity of the surety to avoid liability to the principal debtor's creditor.

Answer (A) is incorrect. A surety may not assert a principal debtor's discharge in bankruptcy as a defense. Bankruptcy is a common reason for a debtor to use a surety. Answer (B) is incorrect. A surety may assert only a limited number of contractual defenses of the principal debtor. A surety may not ordinarily assert a defense personal to the principal debtor. Answer (D) is incorrect. A surety may not assert the incapacity of the principal debtor as a defense. A debtor's incapacity is a common reason to use a surety.

27. If a debtor defaults and the debtor's surety satisfies the obligation, the surety acquires the right of

A. Subrogation.

B. Primary lien.

C. Indemnification.

D. Satisfaction.

Answer (A) is correct.

REQUIRED: The surety's right after (s)he satisfies the principal debtor's obligation.

DISCUSSION: Subrogation is the right of a surety, after paying the obligation of a debtor who has defaulted, to succeed to the legal rights of the creditor against the principal debtor, cosureties, or any collateral.

Answer (B) is incorrect. The surety stands in the shoes of the creditor, who may or may not have had a senior security interest or a priority in bankruptcy. Answer (C) is incorrect. A right of indemnification arises from a contract by which one party agrees to hold another party harmless. Indemnity (e.g., insurance) protects a debtor from loss. A suretyship contract protects a creditor. Answer (D) is incorrect. Satisfaction is the creditor's acceptance of a performance stipulated in an accord, which is an agreement to accept some performance by the debtor that is different from, and usually less than, what was originally agreed.

28. Which of the following events will release a noncompensated surety from liability to the creditor?

A. The principal debtor was involuntarily petitioned into bankruptcy.

B. The creditor failed to notify the surety of a partial surrender of the principal debtor's collateral.

C. The creditor was adjudicated incompetent after the debt arose.

D. The principal debtor exerted duress to obtain the surety agreement.

Answer (B) is correct.

REQUIRED: The event that will release a noncompensated surety from liability to the creditor.

DISCUSSION: The creditor's impairment of collateral, for example, by returning it to the principal debtor or failing to maintain a perfected security interest in it, discharges the surety to the extent of the value of the lost collateral. The reason for permitting this defense is to protect a surety who assumed the obligation solely because the creditor held the security for the debt.

Answer (A) is incorrect. The manner in which the principal debtor entered into bankruptcy proceedings is irrelevant. It is one of the reasons a creditor enters into a surety contract. Answer (C) is incorrect. The mental capacity of the creditor after the debt arose is irrelevant. Answer (D) is incorrect. The principal debtor is not a party to the surety agreement. Accordingly, the duress defense is not valid.

29. Sklar borrowed $360,000 from Rich Bank. At Rich's request, Sklar entered into an agreement with Aker, Burke, and Cey to act as cosureties on the loan. The agreement between Sklar and the cosureties provided that the maximum liability of each cosurety was Aker, $72,000; Burke, $108,000; and Cey, $180,000. After making several payments, Sklar defaulted on the loan. The balance was $240,000. If Cey pays $180,000 and Sklar subsequently pays $60,000, what amounts may Cey recover from Aker and Burke?

A. $0 from Aker and $0 from Burke.

B. $60,000 from Aker and $60,000 from Burke.

C. $48,000 from Aker and $72,000 from Burke.

D. $36,000 from Aker and $54,000 from Burke.

Answer (D) is correct.

REQUIRED: The amounts recoverable from cosureties.

DISCUSSION: A cosurety who has paid more than his or her proportionate or agreed share of the debt has a right to proceed against the other cosureties for their proportionate or agreed share. A cosurety's contributive share is determined by dividing the maximum liability of that cosurety by the sum for all the cosureties and then multiplying by the amount of the default.

Aker	$ 72 ÷ ($72 + $108 + $180) = 20% × $180 = $36
Burke	$108 ÷ ($72 + $108 + $180) = 30% × $180 = $54
Cey	$180 ÷ ($72 + $108 + $180) = 50% × $180 = $90

Hence, Cey should receive contributions of $36,000 and $54,000 from Aker and Burke, respectively. Although the suretyship agreement is between the debtor and the cosureties, the cosureties are liable on the contract to the creditor. The creditor can sue on the contract because it is a third-party beneficiary.

30. When approached by Bob Lanier regarding a $2,000 loan, Dina Dustin demanded not only an acceptable surety but also collateral equal to 50% of the loan. Lanier obtained King Surety Company as his surety and pledged rare coins worth $1,000 with Dustin. Dustin was assured by Lanier 1 week before the due date of the loan that he would have no difficulty in making payment. He persuaded Dustin to return the coins because they had increased in value and he had a prospective buyer. What is the legal effect of the release of the collateral upon King Surety?

A. It totally releases King Surety.

B. It does not release King Surety if the collateral was obtained after its promise.

C. It releases King Surety to the extent of the value of the security.

D. It does not release King Surety unless the collateral was given to Dustin with the express understanding that it was for the benefit of King Surety as well as Dustin.

Answer (C) is correct.

REQUIRED: The legal effect on the surety of the release of the collateral by the creditor.

DISCUSSION: When a debtor has put up security or collateral, the surety (after payment) succeeds to it if the creditor has not sold it to satisfy the debt. Thus, a creditor who releases collateral interferes with the subrogation rights of the surety to the collateral. This interference releases the surety. When Dustin released the $1,000 (or greater) coin collection, she also released King Surety to that extent.

Answer (A) is incorrect. Release of collateral by the creditor only releases the surety to the extent of its value. Answer (B) is incorrect. A surety has subrogation rights to the collateral no matter when pledged. Thus, its release prejudices the surety, and (s)he is released. Answer (D) is incorrect. The surety has subrogation rights to the collateral automatically under law.

20.7 PRACTICE TASK-BASED SIMULATIONS

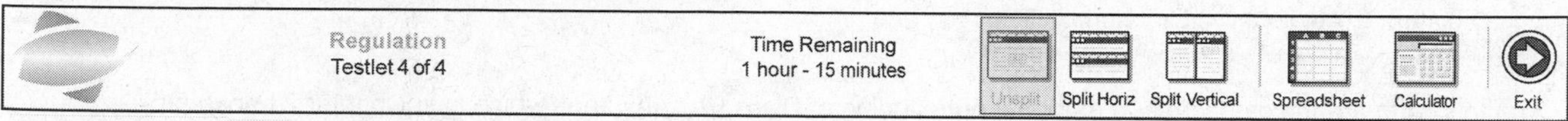

DIRECTIONS

Note: If you believe you have encountered a software malfunction, report it to the test center staff immediately.

Navigation

To navigate from task to task, use the controls at the bottom of the screen. Click on the **Next** button to advance to the next task, or the **Previous** button to go to the previous task. To go directly to any task, click on its number.

If you would like a reminder to revisit a task, or want to indicate that you are finished with it, click on the reminder flag below the task number. To clear the flag, click on it again. Reminder flags are for your use only – they do not contribute to your score.

Tabs

In this part of the examination, you will be asked to complete various tasks. Every task has one or more **Work Tabs**. Some tasks have one or more **Information Tabs**, others may have none. Every task has a **Help** tab.

If a task has **Information Tabs**, you may use the information in them to complete your responses in the **Work Tabs**.

Work tab **Information tab** **Help tab**

Work Tabs:

- **Work Tabs** are identified with a pencil icon. This is where your responses are expected.
- Each task has one or more **Work Tabs**.
- **Work Tabs** contain directions for completing the task – be sure to read these directions carefully.
- The **Work Tab** name in the example above is for illustration only – yours will differ.
- You must complete all of the **Work Tabs** in each task to receive full credit.

Information Tabs:

- The Authoritative Literature will be provided in all tasks in the AUD, FAR, and REG sections for your reference.
- Your simulation may have one or more additional **Information Tabs**. Like the Authoritative Literature tabs, **Information Tabs** do not have a pencil icon.
- If your task has additional **Information Tabs**, go through each to familiarize yourself with the task content.

Help Tab:

- The **Help Tab** provides assistance with the exam software that is used in this task. For example, if the task is to compose a memorandum, **Help** will provide information about the word processor.

The Toolbar

The toolbar at the top of the screen shows the amount of time remaining for you to complete the tasks. In addition, the following tools are available. Note that only the **Exit** button is displayed when Directions are visible - the others will appear when you begin the tasks.

Click on these buttons to split or unsplit the screen. You can split the screen vertically or horizontally.

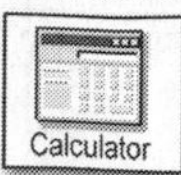

Click on this button to display the calculator; click on it again to hide the calculator. To move the calculator, click on the calculator title bar and drag the calculator to the desired location.

Click on this button to use the spreadsheet; click on it again to hide the spreadsheet. To move the spreadsheet, click on the the spreadsheet title bar and drag the spreadsheet to the desired location.

Click on this button to go on to the next part of the examination. You must complete all of the tasks to receive full credit. Once you click on **Exit** and confirm the action, you will NOT be able to return to this testlet.

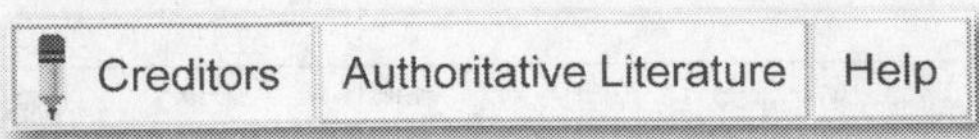

The following are the creditors and amounts outstanding of Disco Records, Inc., which is in Chapter 7 bankruptcy:

- National Bank: Mortgage on Disco's store in the amount of $125,000. The fair value of the store is $110,000.
- Disco's employees: Wages due of $4,500.
- Federal Government: Taxes due of $8,000.
- Eureka Electric: $1,500 for outstanding electric bills.
- Glover Corporation: $22,000 loan secured by equipment with a fair value of $25,000.
- Holly Plastics: $30,000 for inventory.

Based on the description of amounts owed by Disco to its creditors, select from the list provided the correct status for each creditor. Each choice may be used once, more than once, or not at all. Assume the amount owed to Holly is still outstanding.

Creditor	***Answer***
1. National Bank	
2. Disco's employees	
3. Federal government	
4. Eureka Electric	
5. Glover Corporation	
6. Holly Plastic	

Choices
A) Secured creditor
B) Priority creditor
C) General creditor
D) Secured and general creditor
E) Secured and priority creditor

The following are the creditors and amounts outstanding of Disco Records, Inc., which is in Chapter 7 bankruptcy:

- National Bank: Mortgage on Disco's store in the amount of $125,000. The fair value of the store is $110,000.
- Disco's employees: Wages due of $4,500.
- Federal Government: Taxes due of $8,000.
- Eureka Electric: $1,500 for outstanding electric bills.
- Glover Corporation: $22,000 loan secured by equipment with a fair value of $25,000.
- Holly Plastics: $30,000 for inventory.

For each creditor, enter in the shaded cell the payment that each will receive if the store and equipment are sold for fair value. After the sales, $37,400 of cash is available to pay the unsecured claims. Assume that the amount owed to Holly is still outstanding.

Creditor	***Amount***
1. National Bank	
2. Disco's employees	
3. Federal government	
4. Eureka Electric	
5. Glover Corporation	
6. Holly Plastic	

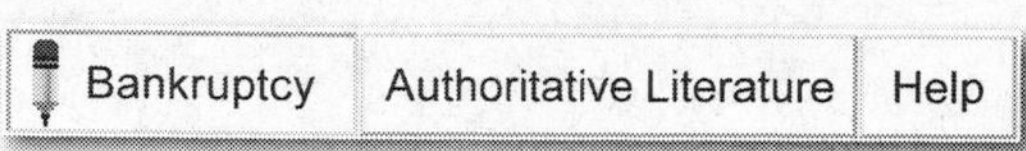

Identify which types of bankruptcy each statement is related to by entering yes or no in the respective column.

Statement	***Chapter 7***	***Chapter 11***	***Chapter 13***
Voluntary only	1.	2.	3.
Applies only to individuals	4.	5.	6.
Individuals are subject to a means test	7.	8.	9.
Railroads can file under	10.	11.	12.
Can involuntarily petition debtors into bankruptcy	13.	14.	15.
Treated as a reorganization, as opposed to strictly debt relief	16.	17.	18.

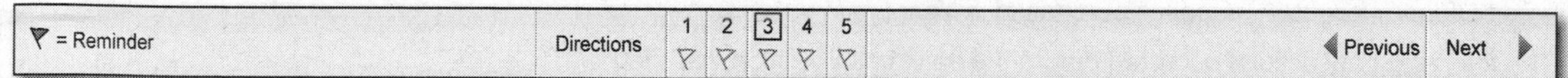

Items 1 through 6 below are descriptive words, phrases, and statements related to surety law. Select the term from the box that best matches each phrase or statement. Each answer may be used only once.

Statement	***Answer***
1. Sued after a judgment is returned unsatisfied	
2. Oral guaranty	
3. Compelling debtor to pay before surety	
4. Primarily liable even though never paid	
5. Diminishes creditor's recovery only if asserted by debtor	
6. Liable to pay debt of person not sued by creditor	

Terms
A) Exoneration
B) Surety
C) Set-off
D) Unenforceable
E) Accommodation surety
F) Guarantor

On April 15, Year 3, Wren Corp., an appliance wholesaler, was petitioned involuntarily into bankruptcy under the liquidation provision of Chapter 7 of the Federal Bankruptcy Code. When the petition was filed, Wren's creditors included

Secured Creditors	Amount Owed
Fifth Bank — 1st mortgage on warehouse owned by Wren	$50,000
Hard Manufacturing Corp. — perfected purchase money security interest in inventory	30,000
TVN Computers, Inc. — perfected security interest in office computers	15,000

Unsecured Creditors	Amount Owed
IRS — Year 1 federal income taxes	$20,000
Acme Office Cleaners — services for January, February, and March, Year 3	750
Ted Smith (employee) — February and March, Year 3 wages	2,400
Joan Sims (employee) — March, Year 3 commissions	1,500
Power Electric Co. — electricity charges for January, February, and March, Year 3	600
Soft Office Supplies — supplies purchased in Year 2	2,000

The following transactions occurred before the bankruptcy petition was filed:

- On December 31, Year 2, Wren paid off a $5,000 loan from Mary Lake, the sister of one of Wren's directors.
- On January 30, Year 3, Wren donated $2,000 to Universal Charities.
- On February 1, Year 3, Wren gave Young Finance Co. a security agreement covering Wren's office fixtures to secure a loan previously made by Young.
- On March 1, Year 3, Wren made the final $1,000 monthly payment to Integral Appliance Corp., one of its suppliers, on a 2-year note.
- On April 1, Year 3, Wren purchased from Safety Co. a new burglar alarm system for its factory for $5,000 cash.

All of Wren's assets were liquidated. The warehouse was sold for $75,000, the computers were sold for $12,000, and the inventory was sold for $25,000. After paying the bankruptcy administration expenses of $8,000, secured creditors, and priority general creditors, there was enough cash to pay each nonpriority general creditor $0.50 on the dollar.

Items 1 through 5 represent the transactions that occurred before the filing of the bankruptcy petition. Indicate whether each transaction would be set aside as a preferential transfer by the bankruptcy court.

	Transaction set aside	***Transaction not set aside***
1. Payment to Mary Lake.		
2. Donation to Universal Charities.		
3. Security agreement to Young Finance Co.		
4. Payment to Integral Appliance Corp.		
5. Purchase from Safety Co.		

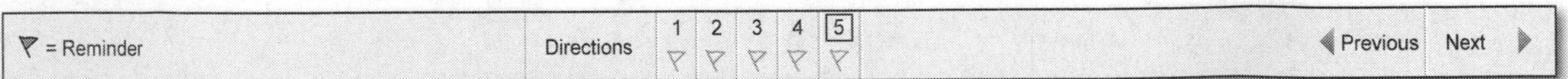

Unofficial Answers

1. Creditors (6 Gradable Items)

1. D) Secured and general creditor. National Bank is a secured creditor up to the amount for which the store can be sold to pay the mortgage. The amount of the deficiency is an unsecured claim. National Bank is a general creditor for the deficiency.
2. B) Priority creditor. Employees are priority creditors for up to $11,725 of unpaid wages earned within 90 days prior to the earlier of the cessation of business or bankruptcy.
3. B) Priority creditor. Claims for unsecured federal taxes are priority claims.
4. C) General creditor. Eureka Electric is a general creditor because the electric bill is not secured by any asset and is not a priority claim.
5. A) Secured creditor. Glover Corporation is a secured creditor because the fair value of the equipment is sufficient to cover the outstanding loan.
6. C) General creditor. Holly Plastic is a general creditor because the inventory bill is (a) not secured by any asset and (b) not a priority claim.

2. Payments to Creditors (6 Gradable Items)

1. $118,032. National Bank receives the full proceeds of the sale of the building ($110,000). National Bank is a general creditor for the additional $15,000 owed by Disco. Disco has $24,900 ($37,400 cash – $12,500 to priority creditors) to pay the general creditors. National Bank will receive $8,032 [$24,900 × ($15,000 ÷ 46,500)] as a general creditor. National Bank receives a total of $118,032 ($110,000 + $8,032).
2. $4,500. Disco employees are priority creditors. They are paid in full before lower-ranking priority creditors and general creditors are paid.
3. $8,000. The Federal Government is a priority creditor. Priority creditors are paid in full before lower-ranking priority creditors and general creditors are paid.
4. $803. Eureka Electric is a general creditor. Disco has $24,900 ($37,400 cash – $12,500 to priority creditors) to pay the general creditors. Eureka's portion is $803 [$24,900 × ($1,500 ÷ $46,500)].
5. $22,000. Glover is paid the full amount of the loan. The proceeds of the sale of the equipment, $25,000, is more than the amount of the loan. Thus, Glover receives the full $22,000, and the additional $3,000 is used to pay the other creditors.
6. $16,065. Holly is a general creditor. Given that $24,900 ($37,400 cash – $12,500 to priority creditors) is available to pay the general creditors, Holly receives $16,065 [$24,900 × ($30,000 ÷ $46,500)].

3. Bankruptcy (18 Gradable Items)

1.-3. No, No, Yes. Of Chapters 7, 11, and 13 bankruptcies, only Chapters 7 and 11 allow for the involuntary filing of a petition.

4.-6. No, No, Yes. Partnerships, corporations, railroads, and debtors qualified for relief under Chapter 7 (except stock or commodity brokers) are eligible for Chapter 11 bankruptcy. Chapter 13 provides for adjustment of debts of an individual only.

7.-9. Yes, No, No. Under the rules for Chapter 7 bankruptcy, abuse by an individual debtor with primarily consumer debts results in dismissal from Chapter 7, or results in conversion to Chapter 13 bankruptcy. Abuse is found when the debtor does not pass the means test, or the general grounds exist for the finding.

10.-12. No, Yes, No. Railroads cannot file for Chapter 7, and they are not individuals, therefore, they can not file for Chapter 13. However, railroads may reorganize under Chapter 11 bankruptcy.

13.-15. Yes, Yes, No. Of Chapters 7, 11, and 13 bankruptcies, only Chapters 7 and 11 allow for the involuntary filing of a petition.

16.-18. No, Yes, No. A Chapter 11 reorganization allows for a debtor to restructure its finances, the business to continue, and the creditors to be paid. Chapters 7 and 13 allow for debt forgiveness.

4. Surety Law (6 Gradable Items)

1. Guarantor. A guarantor is secondarily liable for the principal debtor's obligation. The creditor may proceed against the guarantor only after the debtor has defaulted and the creditor has sued the principal debtor and obtained a judgment that is returned unsatisfied.

   Author's Note: The AICPA has specified "guarantors" as a CPA exam testing area. Surety, however, is a more general term describing one person's obligation to pay the debt of another. A guarantor is one type of surety. The law of some states no longer distinguishes between a surety and a guarantor.

2. Unenforceable. Under the statute of frauds, a contract to answer for the debt of another must be in a writing signed by the party to be charged. Thus, an oral suretyship agreement is unenforceable.
3. Exoneration. Exoneration occurs when a court of equity compels an able but reluctant debtor to pay the debt before the creditor collects the debt from the surety.
4. Accommodation surety. An accommodation (gratuitous or voluntary) surety is one who is not paid. Consideration to support enforceability of the contract of the accommodation surety is found in the legal detriment to the creditor (and the benefit to the debtor).
5. Set-off. Set-off diminishes the creditor's recovery by the amount of an obligation of the creditor to the debtor. Set-off is a personal defense of the debtor. It may not be asserted by the surety. Nonpersonal defenses of the debtor may be asserted by the surety.
6. Surety. A surety has primary liability for the principal debtor's obligation. The creditor is not required to sue the principal debtor before proceeding against the surety.

5. Prefiling Transactions (5 Gradable Items)

1. Transaction set aside. The payment to Mary Lake is a preferential transfer because she is considered an insider. A trustee may set aside preferential transfers and grants of security interests to insiders within 1 year before the petition, provided the debtor was insolvent at the time of the transfer or grant. In a case filed by a debtor whose debts are not primarily consumer debts, the aggregate value of all property affected by such a transfer must exceed $6,225 in order for the trustee to set aside the preferential transfer. The value of property transferred to Mary Lake exceeded $6,225.
2. Transaction not set aside. The donation to Universal Charities is not a preferential transfer because it was not for, or on account of, an antecedent debt.
3. Transaction set aside. The security agreement to Young Finance Co. is a preferential transfer. It was (a) for the benefit of Young, (b) given when Wren was insolvent, and (c) given within the 90 days prior to filing the bankruptcy petition to secure an antecedent debt.
4. Transaction not set aside. The payment to Integral Appliance Corp. is not a preferential transfer because it is a payment in the ordinary course of business to a supplier.
5. Transaction not set aside. The purchase from Surety Co. is not a preferential transfer because asset transfers for current consideration are not voidable by the trustee.

Gleim Simulation Grading

Task	Correct Responses		Gradable Items		Score per Task
1	____	÷	6	=	____
2	____	÷	6	=	____
3	____	÷	18	=	____
4	____	÷	6	=	____
5	____	÷	5	=	____
			Total of Scores per Task		____
		÷	Total Number of Tasks		5
			Total Score		____ %

APPENDIX A
AICPA CONTENT SPECIFICATION OUTLINES (CSOs) WITH GLEIM CROSS-REFERENCES

The AICPA has indicated that the content specification outlines have several purposes, including

1. *Ensure that the testing of entry-level knowledge and skills that are important to the protection of the public interest is consistent across examination administrations*
2. *Determine what kinds of questions should be included on the CPA Examination so that every version of the examination reflects the required distribution and balance of knowledge and skill components*
3. *Provide candidates preparing for the examination with information about the subject matter that is eligible to be tested*

For your convenience, we have reproduced verbatim the AICPA's Regulation CSOs. We also have provided cross-references to the study units and subunits in this book that correspond to the CSOs' coverage. If one entry appears above a list, it applies to all items.

<u>AICPA CONTENT SPECIFICATION OUTLINE</u>

Regulation

I. Ethics, Professional, and Legal Responsibilities (17%)

A. Ethics and Responsibilities in Tax Practice

1. Treasury Department Circular 230 - 1.1
2. AICPA Statements on Standards for Tax Services - 1.2
3. Internal Revenue Code of 1986, as amended, and Regulations related to tax return preparers - 1.3

B. Licensing and Disciplinary Systems - 1.4

1. Role of state boards of accountancy
2. Requirements of regulatory agencies

C. Legal Duties and Responsibilities

1. Common law duties and liability to clients and third parties - 2.4
2. Federal statutory liability - 2.3
3. Privileged communications, confidentiality, and privacy acts - 2.5

II. Business Law (19%)

A. Agency

1. Formation and termination - 16.1, 16.4
2. Authority of agents and principals - 16.2-16.3
3. Duties and liabilities of agents and principals - 16.2-16.3

B. Contracts

1. Formation - 17.1-17.8
2. Performance - 17.9
3. Third party assignments - 17.11-17.12
4. Discharge, breach, and remedies - 17.9-17.10

C. Uniform Commercial Code

1. Sales contracts - 18.1-18.6
2. Negotiable instruments - SU 19
3. Secured transactions - 18.7-18.10
4. Documents of title and title transfer - 19.7

D. Debtor-Creditor Relationships

1. Rights, duties, and liabilities of debtors, creditors, and guarantors - 18.10, 20.1-20.2, 20.6
2. Bankruptcy and insolvency - 20.3-20.5

E. Government Regulation of Business

1. Federal securities regulation - 2.1-2.2
2. Other federal laws and regulations (antitrust, copyright, patents, money-laundering, labor, employment, and ERISA) - 16.5-16.8

F. Business Structure (Selection of a Business Entity) - SU 14-SU 15

1. Advantages, disadvantages, implications, and constraints
2. Formation, operation, and termination
3. Financial structure, capitalization, profit and loss allocation, and distributions
4. Rights, duties, legal obligations, and authority of owners and management

III. Federal Tax Process, Procedures, Accounting, and Planning (13%)

A. Federal Tax Legislative Process - 13.1

B. Federal Tax Procedures - 13.2

1. Due dates and related extensions of time
2. Internal Revenue Service (IRS) audit and appeals process
3. Judicial process
4. Required disclosure of tax return positions
5. Substantiation requirements
6. Penalties
7. Statute of limitations

C. Accounting Periods - 3.3, 7.1, 10.1, 11.1

D. Accounting Methods

1. Recognition of revenues and expenses under cash, accrual, or other permitted methods - 3.3-3.5, 6.1, 7.1-7.3, 13.4
2. Inventory valuation methods, including uniform capitalization rules - 13.4
3. Accounting for long-term contracts - 13.4
4. Installment sales - 6.5

E. Tax Return Elections, Including Federal Status Elections, Alternative Treatment Elections, or Other Types of Elections Applicable to an Individual or Entity's Tax Return - 3.1, 7.1, 10.1, 11.1

F. Tax Planning - SU 5, SU 8, 13.3

1. Alternative treatments
2. Projections of tax consequences
3. Implications of different business entities
4. Impact of proposed tax audit adjustments
5. Impact of estimated tax payment rules on planning
6. Role of taxes in decision-making

G. Impact of Multijurisdictional Tax Issues on Federal Taxation (Including Consideration of Local, State, and Multinational Tax Issues) - 13.5

1. General concepts of state and local tax (non-state specific – for example – nexus and apportionment)
2. U.S. taxation of multinational transactions

H. Tax Research and Communication - 13.1

1. Authoritative hierarchy
2. Communications with or on behalf of clients

IV. Federal Taxation of Property Transactions (14%)

- **A.** Types of Assets - 6.1, 6.3, 6.5
- **B.** Basis and Holding Periods of Assets - 6.1, 6.3
- **C.** Cost Recovery (Depreciation, Depletion, and Amortization) - 6.2
- **D.** Taxable and Nontaxable Sales and Exchanges - 6.4. 6.6
- **E.** Amount and Character of Gains and Losses, and Netting Process - 6.3, 6.7
- **F.** Related Party Transactions - 6.4
- **G.** Estate and Gift Taxation
  1. Transfers subject to the gift tax - 12.3, 12.5
  2. Annual exclusion and gift tax deductions - 12.3
  3. Determination of taxable estate - 12.4
  4. Marital deduction - 12.3-12.4
  5. Unified credit - 12.4

V. Federal Taxation of Individuals (16%)

- **A.** Gross Income - 3.3-3.5
  1. Inclusions and exclusions
  2. Characterization of income
- **B.** Reporting of Items from Pass-Through Entities - 10.3, 11.1-11.5
- **C.** Adjustments and Deductions to Arrive at Taxable Income - SU 4-SU 5
- **D.** Passive Activity Losses - 5.5
- **E.** Loss Limitations - 5.5
- **F.** Taxation of Retirement Plan Benefits - 3.5
- **G.** Filing Status and Exemptions - 3.1-3.2
- **H.** Tax Computations and Credits - 5.1-5.3
- **I.** Alternative Minimum Tax - 5.4

VI. Federal Taxation of Entities (21%)

- **A.** Similarities and Distinctions in Tax Treatment Among Business Entities
  1. Formation - 7.1, 9.1, 10.1, 11.1, 11.7
  2. Operation - 7.2-7.5, 10.2, 11.3-11.4
  3. Distributions - 9.2, 10.3, 11.5
  4. Liquidation - 9.4-9.7, 10.1, 11.6
- **B.** Differences Between Tax and Financial Accounting - 7.5
  1. Reconciliation of book income to taxable income
  2. Disclosures under Schedule M-3
- **C.** C Corporations
  1. Determination of taxable income/loss - 7.2-7.4
  2. Tax computations and credits, including alternative minimum tax - 8.1-8.2, 8.5-8.8
  3. Net operating losses - 7.4
  4. Entity/owner transactions, including contributions and distributions - 9.1-9.3, 9.8-9.9
  5. Earnings and profits - 7.3, 8.7
  6. Consolidated returns - 8.3-8.4
- **D.** S Corporations
  1. Eligibility and election - 10.1
  2. Determination of ordinary income/loss and separately stated items - 10.2
  3. Basis of shareholders' interest - 10.2
  4. Entity/owner transactions, including contributions and distributions - 10.3
  5. Built-in gains tax - 10.4

E. Partnerships

1. Determination of ordinary income/loss and separately stated items - 11.1-11.2
2. Basis of partner's/member's interest and basis of assets contributed to the partnership - 11.1-11.3
3. Partnership and partner elections - 11.1-11.2
4. Transactions between a partner and the partnership - 11.3
5. Treatment of partnership liabilities - 11.4
6. Distribution of partnership assets - 11.5
7. Ownership changes and liquidation and termination of partnership - 11.1-11.2, 11.6

F. Trusts and Estates

1. Types of trusts - 12.1
2. Income and deductions - 12.1
3. Determination of beneficiary's share of taxable income - 12.2

G. Tax-Exempt Organizations - 11.8

1. Types of organizations
2. Obtaining and maintaining tax-exempt status
3. Unrelated business income

INDEX